Government and Professional Organization Labor Web Sites

Department of Labor	www.dol.gov
Wage and Hour Division	www.dol.gov/esa/whd
Bureau of Labor Statistics	www.bls.gov
National Labor Relations Board	www.nlrb.gov
EEOC	www.eeoc.gov
Federal Mediation and Conciliation Service	www.fmcs.gov
Federal Sector Labor Relations & HR	www.members.aol.com/cfr5
Society for HR Management	www.shrm.org
American Society for Training and Development	www.astd.org
Bureau of National Affairs	www.bna.com
Commerce Clearing House	www.cch.com
William M. Mercer Companies	www.mercerhr.com
Towers Perrin	www.towers.com
HR Magazine	www.shrm.org
Workforce Online (Personal Journal)	www.workforceonline.com
Employment Law Central	www.employmentlawcentral.com
Cornell University's Employment Law Documents	www.hrsolutionsinc.com/links/ legalgeneral.htm

EIGHTH EDITION

LABOR RELATIONS AND COLLECTIVE BARGAINING

Cases, Practice, and Law

Michael R. Carrell

Dean
College of Business
Northern Kentucky University

Christina Heavrin, J.D.

Labor Negotiator and Special Counsel to the Mayor
Louisville/Jefferson County Metro Government
Louisville, Kentucky

PEARSON

Prentice
Hall

Upper Saddle River, New Jersey 07458

Library of Congress Cataloging-in-Publication Data

Carrell, Michael R.
 Labor relations and collective bargaining : cases, practice, and law /
Michael R. Carrell, Christina Heavrin. -- 8th ed.
    p. cm.
 Includes bibliographical references and index.
   ISBN 0-13-186872-1
 1. Collective labor agreements--United States. 2. Collective
bargaining--United States. 3. Industrial relations--United States. I.
Heavrin, Christina. II Title.
   KF3408.C37 2007
     344.7301'89--dc22

2006018095

Senior Acquisitions Editor: Michael Ablassmeir
VP/Editorial Director: Jeff Shelstad
Product Development Manager: Ashley Santora
Editorial Assistant: Stephanie Kamens
Media Project Manager: Ashley Lulling
Marketing Manager: Anne Howard
Marketing Assistant: Susan Osterlitz
Associate Director, Production Editorial: Judy Leale
Managing Editor, Production: Renata Butera
Production Editor: Kelly Warsak
Permissions Coordinator: Charles Morris
Associate Director, Manufacturing: Vinnie Scelta
Manufacturing Buyer: Michelle Klein
Cover Design: Bruce Kenselaar
Illustration (Interior): Techbooks
Director, Image Resource Center: Melinda Patelli
Manager, Rights and Permissions: Zina Arabia
Manager, Visual Research: Beth Brenzel
Manager, Cover Visual Research & Permissions: Karen Sanatar
Image Permission Coordinator: Debbie Hewitson
Photo Researcher: Kathy Ringrose
Composition: Techbooks
Full-Service Project Management: Penny Walker/Techbooks
Printer/Binder: Hamilton Printing Company
Cover Printer: Lehigh Press
Typeface: 10/12 Times Ten Roman

Credits and acknowledgments borrowed from other sources and reproduced, with
permission, in this textbook appear on appropriate page within text.

Pearson Education LTD.   Pearson Education Australia PTY, Limited
Pearson Education Singapore, Pte. Ltd   Pearson Education North Asia Ltd
Pearson Education, Canada, Ltd   Pearson Educación de Mexico, S.A. de C.V.
Pearson Education—Japan   Pearson Education Malaysia, Pte. Ltd.

10 9 8 7 6 5 4 3 2
ISBN: 0-13-186872-1

DEDICATION

This work is dedicated to Colonel Everett Mann of Bakersfield, California, a public servant, soldier, teacher, scholar, mentor, swimmer, coach, artist, and humorist. He is also as good a friend as a person could ever hope to have on this Earth.
Mike Carrell

As always, this is dedicated to my husband Mike Ward, my son and his wife, Jasper and Amanda Ward, and my son, Kevin Ward. And a special thanks to my sisters, Marilyn, Margie, Susan, Andrea, and Nancy.
Christina Heavrin

Brief Contents

Contents

Preface

Labor Relations and Collective Bargaining: Cases, Practice, and Law, Eighth Edition, introduces students to collective bargaining and labor relations with an emphasis on real-world situations. The changing relationships in the workplace have taken their toll on the traditional collective bargaining and labor relations processes. Although the nation's laws still protect collective bargaining as a way to promote commerce, the realities of a changing economy, a decrease in union membership, an increase in government regulations, and a diverse workforce have complicated labor relations.

Drawing on over 60 years of experience in negotiating, labor law, and teaching, we have developed a text for readers who need a practical working knowledge of labor relations and collective bargaining terms, practices, and law. This text introduces students to collective bargaining and labor relations with an emphasis on the "real-world" situations they will face on the job. Sections of actual labor agreements as well as arbitration cases and decisions of the National Labor Relations Board (NLRB) and the courts illustrate and emphasize contemporary issues of collective bargaining and labor relations. In addition, experts in the fields of labor law and arbitration have contributed "tips" on how the concepts learned can actually be applied. In this edition, we have included a new chapter on global comparative labor relations.

This text begins with a treatment of the historical and legal basis for labor relations and collective bargaining in the United States. The labor history section adds to the students' understanding of the collective bargaining process in the United States by profiling both the people and the events that shaped this process. In addition, the students are exposed to the economic realities in the past, present, and future that have and will affect the workplace. Changes in the application of labor laws due to court decisions, NLRB rulings, and changes in the environment of union and management relations are covered throughout the text and include the latest decisions and rulings as well as an analysis of what these changes might mean in the workplace. The text also includes ways of estimating wage and benefit items and computerized costing methods. It describes negotiating techniques and covers items in depth, giving students direct exposure to how negotiating theory is applied in actual situations. This edition has a collective bargaining simulation online that enhances the traditional lecture and case approach to teaching collective bargaining with "hands-on" experience in contract negotiation. There are detailed explanations of contract enforcement, grievance, and arbitration procedures.

PEDAGOGICAL FORMAT

A student-oriented chapter format was designed to integrate theory with the "bread-and-butter" issues at the core of most actual negotiations. This integration, which includes the following material, provides a sense of how issues in the real world are resolved:

- **Labor News.** These chapter-opening articles summarize current labor relations activities. The purpose of the articles is to help students relate current events to the day-to-day labor practices discussed in the chapter.

- *Chapter Cases.* Several short cases, which include the decisions of the arbitrator or judge, illustrate those points discussed within each chapter while bridging the gap between theory and practice.
- *Tips from the Experts.* In Chapters 3 to 8, labor relations professionals answer questions about the collective bargaining process and point out pitfalls for employers and employees involved in the labor relations field. In Chapters 9 to 11, a labor arbitrator gives tips on how employers and employees can avoid labor disputes.
- *Labor Profiles.* In several chapters, a number of profiles of labor leaders or of innovations in the labor relations process help the student understand the concepts in the chapter and the history of labor relations in the United States.
- *Public Sector.* In each chapter, there are one or more sections that compare and contrast labor relations and collective bargaining in the public sector. Unionization in the public sector is increasing, and students need to understand how unionization here differs from that in the private sector.

Chapter-end and end of text materials include the following:

- *"You Be the Arbitrator."* A "real-world" arbitration case at the end of each chapter allows students to assume the role of arbitrator who is presented with the facts, relevant provisions of a labor agreement, and the positions of the union and management. Then they are asked to decide an award and opinion, cite the most relevant facts, and decide what actions the employer and/or union might have taken to avoid the conflict.
- *Case Studies.* Case studies help students understand both sides of the issues. The case studies describe the facts and lawsuits, but actual decisions are not provided. These cases are taken from court and NLRB decisions and allow students to play the role of the arbitrator or judge in deciding cases.
- *Key Terms and Concepts.* A list of the important terms and concepts discussed in the chapter, including much of the vocabulary unique to labor relations, is provided. The student should be able to recognize, define, and discuss the terms after completing the chapter. Key terms appear in boldface and are defined in context.
- *Review Questions.* Straightforward questions focus on the major areas covered. If the review questions present any difficulty, the student should reread the appropriate material.
- *Experiential Exercise.* An exercise is included at the end of each chapter that requires students to apply what they have learned from the chapter to practical and realistic situations. Many of the exercises require that students go outside the classroom and visit work sites and/or contact union and management representatives in the community for information.
- *Glossary.* At the end of the book is a glossary of all key terms that appear in bold print in the chapters.
- *Texts of Major Labor Legislation.* The text of the National Labor Relations Act and the Labor Management Relations Act, as amended, is included at the end of this book to provide a ready reference to these important documents.

COMPREHENSIVE COVERAGE

This text comprehensively treats the environment of labor relations, the activity of collective bargaining, and the need for administrating an agreement after it has been signed. The text also explores labor relations issues in the public sector, the impact of diversity in the workplace, and how global labor relations affects U.S. interests.

Part One traces the development of collective bargaining. Chapter 1 focuses on the roots of the American labor movement and discusses the laws that led to and finally established the collective bargaining process. Chapter 2 takes the student through the development of the workplace and how that development has affected modern labor relations. This chapter explores both the causes and the solutions to the challenges that unions face in representing workers, including the challenges of decreasing union participation, globalization and diversity of the American workforce.

Part Two examines the collective bargaining process. Chapter 3 discusses provisions of the National Labor Relations Act, how bargaining units are formed and chosen, and the types of units in the workforce. The rights of unions to represent members as well as the obligations of unions to their members are also explored in this chapter. Chapter 4 describes the ways unions organize a workplace for representation and discusses what conduct around such campaigns is construed as an unfair labor practice, both by employers and by labor unions. Unfair labor practices surrounding the duty to bargain are also discussed. Chapter 5 deals with content of labor agreements, negotiating techniques, and overcoming an impasse.

Part Three covers the costs of collective bargaining agreements. Chapter 6 deals with wages and the different ways in which wages are negotiated and paid under collective bargaining agreements. Chapter 7 looks at the benefits negotiated in most contracts, from vacations to health-care coverage. Chapter 8 presents issues of job security and employee seniority.

Part Four presents the operational processes involved in enforcing collective bargaining agreements. Chapter 9 explores the basic principles of collective bargaining agreements, methods of enforcement, the NLRB and court intervention, grievance and arbitration procedures, and pressure tactics such as strikes and lockouts. Chapter 10 defines individual rights under collective bargaining agreements and presents widely used procedures to resolve grievances between employers and employees. Chapter 11 expands on these issues to describe the arbitration process that generally follows an unsuccessful grievance procedure.

Chapter 12 is a timely look at globalization and its impact on U.S. workers. Globalization, which is the integration of national economies into a single market, the creation of new world production systems, and the increased investment by multinational companies across national borders, brings more and more people into direct contact with the global economy. The traditional roles and responsibilities of both management and labor are being challenged by the creation of a global fiber-optic network that makes "work" more mobile than ever before. The chapter contains a comparative review of industrial relations in 10 countries, including Great Britain, Germany, Japan, and China, as well as a brief look at the International Labour Organization and the European Union.

FACULTY RESOURCES

INSTRUCTOR'S RESOURCE CENTER: Register. Redeem. Login.

www.prenhall.com/irc is where instructors can access a variety of print, media, and presentation resources available with this text in downloadable, digital format. For most texts, resources are also available for course management platforms such as Blackboard, WebCT, and Course Compass.

It gets better. Once you register, you will not have additional forms to fill out or multiple usernames and passwords to remember to access new titles and/or editions. As a registered faculty member, you can log in directly to download resource files and receive immediate access and instructions for installing Course Management content to your campus server.

Need help? Our dedicated Technical Support team is ready to assist instructors with questions about the media supplements that accompany this text. Visit: http://247.prenhall.com/ for answers to frequently asked questions and toll-free user support phone numbers. The following supplements are available to adopting instructors.

For detailed descriptions of all of the supplements listed below, please visit: www.prenhall.com/irc

Instructor's Resource Center (IRC) Online—visit prenhall.com/carrell
PowerPoints—Visit the IRC Online
Printed Instructor's Manual with Test Bank—ISBN: 0-13-186871-3

STUDENT RESOURCES

Companion Website

www.prenhall.com/carrell features an interactive and exciting online student study guide. Students can access multiple-choice, true/false, and Internet-based essay questions that accompany each chapter in the text. Objective questions are scored online, and incorrect answers are keyed to the text for student review.

Mock Bargaining Exercise

A mock bargaining exercise to be used with this text has been added to **www.prenhall. com/carrell** for this edition. This bargaining exercise is based on an actual negotiation involving the merger of two bargaining units within a local government with adequate, but not excessive, financial resources. These bargaining units came into the merger with an equal number of employees, but the employees had significant differences in pay, benefits, and working conditions. Students must negotiate an agreement in which differences in pay and benefits have to be reconciled and noneconomic issues such as mandated overtime and new work schedules have to be addressed. Both units had collective bargaining agreements in place at the time of the merger, so conflicting contract provisions have to be renegotiated. Your instructor will have access to the actual contract negotiated by the parties to share with you after negotiations have been completed.

Collective Bargaining Simulated, Fifth Edition

This supplement, by Jerald B. Smith, Michael R. Carrell, and Peggy Golden, is an award-winning classroom-tested simulation of an actual private-sector labor agreement that involves students directly in a labor contract negotiation. The entire text of the current contract, history of the company, relevant financial data, employee desires, and player roles are provided. In addition, an online costing program is provided to enable students to easily and quickly cost out economic proposals.

SafariX eTextbooks Online

Developed for students looking to save on required or recommended textbooks, SafariX eTextbooks Online saves students money off the suggested list prices of the print text. Students simply select their eText by title or author and purchase immediate access to the content for the duration of the course using any major credit card. With a SafariX eText, students can search for specific keywords or page numbers, make notes online, print out reading assignments that incorporate lecture notes, and bookmark important passages for later review. For more information, or to purchase a SafariX eTextbook, visit *http://www.safarix.com*.

FEEDBACK

The author and product team would appreciate hearing from you! Let us know what you think about this textbook by writing to college_marketing@prenhall.com. Please include "Feedback about Carrell/Heavrin 8e" in the subject line. If you have questions related to this product, please contact our customer service department online at www.247.prenhall.com.

Acknowledgments

We wish to thank the labor law and arbitration experts who so graciously agreed to answer our questions for inclusion in chapters 3 to 11 of the text. They are Kay Wolf and Thomas C. Garwood, Jr., formerly of Garwood, McKenna & McKenna, P.A., Orlando, Florida; Nancy E. Hoffman, general counsel, Civil Service Employees Association, Inc., Local 1000, AFSCME, AFL-CIO, New York; Phyllis Florman, arbitrator, arbitration office of Volz & Florman, Louisville, Kentucky; Scott D. Spiegel of Lynch, Cox, Gilman & Mahan, P.S.C., Louisville, Kentucky; and Steve Barger, executive secretary-treasurer, Kentucky State District Council of Carpenters, AFL-CIO.

A special thank you to Louisville/Jefferson County Metro Mayor Jerry E. Abramson and the members of the labor relations negotiating team for Louisville/Jefferson County Metro Government: Bill Summers, Greg Reddington, Bill Hornig, Lynne Fleming, and Marlene Ater. A very special thank you to Kenzie and Mary Baker, as well as Connie and Amberly Hurst.

We are grateful to the following people who reviewed prior editions of this text and to those who gave us their suggestions on how we could improve this eighth edition: Anthony Chelte, Western New England College; Dawn Addy, Florida International University; James Browne, Colorado State University–Pueblo; Ross Prizzia, University of Hawaii West; Jim Hall, Santa Clara University; Jack Dustman, Northern Arizona University; Douglas McCabe, Georgetown University; Mel Schnake, Valdosta State University; James Kyle, Indiana State University; James Castaghera, Rider University; Joe Benson, New Mexico State University; Ronald Atkins, Salve Regina University; Katie Laskowitz, Purdue University; Jeffrey Bailey, University of Idaho; Kenneth Kovach, George Mason University; Richard Posthuma, University of Texas–El Paso; James Wanek, Boise State University.

Michael R. Carrell
Christina Heavrin

CHAPTER I

History and Law

The Roots of the American Labor Movement
Growth of National Unions
Early Judicial Regulation
Pro-Labor Legislation
The Creation of a National Labor Policy
Public-Sector Collective Bargaining

UFCW International President Joe Hansen speaks at the Change to Win founding Convention in St. Louis, MO.

Labor News

RIVAL UNIONS SPLIT FROM AFL-CIO, END 50 YEARS OF UNITY

On the eve of the 50th anniversary of the historic 1955 merger of the two major American unions, the American Federation of Labor and the Congress of Industrial Organizations, seven national unions split from the AFL-CIO to form a rival labor organization, **Change to Win** Coalition. Led by the Teamsters Union and its powerful president, James P. Hoffa, the Service Employees International Union, the largest AFL-CIO union, the United Food and Commercial Workers (UFCW), and UNITE (textile, restaurant hotel employees) boycotted the 2005 AFL-CIO annual convention in Chicago and announced the creation of their new labor coalition. Other unions began to follow, and the AFL-CIO lost over 4 million of its 13 million members and 7 of its 56 national unions.

Why the split? At a time when organized labor is fighting to remain an important force in American society, many labor experts questioned the motive behind the split. UFCW President Joe Hansen claimed, "The world has changed and workers' rights and living standards are under attack . . . and tradition and past successes are insufficient to meet new challenges." Hansen further stated that a primary goal of the new coalition is to organize employees and bring new members into organized labor, and that the split was more about strategies than goals. The AFL-CIO in the past placed too much emphasis on backing political candidates in Washington.

A second possible cause for the split is the rivalry between AFL-CIO President John J. Sweeney, who was reelected at the convention in Chicago, and Andrew L. Stern, president of the Service Employees International Union, who had been mentored by Sweeney when he headed the union. Stern began a campaign several months before the convention to convince members of his own union and other unions to leave the AFL-CIO.

Leo Gerard, president of the United Steelworkers of America, agreed that the split was a power struggle between the two union leaders, Sweeney and Stern, and stated: "This is not about creating better lives for our children and grandchildren. This is nothing but a disguised power grab. They [the unions that split] should be ashamed of it."

Yet a third major cause of the split may have been national politics. National Republican leaders may have prompted Stern and other leaders of Change to Win Coalition to make their historic move. Sweeney and the AFL-CIO have been major supporters of Democratic presidential and congressional candidates for several decades, and thus splitting it up can only help Republicans.

SOURCE: Adapted from Steven Greenhouse, "Ambitions Are Fueling a Division of Labor," *The New York Times* (July 26, 2005) A1, 17; and Will Lester, "UPCW Is Third Union to Abandon AFL-CIO," *The Associated Press* (July 29, 2005).

Everyday in millions of workplaces throughout the United States, employers and employees interact in what is referred to as *labor-management relations*. For some, in addition, their working relationship has been structured around a process known as *collective bargaining*. This process has existed in the United States for more than 200 years. It began in 1792, when the Philadelphia Cordwainers

TABLE 1-1   U.S. Union Members by Selected Industry, 2004

	Union Members (in Thousands)	Members as a Percentage of Wage and Salary Workers
Total union members	15,472	12.5
Agriculture	23	2.2
Private nonagricultural	8,182	8.0
Mining	57	11.4
Construction	1,110	14.7
Manufacturing	2,036	12.9
Transportation	1,218	25.9
Communication, public utilities	433	24.0
Wholesale trade	189	4.6
Retail trade	839	5.7
Finance, insurance, real estate	171	2.0
Services	2,371	11.4
Government	7,267	40.0

SOURCE: U.S. Department of Labor, Employment and Earnings, January 2004.

(shoemakers) formed a local trade union to bargain for higher wages. The history of the labor movement in the United States is the story of people who sought to find balance between the needs of employers and the needs of employees. Early struggles threatened a nation on its rise to become an industrial giant and resulted in excesses on both sides.

Collective bargaining as it exists today was formed largely by federal statutes enacted in the 1930s and 1940s and court decisions interpreting those statutes. This legal framework for labor-management relations can best be understood when viewed within its historical context.

Collective bargaining in government workplaces developed much later than in the private sector and largely because of the success of labor unions in improving the lot of its members. As the labor movement moves into the twenty-first century, public-sector labor relations has become a major factor in its continuing story.

Today unions represent 15.4 million workers, or 12.5 percent of the labor force. Their presence varies greatly by industry, as illustrated in Table 1-1, with the greatest concentration in government (40 percent of all government workers), transportation (26 percent), telecommunication (24 percent), construction (15 percent), and manufacturing (13 percent). From 1994–2004, union membership nationally dropped 9.4 percent.

THE ROOTS OF THE AMERICAN LABOR MOVEMENT

Pre-Revolutionary America was overwhelmingly rural, with nearly 90 percent of the population living in the countryside.[1] A majority of the population earned their living as farm owners, tenants, or hired hands. Supporting these agricultural workers, however, was a workforce of craftspeople and unskilled laborers. Craftspeople included carpenters and masons, shipwrights and sailmakers, tanners, weavers, shoemakers, tailors, smiths, barrel makers, glassmakers, and printers. These artisans at first plied their trades independently, but as demand increased, a master worker would set up a small retail shop and employ journeymen and apprentices in America's original workplace. Prior to permanent trade unions, these workers joined together in combinations of master workers to maintain monopolies.

The original craftspeople came from free laborers, those immigrants who paid their way to the New World and established homes and families and passed on their trade to their children. The increased need for such skilled workers, however, led to the London Company's recruitment of indentured servants for colonial America. Many of these indentured servants were eager to leave England and northern Europe because of the homelessness and unemployment caused by their declining economy. Convicts willing to migrate as an alternative to English prisons also joined the indentured servant pool. Many of these laborers supplemented the craftsmen's workers and learned, by the end of their indentured period, a marketable skill.

Indentured servants, as well as slaves brought from Africa, also supplied the unskilled workforce necessary for farming, the expansion of the colonies into the wilderness, and the distribution of goods. The craftspeople of colonial America supplied some familiar names in the American Revolution: Benjamin Franklin (printer and inventor), Paul Revere (silversmith), and George Washington (surveyor).

After the American Revolution, craftspeople also supplied the first labor unions in America. The Federal Society of Journeymen Cordwainers (shoemakers), formed in 1792; the Journeymen Printers in New York (1794); and New York Cabinetmakers (1796) are prime examples. These "trade societies," as the craftsmen's unions were called, grew of necessity as the volume of goods produced caused a clear separation between worker and employer. Thus, the employers and workers began their struggle for control over the bottom line. The availability of competing craftspeople meant that consumers would no longer pay any price for the crafted goods.

To increase profits, the employer needed to decrease cost, and to do that, the employer needed to decrease wages. The organization of skilled craftspeople allowed wage security for the artisans. When all available shoemakers committed to work only for the wage they believed fair, the solidarity of the worker, so necessary for success, was born. As the employer moved away from hands-on involvement with the making of the product, the merchant–capitalist emerged. That merchant–capitalist expanded the manufacturing of handicrafts.

These expanded workplaces were the first sites for American unions and consisted primarily of craftspeople that were white males. In the early 1800s, slavery still found African Americans in servitude, primarily on plantations in the South. Women worked primarily in the home—their own or someone else's. Even though the demographics of the American workforce for the past two centuries have undergone great transition, the profile of American unions has stayed amazingly homogeneous. As the number of workplaces for skilled laborers increased, so did the need for organizing those workers. During the 1830s, the American factory system was emerging, and the struggle between employer and employee intensified. Factories substituted mechanical power and machinery for muscle power and skills. Industrialization necessitated large capital outlays and a concentration of labor. Mass production for national and even international markets began to develop. By the time the Civil War erupted, the textile, boot and shoe, and iron industries were ready to take the final step to a modern mechanized operation.

In the Northeast, textile mills opened, and in contrast to skilled labor operation, unskilled laborers peopled an American factory in significant numbers. The workers chosen for these factories were often young women recruited from the neighboring rural areas. In the 1840s, these young women found a relatively safe and promising environment in textile mills such as those in Lowell, Massachusetts, and Pawtucket, Rhode Island. Originally, these young women came from the rural New England countryside to work to save enough money for a marriage dowry, to move west, or to preserve the family farm. The work was hard and consumed their days with 11- to 13-hour schedules. But the time of their lives devoted to this work could be measured in months, not years. The 1850s, though, saw an influx of women immigrants from Ireland and Germany who took these hard, low-paying jobs with little, if any, chance to move on to something better.[2]

The impact of this influx of immigrant labor on American workers between 1846 and the Civil War was not limited to young women in New England. Almost three million immigrants entered the country between 1846 and 1855, providing an abundant supply of both skilled and unskilled labor. Workers who had previously protected their wages by agreement not to work for less than their fellow workers were faced with competition from immigrants willing to work for much less. As skilled trades became mechanized, the availability of cheap labor to run that machinery greatly reduced wage rates.

This influx of millions of immigrants over a hundred years ago may be equaled in America today and in the near future. After an initial resistance to these intruders, American labor formed a partnership with some of those immigrant groups.[3] The challenge to today's labor movement may be to repeat that alliance.

After the Civil War, there was another influx of immigrants to the United States. Nearly five million immigrants arrived in the last decade of the nineteenth century. These immigrants arriving on the East Coast were, by and large, from southeastern Europe—Italians, Poles, Czechs, Slovaks, Hungarians, Greeks, and Russians. On the West Coast, immigrants from China were welcomed to help build the Transamerican Railroad. During this period the United States grew rapidly, primarily as a result of the creation of national corporations, such as E. H. Harriman's railroads, Andrew Carnegie's steel mills, and John D. Rockefeller's oil refineries.

The monopolistic practices of the employer encouraged the employees to unionize.[4] The need for the joint action of laborers in this newly mechanized environment was expressed by Jonathan C. Fincher, an organizer of a union for machinists and blacksmiths:

> In the early days of mechanism in this country but few shops employed many men. Generally the employer was head man; he knew his men personally.... If aught went astray, there was no circumlocution office to go through to have an understanding about it. But as the business came to be more fully developed, it was found that more capital must be employed and the authority and supervision of the owner or owners must be delegated to superintendents and under foremen. In this manner men and masters became estranged and the gulf could only be bridged by a strike, when, perhaps, the representatives of the working men might be admitted to the office and allowed to state their case. It was to resist this combination of capital, which had so changed the character of the employers that led to the formation of the union.[5]

GROWTH OF NATIONAL UNIONS

Unions, People, Incidents

It was at this point that the unionization of workers left its infancy of informal local communities of like-skilled laborers and tried to find its place in the changing American economy. The idealism of those leaders credited with creating the American labor movement can be seen in the original national unions. For years, **trade unionists** had tried to develop a national trade union. In 1866, 77 delegates from various local organizations attended the first National Labor Congress held in Baltimore, Maryland. The Congress resulted in the formation of the **National Labor Union**, which allowed membership for skilled and unskilled workers alike. The National Labor Union saw itself as a political force nationwide and advocated the creation of local unions of workers.

Active at a time when reformists such as Elizabeth Cady Stanton and Susan B. Anthony advocated women's suffrage, a Farmers' Alliance sought government support for farmers' produce, and religious organizations worked in tenements to save lives as well as souls, the National Labor Union advocated reforms to help the workers. It demanded adoption of laws establishing an eight-hour workday and sought restrictions on immigration and the abolition of convict labor. It was the first to ask for the creation of a Department of Labor at the national level. It initially supported women's unions, and it recognized the need to organize African Americans, although it did not invite them to join the National Labor Union. As the suffragettes' cause gained ground, the willingness to accept women's trade unions in the National Labor Union diminished. And by 1872, most of the women's labor organizations disappeared. The National Labor Union's reluctance to admit African Americans to full membership led to the creation of the National Colored Labor Union (NCLU). The NCLU hoped to affiliate with the National Labor Union but was refused in the 1870 Congress.[6]

As the National Labor Union's political agenda grew, its effectiveness as a "national union" diminished. When it finally converted to the National Labor Reform Party in 1872 and nominated a candidate for the presidency who withdrew from the election, the National Labor Union ended its days.

Although the National Labor Union could not boast of passing many of the reforms it advocated, it did spur the formation of numerous national trade unions, including spinners, shoemakers, railway conductors, locomotive firemen, and coal miners. When the depression of 1873 hit, these trade unions formed the core of two major national unions and nurtured two legendary labor leaders: Eugene Debs and Samuel Gompers. The depression of 1873 placed employees at the mercy of their employers and ushered in a violent period for the American labor movement. Following are some examples.

Molly Maguires

In January 1875, miners who were members of the Miners' and Laborers' Benevolent Association went on strike against the anthracite mine owners. Because of hunger, the miners went back to work in June 1875 and took a 20 percent pay cut. The Benevolent Association's leaders were forced to leave the area, and the local miners' unions essentially ceased to function.

After the strike there were a series of murders, assaults, robberies, and acts of arson around the minefields. Authorities blamed a legendary group of union organizers

---

PROFILE 1-1

"LABOR SPIES"

The use of the Pinkerton Agency by employers to infiltrate labor unions in 1875 was just the beginning of more than 65 years of such activities in the United States. Robert Pinkerton, son of Allan Pinkerton, the agency's founder, realized the potential for industrial espionage work and began sending operatives to union meetings.

Between 1890 and 1910, business was so good that he established 15 new offices. The activities of the labor spies included gathering advance warning of strike plans, investigating labor incidents, listing union sympathizers for retaliation purposes, and sowing dissent and unrest within the union ranks.

The Pinkerton Agency was not alone in this type of work. Between the late 1890s and the early 1940s, various governmental or labor investigatory bodies had documented extensive spy activities. In 1912, the U.S. Commission on Industrial Relations reported approximately 275 detective agencies with active antiunion operatives. And in 1936, a congressional investigative committee headed by Senator Robert M. LaFollette, Jr., uncovered the following costs

paid by employers for the detective agency's services:

- General Motors, January 1934–July 1936: $994,000
- Chrysler Motor Company, 1935: $72,000
- Remington Rand Corporation, 1936: $81,000

The committee also reported the income of various agencies:

- Burns Agency, 1934: $580,000
- Pinkerton, 1935: $2,300,000

The LaFollette committee documented the correlation between increased espionage activities and union membership drives. At the end of its investigation, the LaFollette committee proposed sweeping legislation to prohibit employers from using such tactics as violations of the Wagner Act. Although the legislation did not pass, the exposure of the detective agencies' tactics caused many employers to stop using them. Later the National Labor Relations Board cracked down on such tactics as unfair labor practices, and at least publicly, the use of espionage ceased.

SOURCE: Adapted from Robert M. Smith, "Spies against Labor," *Labor's Heritage* 5, no. 2 (Summer 1993), pp. 65–77.

---

known as the **Molly Maguires** for the criminal acts. Twenty-four members of the Molly Maguires were brought to trial after the Philadelphia and Reading Railroad hired a Pinkerton private investigator to infiltrate the group. Ten were convicted and executed, the rest sentenced to prison. The fairness of the trial was suspect, but the result was plain. The labor movement was portrayed as a violent and criminal movement.[7] Throughout this period, as seen in Profile 1-1, owners used hired detectives to challenge the labor movement.

Railway Strike of 1877

The treatment of workers by railroad companies is another good example from this period. Railroad companies had, through various capitalization schemes, produced large dividends for wealthy stockholders while consistently losing money. To compensate, the companies increased railway rates and reduced wages. The workers' discontent reached desperation after a 35 percent wage cut in three years, irregular employment, increases in railway, hotel and transportation costs (the use of which was necessitated by work schedules), and a suppression of union activities.

In 1877, numerous eastern lines announced a new 10 percent cut in wages, and the workers in Maryland began a strike. The railway strike spread quickly and violently to West Virginia, Kentucky, Ohio, Pennsylvania, New York, and Missouri. State militia dispersed one gathering in Pittsburgh, killing 26 people. A militia was called out in Kentucky, and federal troops fought with workers in Maryland, Ohio, Illinois, and Missouri. The strike lasted less than 20 days, but more than 100 workers were killed and several hundred badly wounded.[8] For the first time in the history of the U.S. labor movement, a general strike swept the country, and federal troops were called out to suppress it.

The embryonic labor movement realized that the failure of the largely spontaneous strike stemmed from lack of organization. Propertied classes, terrified by the events of 1877, strengthened support of the state militia. The construction of armories in major East Coast cities coincides with this period.[9]

The Railway Strike of 1877 ignited a wave of work stoppages between 1880 and 1900. As America's labor force quickly became more centralized in big cities, it also became more organized—and the Railway Strike gave it a new weapon to achieve its goals. The U.S. Labor Bureau's first estimate of strikes and lockouts is for the period of 1880–1900, which was included in the 1900 census. The estimate was astounding—from the first strike in 1877, the total for the 20-year period was 117,000 strikes and other work stoppages at U.S. employers. One of the first methods employers sought in response to strikes was to purchase strike insurance. But only one insurer—Mutual Security Company of Waterbury, Connecticut—would write strike insurance, and it was expensive.[10]

The Haymarket Square Riot

The **Haymarket Square Riot** took place in Chicago in 1886. Laborers had called a general strike on May 1, 1886, to demand an eight-hour day. The May 1 daylong strike passed quietly, but a subsequent demonstration on May 3 at the McCormick Harvester plant in Chicago caused a confrontation with police and resulted in the deaths of four strikers. A peaceful meeting, held to protest the police shooting, ended when a bomb was thrown into a group of police, killing one policeman and injuring others. The police opened fire, and more strikers were killed or injured. Eight so-called anarchists, some of whom had not even been at the meeting, were tried and found guilty not because of complicity in throwing the bomb but because they held political beliefs that threatened accepted ideas.[11] One account describes the trial as follows:

> Proceedings began before Judge Joseph E. Gary on June 21. The jury, consisting largely of businessmen and their clerks, was a packed one and the trial judge prejudiced. . . .
>
> These witnesses, all of them terrified and some of them paid, testified that the defendants were part of a conspiracy to overthrow the government of the United States by force and violence and that the Haymarket bomb and Degan's murder were the first blow in what was to have been a general assault on all established order. But their testimony was so filled with contradictions that the State was compelled to shift its ground in the midst of a trial. The core of the State's charges then became the allegation that the unknown person who had thrown the bomb was inspired to do so by the words and ideas of the defendants.
>
> Thus, the trial was transformed into a trial of books and the written word, a procedure that was later to be repeated in the United States. Endless editorials by Parsons and Spies were read. Interminable speeches by the defendants were recited to the jury. Excerpts were torn from the context of involved works

on the nature and philosophy of politics and described as damning evidence against the conspirators. The political platform of the Working People's Association, its resolutions and statements, were regarded as evidence involving the defendants in the murder of Degan. . . .

The press was there, of course, in all its glory, from every great city of the country. Thousands of words were printed daily in all parts of the country. From these dispatches we learn of the graceful, laughing society people beside Judge Gary on the bench, learn of the wives of the defendants, pale and haggard, their restless, bewildered children clinging to them, as they crowded together in the front row. We are informed that the courtroom was hot and suffocating, that the people packed together had scarcely room enough to wave the fans with which they had supplied themselves, and that the length of trial, dragging on week after week, reflected the justice of American jurisprudence wherein even the guilty get all the impressive forms of the law before hanging. . . .

The verdict was almost a formality, and the trial's big day arrived when the condemned men arose in court to accuse the accuser, to say why a death sentence should not be passed upon them by Gary, and why it was not they but society that was guilty. They dominated the courtroom and they dominated the country that day. No newspaper was so conservative that it did not admit that the defendants in defying death and in defending the working class were both dignified and impressive.[12]

Four of the eight defendants were executed, one committed suicide, and the remaining three were sent to prison.[13]

Knights of Labor

Although the **Knights of Labor** (KOL) was formed in 1869, the KOL grew to prominence between the Railway Strike of 1877 and the Haymarket Square Riot of 1886. Once seen as the future of the American labor movement, it sought to promote a national union embracing both skilled and unskilled workers in a single labor organization. It recognized that industrial workers, the so-called unskilled workers, would soon outnumber trade unionists. The KOL was begun by trade unionists, who had decided it was safer to keep its membership secret. Members were less likely to be blackballed by antiunion employers. The secrecy of the organization both limited its growth and brought it under suspicion. When it was forced to go public in 1881, it benefited from a rash of labor victories brought about by strikes against the Union Pacific Railroad, the Southwest System Railroads, and the Wabash Railroad. The latter resulted in face-to-face negotiations between powerful financier Jay Gould and the KOL—the first instance of bargaining with a specific employer by a nationwide labor organization.

The success of the KOL led to a huge influx of members—so many that the president, Terence V. Powderly, felt overwhelmed.[14] Unfortunately, the KOL began experiencing a number of defeats in 1886, when some 100,000 workers were involved in unsuccessful strikes and lockouts attributed to their organization. The KOL was also blamed for the Haymarket Square Riot, which contributed to its continuing decline. And finally, although the KOL had advocated an eight-hour workday, its leadership refused to support the May 1, 1886, general strike of some 170,000 workers that was called to pressure employers to institute it. Membership in KOL dropped dramatically when trade unionists turned to the American Federation of Labor for a national union and industrial workers simply disbanded the locals they had formed.

Homestead, Pennsylvania, 1892

The Amalgamated Association of Iron and Steel Workers and the Carnegie Steel Company's plant in **Homestead, Pennsylvania**, had enjoyed a relatively friendly relationship while under a three-year agreement that expired in 1892. Andrew Carnegie, although professing satisfaction with the relationship between his plant and the union, turned negotiations over to the local plant manager, Henry Clay Frick. Frick's preparation for negotiations included arranging for both strikebreakers and more than 300 armed guards. With a declared goal of breaking the union, Frick locked the workers out when they refused the wage cuts proposed at the bargaining table and then brought in the armed **Pinkerton Agency** guards.

The guards and the workers engaged in a gun battle resulting in three dead Pinkerton guards and seven casualties on the workers' side. After an uneasy cease-fire, the governor of Pennsylvania sent 8,000 state militiamen to Homestead and established martial law. The plant reopened under militia protection with strikebreakers replacing the union workers. The union organizers were prosecuted for rioting and murder. The Carnegie Steel Company had successfully crushed the steel workers union not only at this plant but also in other Pennsylvania mills. In Profile 1-2, the spirit of the labor movement in Homestead is remembered.

Pullman Strike, 1894

Interest was again focused on the railroads when workers in Illinois went on strike in 1894. These workers lived in Pullman's town, where wages were low and rents high. A group of employees who made the Pullman cars demanded wages be restored to previous levels and rents be lowered. When the demands were refused, these workers struck. In sympathy, another group of workers refused to switch Pullman cars. When switchers were fired, even more classifications of railway workers went on strike. This new solidarity among railway workers was the result of the establishment of the **American Railway Union** in 1893 by Eugene V. Debs. His was a new kind of industrial union that placed all workers into one organization, instead of dividing them into hostile craft unions, fulfilling the goal of KOL.

The **Pullman strike** was peaceful and well organized under Debs's leadership. It shut down Illinois Central along with the Southern Pacific and Northern Pacific railroads. The boycott spread from Illinois to Colorado.

With the help of the federal government, railroad owners added mail cars to all trains. The strikers were then charged with interfering with mail delivery. Federal troops were brought in to break the strike. Although violence ensued, the strike continued. The court ordered the strikers back to work by applying the Sherman Antitrust Act.[15] This 1890 act declared that contracts, combinations, and conspiracies formed in restraint of trade and commerce were illegal. Theoretically directed at business, the court's injunction caused much controversy when applied to labor unions. Yet, along with contempt-of-court sentences and fines, the injunction finally broke the Pullman strike. Debs was sentenced to six months in prison for contempt of court as a result of his participation.

Eugene Debs

Eugene Debs was the son of an immigrant. He left school when he was 14 years old and became a railroad shop worker for 50 cents a day. At age 16 he joined the Brotherhood of Locomotive Firemen and began his work as a union organizer. Although he served as both a city and state elected official, his devotion was to the labor movement. In 1893

"OLD BEESWAX" TAYLOR (1819–1892)

Thomas W. Taylor, nicknamed Old Beeswax, was a colorful leader of the U.S. labor movement at the height of the power of the Knights of Labor. He was also a founding member of the American Federation of Labor (AFL). In 1892, he was serving as mayor of Homestead, Pennsylvania, one of the nation's preeminent labor towns.

In June 1882, 10 years before the Homestead lockout, the Amalgamated Association of Iron and Steel Workers and the Knights of Labor had organized a peaceful "Grand Labor Demonstration" in which 30,000 workers marched and a crowd of 100,000 attended. Old Beeswax rode at the head of the parade. The demonstration, which some call the first Labor Day in the United States, was held to rally support for ironworkers who had recently won a bitter strike with the local mine owners.

Old Beeswax, with many of his contemporaries, believed that the struggle undertaken by labor was one of freedom—a freedom from slavery imposed by the owners. The rally song penned by Old Beeswax and sung on that first Labor Day captured the spirit of the cause.

"STORM THE FORT"

Toiling millions now are walking,
See them marching on,
And the tyrants now are shaking
Ere their power is gone.

Chorus:
Storm the fort, ye Knights of Labor,
God, defend our cause;

Equal rights for self and neighbor,
Down with unjust laws.

'Tis labor that sustains the nation,
And 'tis just and fair
That all should help, whate'er their station,
To produce their share.

But now the drones steal all the honey,
From industry's hives;
Banks control the nation's money
And control our lives.

In time of war the workmen rally
At their country's call;
From the hilltops and the valley
Come they one and all.

In time of peace the loom and anvil,
Reaper, plow and spade.
Join their chorus with the mandril;
Each man at his trade.

Do not load the workman's shoulder
With an unjust debt;
Do not let the rich bondholder
Live by blood and sweat.

The land and air by God was given,
And they should be free,
For our title came from heaven—
Not by man's decree.

Why should those who fought for freedom
Go in bonded chains?
Workingmen no longer need them
When they use their brains.

SOURCE: Adapted from Paul Krause, "The Life and Times of 'Beeswax' Taylor," in *Labor History* (New York: Taiment Institute, New York University), pp. 32–54.

---

he broke away from the Brotherhood and formed the American Railway Union. Frustrated by the inability of the numerous railroad craft unions to maintain solidarity during a strike, Debs hoped this union of employees across craft lines would prove able to sustain a job action. The resulting success and then failure of the Pullman strike was a watershed for both Debs and the labor movement. The labor movement realized that government involvement in support of employers was their nemesis. At that point the focus of national unions turned to creating a different government agenda.

The six months in prison radicalized Debs. There he read Marx's *Das Kapital* and came to believe that the labor struggle in the United States represented a struggle between the classes. "The issue is Socialism versus Capitalism. I am for Socialism because I am for humanity."[16]

When Debs started out as a labor organizer, he decried strikes and violence. But years of strikebreaking by Pinkerton agents and rival unions and the futility of intra-union struggles led to a change of heart. He is quoted as saying, "The strike is the weapon of the oppressed, of men capable of appreciating justice and having the courage to resist wrong and contend for principle."[17]

For the next 30 years, Debs led the democratic socialist movement among the workers of America. He espoused industrial unionism in the economic realm and social-ism in the political realm to protect workers from the unbridled capitalism facing the United States in the last decade of the century. As the Socialist Party of America's pres-idential candidate in 1900, 1904, 1908, 1912, and 1920, he waged a campaign for such "radical" ideas as the abolition of child labor, the right of women to vote, a graduated income tax, the direct election of U.S. senators, an unemployment compensation law, a national Department of Education, and pensions for men and women.

Debs's objection to U.S. entry into World War I was stated frequently in speeches around the nation. In Canton, Ohio, in 1918, his speech pointed out that the burden placed on the workers during a war far exceeded that placed on the business owners. The federal government indicted Debs for that speech under the Espionage Act and convicted him. Debs was again incarcerated and, in fact, was in jail during the 1920 presidential election, in which he received a million votes. Although Debs continued to espouse democratic socialism until his death in 1926, he rejected the Communist Party, which had come into power in 1917 in Russia after overthrowing the czar.[18]

American Federation of Labor

The **American Federation of Labor** (AFL) was formed in 1886 under the leadership of Samuel Gompers. Its sole policy was to improve the position of skilled labor. The AFL's program included standard hours and wages, fair working conditions, collective bar-gaining, and the accumulation of funds for union emergencies. More important, the AFL introduced the concept of business unionism to union management and leader-ship. A decentralization of authority allowed trade autonomy for national unions, enabling them to make decisions for themselves. A particular craft or trade union had exclusive jurisdiction to ensure protection from competition. The AFL rejected formation of a political labor party, preferring to work as a voting bloc within existing parties. At one of its initial meetings, the AFL prepared the following declaration of principles that embodied the spirit of the national labor movement:

> Whereas, a Struggle is going on in the nations of the civilized world, between the oppressors and the oppressed of all countries, a struggle between capital and labor which must grow in intensity from year to year and work disastrous results to the toiling millions of all nations, if not combined for mutual protec-tion and benefits. The history of the wage workers of all countries is but the his-tory of constant struggle and misery, engendered by ignorance and disunion, whereas the history of the nonproducers of all countries proves that a minor-ity thoroughly organized may work wonders for good or evil. It behooves the representatives of the workers of North America in congress assembled, to

adopt such measures and disseminate such principles among the people of our country as will unite them for all time to come, to secure the recognition of the rights to which they are justly entitled. Conforming to the old adage, "In union there is strength," a formation embracing every trade and labor organization in North America, a union founded upon the basis as broad as the land we live in, is our only hope. The past history of trade unions proves that small organizations, well conducted, have accomplished great good, but their efforts have not been of that lasting character which a thorough unification of all the different branches of industrial workers is bound to secure.[19]

It was perhaps ironic that the unification of workers during the Haymarket Square Riot caused the AFL to monopolize the labor scene, overshadowing its predecessors. Although the KOL had participated in neither the general strike nor the Haymarket Square incident, their notoriety for other successful strikes led to the assumption that they had engineered the Haymarket upheaval. The public began to associate the KOL with violence and anarchy. Such criticism caused the KOL to lose support. The AFL began to dominate the labor movement.[20]

With the AFL in a dominant position, labor's goals jelled. Leaders kept labor's ultimate goal—participation in the decision-making process—in sight. This goal meant collective bargaining and an arbitration system to resolve disputes with individual employers. On a national level, labor sought legislative actions to gain an eight-hour day, to prohibit child labor, and to provide for workers' compensation in case of injury on the job. Thus, the American labor movement was largely based on two competing ideas. One was community: People with common interests can best collectively work to solve their problems—that is, there is strength in numbers. The second idea was individualism: People can become successful through their own hard work and ingenuity. The founders of the AFL were distrustful of the KOL's belief that only the elimination of the wage system could guarantee individual respect within one collectively active political community. The AFL founders believed instead that individual respect and dignity could be achieved through economic rewards for work and that a better life could be achieved through a new class of skilled workers. Thus, through collective action, individuals could achieve better individual rewards, such as higher pay, better hours, and better working conditions. The KOL was pursuing political equality, not individual equality, through collective action.[21]

Samuel Gompers

Samuel Gompers, at age 13, emigrated with his family from England in 1863. His father was a cigarmaker, and Samuel joined his first cigarmakers' union in 1864. Steeped in British trade unionism, Gompers saw the burgeoning labor movement in the United States go from an idealist, reformist cause to a daily bread-and-butter struggle for an improved workplace. It was this focus he brought to the AFL that caused it to survive when the KOL and the Socialist Labor Party lost ground. Gompers, with two other labor leaders, began the AFL after reorganizing the Cigarmakers International Union in 1875. This reorganized union charged initiation fees and dues to fund sick and death benefits for its members, thus ensuring a stable membership base. Members of the trade locals wanted to copy the revitalization of the Cigarmakers Union, and Gompers supplied the model.

In 1881, the same year the KOL decided to go public with its organization, a meeting of labor leaders from national and international trade unions and the KOL was held in Pittsburgh. Originally, and against Gompers's wishes, the vision for an alliance

Samuel Gompers,
Founder and President of the
American Federation of Labor.

of unions as a result of this meeting was to include both trade and industrial unions. The resulting Federation of Organized Trades and Labor Unions embraced the idea of the solidarity of all workers and the single-mindedness of the trade unionist who chose a workplace agenda as opposed to a societal overhaul agenda. Although the federation did not survive five years, it was a transition from the KOL's organization to the new unionism espoused by Gompers.

Gompers's AFL placed the major emphasis on economic or industrial action as opposed to political action. Although the member trade unions retained their autonomy, the unity of labor was promoted through education and through support of striking locals. Gompers is credited with practically forming the federation by himself. He worked tirelessly, traveled extensively, and devoted his entire life to it for 38 years until his death.

Bunker Hill & Sullivan Mining Incident, Coeur d'Alene, Idaho

In contrast to the demise of the trade unionists in the steel mills of Pennsylvania after Homestead, a similar confrontation led to a strengthening of union organizations in the mining country of the West. In 1892, miners in the Coeur d'Alene area of Idaho were locked out when they refused significant wage reductions. The mine owners brought in strikebreakers and armed guards who were confronted and driven out by the miners. Armed federal troops were called in, and they restored order, reopened the mines with strikebreakers, and arrested the union men.

The reaction from union members was to form the Western Federation of Miners (WFM) and begin a series of strikes: Cripple Creek, Colorado, 1894; Leadville, Colorado, 1896; Coeur d'Alene, Idaho, 1899; and Telluride, Colorado, 1901. Each strike involved a determined reaction from mine owners, who employed strikebreakers and armed guards and finally the state militia, when necessary, to squelch the strike. The union members were arrested and blacklisted. Nevertheless, the WFM continued to grow.

The **Coeur d'Alene incident** is of particular interest because the unprecedented acts there came to occupy an important and unique role in the history of the American labor movement. In 1885 Noah S. Kellogg, looking for gold in the South Fork of the Coeur d'Alene River, discovered lead ore in what became known as the Bunker Hill lode in Milo Gulch. In 1898 the Bunker Hill & Sullivan Mining and Concentrating Company purchased interest in a manufacturing plant and expanded it into a facility for smelting ores. Almost immediately, trouble with the Western Federation of Miners began—and continued for 12 years. The conflict peaked in 1899, when the WFM demanded that Bunker Hill & Sullivan Mining, the last holdout that employed nonunion workers, recognize the WFM to represent its miners. The owners refused by firing all WFM miners at other mines. The WFM then responded by dynamiting the mine—the largest in the world. Governor Frank Steinenberg, once a friend of the union, declared martial law and asked President McKinley to send in federal troops from Montana to restore order. The miners were rounded up into barracks that were surrounded by barbed wire—an area referred to as the **Bull Pen**—a term later used in baseball to refer to the enclosed area for relief pitchers. The miners never forgave Governor Steinenberg, who constantly received threatening letters. Then in 1905, as he opened the garden gate at his home, a bomb exploded. As he lay dying in his home, he told family members that the miners finally got him. Three WFM leaders were arrested for the murder.[22]

Despite these incidents, the WFM continued to organize and work for their members' betterment. Its work included efforts to pass legislation for an eight-hour workday for miners. However, even though it succeeded in passing an amendment to the Colorado State Constitution for the eight-hour day, it could not get the legislation passed. The WFM then decided to call a strike at a Cripple Creek, Colorado, mill in 1903 to push for the eight-hour day. A sympathetic walkout at neighboring mines caused mine owners to bring in the state militia once again. What followed was a year of pitched battles, arrests, civil disorder, martial law, and a suspension of usual constitutional protections. The strike was crushed in 1904, and the WFM looked as if it would suffer a similar fate. In an attempt for self-preservation, the WFM convened a meeting of activists from trade and industrial unions as well as representatives of the democratic socialist arm of the labor movement.

Industrial Workers of the World

What emerged from the meeting in 1905 was the Industrial Workers of the World (IWW). Forming the nucleus of the IWW, the WFM joined with 42 other labor organizations with an aim of uniting all skilled and unskilled workers into one great industrial union of the workforce. Like the National Labor Union, the KOL, and the Socialist Labor Party, the IWW embraced both a workplace agenda—to organize all labor into industrial unions—and a political agenda—to overthrow capitalism for a cooperative society. The IWW's members, who were commonly called **Wobblies**, organized industrial workers in a Lawrence, Massachusetts, textile mill and led a long and bitter strike there in 1912. The Wobblies, however, suffered the same fate as its predecessors, who had dual agendas, when its membership went from a strength of at least 30,000 at the time of the Lawrence strike to 10,000 in 1930 to less than 1,000 in the mid 1990s.[23]

From the turn of the century to the end of World War I, the labor movement struggled through any number of victories and defeats: strikes that broke unions and strikes that solidified union membership, political victories for its reform agenda and a significant split with other reform movements, and court injunctions and the passage of protective laws. By the end of the war, the IWW was no longer a leading association, but its stated objective—to organize industrial workers—resulted in the creation of major national industrial unions, such as the United Mine Workers, the Ladies Garment Workers, and the Amalgamated Clothing Workers.[24] The tragic turn of many labor struggles can be seen in the life of Fannie Sellins (Profile 1-3).

PROFILE 1-3

FANNIE SELLINS (1870–1919): LABOR'S MARTYR

The story of Fannie Sellins's life is not so different from that of other workers in her time. Sellins was of Irish descent; she lived and worked as a dressmaker in St. Louis at the turn of the century. As recorded in the 1910 census, she was a widow, with three children at home and one already living away from home. She was a union member; in fact, she served as president of the St. Louis Local 67 of the United Garment Workers of America (UGWA). She came to national prominence as a result of a lockout of the members of the UGWA locals by the firm of Marx & Hoas in 1909. Sellins traveled to Chicago to solicit support for the striking union members. Her eloquent and inspirational pleas gained assistance from the Women's Trade Union League, Jane Addams of Hull House, and the United Brotherhood of Carpenters. The striking union was able to stand its ground during the lockout, and in 1911 agreement was reached with the company on union recognition.

Fannie Sellins's leadership in that work stoppage led to her taking a key role in an organizing campaign at the Schwab Clothing Co., also located in St. Louis. Sellins appeared before the 23rd convention of the United Mine Workers and begged for their assistance—and pledged that the UGWA would never forget their support. The UAW sent money at a critical point in the effort. The boycott of Schwab eventually put the firm out of business.

Fannie Sellins, by this time, had become a full-time labor organizer for the UGWA. While working with garment workers in West Virginia and Pennsylvania, her attention shifted to mine workers in 1913, and she began organizing in the West Virginia and Pennsylvania coal mines. Initially her work focused not on direct organization but on offering support to the families of coal miners. Her presence as a labor leader in the Hutchinson Coal Mine strike resulted in a six-month jail sentence for disobeying a court injunction against union organizing. After being pardoned by President Wilson in 1917, Sellins began again organizing coal miners in earnest.

A 1919 strike of Allegheny Coal & Coke Company miners brought Sellins to the Alle-Kishe region of Pennsylvania. Deputies hired by the coal mine owners to protect company property engaged in a number of confrontations with the striking workers. Sellins witnessed an assault by a deputy of a mine worker and took pictures of it. A melee ensued when Sellins attempted to leave the area with the pictures to have the deputy arrested. An investigation of the incident found that Sellins was shot in the back and killed while trying to get away from the deputies. The story the deputies told was that Sellins was shot while attacking the deputies.

Fannie Sellins became a martyr of the labor movement. Pictures of her lifeless body were used as propaganda material in coalfields and steel mills from Gary, Indiana, to West Virginia. She was buried in Union Cemetery, Pennsylvania.

SOURCE: Adapted from John Cassedy, "A Bond of Sympathy," *Labor's Heritage* 4, no. 4 (Winter 1992), pp. 34–47.

Women's Trade Union League

The first national association dedicated to organizing women, the **Women's Trade Union League** (WTUL), emerged after a 1903 meeting of the AFL at which some women labor leaders believed the AFL did not intend to fully involve women within its ranks. Samuel Gompers shared society's belief that a woman's place was in the home. He stated that "it is wrong to permit any of the female sex of our country to be forced to work, as we believe that men should be provided with a fair wage in order to keep his female relatives from going to work."[25] The WTUL was a community-based network formed through an alliance between elite and working class women to investigate women's working conditions and promote the creation of women's trade unions. Mary Kenney O'Sullivan, an organizer for the AFL; Mary McDowell, founder of a Chicago settlement house; Lillian Wald, founder of the Visiting Nurse Service; and Jane Addams, founder of Hull House, among others, founded the League as a way of uniting women from all classes to work for better working and living conditions. The WTUL advocated for an eight-hour workday, a minimum wage, and the abolition of child labor.

Ludlow, Colorado, Massacre, 1914

April 20, 1914, has been called "a day that will live in infamy" in the history of the American labor movement. Coal miners in Colorado and other western states had been trying to join the United Mine Workers of America. The coal operators, however, had strongly opposed their joining the UMWA. In April 1914 in **Ludlow, Colorado**, the miners went on strike, and the coal operators evicted them and their families from their company-owned houses. The miners, in response, quickly erected a tent colony on public property. The coal operators called in the Colorado militia, and together with an army of thugs hired as strikebreakers, they staged a well-planned attack. At 10:00 A.M. on April 14, 1914, without warning, they surrounded the tents and massacred 20 men, women, and small children in the tent colony. Many others were seriously injured. Kerosene was poured over the tents, which were set on fire. Some died from randomly fired gunshots, others were found burned to death in their tents. The gunshots were from machine guns mounted on an armored car—called the "Death Special." The exact date of April 14 was chosen because the miners had planned a celebration—it was Greek Easter. Many of the miners who survived were blacklisted by the coal operators and never worked in the coal industry again. Not one of the militia or hired thugs was ever prosecuted.[26]

John L. Lewis

The 1920s were seen as a crisis period for the labor movement. The postwar prosperity, coupled with completing their economic shift to mass production, left U.S. bureaucratic firms in a dominant position. Workplaces with large craft unions became overshadowed by workplaces with unskilled and unorganized industrial workers. The inability of the AFL to change and organize the industrial worker doomed it to lose membership during this decade.

The antiunion position of many employers also crippled attempts of national industrial unions to increase their membership. The United Mine Workers was one such industrial union. Emerging from its leadership in 1924 was John L. Lewis, the next giant in the history of the American labor movement. Lewis was a great labor leader who inspired millions to join America's new industrial unions. However, in

John L. Lewis (standing at the left) founded the Congress of Industrial Organizations (CIO) for workers who did not have the advantages that craft skills gave workers in other unions.

the 1920s some labor leaders viewed Lewis as a ruthless autocrat who was as intent on stifling rank-and-file union members who dared to challenge him as he was intent on defeating the coal companies. In 1926, for example, John Brophy challenged Lewis in his campaign for president of the Mine Workers Union. Powers Hapgood, a Brophy supporter at the miners' convention, challenged the election. Hapgood was first pummeled in his hotel room by Lewis men, and then on the convention floor until he fell silent. Lewis saw the stock market crash of 1929 and the ensuing Great Depression as an opportunity to organize the unorganized workforce. With the passage of the Wagner Act in 1935, which gave government protection to collective bargaining, industrial unionism became possible. Lewis set out to make that possibility a reality.

Lewis was the son of Welsh immigrants. He, along with his father and two brothers, worked in the coal mines of Cleveland, Iowa. He joined the United Mine Workers in 1900. He left mining and, after failed attempts at other careers, ended up as an organizer for the AFL (1910–1916) and then an official of the United Mine Workers (1916–1920).

Congress of Industrial Organizations

In 1935, John L. Lewis and leaders of the Ladies Garment Workers and the Clothing Workers set up the **Congress of Industrial Organizations** (CIO). Industrial workers, unlike their fellow craft workers, could not rely on the solidarity based on their skill for union strength. Industrial unions had to build such loyalty from the results of their organization. Reacting to the trade unionization of the AFL, Lewis led the formulation of the CIO. The CIO focused on a workplace agenda, as did the AFL, but unlike the AFL it organized and encouraged industrial unions. Although originally associated with the AFL, by 1938 the CIO was a separate and growing organization. The CIO also differed from the AFL by promoting solidarity with African American workers and with the women and immigrants in the workforce.

The CIO attracted the autoworkers, and in Flint, Michigan, in 1936 the United Auto Workers (UAW) staged the first sit-in strike. The nation watched for weeks as this first display of passive resistance by the union members caused General Motors major problems. When the governor of Michigan was asked to intervene with the militia, he instead called for a meeting between General Motors and Lewis, representing the UAW. A compromise was reached, and although General Motors did not recognize the UAW as the exclusive representative of its employees, it did recognize representation of UAW members to management.

After the auto industry experience, the CIO had similar successes in the steel industry when U.S. Steel recognized the union and signed a contract without the need for a strike. The use of the "sit-down strike" during this brief period forced management to honor the collective bargaining process put into law by the Wagner Act. Most workers identified these successes with the CIO and Lewis. CIO union membership began to increase, but even the AFL membership grew. The competition for union members between the leadership of the CIO and the AFL intensified.

The political activities of the labor movement that resulted in pro-labor legislation are detailed next. The results can be seen in the rise of union membership from the 1930s to its high in the 1950s, when 33 percent of all nonagricultural workers were part of a labor union.

EARLY JUDICIAL REGULATION

As previously discussed, pre-Revolutionary America saw little division between the employers and employees. The economy of the colonies was primarily agricultural, with some handicraft trade. Basic goods were supplied by skilled laborers: shoemakers, tailors, carpenters, printers, smiths, and mechanics. The growth of the economy benefited these laborers, who, because their skills were scarce, could enjoy relatively high wages and job security. They were largely self-employed and dealt with consumers on an equal footing. After the American Revolution, some of these skilled workers became shop owners, employing others to fill orders that became more frequent as the economy began to build. Their need to produce goods in an increasingly competitive market demanded cheaper production costs and lower wages. Thus, a clearer distinction between employer and employee began. Skilled workers of a single craft formed associations and societies to protect their handiwork and their livelihood. Their method of action was to agree on a wage scale and then pledge to work only for an employer who would pay those wages. The response from the employer to this erosion of management rights was swift and decisive. Using a very supportive court system, those workers were charged with criminal conspiracy in a series of cases known as the Cordwainers conspiracy cases.[27]

The Cordwainers Conspiracy Cases

In the **Cordwainers conspiracy cases**, the state courts stated that the common law of criminal conspiracy was the law of the United States. In other words, if two or more people conspired to commit an illegal act, they were then guilty of conspiracy whether or not they ever completed the particular illegal act. Early American labor law was interpreted by judges and based on English common law. Whereas English judges had relied largely on statutes to find criminal conspiracy in labor cases, U.S. judges, who often shared a common background with employers, chose to find legal precedents in the common law for protecting the employer's property rights over the employee's job rights.[28] In the 1806 Philadelphia Cordwainers case, the court considered the mere "combination" of workers to raise wages an illegal act. The court felt that such combinations were formed to benefit the workers and to injure nonparticipants. Public outcry over judicial interpretation of combinations led later courts to find other grounds for declaring them illegal.

In a New York Cordwainers case three years later (*People v. Melvin*), the court dismissed the idea that it was illegal merely to combine. But it denounced using a combination of workers to strike because it deprived others, primarily the employers, of their rights and property. Further, in an 1815 Pittsburgh case, the court clearly characterized the offense involved in organizing workers as conspiracy to impoverish a third person, be it the employer or another worker willing to work against the combination's rules. The threat of criminal conspiracy charges and the depression following the War of 1812 practically destroyed the fledgling labor movement. When prosperity returned, the demand for skilled labor put the employees in a better bargaining position, and combinations of skilled laborers began again.

Employers responded to this attempt by labor to again enter the decision-making process by taking employee combinations to court. Conspiracy cases against the New York Hatters (1823), Philadelphia Tailors (1827), and Philadelphia Spinners (1829) questioned the legality of the means used to force the employer to meet labor's demands—picketing, circulation of scab lists, and the sympathetic strike. Before labor could rally from such attacks by the courts, another depression weakened the demand for labor, and the combinations lost their bargaining power.

The development of the American factory system and the monopolies created by the robber barons in the later part of the nineteenth century softened public opinion for a while; to some extent there was sympathy to the needs of the worker. Because of this need for the worker to meet the employer as an equal, the courts began to move away from finding workers guilty of criminal conspiracy.

The conspiracy doctrine was further narrowed during *Commonwealth v. Hunt* (1842), which involved a stubborn journeyman who worked for less than union scale and repeatedly broke other union rules.[29] Union members caused his dismissal by refusing to work with him, and his complaint led to the criminal conspiracy charge. The court found that criminal conspiracy required either an illegal purpose or a resort to illegal means. In this instance, the purpose was to induce workers to become union members and abide by union rules; hence, it was not illegal. In addition, the means—refusing to work with a worker who did not comply—was not unlawful because no contract was breached. The court upheld the workers' right to organize and to compel all workers to comply with the union scale.

Use of Labor Injunctions

Abandonment of the criminal conspiracy doctrine by the courts did not signal judicial acceptance of unions, nor did it enhance the employers' relationships with unions. Indeed, judicial and business attitudes toward union activities became even more hostile as viable union organizations sought to use economic measures to regulate the terms

INJUNCTION

The Hitchman Coal & Coke Company had reluctantly accepted unionization in 1903. For the next three years it was plagued with strikes over mine workers' pay scales, causing considerable losses to the company. A two-month strike in 1906 prompted a self-appointed committee of employees to inform the company that they could not afford to stay off the job, and they asked the company upon what terms they could return to work. The company said they could come back—but without the union. The employees agreed and returned to work.

Prospective employees were told that, although the company paid the same wages demanded by the union, the mine was nonunion and would remain so, that the company would not recognize the United Mine Workers of America, and that the company would fire any worker who joined. Each worker employed assented to those conditions.

The United Mine Workers of America wanted to expand union mines in the area because nonunion mines tended to keep the cost of production low. Union mines could not compete and still grant workers the pay increases they demanded.

Union organizers repeatedly declared the need to organize the nonunion mines by means of strikes. They were determined to protect themselves from the unorganized mines. A plan was devised whereby the unionized mines would stay open while the nonunion mines would strike. The working miners would provide strike benefits for the strikers to ensure their cooperation.

The Hitchman Company refused to grant recognition when approached by union officials and informed the union of the employment agreements not to unionize. Representatives of the union began organizing the miners with the express intent of shutting down the mine until the company recognized the union. Their organizational means were limited to orderly and peaceful talks with individual workers and a few unobtrusive public meetings. The company sought and received an injunction against the union's activities. The union appealed.

DECISION

The injunction was upheld on appeal. The U.S. Supreme Court reasoned that the company was within its rights in excluding union workers from its employ and that even though the union was within its rights in asking workers to join, it could not injure the company when exercising that right. The court found that the express intent of the union—to organize the workers to strike for recognition—would injure the company in two ways. It would interfere with the employer–employee relationships, and it would cause a loss of profits.

SOURCE: Adapted from *Hitchman Coal & Coke Co. v. Mitchell*, 62 L.Ed. 260 (1917).

and conditions of worker employment, as demonstrated by the Court's decision in Case 1-1.

The labor incidents cited earlier coincided with the growth and development of national labor organizations. Employers' use of court **labor injunctions** to stop these acts, supported by court reaction to these incidents, took on national importance and to a large extent created the need for a national labor policy.

The ability of railway workers to cripple the national railroads during the Pullman strike caused alarm in the government and among employers. A state court invoked the Sherman Antitrust Act, which declared monopolies illegal against the striking workers. The U.S. Supreme Court later confirmed the lower court's application of the Sherman Antitrust Act to the Pullman strike in the *Danbury Hatter's* case.[30] The Supreme Court stated that the act was designed to prevent conspiracies in restraint of interstate commerce and that a boycott was a form of this interference and therefore prohibited.

The Erdman Act

A key by-product of the Pullman strike was the passage of the Erdman Act of 1898.[31] President Grover Cleveland had formed the U.S. Strike Commission to investigate the cause and results of the Pullman strike. The commission recommended a permanent federal commission to conciliate and, if necessary, decide railway labor disputes. Congress used this recommendation as its basis for passage of the Erdman Act. This act gave certain employment protections to union members and offered facilities for mediation and conciliation of railway labor disputes. Although the legislation was limited to employees operating interstate trains, its mere passage suggested that federal regulation of the employer–employee relationship might be necessary to ensure peace in interstate industries.

Unions Gain a Foothold

The courts continued to use the injunction as a way to regulate union activity. But not all court actions against organized labor were successful in discouraging union actions. In 1902, the United Mine Workers organized a strike of anthracite coal miners, demanding an increase in wages and union recognition. With the widespread support of boycotts and money for the workers, the United Mine Workers withstood federal troops and antitrust lawsuits. President Theodore Roosevelt stepped in and offered to establish a president's commission to arbitrate. The workers accepted the offer almost immediately, but the mine owners balked. Threatening to seize the mines unless the coal operators accepted a plan of arbitration, the president gained acceptance of his offer.[32] The commission's recommendation included wage increases but fell short of union recognition. Textile workers conducted another successful strike during this period in Lawrence, Massachusetts, in 1912. Again the strikers were supported by contributions from around the country. After nine and one-half weeks, mill owners capitulated and met most of the workers' demands.

A 1913 strike by mine workers in Ludlow, Colorado, spurred the start of **company unions**. The mine owner, John D. Rockefeller, Jr., realized the inevitability of such workers' organizations. By instituting his own recognized employee organization and initiating reforms such as health funds and better living conditions, Rockefeller sought to eliminate the need for union recognition. Such company unions created the illusion of participation but lacked the essential element whereby labor and the employer meet as equals at a bargaining table.

These successes increased the resolve of organized labor to establish viable collective bargaining relationships with employers. But the employers were not ready to yield control to their employees. When faced with an employee strike, employers resisted, seeking and often receiving support from the courts in the form of labor injunctions (see Figure 1-1 for events in the era of strong union opposition).

Era of Union Opposition

1790   *New York Printers strike.* First strike by employees.

1790s   *First unions.* Craft workers formed first known unions, including printers, shoemakers, tailors, carpenters, and bakers.

1806   *Philadelphia Cordwainers case.* Court found combination of employees illegal.

1837   *Severe depression.* Mass unemployment reduced union membership.

1842   *Commonwealth v. Hunt.* The conspiracy doctrine greatly narrowed.

1860s   *Civil War.* Buildup of coal, steel, and other war-related industries.

1866   *National Labor Union.* Advocated consumer cooperatives, immigration restrictions; disbanded in 1872.

1869   *Knights of Labor.* National social union formed to organize farmers and skilled and unskilled workers.

1875   *Molly Maguires.* After a strike by coal miners, union organizers were tried and executed for strike-related violence.

1877   *Railway strike.* More than 100 workers were killed, and several hundred were wounded in the first national strike.

1886   *American Federation of Labor (AFL).* Samuel Gompers led the first national trade union to advocate collective bargaining, trade autonomy, exclusive jurisdiction, standard hours, and better wages and working conditions.

1886   *Haymarket Square riot.* Several workers were killed; others were found guilty of anarchism. The Knights of Labor suffered the blame for the riot, shifting much of their support to the AFL.

1890   *Sherman Antitrust Act.* Designed to break up corporate monopolies.

1892   *Homestead, Pennsylvania.* A strike by steel workers against Carnegie Steel Company ended with the town being placed under martial law.

1894   *Pullman strike.* Rail workers demanded higher wages and lower rents. The strike was ended by court orders under the Sherman Act. The strike led to passage of the 1898 Erdman Act giving railroad employees employment protection.

1905   *Industrial Workers of the World (IWW).* The "Wobblies" were organized in response to the strong opposition to the labor movement. They advocated including all workers in one union and the end of capitalism.

1914   *Ludlow, Colorado, massacre.* Twenty men, women, and children killed by fire and bullets in a tent colony.

Era of Union Support

1914   *Clayton Act.* Congress attempted to limit use of court injunction. First national pro-union legislation.

1914–1918   *World War I.* President Wilson created the National War Labor Board to mediate labor disputes. The board also recognized employee collective bargaining rights during the war.

1926   *Railway Labor Act.* Railroad employees were given collective bargaining rights and the right to use voluntary arbitration.

1929   *Stock market crash.* Beginning of Great Depression and 33 percent national unemployment.

1931   *Davis-Bacon Act.* Required federal contractors to pay "prevailing wages," which are usually union wages.

continued

FIGURE 1-1   Chronology of the Most Significant Events in U.S. Labor Relations

Era of Union Support *(continued)*

1932   *Norris–La Guardia Act.* Limited use of court injunction, made yellow-dog contracts unenforceable.

1935   *Wagner Act.* The Magna Carta of U.S. labor history. Within 12 years, union membership tripled in the United States. Upheld by the Supreme Court in 1937. Created the NLRB.

1935   *Committee for Industrial Organizations.* John L. Lewis led industrial unions to split with the AFL.

1936   *Flint, Michigan.* The UAW staged the first "sit-in" strike, occupying the GM auto plant.

1936   *Walsh-Healey Act.* Required federal contractors to pay time and one-half for overtime, over an eight-hour day.

1938   *Fair Labor Standards Act.* Provided minimum wage, 40-hour week, overtime pay, and the abolition of child labor.

1941–1945   *World War II.* Widespread labor strikes during and after the war harmed the war effort and caused strong antilabor public sympathy.

Era of Union Stabilization

1947   *Taft-Hartley Amendments.* Amended Wagner Act to equalize the balance between labor and management. Also created the Federal Mediation and Conciliation Service (FMCS) and right-to-work states.

1952   *No-raiding pact.* After 17 years of bitter fighting, new labor chiefs in the AFL and CIO signed a no-raiding pact.

1955   *AFL-CIO merge.* New unity spurred labor hopes for membership gains, which failed to materialize (25 percent of labor force in 1955, 12.5 percent in 2004).

1959   *Landrum-Griffin Act.* U.S. Senate hearing on labor union corruption led Congress to establish stricter controls on union operations.

1962   *President Kennedy's Executive Order 10988.* The order gives federal employees the right to collectively bargain and join or refrain from joining unions. Begins period of substantial growth by public unions.

1978   *Civil Service Reform Act.* Creates Federal Labor Relations Authority, which oversees labor practices in the federal government.

1981   *Air traffic controllers (PATCO) strike.* President Ronald Reagan uses replacement workers to end the first declared national strike against the federal government. The success of his action spurs a period of increased use of replacement workers in private and public sectors, reducing the number of strikes.

1986   *President Reagan's Executive Order 12564.* The order initiates random drug testing of federal employees and contains "zero tolerance" of illegal use.

1987   *Teamsters Union.* Rejoins AFL-CIO after 30 years of separation. Many other unions merge in the 1980s to increase their strength.

1993   *Family and Medical Leave Act.* Law requires employers to give employees up to 12 weeks of unpaid leave for family reasons. The act was strongly supported by unions.

1994   *Baseball players' strike.* The most unpopular strike in sports history cancels the 1994 World Series and costs the industry many fans.

FIGURE 1-1   Chronology of the Most Significant Events in U.S. Labor Relations (Continued)

> **Era of Union Stabilization** *(continued)*
>
> 1997   *UPS strike.* The Teamsters union strike idled over 180,000 workers, crippled delivery of packages worldwide, and focused national attention on the plight of part-time workers.
>
> 2002   *West Cost dock strike.* Over 10,500 longshoremen stage a costly strike ($1 billion/day) that closes 29 West Coast docks. President Bush invoked the Taft-Hartley Act to temporarily reopen the ports. A new six-year agreement ended the strike and provided higher wages and pension benefits, as well as the use of new technology on the docks that will replace jobs over time.
>
> 2005   The *AFL-CIO split.* During its 50th anniversary year, the AFL-CIO endures a major split as seven national unions, including the Teamsters, SEIU (the largest union in the AFL-CIO), and UNITE create a rival federation, the Change to Win coalition.

FIGURE 1-1   Chronology of the Most Significant Events in U.S. Labor Relations (Continued)

PRO-LABOR LEGISLATION

The Clayton Act

Public criticism of the use of the injunction against labor unions caused Congress to pass the Clayton Act in 1914.[33] This act sought to limit the court's injunctive powers against labor organizations. The **Clayton Act** stated that labor was not a commodity, that the existence and operation of labor organizations were not prohibited by antitrust, and that individual members of unions were not restrained from lawful activities. The act provided that neither the labor organization nor its members were considered illegal combinations or conspiracies in restraint of trade.

Still, courts continued to apply the Sherman Antitrust Act after passage of the Clayton Act by narrowly interpreting its provisions. The courts felt that secondary strikes, boycotts, and picketing were not covered by the Clayton Act because of the employee–employer language and because legitimate objects of labor would not include strikes and activities if their purpose or effect was the unreasonable restraint of trade. Though the Clayton Act was practically ineffective, its passage signaled a hopeful period for labor organizations. With other political victories behind them, such as child labor laws, workers' compensation, and some limitations on working hours, members of the labor movement believed that a new era was upon them.

The National War Labor Board

During World War I, President Woodrow Wilson formed the **National War Labor Board** to prevent labor disputes from disrupting the war effort. Formed to provide a means of settlement by mediation or conciliation of labor controversies in necessary war industries, it adopted self-organization and collective bargaining as its basic policy.[34] Federal recognition of labor rights continued and expanded when the federal government began to operate the railroads. After World War I, the National War Labor Board was abolished, and railroads were returned to their owners. Despite the economic sense of avoiding labor disputes through cooperation, the federal government no longer protected collective bargaining.

The labor movement sustained losses in the early 1920s. Another postwar depression and labor's alleged association with American sympathizers for Russian communism eroded public support. Even though the Clayton Act supposedly exempted labor unions from injunctions, the courts interpreted the Clayton Act as granting immunity only if an injunction was not necessary to prevent irreparable injury to property or its rights. In the broadest sense, any labor action could injure property or property rights.[35] Trade union leadership and the rank and file turned to political action and industrial unionism to counteract their losses. They allied with the Progressive movement, a loose coalition of farmers, socialists, and reformers who represented a populist view. Many people, fearing that the use of militia, federal troops, and court injunctions against unions represented a threat to the democratic process, adopted the Progressive doctrine. That doctrine espoused the control of the political activities of corporations, graduated income and inheritance taxes, stringent conservation measures, federal regulations of the labor of women and children, and workers' compensation laws. The movement, although not widely embraced, successfully supported the passage of the Railway Labor Act. In 1942, President Roosevelt reestablished the National War Labor Board to oversee labor issues during World War II. Many of its members became instrumental in the creation of the postwar labor policies (see Profile 1-4).

PROFILE 1-4

THE "IRRA"

In 1946, J. Douglas Brown and Richard Lester of Princeton University proposed the establishment of "a learned society on industrial relations." Their proposal came at a time when the largest wave of labor strikes in American history, high unemployment, and other labor issues dominated newspaper headlines. Labor economists responded to the letter sent by Brown and Lester by setting up an organizational committee, drafting a constitution, and electing officers for the new "Industrial Relations Research Association" (IRRA), which held its first meeting in 1948. In the next 14 months, 1,025 members joined the young organization!

Many of the new members, including Brown and Lester, were veterans of the National War Labor Board (NWLB), which was created in 1942 by President Franklin Roosevelt to prevent strikes and control inflation during World War II. Many of the NWLB veterans, including noted Theodore Kheel, became full-time arbitrators; others joined university faculty or became negotiators. Almost all continued the same function in industry as they had performed during the war—labor-management relations. They had a great influence on American collective bargaining practices in the postwar era. For example, the NWLB required unions and employers to use arbitration to resolve grievances and avoid strikes; and within 40 years, 89 percent of all labor agreements in the United States included binding arbitration agreements.

The IRRA was a different organization. Not a professional association, nor a political organization, it was the postwar intellectual equivalent of the War Labor Board. It brought together professors of industrial relations, corporate managers, union negotiators, government officials, and arbitrators.

The executive committee chose the awkward name "Industrial Relations Research Association" not to differentiate the Association from other learned societies but to emphasize the impartial character of the organization. "Workable policies were of central interest," Clarke Kerr wrote in 1977. "What would work among the bumps and grinds of the real world; not what might work in the best of all possible worlds. Reality is more complex than theory or ideology once supposed." The goals of the IRRA founders were to (1) reduce violence in the workplace, (2) raise the standard of living for workers and their families, and (3) lead members of management and labor to respect each other.

SOURCE: Adapted from Ronald Schatz, "A Portrait of the IRRA's Founders as Young Men," *Labor Law Journal* (September 1998), pp. 1157–1162.

The Railway Labor Act

In an effort to avoid the interruption of commerce, the Railway Labor Act (RLA) passed in 1926 with the support of both labor and management.[36] It required railroad employers to negotiate with their employees' duly elected representatives. It provided for amicable adjustment of labor disputes and for voluntary submissions to arbitration. As a result of the RLA, Congress again fostered peaceful settlement of labor disputes through negotiation and mediation. The Supreme Court case upholding that act removed major judicial obstacles by supporting a national labor policy based on the affirmative legal protection of labor organizations.[37] Under the umbrella of the commerce clause of the U.S. Constitution, the Court said that Congress could facilitate settlements of disputes and that

> the legality of collective action on the part of employees in order to safeguard their proper interests is not to be disputed. . . . Congress . . . could safeguard it and seek to make their appropriate collective action an instrument of peace rather than of strife.[38]

In 1936, the RLA was expanded to include the fledgling airline industry. The RLA listed four purposes: avoid interruptions to commerce, protect employee right to join a union, ensure independence of carriers and employees to resolve issues between them, and settle grievances and disputes growing out of the RLA contracts. Because RLA contracts do not expire but can be modified only through negotiations, the RLA set up a multistage mediation procedure that included a "cooling-off" period and the appointment of presidential boards to investigate disputes and push for settlements.[39]

THE CREATION OF A NATIONAL LABOR POLICY

In 1929 the stock market crashed, and the United States plunged into a major depression. The impact of the Great Depression on the workers was devastating. One-third of the country's workforce was unemployed. President Hoover's programs to combat unemployment served mainly to highlight the deprivation. The labor movement made more emphatic efforts to organize and demand recognition and became more politically active. The severity of conditions led to public sympathy for workers' problems. For years the nation struggled over the right of workers to organize and to negotiate collectively with employers. Judicial solutions to the struggle were ineffective. Court decisions, by their nature, were confined to particular parties, to narrow situations, and to fixed time frames. Such decisions could not give national guidance. The judicial process was also time consuming; neither labor nor management wanted disputes to drag on while the wheels of justice ground to a decision.

State legislation was also ineffectual because organized labor transcended state boundaries. With few exceptions, the disruption of an industry in any one state affected industries throughout the country.

The Norris–La Guardia Act

Congress recognized the need for a national labor policy. The Erdman Act and the Clayton Act were the first steps in ensuring industrial peace based on the balanced bargaining relationship of worker to owner. The Davis-Bacon Act, passed in 1931, was another attempt to support the fledgling union movement. This act put into place a requirement that companies using federal dollars for construction projects use the "prevailing wage rate" of the area as the minimum-wage rate on their construction project. Because the trades needed for construction—carpenters, plumbers, and electricians—were generally organized, the prevailing wage rate would most often be the union wage rate. Companies are selected to do federally funded jobs through a competitive bidding process. The Davis-Bacon Act meant that companies who use union labor did not lose their competitive advantage when bidding on federal jobs by paying their workers union wages.[40]

The **Norris–La Guardia Act** (1932) was the next step in formulating a comprehensive national labor policy.[41] This act, like the Clayton Act, sought to restrict federal judicial intervention in labor disputes, thereby giving the unions an opportunity to grow. Courts could not enjoin strikes without actual violence, nor could they restrict the formation of a union or associated activities. The act also made illegal "yellow-dog" contracts, in which employees pledged to refrain from union membership. These protections were extended to secondary boycotts and strikes by expanding the employer–employee language of the Clayton Act.

The National Labor Relations Act (The Wagner Act)

The Great Depression and the election of Franklin D. Roosevelt with strong labor support set the stage for passage of national legislation. Roosevelt quickly proved his interest in the plight of the worker. The National Industrial Recovery Act (1933) recognized workers' rights in selecting their own representatives.[42] Well intentioned but poorly constructed, the National Recovery Administration had no power to enforce the act, and industry largely ignored it. Within two years the National Industrial Recovery Act was declared unconstitutional.[43]

Relief of the unemployment problem continued by creation of such New Deal programs as the Civilian Conservation Corps, unemployment insurance, the Social Security program, and the Works Progress Administration. But these measures alone were not enough.

By 1935, the judiciary policy toward labor was one of selective suppression of organized labor's activities whenever they trenched too heavily on the interest of any other segment of society. Commercial interests must not be injured by disruption of the interstate flow of goods, consumers and unorganized laborers must not be injured by wage standardization, and employees and the public at large must not be injured by expansion of labor disputes through secondary boycotts.[44]

Senator Robert Wagner, a champion for labor, proposed an act that recognized employee rights to organize and bargain collectively. A quasi-judicial tribunal with the power and authority to enforce its own orders would be created. Although the act was purported to protect the public from the disruption of interstate commerce resulting from labor disputes, Senator Wagner stated that the act would also give the employee freedom and dignity.[45]

The **National Labor Relations Act** (also known as the **Wagner Act**) gave most private-sector employees the right to organize.[46] It required employers to meet with accredited representatives of a majority of their employees and to make an honest effort to reach agreement on issues raised. Employees now had the right to strike, and the employer's retaliatory powers were limited under the act's unfair labor practice provisions. The **National Labor Relations Board** (NLRB) was created to enforce provisions of the act.

By legislating the recognition of employee representatives and protecting the right to strike, Congress forced the employer to share the decision-making power with employees. Labor no longer depended on work stoppages to get to the bargaining table or on economic factors to determine its equality.

The entire thrust of the Wagner Act was to protect employees from employers and to establish a balance of bargaining power between the two. Later it was criticized for its one-sided nature, but at the time it was passed, organized labor had no leverage to pose a threat to management; thus, equal protection for management seemed unnecessary. Critics claimed that the act was unconstitutional because, although it was based on the

---

Findings and Policy
- Denial by employers of employee collective bargaining leads to strikes, industrial unrest, and obstruction of commerce
- Inequality of bargaining power between employees and employers affects the flow of commerce and aggravates recurrent business depressions
- Protection of the right of employees to organize and bargain collectively safeguards commerce
- Policy of the United States to encourage practice and procedure of collective bargaining and the exercise of employees of their right to organize and negotiate

Rights of Employees
- To organize into unions of their own choosing
- To assist such labor unions
- To bargain collectively with their employer through representatives of their own choosing
- To strike or take other similar concerted action

Employer Unfair Labor Practices (illegal)
- Interfering with employee rights guaranteed by the act
- Refusal to bargain in good faith with employee representatives
- Discrimination against union members or employees pursuing their rights under the act, including retaliation for exercising rights under the act
- Any attempt to dominate or interfere with employee unions

Representatives and Elections
- Employee representatives shall be exclusive representatives of the appropriate unit
- NLRB decides appropriateness of unit for bargaining purposes
- NLRB shall conduct secret ballot elections to determine employee representatives

National Labor Relations Board
- Members appointed by president of the United States
- Conducts elections to determine employee representatives of appropriate unit
- Exclusive power to prevent employer unfair labor practice

FIGURE 1-2 Major Provisions of the Wagner Act

---

commerce clause, the latter did not specifically allow Congress to dictate the relationship between employers and employees. The NLRB was careful in its activities, delaying adjudication on the constitutionality question until the Supreme Court upheld the act in the 1937 case of *Jones and Laughlin Steel Corporation*.[47] Labor-management relations improved somewhat under the Wagner Act but still remained uneasy. Figure 1-2 outlines the major provisions of the Wagner Act.

The creation of a national labor policy dominated the labor scene in 1935, but the character of the national labor union was also undergoing changes. The AFL, a confederation of craft unions, had been the principal union model for half a century. However, in 1935 the Committee of Industrial Organizations, later called the Congress of Industrial Organizations (CIO), challenged the leadership of the AFL by successfully supporting industrial unions. Membership in industrial unions was based on employment in a particular industry, such as automobile, steel, or clothing, rather than on a particular skill.

The CIO grew to five million members in less than 20 years under the leadership of John L. Lewis. This growth was attributed to the passage of the Wagner Act, the increased shift of the American economy from agriculture to manufacturing, and the heightened economic activity of World War II and the Korean War.

The Fair Labor Standards Act

The National Labor Relations Act was followed by the passage of the Walsh-Healey Act and the Fair Labor Standards Act (FLSA). The Walsh-Healey Act, passed in 1936, foreshadowed the passage of the FLSA. It again imposed rules on employers who received federal dollars. It required those employers with federal contracts to pay time and a half to any employee working more than eight hours per day.[48] The Fair Labor Standards Act, passed in 1938, applied primarily to employees engaged in interstate commerce and provided a federal minimum wage and a 44-hour week to be reduced to 40 hours in three years.[49] Passage of the act secured three main objectives of the labor movement: wages adequate to maintain a decent standard of living, shorter hours, and the abolition of labor by children under the age of 16.

World War II and the war effort resulted in a shortage of labor and more labor demands. Strikes brought charges that labor unions were unpatriotic. Congress, reacting to pressure, passed the Smith-Connally Act to control strikes injurious to the war effort.[50] Passage of this act showed a shift in political forces against strong federal support of union activities. The Wagner Act, however, was still in place at the end of the war, and labor entered the postwar economic slump with considerable legal protection. The collective bargaining rights mandated by the act forced business to deal with labor on an equal footing. Supported by two Supreme Court decisions in the early 1940s, labor unions were allowed the use of peaceful picketing to inform the public of their alleged grievances and to elicit support for their cause.[51]

The Fair Labor Standards Act has been amended several times since 1938. The minimum wage has been raised several times and is currently $5.15. In 1989, a "subminimum," or "training," wage was created as a concession to employers. It had primarily allowed teenagers to be paid 64 cents per hour less than minimum wage during training to make up to employers for the imposition of a higher minimum wage. In 1993, as a concession to unions, the subminimum wage was not continued.[52] But in August 1996 it was reenacted as a "youth minimum wage." Employees who have not reached their 20th birthday can be paid $4.25 per hour for their first 90 days of employment.[53]

In 2004 the FLSA received a major amendment by the Bush administration and the U.S. Congress. The amendment strengthened and clarified the criteria for the "exempt" classification adding both a salary level test and a duties test. To be exempt from the overtime provision (time and a half for hours worked over 40 per week), a worker must be paid a salary of $455 per week ($23,660 per year) and meet a bona fide job duties test. Specific job exemptions include executive, administrative, professional, outside sales, and some computer-related jobs in which the employee's primary duty includes exercising discretion and independent judgment.[54]

The Labor-Management Relations Act (Taft-Hartley Amendments)

For 12 years the Wagner Act gave unions the time and ability to grow strong. From 1935–1947 union membership went from 3 million to 15 million, with some industries having 80 percent of their employees under collective bargaining agreements.[55] The image of organized labor in Congress was one of power—power to stop coal production during World War II and to shut down steel mills, seaports, and automobile assembly plants after the war. That image was personified by isolated instances of placket-carrying strikers attempting to stop **scabs** or strikebreakers from passing through a picket line. As seen in Case 1-2, some of those strong feelings persist today.

DEFINITION OF A "SCAB"

The employees had just completed a bitter strike in which between one-third and one-half of the employees had crossed the picket line and returned to work before the strike was over. This caused animosity between the strikers and the nonstrikers. Within days of returning to work, someone put the following "definition of a scab" poster on a union bulletin board located on company property. Jack London's "definition of a scab" reads as follows:

After God had finished the rattlesnake, the toad, and the vampire, he had some awful substance left with which he made a SCAB. A SCAB is a two-legged animal with a corkscrew soul, a waterlogged brain, and a combination backbone made of jelly and glue. Where others have hearts, he carries a tumor of rotten principles.

When a SCAB comes down the street men turn their backs and angels weep in Heaven, and the devil shuts the gates of Hell to keep him out. No man has the right to SCAB, so long as there is a pool of water deep enough to drown his body in, or a rope long enough to hang his carcass with. Judas Iscariot was a gentleman.... compared with a SCAB; for betraying his master, he had the character to hang himself a SCAB hasn't.

Esau sold his birthright for a mess of pottage. Judas Iscariot sold his Savior for thirty pieces of silver. Benedict Arnold sold his country for a promise of a commission in the British Army. The modern strikebreaker sells his birthright, his country, his wife, his children and his fellow men for an unfulfilled promise from his employer, trust or corporation.

Esau was a traitor to himself. Judas Iscariot was a traitor to his God. Benedict Arnold was a traitor to his country.

A strikebreaker is a traitor to himself, a traitor to his God, a traitor to his country, a traitor to his family and a traitor to his class.

THERE IS NOTHING LOWER THAN A SCAB

The employer removed the poster from the union bulletin board and prohibited the employees from reposting the definition under threat of disciplinary action. The employer contended it had a business justification for removing the poster because it feared that the hard feelings between the striking and nonstriking employees would erupt into a disturbance.

The union appealed the action of the employer, claiming that it had no right to remove the poster from the union bulletin board and that removing the poster was an unfair labor practice, as it interfered with the employees' right to bargain collectively under the NLRA. The union pointed out that there was no company rule concerning the posting of *literature* on the union bulletin boards located on company premises. When an employer allows a union unrestrained access to its bulletin boards for the posting of notices, the employer violates Section 8(a)(1) if it removes a notice it merely finds distasteful. Furthermore, the employer did not prove that any actual confrontation or disturbance in the workplace happened as a result of the posting of the "definition of a Scab."

The employer contended that unions have no statutory right to post notices on an employer's premises and that it had the right to remove the "definition of a scab" because the poster was disruptive to the workplace. According to the employer, employees were "milling around" or "talking in huddles" instead of working independently at their stations as they normally did. Furthermore, various employees had complained to the employer that there was

continued

CASE 1-2 — DEFINITION OF A "SCAB"—continued

something distasteful on the bulletin board. The employer contended that it took no more than common sense to conclude that the "definition of a scab" was likely to provoke confrontations between striking and nonstriking employees and to prolong ill will between the two groups.

DECISION

The Court found in favor of the union, holding that the employer had indeed engaged in an unfair labor practice by removing the offending poster from the union bulletin board. The judge was not convinced that the employer had demonstrated the necessary "special circumstances" that would justify the employer removing it from a union bulletin board. Although the judge noted that the employer had responded to some employees who had complained about the poster, it noted "an employer, however, does not prove 'special circumstances' merely by reference to the sensibilities of one or two employees."

SOURCE: Adapted from *Southwestern Bell Telephone Co. v. Communications Workers, Local 12222, AFL-CIO*, 120 LRRM 1145 (September 30, 1985).

Widespread strikes during 1945–1946 and wage drives in 1946–1947 caused critics of the Wagner Act to increase the political pressure for amendment. The amendment's stated goal was to equalize its impact on employers. The relentless campaigning of the Chamber of Commerce and the National Association of Manufacturers, resentment over wartime strikes, and internal union irregularities began to turn the tide against organized labor.

Numerous bills were introduced to change the Wagner Act, to weaken the powers of the NLRB, to redefine appropriate bargaining units, to outlaw a closed union shop, to subject unions to unfair labor practices charges, and to limit strikes and other concerted activities. Although these bills did not pass, they laid a foundation for the passage of the Taft-Hartley Amendments in 1947. Figure 1-1 includes a brief chronology of the era of strong union support in the United States.

A Republican Congress in 1946 introduced 200 bills on labor relations during its first week, and President Harry Truman proposed some revision of the nation's labor laws in his State of the Union Address. After extensive hearings by both the House and the Senate, the 1947 Labor-Management Relations Act (known as the **Taft-Hartley Amendments**) was passed.[56] Although President Truman vetoed it, Congress overrode his veto, and the bill became law on August 22, 1947. In Profile 1-5 a participant in that process recalls the passage of the Taft-Hartley Amendments.

Management saw the Taft-Hartley Amendments as a shift to a more balanced approach to labor relations. Labor unions were subjected to many of the same duties as employers. Whereas the Wagner Act gave employees the right to organize, the Taft-Hartley Amendments recognized their right not to organize. Under the Wagner Act employers were required to bargain in good faith; under Taft-Hartley that duty was extended to unions. The unfair labor practices section protected employees and employers from labor unions' unfair labor practices. The Wagner Act had protected employees from being fired for joining a union; the Taft-Hartley Amendments protected employees from losing their jobs for not joining a union. The 1947 amendments

MACK SWIGERT

Ohio Senator Robert Taft was installed as majority leader of the U.S. Senate in 1946. He immediately asked to dinner Mack Swigert, a lawyer in the Cincinnati law firm of Taft, Stettinius and Hollister. Senator Taft told him, "I'm under a lot of pressure to repeal the Wagner Act. People are steamed up. What do you think about that?" Repealing the Wagner Act would have been difficult if not impossible politically. Swigert suggested that rather than push to repeal the Wagner Act, a number of amendments could substantially change the act, including giving workers the right to stay out of unions (closed shops) and giving the federal government the ability to end strikes that threaten national security. Several days later Swigert gave Senator Taft three pages of amendments to the Wagner Act— which became the heart of the Taft-Hartley Act of 1947, an amendment to the Wagner Act that dramatically halted the rise of organized labor in the United States and remains the anchor of U.S. labor law.

The year before Taft-Hartley, 1946, 4.6 million union workers staged over 5,000 strikes, often shutting down entire industries. The first year under Taft-Hartley the number of strikes dropped by more than one-third, and the decline continued until, by the year 1998, the number of U.S. strikes was only 25, or less than 1 percent of the record 5,000 in 1946.

Swigert, in a 2000 interview, stated that he is proud of the Taft-Hartley Act that he helped to conceive and believes the reforms it brought were critical to the prosperity enjoyed in the United States today. Without it, he noted, millions of man-hours lost to strikes and other work stoppages would have severely limited U.S. productivity. Before Taft-Hartley, unions could strike, and owners were at their mercy because they were compelled by the Wagner Act to deal with the union and in many cases, because of closed shops, hire only union workers. Taft-Hartley achieved a greater balance between the power of unions and the power of management.

SOURCE: Adapted from Cliff Peale, "Local Lawyers Had Role in Labor Law," *Cincinnati Enquirer,* September 4, 2000, Al, p. A6.

recognized and gave preference to state right-to-work laws over bargained-for provisions in collective bargaining agreements that required union membership as a condition of employment. Figure 1-3 outlines the major provisions of the Taft-Hartley Amendments.

Organized labor immediately began to work for the repeal of Taft-Hartley. Labor had, by opposing any change to the Wagner Act, shut itself out of congressional decision making and demanded that Taft-Hartley be repealed before even discussing possible changes in the Wagner Act. This all-or-nothing approach backfired, and Taft-Hartley was left unchanged. Labor legislation did not receive national attention again until 1957.

Certainly one response of the labor community to the passage of the Taft-Hartley Amendments was a reemergence of the "in union there is strength" approach to organized labor. The AFL-CIO merger in 1955 ended a 20-year separation of the two dominant national labor organizations and enabled the united group to claim a total membership of 16.1 million workers: 10.9 million members from 108 AFL unions and 5.2 million members from 30 CIO unions.

Besides fear of antiunion sentiment represented by the Taft-Hartley Amendments, the merger was prompted by a desire to end union raiding, in which one union pirated members from another. A change in leadership in both, as well as internal housecleaning by the CIO to rid itself of 11 communist front unions and by the AFL to expel the

---

Findings and Policy
- Certain practices of labor organizations, such as secondary strikes, burden and obstruct the free flow of commerce
- Elimination of such practices is necessary to guarantee rights of act

Rights of Employees
- To refrain from any and all union activities except union shop provision (which a majority must approve) in valid collective bargaining agreements
- Closed shops requiring workers to join unions before being hired became unlawful

Union Unfair Labor Practices
- Restraint or coercion of employees in exercise of their rights
- Refusal to bargain in good faith with employer
- Discrimination against employee for not engaging in union activities
- Unions can be sued for breach of contract

Restrictions on Strike Activities
- No secondary strikes and boycotts
- Prohibits strikes conducted by one labor union to dislodge another labor union
- Outlaws strikes to force employers to make work for union members
- Prohibits strikes during the term of a valid collective bargaining agreement unless employees give 60 days notice to employer and 30 days notice to the Federal Mediation and Conciliation Service (FMCS)
- Provided 80-day injunction for strikes that threaten national security

Right-to-Work Laws
- Give states the right to outlaw union shop requirements in collective bargaining agreements so employees can refrain from joining the union representing them at the bargaining table

---

FIGURE 1-3 Major Provisions Of The Taft-Hartley Amendments

racket-ridden International Longshoremen's Union, created the mutual respect necessary to overcome past differences.

The Labor-Management Reporting and Disclosure Act of 1959

The internal affairs of unions from the early 1800s until 1959 were not the subject of any federal law. Thus legal disputes were settled inconsistently through the application of common law and state court interpretation of union constitution. The 1959 Labor-Management Reporting and Disclosure Act abruptly changed that situation. It was the first federal law passed with the objective of regulating the conduct of internal union affairs. At first the Act covered only private-sector employees, but a 1978 amendment included public employees. The major provisions of the Act include

- Member freedom of speech
- Member right to participate in union activities
- Mandatory secret-ballot election of officers
- Limits on the use of union funds[57]

The famed McClellan hearings in 1957 set the stage for the second major change to the national labor policy since the Wagner Act. Initiated to investigate wrongdoings in the labor-management field, the Senate committee soon unearthed corruption in some major unions. Charges of racketeering centered on threats that strikes would be called against employers and on incidents in which union officials sold out the interests of union members for cash.[58] The public outcry for labor legislation to protect the internal operations of unions was noticed by political leaders, and congressional bills offering sweeping reforms were introduced. Labor supported reforms as long as amendments to Taft-Hartley were included. Management also supported them as long as their amendments to Taft-Hartley were included. The mood created by the McClellan hearings was in management's favor, and the **Labor-Management Reporting and Disclosure Act of 1959** (known as the **Landrum-Griffin Act**) was passed.[59]

The Landrum-Griffin Act provisions amending the Wagner and Taft-Hartley Acts further eroded the power of labor unions by limiting such economic activities as boycotts and picketing. In regulating the internal operation of labor unions, the Landrum-Griffin Act introduced controls on internal handling of union funds. It established safeguards for union elections and in certain cases gave members the right to bring suit against the union. Under the act, unions were required to have a constitution and bylaws and to file these and other disclosure documents with the secretary of labor. It also established due process rules for disciplining members. For example, in 1995 a union member was expelled from his union after working to remove his union and put another in its place. After he was expelled from the union, he stopped paying dues. The union notified him that under the collective bargaining agreement, they would have him terminated for failure to pay dues. He appealed, and the NLRB upheld the union.[60]

The Landrum-Griffin Act protects the democratic nature of unions. The act ensures full and active participation by the rank and file in the affairs of the union. It accords protection of union members' rights to participate in the election process. It requires high standards of responsibility and ethical conduct by union officials and protects members from the arbitrary and capricious whims of union leaders. The first major case involving the rights of union members in an election was in *Wirtz v. Local 6*. The issue in that case was whether a union could require a member to have been elected to a lesser office within the union before standing for a higher office. The U.S. Supreme Court found that to be an unreasonable requirement and thus a violation of the Landrum-Griffin Act.[61]

The Bill of Rights of Members of Labor Organizations established the machinery necessary to enforce this act. The rights under this Title I section include the right to nominate candidates and to vote in union elections, to attend membership meetings, and to participate in the deliberation of those meetings. Freedom to speak about union affairs and to assemble with union members was also reaffirmed. Title I protects union members from excessive charges because dues, fees, and assessments are decided by a majority vote of the membership. Members are given the right to sue the union and are ensured due process protections in the union's disciplinary actions.

Under subsequent titles of the Landrum-Griffin Act, union members gained access to union financial reports, local unions received protection from their national organization in the assertion of trustee rights, the fair and democratic conduct of union elections was ensured, and the fiduciary duty of union officials to their members was clearly outlined. With passage of the Landrum-Griffin Act the legislation that established the national labor policy—a policy characterized by strong support of collective bargaining as a means of ending industrial strife—was in place. Successive chapters will discuss how that bargaining process is to be carried out under the provisions of the act. See Figure 1-1 for highlights of events in the modern era of unionization.

PUBLIC-SECTOR COLLECTIVE BARGAINING

The National Labor Relations Act established a national labor policy recognizing the need for collective bargaining as a way to eliminate and mitigate industrial strife. The act established equality of bargaining power between employers and employees and gave employees substantive rights to organize into labor unions, presenting themselves to the employer for recognition. Employers were required to meet with their employees at the bargaining table to discuss the terms and conditions of the job. The right to strike was given government protection and served as an economic equalizer for the employee.

Public employees, however, were not guaranteed rights under the National Labor Relations Act. The development of labor relations in the public sector has followed a completely different route. How the rules, the parties, and the interests differ from those in the private sector and how disputes are resolved will be explored throughout the text.

The unionization of public employees has borne witness to a basic change in the character of the American labor movement. For instance, in 1953, public employees constituted only 6 percent of union membership. Then in 1968 the Memphis Sanitation Strike ignited a burst of public-sector union organizing efforts at all levels of government. The Memphis strike was staged by African American garbage men who refused to work until they were paid—minimum wage! Their success gave momentum to the public-sector union movement.[62] By 2002, approximately 44 percent of union members were public employees, and in 2005, with 7.4 million union members working in all levels of government, 40 percent of the public workforce is unionized.[63]

Evolution of Public-Sector Labor Relations

Congress excluded federal, state, and local government employees from the provisions of the National Labor Relations Act until the Postal Reorganization Act of 1970 allowed postal workers to come under the National Labor Relations Act's provisions.[64] In the traditional sense, Congress viewed government not as an employer but as a representative of the people, supplying certain necessary services. Therefore, people employed by the government were not employees but public servants, and they were protected from the arbitrary actions of private employers by already existing systems. Such systems addressed basic employee concerns—wages, benefits, and job security—even as the sovereignty of the government was maintained.

Such was not always the case. In the early 1800s, citizens were scandalized by the use of party patronage in federal, state, and local governments. This **spoils system** caused a turnover of government workers on the basis of their political affiliation, not on their ability or dedication. Government workers were expected to support political candidates with time and money or fear losing their jobs. The government lost continuity and efficiency because of the repeated replacement of trained employees.

In 1871, the first Civil Service Commission was established to propose reforms in the national government. Congress, however, failed to make an appropriation for the commission, and it disbanded. In 1883, an outgoing Republican Congress passed the **Pendleton Act**, which provided for a bipartisan three-member Civil Service Commission to draw up and administer competitive examinations to determine the fitness of appointees to federal office. The act protected federal employees from being fired for failure to make political contributions and actually forbade political campaign contributions by certain employees. The Pendleton Act affected only about 10 percent of the federal employees at the time, but it enabled the president to broaden the merit system and was the foundation of the present federal civil service system.

Many states followed the federal government's lead and instituted civil service merit systems for their employees. Thus, the civil service system provided job security for government workers. Rules governing hiring, firing, and discipline protected the worker from arbitrary actions. Due process hearings gave workers a forum to protest an employer's actions.

The Pendleton Act also gave Congress the right to regulate wages, hours, and working conditions of public employees. These employees began to lobby Congress for wage increases and improved benefits. In the early 1900s, Presidents Theodore Roosevelt and William Howard Taft issued restrictive executive orders aimed at preventing such lobbying. But in 1912, Congress enacted the Lloyd-LaFollette Act allowing unaffiliated organizations to present their grievances to Congress without fear of retaliation.[65] In the public sector, organizations of government employees, such as the National Federation of Employees formed in 1917 and the American Federation of Government Employees formed in 1932, concentrated on lobbying to obtain legislation favorable to their members. For most government workers, such lobbying proved to be successful. Although income was modest, fringe benefits such as vacations, paid holidays, paid sick leave, and pensions offered the public employee rewards not found in the private sector.

Before the National Labor Relations Act was passed, public employees, represented by employee associations and organizations, could boast of an indirect participation in decisions affecting their employment. Unlike their counterparts in the private sector, their employer also could be reached in the legislatures and at the ballot box. However, the growth of public employment at every level soon began to erode that accessibility.

The Rise of Public-Sector Unions

During the 1930s and 1940s, private-sector unionization flourished under the protection of the National Labor Relations Act. These unions sought job security, higher wages, improved benefits, grievance procedures, arbitration rights, and more important, recognition as participants in the decision-making process. Because many public employees already had these conditions, unionization held no attraction for them. The successes of private unions, however, began to surpass the public employees' ability to lobby, and changes in their job classifications and numbers gave an impetus to public-sector unionization.

In the private sector, wages and benefits improved year after year, and job security was increased through the establishment of grievance and arbitration procedures in collective bargaining agreements. The organized worker also became cognizant of the respect a union could demand from an employer. Because strikes were protected under the act, the employer did not hold all the bargaining strength.

Public employees discovered that lobbying efforts alone could not provide them with the controls and benefits of collective bargaining. Their swelling ranks made the lobbying process increasingly cumbersome and contributed to the rise of public-sector unionism.[66] The organizational size and complexity of government contributed to mismanagement and job dissatisfaction. It became increasingly difficult for employees to influence legislative action because the numerous layers of bureaucracy freed politicians from responsibility. In addition, the **civil service systems**, developed to protect public employees, were perceived as employer-recruited, employer-directed personnel mechanisms. As one expert observed, "It is the labor-management inadequacy of the civil service system that has been a prime cause of the remarkable thrust of union organization among public employees in recent years."[67] The 1939 **Hatch Act** also limited the political activities of most public workers (see Profile 1-6).

HATCH ACT (1993 AMENDMENT)

In 1993, President Bill Clinton signed a bill amending the Hatch Act and removing restrictions on federal workers' partisan political activity that had been in place for over 50 years. The Hatch Act was passed in 1939 after politicians used their control over Works Progress Administration (WPA) programs to influence elections. Workers were solicited for contributions and were pressured to change their party registration and to work for the election of candidates selected by the WPA politicians. In an effort to clean up the WPA, the Hatch Act was proposed. The act placed prohibitions on the federal employees, limiting their rights to take an active part in partisan elections rather than placing any strictures on those who solicited the employees. The act passed and was signed into law by President Franklin Roosevelt. Almost immediately it was amended to include state and local government employees working under federal contracts and was put under the U.S. Civil Service Commission for enforcement.

Labor unions seeking to organize federal employees in the 1950s found the Hatch Act to be a deterrent. The threat, or perceived threat, of being accused of violating the Hatch Act because of union organizing activities became a major issue. One union, the United Federal Workers of America, decided to challenge the law. Arguing the case two times to a divided Supreme Court, the union contended that the Hatch Act went too far. The act's infringement on the First Amendment rights of federal employees was not necessary in order to guard against corruption. The Court disagreed and upheld the act as a reasonable restriction on activity necessary to ensure orderly management of the federal government free of political partisanship.

After years of seeking amendment, federal employees can now engage in a wider range of political activities off duty, including managing political campaigns. In addition, federal-sector union members may solicit other union members for contributions to union-based PAC funds. However, federal employees are still barred from running for office and from soliciting for other types of political contributions.

SOURCE: Adapted from Gilbert Gall, "The CIO and the Hatch Act," *Labor's Heritage* 7, no. 1 (Summer 1995), pp. 4–21; "Federal Service Labor and Employment Law," *Labor Lawyer* 10, no. 3 (Summer 1994), p. 373.

The Sovereignty Doctrine

As discussed earlier, the key to employers' resistance to collective bargaining in the private sector was the desire to protect their private property rights. The National Labor Relations Act tried to balance the employer's private property rights against the employee's right to organize and to bargain collectively. Although the purpose of the act was to place employees in an equal bargaining position, employers still held all rights not taken from them at the bargaining table.

In the public sector, governments were able to resist collective bargaining because of the **sovereignty doctrine**. Sovereignty is defined as "the supreme, absolute, and uncontrollable power by which an independent state is governed."[68] In a democracy, the source of that supreme power is the people who have vested their government with rights and responsibilities as caretakers of that power. The sovereignty doctrine requires that the government exercise its power unfettered by any force other than the people— all the people. Collective bargaining was seen as a threat to that sovereignty doctrine if government were to share decision-making authority with employees. Obviously, decisions made at the collective bargaining table would affect the way government provides services and the amount those services would cost the taxpayer. But the sovereignty

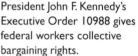

President John F. Kennedy's
Executive Order 10988 gives
federal workers collective
bargaining rights.

doctrine had numerous weak points. Government contracts extensively with members of the private sector, and negotiation of those contracts takes place bilaterally. This practice disputes the claim that government must make its decisions unilaterally. Government's voluntary recognition of the employee's right to bargain collectively with it has also weakened the sovereignty doctrine. And the sovereignty doctrine can no longer be used to support the theory that government—the ruler—can do no wrong when numerous court decisions have ruled against the sovereign. The Supreme Court has allowed citizens to claim civil rights, torts, and contract violations against state and local governments, subjecting such institutions to monetary damages and remedial actions. In some states, federal judges have taken over the responsibility for administering the prison system until court-mandated improvements are made.

Laws for Public-Sector Collective Bargaining

Executive Orders

In January 1962, the President's Task Force on Employee-Management Relations reported that one-third of the federal employees belonged to labor organizations. It recommended that the government officially acknowledge this fact and respond affirmatively to employees' desire for collective bargaining. President John F. Kennedy signed **Executive Order (E.O.) 10988**, which recognized the rights of federal employees to join or to refrain from joining labor organizations, granted recognition to those labor organizations, and detailed bargaining subjects. Although this executive order can be cited as having established the framework for labor-management relations in the federal government, comparison to its private-sector counterpart, the National Labor Relations Act, showed glaring deficiencies.

What is important about Kennedy's original order of 1962 is the lightning effect it had on organizing drives among federal, state, and municipal employees. The order served as a signal to organize public workers as much as the Wagner Act of 1935 had stimulated the growth of industrial union membership in the CIO and AFL. The effect of E.O. 10988 was to send public-sector union membership rolls soaring. Before 1962, only 26 union or association units in the executive branch of the federal government had union shops, and they represented only 19,000 workers. Six years after the Kennedy order, there were 2,305 bargaining units, with a total membership of 1.4 million employees. A number of unions represented federal workers, the largest being the American Federation of Government Employees (AFGE). From 1962–1972, the AFGE grew from 84,000 members to 621,000. The Postal Workers and the Letter Carriers also experienced growth in that period. For state and local public employees, the 1962 Kennedy order also spawned growth in unionization, although the order did not apply to them directly. The fact that union membership grew, however, did not mean that all state or local governments recognized or bargained with unions.[69]

As in the National Labor Relations Act, the right to organize was granted to federal civilian employees under E.O. 10988. However, the head of an agency could determine that a bureau or office was primarily performing intelligence, investigative, or security functions, and the employees of that bureau or office could be excluded from the executive order for national security reasons.

Under the National Labor Relations Act, a labor organization receiving a majority vote of the members of the bargaining unit gains exclusive recognition. Under E.O. 10988, exclusive recognition could be gained in the same manner, but two other types of recognition were also proffered. The first type granted formal recognition if there was no exclusive representative for the bargaining unit and the organization had at least 10 percent of the employees in the unit. Such an organization would represent only its members. A second type consisted of informal recognition of an employee organization that did not meet the majority vote or 10 percent of membership qualifications. This system generated much confusion because an agency might have to deal with two unions representing the same class of employees. For example, 10 percent of the service personnel could gain formal recognition, whereas a different 8 percent could claim informal recognition. The agency would be negotiating with two unions consisting of 18 percent of one class of employee.

In the private sector, bargaining subjects protected by the act included wages, hours, and conditions of employment. Under E.O. 10988, bargaining subjects were limited. The employees could not mandate negotiations on economic issues. A management rights clause reserved the government's power to direct and discipline employees. And the grievance procedure could not result in binding arbitration.

Another deficiency in E.O. 10988 was the lack of a central authority to determine bargaining unit recognition and to resolve disputes. Many decisions were left to agency heads who were the immediate employers of the labor organization's members. The most significant difference between the National Labor Relations Act and E.O. 10988 was the right to engage in work stoppages. Strikes were specifically denied the public labor organizations.

The Civil Service Reform Act of 1978

Currently, Title VII of the **Civil Service Reform Act of 1978** and Reorganization Plan No. 2 of 1978 govern federal employee labor relations. Title VII, known as the Federal Labor Relations Act, is modeled after the National Labor Relations Act. Central authority was placed in a three-member panel, the Federal Labor Relations Authority. This panel oversees labor-management relations within the federal government; its three members are appointed by the president of the United States. The president also appoints a general counsel empowered to investigate alleged unfair labor practices and to file and prosecute complaints.

The Federal Labor Relations Authority oversees creation of bargaining units, conducts elections, decides representation cases, determines unfair labor practices, and seeks enforcement of its decisions in the federal courts. The Federal Service Impasse Panel was continued by the act and provides assistance in resolving negotiation impasses. The unfair labor practice provision of Title VII generally mirrors the unfair labor practice provision in legislation for private employers and employees. The government is prohibited from the following practices:

1. Restraint and coercion of employees in the exercise of their organizational rights
2. Encouragement or discouragement of union membership
3. Sponsorship of labor organizations
4. Refusal to bargain in good faith with a recognized organization
5. Refusal to cooperate in impasse procedures
6. Discipline of a union member who files a complaint
7. Enforcement of a new regulation that conflicts with an existent collective bargaining agreement

A labor organization is prohibited from these actions:

1. Interference with an employee's right to organize or to refrain from organizing
2. Discrimination against or causing the employer to discriminate against employees because of union activity
3. Refusal to cooperate in impasse procedures
4. Refusal to bargain in good faith
5. Calling for or engaging in a work stoppage or slowdown

Unlike private-sector labor laws, Title VII mandates inclusion of a grievance procedure with binding arbitration as a final step in all federal collective bargaining agreements:

(B) Any negotiated grievance procedure referred to in subsection (A) of this section shall

1. Be fair and simple
2. Provide for expeditious processing
3. Include procedures that
   a. Assure an exclusive representative the right, in its own behalf or on behalf of any employee in the unit represented by the exclusive representative, to present and process grievances
   b. Assure such an employee the right to present a grievance on the employee's own behalf, and assure the exclusive representative the right to be present during the grievance proceeding

1871	The first Civil Service Commission was established to prohibit public employees from losing their jobs with every change of administration.
1883	The Pendleton Act was passed protecting about 10 percent of federal employees from being fired for failure to make political contributions and forbade political activities by certain employees.
1912	Lloyd-LaFollette Act was passed; it allowed public employees to lobby Congress for better wages and working conditions.
1932	The American Federation of Government Employees, one of the first public-sector unions, was formed to lobby for legislation favorable to their members.
1939	The Hatch Act was passed limiting the political activities of most federal workers.
1962	Executive Order 10988 was signed by President John F. Kennedy. The order recognized the rights of federal employees to join unions and granted recognition to those unions and allowed limited bargaining rights.
1970	The Postal Reorganization Act was passed allowing postal workers to come under the National Labor Relations Act.
1978	The Civil Service Reform Act replaced previous executive orders concerning federal employee bargaining rights. Title VII of that act established the Federal Labor Relations Authority and modeled bargaining rights in the federal government after the NLRA.
1993	The Hatch Act was amended to lift some of the restrictions against political activities of public employees.
1993	Executive Order 12871 was enacted by President Bill Clinton as part of the reengineering of government programs, creating a National Partnership Council to change the way management and unions relate in the public sector.
2001	Executive Order 13203 was signed by President George W. Bush and effectively repealed President Clinton's 1993 E.O. 12871.

FIGURE 1-4 Public-Sector Collective Bargaining

    c. Provide that any grievance not satisfactorily settled under the negotiated grievance procedure shall be subject to binding arbitration, which may be invoked by either the exclusive representative or the agency[70]

Title VII codifies presidential policies toward federal labor-management relations and improves the opportunities for the growth of collective bargaining in the public sector. Major events in the development of public sector labor relations are noted in Figure 1-4.

National Partnership Council, 1993

In 1993, President Bill Clinton enacted Executive Order 12871 as part of the reengineering of government programs. It was hailed as a significant and fundamental change in federal-sector labor-management relations. The goal was to change the relationship and alter the process by which the managers and unions reached decisions. A team of federal managers and union representatives worked on the plan. It created a National Partnership Council (NPC) to advise the president on labor-management issues. The NPC is made up of union leaders, representatives from the Federal Labor Relations Board, the Federal Mediation and Conciliation Service, and executive branch directors.

The order directed each agency to establish labor-management partnerships at appropriate levels to change the way government operates.[71] The 1993 NPC allowed federal unions to organize new bargaining units and increase membership, as well as designing and implementing methods of increasing productivity. In 2001, however, President George W. Bush issued Executive Order 13203, which abolished the labor-management partnerships. The Bush order ended a period of federal union growth (61 percent) of all federal workers and 80 percent of all federal employees eligible for union representation. This change came at a critical time for federal unions—when over half of their membership will retire before 2010, and thus they must appeal to younger workers, 70 percent of whom work in "knowledge" positions that have not been an easy target for unions in general.[72]

State and Local Government Laws

Title VII does not cover state and local employees, who must look to state and local laws for their collective bargaining rights. More than two-thirds of the states have enacted legislation granting public-sector collective bargaining rights to some groups, such as teachers, police, and firefighters. Local, county, and municipal governments may also adopt collective bargaining laws or, by practice, recognize and bargain with employee organizations.

Although state and local laws differ as to particulars, some patterns do emerge. Legislation is more favorable to collective bargaining in the northern, northeastern, midwestern, and far western parts of the United States. The Sunbelt states located along the lower Atlantic coast, the Southeast, the Southwest, and the southwestern Rocky Mountain states generally do not have comprehensive public-sector labor laws.

State legislation usually includes bargaining over wages, hours, terms of employment, and working conditions. Unfair labor practices and limits on or prohibitions of the right to strike also are legislated. The bargaining obligation is enforced by an administrative agency, and procedures are established should there be an impasse.[73]

A developing campaign to include state and municipal employees under federal legislation was substantially undermined by the Supreme Court decision in *National League of Cities v. Usery*.[74] That case reconfirmed the specific state's sovereignty over its own employees and denied that the commerce power of the federal government could be invoked to regulate that relationship. A recent study of the growth of teacher bargaining concluded that, although teacher bargaining in large cities typically starts before collective bargaining laws are passed, the passage of the laws spurs subsequent union growth.[75]

SUMMARY

The labor union movement in the United States is the history of individuals struggling to survive. As the country grew and developed, the needs of owners and workers intertwined, and the struggle for control caused both strife and cooperation. During that struggle, the labor movement faced hostile court decisions, economic depressions, and internal power struggles. Labor unions had to decide whether to follow a social, political, or economic agenda. The emergence of the AFL and the CIO, with collective bargaining as their most important goal, meant that labor unions picked an economic agenda.

In 1935, Congress articulated the foundation of today's national labor policy with the passage of the Wagner Act (National Labor Relations Act [NLRA]). That act was the culmination of more than 100 years of organized labor's efforts to recognize the employees' rights in the workplace. The disruptive nature of work stoppages caused political leaders to seek a national solution to labor's problems. Under the NLRA, employees were free to organize and bargain collectively and were given the right to strike, and employers were required to bargain with employee representatives. The Great Depression and the New Deal set the stage for Congress to pass legislation that not only protected organized labor but also promoted its growth. Although the Taft-Hartley Amendments and the Landrum-Griffin Act modified the NLRA, its basic support of collective bargaining was not changed.

Widespread unionization in the public sector developed later than in the private sector. Presently, public-sector unionization is still somewhat limited because of the sovereignty doctrine curtailing the scope of collective bargaining in the public sector. Under Executive Order 10988, as updated under the Civil Service Reform Act of 1978, federal employees are granted limited collective bargaining rights, whereas public employees in state and local governments must look to individual state and local legislation for those same rights.

CASE STUDIES

Case Study 1-1 Interfering with the Employee's Right to Unionize

The employer sells automotive replacement parts at wholesale from warehouses and distribution centers in the eastern United States. Ms. Fortin began work at the company's Miami warehouse in 1986, and from that time until her layoff in October 1994, she held a number of customer service positions. Because of her excellent reputation for providing service to customers, she was assigned to staff the Metro-Dade account, a separate account established to provide exclusive service to approximately 24 governmental customers in the metropolitan Dade County area. In 1994, Fortin had been commended for increasing sales in the Metro-Dade account.

On June 1, 1994, Fortin appeared under subpoena to testify on the union's behalf at a representation hearing concerning the organizational efforts being undertaken at her workplace and was quoted in the *Miami Herald* as saying the workers "want to better ourselves."

When she returned to work later that day, she received her first disciplinary warning ever. The employer issued four additional disciplinary warnings to Fortin during June, three within two days of the hearing. The employer also removed an exclusive telephone number with its voice mail capabilities used by the customers of the Metro-Dade County account to reach Fortin directly and ceased the special van deliveries to those customers. Fortin was held accountable for the ensuing decreased sales in that account. Notwithstanding this discipline, Fortin remained one of the union's most prominent vocal supporters, appearing in a group photo on a union flyer distributed during the campaign, passing out leaflets and petitions, and serving as one of the union's two observers at the election held July 7 and 8, 1994.

In early August 1994, her supervisor gave Fortin a negative performance evaluation in which she received an overall rating of "2," indicating "improvement needed." On October 27, 1994, Fortin was laid off. Her new supervisor relied on the negative performance evaluation in deciding to lay her off.

The union charged the employer with an unfair labor practice for fabricating disciplinary actions and a poor performance evaluation and for unlawfully laying off Fortin because of her union activities.

The employer contended that each of the disciplinary actions it took against Fortin was *unrelated* to her union activity and that in each case Fortin was disciplined for being away from her workstation and in an area of the warehouse where she did not belong. Furthermore, one of the employer's outside salesmen told Fortin's supervisor that customers were complaining of poor service from her. And finally, Fortin's new supervisor based his layoff decision on her poor performance evaluation and was not even aware of her union activity.

The union contended that Fortin had business reasons to visit the warehouse and had done so routinely in the past and that the employer began to restrict her movements only after it learned of her support for the union. Moreover, other employees were not similarly disciplined, even those employees who were talking to Fortin on the very occasion for which she was disciplined. Given this disparity of treatment and the fact that Fortin's movements were not restricted before the employer learned of her union activity, the reasonable inference, according to the union, is that Fortin's union activity was a motivating factor in the employer's discipline of her. As to the poor performance evaluation, the union noted that the evaluation covered a one-year period from August 1993 to August 1994, during which time Fortin was selected for the Metro-Dade account and commended for increasing the Metro-Dade sales. If there was any problem with the Metro-Dade account, as noted above, the employer caused it by removing the special phone line, voice mail service, and special delivery van dedicated to Metro-Dade customers rather than any fault of Fortin. Finally, because the performance evaluation was based on the employer's union animus, basing the layoff on it was unlawful, even if the supervisor knew nothing of her union activities.

SOURCE: Adapted from *Parts Depot Inc. v. NLRB*, 170 LRRM 1005 (September 29, 2000).

QUESTIONS

1. Do you believe Fortin was the victim of antiunion discrimination by her employer? Why or why not?
2. Fortin's supervisor had no knowledge of her union activity but laid her off on the basis of her poor performance evaluation. Give reasons why a court should uphold or override the supervisor's decision.
3. Explain why you think employers still resist unions 70 years after the passage of the National Labor Relations Act.

Case Study 1-2 Discriminating Against Union Members

The company, a nursing home, provides nursing, rehabilitation, and therapy services. The union represents all regularly scheduled nonprofessional employees, including nurse aids, housekeeping employees, laundry employees, dietary employees, medical records clerks, and janitor-maintenance employees. The company employs 80 full-time personnel to operate the facility, of which about 50 are included in the bargaining unit. The company and the union had a long-standing collective bargaining relationship, but the current contract was due to expire on September 10, 1999, and negotiations were not going well.

In the midst of the negotiations, the grievant, a nurse's aide, a longtime employee of the company and *a member of the union negotiating team,* was injured on the job. After a doctor's examination, she was placed on "light duty" and referred to physical therapy. At the time, the company did not have a light-duty policy. However, the company ordered the grievant back to work for assignment to light duty and threatened to fire her if she did not return. Grievant did not report to work for light duty. She claimed that because the contract contained no light-duty provision, the company did not have the authority to unilaterally institute such a policy.

In addition, the company scheduled members of the union negotiating team, including the grievant, for part-time work on days when contract negotiations were to take place. The grievant did not report for work on days when negotiations were to take place because she claimed that under the "past practice" of the company and union, union negotiating team members were not required to work the day of negotiations but rather were allowed to meet to prepare for the actual negotiations session. The grievant

was terminated for failure to report for work as ordered.

The union filed a grievance protesting the discharge as unjust and in violation of the National Labor Relations Act. The union contended that the company's imposition of light duty on the grievant and the scheduling of members of the negotiating committee to work on the day of negotiations were unfair labor practices.

According to the union, historically members of the negotiating committee have been scheduled off—unpaid—on the days of contract negotiations, thereby establishing a "past practice" the company had to honor. The union asserts that members of the negotiating committee were improperly scheduled to work on November 1 and November 2, and when they rightfully attended to union business as they had always done in preparation for bargaining sessions, they were severely disciplined for not reporting to work as directed. As noted by the union, had the negotiating team members worked those days, it would have interfered with their duties as members of the negotiating committee. Furthermore, the company did not have the right to unilaterally institute a light-duty policy and impose it on a union negotiating team member. Such a policy affected the terms and conditions of the employees' work and is therefore a mandatory subject for bargaining.

The company argues *economic privilege* in the preceding instances of unilateral action. According to the company, the purpose of the change in the scheduling and attendance policy was to require people to come to work to make certain that adequate staffing was maintained. The purpose of requiring union officials to work part-time on days of union negotiations, although perhaps previously unnecessary, was to fill the work schedule, not adversely affect union negotiators, and the purpose of the light-duty work assignments was to save money by having medically restricted employees on the job. The policy was not instituted for or directed at the members of the negotiating team. Thus, the company has not violated the NLRA

SOURCE: Adapted from *HCM, Inc. v. United Food and Commercial Workers Union, Local 1529,* 116 LA 1200 (January 8, 2002).

QUESTIONS

1. Active union members often have two jobs to do—as an employee and as a union member. How far do you think an employer should be required to go to allow the member to do both jobs?
2. The nonprofessional jobs at a nursing home are often hard to fill, and there can be a lot of employee turnover. Do you think having a union at a nursing home helps or hinders in the employment and retention of employees?
3. Do you think the company has evidenced an antiunion attitude by instituting in close proximity a light-duty policy that directly impacts one of the union negotiators and by requiring the union negotiating team to work part time on negotiating days?

KEY TERMS AND CONCEPTS

- American Federation of Labor
- American Railway Union
- Bull Pen
- Civil Service Reform Act of 1978
- civil service systems
- Clayton Act
- Coeur d'Alene incident
- company unions
- Congress of Industrial Organizations
- Cordwainers conspiracy cases
- Executive Order (E.O.) 10988
- Hatch Act
- Haymarket Square Riot
- Homestead, Pennsylvania
- Knights of Labor
- labor injunctions
- Labor-Management Reporting and Disclosure Act of 1959
- Landrum-Griffin Act
- Ludlow, Colorado
- Molly Maguires
- National Labor Relations Act
- National Labor Relations Board
- National Labor Union
- National War Labor Board
- Norris–La Guardia Act
- Pendleton Act
- Pinkerton Agency
- Pullman strike
- scabs
- sovereignty doctrine
- spoils system
- Taft-Hartley Amendments
- trade unionists
- Wagner Act
- Wobblies
- Women's Trade Union League

REVIEW QUESTIONS

1. What factors in the 1800s contributed to the growth of the American labor agreements?
2. Did the Great Depression have any impact on the U.S. labor movement? If so, what?
3. Why is Fannie Sellins called "Labor's Martyr"?
4. Describe the federal and court actions against union workers in the 1800s.
5. Why did the Wagner Act have a major impact on employees' rights?
6. What is the general role of the NLRB? How and when was the NLRB created?
7. What circumstances prompted Congress to pass the Taft-Hartley Amendments? The Landrum-Griffin Act? What are the key provisions of these acts?
8. How are public employees provided the right of collective bargaining? Do state and local government employees have the same rights as federal employees?
9. Why did the federal government resist collective bargaining?
10. How do public employees' rights generally differ from those of private-sector employees?

YOU BE THE ARBITRATOR
Should an Employee's File Be Expunged?

ARTICLE XV
DISCIPLINE/DISCHARGE PROCEDURES

The Employer shall not discipline or discharge any Employee without just cause.

The following procedure of progressive discipline shall be applied by the Employer, except the Employer need not follow progressive discipline before suspension or discharge if the suspension or discharge is for theft, deliberate damage to Company property, gross insubordination, physical violence or other similar offenses.

The Employer may issue an oral warning(s) prior to written warnings or suspensions, which shall be imposed for related offenses as follows:

> First Offense: Written warning(s)
>
> Second Offense: One (1) day suspension without pay
>
> Third Offense: Suspension of up to three (3) days without pay
>
> Fourth Offense: Further suspension or discharge

Warnings and one-day suspensions as herein provided shall be null and void after six (6) months and shall not be used as a basis for further disciplinary action. Suspensions of more than one day as herein provided shall be null and void after nine (9) months and shall not be used as a basis for further disciplinary action.

These procedures herein provided are subject to the terms of the grievance procedure.

Facts

An Alternative Calendar Committee (ACC) of the employer's college met to discuss a proposal to shorten the calendar at the college from 17½ to 16-week semesters. Professor L testified that the proposal to shorten the calendar had been discussed at an Academic Senate meeting and that he had been appointed chair of the ACC. The grievant, Professor W, was president of the Faculty Association at that time. Although he was not a member of the ACC, the meeting was open. The proposal to shorten the academic calendar was considered controversial by the faculty. During the meeting, there was a discussion of whether the ACC or the Faculty Association should survey the faculty on the issue. There was a considerable amount of discussion regarding this issue. At the end of the meeting the other faculty members had moved to the other end of the room.

There is general agreement that L and W stayed at the back of the room and engaged in a heated discussion. W said that L was trying to circumvent the contract by having ACC survey the faculty rather than the Faculty Association. L retorted that the contract the Faculty Association had negotiated was lousy. L admitted stating at the meeting that W "was acting like a jerk" and that he had criticized the contract W had negotiated. At the end of the discussion they grabbed their things and walked to the end of the room to join the other faculty members. According to witnesses, during the heated discussion L and W were loud but not shouting. No one witnessed W using inappropriate language nor was he observed making any threatening gestures. No one witnessed W shove a chair into L. However, according to L, W had shoved a chair into him.

L reported the incident, and W was sent a warning memorandum regarding the incident that stated:

> An incident was reported and investigated that occurred on Tuesday, August 28, 2001, at the end of an Alternative Calendar Committee meeting in the Staff Lounge. Apparently, your behavior towards L was physically menacing, as you were shouting inches away from his face while continually pushing a chair against L. Both Security personnel and my office took statements from those present at the meeting.
>
> W, this memorandum is intended as a warning. The College is concerned about the safety of its employees. Another incident of this kind of behavior may warrant disciplinary action. You are to conduct yourself in a professional and respectful manner, even though you may not agree with others.
>
> This memorandum will be placed in your personnel file. I trust you will see that any form of physical intimidation is not to be tolerated on campus.

W grieved the warning memorandum, and a meeting was held. At the end of the meeting the supervisor issued the following grievance memorandum:

> At the grievance meeting held Monday, October 22, 2001, there was agreement that an altercation occurred in which you and L exchanged statements related to the proposed alternative calendar. There was not agreement that you pushed a chair into the legs of L.
>
> You insist you did not push a chair. Upon further discussions with L, he insists that you did push a chair into his legs. The incident could have resulted in an injury. Since there is no corroboration that a chair was pushed into L's legs, it would be inappropriate for disciplinary action to be taken. However, a memorandum of warning to you is appropriate and appropriately included in your personnel file. Placing the memorandum of warning in your personnel file does not violate the contract agreement in any way.
>
> If there are no subsequent altercations or incidents of a similar nature the memorandum of warning will be removed from your personnel file on June 30, 2003.

In light of the finding at the grievance meeting, W appealed the decision to leave the warning memorandum in his personnel file.

Issue

Should a warning memorandum in an employee's file that contains false and/or erroneous information as to facts or conclusions be expunged?

Position of the Parties

The grievant's position is that the warning memorandum should be removed from his file immediately. If the warning memorandum is read together with the grievance memorandum, it is clear that the warning memorandum is defective, as the grievance memorandum states that there was no corroboration that a chair was pushed against L. Grievant contends that the warning memorandum cannot be minimized as "a mere warning." In progressive discipline, disciplinary action progresses from verbal or written warnings to more serious discipline such as suspension and, ultimately, discharge. The purpose is to put an employee on notice that if the behavior continues, more serious discipline may follow. The contemplation of further disciplinary action is set forth in the warning memorandum, in which it is stated that the warning will remain in the grievant's personnel file until June 30, 2003, and will then be removed if, and only if, "there are no subsequent altercations or incidents of a similar nature." As there was no "incident" as alleged by L in the first place, the grievant should not be left on an initial stage of a disciplinary action by having the memorandum left in his file.

The college's position is that the warning memorandum and the grievance memorandum read together create an accurate report of the incident. Even though the "shoving" was not proven, there was significant evidence that the grievant and L engaged in a verbal altercation. The college does not agree that leaving the information in the grievant's file is an inappropriate disciplinary action under the CBA.

SOURCE: Adapted from *Citrus College Community Dist.*, 117 LA 26 (Arb. 2002).

QUESTIONS

1. As arbitrator, what would be your award and opinion in this arbitration?
2. Explain why the relevant provisions of the CBA as applied to the facts of this case dictate the award.
3. What actions might the employer and/or the union have taken to avoid this conflict?

Exercise

Sources of Labor Relations Information

PURPOSE:

For the student to gain practice in the library research of labor relations topics.

TASK:

Choose a labor relations topic of interest to you (or you may be assigned one by your instructor) from the following list. After choosing a topic, complete the following steps:

1. Find at least six recent references (or more, depending on your instructor's wishes) that pertain to your topic. Do not use a reference (e.g., *Monthly Labor Review*) more than once.
2. For each reference, indicate the title of the book, journal, and so on; the title of the journal article (if applicable); the author's name; and the publisher and the publication date. In addition, indicate how you located each reference (e.g., *Business Periodicals Index*).
3. Write a one-paragraph abstract for each source. (If your source is a book, review at least one important chapter and write the abstract for that chapter.)

TOPICS:

AFL-CIO	Permanent replacement workers
Airline industry/unions	Plant closing
Boycotts	Professional sports unions
Change to Win Coalition	Profit-sharing plans
Cost-of-living adjustments (COLAs)	Public-sector unions
Craft unions/industrial unions	Recent strikes
Drug testing	Right-to-work states
Duty of fair representation	Rolling strike
Grievance arbitration	Salting
Health-care issues	Seniority systems
Job security issues	Sick leave provisions
Just cause	Subcontracting
Mediation	Successorship
NHL 2004-05 season	Termination at will (employment at will)
NLRB certification/decertification elections	Trends in union membership
Outsourcing	Two-tier wage contracts
Pension issues	UPS/Teamster 2002 agreement
	Wages (newly contracted)

CHAPTER 2

Challenges and Opportunities

Wal-Mart, which is non-union, is now the largest U.S. food retailer, and thus presents a major challenge to The Kroger Company & the United Food & Commercial Workers Union.

Labor News

UNIONS FAIL TO ORGANIZE WAL-MART STORES

In 2004 a Wal-Mart store in Quebec, Canada, became the first such store to become unionized. The world's largest retailer, Wal-Mart, had successfully fought other union drives and pays lower wages and benefits than major competitors. Kroger, the second largest food retailer (Wal-Mart is the largest) and the United Food & Commercial Workers union negotiated a new agreement in 2004 that pays its union workers about 30 to 40 percent more in pay and benefits than the nonunionized workers at Wal-Mart receive in compensation.

Union organizational drives started at other Wal-Mart Canadian stores, spurred on by the victory in Quebec. In a key legal battle the workers won a decision by a Canadian Labor Relations board forcing Wal-Mart to turn over internal documents that the union claimed showed a potentially unlawful corporate campaign to stop the union drives. In 2005, Wal-Mart announced its decision to close the Quebec store—the only unionized one out of thousands of stores in North America. In addition, several Wal-Mart employees were fired as news of the "union project" was released. The project apparently was an antiunion campaign and possible violation of the federal Taft-Hartley Act. One of the employees fired was Jared Bowen, an accountant who "blew the whistle" on expense accounts that provided funds for the "union project."

Adapted from: The Associated Press, "Union Efforts Beat Wal-Mart in Court," *The Cincinnati Enquirer* (Nov. 24, 2004), D5; and James Bandler and Ann Zimmerman, "A Wal-Mart Legend's Trail of Deceit," *The Wall Street Journal* (April 8, 2005) A1, 10.

The labor movement in the United States struggles to adapt to changed workplaces and a changing profile of workers. The history of labor unions in the last half of the twentieth century reveals both the challenges they face and the opportunities they have. "One thing is certain: organized labor must change—and soon," according to noted *HR Magazine* editor Robert J. Grossman. Why? Organized labor has been too complacent, as its market share has declined every year for over 30 years. It has a major problem.

And the 2004 organizational efforts by the AFL-CIO were the least productive in its history—and led to the split of the AFL-CIO in 2005, as seven major national unions created CHANGE TO WIN, a new international federation of unions largely dedicated to reversing the loss of market share and number of union members. The International Association of Machinists and Aerospace Workers (IAMAW) lost over 100,000 members in 2004 alone. How can a turnaround be accomplished? Many union members point to political and legislative change. Former NLRB general counsel Fred Feinstein agrees that new legislation is critical to making it easier for unions to organize, but also points out that many members of UNITE believe that internal changes by union leaders are also critical—to stop the complacent attitude.

Another strategy is to follow the example of big business and merge smaller unions into a few large ones to give them more power. Such strategy led to the 2005 merger between the U.S. Steelworkers and the Paper, Allied-Industrial Chemical and Energy Workers International (PACE, International) to form a union with 850,000 members—

the largest industrial union in North America. Now with workers in diverse industries, a strike by one group of workers can be supported by many others who continue working in other industries. But Andy Stern, SEIU president, believes in one national union in each industry—one in health care, one in manufacturing, one in education, and so on to provide higher wages and benefits to all employees—and then the costs get passed along to consumers. A third strategy is to focus on industries that are growing and cannot send jobs offshore—such as health care, education, and custodial services. Yet another strategy is to seek successful cooperation with management. Southwest Airlines, for example, is one of the most profitable carriers and has a history of cooperation with the IAMAW, which provides job security, productivity, and efficiency.[1]

WORKPLACE CHANGES

Union Membership Rise and Fall

It is easy to understand why workers in many manufacturing industries chose to unionize after the passage of the 1935 Wagner Act. At that time many of the manufacturing plants were oppressive places of employment. Each morning men lined up at the gate. If there was no work, they were sent home; if they were hired, it was for that day only. There was no continuous employment. The men never knew when their workday would end until the whistle blew. One autoworker recalls that some foremen were so intimidating that workers had to do the foremen's yard work on the weekends and had to bring along their daughters to provide sexual services. The foremen managed by terror and hired prizefighters to keep control. Workers could not talk during lunch and had to raise their hands to go to the bathroom. The bathrooms did not have doors, and foremen followed workers who took a bathroom break to make sure the break was needed; such indignities, as well as poor wages and unsafe working conditions, made workers ready to join unions.[2]

In response to these conditions and in frustration over issues such as wages, benefits, and fair treatment, union membership grew quickly in the 1930s, from 3.4 million members in 1930 (12 percent of nonfarm payrolls) to more than 10 million in 1941. "Union density" peaked in 1945–1946 and in 1954, when 35 percent of workers were union members (see Figure 2-1). Although the percentages began to fall, the number of union members continued to grow, from 17 million in 1954 to a peak of 20.2 million in 1978.

But the American workplace and its workforce were changing, and labor unions were failing to keep up with those changes. By 1983, union membership had dipped to

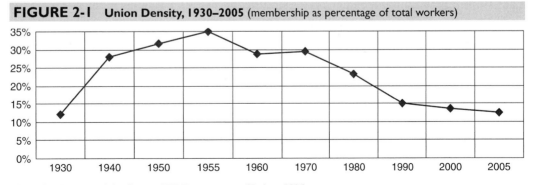

FIGURE 2-1 Union Density, 1930–2005 (membership as percentage of total workers)

SOURCE: Bureau of the Census, U.S. Department of Labor, 2005.

TABLE 2-1   Union Membership and Earnings by Industry, 2004

Industrial sector	Union Membership	Percent of Total Sector	Mean Weekly Earnings of Union Members
Total union members	15,472,000	12.5%	$781
Manufacturing, mining & construction	3,358,000	14.1%	$895
Commerce (wholesale & retail trade)	1,130,000	6.2%	$596
Transport & utilities	1,294,000	26.2%	$854
Information (media, entertainment, & telecom)	543,000	10.7%	$893
Finance	176,000	2.1%	$657
Professional & business services	243,000	2.3%	$679
Private education & health	1,324,000	8.0%	$717
Government (state & local, federal, & postal)	7,324,000	39.2%	$832
Other services	236,000	2.6%	$749

SOURCE: Bureau of Labor Statistics, *Employment and Earnings,* February 2005.

17.7 million (20.1 percent of workers). Since 1983, the union share of wage and salary workers has declined in private nonagricultural industries from 17 percent to less than 9 percent, but the share has increased slightly in government, where it stands at 40 percent.

Today 15.5 million U.S. wage and salary workers—12.5 percent of all nonfarm workers—belong to unions. About one in four wage and salary workers in the transportation and the communication/public utilities industries is a union member. The greatest growth in union membership in recent years has occurred in the government sector, where 40 percent of all employees in 2005 were union members (see Table 2-1). The two industries or sectors with the highest rates of unionization, at 37 percent, are education and protective service occupations. The next highest rates are transportation and utilities, at about 25 percent. Other industries with higher than average rates are construction (15 percent), information/communications (14 percent), and manufacturing (13 percent).[3]

In the traditional union stronghold—production jobs in metropolitan areas—the proportion of union to nonunion employees declined from 73 percent to 17 percent from 1961 to 2005. The substantial drop in the nation's large cities was not limited to production workers; nonsupervisory office clerical workers in unions also declined.

Why has union membership in the United States declined? A 2005 Stanford University study provided several key reasons. First, it noted that declining union membership is not unique to the United States. In fact, of the 20 major industrial countries of the world, only 3 did not record a decrease in the percentage of workers belonging to unions **(union density rate)** from 1985 to the late 1990s (see Table 2-2). In addition, most of the developing regions of Asia, Africa, and Latin America experienced declining union membership. The study found major reasons for the decline in union membership in the United States:[4]

- The growing attrition of existing members from their unions. This may be caused by frustration with union leadership or be due to a surprising result of the study: union workers feel they have *less* at the workplace than do nonunion workers. In

TABLE 2-2   Union Density Rates, Major Industrial Countries (percent)

	1970	*1985*	*Late 1990s*[b]	*Change (1985– late 1990s)*
Australia	50.2	45.6	24.7	−20.9
Austria	62.2	51.6	38.0	−13.6
Belgium	45.5	50.7	53.4	2.7
Canada	31.0	34.6	29.9	−4.7
Denmark	60.0	78.2	75.4	−2.8
Finland	51.4	69.1	76.1	7.0
France	22.3	13.9	10.0	−3.9
Germany, W.	33.0	34.3	32.1	−2.2
Ireland	53.1	48.3	43.5	−4.8
Italy	36.3	42.5	38.0	−4.5
Japan	35.1	28.8	21.5	−7.3
Netherlands	38.0	25.2	24.5	−0.7
Norway	51.4	57.5	55.6	−1.9
New Zealand	n.a.	53.1	21.4	−31.7
Portugal	60.8	51.4	25.1	−26.3
Spain	27.4	9.3	16.4	7.1
Sweden	67.7	83.7	81.3	−2.4
Switzerland	30.1	28.6	21.7	−6.9
United Kingdom	44.8	39.0	30.7	−8.3
United States	23.2[a]	17.4	13.0	−4.4

[a]1977 data. [b]2000: Japan, United States. 1999: Austria, Denmark, Netherlands, New Zealand, Switzerland. 1998: Canada, Finland, France, Italy, Sweden, United Kingdom. 1997: Ireland, Norway, Spain. 1996: Australia. 1995: Belgium, Portugal. 1990: West Germany, n.a. not available.

SOURCE: 1970–80: OECD, 1994, Table 5.7, p. 184. 1985—Visser, 2003, Tables 1A, 1C, 1D, compiled by Robert J. Flanagan, "Has Management Strangled U.S. Unions?" *Journal of Labor Research,* 26, no. 1 (Winter 2005), p. 35. Used by permission.

addition, union workers have increasingly witnessed layoffs and the use of replacement workers that may have eroded their belief that unions can provide job security.

- Reduced nonunion member interest in joining a union, possibly due to increased similarity between union and nonunion employers.
- Increased efforts by management to remain nonunion through worker-friendly human resource management policies and actively fighting organizing efforts.
- Union organizing efforts have largely been the responsibility of individual national unions while the AFL-CIO pursued labor's political agenda in Washington, D.C. This issue was largely responsible for the 2005 split from the AFL-CIO by several national unions that formed Change to Win Coalition, a new union federation focused on increasing membership.
- Global marketplace changes including increased competition from non–U.S. employers and the rapid, continued practice of sending U.S. jobs to other nations have negatively affected U.S. unions.

Union leaders in the United States, however, point out that in 1999 total membership grew by 265,000—the largest increase in 10 years. The gain, however, was followed by a loss in 2000.[5] In addition to the 1999 total growth in the government sector (40 percent in

2000), some private-sector unions have increased membership in recent years by organizing health-care workers, lawyers, janitors, cleaners, and hotel and restaurant employees. The Hotel Employees and Restaurant Employees Union organized 9,000 new members in 2001, and the Service Employees International Union added 81,000 members.[6] However, from 2001–2005, in just four years under President George W. Bush, the member gains of 1999–2000 were eliminated as total U.S. union membership declined by over 5 percent. During those years the real wages of union workers also declined by about 1 percent, the percentage of all employees receiving health insurance decreased, and the pensions of many workers were challenged. However, a bright spot for union workers is they still enjoy a higher annual salary (compared to nonunion workers) of about $9,000 and significantly higher health care and pension benefits.[7]

Union–management relations in the United States are in a divisive period, which is evident by a series of significant strikes and other actions in several industries that have traditionally had strong union bases, such as the airlines, newspapers, grocery/food stores, and communications. The central question in all the current labor problems: Is this simply a passing phase caused by economic problems, which started with the 2000 downturns in the U.S. stock market and was enhanced by the terrorist events of September 11, 2001, **OR** is it a fundamental restructuring in the U.S. workplace similar to that of the 1970s and 1980s? During that period, about 30 years past, the rapid changes caused by technology—such as robotics in manufacturing and the introduction of computers in several industries, which replaced many clerical/office jobs, caused a significant downsizing in many U.S. industries, which then enabled many companies to operate more "lean and mean" and fuel the economic boom of the 1990s. Today, however, according to Peter Rachleff, a labor consultant, pressures on these unionized industries are "both cyclical and, as they say in MBA classes, secular: We're . . . struck at this . . . intersection between secular or structural changes in the economy . . . the lack of real growth of good jobs and the increased global competition. . . . ." Is this period only a cyclical adjustment, or is it another true secular, permanent change as the economy experienced in the 1970s and 1980s? Only time will determine.[8]

Historical Perspective

To understand the labor–management relationship in today's world, one must understand how it developed. The influences of the marketplace in developing the modern workplace can be traced back to the late 1700s. It was during this period of political democratic revolutions—the American Revolution, the French Revolution, and the rise of the English Parliament—that other revolutions began: the agricultural revolution, the industrial revolution, and the capitalist revolution.

During the 1700s a combination of factors caused a population boom in England, Europe, Russia, and China. The decline of diseases such as smallpox, the increase in the use of vaccination, improvements in diet, and a younger marriage age for women who therefore produced more children were all possible causes.[9] People at first feared that the increase in population would strain the resources of the societies they inhabited. The shift of population from farms to urban centers, especially in England and on the Continent, increased the need for solutions to this larger population. England led the way and responded in three ways. First, a major emigration occurred. The creation of the British Empire, on which it was boasted that the sun never set, was a creature of necessity. If not for the emigration between 1815 and 1914 of more than 20 million Britons to every corner of the world, the population boom in England would have seriously threatened its existence.

The second response to the needs of an increased population was the agricultural revolution that took place roughly between 1750 and 1880. The agricultural revolution refers to the changes made in farming during that century, including rotation of crops to keep the soil fertile, new breeding techniques of animal stock, and the expansion of farmland—in England both through enclosure of common lands and draining of wetlands and through settlement of England's colonies. Advances in communications and transportation put these new techniques within the reach of farmers throughout Europe and the colonies and put the food they produced on tables around the world.

Finally, the industrial revolution gave England and then the rest of the developed world a way to handle the population boom. The substitution of mechanical devices for human skills and of inanimate power for human or animal strength caused a vast leap forward in productivity. The new workplace first benefited the masses in urban centers by providing them with jobs, albeit jobs with meager rewards. But the needs of this newly urbanized workforce were few. Consumer consumption came later and was, in fact, a result of the industrial revolution. High-volume production of affordable goods created a middle class that both produced and consumed those goods.

As modern nations emerged from these political, agricultural, and industrial revolutions, nation–states arose and became identified with the economic needs of their citizens. The growth of materialism in the 1800s was a reflection of the political shift from monarchy to representative government and the creation of a middle class. This middle class depended on partnerships between business and labor, business and capital, and business and government.

Before the turn of the twentieth century, the United States faced the challenges of converting from an agrarian to an industrial nation and accepting and accommodating more than 26 million immigrants who had come to this country during the half century after the Civil War.[10] At first these immigrants were primarily of western European origin—Irish, Scandinavian, English, and German. Soon, however, word spread of the opportunities for work and religious freedom, and masses of immigrants came from Italy, Poland, Austria, Hungary, and Russia. From all these countries groups migrated to escape direct and persistent discrimination in their native lands.[11] This second wave of immigrant workers from southern and eastern Europe also came about because of the need for cheap, plentiful labor to fill the factories and mines that multiplied during the industrial revolution.

Business in the 1890s had to create working environments that would enable people with limited industrial work experience and limited knowledge of English to function in the mines and factories. Frederick Winslow Taylor, author of *Principles of Scientific Management* (1911), and Henry Ford, whose success with the assembly line at the Ford Motor Company in the early decades of the twentieth century is legendary, are credited with establishing in organizations work principles still largely in use in American workplaces today. These principles are the following:

- *Fractionalization of work,*   in which workers could be taught discrete, repetitive tasks regardless of language barriers or educational achievement
- *"One best way" theory*   in which the most efficient way to perform a job is determined by use of a clipboard and a stop watch (see Profile 2-1)
- *Dividing the workforce,*   by clearly separating those who are hired to "think" (manage, direct, plan) and those who are hired to "do" (produce, perform)
- *Protecting the process from the worker,*   with a system of controls and compliance

---

"ONE BEST WAY" THEORY

Frederick Winslow Taylor, in his work *Principles of Scientific Management,* proffered his theory that there is "one best way" to perform a job and that it is determined by using a clipboard and a stopwatch. Taylor's theory did not go unchallenged, even in his own time. Labor unions criticized Taylor's attitude that systems should drive the work rather than people. They complained that scientific management ignored workers' skills and know-how, that it failed to address the motivation of workers, and that the monotonous jobs were detrimental to workers' performance. At that same time, Frank and Lillian Gilbreth, credited with being the first "efficiency experts," were leading scientific management into a far more humanistic era.

Frank Gilbreth was an apprentice bricklayer who rose through the ranks to become a successful owner of a construction company. His observations of the varied ways in which construction workers performed their tasks convinced him that by observation and by addressing what motivates employees, he could arrive at a better system for construction. Lillian Gilbreth, as a student of industrial psychology, brought an academic's discipline and scientific protocol to her husband's practical knowledge. Between 1912 and 1924, the Gilbreths advised manufacturing companies on improving their work processes. Their approach, unlike Taylor's, included sensitivity to the concerns of the workers.

One noted innovation they used to study the workplace was micromotion, utilizing the new motion picture camera. The Gilbreths refined the technique by using cyclegraphs in which workers had small lights attached to hands, feet, and head and photos were taken of them with long-exposure techniques. This innovation enabled the Gilbreths to analyze the motions for wasted, strained, or duplicative efforts. These studies led to suggestions of changes in processes, such as where to place key equipment used in production, as well as how to improve worker stations, for example, by raising or lowering benches or using chairs on springs to reduce vibration. The Gilbreths' work led to their alternative theory of the "one best way" based not on a clipboard and a stopwatch but on the 17 "pure motions" recorded by their cameras, which they believed any job included.

The growth of labor unions before and immediately after World War I, which coincided with Taylor's and the Gilbreths' work, caused many industrialists to start internal industrial relations departments and company unions. Personnel management began to decrease the use of scientific management, at least by that name.

SOURCE: Adapted from Peter Liebhold, "Seeking 'The One Best Way,' " *Labor's Heritage* 7, no. 2 (Fall 1995), p. 19.

These work principles created the "top-down" management organization typical of U.S. corporations. The growth of the labor union movement in response to the industrialized society of early twentieth-century America was one result of this corporate organization.

Business and government joined together to ensure the profitability of the emerging industries by limiting foreign competition through trade tariffs. By keeping cheap foreign products out of the United States, government enabled business to run marginally profitable businesses. But trade tariffs imposed by other countries in response to the U.S. tariffs kept U.S.-manufactured goods out of the international market. So, to ensure that profits were sufficient to keep production going, business and capital entered into a partnership. The partnership of business and capital was reflected in the creation of national corporations. They were created to reduce domestic competition and thereby keep profits high enough to keep businesses operating. The so-called **robber**

barons, who built the railroads, produced steel, and mined minerals, became the focus of both admiration and contempt.

The United States had always suspected monopolies, having suffered in colonial days from the abuse of royally protected monopolies such as the East India Company.[12] The Sherman Antitrust Act of 1890 prohibited price fixing by American firms. But in effect the act promoted the acquisition of smaller companies by large conglomerates because when U.S. Steel, for example, had to pay more for domestic than foreign iron and coal, it simply bought the companies that produced iron and coal domestically.

The laborers who organized to counter the power of the Carnegies, Rockefellers, and Goulds had little success until the passage of the Wagner Act. By forcing big business to sit down at a bargaining table with representatives of the workers, the government was able to create more equal partners where previously only inequality had existed.

This protection by and promotion of unions by government led to the heyday of union organizing. By 1955, 35 percent of the nonagricultural workers in the United States were represented by unions. The ability of labor to organize and support strikes before, during, and after World War II caused business to seek restraints on labor's legal protection. When the Taft-Hartley Act was passed in 1947 to curb unions' right to strike, organized labor was not able to prevent its passage or to affect its repeal.[13]

THE CHALLENGES

Manufacturing in the United States in the 1960s was at its peak as the mass producer of goods for a global consumer market. The reason was clear. Except for the bombing of Pearl Harbor, World War II had not taken place on U.S. soil. Unlike Europe and Japan, the United States emerged from World War II with its industrial base intact. Its production system was geared to turn out standard, assembly-line products in high volume. For the United States, a buyer's market existed worldwide. Plenty of customers, domestic and international, were ready to absorb its goods while other industrial nations sought to rebuild from the war. If one imagines national production as the progress of a locomotive, the United States stayed on track through the war and was still moving forward after the war. Other nations had been derailed by the war, and it would take years for them to rebuild.

But the advantage the United States had from readily available national resources and a large domestic market began to erode in the last quarter of the twentieth century when transportation costs fell, European integration and trade liberalization advanced, and Japan discovered quality control. Japan's straight-line assembly plants were converted into team assembly plants that utilized engaged workers and automation to increase the quality and the efficiency of the manufacturing process. The Japanese plants coupled automation with a **just-in-time** inventory system that delivers parts to a production area exactly when needed. As a result, by the 1980s Japan challenged U.S. production with superior production capabilities in standardized goods and in industries such as automobiles and electric appliances.

Figure 2-2 shows the decline in the growth rate for domestic products in the United States in the 1970s, 1980s, and early 1990s. The United States rebounded some in the latter 1990s as U.S. manufacturing instituted "lean and mean" management, adopted new technologies, and encouraged self-managed employee teams. It rebounded again in 2004 as a result of the cyclical reinvestment by businesses in creating inventories.[14]

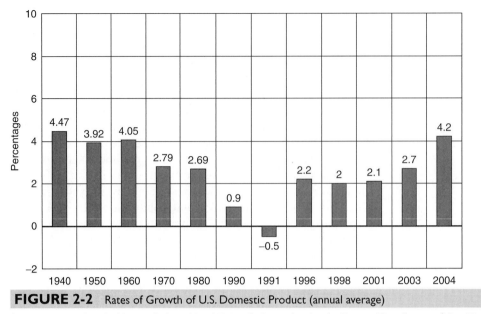

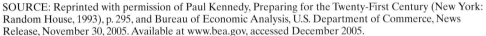

FIGURE 2-2 Rates of Growth of U.S. Domestic Product (annual average)

SOURCE: Reprinted with permission of Paul Kennedy, Preparing for the Twenty-First Century (New York: Random House, 1993), p. 295, and Bureau of Economic Analysis, U.S. Department of Commerce, News Release, November 30, 2005. Available at www.bea.gov, accessed December 2005.

However, the exodus of American manufacturing jobs to cheaper overseas labor markets, regardless of how "lean and mean" U.S. companies have become in their efforts to compete, continues: by 2004, the number of U.S. manufacturing jobs hit a 53-year low after losing 2.8 jobs from 2001–2004. The three states hardest hit by the decline each lost over 100,000 jobs from 2001–2004: Pennsylvania, Michigan, and Wisconsin. And even though the average hourly compensation costs for production workers in 31 foreign countries climbed to 78 percent of the U.S. level in 2004, only European countries had higher hourly compensation costs than the United States. (See Figure 2-3.)

The U.S. economy underwent a dramatic structural change during the 1980s—away from manufacturing and toward services. Since 1960, employment in the service sector grew by 182 percent while employment in the goods sector only increased by 19 percent. The occupational composition of the workforce has shifted as well from blue-collar to white-collar workers. And the wage premium for private-sector union members over nonunion workers has declined from 40 percent in 1983 to 28 percent in 1996. The shift from a manufacturing-based to a service-based economy has decreased company size, making organizing activities more difficult.[15]

Employment legislation protects workers and allows them to challenge unsafe working conditions, job discrimination, and unjust dismissals without the assistance of unions. And the ability to substitute unemployment insurance and welfare benefits for union-provided benefits and services further decreases interest in unionization. In addition, new technologies alter production processes and typically increase productivity and reduce the cost of production. Because fewer employees produce more products and technology changes require highly skilled rather than unskilled workers, new technologies reduce the base for unionization in manufacturing industries.[16]

Hourly compensation costs in U.S. dollars for production workers in manufacturing, 1974–2004

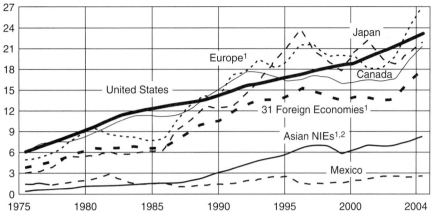

[1] Trade-weighted average.
[2] The Asian NIEs are Hong Kong SAR, Korea, Singapore and Taiwan.

Indexes of hourly compensation costs in U.S. dollars for production workers in manufacturing, 2004 (US = 100)

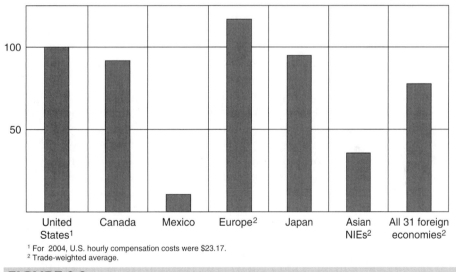

[1] For 2004, U.S. hourly compensation costs were $23.17.
[2] Trade-weighted average.

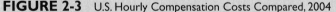

FIGURE 2-3   U.S. Hourly Compensation Costs Compared, 2004

SOURCE: "International Comparisons of Hourly Compensation Costs, 2004," Bureau of Labor Statistics, November 18, 2005.

Globalization

The economic expansion of the 1990s across geographical and political boundaries created a new economic order, popularly termed **globalization**. Globalization is characterized by increased mobility—in goods due to improvements in transportation, in investment by relocating production sites in foreign countries, and in information due to digitization. The emergence of air cargo companies that provide speedy and cost-effective means of transport, UPS and Federal Express for example, has dramatically improved international trade. International financial institutions and trade agreements promote investment liberalization and privatization of services, creating new opportunities for U.S.

corporations in overseas markets. Communication costs for voice, text, and data have dropped dramatically making it possible to outsource many types of services. Massive amounts of information can now be transmitted across the world at low cost, making geographic distances less important.

Outsourcing, once the bane of U.S. blue-collar workers, has become a major challenge to white-collar workers. One study estimated that as many as 830,000 U.S. service jobs moved to low-wage countries such as China, India, and Mexico by the end of 2005, and 3.4 million jobs and $136 billion in wages will move offshore by 2015.[17] Outsourcing service jobs is akin to companies subcontracting parts of business operations to nonunion shops within the United States. The practice has gone global, in part because of technological changes. It is estimated that U.S. companies make up about 70 percent of the global outsourcing market.[18]

Foreign-Owned Southern Auto Plants

One new global reality is the rise of successful foreign-owned automobile plants, located in the United States, primarily in the South. The plants have remained nonunion, and the United Auto Workers (UAW) union has managed several organizing campaigns, with no success. Between the split of the Canadian UAW members in 1986 and the decline of Detroit's "Big Three" automobile companies' share of the market and thus union members, the UAW has sustained an almost unbelievable loss of over one million members in a 30-year period from its membership peak in 1971 to 2001. The new foreign-owned auto plants include Toyota (Kentucky, Indiana, West Virginia), Honda (Ohio), BMW (South Carolina), Nissan (Tennessee), and the Daimler Chrysler Mercedes-Benz plant in Alabama. The UAW in 2000, after repeated organization campaign failures in other states, targeted the new German-owned Mercedes-Benz plant. After several months of trying to collect authorization cards from enough workers, the union gave up. Why?

According to "Wa Wa" Walters, president of a United Steelworkers of America local union in an Alabama tire plant, "It's kind of hard to organize a guy driving a Mercedes to work every day." For example, Wade Smith, a 32-year-old worker at the Mercedes plant, made over $100,000 in 1999, including overtime, and drives a Mercedes Sport Utility Vehicle to work. Another reason, however, was the continuing campaign organized by the local business community that included billboards that read, "No UAW: Save Our Jobs for Alabamians," which refers to the suspicion that if the UAW won, future new jobs might be filled by UAW members from Detroit or other cities who could bid on the jobs.[19]

The New Economy

Organized labor has also not been successful in organizing the workers of the "new economy," which includes high technology from computer hardware and software to cable television. In fact, about 98 percent of technical positions in the growing cable television industry are nonunion. This is particularly surprising because union members hold a majority of the jobs in the broadcast network industry. Some unions have tried to organize new economy workers, but mostly without success. The National Association of Broadcast Employees and Technicians Local 11, for example, tried to organize technical workers at CNBC, many of whom were paid less than half of what their NBC unionized counterparts were paid. The effort gained little support. Other attempts at organizing new economy workers have had similar results. Why? Marcus Courtney, a former Microsoft employee and union sympathizer, claims it is hard to convince high-technology workers to join a union, even though fundamental issues—wages, retirement and health care, and job security—are the same as in other industries. Many new economy employers, for example, classify thousands of employees as temporary workers or independent contractors to avoid paying their health care or retirement benefits. New economy workers in the American economy are often recent college graduates who are thrilled to be working in television or the computer industry and thus do not think they need the security or economic benefits promised by unions.[20]

Unions and Technology

In the early years of information technology, unions opposed the intervention of computers and similar technology on the job floor, in offices, and elsewhere in the workplace because they were viewed as threats to the job security of union workers. However, a 2002 survey study of 75 national U.S. unions found that union opposition to information technology that increases worker productivity is almost completely absent today. In fact, unions have become users themselves: About 70 percent of the surveyed national unions use Web sites to provide information to members and the public, 98 percent use e-mail and spreadsheets for bookkeeping and membership data, 59 percent use technology to track organizing efforts, 32 percent use spreadsheets and word processing in negotiating contracts, and 16 percent use videoconferencing. Unions also reported that it has become commonplace to use laptops and Web links to aid in rapid response during fast-paced organizing campaigns. Online links to video clips featuring current members' views of the benefits of union membership provide important tools in persuading potential members in a campaign. In addition, the ability to post proposed or new contracts online and thus provide thousands of members with instant access has provided a critical means of real-time communication. In the Boeing Company strike of 2001, in an unusual example of a union's use of information technology, union activists even posted the names of "scabs" on the Web.[21]

THE OPPORTUNITIES

The effect on the American workforce of these major changes in the way business is done has been predictable. Layoffs, subcontracting, and relocations have hit every manufacturing industry. Because union jobs had been concentrated within trades and manufacturing industries, since the 1950s unions have lost thousands of members and influence. Unions, however, have tried to address the changes happening in the workplace in a number of ways.

Strategic Industry Focus

In 2005 Andrew Stern, president of the 1.8-million member Service Employees International Union (SEIU) together with several other national union presidents challenged the AFL-CIO to focus more resources and efforts on organizing new members. When AFL-CIO president John Sweeney did not endorse Stern's new focus, Stern led several national unions in a historic break from the AFL-CIO to a new federation—CHANGE TO WIN. Stern's vision for the new union federation is to build membership and union strength by focusing on a few strategic industries—building services, hospitals, long-term health-care providers, express shipping, and the leisure/hotel/lodging industry. Stern believes the labor movement should reorganize from a few large unions and many small ones (40 AFL-CIO national unions have fewer than 100,000 members) to about 15 to 20 large unions, each concentrated on a specific industry or sector. This could provide the unions with greater leverage in negotiations as well as the ability to organize new members. The strategy is very similar to the early craft unions of the AFL and industrial unions of the CIO.[22] One industry target, for example, is express shipping, which is dominated by three large carriers: UPS, DHL, and FedEx. The International Brotherhood of Teamsters in 2004 began an organizational effort to organize DHL's delivery workforce of about 25,000 employees. The Teamsters already represents thousands of UPS workers (FedEx is nonunion). In less than a year the Teamsters recruited over 1,500 new DHL workers by stressing salary, health-care and pension issues, to represent about 9,000 total DHL employees in the United States. The organizational effort at DHL, however, will be difficult because the union will need to organize about 420 local DHL employers, and the delivery agents are independent cartage contractors (ICCs), not full-time DHL employees. At UPS, by comparison, the delivery agents are direct employees of only one employer—UPS.[23]

In recent years the North American hotel and lodging industry has become a target for union organizing. This focus is probably due to historically low wages and benefits for work that is needed 24 hours per day, seven days a week, 365 days a year. In the past a union would negotiate an agreement with a council of hotel owners in a metropolitan market. The owners could withstand a work stoppage in one area because they operated hotels in ten or more markets. However in 2004 the national hotel union, Unite Here, began a movement to "consolidate contract expiration dates" so most or all of the contracts with the major hotel companies—Marriott, Starwood, Hilton— would be renegotiated at the same time. The strategy is that it would be much harder for these hotels to face a strike in the same year in several major markets—Las Vegas, New York, Los Angeles, Washington, San Francisco, Atlantic City, and Detroit. This innovative union strategy will most likely be successful only if public response is supportive and convention and vacation trade in those cities is affected.[24]

Health-Care Industry

The health-care industry, and in particular long-term care, has experienced an unprecedented growth in recent years as the "baby boomer" generation enters the market in large numbers. The unions in the health-care industry have also experienced substantial growth. The Service Employees International Union (SEIU), for example, grew by over 150,000 new members in one year! Health care, along with the government sector (all levels) has been called the "shining exception" to the decline in union membership experienced in other industries. In addition, the rate at which unions are winning NLRB representation elections is climbing, from less than 50 percent in 1995 to almost 69 percent in 2005. Why has the health-care industry become the "shining example"? According to John Lyncheski, director of the Healthcare Practice Group of the Cohen and Grigsby law firm, there are several reasons: First, employers are driving employees to unions by providing low take-home pay and turning away from employee demands for better working conditions and patient care, as well as less overtime. Second, unions are using more sophisticated organizing methods including "home visits," professionally produced ads, DVDs, and "salts" (union members presenting themselves as applicants, then upon hiring organize from within the employer). Third, some employers forget that their supervisors are the key to positive employee relations and should be attuned to the warning signs of union activity.[25]

TABLE 2-3 Unions with 100,000 or More Members, 2002

Union	Members	Union	Members
National Education Association	2,679,396	Union of Needletrades, Industrial and Textile Employees	209,876
Service Employees International Union	1,464,007	American Federation of Government Employees	200,600
United Food and Commercial Workers International Union	1,380,507	American Guild of Variety Artists	182,597
International Brotherhood of Teamsters	1,350,000	United American Nurses	152,000
American Federation of State, County, and Municipal Employees	1,350,000	Office and Professional Employees International Union	150,882
Laborers' International Union of North America	840,180	Sheet Metal Workers International Association	148,378
American Federation of Teachers	770,090	International Association of Bridge, Structural, Ornamental and Reinforcing Iron Workers	130,928
International Brotherhood of Electrical Workers	700,548	International Union of Painters and Allied Trades	115,511
International Association of Machinists and Aerospace Workers	673,095	Bakery, Confectionery, Tobacco Workers and Grain Millers International Union	114,618
International Union, United Automobile, Aerospace, and Agricultural Implement (UAW)	638,722	Transport Workers Union of America	110,000
Communications Workers of America	557,136	American Association of Classified School Employees	109,188
United Steelworkers of America	532,234	International Alliance of Theatrical Stage Employees, Moving Picture Technicians, Artists and Allied Crafts of the United States and Canada	104,102
United Brotherhood of Carpenters and Joiners of America	531,839	American Federation of Musicians of the United States and Canada	102,000
International Union of Operating Engineers	390,388	National Rural Letter Carriers' Association	101,810
National Postal Mail Handlers Union	388,480	International Union of Bricklayers and Allied Craftworkers	101,499
United Association of Journeymen and Apprentices of the Plumbing and Pipe Fitting Industry of the United States and Canada	325,914	Transportation Communications International Union	101,228
National Association of Letter Carriers	294,315	United Mineworkers of America	100,570
American Postal Workers Union	292,901		
Paper, Allied-Industrial, Chemical Employees International Union	274,464		
International Association of Fire Fighters	261,551		
Hotel Employees and Restaurant Employees International Union	249,151		

SOURCE: U.S. Department of Labor

Public Sector

One of the brighter aspects of the total membership picture is the potential growth of unionism among workers in the public sector. By 2000, three public unions were among the nine largest U.S. unions: The National Education Association ranked first; the American Federation of State, County and Municipal Employees (AFSCME) ranked fourth; and the American Federation of Teachers ranked ninth. See Table 2-3 for a listing of all U.S. unions with 100,000 or more members.

The American Federation of Teachers, an international organization of teachers and other nonsupervisory educational employees affiliated with the AFL-CIO, added nearly

300,000 members in the 1990s. Membership in the American Federation of Government Employees (AFGE) reached over 200,000 in June 2002. The AFGE is the largest federal employee union, representing over 600,000 federal government workers.

Public-sector collective bargaining is not without challenge, however, as the workforce is made up largely of groups not traditionally supportive of unions: female, professional, white-collar, and minority workers. A recent study regarding public employment noted that women and older workers make up a larger share of the public-sector workforce than the private-sector workforce. The Nelson A. Rockefeller Institute of Government report, released in August 1999, found that 44 percent of government workers in 1998 were over age 45 compared to 30 percent in the private sector and that women accounted for 55.5 percent compared with 45.5 percent of the private-sector workforce.[26]

Professional Workers

A professional and technical workforce requires union organizers to become attuned to changing worker concerns and aspirations. Those changes may be having an effect. The historic resistance of professional workers to unionism may be weakening, as evidenced by higher union success rates in professional unit elections than in all other units.[27] The 1999 unionization of doctors in Los Angeles County and nurses in Cleveland, Ohio, signaled to many labor leaders the change in attitudes toward unions by health-care professionals. At the 1999 American Medical Association convention, physicians voted to unionize, claiming that then they could better negotiate with the managers of hospitals, HMOs, PPCs, and so on. The move came only a month after the doctors in Los Angeles voted to unionize. In the nation's largest election for physicians in 18 years, nearly 800 physicians employed by Los Angeles County voted overwhelmingly to join the Union of American Physicians and Dentists (UAPD), an Oakland-based affiliate of AFSCME. With the victory, the UAPD boosted its membership to 6,000 doctors, making it the nation's largest union of postresidency physicians.

The Service Employees International Union (SEIU) in recent years has successfully organized thousands of service workers who often receive low wages and no medical or pension benefits. In 2005, for example, the SEIU began organizing 1,300 janitors working for commercial cleaning employers in Ohio. The janitors typically work about 20 hours per week for $7,200 annual income, which is below the federal poverty level of $18,660 annually for a family of four. Most janitors work two or three part-time jobs for $6 to $8 per hour.[28]

Immigrant Workers

Immigrant workers are the fastest-growing segment of the working class. Unions recognize the potential substantial number of new members in these workers and are pouring resources into organizing them. They include Mexican construction workers in Seattle, Dominican hotel and nursing home workers, and Haitian cab drivers in Connecticut. A major win for unions was the 1999 victory in Los Angeles to represent 75,000 home health-care workers, mostly immigrants. But immigrant organizing efforts can run into unique cultural and language problems. For example, Russian workers often had bad experiences with unions in Russia, Vietnamese workers in Georgia were afraid the union organizers were part of the U.S. government and would send them home, and some so-called union members in Europe persecuted Hungarians and Poles.[29]

Labor–Management Cooperation

In 2005, about 20 percent of all major collective bargaining agreements provided at least one cooperative article. Typical of agreements that exhibit labor–management cooperation is the 2005–2010 agreement between AK Steel and United Steelworkers Union Local 1865. AK Steel CEO James L. Waincott called it a model for "new era" agreements because both sides gained their primary objectives and the company will be more competitive. The management gains included (1) the consolidation of 100 job classifications into only five, which provides greater workforce flexibility; (2) the elimination of a workforce guarantee (minimum number of workers), which allows for a reduction in force; and (3) greater health-care cost sharing by workers, while the union gains included (a) an enhanced profit-sharing plan, which should provide increased worker pay, and (b) a guaranteed defined pension plan, which preserves future pension payments through higher pension contributions.[30] Other examples of labor-management cooperation include the NUMMI plant and the Beiersdorf, Inc. Sewing Plant discussed next.

NUMMI Agreement

In 1962, General Motors (GM) built a new Chevrolet plant in Fremont, California. By 1982, the plant's constant labor problems were blamed for poor quality, low productivity, high absenteeism, and GM's decision to close the plant. But the plant reopened in 1983 as New United Motor Manufacturing, Inc. (NUMMI), a unique international joint effort between GM and Toyota. It was the United States' first taste of the Japanese-style team management. Over the next several years the new Japanese management combined with UAW members to make U.S. labor history. For years, GM had complained that the UAW was the cause of its problems at the Fremont plant. But 85 percent of the NUMMI workers were those same union workers who, when combined with Japanese management, produced high-quality Toyota Corollas and Chevrolet Novas (now Prizm). The NUMMI plant convinced many Americans that the old problems were with American management, not with American labor. GM, however, did learn a great deal about Japanese management and manufacturing methods. Many of the NUMMI techniques, especially employee involvement teams, were incorporated into GM's highly regarded Saturn plant in Tennessee.

Exactly how did the new Japanese management change one of the least-productive U.S. auto plants into one of the finest? Several factors combined may provide the answer:

- *Cooperation.*   The most significant change was the spirit of cooperation that began with the UAW/NUMMI "letter of intent," including these broad guidelines:
  1. Management and labor should work together as a team.
  2. Management and labor should build the highest-quality automobile at the lowest cost.
  3. Management should provide workers a voice in decision making.
  4. Management and labor should constantly seek quality improvement.
  5. Management should maintain a profitable business and provide fair wages and benefits, job security, and opportunity for advancement.
- *Training.*   The initial 240 NUMMI production workers were sent to Japan for three weeks of training on a Toyota production line and in the classroom. Subjects included the following:
  1. Kaizen (continuous improvement)
  2. Jidoka (the pursuit of superior quality)
  3. Just-in-time inventory
  4. Teamwork
  5. Union–management relations

Since 1983, the GM-Toyota NUMMI Plant has demonstrated that American union workers can compete successfully with Japanese and European workers.

- ***Fewer job classifications.*** In the old GM plant there were 95 job classifications that generally produced routine, boring jobs. NUMMI has four classifications—one unskilled and three skilled.
- ***Fewer supervisors.*** With teams performing routine management functions and a focus on building quality (rather than inspecting for it), fewer supervisors and inspectors were needed.
- ***Work teams.*** The 2,400 hourly employees were organized into teams of 5 to 10 members who rotate among as many as 15 tasks.

The NUMMI plant has been so successful that in 1991 Toyota opened a new $350 million compact-truck line on the same site.[31]

Beiersdorf, Inc., Sewing Plant

The Beiersdorf, Inc., plant in Mariemont, Ohio, makes an assortment of medical aids, primarily elastic knee, ankle, and wrist braces. It is one of the few "cut-and-sew" operations left in the United States. Most of the industry has moved overseas for cheap labor. The Ohio plant almost moved overseas in 1996. Owned by a German conglomerate—Beiersdorf AG—the managers and employees were told that costs were too high and that a move was necessary, and a shutdown date was set.

But a determined plant manager, Larry Kessler, and members of the Union of Needletrades Industrial and Textile Employees (UNITE) asked for a chance to match the $6 million savings projected by an overseas move, and the German executives agreed. A plan was developed by Kessler, which included the following:

- A new labor contract with UNITE, which accounted for half of the $6 million cost savings, was approved by 79 percent of the membership. It included a cut in wages for only one-third of the workers and a reduction in insurance and other benefits. Both the union and the plant's management reduced their numbers in the plan. The union also agreed to an entirely new production process—the Toyota Sewing System.
- The Toyota Sewing System was implemented to increase productivity by changing from a "batch" system with a single-piece flow to a small team process. The teams of two to five workers sew complete products and put them in boxes for shipping.

It is a more efficient process because the handling, storing, and moving of parts is reduced, and workers enjoy a greater freedom of movement and autonomy. The system was developed in the 1970s by Toyota Motor Manufacturing to produce automobile seat covers.

- The plant's landlord agreed to a one-third cut in the lease to keep the facility locally.
- The plant's 25 vendors agreed to price cuts that reduced the costs of 90 percent of the materials.

Within three years the new plan not only kept the plant in Ohio but also accomplished the following:

- Cost cuts exceeded $10 million—well above the $6 million goal.
- The company was realizing a profit, introduced six new products, and won the Beiersdorf's innovation award.
- Exports, only 10 percent of sales in 1996, were 25 percent of sales in 1999.
- Production increased by 50 percent from 5.7 million pieces to 8.6 million.
- Employment increased by 60 workers.

In 1999 *Industry Week* included the Beiersdorf plant in its Top 25 manufacturing list.[32]

Quality of Working Life

Many different programs often referred to as **quality of working life** (QWL) are designed and implemented to increase employees' satisfaction with their work environment along with their productivity. Quality of working life is a catchall phrase characterizing the process by which management, union, and employees determine together what action, changes, and improvements can better the quality of life at work for all members of the organization and the effectiveness of both the company and the union.[33] QWL programs attempt to establish practical relationships outside the traditional union–management means of negotiations, grievance handling, and joint committees.

QWL programs, some workers and employers believe, have significantly altered the conduct of labor relations. Unlike past efforts, QWL programs try to establish direct channels of communication between workers and their supervisors and give workers a greater voice in decision making. One of the most widely heralded QWL programs was introduced by GM and the UAW. This program was adopted by 18 similar GM plants and was subjected to careful empirical review. It was designed to enrich jobs by removing the most boring, repetitive tasks and by increasing employee autonomy. Results of plant-level data from 10 years showed that more intensive QWL programs were associated with product quality and lower grievance and absentee rates. It was then concluded that QWL efforts represent one possible strategy for breaking the traditional union–management cycle of high conflict and low trust.

Such change might be evident in a displacement of resources and energies from dealing with conflicts to concentrating on work problems, increased worker motivation because of greater participation in job-related decision making, and greater flexibility in human resource management resulting from less reliance on strict work rules and assignments. Although the GM experience with QWL programs has been quite positive, such efforts will not likely produce an end to all labor–management differences, as is sometimes predicted.[34]

Quality Circles

One employee participation technique that quickly became popular is **quality circles** (QC). William Ouchi, author of *Theory Z*, correctly predicted that quality circles would become the "management fad of the eighties." He further stated that QC success would be longer lived than management by objectives or zero-based budgeting.[35]

The QC concept is generally one of "people building" rather than "people using." Usually 5 to 10 employees with common work interests meet voluntarily in groups once a week. The purpose of their meeting is to identify, analyze, and develop solutions to work problems. Solutions are presented to management for final approval. There is no reward for the circle members other than the recognition and satisfaction they receive from helping increase the efficiency of the organization. QC programs generally start with only two or three circles and add circles as more employees become interested. Circles are independent; they are not part of the organizational chart, members volunteer to participate, and they choose what problems to address and how to analyze them.

Quality circles began in Japan in the 1960s as a major effort for Japan to overcome its image as a producer of cheap, inferior goods. By the 1980s, there was no question that Sony, Panasonic, Toyota, and others had built a reputation for excellence. It has been estimated that 80 percent of Japanese production workers belong to quality circles. A 2004 study noted that in the United States the percentage of firms using quality circles almost doubled from 27 percent in 1992 to 58 percent by 2000, even while the use of employee teams reached their plateau during the same period.[36]

The most obvious advantage to quality circles is that they produce solutions to work-related problems and thus increase quality and efficiency. However, managers and employees have been amazed at the intrinsic rewards—personal satisfaction and peer recognition—that also result.

Thus far, unions in the United States have adopted a neutral attitude toward the QC concept. They probably recognize that circles do increase efficiency, helping the job security of their members. However, they also are aware that employees may not directly share in the reduced costs.

EMPLOYEE TEAMS

A large portion of the work within most organizations occurs within groups. Most jobs do not exist in isolation but instead involve both formal work groups (departments, sections, and so forth) and informal groups of employees whose strong friendships affect their working relationships. The effectiveness of these employee groups or teams can be critical to the success of the entire organization.

A major reason for the frequent utilization of groups is synergy; synergy occurs when the production of the whole (group) is greater than the sum of the parts (individuals). When people work together in a group, they exchange ideas, learn from each other, and motivate each other to achieve more than they typically achieve when working in isolation. The heart of this interaction is the social mingling of the group. Employees build strong friendships with each other; in fact, often their best friends are their coworkers. Thus, when a group develops a successful working interaction, synergy occurs, and more can be achieved as a group than the members could achieve working individually. This enhanced productivity occurs in three primary areas:[37]

1. ***Decision making.*** Without a designated leader who is looked to for most decisions, groups often make better decisions than the member would if acting alone.

Employees working in teams were called the "Productivity Breakthrough of the 1990s".

2. *Problem solving.* Through the exchange of ideas and sharing of information, groups usually solve common problems better than individuals who are limited to their own knowledge and experience.

3. *Creativity.* Groups are more willing to make innovative or creative changes in their tasks because they have the support of members.

In many organizations, formal groups of employees responsible for an identifiable work process, a specific project, or solving a problem are called employee teams or committees. These groups were once called the "productivity breakthrough of the 1990s," even though the first ones—such as those at General Foods in Topeka, Kansas, had been in existence for more than 20 years.[38] A 2004 study on employee teams noted that surveys of *Fortune* 1000 companies indicate at least 68 percent to 70 percent utilize employee teams. Major users include Ford, Proctor & Gamble, Federal Express, Levi Strauss, and Westinghouse. Most companies have reported that teams increased productivity, quality of products, and innovation. However, others have reported no gains in these areas and even negative outcomes from changing to teams. The research study found that the level of autonomy provided to a team and the structural context—work rules, policies, and procedures—might be significant predictors of the success of teams within an organization.[39] We refer to all these groups as teams.

Types of Teams

Formal employee teams can generally be divided into three categories: special project teams, problem-solving teams, and self-managed teams (see Table 2-4). Self-managed teams are characterized as permanent groups of employees who perform all tasks required of one general activity and perform the supervisory duties related to their work. Special project teams are usually formed by combining people from different functions to design, develop, and produce new products or services. Problem-solving teams usually meet on a regular basis to analyze, recommend, and implement solutions to selected problems.

TABLE 2-4	What Is a Team?	
Problem Solving	***Special Project***	***Self-Managed***
Usually 5 to 12 volunteers who meet a few hours a week to discuss ways of improving quality, efficiency, and work environment.	Usually 10 to 15 people from different functional areas. May design and introduce work reforms or new technology or meet with suppliers and customers. In union shops, labor and management collaborate at all levels.	From 5 to 15 workers who learn all production tasks and rotate from job to job. Teams do managerial duties such as schedule work and order materials.

SOURCE: Aaron Bernstein, "Putting a Damper on That Old Team Spirit," *Business Week,* May 4, 1992, p. 60. Reprinted by special permission, copyright © 1992 by the McGraw-Hill Companies, Inc.

In the 1980s, a handful of U.S. companies began using a new approach to new product development—**special project teams**. They most often consist of 10 to 15 people from different functions, such as research and development, engineering, manufacturing, and marketing, brought together to design and develop a new product quickly and successfully. The project team is viewed as an autonomous group operating independently within the organization. Some of the early project teams' successes include the IBM Personal Computer, 3M's Post-it™, and Jell-O's Pudding Snacks.[40]

The need to improve the safety record and reduce workers' compensation costs was the cause for special project teams in a unionized Ohio automotive finishing plant. The work injury rate had increased to a level deemed "unacceptable" by the state of Ohio. The company was on the verge of being shut down because of its insurance status. A safety committee of management and union representatives was formed and completed intensive team building, brainstorming, ergonomics, and consensus decision-making exercises. The team developed several programs and measures of effectiveness—number of safety incidents, lost employee time, the number of safety violations, amount of scrap, and the number of rejected units. Within only two years significant progress was made in all areas. Not only did all measures of safety improve and the company was again insurable, but employee turnover, product quality, and productivity improved as well. As a result of the team's success, permanent management/union employee teams were formed to continue to focus on safety, and by 2002, the number of lost days due to injuries was less than 24 percent from the year before the teams were established.[41]

Problem-solving teams have increased in popularity but are generally used less than special projects teams are. They can, however, be highly successful. Many problem-solving teams have their roots in quality circles and may be characterized as mature, fully empowered quality circles. The creation of permanent problem-solving teams should not be surprising; an American Society for Training and Development survey of organizations with employee teams found that the most common objective of the teams was problem solving (72 percent of those responding listed as an objective), team building was second (61 percent), and improving quality was third (58 percent).[42] Thus, many organizations with positive experiences with quality circles and with problem solving as an ongoing concern allowed the evolution of quality circles or similar groups into permanent problem-solving teams.

Self-managed employee teams (also called employee or worker involvement groups, autonomous work groups, or self-directed teams) have become commonplace in many American organizations. Special project teams and self-managed teams are the most common and perhaps best publicized types of employee teams. They have been called "the new American industrial weapon" in cover stories in *Business Week, Fortune,* and other business publications.[43]

Exactly what are self-managed employee teams? Although no universal definition exists, the following is accurate:

> A self-managed team is a small group of employees responsible for an entire work process or segment. Team members work together to improve their operation or product, plan their work, resolve day-to-day problems, and manage themselves.[44]

Thus, self-directed teams are groups of employees who normally work together on a daily basis. They are not groups formed to design and develop special projects or new products or to analyze and solve problems as discussed previously. Their members have not been selected from functional areas to work together as a team. Instead, these teams are permanent components within the organization that "get the work out" on a daily basis. The key difference is that their work is assigned to a team, whereas in traditional organizations it would be assigned to a department with a supervisor or head, who then assigns portions of the work to individuals within the department.

The successful creation and utilization of self-directed teams (both union and nonunion) have been reported by a large number of U.S. companies, including Ford Motor Company, Procter & Gamble, Digital Equipment, IDS, Honeywell, Cummins Engine, General Electric, Boeing, and LTV Steel. In general, these companies all report many positive benefits from their experience with self-directed teams, including higher productivity, improved quality (usually the major goal), improved employee morale, better attendance, and lower turnover.[45] A survey of top managers of these and other companies using self-directed teams asked why these organizations should consider developing teams. The major reasons cited were the following:[46]

- *Improved quality, productivity, and service.*   To stay competitive, most organizations must continually improve quality, service, costs, and speed. The day-to-day attention of all employees is required. The Japanese call this principle kaizen—continuous improvement. The sense of ownership that members of a team develop makes continuous improvement possible.

- *Greater flexibility.*   Organizations must be able to respond constantly to changing customer needs. Work teams communicate better, identify new opportunities faster, and implement needed changes more quickly because they do not need to wait for approval from a traditional hierarchy. The team members are more alert to customer needs and are proactive because they realize they can make the difference between success and failure.

- *Reduced operating costs.*   Self-directed teams enable organizations to reduce costs by eliminating layers of middle management. The teams make the decisions, plan the work, and solve problems that are "passed up" the organization in traditional companies.

- *Faster response to technological change.*   New technologies demand greater skills, communication among workers, and coordination among work activities. Thus, workers who previously worked alone must work more closely together. Teams provide a natural environment for such coordination.

- *Fewer job classifications.* Increased technology demands multiskilled employees with greater flexibility to perform many related job functions. Traditional organizations often have many job classifications, each with one or two employees. Self-directed teams train their members to perform all tasks. Thus, each work team has only one job classification. In addition, the reduced number of management layers, as previously discussed, also reduces the number of classifications. The Toyota plant in Georgetown, Kentucky, for example, has only three job classifications, compared with an average of 150 in most U.S. plants.

- *Ability to attract and retain good people.* Employees in today's workforce want greater autonomy, challenge, and responsibility in their jobs. Teams offer the type of jobs desired by the most creative and talented members of the workforce.

Union Response to Teams

Union leaders and members have varied greatly in their responses to the creation of self-directed employee teams. At a Ford Motor Company assembly plant, the creation of self-directed teams has made the facility "a much better place to work," according to J. R. "Buddy" Hoskinson, union cochairman of the UAW–Ford Education Development and Training Programs. "In the old days we punched a time card and had no say in what was going on. . . . We'd just do what we had to get by." But today Hoskinson credits the self-directed teams, which have no direct supervision and devise their own work schedules, with creating a "new sense of pride. . . . We know we're doing the best we can do."

The feeling is similar on a project team at the Ford assembly plant. It consists of 10 hourly union workers who implemented the plant manager's idea of modifying the Ford Explorer sport utility vehicle for export. Ralph Wiseman, a project team member, noted that in the past the modification would have been done by an outside firm (a nonunion one most likely). For the project, the 10 members received special training that was unheard of for hourly workers in the past. Wiseman, who bid for a place on the project team, said, "I've never worked so hard, or had a job I liked so much." He emphatically explained his interest in the project: "Our jobs depend on it."[47]

Many other unions, however, view teams as a threat to union strength. They see employee involvement groups and teams as a bridge between management and employees, and once the gap has been bridged, the obvious question may become, "Why do we need a union?" Lewis Maltby, director of the Workplace Task Force of the American Civil Liberties Union, claims that union concerns are justified and that employee teams or involvement groups have no place in a union setting because "employees have already chosen a union to speak for them." Citing this concern over duplication of interest, the United Transportation Union decided its 8,000 Union Pacific members would not participate in quality improvement teams.[48] In 1998 the Teamsters union won a long-sought agreement from United Parcel Service to end "Team Concept" programs. The Teamsters believed the "real purpose (of the teams)" appeared to restrict workers' rights under collective bargaining.[49] The National Labor Relations Board and the courts have generally agreed with critics who have considered employee involvement programs and self-directed work teams as potentially unlawful under Section 8(a)(2) of the Wagner Act. In general, for a violation to occur it must be shown that (1) the entity created by the program is a "labor organization" and (2) the employer dominates or interferes with the formation or administration of that labor organization or contributes support to it. A committee or group is generally considered a "labor organization" if employees participate in it and at least one purpose is to "deal with" the employer on issues of grievances, labor disputes, wages, work rules, or hours of employment.

The "dealing" must involve give and take—as in collective bargaining. If the employer simply says yes or no to employee proposals (often the case with committee quality circles) or if an employee group can decide such issues by itself (often the case with self-directed teams), then the element of dealing is missing, and the group is probably not a labor organization.

With regard to the second criterion for violation—employer domination or interference—Section 8(c) of the Wagner Act allows an employer to voice an opinion on labor–management issues but not to create or initiate a labor organization. Thus, an employer can suggest the idea of committees or work teams, but employees must be free to adopt or reject the concept (as did the Union Pacific workers). In cases involving employers' suggesting the creation of employee teams, motive may be considered a factor, although Section 8(a)(2) of the Wagner Act does not require the presence of an antiunion motive; it condemns any interference or domination.[50] Some "employee–management" teams have been in existence for years and avoid any criticism. How? See Profile 2-2.

PROFILE 2-2

CHRYSLER/UAW EMPLOYEE TEAMS

Why do employee teams in some unionized organizations succeed while others are less successful? In 2002, research on employee teams established through the collective bargaining agreement between the Chrysler Corporation and the United Auto Workers provides some answers. Beginning in the late 1980s Chrysler and the UAW attempted to improve the labor climate at six of the operating plants through a new collective bargaining agreement that (1) created employee shop-floor teams, (2) reduced the number of pay classifications, (3) tied pay to skills within those classifications, and (4) established joint labor–management consultation committees. An anonymous survey of workers who had experienced the old system of "obey-now-and-grieve-later" conflict resolution and leave all decisions to management as well as the new teams produced interesting results. First, when asked, "Do you prefer teams to the old system?" 77 percent responded that they agreed or strongly agreed, and only 22 percent disagreed. Second, when asked, "How satisfied are you with the (new agreement)?" 58 percent responded satisfied or very satisfied, and 34 percent responded dissatisfied or very dissatisfied. Third, when asked, "Do you prefer the (new agreement with teams) to the previous system?" 68 percent responded they agreed or strongly agreed, and 27 percent responded they disagreed or strongly disagreed. These positive worker attitudes were reported despite the fact the new employee teams were forced on workers in plants by the national union and Chrysler, and thus the teams began with a "rocky start."

The research also indicated, however, that workers will remain supportive of teams only if the promised benefits continue to be delivered. Specifically, workers who believed their teams had significantly improved the economic performance of the plant and those who believed their teams continued to have real influence on work processes were more favorable toward the new agreement and the use of employee teams. Overall, the research indicated that the union employees were supportive of the new teams because (1) they were secured through the national contract, (2) they enhanced their economic self-interest by increasing their job security and profit sharing, and (3) they made the work more intrinsically motivating by increasing their level of input and decision making.

SOURCE: Adapted from L. W. Hunter, J. P. MacDuffie, and L. Doucet, "What Makes Teams Take: Employee Reactions to Work Reforms," *Industrial and Labor Relations Review* 55, No. 3 (April 2002), pp. 448–472.

The National Labor Relations Board (NLRB) in two historic decisions has limited the creation of employee committees or teams by its strict interpretation of the Wagner Act as just described. In the *Electromation* case, the board found that the company illegally created and dominated a labor organization.[51] The case involved the Electromation Company of Elkhart, Indiana, a nonunion electrical parts manufacturer. The employer crafted six "action committees" to deal with the employees on various issues. The committees contained members of both management and hourly workers and were charged with developing proposals for management's consideration. Issues considered by the action committees included pay, absenteeism, and attendance bonus programs. The Teamsters union had begun an organizing drive at the company about the time the committees were created. The NLRB ruled that the company clearly violated Section 8(a)(2) of the National Labor Relations Act by creating the action committees. The board decided that the committees had been formed for the purpose, at least in part, of "dealing with" the employer over conditions of employment.

In the 1993 landmark *duPont* case, the NLRB ordered the company to dismantle seven committees of labor and management representatives that had been established to work on safety and recreation issues at the Deepwater, New Jersey, plant.[52] The board ruled that the company had illegally bypassed the plant's union by setting up the committees and thus violated the Wagner Act. This was the board's first ruling on labor–management committees in a unionized plant. The board did note that "brainstorming" sessions might be held if decisions are made by a majority vote and management representatives are in the minority.

From these cases and others, it can be concluded, in general, that employee teams having the authority to make decisions and act without obtaining employer approval are not illegal labor organizations.[53] If joint labor–management teams or committees are created to consider employment issues and a union represents the employees, the union must be involved in the creation of the groups. If such groups are created, they should be voluntary and contain more union members than management.

After the *Electromation* and *duPont* decisions, an attempt was made to amend the National Labor Relations Act to allow for employee work teams. The **Teamwork for Employees and Managers (TEAM) Act** passed Congress in 1996 but was vetoed by President Clinton. If adopted, the act would have allowed an employer to establish or participate in any organization in which employees participate to address matters of mutual interest, as long as the organization does not seek to be the exclusive bargaining representative of the employees.

A decision by the NLRB, however, appears to signal a possible departure from the board's holdings in *Electromation* and *duPont*. Under *Electromation* the board had a consistent, restrictive approach to employee committee issues. This approach lasted throughout the 1990s and until mid-2001, when *Crown Cork & Sea*[54] was decided. Crown Cork & Seal Company, an aluminum can manufacturing plant, employed approximately 150 employees who were not represented by a union. From the time the plant opened, it operated under an employee–management system in which substantial authority was delegated to employees to operate the facility through their participation on numerous standing committees. These employee participation committees consisted of employees and managers and made decisions concerning a broad range of matters, including production, quality, training, attendance, safety, and maintenance. Committees also decided certain disciplinary issues. The board found the employee committees lawful on the grounds that none of the committees were "dealing" with management because "dealing" is not present where a committee's purpose is to perform managerial functions. Indeed, the board found that an employee committee with delegated managerial authority does not "deal with" management because they are management.

WHY UNIONIZE?

The labor union developed as a means by which individuals could unite and have the collective power to accomplish goals that could not be accomplished alone. Whether that power was used to increase take-home wages, to ensure job protection, to improve working conditions, or simply to sit across the bargaining table as an equal with the employer, members believed that in unions there is strength.[55]

Unions have been seen as pragmatic organizations seeking to improve the economic and social conditions of their members. Their ability to achieve economic gains for their workers is demonstrated by the comparison of union and nonunion workers' earnings and major benefits in Table 2-5. The success of their activities can be measured by the improvements in members' work conditions and the perception members have of the union's effectiveness. As the workforce changes, unions needed to change the way they attract members. But first, they need to understand what has attracted workers to unions in the past and why many of those now in the workforce have not been attracted to unions.

Numerous studies have tried to quantify the subjective reasons a worker will vote for union representation. The obvious reason most union members today might suggest is money. A Lou Harris & Associates poll done on behalf of the AFL-CIO concluded that a decision by a worker to vote for union representation includes the following:

1. A deep dissatisfaction with current job and employment conditions
2. A view that unionization can be helpful or instrumental in improving the job or the employment condition
3. A willingness to overlook the image of unions as "big labor" out for themselves and not for the workers
4. Viewing unions as having a significant and substantial role for more altruistic endeavors that improve the lot of members and nonmembers alike by promoting social advances[56]

In addition to the economic benefits unions provide their members, in comparison to nonunion workers, Joe Twarog, Associate Director of Labor Education, has summarized

TABLE 2-5   Union v. Nonunion Wage & Benefit Differences, 2004 (average of U.S. workers)

Per Hour Compensation	Union	Nonunion	Difference (%)
Total compensation	$32.04	$22.38	43%
Wages and salaries	$20.25	$16.29	24%
Paid leave (holiday, vacation, etc.)	$2.16	$1.42	52%
Supplemental pay	$1.04	$0.59	76%
Insurance (health, life, disability)	$3.36	$1.46	130%
Retirement & savings	$2.27	$0.65	249%
Required benefits	$2.85	$1.94	47%
Other	$0.10	$.03	300%

SOURCE: U.S. Bureau of Labor Statistics.

TABLE 2-6 Noneconomic Union Benefits

Benefit	Union	Nonunion
Due process	The union contract provides each bargaining unit member with access to "due process" through the grievance and arbitration procedure.	No formal grievance process with arbitration. In some cases, there may be an internal, self-policing "appeals" process that is ultimately unenforceable.
Wages, benefits, and working conditions	These are negotiated. All members have the opportunity to improve their working conditions through contract negotiations at the bargaining table.	All are unilaterally set by the employer. No avenue for employee input. Management gives what it wants to.
Hiring, promotions, transfers, layoffs	All are governed by the contract. Seniority and other objective standards apply.	All are determined unilaterally and subjectively by the employer.
Changes in working conditions	The negotiated contract establishes all working conditions. These can only be changed by negotiations between the parties.	Changes can be made at any time, without warning, by the employer alone.
Discipline	Any disciplinary action is usually subject to the "just cause" standard, meaning that there is a burden of proof on the employer to justify the discipline.	Workers are "employees at will" meaning that they are subject to discipline and termination for no reason at all, depending on the desires of the employer. No just cause standard applies.
Weingarten rights	These rights allow an employee to have a union representative present during investigatory meetings when discipline may result.	No such rights. Recently, the National Labor Relations Board reversed its position and took away these rights in nonunion facilities.
Voice in the workplace	Employees have a real and formal voice in their working conditions at the bargaining table.	Employers may listen to the employees and then do whatever they choose to do, regardless.
Access to information	The union, through its officers and representatives, has access to information to investigate grievances and for contract negotiations.	Employees have no rights of access to information. The employer tells employees what it wants to do. Information is closely guarded.
Voice in patient care	Through the contract, RNs can negotiate enforceable language on staffing levels, mandatory overtime, floating, and other issues that impact directly on patient care and the quality of health care.	In some facilities, RNs may be afforded the opportunity to make suggestions on some issues, that management is then free to ignore. None of the nurse input is enforceable.

SOURCE: Joe Twarog, "The Benefits of Union Membership: Numerous and Measurable," *Massachusetts Nurse*, 76, no. 4 (May 2005), p. 6. Used by permission.

other benefits. These noneconomic benefits generally include job security, protection against discretionary actions, and due process and are summarized in Table 2-6.

In a survey of labor leaders around the country, the four most important factors affecting the health of the American labor movement were the following:

1. Collective bargaining rights
2. Leadership in the labor movement
3. Union member solidarity
4. Action of the NLRB

The assessment of these labor leaders certainly coincides with the demands of the workers.[57] The Louis Harris survey of 1,500 union and nonunion workers tried to answer the basic questions of how members believe they benefit from union representation. The following questions were asked of individuals of both groups: What conditions in the workplace would change if workers lost their unions? Would conditions get better, worse, or stay the same? The results showed a substantial difference between union and nonunion workers.

Union leaders view the active participation by members in union activities as critical to maintaining strong unions. Union participation, according to a significant body of research, is determined largely by members' commitment, which is determined by two factors: their prounion attitudes in general and their belief that the union is instrumental in improving their economic well-being (wages and benefits) and general working conditions.[58] Prounion attitudes are generally developed over several years and are influenced by external factors, including family members, work history, the media, and direct observation. Their instrumental beliefs can more easily be affected by direct union efforts at the negotiating table and in resolving grievances.

Although most supervisors believe that employees are initially attracted to unions over wage and benefit issues, according to noted labor attorney Jonathan A. Segal, it is the "soft" issues that lead employees to unionize. The soft issues include the following:

- *Recognition.*   Many employees feel overworked and underappreciated. If supervisors do not give them recognition, a union might give them the recognition they desire.
- *Protection from humiliation.*   Some supervisors discipline or correct employees in the presence of their peers. The humiliated employee can easily become a union organizer.
- *Hopelessness.*   Many employees, especially Generation X members, feel they will never be promoted. The pie of good career jobs is shrinking, but the union organizational positions offer an alternative career.
- *Double standards.*   Reserved parking spaces for management, executive dining rooms, country club membership, and paid noontime lunches are visible manifestations of a double standard that union organizers can easily point out during an organizing campaign.
- *Lack of control.*   Many managers still do not "empower" employees to make decisions about their jobs, but collective bargaining can give them some control.
- *Job insecurity.*   Most nonunion employees work "at will," whereas union employees can be terminated only with "just cause." Only one perceived unfair firing could cause employees to question their own job security.
- *Broken promises.*   Once an organizing campaign is under way, employers cannot make promises to influence a union election and can only ask for a "second chance" if they have broken promises in the past.
- *Representation.*   If supervisors and human resource professionals do not represent employee needs and stand behind them when asked, employees may seek help from an outside source, such as a union.[59]

Overall, does it pay to belong to a union? The primary pros and cons are discussed in Profile 2-3. Certainly today that is a question asked by more workers.

One reason often given for why workers do **not** unionize is that labor laws advocated by unions since the 1938 Fair Labor Standards Act, which provided for a minimum wage, a 40-hour week, overtime pay and the abolition of child labor, have

---

PROFILE 2-3

DO UNIONS PAY?

Employers say unions no longer present an attractive value proposition to most private-sector workers.

"Why pay union dues?" asks Lawrence Lorber, a partner at the law firm of Proskauer Rose in Washington, D.C. "What are you buying where it's not already provided somewhere else?" Lorber says the protections unions used to seek, such as from unfair dismissal and dangerous workplaces, have—with labor's ardent support—been taken over by government. "These bedrock issues, which inspired people to organize 50 years ago, are now off the table. The one major thing unions offer is making you a 'for cause' instead of an 'at-will' employee, which guarantees a hearing and arbitration if you're fired," says Lorber. "But in the final analysis, can a union preserve your job?"

Unions concede that external factors like outsourcing and globalization have sapped their power, but they argue that they will have much to offer: higher wages, better benefits, protection from dismissal without a hearing. And, on average, the facts bear them out: From professional athletes to janitors, union members fare better than their nonunion peers.

"You find about a 15 percent advantage for union members across sectors in pay and fringes," says John Heywood, director of the Graduate Program in Human Resources and Labor Relations at the University of Wisconsin at Milwaukee. "In return, unions take about one or two percent of salary— not a bad trade-off."

According to the Bureau of Labor Statistics, the advantages are even greater. In 2004, union workers' median weekly earnings were 27 percent higher than their nonunion counterparts. What's more, 70 percent had defined benefits pensions, compared with 16 percent for nonunion workers, and 89 percent had health benefits, compared with 67 percent nonunion.

SOURCE: Robert J. Grossman, "Unions Follow Suit," *HR Magazine* 50, no. 5 (May 2005), 49. Used by Permission.

---

provided workers with enough job protections that unions are no longer needed. These laws include:

- In 1963, Congress amended the 1938 Fair Labor Standards Act with what is often termed the **"Equal Pay Act."** This act contains the principle of **equal pay for equal work** regardless of gender. Equal pay for equal work does not, in fact, require that jobs be identical to receive equal wages, nor does it require that jobs that are not exactly identical be placed in separate wage categories. Instead, the act as prescribed by Congress requires that organizations pay men and women approximately the same wages for substantially equal work. The concept of substantially equal refers to jobs containing similar skill, effort, responsibility, and working conditions.[60] The Equal Pay Act does provide for legal variances in wages paid to individuals performing identical jobs. Employees may receive different wage rates while performing the same work if such differences are based on seniority, merit, quantity or quality of production, or factors other than gender.[61] Many employers developed new wage and salary systems based on formal job analysis and job evaluation programs to comply with the Equal Pay Act. Such programs provide legislative protection for employees so that they are paid according to the content of their jobs and not according to other factors, such as sex, supervisory bias, or job titles.

- **The Civil Rights Act of 1964** prohibits discrimination in employment and compensation of employees based on race, color, religion, sex, or national origin.[62] It requires the removal of artificial, arbitrary, and unnecessary barriers to employment when the barriers discriminate on the basis of racial or other nonpermissible classifications.[63] Such barriers identified by the Supreme Court and other federal courts include practices and policies of recruitment, selection, placement, testing, transfer, promotion, and seniority as well as other basic terms and conditions of employment.

- Discrimination based on religion is also prohibited by the Civil Rights Law and various state and local laws. The laws define religion to include "all aspects of the religious observance, practice, and belief." Issues that have arisen under the laws include the following:
  a. *Work schedules.* Employers are required to make "reasonable accommodations" for all employees who request time off for religious observances if no undue hardship is placed on the business or on other employees.
  b. *Dress policies.* Employers and unions can generally enforce uniform and dress codes for purposes of public image and employee safety.
  c. *Harassment.* Prohibited actions include jokes, slurs, taunts, or tricks by supervisors, coworkers, or others. Repeated actions may be viewed as creating a "hostile environment" and thus are prohibited.[64]

- The Civil Rights Act also protects workers from sexual harassment, a form of illegal sex discrimination. Sexual harassment constitutes a form of behavior directed toward an employee specifically because of his or her sex.

- In 1993, the **Family and Medical Leave Act (FMLA)** became law. It requires that employers (with a minimum of 50 employees) provide up to 12 weeks of unpaid family leave to employees in cases of childbirth, adoption, or care of a family member. The law guarantees the employee the opportunity to return to the same job or a job of equal status and pay. The law also requires that the employer continue the employee's health benefits during the leave period.

- With the passage of the **Americans with Disabilities Act (ADA) of 1990**,[65] people with disabilities have legal protection from discrimination. A person is considered disabled under the ADA if the following apply to that person:
  a. has a physical or mental impairment limiting substantially one or more of the major life activities of the person
  b. has a record of such an impairment or
  c. is regarded as having such an impairment

- The **Age Discrimination in Employment Act (ADEA)** makes it illegal for employers to discriminate against individuals over the age of 40. Employers cannot refuse to hire or discriminate in terms of compensation, promotion, or other conditions solely on the basis of an individual's age. Employers are also prohibited from using age as a preference in their recruiting practices.

- The **Older Workers Benefit Protection Act (OWBPA)** provided additional protection for older workers by instituting the "equal benefit, equal cost" test, which meant that employers could not deny older workers the same benefits that younger workers received if (any) such benefits cost the same. The OWBPA also incorporated guidelines for early retirement incentive plans.

UNIONS TODAY

As noted in Chapter 1, skilled craft workers formed the original unions in America. **Craft unions** represent a group of workers who share a skill or an occupation, such as electricians, carpenters, and bricklayers. Unions such as the United Brotherhood of Carpenters and Joiners of America and the International Brotherhood of Electrical Workers are examples of such craft unions. **Industrial unions** found their start in factories where largely unskilled laborers worked. Organizing the entire plant in one union gave the workers the necessary leverage to counteract the availability of unskilled nonunion workers. Industrial unions include the UAW and the United Mine Workers.

In the public sector and in professions where unionization is growing, unions also tend to fall into these same two categories. **Public-sector unions**, such as the National Education Association and the Fraternal Order of Police, organize within particular professions in the public sector—teachers and police officers. Other unions, such as AFGE (federal) and AFSCME (local), are industrial-type unions that organize government employees by location. Over 98,000 professional actors are represented by the Screen Actors Guild (SAG) (see Profile 2-4).

As discussed later in this chapter, **professional sports unions** have been organized to represent professional players in collective bargaining with team owners. These unions resemble craft unions, as they are organized around one sport, such as the Major League Baseball Players Association and the National Football League Players Association.

PROFILE 2-4

MELISSA GILBERT, UNION PRESIDENT

Many fans know her as the adorable Laura Ingalls from the television series *Little House on the Prairie*, which also starred Michael Landon as her father. That identity, however, was not helpful to her as past president of the powerful Screen Actors Guild (SAG) union. Ms. Gilbert claimed, "Not only do people still perceive that I'm going to be a doormat, they perceive I'm still 12!" President Gilbert won her office in a hard-fought 2002 election with Valerie Harper—also known as "Rhoda" of the television sitcom *Mary Tyler Moore*. Ms. Gilbert headed the large, powerful union with 98,000 members; a small percentage of whom are multimillionaire actors, but the majority can be unemployed on any given day. Former SAG President William Daniels believes that contrast in membership income is unique—and unlike members of other unions most SAG members work in other occupations—as waiters, accountants, etc.

At age 38, Ms. Gilbert displayed determination and commitment to the job. Gordon Drake, a SAG board member who supported Gilbert's opponent, has noted, "She works hard . . . and shows up at the guild every day." Ms. Gilbert and the union leadership were faced with several difficult issues similar to some other U.S. industries, such as textiles, electronics, and appliances. Many film and television companies have moved production to other countries to save labor and other costs, which cost Hollywood thousands of union jobs. Ms. Gilbert negotiated with MGM, Warner, Paramount, and other studios on a film-by-film basis to maintain SAG contracts when movies and shows are produced abroad.

SOURCE: Adapted from Gary Gentile, Associated Press, published in *Cincinnati Enquirer,* June 13, 2002, pp. 1, 3.

Former Screen Actors Guild President Melissa Gilbert defeated Valerie Harper in a heated 2002 election to head the powerful union.

Transportation unions in the railroad and airline industries, such as the United Transportation Union and the Air Line Pilots Association, are governed by the Railway Labor Act, which differs some from the National Labor Relations Act. After the 1981 strike by the Professional Air Traffic Controllers Organization, the public became more aware of the impact of unionization on the airline industry.

Finally, unions of **agricultural workers**, like the **United Farm Workers** founded by Dolores Huerta and Cesar Chavez, do not have the protections of the National Labor Relations Act, but they still organize and gain recognition through concerted activities, as discussed in Profile 2-5.

UNIONS IN PROFESSIONAL SPORTS

As the numbers of jobs in most traditionally unionized industries continue to drop, a generation of Americans is learning about collective bargaining through the news media instead of around the dinner table. For example, collective bargaining and unions have had a substantial impact on Americans through professional sports. Through contract negotiations players in recent years have received an increasing share of gate receipts and television revenues. Some sports fans may complain that the days when athletes "played because of their love for the game" are gone forever; however, others recognize

---

CESAR CHAVEZ AND THE RISE OF THE UNITED FARM WORKERS

Although the passage of the Wagner Act gave most employees the right to organize and collectively bargain over wages and the conditions of their employment, agricultural workers were excluded from the act. In 1962, **Cesar Chavez** founded the National Farm Workers Association (later called the United Farm Workers [UFW] after merger with the Agricultural Workers Organizing Committee) and began his lifelong struggle to gain collective bargaining rights for these unrepresented workers. Using techniques of nonviolence such as boycotts, pickets, and strikes, Chavez spearheaded *La Causa* (the cause), the struggle for decent wages and working conditions for the mainly migrant workforce in California's agribusiness farms.

One of his most successful boycotts involved a nationwide boycotting of grapes. In the summer of 1965, grapes were ripening in the fields around Delano, California. Getting the grapes picked and to market quickly is crucial to the grower's profit. A group of migrant farm workers who were coming from harvesting grapes in southern California demanded a wage of $1.25 an hour, but the growers would not agree. A strike of nine farms organized by the Agricultural Workers Organizing Committee, an AFL-CIO organization, was begun. Chavez's union joined the strike, and within a month the strike had spread to more than 30 farms. Under pressure from the strikers, the growers, who had always been able to end strikes with a small wage concession, offered to raise wages to $1.25. This time the workers said no.

Shortly after the strike began, Chavez called on the public to refrain from buying grapes without a union label. Union volunteers were sent to big cities where boycott centers were established. These centers would identify union-friendly groups, churches, and civil rights and women's rights organizations, and ask them to publicize and join in the boycott. The civil rights movement, which had been focusing attention on the treatment of African Americans in the south, helped consumers recognize the racism in the treatment of largely Chicano and Filipino farm workers, and millions of them stopped buying table grapes.

The strike was still on when in March 1966, Chavez lead strikers on a 340-mile march from Delano to Sacramento, the state's capital. The walk started with 70 strikers, but by the end of the 25-day walk, Chavez addressed a crowd of 10,000 who rallied in support of the farm workers. One of the two major growers bowed to the pressure and signed an agreement with the NFWA. The other major grower agreed to hold a representation election. However, before the election could be held, the International Brotherhood of Teamsters offered itself as an alternative to the UFW (the union resulting from the merger of the NFWA and AWOC). Angered by this betrayal by another union, Chavez called for a boycott of the election. More than half the workers refused to vote, and the issue was sent to an arbitrator appointed by California's governor. Another election was held under the auspices of the arbitrator, and the UFW won the election. By 1970 the UFW had effectively organized most of the grape growers industry, claiming 50,000 dues-paying members. Chavez's vision of an organization that was both a union and a civil rights movement gave its members both a sense of mission and a depth of moral pressure to enable it to succeed.

SOURCE: Adapted from "The Rise of the UFW" and "The Story of Cesar Chavez," www.ufw.com (2002).

---

that today's players are able to make a career from their profession and are sharing in the wealth they generate through their accomplishments. Still other sports fans blame the high players' salaries (see Figure 2-4) for the high stadium prices, and they miss the days when players stayed with one team for their entire careers. In addition, collective bargaining has resulted in long strikes and lockouts and has disrupted several seasons.

Many working men and women could have trouble sympathizing with baseball players because the average player's salary is 75 times that of an average worker and the average basketball player's salary is 132 times that of an average worker. How does your salary compare with these national averages?

Occupation	2005 Average Salary
U.S. worker	$37,020
Baseball player	$2,800,000
Football player (NFL)	$2,300,000
Basketball player (NBA)	$4,900,000
Hockey player (NHL)	$1,800,000

SOURCE: U.S. Department of Labor, Major League Baseball Players Association, National Football League Players Association, National Basketball Players Association, and National Hockey League Players Association.

FIGURE 2-4 How Does Your Salary Compare?

In general, the sports industry can be viewed as a part of the larger entertainment industry, which enthralls the American public. In this respect, star athletes are similar to musicians, stage bands, actors, and other performers. The principal common features among these professionals are technology, media, market constraints, and societal power. The televising of sporting events, including cable and satellite distribution, has become the largest source of revenue for professional sport franchises. Schedules, locations, and times of games are quickly changed to meet the needs of the television industry. Similar influences can be found in other entertainment fields. Both sports and other professional entertainment areas are highly subject to the "star system," in which a few stars command a substantial influence on their professions and derive substantial income from outside sources such as product endorsements. Like the older unions in entertainment—the Screen Actors Guild, the National Association of Broadcast Engineers and Technicians, and the American Federation of Television and Radio Artists—sports unions are concerned about the welfare of the other players (nonsuperstars), who are more subject to the desires of management.[66]

The key elements of labor relations in professional sports are shown in Figure 2-5. The three principal participants are management (leagues and team owners), labor (players and unions), and government. The federal government performs the regulatory function under the National Labor Relations Act in the same capacity that it oversees all private commerce. A body of NLRB and court decisions unique to collective bargaining in professional sports has been compiled since 1935. In this respect, the sports industry is similar to many other American industries—steel, auto, service, and clothing—in that it falls under the NLRB, but it contains past practices, unions, and historical events unique to the industry.

Management in the sports industry operates through league structures. The leagues negotiate collective bargaining agreements, set rules for drafting players, determine management rights, and negotiate national television agreements. Thus, club owners yield a great deal of the traditional management authority to the leagues. They do, however, retain decision making over front-office personnel, local television contracts, and stadium management, and they negotiate individual player contracts.

Labor unions in the sports industry operate much as other unions do. They organize the players for the purpose of collective bargaining, promote solidarity, negotiate

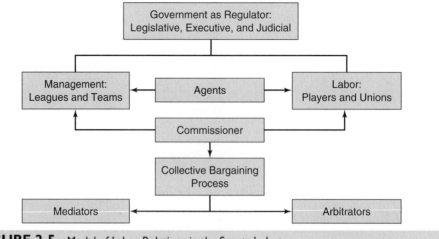

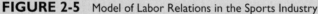

FIGURE 2-5 Model of Labor Relations in the Sports Industry

SOURCE: Reprinted from *Industrialization and Labor Relations: Contemporary Research in Seven Countries,* edited by Stephen Frenkel and Jeffrey Harrod. Copyright © 1995 by Cornell University. Used by permission of the publisher, Cornell University Press.

contracts, utilize power tactics such as strikes and picketing if necessary, file and administer grievances, collect dues, and lobby for the interests of their members. The roles of the commissioners and agents are unique to the sports industry. In general, commissioners serve both management and labor and act as the public spokespeople for the league. Because they are hired and paid by management, however, they tend to be viewed as part of the management structure.

Agents serve as representatives of individual players and negotiate their contracts with individual team owners. Some agents also manage the assets of their players and negotiate their outside contracts. Many observers believe that agents have become a destructive force in the sports industry and have caused the colossal salaries of some players, while the unions have concentrated on increasing the salary, benefits, and working conditions of all players. Unless the unions take over the role of negotiating individual contracts, a change that superstar players are unlikely to support, the influence of players' agents is likely to continue to grow. The other major participants are the mediators and arbitrators. The common use of individual player **salary arbitration** in the sports industry has had a significant influence on player salaries and has developed a highly specialized field of collective bargaining.[67]

Baseball

The National and American Leagues of Professional Baseball Clubs represent management for purposes of collective bargaining. The Major League Baseball Players Association (MLBPA), formed in 1952, has represented players for collective bargaining since 1966. Under a 1922 Supreme Court decision, upheld in the 1972 *Curt Flood* decision, the Court excluded professional baseball from federal antitrust acts. The Court cited baseball's unique needs as an industry and its place in U.S. history.[68] For many years the collective bargaining agreements for professional baseball teams limited the areas of negotiations to primarily salary, insurance, and pensions. Then in 1970 a new provision provided for a tripartite grievance arbitration panel to replace the commissioner as the last step in resolving disputes.

The "modern era" of professional sports and collective bargaining began in the mid-1970s. Arbitration of salary disputes in baseball (after three years of service) was first

TABLE 2-7 Major League Baseball Salaries, 1970–2005

Year	Average Salary
1970	$29,303
1975	$44,676
1980	$143,756
1985	$371,157
1990	$597,537
1996	$1,156,666
2001	$2,138,896
2005	$2,800,000

SOURCE: Major League Baseball Players Association

provided in the 1973 agreement. The arbitrator, however, must choose the final salary offer of either the player or the team without any compromise. The 1976 baseball agreement first allowed players to become **free agents** (after six years of service) and thus limited to newer players the "reserve clause" status, under which teams reserve the sole right to negotiate a contract with the player. The reserve clause is a most unusual labor–management principle in that it takes from players a basic right enjoyed by other American workers—to sell their services to any employer. The NBA limited its reserve clause contract language in 1980, the NFL in 1993. As a free agent, the player can sign with the highest bidder or whomever he chooses. These major changes in the 1970s began what is called the "modern era" of professional sports as other sports unions followed the lead of baseball.[69] In 2005 baseball player salaries averaged over $2.8 million, 50 times what they received in 1975, the last year before free agency. By comparison, the average U.S. worker's 2005 income of $37,020 was only four times what it was in 1975.

The effect of free agency and salary arbitration on average players' salaries can be seen in Table 2-7.

In 2005, 89 baseball players utilized arbitration and received an average salary of $2.8 million. Although this amount is about five times larger than the average player's salary only 15 years earlier, it was down 126 percent from 2004, which is important to note because players sometimes lose when they use arbitration. In fact, in about 66 percent of the cases the arbitrator award was lower than the owner's last offer. For example, Jeremy Affeldt was awarded $950,000 rather than the Kansas City Royals' last offer of $1.2 million. Cincinnati outfielder Adam Dunn received the largest percentage increase through arbitration, 934 percent (from $445,000 to $4.6 million), and Houston Astros pitcher Roger Clemens won the largest single-season salary for a pitcher in baseball history—$18 million![70]

Baseball Strikes

The first major league strike that affected season play occurred in 1972. The MLBPA struck over a pension issue, and 86 games were canceled. The first costly and most significant strike in professional sports, however, occurred in baseball in 1981. The issue was players' free agency rights, with owners demanding a replacement player for teams that lost a player because of free agency as a means to reduce the use of the free agency process. The players' union held fast to protect the free agency process, which had significantly increased players' salaries. At the last minute, the NLRB petitioned the U.S. district court for any injunction, but the court refused, and on June 12 a 50-day strike began.

In 1994, for the first time in history, the World Series was canceled. A union-called strike did what two world wars, a depression, and an earthquake (1989 in San Francisco)

> **What the Players Association Wanted**
>
> Free agency. Eliminate the restriction on repeat free agency within a five-year span if a player's club offers salary arbitration at the end of his contract
> Salary arbitration. Reduce the threshold to two years of major league service, its level from 1974 to 1986; it had been three years
> Minimum salary. Increase from $109,000 to $175,000 to $200,000
>
> **What the Owners Wanted**
>
> Revenue. A 50-50 revenue split with players, with a $1 billion total guaranteed over seven years
> Salary cap. After a four-year phase-in period in the seven-year agreement, clubs could not have payrolls more than 110 percent of the average or less than 84 percent of the average
> Arbitration. Salary arbitration eliminated
> Minimum salary. Escalating scale of minimum salaries for players with fewer than four years' major league service, but they would be allowed to sign for more than the minimum

FIGURE 2-6   Players' and Owners' Issues: 1994 Major League Baseball Strike

could not—cancel the World Series. It was the eighth work stoppage since 1972 and by far the most damaging to the game, its players, and its owners. The strike began on August 12, 1994, and eventually caused the World Series to be canceled. By the spring of 1995, the owners had assembled teams of replacement players, but at the last minute the MLBPA agreed to let its players on the field without a new contract and thus kept out the replacement-player games. The 1994 issues all centered on money—or greed, as outlined in Figure 2-6.

The National Football League

Although the National Football League (NFL) shares some cost and revenue factors with major league baseball, there are several important differences. On the cost side, the NFL does not maintain an expensive farm system of minor league teams. However, each NFL team has 45 players, and the NFL has about 1,500 players compared with only 600 major league baseball players. On the revenue side, each NFL team plays only 20 regular-season and preseason games, compared with 162 for each major league baseball team. The NFL, however, has built a strong television audience. Of all professional sports, only the NFL has been able to command network contracts for all its televised games. Baseball, basketball, and hockey, for example, have most of their games televised on free local television or cable.

The National Football League Players Association (NFLPA) is the union that represents professional football players. It was first registered with the U.S. Department of Labor in 1968. The players, in selecting the NFLPA, also rejected the Teamsters union, which tried to organize them. In 1974 the NFLPA became the first sports union to receive a charter from the AFL-CIO. The union, however, had difficulty negotiating with the NFL. One major break occurred when the NLRB ruled that playing on artificial turf was a mandatory subject for collective bargaining.

In 1993 the NFL and the union signed a historic contract that ended five years of negotiations and a landmark court decision, *McNeil et al. v. The National Football League.* The primary issue was the owners' reserve clause and the players' free agency rights. In the new agreement, players will receive true free agency status after six years of service, and thus owners lose their reserve clause that binds players to one team. In return the owners received the first salary cap in football that limits total players' pay to 67 percent of designated gross revenues (61 percent after three years). In the first NFL "free agency derby," 120 players changed teams, and a new era in NFL collective bargaining had begun.[71] Whether the new free agency provision will drive up NFL salaries to equal those in baseball and basketball is a question only time can answer.

In 1996, the Supreme Court, in *Brown v. Pro Football,* made it clear that the NFL was a legitimate multiemployer bargaining group under labor law statutes and that negotiations by the league were not in violation of the Sherman Antitrust Act.[72]

The National Basketball Association

In a process similar to baseball, professional basketball players have a union, the National Basketball Players Association (NBPA), which negotiates a general contract with the league—the National Basketball Association (NBA). Also as in baseball, outside agents negotiate individual player contracts with the team owners. Compared with baseball and football, basketball has the unique advantage of requiring only 12 players per team. This factor, combined with an 82-game season, has resulted in the teams' profitability largely depending on home-game attendance. Perhaps because of the competition from college games, however, professional basketball has consistently ranked a distant third behind baseball and football in television ratings. Overall, however, the combination of a relatively small number of players (300) in a game that has many individual stars and far more home games than football has enabled NBA players to negotiate high salaries. In fact, in the 1980s the NBA average player's salary surpassed that of players in all other professional sports.

Other major factors that have escalated NBA salaries include competition from other leagues (starting with the old American Basketball Association) and the 1981 NBA contract that provided players with free agency status. The NBA was the first sport to adopt the "hardship rule," which allowed young players to be drafted before their college senior year if they could prove financial need.

The most important labor relations case in NBA history is *Robertson v. NBA*[73] (see Profile 2-6). The players involved, led by Oscar Robertson, filed suit against the NBA, contending that the draft, uniform contract, and reserve clause together were a violation of the Sherman Antitrust Act because they eliminated competition among the teams for the individual players. A final settlement of all issues was reached through collective bargaining between the NBA and NBPA in 1976. The historic contract provided a first right of refusal for players with expired contracts (the original team can keep the player if it matches the offer of another team), and the college draft was amended to allow a player who chooses not to sign with his drafting team the right to be selected by any team in the following year's draft.[74]

The issue of antitrust violations in professional basketball was litigated again in 1995. In *Caldwell v. NBA,* Caldwell, a professional basketball player, charged the NBA with an antitrust violation for failure to play him. He alleged that they failed to play him because of his activities as president of the NBPA. The Court dismissed his case, saying that the association's activities were exempted from the Sherman Antitrust Act because they fell under the National Labor Relations Act.[75]

1998 NBA Lockout

On July 1, 1998, the NBA owners began a lockout when contract negotiations reached an impasse. Players were not paid, and teams did not negotiate with new players or trade existing ones. In the end, three months of the NBA season and the All-Star game

---

OSCAR ROBERTSON, NBA UNION PIONEER

Oscar Robertson was president of the National Basketball Players Association (NBPA) from 1965 to 1974. It was under his leadership that the NBPA decided to take a very risky but historic step and filed suit against the NBA, challenging the league's practices of a draft, uniform contract, and reserve clause as a violation of the Sherman Antitrust Act. The settlement of *Robertson v. NBA* ended the reserve clause and opened the door to free agency and the highest average salaries in all professional sports.

Robertson was the first collegiate basketball player to be named Player of the Year three times (1958–1960) and then became a 12-time NBA All-Star with the Cincinnati Royals and Milwaukee Bucks. Thus, as a player he was too valuable for any team to not play him. However, after his NBA career Robertson believes he was "blacklisted" by the NBA and team owners: "There's no doubt about it. They couldn't do anything to me during my playing days, but at some of the depositions we had against them later, they alluded to [the

blacklisting]." In addition Robertson says he saw fellow NBA players cut or traded because they were union leaders.

In the 1950s NBA players had no minimum wage, pension plan, or health benefits—and an average salary of $8,000. At first the NBA refused to recognize or negotiate with the players union. Player representatives became a target and were cut from teams or not played, according to Robertson, and thus the union sought players like himself and Tom Heinsohn, a Boston Celtics star, who served as NBPA president prior to Robertson. The first collective bargaining agreement was not reached until 1964, when the players threatened to not play in the first televised NBA All-Star game.

Today Oscar Robertson is principal owner of three successful companies in Cincinnati, Ohio. He is a living legend in Cincinnati who is engaged in many civic and charitable organizations but not the NBA. How does he feel about his union activities? "I did what I had to do . . ., I would do it again."

SOURCE: Adapted from Tom Groeschen, "Robertson, an NBA Union Pioneer, Says League Made Him Pay Price," *Cincinnati Enquirer* (August 15, 2002), pp. A1, A7.

---

were lost as well as over $500 million in salaries. On the day before the date Commissioner Stern had set by which he would cancel the entire season, both sides made compromises, and a settlement was reached. The owners, in general, had won a better agreement. A key provision was the union accepting 55 percent of league revenues. The players approved the new contract by a vote of 179 to 5.[76]

The National Hockey League

The National Hockey League (NHL) for many years was the least economically successful of the four major professional sports because it had limited television contracts and small arena seating capacities (average about 15,000) for the 80-game season. Cooperation between the NHL and the National Hockey League Players Association (NHLPA) has historically been good, and thus the difficult task of requiring joint U.S.–Canadian collective bargaining laws for professional hockey has been limited. The NHL drafts new players from amateur hockey leagues in a process similar to the NFL draft, except that the players gain experience in minor leagues instead of college.

Collective bargaining in hockey is unique in that negotiations begin spontaneously as new issues arise, resulting in modifications to long-term agreements. As in other sports, agents negotiate individual contracts with team owners, and salary arbitration is utilized if either side requests it. However, the practice is used far less often than it is in baseball. Contractual grievances also go to arbitration in hockey if unresolved in earlier steps. Hockey players have gained free agency rights, with teams retaining the right of first refusal on those who might leave.[77]

The 1990s witnessed a substantial rise in the fortunes of professional hockey. Under NHL Commissioner Gary Bettman, the league has enjoyed greater revenues through new television contracts and two new expansion teams—the Anaheim Mighty Ducks and the Florida Panthers. Bettman also helped improve the sport's image by reducing violence in the game by negotiating strict penalties for unnecessary violence.[78]

2005 NHL Lockout Cancelled Entire Season

The National Hockey League became the first North American professional sports league to cancel an entire season due to a labor dispute. In February 2005 NHL owners officially called an end to the 2004/05 season five months after they locked out the 700 union members of the NHLPA. The cancellation of the entire season cost the players over $1 billion in salaries and the owners of 24 U.S. teams and 6 Canadian teams over $2 billion in revenue from ticket sales, concessions, sponsors, and media contracts. The long-term loss of fans and media support will not be known for years. NHL Commissioner Gary Bettman noted, "We're going to have to earn back the trust and love and affection of everybody who's associated with the game." ESPN replacement programming of men's college basketball games drew twice the ratings as NHL games—and thus raised the question of how much the media will pay to televise future hockey games.

The central issue was player salaries that had tripled in the previous ten years to an average of $1.8m in 2003/04. The NHL owners claimed players' salaries accounted for over 75 percent of total revenues and demanded "cost certainty," which would directly link total player salaries to total revenues. The players' union steadfastly refused any type of salary cap, which exists in the NFL and NBA. The union did offer a 24 percent cut in player salaries, but the owners rejected the offer. Then, right before the lockout in December 2004, the union offered a salary cap of $52 million per team, but the league asked for a $40 million cap, and the talks ended.[79]

WORKFORCE DIVERSITY

The history of the labor movement in America is one of competing agendas. Focus on societal changes doomed the National Labor Union, the Knights of Labor, and the Industrial Workers of the World, whereas focus on trade and industrial unionization and workplace representation preserved the AFL and CIO. Although studies show that the altruistic nature of labor unions is a factor in workers' approval, the bread-and-butter issues of collective bargaining rights are of more importance.

The labor movement, then, has been caught between the proverbial "rock and a hard place" in its relations with the groups that make up the new diverse workforce. In the past, the labor movement had a number of opportunities to react to these groups: for African Americans during abolition and the 1960s civil rights movement, for women during the suffrage movement and the various stages of the women's movement, and for immigrants at the turn of the twentieth century and after World War I.

Union leaders know that minorities and women benefit economically from union membership. Union workers earn 25 percent more in annual wages than nonunion workers, according to the Department of Labor's Bureau of Labor Statistics. The union wage difference is even greater for minorities and women. Union women earn 30 percent more

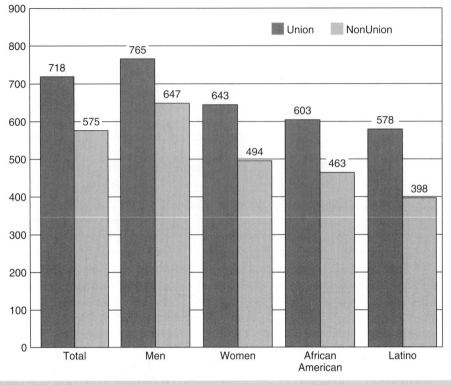

FIGURE 2-7 Median Weekly Earnings of Full-Time Wage and Salary Workers, 2002

SOURCE: U.S. Department of Labor, Employment and Earnings, January 2002. Prepared by the AFL-CIO, www.aflcio.org (June 18, 2002).

than nonunion women; African American union members earn 31 percent more than their nonunion counterparts, and for Latino workers the union advantage totals 45 percent (see Figure 2-7).[80]

Unions today, according to the AFL-CIO, strive to give working people a voice on the job, in their local communities, and in their government. Union workers earn an average income that is higher than their nonunion counterparts and are more likely to receive paid health-care and pension benefits (see Figure 2-8). So why has it been so difficult for unions to organize women and minorities? Some of the reasons can be found in the history of unions with these groups.

African Americans and Unions

The abolitionist movement could not claim major support from American white workers. Trade unionists protested the move the federal government was making toward war over the issue of slavery in 1861 with the slogan "Concession, Not Secessions."[81] After the Civil War the labor movement struggled with the influx of cheap labor into the labor pool, eroding its power to keep wages high. Freed slaves and immigrants were a part of that cheap labor pool. The National Labor Union (NLU) originally encouraged freed slaves to unionize, but they were not invited to actually join the NLU.[82] The relationship between the freed slaves and the white workers in the industrial centers deteriorated. African Americans began forming their own trade union locals, including the **National Colored Labor Union** (NCLU). Headed by Isaac Myers, the NCLU organized in the South in 1870 and applied for affiliation with the NLU, stating, "The day

Labor unions are made up of working people working together to solve problems, build stronger workplaces, and give working families a real voice. Unions stand for fair treatment of all working people on the job, in our communities, and in the economy.

Unions give working people a voice in government. They represent working families before lawmakers, and make sure politicians never forget that working families voted them into office.

Machinist Mike Gunarich, of York, Pennsylvania, is proud of his union and of his company. Working together, they pulled Harley-Davidson through tough economic times and put the company back in the black.

Unions give workers a voice on the job about safety, security, pay, benefits, and about the best ways to get the work done. That helps working families, the companies that employ them, and the customers who use their products and services.

Unions work for equal treatment and fight discrimination. We marched with Dr. Martin Luther King, Jr., in the 1960s, and we continue to fight for justice for women and minorities in collective bargaining as well as legislation.

For Erin McCarthy, a Las Vegas food services worker, being a union member means she has the job security, flexibility, and benefits she needs to raise her family.

When Chicago construction worker Michael Vukasovic is 30 stories up, he knows he can count on his trained union coworkers to be a solid, skilled, safety-minded team.

Unions help working families get a fair shake in today's economy. Union workers earn an average of $155 (or 33 percent) more each week than nonunion workers and are much more likely to have health and pension benefits. On the job and in national policy debates, we are committed to seeing that working families, not just rich CEOs, benefit from our labor.

Unions strengthen communities. We promote economic development, partner with community groups, and pitch in when disaster strikes.

Arthereane Brown, a Los Angeles nurse, says patients are well cared for because her union gives her a voice on the job about staffing levels and patient care.

FIGURE 2-8 Today's Unions

SOURCE: www.aflcio.org (July 23, 1999).

has passed for the establishment of organizations based upon color."[83] Unfortunately, the white labor movement did not agree.

Rebuffed by the white labor unions, the NCLU joined forces with the Republican Party in the South in hopes of gaining ground in its racial emancipation movement. Labor eventually joined forces with the Democratic Party, the party seen as the "working man's party," as a reaction to big business. The split between African American workers and white workers widened when African Americans were used as strikebreakers. Because racial discrimination in the South limited African Americans' job opportunities, they fell victim to the opportunities big business offered when they were recruited to go north and west to provide scab labor to break union-supported strikes.[84]

The antagonism between African American workers and white workers continued as the labor movement matured. The effects of racial discrimination and the use of blacks as strikebreakers drove an almost insurmountable wedge between the two. In addition, at the same time the white upper classes in the South created the "Jim Crow" laws. These segregation laws kept African Americans at the lowest rung of the economic ladder by convincing poor whites that their place one step up the ladder was dependent on keeping blacks down. Institutional racism kept white and black workers apart.

As trade unions began to gain strength in the 1920s and 1930s and came to the South to organize workers, the unions did not include African American workers. AFL unions in Memphis, Tennessee, for example, excluded black carpenters, and white railroad brotherhoods organized teams of assassins to shoot black workers. The CIO's performance was not much better, although African Americans were allowed to participate in the unions of the lowest level of unskilled laborers, such as hod carriers and construction laborers. Despite the lack of acceptance, African American industrial workers, such as those in Memphis in the 1930s, supported the union movement.

They saw the union movement as a chance to change the power relationship between them and their employers. One example of how they were treated can be seen in an "A, B, C" wage system instituted in one Firestone factory in 1937: "Adult white males (A) received 32 cents an hour while boys (B) between 18 and 21 and the 'colored' (C) made 28 cents an hour."[85] But because the Jim Crow system continued to give white workers an advantage, unions excluded African Americans. This exclusion gave AFL-organized unions dominance over CIO-organized unions in union elections through the 1930s. However, white industrial workers began to abandon the AFL for the CIO when it began to dominate the labor movement under John L. Lewis. Because black workers made up a significant part of the unskilled labor force, some African American participation resulted. However, even black labor leaders suffered from discrimination when a hotel, in 1948, which was to house a labor negotiation session, refused admission to a black member of the union's negotiating team.[86]

African American workers experienced a series of advances and defeats in the pre–civil rights days. When the growth of the CIO began to slow down and the AFL-CIO united to preserve the labor movement, the AFL's exclusionary policies seemed to dominate so that identification of unions with the civil rights movement declined.

The labor movement was again confronted with the needs of African American workers during the 1960s civil rights movement. The civil rights movement was to give African Americans shut out from the job market by segregation and discrimination an opportunity to work. Their need to integrate workplaces was coupled with their need to integrate unions.

Although labor leaders were seen as supportive of the civil rights movement, such support did not go deep into union membership. Trade unions that sponsored apprenticeship programs excluding African Americans were not alone in their discrimination.

Industrial unions did not help the African American worker. Reacting to this treatment, civil rights leaders and organizations simply regrouped and organized African American workers into unions as part of their civil rights activities. The **Maryland Freedom Union** (MFU) and the **Mississippi Freedom Labor Union** organized and engineered strikes and demonstrations to improve the lot of African American workers who had been shunted to low-paying jobs. A boycott of a small retail chain in a white neighborhood of Baltimore, Maryland, in 1966 led to the MFU's first success. When AFL-CIO officials learned that the MFU had been recognized as the exclusive bargaining agent for the employees of the retail chain, they objected. Walter Reuther, then head of the AFL-CIO's Industrial Union Department, pressured the leadership of the Congress of Racial Equality, a major civil rights organization, to sever its support of the MFU.[87] The MFU, like the activist civil rights organizations, peaked in the late 1960s and disappeared in the 1970s.

Although the AFL had supported African American membership in affiliate unions, it was not until 1964 that the last affiliate of the AFL-CIO removed the "whites only" clause from its bylaws and constitution. African Americans today are more unionized (15 percent of organized labor) than the workforce as a whole (11 percent of the population). Union membership has been rewarding for African American workers, who average about 50 percent more income than African American nonunion workers. In the future, African Americans are likely to increase their role in union leadership and membership. The labor movement has been an important vehicle in the growth of the African American middle class and partially explains the proclivity of black Americans to join unions. At the same time, there is a shift away from heavy industry and manufacturing in the American economy, and union workers are losing their jobs and being left unprepared for the new high-skilled labor market.[88] Whereas blacks in 2001 have shown a greater preference for union membership than whites, 17 to 13.1 percent, Hispanics trailed with 11.3 percent membership. Membership among women, 11.7 percent, has always trailed that of men, which was 15.1 percent in 2001.[89]

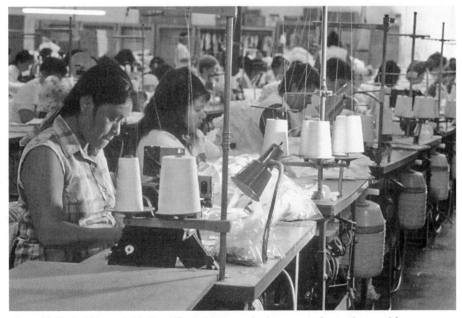

Since 1907, the Women's National Trade Union and other groups have advocated for women to receive equal pay for equal work.

Women and Unions

To begin to improve women's participation in unions, women within the U.S. labor movement organized the founding conference of the **Coalition of Labor Union Women** (CLUW) in 1974. Recognizing that less than 12 percent of the women in the labor force are unionized and that most workingwomen are suffering economically, the CLUW was formed to promote unionism. Following is the statement of purpose adopted at the CLUW founding conference:

> It is imperative that within the framework of the union movement the Coalition of Labor Union Women take aggressive steps to more effectively address the critical needs of millions of unorganized sisters and make our unions more responsive to the needs of all women, especially the needs of minority women who have traditionally been singled out for particularly blatant oppression. Union women work in almost every industry, in almost every part of the country. Despite their geographical, industrial, and occupational separations, union women share common concerns and goals. Full equality of opportunities and rights in the labor force require the full attention of the labor movement . . . and especially, the full attention of women who are part of the labor movement. The primary purpose of this National Coalition is to unify all union women in a viable organization to determine our common problems and concerns and to develop action programs within the framework of our unions to deal effectively with our objectives. This struggle goes beyond the borders of this Nation and we urge our working sisters throughout the world to join us in accomplishing these objectives through their labor organizations.[90]

Women today provide almost two-thirds of the new entrants into the job market. The two major areas of potential growth for unionization are in the health industry and among clerical workers. Both of these industries are made up mostly of women workers. The reluctance of unions to include women fully and women's reluctance to unionize may have the same basis. During the post–Civil War period, women who had entered the workforce during the war continued to work. The NLU found itself in the center of controversy for recognizing representatives of women's unions into its congress. Because unions did not welcome women into their organizations, protective unions and trade associations for women were formed. Sometimes women and men working right next to each other had separate unions. Most men workers viewed women as competition, so they decried their employment. The NLU allowed representatives of a number of the women's protective unions to join their 1868 congress, including Susan B. Anthony, the most famous suffragette. When Anthony admitted that her protective union was used as a strikebreaking organization because the women's movement needed to do so, the NLU expelled her. After that, protective unions for women lost support from their fellow male workers, and by 1872 most had died out.[91]

In the years between 1903 and World War I, new women's labor unions emerged, mostly founded by middle-class reformers and working-class women. The reformers had gathered and organized around settlement houses in major urban areas. These settlement house reformers and active workingwomen met with male union leaders in 1903 to form the Women's Trade Union League, described in Chapter 1.[92] The league's first convention in 1907 adopted the following six-point platform:

1. Equal pay for equal work
2. Full citizenship for women
3. An eight-hour workday

4. A minimum wage

5. Organization of all workers into unions

6. The economic programs of the American Federation of Labor

During the early 1900s, the league supported unionization of women workers in many industries, but it had its major successes in the garment industry. Unfortunately, the AFL, led by Samuel Gompers, gave no more than lip service to support of the league's activities.

During World War I, women entered industries in huge numbers to support the men at war. The workingmen left in those factories resented the influx of women because it caused them to have to compete and because they believed it lowered wage rates.

The Great Depression, which started in 1929, caused unemployment to rise from three million in 1930 to nearly 15 million in 1933 and wages to drop 45 percent. Among the casualties of the Depression were workingwomen, especially married working-women. In response to such high unemployment, they were targeted for discharge because they were taking jobs away from men. Laws were passed or policies instituted to lay off women in favor of men, the false assumption being that married women did not have to work, whereas married and single men did.

The Depression greatly damaged the Women's Trade Union League, which had no convention from 1929 to 1936. Following the passage of the Wagner Act and the strong growth of the CIO, women's auxiliaries to CIO unions became a major factor in the success of the CIO's organization. The famous and effective sit-down strikes of that period in the auto, steel, and mine industries were possible because of the support that wives, mothers, and sisters gave to the strikers. These women were rewarded by a promise from the CIO that women should be taught about unionism as "an effective means of mobilizing support for unionism among the families of union members."[93] Although the CIO never overtly denied admission of women into unions, as had the AFL, neither had it ever encouraged women to organize.

During World War II, women continued to invade the man's working place—first of necessity and then by choice. When the war ended, men expected women to go back home and give the jobs to men, just as had occurred previously. Many women tried not to do that, but the pattern of layoff was such that twice as many women as men lost their jobs during the spring and summer of 1945. The CIO's Reemployment Plan, adopted at its 1944 convention, failed to mention women workers. Despite layoffs, women did not leave the job market, although to a large extent they did leave the factories. The real expansion in women's employment took place in clerical and service operations such as education and the health fields. As those workers were not targets of union organizing, the history of the women's movement for equality and their interest in labor unions began to branch off into different directions.

As the women's movement focused on improving the position of women in the United States, including women in the workforce, the goal was legislation to ensure equal treatment, equal pay, and equal rights. The success of that movement can be seen in the passage of Title VII to the Civil Rights Act of 1964, which prohibited job discrimination on the basis of gender (among other things).

With that law theoretically protecting women in the workforce from employers, women had the ability to turn to unionization again to increase their power in the workforce. The Coalition of Labor Union Women, formed in 1974, was the manifestation of this renewed interest among women to unionize.

Immigrants and Unions

Except for American Indians and their descendants, all the people of the United States are immigrants or descendants of immigrants. Despite this fact, the history of the

American labor movement chronicles both the inclusion and the exclusion of immigrants from the ranks of organized labor.

Skilled laborers of whatever background were included in trade unions in the earliest days of organization. But as the industrial revolution converted many trade industries to industrial factories, competition with immigrant labor was keenly felt. When trade unionism first experienced the challenge of industrial unionism, the organizing of immigrants, who had largely migrated from England, Iceland, and northern Europe, swelled the ranks of those unions. It was not until after World War I that industrial labor unions took a negative stand on immigration, especially regarding people from Italy and southern Europe. Unionists supported the Immigration Acts of 1921 and 1924, which restricted immigration, because those acts reduced the nation's labor supply. Union members believed that they would reap the benefit of these policies with higher wages and job security.

The rise of industrial unionism after World War II signaled a more open time for immigrants and unions, as it had for women and African Americans. Many CIO unions established ethnic locals and targeted various Catholic immigrants to disregard their ethnic differences in joining industrial unions.[94] In the 1980s and 1990s, the United States supplemented its shrinking workforce base just as it did in the last century: by an influx of immigrants. One-fourth of the new immigrants coming into the United States are college graduates; one-third are high school dropouts. The immigrant workforce in that respect is like the American workforce—split between the highly skilled and well educated and those with minimal skills and little education. American business is taking advantage of both groups.

For the skilled immigrant, the United States is seen as a place of opportunity. As immigrants gravitate to America's urban centers, some cities have seen a rebirth in older sections and suburbs, where immigrants start businesses, buy homes, and pay taxes. In Dallas, Texas, Hispanics turned around Jefferson Boulevard, which had been a dying inner-city business district.

Today both American employers and unions recognize that new unskilled immigrants are changing workplaces across the United States. Union leaders and managers are realizing they must abandon old assumptions of how these new workers will view organized labor and instead adopt new strategies to gain the loyalty of each new wave of immigrants (see Profile 2-7 for an example of this dilemma).[95]

The 1999–2001 strike by 750 Mexican immigrants members of Teamsters Local 890 in King City, California, against Basic Vegetable Products is an excellent example of a new strategy that has been viewed as a "model of labor movement revival." The strike lasted 27 months and was successful against not one but two formidable employers (Basic Vegetable Products was sold to ConAgra Corporation during the strike). The union and its workers employed several key strategies to retain representation as well as wages and benefits:

- "Reframing" the issue to one of workers rights to unionism and racial justice.
- Making the work stoppage "a strike for our families and our community" to preserve jobs for future generations.
- Building coalitions with regional Chicano and Mexican merchants to oppose the permanent replacement workers.
- Affiliating with the regional labor council and the National Teamsters Union to raise over $2M in benefits for the strikers.
- Building a successful boycott of Basic potato products in regional schools, cafeterias, hospitals, and jails.

"SCAB" BOSNIANS REPLACING IMMIGRANT LAOTIANS IN IOWA

Immigrants have been coming to the United States and entering the American workplace for over a century. Today thousands of new immigrants from all over the world work on conveyor belts in meatpacking plants in the Midwest, assemble circuit boards in California's Silicon Valley, and work on tobacco farms in North Carolina. Some are from countries where unions are well established, and thus they recognize their roles in organizations. But others are from countries that have no history of unionism, and thus they lack any knowledge of what unions provide to their members and may confuse unions with people from the government, management, military, or organized crime. This can cause problems for unions and management. In 2001, for example, Titan Tire Corporation in Des Moines, Iowa, had recently hired 410 replacement workers after the former workers (United Steelworkers Union) went on strike. In recent years this would not be an uncommon situation for an American manufacturing plant, except that the former workers were mostly immigrants—largely from Southeast Asia, and the replacement workers were also mostly immigrants—largely from Bosnia and Sudan.

Phanh Cavan, a striking worker from Laos, worked the picket line and shouted "scab" and "cockroach" at the replacement workers entering the Titan plant. He considered himself a solid union man and proud to be an American but is upset because the new replacement workers "don't understand" the role of the union and what it is fighting for at Titan. The picket lines and "Scab of the Week" signs posted outside the plant do not bother the Bosnians. Why? Many recently had experienced a war in their country, so picket lines are nothing by comparison. One Bosnian is Velhudinka Dizdarevic, a 34-year-old mother of four who previously worked for $6.70 an hour in a car parts factory, but at Titan she makes $14 an hour. The Bosnian replacement workers remain loyal to the company, which has worked hard to accommodate them by using trilingual signs (English, Spanish, and Bosnian) and by sponsoring a Bosnian soccer team. In response, to find a way to reach the Bosnians, the union has begun working with local Quakers and other church groups who support the new immigrants. In past decades unions would never have gone to such lengths to reach potential members. But now the Titan union views such community alliances as a critical means of educating immigrants about their cause.

SOURCE: Adapted from Timothy Aeppel, "Replacing Picketing Latinos, Company Hires Bosnians: Outburst of Ethnic Slurs," *Wall Street Journal*, June 12, 2001, pp. B1, B4.

- Defeating a decertification election by encouraging enough strikers to return to work so they could vote.
- Building support from ConAgra unions and top corporate management as well as shareholders until ConAgra changed course and returned to the bargaining table to negotiate a settlement and hire back the strikers to replace the permanent replacement workers.[96]

SUMMARY

The U.S. workplace was designed for and supported the industrial revolution. In that context, a labor union organized and represented workers to make sure they shared in the profits of those industries. The roles of owner and worker were clearly defined.

Times have changed, and the workplace must change with it. The industrial revolution has been replaced by the technological revolution, and the challenges and opportunities for unions in these changing times cannot be dismissed.

Examples of union–management cooperation included QWL, quality circles, and employee teams. At first unions viewed teams as a threat, but today they most often view teams as a positive means of working with management to cooperatively solve problems and make decisions.

The workforce of the new millennium poses its own challenges and opportunities for unions, which have historically attracted blue-collar, white males. Professional men and women, people of color, and those of diverse ethnic backgrounds are the workforce of today. The concerns of workers continue to be wages, working conditions, job security, and respect. It remains to be seen if unions can step into today's workplaces and represent today's worker with the same kind of success they experienced in the past.

CASE STUDIES

Case Study 2-1 Job Performance

The company manufactures ovens. During the period 1982–1996, nonbargaining unit, salaried employees did the testing of the ovens. In 1996, the company told the union they would like to see the oven testing work done by members of the bargaining unit. The union reluctantly agreed. The company and union entered into a "sidebar agreement" that provided that "the move of the oven tester position from salaried to hourly is contingent upon a smooth transition with no reduction in product quality. (We are confident that this will be the case.)" By 1997, when the collective bargaining agreement (CBA) expired, there were four bargaining unit testers. The company and union successfully negotiated a new contract, and the only discussion regarding the testers in those negotiations was where to place them in the new agreement.

In 1999, however, the company met with the union and voiced concern about the job performance of the testers. The company contended that because the testers were not doing their jobs, oven quality problems had risen significantly. The company told the union it was taking the tester positions out of the bargaining unit. The union objected. It was the union's position that the company could not unilaterally take the job classifications at issue out of the bargaining unit. It was the company's position that under the "experimental" language in the December 31, 1996, sidebar agreement, an agreement that was in effect when the current CBA was negotiated and remained in effect, the company had the authority to take the jobs out of the bargaining unit because the experimental program had failed. The union filed an unfair labor practice charge, and a hearing was held.

At the hearing, the company testified that after the job classifications were put into the bargaining unit, there were ongoing problems with output, qual- ity, refusals to work overtime, neglect, and possible sabotage. After the jobs were removed from the bargaining unit, quality improved. It was undisputed that the four testers were properly trained to perform the full range of job duties of a tester/assembler. Given this fact, the company attributed their poor job performance to behavioral problems as opposed to competency deficiencies. The company contended it never disciplined the testers for anything related to job performance because it could never get sufficient proof to identify specific individuals who might be responsible for the problems. The record very convincingly shows that the company believed that by taking the job classifications at issue out of the bargaining unit, they could better control the people who would fill the jobs.

The union testified that not only did the company never discipline the four testers for poor job performance but it also offered the jobs to these same four testers after the jobs were removed from the bargaining unit. Furthermore, the union contended that although the job classifications were put into the bargaining unit on an experimental basis and the company retained the sole authority to take them out of the bargaining unit if the experiment failed, the company had an obligation to negotiate that change in the new CBA. The evidence showed that the company knew the experiment was not going well before negotiations for the current CBA commenced. The record clearly established that at no time during the negotiations did anyone in the company tell the union that the experiment was not going well and could be declared a failure. Given the company's silence in this regard during the negotiations, the union believes that the sidebar agreement was replaced by the CBA, which included the tester positions as regular positions.

SOURCE: Adapted from *Lincoln Foodservices Products, Inc. v. Sheet Metal Workers International Union Local 237*, 114 LA 1745 (October 19, 2000).

QUESTIONS

1. Why would the placement or removal of the job classifications in a bargaining unit have any impact on the quality of the job performed?
2. If the company knew that the tester "experiment" was not going well during the negotiations on a new contract, should it have negotiated the issue?
3. Was the company justified in attempting to remove the positions from the union?

Case Study 2-2 Company Unions

In January 1991, the company was not unionized but had established a "Plant Council," which consisted of three managers and five employees elected by the plant's workers. The council was created and designed by the employer to offer recommendations to management about proposed changes in working conditions. The employer had agreed to consider those recommendations, recognizing that if the managers and employees on the council reached a consensus, then that idea would likely be acceptable to both management and employees. In February 1991, the union began an organizing campaign to try to establish a collective bargaining unit for the company. During the campaign, the employer emphasized the role of the Plant Council when urging employees to vote against the union. In addition, the employer told employees that their vote was a choice between an "employee involvement process" and selecting a union as a representative. After the union lost the election, it filed an unfair labor charge against the employer for interfering with the election and for creating a "company union" in violation of the National Labor Relations Act.

SOURCE: Adapted from *Webcor Packaging Inc.,* 151 LRRM 1221 (1995).

QUESTIONS

1. Do you think the union should or should not have challenged the election? Why?
2. One of the techniques used by companies in the late 1800s to discourage union organizing was to create company unions, as discussed briefly in Chapter 1. This case would seem to suggest that nothing about the workplace had changed in over 100 years. What decision do you think the judge made in this 1991 case and why?
3. The employer obviously wanted the employees to participate in the decisions in the workplace because such buy-in would result in better decisions. Why then did the employer prefer the council to the union?

KEY TERMS AND CONCEPTS

- Agricultural workers
- Americans with Disabilities Act (ADA) of 1990
- Cesar Chavez
- Civil Rights Act of 1964
- Coalition of Labor Union Women
- craft unions
- Equal Pay Act
- equal pay for equal work
- free agents
- globalization
- industrial union
- just-in-time
- Maryland Freedom Union
- Mississippi Freedom Labor Union
- National Colored Labor Union
- "one best way" theory
- problem-solving teams
- professional sports unions
- public-sector unions
- quality circles
- quality of working life
- robber barons
- salary arbitration
- self-managed employee teams
- special project teams
- Teamwork for Employees and Managers (TEAM) Act
- transportation unions
- United Farm Workers
- union density rate

REVIEW QUESTIONS

1. How did the organization of work in the late 1800s contribute to the way unions organized?
2. What factors are contributing to the decline of union membership?
3. How have the concerns of workers changed since the 1930s? Which issues are still critical today?
4. What do union members believe they gain from unionization? What do they lose?
5. How do quality of working life programs differ from past union–management communications?
6. Why has the use of "employee teams" been so controversial? What are the pros and cons?
7. Why was the relationship between unions and African Americans one of advances and defeats?
8. In which industry did women enjoy the most organizing success in the early 1900s?
9. Although "stars" in professional sports obviously benefit from union activities on their behalf, how do all players benefit? Is the benefit out of proportion to the work they do?

YOU BE THE ARBITRATOR
Can a "Just Cause" Standard Be Satisfied Without Proving Fault?

ARTICLE XXIII
DISCIPLINE

A. The Employer may establish and publish reasonable rules and regulations governing the conduct of employees, as are necessary for the proper operation of the facilities and the proper care of residents.

1. Any discipline imposed for infractions of these rules and regulations will be corrective and progressive in nature with the objective of helping the employee improve. . . .

D. Should it be determined by the Home, or by the arbitrator appointed in accordance with the arbitration procedure, that the employee has been suspended or discharged unjustly, the Home shall reinstate the employee and pay full compensation at the regular rate of pay for the time lost. . . .

Facts

The employer is a nursing home in the state of Minnesota. The state of Minnesota has implemented a policy for the return of unused Schedule III medications from nursing homes to pharmacies, a protocol to ensure the integrity of the drug being returned. When drugs for one reason or another are left over at the end of a one-week cycle at the employer's nursing home, they are returned to the dispensing pharmacies in accordance with that protocol.

During the Thursday to Friday night shift, the four drug carts, one from each wing of the nursing home, are collected by the charge nurse and (at least until recently, with the assistance of a Trained Medication Aid) the drug trays are then sorted and the amounts being returned recorded and then placed in large blue canvas transfer bags for return to the dispensing pharmacies. Prior to their return to the pharmacies, the bags are stored in the 400 wing "med room." The room contains a locked drug cabinet for storing Schedule II medications and also has a lock on the door to the room. The nursing home stores the unlocked bags for pickup in the locked med room.

It came to the attention of the employer that there was a discrepancy in the records concerning how much medication had been returned to the pharmacies from one of the grievant's shifts. The grievant was a charge nurse on the graveyard shift. An investigation was initiated. Witnesses were questioned regarding access to keys to the meds room. Testimony indicated that the investigation concluded that each LPN charge nurse had a key, as did the four LPNs on the day shift and the RNs and DK, the nurse secretary; there was no inventory of the total number of keys, nor was there any sort of "sign-in/sign-out" system for the keys. No other conclusion regarding the missing medication was reached. The grievant received a letter from her employer indicating that she was being terminated "due to discrepancy in the amount of medication returned to the pharmacies after the exchange done on the nights you were charge nurse. Records indicate that the number of individual pills documented for return is less than the amount received by the pharmacy." The grievant appealed her termination.

Issue

Can the "just cause" standard, which governs discipline and discharge of employees in the bargaining unit, be satisfied without proving fault on the part of the grievant?

Position of the Parties

The employer contended it had just cause to dismiss the grievant. It did not contend that the grievant took the missing medications or knows who did. Rather, it contends that as charge nurse she had the responsibility to correctly account for and return unused medications and her failure to do so or to supervise others to do so properly put the nursing home's license at risk. The employer pointed to the grievant's job description, which requires her to be licensed and to function under the standards of the nursing profession and in compliance with all the nursing home's rules and regulations. The employer held the grievant to a "strict liability" theory; that is, if there were discrepancies in the tallies, no matter what the explanation might be for such discrepancies, the grievant was responsible.

The union's position was that the employer did not have just cause to discharge the grievant. Although the grievant acknowledged that as the nurse in charge of the building at night she had a duty to try to explain any discrepancies in the drug tallies, she testified that it had not been her understanding that her failure to be able to explain the discrepancies was grounds for termination. The discrepancies in the drug count could have been caused by any number of things not under the control of the grievant. There is no meaningful difference between "for cause," "just cause," "discharged unjustly," and similar such phrases. "Just cause" references and provisions have evolved in the workplace and in arbitration decisions over time to the point of having certain characteristics and requirements in common, which are generally applicable to all grievance disputes. As a general proposition, expressions in contracts referring to "just cause" exclude discipline and discharge for mere whim or caprice. They are, obviously, intended to include those things for which employees have traditionally been fired. The employer in this case has disciplined the grievant for something that occurred—discrepancy in drug count—without proving that the grievant did anything wrong. The grievant should be returned to her position.

SOURCE: Adapted from *Lutheran Care Center*, 116 LA 1795 (Arb. 2002).

QUESTIONS

1. As arbitrator, what would be your award and opinion in this arbitration?
2. Explain why the relevant provisions of the collective bargaining agreement as applied to the facts of this case dictate the award.
3. What actions might the employer or the union have taken to avoid this conflict?

EXERCISE

Attitudes Toward Unions

PURPOSE:

To examine your general attitude toward unions and discuss the possible causes for any positive or negative feelings.

TASK:

Divide into small groups. Complete the following survey. The statements in this survey are listed in pairs. Put an X next to the statement that you agree with more firmly. If you strongly agree with the statement, put two Xs next to it. You may not entirely agree with either of them, but be sure to mark one of the statements. Do not omit any item. When you have completed the survey, add the "a" Xs and the "b" Xs and compare.

After the completion of the survey, your instructor will ask a group with more "a" answers and a group with more "b" answers to lead a discussion of attitudes toward unions and labor–management relations.

1. (a) Unions are an important, positive force in our society.
   (b) The country would be much better off without unions.
2. (a) Without unions, the state of personnel management would be set back a hundred years.
   (b) Management is largely responsible for introducing humanistic programs and practices in organizations today.
3. (a) Unions help organizations become more productive.
   (b) Unions make it difficult for management to produce a product or service efficiently.
4. (a) Today's standard of living is largely due to the efforts of the labor movement.
   (b) The wealth that people are able to enjoy today is largely the result of creativity, ingenuity, and risk taking by management decision makers.
5. (a) Most unions are moral and ethical institutions.
   (b) Most unions are as corrupt as the Mafia.
6. (a) Unions afford the worker protection against arbitrary and unjust management practices.
   (b) Managers will treat their employees fairly regardless of whether a union exists.
7. (a) Unions want their members to be hardworking productive employees.
   (b) Unions promote job security rather than worker productivity.
8. (a) Unions promote liberty and freedom for the individual employee.
   (b) With the union, employees lose their individual freedoms.
9. (a) Section 14(b) of the Taft-Hartley Act (which allows individual states to pass right-to-work laws) should be repealed.
   (b) Congress should pass federal right-to-work legislation.
10. (a) Unions are instrumental in implementing new, efficient work methods and techniques.
    (b) Unions resist management efforts to adopt new, labor-saving technology.
11. (a) Without unions, employees would not have a voice with management.
    (b) Labor–management communication is strengthened with the absence of a union.
12. (a) Unions make sure that decisions about pay increases and promotions are fair.
    (b) Union politics often play a role in deciding which union employee gets a raise or is promoted.
13. (a) The monetary benefits that unions bargain for are far greater than the dues the member must pay to the union.
    (b) Union dues are usually too high for what the members get through collective bargaining.
14. (a) Employee discipline is administered fairly if the organization is unionized.

   (b) Union procedures generally make the disciplinary process slow, cumbersome, and costly.
15. (a) Without the union, the employee would have no one with whom to discuss work-related problems.
   (b) The best and most accessible person for the employee to discuss work-related problems with is the immediate supervisor.
16. (a) Union officers at all levels carry out their jobs in a competent and professional manner.
   (b) Union officers are basically political figures who are interested primarily in their own welfare.
17. (a) Most unions seek change through peaceful means.
   (b) Most unions are prone to use violence to get what they want.
18. (a) Unions are truly domestic institutions with full participation of the rank and file.
   (b) Unions are controlled by the top leadership rather than by the rank and file.
19. (a) Union members do the real work in our society and form the backbone of our country.
   (b) Union employees are basically manual laborers who would flounder without management's direction and guidance.
20. (a) Unions are necessary to balance the power and authority of management.
   (b) The power and authority of management, guaranteed by the Constitution and the right to own private property, are severely eroded by the union.

Note to Instructor: The participants of this exercise should be identified by name, ID, Social Security number, or the like on the completed surveys. Then at the end of the course (see Chapter 12), the survey can be repeated and changes in attitudes noted for comparison purposes.

CHAPTER 3

Establishing a Bargaining Unit

What Is Collective Bargaining?
The National Labor Relations Board
Bargaining Unit Determination
Bargaining Unit Determination in the Public Sector
Union Structure
Public-Sector Unions
Representation Elections
The Organizing Drive
Union Security
Individual Rights within Unions

In 2004, the NLRB reversed a landmark 2000 decision by ruling that graduate students, who do most classroom teaching on some college campuses, are students and not workers and therefore cannot unionize.

Labor News

2004 NLRB DECISION HALTS GRADUATE STUDENT UNION RISE

In April 2005 teaching assistants at Columbia and Yale Universities staged the first joint strike ever at the Ivy League institutions. During the same week teaching assistants at New York University held a rally. The assistants staged what might be called a "solidarity action" to show the New England schools they stand together seeking higher pay, child care, and medical benefits. Their goal is to bring the universities to the negotiating table voluntarily through public pressure.

The 2005 solidarity action was in response to a 2004 National Labor Relations Board (NLRB) ruling that overturned a 2000 NLRB ruling that required New York University to recognize a graduate teaching assistants union. The 2000 NLRB ruling sparked a wave of union organizing efforts on private university campuses across the Northeast including Brown, Columbia, Temple, Harvard, Cornell, Tufts, and the University of Pennsylvania. Then, in 2004, a new NLRB "loaded with Bush appointees reversed the 2000 ruling." Following the 2000 ruling the number of graduate teaching and research assistants represented by unions had more than doubled to over 40,000 on 24 American university campuses.

The solidarity action in 2005, according to Melissa Stuckey, a Yale University graduate student, was intended to demonstrate that "We've just basically been getting stronger because of the NLRB ruling." However, at a coffee shop near the Yale Campus a group of graduate students gathered to oppose the Graduate Employees and Students Organization (GESO) strike. After the 2000 NLRB decision Yale increased graduate stipends by 20 percent to $17,000. Allison Alexy, a graduate anthropology student, commented that she does not feel abused by Yale after the raises.

SOURCE: Adapted from John Graves, "Scenes From the Picket Lines," *The Chronicle of Higher Education* (May 13, 2005), A8–10.

The collective bargaining process is at the heart of the employer-employee relationship. That process, however, is not a simple one. The 1935 National Labor Relations Act, as subsequently amended, defines the process and limits the parties to it. A group of employees cannot simply present their requests to the employer. Procedures must be followed to determine if those particular employees are protected by the act. A union purporting to represent the employees must prove that it does indeed represent them. And any particular group of employees who feel that they have the same interests and desires and therefore should negotiate together may not satisfy the requirements of the act as an "appropriate" unit of employees for collective bargaining purposes. This chapter explores the particulars of the act to learn when and how it can be used to determine parties subject to its provisions.

WHAT IS COLLECTIVE BARGAINING?

Collective bargaining is the process by which union leaders representing groups of employees negotiate specific terms of employment with designated representatives of management. The term **collective bargaining** originated in the British labor movement. But it was Samuel Gompers who developed its common use in the United States. The following is a modern-day definition:

Collective bargaining is defined as the continuous relationship between an employer and a designated labor organization representing a specific unit of employees for the purpose of negotiating written terms of employment.[1]

According to the definition, collective bargaining must be recognized as a continuous process, beginning with the negotiation of a contract through the life of the contract with almost daily interpretation and administration of its provisions. In recent years the process has also come to include the handling of employee grievances in most labor agreements and, if necessary, arbitration of such grievances in a final and binding decision.

The *employer* referred to in the definition may be one or more related employers joined together for purposes of collective bargaining.

The *labor organization* or union is selected by a group of employees to represent them at the bargaining table. Later in this chapter the election process undertaken to select a union is explained. And, although employees select the union they wish to represent them, the specific group of employees, or **bargaining unit** to which employees belong, must be recognized by the NLRB. Under U.S. law, the labor organization is given the right to represent all employees of the bargaining unit. This right gives the union leadership leverage in negotiation because management cannot seek competing unions to negotiate other agreements.

The **terms of employment** negotiated generally include the price of labor, for example, wages and benefits; work rules, including hours of work, job classifications, effort required, and work practices; individual job rights, such as seniority, discipline procedures, and promotion and layoff procedures; management and union rights; and the methods of enforcement and administration of the contract, including grievance resolution.

Confrontation—the "screw the boss" and "keep the union in its place" syndromes—have sometimes characterized the American system of collective bargaining and labor relations.[2] However, most union and management officials view collective bargaining as a rational, democratic, and peaceful way of resolving conflict between labor and management. Of approximately 150,000 collective bargaining agreements negotiated by affiliates of the AFL-CIO, only 2 percent have resulted in strikes. Ninety-eight percent of all cases involving collective bargaining have ended in successful, peaceful negotiations. This record is the result of years of fine-tuning the collective bargaining process in the United States.[3]

The news media usually report only those cases involving picketing, strike activities, or other work disruptions. Seldom do we see reports on cases such as the Bagdad Copper Mine in Arizona, in which the company has offered guaranteed lifetime employment since 1929 and has never experienced significant labor unrest. The U.S. Bureau of Labor Statistics has reported a steady decline in both the number of strikes and the number of workers involved in strikes since a peak in 1946. In fact, the 1990s was the most peaceful labor decade in the modern era of labor relations.[4]

Collective bargaining can be found in countless meeting rooms countrywide. Representatives of management and labor sit across from each other at a bargaining table negotiating a labor contract. Teams of negotiators haggle over appropriate wage levels, hours of work, and other conditions of employment. If the industry is large enough, the public may be aware of the progress of the negotiations. In 1997, for example, when the Teamsters struck United Parcel Service (UPS), not only were millions of businesses and customers affected but also the media and the entire nation focused their attention on the issue of part-time workers wanting to work full time. By 2002, UPS had converted 10,000 part-time jobs to full time and then agreed in negotiations that year to convert another 10,000 part-time jobs to full time during the 2002–2008 agreement. So in 2002, another costly strike, such as the one in 1997, was avoided, and both sides met some of their negotiating priorities. However, in 2005 when the National Hockey League (NHL) owners cancelled the season due to a labor dispute, millions of fans of its 30 teams were affected.

THE NATIONAL LABOR RELATIONS BOARD

The stated purpose of the National Labor Relations Act was to minimize industrial strife interfering with the normal flow of commerce. Using the authority of the commerce clause of the U.S. Constitution, Congress legislated a federally protected interest in the internal operations of certain industries.[5] That interest was in setting the legal process by which labor and management would bargain. The act created a five-member National Labor Relations Board (NLRB) to administer its provisions. These board members are appointed for five-year terms by the president of the United States, with the advice and consent of the Senate.

The NLRB members' authority under the act enables them, through a wide range of remedies, to effectuate the purposes of the act and "to protect the rights of the public in connection with labor disputes affecting commerce."[6]

Four basic principles of the act guide the NLRB's administration:

1. Encouragement of labor organizations and collective bargaining
2. Recognition of majority representation
3. Establishment of prompt administrative machinery for enforcement instead of criminal sanctions
4. Imposition of sanctions or punishments even if other sanctions or punishments are found in other jurisdictions[7]

Jurisdiction of the NLRB

Congress established certain jurisdictional tests to satisfy expected practical and legal criticisms of the act. The NLRB has jurisdiction over persons when there is a labor dispute affecting commerce or when there is a controversy involving an employer, employee, or a labor organization.[8] This jurisdiction has been found broad enough to include all representation and unfair labor practice proceedings. The tests must be met before the board is empowered to act.

Persons

The definition of a person under the National Labor Relations Act is all-inclusive and involves "one or more individuals, labor organizations, partnerships, associations, corporations, legal representatives, trustees, trustees in bankruptcy, or receivers." Because the definition is so broad, few problems arise with finding a person in most disputes. However, entities otherwise exempt from the act because they are not considered "employers" (namely, political subdivisions and railroads) have been able to invoke protections of the act against union-sponsored activities.[9]

Labor Dispute

A labor dispute must exist for the board to exercise jurisdiction. The act defines *labor dispute* as "any controversy concerning terms, tenure, or conditions of employment." Labor disputes have been held to include employee-concerted activities such as strikes, walkouts, and picketing; unfair labor practices, such as employers' refusal to bargain; and interference in employee rights. The term has also been interpreted to include investigation of the health and safety facilities of a work environment. Included in the definition are controversies "concerning the association or representation of persons in negotiating, fixing, maintaining, changing, or seeking to arrange terms or conditions of employment." The NLRB in its representation cases usually addresses these controversies.

Affecting Commerce

A broad definition of *commerce* under the statute gives the board authority in all but purely local disputes. The board has jurisdiction if the labor dispute directly affects commerce. In addition, if the employer's operation affects commerce, any labor dispute involving that employer falls within the board's jurisdiction. The NLRB, using this authority, has taken jurisdiction over a manufacturer whose goods were to be transported interstate, even though the manufacturer was not engaged in out-of-state commerce.

To judge the substance of a dispute, the board has established jurisdictional standards using annual specific dollar amounts for different types of businesses. For example, for nonretail enterprises, a gross outflow or inflow of at least $50,000 in revenue is required for the NLRB to take jurisdiction, whereas retail establishments need gross business volumes of at least $500,000 per year and substantial interstate purchases or sales. This limitation is not absolute, however, and the board may enter cases of significant impact regardless of the dollar volume involved. An example is the NLRB's decision to examine handicapped workshop operations on a case-by-case basis. If the NLRB determines the operation is essentially rehabilitative, it will not take jurisdiction, but it will if the workshop is primarily industrial with an economic purpose.[10] In a 2004 decision, the NLRB reiterated this holding in a 3–2 opinion involving disabled workers employed as janitors at Cape Canaveral. The dissenting members of the board argued that the company had failed to demonstrate that its operation was essentially rehabilitative because it required its disabled workers to perform the same job functions as its nondisabled workers and did not require they to attend any rehabilitation sessions.[11]

The board has also judged the substance of a case and has removed itself from some controversies because of the type of employer involved, for example, employers whose employees are subject to laws of a foreign country.[12] In one case when the board asserted jurisdiction over a complaint from two discharged employees, whose permanent employment was in the U.S. but who had volunteered for a two-week work assignment in Canada, the federal court reversed. The court disregarded the board's policy argument that not protecting these employees would undermine the act's purpose, noting rather that the act's jurisdictional language clearly did not provide for extraterritorial application.[13]

The board at one time removed itself in a case in which a company did not have sufficient control over employment conditions because of its contractual arrangement with the U.S. Department of Labor.[14] However, subsequent board decisions reversed that trend, and the board has determined that even in circumstances in which some of the conditions cannot be negotiated, other areas can be.[15]

The NLRB is often called on to decide the limit of its own jurisdiction. In *San Manuel Indian Bingo and Casino*,[16] the NLRB reversed previous board decisions and asserted jurisdiction over a casino owned by an Indian tribe and located on its reservation. The board reasoned that the act did not expressly exclude Indian tribes as employers and that because the particular undertaking was a typical commercial enterprise employing and catering to non-Indians, it was within the "affecting commerce" clause of the act.

Employees

Employees, as included in the statutory definition, are entitled to the rights guaranteed by the act. Those include the right to self-organization, to form labor organizations, to bargain collectively, to engage in concerted activities for purposes of collective bargaining, and to refrain from such activities, unless there is a contract requirement to pay labor organization dues as a condition of employment. The definition of employee is liberally construed, so stated exclusions in the definition become important in determining who is not an employee. The types of workers not covered are agricultural workers, domestic servants, persons employed by a spouse or a parent, independent contractors, supervisors, individuals who work for employers subject to the Railway Labor Act, and employees of the U.S. government, the Federal Reserve Bank, the states, or their political subdivisions. In Case 3-1 the NLRB had to determine whether certain workers were employees or independent contractors.

Employers

Employers under the act are subject to the unfair labor practices section, which emphasizes the duty to bargain collectively with employee representatives. The definition of *employer* also takes on broad connotations by listing those persons who are not employers: the U.S. government or a wholly owned government corporation (with the exception of the U.S. Postal Service by virtue of another federal law), the Federal Reserve Bank, a state or political subdivision, anyone subject to the Railway Labor Act, or any labor organization.[17]

Labor Organizations

Labor organizations are most commonly labor unions, but the NLRB recognizes other kinds of employee committees that represent their employees to employers.[18] Labor organizations are also subject under the act to the unfair labor practices section that places some limitations on strikes supported by the organization.

Preemption

A question of **preemption** arises when a field of activity, such as collective bargaining or labor relations, is subject to regulation by both the federal and state governments and a decision must be made as to whether concurrent jurisdiction exists or if the federal government enjoys exclusive jurisdiction. The Constitution is clear that federal law is the supreme law of the land, so a factual determination must be made as to whether Congress has entered and completely covered a field or activity.

If Congress has entered and completely covered the field, then an individual who wants to bring a lawsuit concerning that issue must bring it in the federal court rather than the state court. Or, even if the individual is allowed to litigate in state court, the law applied will be the federal law. In many instances, an individual might consider the state court procedure more "user friendly" than that of the federal court or the remedies provided under a state law more generous than the federal law. Preemption, however, is a legal determination that only the federal law applies and an individual is not allowed to make that determination—the court makes it.

The U.S. Supreme Court decided the preemption issue as it relates to the labor-management relationship in a series of cases.[19] If an activity is clearly protected

EMPLOYEES OR INDEPENDENT CONTRACTORS?

CASE
3-1

Corporate Express Delivery Systems engaged two types of drivers to deliver packages in Oklahoma City: those who drove company vehicles and those who operated their own vehicles. In February 1999 several owner-operators held a meeting to discuss forming a union. Soon thereafter two company managers told certain owner-operators the company would close its Oklahoma City branch rather than deal with a union. A third manager then fired three of the union organizers. When the owner-operators held a second meeting, this manager drove twice around the meeting hall in an apparent effort to learn who was attending. The union charged Corporate Express with violating Section 8(a)(1) and (3) of the National Labor Relations Act by threatening and firing employees for engaging in union activity and by monitoring such activity. The company argued that its owner-operators were independent contractors and not employees and therefore were not protected by the Act. The NLRB determined that the drivers were employees, and because Corporate Express had interfered with their right to organize a union, it violated the law. Corporate Express appealed.

DECISION

The Court noted that the key question before it was whether the drivers were *employees,* protected by the act, or *independent contractors,* who would not fall under the act's provisions. The Court explained that generally it determines whether a person is an "employee" by the control an employer had over the means and manner of the work being done. In this instance, the drivers were free to choose their own routes, break times, and the type of vehicle they used. They were also responsible for the maintenance of their vehicles. Corporate Express, however, decided the order of their deliveries, required them to carry pagers to call in for scheduling changes, and required them to wear a uniform. The Court noted that the distribution of authority between Corporate Express and the drivers as to how they did their job was fairly even. So the Court employed another test, which was to determine whether the alleged "independent contractors" had a significant entrepreneurial opportunity for gain or loss. That is, did the drivers assume any economic risk or have an opportunity to profit from the work? In addition to supplying their own vehicle, did the drivers hire subordinates to help them, or did the driver work for more than one employer? In this instance, the Court found, that the drivers did not in fact share any risk or opportunity. The drivers were not allowed to subcontract the work by allowing others to drive their vehicles for Corporate Express. Nor were the drivers allowed to work for other companies.

In light of these facts, the Court found the drivers were not independent contractors but rather employees with the right to unionize and that the actions by Corporate Express violated the National Labor Relations Act.

SOURCE: Adapted from *Corporate Express Delivery Systems v. NLRB,* 170 LRRM 2193 (June 11, 2002).

under Section 7 of the National Labor Relations Act, the state is totally preempted from the field and federal law controls. Section 7 provides employees the rights to self-organization; to form, join, or assist labor organizations; to bargain collectively; to engage in other concerted activities; or to refrain from doing all of these.

Also, if Section 8, the unfair labor practice section, clearly prohibits the activity sought to be regulated by the state, the state is totally preempted from the field. The

Court went even further when it decided that the state would be preempted if the activity was arguably protected or prohibited by the act. However, the *arguably protected or prohibited* test was not to be applied in what the Court described as a rigid manner.[20]

For example, in *Lingle v. Norge Division of Magic Chef, Inc.,* a union employee, allegedly fired for making a workers' compensation claim, wanted to proceed under a state law that protected employees from retaliation by an employer rather than following the union contract. The remedy for the employee under the union contract and federal labor law was limited to reinstatement to the job lost and back pay, whereas the state law allowed for money damages. Reversing previous holdings, the Supreme Court allowed the worker to bypass the contractual remedies and the application of federal law for the remedies sought under the state law.[21] The Court's reasoning was that the state court cause of action—retaliatory discharge under a specific state law—could be adjudicated without any examination, interpretation, or discussion of the labor contract or established labor–management relations law. Therefore, allowing the employee a choice in forums did not undermine the public policy issues supporting the preemption doctrine.[22]

BARGAINING UNIT DETERMINATION

The NLRB, in carrying out its lawful responsibilities, decides representation cases. That is, Section 9(b) of the Labor-Management Relations Act authorizes the board to decide on a case-by-case basis the **appropriate bargaining unit** of employees for collective bargaining purposes. The board exercises this power to guarantee employees the fullest freedom under the act—mainly, the right of self-organization. The NLRB does not have rigid or constrictive regulations for dealing with recognition cases. It has wide discretion in its decisions, which courts will uphold unless they find that the board acted arbitrarily.[23] Both the board and the courts recognize that more than one unit sometimes may be appropriate for collective bargaining. The board is not required to choose the *most appropriate unit,* only an *appropriate unit,* as demonstrated in Case 3-2.

Although there are no hard-and-fast rules in the act to determine appropriateness, there are certain limitations on the types of units and on workers to be included and excluded from units. Certain fundamental and logical policies should be followed in determining a unit.

Bargaining Unit

The bargaining unit is defined as "that group of employees that is represented by the union in collective bargaining. The union has exclusive bargaining rights for all employees within the unit, and it has no rights for those employees outside, including managerial and non-managerial." The determination of exactly which employees are within the bargaining unit may have a great effect on the outcome of the organizing campaign. The union seeks a unit in which it feels it can win a majority of the vote in a representation election. When the employer and union cannot agree on the unit, the NLRB, under Section 9 of the National Labor Relations Act, decides on "the unit appropriate for the purposes of collective bargaining."[24]

Appropriate Unit

The basic underlying principle for the NLRB's determination of an appropriate unit is that only employees having a substantial mutuality of interest in wages, hours, and

APPROPRIATE UNIT

The company is a truck dealership that sells, modifies, and services light-duty and heavy-duty trucks. The company operates two facilities. The Main Facility is the primary location for sales and service of trucks. The second, known as the Annex, is across the street and operates under a different name. The Annex specializes in servicing, equipping, and modifying trucks. The central issue in dispute is whether the union designated an appropriate collective bargaining unit under the National Labor Relations Act.

At the Main Facility, the service department consists of several service advisers who deal with customers seeking truck service, approximately 14 service technicians who diagnose and repair trucks, and two lube workers who perform lubes, oil and filter changes, and the like. The service technicians work either day or evening shifts. They are responsible primarily for the actual servicing and repairing of customer vehicles. Service technicians are paid an hourly wage, receive commissions based on their efficiency, and can receive commissions for additional work authorized by a customer on a technician's recommendation. Service technicians are certified and are required to provide their own tools, wear blue uniforms with a company logo, and attend regularly scheduled meetings with management. The lube workers also work either day or evening shifts. They work alongside the service technicians and are responsible primarily for oil and filter changes and lubes. The lube workers are not certified and are paid hourly. One lube worker owns his tools; the other does not. The lube workers report to the same supervisor as the service technicians.

At the Annex, there are several installer/fabricators, a parts employee, and an estimator. The installer/fabricators are technically part of the company's service department. The Annex employees are responsible primarily for installing custom beds and other features on trucks sold by the company and those brought in for service or other work. Sometimes work will be performed on the same truck at both locations, as when modifications are made to trucks bought at the main location, and some of the work will be performed at the Annex, such as air conditioner and hitch installation. Installer/fabricators employed at the Annex must be able to weld and are administered a welding test prior to employment. Like the service technicians, the installer/fabricators are required to provide their own tools. There is only one shift at the Annex, however, and Annex workers have a different supervisor than the service department employees. Annex employees wear a different uniform and are paid an hourly wage without any commission or bonuses.

The company employs one human resources manager for both facilities. The company's parts and service director also interviews all applicants for either facility. Employees at both facilities are on the same payroll and have the same vacation and benefit policies as well as use the same break room, though there is an additional break room in the Annex. Employees are rarely transferred from one facility to the other. All the company employees attend occasional safety meetings and company functions.

The union filed an election petition to represent a unit of employees at the Main Facility consisting of all full-time and regular part-time service technicians and lubricators. The NLRB certified the 16 employees at the Main Facility as an appropriate unit, and an election was held. The union won by a vote of nine to seven and was certified. The company, however,

continued

APPROPRIATE UNIT—continued

refused to bargain, contending that the group of employees designated as the bargaining unit was not the appropriate unit for collective bargaining.

The company claimed that the board erred in its unit determination because there were other appropriate units. For example, the company believed that a pure "craft" unit consisting of the service technicians was a more appropriate unit because the lube workers have limited responsibilities and do not receive technician training or that a broader unit that included all the service department personnel at both locations would be a more appropriate unit because the employees performed functions related to the repair of trucks.

DECISION

The Court noted that the National Labor Relations Act delegates to the NLRB the power to determine what an "appropriate" employee unit for collective bargaining purposes. The Court will uphold an NLRB's

unit determination as long as the identified unit is appropriate and the decision is supported by evidence. The company's complaint was that the unit certified by the NLRB was not appropriate because there were other potential units that could also be appropriate. But the existence of other "appropriate" units will not in and of itself invalidate a finding of the NLRB that the unit requesting recognition is an appropriate unit. In this case, placing the lube workers in the same unit as the service technicians made sense because of all the workers at the Main Facility, these were two groups of workers who actually performed mechanical work. And although there might have been similarities between the workers in the Main Facility and in the Annex, there were also differences. The Annex workers performed different functions and were required to have different skills. They worked different shifts and were compensated differently. The Court upheld the NLRB decision that the service technicians and the lube workers were an appropriate unit.

SOURCE: Adapted from *Country Ford Trucks, Inc. v. NLRB and International Assoc. of Machinists and Aerospace Workers, AFL-CIO, Local 1528*, 165 LRRM 2649 (October 27, 2000).

working conditions can be appropriately grouped in that unit. The logic is that the greater the similarities of working conditions, the greater the likelihood the unit's members can agree on priorities and thus make the collective bargaining process successful.[25]

The following criteria are most often used in deciding what constitutes a rational unit:

1. Community of interest
2. History of bargaining
3. Desire of employees
4. Prior union organization
5. Relationship of the unit to the organizational structure of the company
6. Public interest
7. Accretion
8. Stipulated units
9. Statutory considerations

Community of Interest

The **community of interest doctrine** attempts to quantify, by means of descriptive criteria, when workers should feel that their individual interests are so similar that collective bargaining will be fruitful. The board has at various times enumerated these criteria: similarity of job functions and earnings, in benefits received or hours worked, and/or in job training or skills required; a high degree of contact and interchange among the employees; and/or geographic proximity and common supervision.[26] All these can indicate a common interest or interests that, coupled with the other listed criteria, establish an appropriate unit.

The NLRB's decisions in this area are subject to change, however. For example, in a 2000 decision, the NRLB ruled that a group of temporary employees at *M. S. Sturgis, Inc.* showed "a sufficient community of interest" with permanent employees to be added to the bargaining unit.[27] The "temporary employees" were subject to the same supervision, worked the same hours, and performed the same work side by side with the permanent workers who were part of a bargaining unit. This ruling reversed a 1990 NLRB ruling and was widely touted as giving about 5.7 million temporary employees collective bargaining rights for the first time.[28] In 2004 the NLRB *reversed* its decision in *M. S. Sturgis* in *Oakwood Care Center* and ruled that full-time employees of one employer could not be in the same bargaining unit as employees who were jointly employed (i.e., as temporary employees with a joint but separate employer). Oakwood, a long-term residential care facility, had its own employees, and it used a temporary service for additional employees. All the employees were supervised and disciplined by Oakwood supervisors, and Oakwood and the temporary service jointly determined the pay and benefits of the temporary employees. The NLRB acknowledged that under the *Sturgis* case, the temporary employees would have been a part of the bargaining unit. In overruling *Sturgis,* the NLRB, in a 3–2 opinion, stated that grouping employees of different employers into the same bargaining unit violates the act's purpose of protecting employee rights by subjecting the employees to fragmented bargaining and inherently conflicting interests.[29]

History of Bargaining

If a bargaining unit and a particular employer have a history of bargaining, the board will recognize the appropriateness of the unit, in the absence of compelling reasons to the contrary, to ensure the employees' right of self-organization and to provide the stable labor relations sought by the board. History of bargaining usually becomes a question when the board receives a request for decertification to allow for smaller or different bargaining units or when a new class of employer has come under the board's jurisdiction, such as when the National Labor Relations Act was extended to the health-care industry.

Although the board favorably considers prior bargaining relationships, such histories are not absolute. The board has disregarded history of bargaining in several cases when that history contravened the board's policy of mixing clerical and production and maintenance personnel, when it was based on oral contracts, and when it reflected racial or sexual discrimination.[30]

Employee Wishes

The *Globe* **doctrine** established the NLRB policy to give weight to employee wishes when determining an appropriate bargaining unit.[31] Although the board cannot delegate the selection of a bargaining unit to employees, it may use the election process as a way to consult employees. In the *Globe* case, the board provided for special balloting to determine the representation wishes of the employees. The situation involved a bargaining unit determination by the board where a smaller craft unit and a larger industry unit were equally plausible. By permitting the employees in the smaller unit to indicate their preference, the board was able to decide whether to leave the craft group in the smaller bargaining unit or to combine it with the larger group.[32] Such consultation is especially helpful if two or more bargaining units are considered appropriate by the board's otherwise objective standards.

Employee Unionization

The NLRB will consider the extent of unionization by a bargaining unit as one factor in unit determination but not as a controlling factor. The question is still one of appropriateness and not of whether the wishes of a union can be honored. If the bargaining unit is otherwise appropriate, prior unionization can again indicate employee wishes. There is no prohibition to recognition as long as the unit is not otherwise prohibited.

The Unit and Company Organizational Structure

As discussed earlier, the considerations used to determine appropriateness are not legally binding formulas but an exercise in rational examination of the facts of an individual case. The NLRB recognized this distinction from its earliest decision. In *Bendix Products Corporation,* the board stated, "The designation of a unit appropriate for the purposes of collective bargaining must be confined to evidence and circumstances peculiar to the individual case."[33] Under such a philosophy, a particular company may, because of its relationship to branch offices or its particular reporting policies, make an otherwise inappropriate unit appropriate for its employees. The board must examine, in some cases, the internal operations of a company to ascertain those peculiarities.

Public Interest

One consideration added by the courts for review by the board is the public interest. Without much guidance provided by the courts, the board is to ascertain when its decision will serve the public interest. In making this determination, the NLRB must not be affected by the desires of the parties involved.[34]

Accretion

The **doctrine of accretion** allows the NLRB to add new groups of employees to existing units if their work satisfies the same criteria as the original unit, that is, community of interests, bargaining history, interchange of employees, geographic proximity, common supervision, and union wishes. However, such a determination is not automatic. If the new class of employees retains a separate identity, perhaps by virtue of its newness, it can be determined an appropriate unit. Accretion usually occurs when an employer expands operations, builds a new facility, or merges with another employer. It is often to the advantage of the union to have an accretion.[35]

Accretion offers the board a conflicting choice. Adding new employees to an established union preserves the stability so important under the act, but squeezing in new employees, under perhaps narrow similarities, constricts the employees' freedom of choice.

Stipulated Units

The board's authority to determine an appropriate unit is not without limitations. A company and a union may stipulate to the board what they consider an appropriate unit. The courts have said that the board may not alter the unit in such cases. However, a stipulated unit may not violate principles in the National Labor Relations Act or established board policy, for example, by including supervisors.[36]

Statutory Considerations

The NLRB is limited by specific sections of the act in determining appropriate bargaining units. Workers not included under the act's definition of employee may not be included in a unit. Moreover, the board may not determine a unit appropriate with both professional and nonprofessional personnel unless a majority of the professional employees has approved such a designation. A craft unit can seek recognition even if it previously had been part of a larger unit unless a majority of the employees in the craft votes against separate representation. Finally, guards cannot be included in a unit with any other employees.[37]

Other types of workers are excluded from appropriate units because of various board and court interpretations. Excluded are managerial employees, defined in board rulings as "those who formulate and effectuate management policies by expressing and making operative the decisions of their employer."[38] Confidential employees are excluded if the nature of their work has a labor nexus, that is, if it involves the formation, determination, or execution of labor relations management policies and if it involves access to confidential information concerning anticipated changes resulting from collective bargaining.[39] Temporary employees and, in some instances, part-time employees may also be excluded from appropriate units.

The lines drawn by court rulings and board interpretations are never totally clear. In *National Labor Relations Board v. Yeshiva University,* it was determined that the faculty members were managerial employees because of their input into the academic product of the university. As managerial instead of professional employees, they did not come under the protection of the National Labor Relations Act and could therefore not be recognized. Such a determination has a negative effect on unionization in the academic sector.[40]

Two Supreme Court decisions, however, expanded the definition of employees. In *Holly Farms Corp. et al. v. NLRB,*[41] the Court upheld a board decision that gave the employees of "live-haul crews" (chicken catchers, forklift operators, and truck drivers), employed by a vertically integrated poultry producer, coverage under the National Labor Relations Act. The Court found that the workers who collected and transported the chickens were part of the company's processing operations not engaged in agriculture. In *NLRB v. Town and Country Electric,*[42] the Court rejected an employer's contention that union-paid organizers who applied for nonunion positions with the employer's electrical company were not employees under the National Labor Relations Act. The employer argued that these union members could not serve two masters and that the union would direct the employees' work. The Court ruled that union employment did not inherently create a conflict. If the employee failed to do the job as directed by the employer, then the employee could be dismissed.

Types of Units

Certain types of units have evolved within the established principles of appropriateness. The act itself lists employer units, craft units, plant units, or their subdivisions.

Craft Units

A **craft unit** is composed exclusively of workers having a recognized skill, such as electricians, machinists, and plumbers. Recognition questions for craft units usually come before the board when a group of craft employees wants to break away from an existing industrial union, an action called *craft severance*. Congress has established the policy that the board cannot determine a craft unit inappropriate on the grounds that a different unit has been established by prior board determination, unless the majority of the

The International Brotherhood of Electrical Workers (IBEW) is known as a craft union because most of the members have a recognized skill—they work with electrical components and equipment as linemen, repairmen, machine operators, meter installers, boiler operators, cable splicers, welders, and the like.

employees in the craft unit vote against separate representation. Despite this legislative policy, the NLRB has severely limited craft severance elections through a number of decisions. Under the *National Tube* doctrine,[43] the board identified certain industries whose operations were so integrated that craft workers could not be taken from the unit without affecting the stability of labor relations. And in the *Mallinckrodt Chemical Works* decision, the board outlined the criteria it would use to allow craft severance; the application of these standards has greatly reduced incidents of craft severance.[44]

The NLRB requires that the craft group be distinct from others in the unit by virtue of the skilled, nonrepetitive nature of its work. The board will examine the extent to which the group has retained its identity or, as the alternative, actually participated in the affairs of the larger unit. The impact of separating the craft unit from the whole is also a factor in the board's determination. Consideration of the particular bargaining history of the larger unit, as well as the history of collective bargaining in the industry as a whole, must be part of the board's deliberations. In some instances, the NLRB decision will be influenced by the degree to which the craft work is integrated with the unskilled work and is therefore essential to the production process. Finally, the board may examine the qualifications of the union seeking to represent the craft union for its experience as an agent for similar groups.[45]

Departmental Units

Similar to a craft unit, a **departmental unit** is composed of all the members of one department in a larger organization. The board uses standards similar to those used for craft severance in determining one department to be an appropriate unit separate from the entire plant or company. An examination of the difference in skills and in training, the degree of common supervision, the degree of interchange with employees outside the department, and different job performance ratings have been used to allow a departmental unit to exist.[46]

One Employer, Multiple Locations

Many employers have plants, facilities, or stores at more than one location. And the NLRB must determine if a single location can be an appropriate unit or whether all locations should constitute a single unit. It is well established that a petitioned-for single-facility unit is *presumed* to be an appropriate bargaining unit.[47] That presumption is, however, rebuttable on a showing that the single facility has so effectively merged into a more comprehensive unit, or is so functionally integrated, that it has lost its separate identity. To determine whether the single-facility presumption has been rebutted, the board looks at such factors as the centralized control over daily operations and labor relations; extent of autonomy of the local management to handle the facility's day-to-day ordinary operations and to supervise the employees' day-to-day work; similarity of employee skills, functions, and working conditions; extent of employee interchange; geographic proximity; and bargaining history, if any.[48] The party *opposing* the single-facility unit has the burden of rebutting its appropriateness. However, the board does not require overwhelming evidence of such integration. In a recent case, the board determined that the employer had successfully rebutted the presumption of a single-facility unit when the union sought to represent employees at one of the employer's two facilities, and the board determined that the two facilities operated as one even though they were 100 miles apart.[49]

In reviewing requests for single-facility units in the health-care industry, the board has relied on Congress's directive to the board to guard against the undue proliferation of units in health-care institutions. In one case the board denied a petition from a union to designate 7 of a company's 29 Patient Service Centers an appropriate bargaining unit noting that the 29 facilities comprised the company's Southern New Jersey Region and that the 7 locations did not comport with any of the employer's administrative or regional groupings. The board found that the management of the 29 facilities was relatively centralized and that there were regular interchanges between the seven petitioning centers and one of the other centers.[50] The board also denied a petition to designate a bargaining unit at one of the employer's 21 family practice clinics because the employer established that the clinics operated as a functionally integrated network.[51]

Multiemployer Units

Although the Wagner Act favors localizing a unit within one employer, collective bargaining can be conducted between a group of related employers and representatives of their employees.[52] Factors to be considered in such a designation are whether there is an express or implied approval of all parties to enter into such bargaining relationship or if the history of the bargaining in the industry implies intent to consent to multiemployer units. The employer can withdraw from a multiemployer collective bargaining relationship before the date for modification or negotiation of a new contract. After bargaining has begun, an employer may withdraw only with the union's consent or on showing unusual circumstances. The union consent ensures the stability necessary under the National Labor Relations Act, and the board has found unusual circumstances when there is a genuine bargaining impasse.[53]

Residual Units

Workers do not always fit into neat packages, and the board has sometimes given recognition to odd collections of employees because of their common working situations or the proximity of their working sites. The NLRB policy is that employees are entitled to separate representation if they are left unrepresented after the bulk of employees are organized. Employees who do not fit anywhere else—such as sales and service personnel, porters, janitors, and maids—are residual units.

Remaining Units

Employee groups that are separate from primary production and maintenance units can be classified as remaining units. Because of exclusions contained in the act itself, professional employees and guards often have professional and guard units. Technical units contain employees with a high degree of skill and training who exercise independent judgment but fall short of professional status. The factors to be considered in determining a technical unit are the desires of the party, the bargaining history, the existence of a unit seeking self-representation, the separate supervision of the technical employees, the location of the workplace, similarity of work hours, and employee benefit packages. It often becomes a question of who should be included on the basis of the level of skill and training, employee contact and interchange, and similarity of working conditions. Departmental units are treated the same as craft units in severance cases. Office clerical units are commonly separated from production and maintenance units in a large plant because the board recognizes the common interest of office clerical employees, regardless of previous bargaining history.

Health-Care Institutions Units

The 1974 Health Care Amendments extended coverage of the act to employees of nonprofit hospitals. In hearings concerning the amendments, Congress directed the NLRB to give "due consideration . . . to preventing proliferation of bargaining units in the health care industry." However, this direction was not specified in the language of the act itself.

Since 1974, the board has applied the usual standards for unit determination and approved eight basic **health-care units** for the health-care industry:

1. Physicians
2. Registered nurses (RNs)
3. All other professional employees, including licensed practical nurses
4. Technical employees
5. Business office clerical employees
6. Skilled maintenance employees
7. Guards
8. All other nonprofessional employees

Health employers accepted exclusive physician units, but RN bargaining units separate from other professional employees were not. The per se acceptance of an exclusive RN unit by the board came under considerable court attack.[54] Unions attacked this attitude and blamed it for stymieing union organizing efforts. In April 1989 the NLRB confirmed its regulations involving the eight health-care units and opened the door to organizing the health-care industry.[55]

In *American Hospital Association v. NLRB,*[56] a health-care employer challenged the ruling of the NLRB that established the eight bargaining units. The Supreme Court, however, upheld the NLRB's decision.[57] In a 1994 decision, however, the Court reversed an NLRB ruling regarding nurses' units and severely reduced opportunities for growth of unions in the health-care industry. In *NLRB v. Health Care & Retirement Corporation,*[58] the corporation had challenged the certification of a nurses' unit on the grounds that the nurses acted as "supervisors" and were therefore exempt from the act. The NLRB disagreed and said that in the case of nurses the assignment and direction of other employees by itself does not make the nurse a supervisor if the activity is to ensure high-quality and efficient service. The Court reversed, however, saying that the

National Labor Relations Act defines a supervisor as someone using independent judgment to assign and direct the work of other employees in the interest of the employer, which a nurse would do. Most nurses were, therefore, supervisors and exempt from the act. Subsequently, the NLRB ruled that nurses were not supervisors exercising "independent judgment" if their judgment was no more than using their professional or technical training or experience to direct less-skilled employees to deliver services in accordance with employer-specified standards. The Court again rejected the NLRB interpretation of the act as to nurses in *NLRB v. Kentucky River Community Care, Inc.,*[59] holding that just because a nurse's exercise of supervision was limited by professional standards did not mean the nurse was not a supervisor.

BARGAINING UNIT DETERMINATION IN THE PUBLIC SECTOR

Under Title VII of the Civil Service Reform Act, the **Federal Labor Relations Authority** must determine an appropriate bargaining unit for federal agencies. Borrowing from court decisions under the National Labor Relations Act, the federal law applies a community-of-interest test to identify an appropriate unit on an agency, plant, installation, functional, or other basis. The criteria used to determine a clear and identifiable community of interest include common skills, similar working conditions, common supervision, common work site, and identical duties. An appropriate unit must promote effective dealings with the agency; the extent of unionization by a bargaining unit is not a factor in its recognition. At the federal level, confidential employees, managers, supervisors, and personnel employees are excluded from the bargaining unit. Professional employees are excluded from nonprofessional units unless the professional employees vote in favor of their own inclusion.

A community-of-interest test is also used in state and local government to determine an appropriate unit. Guidelines for such determination may or may not be outlined in the legislation. The following criteria have been developed by the Advisory Committee on Intergovernmental Relations to define community of interest:

1. Similar wages, hours, working rules, and conditions of employment
2. Maintaining a negotiating pattern based on common history
3. Maintaining the craft or professional line status
4. Representation rights, which involve the inclusion or exclusion of supervisors or nonprofessionals (this refers to organizations such as police or fire departments)[60]

On the state and local levels, the inclusion of supervisory personnel within the bargaining unit has presented a difficult question. Those in favor of such inclusion point to the need to consolidate employees and to limit the number of unions involved. It has been suggested that supervisors moderate demands and create less-militant organizations. In some instances, supervisory titles in the public sector do not reflect actual supervisory authority because of the way decisions are made in the public sector. In addition, all supervisory and nonsupervisory career employees share common interests, especially in financial issues. Those who oppose the inclusion of supervisory personnel point out that supervisors face a potential conflict of interest when they themselves are affected by a contract they must enforce. Also, in pursuing grievance procedures, the distinction between management and employee needs to be clear, and supervisors may need to continue an operation during a work stoppage by the bargaining unit.

The size of a public employee unit can give a strategic advantage to either side. The public employer may encourage a larger unit, hoping the diverse interests and backgrounds of a larger unit will prevent the union from gaining majority status. Larger units prevent or reduce the possibility that multiunion negotiation will be used against the employer. The time and cost of bargaining are greatly reduced with larger units. Still, employers realize that the political power of public employee unions may be increased if the unit is very large. Because unions seek to represent the unit most likely to give it majority status, size is not the only determining factor in their organization efforts. In addition, because of the mix of service and clerical employees being organized on a local or state level, the employees often have to choose between two labor organizations—a trade union and an employee association. Their choice will have significant impact on the labor–management relationship.[61]

UNION STRUCTURE

The structure of labor unions reflects the reasons they were formed and the influences of the times in which they grew. Unions seek to secure a better living standard for their members through higher wages and fringe benefits and to enhance job security through tenure, layoff provisions, and seniority rights. In addition, labor organizations have broadened their interests to seek legislative protections for workers such as occupational health and safety laws, workers' compensation, and unemployment insurance. To advance the welfare of all workers, unions also support social legislation such as Social Security, funding for public education, and environmental laws. To meet the unions' objectives, a two-tiered labor organizational structure has evolved. On the local level, job-oriented units form the basis for bargaining with employers. On the national level, a network or federation of unions pursues broader goals.

Types of Unions

Craft Unions

The U.S. labor movement began when associations and combinations of skilled workers joined together for short periods of time to confront an employer on a specific job action. These associations were the bases of the **craft unions**. Craft unions are made up of workers who have been organized in accordance with their craft or skill. "One craft, one union" is their slogan. For example, in the building construction industry, skilled workers include electricians, carpenters, bricklayers, and ironworkers; in the printing industry, printers, typesetters, and engravers; in the service industry, barbers, cooks, and telephone workers; and in the manufacturing industry, millwrights, machinists, and tool-and-die makers.

The craft union, as an organization of skilled workers, is able to approach an employer on a much different footing than the industrial union. A craft union local typically seeks to organize all practitioners of its trade employed by a certain employer or within a specific geographic area. By doing so successfully, the craft union creates a union shop. Employers who need the services of a skilled laborer must employ a union member. Craft unions also seek to restrict the supply of skilled laborers so they can demand higher wages. Stringent apprenticeship programs consisting of several years of classroom instruction and on-the-job training limit craft union membership. State or local licensing boards composed of members of the trade union can often restrict the number of licenses issued.

Union members enter the craft union after an apprenticeship of several years. Craft unionists remain members for their working lifetimes, moving from job to job as required but always remaining a part of their craft union. Even after retirement, their contact with the union remains as a tribute to their craft.

Labor agreements entered into by craft unions usually cover a geographic region rather than one employer. Union members may work for more than one employer within a year and still be covered by that same agreement. This practice is common when the building trade unions have negotiated a labor agreement with all the major construction companies in the area. Electricians, plumbers, drywallers, and other trades can go from job to job under the same agreement.

The **business agent** of the craft union is usually a full-time administrator paid by the union to handle negotiation and administration of the union contracts as well as the day-to-day operation of the union hiring hall. On the job, one union member performs the role of steward; he or she may be the first person hired for that construction project, the most senior member of the construction crew, or a person chosen by the business agent. **Stewards** are the eyes and ears of the business agent. The steward's job is to make sure the contractor lives up to the agreement and to report to the business agent if he or she does not. This arrangement ensures the business agent an active contact at each job site at which the craft union is supplying laborers. There is, however, no continuing role for any particular steward in the craft union local. The steward's authority is limited to the job site, and when that job is finished, the steward returns to regular union membership.

Industrial Unions

Whereas craft unions can be traced to the earliest days of this country, industrial unions have a wider and stronger base of mostly unskilled laborers. The slogan "One shop, one union" typifies the **industrial union** seeking to organize workers at one workplace with the same employer, regardless of their jobs. The industrial union seeks to increase membership to ensure its influence.

Typical industrial unions include organizations of autoworkers, rubber workers, textile workers, commercial workers, steelworkers, miners, and truck drivers. Increasingly, government employees such as firefighters, police, and hospital workers are organizing industrial-type unions.

The local union most often is affiliated with a national or international union. Some national unions will negotiate master agreements, which are regional or national labor agreements covering wages, transfers, pensions, layoffs, and other benefits. The local agreement must be negotiated separately to cover matters of specific concern to the local union and the plant. An example of such a two-tiered agreement is the labor agreement between the United Auto Workers and Ford Motor Company. The table of contents in this particular master agreement includes the following:

Article I	Recognition
Article II	Union Shop
Article III	Dues and Assessments
Article IV	Company Responsibilities
Article V	Strikes, Stoppages, and Lockouts
Article VI	Representation
Article VII	Grievance Procedure
Article VIII	Seniority and Related Matters
Article IX	Wages and Other Economic Matters
Article X	Miscellaneous
Article XI	Duration of Agreement

The local agreement negotiated by Local 862, UAW Unit No. 2, includes the following:

Day-off program
Employee information
Job-posting agreement
Letters of understanding
Line spacing
Manning of medical facility
Miscellaneous agreement
Other miscellaneous agreements
Overtime agreement
Paid holidays
Seniority agreement
Shift preference agreement
Shift starting time

Members of an industrial union often join the union after being hired simply because of a union shop provision in the contract. Members regard their union as their voice with the employer, and when employment ends, their membership usually ends as well. Elected officials who are also full-time employees at the workplace typically administer the work of local industrial unions. Their duties include negotiation and administration of the local union contract, normally with the assistance of a representative of the national or international union. Elected shop stewards who form a permanent tier in the local industrial union hierarchy aid this work. At the departmental, shift, or line level, the shop stewards are the eyes and ears, voice, and strong right arm

The United Auto Workers (UAW) is known as an industrial union because it represents almost all the employees in one workplace: "One shop, one union."

of the union. Their position enables them to communicate members' desires and complaints to union officials and to relay information back to the membership. Stewards participate in grievance adjustment and, through steward councils, assist in contract negotiations.

Levels of Unions

The four levels of unions are local unions, national (or international) unions, intermediate unions, and the federation of unions.

Local Unions

Unionized workers are members of a local union, which is the organizational component of the labor union. It handles the day-to-day operations of the collective bargaining agreement, disposes of most grievances, manages strikes, and disciplines members. A local union may fill a social role in the lives of its members, sponsoring dances, festivals, and other functions. It may be the focal point of the political organization and activity of its members.

A local union usually meets once a month to conduct business. At such meetings, annual elections are held, union issues are discussed, and activities are organized. Although this level is the most important to its members, attendance at the union meetings varies and is highest at times of crisis. Unlike paid business agents for craft unions, elected officials of local industrial unions are compensated by being given time off the job when conducting union business. Local unions usually adopt bylaws that specify their jurisdiction, meetings, and election process, as well as the duties and salaries of officers (see Figure 3-1).

National (or International) Unions

Typically, but not always, the local union is affiliated with a national or international union. Craft and industrial unions organize on a national basis and designate local unions by region. The national union serves as the local's parent, having created it. But a local union is considered a separate and distinct voluntary association owing its existence to the will of its members. The union's constitution, bylaws, and charter determine the relationship between a national union and its subordinate local unions. The charter is a contract between the national and local organization and its members. The constitution and bylaws authorize the national union not only to function but also to protect individual rights.

Constitutions are adopted or changed at conventions of representatives of member locals. Officers and executive boards are elected to take action consistent with policies established by the convention. Most national unions allow their elected officials to hire and organize the union's administrative staff. Most unions have the following operational departments: executive and administrative, made up of president, vice president, secretary-treasurer, and assistant; financial and auditing; organizational and service (to serve local unions); and the technical staff, which gives expert assistance in arbitration, labor laws, and data research.

The national union provides services to the locals, and the fundamental relationship is based on the services rendered. Services include organizing the nonunion workers within the jurisdiction of the local union. In appropriate circumstances, the national negotiates master agreements with nationwide employers and assists the local union in its local agreement. Even if no national contract is entered into, the national union assists the local unions in their contract negotiations through its research and educational services and may provide an expert negotiator. A national union helps with grievance

**BY LAWS
OF
LOCAL UNION 1347
INTERNATIONAL BROTHERHOOD
OF
ELECTRICAL WORKERS
CINCINNATI, OH**

INDEX

FIGURE 3-1   By Laws of Local Union 1347, IBEW

SOURCE: Kenzie Baker, IBEW Local Union 1347, permission granted by Stephen Feldhaus, Business Manager, Dec. 2005.

and arbitration administration and provides support in strike activities. National unions play an important political and representative role on behalf of their locals in national and statewide political action, such as protecting members' financial interests as in Profile 3-1. Local unions support the national unions with dues and fees.

Intermediate Organizational Unions
Intermediate organizational unions consisting of regional or district officers, trade councils, conference boards, and joint councils lie between national and local unions.

PROFILE 3-1

ENRON SCANDAL: RESPONSE BY CARPENTERS UNION

The Enron scandal in 2002 drew national media attention for months and cost thousands of workers their jobs and millions of dollars in 401(k) savings. It also caused countless changes in the accounting profession. Enron, the Houston-based energy company, filed the largest bankruptcy in U.S. history after admitting to overstating profits by $586 million over four years. The resulting investigation discovered that Enron had paid its auditor, Arthur Andersen, more for nonaudit management consulting ($27 million) than for audit services ($25 million). The revelation caused many U.S. companies, to avoid any conflict of interest, to split the two services to different firms. Why? Fees paid to an audit firm for lucrative consulting work may bring into question the integrity and accuracy of the audit. The U.S. Securities and Exchange Commission began requiring that companies report the two services separately.

The United Brotherhood of Carpenters and Joiners of America union, in response to the incidents, filed shareholder resolutions with 35 national companies seeking that they limit their use of auditors for nonauditing services. Carpenters union director Ed Durkin stated that the "whole stock market system of publicly buying and trading shares (of stocks, bonds, mutual funds) relies on the information of the financial reporting system. If you can't trust the documents there's a complete lack of confidence in the system." Other national unions, with billions of dollars worth of shares, filed similar actions. Some sought to directly prevent companies from hiring their audit firms as consultants.

SOURCE: Adapted from Amy Higgins, "Public Firms Blur Accounting Borders," *Cincinnati Enquirer,* June 23, 2002, pp. D1, D2.

For industrial unions, the intermediate office serves to bring the national office closer to the local unions to provide better services. For craft unions, joint councils often bring the various crafts together to give them better negotiating power with local construction employers, to coordinate their activities, and to assist in resolving jurisdictional disputes between craft unions.

Federation of Unions

From 1955, when the American Federation of Labor (AFL) and Congress of Industrial Unions (CIO) merged to create the AFL-CIO, until 2005, the AFL-CIO was the only **federation of unions** in the United States. In 2005, however, seven national unions split from the AFL-CIO to create Change to Win, a new federation of national unions dedicated to growing their membership through strategic organizational campaign and improving the living standards of workers. The three national unions that led the split were the International Brotherhood of Teamsters, the Service Employees International Union, and the United Food and Commercial Workers.

The AFL-CIO is composed of approximately 53 national and international unions; the AFL-CIO has 39,000 local unions and 9 million members. Figure 3-2 illustrates its structure. Federations were formed to increase union power. Although the AFL-CIO is itself not a union, it represents U.S. labor in world affairs and coordinates union activities such as lobbying, voter registration, and political education. For example, the AFL-CIO worked with local unions to defeat two Los Angeles campaigns to break up the city. The secession issues appeared on the November 5, 2002, ballots in Hollywood and San Fernando Valley. Supporters hoped to create new, smaller cities and cut the costs and taxes for municipal services such as police, fire, sanitation,

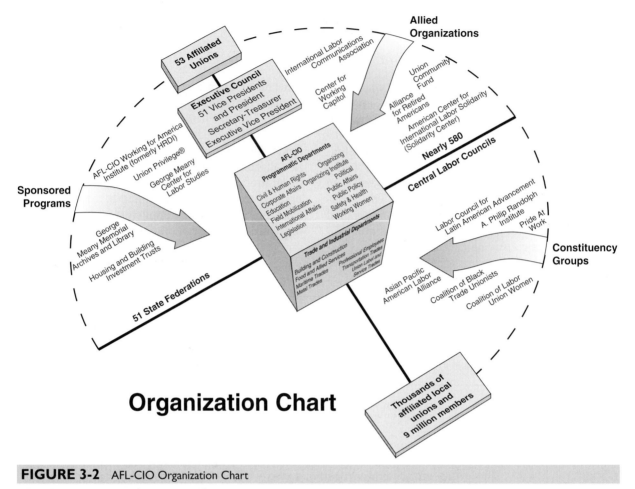

FIGURE 3-2 AFL-CIO Organization Chart

SOURCE: www.aflcio.org (August 1, 2002).

public works, and housing. The City of Los Angeles at the time had 35,500 workers, most of who belonged to labor unions. Miguel Contreras, head of the Los Angeles County Federation of Labor, AFL-CIO, noted that Los Angeles had "progressive" labor laws, which might not be passed in the new cities. The new cities would be required to honor existing union contracts for one year only. With over 810,000 California members, the federation distributed leaflets and manned telephone banks against the succession ballots.[62]

In 2005, seven national unions, which split from the AFL-CIO, formed **Change to Win Coalition**, a new union federation. The new federation started with six million members and elected Anna Burger as the first woman in history to lead a labor federation in the U.S.

As with national unions, the officers, policies, activities, and business of the AFL-CIO are voted on at periodic conventions to which each national union sends delegates. Between conventions, the executive council, consisting of the president, secretary-treasurer, and 33 vice presidents, convenes to handle such items as charters of new internationals, judicial appeals from member unions, and union corruption. The general board is composed of the executive council plus the chief executive officer of each affiliated union. The general board rules on questions referred by the executive council that include items deemed to be politically sensitive and those requiring council action by the AFL-CIO Constitution.

Independent Unions

As stated earlier, not all local unions are affiliated with a national or an international union that in turn is a part of the AFL-CIO. These local independent unions are characterized by smaller memberships, more limited funds, and a lower profile. They are, however, growing. One major reason for their growth is that these independent unions find their membership primarily among government and white-collar workers.

Independent unions are generally not designed along either the craft or the industrial unit model, preferring to open their membership to employees of a specific professional occupation. The independent unions resemble other unions in that they do target membership, albeit often a wider target. They hold national conventions and elect national officers, although the conventions are more frequent and seemingly more democratic among the independent unions. The election of their national officers reflects the smaller size of these unions in that the membership often elects the national officers themselves, not the delegates to the conventions. In union disciplinary procedures, the independent unions are more likely to invoke outside arbitrators or hearing panels than are the traditional affiliated unions. This approach to union self-regulation keeps union officials from becoming too autocratic and powerful.[63]

PUBLIC-SECTOR UNIONS

Many public-sector unions have their roots in professional organizations that developed prior to widespread public-sector collective bargaining. The National Education Association, incorporated in 1906, was organized to advance the interests of educators. It is the largest professional organization in the world with over 2.6 million members and affiliates in every state as well as in over 13,000 communities.[64] The American Federation of Teachers (AFT), which in the 1960s pioneered collective bargaining for teachers, began as a labor union and has grown into a trade union representing workers in education, health care, and public service. The AFT has over three quarters of a million members and is affiliated with the AFL-CIO.[65]

The American Federation of State, County and Municipal Employees (AFSCME) is the second-largest public union in the United States and the fifth-largest national union in the AFL-CIO, with over 1.3 million members. It represents public employees and health-care workers throughout the United States, Panama, and Puerto Rico. They include employees of state, county, and municipal governments; school districts; public and private hospitals; universities; and nonprofit agencies that work in a cross section of jobs ranging from blue collar to clerical, professional, and paraprofessional.

AFSCME began as a number of separate locals organized by a group of Wisconsin state employees in the early 1930s. By 1935, 30 locals had become a separate department within the American Federation of Government Employees. In 1936, the American Federation of Labor chartered AFSCME. By 1955, at the time of the AFL-CIO merger, AFSCME had 100,000 members. The following year, the union merged with the 30,000-member CIO Government and Civic Employees Organizing Committee.

AFSCME's organizational structure is typical of public-sector unions. AFSCME is organized into more than 3,500 local unions, most of which are affiliated with one of 61 councils. Local unions and councils have their own constitutions, elect their own officers, and administer a wide variety of local affairs. The international union coordinates issues of concern to AFSCME members and provides research, legislative, legal, organizational, educational, public relations, and other services.[66]

REPRESENTATION ELECTIONS

The NLRB's duties include the regulation of representation elections and campaigns. The board's objective is to preserve the right of employees to self-organization without outside and unwanted influences. Under the National Labor Relations Act, the bargaining agent is selected by a majority vote of unit members to be the exclusive representative for negotiation and administration of the agreement. The procedures for conducting employee elections are codified. Cases decided by the NLRB have provided rules to supplement those procedures. The board is empowered to conduct elections by secret ballot and to certify the results. The main purpose and benefit of board certification is to resolve any question of representation. A detailed look at how such elections may and may not be conducted can be found in Chapter 4.

THE ORGANIZING DRIVE

The impetus to organize employees may come from two sources. First, the workers may be dissatisfied with their pay or work conditions and initiate contact with the union. Although some supervisors believe that most organizing drives focus on wages and benefits, in reality most drives are caused by "soft issues," such as employees feeling overworked and underappreciated; humiliation or harassment by supervisors, clients, or coworkers; employees' sense of double standards for management and workers; perceived job insecurity possibly caused by the unjust termination of a worker; or simply protection from change or broken promises by management.[67]

Second, a **union organizer**, a full-time, salaried staff member who generally represents a national union, may contact workers. As the job title suggests, the union organizer increases union membership and strength by organizing groups of workers who are not presently unionized. An **organizing drive** usually follows the series of events shown in Figure 3-3.

The union's goal is to organize workers and bring them into the union. Labor's strategy is to convince the workers that union membership will bring them benefits they do not presently enjoy. Union organizers may suggest that union representation will result in higher pay, more benefits, better working conditions, and greater fairness in promotions, job transfers, and layoffs. Speaking proudly of the benefits and work improvements they have achieved for other workers, union organizers often cite impressive and convincing statistics about wage gains achieved through collective bargaining. Labor advocates hold formal meetings at the local union hall and encourage supporters to spread the word informally about the benefits a union would bring to the employees' place of work. Prounion handbills and flyers are often passed to workers as they leave work or go to lunch.

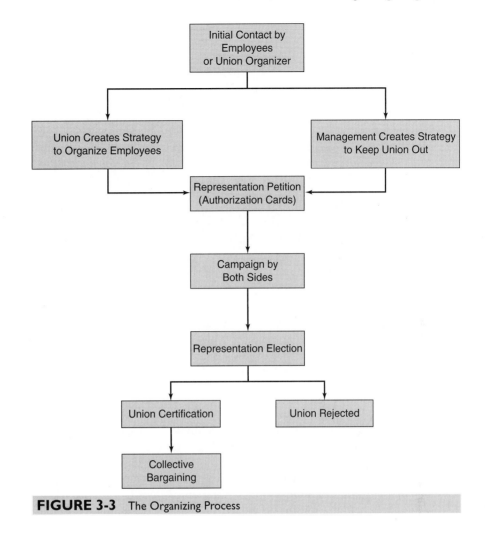

FIGURE 3-3   The Organizing Process

If management's goal is to keep the union out of the workplace, then its strategy may be to convince the workers that unionization will do them more harm than good. Management may attempt to ensure workers that their present pay and benefits are competitive and may show data to prove it. Emphasizing a philosophy of fair dealings with all employees, management may discuss the union's involvement in violent or corrupt activities if such has been the case. Management will also enumerate the costs of union membership, which include initiation fees, dues, and other assessments. The workers will be reminded that wages will be lost should a strike occur. A discussion of how far management can go to discourage unionization and not violate the National Labor Relations Act can be found in Chapter 4.

Election Procedures

The steps in a representation election are described in the following paragraphs.

Step 1: *Representation Petition*   The first step in the election process is to file a representation petition at the office of the appropriate regional director (see Figure 3-4). A union must present evidence of employee support before a representation

Dr. Robert Weinmann, M.D. gave the victory speech after successfully winning the representation election for 800 Los Angeles County doctors, who voted to join the Union of American Physicians and Dentists (UAPD).

election will be held. The NLRB requires designation by at least 30 percent of the bargaining unit employees, usually in the form of signed and dated authorization cards. The NLRB also accepts designations in the form of signed petitions and union application cards.[68]

Board actions have several kinds of petitions. An employee, a group of employees, or a union representing employees can file an **RC petition** seeking certification of an appropriate unit. An employer can file an *RM petition* if one or more labor organizations claim representation status in an appropriate unit and the employer questions the representative's status. Also, when an employer has objective proof that the union no longer represents the majority of the employees, he or she may file an RM petition. An employer, employee, other individual, or a union may also use a decertification or *RD petition* to determine whether a recognized union still has the support of employees.

Other types of petitions available are the *UD petition,* which 30 percent or more of the employees file to rescind a union shop agreement; a *UC petition,* requesting clarification of the composition of a bargaining unit currently certified; and an *AC petition,* requesting that a change of circumstances be recognized, such as a change of union name or affiliation on a previous NLRB certification.

Petitions demonstrate sufficient employee interest or the actual type of representation case so that the board may decide if it has jurisdiction. The board will assume the requisite employee interest and will accept an expedited election petition if it is filed within 30 days of the beginning of a recognitional or organizational picket. The board will normally accept petitions requesting certification or decertification only if 30 percent of the employees in a unit favor such an election. Presenting cards authorizing the union to act as the employees' agent for collective bargaining usually demonstrates this

INTERNET
FORM NLRB-502
(3-96)

UNITED STATES GOVERNMENT
NATIONAL LABOR RELATIONS BOARD
PETITION

FORM EXEMPT UNDER 44 U.S.C. 3512

DO NOT WRITE IN THIS SPACE	
Case No.	Date Filed

INSTRUCTIONS: Submit an original and 4 copies of this Petition to the NLRB Regional Office in the Region in which the employer concerned is located. If more space is required for any one item, attach additional sheets, numbering item accordingly.

The Petitioner alleges that the following circumstances exist and requests that the National Labor Relations Board proceed under its proper authority pursuant to Section 9 of the National Labor Relations Act.

1. **PURPOSE OF THIS PETITION** *(If box RC, RM, or RD is checked and a charge under Section 8(b)(7) of the Act has been filed involving the Employer named herein, the statement following the description of the type of petition shall not be deemed made.)* **(Check One)**

☐ **RC-CERTIFICATION OF REPRESENTATIVE** - A substantial number of employees wish to be represented for purposes of collective bargaining by Petitioner and Petitioner desires to be certified as representative of the employees.

☐ **RM-REPRESENTATION (EMPLOYER PETITION)** - One or more individuals or labor organizations have presented a claim to Petitioner to be recognized as the representative of employees of Petitioner.

☐ **RD-DECERTIFICATION (REMOVAL OF REPRESENTATIVE)** - A substantial number of employees assert that the certified or currently recognized bargaining representative is no longer their representative.

☐ **UD-WITHDRAWAL OF UNION SHOP AUTHORITY (REMOVAL OF OBLIGATION TO PAY DUES)** - Thirty percent (30%) or more of employees in a bargaining unit covered by an agreement between their employer and a labor organization desire that such authority be rescinded.

☐ **UC-UNIT CLARIFICATION** - A labor organization is currently recognized by Employer, but Petitioner seeks clarification of placement of certain employees: *(Check one)* ☐ In unit not previously certified. ☐ In unit previously certified in Case No. _____

☐ **AC-AMENDMENT OF CERTIFICATION** - Petitioner seeks amendment of certification issued in Case No. _____ *Attach statement describing the specific amendment sought.*

2. Name of Employer	Employer Representative to contact	Telephone Number
3. Address(es) of Establishment(s) involved *(Street and number, city, State, ZIP code)*		Telecopier Number (Fax)

4a. Type of Establishment *(Factory, mine, wholesaler, etc.)*	4b. Identify principal product or service

5. Unit involved *(in UC petition, describe **present** bargaining unit and attached description of proposed clarification.)*	6a. Number of Employees in Unit:
Included	Present
	Proposed *(By UC/AC)*
Excluded	6b. Is this petition supported by 30% or more of the employees in the unit?* ☐ Yes ☐ No *Not applicable in RM, UC, and AC

(If you have checked box RC in 1 above, check and complete EITHER item 7a or 7b, whichever is applicable.)

7a. ☐ Request for recognition as Bargaining Representative was made on *(Date)* _____ and Employer declined recognition on or about *(Date)* _____ *(If no reply received, so state.)*

7b. ☐ Petitioner is currently recognized as Bargaining Representative and desires certification under the Act.

8. Name of Recognized or Certified Bargaining Agent *(If none, so state.)*	Affiliation
Address, Telephone No. and Telecopier No. (Fax)	Date of Recognition or Certification

9. Expiration Date of Current Contract. If any *(Month, Day, Year)*	10. If you have checked box UD in 1 above, show here the date of execution of agreement granting union shop *(Month, Day, and Year)*

11a. Is there now a strike or picketing at the Employer's establishment(s) Involved? Yes _____ No _____	11b. If so, approximately how many employees are participating?

11c. The Employer has been picketed by or on behalf of *(Insert Name)* _____, a labor organization, of *(Insert Address)* _____ Since *(Month, Day, Year)* _____

12. Organizations or individuals other than Petitioner *(and other than those named in items 8 and 11c)*, which have claimed recognition as representatives and other organizations and individuals known to have a representative interest in any employees in unit described in item 5 above. *(If none, so state.)*

Name	Affiliation	Address	Date of Claim
			Telecopier No. (Fax)

13. Full name of party filing petition *(If labor organization, give full name, including local name and number)*

14a. Address *(street and number, city, state, and ZIP code)*	14b. Telephone No.
	14c. Telecopier No. (Fax)

15. Full name of national or international labor organization of which it is an affiliate or constituent unit *(to be filled in when petition is filed by a labor organization)*

I declare that I have read the above petition and that the statements are true to the best of my knowledge and belief.

Name *(Print)*	Signature	Title *(if any)*
Address *(street and number, city, state, and ZIP code)*		Telephone No.
		Telecopier No. (Fax)

WILLFUL FALSE STATEMENTS ON THIS PETITION CAN BE PUNISHED BY FINE AND IMPRISONMENT (U.S. CODE, TITLE 18, SECTION 1001)

FIGURE 3-4 U.S. Government National Labor Relations Board Petition

30 percent. It can also be shown by a certification listing at least 30 percent of the employees of the represented unit as members in good standing of a union.

Another union may enter an election with a **showing of interest** that represents 10 percent of those in the unit in question. A cross petition from another union may also be filed claiming representation of an appropriate unit different from the original unit but including some of the same people.[69]

Step 2: *Investigation*   The second step occurs when the regional director conducts investigations and a hearing, if necessary, to determine whether to proceed with an election. The employer's business must sufficiently affect commerce so as to rest jurisdiction in the NLRB. An actual representation question must exist, and sufficient employee interest must be demonstrated. The requested unit is deemed appropriate and the bargaining agent qualified. Certain statutory time periods must be honored.

Once the NLRB has determined an election petition is valid, the employer is obligated to furnish to the petitioning union a list of eligible voters' names and addresses. In an unusual case, the union requested e-mail addresses because the bargaining unit members were crewmembers on a ship and would be at sea during the preelection period.[70]

Step 3: *Secret Ballot Election*   The third step is the secret ballot election (see Figure 3-5). The NLRB has the responsibility to ensure that a representative election is fairly and honestly conducted. In a 1948 case, the board stated that its function in representation proceedings was "to provide a laboratory in which an experiment may be conducted, under conditions as nearly ideal as possible, to determine the uninhibited desires of the employees."[71] But the board recognized that the standards for election cases had to be judged against realistic standards of human conduct. When improprieties occur, certain factors should be weighed, such as the size of the unit, the circumstances of any alleged misconduct, and the real or apparent influence of the interfering party. In general,

---

FIGURE 3-5   Request to Proceed with Election

Internet Form NLRB-4551
    (11–94)

UNITED STATES OF AMERICA
NATIONAL LABOR RELATIONS BOARD

REQUEST TO PROCEED

In the matter of _____   _____
                            (Name of Case)   *(Number of Case)*

The undersigned hereby requests the Regional Director to proceed with the above-captioned representation case, notwithstanding the charges of unfair labor practices filed in Case No. _____.
The alleged unlawful conduct in the above (unfair labor practice) case that occurred after the filing of the petition may constitute the basis of objections.

Date _____   _____

                    By_____

                         _____

                                              (Title)

the NLRB will consider objectionable conduct in determining the validity of an election only if it occurs during the critical period, that is, between the filing of an election petition and the election itself.

The NLRB has traditionally favored direct or manual ballots (voting machines, voting boxes, and so on) over mail ballots in representational elections. The board's policy has been to use only mail ballots when manual ballots are "infeasible." Manual ballots are favored because they provide (1) greater secrecy, (2) integrity of the voting process, (3) absence of coercion, and (4) greater participation by employees. Mail balloting is cheaper than manual balloting, but the National Labor Relations Act clearly states employees should be given a "free choice" in representational elections—which can be more easily guaranteed in manual balloting. Yet in recent years the NLRB has used mail balloting more often, establishing appropriate procedures to ensure the fairness and validity of the election. These include precise procedures for casting and returning the ballots and when those procedures are not followed, the election may be set aside. For example, in a run-off election between two unions, the election was set aside when a union representative collected the ballots from the employees rather than have them mailed in as directed.[72]

An employer may cause an election to be invalidated by offering promises of benefits during an election. For example, the NLRB has ruled that employers could not pay employees who were not scheduled to work on the day of a union certification election to get them to come in to vote. In one case, the employer paid for two hours of work and in the other four hours of work.[73] Although a previous NLRB ruling allowed for such compensation as a reasonable reimbursement for travel and time costs,[74] the board said it believed that these offers were more substantial than merely reimbursement and that employees might feel obligated to vote against the union because of the employer's action. Later the board clarified the issue further when it ruled that it was all right for a union to give employees $25 to reimburse them for their time and travel because that amount was reasonably related to an actual cost.[75] Nor are employers allowed to threaten reprisals against employees or state that a successful election will result in strikes and layoffs, although an employer is free to communicate his general views about unionism, even if the employer references a recent, concrete example of a negative outcome for employees who were represented by the same union seeking recognition.[76]

Some employers have used increased one-on-one contact with employees during an election campaign to discourage unionization. Frito Lay, for example, instituted "ride-alongs" with its drivers by managers and nonunion drivers from other locations. The ride-alongs averaged 10 to 12 hours and three per driver during the election campaign period.[77] Wal-Mart urged managers to spend time with employees under a practice of "coaching while walking around" during a union campaign.[78]

Employee actions may also influence the election certification. A union's agreement to waive union fees before an election has been considered an unfair labor practice. And, in another case, a union was held to have invalidated an election by offering free medical screening characterized as the "first union benefit" two days before an election.[79]

Elections may be voided because of misrepresentation or trickery, but they will not be set aside solely because of misleading campaign statements or misrepresentation of fact. However, if parties use forged documents so that the nature of the publication cannot be discerned or if NLRB documents are altered to indicate its endorsement, the election can be voided.[80]

Actions of third parties also may influence and invalidate an election. Employees who are not union agents will not influence an election if the union neither authorizes nor condones the conduct. Supervisors may exhibit prounion sentiment unless it leads employees to believe that the employer favors the particular union and they are expected to support it. Outside groups, newspapers, and public interest organizations may be considered in board hearings on elections if their activities have exacerbated employee fears of employer retaliations or reprisals. Even the NLRB agent may cause an election to be set aside if his or her action tends to destroy confidence in the election process or can be reasonably interpreted as impinging on the board's impartial election standards.

24-HOUR RULE

The board's rules prohibit both unions and employers from making speeches to mass groups of employees on company time within 24 hours of an election—the **24-hour rule**. However, such meetings within 24 hours of an election do not violate these rules if voluntarily attended on the employee's own time. Employers may assemble their employees and speak to them on company time if it is prior to 24 hours to the election and if the employer does not prevent, by rigid no-solicitation rules, access to the employees by the union representatives.

On election day, prolonged conversations between either party and the voters are prohibited, as are traditional campaign activities at the polling place. For example, election-day raffles have been held to be illegal because of the potential to taint an election as demonstrated in Case 3-3. In recent studies of employee participation in representative elections, some questions have been raised as to what degree even a legal

CASE 3-3	ELECTION-DAY RAFFLES

An election was conducted at a hotel in Atlantic City to determine whether the employer's unit employees wanted to be represented by the union for the purposes of collective bargaining. Approximately five days prior to the election, the employer distributed a flyer to all employees eligible to vote in the election titled "Election Day Raffle! Election Day Raffle!" The flyer announced that the employer would hold a raffle following the election and that the winner of the drawing would receive a color television with an integrated videocassette recorder. According to the employer's flyer, the TV/VCR was "approximately equal in value to what your union dues and initiation fees could be for the first year." The flyer also stated that the "sole purpose of the raffle is to encourage everyone to vote" and that participation in the raffle was voluntary.

On the day of the election, the balloting area was established in a room in the rear of the hotel. The raffle was set up at a table in the hotel's middle lobby, and the voting area could not be seen from the raffle area. Voters entering the hotel through its front entrance inevitably passed through the raffle area in the middle lobby to get to the voting area, but voters entering through the hotel's restaurant could avoid the raffle area altogether. The employer paid the raffle attendant, a friend of a nonunit employee, $100 for the single day to conduct the raffle. The raffle attendant did not know, and made no attempt to learn, the voters by name or face, nor did he consult any sort of voter list. He was instructed by the employer's president to distribute a raffle ticket to each person who approached the table and indicated a willingness to participate. The TV/VCR was displayed on the raffle table, which also held the box in which voters dropped their raffle tickets. The employer's flyer announcing the raffle was affixed to the raffle box.

continued

ELECTION-DAY RAFFLES—continued

Ballots counted after the polls closed indicated that the majority of the voters voted against representation by the union. The union filed a complaint citing the employer's election-day raffle as an unfair labor practice. The union argued that the raffle constituted a conferral of benefits and created an inappropriate "circus atmosphere" that warranted setting aside the election. The regional director conducted an investigation, overruled the objection, and certified the results of the election.

Specifically, the regional director found that the raffle satisfied prior board rulings because the raffle was not used as a means to determine how or whether employees voted, participation in the raffle was not conditioned on how the employee voted in the election or on the election's outcome, and the $350 prize was not so substantial that it diverted employees' attention away from the election or induced voters to support the employer's position. The union appealed the regional director's finding to the NLRB.

DECISION

In order that employees may exercise **freedom of choice** on questions concerning union representation, the board seeks to create and preserve for its elections an atmosphere free of undue advantage or improper influence. In applying this principle to a variety of factual settings, the board has imposed restrictions on the parties' preelection conduct. Such restrictions have included, for instance, a strict rule against prolonged conversations between representatives of any party to the election and voters waiting to cast ballots, a prohibition of election speeches on company time to massed assemblies of employees within 24 hours before the scheduled time for conducting an election, a rule barring changes in the payroll process for the purpose of influencing the employees' vote in the election during a period beginning 24 hours before the scheduled opening of the polls and ending with the closing of the polls, and a prohibition on the bestowing of economic benefits that have a tendency to influence the outcome of the election. The board has reviewed the question of whether election-related raffles impair employee free choice in representation elections on a case-by-case basis using the multifactor test employed by the regional director in this case. The board has found, however, that this case-by-case approach is confusing. Therefore, the NLRB adopts a new rule concerning election-day raffles.

The new rule prohibits employers and unions from conducting a raffle if (1) eligibility to participate in the raffle or win prizes is in any way tied to voting in the election or being at the election site on election day or (2) the raffle is conducted at any time during a period beginning 24 hours before the scheduled opening of the polls and ending with the closing of the polls. The term "conducting a raffle" includes the following: (1) announcing a raffle, (2) distributing raffle tickets, (3) identifying the raffle winners, and (4) awarding the raffle prizes. If there is a showing that such a raffle has occurred during the proscribed period, the election will be set aside. The parties should not attempt to circumvent this rule by, for example, announcing a raffle more than 24 hours before the opening of the polls and then completing the raffle immediately after the closing of the polls.

Under these new guidelines, the employer's election-day raffle was held to have violated the National Labor Relations Act. The election results were set aside, and a new election was ordered.

SOURCE: Adapted from *Atlantic Limousine Inc. v. Teamsters Local 331*, 165 LRRM 1001 (August 14, 2000).

campaign discourages participation.[81] If an employee perceives that an election will be won or lost regardless of his or her vote, that employee may choose not to vote at all.[82]

In cases in which an election involves three choices—for example, Union A, Union B, or no union—a **runoff election** may be required if none of the choices receives a majority of the votes cast. The two top vote getters are placed before the members of the bargaining unit again, and the one receiving a majority vote can be certified:

> Under NLRB rules and regulations, "A runoff election is conducted only where: (a) the ballot in the original election contained three or more choices [i.e., two labor organizations and a *neither* choice]; and (b) no single choice received a majority of the valid votes cast. Thus there can be no runoff where the original ballot provided for: (1) a *yes* and *no* choice in a one-union election; or (2) a *severance* election." The ballot in the runoff election provides for a selection between the two choices receiving the largest and second largest number of votes in the original election.[83]

In 2002, for example, a representation election was held for office and service employees at the University of Baltimore. The initial ballot had three options: (1) no representation, (2) AFSCME, and (3) the MCEA, a local independent union. None of the three won a majority, and thus a second, runoff election was held, and AFSCME won with 64 percent of the runoff vote to 35 percent for MCEA.[84]

Step 4: *Certification of Election Results* If the board is satisfied that the election represents the employees' free choice, the election is certified, the fourth step. Either no union is victorious or, if a union has gained a majority of those voting, that union is certified as the bargaining agent for the unit.

Certification benefits a union in a number of ways. It closes any challenges to the union's status as the exclusive bargaining agent for the particular unit. Its status is binding on the employer for at least one year, during which time the employer must bargain with it. After the first year the employer must continue to bargain unless there is reasonable doubt that the union will continue to enjoy a majority vote of the unit. The board will not entertain petitions regarding rival certification for that unit within the one-year certification or within three years if a valid contract is in effect. The certified union may strike against the employer under certain circumstances without fear of an unfair labor practice charge. A 2005 study of newly certified bargaining units found that about 90 percent of the time the union was successful in negotiating the first contract with the employer within the first year. In previous years between 1996 and 2003 the annual success rate ranged between 73 percent and 95 percent, with a trend of higher rates in recent years. In previous decades the annual rates were as low as 60 percent. First contract negotiations are often more contentious than renewals because the NLRA provides no penalty for failure to reach a contract and no mandate for mediation.[85]

The number of representation elections held each year varies greatly by state. In 2000, for example, the five states with the most elections were California, 309 (55 percent won by the union); New York, 272 (58 percent); Illinois, 209 (48 percent); Pennsylvania, 207 (49 percent); and Michigan, 148 (54 percent). The five states with the fewest elections were Idaho, 5; South Dakota, 6; Vermont, 6; Wyoming, 6; and New Hampshire, 8. In all 50 states, 2,799 representation elections were held in 2000, and unions won 52 percent.[86]

A union may seek recognition by the board to obtain the benefit of certification even if its status as an exclusive bargaining agent has not been challenged and the employer has agreed to bargain. The NLRB considers such a request as raising a question of representation.

Voluntary Recognition

Election, although the most accepted way by which employees select their representatives, is not the exclusive method condoned by the NLRB. An employer may recognize the union as the bargaining agent without an election—this **voluntary recognition** is rare but increasing in use by some unions. By publicity, picketing, friendly politicians, or boycotts, these unions pressure employers into recognizing a union without an election. In one such 2001 case, the Union of Needletrades, Industrial and Textile Employees, with the support of hotel and medical center workers (major clients of the targeted employer and the Baltimore City Council), convinced the laundry to recognize the union voluntarily and then negotiated a $1.25-per-hour raise for the $6-per-hour employees as well as better health and pension benefits.[87] As another example, in 2002 the University of California at Los Angeles (UCLA) voluntarily recognized AFSCME to represent food and service workers. The university agreed to recognize the union after several weeks of student and worker protests and a heated UCLA board meeting. AFSCME represents over 15,000 food and service workers on nine University of California campuses and five medical centers.[88]

In a Supreme Court decision upholding a board bargaining order, the Court recognized two other valid means by which a union may establish majority status and thereby place a bargaining obligation on the employer: (1) through a show of support through a union-called strike and (2) when a union collects authorization cards from a majority of the unit members. The cards must be submitted to a third party for a "**card check**" to verify the names against payroll. If an employer agrees to the card check, then, if the third party finds a majority for the union, the employer must bargain.[89] In recent years employers agreeing to a card check include Marriott, Freightliner, Cingular, and Rite-Aid. Examples of Union Authorization Cards can be seen in Figure 3-6. Some labor experts believe that NLRB–conducted secret ballot elections are "the gold standard" of employees' freedom of choice and view the card-check process as open to manipulation. They believe the neutrality/card-check recognition agreement process creates a tension between two important principles of federal law—the freedom of employers and unions to sign contracts and employee free choice of union representation.[90]

For example, in September 1996, in a small town near Boston, a small group of Latino workers showed up for work at the Richmark curtain manufacturing plant. They began distributing leaflets supporting an organizational campaign and were immediately fired. Then, in support of the fired workers, 40 others walked off the job in an unfair labor practice strike. Over the next several weeks, all the 170 women who worked at the plant picketed and united community support for "direct action" and presented Richmark a demand for card-check recognition. The picket lines kept up a daily protest, local churches collected money and food for the striking families, and Latino centers provided assistance and facilities. Finally, on October 8, 1996, 13 community leaders met with the Richmark president—and were arrested for refusing to leave. Only two days later the company agreed to recognize the union without an election, reinstate the strikers, and give them full back pay.[91]

The NLRB has agreed to review a card-check case in recognition of the trend toward determining employees' desire for union representation through voluntary recognition as opposed to "secret vote under laboratory conditions and under the supervision of a Board agent."[92]

IWW AUTHORIZATION CARD

We believe that through collective bargaining we can gain a legal voice in our workplace, achieve fair treatment for all, establish job security and better benefits, wages and working conditions. Therefore, this will authorize the Industrial Workers of the World solely and exclusively to represent me in Collective Bargaining with my employer.

PLEASE PRINT:

NAME   DATE

ADDRESS

CITY   STATE   ZIP CODE   PHONE

EMPLOYER NAME   HOURLY WAGE

SHIFT   DEPARTMENT

SIGNATURE

IMPORTANT: This Authorization was signed and dated in the employee's own handwriting. YOUR RIGHT TO SIGN THIS CARD IS STRICTLY PROTECTED BY FEDERAL LAW.

SOURCE: www.iww.org (December 2005). Used with permission.

IAEP AUTHORIZATION CARD

I hereby authorize the **INTERNATIONAL ASSOCIATION OF EMTS & PARAMEDICS (IAEP) (NAGE, SEIU)** to act as my representative and exclusive bargaining agent for the purpose of collective bargaining.
SIGNATURE DOES NOT COMMIT YOU TO MEMBERSHIP

Name (print): _____ Email: _____
Address: _____
City: _____ State: _____ Zip: _____
Employer: _____ Worksite/Station: _____
Signature: _____ Date: _____
Home phone: _____ Shift: _____
Job Classification: _____

FIGURE 3-6   Typical Union Authorization Cards

SOURCE: http://www.iaep.org (December 2005) Used with permission.

In the *Gissel* **doctrine**,[93] the Court gave a stamp of approval for authorization cards as a substitute for an election *when an employer's actions amounted to an unfair labor practice.* The Court recognized that if traditional remedies could not eradicate the lingering effects of the employer's conduct and permit the holding of a fair election, the union's authorization cards were a more reliable indicator of the employees' desires than an election, and a bargaining order should be issued. The board is strictly limited in imposing a *Gissel* bargaining order to cases in which the union actually gained majority status through the authorization cards. Regardless of how outrageous the employer's actions, unless such a majority is demonstrated, no order to bargain can be issued.[94] The board has also issued bargaining orders when the employer has gained independent knowledge of the union's majority status or has acknowledged the union's right to represent employees or, as in Case 3-4, when it is demonstrated that the employer hoped that if it ignored the union, it would just go away.

AUTHORIZATION CARDS HONORED FOUR YEARS AFTER SIGNING

CASE 3-4

The company operates a plastics recycling facility. Its business is to recycle used plastic containers into plastic pellets that are then sold as raw material to manufacturers. The company employed 64 people at its inception and reached a peak workforce of 92 in February 1994. At the time of the events that were the subject of the instant complaint, the company employed 68 nonsupervisory employees, but since then the workforce has dwindled to 36.

In the fall of 1994, some of the company's employees contacted the International Ladies Garment Workers Union (ILGWU). In early October, the ILGWU began a campaign to unionize the company's workers. In January 1995, the company laid off 29 employees and then another 10 in July. Since 1995, the workforce of the company has remained at around 35 employees.

The ILGWU filed a charge with the NLRB, alleging various unfair labor practices, including charges that the layoffs were motivated by a desire to quash the unionization campaign. The general counsel of the NLRB issued a complaint against the company on March 21, 1995. The complaint was heard in 1995 and a decision issued in 1996. The administrative law judge (ALJ) found that the company had committed numerous violations of the NLRA and recommended the imposition of a bargaining order under the *Gissel* doctrine. The company timely appealed the ALJ's decision to the NLRB.

For some unexplained reason, the NLRB did not issue its decision and order until 1999, more than three years after the ALJ's decision. The board affirmed the ALJ's findings. The board agreed with the ALJ that the severity of the company's conduct required the imposition of a bargaining order under *Gissel*. Under the bargaining order, the company was directed to bargain with ILGWU's successor union, the United Needletrades, Industrial and Textile Employees (UNITE).

When the board's order was issued, the company's original attorney on this matter had retired, and the company was in the process of finding a replacement. The company filed a motion to reopen the case, arguing that circumstances had changed since the ALJ's decision, including the restructuring of its business, a high turnover rate (only five employees who were working at the time of the complaint still worked for the company), and the passage of four and a half years. The company asked for reconsideration of the bargaining order in light of these changed conditions. The board refused, and the company contested the order in court.

DECISION

Courts are almost unanimous in holding that the NLRB must take current conditions into account when it determines whether to issue a bargaining order under the *Gissel* doctrine. Relevant changed

continued

AUTHORIZATION CARDS HONORED FOUR YEARS AFTER SIGNING—continued

circumstances include passage of time and turnover in the workforce. If the board had before it evidence that circumstances at the company's plant were in relevant respects significantly different from those at the time of the ALJ's decision recommending a bargaining order, the board erred when it refused to take the changes into account in determining whether a bargaining order should issue.

However, the Court found that the board was not required to seek out changed circumstances. Both the company and the NLRB agreed that the board's procedural rules would have permitted the company to update the record at any time after the ALJ's recommendation and prior to the board's decision. The company made no such motion until a month after the board's decision. The Court held that the party seeking to benefit from changed circumstances bears the burden of providing the information to the board. The board is entitled to assume, in the face of the party's silence, that the facts are as initially presented. As the changes to the company were gradual over a number of years and not a sudden event, the company had no excuse for its failure to so inform the NLRB.

SOURCE: Adapted from *NLRB v. U.S.A. The Company Corporation,* 168 LRRM 2897 (November 6, 2001).

Representation Elections in the Public Sector

Although modeled after private-sector campaigns, union elections conducted in the public sector have some differences. Public-sector employers may not be able to prohibit nonemployee union agents access to the workplace because the workplace is a public area.[95] Rules governing public employer preelection activities during an organizational campaign generally mirror private-sector restrictions, although some state and local governments have encouraged less-restrictive standards, particularly when applied to employers expressing an opinion on the effect of unionizing. In effect, this approach balances the employer's right of free speech with its duty not to be coercive.[96]

Decertification Elections

Also allowed under the act and supervised by the NLRB are decertification elections, whereby the members of the unit vote to terminate an existing union's right to represent them in collective bargaining. Decertification elections most commonly occur when the initial year of union representation ends with no collective bargaining agreement, an existing contract will expire within 60 to 90 days, or a contract has expired and no new agreement is being negotiated. The NLRB is currently considering whether union representation based on voluntary recognition or a card-check procedure should be considered the same bar to a decertification election within the first year of representation as a secret vote election.[97]

The rules for a **decertification election** are similar to those for certification, with some exceptions. Only employees can file a decertification petition, which must include 30 percent of the eligible members of the unit. Again, the NLRB investigates the validity of the petition. If the union feels that there is a problem with the petition or that an employer has unlawfully helped in the petition, it may file a blocking charge and delay the election until the unfair labor charge is resolved.

Although an employer can in no way aid the filing of a petition, afterward, the employer, the employees who filed the petition, and the union may all engage in an election campaign. The rules for conducting a decertification election are the same as those for a representation election.

After the votes are counted, if a majority of the employees vote against the union, it is decertified. A tie vote counts against the union because it no longer enjoys a majority status. If the union wins, it continues to represent the unit, and another election is barred for at least a year.

Why do workers vote to decertify their union? One or more of the following factors are usually present in situations in which unions are decertified:

1. The employer has recently treated employees better.
2. The employer waged an aggressive antiunion campaign.
3. The employer moves to a traditionally nonunion geographic area.
4. The union is perceived by a majority of its members as being unresponsive.
5. Female, minority, and younger workers lose confidence in the union because of its declining public image and aging leaders.[98]

The decertification election or representatives' decertification (RD) is similar to, but different from, a **deauthorization election** or union deauthorization election (UD). In a deauthorization election (UD) the bargaining unit members decide if they desire to nullify the union shop provision in their agreement. Thus if a union loses a deauthorization election (UD), the union still represents the employees in the bargaining unit and the rest of the collective bargaining agreement remains intact. However, if a union loses a decertification (RD) election it no longer represents the employees in the bargaining unit, obviously a much more serious outcome. The deauthorization (UD) election process in the NLRA is unique in that a majority of the employees in the bargaining unit must vote to rescind the union shop provision, compared to only a majority of those voting required in certification and decertification elections.[99]

A 2003–04 study by Clyde Scott and Edwin Arnold of decertification (RD) elections and deauthorization (UD) elections as well as certification of representation (RC) elections for a 40-year period (by decades, 1959–1998) indicated a few election trends: (1) although decertification (RD) elections and deauthorization (UD) elections together account for under 20 percent of all elections held by the NLRB, the percentage of RDs more than tripled (from 5.6 percent to 16.5 percent) and the percentage of UDs more than doubled (from .8 percent to 2 percent); (2) the number of RD and UD elections peaked in the 1980s (RD = 18.7 percent, UD = 2.8 percent); the number of representation elections (RCs) peaked in the decade of the 1970s (133,506) and fell by over half during the 1990s (61,515); (3) union victories in RDs rose from 34.8 percent during the 1960s to 56.5 percent during the 1990s while union victories in UDs remained stable around 31 percent; (4) unions were generally more successful in winning UD and RD elections in larger bargaining units.[100]

Exclusive Representation

When a labor union is recognized as the exclusive bargaining agent for a unit of employees, two major issues come into play. The first is union security, which is preserving the union's continued representation of the employees. The second is what representation by a union means to an individual employee.

Exclusive representation is both a practice and a principle of law. The practice predates the law. As discussed in earlier chapters, the very roots of the labor-management relationship depended on the workers' agreement to join together to make demands on the employer. Without such solidarity, employers would have gone to other workers willing to work for what the employer wanted to pay. Before this practice became law in the Wagner Act, labor organizers and union members had to "strong-arm" some employees who might otherwise break ranks.

Because part of the goal of the Wagner Act was to eliminate labor unrest, the lawmakers agreed that if a majority of the employees working in a defined unit voted to be represented by a union, then all the employees would be covered. This rule gives real power to the union's bargaining position and simplifies the bargaining process. The value of exclusive representation in negotiating collective bargaining agreements cannot be overemphasized. Without it, the process simply will not work. If even a few employees ignore the union and gain individual benefits from the employer, the need for a union can be questioned. Or if individual members of a bargaining unit take unsanctioned action—such as a wildcat strike—an employer's confidence that the union's agreement not to strike if gains are made at the negotiation table may be destroyed. And if exclusive representation were not the rule, the administration of a contract among like employees in an inconsistent manner would be disruptive to the labor–management relationship.[101]

Tips from the Experts

UNION

A union organizer can generate sufficient interest at a workplace to organize employees in the three following ways.

Organizing at the workplace is not much different from organizing in the community, on campus, or anywhere else for that matter. The key to successful organizing efforts is finding the connection between the prospective "members" and the "organization" seeking their allegiance. For employees, traditionally this connection was easy: better compensation for their labor, health benefits, and job security. As we go into the twenty-first century, this connection must be based on other things as well. The basics exist for many workers, whether by existing collective bargaining or by legislation. Where the basics do exist, the emphasis must shift to (1) employment security, (2) employee–employer partnership in providing quality products and services, and (3) employee political power in the elective and legislative processes. It is necessary to find out what the workers want and to show them how the union is the vehicle for attaining what they want.

MANAGEMENT

What are three ways an employer can legally discourage employees from organizing?

a. Good communication, from suggestion programs (boxes for employees to write questions to be answered by top management, e.g., Winn-Dixie's "I want to know" program, in which the Chief Executive Officer personally responds to any question within 24 hours; anonymous questions can be answered in company newsletters or publications specifically geared for that purpose) to reward programs in which employees compete for the best idea for cost-cutting or similar measures to simply training supervisors in how to best field questions and issues around which union organizing attempts focus and how to proclaim the company's union-free philosophy without interrogating the employee in the process.

b. Active participation, from joint employee–management quality teams dealing with specific workplace issues to bonus incentives for every employee when both the company and the individual employee exceed their performance objectives to employee representation in the development of critical personnel policies (such as the disciplinary system).

c. Instituting an internal grievance appeal process to remove the last (assuming a and b are followed) appeal the union has.

UNION SECURITY

The preservation of existing strength and influence is a major issue facing unions. Security and the structure of the present organizations affect union preservation.

Union security refers to a union's ability to grow and to perform its exclusive collective bargaining role without interference from management, other unions, or other sources. A key element to a union's security is a provision in the collective bargaining agreement requiring employees to join the union and pay union dues as a condition of continued employment. Such a provision assures the union and its members that all the employees who share the benefits of collective bargaining agreements pay for the union's cost. Required union membership increases the financial base of the union and may increase its ability to represent its members at the bargaining table.

Unions are concerned about their security for many reasons. For instance, a union is certified as the exclusive bargaining agent for only one year following a representation election. Rival unions may not seek to organize its members during that short time. Although a union security provision cannot prevent such raiding after the year, loyalties are developed and strengthened by participation in the union for that year.

Union Security Clause

Most collective bargaining agreements contain a union security clause similar to the one in Figure 3-7. The clause requires that all employees within the bargaining unit become and remain members in good standing as a condition of employment. This phrase "members in good standing" means that employees have the option to choose either *full membership,* which includes the payment of all dues, fees, and assessments as well as prescribed membership obligations, or *limited membership,* which requires the payment only of those dues and fees directly needed to support the union in performing representation duties such as collective bargaining and grievance settlement. Thus, the costs of limited memberships are normally lower than those of full membership. The union, as the exclusive bargaining representative of all employees in the bargaining unit, is required to inform employees of their membership rights. These rights include the option to refrain from supporting union activities other than those involved in collective bargaining, contract administration, and grievance arbitration. The employer is not the representative of the employees and thus has no obligation to inform employees of their membership rights. Unions, to maintain solidarity and secure greater funding strongly encourage employees to maintain full membership.

FIGURE 3-7 Union Security Clause

All employees in the bargaining unit who are members of the Union in good standing on the effective date of this Agreement, or on the date of its execution, whichever is the latter, must as a condition of employment maintain their membership in good standing for the life of this Agreement.

Any employee who is not a member of the Union and any employee who is hired on or after the effective date of this Agreement or the date of its execution, whichever is the latter, shall be required to apply for membership in the Union on or after the eighth (8th) day of employment, following the effective date of this Agreement. Employees who become members of the union must as a condition of employment maintain their membership for the duration of this Agreement.

SOURCE: Agreement between AFL-CIO State District Council of Carpenters and Millwrights, Conveyors and Machinery Erectors Local Union 1031, 2000–2003.

Legal Background

The 1935 National Labor Relations Act protected union security in several ways. Company unions were prohibited because the act's proponents saw them as a major threat to employee rights.[102] Yellow-dog contracts, whereby employees agreed not to join unions to get hired, and blacklisting of union sympathizers were made illegal. The act allowed an employer to make an agreement with the union requiring union membership as a precondition to employment. As a result, the closed shop clause became common.

Union security increased union membership. Automatic **checkoff** provisions in the contract authorizing the employer to withhold dues from a member's wages ensured that the union would receive payment. Dues "checkoff" is the method by which the union collects the monthly dues and fees from members through payroll deduction. Employees must voluntarily authorize the payments, in writing, and their authorization cannot be irrevocable for more than a year or the life of the contract, whichever is shorter. Normally after an employee signs a checkoff authorization, it is renewed automatically each year unless he/she revokes it.[103]

Public reaction to the growth of union membership and numerous labor-management conflicts following World War I led to the 1947 passage of the Taft-Hartley Amendments to the National Labor Relations Act. Added to Section 7, which guaranteed freedom of organization, was a guarantee of the employee's right not to organize and engage in union activity. The closed shop was outlawed, although the amendments allowed union shops to be negotiated in future contracts. A union shop required union membership on or after 30 days of employment. The hiring power was, therefore, restored to the employer. However, although the act allowed union shops, it also permitted states to outlaw union shops. The so-called **right-to-work laws** permitted states to prohibit agreements requiring membership in a labor organization as a condition of employment. The Taft-Hartley Amendments also limited the dues checkoff practice by requiring a written authorization from each union member.

Finally, court decisions have limited the application of a union shop provision by narrowing the meaning of union membership. The Supreme Court has long held that being a union member for the purpose of complying with a union shop provision could not require more of a person than paying dues or limited membership. A union could not require attendance at meetings or participation in union activities.[104]

In a historic 1988 decision, *CWA v. Beck,* the Supreme Court limited a union shop requirement for the paying of dues as a union member to only that portion of the union's dues that represented the cost of bargaining and representation. The decision covered both private and public unions. Individual union members can choose not to pay any funds to support "noncore" matters such as political contributions or lobbying efforts.[105] In 1995, the NLRB expanded the *Beck* holding to include an affirmative duty on the part of a union to inform its members of their rights under *Beck* to object to the expenditure of their dues for political or fraternal activities.[106]

Forms of Union Security

Union security clauses may take several basic forms:

1. *Closed shop.*   Outlawed by the Taft-Hartley Amendments, the **closed shop** provision allowed the employer to hire only union members. To get a job, a person first had to join the union.

2. *Open shop.*   No employee is required to join or to contribute money to a labor organization as a condition for employment under the **open shop**.

3. *Union shop.* A **union shop** provides that within a specific period of time, usually 30 to 90 days, an employee must join the union to continue the job with the company. Union membership under such a provision must be available on a fair and nondiscriminatory basis, and fees and dues must be reasonable and can be limited to an amount reflecting only the cost of bargaining and representation.

Although the National Labor Relations Act seems to allow a union to negotiate contracts requiring membership in the union as a condition of employment, in *NLRB v. General Motors Corporation,* the Supreme Court held that "membership" means paying union dues—the amount needed by the union to pay the costs to conduct collective bargaining. Thus, an employee cannot be required to sign a membership card or take an oath of membership. Despite the *General Motors* decision, many union leaders tell employees they must join the union.[107]

The National Labor Relations Act allows a majority of employees to vote to rescind the union shop authorization. This form of union security clause, along with the checkoff provision, is most commonly found in collective bargaining agreements.[108]

4. *Union hiring hall.* A **union hiring hall** provision is typical of the construction, trucking, and longshoring trades. This form requires an employer to hire employees referred by the union, provided the union can supply a sufficient number of applicants. As long as the union refers union and nonunion members alike and does not require membership before the seventh day of employment, such provisions are legal. A hiring hall run by the International Brotherhood of Electrical Workers Local 48 (IBEW) in Portland, Oregon, was determined to be illegal by the NLRB because it dispatched workers based on their willingness to (1) engage in union organizing, (2) leave a nonunion employer and join the union, and (3) reward those who join the union with additional jobs.[109]

5. *Agency shop.* **Agency shop** provisions require employees to contribute a sum equal to membership dues to the union, but they are not required to join the union. The union is provided with the financial support of employees who benefit from their collective bargaining, but the employee's right not to join the union is retained.

6. *Maintenance of membership.* The **maintenance of membership** provision requires those who are union members at the time a union contract is entered into to remain union members but only for the duration of the agreement. Nonunion members are not required to join.

7. *Miscellaneous forms of union security.* A *preferential shop* requires the employer to give hiring preference to union members. The *checkoff* of union dues from an employee's paycheck operates as a union security form because it protects the source of union funding and automatically keeps the employees in good standing with the union. This form of union security is often the only legal device available in right-to-work states. *Superseniority* gives union leaders top seniority for layoff purposes and indirectly increases union security by ensuring the continuity of its leadership.

NLRB and court decisions have altered some of these traditional areas of union security. Superseniority rights are now limited to those union officials who are necessary to the actual administration of a collective bargaining agreement; being an officeholder is not enough.[110] In addition, agency shop nonunion members are increasingly challenging the amount of representation fees they are charged. A 1998 Supreme Court decision, *Air Line Pilots Association v. Miller et al.,* held that such challengers may not be required to use the arbitration process provided in a contract but can challenge a union's calculation of agency shop fees in a federal court. Citing its previous ruling in

Teachers v. Hudson, the Court outlined three procedural protections for nonunion workers who object to the agency-fee calculation: (1) they must be given sufficient information to determine the fees estimation, (2) the escrowing of any amount in dispute driving the challenge, and (3) and a reasonably prompt opportunity to challenge the amount of the fee before an "impartial decision maker." According to the Court, the impartial decision maker can be a federal judge.[111]

Right-to-Work

Section 14(b) of the National Labor Relations Act states,

> Nothing in this act shall be construed as authorizing the execution and application of agreements requiring membership in a labor organization as a condition of employment in any state or territory in which such execution or application is prohibited by state or territorial law.

This provision allows states to enact laws prohibiting the union or agency shop forms of union security as seen in Case 3-5. Only 22 states, mostly in the West and the South, have done so (see Figure 3-8). Right-to-work legislation understandably evokes great emotions from both proponents and opponents.[112] A significant research study published in 2004, however, concluded that states with right-to-work laws have 9 percent

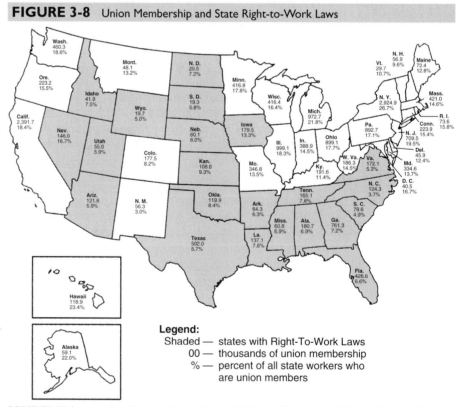

FIGURE 3-8 Union Membership and State Right-to-Work Laws

Legend:
Shaded — states with Right-To-Work Laws
00 — thousands of union membership
% — percent of all state workers who are union members

SOURCE: Union membership data derived from Additional Earnings and Union Membership Data, Companion to *Union Membership and Earnings Data Book:* Compilations from the Current Population Survey (2002).

lower levels of union membership (union density) with all other significant factors held constant. Union membership varies greatly from state to state with the highest levels in New York (24.6 percent), Alaska (22 percent), Michigan (21.8 percent), California (18.4 percent), and the lowest levels North Carolina (3.1 percent), South Carolina (4.2 percent), Utah (5.2 percent), and Arizona (5.2 percent). Although several factors influence union density, including "social capital" or workers' attitudes toward unions, and other social and political factors, the existence of a right-to-work law within a state has the most significant impact on the level of union membership within the state, and therefore it is an issue that raises strong emotions.[113]

Opponents contend that right-to-work legislation is an attempt to change the bargaining power at the negotiating table in management's favor. In addition, "right-to-work" as a slogan is misleading. Such laws guarantee no one a job and in their opinion confer rights only on employers.[114] The phrase implies the union's concomitant right to prevent a person from working. According to union advocates, the requirement of union membership as a condition of employment is no more restrictive of an individual's freedom than the requirement of specific hours of work or of certain minimal job qualifications. Union members contend that employees should support the union primarily because of the benefits that union and nonunion employees alike receive through collective bargaining agreements.[115] Finally, opponents point out that the per capita income in states not having right-to-work laws is higher.

Proponents of the right-to-work legislation believe that it affirms the basic rights of a person to work for a living whether he or she belongs to a union or not.[116] They contend

RIGHT-TO-WORK LAWS

CASE 3-5

Four nonunion employees who sought injunctive relief against an employer and a union that had agreed to an agency shop arrangement in a collective bargaining agreement instituted a class-action suit in a Florida state court. The agreement did not require the employees to join the contracting union, but it did require them to pay an initial service fee and monthly service fees to the union as a condition of employment. On the basis of the Florida right-to-work law, the Florida Supreme Court held that the agency shop clause involved was illegal. The union appealed on the grounds that the National Labor Relations Act specifically allows agency shop provisions in collective bargaining agreements, prohibiting only agreements requiring membership. Because this agency shop agreement did not require membership in the union, the state's law should not be allowed to forbid it.

DECISION

The Supreme Court upheld the Florida court's decision in finding that the agency shop clause was prohibited by Florida's right-to-work law. The Court found that Section 14(b) of the National Labor Relations Act, which allows states to prohibit agreements requiring membership in a labor organization as a condition of employment, could not be so narrowly construed as the union had requested in this case, or else the section would have no meaning. The state's right-to-work law had to be interpreted to preclude any type of union security agreement allowed under federal law if the purpose of the act and the Taft-Hartley Amendments were to be effective.

SOURCE: Adapted from *Retail Clerks International Association v. Schermerhorn,* 375 U.S. 96 (1963).

that no private organization should be able to tax a person and use that money to support causes with which all the members may not agree. Compulsory union membership can mean that a union does not need to be responsive to its members. And, according to proponents, right-to-work legislation encourages economic development because employers are not as likely to lose income from strikes over union security issues. A 2004 study confirmed that union membership density is significantly lower in right-to-work states in comparison to non-right-to-work states. The study also confirmed the belief that right-to-work states have lower wages overall in comparison to other states.[117]

A 1986 right-to-work referendum (RTW) election was held in Idaho. Both sides waged extensive media campaigns and focused the debate on the issues of lower wages and growth in the Idaho economy. Whether someone should be forced to join a union became a peripheral issue in the campaign. The National Right to Work Committee had targeted Idaho since 1976, when it successfully pushed passage of the Louisiana right-to-work law.[118] Right-to-work states have several characteristics that differ from union shop states. These characteristics include (1) low union membership, (2) little heavy industry, and (3) a high level of agriculture. Idaho shared these characteristics with the 20 right-to-work states.[119]

Union membership in Idaho was about 70,000 out of a population of one million. Idaho is surrounded by other right-to-work states: Wyoming, Utah, and Nevada. The referendum election was initiated by organized labor in an effort to overturn a 1985 law that was passed despite the governor's veto and made Idaho the 21st right-to-work state. Opponents of right-to-work began their campaign with the message, "The real intent of right-to-work is to damage unions and lower wages for all Idaho employees—both union and nonunion." Supporters of right-to-work pushed the message, "Should you be free to hold a job . . . whether you belong to a union or not?" Each side then began to muddle the issues by bringing in actors from Hollywood—Charlton Heston for the right-to-workers, Patty Duke for the opposition. The final vote was in favor of retaining the new right-to-work law by 30,514 votes of the 385,324 total votes cast.[120]

How did the new RTW law affect Idaho? A 2002 study published by the Federal Reserve Bank of St. Louis concluded: (1) Idaho is "an interesting case study" because it was a late adopter of a RTW law and because it is bordered by three RTW states and by three non-RTW states; (2) a decline in the unionization within Idaho began in 1981, four years prior to the law, and continued after passage until now it is similar to the border RTW states, but this decline was significantly faster after passage of the law; and (3) Idaho realized a significant and constant growth in manufacturing after passage of the law, suggesting that the state became more attractive to plants in comparison to the rest of the region.[121] A 2005 report on wages in Idaho for the 15-year period following the 1985 passage of its right-to-work law concluded that the wages of nonunion workers in the state fell by 4.2 percent, while the wages of union workers remained unchanged. This result supported the hypothesis that the law reduced the level of unionization and the wages of nonunion workers, resulting in an increase in the union–nonunion wage gap in the state.[122] In 2002, Oklahoma became the 22nd right-to-work state.

Court rulings and right-to-work states have had the effect of creating two new categories of employees: free riders and cheap riders. **Free riders** are employees who are in a unit represented by a union and are covered by a collective bargaining agreement but do not join the union. The collective bargaining agreement is binding on them, but they may not have any influence over its creation. Because unions are prohibited from negotiating union-shop and agency-shop agreements in right-to-work states, these states tend to have more "free riders," which pose a problem for unions because they cannot collect dues from them but must provide them the same benefits as union members.[123] **Cheap**

riders are employees who, again, are covered by a collective bargaining agreement but are not union members, but they are required to pay something to the union for the bargaining and representation services they receive. The share employees pay under union and agency shops where nominal membership or financial support is required ranges from 20 to 85 percent of a regular member's dues.

INDIVIDUAL RIGHTS WITHIN UNIONS

Duty of Fair Representation

The certified union for a bargaining unit is granted an exclusive right under the National Labor Relations Act to represent all the employees in that unit, members and nonmembers alike. Individuals within that bargaining unit may not contract privately with the employer but must be represented by the recognized bargaining agent. In the traditional factory setting this exclusivity rule posed no particular problem for the individuals as long as the bargaining unit was appropriately formed. But today, nontraditional union members, such as pro football players, lawyers, and architects, may find representation by the bargaining agent disadvantageous if the member is considered a superstar. Under this rule, a famous quarterback may have to accept the same salary as a member of the forward line if that was the negotiated agreement. The exclusivity rule giving the union the right to represent all members, however, is essential to the union's ability for proper representation at the bargaining table. Along with this right goes the duty to represent fairly all the employees of the unit. Fair representation must be found both in the negotiation of the collective bargaining agreement and in its enforcement. In some situations, however, the issue of fair or exclusive representation can be difficult. As Profile 3-2, "University of Akron: Union In, Faculty Governance Out?" discusses, on a college campus, exclusive representation for a faculty union may require that faculty lose their traditional shared governance role.

In a leading Supreme Court case, *Steele v. Louisville and N.R.R.,* a black railroad fireman asked the Court to set aside a seniority agreement negotiated by his union because it discriminated against minorities who were part of the bargaining unit.[124] Although the Railway Labor Act under which the union had exclusive rights to bargain for the employees did not explicitly do so, the Court held that the act implicitly imposed a duty on the union to exercise its powers fairly on behalf of all those it acted for. Later court decisions found that the National Labor Relations Act imposed that same duty on its unions.

However, court decisions have acknowledged that contracts may have unfavorable effects on some members of the unit. The law does provide that such unfavorable effects cannot be the result of discriminatory treatment based on irrelevant or insidious considerations such as union membership or race. Guidelines on the resolution of such thorny issues as seniority, access to training programs, or promotion, without a breach of the fair representation duty, basically come from court decisions. A union must consider all employees and make an honest effort to serve their interests in good faith and without hostility or arbitrary discrimination. The courts have held, in fact, that absent such a finding, the courts may not question the actual bargain struck by the union. It cannot be a breach of duty unless it is so far outside the range of reasonableness as to be wholly irrational.[125]

An employee must use the grievance procedure controlled by the union, but the employee does not have an absolute right to have a grievance pursued. In *Vaca v. Sipes,* the Supreme Court noted that a procedure giving the union discretion to supervise the grievance machinery and to invoke arbitration establishes an atmosphere for both parties to settle grievances short of arbitration.[126] The parties are assured that similar grievances

UNIVERSITY OF AKRON: UNION IN, FACULTY GOVERNANCE OUT?

Faculty governance is the cornerstone of most universities. It means that the faculty has input into the selection of department chairs and deans, and most importantly it means that through a governing body—usually the Faculty Senate—the faculty has a voice in the governance of the university. In August 2003, the University of Akron Board of Trustees removed most of these powers, and faculty governance was, according to some observers, "gutted."

Why would the stewards of a major university take such drastic action? It was because the faculty had exercised their right to be represented by a union. In March 2003 by a vote of 388–220, the faculty chose the American Association of University Professors (AAUP) to represent them. The trustees reasoned that because the faculty had chosen a union to represent them on issues such as wages, benefits, working conditions, and hours, they could no longer be represented by the Faculty Senate and committees on the same issues—thus giving them two and possibly conflicting voices. Certainly this was a position to be given serious consideration. However, the issue of "two voices" has been successfully handled on hundreds of college campuses for decades. Over 250,000 faculties are represented by unions and still maintain traditional faculty governance mechanisms—from the California State University System (CSU) to the University of Cincinnati.

Patrick Graves, Chair of the University of Akron Board of Trustees, responded to the question of retribution as a possible motive by saying: "I have no comment ... We are doing what we are told to do by our legal counsel." Sidney C. Foster, Assistant Vice President for Labor Relations, responded that the changes were "arguably legally necessary." Larry Glenn, an AAUP official, reasoned, "They want the union to have to squander more chips at the table to get back what they already had."

SOURCE: Adapted from, Scott Smallwood, "Union In, Governance Out," *The Chronicle of Higher Education* (October 10, 2003), A10–11.

receive similar treatment; thus, problem areas under the collective bargaining agreement can be isolated and perhaps resolved. Therefore, a breach of the duty to represent an employee fairly occurs only if the union's conduct toward the member is *arbitrary, discriminatory, or in bad faith.* In 1998, the Court upheld its decision in *Vaca* in *Marquez v. Screen Actors Guild, Inc., et al.,* and held that a union does not breach the duty of fair representation by negotiating a union security clause. The union security clause should, however, contain statutory language that incorporates an employee's right not to "join" the union and to pay only for (with fees and dues) representational activities.[127]

In a historic Supreme Court case, *Bowen v. The U.S. Postal Service,* the Court apportioned the damages due the wrongfully discharged employee between the union and the employer by using the date of a hypothetical arbitration decision.[128] All back pay prior to that hypothetical date was due from the employer; all back pay from that date to the time of settlement was due from the union. The Court reasoned that if the employee had been properly represented, the employer's liability would have ended at the arbitration decision. All back-pay benefits from that point forward were caused and should be paid by the union.

Employees' "right to refrain" from supporting a union includes (1) the right to refrain from joining a union, (2) the right to resign union membership at any time, and (3) the right to stop paying full union dues and pay only the financial core, which includes only the costs of collective bargaining. When an employee joins a union, however, he or she is subject to the internal rules of the union and may be fined and even sued in court. As an example, unions often fine members who cross a picket line during a strike. However, unions can discipline only their voluntary members, and those members are free to leave the union at any time. Many employees wrongfully believe that they must remain a union member to keep their jobs. However, formal union membership cannot be required—they can only be required to pay the financial core or agency fee. But union members and nonmembers are still within the bargaining unit and thus covered by the terms of any negotiated agreement, including wages, benefits, and working conditions. Because a union can discipline only those employees who are voluntary members, those who refrain from joining or leave a union are not subject to any form of discipline a union may impose on its members.[129]

SUMMARY

The National Labor Relations Act regulated the industrial relations of employers whose activities affect interstate commerce. The act guaranteed employees the right to self-organization and required the employer to bargain collectively with employee representatives. The NLRB was established to enforce the act. The board, in order to protect the employee rights guaranteed by the act, determines on the appropriateness of the selected bargaining units. The board also regulates and conducts union elections to ensure that employees exercise their freedom of choice.

Labor relations, as regulated by the National Labor Relations Act, is considered the exclusive domain of federal law. With a few exceptions, the NLRB has primary jurisdiction in any labor dispute affecting commerce. State laws and regulations are not controlling. Unions seek to improve their members' living standard through better wages, job security, and social legislation. To do this, unions must seek their own security as the exclusive representative of the worker.

The organizing drive conducted by a union wishing to represent a unit of employees is very important. Tactics used by unions to organize and by companies to resist unionization have become much more sophisticated. In recent years unions have had a decreasing rate of success in certification elections and in defeating decertification elections. That trend, along with the erosion of union security protections, has had a very negative effect on unionization.

A union seeks union security clauses in collective bargaining agreements, ranging from union shops to dues checkoff provisions, to ensure both the exclusive nature of its representation and its financial security. State right-to-work laws undermine that security and pose a great threat to unionization.

Individual employees have certain protections as members of labor unions, including guidelines on how they are to be represented in negotiation with the employer and in grievance procedures.

CASE STUDIES

Case 3-1 Duty of Fair Representation

In 1981, the company laid off more than 100 employees because of an economic recession. The existing contract already provided that laid-off employees would accrue "continuous service" credit for two years and would retain continuous service credit for an additional five-year period. In addition, the union negotiated additional benefits for these laid-off employees. One of the benefits was a commitment by the company that these laid-off employees would be "offered future employment opportunities" with the company in the event positions opened up.

Eleven years later, in 1992, the company needed employees, and it notified the former employees and offered them interviews. Some were rehired. However, 16 former employees who were still union members were not rehired. They sought the help of their union in filing a grievance against the company, claiming that the company had violated the contract by not rehiring them. The union declined, saying that because these union members were no longer employees of the company, they were not part of the bargaining unit and the union had no duty to represent them. The 16 former employees argued that under the agreement negotiated by the union while they were employees, they had acquired certain protections and that it was now the union's duty to enforce those protections. Because the former employees could not pursue the grievance without the union, the negotiated protections would be meaningless if the union failed to represent them. The 16 former employees sued the union.

SOURCE: Adapted from *Smith v. ACF Industries,* 149 LRRM 2693 (1995).

QUESTIONS

1. If the court rules that the union has no duty to represent these former employees, they cannot pursue their grievance against the company. Discuss why this result is fair or unfair to all three parties: the company, the union, and the former employees.
2. When the union bargained for the laid-off employees, the employees were told they would have future employment opportunities with the company. Do you think it was unreasonable for these laid-off employees to expect the union's help 11 years later? Why or why not?
3. If the company and the union had known that 11 years would pass before positions opened up at this plant, do you think they would have provided the "future employment opportunities" provision?

Case 3-2 Employer's Unlawful Assistance to Union

The incumbent union, Organized Workers of Legal Services, Local 2 (OWLS II), was certified in 1978 to represent a unit of the company's clerical and paralegal employees. The parties' last collective bargaining agreement was effective until October 1, 1994, but was automatically renewed for one year when neither party sought to modify its terms. On July 6, 1995, Office and Professional Employees International Union (OPEIU) Local 42 petitioned for an election in a unit of the company's full-time and regular part-time nonprofessional employees. The regional director ordered an election in which the employees would vote for OPEIU, OWLS II, or no union. The election was held on September 13. Of approximately 106 eligible voters, 38 voted for OPEIU, 19 voted for OWLS II, and 20 voted for no union. Because no choice had received a majority of the valid ballots cast, the regional director ordered a runoff election in which employees would vote on whether they wished to be represented by OPEIU or no union.

Despite the fact that OWLS II had received the fewest votes in the election and had been eliminated from further contention, the company continued to withhold dues from unit employees' paychecks pursuant to the contract with OWLS II until some time in February 1996. It also stated, in a letter to employees in early November, "We have been a unionized company for more than 17 years. OWLS II *is still* the collective bargaining representative of certain employees. OWLS II *will continue* to be that representative unless the National Labor Relations Board determines differently." OPEIU charged the company with an unfair labor practice for supporting a union.

The company argued its conduct was not unlawful. Even though OWLS II had been eliminated from contention in the September election, no choice received a majority of the votes cast in that election, and a runoff was necessary to determine whether the employees wanted continued representation by a union. Thus, in its view, OWLS II had not been decertified before the runoff election because not until then would the employees make their ultimate choice between OPEIU Local 42 and no union. In those circumstances, it would be "unduly harsh" to require the company to cease recognizing OWLS II because that would invalidate the existing collective bargaining agreement and deprive the unit employees of union representation before they chose whether to have continuing representation (by another union) in the runoff. The company believed that the intent of the act would best be served by maintaining the existing collective bargaining relationship during the period before the runoff.

The OPEIU argued that the results of the first election demonstrated that OWLS II had lost the support of a majority of employees and that when OWLS II was eliminated from contention as a result of the initial election, the company violated Section 8(a)(2) and (1) of the National Labor Relations Act by thereafter continuing to recognize OWLS II as the employees' bargaining representative and continuing to deduct dues. In the September 13 election, OWLS II received only 19 out of 77 votes, compared with 38 for OPEIU and 20 for no union. No party filed objections. When the ballot tally became final, it was manifest that OWLS II would no longer be the bargaining representative of the unit employees. True, the final outcome of the representation proceeding was not known at that time because not until the runoff election had been held would it be clear whether the employees would choose OPEIU as their representative. But as far as OWLS II was concerned, the outcome was known. Three-fourths of the employees who voted and a majority of the 106 employees in the unit had rejected OWLS II as their bargaining representative. There was no prospect that they would reconsider their decision in the runoff because OWLS II would not be on the ballot in that election.

SOURCE: Adapted from *Wayne County Neighborhood Legal Services Inc. v. Office and Professional Employees Local 42*, 166 LRRM 1169 (January 31, 2001).

QUESTIONS

1. What reasons could the company have for continuing to recognize OWLS II?
2. Should OWLS II be allowed to continue to represent the employees until the runoff election is held?
3. How do you think the company's support for OWLS II might influence the runoff election?

KEY TERMS AND CONCEPTS

- agency shop
- appropriate bargaining unit
- bargaining unit
- business agent
- card check
- certification
- Change to Win Coalition
- cheap riders
- checkoff

- closed shop
- collective bargaining
- community of interest doctrine
- craft unions
- craft unit
- deauthorization election
- decertification election
- departmental unit
- doctrine of accretion
- exclusive representation
- Federal Labor Relations Authority

- federation of unions
- free riders
- freedom of choice
- *Gissel* doctrine
- *Globe* doctrine
- health-care units
- industrial union
- maintenance of membership
- open shop
- organizing drive
- preemption
- RC petition

- right-to-work laws
- runoff election
- showing of interest
- stewards
- terms of employment
- 24-hour rule
- union hiring hall
- union organizer
- union security
- union shop
- voluntary recognition

REVIEW QUESTIONS

1. What are the purpose and the jurisdiction of the NLRB?
2. Summarize the rights of employees and employers as provided by the National Labor Relations Act.
3. When are states totally preempted from regulation of the labor field, according to Supreme Court decisions?
4. What criteria does the NLRB consider when determining whether an appropriate unit of employees has a substantial mutuality of interests?
5. How does the National Labor Relations Act limit the board's determination of the appropriate bargaining unit?

6. What are the steps the NLRB follows in a representation election?
7. How does certification benefit a union? Under what circumstances might the NLRB invalidate a certification election?
8. What factors might contribute to employees' voting to decertify a union?
9. Define *union security* and explain its importance to labor leaders.
10. Discuss why labor leaders have tried to repeal Section 14(b) (the right-to-work section) of the Taft-Hartley Amendments since its passage in 1947.

YOU BE THE ARBITRATOR
"Just Cause" for Termination

ARTICLE VII
SENIORITY

Section 2. Seniority shall be lost for the following reasons:
 b. if the employee is discharged for cause.

ARTICLE XVII
GRIEVANCE AND ARBITRATION PROCEDURE

Section 3. Step 3.
 4) The arbitrator shall not have the authority to amend or modify this agreement or establish new

terms or conditions under this agreement. The arbitrator shall determine any question of arbitrability.

ARTICLE XXII
DISCHARGE OR SUSPENSION

Section 1. The following disciplinary policy is hereby established:
Step 1: A written notice describing the nature of the employee's problem(s) will be given to the employee, an opportunity will be provided to correct these problems.
Step 2: A second written notice will be sent and a two (2) day suspension without pay will be imposed,

affording the employee some time to reflect on the problem and on ways to correct them. . . .

Step 3: Termination—Management reserves the right to waive this policy, if, in their opinion, it is in the best interest of the company to do so. . . .

Facts

A truck driver was discharged for failing to make timely deliveries and not using the quickest, most direct route as previously instructed. The company warehouses and distributes wholesale floor covering products and operates from several locations. The driver was hired in November 2000 and during his relatively short, eight-month tenure with the company received a total of four other employee warning reports. According to the employer, the driver demonstrated a continuing pattern of failing to follow orders, company policies, and supervisory instructions involving the use of a global positioning system (GPS) mounted in his truck, completing daily driving logs, and utilizing toll roads for the best way to make deliveries in a timely fashion. On two occasions the employee simply failed to complete his deliveries, costing the company extra expense and a loss of customer satisfaction. The triggering event for his termination was his refusal to use the toll road to make a delivery even though he was offered an advance of the toll road fee. In response, the union claims that the employee's failure to use toll road was justified because he was already owed $87.32 in post-toll reimbursements. One of the employee's prior warning reports was grieved and settled in his favor, and he was disputing the remaining three at the time of his discharge. In this grievance he is challenging his discharge, seeking reinstatement with back pay, seniority, and benefits.

Issue

Does the collective bargaining agreement (CBA) require the employer to have "just cause" to fire an employee, even if the language is not in the CBA?

Position of Parties

The employer argues that this discharge is not subject to arbitration because the CBA does not contain a "for cause" requirement (see Article XVII, Grievance and Arbitration Procedure, and Article XXII, Discharge or Suspension, printed earlier). Therefore, there is no standard against which the arbitrator may test the employer's actions.

In response, the union argues that the company position ignores the plain language of the agreement stating that seniority "shall be lost. . . . if the employee is discharged for cause." According to the union, in a unionized work environment, the termination of seniority equates to the termination of employment (see Article VII, Seniority).

SOURCE: Adapted from *Superior Products,* 116 LA 1623 (Arb. 2002).

QUESTIONS

1. As arbitrator, what would be your award and opinion in this arbitration?
2. Explain why the relevant provisions of the CBA, as applied to the facts of this case, dictate the award.

3. What actions might the employer and/or the union have taken to avoid this conflict?

EXERCISE

Certification Election

PURPOSE:

To understand various factors that may be considered in determining bargaining units.

TASK:

AmberCraft Toy Co. manufactures, sells, and distributes toys in eight Western states. They have the following job classifications:

Administrators	Assembly-line workers	Inside sales
Managers	Truckers	Outside sales
Supervisors	Maintenance workers	Security guards
Clerical workers	Janitorial workers	

AmberCraft has four manufacturing plants (with about 300 employees in each) located in California (San Diego, Fresno, Oakland, and Fort Bragg). BEST union wants to organize the AmberCraft employees in the San Diego location. AmberCraft has no previous union history. A plant manager largely runs each location independently, but the central office in Fresno sets all personnel policies. The plant managers conduct hiring and other labor activities.

1. Does the San Diego plant meet the 1995 NLRB rules for one employer, multiple locations?
2. Do you think that the San Diego plant is an appropriate unit?
3. If BEST were organizing all four sites, which job classifications would be combined into the appropriate bargaining unit(s)? Which job classifications would likely be excluded from any units?

CHAPTER 4

Unfair Labor Practices

Cintas workers picket a Starbucks shop in Detroit. Starbucks has a nationwide contract with Cintas for apron and linen services.

Labor News

THE MOST SIGNIFICANT U.S. ORGANIZING CAMPAIGN: CINTAS CORPORATION

Kate Brofenbreuner, Director of Labor Education Research at the New York State School of Industrial and Labor Relations at Cornell University, calls the effort to organize Cintas Corporation, the largest uniform supplier in the United States, the "most significant organizing campaign in the United States." UNITE, formerly the Union of Needletrades, Industrial and Textile Employees, is trying to organize 10,000 Cintas Corporation laundry workers, and the Teamsters are trying to organize the 7,000 Cintas truck drivers. The organizing effort extends to 365 U.S. cities where Cintas operates in North America.

UNITE has asked CINTAS to sign a "card-check neutrality" or "neutrality agreement," which would require the employer to recognize the union as the official bargaining agent for the laundry workers after a third party (usually the NLRB) verifies that 50 percent or more of the workers signed union membership cards, and then be recognized by the NLRB without a time-consuming and costly election. Neutrality agreements, or "card checks," have become increasingly popular in recent years in situations where traditional secret ballot elections are avoided by unions. However, Stefan Gleason of the National Right to Work Foundation claims such agreements are "sweetheart contracts" between unions and employers and deny workers their right to an election to determine if a union should represent them.

UNITE staged successful protests from New York to Las Vegas at one of Cintas' best-known customers, Starbucks, in an effort to put pressure on the company. At the start of the campaign, UNITE filed over 100 unfair labor practice complaints against Cintas. However, Robert Kohlhepp, Cintas vice-chairman and former CEO, noted that more than half of the complaints have been dismissed and that the issue isn't about unionization, but about "how people become unionized"—a reference to the UNITE demand for a card check to achieve a voluntary recognition without an election.

Cintas officials say a union is not needed and note that its culture earned it a place on the *Fortune* magazine's list of "America's Most Admired Companies." Kohlhepp said, "Our feeling is that our people are better off without a union." UNITE president Bruce Raynor disagrees, citing what he claims are Cintas' "poverty-level" wages of $8 to $9 per hour and lack of health-care and pension benefits. Kohlhepp says Cintas' wages are as high or higher than competitors and notes the company offers profit sharing, 401(k) matching retirement benefits, and a stock ownership plan as well as a health-care plan for all employees.

UNITE, in addition to seeking employees to sign authorization cards, also used the Cintas annual shareholder meeting to win support. Four shareholder resolutions were introduced to change the membership of the Board of Directors' nominating committee. Although the resolutions failed, UNITE did gain support from half the stock not controlled by management. UNITE has had success with the card-check strategy, winning the right to represent 800 workers at Brylane, a catalog-clothing distribution center in Indianapolis. Employers that agree to the card-check neutrality usually do so to prevent picketing outside their operations, alienating union members at other branches of their operations, or avoid the cost of a strike or election campaign.

SOURCE: Adapted from, Mike Boyer, "Unions Put Heat on Cintas," *The Cincinnati Enquirer* (August 23, 2003), pp. B1, 4; and Andy Meisler, "Who Will Fold First?" *Workforce Management* (January 2004), pp. 29–38.

The collective bargaining process requires the employer and the employee to meet and negotiate terms and conditions of employment. It is an uneasy relationship that requires give and take. Often one side does not choose to participate or to participate fully. The National Labor Relations Act recognizes that reluctance and by its terms seeks to legislate the behavior of the parties. Certain actions are deemed to be unfair if they run counter to the purposes of the act, and bad faith might be evidenced in the negotiation process by other actions. This chapter explores aspects of unfair labor practices and breaches of the duty to bargain in good faith to see how such behavior frustrates successful collective bargaining.

One of the primary objectives of the National Labor Relations Act was to encourage collective bargaining to minimize the industrial strife adversely affecting the free flow of commerce. To that end, the National Labor Relations Board (NLRB) gave employees certain protected rights. Section 7 of the act, as amended by the Taft-Hartley Amendments, enumerates these rights:

1. To self-organize
2. To form, join, or assist labor organizations
3. To bargain collectively through representatives of their own choosing
4. To engage in other concerted activities for the purpose of collective bargaining or other mutual aid or protection
5. To refrain from any or all of the above[1]

The act also lists employer activities considered unfair labor practices in violation of those rights:

1. Interference with, restraint, or coercion of employees in rights guaranteed under Section 7
2. Domination or interference with the formation or administration of a labor union
3. Discrimination against union members for their union membership
4. Discrimination against an employee for pursuing the rights under the act
5. Refusal to bargain collectively with representatives of its employees[2]

The basic right of employees to join together has always been protected under the freedom-of-association provision of the First Amendment to the U.S. Constitution. Prior to the National Labor Relations Act, however, no federal law protected the employee in the exercise of that right. The National Labor Relations Act balances employers' property rights with employees' organization and recognition rights. A violation of the act is an unfair labor practice. It may be helpful to think of unfair labor practices in two major categories: those that occur during a union organizational campaign and those that occur in collective bargaining or during the life of a contract.

ORGANIZATIONAL CAMPAIGNS

Union Organizing Campaigns

Employer Interference with Employee Rights

Section 8(a)(1) of the National Labor Relations Act prohibits interfering, restraining, or coercing employees in the exercise of their right to unionize.

To determine an unfair labor practice by an employer of this right, the NLRB must find that the act interfered with, restrained, or coerced an action protected under the law. It must also be determined, under a reasonable probability test, that the employer's conduct could have an interfering, restraining, or coercive effect on employees. Within some constraints, the employer's motivation also must be weighed.

The NLRB's reasonable probability test eliminates the need to prove actual interference, restraint, or coercion by the employer if it can be shown that the activity tends to interfere with the free exercise of protected rights.[3] The courts, however, distinguish between inherently discriminatory or destructive violations of employee rights, when an employer could foresee the unlawful consequences, and those not so blatantly in violation. A hostile motive may be necessary to establish proof of an unfair labor practice if the activity itself can be objectively viewed as nondestructive. The kind of practice that most often evokes the need to prove intent is one motivated by a legitimate and substantial business justification.[4] In such cases, an actual intent to frustrate the purposes of the act must be found to warrant an unfair labor practice charge.

Organizing at the Workplace

The right of self-organization and participation in a labor union includes the right to engage in organizational campaigns. In many cases, the exercise of that right directly opposes the employer's right to maintain a work environment. The courts have devised rules based on the NLRB's opinion that working time is for work, to balance the two interests. However, time outside working time is personal and may be used without unreasonable restraint, even on the employer's property. This includes lunchtime, break time, rest periods, and before and after the regular workday. The Supreme Court upheld this opinion in ***Republic Aviation***, stating that rules prohibiting union solicitation by employees outside working time, even on the employer's property, were an unreasonable impediment to self-organization.[5]

The courts, however, have long viewed organizing by an employee and organizing by a nonemployee as distinct when deciding on the right of access to employer premises. Rules prohibiting nonemployee union organizers from solicitation on the employer's property have not been considered an unfair labor practice if there were other *reasonable means* to reach employees. With a Supreme Court decision in 1992, however, this standard has changed. In the *Lechmere* case, the Court decided that an employer would not be committing an unfair labor practice when barring a nonemployee access to its property if there was *any other means* to reach the employees.[6] In the *Lechmere* case, the employer banned union organizers from leafleting cars in the employer's retailer parking lot, which was clearly open to the public. But because the union organizers were able to picket on a public space outside the parking lot, Justice Clarence Thomas wrote in his opinion that the nonemployee union organizers had reasonable access to the employees *outside* the employer's property. Because such access existed, there was to be no "balancing" of the employer–employee rights used in other cases.

A 1996 federal appeals court decision reaffirmed the *Lechmere* decision and, to a certain extent, expanded it. In *UFCW Local No. 880 v. NLRB,* the court ruled against a union's request to find the employer, a retail store, guilty of an unfair labor practice when the employer refused the union access to its parking lot to distribute boycott information to the store's customers. Relying on the *Lechmere* reasoning, the court noted that the availability of mass media alone to reach the store's customers gives the union a reasonable alternative to what the court termed "trespass access."[7]

Organizing activities protected under the National Labor Relations Act include the following:

1. ***Solicitation and distribution.***   Oral solicitation by employees is allowed on the work premises during nonworking times. But distribution of union literature is restricted to nonworking times and areas. The board based this decision on employers' representations that such literature could clutter the workplace. No rule, however, is without exceptions. If justified by the nature of the business, a no-solicitation rule restricting employees even on nonworking time can be defended. Examples include department stores, restaurants, and patient care areas of hospitals where the public nature of the working area would prohibit normal interaction between employees. An employer may implement a "no-solicitation" policy for both employees and nonemployees in effect during work or nonwork hours if that policy extends to all types of solicitation. If it is applied only to union solicitation, it is likely to be an unfair labor practice. For example, several employees at an Oklahoma manufacturing plant were disciplined for soliciting support for the United Steelworkers union on company time. The employer had a nonsolicitation policy that prohibited workers from distributing literature or soliciting during work hours. The court in *Webco Industries, Inc. v. NLRB*[8] upheld the NLRB decision that the employer had committed an unfair labor practice not because the policy was unlawful, but because the employer allowed other types of solicitation such as group sales of candy and cookies, sports pools, and fantasy football.[9] However, in *Cleveland Real Estate Partners v. NLRB,*[10] the federal court held that the employer did not discriminate against unions when it excluded handbillers favoring one union over another or employer materials over union materials, but allowed charities to solicit on its property.

2. ***Union buttons or insignias.***   Another protected activity is the wearing of union buttons or insignias. This right is balanced against the employer's right to conduct business. If a button or insignia should in particular circumstances cause a disturbance, present a health hazard, distract workers, cause damage to a product, or offend or distract customers, it may be prohibited. The NLRB in 1985, however, refused to allow an employer to discharge a construction employee who had a union insignia sticker on his helmet because no special circumstance existed to make the removal necessary to maintain production or discipline or to ensure safety.[11]

3. ***Bulletin boards and meeting halls.***   Employees have no statutory right to use an employer's bulletin board. However, if the employees are allowed access to the bulletin board, the employer cannot censor the material to exclude union solicitation. Meeting halls fall under the same rule. If access has been allowed to employees on an unrestricted basis, use by employees for union organization cannot be the only exception. Also, if the physical location of the business makes other meeting places inaccessible and the employer does not normally give employees access to the hall, his or her

An employee has the right to wear union buttons or insignias in most circumstances.

subsequent refusal might result in an unfair labor practice charge. In one 1986 case, the NLRB found an unfair labor practice when the company denied the union access to employee mailboxes that the union had been using to distribute literature for 40 years. Although the company claimed that the union could reach employees by other means, their denial was found discriminatory because other groups were allowed access to the mailboxes.[12]

4. *E-mail solicitation.*   Section 7 of the NLRB clearly affects employer rights to regulate electronic mail (e-mail) use. Employees have the right not to be discriminated against by their employer for engaging in discussions relating to wages, hours, and working conditions, assuming the discussions do not violate a legitimate employer policy regarding the use of work time or equipment. An NLRB decision in 1993 found that an employer policy that had prohibited employee access to an e-mail system for union purposes, while allowing many other nonwork uses of the e-mail system, violated the NLRA. In a similar case, *E.I. duPont deNemours Co.,* the employer had certain "authorized employee committees" that were permitted e-mail access, but its use by employees for union purposes was prohibited. The NLRB found the policy, which singled out union purposes, to be a violation of the National Labor Relations Act.

In general, if the use of workplace e-mail is significant, it can be considered a "work area" under the National Labor Relations Act, and thus employers may not totally restrict employee e-mail use because it is equivalent to oral solicitation, which is protected by Section 7 of the act. However, special circumstances, such as maintaining production or not overburdening the computer network, may make it necessary to limit the use of e-mail. This ban may be upheld even if it includes union business. In general, however, a total ban on nonbusiness use of e-mail just to prohibit union activity is a potential violation of the act, especially where employees rely on e-mail as a significant avenue of communication.[13]

UNION ORGANIZING STRATEGIES

Although every workplace is different, there are some basic steps involved in launching a union organizing campaign as seen in these steps suggested by the Industrial Workers of the World.[14]

Step 1: *Build an Organizing Committee* Identify the leaders and establish an organizing committee representing all major departments and all shifts, which reflects the racial, ethnic, and gender diversity in the workforce. Committee members must be prepared to work hard to educate themselves and their coworkers about the union and to warn and educate coworkers about the impending management antiunion campaign. The employers will most likely engage in a well-organized, well-funded antiunion campaign. The organizing committee must be educated about the workers' right to organize and must understand their union's policies and principles of democracy and rank-and-file control. Also at this step, basic information about the workplace must be gathered, including the following:

- Workplace structure: departments, work areas, jobs, and shifts.
- Employee information: name, address, phone, shift, job title, and department for each worker (employee list).
- Employer information: other locations, parent company, product(s), customers, union history, financial assets, and economic strengths and weaknesses.
- Intangibles: informal cliques, social networks, and existing relationships—the employer will try to use these to its advantage to try and disrupt union organizing activities. An organizing committee must accommodate for these existing relationships.

Step 2: *Determine the Issues* The committee develops a program of union demands (the improvements they are organizing to achieve) and a strategy for the union recognition campaign. A plan for highlighting the issues program in the workplace is carried out through various organizing campaign activities.

Step 3: *Choose a Union Recognition Strategy* Workers are asked to join the union and support the union program by achieving union status. A union recognition strategy needs to be chosen:

- Card-check recognition: The Organizing Committee and/or a representative from the union informs the employer that a sizable majority (at least 50 percent plus one person but ideally 60 percent or more) has signed union authorization cards. If successful, the employer will voluntarily agree to recognize the union as the legal bargaining agent for the designated bargaining unit.
- Strike for recognition: A sizable majority (at least 50 percent plus one person but ideally 60 percent or more) may agree to a short strike to force the employer to recognize the union. If successful, the employer will voluntarily agree to recognize the union as the legal bargaining agent for the designated bargaining unit.
- Call for an NLRB-sponsored election: The Organizing Committee manages to convince coworkers to sign union authorization cards. The goal is to sign up a sizable majority. Only 30 percent of the workforce needs to sign authorization cards to have an NLRB-sponsored election. This "card campaign" should proceed quickly once begun and is necessary to hold a union election. If successful, the employer is legally required to recognize the union as the legal bargaining agent for the designated bargaining unit.

Step 4: *Achieve Union Recognition or Status*   To hold an election, the signed authorization cards are used and are required to petition the state or federal labor board to hold an election. The labor board will determine who is eligible to vote and schedule the election. The union campaign must continue and intensify during the wait. If the union wins, the employer must recognize and bargain with the union. Not only does winning a union election require a strong, diverse organizing committee and a solid issues program, but there must also be a plan to fight the employer's antiunion campaign.

Salting

In the early 1980s, employers became more aggressive in fighting unionization. By hiring replacement workers, relocating operations to less-unionized states, and seeking concessions during negotiations, employers made union organizing more difficult, time consuming, and expensive. Total union membership dropped, and with it union dues income, which reduced the union's resources and its ability to organize. When a union won an election, an employer would frustrate the union's ability to negotiate an initial contract by demanding concessions and hiring striker replacements if the union went on strike. After a year without an agreement, the employer would seek to have the union decertified.[15]

In response to union membership decline in the 1980s, unions initiated a program commonly called **salting**. Union members are encouraged to seek employment with target companies that are not unionized. The union members receive permission from the union through "salting resolutions" to work nonunion without being subject to disciplinary action by their union.

There are three types of salting. In cases in which union jobs are not available, the union members are urged to seek employment at nonunion companies, and on their own time, they talk with their fellow workers about the benefits of unionizing. In these cases, the union members are not compensated by the union for their activities. Occasionally, union members seek employment with nonunion companies at the request of the union. Again, on their own time, they promote unionization. As compensation, the union will supplement the regular pay they get from the employer to equal a "union" wage. Often, when union jobs open up or when it is clear that the company will not become unionized, the union encourages these members to move on. Finally, in some instances regular, full-time employees of a union will seek employment with a nonunion company for the sole reason of organizing the workers. The union makes up the difference between their organizers' pay and what the employer pays the employees of the union while being employed at the nonunion company.

The Supreme Court ruled in *NLRB v. Town and Country Electric*[16] that regardless of one's relationship with one's union, each employee of the nonunion company has rights under the National Labor Relations Act. If the employee is doing the work asked by his or her employer, union activities cannot be used against the employee.[17] The lower court had ruled that paid union organizers, or "salts," were not employees in the true meaning of the act and thus did not have the right to organize and engage in collective bargaining. The rationale provided by the appeals court was that paid organizers served the union's interests and not the interests of the employer.

In disagreeing, however, the Supreme Court noted that: (1) paid union organizers fall within the definition of "employee"; (2) individuals can be employed by two employers without losing their employee status; and (3) an employee has the right to attempt to persuade fellow employees to support or join a union.[18] A former salt, Scott Lyman, explained how he operated: "I used to get hired at a company to organize and report information back to the union. The big thing you look for is unfair treatment—like a supervisor who's unfair—so you can galvanize the workers together as a group."[19] The future success of salts, however, may be in question for a number of reasons. First, some employers have initiated a policy preventing salting by not hiring anyone who adds information to their application, such as "voluntary union organizer." Thus the employer cannot be accused of discriminating against an applicant because of their union sympathies if they are unaware of those sympathies. Second, a 2004 NLRB decision may indicate a shift in the board's support of salting. In *I.B.E.W. Local 48* the NLRB ruled a union violated the NLRA, Section 8(b)(1)(A) by granting salts (and "peppers"—current employees who are hired to support the union) preference over other members who were not willing or able to act as salts.[20] And third, a federal court refused to hold an employer liable for refusing to consider a union applicant for a job, even though it was motivated by antiunion animus, because there was no job available that the applicant could fill.[21]

New Organizing Tactic

Some unions are trying to gain recognition by becoming part of the corporate governing body. In 1998, an organizer for the Hotel Workers and Restaurant Workers International Unions called a meeting with bondholders of the Santa Fe Gaming Corporation and asked them to elect two of its members to the corporation's board of directors. At the time, a key supporter for the two new union directors was from the head of a New York investment group that held one-third of the preferred stock and was receiving no dividends. Although the investor claimed he was not a "prounion person," he agreed with the union organizer that a change was needed. The members won and led the effort to remove the corporation president, who had been so resistant to collective bargaining.

This new organizing tactic of becoming part of the corporate structure is showing mild success. In one instance, Marriott International Inc., a union led a successful fight to stop the issue of a new class of stock that would have protected the Marriott family's control of the stock and defeated union interests.[22]

UNION AVOIDANCE STRATEGIES BY MANAGEMENT

In many workplaces, management's goal is simply to keep the union out, and as the example shows in Profile 4-1, a company need not be shy about saying so. The strategy is to convince the workers that unionization will do them more harm than good. Management may attempt to ensure workers that their present pay and benefits are competitive and may show data to prove it.

Emphasizing a philosophy of fair dealings with all employees, management may discuss the union's involvement in violent or corrupt activities if such has been the case. Management will also enumerate the costs of union membership, which include initiation fees, dues, and other assessments. The workers will be reminded that wages will be lost should a strike occur.

Such activities seem to have an effect on union organizing. A thorough study of NLRB-supervised representation elections held over a 46-month period indicated three important facts: (1) the number of elections held annually rose continuously until the late 1970s, and then began a decline that has continued; (2) the percentage of elections won by unions declined slowly over the entire period (see Figure 4-1); (3) unions are less likely to win elections in larger units than in smaller ones, probably due to greater organized resistance by the employer in larger units.[23]

PROFILE 4-1

UNION AVOIDANCE PROGRAM AT WAL-MART

Wal-Mart, Inc. is the world's largest employer, with over 1 million workers in 3,372 stores, and the world's largest retailer, with over $220 billion in annual sales. In fact, Wal-Mart revenues are over 2 percent of the entire Gross Domestic Product of the United States. Sam Walton opened his first Wal-Mart in 1962 on the philosophy of "Service to our customers."

In 1970 the Retail Clerks Union (RCU) initiated the first serious organizational campaign of Wal-Mart stores in Missouri. Sam Walton hired a professional union buster, John Tate, who lectured workers on the negative aspects of unions and encouraged Walton to implement a profit-sharing program. After defeating the union, Walton hired a consulting firm to develop a union avoidance strategy. Martin Levitt describes the program as "whatever it takes to wear people down and destroy their spirit. Each manager is taught to take union organizing personally . . . anyone supporting a union is slapping the supervisor in the face."

In 2000, the United Food and Commercial Workers Union (UFCW) initiated a new union organizing campaign. The union won the representation election—and the meat cutting department of Wal-Mart in Jacksonville, Texas, became the first in the history of the company to successfully organize a union. Two weeks later, however, Wal-Mart announced the elimination of the meat-cutting departments in all its stores, and fired four of the workers who voted for the union. Dotty Jones, a former Jacksonville meat-cutter, said Wal-Mart managers held a meeting and told the employees there was nothing they could do; "they would hold it up in court until we were old and gray."

Despite Wal-Mart's successful union avoidance program, in recent years workers in over 100 stores in 25 states have started organization campaigns. Why? Greg Denier, an official with the UFCW union says, "Americans can't live on a Wal-Mart paycheck . . . and Wal-Mart is the dominant employer, and what they pay will be the future of working America." The average Wal-Mart employee earns $18,000 a year—only about 40 percent receive health-care coverage—which costs employees up to $2,844 a year plus deductibles.

Another issue is the employment of women in top store positions. Although women account for two-thirds of all Wal-Mart employees, they account for less than 10 percent of top store managers, the same percentage as in 1975.

Can unions successfully organize Wal-Mart in the future? Not according to Bernie Hesse, a UFCW organizer in Minneapolis, who claims, "They'll close the frigging store," or Martin Levitt, author of *Confessions of a Union Buster;* "In my 35 years in labor relations, I've never seen a company that will go to the lengths that Wal-Mart goes to, to avoid a union."

SOURCE: Adapted from: Karen Olsson, "Up Against Wal-Mart," *Mother Jones* (March, April 2003), pp. 54–59.

One company that had a corporatewide policy against unionization instructed its managers on how to avoid unions legally by enumerating certain do's and don'ts. These instructions have been put into useful acronyms for managers and supervisors facing union organizing campaigns. For the things a manager *may not do,* they are told to remember **"TIPS"**: threaten, interrogate, promise, spy. Or, as the management consultant in Profile 4-2 terms it: "SPIT"—spy, promise, interrogate, or threaten. For the things a manager *may do,* they are told to remember **"FORE"**: facts, opinions, rules and experience.[24]

Among things managers **cannot** do to discourage unionization are the following:

T—Threaten
- Don't threaten or imply the company will take *adverse action* of any kind for supporting the union.

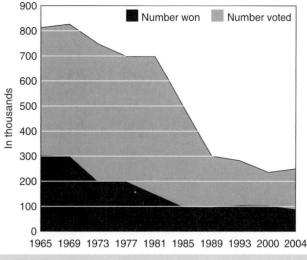

FIGURE 4-1 Union Representation Elections Drop

SOURCE: *Organizing for Change, Challenging to Organize.* Report from the AFL-CIO Leadership Task Force on Organizing (Washington, DC, 1996), p. 5; Bureau of Labor Statistics, 2002, and "Sixty-Ninth Annual Report of the National Labor Relations Board for Fiscal Year ending September 30, 2004."

- Don't threaten to *terminate* employees because of their union activities.
- Don't threaten to *close the facility* if a union is voted in.
- Don't threaten to *transfer employees* to other locations because of their union affiliation.
- Don't threaten employees with *loss of their wages* and benefits during negotiations.
- Don't threaten employees with *loss of their job* if they sign a union authorization card.
- Don't threaten employees by saying, "With the union there will be *a strike.*"
- Don't threaten to penalize employees who actively support the union for *violations of company policies* that nonunion employees are permitted to commit without being disciplined.
- Don't make *work assignments* with the intent of causing an employee who has been active on behalf of the union to quit his or her job.
- Don't take any action that is intended to *impair the employee's job or pay* because of his or her activity on behalf of the union.
- Don't intentionally *assign work or transfer employees* so that those active on behalf of the union are separated from those you believe are not interested in the union.
- Don't *reduce hours* of employees with the intention of curtailing the union's strength of organizing.

I—Interrogate
- Don't interrogate or ask employees their *position concerning unions.*
- Don't ask employees how they are *going to vote in an election.*
- Don't ask employees if they or anyone else *signed a union authorization card.*
- Don't ask employees if they are *going to the union meeting* or who else may be attending.

UNION BUSTER

Peter List's job title is not "union buster," but that is how many of his employers refer to him. List is hired by employers to persuade workers not to join a union because it is not in their best interests. His background is surprising. For eight years his career was handling heavy spools of telephone cable on the factory floor of an AT&T factory in Phoenix, Arizona. He joined the Communications Workers of America his very first week at AT&T, rose to the rank of chief shop steward within the union, and edited the local union newspaper.

Today, however, List is hired to fight union organizing campaigns, and in 2003 he won 32 of 35 campaigns. List estimates that 60 percent to 70 percent of his clients are small-business owners because unions have sought to organize more small businesses in recent years, and he averages a 57 percent "win rate" against them. Why did List switch sides? In 1992 AT&T outsourced his job to Mexico and thus he went back to college to complete a degree in labor relations. In his senior year he had an "epiphany" when researching a thesis on the history of unions. List decided unions blamed their decline on everyone—but themselves. He developed a strong procapitalist, Ayn Rand philosophy of radical individualism and opposed all governmental regulation of labor relations. List then started his own company, the North American

Employers Group, which advises employers who are engaged in an organized campaign.

For example, in 2001, the Teamsters collected authorization cards from a majority of 35 employees at Mazza & Sons in Tinton Falls, New Jersey. The recycling and demolition firm had hired a "salt," or Teamster member, who began organizing from the inside. The company had not given workers a raise in several years and thus was vulnerable. The Teamsters began picketing Mazza & Sons and created what Dominick Mazza called a "battle zone" that disrupted business. Mazza called List, who immediately started distributing handouts to the employees. List also coached Mazza on what he legally could and could not say or do during the organizational campaign. For example, List emphasized that a manager or owner should never "SPIT" on workers: *S*py, *P*romise, *I*nterrogate, *T*hreaten. In addition, List suggested that managers explain critical facts such as: If a union is certified management is under no obligation to sign an agreement; if negotiations reach an impasse, management has the right to impose its final offer unilaterally; and if the workers strike, management can hire permanent replacement workers. After a few months the picketing stopped, and the Teamsters lost interest in Mazza & Sons.

SOURCE: Adapted from Richard Murphy, "The Persuaders," *Fortune Small Business, 14,* no. 4 (May 2004), pp. 74–82.

- Don't ask employees their *opinion of the union organizer.*
- Don't *visit employees' homes* for the purpose of asking questions about the union or urging them to reject the union.

P—Promise

- Don't promise employees a *pay increase, better benefits,* or *special favors* if they vote against the union.
- Don't promise employees a *promotion* if they vote against the union.
- Don't promise employees that *all the concerns* they brought to management before the election will be corrected to their advantage if they vote against the union.
- Don't engage in *favoritism* of employees who are antiunion.

S—Spy

- Don't spy on any *union activities* the employees may be involved in, such as attending union meetings.
- Don't *attend a union meeting,* even if invited.

Among the things managers **can do** to discourage unionization are the following:

F—Facts

- Do tell employees that by signing a union authorization card, they may have authorized the union to become their *legal representative* in all matters pertaining to wages, hours, and working conditions.
- Do tell employees that if they sign a union authorization card, it *does not mean they must vote for the union* in an election. An election is a secret ballot process.
- Do tell employees that if a union is voted in, everything (their wages, benefits, and working conditions) would go *on the bargaining table.* It is much like the game show *Let's Make a Deal!* They could get more, they could get the same, or they could get less. Regardless, they will be responsible for dues, fees, fines, and assessments.
- Do tell employees that they *can actively campaign against the union*—you just cannot help them in any manner.

O—Opinion

- Do tell employees that *management does not believe the employees need* third-party representation.
- Do tell employees that *management believes in the open-door policy* and are willing to discuss any subject with them.

R—Rules

- Do tell employees that the *law permits the company to permanently replace them* if there is a strike.
- Do tell employees that the *union cannot make the company agree to anything it does not want to* during negotiations.

E—Experience

- Do share any *personal experiences* you may have had with a unionized workplace.

Countersalting Steps

Companies that have been "salted" have also come up with countermeasures. For example, one company suggests that employers take the following steps to prevent hiring "salts":[25]

1. Prescreen as many applicants as possible to ensure you are hiring the most qualified person for any opening you have available. The National Labor Relations Act prohibits an employer from refusing to hire an applicant because of his or her union affiliation. However, the law does not prevent a company from selecting the most positive, dedicated, enthusiastic applicant available.

2. Utilize "consensus" interviewing. Several members of management should interview applicants and then compare notes and recommendations for hiring.

3. An application should say, "List entire employment history, starting with present employer. For any unemployed or self-employed periods, show dates and locations. (Attach additional sheets when necessary.)" If there are only three spaces on the application to list existing or former employers, ask applicants if they have completed their entire employment history. If they have not, ask them to attach additional sheets.

4. Ensure that applications show entire work history with no gaps in employment. If you notice gaps, question them. Then ask applicants to fill in those gaps.

5. Check references thoroughly.

Prohibited Conduct

Through its rulings over the years, the NLRB has determined that activities that constitute violations of the act, or **prohibited conduct**, include the following:

1. ***Campaign propaganda and misrepresentation.*** In the conduct of representation elections, the board routinely ignores rhetoric, realizing that it is part of any election campaign and usually will be disregarded by employees in making decisions. But such an attitude is flexible if the rights of the parties to an untrammeled choice are in jeopardy. In *Midland National Life Insurance Company,* the NLRB stated that it would intervene in cases in which forgery would render the voters unable to discern the propagandistic nature of a publication.[26] Also, an employer was found to have interfered with an election when it provided a $250 prize to the employee who scored highest on a test that determined knowledge of the process used in decertifying a union.[27]

The board often sees misleading information on wage and fringe benefit data, proffered by the union to encourage unionization, as exaggeration, but if viewed by the courts as more serious, it can cause the election to be invalidated.[28] The board has also found that a flyer circulated by the union that guaranteed that it was illegal for the company to close or threaten to close the plant if the union won the election a piece of union campaign literature that the voters could evaluate for themselves and not a reason to void an election.[29]

2. ***Threats and loss of benefits.*** Unlike mere campaign rhetoric, the actual reduction or withholding of benefits as a method of combating an organizational drive constitutes interference. Direct threats of economic reprisals issued to thwart a representation election will result in an unfair labor practice finding. These include discharge, loss of pay or benefits, more onerous working conditions, and threats of plant closure, physical violence, or permanent replacement of strikers. It is more difficult to ascertain an unfair labor practice when threats of reprisals or promises of benefits are merely implied. In 2000 in *Springs Industries,* the NLRB ruled that when an employer threatens to close a plant if the union wins a representation election, that the assumption is the threat will make the rounds of the workplace, thereby tainting an election. However, in a 2004 NLRB (3–2) decision, *Springs Industries* was overruled. In *Crown Bolt, Inc.,* the NLRB decided that if a threat of plant closure were made to a single employee, an election would not be overturned without evidence that the threat was actually disseminated throughout the workforce.[30]

Under the *Gissel* case, an employer is not prohibited from communicating general views about unionism or predictions of the effect of unionization on the company as long as such predictions involve consequences outside the employer's control.[31] The

Supreme Court added a subjective test of what the speaker intended and the listener understood to ensure that veiled threats would not coerce employee actions. To determine the coercive nature of a statement, a court should examine the total context in which the statement is made. Elements to be reviewed include the presence or absence of other unfair labor practice incidents, the actual content of the communication, the exact language used, the employer's history of dealing with unions, and the identity of the speaker.[32]

A 1996 NLRB decision outlined a new test to be utilized in cases involving employer threats of loss of benefits during a representation election. The new test provides that employers may not distribute propaganda regarding possible loss of benefits if workers are unionized *within 24 hours of the opening of the polls* in an election. In *Kalin Construction Co.,* the employer distributed two separate "paychecks" to workers as they approached the polls in a representation election. One "check" showed what the average worker would earn if the union won, the second showed those benefits that would be lost if the union won. The union lost the election and filed an unfair labor charge. The NLRB agreed that workers' freedom of choice had been affected and ordered a new election.[33]

3.   *Promise or grant of benefit.*   The promise of economic benefits by the employer if employees reject unionization will violate the National Labor Relations Act, as will the promise or grant of economic benefits during an organizational campaign to influence the outcome of an election or to discourage organizational activities. The fact that there is no direct link between receipt of the benefit and a vote against the union is unimportant; the courts look to the implication of such largesse. The employee may be impressed with the power of the employer's discretion to give and presumably take away benefits. However, the granting of benefits during a union campaign has not always been held a violation of the act. The board does not favor a per se approach but will examine each case within context. For example, the board refused to assume without specific proof that an employer's unilateral grant of improved health insurance caused a decertification of the union.[34] Clearly, offering money while urging a vote in a particular way will be considered coercive. In other cases, the board has found interference when salary increases were made in the context of repeated references to unionization, made effective just before an election, or announced before an election when there was no particular reason to do so.[35] On the other hand, a salary increase has been found not to interfere with the employee's right to organize when the timing, amount, and application of the increase were consistent with past practice.[36]

Some employers' benefits, such as free access to vending machines, have been found to be too minimal to affect the outcome of an election. Also, benefits provided to multiple locations—including some outside a campaign—can be permitted.[37] Unions can also be charged with unfair labor practices pertaining to promises. If the promise is within the bounds of what union representation can do for employees in relationship to their employer, it is probably not legally objectionable. However, promising economic benefits from the union itself, such as life insurance coverage or a waiver of union dues, has been found to be coercive.

4.   *Interrogation and polling of employees.*   The NLRB originally viewed all employer interrogation of employees as to union sympathy as unlawful per se for two reasons: Such interrogation instills a fear of discrimination in the mind of the employee, thereby restraining freedom of choice, and no purpose could be served by such inquiry except to identify employees with union sympathies.

The courts, however, chose not to view employee interrogation as a per se violation and instead examined it within the context of the inquiry. As a result, the board set its standard for polling of employees in *Struksnes Construction Co.:*

> Absent unusual circumstances, the polling of employees by an employer will be violative of Section 8(a)(1) of the act unless the following safeguards are observed: the purpose of the poll is to determine the truth of a union's claim of majority, this purpose is communicated to the employees, assurances against reprisals are given, the employees are polled by secret ballot, and the employer has not engaged in unfair labor practices or otherwise created a coercive atmosphere.[38]

A long-standing NLRB precedent provides that an employer who entertains a **good-faith reasonable doubt** whether a majority of its employees supports an incumbent union has three options:

- To request a formal, board-supervised election
- To withdraw recognition from the union and refuse to bargain
- To conduct an internal poll of employee support for the union

In the 1998 decision of *Allentown Mack Sales & Service, Inc. v. NLRB,*[39] the Supreme Court held the "good-faith reasonable doubt" test for employer polling to be consistent with the National Labor Relations Act. The reasonable doubt standard is the same one used to support an RM petition that is used when an employer questions if a labor organization continues to represent a majority of the employees.[40] And the NLRB held that in determining whether an employer had a good-faith uncertainty under *Allentown Mack,* statements by known union opponents to the effect that other unnamed employees opposed union representation were entitled to "little weight."[41]

Individual or isolated questioning of employees is not a per se violation of the act. Tests of noncoercive questioning are whether an employer has a legitimate interest in the information sought, the employee is assured that no reprisals will result from the answer, and there is no evidence of coercion in the interrogation itself. Such interrogation can arise when an employer attempts to prepare a defense for an NLRB unfair labor practice proceeding. However, if under all the circumstances the interrogation reasonably tends to restrain or interfere with employees in the exercise of their rights, it will be held unlawful (see Case 4-1). Previously, the board had held that questioning of open and well-known union adherents was inherently coercive, but under its decision in *Rossmore House,* the totality of the circumstances must now be examined to determine if a violation has occurred.[42]

The board has developed the following detailed criteria to protect the interests of both parties:

a. The purpose of the questioning must be communicated to the employee.
b. An assurance of no reprisal must be given.
c. The employee's participation must be obtained on a voluntary basis.
d. The questioning must take place in an atmosphere free from antiunion sentiments.
e. The questioning itself must not be coercive in nature.
f. The questions must be relevant to the issues involved in the complaint.
g. The employee's subjective state of mind must not be probed.
h. The questions must not otherwise interfere with the statutory rights of employees.[43]

UNLAWFUL INTERROGATION

The company is in the business of selling automotive replacement parts at wholesale from 11 warehouses and distribution centers in the eastern United States. Early on the morning of May 12, 1994, the plant manager summoned an employee to his office and asked whether she had heard rumors about the union. When she replied that she had, the plant manager asked what he could do to stop the union and if getting rid of a particular supervisor whom the workers disliked would help. The employee said she did not know, and the conversation ended.

The union charged the company with an unfair labor practice because asking the employee whether the union could be stopped if he terminated the disliked supervisor constituted an unlawful offer to improve working conditions in violation of Section 8(a)(1). In addition the union alleged that the conversation was an unlawful interrogation.

The company contended that there was no coercion during this conversation inasmuch as the plant manager was unaware that the employee had signed a union card, he had spoken with her a number of times over the years, and he "trusted" her.

An employer violates Section 8(a)(1) when it interrogates an employee about the union where the questioning reasonably tends to restrain, coerce, or interfere with employees' rights guaranteed by the act. To determine whether the inquiry is coercive, the board considers the following factors: the background, the nature of the information sought, the identity of the questioner, and the place and method of interrogation.

DECISION

Applying these factors to the plant manager's interrogation of the employee, the board found that the union amply demonstrated coercion on the part of the company of the type prohibited by Section 8(a)(1). As of May 12, 1994, the employee was not an open and active union supporter. On that date, plant manager, the highest management official at the facility, summoned her to his office for no purpose other than to ask her about the union and, during the course of the brief conversation, unlawfully promised to improve working conditions in order to stop the union effort. Where the interrogation is accompanied by threats or other violations of Section 8(a)(1), as this one was, there can be no question as to the coercive effect of the inquiry.

SOURCE: Adapted from *Parts Depot, Inc. v. NLRB*, 170 LRRM 1005 (September 29, 2000).

5. *Surveillance.* Surveillance in almost any form has been held a violation of the unfair labor practices section of the National Labor Relations Act. The board has such an aversion to surveillance that it will uphold findings even if the employees know nothing about it or the surveillance was only an employer's attempt to foster an impression of scrutiny. Encouraging surveillance and eavesdropping by union members has also been condemned by the NLRB.

6. *Poll Activity.* The NLRB prohibits any electioneering at or near the polls in a campaign. In fact, in *Milchem, Inc.,* the board applied a strict rule that conversations between company or union officials in the polling area are prohibited regardless of what is discussed. Although the exact distance within this rule varies, the board often

MANAGERS AND SUPERVISORS SHOULD FOLLOW THESE **TIPS** AND **FORE** GUIDELINES:

DON'T	DO TELL
THREATEN	**F**ACTS
INTERROGATE	**O**PINION
PROMISE	**R**ULES
SPY	**E**XPERIENCE
These actions are **prohibited** by the National Labor Relations Act.	These actions are **permitted** by the National Labor Relations Act.

FIGURE 4-2   Union Organizing Campaign: TIPS and FORE

sets a radius of 100 feet around the polls.[44] And in a 1953 case, *Peerless Plywood Co.*,[45] the board detailed a **24-hour rule**, which it has maintained for more than 40 years. The 24-hour rule prohibits employers and unions from making organizational campaign speeches on company time to large assemblies of employees within 24 hours of a scheduled election. It does not prohibit voluntary assemblies on or off company time or the distribution of written material.[46]

In general, supervisors are advised to follow the TIPS and FORE guidelines shown in Figure 4-2.

UNFAIR LABOR PRACTICES BY EMPLOYERS

Under the National Labor Relations Act, in addition to campaign-related violations, employers' domination of and assistance to labor organizations are also **employer unfair labor practices**. This provision obviously reflects the historical aversion to company unions of the 1930s that were used to discourage outside union organization. The National Labor Relations Act views employer interference in the internal workings of a union as a threat to the employees' free exercise of guaranteed rights.

The unlawful domination and assistance pertains only to labor organizations. Employee recreation committees, credit unions, social clubs, and the like may be initiated and supported by the employer without violation.

Employer Domination and Interference

Once a labor organization is identified, the board will look for prohibited domination or support. *Support* is mere assistance to a favored union, whereas domination means actual control of the union. An employer-created organization falls within the prohibited controls section of the act.

Domination of a union may also be found when the employer does not create a union. The employer's behavior toward an existing union may result in the employees' freedom of choice being unlawfully infringed. Courts have found domination when supervisors solicited union membership, the employer's attorney acted for the union in drafting its constitution and bylaws, and the employer allowed union officials on company time and property to pursue a union organization drive. Tests for domination are subjective from the standpoint of the employees.[47] Another violation of this section is employer interference by friendly cooperation with the creation or operation of a labor organization. A suggestion in and of itself by an employer that a union be formed is not an unfair labor practice, but interference may be found if the suggestion is timed to counter an organizational drive by an outside union. After a union has been recognized, a violation may occur if supervisors and company executives who gained membership status prior to their promotions remain in the union.

Employer Support and Assistance

Although domination and control of a labor organization clearly violate the act, support and assistance of a labor organization by the employer present a different problem. Often the suspect activities may be a manifestation of the employer's legal cooperation with the union. If the support does not have any effect on the employees' exercise of their rights guaranteed by the act and is trivial, no violation will be found.

Assistance or support that does violate the act is employer aid to one of two competing unions. The employer can unlawfully favor one union by giving direct assistance to its campaign drive, by allowing it exclusive use of company facilities, by supplying the union with employee names to aid in a raid of the other union's membership, and by assessing and collecting union dues without signed authorization cards. Prior to 1982, continuing to recognize an incumbent union when an election challenge is pending would have been a violation of the act. The board determined in that year that the mere filing of a representation petition by an outside union does not require or permit an employer to withdraw from bargaining with the incumbent union.[48] Financial support of a union, either directly by donating money or indirectly by, for instance, allowing the union to receive the profits from company-owned vending machines, are other violations of the support and assistance provisions.

Employee Teams

The emergence of total quality management and teamwork principles in the workplace, as discussed in Chapter 2, has created a new area for charges of unfair labor practices. The NLRB decided in two publicized cases in 1992, *Electromation*[49] and *DuPont*[50] that the employer–employee committees formed to make recommendations on improvements to the workplace violated the domination provision of the National Labor Relations Act.

In *Electromation*, a nonunion company announced several changes in its personnel policies, including no wage increase for the upcoming year. In reaction to employee complaints over these changes, the employer established five action committees made up of management representatives and employees who volunteered to participate. The employer scheduled the meetings during the regular workday. It was anticipated that the recommendations of the committees would be implemented. A union organizing campaign was begun after the action committees were functional. The union brought an unfair labor charge, and the NLRB ruled in the union's favor, noting that the committees were obviously labor organizations under the act and dominated by the employer.

In the *DuPont* case, an employer-sponsored employee participation program with unionized employees was also found to have been an unfair labor practice. DuPont created employee–management committees to deal with safety and recreation issues at one of its plants. The union charged DuPont with an unfair labor practice for creating and dominating a labor organization. Again, the NLRB agreed and ordered the committees to disband.[51]

The board, however, did not foreclose every conceivable form of employee participation committee. As pointed out in *Polaroid Corp.*,[52] Section 8(a)(2) is designed to ensure that employer-dominated groups "do not rob employees of their right to select a representative of their own choosing." In *Electromation* and *DuPont*, the board identified several examples of specific types of communication mechanisms that did not rise to the level of "dealing," for example, "brainstorming" groups that merely develop ideas for management's consideration, "information-sharing" committees, suggestion boxes, groups that serve a purely "clerical" or "ministerial" function, and groups in which management served only as an observer without any right to vote on proposals. More recently in *Crown Cork & Seal,* the board ruled that an employee committee with delegated managerial authority does not "deal with" management because they are management.[53]

Could, in fact, participation by employees in such programs or teams affect their attitudes toward unions and the need for collective bargaining? In a survey of 200 organizational campaigns, Professor James Rundle of Cornell University found that 7 percent of the companies had employee participation programs in 1988 and 32 percent in 1994. He also found that in almost half the elections in companies with no employee organization, the union won the organizational campaign, whereas in companies with employee participation groups, the success rate was less than one-third.[54]

Remedies

If employer control or interference in a labor organization is so extensive that it results in employer domination, the board will disestablish the union. To ensure the removal of the employer from union activities, the board requires a public announcement that the company will cease bargaining with and will withdraw its support from the union. The employer must take no part in any reorganization by employees.

If only support and not domination is found, the NLRB applies a less-stringent remedy. Union recognition is withdrawn until the employer's support is eliminated and a new certification election is held.

Discrimination in Employment

Discrimination against employees, based on their union activities, is an unfair labor practice and an obvious deterrent to successful collective bargaining. A violation of the act occurs when an employer encourages or discourages membership in any labor organization by hiring or tenure practices or by using membership as a term or condition of employment.

Discrimination occurs when a union member is treated differently from a nonunion worker because he or she is involved in union activity. In general, the fact that a particular incident took place is not an issue. It is easy to ascertain that a refusal to hire, a discharge, or a change in an employment condition has occurred. The question for the board to resolve is whether the action was motivated by a desire to encourage or discourage union membership and thereby discriminate against the member. **Antiunion animus** is found when the employer's conduct is not motivated, or at least is not entirely motivated, by legitimate and substantial business reasons but by a desire to penalize or reward employees for union activity or the lack of it.

An employer has a right to select employees and take disciplinary action to maintain good business conditions. The NLRB must weigh claims of discrimination by the employee against claims by the employer that certain actions were taken for cause.

Discrimination cases fall into two categories. In a **dual-motive discrimination case**, two explanations for the action complained of can be offered by the employer. One constitutes a legitimate business reason, and the other is a reason prohibited under the act. In a **pretext discrimination case**, the employer puts forth only the legitimate business reason, but the complainant asserts that the prohibited reason is the true cause for the action. Approximately 60 percent of the unfair labor practice cases presented to the board involve a charge of discrimination for union activity. Prior to 1980, the board's test in these cases was to decide if the antiunion animus of the employer played a part in the complaint. If so, the employer was found to have violated the act. Since then, however, the board has required the employee to present a prima facie case that the antiunion animus of the employer played a substantial or motivating role in the complaint before requiring the employer to justify the action taken.[55]

Discriminatory acts by the employer in compliance with a union shop provision in a collective bargaining agreement do not violate the act. The act specifically allows a collective bargaining agreement to require that new employees join the union within 30 days of employment.

Applicants for jobs as well as persons already employed are protected by the act. The language "discrimination in regard to hire" could stand no other interpretation. Therefore, it is an unfair labor practice for an employer to refuse to hire an applicant because of union activities. It is also a violation to offer employment on the condition that the applicant will not join or participate in a union.

Obvious acts of discrimination against employees regarding wages, hours, and working conditions will lead to charges of unfair labor practices. As discussed earlier, withholding benefits pending union recognition elections is an unfair labor practice if the purpose is to influence the election.

Discrimination can arise when an employer treats striking employees differently from nonstriking employees. For example, discrimination may be found if an employer announces that he or she will pay vacation benefits under an expired agreement to returning strikers, nonstriking workers, and strike replacements but not to strikers.

Concerted Activities

Employers that discriminate against employees for engaging in concerted activities violate the interference, restraint, or coercion provisions of the unfair labor practices section of the act and also violate the discrimination for purposes of discouraging union membership provision.

Concerted activity is any action by employees to further legitimately their common interests pursued on behalf of or with other employees and not solely by and on behalf of an individual.[56] The most common form of concerted activity is the strike. Concerted activity need not involve union leadership or membership to be protected. To establish concerted activity, certain elements must exist: The issue involved must be work related, the goal is to further a group interest, a specific remedy or result is sought, and the act itself must not be unlawful or improper.

The work-relatedness requirement is not stringently applied. The board has found many activities protected under the act:

1. Employees assisting another employer's personnel to unionize
2. Union resolution condemning employer's opposition to another union's strike
3. Union support of workers' compensation law changes
4. Union lobbying against the National Immigration Policy
5. Union lobbying against right-to-work laws[57]

However, as seen in Case 4-2, the courts do not always agree with the NLRB's findings.

Unprotected concerted activities occur when the employees are violent, act in breach of contract, or engage in activities otherwise prohibited by the act, such as jurisdictional strikes or secondary boycotts. Employees can lose the protection of Section 7's concerted activities if they take actions disproportionate to the grievance involved. Disparaging an employer's product without clarification of the context of the dispute is such an action.

EMPLOYER'S UNFAIR LABOR PRACTICE—RETALIATION

The company, an industrial general contractor, received a contract to modernize a steel mill near the beginning of 1987. According to the company, various unions attempted to delay the project because the company's employees were nonunion. The company and the mill operator filed suit against those unions based on the following basic allegations:

1. The unions had lobbied for adoption and enforcement of an emissions standard despite having no real concern the project would harm the environment.
2. The unions had handbilled and picketed at the company's site—and also encouraged strikes among the employees of the company's subcontractors—without revealing reasons for their disagreement.
3. The unions had filed an action in state court alleging violations of the Health and Safety Code to delay the construction project and raise costs.
4. The unions had launched grievance proceedings against the company's joint venture partner based on inapplicable collective bargaining agreements.

Initially, the company and the mill operator sought damages under Section 303 of the Labor-Management Relations Act, which provides a cause of action against labor organizations for injuries caused by secondary boycotts prohibited under Section 158(b)(4). But after the court granted the unions' motion for summary judgment on the company's lobbying- and grievance-related claims, it amended the complaint to allege that the unions' activities violated Sections 1 and 2 of the Sherman Antitrust Act, which prohibit certain agreements in restraint of trade, monopolization, and attempts to monopolize.

The court dismissed the amended complaint because it realleged claims that had already been decided. The appeals court affirmed the dismissal of the company's antitrust claim because the unions had antitrust immunity when lobbying officials or petitioning courts and agencies, unless the activity was a sham. The company did not argue that the unions' litigation activity had been objectively baseless but maintained that "the unions had engaged in a pattern of automatic petitioning of governmental bodies . . . without regard to . . . the merits of said petitions."

In the meantime, two unions had lodged complaints against the company with the NLRB, and after the federal proceedings ended, the board's general counsel issued an administrative complaint against the company, alleging that it had violated Section 8(a)(1) of the National Labor Relations Act by filing and maintaining the federal lawsuit. Section 8(a)(1) prohibits employers from restraining, coercing, or interfering with employees' exercise of rights related to self-organization, collective bargaining, and other concerted activities.

The NLRB ruled that the company's federal lawsuit had been unmeritorious because all of the company's claims were dismissed or voluntarily withdrawn with prejudice. The board then examined whether the company's suit had been filed to retaliate against the unions for engaging in activities protected under the National Labor Relations Act. The board first concluded that the unions' conduct was protected activity and then decided that the company's lawsuit had been unlawfully motivated because it was directed at protected conduct and necessarily tended to discourage similar protected activity. The NLRB also found evidence of retaliatory motive because the company's Labor-Management Relations Act claims had an utter absence of merit and had been dismissed on summary

continued

EMPLOYER'S UNFAIR LABOR PRACTICE— RETALIATION—continued

judgment. The NLRB found that the company had committed an unfair labor practice because the suit it brought was unsuccessful and retaliatory. The company appealed to the Supreme Court.

DECISION

The Supreme Court reversed the judgment, however, holding that the same application of the First Amendment that kept the unions from being found in violation of the Sherman Antitrust Act for lobbying efforts prevented the company from being charged with an unfair labor practice. Under the First Amendment, citizens are allowed the right to "petition" their government. Joining together to lobby elected officials, which certainly unions do, is a protected activity and cannot be found to have violated the Sherman Antitrust Act. Likewise, "petitioning" the government includes the right to seek redress with the court system. So that filing a well-founded, albeit unsuccessful, lawsuit, even if it would not have been commenced but for the company's desire to retaliate against the unions for exercising rights protected by the National Labor Relations Act, is a protected activity under the First Amendment.

SOURCE: Adapted from *BE & K Construction Company v. NLRB,* 170 LRRM 2225 (June 24, 2002).

A **primary strike** is a type of concerted activity protected under the act if it is called for economic reasons or to protest unfair labor practices. Any retaliation against employees participating in a primary strike is therefore an unfair labor practice. However, if the employer has replaced strikers participating in an economic strike, he or she need only reinstate those for whom there are vacant positions. In contrast, employees participating in a strike to protest an unfair labor practice are entitled to reinstatement and back pay, even if they have been replaced. Unlawful activity during a strike may be grounds for discharging an employee and would not subject an employer to an unfair labor practice charge. Nor is an employer who discharges employees for breaching a collective bargaining agreement guilty of an unfair labor practice. However, discharging or otherwise discriminating against an employee for filing charges or giving testimony is, under the National Labor Relations Act, specifically designated as an unfair labor practice.

Other employee-concerted activities protected under the act are bringing a civil action against the employer unless done with malice or in bad faith, circulating a petition among coworkers calling for a union meeting to discuss current contract negotiations, complaining to local government authorities, and under some circumstances, refusing to cross a picket line.[58] In addition, under the *Weingarten* **rule**, an employee's insistence on union representation at an investigatory interview, which the employee believes might result in disciplinary action, is protected concerted activity.[59]

However, the original *Weingarten* decision has been narrowed by subsequent board decisions. For example, the union employee cannot refuse to attend a meeting with management without a union representative because until the meeting begins, the employee cannot know it is an investigatory interview,[60] and a union steward can

Tips from the Experts

UNION

What are the three most common unfair labor practices committed by employers, and how should a union respond?

In the public sector right now, we find that a lot of our unfair labor practices involve giving away our unit work: subcontracting and privatization. We also find that there are numerous times where management treats union activists differently from other employees (antiunion animus) in efforts to silence or dampen the enthusiasm of union activists. Third, I guess we do see a lot of unilateral changes of terms and conditions of employment without management's meeting its bargaining obligations. As for the union response: It can only be to press the issue through whatever informal and formal mechanisms it has under its contract, before its labor board and even in the courts if appropriate. For a union to "sit on its rights" is to "sow the seeds" of its own undoing.

MANAGEMENT

What are the three most common unfair labor practices management should avoid, and how can it do so?

a. Charge: 8(a)(3), discriminating against a union sympathizer/organizer/officer as regards discipline, especially termination. Avoid by either not touching those persons for violations of work rules (which makes managing the workforce very difficult) or (preferably) being doubly cautious in enforcing violations of work rules by such persons, that is, making absolutely certain that the violation and similar treatment for nonunion violators is well documented before taking action.

b. Charge: 8(a)(5), refusal to bargain/surface bargain intentionally or inadvertently, such as in unilaterally implementing a drug and alcohol policy. Avoid by scheduling sufficient numbers of negotiation sessions, being prepared and willing to make and listen to proposals, making some movement on at least some issues, not making public announcements either before bargaining commences or during the process (prior to impasse) that "X" is the company's position and that the union can go fly a kite or whatever if it thinks it will get any more, and so on. With respect to the inadvertent stuff, make sure human resources and legal are working together in the implementation of any new or major changes to current policies or benefits to ensure no unintentional unilateral changes in terms or conditions of employment.

c. Charge: 8(a)(1), interference with employees in the exercise of their Section 7 rights. Avoid through soliciting information, spying, or crossing over the line in an organizing campaign. Make sure thorough supervisory training is repeated regularly and supported by an adequately staffed and respected labor relations department available for immediate assistance when necessary.

be expelled from an investigatory interview if the steward interferes with the employer's legitimate right to investigate.[61] Thus, management can request meetings with employees without a steward present and is not obligated under *Weingarten* to tell employees when they do have the right to have their steward present. Recently the board refused to invalidate two employees' suspensions because they were allowed only one union representative at an investigation meeting although they had requested two.[62]

The general purpose for having a steward present when a disciplinary situation may be discussed is to (1) provide a witness, (2) provide the employee with assistance of a person experienced in such situations, and (3) advise the employee about what to say and not say. The International Brotherhood of Teamsters provides their members printed cards with language to use if management asks about a potential disciplinary situation. The card reads, "If this discussion could in any way lead to my being disciplined or terminated, or affect my personal working conditions, I request that my union representative, officer, or steward be present at the meeting. Without representation, I choose not to answer any questions."[63]

In 2004, in a 3–2 decision, the NLRB reversed a previous NLRB decision, *Epilepsy Foundation v. NLRB,*[64] which had extended the *Weingarten* right to employees in nonunion workplaces. That previous opinion found such activity protected under the act for all employees because it provided employees with the opportunity to act in concert to address their mutual concerns. The board in *IBM, Corp.,*[65] however, asserted that in nonunion workplaces coworkers do not represent the interests of the entire workforce, have no official status as a union representative so they cannot redress the imbalance of power between employer and employee, and may compromise the confidentiality of the interview.

Concerted activities not considered protected are serious trespass, destruction of property, violence, and participating in an unlawful strike in violation of a no-strike clause in an applicable collective bargaining agreement.[66] In a recent arbitration, an employee became threatening to a supervisor. The supervisor suspended him and instructed him to leave the plant while management determined what discipline might be assessed. The employee stopped on his way out to confer with a union steward, who told him he was entitled to a written disciplinary report before leaving. The supervisor saw that the employee had not left the plant and again ordered him out. This resulted in a shoving match. When the employee grieved the incident, the arbitrator held that the supervisor was in the right in ordering the employee out of the plant. There was no *Weingarten* violation because there was no disciplinary interview being conducted. It was clearly within the employer's prerogative to "suspend pending investigation," as was done here.[67]

UNFAIR LABOR PRACTICES BY LABOR ORGANIZATIONS

The Taft-Hartley Amendments to the National Labor Relations Act were a response to the perceived power of organized labor during the 1940s to dictate to the employer instead of meeting at the bargaining table as an equal. One aspect not previously covered by the act was the imposition of **unfair labor practice standards against labor organizations**.

Restraint or Coercion of Employees

Unfair labor practice standards were applied to labor organizations to enforce an employee's right to refrain from union activities, which was granted by the Taft-Hartley Amendments. This right includes protection to work without restraint from strikes, to refuse to sign union dues checkoffs, and not to be coerced into accepting a particular union or any union at all.

The amendments did not impair the right of a labor organization to prescribe its own rules on members in good standing. And if a union shop provision is part of a current collective bargaining agreement, an employee can be compelled to join the union after being hired and to pay dues or fees to retain employment. Nonetheless, in *Pattern Makers League v. National Labor Relations Board,* the Supreme Court held that a union was guilty of an unfair labor practice when it attempted to fine its members for resigning from the union and returning to work during a strike. The Court believed that such fines were an attempt to compel membership in the union in violation of Section 8(b)(1)(A) of the act.[68]

Only a labor organization or its agent can violate the section of the amendments prohibiting unfair labor practices by unions. Actions by individual employees not sanctioned by a union cannot subject the employee to an unfair labor practice charge.

The unfair labor practices provision prohibiting a union from restraining or coercing employees in the exercise of their guaranteed rights is not as broadly stated or as strictly enforced as the mirror provision affecting employers. Violent or otherwise threatening behavior or clearly coercive or intimidating union activities are necessary before the NLRB will find an unfair labor practice. Union propaganda and peer pressure present in a situation in which employees belong to a union will not cause an unfair labor practice charge.

Specific activities are deemed to be in violation of the amendments:

1. Physical assaults or threats of violence directed at employees or their relatives
2. Threats of economic reprisals
3. Mass picketing that restrains the lawful entry or leaving of a work site
4. Causing or attempting to cause an employer to discriminate against employees
5. Discriminating provisions in collective bargaining agreements (union shop being an exception), for example, superseniority clauses for union members that do not exist for a legitimate purpose[69]

Union Interference with Elections

The activities that concern representation elections, including the 24-hour rule, electioneering near polls, and coercion, apply equally to unions and employers. In addition, unions, under Section 8(b)(1)(A) of the National Labor Relations Act, are prohibited from the threat or use of violence against unsupportive employees. Threats, if made by union organizers or merely supportive employees, may cause the NLRB to overturn an election.[70] For example, in *United Broadcasting Co. of New York,* a union steward told an employee he would be blacklisted and could never work again in New York—the union victory was overturned.[71]

Negotiators bargaining in "good faith" exchange proposals at a negotiation table in 2005.

DUTY TO BARGAIN IN GOOD FAITH

The National Labor Relations Act established a national policy to encourage collective bargaining as a way to eliminate or to mitigate industrial strife obstructing commerce. Employees seek strength in numbers by joining employee organizations to ensure equal bargaining powers. Under the act, employee organization is a right—protected and preserved. However, once that right is exercised, a duty is placed on both the employee organization and the employer to proceed to bargain in good faith. Management's very first obligation to a new union representing a bargaining unit is to bargain in good faith. That obligation does not, however, mean that management must make a concession on any issue. Good-faith bargaining, in general, does mean meeting and exchanging proposals and explaining reason(s) for rejecting a proposal.[72]

Nature of the Duty

The Wagner (National Labor Relations) Act itself made it an unfair labor practice for an employer to refuse to bargain with representatives of his employees.[73] The NLRB, in enforcing that provision, imposed a good-faith efforts test as a condition for compliance with this duty. The criteria established by the board includes the following:

1. Active participation in deliberations with an intention to find a basis for agreement
2. A sincere effort to reach a common ground
3. Binding agreements on mutually acceptable terms[74]

The board found indications of less than good faith when employers met directly with employees outside the bargaining process to reach an agreement not sanctioned by their representatives, when an employer refused to put the agreement in writing even after all issues were agreed to, or when an employer refused to make counterproposals.[75]

The comprehensive inclusion of unions in the unfair labor practices section of the National Labor Relations Act by the Taft-Hartley Amendments placed an equal obligation to bargain in good faith on employees. In addition, the board-imposed test of good faith to determine whether either party had refused to bargain was included in the amendments.[76]

The amendments also clarified what was meant by bargaining: to meet at reasonable times; to confer in good faith with respect to rates of pay, wages, hours of employment, or other conditions of employment; and to execute a written contract if the parties reach an agreement. However, the obligation to bargain does not compel either party to agree to a proposal or to make a concession.

In addition, the amendments imposed on the employer the duty to bargain in good faith when the collective bargaining representative requests that the employer meet for purposes of collective bargaining. The completion of a representation election alone does not trigger the bargaining process. Until the employer has been asked, there can be no breach of the duty to bargain. When the duty to bargain has arisen, the amendments require that negotiations be conducted in good faith with the view of reaching an agreement. Merely going through the motions without actually seeking to adjust differences does not meet this stipulation.

Totality of Conduct Doctrine

A **totality of conduct** test is applied to determine the fulfillment of the **good-faith bargaining** obligation. If, in total conduct, a party has negotiated with an open mind in a sincere attempt to reach an agreement, isolated acts will not prove bad faith. On the other hand, actions that are not per se unfair labor practices may indicate bad-faith bargaining when viewed in the totality of the bargaining process.

Boulwarism

Boulwarism is a "take-it-or-leave-it" bargaining technique. Its name derives from Lemuel R. Boulware, a vice president for the General Electric Company, who negotiated for that company in the late 1940s. Using this technique, a company presents a comprehensive contract proposal that, in its opinion, has included all that is necessary or warranted. This form of negotiation eliminates any need to compromise in the employer's mind. Such a proposal is presented at the outset with the understanding that nothing is being held back for later trading, and employees are notified it is a final offer. This practice places the employer in the untenable position of not being able to negotiate. The NLRB declared an attitude of boulwarism a violation of the duty to bargain. It noted that although the formality of bargaining is followed—no illegal or nonmandatory subjects are insisted on, and an intent to enter into an agreement is exhibited—there exists no serious intent to adjust differences and to reach a common ground.

A 1964 decision (confirmed in 1969) involving this procedure as practiced by the General Electric Company gave the NLRB a chance to examine the technique in detail. The company had examined all relevant facts and had anticipated union demands. It actively communicated its position to employees prior to the negotiation session. It presented what it considered a fair and firm offer; although representations were made that new information could alter its position. The company was found to have failed in its duty to bargain in good faith because it failed to furnish information requested by the union; it had attempted to bypass the international union and to bargain directly with local unions; it had presented a take-it-or-leave-it insurance proposal; and it had, in its overall attitude and approach as evidenced by the totality of its conduct, failed in the good-faith test.[77]

By the examination of the totality of conduct, the court expanded the understanding of the duty to bargain collectively by emphasizing the collective nature of the duty as contained in the National Labor Relations Act. Involvement is a bilateral procedure, allowing both parties a voice in the agreements reached. It is in direct opposition to the intent and purpose of the act for a party to assume the role of decision maker; an exchange of options must be presented and received with an open mind.

The technique of boulwarism, although most often used by an employer, has also been used by unions. In *Utility Workers (Ohio Power Company),* the board found a union violating the duty to bargain in good faith when the union insisted that identical offers be made to several bargaining units and conditioned acceptance in any single unit on submission of identical offers to all units.[78]

Surface Bargaining

Another violation of the good-faith duty can be evidenced by **surface bargaining**, that is, simply going through the motions without any real intention of arriving at an agreement. A totality test is used to determine surface bargaining. Surface bargaining can occur when a party has rejected a proposal and offered its own and does not attempt to reconcile the differences, or it can be used when a party's only proposal is the continuation of existing practices.[79]

Extensive negotiation in and of itself will not justify a finding of surface bargaining because the National Labor Relations Act does not compel parties to agree to proposals or to make concessions. Hard bargaining on a major issue does not exhibit bad faith because a party is not required to yield on a position fairly maintained. Even if the parties exhibit open hostility, surface bargaining may not be charged if the totality of the bargaining process complies with the dictates of the act.

The NLRB uses these factors when considering an unfair labor charge for surface bargaining:

1. Prior bargaining history of the parties
2. Parties' willingness to make concessions
3. The character of exchanged proposals and demands
4. Any dilatory tactics used during negotiations
5. Conditions imposed by either party as necessary to reaching an agreement
6. Unilateral changes made during the bargaining process in conditions subject to bargaining
7. Communications by employer to individual employees
8. Any unfair labor practices committed during bargaining[80]

Although the National Labor Relations Act does not require a party to make concessions, courts have consistently viewed a willingness to make concessions as evidence of good faith. Parties are encouraged to engage in **auction bargaining**, in which parties state their positions, make proposals, and then trade off on those proposals to arrive at agreeable terms. Refusal to make any concessions, evidenced by inflexibility on major issues, can be held as bad faith. An intransigent attitude on some issues may be acceptable if bargaining continues on other issues.[81]

The NLRB in its totality review considers the degree to which either party stalls or uses **delaying tactics** to avoid collective bargaining. Obviously, a complete refusal to meet and to bargain violates the act. Scheduling meetings infrequently or canceling scheduled meetings can also evidence bad faith. Prolonged discussions on formalities designed to thwart the collective bargaining process will be considered bad faith. The number or length of negotiation sessions alone cannot determine good or bad faith, but the NLRB frequently reviews meeting history to determine an employer's charge of bad faith. Also, although there is no hard-and-fast rule as to how many or how long, a review of case decisions shows the board's preference for frequent meetings—79 in 11 months, 11 in 5 months, 11 in 4 months, and 37 in 10 months.[82]

Employers may be guilty of bad faith if they unilaterally change conditions, such as employees' wages, rates of pay, or hours of employment, during contract negotiations. One employer violated the act when it unilaterally rescinded a long-standing practice of allowing employees to participate in blood drives during paid work time after an impasse.[83] If such changes in benefits are considered better than those being offered at the table, bad faith may be evidenced.[84] The NLRB has ruled in decertification situations, however, that there must be a causal connection between the unilateral change in benefits and the employee dissatisfaction with the union.[85] The act seeks to avoid this attempt to bypass the union and to deal directly with employees. However, there are exceptions to this rule. If an impasse is reached that is not the result of the employer's bad faith, a unilateral increase of benefits is not evidence of bad faith. The NLRB has held that it is a violation of the act to put into place a wage proposal on impasse that allows for continual adjustments by the employer based on "marketplace pay."[86]

An increasing number of employers have tried to present a "business necessity" defense for making unilateral changes when a collective bargaining agreement is not in effect. Such a defense has been successful in limited cases in which the employer demonstrated a good-faith inability to maintain the status quo because of necessary business considerations.[87]

Bypassing the bargaining representation by attempting to **negotiate directly with employees** will often be held as a violation of the duty to bargain in good faith. The courts, in reviewing the National Labor Relations Act, found it was the employer's duty to recognize the union and conduct negotiations through the union rather than deal directly with employees. This is an obligation even if the employer traditionally had contracts with individual workers. The collective bargaining contract will supersede such contracts.[88] One exception to this rule is that if a union refuses a final offer, the employer may communicate that offer directly to employees.

The good-faith test includes the duty to send negotiators to the table with sufficient **authority** to carry on meaningful negotiations. All attempts to delay commitment by the recourse of management representatives to check with some final authority are scrutinized closely for evidence of bad faith. However, the obligation of the union representative to take a contract back for a vote of union members before acceptance is not a violation of the duty to bargain in good faith.

Unfair labor practices during contract negotiations evidence bad faith. Threats to close a plant or to engage in discriminating layoffs during bargaining have been held to be in bad faith. To encourage the decertification of a union or to assist employees in the decertification process has also been found to obstruct the bargaining process.

DUTY TO FURNISH INFORMATION

The employer has a duty to furnish information to the union enabling it to carry on the negotiation process. Often, the employees are unable to collect relevant data about an employer's business without the employer's cooperation. If the National Labor Relations Act did not support this duty to furnish information, much of the collective bargaining process would be futile. As with the duty to bargain, the duty to furnish information arises only after a request for information is made in good faith. A union may be subject to a charge of an unfair labor practice if it requests information only to harass or humiliate the employer.

1. *Relevancy.*   Within liberal interpretations, the NLRB has said that information requested must be relevant to the union's right to represent its members. The union need not prove that the particular information requested is related to a currently discussed item if the subject matter is part of the overall negotiations.

2. *Financial information of company.*   When an employer claims financial inability to meet a union wage demand, the financial information of the employer's company becomes relevant. The Supreme Court held that if such a claim by the employer is important enough to be made at the table, it requires some proof of its accuracy.[89] The board has extended this rule to actual claims of financial inability. Refusal to grant wage increases because the employer claims it could not stay competitive or would lose the profit margin was held by the board to invoke financial inability. Therefore, financial data become relevant. In the absence of such a claim, an employer's financial records can be denied the union's bargaining team. The employer may see nondisclosure of financial information as a reaffirmation of management prerogative and by the employees as an obstacle to effective bargaining.[90] In a very narrow interpretation of previous Court decisions, the NLRB has denied a union's right to financial information when the employer merely claimed it could not meet the union's wage demands and stay competitive.[91] A later federal court opinion, however, ruled that an employer had asserted an "inability to pay" when it said that "competitive pressures" prevented it from agreeing to union contract demands.[92]

3. *Prompt delivery of information in workable form.* Bad faith may be evidenced if requested information is not delivered in a timely manner or is delivered in an unreasonable, useless form. An employer may claim that compiling requested data is unduly burdensome, but he or she must be flexible and should suggest alternatives. If the information is given in a form generally accepted in business, a union's request for a different form will not be binding on the employer. And when the employer allows the union access to all its records, it need not furnish information in a more organized form.

4. *Information that must be furnished.* Almost all areas touching on mandatory bargaining have been open to union requests for information. However, employers frequently refuse requests by the union to furnish wage information. The board, supported by lower courts and the Supreme Court, has found little if any justification for such refusals. The statutory requirement that wages be subject to collective bargaining extends to wages paid to particular employees, to groups of employees, and to methods of computing compensation. The union's right to information may include employees even outside the bargaining unit or in other plants operated by the employer.

Refusal to Bargain

The labor organization, like the employer, is charged with a duty under the Taft-Hartley Amendments to bargain in good faith. Failure to do so can result in an unfair labor practice charge. Basically, the good-faith requirement is the same as for employers and involves having an open mind in meeting and conferring with employers to reach an ultimate agreement. Refusal to sign an agreement the union and employer have come to terms on is an unfair labor practice. Insistence on being recognized as the exclusive bargaining agent for an inappropriate unit or when majority status is not held is also an unfair labor practice. Other unfair labor practices charged against a union are explored in the contract negotiations discussed in the next chapter.

THE AUTHORITY OF THE NLRB

An unfair labor practice charge comes to the NLRB through procedures similar to election petitions. The party claiming injury files an appropriate form with a regional office of the NLRB (see Figure 4-3). An initial investigation is held, and if merit is found to the charge and the regional director cannot convince the parties to settle, a hearing is held before an administrative law judge. The decision of the administrative law judge may be appealed to the NLRB, which will decide the case through a subpanel of three members randomly selected by its executive secretary.[93]

A party who disagrees with an NLRB decision can appeal to a federal court. Recent statistics, however, show that less than 3 percent of the unfair labor practice cases brought to the NLRB actually ended up in a litigation process, either in the NLRB or in federal court. The study demonstrated how cases are resolved through the NLRB process. When a complaint is filed, it is assigned to an agent of the regional director in the NLRB region with jurisdiction over the parties. The agent is under tight time restraints to investigate the charges and make a recommendation to the regional director. Statistics show that the decision of a regional director to issue a complaint or not almost always determines the ultimate outcome of the charges. With that in mind, the practice of the NLRB regional directors is to let the parties know which way the decision is going to go and to give the losing party a choice of withdrawing (if the charging party is going to lose) or offering a settlement (if the charged party is going to lose).[94]

FORM EXEMPT UNDER 44 U.S.C. 3512

UNITED STATES OF AMERICA
NATIONAL LABOR RELATIONS BOARD
CHARGE AGAINST EMPLOYER

DO NOT WRITE IN THIS SPACE	
Case	Date Filed

INSTRUCTIONS:
File an original and 4 copies of this charge with NLRB Regional Director for the region in which the alleged unfair labor practice occurred or is occurring.

1. EMPLOYER AGAINST WHOM CHARGE IS BROUGHT

a. Name of Employer	b. Number of Workers Employed

c. Address *(street, city, State, ZIP Code)*	d. Employer Representative	e. Telephone No.
		Fax No.

f. Type of Establishment *(factory, mine, wholesaler, etc.)*	g. Identify Principal Product or Service

h. The above-named employer has engaged in and is engaging in unfair labor practices within the meaning of Section 8(a), subsections (1) and *(list subsections)* _____ of the National Labor Relations Act, and these unfair labor practices are unfair practices affecting commerce within the meaning of the Act.

2. Basis of the Charge *(set forth a clear and concise statement of the facts constituting the alleged unfair labor practices.)*

By the above and other acts, the above-named employer has interfered with, restrained, and coerced employees in the exercise of the rights guaranteed in Section 7 of the Act.

3. Full name of party filing charge *(if labor organization, give full name, including local name and number)*

4a. Address *(street and number, city, State, and ZIP Code)*	4b. Telephone No.
	Fax No.

5. Full name of national or international labor organization of which it is an affiliate or constituent unit *(to be filled in when charge is filed by a labor organization)*

6. DECLARATION
I declare that I have read the above charge and that the statements are true to the best of my knowledge and belief.

By _____
(Signature of representative or person making charge)

_____
(Title, if any)

Fax No. _____

Address _____

_____ _____
(Telephone No.) Date

WILLFUL FALSE STATEMENTS ON THIS CHARGE CAN BE PUNISHED BY FINE AND IMPRISONMENT (U.S. CODE, TITLE 18, SECTION 1001)

FIGURE 4-3 United States of America National Labor Relations Board Charge Against Employer

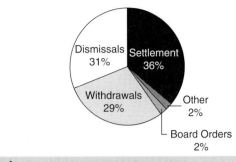

FIGURE 4-4   Dispositions of NLRB Cases, 2004

SOURCE: Adapted from the "Sixty-Ninth Annual Report of the National Labor Relations Board for Fiscal Year ending September 30, 2004" at page 15.

The success of this precharging process can be seen in the statistics in Figure 4-4 showing the disposition of NLRB cases in a typical year in which some withdrawals and dismissals were resolved before complaints were issued.

As presidential appointees, board members are part of the political process, and their decision making should not be viewed as a pure exercise in administrative law. Recent studies indicate a high probability that board decisions in unfair labor practices reflect the appointing president's political philosophy toward labor–management relations. Frequent board turnover can influence the stability of decisions, having a negative impact on the national labor-management relations policy.[95] Critics and supporters alike noted a dramatic shift in board decisions beginning with the administration of Ronald Reagan in 1980. Union attorneys cite a number of those decisions as undermining employees' basic rights under the National Labor Relations Act,[96] whereas management attorneys saw the shift as the proper return to a middle ground with the board recovering from a prounion bias.[97] Union advocates cheered the return of a Democrat to the White House in 1992 as the opportunity to change the direction of the NLRB. They stopped cheering with the return of a Republican to the White House in 2000, as seen in Profile 4-3.

Unfair Labor Practice Settlement Program

In 1995 the NLRB gave its administrative law judges (ALJs) a new authority in addition to their traditional one of serving as judges in trials to resolve labor disputes. The NLRB created the Unfair Labor Practice (ULP) Settlement Program, which was instituted to speed up the resolution of disputes between unions and employers. Under the program the ALJ does not serve as a trial judge, but instead serves as a facilitator (mediator) who arranges conferences between the parties in an effort to reach a voluntary settlement. Therefore, in general the ULP settlement judge is assigned to a case "to conduct settlement negotiations" in an open-ended, informal process similar to other Alternative Dispute Resolutions (ADR) processes that are a fast-growing alternative to court proceedings. A 2005 study of the effectiveness of the NLRB's new ULP Settlement Program found that the parties that have utilized the program reported several positive perceptions including the speed, cost, and process (see Table 4-1).[98]

Section 10(J): Court Injunctions

Section 10(j) of the National Labor Relations Act permits the NLRB to seek a federal court injunction in situations in which the action of the union or employer might cause

POLITICS AND THE NLRB

Congress created the NLRB during Franklin Roosevelt's New Deal era to administer the law that guarantees employees the right to organize into unions and bargain collectively—or to refrain from organizing. Congress thought it should be made up of impartial government members.

But nowadays the agency is stacked with labor-side and management-side attorneys who hew closely to their ideological backgrounds, legal scholars say. "It's become almost purely politics," said Joan Flynn, professor of law at the Cleveland-Marshall College of Law at Cleveland State University. Craig Brown of Duvin, Cahn & Hutton, a management-side Cleveland law firm, said the board "has succumbed to a terrible political bias. . . . You see it in its very strident decisions."

Fred Feinstein, the NLRB's general counsel under President Clinton, thinks consensus appointments are a thing of the past. "The model is no longer a board of people in the middle," said Feinstein, now a senior fellow at the University of Maryland's School of Public Policy. "It's like, two for you and three for me."

These observers say they are not singling out current members but rather noting a trend that started about 20 years ago. Board Chairman Robert Battista, a Bush appointee who came from a 35-year practice with a Detroit firm representing employers, said the NLRB has historically been a contentious agency, with "two fairly significant power groups" vying for dominance. But he said today's Republican-controlled board is not biased. "We look dispassionately at our cases," he said. The board has five seats, usually three Republicans and two Democrats or the opposite ratio, depending which party holds the White House. Even the board's critics say it has a long, legitimate tradition of swinging toward management when a Republican is president and toward labor when a Democrat is. The board was meant to be politically responsive, Flynn said.

Until the 1950s, though, board members were government and university officials with at least the appearance of neutrality. President Eisenhower broke with tradition and nominated the first pro-management lawyer. What really galled labor, though, was another Eisenhower choice—an industrial-relations director for two companies who would cast the deciding vote on many hot issues awaiting board rulings, Flynn says in a recent *Ohio State Law Journal* article on the NLRB's transformation. Flynn said another NLRB watershed came when President Nixon chose an Illinois man who had spent almost his entire 23-year career as a management lawyer.

The AFL-CIO's George Meany fought the nomination, arguing that partisan appointments should be banned on both sides. Meany noted that members often returned to the private sector after a few years at the NLRB and could hardly be expected to vote against their imminent self-interest. Nixon's candidate cleared the Senate by unanimous vote, though—with even labor allies such as Sen. Edward Kennedy approving—and unions apparently concluded that it was fruitless to oppose partisan nominees, Flynn said. In short order, "the old rules were off," with both sides backing candidates from the ideological poles, she said.

Politics at the board were heightened by a shift to greater Senate control over the choice of board members (in practice, a small number of senators or even one senator drives the process) at the expense of the president, who has a bigger constituency and stronger incentive to be moderate, Flynn said. Senate-led appointments also are more prone to being hijacked by narrow interest groups such as the right-wing National Right to Work Committee, which today can seize the lead over mainstream organizations such as the Business Roundtable, she said.

Academic experts and labor lawyers who study the board say hardened party lines have led to a string of recent decisions that make it harder to organize workers. The Bush board in recent cases reduced temporary workers' ability to unionize. It also gave companies expanded leeway to lock out workers during labor disputes (an appeals court later refused to enforce the decision). The board

(*continued*)

made it more difficult for unions to get financial information from companies that said they couldn't afford union demands. The board also decided that disabled workers employed as janitors could not join a union with able-bodied janitors because their relationship with their employer was "primarily rehabilitative." And the board said nonunion employees don't have the right to have a coworker present at disciplinary hearings—a decision that affects the 87 percent of American workers who are not in unions. Defenders of the current board say it is merely restoring sense to out-of-kilter NLRB decisions that came from the Clinton board.

"Beauty is in the eye of the beholder," said John Raudabaugh, who was tapped by the first President Bush and served in the early 1990s. "Is it really fair to complain about overturning precedent when you're just returning to the way it was for decades?" Board chairman Battista rejects complaints that the board is unbalanced or heedlessly overturning prior decisions. He said the Bush board has reversed eight times—far fewer than the 54 cases overturned by the Clinton panel. Raudabaugh points out that some of the recent reversals are merely a return to previous decisions that the Clinton board had overturned. For example, a decision by the Bush board concerning graduate students reverted to an earlier case that found graduate teaching assistants were ineligible for unions. Raudabaugh agrees, saying that grad assistants' wages are, in essence, a scholarship grant to help finance their education.

Raudabaugh worries, though, that the board is losing respect because of its reversals. In fact, neither management- nor labor-side lawyers are happy with how the labor board oscillates, Flynn said. "It makes it very difficult to counsel their clients," she said. "What's legal today may be illegal tomorrow."

In fact, the NLRB is prepared to take up one of the most explosive issues in its history: The board has agreed to hear several cases that would severely curb card check. Unions of late have had much better success in organizing workers with card check than with campaigns that end in secret-ballot elections overseen by the NLRB. Unions say elections give employers months, even years, in which to coerce and intimidate employees. Employers say card check is coercive because workers don't get the privacy of a secret ballot. Battista, the board chairman, says the issue is at the top of his agenda for 2006. "This is huge," Flynn said. "If they do what they have suggested they might do, it would turn 40 years of labor law on its head."

SOURCE: Alison Grant, "Tipping the Scales or Restoring Balance?" *The Plain Dealer* (December 16, 2005). Used with permission.

TABLE 4-1 The NLRB Unfair Labor Practice Settlement Program (Participant Perceptions)

Variable	Mean (5-pt. scale)
1. Fairness	3.76
2. Impartial judge	3.86
3. Judge understood position	3.69
4. Provided opportunity to present my views	3.57
5. Not too formal or informal	3.80
6. Satisfied with outcome	3.25
7. Judges' skill	3.41
8. Process saved costs	3.29
9. Satisfaction with speed	3.62
10. Would recommend process to others	3.65

SOURCE: Lamont Stallworth, Arup Varma, and John T. Delaney, "The NLRB's Unfair Labor Practice Settlement," *Dispute Resolution Journal,* 59, no. 4 (Nov. 2004–Jan. 2005) pp. 22–29. Used by permission.

INTERNET
FORM NLRB-508
(6-90)

FORM EXEMPT UNDER 44 U.S.C. 3512

UNITED STATES OF AMERICA
NATIONAL LABOR RELATIONS BOARD
**CHARGE AGAINST LABOR ORGANIZATION
OR ITS AGENTS**

DO NOT WRITE IN THIS SPACE	
Case	Date Filed

INSTRUCTIONS: File an original and 4 copies of this charge and an additional copy for each organization, each local, and each individual named in item 1 with the NLRB Regional Director of the region in which the alleged unfair labor practice occurred or is occurring.

1. LABOR ORGANIZATION OR ITS AGENTS AGAINST WHICH CHARGE IS BROUGHT

a. Name	b. Union Representative to contact

c. Telephone No.	d. Address *(street, city, state and ZIP code)*

e. The above-named organization(s) or its agents has *(have)* engaged in and is *(are)* engaging in unfair labor practices within the meaning of section 8(b), subsection(s) *(list subsections)* _____ of the National Labor Relations Act, and these unfair labor practices are unfair practices affecting commerce within the meaning of the Act.

2. Basis of the Charge *(set forth a clear and concise statement of the facts constituting the alleged unfair labor practices)*

3. Name of Employer	4. Telephone No.

5. Location of plant involved *(street, city, state and ZIP code)*	6. Employer representative to contact

7. Type of establishment *(factory, mine, wholesaler, etc.)*	8. Identify principal product or service	9. Number of workers employed

10. Full name of party filing charge

11. Address of party filing charge *(street, city, state and ZIP code)*	12. Telephone No.

13. DECLARATION
I declare that I have read the above charge and that the statements therein are true to the best of my knowledge and belief.

By _____
(signature of representative or person making charge) _____ *(title or office, if any)*

Address _____ _____
(Telephone No.) *(date)*

WILLFUL FALSE STATEMENTS ON THIS CHARGE CAN BE PUNISHED BY FINE AND IMPRISONMENT (U. S. CODE, TITLE 18, SECTION 1001)

*U.S. GPO: 2000-464-640/29074

FIGURE 4-5 U.S. National Labor Relations Board Charge Against Labor Organization or its Agents

substantial harm to the other side. The court, in response, can then order either party to resume or desist from a certain action. In general, the NLRB must demonstrate that the unfair labor practice, if left alone, will irreparably harm the other side before a final NLRB decision can be administered, or "justice delayed is justice denied." In the 1994–1996 baseball strike, for example, players would have found their abilities slipping with increasing age, so a U.S. district court ordered the owners to abide by the old contract and to "play ball" until a new one was reached. Some baseball fans believed that the NLRB saved the game. Most Section 10(j) cases fall within the following 13 categories:[99]

1. Union organizing campaign interference
2. Subcontracting work to outside employers
3. Withdrawing recognition of the union
4. Undermining or denigrating the members of the union's bargaining team
5. Granting exclusive representation to a minority union
6. Successor employer refusing to recognize and bargain
7. Bad-faith conduct during negotiations
8. Picketing violence
9. Strike or picketing notice or waiting period violations
10. Employer refusal to allow protected activity on private property
11. Retaliation for NLRB processes
12. Closedown of operations during litigation
13. Union coercion to achieve unlawful object

Figure 4-5 is a form used in filing charges against unions.

UNFAIR LABOR PRACTICES IN THE PUBLIC SECTOR

For 1.9 million federal government employees worldwide, the Federal Labor Relations Authority (FLRA) is the independent government agency charged with administering federal labor–management relations programs. Included in that role is adjudicating unfair labor practice claims involving federal government agencies. Modeled after the National Labor Relations Act, the Federal Labor Relations Act creates rights and obligations on the part of management, unions, and employees in a federal government workplace represented by a labor union. As shown in Case 4-3, the employees of the NLRB appeal their complaints of unfair labor practices under the Federal Labor Relations Act also.

REFUSAL TO BARGAIN—*NLRB V. FLRA*   CASE 4-3

This case arises under Title VII of the Civil Service Reform Act of 1978, commonly known as the Federal Service Labor-Management Relations Act (see Chapter 1). The act, modeled after the National Labor Relations Act, confers on federal employees the right to engage in collective bargaining with respect to conditions of employment through their chosen representatives. The act requires each agency to "negotiate in good faith" with the exclusive representative of its employees for the purpose of arriving at a collective bargaining agreement. The range of subjects over which agencies are required to bargain is not unlimited. In particular,

continued

REFUSAL TO BARGAIN—*NLRB V. FLRA*—continued

the act establishes certain "management rights" that are exempt from the negotiation process.

The NLRB's employees, as federal employees, are covered by the act. Disputes between the NLRB and its employees are taken to the Federal Labor Relations Authority (FLRA). This dispute concerns a change in the NLRB's approach to conducting performance appraisals of professional and clerical employees in its field offices. Under the "old" system, an employee's immediate supervisor would prepare a written appraisal and would then meet with the employee to discuss the appraisal. Thereafter, the supervisor would forward his evaluation to higher-level officials, including the regional director, who in turn would supply an assessment of the employee's performance. The employee would receive copies of the assessments and be allowed to comment before they were finalized and sent to the board's Washington headquarters. Under the "new" review process, the appraising officials and the regional director meet in advance to determine the performance rating each employee will receive. Once the regional director, who is now the sole "reviewing official," determines the outcome of the appraisal, a written report is prepared and furnished to the employee in "one voice," that is, without dissenting opinions.

During collective bargaining negotiations, the union sought to negotiate the performance appraisal process by proposing a return to a modified version of the "old" appraisal process, giving employees more of an opportunity to respond to the appraisals either before or as soon as they became final. The NLRB refused to bargain over the union proposal on the ground that it infringed on the rights reserved to management under the act. The union appealed to the FLRA.

The FLRA agreed that the NLRB was partly correct in that *some* of what the union proposed was not negotiable because it impinged on the NLRB's management rights. However, some of what the union proposed was negotiable under a section of the act that allowed for negotiating appropriate arrangements for employees *adversely affected* by the exercise of management rights. The FLRA determined that the proposal, which would require the NLRB to change the manner in which it conducts employee performance appraisals, was negotiable under that exception. The FLRA ordered the NLRB to negotiate with the union.

The NLRB filed suit and requested the court to review the FLRA order. The NLRB pointed out that the "adversely affected" exception in the act was to be narrowly applied so that the scope of negotiations was limited to arrangements tailored to redress only those employees adversely affected, not an arrangement to address potentially adverse effects to all employees.

DECISION

As the proposal from the union was to negotiate a change in the appraisal process affecting all employees, those who received positive as well as negative evaluations, the court found that the proposal might not be sufficiently tailored to redress the harms suffered by the particular employees who are in fact adversely affected by the performance appraisal process. Therefore, the court agreed to grant the petition for review and denied the FLRA's cross petition for enforcement of its order.

SOURCE: Adapted from *NLRB v. FLRA*, 144 LRRM 2129 (August 31, 1993).

In the public sector, unfair labor practice charges fall into the same type of areas as in the private sector. It is an unfair labor practice for agency management to threaten or retaliate against employees for seeking union representation or for refusing to provide a union information necessary to fulfill its representational responsibilities. Similarly, unions cannot discriminate against unit employees because they fail to join the union. And both parties must negotiate in good faith. Although individuals and agencies may file unfair labor practice charges, historically unions have filed 95 percent of all unfair labor practice charges filed with the FLRA.[100]

The FLRA launched an innovative approach to resolving unfair labor practice charges. Regional directors who investigate unfair labor practices were directed to undertake "intervention" techniques to assist the parties in resolving the underlying dispute rather than determining the merits of the charge. The following criteria are to be used to determine whether to offer intervention as an alternative case-processing technique to the parties:

1. If there are numerous charges filed within the same time frame involving the same parties, it is an indication that the dispute arises from a lack of communication and understanding between the parties rather than a legal dispute over statutory rights and obligations.
2. Both parties must agree to participate in the intervention process, or else the FLRA cannot suspend its statutory duty to investigate and adjudicate unfair labor practice charges.
3. Both parties must be committed to resolving their dispute and must send representatives to participate in the process who have the authority to resolve the dispute.
4. The charges should concern institutional and relationship issues, such as the duty to bargain, rather than individual statutory rights to engage in protected activity. The things supervisors and managers generally may and may not do in organizational campaigns are summarized by the "TIPS" and "FORE" guidelines.
5. The experience of both parties in federal sector labor management relations may dictate whether they can benefit from intervention. A "newer" relationship could probably benefit more.
6. Some disputes are not "ripe" for resolution through an intervention. For example, either the union or the agency may be on the verge of changing its officials for various reasons. The process could be frustrated by the presence of "lame-duck" officials.
7. The ability of the central office of the FLRA to provide follow-up support to the regional directors after the dispute is resolved.[101]

SUMMARY

Employer unfair labor practices impede the collective bargaining process. Unfair labor practices, as contained in the National Labor Relations Act, include interference with employees in the exercise of their rights, domination of an employee union, discrimination against union members, and refusal to bargain. The act imposed a duty in good faith on the employer and the labor organization, subject to its provisions. That good faith is evidenced by the total conduct of the parties toward the collective bargaining process.

Because the act guarantees employees the right to refrain from union activities, attempts by labor unions to coerce employees to join is a violation. A union must fairly represent all its members, and a breach of that duty is an unfair labor practice. The same is true of a union's duty to bargain in good faith with the employer.

The FLRA has a role similar to the NLRB in adjudicating unfair labor practices in the federal government. Federal agencies cannot interfere with employees' right to join together for collective bargaining purposes, and public-sector unions cannot violate an employee's right not to join a union.

CASE STUDIES

Case Study 4-1   Unfair Labor Practice by an Employer

The employer manufactures automobile parts and supplies those parts to major auto manufacturers. The UAW filed a representation petition to unionize the employer's workforce. Between November 14, 1994, when the petition was filed, and January 12, 1995, when the election was held, the employer did the following:

1. The human resources director distributed a letter to employees asserting that two-thirds of the 600 plants that had closed in their state over the past 20 years had been unionized.
2. The employer distributed an article concerning Ford's decision to move a parts contract from a supplier whose workforce had gone out on strike, emphasizing that the striking union was the UAW.
3. Around Christmas, the employer relocated production of a Ford part to another one of its plants at a location not subject to the pending election petition. The employer offered no explanation for the move.
4. The employer told the employees that negotiations on a renewal contract with a customer were being held in abeyance until the outcome of the union election, although the customer also had issues of quality and delivery to discuss.
5. The employer displayed large photo posters of closed manufacturing plants and distributed a letter noting that all the plants had been unionized.
6. On January 9, 1995, the president of the company sent a letter to employees telling of his concern that its manufacturing partners would become nervous and go elsewhere if the company developed "a reputation for not being dependable because of labor problems, a UAW-led strike, or even the possibility of a strike every time the contract comes up for renewal."
7. On January 10, 1995, the division manager told employees that the employer was concerned about the impact of the union vote on its manufacturing customers. On January 9 and 10, one such customer did a very visible "walk-through" inspection of the facility accompanied by numerous managers.

When the ballots were counted, the union lost 196 to 154. The union filed an unfair labor charge against the employer, charging that its campaign tactics had violated the National Labor Relations Act and invalidated the results

SOURCE: Adapted from *SPX Corporation*, 151 LRRM 1300 (1995).

QUESTIONS

1. Which, if any, of the employer's actions might the court find violated the National Labor Relations Act and therefore might cause the election to be set aside?
2. Recognizing that this election took place in 1995, do you think the court might find that the employees could have seen through the employer's tactics and voted the way they wanted despite the employer's actions?
3. Would you have been swayed by the employer's actions to the point you could not have voted with "freedom of choice"?

Case Study 4-2 Unfair Labor Practice by a Union

A decertification election was held at a plant owned by a Japanese company. The appeal to the NLRB by the company and one employee was that the election, in which the decertification petition was defeated, be set aside on the basis of the union's unfair labor practice. The company and the petitioning employee charged that the union's patterns of threats and intimidation, as well as its racially oriented acts, were so extensive and persuasive that they prevented the employees' exercise of free choice.

The company presented testimony at the hearing regarding the following activities:

1. An employee's tires were slashed after he had been identified in the union's newsletter as withdrawing his union membership. In addition, one of his wheels fell off when he left work; he discovered that the lugs had been removed and were only a few feet from where the car had been parked.
2. Another employee, who had headed up the decertification petition, received numerous anonymous obscene telephone calls.
3. A union steward intimidated an employee along the roadway by slowing down so the employee would pass and then speeding up and quickly slamming on the brakes, causing the employee to do the same and swerve in order to avoid an accident. The union steward had used the same harassing highway tactics on another employee who was driving with her daughter and five grandchildren.
4. One employee was followed home and found her fuel line cut the next day.
5. Another employee discovered a scratch down the entire side of her car, which had been parked at the plant.

6. An employee wearing a "Vote No" button was threatened with physical harm by a fellow employee.
7. Several employees received intimidating telephone calls at their homes from both union agents and anonymous callers. The employees' children answered some of the calls, and threatening statements were then made to the children.
8. Two employees were overheard discussing the rumors of threats surrounding the campaign, and one of the employees said, "Sometimes it takes this kind of thing to get the point across."
9. At two union organizing meetings, at which more than 100 employees were present, a union official ended his speech with the following quote: "We beat the Japs after Pearl Harbor, and we can beat them again." Anti-Japanese graffiti appeared on bathroom walls, and a steward wore a shirt and work tags printed with the phrases "Remember Pearl Harbor" and "Japs go home."

The union's position was that it should not be charged with an unfair labor practice because of the alleged activities of individuals who were not acting at the union's direction. Union membership and support for the union can cause emotions to run high; it happens in every election. But there was no evidence that the employees were prevented from exercising their free choice in the election itself. The anti-Japanese statements were unfortunate but mere rhetoric. Such rhetoric violates none of the established NLRB standards for conducting a fair election.

SOURCE: Adapted from *YKK (U.S.A.), Inc.,* 115 LRRM 1186 (1984).

QUESTIONS

1. Would you set aside the election results and order another election? Explain your answer.
2. How could the union have stopped individuals from the intimidating actions that allegedly went on in this case?
3. Does the racial nature of the rhetoric involved in this case put a heavier burden on the union than does the usual rhetoric about an employer? Explain your answer.

KEY TERMS AND CONCEPTS

- antiunion animus
- auction bargaining
- authority
- boulwarism
- concerted activity
- delaying tactics
- dual-motive discrimination case
- *Electromation* case
- employer unfair labor practices

- FORE
- good-faith bargaining
- good-faith reasonable doubt
- labor organization unfair labor practices
- negotiate directly with employees
- pretext discrimination case
- primary strike

- prohibited conduct
- *Republic Aviation* case
- salting
- Section 10(j)
- surface bargaining
- TIPS
- totality of conduct doctrine
- 24-hour rule
- Weingarten rule

REVIEW QUESTIONS

1. What might the NLRB consider to be a breach of the good-faith bargaining principle?
2. How does the NLRB review an unfair labor practice charge of surface bargaining?
3. Is an employer always required to furnish any data requested by a union during negotiations? If not, list some exceptions.
4. What are the rules that employers and union organizers must follow during an organizational campaign?
5. Under what circumstances can an employer poll employees to determine their desire to join a union?

6. What is the difference between an employer's support of and domination of a union?
7. When is an employer illegally discriminating against employees because of their union activities?
8. What union activities are prohibited under the Taft-Hartley unfair labor practices provision?
9. Are federal government employees protected from unfair labor practices in the same way as private-sector employees?
10. How do "intervention" techniques in federal labor-management relations differ from the process under the NLRB?

YOU BE THE ARBITRATOR
Bereavement Leave

ARTICLE 23
BEREAVEMENT LEAVE

Section 23.1. If a death occurs in the employee's immediate family (spouse, children), employee's family (mother, father, step-parents), a grandfather, grandmother, father-in-law, mother-in-law, person in loco parentis, and any member of the employee's family residing in the employee's residence, such employee shall be granted three (3) days' funeral leave, consecutive and contiguous to the death without loss of pay, benefits, days off, holidays, or vacation time, provided that such leave may be extended, within discretion of the Sheriff, based on individual circumstances. If the death requires that the employee travel more than 200 miles, the Sheriff may, at the request of the employee, allow up to two (2) additional workdays as a bereavement leave.

Facts

The employer provides the statutory law enforcement services to the citizens of Fulton County, Ohio. The grievant is a deputy. The grievant worked on the night shift, and his days off were Wednesday and Thursday. On the evening of Thursday, June 21, the grievant's paternal grandmother died. The grievant was not informed of her death until after he had finished his shift on Friday, June 22. He was also informed that the funeral was going to be Sunday, June 24. The grievant reported for work for his regular shift on Saturday, June 23. The grievant then informed his supervisor of the death and indicated that he would be taking Sunday, June 24, off to attend the funeral. The grievant's request was approved, and the grievant then requested two additional days of bereavement leave, that is, Monday, June 25, and Tuesday, June 26, which was made known to the grievant's supervisors. The grievant filled out a "Request for Leave" form as required. However, after the fact, the employer reviewed his request in light of the collective bargaining agreement (CBA) and decided the grievant was not entitled to bereavement pay for Tuesday on the ground that the three days of bereavement leave here should have been Friday, Saturday, and Sunday. Nevertheless, the employer chose only to disallow the Tuesday bereavement pay. The grievant appealed.

Issue

Did the employer violate the provisions of the CBA when it denied bereavement leave to the grievant?

Position of the Parties

The employer argues that under the CBA, the grant of three days' funeral leave must be consecutive and

contiguous to the death (see Article 23, Bereavement Leave, above). So grievant was entitled to bereavement pay only for Sunday, as the death occurred on Thursday. The approval of any extension of that leave is within the discretion of the sheriff, who in this instance approved one day of the extension, Monday. Therefore, the grievant is not entitled to bereavement pay for Tuesday.

The union argues that the CBA does not require that the three bereavement days begin on the "first day" after the death, just that the days be near the death and be consecutive and contiguous to each other. When the employer approved the grievant's request for Sunday off, the three days of bereavement began, which means Monday and Tuesday should also count as bereavement days.

SOURCE: Adapted from *Fulton County Sheriff*, 116 LA 1773 (Arb. 2002).

QUESTIONS

1. As arbitrator, what would be your award and opinion in this arbitration?
2. Explain why the relevant provisions of the CBA as applied to the facts of this case dictate the award.

3. What actions might the employer and/or the union have taken to avoid this conflict?

What Do You Really Know About Organizational Campaign Unfair Labor Practices?

PURPOSE:

To give students an understanding of employer rights during an organizational campaign.

TASK:

Managers often have a great deal of influence with their employees. Thus, knowing what managers lawfully may and may not tell employees during a union organizing campaign is very important. They should be certain their actions do not unintentionally cause an unfair labor practice. You must determine if managers are generally allowed or prohibited from each of the following. Place an X in the most appropriate column:

	Allowed	Prohibited	
1.	_____	_____	Managers can ask employees how they intend to vote.
2.	_____	_____	Managers can promise employees a pay increase if the union is defeated.
3.	_____	_____	Managers can tell employees that the law allows the employer to permanently replace them if they strike.
4.	_____	_____	Managers can tell employees about the bad personal experiences they have had with unions.
5.	_____	_____	Managers can say, "If the union wins, there will be a strike."
6.	_____	_____	Mangers can visit the employees at home to discuss the campaign with their families.
7.	_____	_____	Managers can tell employees they can vote against the union even if they signed an authorization card.
8.	_____	_____	Managers can tell employees that management does not think the employees need a union to represent them.
9.	_____	_____	Managers can tell employees the plant will be closed if the union wins the election.
10.	_____	_____	Managers can tell employees that if a union is victorious, all current wages and benefits must be negotiated and could be reduced.

CHAPTER 5

Negotiating an Agreement

The Bargaining Process
Bargaining Techniques
Impasse
Bargaining in the Public Sector

Northwestern mechanics picket at St. Paul International Airport in September 2005.

Labor News

NORTHWEST AIRLINES THREATENS UNION WITH REPLACEMENT MECHANICS

On August 11, 2005, Northwest Airlines announced that it had 1,500 *trained* and *ready* replacement workers should the Aircraft Mechanics Fraternal Association Union decide to strike. The announcement came nine days before the union would be free to strike when the current contract expired. The bold strategy by Northwest was highly unusual because mechanics are highly skilled, licensed workers who repair and maintain airplanes. Most employers would find it extremely difficult if not impossible to find and train such a large number of highly skilled workers.

How did Northwest accomplish this feat? For 18 months management contacted mechanics laid off by other airlines and trained some of its own management personnel. In addition, Northwest announced it had 1,500 replacement flight attendants ready should its own flight attendants call a sympathy strike in support of the mechanics union. Again the replacements were managers and attendants laid off by other airlines.

Why did Northwest make the announcement and stage such a bold strategic move during contract negotiations? By announcing that it had over 3,000 replacement workers ready should the mechanics and flight attendants strike, the company hoped to convince those union members that a strike could cost them their jobs—and thus a strike might be avoided. The root cause for the move was Northwest's demand for $176 million in wage and benefit concessions from the union, as well as job cuts. Northwest claimed the cuts were needed to avoid the fate of bankruptcy that had already claimed United and US Airways and threatened Delta Airlines.

Ted Ludwig, president of the AMFA Local 33, was quoted as saying that Northwest had already "cut the union to the bone" from 9,500 members in 1999 to 2,900 in 2005 by shipping maintenance work to Hong Kong.

One major concern for Northwest, one might assume, was how the public might respond to the idea of flying in planes being repaired and maintained by replacement workers. One industry analyst, Terry Trippler of Cheapseats.com, noted that passengers might not notice the difference—if they continued to fly the 400 aircraft in the Northwest fleet.

SOURCE: Adapted from Robert Manor, "Northwest Says Replacements Ready If Mechanics Walk Out," *The Chicago Tribune* (August 12, 2005), pp. 3-1, 3-8.

Central to the collective bargaining process are the actual **negotiations** carried out by the parties to reach an agreement. Artful use of this process can improve the relationship between an employer and the employees and result in a profitable agreement for both parties. Unsuccessful negotiations can lead to work stoppages and a loss of profits and benefits. This chapter examines different techniques of bargaining, details of the bargaining process, and solutions to the bargaining impasse.

The bargaining process usually begins when one party wants to terminate or amend an existing contract. Most agreements provide for the automatic extension of an existing contract past the expiration date, usually for one year. Either party may initiate new negotiations by providing written explicit notice to the other party. A clause specifying automatic renewal and the process to begin new negotiations is included in 90 percent of labor agreements.[1]

THE BARGAINING PROCESS

The collective bargaining process begins long before the parties meet across the bargaining table. As discussed in previous chapters, the organization of units and the selection of the agent is a lengthy process necessary in determining the parties to a collective bargaining relationship.

People Who Bargain

Union Representatives

Although there are as many types of negotiators as there are negotiations, some generalizations can be made. National agreements require large negotiating teams, with members from several union offices, staff, and locals (see Figure 5-1 for the 2003 UAW–Ford national negotiating team and the 2003 UAW–DaimlerChrysler national negotiating team). The majority of negotiating takes place at the local level—either after a national agreement decides certain issues or because no national agreement exists.

A local union's negotiating team is made up of certain ex officio members, such as the president or one or more elected officers of the local union, and a chief steward or grievance committee member. In most negotiations involving craft unions, the business agent is part of the negotiating team and often the chief negotiator. For industrial unions, an international union representative who is a professional negotiator is often available to guide and counsel local union officials.

Although international representatives have no official status during local negotiations, their experience often puts them in a leadership role. They give guidance on the grievance process and set the tone for negotiations and, in the case of impasse, for pressure tactics. They play the role of mediator or assume a militant stand to allow the local representatives to appear reasonable.

Whatever the makeup of the union's negotiating team, its authority is somewhat limited by the membership. The union members usually delegate only provisional and temporary authority to the negotiating team to make a settlement. Usually, any final settlement must be presented to the total membership for a vote.

Management Representatives

The authority of the management negotiating team comes from top management and is generally a more complete delegation. Policy makers are often a part of the team. In negotiations involving a single employer, representatives may be the company's labor relations director or a production person and line executive, or there may be staff advisers such as the personnel director, financial officer, and a company lawyer. When a multiemployer association is involved, the companies often employ a labor relations adviser and negotiator who is equivalent to the international representative. This professional serves a role similar to that of the union counterpart by promoting the multiemployer organization, by preparing management counterproposals, and by conducting negotiations.

United Auto Workers (UAW) from left, Vice Presidents Nate Gooden, Gerald Bantom, Richard Shoemaker, President Ron Gettelfinger, and secretary-treasurer Elizabeth Bunn are shown at the negotiating table at Ford World Headquarters in 2003.

United Auto Workers President Ron Gettelfinger, center, with the union bargaining team at the start of contract negotiations with DaimlerChrysler in 2003.

FIGURE 5-1   UAW National Negotiating Committees, 2003

SOURCE: United Auto Workers, www.uaw.org Used by permission.

Negotiating Skills

Successful negotiations depend on the knowledge and skill of the negotiators. They must, through careful preparations, become knowledgeable about their own and the other side's positions on the bargaining issues. They prepare and propose workable, attainable, and realistic issues within the framework of the negotiations. For example, negotiators may develop strong economic positions to give the parties bargaining room during the negotiation process.

To use the acquired knowledge wisely, a negotiator develops an understanding of the opposition. Listening skills and the ability to communicate clearly are two cultivated techniques. A thick skin may be helpful because the other side may engage in personal attacks at some point in the negotiations. A negotiator realizes that such attacks are often necessary in satisfying a constituency.

The successful negotiator possesses personal integrity and courage.[2] At some point in the negotiations, agreements must be made. A negotiator's word or handshake is the basis for the agreement until it is committed to paper. The untrustworthy or faint of heart cannot bring collective bargaining negotiations to a successful conclusion.

Suggested attributes of the successful negotiator include the following:

1. Sets clear objectives
2. Does not hurry
3. Calls for a caucus when in doubt
4. Is prepared
5. Remains flexible
6. Examines continually why the other party acts as it does
7. Respects face-saving tactics employed by the opposition
8. Attempts to ascertain the real interest of the other party by the priority proposed
9. Actively listens
10. Builds a reputation for being fair but firm
11. Controls emotions
12. Remembers to evaluate each bargaining move in relation to all others
13. Measures bargaining moves against ultimate objectives
14. Pays close attention to the wording of proposals
15. Remembers that compromise is the key to successful negotiations; understands that no party can afford to win or lose all
16. Tries to understand people
17. Considers the impact of present negotiations on the future relationship of the parties[3]

Preparation and Choice of Bargaining Items

Many unions affiliate with larger international unions. If a master agreement is negotiated by the international, then the international controls all but local concerns. Preparation for negotiations on a master agreement is virtually nonstop, and preparations for the next negotiation begin as soon as a contract is signed. Preparation for contract negotiation on a local level, although not that extensive, is still necessary.

The first stage, preparation, involves analysis and planning. In analysis, information is gathered, and bargaining items are decided on, narrowing the issues to a manageable size. Planning forces the parties to evaluate and set priorities and to make realistic decisions about their demands. The parties' attention is focused on achievable goals. The parties are then ready for the second stage, the bargaining stage, which leads to the final stage, resolution (see Figure 5-2).

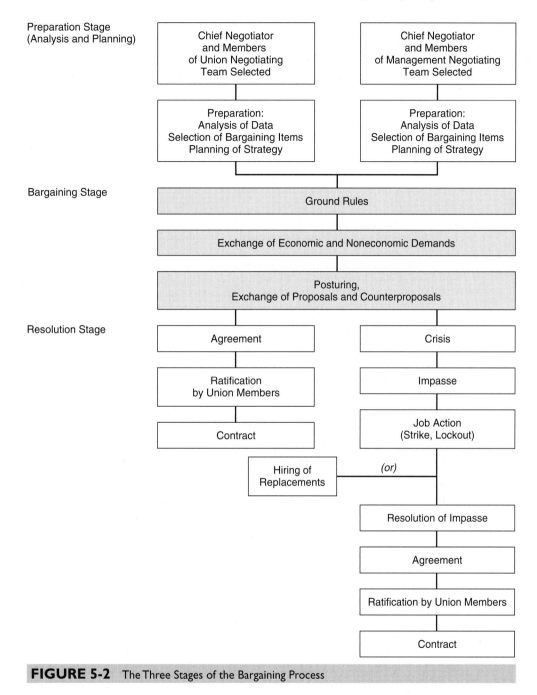

Preparation Stage
(Analysis and Planning)

Chief Negotiator
and Members
of Union Negotiating
Team Selected

Chief Negotiator
and Members
of Management Negotiating
Team Selected

Preparation:
Analysis of Data
Selection of Bargaining Items
Planning of Strategy

Preparation:
Analysis of Data
Selection of Bargaining Items
Planning of Strategy

Bargaining Stage

Ground Rules

Exchange of Economic and Noneconomic Demands

Posturing,
Exchange of Proposals and Counterproposals

Resolution Stage

Agreement

Crisis

Ratification
by Union Members

Impasse

Contract

Job Action
(Strike, Lockout)

Hiring of
Replacements

(or)

Resolution of Impasse

Agreement

Ratification by Union Members

Contract

FIGURE 5-2 The Three Stages of the Bargaining Process

Analysis

It is a function of law and common practice to decide what items to include in the collective bargaining session. The National Labor Relations Act provides that bargaining shall include rates of pay, wages, hours of employment, and conditions of employment.[4] Under enforcement of the unfair labor practice charge of refusal to bargain, the National Labor Relations Board (NLRB) determines which subjects fall under the law.

Tips from the Experts

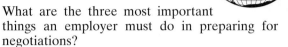

UNION

What are the three most important things for a union to do to prepare for negotiating a collective bargaining agreement?

1. Its homework as far as defending its own proposals
2. Its homework as far as anticipating management's proposals
3. Its homework as far as the politics of the negotiations: its own negotiating team as well as management's

You can never be overprepared for negotiations. Whether it is an art or a science, effective negotiation takes tremendous understanding of the substantive issues, a lot of creativity, and thoroughness as well as keen understanding of people and power. Successful negotiations require looking beyond what is in place to what is possible to create to achieve a result that gives everyone what they need in a way that they can say "yes."

MANAGEMENT

What are the three most important things an employer must do in preparing for negotiations?

1. Select a spokesperson both for the team and for public statements; someone familiar with labor law as well as the company/industry/labor relations issues and someone who has the respect of both the union and management teams (whether in-house or an outside counsel or consultant).
2. Establish specific goals and directions, including "drop-dead" points.
3. Gather input from line management in terms of what is or is not working in current collective bargaining agreement (or practice, if this is the first collective bargaining agreement to be negotiated) and from budget folks as to cost of changes and impact of same.

The board and later the courts recognized three categories of bargaining subjects: those that will be discussed, those that might be discussed, and those that cannot be discussed.

In the early years of the act, the board based its decisions on what constituted bargaining subjects by evaluating the history of the agreements. However, to protect unions and the collective bargaining process in its formative stage, the board found the discussion of union recognition clauses compulsory. Hence, union shops, dues checkoffs, and the treatment of employees after a strike became part of the collective bargaining discussion.

In a case-by-case method, the board began to establish the list of subjects to be covered. In 1958 the Supreme Court decided the ***Borg-Warner*** case, which distinguished between the treatment accorded subjects determined by the board to be mandatory and the treatment accorded subjects determined to be permissive or illegal. The Court noted that although the attitude of the parties is important in determining the good faith required by the act, the issues being discussed are also important.[5] It became a legal question of whether a proposal was one the parties were obliged to discuss.

If the subject is **mandatory**, a party may insist on its inclusion, and the other party cannot refuse to discuss it. Although compelled to bargain in good faith, neither party is legally obligated to compromise its stated position on a mandatory subject, and each party may even push the bargaining situation to an impasse. A legal impasse in negotiations can occur only when the parties cannot agree on a mandatory issue. The employer can, if there is a bona fide impasse, unilaterally implement its final offer to the union. If any permissive issues are also unresolved at the time of impasse, they can be implemented with the mandatory issue.[6]

Subjects deemed mandatory by the NLRB include those issues actually listed in the act: rates of pay, wages, hours of employment, and other conditions of employment. Also included are issues the NLRB considers related to the subjects listed in the act. After the *Borg-Warner* decision, the Supreme Court refined the definition of mandatory bargaining subjects to include subjects that "vitally affect" employees.[7] In recent years, several issues critical to unions, such as liquidation of a business, partial plant closings, subcontracting work, and plant relocations, have been litigated to determine whether they are mandatory or permissive subjects of bargaining.

After some confusion that was generated by board decisions during Ronald Reagan's presidency, board rulings listed subcontracting and plant relocations in the mandatory list if such are a means to substitute other workers for the bargaining unit members. Partial plant closings or other "going-out-of-business" decisions are not subjects of mandatory bargaining because there is no intention to replace the bargaining unit members.[8] Table 5-1 delineates mandatory, permissive, and illegal subjects.

Concessions are seldom made regarding permissive subjects because the parties cannot bargain to an impasse over them.[9] Designating plant closings and other business issues that focus on the economic profitability of a business as permissive[10] has had a

TABLE 5-1   Bargaining Items

Mandatory	*Permissive*	*Illegal*
Rates of pay	Indemnity bonds	Featherbedding
Wages	Management rights as to union issues	Whistleblowing
Hours of employment		Discrimination by race, creed, color, religion, or national origin
Overtime pay	Preferential hiring	
Shift differentials	Pension benefits of retired employees	
Holidays	Scope of bargaining unit	Interfering with union affairs or officials
Vacations	Including supervisors in the contract	Closed shop
Severance pay		Hot cargo clause
Pensions	Additional parties to the contract, such as the international union	Separation of employees by race
Insurance benefits		
Profit-sharing plans		Discriminatory treatment
Christmas bonuses	Use of union label	
Company-provided housing, meals, and discounts	Settlement of unfair labor charges	
Employee security	Prices in cafeteria	
Job performance	Continuation of past contract	
Union security	Membership of bargaining team	
Management–union relationship	Employment of strike breakers	
Drug testing of employees	Employer child care	
Subcontracting or relocating union members' work	Plant closings	

SOURCE: Adapted from Patrick Hardin, John E. Higgins, Christopher T. Hexter, and John T. Neighbors, *The Developing Labor Law* (4th ed.) (Washington, DC: Bureau of National Affairs, 2001).

profound impact on unions' ability to win concessions on such issues at the negotiating table or to alter major decisions affecting union security.

The board has defined wages as "direct and immediate economic benefits, flowing from the employment relationship."[11] Included in the discussion of wages are hourly pay rates, overtime pay, piece rates, incentive plans, shift differentials, paid holidays and vacations, and severance pay. Other forms of compensation are also included by the NLRB under the wage category and are therefore considered mandatory; they include the following:

1. ***Pensions and insurance benefits.***   Whereas employers considered pensions and insurance benefits as separate from wages, the NLRB considered them as payment for services rendered and found an inseparable nexus between employees' current compensation and future benefits. However, retirement and pension plans are mandatory subjects for active employees only and not for retired members.

2. ***Profit-sharing plans.***   Profit-sharing plans are also considered as payment and enhancement of economic benefit. Such plans are usually structured to increase benefits to employees when company profits go up.

3. ***Christmas and other bonuses.***   A one-time or performance bonus may be a mandatory subject. The board has devised a test to determine whether such a bonus is a gift or part of the employees' compensation. The decision is based on the following:

   - The consistency or regularity of the payment
   - The uniformity of the amount of payment from bonus to bonus
   - The relationship between the amount of the bonus and the pay scale of the employee
   - The taxability of the payment as income
   - The financial condition and ability of the employer to give the bonus

   The board will determine it is a gift if the following is true:

   - The bonus has been awarded intermittently over a very few years.
   - The amount of the bonus is not uniform from year to year.
   - The amount is not tied to the employees' salary.
   - The awarding of a bonus depends on the present financial condition of the employer.

4. ***Stock purchase plans.***   Employers contend that stock purchase plans are not employee benefits but simply an incentive for the employee to invest in the company. The NLRB rejects that argument and deems such plans a form of compensation that is a mandatory subject for collective bargaining.

5. ***Merit wage incentives.***   A company may consider merit increases management's prerogative, but the NLRB has said that because merit raises involve the formation and application of standards affecting all wages, they must be considered a mandatory bargaining subject.

6. ***Company housing, meals, and discounts.***   The inclusion of these in the list of mandatory subjects depends on the situation. Such items would be mandatory if the job required living or eating on company-owned premises.

Provisions detailing hours, daily and weekly work schedules, and requirements for overtime premiums are found in virtually all contracts.[12] Specific start and stop times, lunch and rest periods, and other scheduling rules are usually included. Although scheduling work is normally a management prerogative, any change from the hours specified in the contract, no matter how minimal, is considered an unfair labor practice, even if it does not affect the employee's pay.

Conditions of Employment

The board has stated that the phrase "conditions of employment" refers to terms under which employment status is given or withdrawn, rather than physical working conditions. Conditions must have a material and significant impact directly affecting the employment relationship. Four major areas include the following:

1. *Employment security.* This covers all aspects of hiring and firing and granting tenure. Hiring and probationary periods, seniority, job-bidding procedures, promotions, and transfers must all be bargained, except for the nondiscriminatory promotion of employees to supervisory positions. The order and manner of layoffs and recalls, issues surrounding the discharge and retirement of employees, and contracting out work normally performed by members of the bargaining unit are also mandatory. In some instances, plant closings and relocations must be bargained. Although courts have said that a company is not required to negotiate an economically motivated decision to close or relocate a plant, the effects of such an action must be bargained.

2. *Job performance.* The day-to-day relationship between employer and employee is a mandatory subject of bargaining and includes absenteeism, work breaks, lunch periods, discipline, and dress codes. Although safety practices must be discussed, management may still have the final say. Decisions concerning workloads and the number of employees necessary for a task are considered mandatory, and under recent board and court decisions, drug testing of employees is considered a mandatory bargaining subject, although the decision to test job applicants is not.[13]

3. *Union security.* The protection of the union's representation status is a mandatory subject for bargaining. Such protection requires a 30-day grace period before an employee must join the union, discontinuance of a union shop according to majority vote, and a prohibition against discharge of an employee for nonmembership in a union for any reason other than failure to pay dues.

4. *Management–union relationships.* All principles governing the discharge of collective bargaining duties and enforcement of collective bargaining agreements, including grievance and arbitration procedures, are considered mandatory.

If the subject is **permissive**, a party must withdraw it from bargaining if the other party does not voluntarily agree to its inclusion in the discussion. Both parties must agree for permissive subjects to be bargained. Examples of permissive subjects include performance or indemnity bonds, which protect the employer from liabilities in the quality of the union's work, and management's right to have an impact on the internal affairs of the union.

Subjects deemed **illegal** by the act or the NLRB may not be proposed for discussion and, even if agreed to by both parties, would not be enforced by any court. These include violations of public policy, otherwise unlawful issues, and items inconsistent with the principles of the National Labor Relations Act. A closed shop requiring union membership before an employee is hired, racial separation of employees, and discrimination against nonunion members are illegal bargaining subjects.

If in the future a portion of the contract becomes illegal under a state or federal law, the **separability clause** in the contract becomes effective. The separability clause usually states that any portion of a contract conflicting with state or federal law is declared null and void without affecting other provisions. Separability clauses appear in

68 percent of all contracts. About half provide that the offending section is null and void; the other half call for renegotiation of the issue.[14]

Sources of Bargaining Items

In general, it is the unions who introduce new items to be discussed at a collective bargaining session, and management reacts to such proposals. Management can, however, initiate new items for discussion.

Union negotiation teams solicit member input in formulating demands. This solicitation can be done at general union meetings, at meetings with union stewards, or through written or electronic questionnaires. The Teamsters survey of member concerns in Figure 5-3 is a typical member survey conducted in preparation for labor negotiations.

Often, bargaining items are formulated through analysis of the types of grievances filed and from recent arbitration awards. Problems detected at a lower level are passed on to be included in the collective bargaining talks. Management will often add line supervisors' suggestions on working conditions to its economic positions during negotiations.

What do You think?

Do you have ideas about how we could work better? What improvements in our pay, benefits and working conditions would you like to see? What job protections would you like to have?

Please complete and return this survey as soon as possible, using the enclosed envelope, or by giving it to a organizer or a coworker who is part of your organizing committee—so everyone's voice can be heard.

AirTran Airlines Issue Survey

(Please fill in the blank or circle your response)

Seniority and Scheduling

1. How long have you worked at AirTran?
   Years _____
2. Do you work full time or part time?
   a. Full time
   b. Part time
3. Who makes the schedules at your station?
   a. Management
   b. You and your coworkers
   c. Administrator
   d. Other _____
   e. Don't know
4. How are schedules determined?
   a. Bidding by seniority
   b. Other bid system?
   c. Arbitrarily by management
   d. Other (describe) _____
   e. Don't know

FIGURE 5-3   2005 Teamster Bargaining Survey

5. Do you feel that the current bidding system is fair?
   a. Yes
   b. No
   c. Don't know
6. Do you feel that seniority is applied fairly when it comes to schedules and work assignments?
   a. Yes
   b. No
   c. Don't know

Benefits

7. What benefits that you currently have do you most want to guarantee in our union contract?
   a. _____
   b. _____
   c. _____
8. Do you feel the current sick-leave policy is fair?
   a. Yes
   b. No
   c. Don't know
9. Have you ever suffered consequences for taking sick leave?
   a. Yes
   b. No

Working Conditions

10. Do you feel that your current workload is reasonable?
    a. Yes
    b. No
11. Are you ever required to work beyond your regularly scheduled time?
    a. Yes
    b. No
12. If overtime is required, how is it allocated?
    a. Decided by you and your coworkers
    b. Ask for volunteers
    c. Assigned by management
    d. Other
    e. Don't know

Training and Retention

13. Is turnover at your station:
    a. High
    b. Moderate
    c. Low
    d. Don't know

continued

FIGURE 5-3   2005 Teamster Bargaining Survey (Continued)

14. Do you have the opportunity for training and promotion that you feel you should have?
    a. Yes
    b. No
    c. Don't know

Wages

15. What is your current hourly pay rate?
    $ _____ /hour

16. Do you consider your current pay to be fair and reasonable for the work you do?
    a. Yes
    b. Somewhat
    c. Not at all

17. Have you received a raise in the past 3 years?
    a. Yes
    b. No

Respect and Voice on the Job

18. How frequently do you receive a job evaluation? _____

19. Are you satisfied that the evaluation was fair and accurate?
    a. Yes
    b. No
    c. Don't know

Contract Priorities

20. How important to you are improvements in the following areas? (please circle your response)

    (1 = very important 5 = not so important)

Scheduling & Bidding	1	2	3	4	5
Sick Leave/FMLA	1	2	3	4	5
Health Insurance	1	2	3	4	5
Retirement Benefits	1	2	3	4	5
Training	1	2	3	4	5
Turnover	1	2	3	4	5
Wages	1	2	3	4	5
Respect and Fairness	1	2	3	4	5
Other	1	2	3	4	5

21. Of the above, which three items are your biggest priorities for improvement in our contract negotiations?
    a. _____
    b. _____
    c. _____

FIGURE 5-3 2005 Teamster Bargaining Survey (Continued)

SOURCE: www.teamster.org (2005). Used by permission.

Both union and management can also look to external sources for bargaining items. Recent contracts within the same industry can give both parties ideas on realistic, attainable proposals. Often the overall economic condition of the nation and that of the particular industry limit or expand bargaining demands.

Information necessary to support proposals and counterproposals can be obtained from such sources as the U.S. Department of Labor (Bureau of Labor Statistics) and the Federal Reserve System, which publish economic data. National organizations, such as the NLRB, the Federal Mediation and Conciliation Service, and the Federal Labor Relations Council, are directly involved in collective bargaining and can contribute primary information. Publications of the Bureau of National Affairs, Commerce Clearinghouse, and Prentice Hall show national trends in contract settlement for comparison with local proposals. Special-interest groups representing both labor and management collect a wide variety of information to help in contract negotiations and include the National Association of Manufacturers and the AFL-CIO.

In addition to general sources, each party is entitled to certain types of information from the opposition. Under the duty to bargain in good faith, a union may demand relevant information from the employer in preparing wage demands.

Planning

Planning may be the most critical element in successful negotiations. In general, negotiators plan effectively in the following ways:

1.   *Anticipation.* Each side, through research and members' input, must correctly assess those issues critical to both sides. The general mood greatly affects the early stages of negotiations. The key issues for each side and the possibility of a strike or other actions should be anticipated and a response prepared. A response, such as a detailed counterproposal or a package of several items, can center the conflict on the issues rather than personal emotions.

2.   *Realistic objectives.* Preparation on all items of interest can help avoid costly mistakes during heated and lengthy negotiations. Negotiators should prioritize all objectives and develop a settlement range. Logical trade-offs among items of interest can be analyzed and prepared.

3.   *Strategy.* Each party must evaluate the opponent's current needs as well as its own, review the bargaining history between the two parties, and prepare an overall strategy for negotiations. Important aspects to consider include personalities of negotiators, current financial and political position of each party, and outside influences, such as the economy, product sales, and public support of unions. Strategy formulation helps both sides develop realistic expectations of how negotiations will proceed and what the final agreement will be. For example, senior union employees may be most unhappy with the current pension program, but a significant increase in the pension formula would require costly increases for all future retirees. Thus, in developing its strategy, management could develop an economic package including alternative combinations of one-time lucrative early retirement options with pay increases loaded toward younger employees.

4.   *Agenda.* Both parties should develop an agenda for discussing all items in a logical manner and incorporate it into the written ground rules. For example, after settling problems with the current contract's wording (which may have arisen through grievance), negotiators can exchange noneconomic proposals and settle as many as possible. They should follow this settlement with an exchange of economic proposals dealing with smaller-cost items first, keeping on the table the highest-priority economic and noneconomic items.

Expectations must be established at the same time priorities are set. Successful collective bargaining may be impossible if the highest priority of one party is an item the other party is unlikely to negotiate.

To establish realistic objectives, the party considers patterns and trends in contract settlements of other employers in the industry and the local community. In an economy where a 4 percent cost-of-living raise is almost universal, a request for 12 percent would be unrealistic. The parties also examine their current and past bargaining relationship along with their relative strength. For example, if contract negotiations have already been concluded with other employers in the same industry and this employer always follows their lead, it may be unrealistic to expect major deviations.

Negotiation Sessions

The parties set the rules of the collective bargaining session usually at the opening session. If the parties have a long-standing relationship, establishing procedures can be very routine. But when the collective bargaining process is relatively new or when the parties have had bad labor relations, setting procedures can be as difficult, and as important, as bargaining on the issues.

Ground Rules

The parties decide where, when, how often, and how long to meet. These and other procedures are often agreed to in writing as **ground rules** for negotiations. Exactly what is included in the ground rules varies greatly according to the desires of the negotiators and the bargaining history of the two parties.
The following are examples of ground rules:

1. All negotiation sessions will commence on the time, date, and location heretofore agreed on by the parties.
2. The chief negotiator for the company and the chief negotiator for the union shall be the chief spokespersons for the respective parties' interests. However, others present may speak as required or called on by the negotiators.
3. Insofar as practical and reasonable, the data introduced by either party at negotiations shall be made available to the other party.
4. If either the company or the union intends to add a new member to its respective bargaining committee, the party adding the new member will notify the other party.
5. Proposals and counterproposals will be made on typed copies as reasonable and will be signed and dated by the appropriate party. The parties shall simultaneously exchange initial noneconomic and economic proposals at the appropriate times.
6. Individual items agreed to by both parties shall be signed and dated and removed from the table. Any attempt to reintroduce or discuss those items shall be viewed as a breach of good faith.
7. The company's chief negotiator and the union's chief negotiator shall have the authority to agree in substance on contract language and provisions. However, any agreement is preliminary and contingent on a final contract. All preliminary agreements made regarding individual contract provisions shall be initialed and dated by both chief negotiators.
8. If mediation is agreed to by both parties, the mediator picked by the parties shall be agreeable to both.

Negotiating teams are established. Neither side may dictate the membership of the other's negotiating team, but rules may be established as to how many members are allowed on each side and as to their official roles, such as spokesperson, recording secretary, and doorkeeper, who makes sure only authorized persons attend the negotiations. Negotiating teams are often kept as small as possible to allow for productive discussion. Each side must have a designated leader who makes commitments for the respective parties. Traditionally, union negotiating teams can only agree to propose the contract to the membership for acceptance.

Exchange of Initial Proposals

A bargaining agenda is set to establish exchange of initial proposals, the order of discussion of bargaining items, and if possible, how long to continue with one item if agreement is not forthcoming. A stalemate in the early stages of bargaining can sour the process, making agreement impossible. The number and length of bargaining sessions may indicate a party's reluctance to bargain in good faith. If feasible, the agenda lists less controversial issues first so that an atmosphere of agreement is fostered.

Economic and noneconomic proposals are usually separated. Noneconomic proposals are often negotiated first. If economic data can be agreed on, economic issues are easier to resolve. In general, economic issues are negotiated as a package to ensure a balanced settlement. Agreement is more easily reached on individual noneconomic issues than on a package.

Usually a decision is made on how to keep records of the negotiations. An accurate record keeps both parties honest during negotiations and when the final contract is proposed. A single outline of items discussed, proposals made on those items, and what was agreed to or where disagreement arose is prepared by one party and initialed by the other.

The negotiation site has private space to allow for a caucus by either party. It is decided in the initial session what the caucus and adjournment rights of both parties are to be. Misunderstanding in this area can lead one or the other party to stage a needless walkout when a strategic retreat could have served as a positive catalyst to settlement. Finally, parties should decide early on the role of a mediator if they intend to resort to one in case of an impasse.

Posturing

The atmosphere of a collective bargaining session depends on the attitudes of the parties involved. Their attitudes are influenced by their prior relationships, the economic circumstances of the employer, the basic employer's attitude toward unionization, and the leadership of the union. The relationship of the employer to the local union's international may also be a factor.

Whatever the particular atmosphere, labor negotiations follow a common pattern. The initial working sessions are no more than monologues wherein both parties present their list of demands. Often these sessions are open to the public, or at least they are well publicized to satisfy the negotiators' constituencies that proceedings are on the right course. The laundry list proposed by the parties purposely includes bargaining items that can and will be bargained away during the negotiations with varying degrees of reluctance. This **posturing** is very important. It allows a certain amount of face-saving to the party who comes to the bargaining table with the least amount of bargaining power.

Within the posturing of negotiations, there are several common aspects of bargaining that should be anticipated by the participants:

A heated bargaining session may be caused by one side's need to "posture" or dramatically present their concerns.

1. *Interdependence.*   One element of negotiations is conflict, which can cause tempers to rise as parties become emotionally involved. However, both sides need to remember that their goals are interdependent. Neither side can achieve success without the other.[15]

2. *Concealment.*   During negotiations, parties often conceal their real goals and objectives from the other side to enhance their opportunity for the best possible settlement. This is a characteristic of the negotiation process and should be expected. Every negotiator must decide how open and honest to be in communicating needs and preferences. If a negotiator is completely open and honest, he or she often will settle for less than if he or she conceals goals and fights harder for a better settlement. However, if a negotiator is completely deceptive about goals, the talks may never move in the direction of a settlement. This dilemma of trust poses a key problem for negotiators: First discussions may reveal little of their true needs, with disclosure offered only in an effort to move discussions forward. As both sides begin to trust each other, this process becomes easier.[16]

3. *Packaging items.*   It is difficult to achieve an agreement on all issues at one time. As many as 50 economic and noneconomic issues may be involved during negotiations; if all are left on the table at the same time, the process may become unwieldy. Instead, a few items may be packaged together, agreed to, and removed from further discussion, allowing both sides to achieve their goal on one or more items and thus establish trust in the process. The number of unresolved issues decreases as more packages are agreed to, moving negotiations toward completion. Packaging may at least narrow the list of disputed items to the high-priority issues for each side. The ground rules may require each chief negotiator to "sign off" on a package—signing and dating a written counterproposal detailing the items agreed to—thereby removing them from further discussions.

4. *Throwaway items.*   Negotiators, in their list of initial demands, may include items of no real value to their side, thus providing items to trade in exchange for others of high

priority to their side. Throwaways can be the basis of a successful bluff if the other side believes it has won a concession on an important item. The throwaway items may have real value, but they simply are not of high priority in comparison with other issues. A throwaway item for one side may, in fact, be a high-priority item for the other side.

5.   *Caucusing.* Much of the negotiating time is spent in the two parties' meeting separately. After a proposal or counterproposal is received, a team usually asks for a caucus. There they can openly discuss the merits of the proposal and their willingness to accept it, or they can formulate a counterproposal. A major part of the strategy may be not to reveal at the table how the party feels about a proposal received from the other side. Even an obviously desirable proposal may lead to a caucus in which the team accepts the proposal without emotion. An expression of happiness over one item may lead the other side to believe they need not give on further items. Caucusing is also used for resolving disagreement among members of the same team and gathering additional information about unanticipated or costly proposals.

6.   *Flexibility.* The successful negotiation process requires the exchange of many proposals and counterproposals. Every proposal received should be studied and responded to by acceptance or a counteroffer. Immediate rejection of a proposal implies inflexibility and a response of "we will only accept our position." This attitude angers the other side and may, in fact, be bad-faith bargaining. Also, most proposals must be carefully evaluated before their merits can be accurately estimated.

7.   *Compromise.* The key to successful negotiations is compromise by both parties. If either side believes they will achieve every goal, then most likely no settlement will be reached. Instead, both parties must realize that their goals are in direct conflict; if one side gains on an issue, the other side loses. If one side loses on too many issues, they may not sign the agreement, or, if forced to sign then, they certainly will be looking to "even the score" during the next round of negotiations.

8.   *Saving face.* It is important to recognize the need for both parties to save face. Former chairman of the National Mediation Board, Patrick J. Cleary, described how the face-saving process at the end of labor-management negotiations typically works: When a tentative agreement is reached, the union negotiator claims victory while management remains silent. Why? Because the union must win ratification by the membership. If management boasted about the gains it made at the table (and both sides always make some gains), then the union negotiators might lose face and the members reject the deal, sending their negotiators back to the table for more management concessions. Most important, notes Cleary, is getting a final agreement. Getting a final deal—the ultimate goal—is also the most effective way of putting all disputes and face-saving issues in the past.[17]

Exchange of Proposals and Counterproposals

After the posturing, the real working sessions begin. Agreements are often made almost immediately on less important items. Usually these are noneconomic items that both parties wish to resolve. When the bargaining on economic issues begins, the parties tend to back away from item agreement and look to total packaging. During negotiations, changing proposals must be analyzed for their cost. Until the total economic agreement is seen, neither party can be sure of its position. Negotiators can use different approaches to reach an actual agreement. Some examples follow:

1. The parties can separate economic and noneconomic issues and agree on the noneconomic issues first. Changes improving grievance procedures, work rules,

Tips from the Experts

What are three classic mistakes to be avoided at the negotiations table?

UNION

1. Make certain that when an employer claims it is unable to meet your wage demands, you demand information on the financial condition of the company. Under the National Labor Relations Act, you are entitled to financial information if the employer claims either a lack of funds, an inability to stay competitive, or the loss of a necessary profit margin.

2. Remember that if negotiations reach an impasse and such an impasse is not the result of an employer's bad-faith negotiations, an employer may unilaterally implement its last offer. Such an action allows the employer to bypass the bargaining unit's representatives and deal directly with employees, thereby undercutting your ability to represent your members.

3. Make certain that any issue brought up at the negotiating table is either completely resolved or explicitly reserved for future negotiations. A so-called zipper clause in many collective bargaining agreements precludes reopening negotiations on any mandatory or permissive bargaining subject that could have been brought up at the negotiations table.

MANAGEMENT

1. Unless you want to provide the union with all the company's financial information, make certain you do not claim a financial inability to meet the union's wage demands. The NLRB includes claims that you cannot remain competitive or maintain a necessary profit margin as a "financial inability to pay" entitling the union to your company's financial information.

2. Make it clear at the beginning of the negotiations what authority you do or do not have to reach a binding agreement on behalf of the employer. If you need to check with higher authorities before making a commitment, make sure you have explained that to the union's negotiators. Otherwise, springing the need to go back to management can be seen as a delaying tactic that may be deemed an unfair labor practice.

3. Take care in labeling a proposal as the "last, best" offer because if an impasse is reached and there is no bad-faith bargaining on the part of the employer, the employer may implement its last offer unilaterally. However, it is not permissible in such circumstances to implement a proposal that is in any way different from what was previously offered to and was rejected by the union.

job evaluations, and similar items are often sought by both parties and can be more readily agreed to than issues involving costs and benefits.

2. The parties can separate and discuss economic and noneconomic issues. Items can then be traded, with each side winning one item and giving up another, until all the issues have been resolved.

3. The parties can discuss each economic and noneconomic issue separately but may not agree to anything until all items are agreed on. This total packaging approach, although perhaps more difficult, allows both parties the opportunity to evaluate the entire collective bargaining agreement before making a commitment.

Point of Crisis

Finally, negotiators reach a decision. Once all the proposals and counterproposals are on the table, the parties either agree or stop talking. If agreement cannot be reached, this may be the point of crisis. Various techniques such as mediation and arbitration are available to bring the parties back to agreement. Job actions such as strikes and lockouts, although they receive a great deal of publicity, are seldom used to resolve contract disputes.

Noted mediator Ted Kheel refers to this crisis point in negotiations as **"the crunch,"** or a point of no return that occurs when both sides realize that "some deadline will cause no decision to become the final decision." Up to this point both parties feel little pressure to move significantly from their position. The crunch, however, is a signal that it is time for a decision or impasse. As an example, Kheel offers the tactic of CIO founder John L. Lewis, who, when negotiating for the United Mine Workers, practiced a "no contract, no work" strategy, meaning that the termination date of the current contract would not be extended. Thus, if a new contract were not reached by that date, the members would immediately strike. Then both sides felt "the crunch" to settle before the old contract expired—management wanted to avoid lost production and workers lost wages. Most UAW negotiations reached a settlement before the termination of the old contract; the others experienced a strike, as Lewis had promised.[18]

Tentative Agreement

As the last paragraph of Profile 5-1 states, and as you can see from Case 5-1, all tentative agreements reached by representatives of management and the union are just that—tentative.

At this point, the union leadership will hold informational meetings to present the details of the tentative agreement to the members and to answer questions.

Then the agreement must be ratified (receive a majority positive vote) by the members of the union. If the union negotiators have done a good job of determining the priorities of the members, keeping them informed during the negotiation process, and estimating what they will or will not accept in a new contract, then this step is routine. To show solidarity with their leadership, members usually accept the contract offered to them as the "last, best, and final" one. The ratification process involves a secret-ballot process that can take several days to allow all members at all locations the

---

PROFILE 5-1

THE NEGOTIATING PROCESS, AS DESCRIBED BY THE UAW

THE UNION MAKES US STRONG: COLLECTIVE BARGAINING

The collective bargaining process gives workers power in decisions that affect their everyday lives on the job as well as the economic security of their families. Collective bargaining has been called the "art of the possible"; and the UAW, more than any other union, has pushed the boundaries of what is possible in collective bargaining.

For example, the UAW negotiated the first fully funded pension plan, the first employer-paid health insurance plan for industrial workers, the first employer-paid health insurance plan for retired workers, the first cost-of-living adjustments (COLA), and the first Supplemental Unemployment Benefit (SUB) program. In the 1980s, the UAW pioneered joint union–company education and training programs. In the 1990s, the UAW won an unprecedented role for workers and their union in decisions affecting product quality and, at the Big 3 U.S. automakers (Ford, GM, and Chrysler), a landmark job and income security program protecting workers against volume-related layoffs.

The UAW's collective bargaining goals are set democratically—by bargaining unit members at the local level and by elected delegates to the Collective Bargaining Convention at the international level. The written collective bargaining agreement typically covers wages, benefits, working conditions, grievance procedures, seniority, union representation, hours of work, vacation and holidays, dues checkoffs, and union security.

All tentative agreements must be voted on by secret ballot by the members. Ratification requires a majority of votes. Informational meetings to review and discuss the tentative agreement are held before the ratification vote.

SOURCE: "How the UAW Works," www.uaw.org/faqs/howuawworks/collective.html (January 7, 1997).

CASE 5-1

GOOD-FAITH NEGOTIATIONS

The company owns and operates a nursing home facility. The employees had been represented by the union since 1996. The most recent collective bargaining agreement (CBA) expired on June 30, 1999. At the June 22 negotiating session, the parties reached a tentative agreement. The employees ratified the agreement on June 24. When the CBA was presented to the company's administrator, he told the union that he had to take the CBA to the company's president for approval. As she was out of the country, he left a copy of the CBA at the president's office and provided a copy—marked as tentative—to the company's payroll officer. The president never approved the CBA. Nonetheless, on July 1, 1999, the payroll office implemented the wage agreement as set out in the CBA. When the president returned from Korea in early August, she told her administrator that she had not approved the wage increase and wanted it rescinded. She met with the employees and told them that the wage increases were not a part of the tentative CBA and that she had not delegated authority to anyone to sign the CBA in her absence. As the wage increases were too costly, she was rescinding them affective August 10. She did not notify the union of this action.

The union filed a grievance. The union also filed an unfair labor practices charge against the company. The president then met with the union over the grievance. It was the union's position that the "tentative" CBA was a binding one and that the company was bound by it to reinstate the pay increases. After numerous meetings, the company finally agreed to reinstate the increases retroactively.

The NLRB's administrative law judge (ALJ) took up the issue of whether the company engaged in an unfair labor practice for failure to agree to the tentative CBA and for rescinding the wage increase without negotiating the issue with the union.

DECISION

The ALJ found that the company did not violate the National Labor Relations Act by refusing to sign the tentative agreement. The ALJ noted that the company's administrator had made it clear to the union that the tentative agreement had to be approved by the president before it became effective. That step never took place. So the company was under no duty to sign the CBA. However, the ALJ noted that if the company had been charged with an unfair labor practice for its failure to appoint negotiators with the authority to carry out meaningful negotiations, it might have been a closer question.

On the issue of rescinding the wage increase, the ALJ did find that the company violated the National Labor Relations Act. The judge recognized that the company had made a mistake in implementing the wage increase and that it had the right to correct the mistake; however, it had to notify the union and bargain over how the mistake would be corrected. And while the subsequent discussions the company undertook with the union as a result of the grievance that the union filed was admirable, it did not change the fact that the company had engaged in an unfair labor practice.

SOURCE: Adapted from *JPH Management,* 169 LRRM 1001 (NLRB 2001).

opportunity to vote. The process can be complicated, however; for example, in 1996 the International Longshoreman's and Warehouse Union rules required a 60 percent majority of all voting members across the United States because the Los Angeles and San Francisco local union leaders vetoed the proposed contract.[19]

Contract

Once an agreement has been ratified, the contract is written. The contract language is very important and should accurately state the parties' agreement because they are expected to abide by it through its duration. Many grievance and arbitration actions stem from ambiguous contract language; the parties may even disagree on whether the language reflects what they negotiated.

The four areas most contracts cover are union security and management rights, the wage and effort bargain, individual security, and contract administration.

BARGAINING TECHNIQUES

Labor and management meet across a negotiating table because of the National Labor Relations Act. The act requires that the parties bargain in good faith but provides that neither party has to agree to any particular proposal as long as it continues to bargain in good faith. Thus, the act establishes the boundaries of the negotiation process but leaves the internal workings to the parties involved.

Over the years, the bargaining process has changed from an adversarial confrontation between the forces of capitalist and worker into a stylized ritual between the representatives of management and labor. Collective bargaining may be nothing but a process by which the negotiators seek to make the main terms of the agreement, which are already decided, acceptable to the parties.

Whether or not that observation is correct, collective bargaining has certainly changed from mere confrontation to a process by which labor and management sincerely attempt to resolve conflicting interests. Respect for the process, however, does not eliminate the conflict. The resolution of this conflict has been analyzed in numerous ways.

Labor negotiation has often been inaccurately compared to playing games. Games have a definite set of values and rules so that parties know when they are winning and, more important, when they are losing. There are no rules in negotiation except for those set by the parties, and the rules are often a part of the negotiation itself. The most important difference, however, is that negotiation is the art of compromise, ensuring that neither party wins or loses everything.

The collective bargaining process is in reality a combination of the three styles. The parties interact on the issues using whatever advantage they have to achieve their goals. The key to successful bargaining lies in flexibility and in understanding and controlling the process. The following approaches are written in a "how-to" style, designed as a starting point for understanding the collective bargaining process.

Distributive Bargaining

Two parties are involved in **distributive bargaining** when they view the negotiations as a "win-lose" situation—the goals of one party are in direct conflict with those of the other party. Resources are viewed by the negotiators as fixed and limited, and each side wants to maximize its share of the limited resources. Every negotiator should understand distributive bargaining because many collective bargaining situations are distributive, and many negotiators use distributive strategies almost exclusively.[20]

In collective bargaining, both sides may view the process as distributive bargaining. The limited resources include the monetary assets of the firm, which can be used for a variety of purposes—new equipment or machinery, divided payments, higher wages, and so on. Another limited resource would be unfilled positions, so deciding who is promoted or transferred can be the subject of distributive bargaining. Other noneconomic issues, such as union security, employee grievances, and plant rules, can also be included. Both labor and management view any positive change from the current contract as something to be gained at the negotiating table and as a loss to the other party.

The distributive bargaining process can best be explained by five key elements:

1. ***Target point.*** The optimal goal or objective a negotiator sets for the issue, the target point, is the point at which the negotiator would most prefer to conclude negotiations.
2. ***Resistance point.*** The resistance point is a maximum or minimum beyond which the negotiator will not accept a proposal. This is the negotiator's bottom line.
3. ***Initial offer.*** This is the first number or offer the negotiator presents as a written formal proposal.
4. ***Settlement range.*** The difference between the resistance points of labor and management is the range in which actual bargaining occurs because anything outside the range will be quickly rejected by one party.
5. ***Settlement point.*** The heart of negotiations is the process of reaching agreement on one point within the settlement range: the settlement point. The objective of each party is to achieve a settlement point as close as possible to its target point.[21]

An example of the distributive bargaining process is illustrated in Figure 5-4. First, both sides develop and keep confidential their target and resistance points. Labor has surveyed its members, reviewed similar contracts recently negotiated, and estimated the company's financial situation. Within a generally favorable economic package, the labor negotiators set 4.5 percent as their target point but are willing to consider any offer above 3 percent, the resistance point, if the total package contains other economic benefits. They honestly believe that the members would vote against any contract with less than a 3 percent increase because inflation since the last negotiation has averaged 4 percent, and recent contracts in the industry have included raises between 3 and 5 percent. Management negotiators set their target point at 3 percent, the lowest increase negotiated by any of their competitors. The company president has authorized negotiators

FIGURE 5-4 Distributive Bargaining Negotiation: First-Year Base Wage Increase (percentage)

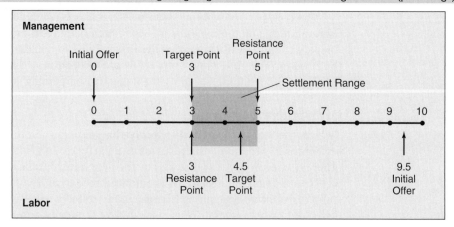

to accept an offer of up to 5 percent, the resistance point, if the total economic package is within a certain dollar amount.

Next, both sides choose their initial offers. Management decides that a proposed wage giveback (decrease in base wage) might be considered bad-faith bargaining because the company is in a reasonably good financial condition, so it initially offers a 0 percent increase, the lowest possible given the circumstances. Labor knows that no similar union has received more than 6 percent and therefore feels that 9.5 percent (just under double digits) is as high an initial offer as can be made within the context of good-faith bargaining. Both sides realize that their initial offers must be different from their target point to allow room for negotiation "give-and-take" while also staying within what the other side would consider a reasonable and good-faith offer. At the same time, both sides realize that the other side's initial offer has left them room to negotiate and is not their last, best, or final offer.

Negotiations between the two sides now center on the 0 to 9.5 percent range. Each side begins trying to convince the other to move from its initial offer. Neither side knows the target or resistance point of the other side. Both sides will, however, through bargaining table discussion, begin to estimate the target and resistance points of the other side to determine if a settlement range exists and therefore a settlement point can be found. At the same time, each side strives to convince the other of the validity of its own position. By presenting factual information such as company records, copies of recent contracts, and industry data—as well as persuasive information such as employee survey data—negotiators hope to influence the perceptions of the other party. Management may try to convince labor that to remain competitive and avoid layoffs, the company cannot afford an expensive settlement and is willing to take a strike if necessary.

Labor may try to convince management of the members' determination to negotiate a high increase and their willingness to put on a successful strike. Eventually, both sides believe that they know, indirectly or directly, the other side's resistance point. For example, management might state, "We will seriously consider an offer under 5 percent if the total package is right," or labor might indicate, "Our members know that no other local has settled for less than 3 percent." Now the negotiations center on the settlement range, both sides realize that there are many possible settlement points within the range.

Now the "hard" bargaining begins. Within the 2 percent settlement range, each side carefully proposes a settlement point that, especially when wages are considered, may include other economic items in a package. And, most important, each negotiator is careful to propose only a settlement that he or she is prepared to accept. Within this range any offer might be accepted if both sides have a settlement point. Once the settlement point has been proposed and accepted, it is too late to "hold out for a little more."

The settlement point is finally reached when one side achieves its target point or when both are willing to accept something less than their target points but within the settlement range. Factors such as the arguments of the other side, the total package, fatigue, or belief that "this is the best we can do" may influence negotiators to accept a settlement different from their target point.

Interest-Based Bargaining

When training new negotiators, the most requested new bargaining technique is **interest-based bargaining** (IBB). The Federal Mediation and Conciliation Service (FMCS) reported in 2000 that IBB was used with increasing frequency in collective bargaining negotiations. The growth is likely based on the realization by unions and management that they both have a fundamental mutual interest in the long-run economic success of the employer. IBB is different from distributive, pressure bargaining and other methods because the negotiators become joint problem solvers seeking a consensus resolution of an issue, not one side "winning" at the expense of the other. The basic principles or steps in the IBB process include the following:[22]

1. Both sides fully share all relevant bargaining information—economic data such as the employer's financial information, industry reports, and the results of other recently negotiated agreements—as well as relevant survey information of workers' priorities.

2. Willingness to forgo power or leverage as the sole determinant of "winning." Instead, both sides strive to find solutions to the other parties' interests as well as their own—similar to "win-win" bargaining.

3. Brainstorming to generate new options and a willingness of both parties to not criticize but objectively analyze each "outside the box" proposed option. The purpose of brainstorming is to focus on the issues. Personalities, often central to "winning" in traditional negotiations, play a minimum role in IBB.

4. Focusing on the present issues and finding solutions that will work in the future contract. Problems and disagreements of the past are not discussed, and there is no objective of "making up for what we lost last time."

5. Focusing on the interests underlying an issue—on both sides. Thus, instead of responding with, "We cannot move from our position on this issue," a party might respond with, "Why did you take that position? Explain what you are trying to achieve." This process often leads both sides to discover mutual goals they otherwise might not realize.

6. Willingness of both parties and all people involved to accept and utilize the IBB process.

However, the FMCS notes that IBB is not a universal replacement for distributive bargaining or other traditional techniques. In fact, only if the parties involved have had a positive labor–management relationship in recent years, received sufficient training in IBB, and are fully willing to accept it as a total method of negotiating will it succeed.[23]

One successful use of IBB occurred in Phoenix, Arizona, where past negotiations between the Salt River Project, the third-largest public utility in the United States, and the International Brotherhood of Electrical Workers had been explosive. When the two again faced a negotiation stalemate in 1995, they agreed to try a new process: IBB. The FMCS trained over 20 representatives from management and the union in the IBB process. The focus of the training was the use of brainstorming to create a menu of possible solutions to the unresolved issues. Issues discussed included compensation, flexible work schedules, preference hiring, performance reviews, and management accountability. Over 90 of the 175 outstanding grievances were resolved, and a settlement was reached before the old contract expired—a first. In addition, the entire mood of the negotiations was changed to a positive one, and for the first time after a new settlement was reached, members from both sides celebrated together.[24]

Principled Negotiations

A process called **principled negotiations** was developed by the Harvard Negotiations Project and published in a book titled *Getting to Yes*. The essential element of the process is to be "hard on the merits, soft on the people."[25] The goal is to decide the issues presented at the negotiating table on their merits rather than through the traditional haggling process that focuses on what each side says it will or will not do. Substituting principled negotiations for the traditional pressure bargaining will theoretically result in a wiser agreement through a more efficient process that improves the relationship of the parties.

By focusing on facts, issues, and options to solve problems, negotiators may minimize "people problems."

The key element in principled negotiations is to separate the people from the problem, an approach that ensures a focus on interests, not on positions; it generates a variety of possible options before a decision on a given position is made; and it insists that the result of the bargaining is based on some objective standard.

People

Under the principled negotiation model, the first objective is to separate the people from the problem. This objective is accomplished by accepting the human element involved in negotiations. An understanding of the attitudes and perceptions of the parties is vital, along with the realization that what is important is not what is true but what the parties believe to be true. Neither party can convince the other of the legitimacy of its position without understanding the other party's perception of that position. Therefore, the first task of a negotiator is to understand the other party's perception. It is best to discuss these perceptions openly and to understand their importance to both parties. For example, during hard economic times, a union's noneconomic demands for job security may be more important to the union than management perceives. If management can understand that importance, it should be easier to reach a mutually satisfactory agreement.

Perceptions can be changed. Consistent with the old adage, "Actions speak louder than words," behavior inconsistent with the other party's perception can help change that perception. Unions expect management to approach the bargaining table determined to maintain the status quo. Thus, if management were to present original proposals to improve employee performance and so give an employee more job satisfaction, the union's perception of management might change.

Finally, negotiating parties must learn to communicate.[26] Too often they are not really trying to converse but are simply going through the motions. To communicate effectively, a party must first actively listen and acknowledge what is being said. If necessary, a party should repeat in its own words what the other party has said to ensure understanding. When speaking, a party should remember that the goal is to persuade. Dialogue should be simple, with each side expressing its own position and then remaining silent so the parties can digest what was said.

People can also be prevented from becoming a problem by building a working relationship before negotiations begin. A not-so-subtle tactic is mixing the seating of the two teams at a negotiating session. This arrangement increases the possibility that the parties will attack the problem rather than each other.

Interests

Attacking the problem is the second objective of principled bargaining. The parties are to focus on interests, not on positions. In general, parties come to the negotiating table with a laundry list of demands. Because a party has invested time, energy, and thought in that list, there is a strong tendency to defend it no matter how absurd it may be.

In principled negotiations, the parties are to develop an understanding of their real desires, concerns, and interests rather than simply list demands. The achievement of those interests is left for future resolution. Both sides have multiple interests, and if those interests can be identified without the parties' hardening into a particular position, conflict is eliminated.

Options

Once interests are identified, the third objective is for both parties to seek as many options as possible in solving their conflicting interests. More often than not, the interests of both parties can be satisfied in numerous ways. If creative thinking is applied, interests can overlap, allowing both parties to reach a successful compromise.

To seek numerous options, both parties must be willing to accept that there is more than one right answer. In seeking new solutions, a party must separate the acts of inventing and judging options. A proposal does not make a hard-and-fast position.

Objective Criteria

The fourth objective in principled negotiating is to have the validity of each party's proposals judged by objective criteria. For example, the parties could agree to ask for expert advice when discussing technological changes that might affect workers' jobs. Working together to understand the expert's advice can more easily lead to agreement than working in opposition can; either party can criticize the other party's proposal or defend its own without destroying the relationship. This approach puts the parties in side-by-side negotiations against an objective third party, the criteria, instead of in a head-to-head confrontation. Agreement becomes easier when the basis of the agreement is recognized criteria.

Pressure Bargaining

An understanding of the use of pressure during labor negotiations is necessary in any study of collective bargaining. The bargaining power model assumes that settlement in the collective bargaining process is determined by the relative bargaining power of each party. Simply stated, if it costs more to disagree than to agree, the party will agree. It is therefore an objective during collective bargaining to determine the costs associated with negotiations. Subsequent chapters discuss how to estimate costs for various contract proposals and provisions. However, the cost of agreeing or disagreeing during the collective bargaining process can be quite different.

The ultimate test of strength in the negotiating process is the union's ability to strike and the company's ability to take a strike. Before such action is undertaken, both sides, either formally or by instinct, decide on a range within which settlement can be achieved. If either party refuses to enter that range, pressure must be applied.

In the **pressure bargaining** model, as with any model for collective bargaining, the parties must make sound assumptions. Miscalculations of the target point can lead to costly and futile actions. Even under the pressure bargaining model, certain techniques such as those that follow lessen the chance of confrontation.

Pressure Tactics

The use of certain tactics during pressure bargaining is often designed to pressure the other party into accepting something they would normally refuse. Often these tactics work, but they can backfire when the members of the other side find them offensive or recognize them for what they are and use a good countertactic. The most frequently used pressure tactics are described here.

- *Good guy/bad guy.* This is similar to the "good cop/bad cop" routine seen on television police shows. One negotiator opens with tough, often unrealistic positions that are presented with threats, foul language, and obnoxious behavior. Then, while the first, "bad" negotiator leaves the room, the "good" negotiator tries to reach a quick agreement on an issue before the bad partner returns. In some negotiations the bad roles are assigned to supervisors or union members on certain issues they are likely to be particularly concerned about, and the chief negotiator plays the good role.

- *Highball/lowball.* This tactic relies on a ridiculously high (or low) opening offer. The other side then reevaluates its position on the issue and moves closer to the resistance point, while the opening negotiator has not moved at all.

- *The nibble.* This tactic occurs when a negotiator asks for a small concession on an item not yet discussed to "close the deal" on a large issue. For example, a union negotiator agrees to accept management's profit-sharing proposal, the last unresolved issue, if management will "throw in" new safety shoes. The union negotiator may claim to be embarrassed about "forgetting" the shoes until the end. Management negotiators must determine whether their profit-sharing proposal would be accepted anyway—or are the safety shoes a "deal buster"?

- *Chicken.* Named for the car-swerving contest, this tactic is a high-stakes game. Management, for example, threatens to close operations and go out of business if the union does not accept its "last, best, and final" offer. It may be a bluff, but can the union risk it? Can management risk not closing down if the union calls the bluff? This may be the strongest pressure tactic of all.[27]

- *Awfulisms.* This relatively new term describes the tactic of proposing something that sounds "awful." If used by one party, the other side must debunk it quickly. For example, one union negotiator claims that a proposal by management would require union airline pilots to be "on call" for up to 12 hours and thus possibly work a 24-hour day. The union responds strongly to the awful proposal. However, it is pointed out that the last daily flights land by 9:30 PM and thus have left hours earlier, meaning that no pilot could possibly work more than 14 hours in a day and most work far fewer hours; thus, the issue is moot. Awfulisms hurt the credibility of those who make them, but they are used, and thus they must be rationally answered to move negotiations forward.[28]

How can a negotiator successfully deal with other negotiators who use one of these pressure tactics? Some proven methods include the following:

1. *Ignore them.* Simply not responding to unwarranted pressure tactics is usually the best response.

2. *Acknowledge and discuss.*   "I see you are using the old good cop/bad cop routine. Well, we can play that routine if that's what you want."

3. *Respond in kind.*   Counter with another hardball tactic, such as walking out while shouting obscenities.

4. *Befriend the other party.*   This tactic often disarms people who might otherwise use pressure tactics. It is far more difficult to attack friends than it is to attack adversaries.[29]

IMPASSE

No matter what method of negotiations is followed, the parties at some point must agree or face an **impasse** (a stalemate). There are many reasons why negotiations could result in an impasse. The most obvious is that the interests of the two parties have not been reconciled. Another reason is that one party has no real intention of settling. Their overall strategy might include going to an impasse to show how inflexible the other party is. Also, during pressure bargaining, a strategic impasse may appear necessary to move the two parties closer together, and a genuine impasse results simply by miscalculating how close the parties really are.

Both parties have numerous options when an impasse occurs. One option is third-party intervention, such as mediation or fact-finding that could keep union negotiations open and workers on the job. Both sides may agree to continue the old contract on a day-to-day basis, maintaining wage and benefit levels and preventing a strike or lockout. Or union members can continue to work without a contract, taking whatever benefits the employer hands them. The employer can continue benefits at the previous contract level or increase them or, theoretically, could decrease benefits. The last usually indicates negotiating in bad faith. Another option is a lockout staged by an employer: He or she withholds employment to resist worker demands or gain concessions. Still another option is a strike called by a union.

Usually, the employees initiate economic pressures during negotiations because the union's goal in contract negotiations is to increase benefits, whereas management's goal is to maintain the status quo or gain concessions. A strike, however, may be called and endured for reasons other than a genuine inability to agree. One party may merely have miscalculated the breaking point of the opposition and increased a demand or refused a request once too often. Errors in strategy or in the interpersonal relations of the negotiator could preclude an opportunity for compromise. Management may want to liquidate surplus inventory while production is stopped by a strike. Union leaders may want to consolidate workers' support for their leadership, proving that a future strike threat has to be respected. Union leaders may feel the need for union solidarity that can be fostered only by a picket line. Often a strike is needed to vent member frustration over an inevitable but unsatisfactory contract settlement.[30]

An impasse may result after the negotiation teams have reached a tentative settlement and union membership rejects the contract. Such rejection may stem from a misjudgment of membership wishes by union officials or an inability to sell the agreement.

Calling a Strike

The right to strike is one of the rights made available to employees expressly provided by the National Labor Relations Act. It "lies at the core" of the Congressional intent to promote collective bargaining. Without the possibility of a strike, the ability of employees to bargain collectively would be seriously undermined.[31] Whatever the reason for an impasse, a decision to strike is not made lightly. In many instances the union negotiating team has called for a strike vote early in the negotiating process to prove its bargaining power when it becomes necessary to apply pressure. Although such a vote strengthens the negotiator's position, it needs to be carefully worked so that a strike deadline is not imposed, thereby tying the negotiator's hands. Slow-moving negotiations could become deadlocked; the deadline could destroy the negotiating atmosphere.

A union must weigh the cost of a strike against the probable benefit. A strike means loss of wages when wages may be quite high after years of successful union negotiations. Strike benefits also can be a drain on union funds. Workers risk losing their jobs, and even if they return to work, a strike can damage or destroy a good relationship with the employer. In addition, a union risks the loss of public sympathy. The success or failure of previous strikes and the availability of other jobs must also be considered. In addition to lost wages, union members today are also almost equally concerned about lost health insurance during a strike, which can leave their family without health-care coverage. For example, in 2002, Smart Papers LLC, a Hamilton, Ohio, company, refused to extend health-care benefits to striking workers as a means of putting added pressure on them to return to the table. The company also did not extend COBRA health-care benefits and began advertising for replacement workers.[32] Today, union leaders are far less likely to call a strike than in past years. In fact, the Bureau of Labor Statistics reports that in 2003 the number of major U.S. strikes (1,000 or more employees) fell to 14, the fewest since 1947, when it began recording strike data, and far less than the 424 in 1974, the modern record (see Figure 5-5). The loss of wages and potential permanent loss of their jobs are reasons why fewer union members and leaders

FIGURE 5-5   Numbers of Major Strikes (Involving 1,000 or More Workers)

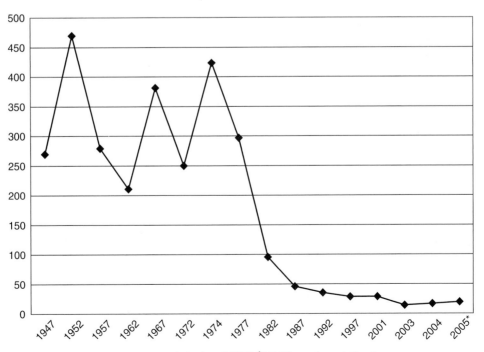

SOURCE: U.S. Bureau of Labor Statistics (April 2005) *2005 figure through October.

are willing to call for a strike. Employers have demonstrated their willingness to hire and train replacement workers to defeat a strike. Finding qualified replacement workers just isn't as difficult as in past years. However, today both sides realize that a strike isn't in either's best interest.[33]

Management Response

The majority of strikes occur when the existing contract expires; then employers have ample notice to prepare a strike plan. However, many wait until negotiations begin to break down, which is too late. A strike plan often focuses on how the employer will shut down operation during the strike, continue to operate with only management personnel, or hire replacement workers. Strikers may not be fired during a strike, but they can be replaced with permanent replacement workers.

Employers may not lawfully discharge a striking worker until they have hired a replacement worker to fill the position. In one case, supervisors telephoned bargaining unit employees to see which would be striking. The employees were told that if they did strike, replacements had been hired. A federal appeals court upheld the company's actions when the union filed an unfair labor practices charge because contract negotiations were underway.[34]

Both sides should keep in mind the possibility of an eventual settlement calling for the recall of striking workers, even after replacements have been hired, and the possibility of "bonuses" being paid to them to compensate them for lost income. Although such events are rare, the Steelworkers Union, in 1996, reached an agreement with Bridgestone-Firestone two years after the union workers went on strike. The agreement provided for the recall of almost all the workers at five U.S. plants and the payment of $15 million in bonuses to them. The Steelworkers charged the Japanese-owned company with illegally replacing the 6,000 striking workers.[35]

Predicting Strikes

Empirical research about the possible causes of strikes has produced conflicting conclusions. To date, a model of the collective bargaining process accurately predicting or explaining strikes in the United States has not been produced.[36] Perhaps the causes are too numerous and unpredictable to be easily explained. Some research has shown that the state of the economy and political forces in labor relations are significant predictors of strike activity. Thus, when negotiators believe that these factors are in their favor, they are more likely to call a strike. These predictors are limited in their usefulness because they do not account for the specific factors involved in each individual strike decision.[37] Other studies have shown that strikes are more likely to occur when either management or labor fails to estimate correctly the other party's level of interest in critical factors.[38] Management, for example, may underestimate the union members' concern over job security and the need for retraining rights or their perceived erosion of real wages due to inflation. Labor may not correctly estimate management's perceived need to adhere to a certain product-pricing policy or pressures from nonunion or foreign market competition.

The cost of a strike has also been shown to affect the likelihood and length of a strike. The employer considers costs such as loss of output, overtime costs to fill back orders, and the possible short-term and long-term effects on consumers and therefore market share. Some consumers may temporarily change to other products or supplies during a strike. Then, because of their satisfaction with the new product or service or as an expression of dissatisfaction with the striking company, they never return as customers. Profits and losses, increased legal and associated fees, and public image are also of concern to employers. The workers are concerned primarily with their loss of income during a strike. Union strike funds and government assistance seldom provide income equal to their previous take-home pay. Also to be carefully considered is the possible permanent loss of their jobs due to the eventual shutdown of the company or replacement by strikebreakers. Both sides consider their own strike costs in comparison to possible negotiation gains resulting from a strike. If the strike costs for the two parties are obviously unequal, that inequality translates into bargaining power for the side facing lower costs.[39]

Why Strikes Occur

Labor relations researchers have presented three basic models that explain why strikes actually occur. The first is the *accident model,* which suggests that negotiators (both union and management) act rationally and have substantial incentives to avoid strikes. Thus, they usually seek to reach a settlement without a strike. Strikes, therefore, occur only accidentally because of bargaining errors, such as unrealistic expectations by union or management leaders, misperception of bargaining goals, or a substantial difference between union negotiators and their rank-and-file membership. The second theory focuses on *joint strike costs* and suggests that strikes are more likely to occur when the joint costs to management and the union are relatively low, for example, when management has substantial inventories and can use management or other personnel to keep operating for a substantial period of time without union members. The third theory views strikes as *rational tactics* in the bargaining process and suggest that they generally occur when the two parties have substantially different information. For example, a firm with a low ability to pay higher wages and remain solvent may have the incentive to endure a lengthy strike and convince the union of its financial condition. Research on strikes in the manufacturing industries from 1982 to 1999 revealed that strikes were most often the result of bargaining errors or the accident model. Examples of strikes under the other two models, however, were also found.[40]

The circumstances that cause workers to strike and form a picket line are often tense and thus can easily provoke strikers to "let off steam," an impulse that can easily lead to serious misconduct. Workers on strike may resort to conduct that the employer believes is improper—conduct that causes damage to property or, in some cases, even bodily harm. The NLRB has held that activities of striking employees constitute serious misconduct when they "reasonably tend to coerce or intimidate employees."[41] The application of this standard has led the courts and the NLRB to consider physical acts or threats of physical harm directed at nonstriking employees (called scabs) to be serious and warrant possible discharge. Actions that have been ruled as serious misconduct include the throwing of rocks or eggs, vandalizing a supervisor's car, carrying a gun or a club on the picket line, and threatening physical harm.[42] In *Clear Pine Mouldings, Inc.,*[43] the NLRB ruled that verbal threats alone could warrant the discharge of a striker who, while carrying a gun, threatened to kill a nonstriking employee. In most cases, the isolated instance of obscenities or name-calling alone will not be considered serious strike misconduct. If an employer fires striking employees because of serious misconduct, the employer is not required to show that all the employees engaged in the activity if they were "actively cooperating" in the misconduct. And violent activity can result in the removal of the participants from the protection of the National Labor Relations Act. An examination of misconduct cases led one labor attorney to conclude that arbitrators are generally tolerant of strikers' misconduct, particularly if the employer provoked the incident.[44]

Types of Strikes

Economic weapons such as a strike are necessary to the collective bargaining process. Many such actions are protected under the National Labor Relations Act. The **primary strike** is a strike between an employer and employee. For employees to be protected under the act, a labor dispute must exist between the striking employees and their employer.

Unions may lawfully conduct a primary strike such as this one at Verizon. However, employers may respond by hiring permanent replacement workers.

The act recognizes two types of strikes and handles them differently. An **economic strike** is called to affect the economic settlement of a contract under negotiation. An **unfair labor practice strike** is called to protest an employer's violation of the National Labor Relations Act. For example, if a union member was fired for union activities, workers could stage a strike until the discriminatory practice was remedied.

Under either strike action the worker retains status as an employee and thereby remains under the protection of the National Labor Relations Act. The worker's right to reinstatement after a strike will depend on the type of strike. After an economic strike, the employee is not entitled to reinstatement if the employer filled the job with a permanent employee during the strike. However, if the job has not been filled or becomes vacant when a replacement leaves, the worker can reclaim it. Employees are entitled to reinstatement after an unfair labor practice strike even if the employer has filled their positions. Strike misconduct by the employee in either case can disqualify the worker from reinstatement.

A strike that begins as an economic strike may become an unfair labor practice strike if the union can prove that an employer is refusing to bargain in good faith. It is obviously to the union's advantage to do so, as it is to management's advantage to keep the strike an economic strike by continuing to negotiate in good faith. Management then has the option to hire replacement workers during the strike and keep the plant open, thereby lessening any adverse impact caused by the strike. At the end of the strike, the replacement workers can be retained, and the employer may have upgraded the workforce with minimal disruption.[45] Or, as in Case 5-2, a strike intended as an economic strike can become an unfair labor practice strike by the union if the goal is not legal. Unlike economic strikers, who may be replaced, unfair labor strikers have a substantially unqualified right to return to their jobs, even if the employer hired replacements. Thus, the type of strike may be a critical issue to both parties and may be in dispute.[46]

HOT CARGO CONTRACT

**CASE
5-2**

On April 21, 1998, the board certified the union as the exclusive collective bargaining representative of full-time and regular part-time building service employees employed by the company. The union and company subsequently met on four occasions in an unsuccessful attempt to negotiate a collective bargaining agreement. At the first meeting, the union representative presented the company representative with a contract proposal containing, among other terms and conditions, the following picket line clause:

> No employee covered by this agreement should be required by the employer to pass picket lines established by any Local of the SEIU in an authorized strike.

During the four bargaining sessions, the parties agreed to various changes in the contract proposal but disagreed as to other provisions. The parties *did not* discuss the picket line clause during any of the bargaining sessions. At the end of the final bargaining session, the union stated that if the company did not accept the proposal then on the bargaining table, the union would strike. It is undisputed that the union's proposed contract included the picket line clause.

After the company refused to sign the proposed contract, the union struck. The union's business agent testified that an object of the strike was to get the company to sign the collective bargaining agreement. During the strike, the strikers informed the union that they wanted to return to work. The agent replied that he "would prefer [the strikers] to stay out for a little longer because we would have a better chance of getting a contract signed." The parties knew that the contract contained the picket line clause, but this clause *was never* a topic of discussion or controversy during the negotiations. Rather, the parties disagreed over other contract terms, and it was those disagreements that provoked the strike.

Nonetheless, the company filed an unfair labor charge against the union alleging that because the union's contract proposal contained a picket line clause prohibited by Section 8(e) of the act and the union engaged in a strike to force or require the company to enter into a contract containing that clause, the strike violated Section 8(b)(4)(ii)(A) (prohibiting secondary boycott agreements).

The administrative law judge found that Section 8(e) prohibited the picket line clause. He nevertheless recommended dismissal of the Section 8(b)(4)(ii)(A) allegation because he did not believe that *the object of the strike* was to force or require the company to enter into an agreement containing the picket line clause. The company appealed.

DECISION

Like the ALJ, the NLRB agreed that Section 8(e) prohibited the picket line clause. Unlike the ALJ, however, the board found

continued

<table>
<tr><td>**CASE 5-2**</td><td>**HOT CARGO CONTRACT—continued**</td></tr>
</table>

that the object of the strike was to force or require the company to enter into a contract containing the picket line clause and therefore that the union violated Section 8(b)(4)(ii)(A). The board noted that it is undisputed that the union engaged in a strike to obtain an agreement. Further, it is well established that a strike constitutes "coercion" within the meaning of the statute. The union proposed an agreement containing a picket line clause prohibited by Section 8(e). The union insisted that the company sign the contract or else the union would strike. When the company refused to sign the contract, the union began a strike. The strike was to compel the company to sign a contract, which, at all relevant times, included the clause prohibited by Section 8(e). Accordingly, the NLRB found that the union's strike, which began on February 22, 1999, had as *an object* forcing or requiring the company to enter into an agreement proscribed by Section 8(e) and that such conduct violated Section 8(b)(4)(ii)(A) of the act.

SOURCE: Adapted from Local 32B-32J, *Service Employees v. Pratt Towers Inc.*, 169 LRRM 1185 (December 20, 2001).

A strike technique that has recently gained favor with unions whose members work at numerous locations for the same employer is the rolling strike. A **rolling strike** targets one location at a time for a union walkout. The location, however, can change daily, making hiring replacements or covering locations with management nearly impossible.[47] For example, on August 11, 2005, baggage handlers and loaders represented by the Transport and General Workers Union staged a one-day walkout at Heathrow Airport in London, England, which stranded about 70,000 summer travelers. The walkout was to demonstrate support for workers fired by the airport catering firm and represented by the same union.[48]

It is interesting to note that courts will not allow an employer to assume that permanent replacement workers hired during a strike are antiunion. In *NLRB v. Curtin-Matheson*, the Supreme Court upheld the board's rule that permanent replacement workers must be treated as any other group of employees when determining whether they wish to be represented by a union. That they took jobs while union employees were on strike does not create a presumption that they are antiunion.[49]

Permanent Striker Replacement

This distinction between how striking employees are treated as a result of either an economic or an unfair labor practice strike was established by a Supreme Court decision in 1938.[50] In the *Mackay* case, the Court decided employers could permanently replace striking workers without violating the (then three-year-old) Wagner Act. The case involved a group of radio employees who decided to go on strike at midnight. The employer, believing it critical to stay "on the air" and provide continuous service, quickly filled the strikers' positions. The strikers then realized their strike was not having the desired outcome and asked for their jobs back. Management decided to reinstate them only if their replacements chose to resign—and 11 replacements did not. The union employees then filed suit claiming the employer had "interfered with, restrained, and coerced" them and thus violated their rights under the National Labor Relations Act. The NLRB agreed with the employees but also agreed with the employer that the act did not prohibit the hiring of permanent striker replacements.

The Supreme Court agreed, and the *Mackay* **doctrine** was established in one of the most important cases in labor law history. The Court noted that although Section 13 of the National Labor Relations Act prohibits the interference with employees' right to strike, an employer has the right to continue the operations of a business and replace strikers. The *Mackay* doctrine has been somewhat limited by three NLRB decisions: (1) employers cannot permanently replace strikers who are striking over an unfair labor practice, (2) strikers who apply for reinstatement unconditionally must be placed on a "waiting list" and hired as jobs become available if they do not acquire other employment, and (3) employers cannot grant pay raises to replacements not offered to strikers.[51]

Before the 1980s, however, companies seldom replaced striking workers with permanent replacements for a number of reasons. Frequently, an economic strike was determined, after the fact, to be an unfair labor practice strike, and the replacement workers were displaced. Often the company used the issue of allowing the strikers to return to their jobs as a way to settle an economic strike.

Economic factors of the 1980s led companies to use **permanent replacement workers** more than ever before.[52] Mergers, downsizing, and companies going out of business provided many employers with available trained workers during a strike. High unemployment and a weakening of union membership caused workers to cross picket lines willingly and to take jobs at wage rates lower than union-bargained rates.

The hiring of permanent replacement workers can also lead to the decertification of a union. The NLRB ruled that workers on strike for over one year are not eligible to vote in a decertification election. Thus an employer, in an effort to win a decertification election, might force a strike, employ permanent replacement workers for over a year, then seek a decertification election knowing the union strikers are no longer eligible to vote in the election. This employer tactic grew in popularity after the 1981 PATCO strike.[53]

A 2002 Bureau of National Affairs survey of management negotiators found that most employers would at least consider hiring replacement workers. However, only 21 percent reported it was a "very likely" event, 30 percent reported it was "somewhat likely," and 49 percent said it was "not likely" or ruled it out totally. Employees in small bargaining units (fewer than 1,000) and those in basic manufacturing, according to the survey, are more likely to be replaced than those of other employers.[54]

However, employers in industries such as the airlines, when trying to avoid losses or even bankruptcy, are increasingly considering replacement workers as a strategy to keep unions from staging a strike or cutting labor costs by hiring replacement workers. As discussed in Labor News, in 2005 Northwest Airlines threatened to employ 1,500 trained and ready replacements if the mechanics union called a strike when their contract expired. Northwest was demanding $1.1 billion in cuts to avoid potential bankruptcy.[55]

In the past several years there has been a growing debate over a proposed amendment to the NLRA that would ban the hiring of permanent replacement workers during a strike. Supporters of the proposal contend that the escalating practice of hiring permanent replacement workers has weakened workers' ability to bargain collectively as expressly provided by the NLRA and has become a significant cause of the decline of unionization in the United States. Opponents of the proposed ban respond that it would tip the scale in favor of unions and even lead to more strikes that would disrupt the economy. Why? Individuals would be less likely to cross a picket line for jobs that were only temporary and end once the strike was settled. Both sides have legitimate points, and the issue may be central to the future of union–management relations in the United States. One "middle-ground" proposal would prohibit employers from hiring permanent replacement workers for a specified number of days after a strike had begun and thus provide both sides some bargaining leverage.[56] Congress, which thus far has chosen not to act, ultimately will decide the issue, and therefore employers remain free to hire permanent replacement workers.

Illegal Strikes

Strikes undertaken by unlawful means or purposes are not legal, and employees can be fired. Unlawful means of conducting a strike include the following:

1. *Sit-down strike.* A takeover of the employer's property. This action is seen as a violation of the owner's property rights.
2. *Wildcat strike.* An economic strike conducted by a minority of the workers without the approval of the union and in violation of a no-strike clause in an existing contract. Although courts try to discourage such actions to ensure the continued credibility of the union, these strikes may be sanctioned if actually called to protect one of the union's aims.[57]
3. *Partial strike.* Various types of job actions, such as a work slowdown or refusal to work overtime. This action is seen as a violation of the owner's property rights.
4. *Sickout.* An organized effort to have workers call in sick. In the 1990s, the fastest-growing type of job action was the **sickout**. In December 1998, for example, Trans World Airlines was forced to cancel 240 flights after the flight attendants all called in sick during the week of Christmas. In an age when most labor unions try to avoid strikes if possible, the sickout is a good alternative job action. The action sends a clear message to the employer and can cause real inconvenience and loss of income. However, unlike when workers go out on an economic strike, they are not out long enough to be replaced with new permanent employees. Public-sector unions, usually under no-strike laws, utilized sickouts more often than private-sector unions in past years. But private-sector unions have increasingly used the tactic as a show of strength and to protest stalled contract negotiations. They can be most effective when utilized by employees who cannot be easily replaced.[58]

In the absence of an absolute strike, the employer cannot replace the workers to keep the operation going, although the employer continues to be responsible for the workers' wages.

The National Labor Relations Act requires that a union desiring to terminate or modify an existing contract may not strike for 60 days after giving written notice to the employer or before the termination date of the contract, whichever occurs later. Also, the appropriate federal and state mediation agencies must be notified within 30 days. Any strike held during the 60-day period is unlawful.

The National Labor Relations Act outlaws some consequences for which workers might strike. The following are unlawful ends that make a strike illegal:

1. *Jurisdictional strike.* Called because two unions are in dispute as to whose workers deserve the work. For example, an electrical union could strike a construction site in protest of laborers being used to unload electrical supplies.
2. *Featherbedding strike.* When a union tries to pressure the employer to make work for union members through the limitation of production, increasing the amount of work to be performed, or other make-work arrangements.
3. *Recognitional strike.* When a strike is called to gain recognition for another union if a certified union already represents employees.[59]

Picketing

The use of picket lines during a strike varies according to the type of union involved. A craft union strike generally uses only two or three pickets. The purpose of the picket is simply to inform other craft union members that a strike is in progress. Because craft union workers are skilled laborers, workers who will not honor a picket line cannot easily replace them. Craft unions may use larger picketing groups when protesting the use of a nonunion contractor.

An industrial union strike, however, often requires an active and large picket line to discourage unskilled laborers from keeping the production lines in operation. Mass picketing generally takes place at least at the start of a strike to persuade union members to join the strike and to keep strikebreakers away. In 2003, for example, almost 2,000 clerical, maintenance, and food service workers at Yale University rallied supporters in New Haven, Connecticut, by picketing. On one day in September, the workers' demonstration closed down the center of the city as well as the university with over 5,000 supporters of the Hotel Employees and Restaurant Employees International Union. As the demonstration became unruly about 100 people were arrested, but the activity led to a new eight-year contract with 4 to 5 percent annual wage increases and sizable pension increases.[60]

An employer may respond to mass picketing by obtaining a court injunction against the union to refrain from certain activities. An injunction, usually in the form of a temporary restraining order, is possible if the strike activities have included incidents of violence, personal injury, or damage to property. In such cases, the court can order specific restraints on the union's use of pickets—limiting, for instance, their number and location.[61]

Today, picket lines have lost the power they once provided unions. In years past, a picket line in front of a plant, store, or construction site could cause a major financial loss to the employer. Union and nonunion workers would "honor" the picket line. Crossing the line was the equivalent of pushing an old lady off a curb. Labor sympathizers would refuse to enter picketed workplaces as employees or customers. When unions represented 36 percent of the labor force, almost every adult had at least one union member in the family—and thus was sympathetic to labor's cause. Today, that just is not the situation. Even Rachelle Pachtman, the daughter of a union man, raised on union wages and benefits, crosses picket lines. "If there's a meeting in a hotel where workers are striking . . . I'm going to the meeting. . . . But I feel terrible."[62]

Prominent U.S. Strikes: 1983–2005

The number of economic strikes has declined sharply in recent years. However, a few significant strikes have attracted the news media and permanently affected U.S. labor–management relations.

The 1983 and 1989 Telephone Workers Strikes

Nearly 700,000 unionized telephone workers broke a 12-year labor peace on August 7, 1983. This strike was partially the result of an order by federal judge Harold Greene to divest AT&T into 22 local operating companies. The federal order, combined with the company's need to increase its use of high technology to remain competitive, gave union members ample reasons to fear future loss of jobs. Thus, their demands centered on employment security, although higher wages and benefits were also issues.

The effects of modern technology at AT&T were strongly felt as a result of the strike. After the first two weeks, the company reported almost no interruption in service except for new installations. Ninety-seven percent of the calls were handled by automated computer systems, which had also enabled management to reduce the ratio of supervisors to workers. By scheduling supervision on 12-hour shifts and by postponing some work, AT&T was able to keep the strike from affecting most of its customers.

Management's ability to endure the strike by means of automated equipment and longer shifts of supervision was something new. Harley Shaiken dubbed it **telescabbing**, that is, using modern technology as a substitute for labor during a strike instead of hiring scab labor.[63] Shaiken further stated that many industries, including oil, steel, and utilities, will be able to maintain high production levels during strikes because of automation, thus taking away the unions' ability to disrupt production by striking.[64] Unions had lost one of their most important collective bargaining tools as a result of high technology. Although repair work, new installations, and some long-distance calls were affected by the strike, union leaders underestimated the ability of the company to continue its normal operations.

When the workers went out on strike again in August 1989, the striking workers faced the same critical problem they first witnessed in 1983—telescabbing.

The 1986–1987 Steel Industry Negotiations

For the first time in 30 years, the major U.S. steelmakers decided in the spring of 1986 not to bargain jointly. The prior use of coordinated bargaining enabled all the major steel producers to negotiate common wage rates and benefits with the United Steelworkers of America. All parties (including 450,000 workers) had also enjoyed relative harmony with an industrywide no-strike agreement. However, foreign competition and weakening demand due to newer and cheaper steel substitutes had caused the industry to lose more than $1 billion in the previous two years. Thus, each steelmaker decided to negotiate separately a contract that could mean survival or bankruptcy.[65] USX and the union had the longest strike in steel history.

The 1989 Eastern Airlines Strike

In March 1989, the International Association of Machinists (IAM) went on strike against Eastern Airlines and was joined by the pilots and flight attendants as Eastern filed for bankruptcy. The strike was triggered by Eastern's demands for large wage concessions from the machinists. In reality, however, the discontent that fueled the strike may have begun when Texas Air Corporation, an obscure airline owned by Frank Lorenzo, staged a takeover of Eastern Airlines in November 1988. In 1983, Lorenzo, a self-proclaimed "union buster," took Continental Airlines into bankruptcy proceedings, imposed significant wage cuts, and broke the pilots' and machinists' strikes. Continental survived as a profitable, low-cost (and low-paying) airline. The machinists and pilots at Eastern saw what was coming and decided to strike even if it broke Eastern.

Late in 1989, the Eastern Airline pilots voted to return to work, leaving only the IAM out on strike. The Eastern strike is a good example of how even highly trained and technical employee unions have a difficult time sustaining a strike.

The 1993 United Mine Workers Strike

In early May 1993, the United Mine Workers began a **selective strike** against coal producers after contract negotiations failed to result in a new master agreement with the Bituminous Coal Operators Association. The primary goal of the union during the talks was to stem the coal operators' practice of opening new, nonunion mines.

The 1994 Baseball Players Strike

The most disastrous strike in sports history canceled the 1994 World Series and cost the sport many fans and significant revenue (see Chapter 2).

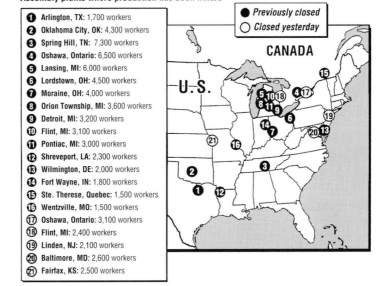

Assembly plants where production has been halted

1. **Arlington, TX:** 1,700 workers
2. **Oklahoma City, OK:** 4,300 workers
3. **Spring Hill, TN:** 7,300 workers
4. **Oshawa, Ontario:** 6,500 workers
5. **Lansing, MI:** 6,000 workers
6. **Lordstown, OH:** 4,500 workers
7. **Moraine, OH:** 4,000 workers
8. **Orion Township, MI:** 3,600 workers
9. **Detroit, MI:** 3,200 workers
10. **Flint, MI:** 3,100 workers
11. **Pontiac, MI:** 3,000 workers
12. **Shreveport, LA:** 2,300 workers
13. **Wilmington, DE:** 2,000 workers
14. **Fort Wayne, IN:** 1,800 workers
15. **Ste. Therese, Quebec:** 1,500 workers
16. **Wentzville, MO:** 1,500 workers
17. **Oshawa, Ontario:** 3,100 workers
18. **Flint, MI:** 2,400 workers
19. **Linden, NJ:** 2,100 workers
20. **Baltimore, MD:** 2,600 workers
21. **Fairfax, KS:** 2,500 workers

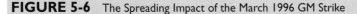

FIGURE 5-6 The Spreading Impact of the March 1996 GM Strike

SOURCE: Rebecca Blumenstein, Nichole Christian, and Oscar Suris, "GM Local Labor Dispute Spins Out of Control," *Wall Street Journal,* March 13, 1996, p. B1. Used by permission.

The 1996 General Motors Strike

A local labor dispute in one plant eventually crippled the world's largest automobile company. UAW local in Dayton, Ohio, went on strike over **outsourcing**—the employer practice of giving business to nonunion suppliers that usually will eventually mean fewer union jobs. The strike gained national prominence and historical significance because the Dayton General Motors plant supplied 90 percent of the brakes for GM cars and trucks. Thus, within weeks more than 72,000 workers at 21 of GM's 29 North American auto assembly plants were idled at a cost of $45 million per day (see Figure 5-6). This method of using a selective strike had been used by the UAW with Ford and Chrysler but not nearly as effectively. The new UAW strategy was to avoid large national strikes by thousands of members that drain support and the strike fund. A selective strike can have the same effect yet pose less risk and cost to a union.[66]

The 1997 UPS Strike

The Teamsters union strike idled over 180,000 workers and crippled delivery of packages worldwide. A central issue was part-time versus full-time jobs. The union won 10,000 new full-time jobs and focused national attention on this issue. After the strike the Teamsters kept pressure on UPS to add the promised new full-time jobs. One successful method utilized by the union was to ask its members online (www.teamsters.org) to help identify exactly where full-time jobs were needed (see Figure 5-7). In 2002, five years after the strike, the UPS/Teamsters contract negotiations received national attention again as other unions looked to their outcome to set the tone for their own negotiations. However, the sluggish economy, combined with the aftermath of September 11, 2001, created a different labor environment. Even in the new environment, popular Teamster president James Hoffa was able to win 10,000 more full-time jobs and "substantial" wage and benefit increases for UPS members already averaging $23 per hour, the highest in the industry.[67]

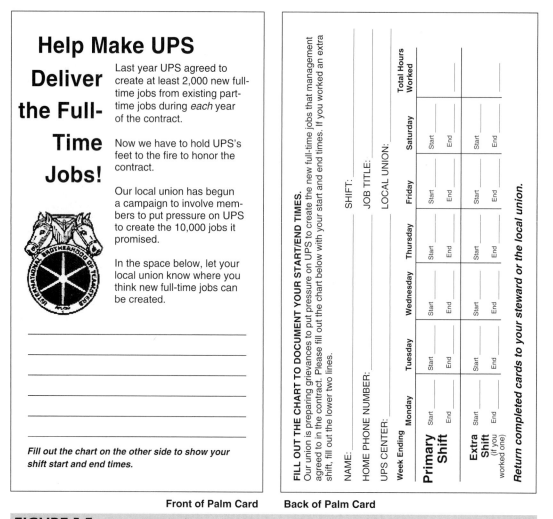

Front of Palm Card   Back of Palm Card

FIGURE 5-7 Teamster Online Appeal to Members

SOURCE: www.teamsters.org/98ups.

The 2001 Comair Strike

Comair, once one of the most successful of the regional U.S. airlines, began an 89-day strike in the spring of 2001 by the Airlines Pilots Association, costing Comair and parent company Delta Airlines almost $500 million in expenses and lost revenue. In addition 2,400 nonpilot employees were laid off because of the strike. With the strike settled in June 2001, Comair had slowly begun to rebuild when the aftermath of September 11, 2001, severely hit the entire airline industry and stalled Comair's recovery. Then in 2002 the International Brotherhood of Teamsters organized the Comair flight attendants, for the first time, as the airline sought to avoid another crippling strike. The company feared that a new strike, combined with the effects of the 2001 pilots' union strike and the industry slump following September 11, might have brought Comair to financial collapse.

The 2003-2004 Southern California Grocery Chain Lockout and Strike

In October 2003 contract negotiations between the United Food and Commercial Workers Union and Kroger's West Coast grocery chains (Albertsons, Vons, Ralphs) broke down over health-care costs. A bitter 20-week strike caused Kroger Company to lose over $337 million in one quarter and cost over 70,000 workers in 860 stores from San Diego to San Luis Obispo almost five months of income. Kroger cited the need to lower operating costs to compete with the nation's largest food retailer, Wal-Mart. Wal-Mart is nonunion and is estimated to have substantially lower personnel costs. The new contract, approved in February 2004, contained a "two-tiered" system of wages and health-care benefits, with employees hired after October 5, 2003 placed on a lower tier. The union tried unsuccessfully to resist the two-tier approach.

Lockout

Although less frequent than strikes, an employer **lockout** may also be used in a labor dispute. The employer may withhold employment to resist union demands or actually to force concessions from the union. Layoffs, shutting down, or bringing in nonunion workers can accomplish the lockout. For example, in July 2005, management at NuTone Inc. in Madisonville, Ohio, notified 450 members of the United Auto Workers Local 2029 that they were locked out of their jobs. The union members were working without a contract after their contract with NuTone expired in June, and they had rejected the company's last offer. The locked-out employees were eligible for unemployment benefits.[68] The employer again must measure the same factors involved in withstanding a strike when deciding to lock out the employees: loss of profits, cost of continued operations, possible loss of customers, and the effect on future labor negotiations. Employer lockouts can be in violation of the National Labor Relations Act as an unfair labor practice if they are invoked to prevent unionization or to preclude collective bargaining before it begins.

Courts have supported both defensive and offensive employer lockouts under the Taft-Hartley Amendments. In defensive actions, employers are justified in a lockout if a threatened strike caused unusual economic loss or operational difficulties. In multiemployer bargaining, a strike against one employer can justify a lockout by the others to preserve the integrity of the multiemployer bargaining unit. Offensive economic lockouts have been justified after an impasse has developed during collective bargaining negotiation or if the lockout was used to pressure employees to end the labor dispute on grounds favorable to the employer. The courts reasoned that an economic strike by employees seeks the same end, and therefore the lockout is protected.[69]

The use of replacement workers during a lockout is governed by the same rule as using replacements during a strike. Permanent replacements may be hired during a lockout to affect the economic outcome of a contract under negotiations but not if the lockout is a result of an unfair labor practice by the employer.[70]

In a recent case, the NLRB was asked to rule on whether a lockout was an unfair labor practice by the employer. The parties were in negotiations but unable to reach agreement on a contract renewal. The employer undertook a lawful lockout and replaced union workers with nonunion workers under a "temporary" agreement. However, as negotiations with the union resumed, the employer decided to permanently replace the union workers. The board found the employer guilty of an unfair labor practice. It ruled that the lockout and permanent replacement of the employees would have been legal had the employer originally taken this action. However, the conversion from temporary to permanent after resuming negotiations was an attempt to pressure the union into accepting the employer's position at the bargaining table and was "inherently destructive" of the rights protected under the act.[71]

No-Strike, No-Lockout Provisions

Most agreements contain provisions restricting the union's ability to call a strike and management's ability to stage a lockout. Usually either both or neither type of provision is negotiated because they are reciprocal in nature. No-strike and no-lockout clauses often contain similar, if not identical, language, falling into two general categories: (1) unconditional bans (63 percent of agreements) on interference with production during the life of the contract and (2) conditional bans that permit strike or lockout under certain circumstances, usually one or more of the following:[72]

Exhaustion of grievance procedure

Violation of arbitration award

Refusal to arbitrate dispute

Noncompliance with portion of agreement

Deadlocked contract reopener

The discipline or discharge of employees participating in illegal strikes under a no-strike provision may be permitted in the agreement. Most of these clauses provide for appeal by the employee.[73]

No-strike clauses are usually highly sought by industry, but severe circumstances may alter their value. As discussed earlier, since 1956 the U.S. steel industry has enjoyed an industrywide no-strike agreement. In 1986 the six major U.S. steelmakers decided to bargain separately with the United Steelworkers of America. The firms' fierce competition for survival forced them to give up the safety of joint negotiations and the continuance of the no-strike pact and led to the longest steel industry strike in history.[74]

Resolution of Impasse

When possible, an impasse should be avoided. Parties to negotiations can decide early on to seek a mediator to encourage joint problem solving. Bargaining techniques such as principled negotiations and interest-based bargaining can be used to avoid pressure tactics. Entering into negotiations long before the contract expiration date can relieve some of the deadline pressure. The use of joint labor–management study committees before and during the contract negotiations also can alleviate much of the conflict present in traditional bargaining sessions.

Still, an impasse often cannot be avoided, and resolution becomes one of the stages of negotiations. Sometimes a pressure tactic works, and one of the parties reactivates negotiations more favorable to the opposing party. Often informal communication through a neutral third party enables the parties to resume talks to a successful conclusion. Traditionally, however, an impasse is resolved by resorting to **mediation** and **arbitration** services.

1.   *Mediation.*   These services are available through the Federal Mediation and Conciliation Service (FMCS) and similar state agencies. A mediator assists in rescheduling negotiation sessions, reopening discussions, and making suggestions on possible areas of agreement. If a mere misunderstanding of the parties' positions has caused an impasse, an unbiased third party can often show them how close they actually are to agreement. If the substantive distance between the parties causes the impasse, a mediator must try to bring the respective proposals closer together.[75]

An empirical study of mediator tactics in 2002 found an array of commonly used methods that can substantially increase the probability of success. For example, mediators in most situations can use the tactics of friendliness and of minimizing negative emotions by those involved. Other tactics included applying pressure in situations where the underlying cause of the impasse is party inflexibility and telling parties their positions are unrealistic and pushing them to a compromise. Another mediator tactic, "inaction," may be the best one to use in some unique situations where mediators suggesting alternatives may actually interfere with the process of reaching a settlement. Overall, these common mediator tactics were positively correlated with moving stalled negotiations to the point of reaching a negotiated settlement.[76] A 2005 FMCS survey of 1,168 pairs of union and management leaders found that mediation is in greater demand today than in past years. The reason is increased polarization of labor–management relations and greater likelihood of strikes and lockouts. Fifty percent of the leaders responded that mediation is needed to resolve differences and prevent work stoppages.[77]

2. *Interest arbitration.* Although infrequently used in the private sector, this method involves the selection of an arbitrator or panel to listen to both sides of a dispute and to make a final and binding decision on the details of the final agreement. This process substitutes a person or panel for the negotiating parties in formulating a written contract.

3. *Final-offer arbitration.* This method requires both parties to submit their final offer to an arbitrator or a panel that has the authority to select one of the proposals. Final-offer arbitration gives the parties the motivation to make their final offers reasonable. Both parties realize that an unreasonable offer will have a lower chance of selection. Therefore, they strive to make their offer appear as fair and reasonable as possible.

In 1987, Detroit Tiger Jack Morris won a $1.85 million contract dispute through final-offer arbitration. The baseball players' union and major league owners had agreed to begin using the impasse resolution technique in 1974 to settle salary disputes. When the Tigers and their star pitcher could not reach a salary agreement, they each presented their final offer to an arbitrator who could choose only one of the two offers and could not choose a compromise. The Tigers' last offer was $1.35 million—$500,000 larger than the previous largest final-offer arbitration award. Morris proposed $1.85 million based on his 123–81 record (most wins in the majors in the 1980s) and his performance in the 1984 World Series. His final-offer salary arbitration began a new era in sports.

4. *Mediation–arbitration.* A combination of items 1 and 2, in this method parties agree to bring in a mediator with authority to arbitrate any unresolved issues. Because the parties must agree to abide by the mediator–arbitrator's decision, they will likely agree on the substantive issues as well.

5. *Fact-finding.* This method lies between mediation and arbitration. A hearing, similar to the one used in the arbitration process, is used to assemble and make the facts public through the media. But the fact-finding panel, like a mediator, can only recommend how an impasse may be resolved. **Fact-finding** can be used to delay a strike, bring an unreasonable demand to the public's attention, create an atmosphere for new ideas, and if reasonable recommendations are made, pressure a party into acceptance. This technique is used mostly in the public sector, where such pressure is useful in forcing the parties to reach an agreement, especially if the facts show that one side is unreasonable.

BARGAINING IN THE PUBLIC SECTOR

Negotiating a collective bargaining agreement in the public sector differs in significant ways from negotiating in the private sector.

The Nature of Public Employment

Essential Services

Unlike employees in the private sector, public employees provide education, police, fire, and sanitation services and maintenance of public improvements. In recent years, legislation has increased government jobs for social workers, clerical and office employees, and computer technicians. Citizens depend on the services of these employees. The nature of the services provided—Social Security checks, food stamps, record keeping—is such that private industry is unable or unwilling to offer them; thus, a government monopoly is created.

Lack of Competition

The lack of competition by the private sector can cause collective bargaining problems. Without consumer control, quality can suffer, subjecting the public employee to adverse public sentiment. The lack of another provider makes the continuation of the public service critical; it prevents the employees from using economic pressure to reach a collective bargaining agreement. The absence of marketplace control on costs might also encourage intemperate collective bargaining settlements by public employers. The public employer, often an elected official, might give more tax dollars than are warranted to a certain project and then let a succeeding administration solve the deficit.

Mostly Professional Employees

Public-sector collective bargaining also differs because of its extensive unionization of professional employees. Measures of productivity are more difficult to devise for professional employees than for production and maintenance employees. In addition, the use of a service in the public sector cannot be related to the need for such service when participating in collective bargaining. Because providing public transportation is necessary, a bus driver should not be expected to have his or her pay affected by the number of people who choose to use that service.

Elected Officials

The public employer represents and provides services to the public. That employer is either an elected official serving for a limited term or someone placed in a position by that official. Although the legislative and executive branches of governments are almost always separate, the government as an employer is a combination of the two. Their roles may be clearly distinguished or may merge as the employee seeks the decision maker for collective bargaining rights. The source of funds available to the public employer may be limited by totally external factors, such as Proposition 13–type taxing limitations or grants of funds from a higher government level with constraints on their use.

The Sovereignty Doctrine

By using the sovereignty doctrine, the public employer may seek to control the collective bargaining process by limiting the issues to be bargained. Also, the public employer can be influenced by a lack of competition in the necessary services.[78]

Limited Scope of Negotiations in the Public Sector

Management Rights

More management rights are reserved for the employer in the public sector than in the private sector. Under the sovereignty theory, government avoids many issues at the bargaining table. For example, in Title VII, an agency is given the right to make a unilateral decision to determine the mission, budget, organization, number of employees, and internal security practices. Questions of hiring, employee assignment, promotions, firings, suspensions, and other disciplinary actions are all at the agency's discretion. A union may be able to negotiate procedures for actions taken by the employer and appropriate arrangements for adversely affected employees, but as stated earlier, the basic content of a grievance procedure is also legislated. Most state and local governments use similar language to ensure that policy and quality of service remain the prerogative of management.

Union Security

As discussed in Chapter 3, union security refers to the ability of the union to grow and to perform its collective bargaining role without interference from management or other unions. As the exclusive representative of certain employees, a union enjoys a high degree of security. In the private sector, union security provisions include automatic dues deductions, a union or agency shop, and maintenance of membership provisions. These ensure a dependable source of revenue.

In the public sector, agency shop provisions are commonly used because they assist the union financially but do not require compulsory unionization. As demonstrated in Table 5-2, agency shop provisions are the most commonly accepted union security clause in public-sector contracts. An agency shop provision requires financial support of the union whether the employee joins the union or not. The agency shop provision came under some question in a Supreme Court decision, *Abood v. Detroit Board of Education,* limiting the amount of dues to be paid by nonunion members to the amount actually spent on collective bargaining, contract administration, and grievance adjustment.[79]

TABLE 5-2 Percentage Distribution of Union Security and Impasse Resolution Provisions by Duty to Bargain: State and Local Government Sample (excluding police and fire)

Variable	Duty to Bargain	No Duty to Bargain
Agency shop		
Right to work	3.6	19.3
No agency provision	9.2	18.8
Agency shop authorized	43.0	2.1
Agency shop mandatory	4.1	0.0
Compulsory checkoff		
No compulsory checkoff	25.9	4.3
Compulsory checkoff	36.1	33.7
Impasse resolution		
No binding method	40.8	0.0
Compulsory arbitration	2.2	0.0
Right to strike	19.0	0.0

SOURCE: Greg Hundley, "Collective Bargaining Coverage of Union Members and Nonmembers in the Public Sector," *Industrial Relations 32,* no. 1 (Winter 1993), p. 76.

Wages and Fringes

In most cases the negotiation of wages and fringe benefits is a union's principal function. Public employee unions, however, often find this subject out of their reach. Under Title VII, the federal statute governing employee rights, the right to bargain collectively is limited to issues concerning conditions of employment and excludes wages and fringe benefits. For most state and municipal employees, the legislative body has determined a budget before or while union contract negotiations are taking place.

Hours

The nature of the job performed often determines the amount of flexibility available in the negotiation of hours. Police, fire, and other emergency services must operate around the clock. Transportation and public utilities cannot be subject to variation. The public employer jealously guards the determination of total hours of work as a management policy decision.

Working Conditions

Unlike in the private sector, negotiation of working conditions in the public sector does not center on promotions, discipline, and production standards. Working conditions directly affect the provision of service to the public. Therefore, issues that may be decided at a negotiating table include the number of police in a patrol car or firefighters on a fire alarm run. Classroom size, the number of bus routes, or the frequencies of trash pickup are issues determined by the public employer, often through negotiations. The public employee is often better able to determine the quality of service than the manager.

Grievance Procedure

Under the federal statute, a grievance procedure must be included in federal contracts. That procedure includes binding arbitration if necessary. State and local government contracts, although containing grievance procedures, frequently stop at advisory arbitration. A review of impasse resolution procedures in state and local government contracts (excluding police and fire departments) found few that called for binding arbitration. Table 5-2 includes those results.[80]

Public employers may believe that the sovereignty doctrine prohibits the delegation of decision-making authority to a nonelected body such as an arbitrator. That legal theory weakens, however, when the binding arbitration concerns only adjudication of contract provisions already negotiated and agreed to by the public employers.

Negotiating the Public Employee Contract

The Bargaining Process

Fundamental ideas regarding bargaining theories and the bargaining process in the private sector hold true for the public sector with a few variations. In the private sector, union negotiators derive their authority to negotiate from their membership. That authority is generally limited in that the contract must be taken back to the membership for a vote. On the other hand, management negotiators have the authority to commit to a negotiated agreement at the bargaining table. This situation is often referred to as **bilateral bargaining**. In the public sector, where management's authority to negotiate flows from the people, the decision cannot be made by one official and is referred to as **multilateral bargaining**.

Multilateral Bargaining

The governmental entities involved in collective bargaining fall into two categories: a council form and an executive-legislative form. For example, an elected or appointed council of a school district acts as a board of directors for a corporation that appoints its own chief executive officer. The public negotiator for management may find his or her role similar to that of the negotiator for labor; that is, he or she is charged with returning a negotiated agreement for approval to the final authority. Such approval is usually given because of the close relationship between the negotiator and the council.

In an executive-legislative form, the executive authority resides with a president, governor, or mayor who is the manager of the governmental entity. The legislative authority resides with a congress, a legislature, or a council that is the lawmaker of the governmental entity. Together, the two parties make up management; both are employers to the public employees. This joint management authority is seldom a problem because the executive manages personnel policies on a day-to-day basis under directives put in place by the legislators. During labor negotiations, however, when the decisions affecting employees are subject to collective bargaining, conflicts can arise. The negotiator is employed by the executive branch and may be understood to be negotiating on behalf of the executive branch. Settlement may be reached by the negotiator and endorsed by the executive (mayor, governor, and so on), but the legislative body must approve it. The legislative body may not approve the negotiated agreement, thereby undermining the collective bargaining process.

Obviously, the disadvantage of multilateral negotiations to the employer is the union's ability to appeal to the legislative body for a more favorable settlement before, during, or after the negotiations, thus undermining the work of the executive. On the other hand, the executive and legislative branches may not agree on a settlement, leaving the union up in the air while each side blames the other for indecision.[81]

The legislative body may seek to play the role of a mediator between the executive branch and the union when an impasse develops.[82] The legislative body is a part of management and, as such, has no legitimate role as mediator. Because the legislature has the authority to determine the budget, involvement at an impasse stage of negotiations represents a new level of negotiation rather than mediation. That level may involve a restatement of the executive's position or a new offer by the legislative branch. Such a practice undermines the public employer's negotiating posture. Intervention after the fact by a third party may destroy the fairness of a negotiated agreement and the commitment to compromise so important to collective bargaining.

Open Negotiations

Public employee collective bargaining makes news. Press coverage of public employee collective bargaining can harm the bargaining process in several ways. If an impasse is reached, the parties may try to explain their side to the media, hoping to influence public opinion and in turn the negotiating process. Rushing for media coverage may cause a party to present proposals publicly before it has presented them to the other party at the negotiating table. By emphasizing the differences between the parties instead of the points of agreement, reporters can actually prolong the posturing stage. In the normal course of events, agreement of public employees and employers at the collective bargaining table is not newsworthy; therefore, media coverage often will be confined to reporting on the items separating the parties and not the items of agreement. Publicity might also encourage the negative tactic of turning to the legislative body for impasse resolution. Coverage reinforces the bad feelings too often present in negotiations in a way the private sector rarely experiences.

Sunshine laws may require that collective bargaining sessions be open to the public, often thwarting the parties' ability to compromise.[83] Sunshine laws require public bodies, such as city councils, to conduct their official business in public sessions open to citizens and the press (see Case 5-3). Some initial posturing is necessary on both sides

NEGOTIATING UNDER SUNSHINE LAWS

During 1985, the city's collective bargaining contracts with its police union and its general employees' union were being renegotiated. Prior to each negotiating session, the city posted notice of the meetings on the city's calendar at City Hall. Additionally, the city's representatives usually communicated directly with the newspaper's reporters concerning such meetings. The city and the unions were unable to agree on a wage level as well as a few other minor economic matters for the new contract. The city and the unions declared that negotiations were at an impasse, and a mediator was appointed to hear the disputes. The mediator scheduled the hearing for the police union on December 10 and the other union for December 11, 1985.

On December 9, the city's bargaining team member contacted his counterpart on the police union's team and arranged a meeting between the representatives for both sides to be held at 7:00 PM in a conference room at City Hall. No notice was posted; the press was not notified. The purpose of the meeting was an attempt to settle the impasse. The meeting was futile.

The city had posted public notice of the mediation, which was convened on the morning of December 10. The reporter and other media representatives were present. Shortly after the mediator convened the hearing, the police union's representative requested a recess so that the city's representative could step out into the hall to speak with him. The reporter, covering his first mediator hearing, did not follow the attorneys as they left the conference room. Out in the hall, the union's representative offered another settlement proposal, which the city's representative accepted. The two representatives agreed not to reveal the terms of the settlement offer until the following day to avoid prejudicing the mediator because

she was to hear the general employees' dispute the next day. The two bargaining representatives reentered the conference room and announced to the mediator that a settlement had been reached. The mediator adjourned the proceedings but retained jurisdiction in the event of a later disruption regarding the settlement. The reporter next asked the two representatives to tell him the terms of the settlement. Both declined, citing the need for confidentiality.

The next day the mediation began with the general employees' union with the same mediator presiding. Once again, the representatives for the city and for the union met outside the hearing room in the hall for a private meeting. The same reporter followed the parties out of the hearing room, and the two representatives made no effort to exclude him from this "off-the-record" encounter. After the second day's mediator hearing was terminated, the reporter was informed of the settlement terms between the city and the police union. The membership of the police union and the general employees ratified the settlements. The city council, at a public meeting with notice, subsequently approved the contracts, including the terms of the settlement agreed to during the private meeting on December 10.

The newspaper sued the city charging that it had violated the Florida sunshine law by carrying out negotiations with the police union on a collective bargaining agreement without notice to the public and an opportunity for the public to attend. The city argued that the Florida sunshine law specified that "collective bargaining negotiations" were to be open to the public, but once an impasse was reached, that provision no longer applied.

continued

NEGOTIATING UNDER SUNSHINE LAWS—continued

DECISION

The court did not accept the city's interpretation of the Florida sunshine law. The court noted that "impasse" only means a deadlock during negotiations when the parties refuse to compromise further to reach agreement. An impasse does not relieve the parties of the duty to negotiate in good faith. An impasse is a part of "negotiations" and, therefore, subject to the sunshine law.

SOURCE: Adapted from *City of Fort Myers v. Newspress Publishing Company, Inc.*, 127 LRRM 3051 (October 28, 1987).

so that the negotiator's constituency is assured that he or she is acting on their behalf. Negotiators may find it difficult to stop posturing if they are under constant scrutiny. At any particular juncture during the negotiation process, it may seem as if one side or the other is winning or losing. A fear of "loss of face" by either side may endanger the fair compromise so necessary to successful negotiations.

However, press coverage of public-sector collective bargaining is necessary because the ultimate decision does rest with the public. Without contribution by the public at some point during the process, the parties will not be able to gauge its reaction. By making the progress of negotiations public, elected officials and union members are able to get a response and so can modify their positions. For example, if a union representing teachers learned through news coverage of their negotiations that the public would support tax increases to improve the teacher–student ratio but not to raise salaries, its posture during the negotiations might change.

The Right to Strike

In the private sector, an impasse in collective bargaining negotiations can result in a strike. The National Labor Relations Act reserves that right to the employee as an economic weapon. In the public sector, the **right to strike** is usually denied to the public employee either by the collective bargaining statute or by court actions.

The right-to-strike issue is to the public sector what the right-to-work issue is to the private sector. Those who believe the public employee should have the right to strike cite the following reasons:

1. Despite legislation to the contrary, public employees do go on strike.[84] Attention is then focused on the strike issue and not on the reason for the disagreement, thereby thwarting resolution of the impasse.
2. Strikes, or at least credible strike threats, facilitate agreement at the bargaining table. Good faith bargaining alone cannot equalize the parties' bargaining power.[85]
3. Strikes test the union's strength as a bargaining representative; this strength can be used as a bargaining strategy.
4. Nonessential public employees should have the same rights as their counterparts in the private sector to strike.[86]

Those who believe that public employees should not have the right to strike cite the following reasons:

1. The primary reason for prohibiting public employee strikes is that the services provided by employees are essential to the general welfare. A distinction between police and fire services and motor pool operations may or may not be made.

2. Under the sovereignty theory, giving unions the right to strike places too much power in the hands of the employees rather than in the elected representatives of the people.
3. Because there are no market controls on government services, the strike threat could cause public employers to make unwise agreements at the expense of the taxpayer.[87]

Despite the traditional bias against public employees' right to strike, some states allow public workers to strike either directly or by not prohibiting it.[88] The percentage of state or local contracts that allow public employees to strike from a sample of public employers is close to 20 percent, as shown in Table 5-2.

The Professional Air Traffic Controllers' Strikes

In 1968 a group of New York controllers formed the Professional Air Traffic Controllers Organization (PATCO). Increased frustration with the Federal Aviation Association's (FAA's) poor management of the air traffic control system led to a slowdown beginning in New York and spreading to other cities. In 1969, PATCO counsel F. Lee Bailey discussed the controllers' frustrations with overcrowding in the skies on *The Tonight Show Starring Johnny Carson* and said, "I'd start walking, if I were you."[89] The next day several hundred controllers conducted a work stoppage, and the FAA suspended 80 of them. In 1970 almost 3,000 controllers informally went on strike; 52 were fired, and 1,000 were suspended. Several other instances gave PATCO the reputation of being an independent and feisty union. Certainly some of their members' feelings of independence were rooted in the belief that they were highly skilled professionals who could not easily be replaced.

Then in 1981, PATCO leaders called the first declared national strike against the federal government. The 13,000 strikers thought they were irreplaceable. President Reagan quickly warned that such direct disobedience of the law against public employee strikes would not be tolerated. He stated, "There is no strike; what they did was to terminate their own employment by quitting."[90] Reagan gave workers a deadline that most ignored; then he fired all but the few who returned to work. Not one controller was given amnesty or rehired until President Clinton took office in 1993.

The success of the Reagan administration in replacing such highly skilled workers, together with widespread public support, left little doubt in the minds of government workers as to what might happen if they went on strike. PATCO miscalculated its ability to gain concessions by striking. It sacrificed a substantial pay increase, a generous benefits package, and its very existence in its attempt to legitimize strikes in the public sector.[91]

Some union leaders point to the PATCO strike as the signal for employers to replace striking workers with permanent employees.[92] An anticipated teachers strike in California in 1990, for example, led the Santa Maria Joint Union School District to advertise for replacement teachers even before the strike began.

Although the most notorious strike, the 1981 PATCO strike had been preceded by at least 22 other strikes unauthorized by law against the federal government.[93]

Resolving Impasse in the Public Sector

Legislation that allows public-sector collective bargaining but prohibits strikes often details the procedures available to resolve an impasse. Certainly, under most public-sector collective bargaining systems, the public employer may unilaterally implement its "last best offer" when an impasse is reached, as seen in Case 5-4.

UNILATERAL ACTION—LAST BEST OFFER

The union and the school board began negotiations in June 1990 for an initial contract for a combined unit of teacher aides and assistants. The negotiations were long and included the parties participating in three mediation sessions and in fact-finding. Thereafter, the parties submitted several issues, including wages, health insurance, and duration of the contract to arbitration. Following a hearing, the arbitration panel issued a report on July 9, 1992, making nonbinding recommendations on wages, retirement payment, and health insurance but imposing a two-year duration of contract for the school years 1991–1992 and 1992–1993.

In September 1992, the school board sent a proposal on wages and insurance to the union. The terms were not in complete accord with the arbitrators' recommendations. The parties met, but the union rejected the offer and made counterproposals. In November 1992, the school board notified the union of its last best offer on wages and insurance. The union immediately filed for mediation. The school board thereafter implemented its wage and insurance proposals. The union filed a prohibited practice complaint with the state labor board alleging that the school board violated the state bargaining act by unilaterally implementing its proposal on wages and insurance.

The labor board ruled that the school board committed no violation of the act by unilaterally imposing its wage and insurance proposals. State law, as well as federal law, imposes the obligation to bargain in good faith as part of the statutory definition of collective bargaining. The law requires employers' and employees' representatives in the public and private sectors to bargain in good faith with respect to the mandatory subjects of bargaining, namely, wages, hours, and other terms and conditions of employment. To support the bargaining process and

prevent it from being circumvented or disparaged, labor law has long been interpreted to prevent either party from unilaterally changing wages, hours, or working conditions. Thus, while bargaining and before impasse, an employer is prevented from "going over the head" of the bargaining agent by unilaterally increasing or decreasing wages. The parties are required to maintain the status quo while bargaining.

When negotiations reach a bona fide impasse, however, a party is allowed to unilaterally implement its last best offer. Once the parties have in good faith exhausted the prospects of reaching an agreement, unilateral change that reasonably relates to the preimpasse proposals does not violate the law. After impasse, however, the duty to bargain is not extinguished. Rather, it is temporarily suspended until changed circumstances indicate that the parties are no longer inalterably deadlocked. Under state law, public employees, who do not have the right to strike or engage in work stoppages, are required to engage in such "peaceful" third-party intervention procedures as mediation, fact-finding, and arbitration. Impasse cannot occur until these forms of intervention have been exhausted. These procedures are designed to provide escalating pressure on both parties to produce a voluntary settlement.

The union argued that allowing the school board to unilaterally put its last best offer in place frustrates the purpose of the collective bargaining act. It is, in effect, forcing the union to accept the terms and conditions of employment that it had affirmatively rejected. It undermines the bargaining process because it says to the school board that the "peaceful" third-party procedures available in the public sector as an alternative to a strike are merely delays in the process, not meaningful impasse resolution measures.

continued

| CASE 5-4 | **UNILATERAL ACTION—LAST BEST OFFER—continued** |

DECISION

The court disagreed with the union and found that the school board did not violate the state law concerning collective bargaining by implementing its last best offer after reaching an impasse. In its opinion, the union missed the point. The wage and insurance provisions implemented by the school board did not end the negotiations between it and the union—it simply created a new "status quo" from which the parties would have to begin bargaining when the duty to bargain was no longer dormant.

SOURCE: Adapted from *Mountain Valley Education Assoc. v. Maine School Admin. Dist. No. 43*, 148 LRRM 2862 (March 2, 1995).

Mediation is provided in almost all states with collective bargaining in the public sector. As with the private sector, the mediator has no independent authority but uses acquired skills to bring the parties back together. It has been suggested that the mediator represent the public's interest at the bargaining table. Such a role does not seem to facilitate resolution of a dispute.

Fact-finding and advisory arbitration can be far more successful in the public sector than in the private because of political pressures. Under fact-finding and advisory arbitration, an unbiased third party examines the collective bargaining impasse and issues findings and recommendations. The findings may move the process simply by eliminating the distrust one party feels for the other party's facts or figures. Reasonable recommendations may also pressure a party to accept an offer that otherwise would not have been considered.

Interest arbitration allows a panel to make a final and binding decision on a negotiation dispute and has been used in the public sector to resolve impasses. However, the legality of allowing a third party to set the terms of the contract has been questioned.[94]

SUMMARY

Individuals representing labor and management are involved in the collective bargaining process. Negotiators prepare for the negotiations, set priorities, and proceed in an honest and thorough manner. The National Labor Relations Act delineates areas of mandatory, permissive, and illegal negotiations. A good negotiator must also understand and value the human element, which is an integral part of the negotiating process. For some parties, the give and take is as important as the end result. Knowing that, although every demand was not met, the position and point of view at least being heard by the other party can be part of a successful negotiation.[95]

Bargaining styles used in the collective bargaining process can focus on the relationship of the parties, on the issues to be decided, and on the relative bargaining power of the two sides. Principled negotiations emphasize getting the people involved in the negotiations to communicate on the issues. Distributive bargaining occurs when the parties view negotiations as a "win-lose" situation and resources as fixed and limited. Parties often use pressure bargaining techniques to further their bargaining objectives.

When the collective bargaining process breaks down, an impasse is reached. The parties can react to that impasse in various ways, with strikes being the most widely publicized reaction. Most often, however, mediation, arbitration, and fact-finding are used to resolve impasses.

Public-sector negotiations differ in a number of significant ways because of the nature of public employment and the responsibility the public employer and employees have to members of the public they serve.

CASE STUDIES

Case Study 5-1 Surface Bargaining

The company was charged with an unfair labor practice for failure to bargain in good faith. The union alleged that the company was engaged in surface bargaining with no intention of entering into a collective bargaining agreement. The company had begun meeting with the union after the NLRB had certified it. Eighteen bargaining sessions were held over an 11-month period. The negotiations did not result in a contract. The parties did reach agreement on a recognition clause; the numbers, rights, and duties of union stewards; the use of a bulletin board by the union; pay for jury duty and other leaves of absence; a procedure for processing grievances and arbitrations; and plant visitation by union representatives.

The administrative law judge hearing the case found that the company met at regular intervals and bore no antiunion animus. The company's conduct away from the bargaining table did not indicate that the company had no intention to conclude an agreement with the union. As there was no evidence of a failure to meet to discuss terms and conditions, the arbitrator had to examine the proposals by the company and by the union to see whether their substance indicated good-faith bargaining. The company's proposals are briefly outlined as follows:

1. *Wages.*   The company insisted that it remain in total control over wages. Wage increases were to be determined on the basis of semiannual merit reviews, in which the union would have no participation. The union had proposed a specific wage schedule, but the company would not adopt it.
2. *Management rights.*   The company retained absolute right to subcontract work, to assign it to supervisors, to abolish jobs, and to transfer, discontinue, or assign any or all of its

operations to others. It required the union to relinquish the employees' statutory right to notice in bargaining over such actions and their effects. Actions taken under the management clause were subject to the grievance procedure only if that right was limited by express contract provision, and there was no such limitation.
3. *Zipper clause.*   The company proposed a zipper clause, which waived the union's right to bargain during the life of the agreement over anything that could have been considered mandatory or permissive under existing law.
4. *No-strike clause.*   The company proposed a no-strike clause, including prohibition against a strike for unfair labor or unfair employment practices.
5. *Discipline and discharge.*   The company rejected the union's proposal of a standard right to discipline an employee for "just or sufficient cause only." The company intended to reserve exclusive authority over discharges and discipline in the management rights clause.
6. *Layoff and recall.*   The company proposed that the layoff and recall of employees would be at the company's sole discretion.
7. *Dues checkoff.*   The company rejected a union proposal that a dues checkoff clause be included in the contract.
8. *Nondiscrimination clause.*   The company rejected a union proposal that stated that the company was not allowed to discriminate against union members. The company's position was that because discrimination was illegal, a clause forbidding it did not need to be included in the contract.

SOURCE: Adapted from *A-1 Kingsize Sandwiches,* 112 LRRM 1360 (1982).

QUESTIONS

1. Was the company bargaining in good faith? Explain your answer.
2. Which company proposal was the most important in determining the "in good faith" issue?
3. Suggest how principled negotiations techniques could be utilized in this case.

Case Study 5-2 Surface Bargaining

The company and the union began negotiations for a new collective bargaining agreement (CBA) on June 17, 1993. The company's representatives initially made a presentation that focused on the company's position and its importance within ConAgra and on the gap between the wages paid by the company under the existing CBA and those paid by the company's competitors in Puerto Rico. The presentation included a chart showing that the company paid an average hourly wage of $17.84 whereas its competitors paid between $5.64 and $13.76, another showing that the company's profits represented 1.6 percent of ConAgra's profits in 1992, and another indicating that the company's sales volume in animal feed had declined sharply during the prior year. After the presentation, the company's chief negotiator presented the union with the company's proposal to cut wages from $17.84 to $11.11.

At the next session, the union representative accused the company of negotiating in bad faith. The company's representative acknowledged that the proposal was "radical," adding that "we need to be competitive" and "we want the company to continue." The union and the company then devoted the next eight negotiating sessions to noneconomic proposals.

The parties returned to the wage proposals at their 11th bargaining session, held on September 14, 1993. The company's representative began by reintroducing the graphs that the general manager had used in his presentation at the first session and soliciting the union's response to the individual components of the company's economic proposals, each of which the union rejected. The union representative then stated that the union wanted to use its own proposal, which called for an increase in hourly wages from $17.84 to $20.00, as the basis for negotiation. The company's representative agreed to consider the union's wage proposal but reiterated that the company needed to reduce its overall labor costs to stay competitive.

At this point, the union requested that the company turn over its certified financial statements for the prior five years and a number of other financial documents, including information on ConAgra. The company's representative asked the union to submit its information request in writing and to explain its relevance to the negotiations, stating, "Our positions are not based on the financial statement but more so on the competitiveness of our costs against a market. . . . The issue that we are bringing is not the company's ability to pay but more so the competitiveness in our market, specifically in our labor costs."

The union's representative acknowledged that he understood the company's assertion: "What you are saying is that the company is not alleging that it does not have the ability to pay." Subsequently, on September 20, the union sent the company a letter repeating its information request and adding a request for the names of all the company's clients for the past three years; the letter included no explanation of the reasons for these requests or of their relevance to the bargaining process.

The parties continued to meet through the end of October but made no substantial progress on the wage issue—the union stood by its demand to increase wages above their existing levels, while the company continued to propose reducing wages below existing levels. The union repeated its request for financial information, while the company continued to assert that it had never claimed that it was in poor financial condition or was unable to pay the wages sought by the union and to ask that the union explain the relevance of the requested information.

On October 27, the company's representative delivered the company's "last and final offer," along with a letter stating that the parties had reached an impasse and giving the union notice of the company's intention to close its facilities that evening. The company locked out the employees on November 1, citing the failure to reach agreement regarding a new CBA. The company had a contingency plan in place to handle a strike and added security for replacement workers.

On November 30, the union demanded financial information from the company again. The company provided the union with information regarding the company's wages, its competitors' wages, its pension plan, and the number of temporary workers employed at the company mills but asserted that the union was "not entitled" to any other information regarding ConAgra companies other than the company. The parties unsuccessfully met with a mediator several times between November 1993 and February 1994.

The NLRB brought charges of unfair labor practices against the company, and on June 13, 1995, an administrative law judges (ALJ) of the board issued a decision finding that the company had failed to bargain in good faith by withholding information it was obligated to provide, purposely creating a bargaining "impasse" and making unilateral changes in the terms and conditions of employment in the absence of a genuine impasse.

Discussion

An employer commits an "unfair labor practice" under Sections 8(a)(1) and 8(a)(5) of the National Labor Relations Act by refusing to bargain collectively with the legitimate representatives of its employees. The duty to bargain collectively includes the duty to meet and confer "in good faith" with employee representatives with respect to wages, hours, and other terms and conditions of employment. When labor negotiations have reached an "impasse" or deadlock, an employer's unilateral changes in working conditions do not necessarily violate the act as they generally do in the absence of an impasse. Predictably, unscrupulous employers can exploit this rule by sabotaging the negotiations to create an impasse while making a show of negotiating in good faith; this practice is referred to as "surface bargaining." The NLRB treats "surface bargaining" as a violation of Section 8(a)(5) of the act. The touchstone for determining whether a genuine "impasse" or deadlock exists is the absence of any realistic possibility that continuation of the negotiations will be fruitful.

The ALJ in this case concluded that the company entered these negotiations with a predetermined resolve not to budge from its initial position and that the company engaged in "surface bargaining" and created a false impasse. She relied heavily for this conclusion on the contents of a "contingency plan" that ConAgra sent to the company prior to the beginning of the negotiations. In her view, the contingency plan revealed that the company prepared its bargaining proposals knowing they would be so unacceptable as to ensure rejection by the union, leading to an impasse followed by a strike. She also rested this conclusion on her findings that the company presented the union with "predictably unacceptable" proposals and merely went through the motions of bargaining, arranged for improved security and replacement workers in anticipation of a strike, and hastily declared an impasse while the union continued to offer compromises.

The duty to bargain in good faith also includes the obligation to provide the union with information relevant to the collective bargaining process in certain circumstances. Although the relevance of information concerning the terms and conditions of employment is presumed, no such presumption applies to an employer's information regarding its financial structure and condition. A union must demonstrate that any requested financial information is relevant to the negotiations to require the employer to turn it over. The Supreme Court has held that, in the context of negotiations over a new CBA, an employer's refusal to attempt to substantiate a claim of inability to pay increased wages may support a finding of a failure to bargain in good faith. The Court emphasized that it was not saying that the union is entitled to supporting information in *every* case in which economic inability is raised as an argument against increasing wages; rather, the Court noted that each case must turn on its particular facts. The inquiry must always be whether, under the circumstances of the particular case, the statutory obligation to bargain in good faith has been met.

Prior to 1986, the NLRB construed the *Truitt* decision to oblige employers to provide unions with supporting financial information even when the employer's only statements tending to put its financial condition in issue consisted of assertions that acceding to the union's wage demands would create or exacerbate a "competitive disadvantage."

Subsequently, however, in response to a decision by the U.S. Court of Appeals for the Seventh Circuit, the board underwent a change of heart. The appeals court rejected the board's finding that the employer claimed an "inability to pay" when an employer asserts that the wages demanded by the union would put the employer at a competitive disadvantage unless the union could show that the employer's claim was for the time period of the CBA being negotiated.

The board announced that it would deal with employer claims of "inability to pay" by distinguishing between employer statements and conduct asserting inability to pay union proposals at some point during the term of the CBA under negotiation and employer statements and conduct suggesting, in a more general fashion, that accession to union demands would create economic difficulties or business losses or the prospect of layoffs someday in the future

SOURCE: Adapted from *ConAgra Inc. v. NLRB*, 155 LRRM 2769 (CA DC 1997).

QUESTIONS

1. Although it is very rare for an employer to begin negotiations with a request to reduce wages, do you think it is always a symptom of bad faith for a company to do so? Would you think differently if it were the first CBA being negotiated?
2. Under the "duty to bargain in good faith" standard articulated by the Supreme Court, did the company commit an unfair labor practice by failing to provide the union with the requested financial information?
3. Was the company engaging in "surface bargaining"? If so, why wasn't the union also guilty of surface bargaining because it would not agree to the company's wage offer?

KEY TERMS AND CONCEPTS

- arbitration
- bilateral bargaining
- *Borg-Warner* case
- "the crunch"
- distributive bargaining
- economic strike
- fact-finding
- ground rules
- illegal bargaining subjects
- impasse
- interest-based bargaining
- jurisdictional strike
- lockout
- *Mackay* doctrine
- mandatory bargaining subjects
- multilateral bargaining
- mediation
- negotiations
- outsourcing
- permanent replacement workers
- permissive bargaining subjects
- planning
- posturing
- pressure bargaining
- primary strike
- principled negotiations
- right to strike
- rolling strike
- selective strike
- separability clause
- sickout
- sunshine laws
- telescabbing
- unfair labor practice strike
- wildcat strike

REVIEW QUESTIONS

1. What are the different styles used by negotiators?
2. Why are perceptions so important during the negotiation process? Why is listening critical to negotiators?
3. Who are the principal parties involved in the collective bargaining process? What are their roles?
4. List some guidelines negotiators can use in aiding the negotiation process.
5. Why do negotiators use posturing during labor negotiation sessions?
6. Distinguish between mandatory, permissive, and illegal bargaining subjects.
7. What types of strikes could result in employees being legally fired?
8. Describe commonly used methods for resolving a negotiation impasse.
9. Explain the significance of a change to the National Labor Relations Act that would prohibit an employer from replacing striking workers with permanent replacements.
10. Why are negotiations in the public sector different from negotiations in the private sector?
11. How is interest-based bargaining different from the other techniques?

YOU BE THE ARBITRATOR
School Bus Drivers

ARTICLE VII
MANAGEMENT RIGHTS, ITEM E

Maintain the efficiency of operations in the New Lebanon School District and the personnel by which such operations shall be carried out.

ARTICLE VII
MANAGEMENT RIGHTS, ITEM F

Exercise any other power or prerogative given it under the Revised Code of the State of Ohio or any reasonable inference to be therefrom.

ARTICLE XXXI
TRANSPORTATION, PARAGRAPH H

All field trips shall be offered on the basis of seniority rotation as follows:

1. There shall be two rotation lists made containing the names of all drivers in order of their seniority (those drivers only desiring to take field trips), the most senior driver being No. 1. One list will consist of daytime trips; the other after school and weekend trips.

2. The first trip of the school year shall be assigned to driver 1. The second being assigned to driver 2 and so on. Driver 1 shall not be eligible for another field trip until all the remaining drivers have had an opportunity to take a field trip on each individual rotation list.

3. If more than one field trip is offered on Monday (or whatever day), driver who is up for the next trip on the seniority list may have their choice of field trips; next drivers will have the same option until all trips have been exhausted.

4. Any driver becoming eligible may have the option to refuse the trip to be passed over in favor of the less senior driver. However, the driver refusing shall not be eligible again until the rotation is complete. There will be no trading of field trips.

5. Field trips shall be assigned to regular classified bus drivers only. In the event that the rotation has been exhausted and no regular drivers are available, the substitute drivers shall be permitted to take field trips.

6. Only classified bus drivers that are contract drivers with the Board shall be assigned to any route or extra trips.

7. When a field trip requires early departure and last all day or overnight, regular school bus drivers will have the option of taking the trip. The school bus drivers will drive their own bus on the trip or the best available. The Supervisor may assign any bus from the fleet to a field trip which is more than 100 miles one way. The regular bus drivers will relinquish their regular pay rate for the field-trip rate. Field trips will stay on the same rotation basis.

8. If a driver has a field trip canceled, they will be offered the first field trip from the same list (either day or after school) as long as they do not have another field trip assigned. Should they already have a field trip assigned, they will be offered the next field trip available. Receiving the makeup trip cannot cause one to lose a trip from the normal list.

9. Every effort will be made to provide drivers with a gas card to those assigned field trips that are beyond a 100-mile round trip.

10. When a field trip is available and after exhausting the regular rotation field trip list and substitute list, that trip becomes an "emergency field trip" situation. Under the above stated guidelines, regular and/or substitute bus drivers may take the participants to the field trip event and return to the school district. At the completion of the field trip, the same driver or an alternate driver may be assigned to pick up these participants and return to the school district; the driver being paid for the time needed to accomplish this.

11. Summer Field Trips/Summer School—For the purpose of determining the rate of pay, a summer field trip is defined as transporting students with a teacher/advisor/designee in charge, and the driver of this trip will be paid FIELD-TRIP RATE. Summer school transportation is defined as transporting students to a school or designated area where the driver has the same responsibility as transporting students to school during the regular school day (no adviser/coach/designee in charge), and the driver of this trip will be paid the REGULAR DRIVING RATE for which they are employed.

Facts

The employer is a public school district. In the past, the superintendent of the district had used his private van to transport students to sporting events. After the district purchased a van, the school van was used to transport students to sporting events. The union grieved the use of the van because the school bus drivers were not being used to drive the van, and the collective bargaining agreement (CBA) required the school bus drivers to drive students on any field trips.

Issue

Did the employer violate its CBA that requires school bus drivers to transport students on field trips when it did not require them to transport students to sporting events?

Position of the Parties

The school district's position was that the CBA's management rights clause gave the superintendent the authority to determine what vehicles to use to transport students when the trip is not a field trip. If the superintendent does not determine that a school bus should be used, then the CBA's provision is not applicable. The CBA does not define "field trip," so "field trip" is defined in the school district's policy as "any planned journey by one or more students away from district premises, which is under the supervision of a professional staff member and an integral part of a course of study." Under the district's definition, no sporting or after school trip is a field trip.

The union's position was that the drivers should be assigned to drive the van whenever school trips are being taken. Even though the CBA does not define "field trip," the union does not accept the use of the definition in the district's policy or the narrow reading of the term "field trip." Any trip taken under the auspices of the district is a field trip for purposes of the CBA.

SOURCE: Adapted from *New Lebanon Local Bd. of Ed.*, 114 LA 952 (Arb. 2000).

QUESTIONS

1. As arbitrator, what would be your award and opinion in this arbitration?
2. Explain why the relevant provisions of the CBA as applied to the facts of this case dictate the award.
3. What actions might the employer and/or the union have taken to avoid this conflict?

Develop Your Own Negotiating Skills

PURPOSE:

To enable students to develop their own negotiating skills that can be used in real-life situations.

TASK:

Make a copy of this list of 10 tactics and carry it with you for one week. As you encounter a potential negotiation situation, refer to the list and try a tactic. Record a description of the situation, the tactic selected, and the outcome. After the week is over, your instructor will lead a class discussion of the exercise and collect the records of the incidents.

Everyone is a negotiator. However, most people do not think of themselves as negotiators, and unfortunately do not often recognize a negotiation situation when confronted with one. Thus, the outcome is less than what they could have achieved had they bargained with the other party. Everyone who has bought a car, home, or piece of furniture; discussed issues like chores and privileges with a daughter or son; accepted a new job or promotion; or even stayed at a hotel or dined at a nice restaurant has been faced with real-life negotiation situations. When faced with such a situation, did you bargain or just accept what was offered? If you wish you had basic negotiating skills, here are 10 proven ones you can easily learn.

First, you need to recognize that you are in a situation where (1) both parties have a mutual goal—you need a hotel room, and the hotel clerk wants your business; (2) the outcome is not certain—the prices of rooms can be changed, discounts given, and so on, and exactly which room is reserved can be negotiated; and (3) the two people who can make the decision are involved—if the clerk says she cannot change the price, ask to see the manager. These tactics were adapted from *The Negotiation Handbook* by Patrick J. Clary, former chairman of the National Mediation Board.

1. *Power and leverage.* Every negotiation is a power struggle, and the side that is perceived (real or not) to have the power advantage has leverage over the other side. But leverage can move back and forth during negotiations—try to keep it balanced.

   Example: The hotel clerk knows there is a convention in town and that every hotel except his is full and thus will not give you a discount. You ask to see the manager, whom you tell that you are on business trip and have a reservation somewhere else, but that you stay at his hotel, always at a lower rate, about 20 times a year. Now you have leverage.

2. *Ego.* Ego is often the core of a dispute and is a driving force during many negotiations: It is "my proposal," "I am the parent," "You are a jerk." Everyone wants to win, and no one likes to lose. But in negotiations, the person with the smallest ego wins. A good negotiator checks his or her ego at the door and can separate emotions from the issue—and may successfully trade an ego "win" for an "issue."

   Example: Two couples are deciding where to make reservations for dinner. One woman says, "They know me at the Shari Inn. I can get us a good table." The other responds, "Well, I'm afraid that is a more expensive place than we had in mind," to which the first woman responds, "No problem, dinner is on us!"

3. *Being right.* In negotiations, what is "right" is whatever is agreed on. There is no exact right, fair, or honest price except the one that is negotiated. The right price for a used car is exactly the price the two parties negotiate. Prices quoted in the NADA Bluebook, Edmunds, and *Consumer Reports* provide only a range of values, not the right price for a particular vehicle. Be willing to let the other party think they are "right" if it saves you money.

   Example: The seller claims that the fair price for his five-year-old Corvette convertible is $40,000 because he has seen that value quoted on four similar vehicles on eBay. The buyer concedes, "You're right, that is a fair price for the average five-year-old Vette! I'll pay that if you will pay a reasonable delivery charge and provide me an allowance for the higher mileage on this car."

4. *Facts.* You need to be prepared with as much relevant, persuasive information as possible. Facts alone may not determine the exact outcome, but they certainly influence it. Today there is an enormous amount of information available on the Internet on the price, availability, selection, and options of many items. If you do not have the relevant facts, you are at an enormous disadvantage when negotiating.

Example: The agent for the home owner warns the buyers that the price is fair and cites the "comps" (comparable prices on homes in the neighborhood that sold recently). She says that other buyers will be looking at the home that day and that they will make an offer. The buyers feel compelled to make an offer—but the fact is the house has been on the market for 180 days, and two other similar houses are for sale in the same neighborhood. If the buyers had all the facts before they began negotiations, they would view the situation quite differently.

5. ***BATNA and principles.***   Always, always know your principles—exactly what you must get on a deal and what cannot be compromised. What will cause you to walk away from the negotiations? The point at which you will walk away is your BATNA—Best Alternative to a Negotiated Agreement. Before you start any negotiation, decide your BATNA and stick to it. Do not get caught up in the heat of the deal, making a deal and agreeing to something just to get a deal. Also, do not confuse your BATNA with a position. Your position, as you tell the seller, is that $126,500 is the highest price you will pay. But you know in your mind that your BATNA is $140,000 and that you will walk away if you cannot get a price below it.

   Example: A new car buyer has driven a Toyota Camry at a Los Angles dealership and likes the car, which has everything she wants. The salesman tells her that his bottom price is $19,400. She, however, says that she will not go above $19,200. He checks with his sales manager and repeats that $19,400 is the bottom price. The buyer walks out and drives to a San Diego dealer to buy the same car for $19,200, having verified its availability by telephone. She decided that $19,200 was her BATNA before she went to the dealer and started negotiating. She was willing to drive an hour and a half to save $200.

6. ***Don't debate the "shape of the table."***   At the end of the Vietnam War, the parties at the Paris Peace Talks argued for months over the shape of the negotiating table. Today when negotiators waste time debating the place, time, length of sessions, and so on, it is said that they are debating the "shape of the table." In reality, they are delaying the discussion—a legitimate tactic if that is the goal. If that is not the goal, give in to such demands and even make a point of it: "In the interest of making a deal, I'll agree to your suggestions." Then focus on the real issues. Normally, such basic issues as who, where, and when are quickly resolved: who—an equal number of people on both sides; where—a neutral site; and when—convenient two- to four-hour sessions.

   Example: A management negotiator insisted on meeting in the company conference room at 7:30 AM the next day for a minimum of five hours. At first hesitant, the union negotiator responded by accepting, "if you will stay at the table until we have a deal." Management had little choice but to agree because it was their proposal, and after a 14-hour session, they were exhausted and agreed to a deal that they had rejected a week earlier.

7. ***List issues and classify as compatible, exchange, distributive.***   A good first step is for both parties to list all the issues to be decided on and their positions on each. Do not assume that you have opposing goals on all issues. Instead, together classify each as (1) compatible—your goals are similar or almost

identical, so that a "common ground" can be found quickly and the issue resolved; (2) exchange—you can easily exchange one issue for another, so that each side gains one goal; and (3) distributive—issues, usually ones involving price or another economic variable in which the gains must be "distributed" between the two parties; that is, a middle ground must be negotiated.

Example: The director of human resources for a large firm wants to hire an applicant who works for another firm and expresses that she is quite content in her job but would move for "the right offer." The director meets with her and says, "Let us identify all the issues that are important to you and/or my firm. Then we will separately list our goals for each issue. Together we can then determine for which issues we have the same goals (compatible) and some where we can trade your goal for mine on another issue so that we each achieve one of our goals (exchange), and finally we can get down to the hard ones where we need to find an acceptable middle ground (distributive)." Over the next two hours, they produce together the following list of issues, identifying each and negotiating an acceptable position. The applicant accepts the position.

Issue	Type	Settlement
1. Annual travel budget	Exchange	Applicant traded her goal to receive a signing bonus (#3).
2. Office location	Compatible	A corner office was acceptable to both.
3. Signing bonus	Exchange	Human resources director traded to get his desired travel budget (#1).
4. Travel days per month	Distributive	A key issue. Both agreed to a 12-day/month maximum.
5. Moving expenses	Exchange	Applicant traded her goal for the enhanced benefit plan.
6. Primary territory	Compatible	Both wanted Phoenix, Arizona, to be their primary territory of the six available.
7. Annual salary	Distributive	The last issue to be resolved. Having settled on the other seven made it easier for both to accept a middle ground.
8. Benefit plan	Exchange	The firm offered three levels of plans, and the human resources director gave her the enhanced plan for no moving expenses (#5).

8. ***Repeat back/empathize.*** As a means of making progress and setting a positive tone, use the classic tactic of repeating back the point made by the other side (not agreeing to it) and emphasizing that you understand their point of view and concerns. At the same time, you should never accuse the other side of a negative motive or misrepresenting the facts—that tactic will only raise their emotions, possibly to the point of not agreeing to any reasonable proposal.

Example: Two coowners of a piece of property are trying to settle a deal in which one would buy out the other's interest. The first repeatedly states his desire to keep only a small portion of the property with a cabin and lakefront. After hours of trying to agree to a partition of the property or a fair price for one to sell out to the other, the two leave in anger. The following day, the second party opens with, "As I think back, you said your primary interest is to keep the cabin your parents built with a small lakefront lot. I can see how you have a lot of emotional attachment to that cabin. Perhaps if we started by agreeing to your goal of keeping the cabin and two acres of land . . ." They reach a deal within two hours.

9. *Use "what-ifs."*   Negotiators often like to float an outrageous proposal to test the water—called "what-ifs." A what-if does not need to be logical. It may be used to find an outer limit by the other party and cause them to think from a new starting point. On rare occasions, a "lowball" what-if might get you a great deal.

> *Example:* Anne is looking for a retirement home in her old neighborhood and loves one of the houses she went through in December. But it is listed at $189,000, and her limit is $129,000, so it was not even in the ballpark—or so she thought. Nine months later at a party, a cousin, an experienced negotiator, asks her how the house hunting is progressing. "No luck," she replied. "What about the one on Redwood you looked at?" he asked. "No way," she responded, "it is $60,000 over my limit." He notes that it is still for sale and that they might come down quite a bit. He convinces her to look at it again and make a "what if I offered $129,000 today, in cash" bid. The sellers reject that lowball offer but counter with $142,000 ($47,000 below the asking price), which she accepts only after finding a lower mortgage rate, and thus her monthly payments are within her BATNA.

10. *Ask, "Can you do any better?"*   It costs nothing to ask—it is simple and direct and often gets a positive response because the other party is prepared to give a little more. Also, the "better" is not limited to price. Terms, color, delivery date, and warranties can be included in the deal. Remember that hotels, airlines, retail shops, restaurants, banks, and car dealers, to list a few, all have different rates but almost never start with their best one.

> *Example:* When checking into an expensive hotel, the clerk assures a man that he is getting the best rate. "So, do you offer any discounts beyond that rate?" the man asked. "Well, yes, AARP and AAA," the clerk replied. The man pulled out his AAA card and saved another 15 percent.

SOURCE: Adapted from Patrick J. Cleary, *The Negotiation Handbook* (Armonk, NY: M. E. Sharpe, 2001), pp. 15–103. Used by permission. Other Suggested Sources: Roger Fisher and William Ury, *Getting to Yes* (2nd ed.) (New York: Penguin Books, 1991); Theodore W. Kheel, *The Keys to Conflict Resolution* (New York: Four Walls Eight Windows, 1999); Michael R. Carrell and Christina Heavrin, *The Everyday Negotiator, 50 Practical Tactics for Work and Life* (Amherst, MA: HRD Press, Inc., 2004).

CHAPTER 6

Wage and Salary Issues

Union Wage Concerns
Management Wage Concerns
Negotiated Wage Adjustments
Wage Negotiation Issues
Wage Surveys
Costing Wage Proposals
Union Wages and Inflation
Public Employee Wage and Salary Issues

Janice Nelson, M.D. led a press conference in Los Angeles, California, when Los Angeles County physicians joined the Union of American Physicians and Dentists. With increasing numbers of health-care professionals joining unions, other unions may be helped in negotiating better wages and health benefits such as health insurance, wellness programs, and dental and vision care.

Labor News

MACHINISTS UNION STRIKES BOEING COMPANY
"WHAT TIME IS IT?" "UNION TIME!"

On September 2, 2005, 18,400 members of the International Association of Machinists and Aerospace Workers Union went on strike against Boeing, the aerospace industry company. The strike idled workers in Seattle, Washington; Wichita, Kansas; and Gresham, Oregon. The strike was the first against Boeing in 10 years, and only the second in 25 years.

The strike halted production of Boeing 737 airplanes and came at a time when Boeing was struggling to compete with Airbus, its European competitor, for international orders for new jet airplanes. What caused the strike? According to Sandi Wiley, a worker on the picket line in Wichita: "You do it for the next generation . . . I am worried she (her 8-year-old daughter, Leslie) will have a worse standard of living than I have." That worry has become commonplace among union leaders who have witnessed a decline in health-care and pension benefits in contracts negotiated in recent years. Employers, however, have pressed for such reductions in benefits to control spiraling health-care and pension costs as the union workforce ages.

The last Boeing contract offer contained a pay and benefit package that was less than the one contained in the 2002 three-year contract, which had expired the day before the strike. The previous major strikes against Boeing by the machinists lasted 69 days (1995) and 48 days (1989).

SOURCE: Adapted from Gene Johnson, The Associated Press, "Machinists Union Strikes Jet Builder," *The Cincinnati Enquirer* (Sept. 3, 2005), D2.

Wages and other economic benefits for employees are undoubtedly the meat and potatoes of collective bargaining in labor relations. To the employee, they represent not only their current income and standard of living but also potential for economic growth and the ability to live comfortably during retirement. Wages are often considered the most important and difficult collective bargaining issue. When negotiated settlements are reported to the public, the first item specified is the percentage wage increase received by employees. In fact, in many cases that may be the only item employees consider critical or an absolute must as they vote to ratify a tentative agreement.

> There is a feeling these days among employees that [the company] is a good place to work and the benefits are good [but] it's just not enough. You can't feed a family on good working conditions. . . . Right or wrong, shortsighted or not—because of inflation money seems to be the prime motivator and driving force.[1]

According to industrial research, pay level is positively related to employee satisfaction.[2] Employees consider their pay to be a primary indicator of the organization's goodwill. Many in our society consider the salary or income one receives a measure of one's worth. Employees can get an exact measure of their salary, which can easily be compared with the salaries of fellow employees and those in other organizations and occupations. Therefore, most of us consciously or subconsciously compare our income levels not only with inflation and our cost of living but also with incomes of other individuals.

Wages and benefits are also a prime collective bargaining issue to the employer. They represent the largest single cost factor on their income statement. Although many management negotiators would like to pay high wages to employees, the reality of competition and the knowledge that competitors may be able to secure less-expensive labor make it difficult to survive. Unlike many costs, such as capital and land, wages constantly rise, and they are not as easy to predict. Wages are the single most important source of tax revenue to federal, state, and local governments and in general are a strong indicator of the economic vitality of a community.

The total economic package of wages and benefits may be negotiated as a complete item rather than treated individually, enabling both sides to estimate accurately the total cost of the contract to the organization in terms of increases over current salary and benefits. In this chapter we discuss wage issues; employee benefits are covered in Chapter 7. Wages and benefits are separated to draw a distinction between the two; however, negotiators consider both a part of the total economic package.

Labor and management negotiators normally define pay by either time worked or units of output. **Pay for time worked**, or an **hourly wage** or **annual salary**, has become the predominant means of employee compensation in the United States. Most labor contracts contain specific job titles and associated wage scales agreed on by labor and management. An example is shown in Figure 6-1.

Pay for units produced, usually referred to as **piecework**, is still utilized in many industries as not only a means of wage determination but also a motivational technique. Many piecework systems today provide a guaranteed salary with an additional rate established for units of output above a certain production level.

	Group	Department
I	Die Repair	Maintenance
II	Maintenance	Maintenance
III	Cage Attendant	Material Handling
	Head Loader	Shipping
	Guillotine Operator	Window and Prime
	Brake Operator	Millroom and Prime
	Crane Operator	Material Handling
	Automatic Bander	Door and Prime
	Automatic Saw-Punch Machine	Millroom and Prime
IV	Material Handler	Material Handling
	Utility	Door and Window
	Thermal Break Operator	Prime
	Large Glass Cutter	Specialty
	Large Punch Press Operator	Door and Millroom
	Loading	Shipping
	Plant Truck Driver	Shipping

continued

FIGURE 6-1 Job Classifications and Wage Rates

V	Salvage	Material Handling
	Material Handler	Material Handling
	Loader-Unloader	Paint Line and Prime
	Schlegeler	Door, Millroom, Prime, and Specialty
VI	(None)	
VII	Glass Cutter	Window, Specialty, Prime, and Insulated Glass
	Sample Builder	Sample
	Glass Washer and Assembler	Insulated Glass
	Spacer Assembly	Insulated Glass
	Sealant Applicator	Insulated Glass
	Parts Puller (Sash, Screen, Frame)	Window
	Belt Line	Door
	Door Prehanger	Door
VII	Screen Pre-Assembler	Door, Window, Specialty, and Prime
	Screener	Door, Window, Specialty, and Prime
	Sash Builder	Door, Window, Specialty, and Prime
	Frame Builder	Window, Specialty, and Prime
VIII	Small Punch Press Operator	Door, Millroom, Specialty, and Prime
	Processor	Door, Millroom, Specialty, and Prime
	Window Wrapper	Shipping
IX	Packaging	Material Handling
XXIII	Equipment Operator	Paint Line
XXIV	Assistant Equipment Operator	Paint Line

Group	Hire Rate Effective June 1, 2005
I	$19.80
II	$19.62
III	$19.30
IV	$18.60
V	$18.30
VI	$17.50
VII	$17.10
VIII	$16.50
IX	$16.20
XXIII	$12.60
XXIV	$10.00

FIGURE 6-1   Job Classifications and Wage Rates (Continued)

As the nature of jobs changes, more agreements provide annual salaries expressed in pay grades. In Figure 6-2, for example, all the clerical, engineering, and technical jobs at DaimlerChrysler Corporation were negotiated to the pay grade that best reflects their value and maintains internal equity. All new employees started at the minimum salary for the grade for their job and each year received an automatic step increase until they reached the top progression rate. To reach the maximum for the grade, they must be given merit pay increases.[3]

Effective September 2003				Effective September 2005				Effective September 2006			
Grade	Minimum	Top Progression Rate	Maximum	Grade	Minimum	Top Progression Rate	Maximum	Grade	Minimum	Top Progression Rate	Maximum
1	$735.94	*	$1,059.29	1	$755.94	*	$1,080.48	1	$786.34	*	$1,112.89
2	$738.15	*	$1,075.04	2	$758.15	*	$1,096.54	2	$788.55	*	$1,129.44
3	$741.41	*	$1,089.10	3	$761.41	*	$1,110.88	3	$791.81	*	$1,144.21
4	$796.13	*	$1,119.95	4	$816.13	*	$1,142.35	4	$846.53	*	$1,176.62
5	$812.71	*	$1,167.62	5	$832.71	*	$1,190.97	5	$863.11	*	$1,226.70
6	$821.78	*	$1,200.88	6	$841.78	*	$1,224.90	6	$872.18	*	$1,261.65
7	$827.73	*	$1,224.39	7	$847.73	*	$1,248.88	7	$878.13	*	$1,286.35
8	$835.36	*	$1,251.86	8	$855.36	*	$1,276.90	8	$885.76	*	$1,315.21
9	$856.03	*	$1,275.10	9	$876.03	*	$1,300.60	9	$906.43	*	$1,339.62
10	$864.17	$1,156.51	$1,312.23	10	$884.17	$1,179.64	$1,338.47	10	$914.57	$1,215.03	$1,378.62
11	$884.14	$1,174.92	$1,335.85	11	$904.14	$1,198.42	$1,362.57	11	$934.54	$1,234.37	$1,403.45
12	$892.34	$1,189.67	$1,363.74	12	$912.34	$1,213.46	$1,391.01	12	$942.74	$1,249.86	$1,432.74
13	$910.50	$1,221.68	$1,390.42	13	$930.50	$1,246.11	$1,418.23	13	$960.90	$1,283.49	$1,460.78
14	$927.55	$1,243.65	$1,432.11	14	$947.55	$1,268.52	$1,460.75	14	$977.95	$1,306.58	$1,504.57
15	$934.17	$1,256.52	$1,455.71	15	$954.17	$1,281.65	$1,484.82	15	$984.57	$1,320.10	$1,529.36
16	$962.78	$1,286.81	$1,493.76	16	$982.78	$1,312.55	$1,523.64	16	$1,013.18	$1,351.93	$1,569.35
17	$980.32	$1,302.73	$1,530.24	17	$1,000.32	$1,328.78	$1,560.84	17	$1,030.72	$1,368.64	$1,607.67
18	$1,027.11	$1,372.82	$1,567.38	18	$1,047.65	$1,400.28	$1,598.73	18	$1,079.08	$1,442.29	$1,646.69

FIGURE 6-2 Chrysler Corporation Clerical—Engineering—Technical 18-Grade Structure

*Automatic progression to the maximum rate in Grades 1, 2, 3, 4, 5, 6, 7, 8, and 9

SOURCE: *UAW-Chrysler Newsgram*, September 2003. Available at www.uaw.org. Accessed December 2005. Used by permission.

UNION WAGE CONCERNS

"A fair day's pay for a fair day's work" is a commonly used phrase summing up the expectations of many employees. Employees expect and even demand to be treated fairly and honestly by the organization. Although most are reasonable in their pay expectations, a few feel that they are being underpaid. If employees perceive that they are unfairly treated by the organization, particularly in pay matters, they typically will react by leaving the workplace either temporarily through absenteeism and tardiness or permanently through seeking employment at another organization, by reducing the quantity or quality of their production, or by filing a grievance or enacting a work stoppage through the union. Eventually their pay dissatisfaction will be brought to the bargaining table, leading ultimately to either higher wages or an economic strike. Or they may change their perceptions by simply accepting the inequity, although this response may become a permanent morale factor.[4]

Obtaining **pay equity** in the workplace is difficult. The slogan "equal pay for equal work" is a guide that union and management leaders follow and that employees expect to be maintained. Obviously not all jobs involve work of equal value to an organization. The first-year bookkeeper does not expect the same pay as a tax accountant; the same is true for a punch press operator and a maintenance attendant. Employees understand that the value of the work leads to different pay grades and classifications for different jobs. As shown in Figure 6-2, labor agreements commonly provide for different job classifications being assigned different pay grades according to level of skill and work demanded. As long as pay grades are fairly structured and evenly applied, employees have no trouble accepting differential pay based on job classification and internal wage levels, unless, as seen in Case 6-1, pay differentials are not based purely on job classifications.

In recent years a new pay equity issue has emerged—the worker/CEO pay gap. The gap is growing, according to a study by the National Bureau of Economic Research. In 1970 the average full-time worker earned $32,522, whereas the average CEO or top corporate executive earned $1.25 million (adjusted to 1998 dollars). By 2000 the average worker's pay increased by 10.3 percent to $35,864 while the average CEO pay increased by more than 2,800 percent to 37.5 million.[5] The difference in CEO pay and worker pay can irritate all workers, but poor timing of pay decisions can further strain management–union relations. For example, in 2003 as American Airlines asked three unions to accept deep pay and benefit cuts of about $10,000 per year per worker, or almost 20 percent of their total compensation, American Airlines disclosed special payments to 45 top executives of about $100 million of the $1.8 billion in concessions gained from the workers. Six top executives received a bonus equal to twice their base salaries. One union member, Joseph Szubryt, who supported the pay cuts to save union jobs exclaimed, "This feels like a stab in the back . . . On the day we voted for all this stuff (pay and benefit cuts) . . . they disclose this? How the heck could these guys do that?"[6]

Some wage systems provide for higher wages to employees with more longevity. Thus, seniority helps employees not only in bidding for open jobs but also in receiving higher pay. Even though less-senior employees perform the same work, everyone realizes that longevity pay serves as an incentive to stay with the organization. But pay inequities can develop for any number of reasons, as seen in the discussion of mergers in Profile 6-1.

Union Wage Objectives

How have unions, as organizations, affected the wages of their workers through the collective bargaining process? What primary objectives have unions held when

WAGES: EXTRA COMPENSATION

The company operated a centralized facility to provide public transportation. The bargaining unit consisted of the vehicle operators, excluding supervisors, substitutes, guards, and office personnel. The collective bargaining agreement (CBA) was in effect from October 1, 1996, to June 30, 1999.

The operation was decentralized in April 1997, when the company opened seven suburban service center locations. Because the company had acted before hiring the management supervisory personnel at each site, it decided to assign certain unit drivers to temporary positions titled "coordinator." These persons had limited supervisory authority but functioned as leaders in each service center. These positions were opened to the company's unit member drivers, who applied and filed the positions. The company paid a $1.00 an hour stipend in addition to the regular contract rates for drivers for the additional leader duties. The additional duties specified for such coordinators were listed as opening and closing the facility, coordinating the work and assignments of drivers, and overseeing that proper service was provided. Additionally, these persons dispatched drivers and handled answering the telephone. This move and the temporary assignments were negotiated with the union, but no agreement was reached, nor was any objection raised to the procedure.

By July 1998, the service centers had been staffed with managers, and the company acted to eliminate the leader duties previously done by coordinators. However, certain duties, such as dispatch and telephone answering, were still assigned to the classification now known as "service provider," which was a change from the former "driver" title. This realignment of duties was not negotiated with the union. When the company made this realignment of duties, those who had previously served as coordinators were continued at the $1.00-per-hour stipend out of recognition of the commitment those people had made to help the company. It viewed this as a grandfathering of the wage for those individuals. However, the company did not apply the $1.00 stipend to other individuals who served thereafter as service providers.

Ultimately, the union grieved extra duties assigned to the former driver classification and that certain employees who were classified as service providers were entitled to the $1.00 stipend because of the duties that they were performing, particularly the dispatching. The union complained that the company violated the contract and the law by unilaterally establishing terms and conditions of a new classification. The effectuation of such terms and conditions, including the assignment of duties and the payment of additional wages, is clearly contrary to the contract. Employees who are assigned such duties as telephone and dispatch should be paid at the same rate as others who formerly performed as coordinators.

The company insisted that it has the management right to assign duties to the drivers that are not inconsistent with the classification and the general purpose of the operation. In establishing coordinators on a temporary basis, it did exactly that and, in addition, compensated them for certain leader/supervisory obligations. When the need for the performance of such duties ended, the company properly removed such assignments. The fact that such employees and others later performed the function of dispatch and telephone should not be considered leader/coordinator duties for which an additional $1.00 stipend was paid but rather normal assignments permitted the company under the contract. All employees are paid equally for the same work within the classification, including dispatching and telephone. The only distinction is that those employees who formerly served as coordinators had been granted a special continuing

continued

CASE 6-1

WAGES: EXTRA COMPENSATION—continued

rate of pay in light of their willingness to make the previous commitment to assist. In no respect did the company ever commit to pay an additional $1.00 for all drivers performing such nonleader/supervisory duties. There is no disparity in pay.

DISCUSSION

A key to this dispute is the question of whether the company would have, in the past, prior to the new service centers, violated the contract by assigning to members of the unit such duties as dispatching and telephone as are now done by certain service providers.

Under the management rights clause, there is certain flexibility and discretion allowing the company to assign related duties. The contract does not have any clear limitation on the assignment of such additional work. As long as such tasks are not supervisory and are reasonably related to the purpose—providing customer transportation—they may be included. In setting up the service centers, the company acted in somewhat of a hurry, so it did not have the managers and, hence, had to make use of drivers by assigning them temporarily to additional duties of a leadership nature. There was no objection to the process of application and interview and placement, nor was there any objection to the fact that the company paid an extra $1.00-per-hour stipend. The company never indicated that this move was intended to be permanent. The company saw certain leadership duties as beyond the scope of the classification and was willing to pay, but that did not create an obligation to continue it indefinitely.

When the company put managers in place, it no longer required the coordinators to perform supervisory tasks. However, there still was a need for nonmanagerial duties, such as dispatch and telephone answering, to be done. The question is whether

after the managers were in place it was improper for the company to assign such duties to unit members without the additional compensation.

The fact that some former coordinators continued to do such tasks and received the $1.00 stipend is not determinative of the company's commitment because, as the company explained, it felt committed to those people who had helped in the transition. Payment to such former coordinators does not, under the circumstances, establish any right of others who are assigned such duties. The issue is whether the company was obligated to "pay equally" everyone within the classification who performs the same duties.

DECISION

The court found that the company did not violate the contract by adding nonsupervisory duties to the service provider classification under its management rights clause because those duties are reasonably connected to the operation of transporting customers and therefore within the scope of the prior driver classification. Furthermore, when the company filled the management positions, the company rightfully discontinued the leader/supervisory duties of the employees designated as coordinators. However, the duties attributable to their status as service providers—dispatch, telephone, and so on—were not leader/supervisory duties and properly were retained within the scope of the service provider classification. Continuing assignment of such work to former coordinators with the $1.00 stipend and to others without such extra compensation did not create a new compensation level or disparate treatment of persons within the classification because the company had the right to continue to pay those individuals $1.00 more an hour in appreciation of their service.

SOURCE: Adapted from *The Mass Transportation Authority v. AFSCME Local 1223,* 115 LA 521 (November 22, 2000).

PAY EQUITY IN COMPANY MERGERS

Mergers and acquisitions are common in today's malleable business climate and have a significant impact on a wide range of employee issues. One major area of concern, of course, is how merging two organizations' compensation plans affect employees' pay. Experts advise that companies need to see the issue as more than just coordinating two payroll systems. "You have to make sure that you're doing it in a holistic way, not just nailing one company to the other," said Ken Ransby, a principal in the San Francisco office of Towers Perrin. Ransby went on to advise that although it might be ideal to use the best aspects of each organization's pay systems, such an approach might be too costly.

Before deciding how to approach compensation issues, the merged company should examine the underlying business reasons for the merger. If full integration of the two or more organizations was the goal, then the compensation systems must be aligned. Aligning pay systems requires a detailed analysis of the pay systems, consideration of how the organizations define pay, and recognition of geographical factors that cause pay disparities.

When Pfizer Animal Health Group acquired SmithKline Beecham Animal Health Business, the two compensation systems offered comparable pay, but Pfizer relied more on base pay whereas SmithKline offered incentive pay. The merged company wanted a single pay system, so it needed to integrate the SmithKline system into Pfizer's without having the SmithKline workers feel they were losing out. The solution was to fold into those former SmithKline workers' base pay an average annual incentive payout based on the three years prior to the merger.

Another common pay problem created in mergers and acquisitions is when similar jobs within the merging organizations have higher or lower rates. Usually, cutting salaries is not an option, and leaving salary discrepancies in place can lead to legal problems. Some companies approach this problem by leaving the higher salaries in place but freezing them for some period of time while at the same time evaluating the lower-salaried positions on a frequent basis. This would enable the positions to reach the same pay in an acceptable time frame without causing the company major cost problems.

Labor law experts warn companies that taking this approach can be hazardous. CoreStates Financial Corp. of Philadelphia found itself liable for $1.5 million in back pay and wage adjustments to 142 workers after 11 acquisitions in seven years left the bank with disparate salary structures in place, many of which resulted in lower wages to women and minorities.

Garry Locke, a principal in Towers Perrin's Minneapolis office, thinks that communication may be the single most important aspect of a post-merger strategy. Communication with employees can minimize employees' discontent about changing pay systems and relieve fears of layoffs or other adverse job actions.

SOURCE: Adapted from "Company Mergers and Acquisitions Present New Pay Equity Considerations for Employers," *Labor Relations Reporter,* 158 LRR 393, (July 27, 1998).

---

negotiating wages? A 2002 extensive review of the related research by Bruce Kaufman, Department of Economics and the W. T. Beebe Institute of Personnel and Employment Relations at Georgia State University, produced eight dimensions of the effects union wage negotiations have caused in the past 50 years:

1. ***Union goals in wage bargaining.*** Lynn Williams, former president of the United Steelworkers Union, summarized union wage goals as (1) "achieving the maximum level of wages and benefits for its members" and (2) "maintain[ing] all the jobs it could within as viable an industry as possible."

2. *The union–nonunion wage differential.* In the United States the size of the union versus nonunion wage differential, on average, is currently 24 percent.

3. *Union wage differentials over time.* From the end of World War II to the early 1980s, the union–nonunion wage differential in the United States continued to increase, but since the early 1980s, it has had a modest decline.

4. *Union wage rigidity and wage concessions.* Unions have historically held to the principle of no "givebacks" or "backward steps" in wages, even to the point of letting a company go out of business rather than accept a cut in wages.

5. *Wage structure.* Unions have also affected the structure of wage scales among workers within one employer or industry, negotiating for differences in working conditions, skills, seniority, age, and job classification. They have typically "flattened" or "compressed" the wage structure among workers in a plant or company and between skilled and unskilled workers.

6. *The form of compensation.* Unions in most cases have bargained for wages based on time or hours worked. They have opposed pay systems based on output, such as a merit or piece-rate systems or merit evaluations by supervisors. They have also bargained for additional forms of compensation that are awarded across the board, such as bonuses based on seniority, overtime, and pensions.

7. *Employment effects.* Unions have in general negotiated for practices and work rules that create or maintain more jobs. Examples include restrictive work rules limiting what duties one person can perform in their job description and "make-work" or "featherbedding" jobs.

8. *Pattern bargaining.* Unions have generally strived to pattern bargain or obtain similar wage gains from separate employers within the same industry or sometimes within similar industries or a community. The extent of pattern bargaining has declined somewhat since the 1980s.[7]

Industrial Differentials

Industrial wage differentials also provide a logical basis for differences in pay among employers in the same labor market. Employees recognize that the relationship between labor and total production costs affects their wage levels. Organizations in highly labor-intensive industries are usually less able to provide wage increases than organizations that are in more capital-intensive industries. For example, if a specialized chemical processing plant that has few competitors increased its wage rates by 10 percent, it would need to raise prices by only 0.6 percent to absorb the wage increase because only 6 percent of its total production costs would be attributable to labor. However, if a southern textile firm raised its wages by 10 percent, it would need to raise prices by 7 percent because its labor costs would equal 70 percent of total production costs. A 7 percent price increase could be disastrous to the highly competitive textile organization. Employees accept and understand that not all employers, because of their profitability or current competitive position within the marketplace, can be the highest-paying organization in the industry. If profits decrease so much that the organization suffers losses, wage demands usually will reflect the reality of the economic times.

Unions affect wages to some extent in many industries. The variation of union power and ability to raise wage levels across industries appears to be related to several factors. Union wage gains are generally greatest where (1) employers' ability to pay is high because of discretionary pricing power and profitability, (2) unions practice centralized bargaining, and (3) unions avoid fragmentation.[8]

MANAGEMENT WAGE CONCERNS

Wage and benefit changes have an impact on the cost of the production of goods and services. Management must consider how a change in wages will affect its pricing policy and ability to compete in the marketplace. It is often mistakenly inferred that management wants to minimize its labor costs for no particular reason or because employees are not appreciated. The reality is that management needs to maintain competitive labor costs to produce and price their products successfully within their industry. Thus, maintaining a competitive position is a primary aim of management in negotiations.

Accurate assessment of competitors' wages and total payroll costs is critical for management in anticipating the future of pricing changes within the industry. Labor-intensive industries find comparable wages to be even more necessary for long-run success. Thus, when national unions seek to negotiate equal pay increases among employers in the same industry, it is beneficial to management from the standpoint of maintaining a current competitive position. Union leaders, of course, find it beneficial to offer all members the same wage increases. More competitive and less organized industries, however, cannot provide this type of consistency.

This practice, known as **pattern bargaining**, can be highly successful for both management and labor. The steel and auto industries, paper, and petroleum, as well as the meatpacking and textile industries, have utilized pattern bargaining. Typically, the union leaders choose what they perceive as the weakest company—the one most susceptible to granting wage increases—and begin negotiations. Once negotiations are completed, the union insists that other firms in the industry agree to equal wage and benefit increases. However, another pattern strategy is to start with the largest employer in an industry, negotiate an agreement, and expect the other, smaller employers to follow suit. In 2001, for example, the United Mine Workers (UMW) ratified a new agreement with the Peabody Coal Company, the nation's largest coal producer, a year before the old contract expired. The early ratification provided a $600 "early signing" lump-sum bonus to workers before the old agreement expired as well as wage, health-care, and pension increases, signaling to all other, smaller coal companies the strength of the UMW. This enabled the union to negotiate similar contracts with smaller companies, calling them "me-too" agreements.[9]

In some situations a single union can use joint bargaining to the same wage package with all major employers simultaneously and thus not advantage or disadvantage any one employer. In 2003, for example, the Teamsters union in Chicago, Illinois, was able to stage a successful strike against the 17 private garbage haulers and then reach a settlement with each that provided a 30 percent increase in wages, up to $25.70 per hour, or an average of $42,000 per year. Instead of negotiating with the 17 employer members of the Chicago Refuse Haulers Association individually, the Teamsters jointly negotiated the same wage package with all the haulers—who were then able to pass the identical increased costs on to their customers and not suffer any competitive disadvantage. The ability to use joint bargaining, like pattern bargaining, gives a union enormous bargaining power, but is not often a realistic possibility.[10]

Pattern bargaining, however, does not prevent firms from negotiating differences according to local labor conditions and the profitability of a particular employer. Instead, when negotiated wage and benefit increases are equal for several employers, they maintain their same relative competitive position with regard to labor costs.

The uncertain economy that followed the terrorist attacks of September 11, 2001, caused a renewed interest in pattern bargaining by some employers. In 2002 about 30 percent of labor professionals negotiating new contracts said they closely watched the patterns set by competitors' settlements. This was significantly more than 10 years earlier in the wake of the Caterpillar strike.[11] For example, in 2003 the United Steel-workers of America signed a five-year agreement with the U.S. Steel Corporation covering 13,000 workers. The agreement was patterned after similar contracts with LTU Steel Corporation and was identical to one with National Steel.[12]

Management is also concerned about the **value added**, that is, labor's theory that wages should equal the contribution of labor to the final product. Out-of-hand labor costs may hamper management's ability to replace and maintain equipment and machinery. It may be tempting in the short run to absorb labor increases by reducing these kinds of expenditures. However, lack of competitive technological improvements and modern machinery can erode productivity. Thus, management wants the value added kept in proportion with the wages paid. The value added by labor to the total product and the value added by capital and equipment cannot be totally separated because of their interrelationship. One is not useful without the other, and each affects the other's increase or decrease in productivity. Determining labor's share of the value added to the product is a difficult and often debated point in labor negotiations. Sometimes subcontracting bids for specific work can be used to estimate the true value that labor has added.

Wage Laws

A number of federal laws outside the National Labor Relations Act affect wage rates. The major compensation legislation regulating employers is the Fair Labor Standards Act (FLSA) of 1938, as amended. It governs the items discussed in the following. Although these laws provided critical help, as seen in Profile 6-2, gaps still exist between many workers and a living wage.

Minimum Wages

Under the FLSA, employers must pay an employee at least a minimum wage per hour, as shown in Table 6-1. The minimum wage per hour in 1938 was $0.25 and has been increased several times to $5.15 in 1997. Exempted from the act are small businesses whose gross sales do not exceed $500,000. Also exempted are organizations that operate within one state. However, several states have minimum wage laws that parallel the federal minimum wage provisions. The 1990 amendments to FLSA also provided for a training wage for employees less than 20 years of age set at 85 percent of the minimum wage. Three studies conducted after the increase in the minimum wage rate and the creation of a training wage for teenagers showed that increases in the minimum wage caused no increase in unemployment.[13] The training wage section of the FLSA amendment expired in April 1993 but was reenacted as a "youth minimum wage" in August 1996. Employees who have not reached their 20th birthday can be paid $4.25 per hour for the first 90 days of their employment.[14]

Overtime Compensation

The FLSA stipulates that certain employees must receive overtime pay of one and a half times the normal rate when they work over 40 hours per week. Certain kinds of employees are **exempt** from the overtime provision of the act. In and of itself, a job title is not a sufficient basis for exemption. Rather, the actual work performed and the primary duties of the employee are what count. A person with an executive title who does not primarily manage a department or a function may not meet all conditions for exemption. In 2004 the U.S. Department of Labor issued new regulations to determine if an employee is classified as exempt. To be exempt an employee must be paid a minimum salary of $455 per week ($23,660 per year). An employee who is paid by the hour or who makes a salary of less than $455 per week is **nonexempt** regardless of the type of work performed. An

MODERN-DAY SWEATSHOPS?

Thousands of immigrants work seven days a week sewing clothes for pennies per garment. They are often treated as machines, not as humans, and they are given 15-minute meal breaks that must be taken at the sewing machine. These immigrant workers may also be subjected to tirades from a boss who will fine someone for asking questions. Minimum wage, overtime, and workers' compensation are unknown concepts in these sweatshops. Is this a scene from the 1930s? No, it is the garment industry in California—today's sweatshops. A study of 69 randomly selected garment factories in California found that 50 percent did not pay minimum wage, 68 percent did not pay overtime, and 90 percent had health and safety violations. They exist from San Francisco to San Diego. Some employees, it was discovered, are paid only $2.97 an hour for 40 of the 60 hours they worked per week. The international labor picture presents an equally troubling scenario, an almost unlimited potential for sweatshop activi-

ties. Some notable examples that have made the news follow:

- Nike, the largest apparel company in the United States, does not own a single piece of equipment for making shoes—not one. Instead, Nike contracts for its products with the owners of over 400 factories in 43 countries. These are often poor, Third World countries where the factory jobs are the best-paying jobs available but far below U.S. pay and safety standards.

- Saipan, a U.S. island territory, uses Chinese "guest" workers who cannot leave because they cannot pay the $7,000 "recruiting fee" that brought them to Saipan. A U.S. congressional delegation found the Chinese workers making clothing with "Made in the U.S.A." labels for 23 companies, including the Gap, The Limited, Gear, and Champions.

- A Honduras garment factory pays workers $20 per 60-hour workweek. The factory has no air conditioning and only two 15-minute breaks per 11-hour day.

SOURCES: Adapted from "Sweatshops Thrive in California," *Omaha World-Herald,* July 31, 1994; "The Shame of Sweatshops," *Consumer Reports 64,* no. 8 (August 1999), pp. 18–20; and Dominic Bencivenga, "1959 Sweatshop Law," *New York Law Journal,* August 13, 1998, pp. 1–4.

employee paid $455 per week must also meet the "duties test" to be exempt from overtime provisions:

- Primary duty is the management of the organization.
- Regularly direct two or more full-time employees or equivalent.
- Authority to hire/fire or recommend the hiring or firing, promotion of others.

OR meet the administrative exemption provision:

- Primary duty of office work directly related to the management of the organization or customers.
- Exercise independent judgment on matters of significance.

TABLE 6-1   U.S. Minimum Wage Changes Under FLSA

1938	1945	1950	1956	1962	1967	1974	
$0.25	$0.40	$0.75	$1.00	$1.15	$1.40	$2.00	

1978	1979	1980	1985	1990	1991	1996	1997
$2.65	$2.90	$3.10	$3.35	$3.80	$4.25	$4.75	$5.15

OR meet the professional exemption provision:

- Primary duty of performing work requiring advanced knowledge in a field of science or learning customarily acquired by a prolonged course of specialized, intellectual instruction; or performing work requiring invention, imagination, originality, or talent in a recognized field of artistic or creative endeavor.

Employees earning over $100,000 per year do not receive overtime if their duties are executive, administrative, or professional.

The new 2004 rules were the first major changes in the 1938 act since 1949 and were hotly debated in Washington, D.C., with labor unions contending they will reduce the number of people receiving overtime by several million, and President Bush and supporters claiming that the new rules will be easier for employers to implement.

About 98 percent of all agreements contain some premium pay for overtime above the FLSA requirement. Daily overtime premiums are provided in 93 percent of agreements. Sixth-day premiums—the sixth consecutive day of work is eligible for a premium payment—and seventh-day premiums are found in about 26 percent of contracts. The **pyramiding** (being paid for more than one premium pay on the same hours) of overtime pay is prohibited in 69 percent of contracts because of management's concerns that the same hours might either become eligible for both daily and weekly overtime or become eligible for more than one type of premium. An example of the latter might be holiday pay plus double time on a seventh day worked. Most agreements also specify how overtime should be distributed among workers: "Equal distribution as far as practical" or on a strict seniority basis are common provisions.[15]

The American 40-hour workweek, with time and a half for hours over 40, may end. President George W. Bush has questioned this workweek standard, which has been in the FLSA since it was passed in 1938. Congress proposed in 1997 a new workweek law that would allow flexible work schedules by employees and that would not be limited by the 40-hour standard. Employees, for example, might work four 12-hour days with a three-day weekend and be paid the standard hourly rate for all 48 hours, sacrificing eight hours of overtime pay. Union leaders strongly opposed the change; they feared that employees would be coerced into working longer hours and giving up overtime pay. Under another proposal, employees could choose time-and-a-half **compensatory time** (hours taken off at a later date) or overtime pay. How do most workers feel about the issue? A Roper poll found that women would prefer the flexible hours (44 versus 32 percent), but men would not (38 versus 42 percent), and about one-third reported that they already have flextime.[16]

In some industries today the aspect of overtime that unions view as a key issue is the use of *mandatory overtime*. They believe that the excessive use of mandatory overtime keeps many of their members from having enough time with their families and can cause shortages of full-time positions as management tries to minimize the total number of employees in certain jobs. For example, in 2002 the Registered Nurses Association of University Hospital in Cincinnati, Ohio, was ready to strike because they believed mandatory overtime had become routine. Nurses were often ordered to work a second shift at the end of their first shift and were commonly called in on their off days. In addition, the union stressed that mandatory overtime may not be good for patient care. The strike was averted when hospital management agreed to end mandatory overtime by 2004.[17]

In 2003 the Communication Workers of America (CWA) walked off the job over forced overtime. The 37,000 CWA members' strike against Verizon was the largest concerted labor action against a telecommunications employer in U.S. history, and it was not over pay or health care—but mandatory overtime. The union eventually won a limited overtime provision. Why do unions today view excessive hours as a critical issue?

AFL-CIO industrial hygienist Bill Kojola says the way work is organized in the United States is changing and requires longer hours. Research, according to Kojola, indicates that longer hours:

- Have an adverse impact on the cardiovascular systems of workers.
- Increase the blood pressure of workers.
- Increase the risk of accidents exponentially to the point it is double for a 12-hour shift compared to an 8-hour shift.
- Increased risk of accident is highest on a night shift, higher on an afternoon shift, and lowest on a morning shift.[18]

In 2005, the U.S. Department of Labor (DOL) approved the use of **prepayment plans** that pay employees overtime in advance of their actual accumulation. To give nonexempt employees a more stable wage, the DOL approved a plan that would pay workers for future overtime hours (at time-and-one-half rate) during weeks when they worked fewer than 40 hours. Then during weeks when employees work over 40 hours, any prepayments they have received will be deducted from their pay. Employees agree to the prepayment plan as a condition of employment. The employer cannot, however, owe an employee any overtime pay. Prepayment plans benefit both employees and employers—with a steady cash flow.[19]

Exactly what counts as "work time" under the FLSA should be carefully determined. The FLSA required employers to "record, and compensate employees for all of the time which the employer requires or permits the employee to work," time spent in principal activities—those that employees were hired to perform regardless of when they are performed! However, some activities may qualify as de minimus—although work, they require so little time that they do not require compensation. The small duties required of an employee before and after their shift can be considered as either de minimus or as a principal activity. For example, in 2005 the Department of Labor, in response to a complaint, investigated Cingular Wireless and found that customer service representatives in 25 call centers in 14 states would begin work prior to their shift, but were "off the clock" and thus not paid overtime. Cingular cooperated with the DOL and agreed to pay 25,351 representatives $5.1 million in back pay and overtime for their preparation time.[20]

The Davis-Bacon Act

The Davis-Bacon Act of 1931 regulates employers who hold federal government contracts of $2,000 or more for federal construction projects. It provides that employees working on these projects must be paid the prevailing wage rate. In most urban areas, the union wage is the prevailing wage for that particular geographic area. If the local union wage for plumbers is $10 per hour, then any plumbers hired to work on federal construction projects in the area must be paid $10 per hour. The reasoning behind the Davis-Bacon Act is that often governments will award contracts to the firm submitting the lowest bid for certain construction specifications. By requiring all employers in construction projects to pay the prevailing wage, the Davis-Bacon Act puts bidders on an equal basis and ensures that craft workers will not be underpaid.[21]

Opponents of the Davis-Bacon Act have consistently claimed that it is difficult to administer and that it substantially increases the cost of public construction projects. Supporters contend, however, that contractors trying to win construction bids will underbid by cutting wages and then hiring less-skilled nonunion labor. In 2001, congressional opponents of the act introduced the Davis-Bacon Modernization Act, which set a much higher threshold and thus would exempt most federal construction projects, rendering the 1931 act almost useless.[22]

Walsh-Healey Act

The Walsh-Healey Act of 1936 covers employees with federal contracts of over $10,000. It requires employers to pay overtime for any hours worked over eight per day at a rate of one and a half times the normal hourly rate. If an employee works days of more than eight hours within a 40-hour week, he or she will receive greater compensation for the same total hours worked.

NEGOTIATED WAGE ADJUSTMENTS

Standard Rate, Pay Range Systems

How wage rates are to be defined in the agreement is a critical issue. Most agreements contain a **standard rate**, or flat rate, of pay for each job classification effective during the life of the agreement, as in Figure 6-1. Some agreements provide a pay range for each job: The person may be paid one of several steps within the range. Usually management will seek flexibility in wage administration by using a range of pay for each grade or category. A common practice in the nonunion sector, this allows management to reward individual differences in employees according to seniority, merit, or quality and quantity of production.

Management usually wishes to hire new, inexperienced employees at the minimum pay rate and allow them to advance during their tenure with the company through merit and seniority increases. Management may argue that it makes little sense to pay exactly the same wage rate for a job regardless of the performance level of the employee. The highest-performing employee and the lowest-performing employee in a standard rate system receive the same wage rate, a system that tends to undermine individual motivation.[23] Union leaders argue that merit increases, which are the primary reason to have pay ranges instead of standard rates, are useful management tools in theory but actually run into severe problems. Union leaders feel that because these systems normally are based on a supervisor's performance appraisal, they are subject to supervisor bias. The subjectivity and imperfections of performance appraisal systems, which cannot be denied by management, lead most union leaders to argue against a merit pay increase system. Management may then counter with the argument that an imperfect performance appraisal system is better than no system of rewarding individual performance.

Piece-Rate Systems

An alternative pay system is a **piece-rate system**. Straight piecework is the most common and easily understood individual incentive plan. If an employee is paid $0.025 per unit produced and completes 100 units in an hour, then the hour's gross earnings will be $2.50. Variations of straight piecework include falling piece rate and rising piece rate. Table 6-2 is a comparison of the various piece-rate plans. If designed effectively, a piece-rate system can reduce labor costs per unit, reward employees based on their productivity instead of the number of hours worked, and help attract and retain dedicated employees. Thus an effective piece-rate system can benefit both the employer and the worker. A field experiment published in 2004, for example, found that when workers were paid piece rates instead of hourly wages, their productivity increased by 20 percent in comparison to workers performing the same job but given a daily production standard, and they received higher compensation.[24]

Plans that use a **falling piece rate** involve a standard time and rate of production. If the employee produces more than the standard, the gain is shared between the employer and the employee. The employee's hourly earnings increase with output above a standard of

In piece-rate incentive plans, workers like these are paid a rate per unit produced rather than an hourly wage.

100, but the rate per piece falls at various predetermined levels. Thus, an employee who has produced 140 units (40 percent above standard) receives only $3.22 (29 percent more) and not $3.50, which would be the case if the $0.025 rate were maintained. The employer receives the remainder of the gain, effectively lowering the overhead cost per piece.

Plans that use a **rising piece rate** also involve a standard time and rate of production. But as Table 6-2 illustrates, the worker who increases output by 40 percent has a greater-than-proportional increase in hourly earnings. After earning $2.50 for the first 100 pieces, the worker earns $2.40 ($4.90 – $2.50) for the next 40 pieces, or 96 percent of the base hourly pay. The increase occurs because the worker earned $0.025 per piece for the first 100 pieces and $0.035 per piece for the next 40. Management benefits nevertheless: The total cost per piece still declines as more pieces are produced because the fixed overhead cost is spread out over more pieces.[25] Why would management agree to a rising piece-rate system? If the higher hourly earnings are sufficiently motivational, the total cost per piece could be cheaper than under a falling piece-rate plan. For example, if under the falling piece-rate plan of Table 6-2 the employee is only slightly motivated and averages 120 units per hour, then management has an average total piece cost of $0.857. But if the rising piece-rate plan is slightly more motivational and the employee averages 140 units per hour, management averages $0.749 total per unit cost whereas the employee averages $4.90 per hour instead of $2.88 (falling rate of 120 pieces).

TABLE 6-2 A Comparison of Piece-Rate Plans ($100 per worker overhead cost per hour)

Standard Piece-Rate Plan

| | | | Per Piece | |
| | | | | |
Number of Pieces	Piece Rate	Worker's Earnings	Overhead Cost	Total Cost
100	$0.025	$2.50	$1.000	$1.025
120	0.025	3.00	0.833	0.858
140	0.025	3.50	0.714	0.739
160	0.025	4.00	0.625	0.650
180	0.025	4.50	0.556	0.581
200	0.025	5.00	0.500	0.525

Falling Piece-Rate Plan

| | | | Per Piece | |
| | | | | |
Number of Pieces	Piece Rate	Worker's Earnings	Overhead Cost	Total Cost
100	$0.025	$2.50	$1.000	$1.025
120	0.024	2.88	0.833	0.857
140	0.023	3.22	0.714	0.737
160	0.022	3.52	0.625	0.647
180	0.021	3.78	0.556	0.577
200	0.020	4.00	0.500	0.520

Rising Piece-Rate Plan

| | | | Per Piece | |
| | | | | |
Number of Pieces	Piece Rate	Worker's Earnings	Overhead Cost	Total Cost
100	$0.025	$2.50	$1.000	$1.025
120	0.030	3.60	0.833	0.863
140	0.035	4.90	0.714	0.749
160	0.040	6.40	0.625	0.665
180	0.045	8.10	0.556	0.601
200	0.050	10.00	0.500	0.550

SOURCE: Leonard R. Burgess, *Wage and Salary Administration* (Columbus, OH: Merrill, 1984), pp. 241–42.

Piece-rate systems have the advantages of being easily understood, simple to calculate, and motivational. But many jobs do not easily lend themselves to such a pay system because the output of the employee cannot be directly and objectively measured. Also, most employees' output is affected by the output of others, so their productivity is not directly proportional to their input. Finally, union and management negotiators may have a difficult time agreeing on what is a fair production standard. Changes in standards by management can easily lead to union grievances.

Standard hour plans are similar in concept to piece-rate plans except a "standard time" is set to complete a particular job, instead of paying the employee a price per piece. For example, an auto mechanic might be given a standard time of two hours to tune up an eight-cylinder car. If the worker's hourly rate is $8.00 per hour and three eight-cylinder tune-ups are finished in six hours, then the employee earns $48.00. If a so-called Halsey 50/50 incentive plan is used, the worker and employer share equally in time saved by the employee. Thus, after completing the three tune-ups in five hours, the employee would be paid $52.00 ($48.00 – $4.00 [1/2 hour saved at $8.00 per hour]), and the employer has an additional hour's work time.

Deferred Wage Increases

Many multiyear collective bargaining agreements provide increases in wage rates that are deferred to later years rather than taking effect immediately. Together with the preferred use of cost-of-living adjustments (see next section), such **deferred wage rate increases** often make multiyear contracts desirable for both sides. Management can predict labor costs further into the future with a greater degree of accuracy, and union members feel that their buying power is protected for a longer period of time and do not have to worry annually about possible strikes.

Deferred wage provisions specify increases in the base pay to take effect on future dates during a multiyear contract. Negotiating multiyear increases often hinges on whether they are evenly distributed over the life of the contract, as in the following example of a three-year contract (5 percent increases) starting July 1, 2006, or whether they are front-end loaded.

Pay Classification	Wage Rate on July 1, 2006	Wage Rate on July 1, 2007	Wage Rate on July 1, 2008
I	$12.00	$12.60	$13.23
II	$10.00	$10.50	$11.03
III	$9.00	$9.45	$9.92

Front-end loading refers to a deferred wage increase with a larger proportion of the total percentage increase in the first year of the agreement. Thus, a three-year total wage increase package might be evenly distributed, with an equal percentage provided at the beginning of each year: 5 percent–5 percent–5 percent; or it could be front-end loaded: 10–3–2. Many contracts provide front-end loading, including providing the total increase in the first year: 15–0–0.

Management generally prefers to spread the increases over the life of the agreement for cash flow purposes and because the total cost of the agreement is substantially less because higher wages paid only in later years are avoided in early years. For example, the two alternatives for the three-year 15 percent increase when applied to a $20,000 current wage produce the following wages paid:

Year	Equal Increases, 5%–5%–5%	Front-End Loaded, 10%–3%–2%	Difference Each Year
0	$20,000	$20,000	—
1	$21,000	$22,000	+ $1,000
2	$22,050	$22,660	+ $ 610
3	$23,153	$23,113	– $ 40
			+ $1,570

Union negotiators often prefer front-end-loaded wage rate increases so that their members receive the additional wages ($1,570) and realize a large increase in pay the very first year. However, negotiators acknowledge from past experience that front-end loading may produce long-term problems. Members who were quite happy with a 10 percent increase during the first year of an agreement can easily become dissatisfied with the two subsequent years of small increases, especially during periods of high inflation. Thus,

"What have you done for me lately?" becomes a real problem for union and management leaders alike. Also, the annual wage rates at the end of the agreement can easily be lower under a front-end-loaded provision than under an evenly distributed provision, as in the previously cited examples. The union may demand a **wage reopener** provision providing for the reopening of contract talks to discuss only wage rates. Such a discussion during the later years of the agreement may become necessary because of unpredictable inflation or company financial success. Management is not obligated to agree to higher wage rates under such a reopener but realizes that this agreement may be necessary to obtain a long-term contract. Also, management negotiators realize that they will likely be faced with the demands, particularly when they are valid, during the next negotiating session anyway.

Before the 1980s, virtually all collective bargaining agreements with multiyear settlements included front-end-loaded wage increases. However, foreign and domestic nonunion competition in the 1980s forced management negotiators to seek a variety of cost-curbing measures including back-loaded contracts. A **back-loaded contract** provides a lower wage adjustment in the first year with higher increases in later years of a multiyear contract. For example, a 10 percent three-year wage adjustment could be 2–4–4. In many back-loaded contracts, workers receive no wage increase in the first year. For example, a 1997–1999 UAW–Chrysler collective bargaining agreement provided for a 0–3–3 distribution with a $2,000 bonus.[26]

Cost-of-Living Adjustments

Union negotiators have for years emphasized the need for **cost-of-living adjustments (COLAs)** during the life of an agreement. They contend that the real wage—the purchasing power negotiated in an agreement as a wage rate—is eroded by inflation during the life of the agreement. Therefore, it is necessary to provide the COLA in an escalator clause so that wage rates will keep pace with inflation. General Motors first proposed a COLA clause during negotiations with the UAW in 1948.

Unions and employers were leery of COLAs until the 1950s. Both feared that COLAs would include pay cuts, which might have occurred because declines in the consumer price index (CPI) were at the time quite possible. Union leaders also disliked COLAs because they represented a "substitute for bargaining," meaning they would receive less credit for increases with a COLA. Unions preferred wage reopeners that put them back at the bargaining table. However, by the mid-1950s, both sides worried less about deflation and more about their ability to estimate correctly rising inflation. In addition, in 1950 General Motors and the United Auto Workers signed a historic wage formula that combined deferred wage adjustments with a COLA—a practice previously avoided by GM but soon followed by many negotiators.[27] The percentage of agreements that contained COLAs steadily increased and peaked in 1979 at 48 percent, but low CPI increases from the 1990s until today have caused the percentage slip to only 18 percent of agreements in 2002.[28] Other reasons for this decline in the use of COLA provisions are (1) the administrative expense for employers to make frequent adjustments in wage rates as specified in most COLA provisions is substantial and (2) the fact that annual base wage adjustments are provided in most multiyear contracts, providing an effective substitute to COLA adjustments as a means of compensating for inflation.[29] Management, to save administrative costs, prefers to make few wage rate adjustments, and unions realize that in periods of low inflation, annual wage rate adjustments are adequate to maintain real income. Thus, the combination of two factors—low inflation rates and the increasing use of multiyear contracts—has decreased the need for quarterly or monthly COLA adjustments to be made if annual base wage rate adjustments have been negotiated in the contract.

Both labor and management negotiators are careful to specify exact COLA provisions during the agreement. Several critical issues must be carefully spelled out.

1. *Inflation index.* Most provisions use the consumer price index determined by the Bureau of Labor Statistics (BLS) as a standard for measuring change in inflation. In 1978 the BLS broke the CPI into two entities: the urban family index (CPI-U) for urban families and the urban wage earner index (CPI-W) for urban wage earners and clerical workers. Starting in January 1999, the BLS changed the CPI-W base from 1967-100 to 1993–1995-100.

Increases in the CPI are linked to increases in wages by an adjustment formula. The two most commonly used formulas are a cents-per-hour increase for each point increase in the CPI or a percentage increase in wage rates equal to some percentage increase in the CPI. The most commonly used formula provides for a 1-cent increase in wages for each 0.26-of-a-point increase in the CPI. An example of this provision is found in Figure 6-3 from the agreement between the UAW and Ford Motor Company.

2. *When the increases are to be provided.* The majority of agreements provide for inflation adjustment four times a year subsequent to the reported increase in the CPI. This quarterly increase provision is also included in the UAW–Ford agreement. Other labor agreements provide for adjustments to be made twice a year (semiannually) or once a year (annually).

3. *Change in base pay.* If COLAs are treated as additions to the base pay, then other wage adjustments, such as shift differential and overtime, will increase after a COLA because they are usually a fixed percentage of a base pay. Thus, the company will find its personnel cost increased by an amount greater than the percentage COLA. The alternative is to treat the COLAs given during the life of the agreement as a benefit and not as an addition to the base pay (see Figure 6-3 for an example).

4. *COLA maximums.* Some labor agreements provide for a maximum COLA increase made by the company during the life of the agreement. This maximum is usually referred to as a cap put on the cost-of-living provision. The cap assures management that wage increases due to CPI increases will not go beyond a certain total.

Critics of COLA provisions state that such provisions fuel inflation. However, only a little more than 10 percent of the civilian nonagricultural workforce in the United States is covered by COLA provisions and is therefore able to keep pace with inflation. Although more than 80 percent of the workforce is thus excluded from COLA provisions, critics still contend that employers who pay COLAs increase their prices to reflect the increase in labor costs. A circular situation develops that ultimately results in increased prices or higher inflation. Inflation causes the CPI to go up, and the higher CPI causes COLA provisions in labor agreements to be enacted; COLA provisions cause an increase in wage rates.

Labor leaders are quick to point out, however, that because only a small portion of the total labor force is covered by COLA provisions, the effect on inflation must not be very great. They also believe that their members should be protected against inflation. Labor leaders point out that government's tying of Social Security increases and federal employee retirement increases to the CPI has much more of an impact on inflation than do labor agreement COLA adjustments.

A significant problem with COLA adjustments that concerns both union leaders and management is that, once given, the increases are taken for granted by employees. Members may believe that the wage increases they receive on the basis of COLA

Section 4. Cost-of-Living Allowance

(a) Payment of Allowance; Effect on Other Payments

Effective **September 30, 1996,** and thereafter during the period of this Agreement, each employee **hired on or before September 30, 1996,** shall receive a cost-of-living allowance as set forth in this Section.

Employees hired or rehired after September 30, 1996, shall receive the Cost-of-Living Allowance amount effective during the three-month period in which they are hired until their first base rate adjustment. Concurrent with each subsequent base rate adjustment employees shall have their Cost-of-Living Allowance amount changed to the then current Cost-of-Living Allowance payable as specified in subsection (d)(2).

The cost-of-living allowance shall not be added to the base rate for any classification, but only to each employee's straight-time hourly earnings (including the earned rate only of employees on an incentive basis of pay).

The cost-of-living allowance shall be taken into account in computing overtime and shift premiums, and in determining call-in pay and pay for vacations, unworked holidays, jury duty, bereavement and short-term military duty.

(b) Basis for Allowance

(1) The amount of the cost-of-living allowance shall be determined and redetermined as provided below on the basis of the Consumer Price Index for Urban Wage Earners and Clerical Workers (revised, CPI-W, United States City Average) published by the Bureau of Labor Statistics (1967 = 100).

(2) Continuance of the cost-of-living allowance shall be contingent upon the availability of the Index in its present form and calculated on the same basis as the Index for July, 1996, unless otherwise agreed upon by the parties. If the Bureau of Labor Statistics changes the form or the basis of calculating the Index, the parties agree to ask the Bureau to make available, for the life of this Agreement, a monthly Index in its present form and calculated on the same basis as the Index for July 1996.

(3) **The Cost-of-Living Allowance provided herein will be determined in accordance with changes in the Consumer Price Index for Urban Wage Earners and Clerical Workers, CPI-W, (United States City Average) published by the Bureau of Labor Statistics, and calculated in accordance with the Letter of Understanding signed by the parties. For the nine adjustments beginning in December 1996 and continuing through December 1998, the BLS's CPI-W (1967 = 100) reference base will be used in such calculations. Thereafter, beginning with the March 1999 adjustment, the BLS's CPI-W (1993–95 = 100) reference base will be used to determine the Cost-of-Living Allowance.**

(c) Redeterminations

Adjustments during the period of this Agreement shall be made at the following times:

Effective Date of Adjustment	Based Upon Three-Month Average of the Consumer Price Index for:
December 2, 1996	August, September, and October, 1996
First pay period beginning on or after March 3, 1997 and at three-calendar-month intervals thereafter to June 7, 1999	November, December, 1996 and January, 1997 and at three-calendar-month intervals thereafter to February, March, and April 1999.

FIGURE 6-3 COLA Provision

(d) Amount of Allowance

    (1) The amount of cost-of-living allowance beginning September 30, 1996, and ending December 1, 1996 shall be five cents (5¢) per hour.

    (2) Effective December 2, 1996 and for any period thereafter as provided in Subsection (c), the cost-of-living allowance shall be in accordance with the following table:

Three-Month Average Consumer Price Index Cost-of-Living Allowance

457.9 or less None
458.0–458.1 1¢ per hour
458.2–458.4 2¢ per hour
458.5–458.6 3¢ per hour
458.7–458.9 4¢ per hour
459.0–459.2 5¢ per hour
459.3–459.4 6¢ per hour
459.5–459.7 7¢ per hour
459.8–459.9 8¢ per hour
460.0–460.2 9¢ per hour

and so forth with one cent (1 ¢) adjustment for each 0.26 point change in the Average Index **(1967 = 100)** as calculated in accordance with the Letter of Understanding signed by the parties **continuing through the adjustment effective in December 1998. Thereafter, beginning with the adjustment effective in March 1999, and beginning with the first next 1¢ that may become payable, the above table will be changed to reflect a conversion in CPI-W reference bases, from 1967 = 100 to 1993–95 = 100, and modified to provide that 1¢ adjustments in the Cost-of-Living Allowance shall become payable for each 0.06 change in the Average Index, as calculated in accordance with the Letter of Understanding signed by the parties.**

FIGURE 6-3 COLA Provision (Continued)

SOURCE: Agreement between UAW and Ford Motor Co., vol. 1, 1997–1999, pp. 99–102.

provisions are not negotiated increases, and therefore they want further wage increases. Union and management negotiators may believe that they are not given credit for these negotiated increases. Because members come to expect automatic adjustments for inflation, they tend to ask labor negotiators and management, "What have you done for me lately?" Finally, management complains that COLA provisions prevent them from forecasting future labor costs. Management contends that it cannot adequately predict the total product cost and that COLA costs hamper the ability to bid successfully on projects or priced items.

History indicates that the percentage of union workers covered by COLAs is most likely to increase in the three-year period following a period of higher inflation as union negotiators strive to regain lost buying power. Because the COLA has been generally intended for this purpose, this is a logical result. However, it appears that recently COLAs have not been a prime negotiating target for labor or management. When either is in a generally strong negotiating position, neither party has significantly altered the percentage of union workers covered by COLAs in the direction expected. This would seem to be the natural result of a few years with low inflation.[30]

Profit Sharing

Compensation systems whereby management agrees to make a lump-sum payment to employees in addition to their regular wages are termed **profit sharing** or bonus plans. The payments may be based on the profits of the company using an agreed-on formula (profit sharing) or an amount specified in the contract based on production or sales levels (see Figure 6-4 for the UAW–Ford formula based on sales). Both are preferred by management over base-wage changes because negotiated increases do not automatically carry over to future years and do not increase the cost of associated benefits such as overtime rates and pension payments, which are typically based on base-wage earnings. Profit-sharing plans appear in about 10 percent of agreements.[31]

Management favors profit sharing to COLAs as a wage supplement for several reasons: (1) payments are made only if the company makes a profit and thus is usually financially strong; (2) unlike COLAs, payments are not tied to inflation, which is not related to the company's financial status and may require increases during difficult times; (3) workers' pay is linked to their productivity and not just to the number of hours they work, giving them a direct incentive to see the company become more profitable; and (4) workers may feel more a part of the company and develop increased interest in reducing waste and increasing efficiency in all areas as well as their own jobs.

In 2001, for example, the Ford Motor Company distributed millions in annual profit-sharing checks to U.S. employees. The average worker received $6,700. Peter Pestillo, Ford's personnel chief and chief labor negotiator, noted, "We think it's money well spent. They get more, and they get more done. We think we get a payback in the cooperation and enthusiasm of the people." The 1984 Ford–UAW master agreement was the first to contain a profit-sharing provision pushed by management as a means of avoiding the UAW-proposed 3 percent annual raises.[32] The concept of profit sharing within the auto industry is not new, however. Douglas Frasier, former president of the UAW, noted that the union first asked for a profit-sharing plan more than 40 years prior to the 1984 agreement and during several other negotiations, but none of the U.S. auto giants were interested until they were losing money in the 1980s.[33]

Scanlon Group Incentive Plans

Joseph Scanlon developed a group incentive plan designed to achieve greater production through increased efficiency with accrued savings divided among the workers and the company. Scanlon at the time was the research director of the United Steelworkers and later joined the faculty at the Massachusetts Institute of Technology.[34] The **Scanlon plan** became the popular standard in U.S. group incentive plans. It has since become a basis for labor–management cooperation above and beyond its use as a group incentive plan. The plan contains two primary features: (1) departmental committees of union and management representatives meet together at least monthly to consider any cost-savings suggestions, and (2) any documented cost savings resulting from implemented committee suggestions are divided 75 percent to employees and 25 percent to the company.[35]

Most other group incentive plans involve programs that set expected levels of productivity, product costs, or sales levels for individual groups and then provide employee bonuses if the targeted goals are exceeded. One widely recognized example is the Nucor Corporation. In one year the company reported a staggering growth of 600 percent in sales and 1,500 percent in profits over 10 years due to a production incentive program. The company actually developed four separate incentive programs: one each for production employees, department heads, professional employees, and senior officers. Their theory was that "money is the best motivation."[36]

Ford Motor Company Profit Sharing Plan for Hourly Employees in the United States

The purpose of this plan is to make provision for profit sharing distributions by the Company to eligible hourly employees, thus affording them a means of participating in the growth and success of the Company resulting from improved productivity and operating competitiveness as well as providing new sources of income for such employees.

  (a) "Eligible Hourly Employee" or "Participant" shall mean, with respect to any Plan Year, any person who met all of the following requirements at any time during such Plan year:

    (i) such person was employed **full-time** at an hourly rate in U.S. Operations on the active employment rolls maintained by the Company in the United States (except that any such person who was so employed on a temporary part-time basis shall be excluded from the definition of "Eligible Hourly Employee" and "Participant"); **and**

    (ii) such person, if represented by a Union, was covered by an agreement making this Plan applicable to such person or, if such person was not represented by a Union, such person was employed in a unit to which the Company had made this Plan applicable;

including any person who met such requirements at any time during such Plan Year and (1) was on layoff or approved leave, including expired medical leave, at the end of such Plan Year, or (2) retired during such Plan Year, (3) died during such Plan Year, or (4) was terminated by the Company during such Plan Year as a result of the sale by the Company of the operation, or a controlling interest in the operation, in which such person was employed; provided, however, that any person who terminated during such Plan Year (without being reinstated at the end of such Plan Year), for any reason other than death, retirement, sale of an operation, or a controlling interest in an operation, or any voluntary termination of employment program developed under the Job Security Program—GEN (Appendix M of the Agreement) shall be excluded from the definition of "Eligible Hourly Employee" and "Participant".

II. Determination of Total Profit Share

For any Plan Year in which there are Profits, the Total Profit Share for such Plan Year shall be determined as hereinafter provided. Such Total Profit Share shall be the sum of the following:

  (a) 6.0% of the portion of the Profits for such Plan Year which does not exceed 1.8% of such Sales;
  (b) 8% of the portion of the Profits for such Plan Year which exceeds 1.8% of Sales for such Plan Year but does not exceed 2.3% of such Sales;
  (c) 10% of the portion of the Profits for such Plan Year which exceeds 2.3% of Sales for such Plan Year but does not exceed 4.6% of such Sales;
  (d) 14% of the portion of the Profits for such Plan Year which exceeds 4.6% of Sales for such Plan Year but does not exceed 6.9% of such Sales; and
  (e) 17% of the portion of the Profits for such Plan Year which exceeds 6.9% of Sales for such Plan Year;

provided; however, that the Total Profit Share for any Plan Year in which there are Profits shall in no event be less than the amount determined by multiplying (3) $50 by (y) the sum of (i) the number of Eligible Hourly Employees for such Plan Year, (ii) the number of persons who would have been Eligible Hourly Employees for such Plan Year except for the fact that they were employed in a unit which was represented by a Union that had not agreed with Ford or a Subsidiary that this Plan shall apply to such unit, and (iii) the number of Salaried Employees for such Plan Year.

III. Determination of Allocated Profit Share

1. A portion of the Total Profit Share, if any, for each Plan Year shall be allocated to this Plan as hereinafter provided. The portion to be so allocated shall be determined by multiplying such Total Profit Share by a fraction, the numerator of which is the sum of (3) the number of Eligible Hourly Employees for such Plan Year, and (y) the number of persons who would have been Eligible Hourly Employees for such Plan Year except for the fact that they were employed in a unit to which the Company had not made this Plan applicable or employed in a unit which was represented by a Union that had not agreed with Ford or a Subsidiary that this Plan shall apply to such unit, and the denominator of which is the sum of (a) the numerator, and (b) the number of Salaried

continued

FIGURE 6-4 Profit-Sharing Plan (selected parts), Ford Motor Co.-UAW Agreement

Employees for such Plan Year. The amount determined pursuant to this Paragraph for any Plan Year is here-inafter called the "Allocated Profit Share" for such Plan year.

2. If any person shall come within the definition both of "Eligible Hourly Employee" and "Salaried Employee" for any Plan Year, such person shall be treated, for all purposes of this Plan, as both an Eligible Hourly Employee and a Salaried Employee.

FIGURE 6-4 Profit-Sharing Plan (selected parts), Ford Motor Co.-UAW Agreement (Continued)

SOURCE: Agreement between UAW and the Ford Motor Company, 1997–1999, pp. 111–21.

Two-Tier Wage Systems

A wage system that pays newly hired workers less than current employees performing the same or similar jobs is termed "two-tier." The **two-tier wage system** was established in 1977 at General Motors Packard Electric Division in Warren, Ohio.[37] The basic concept is to provide continued higher wage levels for current employees if the union will accept reduced levels for future employees. Union leaders believe that they must accept the two-tier system or face greater layoffs in the future. Management usually claims that the system is needed to compete with nonunion and foreign competition. Two-tier systems have declined in usage in recent years. They appeared in about 41 percent of manufacturing contracts in 1995 but fell to only 33 percent by 2002 and in 2005 appeared in only 27 percent of all contracts. Industries in which the systems are most common include food retail, airlines, manufacturing, chemical, rubber, plastic, and transportation. They are rare in governmental and educational institutions contracts.[38] However, in highly competitive industries such as food retailing, where nonunion employers such as Wal-Mart compete directly with unionized employers, two-tier agreements are gaining ground. In 2005, for example, members of the United Food and Commercial Workers union in Colorado voted (60 percent to 40 percent) to accept a two-tier agreement with King Soopers and City Market Stores to avoid a strike. The union's negotiating committee had recommended rejecting the contract and going on a strike. Management maintained the two-tier pay system could have provided cost savings to remain competitive. Top-pay-scale union workers were required to pay higher health insurance premiums as their concession.[39]

Although a two-tier system is contrary to the historical union doctrine of "equal pay for equal work," or pay equity, when a system is first negotiated, the union representatives can claim that they have avoided disaster and saved the jobs or wage levels of current members (who must vote on the contract). It is relatively easy to sell such a concept because no workers at that point are accepting the "lower tier." However, 5 or 10 years later, when many workers are paid lower wages for the same work as their affiliated union members, it can become a source of conflict and resentment. In some cases the lower-paid workers express their feelings with lower product quality and productivity records than their higher-paid counterparts.[40] In these bargaining units, the conflict could present even greater problems to both union and management leaders as the number of lower-tier workers approaches 51 percent of the bargaining unit and they demand equity.

Examples of two-tier agreements that were negotiated in the past include the following:[41]

- At Packard Electric, new hires were brought in at 55 percent of the wages of current employees.

- At General Motors' Delco Products plant in Rochester, New York, new assemblers earned almost $3.00 per hour less than current employees.
- Newly hired journeymen at the Ingalls Shipbuilding Company in Pascagoula, Mississippi, earn $1.00 less than the senior employees. The wages of new hires were to catch up after 2,000 hours.
- Giant Food negotiated a new entry-level wage of $2.00 less an hour than the old contract.
- The Allied Industrial Workers of America union accepted from Briggs & Stratton a wage rate almost $3.00 less for new workers on a lower tier.

Do employees hired into a lower-tier pay position perceive their treatment as equitable? A study of about 2,000 employees found that low-tier employees perceived the employer as being significantly lower in pay equity and perceived the union as being of little use in obtaining fair pay for its members. In addition, compared with the high-tier employees, the low-tier employees felt a lower level of commitment to their employer, which might affect their productivity and tenure with the organization. These perception problems can be controlled, the research results suggest, if low-tier employees are assigned to new work locations where there are few high-tier employees and if they are hired to part-time instead of full-time work. Employees hired under these conditions do not report equity perception problems.[42] Another method of minimizing the morale problems of low-tier employees is to provide eventual merging of the two tiers.

Studies also indicate that the high-tier employee is dissatisfied with the two-tier system. In a survey of over 1,000 employees in a 14-store food outlet company, researchers found that employees at the high end of a two-tier pay scale feared replacement by the lower-tiered employees. In addition, they believed the two-tier system had a detrimental effect on any wage increases they might feel entitled to receive.[43]

Temporary two-tier wage systems allow newly hired employees to reach the higher tier within 90 to 180 days or more. Some two-tier systems are permanent because the contract does not provide for any means by which employees hired at the lower-tier wage can progress to the higher tier. The presence of permanent systems in a contract puts a great deal of pressure on union negotiators to achieve a merger of the two tiers, which is found in 60 percent of all two-tier contract clauses.[44] For example, the two-tier provision in the UAW–Ford Motor Company 1993–1996 contract stated that new employees are hired at 75 percent of the current workers' rates with a merger after three years. The UAW was able to retain full employer-paid health-care benefits in exchange for the two-tier provision.[45]

Table 6-3 outlines the pros and cons of the two-tier wage system, and Profile 6-3 gives a variation on the two-tier wage system that has proven useful for traditionally nonunion positions.

TABLE 6-3 Pros and Cons of the Two-Tier Wage System

Pros	*Cons*
Significantly reduced labor costs	Resentment, low quality, and low productivity from low-tier employees
Maintenance of higher employment levels	Higher absenteeism and turnover of low-tier employees
Relief from wage compression between senior and junior employees on the same job	Intensification of the preceding problems as low-tier employees increase in number

"DUAL-CAREER LADDER" SYSTEMS

Some employers have found it necessary to institute **dual-career ladder pay systems** to retain, recognize, and reward their best technical employees to not lose them to other organizations or to management positions.

Dual-career ladders are separate but equal career tracks within an organization with corresponding jobs and salaries for management and nonmanagement employees. The goal is to make technical, nonmanagerial jobs more appealing by rewarding those workers without kicking them upstairs.

Dual-career ladders are most prevalent in high-tech professions where it is in the best interest of the organization to allow its best and brightest employees to continue to do the innovative work they like without sacrificing advancement.

But as effective as dual-career ladder systems may have been, some observers warn that in the age of downsizing, a leaner organization is looking for workers with multiple skills who can expand "horizontally" rather than just up. Also, some systems became nothing but step systems in disguise, rewarding employees on how long they stayed with the organization.

A properly administered dual-career ladder system should do the following:

1. Be confined to limited areas of an organization, such as the research and development unit.
2. Have clearly defined differences in the job content of each "rung" of the ladder to avoid a step system.
3. Perform continual skills assessment on the employees in the ladder system, as technical skills have a limited "shelf life."
4. Create a learning environment that entails not only training and education programs but also a corporate culture that values the intellectual capital of the employees.

SOURCE: Adapted from "Lawsuit Focuses Attention on Issues Raised by 'Dual Career Ladder' Systems," *Labor Relations Reporter,* 158 LRR 265 (June 29, 1998).

Lump-Sum Payments

As illustrated in Table 6-4, **lump-sum payments** and two-tier systems are methods to provide general wage increases and are increasing in their use, whereas COLAs and wage reopeners have declined in use.

In fact, the 2005 collective bargaining agreement between Caterpillar, Inc. and the United Auto Workers was heralded as a landmark "return" of two-tier pay systems combined with lump-sum increases as a major change in direction for negotiated wage increases. In highly competitive industries such as retail grocery, airlines, and manufacturing, employers seek a means lowering or "resetting" wage rates to meet low-wage

TABLE 6-4   Wage Trends in Contracts (frequency expressed as percentage of contracts)

	1954	*1961*	*1971*	*1979*	*1986*	*1992*	*1995*	*2004*
Deferred increases	20	58	87	95	80	89	88	77
Cost-of-living adjustments	25	24	22	48	42	34	34	18
Wage reopeners	60	28	12	8	10	5	8	7
Lump sums	—	—	—	—	—	23	22	17
Two-tier pay	—	—	—	—	17	27	41	27

SOURCES: Bureau of National Affairs, *Basic Patterns in Union Contracts* (14th ed.) (Washington, DC: BNA Books, 1995), p. 111; and Bureau of National Affairs, *2005 Source Book on Collective Bargaining* (Washington, DC: BNA Books, 2005). Used by permission.

Two-tier wage systems can save substantial payroll costs and jobs during poor economic times. But they can also cause tension between employees performing the same jobs, working side-by-side, and being paid different wage rates.

global competition. By negotiating lump-sum increases for current employees together with a two-tier system for new employees, an employer can effectively lower base wage rates and total labor costs.[46] Management often prefers lump-sum payments to COLAs, profit-sharing plans, or higher wages because their total cost during the contract is easier to predict, and they do not increase hourly wage rates. Unions may prefer they be paid early in the weeks of a new contract to provide quick benefit to members. Lump-sum payments do not preclude the negotiation of a wage rate increase, but usually management will offer a larger total compensation package in the first year if a lump sum is included instead of a larger base-wage increase. Common lump-sum awards include "signing" or "ratification" bonuses designed to give workers an immediate one-time payment between when the agreement is ratified and the first paycheck is issued under the new contract. In 2004 lump-sum payments were most common in manufacturing contracts (28 percent) versus nonmanufacturing (13 percent).[47]

WAGE NEGOTIATION ISSUES

During the negotiation process one or both sides may utilize different wage-level theories to stress their economic proposals. One or both sides will bring to light one or more wage theories and issues having an impact on the negotiation of rates. Which issues might be stressed during negotiations and whether they are even presented depend on the history of the company's labor relations and the personalities of the negotiators. In general, either side would utilize an issue it felt was valid or simply useful in providing a significant point for its list of arguments.

Productivity Theory

One of the oldest and broadest negotiation issues concerning wages involves the **productivity theory** that employees should share in increased profits caused by greater productivity. At the heart of the issue is the commonly accepted proposition that the organization's production is a combination of three factors: machinery and equipment, employee labor, and managerial ability. Union and management leaders agree that all three share in the creation of profits because they contribute to the organization's productivity.

Whenever figures show that productivity or profits have risen, then the question becomes, What percentage is attributable to employees' labor as opposed to machinery and equipment or managerial ability? Labor leaders commonly request that their members get their fair share of the increased profits. Management may request that the value-added concept be applied.

Determining labor's fair share then becomes the problem. Management may contend that all it asks is for employees to perform assigned work at stated times and at accepted levels of performance. The union usually counters that employees seek to improve the quality and quantity of output, reduce cost, and minimize the waste of resources. If specific production standards are established through negotiation, it is much easier to negotiate accepted wage increases. Yet separating out and measuring profit resulting from individual and group productivity as compared with management and capital equipment is almost impossible.

Ability to Pay

The issue of **ability to pay** is commonly expressed during wage negotiations. In principle, this issue is similar to the productivity theory. Union leaders emphasize that labor is one of the primary inputs into a company's productivity and therefore profitability. Labor negotiators conclude that if the company is experiencing high profits, it can better pay its employees who have contributed to the good financial conditions. For example, 1996 was the most profitable year in the history of the airline industry. Thus, when it came time to renegotiate labor contracts, "a spirit of militancy" swept through the ranks of airline workers. "American Airlines is making record profits, and it's time our wages reflect that," said Rob Held, a pilot. American Airlines pilots, in fact, overwhelmingly rejected a contract offer that their own union leaders had called generous. United Airlines mechanics rejected an offer of a 10 percent wage increase. However, only a few years earlier these same unions had accepted layoffs, wage cuts, and longer hours during hard financial times in the airline industry.[48]

The ability to pay concept, however, has severe limitations according to management negotiators. First, unions will not press this issue during hard times when profits have decreased or when the company is suffering temporary losses. Unions seldom want to apply the ability-to-pay doctrine consistently in both good and hard times; instead, they expect wage levels to be maintained during hard times and increased during good times. Second, management will argue that higher profits must be applied back into the company in capital investments. Finally, although profit levels fluctuate greatly, negotiated wage rates do not vary accordingly. If higher wage rates were negotiated on the basis of a six-month crest of high profits, the company might find it extremely difficult to maintain the higher wages during a period of sluggish profitability. Unfortunately, wage rates are negotiated for the future, and profit information is available only for the past. Thus, estimating the company's future ability to pay during the life of the new contract is quite difficult.

Companies are usually reluctant to share extensive financial information with the union during collective bargaining sessions. Unless a company claims that it is unable to pay the demanded wage rates, the union is not entitled to the financial information. If a company merely chooses to say at the negotiating table that it does not want to pay the demanded wage rates, the union cannot get the financial information from the company.[49]

One very important number in contract negotiations is the estimated total profits available during the term of the new contract. Table 6-5 provides a sample calculation of total profits available for a metals firm. During their preparations, both management and labor will project sales, production costs, overhead, changes in productivity, and so

TABLE 6-5 Estimated Profits Available under a New Contract[a]

Potential Profits Available from Current Operations		
	Current	*Projected*
1. Sales revenue	$46,324,064	$52,056,000
2. Production costs	−23,100,000	−26,565,000
3. Labor costs (wages and benefits)	−14,390,064	−15,890,000
4. Labor costs as a percent of sales	30.4%	30.52%
5. Administrative and selling costs	−2,800,000	−3,080,000
6. Overhead	−1,550,000	−1,705,000
7. Net profits before taxes	5,484,000	4,816,000
8. Income tax	−2,020,000	−1,774,000
9. After-tax profit	3,464,000	3,042,000
10. Dividends paid	−400,000	−400,000
11. Profits with current operations	3,064,000	2,642,000

Potential Increased Cost Savings Due to New Equipment		
	Current	*Projected*
12. Increased output: 10% (reduced product costs: $23,100,000 x 0.10)	2,310,000	2,656,500
13. Costs of new equipment = $6,400,000 x 0.10 (current interest rate)	−640,000	−640,000
14. Related new equipment costs	−640,000	−660,000
15. Total cost of new equipment	−1,280,000	−1,300,000
16. Savings due to new equipment (savings available to all organizational needs)	1,030,000	1,356,500

Potential Profits Available from Future Operations and Savings Due to New Equipment	
	Projected
17. Potential profits available for all corporate needs (11 + 16)	$3,998,500
18. Percent of profits available for labor	35%
19. Profits available for increased labor costs under new contract	1,399,475

[a]This example might be used by either management or labor to calculate the dollar amount each believes will be available for labor under the new contract. Of course, each side might make different assumptions about the firm's future sales, profits, and productivity.

on that will occur during the life of the new contract. They can then project the total profits available to pay increased wages and benefits that might be negotiated. Determining labor's fair share of the total profits available is a difficult task; a starting point is usually the current labor cost as a percentage of total revenue (30.4 percent in Table 6-5). The union will try to negotiate a higher percentage using the productivity theory based on management's ability to pay (35 percent in Table 6-5).

Management may cite higher production costs, the cost of new equipment, or additional management costs as reasons to keep the percentage the same or even to lower it under the new contract. Both sides, therefore, enter negotiations with this dollar figure playing an important role in their negotiation strategy. Management uses it as an absolute maximum cost of the new contract that they cannot exceed without endangering the future profitability of the organization. The union uses the figure as a goal that they hope to achieve to realize for their workers a fair share of future profits. During negotiations, both sides carefully keep a running total cost of all economic items negotiated and compare that figure with an estimated amount available developed before negotiations. If management produced these estimates, it would set $1.4 million as a maximum cost for the entire economic package, essentially wages and benefits, for the first year of a new contract. Thus, management might accept a total economic proposal that was far less than $1.4 million. If the union produced these estimates, it would set $1.4 million as a realistic target for negotiations, hoping to achieve at least that amount in new economic items.

Job Evaluation

Job evaluation is the process of systematically analyzing jobs to determine their relative worth within the organization. The process is generally part of job analysis—the personnel function of systematically reviewing the tasks, duties, and responsibilities of jobs, usually to write job descriptions and minimum qualifications as well as to provide information for job evaluation. In general, the result of a job evaluation effort is a pay system with a rate for each job commensurate with its status within the hierarchy of jobs in the organization.[50]

Job evaluation procedures do not include analyzing employee performance; that is referred to as performance evaluation or performance appraisal. Nor is job evaluation an attempt to review the employees within a position. Rather, the position is reviewed for several carefully selected criteria to determine the relative worth of the job to the organization in comparison with other jobs in the labor market. Union leaders as well as members of management can use job evaluation techniques as guides to negotiate wage agreements and explain paid differentials to employees. An example of how an agreement can provide for the use of job evaluation procedures during the life of a labor contract is shown in the following labor agreement between the Lockheed-Georgia Company and the International Machinists and Aerospace Workers:

> The job descriptions for each of the factory and for each of the office and technical classifications which are in effect on the date of execution of this agreement, or which are placed into effect pursuant to Paragraph 2 [next paragraph] herewith, shall be a part of this agreement.
>
> In the event that a new job or position is established or there is a substantial change in the duties or requirements of an established job, the company shall develop an appropriate job description and establish within the existing

rates structure provided in Section 2 of this article, the basic rates to apply to such job. The company shall furnish the union with the new job description and shall submit for its approval the rate established for such job. In the event that an agreement is not reached within seven calendar days from the date of such submission or within such additional days as may be mutually agreed upon, the company may place the new job description and rate in effect subject to continuing negotiation of rate. Within five working days from the date the job was placed into effect, the union may proceed in accordance with Step 3 of the grievance procedure established in Article 3, Section 1 of this agreement.[51]

Job classification is common in labor agreements, and when an agreement contains a rigid classification, the employer may not unilaterally change it. When no explicit provision exists, it is generally recognized that management has the right to make classification changes or to add new jobs. However, even if the agreement contains a job classification, arbiters have recognized management's need—and right—to make changes as long as established pay rates are used, the union is allowed to file complaints through the grievance procedure, and management follows any procedures agreed to in the contract.[52] Case 6-2 illustrates a typical dispute over job classification.

RECLASSIFICATION OF JOBS

CASE
6-2

The company manufactures refrigerators and dehumidifiers. The grievance concerns assembly-line workers who installed foil wrap around the wired socket on certain food liner tops. The company instituted an operational modification that substituted fiberglass insulation for foil in the assembly operation. The grievants were classified as Class III Assemblers. Their grievance was a request to be reclassified to the high classification of Hand Pack Insulation workers. The Hand Pack Insulation classification was specifically created in the early 1960s to cover personnel who must work with fiberglass insulation.

It was the union's position that the grievants regularly worked with fiberglass insulation and therefore should be classified to the higher classification. The workers do not have to spend more than 50 percent of their time handling fiberglass insulation before they can be classified as Hand Pack Insulators because there are Hand Pack Insulators who cut up fiber-

glass insulation on only two days per week. By creating the new classification, the parties had recognized that employees generally do not like to work with fiberglass insulation because it causes the workers to itch.

Using the management rights clause as its basis, the company contended that it had the right to change the materials being used in particular operations and to assign different tasks to appropriate classifications. The company pointed out that many assembly-line workers had occasionally come into contact with fiberglass materials during the 20 years preceding this grievance and that no prior claims or grievances had been made regarding reclassification. It contended that the jobs performed by the two grievants were not meaningfully changed by the substitution of fiberglass for foil. In fact, the job description for the Class III Assemblers mentions that the personnel must deal with insulation, indicating that they may be expected to handle some fiberglass.

continued

CASE 6-2	**RECLASSIFICATION OF JOBS—continued**

DECISION

The arbitrator found that, although it is apparent that the Hand Pack Insulation classification was created to cover personnel who spend a significant amount of their time handling fiberglass insulation, the history of the plant indicates that there were numerous assembly-line workers in other classifications who continued to handle some fiberglass insulation without job reclassification. The arbitrator cited the basic rule that when jobs are classified by titles and the parties have not negotiated a detailed description of job content, management will be permitted wide authority to assign work that is reasonably related or incidental to the regular duties of the job. The arbitrator also put heavy emphasis on the fact that other personnel had not previously sought reclassification of their jobs to Hand Pack Insulator, even though they did handle some fiberglass insulation.

SOURCE: Adapted from *Magic Chef, Inc.*, 84 LA 15 (1984).

WAGE SURVEYS

Both labor and management conduct their own **wage surveys** to provide information on external labor market conditions. The job evaluation process is utilized to maintain internal equity for wage rates, but it is also important to maintain external equity. That is, both sides want to offer wages competitive with the labor market and industry so that the firm can attract and retain qualified, productive employees.

Union leaders want to provide evidence during negotiations to management and their own members that the wage rates they are negotiating are fair and justified by market conditions.

Negotiators seek wage survey information from three general sources. The first source is published labor market information from federal agencies, primarily the U.S. Department of Labor, which provides wage and salary information to all organizations by metropolitan statistical area. In general, the government's employment information is considered complete and accurate. Negotiators in specialized industries may wish to use the second source, industry wage surveys, published by various interested parties within the industry. Or negotiators may choose a third source, their own survey, which is a costly and time-consuming process. One side of the table is less likely to accept the figures produced by the other side unless they have a very strong working relationship or have participated in the survey process.

Conducting their own wage survey can be expensive and difficult for either negotiating team. Job titles alone are no longer acceptable in comparing positions among other organizations. Instead, the surveyor must compare job descriptions and receive detailed information on the duties and responsibilities of various jobs reported in the survey. The wages paid for each job included in the survey must be specifically defined. Information such as initial hiring salary ranges, the value of related benefits, and cost-of-living increases as well as other wage increases must be specified so that wage rates among different organizations can be compared fairly. Information concerning seniority provisions, paid vacations, sick leave, and other paid time off work is critical for a valid analysis. Any other paid benefits, such as uniform allowance or tuition reimbursement, must also be included.[53]

Using wage surveys in negotiations involves primarily two types of problems. First, because survey information is available from many sources, including industry data, the BLS employer associations, and union groups, it is often difficult to agree which source contains jobs and data applicable to a particular firm. This problem may be compounded if negotiators use survey information from different cities and therefore must agree on an acceptable cost-of-living difference between the areas as well. One solution is to combine relevant data of two published surveys to determine averages.[54] But even if negotiators agree on wage survey information, a second problem involves the question of how the negotiating company should compare itself with other firms. Survey information usually provides an average as well as a range of wages paid for different jobs. Negotiating parties must then agree on whether they want to pay higher, average, or lower wages than the competition.

Thus, wage survey information will not resolve the issue of appropriate wage rates but will at least provide ballpark information to negotiators. Management may argue that what it lacks in wages it makes up in liberal benefits, working conditions, or advancement opportunities. Labor leaders may counter that these advantages are available in higher-paying organizations and do not make up for the lack in take-home pay.

COSTING WAGE PROPOSALS

Many of the changes in contract language may result in indirect or direct long-range cost to the company. However, most changes in wages, benefits, and COLAs are direct and usually substantial cost increases. Other types of changes, such as layoff provisions, seniority determination, and subcontracting, may result in indirect cost increases to the company. The process of determining the financial impact of a contract provision change is referred to as **costing**.

The costing of labor contracts is obviously a critical aspect in collective bargaining negotiations. Both sides need to estimate accurately the cost of the contract provision so that it can be intelligently discussed and bargained for by either side. If it is an item that ultimately is given up by one side so that another provision can be gained, then its relative weight is best estimated by knowing its costs.

All economic provisions can be reduced to dollar estimates, whereas noneconomic items cannot be as easily valued by either side. The costing process enables both sides to compare the value of different contract provisions and, it is hoped, helps them arrive at a contract agreement. In most cases, accurate costing processes will be accepted by both sides with little disagreement over the methods employed.

The largest single cost incurred by most corporations is labor cost. Even in capital-intensive organizations such as commercial airlines, labor costs account for about 42 percent of total cost; but in labor-intensive organizations, such as the U.S. Postal Service, labor may account for more than 80 percent of total cost. For most organizations, labor's impact on profits is critical, and relatively small changes in labor costs greatly affect profitability. Therefore, accurate costing of wage proposals in contract negotiations is critical to future cost control for many organizations.[55] Figure 6-5 shows how a typical company might cost the wage provisions of a contract.

Accountant Michael Granof outlines the four most commonly used methods of costing union wage provisions:

1. **Annual cost.** This is the total sum expended by the company over a year on a given benefit; usually the sum excludes administrative costs. Most companies

Data

90 employees at $8.00/hr
60 employees at $6.50/hr
20 employees at $5.75/hr

Proposed wage increase = 6% across the board = 1,900 average number of production hours per year

Annual Cost

Current: 90 × $8.00 = $720
60 × 6.50 = 390
20 × 5.75 = 115
$1,225/hr

Current annual cost is $1,225 × 1,900 hr = $2,327,500

Proposed: 90 × $8.48 = $763.20
60 × 6.89 = 413.40
20 × 6.09 = 121.80
$1,298.40/hr

Proposed annual cost is $1,298.40 × 1,900 = $2,466,960
Total cost of proposed increase is $2,466,960 − $2,327,500 = $139,460

Cents per Hour

$8.48 − 8.00 = $0.48/hr for 90 employees
$6.89 − 6.50 = $0.39/hr for 60 employees
$6.09 − 5.75 = $0.34/hr for 20 employees

Roll-up (Average ÷ Employee)

Cost of benefits per person = $2.00/hr
$1,225 current cost ÷ 170 employees = $7.20 cost of wages/hr
$2.00 benefit cost ÷ $7.20 wages = 27.77% roll-up

Total Cost of Proposed Wage Rates ÷ Roll-up

$139,460.00 + 38,728.04 (27.77% × 139,460.00) = $178,188.04 wages + roll-up

FIGURE 6-5 Costing a Wage Proposal

make computations similar to those illustrated in Figure 6-5 to arrive at the annual cost of a wage agreement or benefit.

2. *Cost per employee per year.* This is determined by dividing the total costs of the benefit by either the average number of employees for the year or the number of employees covered by a particular program.

3. *Percentage of payroll.* This is the total cost of the benefit divided by the total payroll. Companies may include all payments to all employees in the total payroll, but some exclude overtime, shift differential, or premium pay.

4. *Cents per hour.* This is derived by dividing the total cost of the benefit or wage provision by the total productive hours worked by all employees during the year.[56]

The two most commonly discussed economic figures are the annual cost figure and the cents-per-hour figure. When the contract is being negotiated, the total value of all additional wages and other economic items is included so that the annual cost of the entire package can be accurately estimated. All sides want to know the exact figure of the negotiated wages and benefits. The management negotiator may even offer a lump-sum amount, giving the union negotiators the choice of how to divide it among the various proposed economic enhancements. The cents-per-hour figure is perhaps the single most important item to employees in the new contract. Because employees can quickly estimate their additional take-home pay by using the cents-per-hour figure, it becomes vital when they vote on contract ratification. Granof found that most management negotiators agree that the primary goal in bargaining is to minimize the cents-per-hour direct wage increase.[57]

Employers are usually aware that any negotiated economic increases will have to be duplicated for nonunion and management personnel. This spillover effect is often quite costly. However, most costing models do not include the spillover costs; unions do not want to consider them part of the contract cost.[58]

Base

The first step in determining compensation costs is to develop the **base compensation** figure. During negotiation, this figure is essential in determining the percentage value of a requested increase in wages. For example, a $500 annual wage increase means a 2.5 percent wage increase on a $20,000 base and a 5 percent increase for an employee with a $10,000 base. The base may be thought of as the employee's annual salary; however, it seldom represents the total payroll costs incurred by the company for that employee. For example, the average salary cost, or base salary, for a nurse in a city hospital was $14,073. Under the terms of the contract, a nurse may have also received an average of the following: longevity pay of $505.00, overtime of $486.75, shift differential of $1,033.68, vacation cost of $636.76, holiday pay of $560.72, hospitalization insurance of $515.72, a clothing allowance of $150.00, and pension benefit of $965.89. The total additional paid benefits were $4,854.52 for each nurse, equal to about 34 percent of base pay. These additional costs, when added to the base of $14,073.00, produced what many think of as the nurse's true gross salary of $18,927.52.[59]

Figure 6-6 illustrates the Chrysler Corporation–UAW agreement on base rates for three jobs. At the end of the old agreement the base rates were $17.44, $17.92, and $21.11 for the janitor, assembler, and tool-and-die job classifications, respectively. At the start of this 1996 negotiation it was agreed to "fold in," or add to the old base rates, the COLAs that had been given, thereby creating new base rates that would stay in effect during the new three-year agreement (1997–1999). If the CPI increased 2.9 percent each year, the new COLA adjustment and negotiated deferred wage increases of 3 percent in the second and third years would cause the hourly wage rates to increase as reflected in Figure 6-6.

The new base rates for each year are determined by adding the wage increase and COLA to the previous year's base rate. For example, the base rates for the janitor job classification start at $18.47 to start the new contract and for the next three years are $18.88, $19.95, and $21.06, respectively.

The one absolutely essential figure that every negotiator should have in mind at all times is how much a wage increase of 1 percent will cost the employer in thousands of dollars per year. Although the overall dollar cost of a contract settlement is important for budget purposes, most negotiators do not consider such costs to be especially pertinent. They find the total cents-per-hour cost of the negotiated wage increase more relevant, and they bargain in those terms. Settlements are also evaluated by their superiors in terms of cents per hour, but they need to be able to convert cents per hour to total dollars for accurate costing.[60]

TABLE A

Examples of Total Hourly Wage Increases

	Janitor	Assembler	Tool & Die
Base Rate - Contract End	**$22.98**	**$23.57**	**$27.70**
Skilled trades tool allowance			.30
COLA Fold-In	2.00	2.00	2.00
New Agreement Base	**$24.98**	**$25.57**	**$30.00**
Beginning COLA float	.05	.05	.05
1st-year COLA	.32	.32	.32
End 1st-year Base Rate plus COLA	**$25.35**	**$25.94**	**$30.37**
2nd-year COLA	.40	.40	.40
End 2nd-year Base Rate plus COLA	**$25.75**	**$26.34**	**$30.77**
3rd-year 2% base rate Increase	.50	.51	.60
3rd-year COLA	.44	.44	.44
End 3rd-year Base Rate plus COLA	**$26.69**	**$27.29**	**$31.81**
4th-year 3% base rate Increase	.76	.78	.92
4th-year COLA	.36	.36	.36
End 4th-year Base Rate plus COLA	**$27.81**	**$28.43**	**$33.09**

(Projected COLA assumes annual nonmedical Inflation averaging 2.2%)

FIGURE 6-6 Chrysler-UAW Examples: Base Rate, COLA Adjustments, and Wage Adjustments

SOURCE: UAW-DaimlerChrysler Newsgram, September 2003. Available at www.uaw.org

Roll-Up

As hourly wages increase, many benefits also directly increase because they are directly tied to the wage rate or base pay of employees. This direct increase in benefits caused by a negotiated wage increase is referred to as the **roll-up**. Roll-up may also be called add-on or creep. All three terms refer to other costs incurred, which automatically increase as wage rates are increased. These costs must be "rolled up into" the total cost of the negotiated wage package to accurately reflect the total costs that will be incurred.

Examples of some of these benefits are the following:

1. *Social Security and unemployment insurance contributions.* The employer's contribution is computed as a percentage of each employee's wage up to a maximum annual figure. Any negotiated wage increase up to this maximum will cause a direct increase in the employer's contribution.
2. *Life insurance.* Often the amount of life insurance coverage paid by the employer is based on the employee's annual earnings. Therefore, as annual earnings are increased, the cost of the insurance automatically increases.
3. *Overtime pay and shift premium.* Overtime compensation and shift premium are often computed as a percentage of base wage. Thus, these also increase with the base wage.
4. *Pension benefits.* The pension benefit formula normally includes employees' average annual wages. An increase in wages increases the employer's funding liability for the pension.[61]

Negotiators often determine an agreed-on percentage attributable to roll-up. The roll-up percentage is computed by dividing the cost of the directly increased benefit by the cost of the wage rate increase. For example, if a $0.50-per-hour increase in the base wage directly causes a $0.10-per-hour increase in benefits, then the roll-up percentage is $0.10 divided by $0.50, or 20 percent. Therefore, if negotiators agreed to increase employees' base wage by $0.50 per hour, from $5.00 per hour to $5.50 per hour, the 10 percent negotiated wage increase would cause a direct cost increase of 12 percent, or $0.60, when the roll-up costs were added.

Total Negotiated Costs

At all times during negotiations, both labor and management maintain their estimated cost of wage and benefit items on which they have reached agreement. Therefore, as additional economic items are proposed, both sides know exactly the total cost of the new contract; they can then decide whether the cost of the new items would increase the total cost of the agreement beyond an affordable level. In Table 6-6, the total cost of all new wage and benefit enhancements for the metals firm example in Table 6-5 is $1,318,049 at some time in the negotiations. Management had previously determined that the profits available for increased labor costs under a new contract were $1,399,475 (also shown in Table 6-5). Therefore, management would likely agree to the total package of items presented in Table 6-6 or might even be willing to agree to additional economic enhancements if their total cost is less than $81,426.

The union might, for example, propose increasing the clothing allowance by another $150 per year to reach a final agreement. Although the total cost of this proposal would be only $100,500, or about one-half of 1 percent of the total wages and benefits that management estimates would be paid under the new contract, it would increase the total costs of all negotiated items to $1,418,549. Thus, the new total would exceed the maximum management believes it can afford under a new contract. In such a situation, management might either (1) reject this proposal and therefore signal to the union that the total cost is close to the maximum; (2) respond with a counteroffer of an additional $50 clothing allowance, which would be less than the $81,426 that management believes it has left to bargain; or (3) accept the final proposal by the union if it would secure a contract and hope that the $19,074 by which management exceeded its estimate will not critically affect future operations. If management believed that the union would press

TABLE 6-6 Estimated Costs of Negotiated Wage and Benefit Increases

Item	First Year New Contract	Estimated Additional Cost
Wages (wage rate + roll-up)	3%	$361,000
Paid holidays	1 new day	40,505
Funeral leave	New provision: 3 days/death	121,515
Health insurance	Increase in employer share: ($120/year)	128,100
Clothing allowance	Additional year: ($50/employee)	33,500
Profit sharing	New provision: 10% of net	399,850
Pension benefits	Additional $50/month	100,000
Paid vacation	Two additional days/year for employees with less than two years service	24,712
Shift differential	Increased from 10% to 12%	108,867
Total cost of negotiated wage and benefit increases		$1,318,049

Tips from the Experts

UNION

What are three wage issues union negotiation team members should look for at the negotiating table?

1. Fairness at both ends of wage/salary scale
2. Rewards for performance as well as for service
3. Equal pay for equal work

MANAGEMENT

What are some practical forms of wage concessions to use at negotiations that will not break an employer?

1. Swap indirect benefits and apply to direct labor (e.g., switch a holiday for a specific wage increase).
2. Lengthen the term of the collective bargaining agreement (perhaps in combination with item 3).
3. Stagger wage increases with minimum or no increase at the front end but load up near the end of contract (perhaps in combination with item 2).
4. Give concessions in an area that will be utilized infrequently but is a big morale booster, such as extended family leave (unpaid, event).

other economic issues after the clothing allowance increase was accepted, management would most likely reject the proposal. Otherwise, the union could keep proposing small additional increases and possibly exceed the maximum cost estimate by a large amount.

UNION WAGES AND INFLATION

Unionized wages are often characterized as the spark behind wage-price spirals in the United States. The general public is made aware of large union wage increase settlements, often after any economic strike. Salary increases received by management and nonunion employees, however, do not receive such publicity. Also, the use of COLA provisions in negotiated settlements has received criticism as being a prime cause of inflation.

Many labor critics have claimed that union wage increases have an effect far beyond the organized portion of the labor force. The contention is that nonunion employers, to remain unorganized, follow the lead set by union contracts. However, survey data suggest that such a practice depends on the size of the employer. Large nonunion employers do tend to match the union scale of all levels of unionism in their industry. Medium-sized nonunion employers tend to match the union scale only if unionism is a strong presence in their industry. Small nonunion employers tend to maintain wage levels below the union scale regardless of the presence of unionism in the industry.[62] Thus, it is difficult to show that union wage increases are followed by a large proportion of employers who may be raising employees' wages for any of several other good reasons.

Daniel Mitchell, director of the UCLA Institute of Labor Relations, suggests that during negotiations employers offer lower wages than they really intend to pay or than they would pay if the companies were nonunion, and then they agree on higher union-demanded wages. Thus, it appears to the public that the final outcome was a victory for the union, which bargained for more than the employer was willing to give. But the outcome might be similar to what the employer's wage determination would have been without a union. Unions may substantially affect only difficult-to-measure, noneconomic items, such as work rules, working conditions, and grievance procedures.

PUBLIC EMPLOYEE WAGE AND SALARY ISSUES

In most cases the negotiation of wages and fringe benefits is a union's principal function. Public employee unions, however, often find this subject out of their reach. Under Title VII, the federal statute governing employee rights, the right to bargain collectively is limited to issues concerning conditions of employment and excludes wages and fringe benefits. However, employees of the federal government in Case 6-3 were able to address a reduction of pay as a result of reduced hours when the reduction had not been negotiated with the union.

HOURS OF WORK: CHANGED SCHEDULE

CASE 6-3

This case pertains to an allegation that management violated the agreement when, after having changed the employees' work schedules on August 1, 1999, from 32 to 40 hours a week, in March 2000 they changed their work schedules from 40 back to 32 hours a week.

Over a period of years certain employees regularly worked beyond the 32-hour limit of their part-time work schedules. At the time the employees were converted to full-time work schedules, August 1, 1999, the change was documented on their SF50 without a not-to-exceed (NTE) date. In late March 2000 the employees were notified that their full-time work schedules were being reduced back to part-time work schedules. The union objected, claiming that management had changed the positions to full time and could not now change them back without negotiating over the changes.

The relevant subsection of the *Federal Personnel Manual* reads as follows:

Work Schedule Tour of Duty
c. New or changed tour of duty. Agencies may establish a new tour of duty for a part-time employee or temporarily change a current tour to meet the needs of the office or the employee. A change must be made in advance of the administrative workweek in which the change is to occur and must be approved by an authorizing official. (See FPM supplement 296-33, sub-Chapter 24, for information on when an SF 50 is required.) An increase in the tour of duty above 32 hours per week is not permitted for more than two consecutive pay periods in keeping with congressional intent to limit regular part-time work schedules to no more than 32 hours per week.

d. Change to full-time work schedule. It is contrary to merit principles to appoint an individual to work part time with the intent to convert the employees to full time after a brief interval. Unexpected increases in workload may, however, require an agency to change the work schedule of a part-time employee to full time on either a short term (i.e., not to exceed a certain date) or permanent basis. If the change would be a hardship to the employee, for example, by affecting the employee's health or disrupting school or child care arrangements, the agency should first determine if there are other ways to accomplish the added work within available resources. If the change is temporary, the not-to-exceed date *should* be specified in the SF-50 remarks.

Management's position is that the employees were properly notified when their

continued

CASE 6-3	HOURS OF WORK: CHANGED SCHEDULE—continued

hours were changed on a temporary basis from 32 to 40 hours per week in August 1999. The employees were notified again that their hours were going to revert back to 32 hours per week in March 2000. This change in schedule was not intended to become a permanent shift; it was done because of allowable budget expenditures. Employees knew that the change in their scheduled work hours was temporary and that there was never any intent to change their status from part-time to permanent full-time employees. If the employees were reclassified as permanent full time, such action would be contrary to merit principles and be in violation of the law. It was management's position that they complied with all applicable regulations and that the omission of the NTE date on the employees' SF-50s was an administrative omission and cannot be translated into a fait accompli for the union.

Paragraph c provides in part that "agencies may establish a new tour of duty for a part-time employee or temporarily change a current tour to meet the need of the office or the employee." Paragraph d provides that it is contrary to merit principles to appoint an individual to work part time with the intent to convert the employee to full time after a brief interval. Unexpected increase in workload may, however, require an agency to change the work schedule of a part-time employee to full time on either a short-term (i.e., not to exceed a certain date) or a permanent basis. If the change is temporary, the NTE date *should* be specified in the SF-50 remarks. *Should* is not mandatory but permissive, and its omission cannot be translated into a fait accompli without following the proper procedure of promoting someone to permanent full time from permanent part time. Paragraph d permits the agency to change the work schedule of a part-time employee to work full time, and by doing so the employee does not become

a permanent full-time employee, as it would be contrary to the merit system principles to do so.

It was the union's position that management failed to comply with the sunset provisions of the manual and in so doing violated Article 4 of the agreement. Federal employment rules do not authorize part-time employees to work beyond 32 hours per week for more than two consecutive pay periods. An NTE date was required if the change was intended to be temporary.

The past practice of adhering to this congressional intent by following the clear and unambiguous guidance contained in the manual requires the agency to change part-time employees who work more than 32 hours per week for two consecutive pay periods to full time because no other category is authorized and to do otherwise subjects employees to denied pay and benefits.

DECISION

Given the length of time, August 1999 to April 2000, that the employees worked full time, the change cannot be construed as a short-term increase in workload requiring a short-term increase in work hours. Rather, it appears that there was a long-term increase in workload that required a long-term increase in work hours. There was no intent to circumvent the merit system's principles. This case is not about filling newly created or open positions. This case is about ensuring that management does not abuse their right to increase the scheduled work hours of part-time employees beyond 32 hours a week for short periods of time to meet changing workload requirements to avoid having more full-time employees on the payroll. What is set forth in paragraph c is clear and unambiguous. An increase in the tour of duty above 32 hours per week is not permitted for more

continued

HOURS OF WORK: CHANGED SCHEDULE—continued

than two consecutive pay periods. The record establishes that with respect to the four aggrieved individuals, this requirement was not followed. Given what is contained in paragraph c, if the two-consecutive-pay-periods threshold is breached, it is appropriate to conclude that the change is intended to be permanent. This conclusion is further strengthened if an NTE date does not appear on the SF-50. Its absence leads to the conclusion that the change is not intended to be temporary.

Clearly, the supervisor was knowledgeable about what information had to be provided on an SF-50. If the absence of the NTE date on the SF-50s in question was an administrative oversight, manage-

ment should have discovered it soon after the SF-50s were created and taken appropriate action to correct the omission. Considering that the agency's personnel office was involved in the creation of the SF-50s for the four aggrieved employees, the court is not inclined to believe that the failure to comply with the manual's plainly stated requirements was an administrative oversight. Based on what is contained in the record in its entirety, the court believes that the omission was intentional. In conclusion, for all the previously mentioned reasons, it is the court's opinion that management violated the agreement when they changed the employees' work schedules back to 32 hours a week.

SOURCE: Adapted from In re: *Defense Commissary Agency and AFGE LOCAL 1138,* 116 LA 1141 (December 24, 2001).

For most state and municipal employees, union contract negotiations take place during or after the respective legislative body has determined a budget. Unions may be limited to a negotiation on how the available dollars are to be divided among classes of employees or distributed as base wages, fringe benefits, bonuses, and incentive pay.

Public-sector unions can, in some cases, effectively utilize their positive public image and general public support to put additional pressure on management negotiations.

However, not all wage and salary issues in the public sector are resolved in the union's favor. In one recent decision, the Supreme Court rejected a police union's request to pay sergeants and lieutenants significant back overtime pay under the FLSA. The argument the union made was that even though these employees were salaried and therefore exempt from overtime pay, they could be disciplined by being docked a day's pay under the *Police Department Manual,* although as a practical matter they seldom were. The secretary of labor determined that a theoretical ability to dock such employees' pay did not automatically put these employees in the nonexempt classification; rather, employers could preserve the exempt status of the employees by reimbursing any who were indeed docked.[63]

Also, in *Central State University v. American Association of University Professors,*[64] the Supreme Court upheld an Ohio statute that required state universities to develop standards for faculty members' instructional workloads and exempted such standards from collective bargaining. The Court held that the legislation, which was passed to address the decline in the amount of time that faculty members devoted to teaching as opposed to research, served a legitimate government purpose, and therefore these public employees could be treated differently than other public employees.

SUMMARY

Wages and benefits represent the heart of the collective bargaining process. Guarantee of a certain standard of living and a reasonable return for their productive efforts is the major concern for most union members. At the same time, management realizes what large percentages of its total costs are wages and benefits. Through job evaluation, wage surveys, and other methods, both sides negotiate either a standard rate or a pay range for each job covered in the agreement. Also, future COLAs are negotiated. Both labor and management begin negotiations by estimating sales, production costs, overhead costs, and other significant economic variables that can then produce the predicted total revenue available for negotiated wage and benefit enhancements. This figure can be used as a target figure during negotiations and can therefore be constantly compared against estimated total cost of negotiated increases. Management can thus ensure that the organization will be able to afford negotiated future labor costs, and the union can obtain a fair share of future profits for its members.

The accurate costing of all negotiated wage changes is critical to successful bargaining and to management's cost-containment efforts as well as to predictions of future labor cost. Roll-up costs must be included in any estimate when wage increases have been agreed on. The computer has given both management and labor a negotiating tool to add speed and accuracy to the costing of proposals.

Although public sector unions do not always negotiate wages and salaries, the positive influence of unionization in the public sector can be seen in higher wages and better benefits.

CASE STUDIES

Case Study 6-1 Premium Pay Rates

For at least 21 years, the company has paid double the straight-time pay rate for work after 50 hours in any given workweek to all plant employees, whether they worked a 5-day, 8-hour schedule ("5/8 employees") or a 4-day, 10-hour schedule ("4/10 employees"). The collective bargaining agreement (CBA) provided for such payment after 50 hours to the 4/10 employees but not the 5/8 employees. The employer, in December 2000, put the union and all hourly personnel on notice that effective January 1, 2001, overtime would be paid in accordance with the CBA; that is, the practice of paying double time after 50 hours to 5/8 employees would cease. The union objected and brought this grievance.

The union argued that the practice of paying 5/8 employees double time for hours worked over 50 hours in one workweek has been in effect for over 20 years. The current CBA has a provision that protects employees from any deduction in pay. It says, "No employee shall suffer a deduction in wage rates or working conditions as a result of this agreement." Allowing the company to change its overtime pay policies while this CBA is in effect violates that term. Furthermore, there have been some five CBAs negotiated since that practice has been in effect, and the company has never sought to negotiate or clarify the practice of how it pays overtime or the CBA provision regarding no reduction. Finally, the union pointed out that the length of time the practice was in place would certainly qualify it as a "past practice" that the company could not change unilaterally.

The company contended that the payment of overtime at double the straight-time rate for 5/8 employees is in direct conflict with the language of the CBA. An employer may abandon past practice that is in direct conflict with the clear language of the CBA. Also, the general CBA provision regarding "no reduction in pay" cannot be interpreted as controlling the specific overtime provision of the CBA.

Discussion

In nondisciplinary matters, the party complaining of a violation of a CBA has the burden to prove that the other party is violating a specific requirement of that agreement. In this case the parties do not dispute that the CBA does not include 5/8 employees in the overtime provision. The union contends, however, that both past practice and the provision of the CBA "maintenance of benefits" clause entitle these employees to the overtime.

The court recognizes the following as primary elements necessary for an activity to qualify as a past practice:

1. A pattern of conduct that is clear and consistent
2. Longevity and recognition of the activity
3. Acceptability and mutual acknowledgment of the pattern of conduct by the parties

Applying those standards to this case, paying double time to 5/8 employees would certainly qualify as a past practice.

The company argues, however, and points to case law to support it, that if it can be proven that a past practice directly conflicts with a provision of a CBA, the company can abandon it unilaterally. Because the CBA's provision specifically excludes the 5/8 employees and because the union has never sought to have them covered under that provision, the union cannot claim that the CBA provides for the overtime pay.

The issue for the court to determine is which side is correct as to which provision of the CBA applies. Both sides presented cases that had been decided that supported its position. The union argued that the court should avoid an interpretation of the CBA that renders the bargained-for benefits meaningless. A long-standing practice of paying double overtime wages would certainly be the type of "wages" the union sought to protect in its "no reduction" clause. The company argued, however, that the court should look to the unambiguous language of the CBA that governs overtime for the 5/8 employees as "trumping" the more general language of the "no reduction" clause. The fact that the company unilaterally paid more than it was required to under the CBA should not bind the company to continue to do so in the future. Those kinds of benefits should be negotiated at the bargaining table, which this was not.

SOURCE: Adapted from *Rod's Food Products v. Teamsters, Local 630*, 116 LA 1734 (April 16, 2002).

QUESTIONS

1. What do you think would be the "fair" way to resolve this case? Should the company be required to pay 5/8 employees double time even though that benefit has never been negotiated, and so, arguably, the company has never received any exchange for this benefit? Or should those employees who have in good faith accepted overtime work believing they would be paid double time, even though their contract did not say they would, have to give up this benefit and get nothing in return?

2. Should the company have waited to bring up this issue when the CBA was being renegotiated? Does it change your answer to know that the CBA was not to be renegotiated for three years?

3. The parties did not know why the company began paying double time to the 5/8 employees. If the practice began as an error on the part of a payroll clerk, would that fact change your opinion as to how to decide this case?

Case Study 6-2 Incentive Pay

The company had an incentive pay rate in place that could increase the employees' pay by 30 percent over their base pay. Citing changed circumstances, the employer eliminated the incentive pay for one department. The union appealed. The collective bargaining agreement (CBA) in place at the time of the grievance reserved all management rights to the company unless restricted by the language of the agreement.

Article V of the agreement established wages to be paid and specifically continued during the term of the agreement "all incentive rates" in existence at the time of the agreement; excepting only the company's right to "establish new incentive rates or to adjust existing incentive rates" under certain conditions listed in the agreement. Those conditions included changes, modifications, or improvements made in equipment involved in an incentive pay area; new or changed standards of manufacturing; and changes in job duties of those affected by incentive pay.

Procedures on how the company was to proceed to establish new or changed incentive rates were also included in Article V of the agreement, unless changes to the incentive rates were a result of the changed circumstances previously cited. If this was the case, employees affected by the changes were given the right to grieve the application of the changed incentive rate. When the incentive pay was totally eliminated for one department, the union grieved on behalf of those affected employees.

It was the company's position that significant changes of equipment and operations in the affected department authorized the unilateral elimination of the incentive pay under the agreement. A new mechanical device had eliminated the need for fracture tests of a furnace. The employees in the department had been reduced from 6 Head Operators, 22 Attendant Carburizing, and 4 Recorder Optical Pyrometers to 3 Head Operators and 4 Attendants. The classification of Recorder Optical Pyrometer was completely eliminated because the duties were no longer needed. The company's interpretation of the contract language was that these changed circumstances allowed the company to eliminate unilaterally the incentive pay for the remaining employees.

The union's position was that the CBA contemplated the incentive pay being kept in place as part of the employees' wages, and the company could not unilaterally eliminate the incentive pay. New or changed rates could be negotiated as circumstances dictated, but eliminating the pay completely was not allowed.

The following are the relevant contract provisions:

Article V—Wages

A. Wage Rates

. . . such hourly wage rates, together with all incentive rates now in existence, which altogether constitute the wage structure applicable to existing occupations in effect on August 28, 1983, shall remain in effect during the term of this agreement, except as any of such rates may be changed, adjusted, or supplemented in the manner prescribed in this Article. . . .

B. New and Changed Rates

. . . It is recognized that the company, at its discretion, may also find it necessary or desirable from time to time to establish new incentive rates or to adjust existing incentive rates because of any of the following circumstances:

1. Changes, modifications, or improvements made in equipment, material, or product. If there is any such change, modification, or improvement in existing equipment or material or on an existing product, the company may change the elements of the rate or rates affected by such change, modification, or improvement but will not change the elements not affected by such change, modification, or improvement.

2. New or changed standards of manufacture in (a) processes; (b) methods; and (c) quality.

3. Changes in the duties of an occupation covered by incentive rates that affect the existing incentive standards.

Whenever it is claimed by any employee that any of the changes or events have occurred that are outlined in Paragraphs 1, 2, and 3 of the preceding Section B of this Article V, any employee who is affected thereby, either (1) by the production of product or (2) by being employed on an occupation affected by such claimed changes or events outlined in said paragraphs, may request the establishment of a new rate by discussing such request with his supervisor. In the event that no agreement is reached in respect to the employee's request, grievance may be filed by such employee within 10 calendar days after such changes or events have occurred.

If, as the result of a grievance being processed under this Section B, it is determined that the company did not have the right to establish a new or adjusted rate, the rate structure in effect prior to the new or adjusted rate shall be reinstated as of the effective date of the new or adjusted rate. The company will calculate retroactive payment to the extent possible under the applicable rate structure.

SOURCE: Adapted from *Timken Co.*, 85 LA 377 (1985).

QUESTIONS

1. Did the changes made in the department satisfy the circumstances cited in the agreement that would allow the company to eliminate the incentive pay?

2. Did the affected employees have a legitimate grievance under the CBA's language?

3. If you were the arbitrator, would you allow the company to eliminate the incentive pay? Explain your answer.

KEY TERMS AND CONCEPTS

- ability to pay
- annual salary
- back-loaded contract
- base compensation
- COLA
- cost-of-living adjustment (COLA)
- costing wage proposals
- deferred wage rate increase
- dual-career ladder pay systems
- exempt
- falling piece rate
- front-end loading
- hourly wage
- job evaluation
- lump-sum payment
- nonexempt
- pattern bargaining
- pay equity
- pay for time worked
- piece-rate system
- piecework
- productivity theory
- profit sharing
- pyramiding
- rising piece rate
- roll-up
- Scanlon plan
- standard rate
- standard hour plans
- two-tier wage system
- value added
- wage reopener
- wage surveys

REVIEW QUESTIONS

1. What are the general wage concerns that management and employee representatives bring to the negotiating table?
2. Why have profit-sharing plans replaced COLAs in some recently negotiated agreements?
3. Why does management often prefer profit-sharing increases or bonuses to deferred wage increases?
4. How can wage surveys be effectively used in collective bargaining?
5. Why are labor and management negotiators likely to respond to consideration of the company's ability to pay higher wages?
6. What are some problems with negotiated COLAs?
7. Why must labor and management be able to determine accurately the cost of wage proposals?
8. How should negotiators treat the roll-up costs when negotiating wage changes?
9. Why might union negotiators favor front-end loaded deferred wage increases? Are there potential drawbacks?
10. Why do you think profit-sharing and lump-sum provisions have increased in usage in recent years while COLAs and wage reopeners have decreased in use?

YOU BE THE ARBITRATOR
Scheduling Saturday as Part of the Workweek

ARTICLE V
WORKING HOURS AND OTHER CONDITIONS OF EMPLOYMENT

Section 5.1—Workday and Workweek—(B) Production Workweek (in pertinent part): The basic workweek for all bakery employees shall consist of five (5) eight (8) hour workdays for a total of forty (40) hours.... The basic workweek shall be from 12:01 AM Sunday and end at midnight (12:00 AM) Saturday.

Section 5.3—Weekly and Daily Guarantees—(B): A minimum of eight (8) hours of work shall be guaranteed to all full-time employees under this Agreement who report for work in any one day, except that the minimum guarantee shall be only four (4) hours with respect to work requested on the sixth and seventh day of the workweek.

Section 5.4—Work Schedules (in pertinent part): The Employer reserves the right to determine working schedules and the number and starting times of working shifts ...

Section 5.5—Overtime and Other Premium Pay—(A) Overtime (in pertinent part): ... Overtime at the rate of time and one-half (1-1/2) the employee's regular straight time hourly rate ... shall be paid for work performed. ... (4) On the sixth consecutive day of work. Overtime at the rate of double (2x) the employee's regular straight time hourly rate ... shall be paid for all work performed on the seventh consecutive day of work. No overtime shall be payable for Saturday or Sunday work as such.

(B) Sunday Work: Any employee who is assigned to a work schedule that does not provide for two (2) consecutive days off shall be credited with one (1) earned work credit share for each Sunday worked under any non-consecutive day work schedule.

(D) Extra Day Work (9): Saturday and Sunday work which is regularly scheduled as part of the basic workweek shall not be considered extra day work for purposes of seniority claiming. Letter of Understanding Calculation of Double Time Pay to Bakery Workers Who Work Seven Consecutive Days (page 50 of the Agreement) (in pertinent part): Section 5.5 of the Collective Bargaining Agreement provides for the payment of double the employee's regular straight time rate of pay for all work performed on the seventh consecutive day of work. It has been the past practice to combine two workweeks in order to allow employees to have seven consecutive days of work. Normally the employee's pay period, as set by Payroll, runs from Sunday through Saturday and then a new week starts ...

Facts

The employer is a wholesale baker and sells bakery products to others. The employer purchased the wholesale bakery assets of the former employer and is a successor employer that assumed the existing agreement. The employer employs 125 production employees, whose basic workweek for at least 14 years has been Sunday, Monday, Wednesday, Thursday, and

Friday, with Tuesday and Saturday as days off. In order to meet increased customer demand, the employer opened a second bun line so that fresh buns would be baked on Saturday for pickup by 5:00 AM Sunday.

The employer posted bids for the new line, which showed the basic workweek for the new production employees to be Sunday, Tuesday, Wednesday, Thursday, and Saturday, and the days off would be Monday and Friday. Seventeen or 18 production employees work the second bun line and were affected by the new workweek. Two employees filed a grievance on behalf of the bakery employees affected by the new workweek schedule. The grievance charges that the employer violated the Article 5, Section 5.1 B, of the agreement by starting the workweek on Saturday at 4:00 PM.

Issue

Did the employer violate the collective bargaining agreement by scheduling Saturday as a part of the basic workweek?

Position of the Parties

The employer contended that it is permitted to make Saturday part of the basic workweek by the clear language of the agreement. The employer argued that pursuant to Article V, Section 5.1(B), the basic workweek is clearly intended to be a seven-day period, beginning at 12:01 AM Sunday and ending at midnight Saturday. Furthermore, the letter of understanding confirms this by stating the workweek runs from "Sunday through Saturday." Therefore, the employer may, under the management rights provision, change the basic workweek to include Saturday. The employer argued that a week is seven consecutive days usually beginning on Sunday and ending on Saturday and uses the *Random House Dictionary* to support that definition. Thus, the workweek necessarily runs through midnight Saturday, just before the 12:01 AM Sunday starting time. According to common usage, midnight is part of the day that is ending, not part of the day that is beginning. Therefore, it argued "midnight Saturday" means the midnight between Saturday and Sunday and not the midnight between Friday and Saturday. "Midnight" Saturday comes at the end of the day and is followed by Sunday. The reference to "12:00 AM" is a misunderstanding of how to designate midnight because noon and midnight are technically neither "AM" nor "PM." Noon is generally considered to be 12:00 PM and midnight to be 12:00 AM. Under a prior arbitration proceeding, the arbitrator found that the collective bargaining agreement prohibited the use of a past practice to change the meaning of the agreement and that because the employer was a successor-employer who adopted the agreement and did not negotiate it, it was even more necessary to interpret and apply the parties' written agreement according to the plain and ordinary meaning of its language.

The union argued that Article V, Section 5.1(B), which provides that "the basic workweek shall be from 12:01 AM Sunday and end at midnight (12:00 AM) Saturday" does not permit the employer to make Saturday part of the basic workweek since Saturday is specifically excluded from the definition of the basic workweek as provided by this clear and unambiguous language. Under this language the production workweek ends 12:00 AM Friday night and begins again at 12:01 AM Sunday morning. If the negotiators had intended to have Saturday as part of the basic workweek, the language would read that the workweek would start at 12:01 Saturday morning. "AM" is morning before noon, and 12:00 AM is the morning of Saturday and not the morning of Sunday. In support of this position, the union cites *Webster's Dictionary*, which defines "AM" as "ante meridian, before noon: used to designate the time from midnight to noon," and "PM" as "post meridian, after noon: used to designate the time from noon to midnight." The union further argues that there has been a long-standing past practice of at least 14 years that establishes that Saturday cannot be a part of the basic workweek because it is a scheduled day off for the production employees. The production employees have always had Saturday as a scheduled day off and have always been paid premium time when they have been required to work on Saturdays. The prior arbitration award did not preclude the examination of past practice in this instance because it is used to support and define the clear meaning of the agreement. Furthermore, the letter of understanding refers to a payroll issue, does not define the basic workweek, and does not override the specific provisions of the agreement that define the basic workweek.

SOURCE: Adapted from *North Baking Co.,* 116 LA 1788 (2002).

QUESTIONS

1. As arbitrator, what would be your award and opinion in this arbitration?
2. Explain why the relevant provisions of the collective bargaining agreement as applied to the facts of this case dictate the award.

3. What actions might the employer and/or the union have taken to avoid this conflict?

EXERCISE

Wage Provisions

PURPOSE:

To help students understand the necessity of using precise language when drafting a contract.

TASK:

Divide the class into management and labor and assign each of the following wage topics for students to write a mutually agreeable contract term.

1. COLA provision for a three-year contract
2. Profit sharing in a small engineering firm
3. Two-tier wage system for a teacher's contract
4. A 0–3–3 deferred wage increase
5. A lump-sum payment of $2,000 to all eligible unit employees

CHAPTER 7

Employee Benefits Issues

Nearly 1500 Machinists went on strike against the Space and Defense Systems unit of Boeing, like these IAM members from LL 2766 in Huntsville, Alabama.

Labor News

HEALTH CARE: THE ISSUE!

Employee health benefits are *the issue* of concern to most union and management negotiators today. Employee benefits were often called "fringe benefits" in the past because their total costs were only a small portion of the total compensation package provided in labor agreements. Skyrocketing increases in the 1980s and 1990s made health care the most common issue behind labor strikes in 2000.

Health care continued to be the central issue from 2000 to 2005 for most negotiators, and the struggle intensified as illustrated by the 2005 contract talks between General Motors and the United Auto Workers union. The GM–UAW contract did not expire until 2007, but GM claimed it could not wait until then to gain substantial cuts in health-care benefits from the employees and from retirees. Demanding cuts in health-care benefits from retirees was an unprecedented demand. Management noted that in 2005 GM posted its worst quarterly loss in 13 years and that health-care costs accounted for $1,500 of the price of every GM car, truck, or SUV—the largest single cost item! In addition, in 2005 GM's debt rating was downgraded to "junk" status. In 2005 GM spent about $5.7 billion on employee and retiree health-care benefits, which are called very generous.

The GM–UAW contract contains a no-strike clause that generally stops unions from declaring a strike during the life of the contract. But the health-care crisis caused Oscar Bunch, president of UAW Local 14 in Toledo, Ohio, to claim, "It's (strike) a tool that we have."

At the annual GM shareholder meeting, CEO Rick Wagoner announced three options for GM: Cut 25,000 jobs or cut health-care costs for GM retirees. The UAW was presented with three poor options, and by including retirees' health-care benefits GM was probably "painting the union into a corner" with a brilliant strategy. Why? Unions cannot legally declare a strike over retiree benefits because they are permissive, not mandatory, bargaining issues. That fact, combined with the reality that employees are more likely to accept reductions in retiree benefits than their own benefits—or jobs—means GM was presenting an option the union would have difficulty refusing in an effort to preserve jobs and members' own health-care benefits. Health-care issues often include (1) coverage, (2) deductibles, (3) copayments, and (4) choice of health-care provider. However, GM is also taking proactive steps designed to improve the health of its employees including adding gyms to some plants, restricting smoking in plants, and introducing programs to reduce obesity.

SOURCE: Adapted from Sharon Silke Carty, "UAW Raises Possibility of Strike Over GM Health Care," *USA Today* (June 16, 2005), 3B.

Today, negotiated employee benefits, once referred to as fringe benefits, represent a critical part of the total economic package. Employers may easily find that between 25 and 45 percent of the total economic package now consists of benefits rather than direct compensation. Yet benefits are not usually designed to meet the same employee objectives as the wage portion of the negotiated agreement. From the employee standpoint, the wage portion of the economic package provides income needed for the necessities of life, such as food, shelter, and clothing, as well as some luxuries. Management views wages as a means of attracting, retaining, and motivating employees and therefore maximizing their productivity.

Benefits, however, often have different objectives for management as well as the union. For example, many benefits are designed to guarantee employees a stream of income regardless of unforeseen circumstances, such as layoff, automation of work, death, or illness. A major effect of a strong benefit package is the reduction of turnover. A substantial cost borne by workers in changing jobs is the loss of associated benefits. A worker leaving behind a pension may forfeit several thousands of dollars of retirement income, along with sizable losses in vacation, insurance, and other benefits.[1]

Does collective bargaining affect the benefits received by union members? A comparison of more than 10,000 union and nonunion establishments found that unionism had a sizable impact on total benefit expenditures as well as on the straight-time wage rate. The average dollars spent per hour on voluntary benefits is 140 percent higher ($0.70 per hour versus $0.29 per hour) in private union firms (versus nonunion).

The 1990s produced dramatic shifts in the two most expensive types of employee benefits for employees in large and medium-sized organizations. The area of health benefit plans saw a substantial shift away from fee-for-service plans, which accounted for over 67 percent of all plans in 1990, to less than 25 percent by 1999. During the same time, nontraditional health-care plans, including health maintenance organizations (HMOs) and preferred provider organizations (PPOs), increased to 73 percent of all plans offered (HMOs: 33 percent, PPOs 40 percent). In most of these newer plans, employees were required to contribute a greater portion of the costs than had been the case in their prior fee-for-service plans. Employers today continue to try to negotiate a shift in health care cost to their employees.

The second dramatic shift in benefits in the 1990s occurred in the area of retirement plans, when a trend that began in the 1980s picked up steam. Although the proportion of all employees covered by an employer retirement plan remained at about 80 percent from 1990 to 1999, the shift away from defined benefit plans and toward defined contribution plans increased during the decade.[2] The shift continued through 2005 when the number of employees covered by defined benefit plans dropped to 60 percent; although more union workers were covered by defined benefit plans (73%) than nonunion workers (16%).[3]

CONCESSION BARGAINING

The 1980s ushered in a new era in negotiated wages and benefits. High levels of unemployment prompted unions in severely affected industries to seek ways to protect jobs. Through collective bargaining, unions seek to stop further layoffs. Employers are willing to agree to increased employment security only at the high price of wage or benefit freezes. In several cases, reductions in benefits, particularly paid time off work, are required to guarantee employment levels.[4] Thus, givebacks, or **concession bargaining** techniques, were born out of necessity. In 2005 the Bureau of National Affairs estimated that over two-thirds of all employers negotiating contracts sought some concessions, primarily in health care, overtime, and pension benefits. In addition, 59 of the employers were willing to trade wage gains for benefit concessions. Table 7-1 illustrates areas in which employers seek to make and gain concessions.[5]

Concession bargaining first gained national headlines in November 1979, when Chrysler negotiated more than $200 million in givebacks. On the brink of bankruptcy,

TABLE 7-1 Areas Where Employers Will Seek to Make and Gain Concessions

| | *Percent of Employers* | | |
	Make Concessions	*Gain Concessions*	*Net Difference*
Wages	59%	28%	+31%
Job Security	19	13	+6
Paid Leave Benefits	22	19	+3
Pensions/Retirement	22	22	0
Health Care/Insurance	21	69	−48

SOURCE: "Employers Will Seek Concessions in Benefits, May Make Them on Wages, BNA Report Finds," *2005 Source Book on Collective Bargaining* (Washington, DC: The Bureau of National Affairs: 2005), pp. 37–38.

Chrysler used the United Auto Worker (UAW) concessions to negotiate more than $1 billion in long-term federal government loans. Although some concessions were in the area of deferred wage increases, the majority of the savings came in the reduced employee benefits of paid holidays, paid sickness and accident absences, and pension funds.[6] In return, Chrysler gave the UAW a seat on its board of directors and a no-layoff guarantee.

The giveback negotiations of the UAW and Chrysler were historic in the labor relations field. The negotiations set a pattern for several other unions and showed that unions preferred reductions in previously negotiated benefits, such as paid time off work, to reductions in wage levels. The negotiations also proved that a giant corporation and a major union could work together to keep the company operating.

Concession bargaining started in the airline industry in the 1990s and continues today, as illustrated in Profile 7-1.

The U.S. economic slump of 2000–2002, combined with the effect that the terrorist attacks of September 11, 2001, had on the economy, created a new climate of concessionary bargaining. Employers pushed for new wage and benefit concessions to aid falling profits and stock prices, whereas unions were hoping to recoup lost benefits negotiated in the past but also sought greater job security. September 11 may have caused workers to have a new sense of insecurity but at the same time an unwillingness to strike. For example, in 2001 the San Francisco United Food and Commercial Workers rejected their union leaders' call for a strike, possibly because, as David Barrz, chairman of the joint Labor-Management Committee noted, people compared their situation to those affected by September 11, and "what was important to them before September 11 was not important to them afterwards."[7]

Successful concession bargaining hinges on management's ability to convince labor of an impending financial crisis that could cause a significant loss of jobs or total shutdown of the operation.[8] If a union is convinced that the employer may, in fact, file for bankruptcy, then it is motivated to agree to concessions in wages and benefits rather than allow a bankruptcy court judge to impose cuts. Courts have made cuts or allowed employers to abandon contracted wages and benefits in about 90 percent of U.S. bankruptcy proceedings.[9] However, economic adversity alone may not be enough to bring about concessions. Union negotiators expect management concessions and programs to enhance labor–management relationships. Thus, employers as well as unions have made concessions during giveback negotiations, many aimed at increasing quality of work life and worker participation in decision making. Economic concessions have often centered on management's sharing of future "good times" through profit sharing or gain sharing in exchange for immediate union givebacks.[10]

In many cases concessions are not called "concessions," so that neither side appears to have lost or won in negotiations. Most negotiations involving givebacks require both labor

---

DOUBLE-DIGIT CONCESSIONS REQUIRED OF UNION MEMBERS

Trying desperately to avoid bankruptcy, Delta Air Lines in 2004 negotiated an unprecedented 32.5 percent pay concession from the Air Line Pilots Association. The pay cut is believed to be the most severe in U.S. history and was combined with a five-year wage freeze at the reduced level of pay and reduced medical, vacation, and pension benefits. Why would the pilots' union agree to such a drastic concession? Delta made public its plan to avoid bankruptcy and possible shutdown, thus the pilots were convinced they needed to accept the cuts to keep the company afloat—and their jobs. Delta had lost $6.2 billion over the three previous years and had already announced plans to cut up to 7,000 jobs from the customer service areas, in addition to the 16,000 job cuts since the September 11, 2001, terrorist attacks. Delta anticipated saving $1 billion as a result of these concessions.

Despite these history-making concessions, Delta filed for bankruptcy in September 2005, opting for a "Chapter 11" filing that allows the company to continue to operate while it reorganizes itself to pay its creditors. One of its first actions under the bankruptcy was to ask for approval to throw out the union contract. The Bankruptcy Court ordered the parties to try to negotiate a wage deal and on December 28, 2005, the Air Line Pilots agreed to **another** pay cut of 14 percent as an interim measure. Delta expected to save $143 million as a result of these latest concessions. Delta and the Air Line Pilots Association were scheduled to continue to meet to try to reach a permanent agreement by March 2006 and if unsuccessful, to turn the matter over to a three-person arbitration panel.

Northwest Airlines pilots followed the Delta union example in 2004 and approved (89 percent to 11 percent) a new contract with a 15 percent pay concession. The International Association of Machinists and the Teamsters agreed to $428 million in labor cost savings through concessions at the bargaining table. The unions agreed to wage cuts from 6 to 12 percent in exchange for a 30 percent equity stake in the company and 3 of 15 board seats. Northwest Airlines had lost $2.1 billion in three years. Northwest stated that the cuts were needed to compensate for higher fuel costs and to purchase new jet planes to increase the number of seats and thus increase future revenues.

But in September 2005, Northwest joined Delta in filing a Chapter 11 Bankruptcy, pilots absorbed another 23.9 percent cut in base pay, and flight attendants accepted pay cuts of 20.7 percent to save Northwest $117 million.

SOURCE: Adapted from Robert L. Rose, "Northwest Wins Pay Concessions from Two Unions," *Wall Street Journal*, May 28, 1993, p. A2; James Pilcher, "Delta Pilots Not Best-Paid Under Plan," and James McNair, "Unions Unhappy, But Cooperative," *Cincinnati Enquirer*, November 8, 2004, D2, D3; Greg Bluestein, "At Struggling Delta, Pilots Accept 14% Cut In Pay," *Louisville Courier-Journal*, December 29, 2005, D1. See also, Michael Kuchta, "Back To 1989: Bankruptcy Judges Clobber Northwest, Delta Workers," *St. Paul Union Advocate* November 28, 2005. Available at www.ilcaonline.org.

---

and management to make some concessions in a true give-and-take process.[11] Often, for example, if management demands givebacks in wages and benefits, union negotiators will demand similar reductions in management salaries and benefits. If management requests greater flexibility in work rules and scheduling, labor negotiators might demand greater union participation in management decisions. The issue of **executive pay** has become a hot negotiation topic in recent years. Union members want senior management executives to "share their pain." For example, in 2004, union employees at US Airways Group Inc. were forced to accept a 21 percent pay cut to save the company from bankruptcy, but CEO Bruce Lakefield didn't lower his own $425,000 salary, which caused union leaders to confront him and ask why they were "asked to make sacrifices and he wasn't even making a token sacrifice." At Delta Air Lines, executives were given a 10 percent pay cut when pilots accepted a 32.5 percent pay cut and five-year wage freeze in 2005. But then six top

Delta executives were given $1.9 million in stock options, causing John Malone, the union leader, to claim: "The generals are dining while the troops are toiling."[12]

In a similar vein, employers may try to protect the investment they have made in their employees by including **payback agreements** in the negotiations. Payback agreements require an employee who voluntarily quits before a specified period of time (usually one year) to pay the employer the cost of certain benefits. The most common benefits specified include relocation costs for newly hired employees, training program costs, and tuition assistance costs. Companies such as American Airlines (pilot training costs of about $10,000), Electronic Data Systems Corporation (relocation costs), and Lockheed Corporation (tuition assistance) have successfully sued employees who refused to honor their agreements.[13]

Some unions have criticized the agreements: The AFL-CIO has noted their similarity to indentured servitude (a person required to work for another as a servant). However, not all unions dislike the concept. The Sheet Metal Workers Union has required those who complete the union training program to repay the program costs if they work for a nonunion shop within 10 years.

Union concessions generally involve wage, benefit, or work rule changes, with reduced benefits generally more acceptable to employees than wage concessions, although future wage increases may be renegotiated. Often work rule changes are easier to sell to employees and have a more lasting effect. Employers, however, must expect to pay the price of these concessions through one or more of five areas of negotiation:

1. ***Increased job security.***   The union will most likely try to extract a promise not to close plants or not to subcontract with nonunion producers. Another example of providing job security is the 2005 agreement between Comair and its pilots union, the Air Line Pilots Association. The agreement provided that Comair would add 36 new jet planes to its fleet and a hiring freeze for three years. The pilots believed the new planes were needed to maintain the current number of Comair flights—and their job.[14]

2. ***Increased financial disclosure.***   The employer will have to make a claim of inability to pay or financial hardship. Although the company's financial information normally need not be disclosed in collective bargaining, when the employer puts profitability or financial condition in contention, the financial data must be provided to substantiate the position.

3. ***Profit-sharing plans.***   Union members generally feel that sharing losses during lean years should mean sharing profits in good years. For example, Chrysler Corporation's employees demanded a share of the record profits after the UAW made major concessions to guarantee the federal loan to Chrysler. Workers were pleased to receive the profit-sharing check during a slumping economy and expressed their feelings to the national union leaders who had negotiated the benefit in an unusual newspaper advertisement on April 13, 2001. The 103,000 hourly Ford workers under the national agreement received an average payout of $6,700 in 2001. The highest payout under the profit-sharing program that started with the 1982 contract was $8,000 in 1999.

4. ***Equality of sacrifice.***   Employers must demand the same sacrifices from management and nonunion employees as union employees. For instance, General Motors tried to increase its executive bonus program just after the UAW made major concessions in 1982. The UAW and its members demanded and got the increases rescinded.

5. ***Participation in decision making.***   Unions may seek greater participation in various management decisions, including plant closings and the use of new

technological methods. If properly utilized, this concession can help develop greater understanding and improve employee relations.[15]

The essence of successful and continued concession bargaining is the development of mutual trust and respect by both parties. The union must be willing to give up some gains made through the years, especially in terms of nonproductive paid time off and other expensive benefits. The employer, in somewhat of a role reversal, must convince the union of the need to negotiate concessions to guarantee survival of the business. The obvious and ultimate proof is that the company is losing money, which usually must be verified by an objective third party, such as an outside auditor.

REQUIRED BENEFITS

Some employee benefits are required by law and are therefore not negotiated. However, both labor and management representatives need to be cognizant of these benefits and their impact on other benefits that can be negotiated. Some negotiated benefit plans are designed to supplement those required by law to guarantee the employee a greater level of benefit.

Unemployment insurance, Social Security, and workers' compensation are three costly and important government-required benefits. Unemployment insurance programs have been operating since 1938. States provide unemployed workers with benefits by imposing payroll taxes on employers. The amount paid normally varies according to the state's unemployment rate. The unemployed person must have worked for a certain period of time and must register with the state bureau of employment to receive benefits.

About 97 percent of all workers are included in the federal–state **unemployment insurance** system. Employers pay a payroll tax on each employee's wages. There are no federal standards for benefits, qualifying requirements, benefit amounts, or duration of benefits; the states each develop their own formulas for workers' benefits. Under all state laws, a worker's benefit rights depend on work experience during a "base period" of time. Most states require a claimant to serve a waiting period before receiving benefits.[16] Workers are usually required to be available for work, able to work, and seeking work actively to receive benefits. Claimants are disqualified for voluntarily leaving without good cause, discharge for misconduct, or refusal to accept suitable work.

In 1935, Congress established the **Social Security** system to provide supplemental income to retired workers. Initially intended to supplement private, often union-negotiated pension plans, Social Security would help retirees live in dignity and comfort. Employers and employees who pay an equal amount of taxes into the system carry the cost of the system, which then uses the funds to pay benefits to currently retired individuals. Technically, Social Security taxes are Federal Insurance Contributions Act (FICA) taxes. Management often points out that the employees pay only half the cost of the system yet receive all the benefits.

Another phase of the Social Security system was added to provide disability, survivor, and Medicare benefits. To become eligible for retirement benefits, individuals born after 1928 must contribute for 40 quarters (10 full years). Required contributions to receive medical benefits vary according to age.

Since the Social Security Revision Act of 1972, the benefits paid to retirement income recipients increase each year by a percentage equal to the increase in the consumer price index. This automatic and liberal increase has been one of the main causes of the shaky financial condition of the Social Security system.[17] It has also provided management's primary weapon in not increasing employees' private pensions. Employers complain that Social Security taxes have increased each year along with raised salaries because the tax is a percentage of the employees' salary. In addition, Congress raised the employers' and employees' Social Security tax rate from 4.8 percent in 1970 to 7.65 percent in 1990.[18]

Laws requiring **workers' compensation** were enacted by states to protect employees and their families against permanent loss of income and high medical bills due to accidental injury or illness on the job. The primary purpose of most state laws is to keep the question of the cause of the accident out of court. The laws ensure employees payment for medical expenses or lost income. Workers' compensation primarily consists of employer contributions into a statewide fund. A state industrial board then reviews cases and determines employee eligibility for compensation for injury on the job.

Union leaders have played an important role in ensuring that workers' compensation laws are updated and employee interests are protected. Their efforts protect not only the interests of the union workers but also those of the nonunion sector.

NEGOTIATED BENEFITS

The law does not require most benefits included in labor agreements, although most are mandatory issues for negotiations. However, any such paid benefits must be gained at the negotiating table. In general, these benefits can be grouped into four categories

FIGURE 7-1   Benefit Issues

Type of Issue	Issue	Relevant Items
Required	Social Security Unemployment insurance Worker's compensation	
Negotiated	Income maintenance plans	Pensions Wage employment guarantees Supplemental unemployment (SUB) plans Guaranteed income stream (GIS) Severance pay Death and disability
	Employee health care	Health insurance Dental, optical, prescription drugs Alcohol and drug treatment Wellness programs Employee assistance programs
	Pay for time not worked	Paid holidays Paid vacations Sick leave Paid leaves
	Premium pay	Reporting pay Shift differential Call-in pay/on-call pay Bilingual skills Travel pay
	Employee services	Flexible benefit plans Child care Credit union Education assistance

as illustrated in Figure 7-1: (1) income maintenance, (2) employee health care, (3) pay for time not worked, and (4) premium pay. A fifth group includes employee services.

INCOME MAINTENANCE PLANS

Income maintenance provisions have become commonplace in collective bargaining agreements. These plans are negotiable and include supplemental unemployment benefits, severance pay (also called dismissal or termination pay), and wage employment guarantees. In addition, these plans protect employees from financial disruptions. Private pension plans provide for income during retirement, along with Social Security.

Pension Plans

A pension is a guaranteed monthly payment to a former employee during retirement. The pension plan benefit began in the United States after the Civil War when former Union Army soldiers were given payments for their service. Then a few companies began offering pensions as a new benefit. One of the first private pension plans was offered by Proctor & Gamble in Cincinnati, Ohio, to employees in its soap plants. Unions began negotiating pension benefits during World War II when a national wage freeze made it impossible to negotiate higher hourly wages, and pension plans gradually became a common benefit in the workplace. Since the 1980s, however, the number of employers offering pension plans has continuously declined. In 1985 about 112,208 plans were covered by the Pension Benefit Guarantee Corporation, whereas in 2005 only 29,651 were covered, a 74 percent drop! Employers striving to cut personnel costs that affect their bottom line have either simply terminated their pension plans or converted them to cash balance plans. In addition, new employers have not started plans. Employers in severe financial trouble have used the U.S. bankruptcy laws to avoid paying pensions owed to retired and current employees. Others, such as AK Steel, have asked unions to agree to major concessions to avoid bankruptcy, and thus preserve their pension plans. Therefore, employee pension plans, a fixture in the American workplace as late as the 1980s, is today a vanishing part of the American dream for union and nonunion workers alike.[19] Private pension plans today are one of the most prized and most expensive employee benefits. In the early stages of the U.S. labor movement, the benefit provided motivation for senior employees to remain with the organization and thus increase their retirement income. Later both labor and management negotiators accepted management's obligation to provide income to employees beyond their productive years. Acceptance of this obligation occurred largely as a result of a 1949 decision by the Supreme Court, *Inland Steel Company v. NLRB*,[20] in which the Court declared that pension plans are mandatory collective bargaining subjects. Today, pension plans are provided in most labor contracts.[21] The number of private pension plans throughout the United States increased dramatically following the *Inland Steel* decision. Fewer than 1,000 private pension plans were in operation in 1940; by the mid-1980s, more than 700,000 were in operation, a peak number.

The two "traditional" types of plans are distinguished by how their benefits are determined. A traditional **defined benefit plan** (73 percent of contracts) on retirement provides a stipulated, fixed amount of income, usually paid monthly. The exact amount is determined by a benefit formula (see page 334) and is based on years of service and base pay. The second traditional type of plan is a **defined contribution plan**, which is less common in labor contracts (27 percent) but far more common in nonunion employers.

Under these plans the employer makes a specified contribution, usually monthly or quarterly, to an account in a managed fund, and the retirement benefit depends on the investment gains or losses by the fund. Thus, the worker is not guaranteed a specific amount of income on retirement. Some contracts provide other pension options in addition to a defined benefit or defined contribution plan. Two other forms of pension plans are tax-deferred retirement savings plans: 401(k) plans and cash balance plans. **Tax-deferred 401(k) accounts** have grown in popularity from their creation so that by 2005, 77 percent of agreements provide for them, usually in combination with a defined benefit plan. The specifics of an IRS Tax Code Section 401(k) vary, but most provide an employer match (at a ratio of one to one or one to two) of a worker's voluntary contribution up to a fixed percentage of salary, usually 6 percent. Employers and unions have viewed 401(k) accounts favorably as a means of increasing a worker's retirement income, but only if the worker chooses to participate by providing funds.

The Enron Corporation, however, in 2001 changed the universal appeal of 401(k) accounts. Enron had matched employee contributions to 401(k) accounts with company stock and then froze those accounts and transferred them to another provider as the company revealed a huge loss of $638 million. Company executives managed to divest most of their own holdings before the fall in stock price, but thousands of workers were left with company stock accounts that were worthless. Thousands of other employers, unions, and their members realized the practical dangers of some 401(k) retirement accounts that put "all their eggs in one basket" as Enron had done. In addition, the substantial fall in stock prices from 2000 to 2002 also caused people to realize the volatility of these accounts.

Cash balance plans are the newest and fastest-growing type of retirement plans and are found in 10 percent of collective bargaining contracts. Under these plans, often designed to supplement a defined benefit plan, the employer contributes a fixed percentage of workers' income to a hypothetical account and guarantees it will grow at a fixed rate. Thus, the benefit grows more quickly than the traditional defined benefit plan and provides a more predictable benefit.[22] Many employers, in recent years, including IBM, AT&T, Xerox Corporation, Cigna, and Delta Air Lines, have converted their traditional pension plans to cash balance plans in efforts to reduce their pension liability. These plans are usually less attractive to employees and typically reduce their retirement benefits by 20 percent to 40 percent in comparison to their former plan.[23]

However, many American workers never collect from their pension plans. For example, Christine Clark was a tobacco worker for more than 30 years for several companies with private pension plans. Yet she could not receive a single penny in retirement benefits. The reason: Clark never became vested—had enough years to become eligible for company pension benefits—with any employer. Although she worked for Liggett & Meyers Tobacco Company in Richmond, Virginia, for 23 years, only seven years counted toward the pension plan—not enough to qualify her for the minimum of 10 years. After several odd jobs, Clark worked for eight and a half years for American Tobacco Company in Richmond—again not long enough to become vested with the pension plan. At the age of 53 and having worked for 34 years, Clark had no retirement income other than her Social Security.[24]

Many U.S. workers will not receive private pensions because they change jobs and leave employers frequently during their productive years. They miss being covered by any one company's pension plan. For other employees, the company either shuts down, lays them off, or dismisses them before they become vested. The lack of pension planning is particularly a problem in the service sector of our economy, which has grown rapidly in recent years.

Union-negotiated pension plans compared with nonunion plans provide beneficiaries the ability to retire at an earlier age, greater benefits when they retire, and larger increases in their benefits after they retire. Combined with the greater inclusion of union workers in pension plans compared with nonunion, union membership is the dominant factor in determining the private pension dollars received by a retired worker in the United States.[25]

Most workers plan to retire at the age when they first become eligible for full private pension benefits.[26] In the past, that age, most commonly 65, was also the mandatory retirement age and the age at which full Social Security benefits would first be available. In the future the typical retirement age may be difficult to estimate. Many workers are living longer and choosing to work longer. The amendment to the Age Discrimination in Employment Act of 1986 made it illegal for employers to require retirement at any age,[27] and the 1983 Social Security Amendment changed the age of full benefits eligibility from 65 to 67. Thus, the worker is faced with a more complex decision when choosing a retirement date.

Employee Retirement Income Security Act

In 1974 Congress passed the **Employee Retirement Income Security Act (ERISA)**, also known as the Pension Reform Act. The law was passed in response to alleged abuses and incompetence in some private pension plans. ERISA provided a sweeping reform of pension and benefit rules. The lengthy and complicated law primarily affects the following aspects of pension planning:

1. Employers are required to count toward vesting all service from age 18 and to count toward earned benefits all earnings from age 21. (Prior to the Retirement Equity Act of 1984, accrual toward vesting began at age 22 and toward earnings at age 25.)
2. Employers must choose from among three minimum vesting standards (Sec. 203).

Secure pension benefits became a new concern for unions after the Enron scandal left many Enron workers with worthless 401 (k) plans and thousands of other Americans worried as their retirement portfolios shrank during the stock market decline.

3. Each year employers must file reports of their pension plans with the U.S. secretary of labor for approval. New plans must be submitted for approval within 120 days of enactment.

4. The **Pension Benefit Guarantee Corporation** (PBGC) was established within the Department of Labor to encourage voluntary employee pension continuance when changing employment. This is accomplished by providing **portability**—the right of an employee to transfer tax-free pension benefits from one employer to another. The PBGC also assumes the pension plans from employers with underfunded plans in financial difficulties. This provides an important "safety net" for retired and active workers who might otherwise lose their entire pension benefits. For example, in 2005 the PBGC assumed the underfunded retirement plans of United Airlines mechanics, ramp workers, and flight attendants. The plans covered over 120,000 workers and included a $9.8 billion underfunded liability, the largest in the 30-year history of the PBGC. UAL took the action to avoid bankruptcy. The PBGC assumption of the pension plans almost guarantees the workers will receive lower benefits than they expected.[28]

5. Pension plan members are permitted to leave the workforce for up to five consecutive years without losing service credit and allowed up to one year maternity or paternity leave without losing service credit.[29]

ERISA substantially reduced the number and scope of pension issues left at the bargaining table. Employers and labor leaders have criticized the law because it is quite complex and may have encouraged some employers to provide no retirement plan at all.[30] However, ERISA gave employees protection when an employer, Continental Can, engaged in a complex nationwide scheme to avoid pension payments by laying off its employees just before they became eligible for benefits. A settlement of $415 million enabled more than 3,000 victims of the scheme to recover benefits.[31]

Issues in Pension Negotiations

Vesting

The conveying of employees' nonforfeitable rights to share in a pension fund is termed **vesting**. As illustrated in the example of Christine Clark, many individuals never receive private pension funds because they leave employers before working enough years to become vested.

Section 203 of ERISA provides that employers choose from among three alternatives of retirement age and service. One alternative is to provide 100 percent vested rights after five years of service. The other two provide less than 100 percent vested rights with fewer years of service. Union negotiators are very interested in the plan chosen by management. However, no single plan is always preferred by employees.

Qualified Plan

A *qualified plan* generally refers to a plan that meets standards set by the Internal Revenue Service (IRS). By qualifying under the IRS provisions, an employer can deduct pension contributions made to the qualified plan as business expenses for tax purposes. This, of course, is a major reason employers seek to qualify their pension plans whenever possible. Employees, however, also benefit because they do not pay taxes on any dollars either they or the employer invest in the plan under current income. Instead, income taxes are paid when the retirement benefits are received. A *nonqualified plan* would not provide the tax advantages of the qualified plan but would be required to meet the strict guidelines set by the IRS.

Contributory Plans

All pension plans are either contributory or noncontributory. In a **contributory plan**, the employer pays a portion of the funding, and the employee pays the other portion. The percentage paid by employer and employee becomes of keen interest during collective bargaining. Also of interest is the type of benefit plan provided. In a *noncontributory plan*, the employer pays all the administrative and funding costs. Therefore, the question of how much is to be paid by the employer does not arise during collective bargaining; rather, the benefit package provided by the plan becomes the central issue.

Age or Service Requirement

Most pension plans require a minimum age or years of service before an employee becomes eligible to receive retirement benefits. The plan may simply require a minimum age such as 55 or 60 at which the retired employee begins receiving benefits or a minimum of 25 or 30 years of service. Other plans require a minimum of both, such as 25 and 60, meaning 25 years of service and 60 years of age. Under such a plan, the employee who began work with the company at age 20 must work for 40 years before becoming eligible to receive retirement benefits, even though he or she could become eligible at age 45 under the service requirement. Some systems provide for an option of retirement minimums. For example, an employee may receive 50 percent of the benefits if he or she retires at age 55, 70 percent at age 60, 80 percent at age 62, or 100 percent at age 65. Management realizes that the percentages and ages can be changed to motivate employees to retire at an earlier age or to stay with the company longer. A similar type of provision can be created for years of service. The minimum age or service requirement is an item of great interest during contract negotiations. If union membership is heavy with senior employees close to retirement, changing the minimum requirement becomes an even greater goal of the union negotiators.

Disqualifications

ERISA allows a pension plan to suspend pension payments of a retired member who reenters the job market to protect participants against their pension plan being used, in effect, to subsidize low-wage employers who hire plan retirees to compete with and undercut the wages and working conditions of employees covered by the plan. In a recent Supreme Court case, *Central Laborers' Pension Fund v. Heitz,* et al.,[32] the anticut provision was interpreted, however, to protect accrued benefits from *after-retirement* changes. Heinz retired from the construction industry after accruing enough pension credits to qualify for early retirement payments under a "service only" multiemployer pension plan that pays him the same monthly benefit he would have received had he retired at the usual age. The plan prohibits such beneficiaries from certain "disqualifying employment" after they retire, suspending monthly payments until they stop the forbidden work. When Heinz retired, the plan defined "disqualifying employment" to include a job as a construction worker but not as a supervisor, the job Heinz took. Subsequent to Heinz's retirement and entry into his job, the plan expanded its definition of disqualifying employment to include any construction industry job and stopped Heinz's payments. Heinz sued to recover the suspended benefits, claiming that the suspension violated the "anticutback" rule of ERISA, which prohibits any pension plan amendment that would reduce a participant's accrued benefit. The Court held that imposing new conditions on rights to benefits already accrued violates the anticutback rule.

Benefit Formula

Perhaps the most important pension item in collective bargaining is the benefit formula, in which benefits due each retiree are calculated. A common benefit would appear as follows:

Benefit dollars = Years of service × Base pay × _____%

The three variables of importance in the formula are years of service, employee's base pay, and a percentage to be applied. The percentage is usually a fixed figure that is seldom negotiated to change; 2 to 3 percent is often used, but the percentage can be as high as 5 percent or as low as 1 percent. The individual employee determines the number of years of service. The determination of the base pay, therefore, becomes critical to many contract negotiations. For many years, base pay was defined to be the average of the employee's annual gross wage received. However, in recent years, with high inflation causing rapid salary increases as well as moves through promotion and transfer, base pay often receives other definitions.

Contracts today commonly define **base pay** as the average yearly salary for the last three or five years worked or the average yearly salary for the highest three of the last five years. The most liberal definition of base pay would be the employee's highest gross salary received in any one year. The more years included in averaging base pay, if one assumes a steadily increasing salary, the lower the average and therefore the lower the benefit. Union negotiators also want to include vacation time and time taken for personal leave as well as time worked in a definition of base pay. Management will naturally resist any redefinition of base pay that would increase its calculated total and the pension benefit in the formula.

Wage Employment Guarantees

In recent years, union negotiators have fought vigorously for an income maintenance benefit previously provided only to white-collar workers—that of guaranteed income throughout the year regardless of available hours of work or actual work performed. Union negotiators feel that their members should also have the security and convenience of regular pay periods. The problems and frustrations of fluctuating income make the guaranteed wage a high priority for many union leaders.

Wage employment guarantees (WEGs) ensure employees a minimum amount of work or compensation during a certain period of time, usually for the life of the contract. Normally all full-time employees who have at least one year's service are eligible. The UAW contracted a guaranteed wage in its agreement with Ford Motor Company in 1967, a major step for union negotiators in the industry. Today WEGs appear in 16 percent of all agreements.[33] A wage employment guaranteed provision might read: "All regular, full-time employees shall be guaranteed a minimum of 40 hours of work per week or compensation in lieu of work being provided."

When negotiating to provide a guaranteed annual wage, management often will insist on an **escape clause** to suspend the guarantee for production delays beyond the control of management, such as natural or accidental disasters, voluntary absences, employee discharge, or strikes.

Supplemental Unemployment Benefits

In the 1950s, steel and automobile industry union leaders began to negotiate for supplemental unemployment benefits (SUB) plans. These plans provide additional income to supplement state unemployment benefits to employees who are laid off. Union negotiators normally contend that state unemployment benefits do not enable employees to maintain adequately their style of living. SUB plans are designed to be directly supplemental; employees receive a certain percentage of their gross pay for a maximum number of weeks when unemployed. For example, if each employee subjected to a layoff during the period of the contract receives 75 percent of normal base pay, with the company providing the additional funds necessary to the employee's state unemployment benefits, an employee making about $266 a week would receive a total of $200. This 75 percent figure would include $150 per week of state unemployment benefits, with the remaining $50 being provided by the company.

Some negotiated SUB plans will provide only 50 to 75 percent of gross pay; few go beyond 75 percent. Most will provide the additional unemployment benefits for at least a period equal to the state's unemployment, often exceeding up to one year in length. Employees must have at least one year's service before they are eligible for SUB benefits; they do not receive such benefits if they are on strike or under disciplinary action. Most SUB plan provisions include the escape clauses discussed in the previous section.

Management usually strongly opposes implementing a SUB plan. Management negotiators emphasize that the company already pays into the state unemployment fund as required by law and that union leaders should lobby their state legislature to increase those funds. Management will also argue that additional unemployment benefits decrease its ability to make technological changes and to provide new equipment and processes because of the additional benefits paid to displaced employees.

Although some SUB plans were negotiated as early as 1923 by Procter & Gamble and 1932 by Nunn Shoe Company, the great increase in the number of plans providing coverage for employees came after the 1955 negotiated SUB plan between the Ford Motor Company and the UAW. Today most plans are within the primary metals, transportation, electrical, rubber, and auto industries.[34]

Guaranteed Income Stream

The relatively high unemployment rate and severe layoffs in the 1970s and 1980s caused job security to become a top priority for union negotiators and members.[35] Several innovative provisions in contracts have the intent of improving employment security. One of the most interesting and publicized is the **guaranteed income stream** (GIS) plan in the auto industry.

The GIS plan is an alternative to the traditional SUB plan, although the goal of income maintenance for employees is the same. The typical GIS plan differs from SUB plans in three important areas. First, GIS plans furnish benefits to eligible workers until they retire and thus have been called a "guaranteed lifetime wage," whereas SUB plans end after a short period of time, usually two years. Second, qualification for a GIS plan is based on earnings, not on employment, thus encouraging laid-off workers to seek other employment. Third, the benefits provided by a GIS plan are only partially offset by outside earnings until a "break-even" point is reached. Under most SUB plans, benefits are completely offset by outside earnings—a deterrent to laid-off workers seeking outside jobs. Thus, GIS plans create incentives for laid-off workers, unlike SUB plans, which tie them to their former employer. Both sides may benefit from GIS plans. If laid-off workers find new jobs, the amount of GIS benefits paid by the former employer may be reduced as they are partially offset by the outside income. However, the employer is encouraged to avoid layoffs by the long-term eligibility aspect of a GIS plan. When layoffs are necessary, the employer has an additional financial incentive to help workers find new employment. The GIS plan may eventually replace SUB plans because both management and labor can realize important advantages.[36]

Severance Pay

Severance pay, sometimes called dismissal pay, is income provided to employees who have been permanently terminated from the job through no fault of their own. Although similar to SUB in its appearance and formula for provision in determining benefits, severance pay is given under quite different circumstances. SUB pay enables the employee who is temporarily laid off to feel minimum impact from the layoff and anticipate a return to work and full pay. Employees who receive severance pay, however, realize that they have no hope for future work with the company. It is not normally provided to employees who are terminated for just cause or who quit.

The purpose of severance pay is to cushion the loss of income due to plant closing, merger, automation, or subcontracting of work. Union negotiators contend that management should shoulder some of the financial burden while the employee is seeking other permanent work.

The provision of severance pay and advance notice of layoffs varies by industry. It is most common in industries that have incurred past layoffs during hard economic times, such as manufacturing (74 percent of all contracts) and utilities; contracts for professional and technical employees seldom (16 percent) provide severance pay and advance notice.[37]

The amount of severance pay is usually specified by a formula guaranteeing a percentage of base pay determined by number of years of service with the company. The percentage normally increases as the employee's number of years increases to a maximum percentage. To be eligible, employees are normally required to have a minimum number of years of service, usually one, except in a case of disability. Management negotiators have been somewhat more sympathetic to severance pay provisions because management controls its cost completely. However, as the economy, technology, and mergers force changes in many of our industries, management negotiators may be likely to resist further increases in severance pay provisions.

If severance pay is included in an agreement, it is considered an employee right. In the case of a merger, plant closing, relocation, or the sale of the company, the liability for severance pay may become a most important issue. Court decisions have upheld the legal right of employees to receive severance pay from the parties involved. In such cases severance pay owed workers is generally regarded as a legal liability of the company.[38] Unions have a legal right to file suit on behalf of employees denied negotiated severance pay under the Labor Management Relations Act, Section 301.[39]

In 2002, for example, the AFL-CIO filed suit and paid all legal fees on behalf of the 4,200 former Enron workers. The unusual support followed the historic financial collapse of Enron after the company refused to pay severance pay to former workers while top executives received millions in bonuses. After several months in federal court, Enron and its creditors agreed to pay $34 million in severance pay, up to $13,500 per worker. Even though the workers were nonunion, the AFL-CIO supported them because "unions exist to improve the lives of working families," according to Vice President Linda Chavez-Thompson.[40]

Death and Disability Plans

Union leaders have also strongly negotiated for death and disability benefits to supplement Social Security. The negotiated benefit may provide for coverage up to a maximum, or it may provide benefits independent of others received by the employee. The need for negotiators to be very specific about what is provided by these benefits is illustrated in Case 7-1, in which misunderstandings about a program led

DISABILITY PENSION

The agency's pension plan and agreement for the employees provided that an applicant for disability pension would be subject to a medical examination and evaluation by the agency doctors to determine whether the applicant was qualified for a disability pension. The decision, however, would be made by the Disability Pension Board, which is made up of three representatives from the company and three representatives from the union.

The employee in this case became disabled and was unable to drive a bus, which was her job. The employee had been diagnosed by her own doctor as suffering from temporomandibular joint syndrome (TMJ). The employee applied for disability pension, and the board voted on her application. The six-member panel was deadlocked: The three company trustees voted no, and the three union trustees voted yes. The position of the union was that the employee suffered from permanent disability and, under the collective bargaining agreement, should be allowed a pension.

The applicable provision of the collective bargaining agreement stated that employees with 10 years or more of service who become permanently physically or mentally incapable of performing their job could retire and begin receiving benefits. Any such pensioner who regains his health or mental capacity shall have his pension discontinued, and he shall be restored to his former position with full seniority rights.

The union pointed out that although the collective bargaining agreement pension rules required an employee to be examined by an agency physician when applying for permanent disability, the decision of whether the employee qualified was left to the trustees. The trustees had admitted that they did not take into consideration the opinions of the employee's private physicians that the employee suffered from TMJ and could be considered permanently disabled.

The position of the company, however, was that the examination by the agency physician failed to decide conclusively the issue of the permanency of the disability. On the basis of one examination, the agency physician determined that the employee was unable to drive a bus at that time but could not find any physical impairment that would justify classifying the employee's condition as permanent disability.

DECISION

The arbitrator found that to rely only on the agency physician, who had admittedly performed a relatively short and cursory exam, was not sufficient. The arbitrator found that the grievant did meet the disability requirement under the pension plan and should be awarded pension benefits.

SOURCE: Adapted from *Bi-state Development Agency*, 90 LA 91 (1987).

to arbitration. However, negotiators are aware of the benefits made available on death or disability to employees by the Social Security system, and employers remind union officials that they contribute to the Social Security system and therefore provide funding for its death and disability benefits as well as those received through the collective bargaining process. An example of the negotiated benefit is included in the following agreement between Anaconda Aluminum Company and Aluminum Workers Local 130 and the Aluminum Workers International Union, AFL-CIO:

Tips from the Experts

UNION	MANAGEMENT

UNION

What are the three best benefits employees can try to get from their employers?

1. Employment security (as opposed to job security)
2. Family coverage (health insurance, appropriate leave opportunities, child care, and elder care)
3. Opportunity for employee growth through retraining, promotion, education, literacy, and recognition for performance

MANAGEMENT

What three benefits should an employer avoid?

1. COLA (cost-of-living adjustment) or any other benefit plan with fixed benefits unrelated to costs or a future plan with fixed entitlement
2. Discretionary overtime
3. Premium pay for time not worked or any other pay for nonproductive time, such as on-call pay

ARTICLE 19

Group Insurance

a. The company will provide without cost to the employee the following group insurance and benefits.
b. Terms and conditions of the coverage called for in paragraph(s) of this article will be contained in the contract between the company and the insurance company with details in a separate booklet which will be furnished to each employee.
c. Life Insurance—On the fifteenth of the month, following the completion of his probational period, the employee will be covered by $12,000 life insurance. Included in the policy are provisions for coverage after retirement, layoff, and in the event of disability. Retiree benefits do not apply for deferred vested pension.[41]

The company commonly bears the entire premium cost of death and disability insurance. However, often it may be negotiated that employees will be offered additional group insurance through the group plan at reduced rates. Union members, of course, often benefit from such a plan by an amount greater than the premium paid by the company in their behalf. Usually the company can obtain group insurance at a rate cheaper than each individual could purchase on his or her own.

Employee life insurance plans are included in more than 65 percent of negotiated plans. Most provide a specific benefit, often $10,000.[42] Another common type of benefit provides an amount directly related to the employees' annual earnings. Plans that relate the amount to earnings most often provide a maximum benefit equal to total yearly earnings; some provide twice the earnings.[43] The cost of life insurance coverage is paid entirely by the employer in most agreements.

HEALTH CARE

Health insurance benefits are found in almost all collective bargaining agreements (97 percent), and in terms of total labor costs they rank second only to wages and salaries for most employers. The most commonly found provisions provide for hospitalization (97 percent), prescription drugs (96 percent), physician visits (96 percent), mental health (93 percent), dental care (90 percent), and vision care (73 percent). Dental and vision care, less common only 10 years ago (43 percent of contracts in 1993), have increasingly appeared in more contracts until today they are provided in 90 percent of 2005 contracts. Overall management negotiators have been willing to negotiate better health insurance benefits—which are then often provided to nonunion employees as well, including management. Both sides recognize the need for employees and their families to have access to health care, which may be unobtainable or very expensive if purchased outside an employer group plan. Health-care plans usually specify an initial deductible, a family deductible, copayments, and maximum coverage. Most employers provide a choice of health insurance plans to employees, including one or more options under each of the three most common forms of coverage:

1. Preferred provider organizations (PPOs) are available to 74 percent of union workers. A PPO is a contract among the employer, insurance carriers, hospitals and health-care providers, dentists, and physicians that provides specific services at a discount in exchange for a guaranteed number of patients.
2. Health maintenance organizations (HMOs) are available to 62 percent of union workers. An HMO is a medical facility that provides routine checkups, shots, and treatments as well as maternity care, vision testing, and so on, usually at a lower total annual cost to families than a typical insurance plan, and that requires a monthly charge per family.
3. Traditional fee-for-service or indemnity plans are available to 48 percent of union workers.[44]

Health-Care Cost Containment

In some years General Motors spends more money for employee medical benefits than for steel from its main supplier. Indeed, employers pay almost half the nation's health-care bills through insurance programs.[45] However, employer-provided health care has

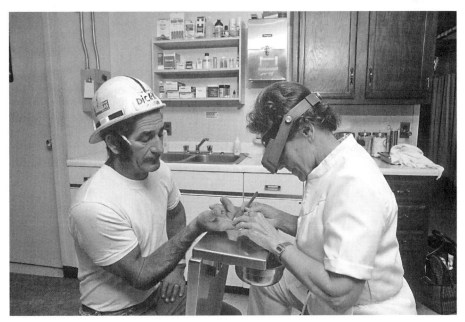

Containing health-care costs is a primary concern for management and union negotiators.

	Percentage of employees				
	All Employers	**By industry**		**By size of bargaining unit**	
		Manufacturing	**Nonmanufacturing**	**Large**	**Small**
Cost-sharing provisions					
Copayments	92%	97%	88%	93%	91%
Deductibles	88	89	86	91	87
Premium contributions	73	79	68	66	77
Cost-containment provisions					
Generic drug requirement	77	79	75	82	73
Preadmission testing	64	71	58	66	62
Pretax spending account(s)	59	58	60	68	54
Utilization review	57	61	54	64	54
Delayed new hire eligibility	54	61	48	59	51
Wellness program	52	58	46	52	51
Outpatient surgery requirement	45	55	37	55	41
Gatekeeper system required	41	42	40	48	36
Second opinion required	38	37	38	50	32
Hospice care requirement	27	31	23	20	28
Home health care requirement	26	34	18	25	26
Hospital billing error detection reward	10	10	11	14	8
No weekend admission	7	11	3	5	9

FIGURE 7-2   Health Care Cost-Sharing and Cost-Containment Provisions in Contracts

SOURCE: Bureau of National Affairs, *2002 Source Book on Collective Bargaining* (Washington, DC: National Affairs, 2002) p. 46.

become "the issue" in collective bargaining as discussed in the chapter-opening "Labor News." Why? Employers in the United States experienced a 147% increase in family coverage health-care premiums ($1,094–$2,713) in only five years, 2000–2005, and that was on top of ten years of significant increases! Thus all parties involved have expressed a new willingness to find cost-containment measures.[46] Provisions designed to lower the cost of health care are included in more than 95 percent of labor agreements—an indication that management and labor are serious about health-care cost containment. Most of the measures are designed to reduce costs by multiple methods, as indicated in Figure 7-2.

The health-care issue on the table is usually what portion of the total cost the employer will pay and what portion the bargaining unit members will pay. For employers, the issue of health-care cost containment is critical because if costs are allowed to increase, they can quickly rise faster than any other personnel cost. Thus, 95 percent of labor contracts require union workers to directly share some of the costs, primarily through three methods: copayments, deductibles, and monthly premium contributions (see Figure 7-2). In addition to these common cost-sharing methods, employers have negotiated a number of other cost-containment provisions; the 13 most common ones are listed in Figure 7-2. Over 95 percent of all contracts include cost-containment methods, and most include several. In recent years the requirement to use generic drugs, preadmission testing for hospital stays, utilization reviews, and pretax spending accounts have rapidly increased because of employer demands. However, at the bargaining table the specifics of the cost-sharing plan typically receive greater attention than the addition or alteration of a cost-containment method. Management negotiators are seldom willing to consider changing a cost-containment method because they are aimed primarily at duplication and unnecessary costs. Union negotiators are generally sympathetic to management's efforts to cut excess costs—as long as the cost-sharing specifics are reasonable from their perspective.[47]

Retiree Health Benefits

Employer efforts to contain health-care costs ignited new tactics in recent years— reducing or eliminating the health-care benefits previously negotiated for workers who are now retired. A 1998 General Motors case court decision allowed the auto industry giant to reduce the health-care benefits it provided to over 50,000 salaried employees in an early retirement program. GM had stated in a brochure that employees who chose to enter the program would be provided health-care coverage "at GM's expense for your lifetime," but the court allowed GM to cut retiree health benefits because a clause in the agreement signed by each employee allowed GM the right to alter benefits. Since that big decision more employers have gone to court seeking similar decisions.[48]

Union retirees' health benefits are generally regarded as more secure because they are provided in negotiated contracts. In 1999, for example, the U.S. 5th Circuit Court denied Masonite Corporation's new "reservation-of-rights clause," which the company claimed overrode the labor contracts clause that gave retirees health benefits "for life." The judge noted that the labor contract language preempted the policy clause. Starting in 2003, however, some employers began suing union retirees and asking judges to allow them to reduce health benefits. Some argue that "lifetime" health benefits mean the life of the contract, not the union retiree. Unions in such cases usually defend the benefits of their retirees. The United Auto Workers and the Steelworkers, for example, have filed suits protecting the benefits of retirees after employers sought to change them. In 2003, for example, Asarco, Inc., told retirees it was raising their health-care premiums and that "duration clauses" in its contracts meant that their agreement to provide retirees health-care benefits expired when the contracts expired. Three unions sued Arasco, Inc. on behalf of the retirees because duration clauses in contracts were meant to cover benefits to current workers, not retirees.[49]

Wellness Programs

Negotiated **wellness programs** have dramatically risen in number. Most are expanded physical fitness or alcohol and drug rehabilitation programs, but many complete wellness programs include stress management, high blood pressure detection, cancer detection and treatment, and individualized exercise programs. Many wellness programs today are created or expanded as a health-care cost containment measure. They focus on individual interventions with employees designed to identify and reduce risky behaviors such as smoking, overeating, and lack of exercise, as well as early detection of illnesses through regular checkups.[50]

The DaimlerChrysler–United Auto Worker's wellness program began in the 1980s with the then Chrysler Corporation and has evolved into a model of labor–management cooperation. The program is run by the six-person labor and management Wellness Advisory Council and involves over 90,000 UAW workers at 35 different DaimlerChrysler locations nationwide. It won the prestigious C. Everett Koop National Health Award in 2000 and was the first labor–management partnership to win the award. The objectives of the program include the number of annual employee health-risk assessments, employee satisfaction surveys, and research by an outside agency. The program provides free on-site awareness, education, and maintenance in several key health areas, including nutrition, exercise, injury prevention, mental health, driver safety, and smoking cessation. Employees may voluntarily attend workshops and receive individual counseling. Family members, retirees, and other workers are also allowed to participate.

The program has been widely accepted by employees and has grown until:[51]

1. Thirty-six percent of eligible employees volunteered to participate in health-risk appraisals.
2. Ninety-five percent of employees who did participate were satisfied with the program.
3. Driving habit risks decreased by 42 percent.
4. Significantly lowered health risks were reported by 4,184 employees.
5. Smoking risks decreased 27 percent.
6. High-risk alcohol consumption decreased by 39 percent.
7. Mental health risks decreased significantly.

Both union and management negotiators view the issue of a company-provided physical fitness plan or wellness program as a desirable addition to the workplace. Thus, the issue at the negotiating table may be reduced to who designs, runs, and pays for the program. What do workers think? A Ford Motor Company employee and UAW member noticed the positive effect on morale: "They've taken out 500 lockers and put in exercise equipment, and two hourly employees get paid to run the room. Those things help make the camaraderie stronger."[52]

Employee Assistance Programs

Beginning in the early 1970s, the number of **employee assistance programs** (EAPs) significantly increased. Today half of all employees have programs in almost every type of service, industrial, and nonprofit organization.[53] The number increased apparently because many labor relations managers believe that they can save money by helping employees resolve personal problems that affect job performance. EAPs also provide the union evidence of management's concern for employees' well-being, which should be a strong boost to employee relations. But the primary reason for more company-sponsored EAPs is that they may enhance a company's profitability by reducing absenteeism, turnover, tardiness, accidents, and medical claims.[54]

Many EAPs grew from alcohol treatment programs. The typical program addresses psychological and physical problems, including stress, chemical dependency (alcohol and drug), depression, marital and family problems, financial problems, health, anxiety, and even job boredom. The procedure in virtually all EAPs is problem identification, intervention, and treatment and recovery.

An example of a successful referral program is the EAP at Bechtel Power Corporation in San Francisco. When a supervisor believes an employee's performance has been adversely affected by personal problems, the supervisor phones the EAP office. (An alternative first step would be an employee self-referral.) Once the supervisor and EAP specialist discuss the particulars of the situation—performance record, absenteeism, and so on—the supervisor is normally advised to suggest that the employee use the EAP. It is carefully explained to the employee that participation is voluntary and does not affect the discipline process, which may be implemented if required by poor work. Strict confidentiality is guaranteed.[55]

Unions have often taken an active role in designing EAPs. Usually both labor and management agree that the troubled employee is a valuable asset and, if rehabilitated, can remain a valuable employee after treatment. However, neither the union nor management views the EAP as an alternative to the disciplinary process, and at some point an employee may be forced to choose between treatment and termination.

The Consolidated Omnibus Budget Reconciliation Act

A federal law titled the **Consolidated Omnibus Budget Reconciliation Act** (COBRA) was passed in 1986. This law provides for the continuation of medical and dental insurance for employees, spouses, and dependents in the event of termination of employment, death of the employee, divorce, legal separation, or reduction of hours, which results in the loss of group health plan eligibility. An employee or the employee's dependents must elect this coverage and pay 100 percent of the full cost of the plan selected. The intent of this law is to alleviate gaps in health-care coverage by allowing the employee or beneficiary to elect to continue medical or dental insurance for up to 18 or 36 months, depending on the circumstances of their employment separation. The passage of the act was a major victory for unions, which had been seldom able to obtain similar provisions from employers at the bargaining table.

Under COBRA, one of the six events requiring an employer to continue group health coverage is termination of employment or a reduction in hours. Under federal regulations, a strike qualifies as such an event; thus, management is required to provide continued health-care coverage to striking employees and their families at the employees' expense. COBRA also requires management to notify in writing each employee and spouse of the right to continue coverage. The employee then has 60 days to choose continued coverage. If the employee chooses to continue coverage, under COBRA, the employer must provide the same group health-care coverage that was provided before the strike.[56]

PROFILE 7-2

2001 LAW BENEFITS FORMER WORKERS AT NUCLEAR PLANTS

In the 1940s and 1950s, the U.S. Department of Energy (DOE) constructed several atomic weapons plants. Upgrades and maintenance of the plants continued for decades. Since then, thousands of workers from those sites, including many International Brotherhood of Electrical Workers (IBEW) members, have suffered major illnesses, especially cancer, which is believed to have been caused by toxic exposure at the DOE plants. In July 2001, a new federal program, the Energy Employees Occupational Illness Compensation Program Act, became law, offering compensation benefits to workers who have suffered from illnesses associated with their work at one of the atomic plants. In less than a year, 1,647 claims totaling $121 million were paid out under the act, with many workers receiving $150,000 lump-sum payments.

One IBEW business manager, Gary Seaz, worked at the Paducah, Kentucky, plant in the 1970s and, like many of the 150 IBEW electricians who worked at the plant, has been diagnosed with cancer. Seaz recalled, "We had no idea of the hazard that existed. Many local union members have come down with cancer." According to the U.S. Department of Labor, workers exposed to radiation may have contracted cancer, beryllium sensitivity, chronic beryllium disease, or chronic silicoses. Claimants can get information at one of nine DOE centers around the nation or at www.dol.gov.

SOURCE: "Benefits Available for Employees of Nuclear Weapons Facilities," *IBEW Journal* (April 2002), pp. 14–15.

PAY FOR TIME NOT WORKED

What has become one of the most sought-after employee benefits by union members is **pay for time not worked** on the job, or paid leave. Employees today have come to expect to be paid for holidays and vacations as well as many other absences. These time-off-with-pay components of labor agreements are many and varied and include the following:

Holidays
Vacations
Jury duty
Civic duty
Military duty
Funeral leave
Marriage leave
Maternity/paternity/family leave
Sick leave
Wellness leave (no sick leave used)
Blood donation
Grievance and contract negotiations
Lunch, rest, and break periods
Personal leave
Sabbatical leave[57]

In general, as illustrated in Table 7-2, a greater percentage of union workers receive paid leave for different reasons than nonunion.

Paid Holidays

More than 99 percent of labor agreements provide for paid holidays. Union negotiators' demand for increased paid holidays has been great and continues to increase the average number of paid holidays provided by the agreements. In 1950, the average number of paid holidays in labor agreements was three; 50 years later the average was closer to 10.5.[58] However, the average number in agreements has remained steady at about 10.5 from 1986–2005. Most contracts provide for between 8 and 13 paid holidays, as illustrated in Table 7-3. Normally, employees required to work on holidays receive double or even triple pay in the contract provision. In the chemical, hotel, and restaurant industries, which operate every day, employees may be given double pay for working holidays and another day off during the following week. If a holiday falls during an employee's paid vacation, the employee usually receives an extra day of scheduled vacation. Employees on layoff during a paid holiday usually do not receive pay for that holiday. Vacation pay provisions can be the source of conflict, as you can see in Case 7-2.

TABLE 7-2 Percent of U.S. Workers with Access to Paid Leave Benefits, 2005

Type of Paid Leave	Holidays	Sick Leave	Vacation	Funeral Leave	Jury Duty	Military	Family Leave Paid	Unpaid
Union	87%	61%	86%	82%	83%	55%	6%	89%
Nonunion	47%	58%	77%	66%	68%	47%	8%	90%

SOURCE: U.S. Bureau of Labor Statistics, *National Compensation Survey* (Washington, DC: 2005) p. 22.

TABLE 7-3   Trend in Number of Paid Holidays (frequency expressed as percent of contracts)

	1957	*1966*	*1975*	*1986*	*1995*	*2005*
None specified	1	1	1	2	1	—
Fewer than 7	36	16	6	3	4	13
$7-7\frac{1}{2}$	48	39	10	6	4	9
$8-8\frac{1}{2}$	12	31	12	8	7	11
$9-9\frac{1}{2}$	4	7	29	9	12	11
$10-10\frac{1}{2}$	4	7^a	20	23	18	15
$11-11\frac{1}{2}$	—	—	12	18	24	13
$12-12\frac{1}{2}$	—	—	10^b	14	16	11
13 or more	—	—	—	19	16	16
Average	**6.2**	**7.6**	**9.1**	**10.4**	**10.5**	**10.5**

[a]10 or more
[b]12 or more

SOURCE: Bureau of National Affairs, *Basic Patterns in Union Contracts,* 14th ed. (Washington, DC: Bureau of National Affairs, 1995) p. 58. See also, The U.S. Bureau of Labor Statistics, *National Compensation Survey* (Washington, DC: 2005) p. 23.

VACATION PAY

CASE 7-2

For many years, the company operated several cigarette-manufacturing facilities in Louisville, Kentucky. In February 1999, the company announced that it planned to phase out the production of cigarettes in the Louisville area. The final production date was in July 2000. However, employees were laid off in various stages prior to the final closing.

The collective bargaining agreement (CBA) between the union and the company provided for a one-week summer vacation and a one-week Christmas vacation for all bargaining unit employees. Generally, production at the facilities was halted during the two vacations, and employees were paid one week of vacation pay pursuant to the CBA. For both vacation shutdowns, the practice of the company has been to pay the vacation pay on the last scheduled day of work prior to the shutdown. The CBA requires that employees be "actually on the payroll at the time of the specific vacation period" to receive shutdown vacation pay. The employer scheduled the summer shutdown so that it included the Fourth of July

holiday. The dates of the vacation period varied, depending on the employee's place in the production process. Those employees who process tobacco at the beginning of the production cycle began their vacation on the Friday prior to the week of the Fourth of July and returned on a Monday, and employees who hold jobs later in the production sequence began vacation on Monday of the week of the Fourth of July and returned on Tuesday.

In 2000, the last day of production prior to the summer shutdown was Thursday, June 29, 2000, so the union understood the shutdown began on June 30, 2000. The employees performed regular duties on June 29. On June 30, the employees being laid off did not perform regular duties but reported to the plant to attend to various administrative matters related to their layoff. These employees were compensated for a full day of work for June 30, 2000, but were not paid vacation pay for the 2000 summer vacation shutdown. The company considered that the effective layoff date for the employees was July 1, 2000. The company concluded

continued

VACATION PAY—continued

that these employees were not *on the payroll during the vacation shutdown period* and therefore were not entitled to the vacation pay for the summer shutdown because the start date for the summer shutdown was Monday, July 3, not Friday, June 30.

In 1999, the Christmas shutdown began on December 24, 1999. A group of employees was laid off in December 1999. Their last day of work was December 23, 1999, with an effective layoff date of January 1, 2000. These employees were paid for the Christmas shutdown because the company considered these employees to be employed during the shutdown.

The union argues that although Article VI, Part 2, of the CBA says that only employees "on the payroll" are entitled to vacation shutdown pay, the term "on the payroll" is not defined in the agreement.

The CBA does not specify whether an employee must be on the payroll during the entire vacation period or only at the beginning of the vacation period. Also unanswered is the question of when a laid-off employee is to be removed from the payroll. For these reasons, Article VI, Part 2, is ambiguous when applied to the facts in this case. Furthermore, the company sent a letter to employees who were to be laid off in June 2000. The letter provided that their last day of work would be June 30, 2000, with a layoff date of July 1, 2000. The "Summer Plant Shutdown Schedule" provides that the shutdown began as of the close of business on June 29, 2000. The employees worked on June 29, 2000, and were scheduled to report for work on June 30, 2000, and were paid their regular wages for that day. Therefore, the company considered the employees to *be on the payroll on June 30, 2000. Because they were on the payroll on the first day of the scheduled summer shutdown, they should have received the vacation pay for that week.*

The company contended that with the practice to vary the "extra" day the employees get during the summer shutdown by including the Fourth of July, the summer vacation shutdown begins on a Friday for some and a Monday for others. So in 2000, the employees who reported to work on Friday, June 30, would start their "summer shutdown week" on Monday, July 3. As the laid-off employees were not on the payroll on Monday, July 3, they were not eligible for the shutdown vacation pay. The laid-off employees who left the company in December 1999 had an effective layoff date of December 31, 1999. The shutdown week at Christmas that year began on December 23. Those employees were clearly on the payroll as of the start date of the winter shutdown.

DECISION

The judge found the position of the company inconsistent. The company notified the laid-off employees that their last day of work would be June 30, a Friday, and they would be removed from the payroll on July 1, a Saturday. And yet the company argued that because the employees worked on Friday, their next "work day" would have been Monday, July 3. The company wanted to use workdays for calculation of the vacation shutdown but used calendar days for determining the date that employees could be removed from the payroll. The judge further noted that there was no indication as to, absent the layoff, which of the employees would have begun their vacation on Friday and which on Monday. The judge determined that the notice to the employees that the "shutdown" would begin on June 30 was binding on the company as to all the laid-off employees and that, because they were on the payroll as of that date, they were entitled to vacation pay.

SOURCE: Adapted from *Phillip Morris USA v. The Bakery, Confectionery, Tobacco Workers and Grain Millers International Union,* 116 LA 1650 (January 30, 2002).

The **personal day**, or **floating holiday**, started in the rubber industry. Floating holiday provisions allow the selection of the day on which the holiday is observed to be left to the discretion of the employee or to be agreed on mutually between management and the employee. Management has resisted the concept of a floating holiday on the theory that there is little difference between a floating holiday and an additional vacation day.

Many labor agreements have observed the **Monday holiday provision** of the federal government. The observance of Monday holidays is, in theory, designed to give employees more three-day weekends during the year for additional rest and relaxation. In practice, however, the Monday holiday has increased absenteeism, the chief administrative problem caused by paid holidays. Employees can easily see that being absent on Friday or Tuesday would provide them a four-day weekend or almost a complete week's vacation.

An agreement provision for a paid holiday should specify the following:

1. *Eligibility.*   As illustrated in the duPont agreement, Figure 7-3, Section 2(b), employee eligibility, which requires employees to work the last working day before the holiday and the first scheduled working day after the holiday, helps minimize the problem of employees stretching holiday periods.
2. *Holiday rate.*   If employees are scheduled to work on what was agreed to be a paid holiday, they will receive premium pay, as in Section 1 of Figure 7-3.
3. *Which days are paid holidays.*   The days determined to be paid holidays should be specified in the agreement as in Section 1 of Figure 7-3.
4. *Holidays falling on nonwork days.*   As specified in Figure 7-3, provisions for the holiday should be made in case the holiday falls on a nonwork day, such as a Sunday.

Paid Vacations

The practice of providing employees with paid vacations in labor agreements has become not only commonly accepted but also expected by union employees. About 86 percent of labor contracts in 2005 provided for paid vacations of two to six weeks' duration.[59] Employers believe that, unlike paid holidays, paid vacations are effective in increasing employee productivity. Employees, by taking a physical and mental break from the workplace, are able to return to work refreshed and rejuvenated.

Four types of vacation plans are commonly negotiated: the graduated plan, the uniform plan, the ratio-to-work plan, and the funded plan. By far the most popular type of plan is the *graduated plan*, which provides an increase in the number of weeks of vacation according to length of service. This is the most common type of vacation plan. The average number of days provided in contracts in 2005 based on service:

Service	*Number of Vacation Days*
1 year	8.9 days
3 years	11.5 days
5 years	13.9 days
10 years	17.6 days
15 years	20.2 days
20 years	22.7 days
25 years	24.5 days

SOURCE: The U.S. Bureau of Labor Statistics, *National Compensation Survey* (Washington, DC: 2005) p. 24.

Holiday Pay

Section 1. An employee who works on any one of the holidays listed below shall be paid, subject to the further provisions of Section 3 of this Article, overtime pay at one and one-half (1) times his regular rate for hours worked in addition to a holiday allowance equivalent to his regularly scheduled working hours not to exceed two and one-half (2) times his regular rate for such holiday hours worked, whichever yields the greater pay.

New Year's Day	Labor Day
*Washington's Birthday	Thanksgiving Day
Good Friday	Day after Thanksgiving Day
Memorial Day	Christmas Eve
**July Third	Christmas Day
July Fourth	

*A Choice of either Washington's Birthday or Martin Luther King's Birthday will be offered provided the COMPANY and UNION have not agreed, prior to December 31 of the preceding year, that another day shall be designated as a holiday in lieu of either Washington's Birthday or Martin Luther King's Birthday.

**July Third shall be one of the recognized holidays except when July Fourth falls on Thursday in which case July Fifth shall be the holiday.

When any of the foregoing holidays, except Christmas Eve or July Third fall on Sunday, the following Monday will be observed as the holiday. When Christmas Eve or July Third falls on Sunday, the following Tuesday will be observed as the holiday. When any of the foregoing holidays fall on Saturday, the preceding Friday shall be observed as the holiday for all employees who normally are scheduled to work Monday through Friday. Saturday shall be designated as the holiday for all other employees. When Christmas Day or July Fourth falls on Saturday, and is observed on Friday by employees normally scheduled to work Monday through Friday, the December Twenty-Fourth holiday or the July Third holiday shall be observed on the preceding Thursday.

Holiday hours shall correspond to the hours of the regular workday.

Employees will be informed at least one (1) week in advance if they are expected to work on a holiday.

Section 2. Pay for hours equivalent to regularly scheduled hours not to exceed eight (8), at the employee's regular rate, shall be paid to an employee for each of the holidays designated above on which he does not work, provided such employee:

(a) Does not work the holiday for the reason that:
    (1) He is required by Management to take the day off from work solely because it is a holiday, or
    (2) The holiday is observed on one of his scheduled days of rest (an employee on vacation, leave of absence, or absent from work for one (1) week or more due to a shutdown of equipment or facilities or conditions beyond Management's control shall not be considered as having "scheduled days of rest" during such periods of absence), and
(b) Works on his last scheduled working day prior to the holiday and on his next scheduled working day following the holiday, except when the employee has been excused from work by Management.

If an employee who is scheduled to work on the holiday fails to work, he will receive no pay for the holiday if his absence is not excused.

Section 3. If an employee works only part of his scheduled working hours on the holiday, and he is required by Management to take off the remaining part of his scheduled

FIGURE 7-3 Holiday Pay Provision, duPont-Neoprene Craftsmen Union Agreement Article VII

hours or is excused by Management because of personal illness, serious illness in his immediate family, or other unusual conditions, he shall be paid overtime pay at one and one-half (1) times his regular rate for the hours worked plus a holiday allowance equivalent to his regularly scheduled working hours not to exceed eight (8) at his regular rate. If the employee works only part of his scheduled working hours and is not required or excused by Management for the above reasons to take off the remaining part of his scheduled hours, the employee shall be paid overtime pay at two and one-half (2) times his regular rate for hours worked but no holiday allowance.

Section 4. Holiday hours paid for but not worked shall not be used in computing hours worked in excess of forty (40) in the workweek.

FIGURE 7-3 Holiday Pay Provision, duPont-Neoprene Craftsmen Union Agreement Article VII (Continued)

SOURCE: Agreement between E.I. duPont de Nemours and Neoprene Craftsmen Union, 1994, pp. 20–22.

The *uniform vacation plan* provides all workers with the same length of vacation. This is most commonly found in manufacturing firms that shut down for specified periods to retool or change product lines, giving employees vacations during the shutdown. The *ratio-to-work plan,* commonly found in the printing and transportation industries, relates the length of vacation to the number of hours or days the employee works during a given time period, usually the year preceding the allocation of vacation. The *funded plan* requires employers to contribute to a vacation fund from which employees may draw vacation pay during periods when no work is available. This is most often found in the construction and apparel industries.

An example of a graduated vacation plan is provided in the following agreement between Anaconda Aluminum Company and the Aluminum Workers International Union, AFL-CIO:

ARTICLE 8

Vacations

a. An employee with one year or more of service with the company and who has worked at least one thousand hours since the employee's anniversary date in the preceding calendar year projecting work hours (if necessary) to the employee's next anniversary date shall receive a paid vacation on the following basis:

Employee's Service	*Vacation Pay*	*Weeks Vacation Leave*
One year, but less than two	$52.00	One
Two years, but less than three	$74.00	One
Three years, but less than five	$100.00	Two
Five years, but less than ten	$168.00	Two
Ten years, but less than fifteen	$180.00	Three
Fifteen years, but less than twenty	$200.00	Three
Twenty years, but less than twenty-five	$210.00	Four
Twenty-five years or more	$240.00	Five

b. The amount of vacation pay for each employee shall be computed at his regular bid rate as of January 1 of each year, multiplied at the appropriate number of hours set forth in the table in the paragraph above.

c. An employee entitled to a vacation shall receive his vacation pay on the payday preceding his vacation leave, but no later than the second pay period in December.

d. Vacation shall be taken during the period from January 1 to December 31 each year. Preference of vacation period shall be according to seniority but subject to planned operation schedule. The company shall discuss a vacation schedule with the union regarding preference by seniority. Nothing in this article shall restrict the company from scheduling all or part of a planned shutdown for vacation purposes, should business conditions permit.[60]

This example includes several provisions that should be specified in the labor agreement, including the eligibility for vacation leave and pay, how long the employee has to be with the company to qualify, and any other requirements for vacation leave. Duration of vacation leave must be determined along with any additional vacation pay, such as premium pay or bonuses. Also, the scheduling of vacations, a critical aspect of the contract, must be specified. Normally, scheduling is done on the basis of seniority; however, management often tries to retain some right in the determination of employee scheduling so that adequate skills and abilities can be maintained in the workplace. In the agreement between Anaconda Aluminum and the union, the company retains the right to schedule vacations during a planned shutdown that might become necessary for business reasons, an important provision for management to retain.

Determining the annual cost of any negotiated increase in the number of vacation days or holidays is relatively straightforward. One common method is to multiply the number of additional vacation or holiday hours by the base wage rate of employees covered. Another method would be to determine the appropriate percentage of the amount charged to the holiday or vacation pay account from the previous fiscal year. For example, if the company estimates that employees averaged 11 days of paid vacation in the previous year at a total cost of $1,200,000, then the average cost per day was $109,090. Thus, if one additional vacation day is negotiated, the total cost for the next year will be $1,309,090.[61] One problem in determining the cost of additional vacation or holiday benefits is that the cost of continuing production as usual is not provided in the two alternatives. Industries such as chemical and utility companies that provide around-the-clock service require many employees to work on holidays for premium rates. Thus, it may be necessary to add additional factors to the estimate of negotiated increases in vacation and holiday pay.[62]

Sick Leave

Sick leave is normally accrued by employees at a specific rate, such as one day per month from the first day of permanent employment. The subject of many arbitration cases, sick leave is intended to provide for continuation of employment when employees are physically unable to report for work. To minimize grievances and other problems associated with sick leave provisions, the labor agreement should specify the procedure for taking sick leave—the time sick leave must be reported by during the beginning of the work shift and what verification by a physician or other individuals is required, a definition of "sick," and the accumulation rights. Some contracts provide that unused sick leave can be accumulated without any maximum to cover employees who require extended sick leave for serious illnesses. A doctor's certification is usually needed only when an employee uses extended sick leave. Many contracts specify a maximum number of days of sick leave that can be accumulated by an employee.

Paid Leaves of Absence

Most agreements provide for paid leaves of absence for a variety of other purposes, including military service, education, and union business as well as personal reasons. Personal leave may result from a variety of causes, such as jury duty, appearing as a witness in a court case, or attending a family funeral. In negotiations for a funeral leave benefit, it is important to specify for which family members the leave should apply. Personal leave may also include the awarding of personal days that employees may take without specifying why they missed work or giving advance notice. Military leave is often negotiated for employees in the United States Armed Forces Reserve Units.

There is little consistency among or even within industries as far as what types of leaves are negotiated and the number of paid days of work provided for. The most commonly negotiated paid leave is for the conducting of union business, with 78 percent of agreements providing this paid benefit. Usually the conducting of union business provision would include contract negotiation as well as handling grievances for arbitration proceedings. Paid leave for military services is included in 55 percent of labor agreements, leave for personal reasons in 46 percent, maternity/paternity leave in 36 percent, and civic duty leave in 83 percent.[63] The provision for paid leave of absence varies greatly by industry but is generally most prevalent in the manufacturing industries.

In general, the labor agreement for paid leave of absence provisions must include employee eligibility requirements; payment received—base wage plus other wages as well as whether additional outside income such as pay for jury duty or reserve pay is to be deducted from the employee's wage; and scheduling considerations.

PREMIUM PAY

Virtually all labor agreements provide a specific work schedule and require **premium pay** for any hours worked beyond the normal schedule. More than 67 percent of labor agreements provide for premium pay for Saturdays and Sundays not part of the normally scheduled workweek, and 99 percent provide for specified overtime premium pay rates on either a weekly or a daily basis.[64] Overtime premiums are often provided on a daily basis for time over eight hours, as shown in Table 7-4. Such additional pay was termed "penalty pay" in the past because it was intended to discourage employers from requiring employees to work additional hours or weekends. Today employers are anxious to maintain their rights in scheduling additional hours so that overtime costs in premium payments can be minimized.

Negotiated increases in overtime in premium pay benefits cannot easily be costed because the actual cost increase per year will be determined by management's scheduling of overtime hours. Therefore, to make the best estimation of negotiated cost increases multiply the percentage increase in the benefit by last year's total dollars allocated to that particular benefit. For example, if management spent an additional $550,000 in overtime pay and the overtime rate is increased by 5 percent during the next year, the additional cost of the increase to management will be $27,500 annually.

The **pyramiding of overtime** pay is prohibited in most contracts. Pyramiding is the payment of overtime on overtime, which can occur if the same hours of work qualify for both daily and weekly overtime payment. In contracts that prohibit pyramiding, provisions specifying how such hours will be paid are usually included.

TABLE 7-4 Premium Pay in Contracts (frequency expressed as percentage of provisions)

| | *Overtime Provisions* | | | | | |
	Daily	*Weekly*	*6th Day*	*7th Day*	*Saturday*	*Sunday*
All industries	93%	72%	26%	29%	51%	64%
Manufacturing	96	74	27	33	63	74
Nonmanufacturing	88	68	25	24	32	48

| | *Second-Shift Differentials* | | | | | | | | | | | |
| | *Cents per Hour* | | | | | | *Percentage of Hourly Pay* | | | | | |
1–10¢	*11–20¢*	*21–30¢*	*31–40¢*	*41–50¢*	*Over 50¢*	*1–3%*	*4–6%*	*7–9%*	*10–12%*	*13–15%*	*Over 15%*
All industries	7%	29%	28%	15%	11%	10%	10%	40%	10%	24%	5%	12%
Manufacturing	5	34	26	18	10	6	10	45	3	31	—	10
Nonmanufacturing	10	11	33	7	13	24	8	31	23	8	15	15

| | *Third-Shift Differentials* | | | | | | | | | | | |
| | *Cents per Hour* | | | | | | *Percentage of Hourly Pay* | | | | | |
	20¢ and under	*21–30¢*	*31–40¢*	*41–50¢*	*51–60¢*	*Over 60¢*	*1–3%*	*4–6%*	*7–9%*	*10–12%*	*13–15%*	*Over 15%*
All industries	16%	24%	22%	15%	11%	13%	3%	12%	18%	39%	15%	12%
Manufacturing	18	26	23	13	9	10	—	14	23	41	9	14
Nonmanufacturing	11	16	16	20	16	20	9	9	9	36	27	9

| | *Reporting Pay* | | | | | | | |
| | *Guaranteed Hours* | | | | | | | |
	1	*2*	*3*	*4*	*5*	*6*	*7*	*8*
All industries	2%	13%	4%	65%	1%	1%	—	13%
Manufacturing	—	5	4	79	1	1	—	9
Nonmanufacturing	5	31	4	31	1	1	—	22

| | *Call-Back, Call-In Pay* | | | | | | | |
| | *Guaranteed Hours* | | | | | | | |
	1	*2*	*3*	*4*	*5*	*6*	*7*	*8*
All industries	—	17%	13%	64%	—	1%	—	3%
Manufacturing	1	14	11	71	1	1	—	3
Nonmanufacturing	—	24	19	50	—	1	—	3

SOURCE: Adapted from Bureau of National Affairs, *Basic Patterns in Union Contracts, 14th ed.* (Washington, DC: Bureau of National Affairs, 1995), pp. 53, 115, 116, 117.

How overtime work is distributed among employees is also discussed in most labor contracts. The most common provision is a general statement to the effect that overtime will be distributed equally as far as practical. Other provisions assign overtime on the basis of seniority or by rotation. Many agreements limit overtime distribution to employees within a department, shift, job classification, or those specifically qualified.[65]

Premium pay for other undesirable work situations may also be negotiated. **Shift differentials** are negotiated additional hourly rates of pay provided to employees who work the least-desirable hours. Usually specified in cents per hour in the labor agreement, the cost of the increase in a shift differential would be calculated similarly to that of an overtime premium pay increase. More than 90 percent of all late-shift factory workers receive a shift differential premium over their day-shift counterparts. Usually

Any employee who reports for work and who has not been notified not to work shall be granted four (4) hours of work or pay therefore. Notice in this Section means that the Company will telephone the employee at the number on file with the Company.

FIGURE 7-4   Article XVI: Report-In Pay

SOURCE: Agreement between Miller Brewing Company and Teamsters Local 97, 2000–2003.

the differential is provided in the contract clause on cents per hour addition to day-shift rates, averaging about 25 cents per hour or 8 percent of the day-shift rate. Third-shift rates often are several cents per hour higher than second shift. Employers are willing to pay the higher personnel costs not only because production volumes can be increased but also because they receive maximum use of plant and equipment and may receive lower utility rates for night usage. Continuous-process industries, such as basic steel and chemical, require 24-hour operation to avoid high start-up and shutdown costs. Thus, shift differentials are most common in capital-intensive industries. On the other hand, workers often resist late-shift employment because of biological, psychological, and social problems related to night work.[66]

Other forms of premium payments similar to shift differentials include reporting pay, call-in pay, and on-call pay. **Reporting pay** is the minimum payment guaranteed employees who report for work even if work is not available. If employees have not been given adequate notice of, usually, 24 hours not to report to work, they are eligible to receive either the minimum amount of work or payment usually equal to four hours of scheduled work (see Figure 7-4).

A supplemental payment given to employees called back to work before they were scheduled is usually termed **call-in pay**. Most labor agreements provide a lump-sum amount or an amount equal to a minimum number of hours of pay for employees called in during other than scheduled work hours. Thus, employees receive a bonus for being called in before their next normal reporting time.

On-call or **standby pay** is given to workers available to be called in if needed. This type of pay is commonly negotiated in companies such as the chemical industry or airlines that must provide continuous production or service. Usually a lump-sum amount is paid to employees on a daily basis when they must be available to work, whether they are called in or not.

Bilingual Language Skills

The 1996 agreement between the National Treasury Employees Union and the U.S. Treasury Department provided premium pay of 5 percent to about 7,000 customs agents who are bilingual. The new premium pay provision was one of the first in U.S. collective bargaining agreements. Other employers agreeing to pay a bilingual premium pay include Delta Airlines to flight attendants and MCI, which pays a 10 percent bonus to workers who are required to speak a second language more than half the time. In general, more unions are pressing for new bilingual premium pay if the skill is needed a substantial percentage of the time in job-related communication.[67]

Travel Pay

In industries that require workers to regularly travel to different job sites, a premium is paid for excessive travel. The construction industry may provide, for example, a specified

---

Article 10-Travel Pay

**Branch Office
Ashland, Kentucky**

Travel pay on all jobs covered by this Agreement are as outlined below, and all miles shall be measured from the office of Millwright Local 1031 by use of the most direct route, using only improved or hard surface, non-toll roads.
5 miles free zone.
All jobs outside the free zone shall be $.25 per hour additional for each hour paid.

FIGURE 7-5 Travel Pay

SOURCE: Agreement between District Council of Carpenters and Tri-State Contractors Association, 2001–2004.

home office and a "free zone" of several miles from that office in which workers will travel to sites for free. Beyond that zone, they receive a premium (see Figure 7-5).

EMPLOYEE SERVICES

A wide variety of employee services have been negotiated in labor agreements. In general, they are not as commonly found as the previously discussed employee benefits; however, most labor agreements provide for at least a few employee services. Some of the more traditional employee services include sponsoring social and recreational activities, such as picnics and athletic events. The cost of these services has been reexamined in recent years because only a relatively small percentage of employees utilize them.

Subsidized food services are a popular employee benefit. Both labor and management feel that providing dining facilities, low-cost meals, or vending machine products minimizes time away from the job spent on breaks or at mealtime in addition to improving employees' diets. Company-sponsored credit unions are another employee service often sought by union negotiators. Although a credit union is normally operated completely independently from the employer, the employer's cooperation in establishing it and providing payroll deductions is critical and must be negotiated.

In recent years, some of the newer employee services negotiated include work-related costs, such as transportation to and from the job; free or subsidized home computers; legal services; and eldercare.

Flexible Benefit Plans

An alternative to negotiating a fixed combination of employer-provided benefits is a **flexible benefit plan**. In a typical flexible benefit plan, employees are allowed to choose the benefits they believe will best meet their needs. Their choices are limited to the total cost the employer has agreed to pay in the collective bargaining agreement. Thus, for example, employees may be given a monthly benefit-dollar figure and told that they can allocate the dollars to the benefits they select from a list. In many programs, employees may exceed their benefit limit, but they must pay the difference between what the employer provides and the cost of what they wish, or if employees choose to allocate fewer dollars than their maximum, they may be allowed to keep all or part of the savings as additional monthly income.

Flexible benefit plans have had an on-again, off-again, on-again life. In the 1960s, **cafeteria plans**, which also allowed employees to choose some benefits from a "menu" of benefits, started to spread among employers. However, the cafeteria approach ran into problems. Employees found it confusing and difficult to make decisions, and employers (without today's computer programs) found the administration of the programs expensive and difficult.

Today, however, flexible benefit plans have become commonplace for several reasons. A 2005 study by TowersPerrin found that 68 percent of employers with plans believe they help provide a positive organizational identity and culture.[68] The primary reason employers are switching from fixed to flexible plans, in addition to better meeting their employees' needs, is to contain their medical costs. In fact, flexible benefit plans may be the most effective means employers have of containing medical costs.

An important feature of a flexible plan is the opportunity for each employee to spend employer dollars as personally desired. By contrast, many so-called flexible plans are fixed. They either offer the employee the opportunity to choose among limited alternatives or offer a "take-it-or-leave-it" approach. For example, the employer offers to pay a portion of an employee's medical insurance if the employee pays the balance. But if the employee does not choose medical insurance (possibly because of a spouse's coverage), then the employer's contribution is lost. A true flexible plan credits the employee with the employer's share, which could be applied to another benefit.

Types of Flexible Plans

There are at least three major types of employee flexible benefit plans. First, the *core cafeteria plan* provides employees with "core" (minimum) coverage in several areas and allows employees to choose either additional benefits or cash, up to a maximum total cost to the employer. In the core cafeteria plan of Figure 7-6, employees have a choice of items 1 through 6 and cash. This plan strikes a balance between giving employees complete freedom to choose among benefits and the employer's need to protect employees against poor decisions. Second, the *buffet plan* starts employees with their exact current benefit coverage and allows them to decrease coverage in some areas (life insurance, medical insurance, and so forth) to earn credits for other benefits (dental care, day care, and the like). Third, the *alternative dinners plan* provides a number of packages ("dinners") from which to choose. For example, one package might be aimed at the employer with a nonworking spouse and children, another at the single employee, and a third at an employee with a working spouse and no children. The total cost of each dinner would be approximately the same as the cost of any other. The employer pays for whatever basic plan is chosen, and the employee can augment the basic benefits package at his or her own expense (contributory benefits options).

Advantages of Flexible Plans

Originally created to better meet the needs of employees, flexible plans have become increasingly effective in matching employees' needs to their benefit plan. Among the advantages of flexible plans are the following:

1. ***Control benefit costs.*** Of employers with flexible plans, 78 percent reported that a major objective in their initiating a plan was to contain rising health-care costs. With health-care costs continuing to rise, this effective containment method is likely to spread among employers.
2. ***Improve benefits offered.*** Employers can better meet the needs of their employees by expanding the variety of benefits offered to employees. Child care is a good example: Employers can pay a portion or all of the cost of providing child care at an

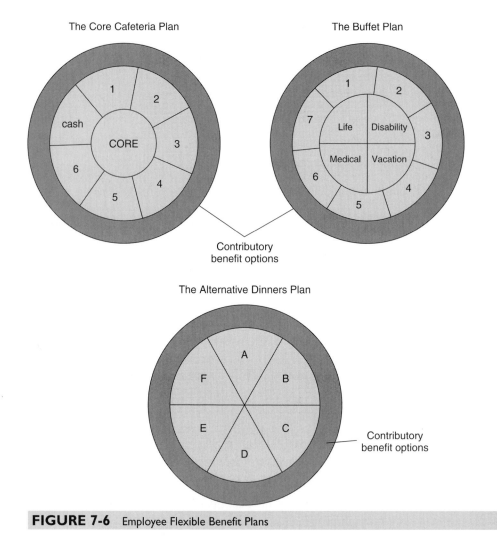

FIGURE 7-6 Employee Flexible Benefit Plans

off-site facility through a voucher system. In choosing the coverage, employees must either reduce the coverage of another benefit or have the increased cost deducted from their pay. (Employers generally, however, provide a portion of child care.)

3. **Attract and retain employees.** The changing workforce is causing employers in some industries to consider flexible benefits as a tool in the recruitment and retention of employees. Just as flexible work schedules can be utilized to attract and keep employees, flexible benefit plans can be included in recruitment and advertising.

4. **Avoid duplicate coverage.** Another aspect of the changing labor force is the increased number of working married couples with duplicate benefit coverage from separate employers. Flexible benefit plans may allow a married couple to save thousands of dollars in wasted duplicate coverage.[69]

Child Care

Although many employers have addressed the child care needs of their employees, child care, according to the National Labor Relations Board (NLRB), is not a mandatory subject for collective bargaining. As the workforce continues to include more single parents and dual-career couples, the direct link between employment and child care might cause the NLRB to reconsider its position. A survey conducted by the U.S. Department of Labor listed the following *employer benefits* from a child care policy:

1. Greater ability of the employer to keep and attract good employees
2. Less employee absenteeism
3. A lower job turnover rate
4. Improved employee morale

Employer-sponsored child care programs are varied.

Child Care Centers

Some employers provide in-house child care services by establishing a child care center in the workplace. The company must have available space and a sufficient number of interested employees for this service to work. Often, smaller employers join together and create a nonprofit center off the premises for all employees.

Financial Assistance

A number of employers choose to participate in their employees' child care needs by providing financial assistance. Employees can afford quality child care with the assistance offered by the employer. Many communities lack the resources necessary to provide quality child care, however, and employers often find it necessary to actually provide the centers.[70]

Elder Care Programs

A relatively new benefit in labor contracts is the support for **elder care programs**. Elder care is defined as assistance for employees who must care for older relatives not able to

Child care is one of the fastest growing employee benefits in labor contracts.

fully care for themselves. U.S. employees are increasingly challenged with caring for aging relatives. Employer-sponsored programs may include:

- Information services including legal, retirement and estate planning
- Referral services for in-home caregiving programs
- Geriatric evaluation and counseling
- Flexible work schedules, part-time work, and time-off policies
- Long-term care insurance for elderly relatives and employees/spouses[71]

Considering the demographics of the American workforce, it is a benefit likely to increasingly appear as a new priority issue for unions. In fact, a 2002 survey of Communication Workers of America (CWA) members found that 20 percent thought they would face elder care needs. Two of the first unions to have negotiated elder care benefits include the CWA and the Hotel and Restaurant Employees (HERE) Union. The benefits negotiated by the two differ in structure and represent two of the more common forms of the negotiated elder care provisions.

First, the CWA and Lucent Technologies in a five-year contract provided for annual contributions to a Family Care Development Fund (FCDF). Employees cannot obtain funds from the FCDF directly but rather can request grants to centers that provide elder care to their family members. Lucent contributes $1.5 million annually to the fund, and more than 330 grants totaling $11 million were awarded from 1998 through 2002. The contract also provides for an elder care referral program to employees seeking assistance. A second major type of elder care provision was negotiated by HERE with over 50 San Francisco hotels. First negotiated in 1994, the provision was partially intended to help the hotels reduce tardiness and absenteeism, which employees reported were partially caused by elder care obligations. Under the contract provision, the hotels contribute 18 cents per hour worked by the employees to a trust fund. Employees with eligible relatives must "win" one of the 100 slots through a lottery to receive the $150-per-month assistance benefit. Eligible relatives include spouse, parent, domestic partner, father-in-law, mother-in-law, or grandparent.[72]

Credit Unions

One of the oldest and most common employee services is the credit union. Most agreements provide that the employer will initiate a payroll deduction process, but the union assumes responsibility for enrolling members, investing funds, and administering the program. In general, employers wish to stay apart from the process and have "the credit union assume complete responsibility."[73]

PUBLIC-SECTOR BENEFITS ISSUES

Public employers provide many of the same employment benefits offered in the private sector. Table 7-5 contains a comparison of the percentage of public- and private-sector full-time workers participating in selected employer-provided benefit plans. For most public employers, income maintenance plans include only pension and death and disability plans. Wage guarantees, supplemental employee benefits, guaranteed income stream plans, and severance pay are not provided to public employees as an acknowledgment that tax dollars cannot be used to pay for nonservice. Medical care plans offered are similar to those in the private sector, and public employers and employees face the same problem with escalating costs as do employers in the private sector.

TABLE 7-5 Private-Sector versus Public-Sector Workers Participating in Selected Benefit Plans

Benefit	Large, Medium Private (1993–1994)	State, Local Government (1992–1994)
Medical care	82%	87%
Long-term disability	41%	30%
Sick and accident insurance	44%	21%
Defined benefit pension	56%	91%
Defined contribution pension	49%	9%
Paid vacations	97%	66%
Paid sick leave	65%	94%
Paid personal leave	13%	38%
Paid funeral leave	50%	62%
Paid holidays	91%	73%

SOURCE: Bureau of Labor Statistics, *Employee Benefit Survey,* 1993–1994.

Vacations, holidays, sick leave, and paid leave of absences for such things as jury duty and military leave are commonly found in public-sector agreements. Premium pay provisions are usually found in agreements covering employees in public safety areas, such as fire, police, and emergency medical services.

One significant area of difference between public- and private-sector benefits is in the prevalence of defined benefit pension plans. Historically, public safety employees did not participate in the Social Security system. Therefore, nearly one-third of all public employees relied solely on their pensions for retirement income. To match the retirement of an employee from the private sector who receives an average of 59 percent of final salary from a combination of benefits from a defined *contribution pension plan* and *Social Security*, the public employee receives 60 percent of final compensation from a defined benefit pension plan.

SUMMARY

Employee benefit costs have constantly risen for several decades. The four most expensive types of benefits in agreements are (1) income maintenance, (2) medical care, (3) pay for time not worked, and (4) premium pay. Still, a variety of employee benefits have increased in recent years as employees and union leaders initiate new benefits in labor negotiations. By necessity, some benefits are unique to particular industries. For example, the agreement between the UAW and Ford Motor Company includes a safety belt user program that pays $10,000 to the beneficiary of a participant who dies in an automobile accident while "properly using a qualified passenger restraint."[74]

Today the top benefit issue in most contract negotiations is health care—who will pay for it, which plans are to be offered, and how spiraling costs will be contained. Retirement plans are a close second, with the concern being, again, who will pay for them and which type of plans will be offered. These two very expensive benefits are often among the top priorities of both union and management.

CASE STUDIES

Case Study 7-1 Paid Leaves of Absence

The collective bargaining agreement between the company and the union contained the following provisions:

> *Overtime/Compensatory Time*:...Employees may elect to use compensatory time off in lieu of a cash payment. Compensatory time is paid at time and one-half. The scheduling of compensatory time, if such be elected by the employee, must be approved by the employee's supervisor....
>
> *Eligibility for Sick Leave*:...Each permanent employee who has earned sick leave credits shall be eligible for sick leave for any period or absence from employment which is due to illness ... of members of the immediate family (defined as ... children of the employee or his/her spouse....)

The company allowed employees who worked overtime to either be paid time and a half for each hour worked or earn time off at the rate of one and one-half hour for each hour worked. The employees accrued 8 sick days and 10 vacation days a year.

Prior to February 13, 1995, employees were allowed to use compensatory time when they were absent because of illness, and prior approval for the use was not always required. However, on February 13, 1995, the company issued a directive stating, "Supervisors will no longer approve utilizing compensatory time for sick leave absences. An exception may be made by a supervisor if the employee does not have

any sick leave hours available but does have a compensatory balance."

The employee's son became ill on February 28, and she left a note for her supervisor that she might not be in on March 1. She did in fact take the day off. On March 2 she called in and said she would not be at work and said she would be using a vacation day. When she filled out her time sheet, she listed March 1 as a compensatory day. On the basis of the company's directive, her supervisor required the employee to use a sick day for March 1 but allowed the use of a vacation day for March 2. The union pursued this grievance on her behalf.

The union's position was that a past practice of allowing the employees to use compensatory time for leaves due to illness without the prior approval of the supervisor had been established and that the company could not change that practice unilaterally. The employees had acquired a "benefit" through that past practice, and the collective bargaining agreement (CBA) did not give the company the right to take away that benefit.

The company position was that the past practice argument was not controlling in this case. Rather, the precise language of the CBA required the use of sick leave for illness and required a supervisor's approval for use of compensatory time. Because the CBA is definitive, past practice does not create additional rights. In addition, the management rights clause of the agreement allows the company to make changes in the way it manages the workplace. Controlling leave time would be included under that clause.

SOURCE: Adapted from *Sheboygan County*, 105 LA 605 (1995).

QUESTIONS

1. The union claimed that the employees lost a benefit when the company changed the use of compensatory time for illness. In light of the fact that the use was permitted if the employee had no sick leave available, how were the employees damaged?
2. The company paid employees the same wage whether the time was credited against accrued

sick leave, compensatory time, or vacation. Why would the employer care which leave was used?
3. As the arbitrator, give your reasons for ruling in the union's favor. Now give your reasons for ruling in the company's favor.

Case Study 7-2 Employee Benefits

The company offers its employees a two-option health and benefit plan. These plans are self-insured by the company, and a third party calculates the health insurance premiums. Premiums are calculated annually in late August on the basis of information from the preceding June–July period. Open enrollment for the employees for the next year are held in October to become effective for the following January.

Premium sharing by employees began on January 1, 1995. Under the collective bargaining agreement (CBA) that expired on August 12, 1999, employees paid an amount equal to 10 percent of the monthly premium. The CBA specified that those rates would be $18 for employees with no dependents (category 1), $36 for employees with one dependent (category 2), and $48 for employees with two or more dependents (category 3). These rates were 10 percent rounded to the nearest dollar of the third-party actuarial calculation of $180 for category 1, $355 for category 2, and $475 for category 3.

The current CBA, which became effective August 13, 1999, changed the premium sharing from 10 to 11 percent for the employees and set out premium sharing rates of $21, $41, and $54, respectively, for the three levels of coverage based on the 1999 premiums. In October 1999, however, the company announced that the premium share levels would be $23, $46, and $61, respectively. The union protested these rates. The union then filed an unfair labor practice charge with the NLRB alleging that the company unilaterally changed the terms of the CBA by increasing the premium sharing amount over the stated amounts.

Discussion

The relevant provision of the CBA stated as follows:

Health Care and Welfare Benefits—Two-Option Plan ("TOP")
Premium Sharing: Effective January 1, 2000, for employees and dependents, there will be a monthly premium sharing equal to 11 per-

cent of the monthly premium for three (3) levels of coverage: (1) employee, (2) employee plus one dependent, and (3) employee plus two or more dependents. Based on 1999 premiums for the TOP, this is (1) $21 for the employee, (2) $41 for employee plus one dependent, and (3) $54 for the employee plus two or more dependents per month. Each year in October the rate for the next year will be announced. In no case shall the premium share dollar amounts increase by more than 10 percent per year rounded to the nearest whole-dollar amount.

The union argued that the company violated that section of the CBA because the amounts announced by the company in October exceeded the amounts in the CBA of $21, $41, and $54, which should have been the 2000 rates. And, the union argued, the amounts in the CBA were the amounts the union membership understood they would be charged for the employee share of premiums for the year 2000, when they voted on and approved the CBA.

The company argued that the operative language in that section of the CBA was "based on 1999 premiums." It was clear from the use of that phrase that the dollar amounts for the employees' share of the premiums in the CBA were there for illustrative purposes only, not to establish the 2000 rates. And even if the CBA was ambiguous, the company's past practice was not. Each year the company counted on its third-party administrator to calculate the health insurance premiums on the basis of information from the preceding year June through July. That calculation was available in October for the open enrollment period, and the premiums took effect on January 1. The initial premiums that would take effect under the CBA approved in August would not be known until October. The union had to know that the rates in the CBA were there as examples only.

SOURCE: Adapted from *Sandia National Laboratories vs. Atomic Projects and Production Workers,* 115 LA 1482 (July 7, 2001).

QUESTIONS

1. Premiums for health insurance have had a tendency to increase appreciatively from year to year. Has the union negotiated a "good" benefit provision for its members? Explain.
2. Do you think that the union's interpretation of the CBA language was reasonable? Explain.

3. Do you think the company should have made the language of the CBA provision more specific so that the union members voting on the contract would understand exactly what the premiums would be? Explain.

KEY TERMS AND CONCEPTS

- base pay
- cafeteria plans
- call-in pay
- cash balance plans
- concession bargaining
- Consolidated Omnibus Budget Reconciliation Act
- contributory plan
- current expenditure system
- defined benefit plan
- defined contribution plan
- elder care programs
- employee assistance programs
- Employee Retirement Income Security Act

- escape clause
- executive pay
- flexible benefit plan
- floating holiday
- guaranteed income stream
- Monday holiday provision
- on-call pay
- pay for time not worked
- payback agreements
- Pension Benefit Guarantee Corporation
- personal day
- portability
- premium pay
- pyramiding of overtime

- reporting pay
- severance pay
- shift differentials
- sick leave
- Social Security
- standby pay
- tax-deferred (401k) accounts
- unemployment insurance
- vesting
- wage employment guarantees
- wellness programs
- workers' compensation

REVIEW QUESTIONS

1. How can negotiators reduce health-care costs and maintain good health-care benefits?
2. In recent years, management negotiators have increased their resistance to increases in private pension plan funding. Why?
3. Why might workers be ineligible for retirement funds from a private pension plan even though they have worked all their lives?
4. What is meant by eligibility in a holiday clause?
5. Why do workers try to negotiate wage employment guarantees? Supplemental unemployment benefits (SUBs)?

6. How does a GIS differ from SUB pay?
7. What type of health-care plans are normally negotiated? How can a health maintenance organization (HMO) be considered as an alternative to such plans? What are the purposes of HMOs?
8. Why do employees today place a high priority on paid time off? How has the Monday holiday caused administrative problems? How can holiday provision problems be minimized?
9. What paid leaves of absence are usually provided by labor agreements?
10. Why does management dislike pyramiding of overtime?

YOU BE THE ARBITRATOR
Not Working a 40-Hour Week

ARTICLE 3
HOURS OF WORK AND OVERTIME:

Employees covered by this Agreement are to work a normal workweek of 40 hours and a normal workday of 8. Each employee shall be entitled to one (1) full day of rest per week, which shall be twenty-four (24) consecutive hours. All work performed in excess of the normal workday or in excess of the normal workweek, or on a day off, shall be paid one and one-half (1½) times the straight hourly wage plus regular day's pay, or one and one-half (1½) times the daily rate of pay, whichever is the higher. Doorman does not get paid for lunch hour.

Facts

The grievant is a night-shift doorman of an apartment building. He is required to work an eight-hour day. Beginning in August 1999, the grievant was sent a letter containing the caption "Second Warning," which spelled out specific instances when he was away from his post for at least a half hour. He was reminded in the letter that his work hours were 3:00 PM to 11:00 PM, with an hour off for dinner and reasonable bathroom breaks. Other than that, he was expected to be at the door. In July 2001, a new collective bargaining agreement (CBA) was entered into that changed the grievant's work shift to 3:00 PM to 12:00 PM, with an unpaid hour for dinner. In August 2001, the company's vice president ("VP") sent a registered letter to the grievant in which she pointed out that he was not working a full 40-hour week. She concluded that letter by stating to him, "Effective immediately, you will work an 8-hour day and a 40-hour week. If you continue to work a short week, you will be suspended without pay." The VP had observed that in addition to the unpaid dinner hour, the grievant was regularly away from his post for 15- or 30-minute periods. This August 2001 letter did not contain any language indicating that it was a warning. In October 2001, the VP asked the building superintendent to document the actual hours being worked by the grievant. The superintendent monitored videotape records from security cameras in the building and documented the grievant's actual hours of work. He showed that the grievant was not working eight hours during his nine-hour shift. The VP sent another letter to the grievant in which she advised him that he was being suspended for a one-week period. The union contends that this suspension was not for proper cause and filed this grievance.

Issue

Was there proper cause to suspend the grievant?

Position of Parties

The company states that the CBA is clear and unambiguous and that it required that employees work an eight-hour day. The grievant has a history of not working the required number of hours in a workday, and he was warned in August 2001 that if he continued not working a full eight-hour day, he would face the consequences of a disciplinary suspension.

It is the union's position that the company is required to provide employees full and adequate notice of an offense before discipline can take place and that it failed to do so in this case. When the grievant received a warning in 1999, the letter was clearly labeled as a warning. The letter the VP sent to the grievant in August 2001 did not spell out that it was a warning letter. Further, under the contract that was in effect prior to July 2001, the grievant worked a shift beginning at 3:00 PM and ending at 11:00 PM. In July 2001, the shift changed, and it ended at midnight with an unpaid dinner hour. The union argues that no one from management ever explained these changes to the grievant and thus that management was to blame for the grievant's misunderstanding of the work hours.

SOURCE: Adapted from *Sagamore Owners*, 116 LA 1574 (Arb. 2002).

QUESTIONS

1. As arbitrator, what would be your award and opinion in this arbitration?
2. Explain why the relevant provisions of the CBA as applied to the facts of this case dictate the award.
3. What actions might the employer and/or the union have taken to avoid this conflict?

Flexible Benefit Decisions

PURPOSE:

To help students gain an understanding of the philosophy behind flexible benefit plans and the individual decision making involved.

TASK:

Management is increasingly striving to negotiate flexible benefit plans as a means of controlling the total cost of employer-paid employee benefits.

If today you were given $1,000 per month in benefit dollars to allocate among the following, what package of benefits would you choose? Complete the following chart by placing a dollar amount for each benefit you choose in the right column:

Benefit	*Benefit Plan Cost*
Pension plan (matched by employer 50/50 up to $500 per month)	
Paid holidays ($50 per day)	
Guaranteed maternity or paternity leave ($50 per day for two weeks per year)	
Medical insurance ($250 per employee, $450 per family)	
Elder care ($50 per week; provides daily care for one adult)	
Health maintenance organization health-care option ($200 per employee, $350 per family)	
Legal insurance ($50 per month)	
Vision care ($50 per month per employee or $75 per month per family)	
Child care ($75 per week per child)	
Cafeteria lunches ($50 per month)	
Tuition reimbursement ($50 per month maximum)	
Funeral leave (three days per death, 6 days per year; maximum, $50)	
Company-sponsored social events (annual picnic, parties, and so on; $10 per month)	
Life insurance ($50 for $100,000)	
Disability insurance ($50 per month)	
Dental insurance ($50 per employee, $75 per family)	
Reserved parking ($50 per month)	

If the total is less than $1,000, the employee and employer split the difference, 50/50. If the total is over $1,000, the employee pays the excess.

CHAPTER 8

Job Security and Seniority

Employers' in the railroad industry proposed in the 2005 contract talks to consolidate engineers, conductors, switchmen, signalmen, firemen, and oilers, into a generic "transportation employee" category. The unions oppose the proposal because it would eliminate minimum crew sizes, which are based on a certain number of each craft working on each train and, therefore, would reduce the number of union jobs. Thus the core issue for the 155,000 union employees and the five largest U. S. railroads was–job security.

Labor News

RAILROAD UNIONS, CARRIERS CLASH OVER JOBS

The 2005 contract talks between the five largest U.S. railroads and the unions that represent about 155,000 employees focused on one issue—job security. Don Hahs, president of the Locomotive Engineers Union, which represents about 30,000 engineers and other railroad workers, said the key issue is the employers' proposal to do away with the traditional crafts, which most unions are based on, and consolidate them into a "transportation employee" category under one collective bargaining agreement. The unions oppose the proposal for three primary reasons: (1) the elimination of minimum crew sizes (based on a certain number of each craft working on each train) would reduce the number of union jobs; (2) the railroad unions are largely organized by crafts (engineers, conductors, switchmen, signalmen, firemen, oilers, and maintenance of way) and the consolidation into one job category would cause conflict among the unions; and (3) safety—the reduction from two workers (engineer, conductor) to one (transportation employee) on most trains may present a public safety problem.

Robert Allen, Chairman of the National Carriers Conference Committee, which represents Burlington Northern and Santa Fe Railway Co., CSX Transportation, Kansas City Southern Co., Norfolk Southern Railway Co., and Union Pacific, believes the current contract requires more workers than are needed on today's modern trains, which are guided by improved technology. Consolidating employee crafts and reducing crew sizes is the goal of the carriers, according to Allen, and "when we can safely operate with one person, that's what we're after."

SOURCE: Adapted from "Unions Fight Freight Rail Carriers' Bargaining Proposals," *2005 Source Book on Collective Bargaining* (Washington, DC: Bureau of National Affairs, 2005), p. 107.

JOB SECURITY

Over the years, workers' interests and demands regarding job security have never waned. Together with wages and benefits, negotiators see job security as a top priority in both good and bad economic times. Job security is viewed by many as simply meaning the guarantee of work. However, in reality it means much more, including the rights to remain employed during times of layoffs, to promotion, and to a fair hearing in cases involving discipline, as well as the need to have work performed by employees within the company rather than subcontracting or increasing the use of automatic equipment. The ultimate job security employment situation occurs in some foreign countries where, after a probationary period, employees are guaranteed a job with good wages and benefits for their entire careers as long as they continue to produce satisfactorily. At the other end of the continuum is the hypothetical lack of job security situations in which management might fire, promote, or lay off employees without rationale or consideration for experience and productivity. Negotiating for better wages or working conditions would be meaningless if management could, without reason or with biased intentions, terminate employees or remove jobs from the workplace.

For example, a three-year-long and often bitter labor dispute between Anheuser-Busch (makers of Budweiser and Michelob) and the International Brotherhood of Teamsters (which includes bottlers, brewers, mechanics, and truck drivers) ended in July 1999 with a new four-year contract. In one case, after more than two years of failed negotiations, Anheuser-Busch imposed its final offer—paying the average Teamster, with overtime, $66,000 a year. Why did the union reject an offer that included the highest pay in the brewing industry? Job security. The members wanted a job security provision and struck the St. Louis plant when negotiations reached an impasse.[1]

The concept of job security has also been termed **industrial jurisprudence** by Sumner Slichter. Slichter's concept contains the primary ingredients of job security in today's collective bargaining: seniority as a determining factor in layoffs, promotions, and transfers; control of entrance to the organization or trade; seniority as a determining factor in job assignments; negotiated management change and work methods and introduction of new machinery; and negotiated wage rates.[2] Industrial jurisprudence generally embodies the principle that a single individual or group of top management officials will not determine the operation of the organization. Instead, the employees are given some rights to guarantee input into important decisions regarding their employment.

Guarantees of work and promotion opportunities are less important in some industries, such as local government and public utilities that have very little variation in the numbers they employ. However, in most manufacturing industries that are heavily unionized, employment variations are great because of changes in consumer demands; thus, job security is a primary concern.

The precedent-setting 1997–1999 UAW–Chrysler agreement, for example, provided a new job employment guarantee program that created a "snapshot" of the workforce at the start of the contract. Then three 100 percent "baseline" employment levels were established at the unit, group, and companywide levels. The agreement then provided that attrition (death, retirement, quitting) cannot allow the employment level to fall below 95 percent of each unit's baseline. The 2003–2007 agreement modified the level to 90 percent, but retained the job security provision. When employment does drop, positions are filled by (1) active employees, (2) a recall of laid-off employees, and (3) new hires.[3]

The ultimate labor–management conflict over job security is a basic and important one. Management believes that it needs to have a free hand in the operation of the workplace to maximize profits and exercise its abilities. In contrast, labor believes that employee experience and skills are critical to productivity. Employees require some protection against unreasonable managers as well as guarantees that important decisions, such as promotions and layoffs, will be made on a rational basis and that favoritism or union busting will be avoided.

Beginning in the 1930s, seniority-based procedures, such as the **last-hired**, **first-fired rule**, became common layoff and recall decision criteria. Various theories support this rule, including the human capital theory, in which employees increase their productivity with experience and rational employers want to retain the more productive employees; the implicit contract theory, in which the career strategy of employers encourages employees to commit themselves to steady productive work (thus, laying off senior employees would cause worker distrust in any career planning); and the internal labor market theory, in which collective bargaining produces rules and procedures to ease the tension between the parties. Seniority-based layoff procedures are a prime example of such rules in limiting management's actions and increasing employee loyalty.[4]

Permanent layoffs are of particular concern to employees because layoffs result in significant reductions in earnings over the course of employees' work lives. Thus, employees

	Percent of Employees				
	All Employers	**By Industry**		**By Size of Bargaining Unit**	
		Manufacturing	*Nonmanufacturing*	*Large*	*Small*
Layoff and recall rights	68%	73%	63%	73%	65%
Promotion	67	72	62	72	64
Subcontracting restrictions	56	52	60	61	55
Advance notice of shutdown	56	63	49	52	59
Transfer rights	45	40	49	64	36
Successorship	38	39	37	39	38
Flexible work scheduling	27	15	40	34	24
Professional development program	16	3	29	27	9
Retraining program	13	15	11	23	
Shared work	5	2	9	11	3

FIGURE 8-1 Job Security Provisions in Contracts

SOURCE: Adapted from The Bureau of National Affairs, *2002 Source Book on Collective Bargaining* (Washington, DC: BNA, Inc. 2002) p. 59. Used by permission. Copyright © 2002 by the Bureau of National Affairs, Inc.

have even stronger expectations that, during economic downswings, employers will reward loyalty.[5] The last-hired, first-fired rule has caused lower permanent separation rates among union workers in comparison with nonunion workers along with more frequent temporary layoffs in the union sector due to senior union members' preference for short layoffs, allowing them to maintain their seniority.[6]

Job security can be provided through a number of contract provisions. About 95 percent of contracts contain one of the job security provisions listed in Figure 8-1, and most contain three or more. In general, contracts with larger unionized workforces contain more job security provisions. Job security, along with wages, health care, and pension benefits, often ranks as one of the top negotiation priorities, especially during hard economic times.[7]

SENIORITY

A seniority system is a set of rules governing the allocation of economic benefits and opportunities on the basis of service with one employer.[8] It is by far the most commonly negotiated means of measuring service and comparing employees for promotion and layoff–recall decisions, thus providing job security.

Seniority is perhaps the most important measure of job security to employees, and the issue of seniority is popular among unions and viewed as critical to job security. Seniority is highly visible because it is so easy to define and measure. Normally, it is calculated in terms of days, beginning with the employee's date of hire and, with a few exceptions, continues over the years during the employee's tenure. Union negotiators will vehemently claim that management, in the absence of a job seniority system, will make promotion, layoff, and other decisions solely on the basis of possible short-run cost savings or individual biases rather than on the objective criteria that seniority easily provides. These criteria include the employee's loyalty to the company and his or her skills and productivity, which increase with time spent on the job.

Management may argue that time worked on the job is only one measure and that the employee's performance record (as well as other criteria, especially performance appraisals completed by supervisors) should be considered. However, performance appraisal systems, even at their best, are heavily dependent on supervisors' objectivity and ability to evaluate honestly and thoroughly individual performance—something that is often very difficult to do. Therefore, performance appraisals are subjective and do not guarantee employees the objectivity and consistency they expect when promotion or layoff decisions are made.

In nonunionized organizations, it certainly is not unheard of for employers to terminate or lay off senior employees who have worked into higher pay grades or junior employees who have unjustifiably suffered a supervisor's contempt. A seniority system provides a means of job security and requires that if a supervisor feels that an employee is unproductive or unable to produce successfully, the supervisor must defend and subject that decision to an agreed-on process. Also, the seniority system utilizes a basic and fair premise that employees who have stayed with the organization longer and provided more service than other employees should be given first preference when all other aspects of the employment decision are equal.

To define fully the concepts of seniority, it may be helpful to distinguish between unionized and nonunionized employer–employee relationships. Seniority is not required by federal or local laws, nor is it an inherent right of employees. However, seniority is a mandatory subject in the collective bargaining process. Strict formal seniority systems are commonplace in virtually all unionized organizations, but they are rare among nonunion employers. In most of the contracts surveyed, seniority played a critical role in the determination of promotion, transfer, and layoff decisions.[9]

CALCULATION OF SENIORITY

In general, seniority is considered to be the process of giving preference in employment decisions on the basis of the length of continuous service with the company. When seniority is involved in promotion considerations, it may be defined as preference in employment on the basis of the length of continuous service and the ability and fitness of the employee to perform the job. New employees generally begin acquiring seniority on the date they are first hired. In the case of two or more employees hired on the same date, the exact time of hire or the alphabetical listing of their last names may determine seniority. Often, however, seniority is not awarded to employees until after the probationary period, even though they begin accruing seniority from their date of first hire.[10] The contract clause that specifically defines seniority can be quite fairly detailed, as in the example of the agreement between E. I. duPont Co. and the Neoprene Craftsmen Union in Figure 8-2. Some clauses may be fairly brief, as the following seniority provision from the agreement between Anaconda Aluminum Company and the Aluminum Workers Trades, AFL-CIO:

Section 1. Plant seniority is defined as an employee's length of continuous service at Anaconda Aluminum Company, division of the Anaconda Company, Columbia Falls reduction plant in Columbia Falls, Montana.

Section 2. Departmental seniority is defined as employee's length of continuous service in a department of the plant.

Section 3. Granted leaves of absence, vacations, and jury duty will not be considered as a break in service. The applicable federal and state laws shall determine re-employment rights of employees who enter the armed forces.[11]

Article IV—Seniority

Section 1. Seniority accrued prior to the effective date of this Agreement shall be that shown on the seniority rosters as of the effective date hereof. Seniority accrued following the effective date of this Agreement shall be an employee's total length of employment acquired since the first day of his last period of unbroken employment or since the effective date of this Agreement, whichever is later, within the bargaining unit, unless otherwise specified in this Article. Such seniority acquired since the effective date of this Agreement shall be calculated and adjusted in the following manner:

(a) The seniority of an employee shall be broken and automatically terminated in case of:
  (1) Discharge for just cause;
  (2) Voluntary quit;
  (3) Absence in excess of sixteen (16) days unless covered by leave of absence;
  (4) Failure to return to work following expiration of leave of absence;
  (5) Termination because of lack of work.

(b) No seniority credit will be given for the time between termination because of lack of work and re-employment. The Plant seniority an employee had at the time of termination because of lack of work shall be used in offering re-employment for a period of three (3) years after date of such termination. A former employee who has been terminated because of lack of work for less than three (3) years will be offered re-employment in accordance with his Plant seniority before new employees are hired, provided such former employee is basically qualified to do the work to be performed. A former employee who has been terminated because of lack of work and who is re-employed shall be credited with the seniority he had prior to his termination; provided that an employee who has not completed his probation period shall begin a new one hundred and twenty (120) day probation period. A former employee who has been terminated because of lack of work will not be eligible for credit of prior seniority nor for other offers of re-employment under the provisions of this Section 1 (b) if he fails to notify the COMPANY of his intent to return to work within one (1) week after notice to return to work has been sent by registered letter to his last known address, or if he fails to report for work within two (2) weeks after notice has been sent by registered letter to his last known address.

(c) Service outside this bargaining unit in other parts of this Plant will be credited only (a) if such credit was given under prior Agreements between the parties and is included in seniority shown on the seniority roster as of the effective date hereof, or (b) if such credit is provided for by other provisions of this Article.

(d) Plant seniority shall be the employee's total creditable seniority within the bargaining unit. If two (2) or more employees have the same Plant seniority date, their names shall be listed in alphabetical order. The name change of an employee shall not affect such listing.

Section 2. An employee shall exercise Plant Seniority only in the Master Division and unit in which he is employed. For the purpose of this Article the four (4) Master Divisions and the units which comprise these Divisions are as follows:

Engineering Master Division
  Each Individual Engineering Unit
Operations Master Division
  Monomer Operations
  Poly Operations
  "Freon" Operations

FIGURE 8-2   Agreement on the Terms of Seniority

> Laboratory
> Power and Refrigeration Operations

Auxiliary Master Division

> Poly Clean-up Operators (Including Water Blasters and Leader-Water Blasters)

Stores Attendants
Monomer Helpers
Diesel Railroad Crew
Labor Unit (Including Power Helpers and Maintenance Helpers)
Service Unit (Including Laboratory Stores Attendant)
Fireman Master Division

Section 3.

(a) An employee may transfer from one Master Division to another only under the provisions of Section 5 (c) pertaining to re-employment and return, or Section 5 (d) pertaining to job bidding, Section 3 (b), or Section 7 pertaining to reduction of force, of this Article except that the transfer of an employee with a disability may be negotiated between parties. On a case-by-case basis the parties may agree on the transfer of an employee from one seniority unit to another.

(b) An employee's "home" unit shall be that unit in which he was first employed. However, if thereafter he has been transferred to another unit because of disability or in accordance with Section 5 (c), (d) or 5 (e) of this Article, then his "home" unit shall be the unit as indicated in these Sections 5 (c), (d), or (e).

Section 4. Seniority rosters shall be maintained by the COMPANY, kept in the Employment Office and shall be available to the UNION. Such rosters shall show each employee's relative position within their Master Division and unit.

Section 5. When job vacancies in a unit occur, they will be filled in the following order:

(a) By Promotions. Promotions shall be made within a given unit on the basis of Plant seniority provided the employees have approximately the same qualifications and are qualified to perform the job.

(b) By the voluntary return of eligible employees within the Master Division to their "home" units. Eligible employees are those who have been involuntarily displaced from their unit. Employees will be offered the vacancy and if they refuse this opportunity, their present unit will become their "home" unit. Employees who volunteer shall be returned to their "home" unit in Plant seniority order, the employee with the most seniority returning first.

(c) By return of employees outside of Master Division to their "home" Master Division.

(d) By job bidding. Job bidding, subject to agreement by the parties on a case-by-case basis, may be limited to the employees of a Master Division, but if not so limited, shall be on a bargaining unit basis. A general announcement regarding vacancies will be posted at least two calendar weeks in advance of selection of successful bidders. Ability, skill, knowledge and training being approximately equal, the candidate having the most Plant Seniority within the bargaining unit shall be selected to fill such vacancy, provided he meets established requirements of the job vacancy. Successful candidates will be transferred to the bid job as soon as it is practical to do so. Each will be notified of his transfer date as much in advance as practical. This provision will not require the COMPANY to drop below a minimum level of experience and skill necessary to properly perform the work in any unit. An employee may job bid to any job with a higher straight-time rate. However, a new employee, or a successful job bidder, may not job bid to a job which does not have a higher straight-time rate for a period of three (3) years from the date they are

continued

FIGURE 8-2 Agreement on the Terms of Seniority (Continued)

declared a successful bidder. All of the above notwithstanding, subject to agreement of the parties on a case-by-case basis, an employee who has been transferred in accordance with his bid may be returned to his former Master Division.

(e) Re-employment shall be in accord with Section 1(b) of this article and in Plant Seniority order with the qualified former employee having the most such seniority returning first. They shall have indefinite return rights to their "home" Master Division and shall be offered one opportunity to return to that Division that (A) vacancy occurs; provided, they are still basically qualified for the vacant job. Eligible employees will be offered the vacant job and if refused, their present unit will become their home unit.

(f) By hiring of new employees (at management's discretion).

Section 6. When new jobs are established on the Plant, they will be filled in the following order:

(a) By job bidding as provided in Section 5 (d) of this Article.
(b) By re-employment and hiring as provided in sections 5(e) and (f) of this article.

Section 7. Plant Seniority shall be used to select employees for transfer in a reduction of force in a Master Division, provided employees to be retained in the Division must have collectively sufficient qualifications to perform all the jobs in the Master Division.

FIGURE 8-2   Agreement on the Terms of Seniority (Continued)

SOURCE: Agreement between E. I. duPont de Nemours and Company and the Neoprene Craftsmen Union (1994).

Seniority List

Most agreements have the company prepare and post a **seniority list** (or roster, as in Section 4 of Figure 8-2) so that there will be no question about employee, department, or plantwide seniority. There must be total agreement as to the exact calculation and order of employees on seniority lists. The method of displaying seniority lists is usually a matter for local negotiation between labor and management. Many contracts provide that seniority lists are updated monthly and that they contain the employee's name, occupational group or department, any specific skilled trades date of entry, and related seniority. Any disputes over seniority lists are taken through the grievance procedure for resolution, as seen in Case 8-1.

Depending on the particular labor agreement, seniority rights are vested within a variety of employee units. The most common unit is **plantwide seniority**, in which an individual employee receives credit that becomes applicable whenever that employee competes with any other employee from another unit for the same position. Plantwide seniority first appeared in the duPont contract in Figure 8-2 in 1943. That year, according to union negotiator Archie V. Carrell, it was the top priority of the members, who wanted job security over members of a new unit. Thus, the provision in 1943 stated that "with respect to reduction of force," seniority shall be determined by "length of continuous service at the plant," therefore providing security to current union members over those of the new unit.[12]

Other common seniority units include departmental, trade, classification, and companywide. In a **departmental seniority system**, employees accrue seniority according to the amount of time they worked within a particular department, and that seniority credit is valid only within that department.[13] For example, an employee with 11 years seniority in department X could not successfully compete with an employee with seven years in department Y for an open position in department Y.

DOVETAILING SENIORITY LISTS

Employees worked for an unincorporated division, Division 1, of the company. The company also operated a second incorporated division in another state, Division 2. Each division had a separate collective bargaining agreement (CBA).

The company announced plans to relocate the Division 2 operations and workers to Division 1. It proposed to "dovetail" (i.e., integrate) the Division 2 seniority list into the Division 1 seniority list. The alternative would have been to "end-tail" the Division 2 workers, that is, treat them as new employees and eliminate their Division 2 seniority. The workers at the Division 1 plant filed a grievance protesting the dovetailing proposal, and the matter was submitted to arbitration.

The basic dispute that drove the arbitration was whether Division 1 and Division 2 were separate "employers" or whether the company should be considered the "employer" of the workers at both divisions. Under both CBAs, the term "employer" was defined as the division, "seniority" as "continuous service with the employer," and the company was not mentioned by name.

The company argued that it was the employer for both divisions. It pointed out that Division 1 was not a separate legal entity. It operated out of the same facility as the company until 1987. The two divisions had the same president and the same accounting and administrative staff. Both divisions had substantially the same working conditions and pay rates. And virtually all the work was interchangeable between workers in the two divisions.

The employees of Division 1 argued that neither of the CBAs provided for the consolidation of the two divisions and that a "no-modification" clause in both contracts precluded the dovetailing of the seniority lists.

DECISION

The arbitrator found, nonetheless, that the company had the authority to dovetail the two seniority lists. First, the arbitrator determined that the company was the de facto employer of the workers at both divisions based on the history of company's development, the shared administrative and executive operations of the two divisions, and the fact that "Division 1" was merely an unregistered trade name, not a separate legal entity.

And although the two CBAs did not explicitly provide for dovetailing, they did not preclude it either. Allowing for dovetailing was a permissible interpretation of the agreement under the changed circumstances presented by the consolidation of work. As the arbitrator noted, the "grievance and arbitration procedures are part and parcel of the ongoing process of collective bargaining. It is through these processes that the supplementary rules of the plant are established."

SOURCE: Adapted from *Division 1 v. R.W.F. Inc.*, 144 LRRM 2649 (1993).

Classification seniority, similar to departmental seniority, provides for employee seniority only within the same job classification. Companywide seniority systems combine all employees from various locations and types of facilities. When two employees compete for an open position in a companywide system, individual experience, length of service, and related departments or job classifications are not considered, only the seniority with the company. This provision makes companywide seniority the most impractical and infrequently used.

Companies often use a seniority system combining plantwide seniority with departmental seniority. Plantwide seniority may be utilized for determining layoffs, vacations, and other specific benefits. Departmental seniority is often used to determine eligibility for a promotion or a transfer so that employees with specific skills and related job experience can be considered for new positions. However, in the case of layoffs, it is often believed that employees' total work experience, and therefore their plantwide seniority, is the most important job security factor.

In situations involving layoffs, seniority systems often use bumping (63 percent of all contracts). **Bumping** occurs when employees with greater seniority whose jobs have been phased out have the right to displace employees with less seniority. Most bumping clauses require that employees be as qualified as the junior employee.[14] For example, in a 2002 case, an arbitrator denied a more senior employee the right to bump a junior employee because the agreement specified that to bump another employee a person must be qualified to perform the work. The senior employee had been fired for poor performance and then reinstated. When he tried to bump a junior employee the company denied his request. The arbitrator upheld the denial citing the agreement language because the senior employee was not as qualified as the junior employee.[15]

Seniority and the ADA

In a historic 2002 decision, the Supreme Court ruled that an employee is not entitled to a job assignment as a reasonable accommodation of his disability under the Americans with Disabilities Act (ADA) if the assignment would conflict with the rules of a seniority system. The decision in *U.S. Airways, Inc. v. Barnett* supported seniority systems when they are in conflict with the ADA in a similar situation. In the case, Barnett, a freight handler injured his back and then used his seniority to transfer to the mailroom. Two senior employees, however, exercised their seniority and bumped Barnett from the mailroom. Barnett asked to remain in the mailroom as a reasonable accommodation of his disability. U.S. Airways declined his request because it would have been counter to the seniority system in the contract. The Equal Employment Opportunity Commission concluded that U.S. Airways had discriminated against Barnett by denying him reasonable accommodation. The Supreme Court, however, held that the requested accommodation was in conflict with the rules of a bona fide and established seniority system and thus was not a reasonable accommodation.[16]

Superseniority

Union officers and committee personnel may be given preferred seniority rights for layoff and recall situations. This is often referred to as superseniority and is granted in the collective bargaining agreement so that union stewards and other labor officials will continue to work during periods of layoff, thus enabling the union to continue to operate effectively. When agreeing to superseniority for the union, management may ensure that certain labor relations personnel be similarly protected against layoffs. Some superseniority clauses require that protected union officials have the ability to perform available work or that superseniority is provided only within departments or job classifications. Others limit superseniority to those union officials who perform steward duties, such as grievance processing and contract administration.[17]

The value of superseniority depends on the frequency and degree of layoffs typically experienced by the company. In some cases, it is virtually meaningless because union stewards and officials have high levels of seniority from their many years of experience with the union and company.

The labor agreement should explicitly specify under what conditions an employee might lose seniority. Virtually all contracts provide that employees lose seniority if they voluntarily quit or are discharged. Employees who do not report back to work after a vacation or other leave of absence for an excessive period of time may also be deprived of their seniority. Usually employees on layoff will retain and accumulate seniority for a period of time specified within the agreement.

PROMOTIONS

Management often disagrees with the use of seniority to determine promotion decisions. The Bureau of National Affairs estimates that seniority is a determining factor in promotional policies as provided by collective bargaining agreements in 67 percent of labor contracts. However, only 5 percent call for promotion decisions based on seniority as the sole determiner. Another 49 percent provide that the most senior individual will receive promotion among those equally qualified, and 40 percent provide seniority as one factor along with "skill and ability."[18]

Some contract clauses that allow promotion according to seniority simply state that promotions to fill vacancies or new job positions on a permanent basis will be based on length of service within the company and employee skill and ability. Determining which employees have the required skill and ability is difficult and subjective. Management generally contends that promotion should be based on an employee's individual performance and required skills rather than on length of service.

When labor agreements provide that promotional decisions will be made according to seniority and job skills, it is difficult to determine the weight of each factor and the measurement of individual skills. Although seniority is a factor in promotion decisions in most labor contracts, it is usually not considered to be as important as ability to perform the job. Quite frequently, ability becomes more dominant. When management decides to promote a less senior employee on the basis of higher demonstrated ability, employee grievances may result, as in Case 8-2. Management must prove that the more senior employee does not have the ability to perform the job.

Managers may argue that making important promotional decisions solely on length of service takes away employee incentive. Employees will tend to perform at the status quo, knowing that they cannot be promoted before all the senior employees and that, when their turn comes, no one can take the promotion away from them. Labor leaders point out that seniority can be objectively and easily measured. Therefore, promotion decisions based on seniority are far less subject to supervisor bias or inability to correctly assess individual performance and skills.

Arbitrators have generally held that management has the right to judge, weigh, and determine qualifications as long as the methods are fair and nondiscriminatory. However, if a clause provides that seniority alone is the deciding factor, then management cannot promote a "better qualified" person if the senior employee is "capable of doing the work." When ability and seniority are equal factors, arbitrators generally allow management the right to make the selection, subject to a union challenge that the decision was unreasonable (given the facts), capricious, arbitrary, or discriminatory. In most disputed cases, the employer's decision is supported, and when the position is a supervisory one, management has unquestioned authority. Contract clauses dealing with promotion apply only to positions within the bargaining unit.[19] Why? It is generally held that management has complete authority to "select its own." And, unless clearly restricted by the Agreement, it is generally held that management has the right to fill temporary vacancies caused by illness, vacations, and so forth.

What weights are given to seniority and ability in actual promotion decisions? Is there a difference between union and nonunion employers? An analysis of more than 600 U.S. firms indicated that 60 percent give the person with greater seniority a preference

PROMOTIONS

The company operates a plant in Mississippi. A position came open as a result of the resignation of the incumbent. The open position was posted, and four employees bid on the job and were interviewed concerning their interest. Employee Studdard, whose plant seniority date was November 17, 1980, was selected. Another employee, Welch, whose seniority date was September 9, 1980, filed a grievance. The union's contentions in Welch's grievance were that management had violated the contract concerning job promotions that stated that the job was to be assigned within seven calendar days to the bidder who had the apparent ability to perform the work and the greatest plant seniority. The union contended that the company had passed over a senior employee without showing that the employee was incapable of performing the job in favor of an employee who was admittedly more qualified. But because the collective bargaining agreement requires only that the bidder with the greatest plant seniority have the apparent ability to perform the work, the company violated the agreement.

The position of the company was that it was not a stringent seniority clause and allowed the company some discretion in selecting the bidder who had the most experience, qualifications, and leadership abilities to perform the job.

DECISION

The arbitrator in this case decided for the union. He found that, although the seniority clause concerning promotions in this contract was a modified seniority clause, it did give the senior employee preference. Although some modified clauses compared the relative ability of a senior and junior employee and promoted the senior only if those abilities were equal, this particular collective bargaining agreement clause required that the senior employee be given preference if he possessed only sufficient ability to perform the job. Therefore, the company was to determine the seniority date of the employees bidding on the job and whether the most senior employee had the apparent ability to perform the work. The interpretation of apparent was understood merely to exclude obviously unqualified bidders and not to allow for comparison among those bidding. If the most senior employee apparently had the ability to perform the job, he would have to be appointed.

SOURCE: Adapted from *American Sawmill Machine Company,* 79 LA 106 (1982).

in promotion decisions. In practice, both union and nonunion employers reported giving length of service more weight in promotion decisions than required by written policy or union contract. Although union employers reported using seniority to a greater extent, the difference in comparison with nonunion employers was not significant.[20]

Nonunion organizations often have promotion policies based primarily on promoting from within to boost employee morale and assure individuals that they can work hard and get ahead. Like union organizations, they hesitate to promote a less senior employee unless there is concrete evidence to show that a more senior employee is less capable. The effect of such a promotion on general employee morale, as well as on the individual involved, also needs to be determined.

Job Bidding

It is quite common for the **job bidding** process to be detailed in the labor agreement to minimize misunderstandings and grievances and to increase employee morale. An example of a detailed job bidding process follows.

1. When a new classification is created or an opening occurs in the existing classification, the opening will be posted on the official bid bulletin boards for a period of four working days, Saturdays, Sundays, and holidays excluded.

2. Bids for such openings will be received from any permanent employee. Temporary employees will not be allowed to bid.

3. Bids will be awarded on an **up-bid**, **down-bid**, or **lateral bid**. An up-bid is a bid classification. A lateral bid is from one classification to another classification in the same pay grade or from one pool position to another regardless of pay grade. A down-bid is from a higher pay grade to a lower pay grade or from a specific line classification to a pool classification.

4. Bids will be based on plant seniority and competency with the following regulations applying:

   a. Bids to be classifications and specific lines of progression: An employee awarded a job bid in one specific line cannot bid again for one year from the date qualified in the specific line job except on an up-bid basis within his specific line progression.

   b. Bids to classifications in the pool: An employee who down-bids from a specific line of progression to a pool position cannot bid again for a period of six months from the date classified except to a specific line. Or an employee classified in a pool position who down-bids or laterally bids to another pool position cannot bid again for a period of six months from the date classified except through a specific line.

   c. Down-bids from classification and pay grades 12 and above will be limited to a maximum of one down-bid per classification in any one 60-day period.[21]

LAYOFF AND RECALL RIGHTS

Employers also question the use of seniority as the sole decision criterion in **layoff** and **recall** situations. Employers argue that ability should be a greater factor in determining layoff and recall of employees. However, because layoff and recall situations are usually seen as temporary, management's argument against the use of seniority is considerably weakened. Also, in layoff and recall situations, there is less of a question of the employee's ability because he or she had been performing the job satisfactorily before a layoff occurred. Thus, management has little room to argue that seniority is not more important in layoff and recall than in promotion decisions.

In most labor contracts, probationary employees will be laid off first, with further necessary layoffs being made in accordance with plantwide seniority. Laid-off employees may be given the opportunity to exercise their plantwide seniority and bump employees at the bottom of the seniority list rather than be laid off. When skilled trades or other specialized job classifications are involved, layoffs will commonly occur by seniority within the trades or classifications. Most agreements also provide that the company gives reasonable notice and reasons for upcoming layoffs to the unions. If the workforce is increased after a layoff, contracts usually provide that laid-off employees will be recalled according to plantwide seniority for appropriate jobs.

Contract layoff procedures may fall into three general categories: layoff based entirely on seniority, layoff based on seniority among those employees who management feels are capable of performing the work, and layoff based on seniority only if ability and other factors are equal among affected employees. When the last two methods of layoff and recall procedures are utilized, grievances are likely to be filed because of the

Seniority is often the sole contract criteria in deciding the layoff and recall order of employees.

subjectivity of determining an employee's ability to perform work, especially when bumping is used and employees are performing new jobs.[22] If a contract provides that seniority and equal ability shall govern in layoff and recall decisions, arbitrators are likely to interpret *equal* as meaning not exactly equal but relatively equal. When contracts provide that ability should be part of the determination in layoff and recall decisions, arbitrators' awards have suggested certain guidelines be considered.[23] Some of the guidelines include the following.

1. When seniority is considered a governing criterion if ability to perform the work is relatively equal, then only the employee's seniority should be considered.[24]
2. A junior employee could be given preference over a senior employee if the senior requires a much greater amount of supervision in performing the job.[25]
3. Senior employees can be required to demonstrate ability to perform the work by passing a test that would qualify them for jobs held by junior employees.[26]

In cases involving temporary or emergency layoffs, management is often given more flexibility in selecting employees than in indefinite layoffs. If the contract does not specify differences in procedure involving temporary layoffs and indefinite layoffs, arbitrators have generally held that ordinary layoff procedures must be followed even where the lack of work lasted only a few hours or one to two days. However, the more common ruling of arbitrators in such situations has been that cumbersome seniority rules need not be followed to the letter in a brief layoff. Arbitrators have even held that in layoffs caused by emergency breakdowns or natural or unforeseen disasters, seniority rules can be disregarded if necessary. However, if the application of seniority rules in the contract does not cause a hardship during the emergency, the employer is advised to follow the contract layoff procedures.[27] The following is a concise layoff and recall contract clause setting forth the procedure and notification requirements and possible emergency exceptions.

ARTICLE 10 REDUCTION OF FORCES

a. The company agrees that in the event of a reduction in force, plant seniority shall govern and employees covered by the terms of this agreement shall be laid off in the inverse order of seniority, provided that the employee retained has the ability to fill the job. He shall have a reasonable length of time to demonstrate his ability to hold the job.

b. If an emergency such as fire, flood, storm, or major breakdown occurs during a workweek, every effort will be made to avoid loss of work and/or to reassign employees on a basis of seniority. However, it is recognized that a layoff out of seniority not exceeding one day may be necessary to avoid a payment of penalty pay.

c. Whenever a reduction in force is necessary, the company will post the names of the employees to be laid off at least three days, excluding Saturday, Sunday, and holidays, prior to such reduction unless cancellation of orders, changes in customer's requirements, breakdowns, or accidents or other emergencies make such notices impossible, in which case a union will be immediately notified.

   When the company again adds to the number of employees, those laid off shall be reemployed in the order of their seniority. A notice of recall or restoration shall be sent by registered mail to the last known address of the employee, and a copy of the notice, before it is mailed, shall be given to the properly designated officer of the union. It shall be the duty of the employee to keep the company informed as to his correct address.[28]

Typically, the only exceptions to the use of seniority as the total or partial determinant in layoff and recall decisions occur when probationary employees are laid off first without any discussion of ability to perform or in cases involving superseniority when union officials are laid off last.

Regarding seniority rights involving layoffs by companies or governmental agencies subject to court-ordered affirmative action plans, the Supreme Court, in *Firefighters Local Union No. 1784 v. Stotts,*[29] upheld a seniority system, even though the resulting layoffs adversely affected blacks hired under a consent decree to remedy past discrimination. The Court would not allow the consent decree, which had not dealt with the layoff issue, to be given preference over a collectively bargained seniority system. Advocates of affirmative action plans fear that this decision, reaffirming the last-hired, first-fired philosophy, will undermine equal opportunity employment strides made in the last few years. Labor leaders, however, defend the protection afforded by seniority systems as necessary to preserve a basic negotiated job right. They argue that changed hiring practices giving women and blacks more job opportunities will eventually lead to their seniority in the various systems. Increased employment and secure job rights will accomplish the desired affirmative action goals without adversely affecting the senior worker.

In some situations, the hiring of temporary workers may be a key to an employer's remaining competitive. Management may negotiate the right to hire a higher percentage of temporary workers. The union may want the ability to add the temporary workers to its membership and collect dues from them. Most contracts will restrict management's use of temporary workers but allow a higher percentage if the union approves. The union is more likely to approve if the temporaries might be transitioned to additional permanent workers within the bargaining unit.[30]

ADVANCED NOTICE OF SHUTDOWN

Worker Adjustment and Retraining Notification Act

In 1989, the **Worker Adjustment and Retraining Notification Act (WARN)**, more commonly known as the Plant Closing Act, became effective.[31] The general purpose of the law is to "warn" workers and local communities of plant closing or mass layoff decisions by requiring employers to provide advance notice in either situation. The AFL-CIO and other labor forces lobbied for a similar bill, which was vetoed in 1988. However, the pressures of the 1988 presidential election contributed to President Reagan's decision to allow WARN to become law without his signature. The U.S. Chamber of Commerce strongly opposed the plant closings bill. However, corporate officials at Ford Motor Company, Eastman Kodak, Whirlpool Corporation, and other companies noted that WARN mandates less notice than most firms have voluntarily given workers.[32]

The act requires employers to provide 60 days' advance written notice of either a plant closing or a mass layoff once the decision is made by management. A plant closing is defined as the permanent shutdown of a single site or one or more operating units that causes an employment loss of 30 days or more for 50 or more employees, excluding part-time workers. The law requires written notification even when other employees remain working if 50 or more are included in the shutdown. Advance notice of a temporary shutdown decision is required if the action affects, for more than six months, at least 50 employees and 33 percent of all employees—or whenever 500 or more employees are affected. Advance written notice of 60 days is also required when mass layoff decisions will affect at least 50 full-time workers and 33 percent of all employees or whenever 500 or more are affected.

Employers covered by the act include most private-sector and nonprofit organizations that employ 100 or more full-time workers. Federal, state, and local government operations are not included in the law. Major exemptions from the law include sudden and unforeseen economic circumstances, natural disasters, and faltering companies actively raising capital to keep a facility open.

These exemptions could bring the effectiveness of WARN into question. For example, one company claimed that it could not give the 60-day warning because of unforeseen circumstances when, in fact, the company had one major client, and that client had begun pulling back its business in late March and continued to do so in increments until late June, when the plant closed. The Court accepted the company's representation that up to the day of the plant closing, it could not have predicted the event.[33] Unions achieved an important section within the law, which provides that the act does not supersede state laws or collective bargaining agreements that require additional notice or assistance to workers. In 2002, about half of all contracts provided additional notice beyond that required by WARN.[34]

The greatest advantage of advance notification is that workers and their community are given time to prepare for the action. For example, workers near retirement may inquire as to the status of their pension and decide to retire without unnecessary psychological strain. Other workers may choose to enter retraining programs offered by the employer or community agencies, and some will secure new jobs and thus avoid weeks or months of unemployment. In some cases, the additional notice can provide the time necessary for community, union, and company leaders to find a means of keeping the plant open. A most persuasive argument is simply the humanitarian issue. Studies show that the incidence of alcoholism, suicide, child abuse, ulcers, and heart attacks increases to an alarming extent when workers are subject to plant closure.[35] In 1982, General Motors Corporation shut down its Fremont, California, automobile assembly plant, giving only three weeks' notice. A year later, Ford Motor Company shut down the nearby San Jose, California, plant, giving six months' notice and an extensive program of counseling, job training, and job search assistance. The total suicides at General Motors was eight—at Ford, none.[36]

In a landmark 1996 decision the Supreme Court recognized a new role for unions under WARN. In *United Food and Commercial Workers Union Local 751 v. Brown Group, Inc.,* the Court ruled that if an employer fails to give sufficient notice of a plant closing, the union may sue on behalf of the affected workers. The decision increased the authority of unions and will likely lead to similar suits because employees are usually hesitant to sue former employers for fear of retaliation. In *Brown,* the company had sent a letter to the United Food and Commercial Workers Union indicating a plan to shut down operations in two months. However, the union filed a suit under WARN because Brown Shoe Company had already laid off some workers. The union won 60 days' back pay for each of its workers.[37]

In another case, the Court found that, because the federal act had no time limitations on the bringing of a suit under it for failure to comply with its provisions, the laws in each state would be applied to determine the timeliness of the lawsuit. This interpretation will mean that in one state an employee might have one year to bring a suit against the employer for failure to notify of a plant closing and that in another state an employee could have five years.[38]

SHARED WORK

Workers who have their work time (and therefore pay) reduced have become more numerous as management strives to cut personnel costs and remain competitive. This **shared work** concept has affected workers who had their hours cut one day per week (short time) but at least retained their jobs and 80 percent of their income. Union leaders pressured to accept this proposal can rationalize that it is preferable for 100 percent of the employees to work 80 percent of their regular hours than to have 80 percent work 100 percent of their regular hours and have 20 percent laid off. Before the 1980s, short-time workers were ineligible for any unemployment insurance benefits because they continued to work a reduced number of hours each week. Thus, a "prolayoff" bias existed because many would prefer total layoff, which would enable them to receive unemployment benefits.

Overall, the AFL-CIO has supported the short-time compensation concept as a means of reducing the number of workers who must experience the extreme hardships of total unemployment. However, the AFL-CIO does not endorse long-term use of shared work or view it as an alternative to the creation of permanent full-time jobs. In general, management has been slow to endorse the concept.[39]

DETERMINING ABILITY

In general, the burden of proof is placed on the employer to show that a bypassed senior employee is not competent for the job during promotions or layoff or recall actions. However, employers are not required to show that junior employees are more competent. When seniority and ability are given practically equal weight in contract clauses, arbitrators expect the employer to prove whether the ability factor was given greater weight than the seniority factor. In general, even though arbitrators may speak in terms of burden of proof when management's decision regarding a passed over employee's ability is challenged, both parties are expected to produce any evidence supporting their respective positions.[40]

Although it is generally agreed that management has the right to determine how ability is to be measured in cases involving promotion or layoff and recall decisions, there is no federal law or agreed-on formula to specify exactly how such decisions should be made. Management generally uses a variety of factors to determine the ability to perform a job, including: performance, tests, a trial period, disciplinary records, merit evaluations, and education, as long as they are job related.[41] The specific factors may be limited by the contract clause prevailing in a given situation. However, the absence of any such clause gives management the freedom to determine its own factors and measurements. The factors or criteria most commonly used to determine an employee's ability to perform the job and make decisions of promotion or recall are summarized here.

1. ***Tests.***   Appropriate written, oral, performance, physical ability, and aptitude tests have been used to determine the ability of competing employees. Most arbitrators look very favorably on the use of appropriate tests as fair and objective means of determining employee fitness to perform the job. Arbitrators have generally held that tests, to be used validly to determine ability, must be
   a. Related to the job requirements
   b. Fair and reasonable
   c. Administered in good faith and without discrimination
   d. Properly evaluated
2. ***Experience.***   This is the extent to which an employee has performed the particular job or relevant type of work and is completely separate from seniority. In most situations, experience is an important related factor considered by management to determine an employee's fitness and ability to perform the job. If other factors are approximately equal and the senior employee has had satisfactory experience performing the job in some capacity, experience may be considered the most important criterion. However, experience on the particular job in question is far more valuable than experience on related jobs.
3. ***Trial period.***   Some contract clauses provide that a trial or break-in period be given to the senior employee so that his or her ability to perform the job is directly tested. The absence of such a specific provision gives management more flexibility in deciding whether to give the senior employee a trial period. Some arbitrators consider a fair trial period the best test of an employee's ability. However, management is not required to give the employee training on the job but instead allows a temporary period to determine whether the employee has the ability. Thus, arbitrators have generally concluded that if there is a reasonable doubt as to the ability of the senior employee, a trial period should be granted unless it would cause serious inconvenience to the company. Most trial periods are 30 days or less.
4. ***Opinion of supervisor.***   The opinion of the supervisor to determine ability is seriously considered only if supported by factual evidence such as production records, merit ratings, or other specific job-related information. Periodic performance evaluations by supervisors are often an essential part of this documentation. Such merit ratings or rating scales generally include factors such as quality of work, knowledge of the job, cooperation with others, ability to accept orders, and attitude. When several levels of supervision reach a similar decision, it is given greater weight.
5. ***Educational background.***   Employee training on or off the job can be considered an important criterion. Such training must be related to the specific job in question. The employee's formal education can also be considered if it is pertinent to the job. Technical training is considered highly pertinent if related to the job.

6. ***Production records.***   Management may rely heavily on an employee's production record as evidence of fitness and ability to perform the job. Certainly, an employee's past output reflects not only skills and abilities but also motivation and effort. If there is a considerable difference among competing employees, arbitrators have held that management can consider production records as the sole factor if the selection is based on ability.

7. ***Attendance records.***   If a senior employee has a particularly poor attendance record, he or she may be bypassed. Arbitrators have generally upheld the promotion of a junior employee over a senior employee on the basis of great differences in their attendance records. The same is true if the senior employee has a poor disciplinary record.

8. ***Psychological and physical fitness.***   Contracts may specify physical and mental fitness as a job requirement. Arbitrators will generally favor recent medical evidence and discard dated medical records. Unless prohibited by contract, management can require competing employees to take physical or mental examinations if all employees are required to take such examinations and the results are job related. A particular physical defect or limitation limiting the employee's ability to perform the job can be considered a pertinent reason to bypass a senior employee. Arbitrators have even upheld management's decision to bypass a senior employee on the grounds of obesity if it has to some extent affected the employee's past work performance. An employee's temperament or nervousness, as exhibited in past job performance, may also disqualify a senior employee.

9. ***Attitude.***   An employee's spirit of cooperation, care for materials, concern for others, and response to instruction may be considered, depending on the job.[42]

COMPANY MERGERS

When separate companies or different entities merge, how the seniority lists of the two are combined is a critical question. The merger must specify which principle of combining seniority lists will be utilized. One of the most commonly used methods is the **Surviving Group Principle**, in which seniority lists are merged by adding the names of the employees of the acquired company to the bottom of the acquiring company. Thus, all the employees of the acquiring company receive greater seniority consideration than any employee of the acquired company.

Another method, the **Length of Service Principle**, is used when an employee's length of service is considered, regardless of which company he or she worked for prior to the merger; therefore, the two seniority lists are combined, with no employee losing any previously earned seniority. With the **Follow the Work Principle**, employees are allowed to continue previously earned seniority on separate seniority lists when their work with the merged company can be separately identified. The **Absolute Rank Principle** gives employees rank positions on the merging seniority lists equal to their rank position on the prior seniority lists. Therefore, two employees will be ranked first, followed by two being ranked second, followed by two being ranked third, and so on.

The **Ratio-Rank Principle** combines seniority lists by establishing a ratio based on the total number of employees in the two groups to be merged. If group A has 150 employees and group B has 50 employees, the ratio is three to one, and of the first four places on the new seniority lists, the three ranked highest in group A will be given positions 1, 2, and 3, and the highest-ranked position in group B will be given rank 4.[43]

Any one principle, especially length of service, may be selected or a combination of methods may be used to combine seniority lists of merged units or companies, with weight being given to the different principles. For example, in merging two airline pilot seniority lists, one-third weight was given to the Ratio-Rank Principle and two-thirds to the Length of Service Principle.[44]

Subcontracting, Outsourcing, and Relocating

Although few problems arise when there are specific contract restrictions on management's rights to subcontract, management's insistence on freedom in this area often leads to grievances. A grievance over management's right to subcontract (or **outsource**) work during the agreement often results in arbitration. In the past, many arbitrators held that management has the right to subcontract work through independent contractors; however, in recent years, this practice has been somewhat restricted by arbitrators.

What is subcontracting? It has been termed the "Twilight Zone" of management rights in collective bargaining and is considered a headache by both labor and management. Basically, **subcontracting** may be defined as arranging to make goods or perform services with another firm that could be accomplished by the bargaining unit employees within the company's current facilities.[45]

Contract provisions against subcontracting may carry over to new employers, as when the Communication Workers of America won a $6 million settlement from AT&T over subcontracting. The 130 workers who won reinstatement of their jobs claimed that AT&T had violated the subcontracting clause contained in their agreement with Pennsylvania Bell. The breakup of the Bell system shifted the workers to AT&T, where they were laid off, and their work, primarily wiring and installation of telephones, was contracted out. The union won reinstatement of their jobs and back pay for the 130 workers and, in addition, won back pay for another 900 workers and resolved more than 100 pending arbitration cases.[46]

Many union leaders and arbitrators believe that the recognition clause recognizing the union as the exclusive bargaining agent implies an agreement that the employer may not remove work from employees in the unit by subcontracting it to others during the life of an agreement. However, others argue that the National Labor Relations Act requires recognition of the union as a representative of people and not work; the purpose of the recognition clause is to enunciate the legal status of the bargaining unit required by the act. The clause merely describes the unit of the employees for whom the union speaks and thus delineates the agreement in terms of those employees covered. Therefore, it does not deal with and has no bearing on any specific employment terms or conditions. The decision was made, however, in a 1964 Supreme Court ruling, *Fibreboard Paper Products Corp. v. NLRB*, that subcontracting was a mandatory subject for collective bargaining.[47]

An example of a contract clause limiting the ability of management to subcontract is provided in Figure 8-3. This example, however, will allow management to subcontract work.

Management could subcontract work currently being performed by employees of the bargaining unit through another employer that has an agreement with the union. Thus, no union jobs are lost to lower-paid nonunion workers.

The historic agreement between the UAW and Ford Motor Company in 1996 included a unique outsourcing provision. As Figure 8-4 describes, the provision requires confidential notification by Ford when outsourcing is considered, the work involved, the reason for outsourcing, the impact on the workforce, and most important, the promise by management to "work with and assist the union at both local and international levels to preserve jobs, replace jobs which may be lost by outsourcing action, and to create jobs for laid-off employees."[48] Outsourcing as a threat to job security is a threat to many unions today and causes them to negotiate a **scope clause** in new contracts.

Article 6—Subcontracting

Section A: The Employer agrees that where portions of the Employer's contracts for construction, repair, or alteration are sublet or assigned to subcontractors, the subcontractor shall be required by the Employer to conform to all of the terms and conditions of this Agreement. The Union will not recognize a contractor's manpower request without first having a signed Agreement.

The Employer will not subcontract any work within the jurisdiction of the Union which is to be performed at the job site except to a subcontractor who holds an Agreement with the Union, or who agrees in writing, prior to or at the time of the execution of his subcontract, to be bound by the terms of this Agreement.

Section B: A contractor, company, or Employer acting in the capacity of a Construction Manager agrees that it, or any of its subcontractors, will not contract or subcontract carpenter work to be done at the site of construction, alteration, repair of a building, or structure except to a person, firm, or corporation party to a current Labor Agreement with the Union.

FIGURE 8-3 Subcontracting Provision

SOURCE: Agreement between the Kentucky State District Council of Carpenters, Local Union 472 and Tri-State Contractors Association (1995–1998).

Ford–UAW Memorandum of Understanding Sourcing

The Company will work with and assist the Union at both the Local and International levels to preserve jobs, replace jobs which may be lost by outsourcing action, and to create jobs for Protected employees in GEN and laid off employees. It is an objective of the Company to grow the business and to continue to rely upon its employees and facilities as the source of its products. During the term of the 1996 Agreement, the Company will advise, in writing, the Union members of the sourcing group of the monthly FAO Sourcing Council meeting results, including the number of potential jobs affected. Additionally, data regarding work brought in-house and work outsourced will be given to the International Union in a quarterly meeting. (The Company will provide this data on a computer disk in addition to providing hard copy.) In this manner, the parties can judge the success of mutual efforts toward improved job security. The Company further agrees to address its sourcing during the 1996 Agreement, in accordance with the guidelines herein.

The rationale for sourcing actions will consider the criteria of quality, technology, cost, timing, statutory requirements, occupational and related environmental health and safety issues, the impact on long-term job stability, the degree to which the Company's resources can be allocated to further capital expenditures, the overall financial stability of affected facilities, and the impact on related facilities. Other factors considered by the Company before a final sourcing decision is made will include the effect on employment, and job and income security costs, on both a short and long term basis. The National parties will jointly further develop the above criteria to be used to address sourcing issues. In developing financial criteria appropriate Corporate return on investment and burden will be considered. Pertinent criteria will be applied consistently in comparisons of internal and external supply capability.

In addition the following specific commitments have been made to address sourcing-related job security concerns of UAW members:

1. **Insourcing**

The National Committee and, where appropriate the Local Committee, will discuss the practicality of insourcing, in whole or in part, work previously outsourced

continued

FIGURE 8-4 Outsourcing Provision

or new work which the Union identifies as that which might be performed competitively within the location based on the criteria outlined above.

If it is established that certain work can be performed competitively, judged by the above criteria, Management will adopt the Committee's proposal and, barring unique or unforeseen circumstances, bring the work in-house. The Union shall thereafter obtain any necessary approval or ratification within 30 days of the decision to bring the work in-house.

2. **Outsourcing**

Outsourcing as used herein means the Company's sourcing of work from Ford-UAW locations, including work connected with current, new or redesigned vehicles, fabricated parts, powertrain, and component products. When a market test is initiated, the International Union and the Local Union at the affected location(s) will be notified in writing by the Company. At such time as the sponsoring activity has received the results of a market test (or a similar point in the sourcing process when a market test is not applicable) and an outsourcing decision is contemplated, the International Union and the Local Union will be given written notice. The notice shall be provided to the Union as far in advance as possible or promptly following FAO Sourcing Council approval, and consistent with the timing requirements of the Ford Product Development System. The notice will provide, on a confidential basis, the reason for the outsourcing, a description of the work involved, the impact on the workforce, the identification of the sourcing authority, the quality status of the recommended supplier, and a copy of all data contained in the financial analysis submitted to the FAO Sourcing Council.

a. When such an outsourcing decision is contemplated at any level of the Company, the written notice will be given to the Vice President and Director of the National Ford Department. A copy of such notice will be given to the Chairperson of the Unit Committee at the same time.

b. When such a contemplated outsourcing decision is initiated by the Company at a level external to the affected location(s), the Company will provide sufficient advance written notice to allow the designated Management representative at the affected location(s) to comply with the notification procedure.

c. Additionally, International Union and Local Union input will be sought by the Company as early as possible in the outsourcing decision-making process. The intent of the evaluation period and Union input being sought as early as possible is to allow for more thorough discussion and to permit the parties to assess better the impact of outsourcing on the long-term job stability of employees and the financial viability of given Company locations.

d. The Company will not enter into a contractual relationship with a non-Ford-UAW supplier until such time as the designated Management representative of the affected location provides written verification that the above notification procedure and discussion by the local Committee has taken place.

Proposals to keep the work in-house will be made by the Union within 90 days of the receipt of the written notice. If it is established that the work can be performed competitively, judged by the criteria listed earlier in this Appendix, Management will, barring unique and unforeseen circumstances, keep the work in-house. The Union shall thereafter obtain any necessary approvals or ratification within 30 days of the decision to keep the work in-house.

e. The Company agrees to a full disclosure to the International Union of the procedures utilized in the sourcing decision-making process.

FIGURE 8-4 Outsourcing Provision (Continued)

SOURCE: Agreement between the UAW and the Ford Motor Company (1996), pp. 236–40.

PROFILE 8-1

LIFETIME EMPLOYMENT GUARANTEE

General Motors in its 1996 contract negotiations with the UAW made a historic offer—lifetime employment guaranteed to current workers—in exchange for the ability to reduce its total workforce as those members retire. Certainly the demographics of GM's aging workforce make the offer reasonable. The ultimate job security proposal, however, would have been unthinkable only a few years ago, even though it would have provided most UAW workers their top job demand. Perhaps ironically the concept of lifetime employment was until recently found only in Japan, whose automakers have taken much of the U.S. market away from the Big 3. The Japanese recession of the 1990s caused many major employers there to end the practice of guaranteed lifetime employment just at the same time that GM proposed beginning the policy in the United States.

SOURCE: Adapted from Rebecca Blumenstein, Nichole Christian, and Angelo Henderson, "GM Offers Lifetime Employment in UAW Talks," *Wall Street Journal,* September 12, 1996, p. A3.

A scope clause like the one negotiated by the International Association of Machinists and Aerospace Workers (IAMAW) with Comair in their 2005–2009 agreement prohibits the company from outsourcing mechanical work while any member of the union is on furlough. The IAMAW had witnessed the Delta Air Lines layoff of 2,000 nonunion mechanics and shift of work to outside companies only a month earlier.[49]

Another related historic first occurred in 1996, when General Motors Corporation offered a lifetime employment guarantee (see Profile 8-1) to the UAW—perhaps the ultimate job security provision.

Management's right to subcontract is usually judged by arbitrators against the recognition of the bargaining unit, seniority, wages, and other clauses within the agreement. Standards of reasonableness and good faith are applied in determining whether subcontracting has violated clauses in the contract. In general, management's right to subcontract is recognized, provided it is exercised in good faith and no specific contract restriction exists. Arbitrators often recognize that signing a contract does not establish an agreement that all the jobs will continue to be performed by members of the bargaining unit unless this condition is specified within the contract. However, the company cannot undermine the unit by subcontracting for the sole purpose of getting rid of work done by union employees in favor of nonunion employees who are paid lower wages. The standards that arbitrators generally apply to subcontracting cases are summarized here:

1. ***Past practices.*** Whether the company has subcontracted work in the past and in good faith.
2. ***Justification.*** Whether subcontracting is done for a business reason such as economy, cost reductions, maintenance of secondary sources for production, plant security, and so on.
3. ***Effect on union.*** Arbitrators look askance if subcontracting is being used as a method of discriminating against the union and substantially prejudicing the status and integrity of the bargaining unit.
4. ***Effect on unit employees.*** Whether members of the union are displaced, laid off, or deprived of jobs previously available to them or lose regular or overtime earnings by reason of the subcontract.

5. *Type of work involved.* Whether it is work that is normally done by unit employees, work that is frequently the subject of subcontracting in the particular industry, or work that is of a marginal or incidental nature are major factors considered by arbitrators.

6. *Availability of sufficient qualified employees.* Whether the skills possessed by available members of the bargaining unit are sufficient to perform the work being subcontracted.

7. *Availability of equipment and facilities.* Whether necessary equipment, technology, and facilities are presently available in the employer's facility or can be economically purchased.

8. *Regularity of subcontracting.* Whether the particular work is frequently or only intermittently subcontracted and for a limited period of time.

9. *Unusual circumstances involved.* Whether an emergency, special job, strike, or other unusual situation exists, necessitating the subcontracting.

10. *History of negotiations.* Whether management's right to subcontract has been the subject of contract negotiations is a significant factor, as well as if a management rights clause gives the employer the right to subcontract.[50]

Case 8-3 is a typical grievance about subcontracting.

CASE 8-3	SUBCONTRACTING

Until January 1982, the company was in the business of installing and servicing equipment on trucks and selling parts. Since the 1950s, the employees were classified as mechanic welders, painters, and utility men and were covered by collective bargaining agreements. It is undisputed that the company was losing money since 1979 and that by 1981 three of the four remaining unit employees were on layoff status.

In 1981, the company was approached by two individuals with an offer to take over the company's mounting and service work under a subcontract. An agreement was worked out, and the company hired the two parties as independent contractors for providing mounting and service work. The company was to lease its facilities and equipment to them. The subcontractor was to pay a percentage of the company's rent and utility bills and to provide various kinds of liability and other insurance. The company reserved the right to hire other subcontractors but reserved no right to exercise control over the employees of the subcontractor. The company notified its employees and the union of the subcontract agreement, citing the dire economic conditions that required the subcontract. The union grieved the layoff of employees as a violation of the contract, protesting that outside employees were performing work normally done by members of the bargaining unit. While the grievance was in progress, the union conducted an audit of the company's books and confirmed that the company was in a poor financial condition. The union offered to consider wage concessions to get the laid-off employees back to work, but the company declined because it deemed the concessions insufficient to address the cash flow problems. The company, citing the reversal by the National Labor Relations Board (NRLB) of the *Milwaukee Spring* decision, stated that before it can be found that a company has violated the act by subcontracting during the

continued

SUBCONTRACTING—continued

term of the contract, a specific term contained in the contract must be identified that prohibits such subcontracting. In addition, under the *Otis Elevator Company* case, a management decision to subcontract was not subject to mandatory bargaining because the essence of the decision turned on a change in the nature or direction of the business and not on labor costs.

The company stated that its decision to contract out service work turned not on labor cost but on a significant change in the nature and direction of the business; therefore, the company had no duty to bargain. The company's decision to subcontract was to reduce its overhead cost across the board so that it could remain in business. To that end, the subcontractor agreed to pay a specified percentage of the rent paid by the company for use of the premises, plus a monthly fee for the rental of the equipment. In addition, the subcontractor agreed to pay a specified percentage of utility bills, to produce liability insurance, and to maintain workers' compensation

and other insurance. The company had made a decision to abandon its service and mounting operations. Therefore, on the basis of *Otis Elevator,* the company had no duty to bargain regarding its subcontracting decision.

DECISION

Although the NLRB agreed that the company did not have to bargain its decision to subcontract, it found that the company unlawfully failed to bargain with the union about the effects of the subcontracting decision on union employees. The NLRB found that the company's notice to the union that the subcontract had been entered into, and its failure to meet with the union and laid-off employees for two months after the subcontract, was not sufficient notice and a meaningful opportunity to bargain with the union about the effect of subcontracting on unit employees. The employees were awarded back pay, as is the customary remedy in such cases.

SOURCE: Adapted from *Gar Wood Detroit Truck Equipment,* 118 LRRM 1417 (1985).

An issue intertwined with subcontracting is management's decision to relocate work previously done at one location by union workers to another location that is generally nonunion. A Supreme Court decision in 1981, *First National Maintenance Corporation v. NLRB*, said that a management decision to eliminate work previously done by union workers was not a mandatory bargaining issue if the decision to eliminate the work was for economic reasons.[51]

The NLRB decided in *Milwaukee Spring II*[52] and in *Otis Elevator II*[53] that the decision to relocate work for economic reasons was akin to eliminating work for economic reasons and, therefore, was not a mandatory bargaining subject. Nonetheless, although a decision to relocate either all or part of the business for economic reasons is not a mandatory subject of bargaining, a company must bargain over the *effects* of such a decision.[54]

In *Dubuque Packing Co. v. NLRB,* however, the NLRB modified its position. Noting that a decision to relocate work, subcontract, or outsource work rather than to eliminate work was not a change in the scope of the enterprise itself, just a decision to do the same work with other workers, the board found that it was a mandatory bargaining subject.[55] Generally, unless an agreement contains specific language barring subcontracting, a union will have difficulty stopping it. They are generally not successful in

Tips from the Experts

UNION

What are some practical protections against employers' relocating, outsourcing, or subcontracting?

Good contract language is the best protection against these employer actions. Good language would ensure no loss of jobs as the result of any of these actions during the life of the contract. It would also include processes for meaningful union input into the debate prior to these decisions being made and into plans to ensure no adverse effects on present employees from such decisions if they are made. These processes would address plans for retraining and redeployment of existing staff if necessary, outplacement services, severance packages, reemployment rights, insurance and pension protections, and reasonable notice of any adverse action.

MANAGEMENT

What are the best ways an employer can outsource, relocate, or subcontract without violating the law or a collective bargaining agreement?

1. Retain specific management rights in each area in the collective bargaining agreement with no restrictions or limitations.

2. Develop a credible business plan for when outsourcing, relocating, or subcontracting is necessary, in conjunction with budgeting, marketing, production, sales organizations, and so on, with buy-in from all who assist in its development, which is defensible to the employees, the media, the public, and whatever board, arbitrator, or judge will ultimately hear the issue.

3. Give timely and appropriate notice to union leadership and then to employees as well.

winning arbitration cases based on a mere implication that it harms the bargaining unit. This view on subcontracting changed in recent years; once consistently limited by arbitrators, now subcontracting is a common practice.[56]

SUCCESSORSHIP

If there is a change in either a collective bargaining representative or an employer, parties to an unexpired collective bargaining agreement may not be certain of their status. This situation may exist when the union becomes decertified; because of a schism, merger, or change in union affiliation; or if the union simply becomes defunct and is replaced. Questions may arise by management when the sale of all or part of a business occurs because of a merger or corporation consolidation or if the corporation is reorganized. The courts refer to these situations as **successorship**.

The law on successorship provides that if there is a genuine change in the collective bargaining representative, the existing collective bargaining contract, even if unexpired, is not binding on the successor representative. If a genuine change of employer exists but the employing industry remains substantially the same, the successor employer is required to recognize the existing collective bargaining unit and its representative but is not bound by the agreement.

The Supreme Court for the first time offered a test for determining the circumstances under which the successorship doctrine applies in *Fall River Dyeing v. National Labor Relations Board*.[57] A new company, Fall River Dyeing, acquired the plant, equipment, and remaining inventory of a textile dyeing and finishing plant (Sterlingware Corporation). The union that had represented the production employees of Sterlingware sought and was refused recognition by Fall River Dyeing. The union filed an unfair

Employees may lose their negotiated wages, benefits, and working conditions when a change in ownership occurs, such as when British Petroleum (BP) replaced Texaco.

labor practice charge, and the NLRB upheld its claim. The Supreme Court upheld the NLRB decision and imposed a bargaining duty on Fall River Dyeing under the successorship doctrine. The Court in its decision suggested three factors that must be present for the successorship doctrine to apply to the purchaser of a business employing union members:[58]

1. **Substantial continuity.** The successor substantially continues the business operations of the predecessor. Factors considered include the purchase of real property, equipment, and inventory; employing workers on essentially the same jobs; employing the same supervisors; and continuing the predecessor's product line. In general, not all factors must be present for substantial continuity.

2. **Appropriate bargaining unit.** The bargaining unit(s) of employees must remain appropriate after the change of employers. Job duties and operational structure are critical in this determination. Significant change in the nature of jobs performed or in the means of operation may mean that the unit is no longer appropriate.

3. **Predecessor's workers.** The new employer hires a majority of its employees from the predecessor.

The new employer has several important rights even as a successor employer, including (1) the right to hire its own workers (although it may not discriminate against workers of the predecessor because of union status), (2) the right to disregard the predecessor's collective bargaining agreement, and (3) the right to set the initial terms of employment, such as wages, benefits, and working conditions, without consulting the union.[59]

A successor employer, however, may also be obligated to remedy an unfair labor practice committed by its predecessor. If it is a true successor, and if it had notice of the unfair labor charge, the NLRB may require the new owner to remedy the unfair labor practice by, for example, reinstating an employee and providing back pay.[60]

A successor employer may be obligated to arbitrate the grievances filed under the predecessor's collective bargaining agreement. So, although a successor employer is not bound by the prior employer's collective bargaining agreement, it is bound to arbitrate violations. If the collective bargaining agreement contained a successor clause that stated that the predecessor employer agreed to "require" a purchaser of the company to honor the collective bargaining agreement and did not do so, a union may be able to force the successor employer to honor that agreement through arbitration.[61]

The NLRB further delineated the successorship doctrine in the *Canteen Company* case in 1996. In this case, the NLRB found that the employer was obligated to bargain with the union about terms of employment. The employer had acquired a unionized plant from another company. The employer then interviewed and offered jobs to some employees and discussed possible new provisions with the union. The NLRB found that by making job offers to some employees and discussing the compensation package with the union, the employer had "demonstrated a clear intention" to hire a majority of its new workforce from among the workforce of the former employer; thus, it had violated the National Labor Relations Act by not bargaining with the union.[62]

And in a recent decision, the NLRB weakened the successorship doctrine by ruling that an incumbent union in a successorship situation is entitled to only a rebuttable presumption of its continuing majority status and that such a presumption will not be a bar to a decertification election or a claim by a rival union.[63]

EMPLOYEE ALCOHOL AND DRUG TESTING

The use of alcohol and drug testing of job applicants and employees has become a complicated and critically important job security issue. Management often claims that employee use of illegal drugs is a problem that is growing out of control.

In the 1980s, President Ronald Reagan launched a federal government "drug-free workplace" campaign that started the testing of job applicants and employees. By 2003 it was estimated that about 25 million people in the United States were tested annually, and millions more were subject to a possible test due to an accident or other cause. Drug test screens typically detect opiates, cocaine, barbiturates, methamphetamine, and marijuana. According to the American Management Association, approximately 61 percent of all employers screen job applicants, and 50 percent test employees. According to the American Council for Drug Education, substance abusers, compared to nonabusers are: ten times more likely to miss work, 3.6 times more likely to be involved in an on-the-job accident, five times as likely to file a workers' compensation claim, have three times the health-care costs, and have 33 percent lower productivity.[64]

In two landmark decisions, the NLRB ruled that the alcohol and drug testing of current employees is a mandatory subject of bargaining; thus, any such program must be negotiated with the union.[65] The NLRB reasoned that the test results could affect a worker's job security and therefore constituted a condition of employment; thus, the testing requires bargaining. However, in another case involving the mandatory testing of all job applicants, the NLRB ruled that management could unilaterally implement such a program without bargaining.[66] The board decided that the testing of job applicants who are not covered by a collective bargaining agreement is a management right.

Therefore, management may generally require any applicant to submit to a drug-screening test, unless limited by a state law. Employers, in a statement of policy, may express their desire to hire only qualified applicants, and because the use of drugs may adversely affect job performance, they can choose to hire only applicants who pass a screening test.

Management's desire to screen all job candidates may increase because of several factors: (1) the increased use of drugs within all segments of society, (2) the reluctance of previous employers to report suspected or known drug usage of former employees for fear of litigation, and (3) the employer's liability for the negligent hiring of employees.

Preemployment testing policies often include clauses such as the following, developed by IBM and other employers:[67]

- *Notification.* Notify applicants of the screening on the physical exam questionnaire. Notification minimizes claims of privacy invasion.

- *No rescheduling of test.* Do not allow an applicant to reschedule a test after he or she appears at the doctor's office and realizes that it is part of the physical exam. The person may be a substance abuser who will refrain from illegal substance use before the next exam.

- *Test validity.* In the event of a positive test result, repeat the test on the same sample to ensure validity. Ensure that test samples are kept by the doctor's office for 180 days in case of litigation.

- *Confidentiality.* Maintain confidentiality by recording positive test results only on the doctor's records. On personnel records, use a code if someone fails the test. Only the applicant should be made aware of the test results, and the person can simply be informed that the results were unsatisfactory. This policy holds true for employees also.

The testing of current employees presents more difficult negotiation issues as well as the need to keep current with court and arbitration decisions. Management will generally test current employees under one of three policies:

- *Random testing.* All employees are tested at random periodic intervals, or randomly selected employees are tested on predetermined dates.

- *Probable cause.* An employee is tested only when his or her behavior causes a reasonable suspicion on the part of supervisors.

- *After accidents.* All employees are tested after any industrial accident or major incident involving employees.

One case illustrates the last point. A worker involved in an on-the-job accident that damaged company property was fired after testing positive for cocaine. It was his second accident in eight months. The contract specified that termination be for "just cause" and that a prior warning was not needed if, while on duty, an employee was tested positive for illegal drugs. The union requested the worker be reinstated and asked for documentation of the chain of custody of the urine sample. The company declined to provide the documentation until the hearing. The U.S. 8th Circuit Court ordered back pay from the date of the discharge to the date of the hearing to the worker because of the company's breach of contract to cooperate in the investigation. The court did, however, uphold the termination because there was sufficient evidence to support just cause.[68] But in Case 8-4, the Supreme Court upheld an arbitrator's award that reinstated an employee who had tested positive for drug use twice because the arbitrator did not believe that the company had just cause to dismiss him.

Employee Attitudes Toward Drug Testing

Unions' institutional response to drug-testing programs originally focused on the struggle over bargaining duties; that is, could an employer institute a drug-testing program unilaterally? After the NLRB ruled that such policies have to be negotiated, unions

DRUG TESTING

The company and union are parties to a collective bargaining agreement (CBA) with arbitration provisions. The CBA specifies that, in arbitration, in order to discharge an employee, the company must prove it has "just cause." Otherwise, the arbitrator will order the employee reinstated. The arbitrator's decision is final.

Smith worked for the company as a member of a road crew, a job that required him to drive heavy trucklike vehicles on public highways. As a truck driver, Smith was subject to Department of Transportation (DOT) regulations requiring random drug testing of workers engaged in "safety-sensitive" tasks. Smith tested positive for marijuana. The company sought to discharge him. The union went to arbitration, and the arbitrator concluded that Smith's positive drug test did not amount to just cause for discharge. Instead, the arbitrator ordered Smith's reinstatement with conditions. Smith had to accept a suspension of 30 days without pay, participate in a substance abuse program, and undergo drug tests at the discretion of company for the next five years. Smith passed four random drug tests.

But in July 1997 he again tested positive for marijuana. The company again sought to discharge Smith. The union again went to arbitration, and the arbitrator again concluded that Smith's use of marijuana did not amount to just cause for discharge in light of two mitigating circumstances. Smith had been a good employee for 17 years and had made a credible appeal concerning a personal/family problem that caused this current relapse into drug use. The arbitrator ordered Smith's reinstatement with new conditions. Smith had to accept a new suspension without pay, this time for slightly more than three months; reimburse the company and the union for the costs of both arbitration pro-

ceedings; continue to participate in a substance abuse program; continue to undergo random drug testing; and provide the company with a signed, undated letter of resignation to take effect if Smith tested positive for drugs within the next five years.

The company brought suit in federal court seeking to have the arbitrator's award vacated, arguing that the award contravened a public policy against the operation of dangerous machinery by workers who test positive for drugs. The district court, although recognizing a strong regulation-based public policy against drug use by workers who perform safety-sensitive functions, held that Smith's conditional reinstatement did not violate that policy. The Court of Appeals for the Fourth Circuit also affirmed the arbitration award, and the company appealed to the Supreme Court.

The Supreme Court considered the company's claims that considerations of public policy make the arbitration award unenforceable. In considering this claim, however, the Court held that the CBA itself called for Smith's reinstatement, because both employer and union have granted to the arbitrator the authority to interpret the meaning of the contract's language. Therefore, the arbitrator's award must be treated as if it represented an agreement between company and the union. The Court then had only to decide whether a contractual requirement to reinstate the employee is so contrary to public policy that it would fall within the legal exception that makes unenforceable a CBA.

The question before the Court, then, was not whether Smith's drug use itself violates public policy but whether the agreement to reinstate him does so. To put the question more specifically, does a

continued

DRUG TESTING—continued

contractual agreement to reinstate Smith with specified conditions run contrary to an explicit, well-defined, dominant public policy?

In the company's view, federal laws regarding drug use by workers in the transportation field embody a strong public policy against drug use by transportation workers in safety-sensitive positions and in favor of random drug testing to detect that use. The company argued that reinstatement of a driver who has twice failed random drug tests would undermine that policy—to the point where a judge must set aside an employer–union agreement requiring reinstatement.

In the union's view, these same federal laws promote rehabilitation as a critical component of any testing program, stating that rehabilitation "should be made available to individuals, as appropriate." The DOT regulations specifically state that a driver who has tested positive for drugs cannot return to a safety-sensitive position until (1) the driver has been evaluated by a "substance abuse professional" to determine if treatment is needed, (2) the substance abuse professional has certified that the driver has followed a rehabilitation program, and (3) the driver has passed a return-to-duty drug test. In addition, the driver must be subject to at least six random drug tests during the first year after returning to the job. Neither the act nor the regulations forbids an employer to reinstate in a safety-sensitive position an employee who fails a random drug test once or twice.

DECISION

The Court noted that the law on drug testing embodied several relevant policies. As the company pointed out, these include policies against drug use by employees in safety-sensitive transportation positions and in favor of drug testing such employees, and as the union noted they also include a policy favoring rehabilitation of employees who use drugs. But these relevant statutory and regulatory provisions must be weighed against the labor law policy that favors arbitration.

The award violated no specific provision of any law or regulation. It was consistent with DOT rules requiring completion of substance abuse treatment before returning to work. It does not preclude the company from assigning Smith to a non-safety-sensitive position until Smith completes the prescribed treatment program. The award is also consistent with the act's rehabilitative concerns, as it requires substance abuse treatment and testing before Smith can return to work.

The Court noted that reasonable people could differ as to whether reinstatement or discharge is the more appropriate remedy in this case. But as both the employer and the union have agreed to entrust this remedial decision to an arbitrator, the Court could find no law or legal precedent of an explicit, well-defined, dominant public policy to which the arbitrator's decision runs contrary. Therefore, the Court affirmed the lower-court decisions in upholding the arbitrator's decision.

SOURCE: Adapted from *Company Associated Coal v. United Mine Workers*, 165 LRRM 2865 (U.S. Sup. Ct. 2000).

were faced with the responsibility of representing their members' views on drug testing at the bargaining table. In the atmosphere created by the government's "War on Drugs," less than a strong antidrug attitude was considered unpatriotic. Knowing that, unions focused no longer on whether drug testing would be done but on how it would be done.

Of the three policies, the use of random testing has raised the strongest criticisms by unions, largely on the basis of an employee's right to privacy. However, as discussed in a later section, because of the random testing policies in the public sector and in industries regulated by the federal government, such as in the defense and transportation industries, the legal barriers to random testing have largely been removed.

Still, private-sector unions in most negotiations will strongly resist random testing programs and insist on a probable-cause or an accident-related program. Drug testing only when there is "probable cause" is a policy that will often be more readily acceptable by employees. Probable-cause testing has also received support from the courts and from arbitrators when the test has been given because of a reasonable suspicion of drug use. A supervisor's reasonable suspicion based on absenteeism, erratic behavior, or poor work performance can generally be accepted as a reason to test.

A major accident involving employees can be considered an immediate probable-cause situation and can thus invoke required testing of all employees involved. The Supreme Court in the *Skinner* case upheld the federal government regulation requiring railroads to test all crew members after major train accidents.[69] The Court held that private railroads subject to federal regulations had to comply with the requirement that all members of a train crew be tested after a major train accident. Both blood and urine tests are required.

Worker drug-testing programs have become common in contracts in recent years. The NLRB ruled that employee drug testing is a mandatory bargaining subject. However negotiation issues such as employee privacy, test validity, and when drug testing should occur make it a complicated issue.

Here are several negotiation issues regarding the probable-cause testing process and the use of test results.

1. ***Valid testing procedure.*** The burden of proof is clearly on management in questions regarding the use of confidential, fair, and valid testing procedures. Proper testing procedures include the use of an approved, certified laboratory with state-of-the-art tests. To guard against "false-positive" results leading to unfair discipline or other actions, a second confirming test should be required. The testing procedure should also specify a "chain of custody" of the specimen. In *Amalgamated Transit Union,* for example, an employee fired for a positive drug test was able to show that the company failed to protect the chain of custody of the drug sample, rendering it useless to the disciplinary proceedings.[70]

2. ***On-the-job impairment.*** In cases involving discipline as a result of a positive drug test, an employee or union may contend that the tests prove the presence of a drug in the employee's body but not on-the-job use or on-the-job impairment. Indeed, in *Shelby County Health Care Center,* the relevant provision of the contract limited drug- or alcohol-related major offenses to drug or alcohol use on the employer's premises or being "under the influence." A fired employee was reinstated because, although his drug test was positive, there was no on-the-job impairment.[71]

   There is concern that positive drug tests involving illegal drugs might be used to discipline an employee for the illegal activity involved in obtaining and possessing the drug regardless of the on-the-job effect. The employer's position is that an employee who engages in such illegal activity is not a fit employee. To date, however, arbitrators and courts often require a nexus between the employee's drug use and the behavior in the workplace before just cause for discipline is found. Such a relationship should not be difficult to find in most cases.

   For example, in *Boise Cascade Corp.,* a drug-screening test was done on an employee after his involvement in an auto accident. Although the test found the presence of marijuana, the level was so low that there was no finding of intoxication. The arbitrator, however, upheld the company's 60-day suspension and requirement that the employee join the employee assistance program. The arbitrator pointed to the employer's drug program, which the union had never challenged, that allowed for disciplinary action "if drugs are detected." No on-the-job impairment was necessary.[72]

3. ***Refusal to be tested.*** Management can usually sustain the termination of an employee for failure to take a drug test in cases of probable cause. In *Warehouse Distribution Centers,* the employer was told that his employee had been seen in a car in the company parking lot "blowing a joint." On the basis of that report, the employee was directed to have a drug test taken, but the employee refused. The collective bargaining agreement provided for disciplining an employee who refused to take a drug test if there is suspicion of drug use. The arbitrator found sufficient grounds for the employer's suspicion and upheld the firing.[73] However, if there is no probable cause for the test, an employee is within his or her rights to refuse to take the test as a protest against an unwarranted invasion of privacy. In *Gem City Chemicals*, management unilaterally added a drug screen to a negotiated annual "physical examination for environmental effects." There was no demonstrated drug problem at the plant. The grievant refused to submit to the test as part of his annual physical and was discharged for his refusal. The arbitrator reinstated the employee because requiring the test under that circumstance was not reasonable.[74]

   And just as with other dischargeable offenses, the employee must be warned that failure to submit to testing will result in discharge. After a truck accident, a supervisor who smelled beer on the driver's breath asked him to take a blood alcohol test. The driver at first agreed and accompanied the supervisor to the hospital. However, before the test he changed his mind and declined to take the test. The arbitrator found no evidence that the supervisor made it clear to the employee that failure to take the test would result in disciplinary action, and the employee was reinstated.[75]

4. ***Supervisor training.*** A program that includes the training of all supervisors to recognize the typical signs of employee drug use is important if probable cause is the basis of testing. Any challenge to the reasonableness of a supervisor's request for a test is likely to be discounted if the supervisor has participated in an appropriate training program.[76] Although many supervisors may be able to detect alcoholic intoxication, detection of drug abuse is more difficult to recognize without training.

Whether unions are indeed representing their members' views in negotiating drug-testing programs was the subject of an interesting survey. In 1989, 930 union members were surveyed on their attitudes toward various drug-testing programs. Approximately 29 percent of those surveyed had drug-testing programs in their workplace; 71 percent did not. The survey hoped to discover whether union members' attitudes regarding drug-testing programs were greatly influenced by their own personal workplace experience or whether the attitudes among union members were fairly uniform.[77]

PUBLIC-SECTOR SECURITY ISSUES

In 2005 the job security and political clout of government employees in California were central issues in a special election called by Governor Arnold Schwarzenegger (see Profile 8-2). The initiatives were opposed by several California unions, including: the

California Nurses Association called for a NO vote on Governor Arnold Schwarzenegger's 2005 Special Election on anti-union propositions.

CALIFORNIA GOV. ARNOLD SCHWARZENEGGER'S 2005 ELECTIONS INITIATIVES DEFEATED

In 2005, Governor Arnold Schwarzenegger of California called for a highly controversial special election. Two of the propositions placed on the ballot by the governor were framed as "antiunion" by the California Nurses Association (CAN), which led the opposition to them:

- ***Proposition 75.*** This initiative would have required unions to obtain annual, written consent from government union employees before union dues could be spent for political purposes.

- ***Proposition 74.*** This initiative would have increased the period required for teachers to become a permanent employee (tenure) from two years to five years. In addition, it would have changed the process by which school boards can terminate a permanent teacher. Thus, opponents criticized the measure as a threat to the job security of teachers.

- ***Proposition 76.*** This initiative, called the "Live Within Our Means" Act, would have limited state and school spending, prohibited state borrowing, and given the governor the power to reduce public employees' compensation.

Governor Schwarzenegger placed the initiatives on the November 8, 2005, ballot despite opposition from 60 percent of California, according to public opinion surveys. The surveys apparently were fairly on target because all three initiatives failed (Prop. 75: Yes 47%, No 53%; Prop. 74: Yes 45%, No 55%; Prop. 76: Yes 38%, No 62%), despite the $250 million spent by supporters. CAN President Deborah Burger, RN, asked voters to "Vote No" on every initiative to "send a clear message to Schwarzenegger and his legions of corporate donors. . . ." Actor Warren Beatty spoke at the CAN convention against the governor, and the League of Women Voters as well as other public employee unions campaigned against the initiative. CAN President Burger noted that if Proposition 75 had passed, the CAN would not have been able to campaign for the Registered Nurse staffing ratio law or other patient protections. Supporters of Proposition 75, however, claimed that without the new law, public employee union members are forced to contribute dues funds to political candidates and campaigns.

SOURCE: Adapted from Charles Idelson, "Special Election: Just Say No!" *Revolution: The Journal for RNs and Patient Advocacy 6,* no. 5 (Sept/Oct 2005) pp. 9–10.

California Nurses Association, the California Teachers Association, and the largest state employee union, the California State Employees Association, as well as other unions. The defeat of the initiatives was viewed as a victory for job security for teachers and support for unions in general.

Privatization

Perhaps the greatest threat to public unions and their members today is outsourcing, or **privatization**. In the past, outsourcing full-time public-sector jobs was unheard of; it was something "big business does, not us." In the 1980s and 1990s, however, as public agencies became strapped for funds, governments looked to lower their personnel costs. In Indianapolis, for example, outsourcing reduced the city's number of public employees by 40 percent in only three years. Sunnyvale, California, used a temporary Manpower company for 25 percent of its workforce. Some states, such as Pennsylvania, have developed their own pool of temporary workers, and large state community college systems use as many as 66 percent contract workers instead of full-time faculty.

Outsourcing has become so widely used so quickly in the 1990s that many public employee unions and some public officials have become alarmed. The most effective response by unions is to negotiate a provision in their agreements that prevents any civil service status employee from losing his or her job to such action. Although legal, these provisions are difficult to negotiate if management intends to outsource. Managers recognize that privatized workers can be treated quite differently from permanent employees; some make as little as one-third the wages of full-time public-sector employees, and they get no health benefits, paid vacations, holiday pay, or sick leave. Some observers see outsourcing as another factor eroding the middle class. "Everyone sees outsourcing as a way of gaining for the government the advantages and flexibility of the private sector, but this creates problems for society," says Frank McArdle, managing director of the General Contractors Association of New York. "When you drive down wages through outsourcing, you undermine your tax base and you add to the burden on government services." Adds Sal Albanese, a New York City Council member, "In the past, the government provided a tremendous opportunity for people to elevate themselves into the middle class. We're in danger of losing that."[78]

Advocates of privatizing government services contend that contracting out public services does the following:

- Produces better management of programs by bringing sophisticated cost-cutting techniques
- Frees public administrators from managing day-to-day operations, giving them more time to plan future programs
- Provides specialized skills otherwise too costly for government to recruit and hire
- Reduces capital outlays for facilities and equipment, which enables government to be more flexible in revising programs
- Motivates private-sector managers to perform well because they are motivated by opportunities for financial gain

Opponents of privatization cite the following downsides to contracting out public services:

- Savings are often illusory because the costs for government to bid, administer, and monitor the results of outside contracts are not considered.
- Depending on outside contractors for facilities and equipment makes government vulnerable to cost increases because it is unable to step in and provide the service.
- Private contractors expect to earn a profit and must also make enough to pay taxes.
- Laying off public employees costs the government unemployment compensation, a loss of tax revenues, and low employee morale.
- Contracting out lowers the quality of services provided because the private contractor's goal is to maximize profits, which often leads to overburdening its employees.
- Contracting out means losing in-house expertise, which makes oversight of contractors more difficult, again resulting in lower quality of services.[79]

American Federation of State, County and Municipal Employees (AFSCME) recommends a number of strategies for employees to fight efforts to privatize public services. The first suggestion is to address the issue in the collective bargaining agreement by either prohibiting any contracting out or severely limiting it. Because such provisions are not always attainable, AFSCME suggests employees try to negotiate a "successorship" clause covering the contracting out of any particular service so that the contractor would have to retain the employees for the duration of the contract and then negotiate with the union.

AFSCME suggests employees explore legal challenges to contracting out. Such unilateral actions on the part of the public employer may violate its duty to bargain if a collective bargaining law similar to the National Labor Relations Act covers it. In some jurisdictions, contracting out has been seen as a violation of civil service laws, which protect public employees from adverse job actions not based on merit. Finally, AFSCME urges public employees to lobby elected officials and to seek community support for maintaining the provision of public services by public servants, as opposed to private, for-profit entities.[80]

School Vouchers

But outsourcing is not the only threat to job security for public-sector employees. Both the National Education Association (NEA) and the American Federation of Teachers (AFT) have cited "school voucher" programs as a major concern for the public employee. Critics of public schools have advocated tuition voucher programs, which provide families with public funds that could be used for private school, including religious-based school, tuition. Advocates of school vouchers contend that giving families a choice will force public schools to improve to stay competitive.[81]

The NEA and AFT raise questions regarding the constitutionality of using public money for religious schools and whether private schools would provide equal access to all children. They cite the lack of public oversight of private schools as undermining the need for accountability to the public for the expenditure of tax dollars or point out that appropriate oversight by government will create a new bureaucracy and erode the autonomy and independence of private and religious schools. NEA President Bob Chase sees the threat of a voucher program not just to public employees but also to the entire public school system:

> America established public education to level the playing field, to provide equity of the most basic opportunity, the opportunity to learn. . . . The children in our country represent great diversity of race, religion, and income, and we cannot afford to replace public education, our single most important and unifying institution, with a system of private schools that pursue private agendas at taxpayer expense.[82]

Despite these concerns, the Supreme Court in July 2002 upheld an Ohio state voucher program in *Zelman, Superintendent of Public Instruction of Ohio, et al. v. Simmons-Harris, et al.*[83] The state of Ohio had established a pilot program designed to provide educational choices to families with children who reside in the Cleveland City School District, which has about 75,000 students, the majority of whom are from low-income and minority families. Cleveland's public schools had been among the worst performing public schools in the nation and had been placed under state control by the federal district court. The district failed to meet the state standards for minimal acceptable performance. More than two-thirds of high school students either dropped out or failed before graduation. Of those students who managed to reach their senior year, one of every four still failed to graduate. Of those students who did graduate, few could read, write, or compute at levels comparable to their counterparts in other cities. Against this backdrop, Ohio enacted its Pilot Project Scholarship Program, which provided tuition aid for students in kindergarten through third grade, expanding each year through eighth grade, to attend a participating public or private school of their parents' choosing and tutorial aid for students who chose to remain enrolled in public school. The Court noted that the Ohio program was enacted for the valid secular purpose of providing educational assistance to poor children in a demonstrably failing public school system. So the only legal question presented to it was whether the Ohio program nonetheless has the forbidden "effect" of advancing or inhibiting religion. The Court did not draw a distinction between government programs that provide aid directly to religious schools and programs of true private choice, in which government aid reaches religious schools *only as a result* of the genuine and independent choices of private individuals.[84]

Public Employee Drug Testing

Random drug testing of employees began in the public sector under President Ronald Reagan's administration. The armed services began random urine testing in 1981, and Executive Order 12564 followed in 1986, extending random testing to various federal employees. Urine testing by the public employer raises the Fourth Amendment constitutional issue of an unreasonable search. The Fourth Amendment provides that

> the right of the people to be secure in their persons, houses, papers, and effects, against unreasonable searches and seizures, shall not be violated, and no warrants shall issue, but upon probable cause, supported by oath or affirmation, and particularly described being the place to be searched, and the person or things to be seized.

Customs department and railroad employees challenged the random drug-testing program as an unreasonable search. The Supreme Court ruled that the tests were searches covered under the Fourth Amendment, but for certain employees whose duties involved public safety or law enforcement, such searches were not unreasonable.[85] This concept had previously been upheld by a Supreme Court decision in *New York City Transit Authority v. Beazer*.[86] In that case the Court ruled that the safety and efficiency of the public transportation system constituted a valid business necessity and a justifiable reason to require drug testing of bus driver applicants.

In a related case, railroad employees challenged Conrail's unilateral institution of a drug-testing program for its employees as a violation of its collective bargaining agreement under the Railway Labor Act. The Court found that, because Conrail's policy of conducting periodic physical exams already existed in the collective bargaining agreement, the inclusion of drug testing in all physical examinations was a minor dispute under the act and, therefore, subject to arbitration, not judicial review.[87]

Two court rulings in cases involving drug policies and public agencies have increased exceptions to the Fourth Amendment prohibitions. A federal court ruled that because the NLRB had determined that drug testing was a mandatory subject for collective bargaining, a public employee union may consent to drug testing on behalf of the employees it represents. Such consent will restrict an employee's right to claim a violation of the Fourth Amendment. The Supreme Court lowered the constitutional test used to determine whether drug testing in the absence of probable cause is legal.

The Vernonia School District instituted a drug policy that authorized random urinalysis drug testing of its athletes. When one student refused, he was not allowed to participate in the school's football program. The Court said that although state-compelled drug-testing programs are subject to the Fourth Amendment's protections against warrantless searches, sometimes "special needs" exist to support suspicionless drug testing. In this instance, the Court found that student athletes have lower expectations of privacy than other students or adults, the procedure used for the testing was not invasive, and the school's interest in not having student athletes use drugs, although maybe not a compelling interest, was "important enough."[88]

SUMMARY

Job security and seniority are vital to collective bargaining agreements. Both labor and management strongly believe that they must maintain certain rights where job security affects the employee's ability to keep his or her job and successfully compete for higher positions. Seniority, or length of service with the organization and the employee's ability to perform the job successfully are the two primary factors considered in layoff and promotion situations for both union and nonunion companies. An effective job security system also requires that the labor agreement contain a fair and just discipline and grievance system so that management's decisions regarding promotion or layoff and recall can be properly disputed by labor.

Seniority systems have generally been utilized because they are easy to develop and provide an objective, unambiguous means of considering employees when job openings occur. The theory behind using seniority is that if the employees are approximately equal in ability, then the employee who has the greatest length of service should be given the opportunity first. This practice is commonplace in nonunion as well as union organizations. Unfortunately, there are not always objective measures of ability to perform. The difficulty lies in determining the relative ability of competing employees. Seniority systems and employee feelings of job security are meaningless unless contract provisions limit management's ability to subcontract work. Without such provisions, management can subcontract work temporarily and force severe hardships on employees, causing them to leave and lose their seniority. Certainly, although union leaders agree that subcontracting is necessary in some situations, it can and has been used to undermine labor unions.

If a change in employers occurs, the successor is not bound by existing collective bargaining agreements. Also, if a genuine change in business has occurred, the new employer is not required to recognize the union. Public-sector unions try to use a successorship provision to make sure its members do not lose their jobs to outside contractors.

The use of an alcohol- and drug-testing program on current employees covered by a collective bargaining agreement must be negotiated at the bargaining table. Unions generally will agree only to probable-cause testing and will strongly object to random testing of all workers. Both sides express great interest in several aspects of any testing program, including the testing procedure, on-the-job impairment, and basis for probable-cause testing. Random drug testing of employees in the public sector who are involved in public transportation, safety, or law enforcement is common. Courts consider such testing as necessary to protect public safety.

Privatization by government is seen as a growing threat to public-sector employees. Public employee unions question the real cost savings or benefits of contracting out public services and urge their members to lobby against privatization and engender community support for maintaining public services by public servants.

CASE STUDIES

Case Study 8-1 Relocating Work Without Bargaining

The company is a family-owned business founded in 1943. Schultz is the company's president and part owner. The company began manufacturing caliper pins, which are used in the production of automobile disc brakes, at its Michigan facility in late 1994. Deciding that caliper pins would be the critical product line for the future of the company, the company received a three-million-dollar industrial development revenue bond from Michigan Strategic Fund (MSF) in March 1996. For federal tax purposes, a borrowing under an MSF agreement must be for a specific project at a specific location. Under the company's MSF agreement, the project site was the Michigan facility, and the project was the renovation of that facility and the purchase and installation of new machinery, including machinery for use in the production of caliper pins. Because the purpose of the MSF was to strengthen the state economy, the company had to give assurances of a reasonable intent to install the machinery at the project site and to maintain it there during the term of the loan. If the company decided to move equipment purchased under the MSF agreement from the site, the company would have to redeem an amount of the bonds equivalent to the value of the relocated machinery "contemporaneously" with the movement of machinery. After receiving the MSF loan, the company renovated its facility and purchased new machinery to meet its goal of increased caliper production. As part of the renovation, the company converted an area of approximately 2,300 square feet in the facility, known as the "blue room," into a caliper pin production area.

In December 1995 the company also applied for tax abatement from Plymouth Township. The tax abatement was to apply to the new machinery that the company would use in its caliper pin production and required that the machinery remain within the township. The company submitted its tax abatement application on May 31, 1996, and the tax abatement was granted January 29, 1997.

On May 10, 1996, the company signed a lease to acquire 10,800 square feet of space in Louisville,

Kentucky. The company sent its caliper pin customer in the Louisville area an announcement of its intent to open a warehouse and distribution facility in Louisville.

In June 1996, the company held a meeting for all employees at the Elks Club across the street from the Plymouth facility to tell them about the company's future plans. Schultz discussed the company's plans for increased personnel and machinery. He forecast that the company's caliper pin sales would go from approximately one and a half million dollars to six million dollars and that the caliper pin business might be relocated to Louisville to be closer to the company's customer base. Shultz did not mention any specific date for the relocation, however, and did not state that a definite decision had been made to move the caliper pin operation.

Between October and December 1996, Schultz said he generally discussed with the caliper pin customer whether it would be prudent to move the company's caliper pin operation to Louisville. Schultz testified that he wanted to know whether the company's largest caliper pin customer thought it would be wise to undertake such a move. Schultz further testified that he independently decided in late December 1996 to relocate the caliper pin operation to Louisville and that he made this decision primarily because Louisville was closer to the company's main caliper pin customer.

In February 1997, the union began its organizing drive at the company's Michigan facility. The union presented Schultz with a signed employee document that set out the rights of employees under Section 7 of the act and explained what specific acts would be illegal during the union's organizing campaign. On March 6, the union filed its election petition with the board. The union gave Schultz a document titled "Sensible Rules for a Fair Election," which was signed by 50 employees. Schultz read the document but would not sign it. It is undisputed that the company was aware of the campaign because employees openly wore union buttons to show their support for the UAW. The election was held on April 17, and the union was certified as the exclusive collective bargaining representative of the unit employees on April 25. In May, a UAW staff representative was assigned to assist the newly certified union obtain its first collective bargaining agreement with the company, which at the time of this grievance had not been done.

Sometime in March, before the election, Schultz walked over to two of the unit employees while they were working in the blue room. He asked, "Do you know what's going on around here?" They both responded no. He then said, "Well, if a union gets in here, a lot of people could be laid off." He placed his hand on one worker's shoulder and said, "If the union gets in here, you can be laid off." In late March or early April, and again prior to the election, the company's comptroller came up to a group of employees as they were discussing the pros and cons of the union and said to the group, "You know that there are changes that are going to be made when the union is voted in, and there may or may not be jobs left. Nothing is in stone, nothing is permanent."

On June 3, a company manager asked the owner of an equipment moving company to come to the Plymouth plant to look at certain machines that were to be moved to another facility. During a tour of the facility, he was asked whether there would be any labor problems if the equipment were relocated. The company manager stated that he did not believe there would be a problem, and he said he wanted the equipment moved from the Plymouth facility to Louisville on July 4.

On June 24, the moving company owner telephoned the union representative and told him of his visit to the company's Plymouth facility and informed him that the company wanted him to move six machines from the Plymouth facility to Louisville on July 4. On June 27, the union representative met with Schultz at the Plymouth facility. During the meeting, he told Schultz that he had heard rumors that the company planned to move some of its equipment and operations to the south. Schultz responded, "That may be something that may have to be considered in the future, but as it stood right then, there were no immediate plans to move anything out of the plant."

On July 2, Schultz informed his customer that the company was relocating its caliper pin operation to Louisville. Then, on July 3, Schultz held an employee meeting at the Plymouth facility. He informed the employees that because of overcrowding in the blue room and since caliper pin customers were closer to Louisville, it was necessary to implement a reduction of employees because of the transfer of the caliper pin operation to the company's Louisville facility. Schultz explained that it would be necessary to lay off 33 employees—those who had been hired since January 1995. Schultz added that applications would be accepted from anyone who was interested in applying for a job in Louisville. Also on July 3, the union representative received a fax transmission from Schultz concerning the move of the caliper pin operation from the Plymouth facility to Louisville.

The union representative responded,

> I specifically asked you [at the June 27 meeting] about any plans the company might have to move work from Plymouth to your facilities in the south. You did not indicate any such plans. Six days later, I now receive your letter announcing the company's "gradual realignment of its core business" and the news you are moving 29 jobs to Kentucky. I find it hard to believe that you were not aware of this plan when we spoke last Friday.

Also on July 3, the union president received a call from a company employee who informed him of the just-announced layoff of company employees. He decided that the union would put up an informational picket line at the Plymouth facility on July 4. Early on July 4, the company manager contacted a moving company and asked them to begin to move the equipment immediately.

A vice president in the commercial loan department of the bank that loaned the company the three million dollars testified without contradiction that he learned in September that the company had acquired a facility in Louisville and that it had transferred machinery valued at over one million dollars to that facility from Plymouth. He advised Schultz that the bonds had to be redeemed to the value of the machinery moved out of state. On November 7, the company redeemed 1.3 million dollars of the bonds with funds borrowed on a short-term loan. On its year-end tax return for 1997, the company notified Plymouth Township that machinery that had been subject to the tax abatement had been moved out of state.

The union filed an unfair labor charge against the company for unilaterally implementing a decision to relocate bargaining unit work and for discrimination because it was clear that the decision to relocate the union work was in response to the employees exercising their right to organize and bargain collectively.

Discussion

Applying the analysis set out in *Dubuque Packing Co.*, the union argued that the relocation decision was a mandatory subject of bargaining; that labor costs, both direct and indirect, were a factor in the company's decision to relocate the caliper pin operation; and that the union could have offered labor cost concessions that could have persuaded the company, had it been notified and permitted to submit bargaining proposals prior to July 3, to retain the caliper pin manufacturing work at the Plymouth facility.

The union further argued that the relocation and layoffs were discriminatorily motivated and therefore violated Section 8(a)(3) of the act. The union pointed out that the evidence does not support Schultz's testimony that he made the relocation decision in December 1996, some two months before the union came on the scene. It was not coincidental that the company implemented the relocation and layoffs on July 3 and 4, less than three months after the union had won the election and been certified as the bargaining representative of the company's employees. Thus, the timing of the relocation and layoffs, shortly after the employees' union activities culminated in the union's election victory and certification, and the company's knowledge of its employees' union activities support the union's contention that the relocation and layoffs were unlawfully motivated.

Furthermore, Schultz and the comptroller implied loss of employment if the union won the election. Their unsupported statements that layoffs could occur and that there might or might not be jobs left if the union got in are evidence of antiunion animus. Schultz was the president of the company and was therefore in a position to carry out the threatened layoffs if the union won the election. In these circumstances, the mere fact that he may have visited the facility only once a week does not lessen the impact of his threat. The company comptroller's threats were credible to the employees because she was fully informed of the company's financial condition.

The union also pointed out that the company originally announced that it intended to use the Louisville facility as a warehouse and distribution center. It was only after the union had been certified and immediately prior to the relocation that the company leased additional space at a second facility in Louisville so that it could relocate the caliper pin machinery from Plymouth to Louisville. The employees' union activities were a motivating factor in the company's decision to relocate the caliper pin operation to Louisville. The company's entering into the MFS agreement in 1996 evidences the company's intention to maintain its caliper pin operation at the Plymouth facility for the indefinite future. It was only after a bank official notified the company of the redemption obligation over two months after the relocation that the company took steps to remedy the problem. Even then, it could only redeem the bonds through a short-term loan. The company's careful preparations to get the MSF loan with its announced intent to keep the caliper pin operation in Plymouth—preparations that occurred prior to the union's appearance—stand in sharp contrast to the company's sudden breach of the terms of the agreement in July—after the union came on the scene—and to its abrupt departure from its avowed intent to keep the caliper pin operation in Plymouth. The union contended that this dramatic change proved that the union's appearance was a motivating factor in the company's relocation decision.

The company's intent to keep the caliper pin operation in Plymouth prior to the onset of the union campaign is also evidenced by its successful efforts to gain tax abatement from Plymouth Township for the caliper pin machinery. Less than six months after receiving the tax abatement, however, and less than three months after the union won the election, the company moved that machinery out of Plymouth Township. This sudden departure from the company's documented intention to keep the caliper machinery in Plymouth proves that the appearance of the union was a motivating factor in the company's decision to relocate that machinery. Finally, the union pointed out the company's stealth in carrying out the relocation—its refusal to inform the union representative that the relocation was imminent despite his request that he be so informed and its sudden secreting of the equipment out of the Plymouth facility over the July 4 holiday—are further evidence of the company's desire to avoid and be rid of the union. The company's stealth in relocating the equipment is further evidenced by its failure to inform its caliper pin customer in the Louisville area of the relocation until only a few days before it occurred.

In its defense, the company pointed out that even if an antiunion animus is found, the company couldn't be found to have engaged in an unfair labor practice if it would have taken the same action regardless of the union activity. The company then reiterated that Schultz discussed the possibility of moving the caliper pin operation to Louisville with

his customer in the fall of 1996, before the organizing campaign, and that he contended that he made the relocation decision in December 1996. And he reminded the court that as early as June 1996, long before the organizing campaign, he informed his employees that there was a possibility that the work would move to Louisville.

Furthermore, Schultz asserted that the reasons for making the relocation decision—that the blue room was overcrowded and that the company's caliper pin customers were in the Louisville area—were valid reasons that supported his decision to move.

SOURCE: Adapted from *Vico Products Co. v. NLRB,* 170 LRRM 1124 (September 30, 2001).

QUESTIONS

1. The union argues that the company's efforts to borrow low-interest bonds and to get tax breaks to build and operate in Michigan support their position that the motivating factor in moving to Kentucky was antiunion animus. Do you agree?

2. The company's defense, that Schultz made the decision to move the company before the organizing campaign got started, was supported only by his own testimony. If you were told that the hearing officer who conducted the hearing

and heard the testimony believed Schultz, would it change your opinion of the defense? Why or why not?

3. Kentucky, like Michigan, is not a right-to-work state, so union organizing in a plant in Kentucky is as likely as in Michigan. The company's decision to move from Michigan seems to have been both complicated and expensive. Do you think that the company made such a decision mainly to avoid a unionized workforce?

Case Study 8-2 Drug Testing

The company and the union had negotiated a typical substance abuse prevention and treatment program in their collective bargaining agreement. It prohibited the use of legally obtained drugs and alcohol if such use adversely affected the employee's job performance. It also prohibited the sale, purchase, transfer, use, or possession of illegal drugs "on the work premises or while on employer business." It allowed for testing in the following circumstances: for reasonable cause, after on-the-job accidents or incidents, for safety-sensitive jobs, and for reinstatement after treatment for drug or alcohol abuse. The collective bargaining agreement also stated, in a separate article, the general principle

that "there is no intent to intrude upon the private lives of employees."

The employee tested positive for an illegal substance after an on-the-job accident and was enrolled in an inpatient treatment program. At the completion of the program, he was reinstated subject to the normal provisions that he would continue with aftercare treatment and submit to random testing for three years. The employee was a member of a work crew that reported to work on a regular schedule and was not subject to being called in. In fact, if he chose not to report to work with his crew, there was no penalty. The employee had been called for a random drug test and had been tested eight times, all of which were negative. The ninth time he was called, he was contacted at home on a day he was not scheduled to work and was told to report for a drug test. In this instance, he tested positive, and the company dismissed him. The union appealed.

The union position was that the collective bargaining agreement prohibited intrusion into the private lives of employees, the drug policy prohibited only on-the-job impairment or abuse, and random testing can be used only in relationship to the workplace (i.e., when the employee is, should, be, or may be reporting to work, at work, or about to leave work). The employee was not scheduled to work, was not on the employer's premises or business, and was not subject to being called in to work. His reinstatement agreement to submit to random drug tests

meant only those types of random tests consistent with the substance abuse policy (i.e., for on-the-job impairment).

The company's position was that because some employees can be called into work at any time, the conduct of random testing needs to be on a 24-hour-a-day, 7-day-a-week basis; the union had not previously objected, and a past practice can be argued; the employee had violated the collective bargaining agreement by drug use on the job and had agreed to submit to random testing for three years in order to be reinstated, so an argument can be made that his testing then is job related; and this employee could elect not to report to work on any given day, so this reinforces the need to be able to test him on his off-duty time.

SOURCE: Adapted from *New Orleans Steamship Association*, 105 LA 79 (1995).

QUESTIONS

1. As the arbitrator, give your reasons for ruling in the union's favor. Then give your reasons for ruling in the employer's favor.
2. Argue for and against a decision by the employer in this case to insist on expanding the drug program to include the prohibition of sale, possession, or use of illegal substances on the employee's own time.

KEY TERMS AND CONCEPTS

- Absolute Rank Principle
- bumping
- departmental seniority system
- down-bid
- Follow the Work Principle
- industrial jurisprudence
- job bidding
- last-hired, first-fired rule
- lateral bid

- layoff
- Length of Service Principle
- outsourcing
- plantwide seniority
- privatization
- Ratio-Rank Principle
- recall
- scope clause
- seniority list

- shared work
- subcontracting
- successorship
- Surviving Group Principle
- up-bid
- WARN
- Worker Adjustment and Retraining Notification Act

REVIEW QUESTIONS

1. Why is seniority considered a critical issue? What are the advantages and disadvantages of using a seniority system?
2. How is seniority generally calculated?
3. Describe the different methods by which labor agreements might consider seniority in a promotion decision.
4. Why is seniority often used in layoff and recall actions? Specifically, how do contract clauses provide for the consideration of seniority in such decisions?
5. Under what circumstances might the employer bypass a senior employee and promote a junior employee when the labor agreement contains a seniority clause?

6. Why is a seniority system important to a labor group's union security?
7. Why has management's right to subcontract work been the subject of many grievances? Compare the issues in private-sector subcontracting to public-sector privatization.
8. What are the key issues in an employee alcohol- and drug-testing program? How do alcohol- and drug-testing programs in the public sector differ from the private sector?
9. How does the successorship doctrine affect union security?
10. When is a successor employer required to recognize a union from the previous employer's business?
11. How do "school voucher programs" threaten public-sector employees?

YOU BE THE ARBITRATOR
Subcontracting Work or Union Busting?

ARTICLE XXV
CONTRACTING WORK

If for any reason the Company desires to contract or subcontract out work, it may do so; however, the Company agrees not to use such contracting or subcontracting as a union-busting tactic.

It is not the Company's intent to contract or subcontract work within a branch location while employees who are qualified to do the work within the branch are on layoff status, except as required by business necessity.

Facts

The employer marketed and sold both large (PBX) and small (key) telephone systems for institutional customers and provided the service and maintenance of those systems after installation. The employer's extensive warehouse and depot operation was responsible for the storage and staging areas for (1) some PBX and almost all key systems; (2) materials and parts stocking for technicians' trucks, and (3) critical spare and replacement parts for both PBS and key systems. In the mid-1990s, in order to become a competitive survivor in the collapsing telecommunications industry, the employer adopted a strategic survival plan that included the dramatic centralization of its distribution operations. The strategic plan called for closing five local warehouses and reducing the size of several others. Following discussions with the union in January 1996, the employer began to implement the centralizing strategic plan. Some material handler positions were eliminated, but although it had no contractual obligation to do so under the terms of the collective bargaining agreement (CBA),

the employer successfully placed all the affected employees within its operations. Around the same time, the employer entered into a number of third-party vendor (TPV) contracts. These TPVs provided services that the employer's warehouse workers could not perform, a 24/7/365 delivery system for critical spare and replacement parts and the storing and staging of PBX equipment. In the fall of 2000, the employer, which had continued to lose money, refined its strategic plan to focus on its service and maintenance agreements and dramatically cut back on its sales and installation role. Ultimately, this led to consolidating the entire employer's 59 warehouses and depots into three locations and the layoff of hundreds of employees. Eleven laid-off material handlers who were not placed within the operation filed a grievance charging that the employer had violated the subcontracting clause of the CBA.

Issue

Did the employer have a business necessity to subcontract work that the laid-off employees could perform, or was it union busting?

Position of the Parties

According to the union, the laid-off employees were fully qualified to provide the services being performed by the TPVs. They had historically performed the full range of work, including the storage and staging of the large PBX equipment, albeit infrequently, and the delivery of critical spare and replacement parts. The union admitted that the employer did not provide the same 24/7/365 operation the TPV did, but the employees were under an "on-call" system so that they could perform timely deliveries just as well as the TPV. The union pointed out that the employer's decision to consolidate and eliminate warehouses resulted in not having the physical facilities that would have allowed the employees to perform their jobs. It was like a taxicab company that sells all its taxis and then subcontracts with another taxi company to transport its customers. Clearly, the employer's actions were nothing but union busting. Further, the union contended that the employer could not prove it had a business necessity for consolidating its warehouse operation and laying off the employees because it still had considerable losses after the 2000 changes. Clearly, according to the union, the real reason for the layoffs and subcontracting was to bust the union.

According to the employer, it had no antiunion animus. It had, in fact, consulted with the union as its strategic plan was put into place and had made an effort to place laid-off employees within the confines of its scaled-back operations. The TPV contracts had been entered into prior to the 2000 consolidation plan and prior to the last CBA negotiations of the employer with the union. The TPV work did not increase after execution of the 2000 strategic plan; rather, the employer's work changed so that its growth was in the service and maintenance operations and not its warehousing operations. In other words, there was a decrease in the employer's overall warehousing operation, and the decrease came totally from the employee side of its operation, not the contractual side of its operation. So although there was a loss on the employee side, there was no gain on the contractual side. Therefore, its subcontracting did not violate the CBA. Furthermore, the TPVs were in place when the current CBA was negotiated. If the union had wanted to "undo" the existing subcontracts, it should have brought it up at the negotiating table. The employer contended that the laid-off workers were not qualified to do the work of the TPVs because the employer did not have the facilities to house/move the PBX systems, and the "call-in" of workers could not meet the efficiency of the 24/7/365 of the TPVs. Finally, the employer contended that the savings in changing its core work from supplying equipment to servicing and maintaining the systems proved that there was a business necessity for the changes it made, including the closing of the warehouses and its subcontracting.

SOURCE: Adapted from *Nexitra*, 116 LA 1780 (Arb. 2002).

QUESTIONS

1. As arbitrator, what would be your award and opinion in this arbitration?
2. Explain why the relevant provisions of the CBA as applied to the facts of this case dictate the award.
3. What actions might the employer and/or the union have taken to avoid this conflict?

EXERCISE

Merging Seniority Lists

PURPOSE:

To utilize a group decision-making process with an issue involving seniority.

TASK:

Covington Custom Window Mfg. Co. recently bought a smaller window firm, Ft. Wright Windows. Both had a job classification, aluminum workers, and were represented by locals of the Aluminum, Brick and Glass Workers International Union. Neither of the agreements, however, contained a provision on how seniority lists should be combined should a merger occur.

Your tasks, in groups of three to five, are to (1) discuss the five merger principles presented in the chapter: Surviving Group, Length of Service, Follow the Work, Absolute Rank, and Ratio-Rank; (2) combine the two lists using each of the five principles; (3) select the method you would recommend in this situation and develop a written explanation of your decision; and (4) review the merged lists and provide a written analysis of what effects the merger principle you recommended may have on the morale of the people involved.

Current Seniority Lists

Covington Mfg. Co. (Est. 1988)

1. Paul Joseph (9 years)
2. Don Willen (9 years)
3. Anne Kling (9 years)
4. Carol King (9 years)
5. Mark Nutter (7 years)
6. Christy Nutter (7 years)
7. Mary Gronefeld (7 years)
8. Bill Gronefeld (7 years)
9. Peggy Gronefeld (7 years)
10. Jeremy Kling (6 years)
11. Sam Brown (6 years)
12. Steve Arvizu (5 years)
13. Gilbert Rojas (5 years)
14. Harvey Sloane (5 years)
15. Bill Stansbury (5 years)
16. Franklin Dixon (5 years)
17. Mary Anne Ryan (4 years)
18. Carolyn Hensley (4 years)
19. Peggy Breeze (4 years)
20. Wasu Chin (4 years)
21. Francis Lamb (4 years)
22. Ping-Ping Woo (3 years)
23. Ev Mann (3 years)
24. Boyd Wang (3 years)
25. Colleen Carrell (3 years)
26. David Banks (2 years)
27. Steve Magre (2 years)
28. Amber Maureen (1 year)
29. Alexis Savannah (1 year)
30. Anna Belle Michaels (1 year)
31. Ralph Swanson (1 year)
32. Sue Clater (1 year)

Ft. Wright Mfg. Co. (Est. 1954)

1. Archie Carrell (37 years)
2. Myrtle Jaggers (35 years)
3. Shari Brown (28 years)
4. Brooks Wilson (24 years)
5. Gary Green (20 years)
6. William Ryan Jr. (17 years)
7. Robert Hatfield (15 years)
8. Donna Shipley (11 years)
9. Johnny Ryan (7 years)
10. Bob Hillard (6 years)
11. Jay Vahaly (6 years)
12. John Nelson (4 years)
13. Beth Davenport (2 years)
14. Bob Shinn (2 years)
15. Sue Vahaly (1 year)
16. Bob Myers (1 year)

CHAPTER 9

Implementing the Collective Bargaining Agreement

Reducing an Agreement to Writing
Contract Enforcement
Rights and Prohibited Conduct
Public-Sector Contract Enforcement Issues

In 2005, the United Farm Workers Union announced a revival of the historic nationwide boycott of grapes, led by Cesar Chavez in the 1960s, to protest Gallo's refusal to bargain in good faith with its seasonal contract workers.

Labor News

UNITED FARM WORKERS BOYCOTT GALLO WINE

In June 2005 the United Farm Workers (UFW) union in California announced a historic boycott of Sonoma, a subsidiary of E&J Gallo Winery. The UFW followed past boycotts organized by Cesar Chavez, the labor leader who organized the union. Chavez founded the UFW in 1962 and led a successful national boycott of grapes in 1965–1966 (see Profile 2-3). These boycotts relied on farm workers and supporters who walked picket lines in front of grocery stores across the United States, urging customers to boycott grapes, wines, and lettuce. Forty years later, in 2005, the UFW are utilizing Internet networks and e-mail lists of union, political, and environmental groups to directly reach consumers and urge them to boycott Gallo wines.

UFW President Arturo Rodriguez called the boycott "the only thing that hopefully is going to bring them (Gallo) to the table." Gallo spokesman John Segale, however, responded that the UFW "delays and their actions continue to hurt the workers they represent." The central issues in the dispute are wages, medical coverage, vacation leave, and grievance procedures for seasonal contract workers. The UFW boycott won support from the Los Angeles City Council as well as national labor leaders. The 1975 UFW boycott led California lawmakers to adopt the nation's only law giving agricultural workers the right to organize.

Rodriguez noted "Cesar always said the good thing about a boycott is that's something you can do every single day . . . Everybody can participate in a boycott."

SOURCE: Adapted from Miriam Pawel, "Union Seeks Boycott of Gallo Wines," *Los Angeles Times* (June 14, 2005).

Although the interest of management and labor is usually focused on the months of negotiations necessary to arrive at a collective bargaining agreement, the negotiated agreement itself is implemented over a much longer period. It is that period of implementation that tests the success of the collective bargaining process. That success is measured not only by the fact that a contract is signed but also by the quality of its terms and the willingness of the parties to administer the contract fairly. This chapter examines implementation and includes an overview of grievance and arbitration issues, economic activity during a contract term, and the rights of labor, management, and individuals under a collective bargaining agreement.

REDUCING AN AGREEMENT TO WRITING

Duty

At some point in the labor–management relationship governed by the National Labor Relations Act, agreement is reached on wages, hours, and other terms and conditions of employment. Today the agreement is written, but when the National Labor Relations Act was passed, the act did not expressly require that a collective bargaining agreement be reduced to writing and signed by the parties. Nor did it address whether bargaining was to be a process of continuing negotiations or even what the legal status of a signed agreement might be. These questions were left to the National Labor Relations Board (NLRB), the courts, and Congress to answer in piecemeal fashion.

As early as 1941, the Supreme Court imposed a **duty to sign**, or a duty on the parties in a collective bargaining relationship to reduce to writing and sign any agreement reached through the bargaining process. A refusal to sign was declared a refusal to bargain collectively and an unfair labor practice because, the Court found, a signed agreement had long been informally recognized as a final step in the bargaining process. The Court thought it obvious that the employer's refusal to sign an agreement "discredits the [labor] organization, impairs the bargaining process, and tends to frustrate the aim of the statute to secure industrial peace through collective bargaining."[1] In the Taft-Hartley Amendments, Congress recognized the need for a written agreement and defined the bargaining duty as including "the execution of a written contract incorporating any agreement reached if requested by either party."[2]

Part of the negotiator's role in the collective bargaining process is drafting the final agreement. The negotiator should try to be clear and concise while accurately reflecting the agreement and the understanding of the parties. One author suggests that before it is signed, the final agreement should be circulated for comment among non-negotiating union and management personnel whom it will affect:

> Once contract provisions are committed to paper, a good test of their meaning is to have a wide variety of different individuals, wholly unfamiliar with what has transpired during negotiations, read and interpret each provision of the contract. Particularly appropriate candidates for this **provisional intent test** are those who enforce, administer, police, or are governed by the terms of the agreement—stewards, foremen, department superintendents, shop chairmen, plant managers, grievance committeemen, rank-and-file members, etc. If provisional meaning is misconstrued, revision is in order.[3]

Nature of the Labor Agreement

The agreement between a union and an employer is not an employment contract. The employment contract is between the employer and the employee. It may be expressed verbally or in writing, or it may simply be a function of the employer's job offer and the employee's acceptance. The union is not a party to this employment contract, but the agreement between the union and the employer does shape the terms of that independent employment contract by establishing company policy in the areas covered by the agreement. The labor agreement also serves to define the union's relationship with management and provides the means to enforce its provisions. Each labor agreement is unique in terms and language, but all have basic similarities. Most labor contracts contain four main sections: union security, wage and effort bargain, management rights, and administration.

Union Security

The contract needs to identify the parties to the agreement, the parties' authority, and the conditions and duration of their authority. The bargaining unit is described generally in terms of employees in job categories included or excluded from coverage under the agreement. By law the union is the exclusive bargaining agent for the unit described. The contract might go further than that and provide for certain union security provisions. These can include the following:[4]

1. **Union shop.**   Requires that a new nonunion employee join a union after a prescribed period. However, under the NLRA, the contract cannot require the employer to only hire union members.

TABLE 9-1 Length of Contract Term

Duration in Years	% of Contracts
1	1
2	5
3	69
4	11
5	9
6 or more	5
	100% all contracts

SOURCE: Adapted from Bureau of National Affairs, *2002 Sourcebook on Collective Bargaining* (Washington, DC: Bureau of National Affairs, 2002), p. 33. Copyright © 2002 by The Bureau of National Affairs, Inc., Washington, DC 20037. Used by permission.

2. *Maintenance of membership.* Requires that union members remain members during the contract term.
3. *Agency shop.* Conditions employment on the payment of union dues and fees but not actual union membership.
4. *Hiring halls.* Require an employer to seek employees through a union hiring hall as an employment agency. Nonunion members can and legally must have access to the referrals, and can be charged a fee by the union.
5. *Modified union shop.* Requires union membership of new hires, but permits current members to remain nonunion.

A contract must run for a specific term. Most contracts contain renewal provisions, with prior notice of termination or of a time for reopening negotiations. Contracts can have **opener clauses** that allow for negotiations to proceed during the term of the contract on one or more items, generally wages.

A majority of contracts (about 67 percent) contain three-year terms, as shown in Table 9-1. The NLRB in a general ruling that extended the contract bar rule (see next section) to a three-year period aided the increase from one-year to three-year terms for most contracts.[5] In recent years, the number of contracts with periods extended to four years or more has steadily increased to 25 percent, up from only 5 percent in 1986. The desire by management negotiators to provide greater long-term stability in labor relations has motivated negotiators toward longer multiyear agreements.[6] For example, in 2003 Yale University and the Hotel Employees and Restaurant Employees International Union signed an eight-year agreement, the longest in the history of the university. The new agreement followed a bitter strike that closed down the center of New Haven, Connecticut, and resulted in 100 arrests. Richard C. Levin, president of Yale University, said he hoped the longer term of the agreement would provide "time to build a more cooperative relationship."[7]

Wage and Effort Bargain

With or without a labor agreement, the employer–employee contract contains a wage and effort bargain. If a union exists, collective bargaining can determine the contents of that employment agreement. Areas primarily covered in this section are as follows:

1. *Pay scales.* Hourly, weekly, or monthly wage or salary paid for the job, usually determined by job classification and compensation schedules or earnings based on work, output such as piecework systems
2. *The effort bargain.* Acceptable standards for the task performance measured in work crew sizes and tasks, quotas, or work rules

3. *Premium pay.*   Includes overtime, call-in pay, shift differentials, and weekend work
4. *Contingent benefits.*   Includes insurance, pensions, paid time off, and severance pay

Management Rights

The area of labor relations known as **management rights** has evoked more emotion and controversy than any other single issue. At the core of the debate is the concept of management's right to run the operation versus the union's quest for job security and other protections for its members.[8] Management rights provisions are found in almost all contracts in a section labeled *management rights*; union rights, however, are usually scattered throughout a contract according to subject matter.[9] The 1999–2003 Ford–UAW contract contained a historic, new way of dealing with the management's right to sell a unit (see Profile 9-1).

Of course, the question of who controls the workplace is of great interest to both management and labor. Management rights generally include decisions governing the working environment, including supervising the workforce, controlling production, setting work rules and procedures, assigning duties, and the use of plant and equipment. Management generally believes that if it is to operate efficiently, it must have control over all decision-making factors of the business. Management usually contends that any union involvement in the area is an intrusion on its inherent right to manage. Union advocates respond that where the right to manage involves wages, hours, or working conditions, labor has a legal interest under federal law.[10] Arthur Goldberg, former secretary of the Department of Labor and Supreme Court justice, summarized the management rights issue:

> Somebody must be boss; somebody has to run the plant. People can't be wandering around at loose ends, each deciding what to do next. Management decides what the employee is to do. However, the right to direct or to initiate action does not imply a second-class role for the union. The union has the right to pursue its

Contract talks between the United Auto Workers union and Ford Motor Co. begin at Ford headquarters in 2003 with a ceremonial handshake between negotiators, UAW President Ron Gettelfinger on the right and Ford negotiator Robert Macin on the left.

FORD–UAW AGREEMENT PROVIDES HISTORIC NEW CONTRACT ENFORCEMENT PROVISIONS

When negotiations between the Ford Motor Company negotiating team, led by Ford President William C. Ford, Jr., and the United Auto Workers, led by UAW President Stephen P. Yokich, began, many important issues were on the table, including wages, the cost-of-living adjustment (COLA) formula, pension benefits, and the number of paid holidays. However, one issue loomed as a potential "deal breaker"—the future of Visteon, one of the largest automotive suppliers in the world. It had been announced that Ford might spin off some facilities to Visteon, thus putting the future rights of the UAW workers and even their UAW representation in question.

Ford might view the decision as a "management right" and thus may not have been willing to discuss it. The UAW was determined to protect the job security and contracted rights of all its union members. The issue was settled with an extraordinary, innovative new provision that provides that if Visteon becomes an independent company, the UAW–Ford workers at Visteon will remain covered by the UAW–Ford national agreement, including the pension plan, in the new contract (1999–2003) as well as the next two contracts, which might extend the life of the provision to 2011. As UAW President Yokich explained, "They can spin off the plants, but they can't spin off the people."

The new provision also covers new hires at Visteon during the three contracts. The 1999–2003 Ford–UAW contract contained several other significant provisions:

1. *Job security.* With the exception of Visteon, Ford will not "close, nor partially or wholly sell, spin off, split off, consolidate, or otherwise disperse of in any form . . . any plant, asset, or business unit of any type constituting a bargaining unit under the Agreement."

2. *Wages.* A total economic package equal to $29,300 in increases over the life of the agreement for a typical assembler: (1) 12% = (3% – 3% – 3% – 3%) base wage increases over the contract, (2) an improved COLA = 1¢/.25 change in the quarterly average of the CPI, and (3) an up-front $1,350 lump-sum contract signing bonus.

3. *New family service and learning center.* The theme of the negotiations was "Bargaining for Families," and the result was a unique provision creating new Family Service and Learning Centers that provide services to workers, spouses, children, and retirees. The centers offer a wide range of services, including child care, health and wellness programs, before- and after-school programs, financial planning, and retirement education.

4. *"Family days."* Two new "family days" that can be taken at the discretion of the worker in addition to two new national election holidays, increasing the total number of paid holidays per year to 17.

5. *Pension benefits.* For the first time in 20 years, pension benefits to a surviving spouse are increased from 60 to 65 percent. A special "catch-up" provision for workers who retired before 1984 is included. Workers who retire under the pension program will receive a $7.45-per-month increase.

SOURCE: Agreement between Ford Motor Company and the United Auto Workers (1999–2003) and UAW Report, October 1999, pp. 1–26.

---

role of representing the interest of the employee with the same stature accorded it as is accorded management. To assure order, there is a clear procedural line drawn: the company directs and the union grieves when it objects.[11]

A management rights clause often appears at the beginning of a contract following the union recognition and security clauses. An example of a common management rights clause follows.

ARTICLE III

Management

The management of the plant and the direction of its working force are vested exclusively in the Company. These functions are broad in nature and include such things as the right to schedule work and shift starting and stopping time, to hire and to discharge for just cause, to transfer or lay off because of work load distribution or lack of work. In the fulfillment of these functions the Company agrees not to violate the following Articles or the intent and purpose of this Contract, or to discriminate against any member of the Union.[12]

Reserved Rights

In addition to explicit management rights specified in the contract (as illustrated in the example), there are also residual, implied, or **reserved rights** not found in the language of the agreement. The reserved rights theory generally contends that management retains all rights except those it has expressly agreed to share with or relinquish to the union.[13] Management, under the reserved rights concept, does not review the agreement to determine which rights it has gained but instead reviews the agreement to ascertain which rights it has conceded to labor. All rights remaining reside with management.[14]

One area of management rights that has received a great deal of attention since the 1980s involves a management decision to *relocate* its operation, in whole or in part. Previous Supreme Court decisions had decided that if a company planned to "subcontract" work currently being done by union workers, that decision was a mandatory bargaining subject.[15] However, if the company was deciding to close down part or all of its operation, such a decision was not a mandatory bargaining subject.[16]

The NLRB, therefore, first likened management's decision to relocate part or all of its facility to the decision to close a plant, and it ruled in *Otis Elevator Co.* that relocating was not a mandatory bargaining subject.[17] After the federal court rejected that comparison, the NLRB, in *Dubuque Packing Co.*,[18] compared relocating to subcontracting and reversed itself, deciding it was a mandatory bargaining subject.[19]

Restricted Rights

Restrictions of management rights are common in contracts (87 percent) as union negotiators strive to delineate the union's rights in specific areas of decision making. The 1999–2003 Ford–UAW Agreement provided a new form of **restricted rights** (see Profile 9-1). Contracts may contain these restricted rights in a general statement restricting management from "taking actions in violation of the terms of the agreement." Specific restrictions of management rights or, conversely, the providing of union rights are most often found in the following contract clauses:[20]

- *Subcontracting of work* to outside firms (contained in 55 percent of all contracts)
- *Supervisory performance* of bargaining unit work, except for training, in an emergency, conducting experiments, and developing new products (58 percent)
- *Technological changes* in work methods or equipment (such as robots) without union approval or the retraining of displaced workers (26 percent)
- *Plant shutdown or relocation* without advance notice and transfer rights to a new location (23 percent)
- *Union rights of access* to bulletin boards, pertinent information, and company premises (94 percent)

Administration

Most contracts provide for the machinery necessary to enforce the terms of the agreement. Union shop stewards and officials give on-the-job representation. External enforcement is provided through arbitration provisions.

"Force Majeure"

The parties to a contract may be released from the provisions of the contract if unforeseeable circumstances prevent them from fulfilling their contractual obligations. This legal concept, known as *force majeure*, may be applied to collective bargaining agreements in rare circumstances. For example, after the terrorist attacks of September 11, 2001, several major airlines laid off pilots and other workers, despite contracts that prescribed employment levels, under the concept of *force majeure*. However, a 2003 arbitrator's decision required Delta Airlines to recall the pilots when revenue passenger miles for any four-month period equaled or exceeded that of the four-month period preceding September 11, 2001.[21]

Contract Bar

Through its decisions over the years, the NLRB established a **contract bar** doctrine stating that a current and valid contract can prevent another union from petitioning for an election and being certified as the exclusive representative. The board developed this doctrine as a balance between two competing interests under the National Labor Relations Act: the right of employees to choose their bargaining representatives and the need to achieve stability in labor relations through negotiation of collective bargaining agreements.

It is the NLRB's theory that if a union has negotiated and signed an agreement on behalf of its members, another union should not be allowed to seek recognition during the life of that agreement. Certain elements must be present to ensure that the contract acts as a bar to a representational election:

1. The contract must be in writing and signed by the parties. An oral agreement cannot be a bar.
2. The contract must be for a fixed term. An indefinite term expiring on some happening in the future cannot bar an election, nor will the board honor a contract with an unreasonably long term. Currently, the NLRB views a three-year contract as reasonable. Any contract of longer term will not bar an election to change representation at the end of the three-year period.
3. The contract must provide substantive terms and conditions to ensure a stable employer–employee arrangement. If a contract covered wages alone, it probably would not operate as a bar.
4. The contract must be duly ratified if ratification by the membership is required.
5. The contract must contain only legal provisions. Clauses that discriminate on the basis of race, religion, and so on or that clearly violate union security provisions of the act cannot bar a new election.
6. The contract must not be prematurely extended. The NLRB allows employees the right to change representation during the **open period**—the first 30-day period in the 90 days before termination of the original contract.

A 1996 case provides an example of the right to change representation. The Supreme Court unanimously ruled that an employer had violated Section 8(a)(1) of the National Labor Relations Act, which protects the union's rights, when the employer disavowed a contract. The union in the case had accepted the company's last contract proposal, but the employer disavowed the contract the next day because 16 (of 23) employees had complained about the union, and 13 had resigned from the union. The Court ruled that to preserve industrial peace and stability, the NLRB presumes that a union has majority support during the term of any contract, once negotiated, up to three years. Only at the end of the contract, during the open period, can employees seek to change representation.[22]

Under the contract bar doctrine, if a rival union wants to win the bargaining rights of a unit, it must petition for an election and win it during the open period—that is, between the 90th and 60th day prior to the contract's expiration. Once the end of an open period arrives without the filing of a petition, the incumbent union becomes insulated from another union's petition, and if a new agreement is reached before the old one expires, the new one presents a new contract bar.[23]

Once contract negotiations begin, the employees cannot petition for a change in representation. This **insulated period** begins 60 days before the contract is due to expire. Therefore, negotiations must not take place during the open period so that employees will have an opportunity to change representation.

CONTRACT ENFORCEMENT

Collective bargaining agreements are enforced through judicial proceedings by either the NLRB or the courts; through adherence to grievance procedures by the parties to the contract and arbitration; or through resorting to economic self-help pressure activities.

Judicial Proceedings

NLRB

The NLRB has the authority to investigate and prevent unfair labor practices as listed in Section 8 of the National Labor Relations Act. Violation of a provision of a collective bargaining agreement is not in and of itself an unfair labor practice. Therefore, enforcement and interpretation of a contract provision might come within the jurisdiction of the board only if the matter also involves a violation of the unfair labor practice provision. The board may be involved in contract enforcement if the contract has incorporated a statutory obligation it already has jurisdiction to enforce or if a contract has incorporated an unlawful provision it is called on to invalidate.

For example, if an employer is accused of refusing to bargain during the term of the contract by making a unilateral change in the wage structure or other term of employment, by subcontracting work, by refusing to supply information the union seeks, and if the employer claims that the contract justifies his or her action, the NLRB can interpret the *lawful contract clause*. The board is called on to investigate and determine the validity of the employer's claim.

The board's interpretive power might also be apparent in a case involving a union security clause or the provisions of a grievance procedure in which a contract is used by an employer or a union to defend the discharge or disciplining of an employee and that employee claims a violation of the National Labor Relations Act.

In representation cases, a party may claim that proper interpretation of a contract places him or her under its protection and provisions. Thus, the NLRB's definition of the parties to a collective bargaining agreement or the appropriate unit of employees who should be represented by a union can have great impact. Although as seen in Case 9-1, not all NLRB decisions are upheld.

CASE 9-1	COURT ENFORCEMENT OF AN NLRB ORDER

The company is in the metal fabrication business. It operates year-round, but it experiences seasonal fluctuations because its business is tied to construction projects. Typically, fall, winter, and early spring are the company's slow times, with production rising in the summer. As production levels ebb and flow, so do the company's staffing levels. In 1996, the company employed between 10 and 12 employees for seven months of the year, 14 employees in June and July, and 7 in November and December. In 1997, the staffing level remained constant at 11 employees throughout the year except for June and July, when it decreased to 10 employees. In 1998, the company employed between 9 and 13 workers for eight months of the year, with a low of 7 in May and a peak of 21 in August. In 1999, the staffing level ranged from a low of 13 in January to a high of 22 in June.

In 2000—the year at issue—the company employed 15 workers in January, 17 from February through April, 19 in May, 24 in June and July, and 26 in August. When the company then received a large order, it added new employees, causing staffing levels to swell to 31 in September and 46 in October.

On November 3, 2000, the union filed a representation petition with the NLRB, seeking to represent all the company's regular and part-time employees engaged in the fabrication of sheet metal. Shortly thereafter, its new customer delayed taking delivery of some of the curbs it had ordered. This caused the company to lay off many of its workers. By November 21, 2000—the day the board held a representation hearing—the company's employee roster had dropped to 13. The board's regional director issued a decision on December 20, 2000, directing an election.

He determined that, in addition to the workers employed at the time of the election, all laid-off employees who had worked a minimum of 15 days in the three-month period preceding his decision had a reasonable expectation of recall and were therefore eligible to vote in the election. This eligibility formula, according to the regional director, indicated that there were approximately 30 employees in the unit. The formula ultimately yielded 40 employees eligible to vote.

The board denied the company's request for review, and the election took place on January 18, 2001. In all, there were 22 votes for the union, 9 votes against, and 5 challenged ballots. The board therefore certified the union as the employees' exclusive bargaining representative. The company refused to bargain, precipitating the unfair labor practice charges. The company argues here, as it did unsuccessfully in defense to the charges, that the board's eligibility formula was arbitrary and contrary to precedent.

DISCUSSION

The NLRB uses eligibility formulas to ascertain which individuals work for an employer with sufficient continuity and regularity to establish their community of interest with other unit employees. Ordinarily the board uses a simple formula to determine who is eligible to vote in a representation election: Employees in the bargaining unit are eligible to vote if they were employed on the date of the election and during the payroll period ending immediately prior to the election. But employment situations may differ, and the board has an obligation to tailor its general eligibility formulas to the particular facts of the case. When employees are temporary or seasonal, the board has attempted to devise alternative formulas designed to permit optimum employee enfranchisement and

continued

COURT ENFORCEMENT OF AN NLRB ORDER—continued

free choice, without enfranchising individuals without continuing interest in the terms and conditions of employment offered by the employer.

Here the board adopted an eligibility formula that looked to (1) whether the employees had worked a minimum of 15 days in the three-month periods immediately preceding the date of the issuance of the direction of election and (2) the employees' eligibility for future employment with company. The board utilized the same eligibility formula used in another case involving a fabricator of ornamental iron. It operated year-round, employing regular full-time welders as well as extra part-time welders that it called on during peak production periods. The part-time welders came from a pool of 27 "on-call" welders, and many of them had substantial histories of employment with the company. The board therefore concluded that it was equitable to include in the unit all part-time employees who had worked a minimum of 15 days in the three-month period immediately preceding the date of issuance of the direction of election.

The company argues that the board erred in applying its eligibility formula without explaining why its laid-off employees had any continuity or regularity of employment or why that particular formula fit this case. There are some similarities, as both the companies were year-round employers with peak production periods. But there are also significant differences between the two cases—the most notable being that unlike the on-call welders in case cited by the board, the employees in this case were hired by the company for a very brief period to meet a short-lived and unprecedented spike in demand. Nowhere did the board explain why it was appropriate to enfranchise these individuals, nor

did it discuss the evidence showing that the company had no plans to increase production to its October 2000 levels ever again. As a general rule, laid-off employees are not eligible to vote when the employer has no plans to recall the employees in the near future. In addition, the board failed to address evidence indicating that the company had reemployed few of the employees the company had laid off in the past.

Finally, the board did not mention the regional director's mistaken assumption that the eligibility formula he devised understated the number of eligible employees by 25 percent: He thought the formula enfranchised 30 employees when it actually enfranchised 40. It is one thing to approve a formula that is expected to yield a unit that includes only four more employees than were working just prior to a one-time surge in the unit's work. It is quite another, however, to approve a formula that, although predicated on the former assumption, actually yields 14 (54 percent) more employees and to do so without explaining why the mistaken calculation does not render the formula inappropriate.

DECISION

The board's decision was devoid of reasoning and explanation; therefore, the court is unable to conclude that the board met its obligation to tailor its general eligibility formulas to the particular facts of the case. Accordingly, the company's petition for review is granted, the board's order is vacated, and the case is remanded to the board for an explanation of why the *particular* formula it applied was appropriate here or for the development of an eligibility formula that is adequately justified and tailored to the facts of this case.

SOURCE: Adapted from *King Curb v. NLRB,* 170 LRRM 2170 (CA DC 2002).

The NLRB may *invalidate a contract or clause* if it finds that the union acted under an erroneous though good-faith claim that it had majority representation, in a successorship situation in which one union has dissolved or merged with another, or when a business has changed hands. Contract clauses impinging on areas prohibited by the act will come before the board for validity tests. Items tested include union security clauses, discriminatory provisions, hot cargo clauses (in which union members refuse to handle goods from a nonunion employer), and breach of a union's duty of fair representation. Also, a petition and election for representation not barred by an existing contract may invalidate an existing contract.

The NLRB may also show support of contracts and contract clauses by interpreting the contract as a waiver of statutory rights. Often, claims that a statutory right of a party has been violated, based on specific language in the collective bargaining agreement, result in a board finding that the party waived those rights when entering into the agreement. Numerous cases have come before the board in which a union is found to have waived the right to bargain over such issues as employee qualifications, employer subcontracting, or administration of a merit rating system. These have been so decided because of specific language in the contract reserving those items to the employer.

The NLRB may even go past the specific language of the contract and explore the bargaining history of the parties to determine whether there has been a waiver of a statutory right. The present law on waiver is summarized as follows:

1. There is a continuing statutory duty to bargain, even during the term of a contract.
2. The continuing duty to bargain embraces not only grievances but also all mandatory subjects that are not contained in a contract for a fixed period.
3. A party may waive his or her right to bargain either by relinquishing a right to bring up a particular subject or by agreeing that the other party may exercise unilateral control over the subject.
4. Such a waiver must be clear and unmistakable and must indicate an acquiescence, agreement, or conscious yielding to a demand.[24]

However, a statutory right to receive information is not waived by waiving a right to bargain over the issue. In one case, the board found that although the union gave the employer the prerogative to discharge for lack of work, it did not in the contract forestall a grievance or a claim for information to justify the discharge when the employer took such action. The enforcement of existing collective bargaining agreements also comes under the NLRB's jurisdiction when it has been claimed that unilateral action by the employer has modified the contract. Or an employer might claim that the union has violated the act by strike action called to force bargaining on a modification of an existing contract. It is an unfair labor practice to terminate or modify an existing contract during its life except under the conditions outlined in the statute.[25]

Court Enforcement

Prior to the Taft-Hartley Amendments, employers and unions could sue in state court for breach of contract if one party believed the other party violated a collective bargaining agreement. Most state courts viewed the collective bargaining agreement as a legally enforceable obligation. Unions could obtain injunctions to restrain employers from violation of wage provisions or to require employers to abide by a union shop agreement. The employer could obtain an injunction against strikes in breach of a valid no-strike clause. Still, contract enforcement for the employer was difficult because many labor unions were not incorporated. In some states such unincorporated organizations could not be sued; thus, the employer had to sue each union member individually. Even if the unincorporated union could be sued for specific injunctive relief, monetary damages might not be available.

The Taft-Hartley Amendments were an attempt to lessen the unions' power by allowing access to federal courts on suits for collective bargaining contract violations. The amendments specifically recognized labor unions as entities that could be sued and held liable for monetary damages. The Senate interpreted the legislative intent of the Taft-Hartley Amendments as follows:

> If unions can break agreements with relative impunity, then such agreements do not tend to stabilize industrial relations. The execution of an agreement does not by itself promote industrial peace. The chief advantage that an employer can reasonably expect from a collective labor agreement is assurance of uninterrupted operation during the term of the agreement. Without some effective method of assuring freedom from economic warfare for the term of the agreement, there is little reason why an employer would desire to sign such a contract.
>
> It is apparent that until all jurisdictions, and particularly the federal government, authorize actions against labor unions as legal entities, there will not be the mutual responsibility necessary to finalize collective-bargaining agreements. The Congress has protected the right of workers to organize. It has passed laws to encourage and promote collective bargaining.
>
> Statutory recognition of the collective agreement as a valid, binding, and enforceable contract is a logical and necessary step. It will promote a higher degree of responsibility upon the parties to such agreements, and will thereby promote industrial peace.
>
> It has been argued that the result of making collective agreements enforceable against unions would be that they would no longer consent to the inclusion of a no-strike clause in a contract. . . .
>
> In any event, it is certainly a point to be bargained over and any union with the status of representative under the NLRA [National Labor Relations Act] which has bargained in good faith with an employer should have no reluctance in including a no-strike clause if it intends to live up to the terms of the contract. The improvement that would result in the stability of industrial relations is, of course, obvious.[26]

Grievance Procedure and Arbitration

Later chapters of this book deal with the practical aspects of contract enforcement through grievance and arbitration procedures. The development of grievance and arbitration as a means of contract enforcement and the relationship and effectiveness of this type of enforcement as compared with court and NLRB enforcement are discussed here.

Development of Arbitration Rights

The American common-law tradition is that an employee is an employee at will, with the terms and conditions of employment established by the employer with virtually no restriction. Although this tradition allowed either party to terminate the relationship and therefore was seen as fair and equitable, the employee had little real protection from poverty. It was in the public interest, therefore, that the government enter into the employer–employee relationship. It could enter either by enacting laws to regulate terms and conditions of employment, including questions of wages, bonuses, fringe benefits, discharge, and employment standards, or by using legislation to regulate the relationship between employer and employee. The National Labor Relations Act reflects the latter choice. Its provisions speak to the requirement for collective bargaining but not to the substantive provisions of the employment contract, and those provisions have resulted in the development of arbitration, a system of private enforcement of publicly protected rights. The act itself did not embody arbitration provisions:

> The real development of labor arbitration as we know it today, and indeed the virtual transformation of the usual meaning of the word, came as a result of World War II, the War Labor Board and the impermissibility of the strike weapon as a method of resolving questions of interpretation and compliance with collective agreements and of providing the interstitial lawmaking which the interpretive process implies. As a result of this development, we have in this country a system of nongovernmental law which provides not only the rules concerning the rights of employees against employers but also the system of adjudication of controversies concerning the applications of those rules.[27]

The public had become responsible for the enforcement of the right to a specific process, but it had not gained the right to substantive protections.

The collective bargaining agreements entered into by parties subject to the act after the War Labor Board Policy of World War II gave each side protective rights enforceable through the use of arbitration. In most contracts, a grievance procedure provides a union the right to seek compliance with a contract provision through a system of formal or informal meetings between union and management. Such procedures may cause the employer to comply simply because the grievance is brought to the employer's attention. However, if the grievance involves disagreement over facts, the meaning of the collective bargaining agreement, application or implementation of the agreement, or the reasonableness of an action, it might not be resolved without the intervention of a third party. Thus, arbitration can also be the resolution by an outside party of a grievance dispute. If the parties to a collective bargaining agreement agree to a grievance arbitration procedure in the contract, the arbitration award enforces substantive rights granted under that contract. Case 9-2 is an example of how the expertise of the arbitrator can lead to a fair result.

Court and Board Enforcement

As discussed earlier, state and federal courts have enforcement powers in collective bargaining agreements. In the ***Lincoln Mills* case**, the Supreme Court, by accepting such enforcement powers, required specific performance of an employer's promise to arbitrate in a collective bargaining agreement.[28] The Court felt that the agreement to arbitrate grievance disputes was the employer's trade-off for the union's agreement not to strike.

The role of arbitration and court enforcement of contract agreements was more specifically outlined in three Supreme Court cases known as the ***Steelworkers Trilogy***.[29] These cases held that the function of a court is limited to a review of whether the issue to be arbitrated is governed by the contract. Any doubt as to the coverage should be resolved

DISCIPLINING A SHOP STEWARD

The employer is a nonprofit corporation that employs social and health-care professionals who do case management for the developmentally disabled by ensuring that they have access to the appropriate resources, living facilities, health-care facilities, and the like. In late March or early April 2000, the supervisor issued an e-mail announcing a change in the daily schedule that also affected compensatory overtime. The supervisor, a long-term employee, had recently been promoted to the position of nursing supervisor.

Two nursing consultants who reported to the supervisor had some concerns about the coming schedule change, namely, its affect on the daily schedule and its impact on their compensatory overtime. The nurses took their concerns to the union's designated shop steward at the facility, also a long-term employee with the facility. She had been active in the union's original organizing drive in 1995 that led to an election in February 1996 and the union's recognition in March 1996. The current collective bargaining agreement (CBA) is the second negotiated agreement between the union and the employer.

The two employees asked the shop steward whether the supervisor could, under the terms of the CBA, make the change in the daily schedule. They also asked the shop steward how the grievance procedure works and how they might initiate a grievance. The shop steward discussed the matter with them and advised them that the CBA gave them the right to orally discuss their concerns with the supervisor with the goal of reaching an accommodation. She told them that they, as employees and bargaining unit members, could either initiate an informal oral discussion with the supervisor on their own or have a shop steward present to assist them during the discussion. The shop steward pointed out

that this oral discussion, as an informal grievance meeting, could be a first step in the negotiated grievance procedure.

A few days later, one of the employees decided to speak to the supervisor and asked the shop steward to go with her. The employee approached the supervisor and asked whether she could meet with her for a few minutes. The supervisor responded with a yes and told her she would meet with her in the nurse's office. When the supervisor entered the nurse's office for the meeting, the shop steward was in the room. The shop steward, with whom she was acquainted, identified herself as a union shop steward. She also informed the supervisor of the issue (schedule changes and compensatory overtime) and informed her that this was a first-level, informal oral meeting as provided for in the agreement. The supervisor said that she felt very uncomfortable, that she was new in her position as a supervisor, and that she "felt the need for an attorney." This was her first grievance, and she admitted that she had not, at the time, read the grievance procedure in the CBA. The shop steward's demeanor was very professional, and the shop steward explained the first step of the grievance procedure to the supervisor, noting that if the matter could be worked out, it would stop here. The supervisor later told her supervisor that she had been caught unaware and "felt blind sided." The entire meeting only lasted a few minutes.

A few days later, the other nursing consultant approached the supervisor and asked whether she could meet with her for a few minutes. The supervisor said yes and told her to wait in her office. The nurse called the shop steward and told her she would be meeting with the supervisor to discuss the change in schedule and overtime and asked that she, as shop steward, be present to assist in the discussion. When

continued

DISCIPLINING A SHOP STEWARD—continued

the supervisor entered her office a few minutes later, the shop steward was waiting in the room with the nurse. The supervisor testified that as she entered her office, she walked past the shop steward and around to the area behind her desk and said to the shop steward, "I have no time for this; I can't do this now." She testified that the shop steward then stepped up to the corner of her desk and announced that she was here in her role as shop steward and that this was a first-level, informal meeting about the compensatory overtime.

The evidence in the record was that the supervisor broke into tears at one point for a moment or so during this meeting but quickly regained her composure. The supervisor ended the meeting by stepping around the shop steward and walked to the door of her office. She stood by the door, and the shop steward and nurse exited her office. The entire meeting lasted only about five minutes, and following the meeting the supervisor was able to make her other appointments and obligations and finish her work for the day.

What followed on that same day, as reflected by the record, provided some insight as to the employer's reasons for and the employer's disciplinary actions taken against the shop steward. About 15 minutes after the meeting, the supervisor mentioned to one of her supervisors and a member of the Executive Management Team (EMT) what had just occurred. He told her to write it up. The supervisor wrote up the incident in the form of an e-mail and sent it to the director, who was also a member of the EMT. A copy of the e-mail was also forwarded to the human resources manager.

The chief executive officer (CEO) learned of the incident on the same day when someone on the EMT telephoned him and relayed the allegations made by the supervisor in her e-mail message. The human resources manager was directed by the CEO to conduct an investigation and to prepare a letter to be given to the shop steward informing her of the allegations and putting her on suspension, without pay, pending the outcome of the investigation. Although the CEO discussed the matter with other members of the EMT, the decision was solely his to conduct an investigation and to put the shop steward on suspension without pay. He was concerned that there had been two verbal altercations and that the meetings that had taken place were not scheduled appointments.

The shop steward was notified that she was to meet with the EMT that afternoon. The union president, also an employee, accompanied the shop steward to the meeting. At the meeting, the shop steward was informed of the allegations and told that she was being placed on suspension without pay pending the outcome of the investigation. The notice, in part, stated,

> You have been placed on suspension pending our investigation under the collective bargaining agreement. Based on the outcome of the investigation, you may be subject to disciplinary action up to and including termination. Should the results of the investigation determine that you are innocent of these allegations, you will be paid for the time you were off on this suspension.

Following their investigation, the EMT decided that the shop steward would be given back pay for the four days she was on suspension. The team also decided that the shop steward would be given a documented counseling/evaluation of performance. Two charges were cited: (1) disrespectful

continued

DISCIPLINING A SHOP STEWARD—continued

conduct and (2) disruptive activity. The documented counseling was the only discipline imposed on the shop steward, who then filed a grievance.

The employer contended that it had just cause to issue the shop steward the documented counseling. The meetings at issue were not scheduled in advance. Her behavior toward the supervisor was disrespectful and disruptive. The shop steward disregarded the supervisor's requests for assistance from others, disregarded the supervisor's requests to reschedule the meetings at some mutually agreeable later dates, demanded that the meetings continue after the supervisor said she did not have the time to meet at that moment, and disrupted her appointments and obligations and schedule.

Both meetings were essentially ambushes by the shop steward. Her behavior was disrespectful and disruptive if not openly insubordinate and a clear violation of the *Personnel Manual, Conduct and Work Rules*. All employees are held to the same standard even if acting in the role of steward. The employer not only had just cause to issue the documented counseling but also would have been justified in issuing a more severe punishment had it decided to do so. The grievance should be denied.

The union contended that the employer did not have just cause to issue the shop steward the documented counseling. The employer violated the CBA and federal law when it issued the documented counseling and when it suspended her without pay pending the outcome of an investigation. The shop steward was just doing her job of representing bargaining unit members and calling the employer's attention to a claim that the agreement was being violated.

Under the "Equity Principle," an employee, when engaging management in grievance proceedings, has parity with the employer. The employee's speech and conduct when functioning in that role are protected activities as long as they do not cross the line between protected and unprotected activities. The shop steward's behavior during the two interactions was never outside the zone of protected speech and conduct. She was simply doing her job as shop steward. The employer should be ordered to cease and desist from interfering, restraining, or coercing unit members by disciplining or threatening to discipline union stewards engaged in their lawful functions. The grievance should be sustained.

DECISION

The arbitrator agreed with the shop steward that the employer had no grounds to discipline her. The employer's action was based on the fact that the shop steward had violated the company's code of conduct in how she approached the supervisor. That is, she attempted to conduct two first-level grievance meetings without scheduling them in advance, she entered the supervisor's office without permission, and she continued the meeting after the supervisor told her she could not meet. The employer characterized the shop steward's behavior as disrespectful.

However, the arbitrator noted that as to being disrespectful, the employer was using the wrong standard. The shop steward, while representing the union, was on equal footing with the supervisor, and as long as she did not conduct herself unprofessionally, she was not required to defer to the supervisor. Furthermore, the arbitrator found no requirement in the CBA that the informal first step of the grievance procedure had to be scheduled.

The grievance was sustained.

SOURCE: Adapted from *Alta California Regional Center v. SEIU*, Local 535, 116 LA 44 (July 20, 2001).

in favor of arbitration. Unless the arbitrator's award is ambiguous, the courts should enforce it even if the court would not have decided the substantive issue in the same way:

> The 1960 *Steelworkers Trilogy* expanded vastly upon the foundation laid in *Lincoln Mills*. Arbitration was acknowledged as the preferred, superior forum for contract interpretation and enforcement. The powers of an arbitrator were held to be bounded by the restrictions of the "four corners of the contract" but arbitral actions were largely immunized from judicial review. As repeatedly stated thereafter, arbitration became the cornerstone of the rapidly arising edifice housing the federal law of the labor agreement.[30]

The Court gave almost complete deference to arbitration as a means of contract enforcement by limiting its own review of an arbitration award to whether the issue under arbitration is in the agreement.

In a study of federal and district court decisions for the 30 years following the *Steelworkers Trilogy,* it was found that the courts deferred to the arbitration process 70 to 74 percent of the time. Case 9-3 is a good example of the Supreme Court's deferral to arbitration.

CASE 9-3

MISCO, INC.

One of Misco's work rules listed as cause for discharge the possession or use of a controlled substance on company property. An employee covered by the collective labor agreement was apprehended by police in the backseat of someone else's car on the company parking lot. There was marijuana smoke in the air of the car and a lighted marijuana cigarette in the front-seat ashtray. A police search of the employee's own car on the lot revealed marijuana gleanings.

Management discharged the employee for violation of the disciplinary rule. The employee grieved, and an arbitrator later upheld the grievance and ordered reinstatement. The arbitrator concluded that the cigarette incident was insufficient proof that the grievant was using or had possessed marijuana on company property. At the time of discharge, the company was not aware of the fact that marijuana was found in the employee's own car, and the arbitrator refused to accept that claim into evidence.

DECISION

The district court vacated the arbitration award, and the court of appeals confirmed, ruling that reinstatement would violate the public policy against the operation of dangerous machinery by persons under the influence of drugs (the grievant operated a slitter-rewinder, which cuts rolling coils of paper).

The Supreme Court reversed, however, holding that the court of appeals exceeded the limited authority possessed by a court reviewing an arbitrator's award under a collective bargaining agreement. The Court stated that absent fraud by the parties or the arbitrator's dishonesty, reviewing courts in such cases are not authorized to reconsider the merits of an arbitrator's award. The Court also stated that the collective bargaining agreement left evidentiary matters to the arbitrator: The arbitrator's finding of fact is conclusive.

SOURCE: *United Paperworkers International Union, AFL-CIO v. Misco, Inc.,* 484 U.S. 29, 108 S.Ct. 364 (1987).

The NLRB also deferred its jurisdiction in certain unfair labor practice cases to an arbitration procedure established under the contract. In the ***Collyer* case**, the NLRB agreed to defer jurisdiction if there was a stable collective bargaining relationship between the parties, the party defending the charge was willing to arbitrate the issue, and the dispute centered on the contract and its meaning.[31] The board also decided to defer to an arbitration award if the arbitration procedure met the following criteria:

1. *Fair and regular proceedings.*   That the proceedings are the equivalent of due process, affording parties an opportunity to be heard, cross-examine witnesses, be represented by counsel, and have an unbiased decision maker.
2. *Agreement to be bound.*   Both parties must agree to abide by the arbitrator's decision. A hearing over the parties' objections would not be honored.
3. *Award not repugnant to purposes and policies of the act.*   Even if due process is followed, the arbitrator's award can be invalidated if it violates the purposes of the National Labor Relations Act. For example, an arbitrator upheld a dismissal of an employee for being disloyal, but his so-called disloyalty was in seeking help from the NLRB. The board did not uphold that award.
4. *Unfair labor practice to be considered by arbitrator.*   The actual issue surrounding the unfair labor practice must be reviewed and decided by the arbitrator, or the NLRB will not defer to the award. Deciding other issues between the parties is immaterial.
5. *Facts are presented.*   The arbitrator was generally presented with the facts relevant to resolving the unfair labor practice.[32]

The courts narrowly construe the ability of a court to provide a public policy exception to the enforcement of an arbitration award. The Supreme Court ruled in the *Misco* case that to vacate an arbitrator's award, it must be clearly indicated that the award violates public policy on the basis of laws and legal precedents and not on general consideration of supposed public interest.[33] Since the *Misco* decision, fewer federal or district courts have overturned an arbitration decision on public policy grounds.[34]

Since the 1971 *Collyer* decision, the NLRB has continued to reaffirm its policy to defer to arbitration in unfair labor cases.[35] A comparison of NLRB awards and arbitration decisions and grievance settlements in one study found that when the unfair labor practice involves a complaint from an individual because of discipline of a union member, the arbitration or grievance procedure often results in the same or nearly the same result as an NLRB award. However, cases involving a charge that the employer has refused to bargain in good faith have less frequently been decided by an arbitrator or settled by the parties in the same manner as similar cases that were decided by the NLRB.[36]

Economic Activity

To use economic pressure as a means to enforce a contract obviously is not the preferred method, as evidenced by the support given arbitration in court decisions. A union slowdown or strike countered by an employer lockout or mass dismissal seems at odds with the National Labor Relations Act's aim of promoting industrial peace. But to use economic activity, or at least the ability to resort to economic activity, is a key element in the success of the collective bargaining process.

Earlier chapters detailed the use of economic weapons, strikes, and other concerted activity during recognition campaigns and during negotiations. Although use of economic power to enforce an existing contract has become increasingly rare because of mandatory grievance and arbitration procedures and no-strike clauses in labor agreements, such action has not disappeared.

EQUAL JUSTICE UNDER LAW

The National Labor Relations Board (NLRB) investigates potential contract violations and has the power to seek the enforcement of a contract in federal court.

The Supreme Court, in the **Boys Market case**, upheld an injunction against a union that struck over an arbitrable grievance despite a no-strike clause and a mandatory grievance procedure.[37] But the Court noted that not all such strikes would be enjoined. It adopted strict standards from an earlier case:

> When a strike is sought to be enjoined because it is over a grievance which both parties are contractually bound to arbitrate, the district court may issue no injunctive order until it holds that the contract does have that effect; and the employer should be ordered to arbitrate, as a condition of his obtaining an injunction against the strike. Beyond this, the district court must, of course, consider whether issuance of an injunction would be warranted under ordinary principles of equity—whether breaches are occurring and will continue, or have been threatened and will be committed; whether they have caused or will cause irreparable injury to the employer; and whether the employer will suffer more from the denial of an injunction than will the union from its issuance.[38]

Thus, a union does have an effective weapon despite a no-strike clause if the grievance does not factually come under the contract arbitration procedure, if the employer is not willing to arbitrate, and if the employer cannot show where he or she has suffered irreparable injury from the breach of the no-strike obligation.

The Supreme Court later upheld the right of a union to engage in a sympathy strike pending an arbitrator's decision on whether such a strike was forbidden under the particular no-strike clause of the labor agreement.[39] The strike had been called in support of another union properly engaged in an economic strike. Although the arbitration procedure could be invoked to decide the scope of the no-strike clause, the Court would not allow the union's strike to be enjoined pending that decision. The NLRB, in its decision in *Indianapolis Power and Light Company*,[40] attempted to create a presumption that broad no-strike clauses were intended to cover sympathy strikes, but the U.S. Court of Appeals overruled that presumption in 1986 in *International Brotherhood of Electrical Workers, Local 387 v. National Labor Relations Board*.[41] The court said a no-strike clause must be interpreted according to the terms of the particular collective bargaining agreement, the bargaining history, and the past practices of the parties to determine its application to sympathy strikes.

RIGHTS AND PROHIBITED CONDUCT

Certain rights and duties arise during the term of a contract. These include the rights of the individual under the collective bargaining process, the duty to bargain during a contract term, and the duty to refrain from prohibited economic activities.

Individual Rights

Right to Refrain from Union Activities

Because of the National Labor Relations Act, labor relations has developed into a stylized system of employer–union relations. In an election decided by majority rule, a union is given the authority to represent all the employees of an appropriate unit in negotiation and administration of a contract. Individual employees who may have voted against the union still find their employment contract affected by the negotiations, and although the union has a duty to represent fairly all employees during the negotiation process, absent a showing of actual hostile discrimination, the court will accept a wide range of reasonableness when a question of a breach of that duty arises.

Originally the National Labor Relations Act allowed an employer to make an agreement with a union to require union membership as a prior condition of employment—that is, the closed shop. All forms of union security were permitted as long as the agreement was made with a bona fide union representing the bargaining unit. Closed shop clauses became common in collective bargaining agreements. Although these clauses protected and promoted the growth of unions, abuses of the system against individuals who were denied job opportunities led to the Taft-Hartley Amendments. These amendments made the closed shop an unfair labor practice and added the right *not* to organize and engage in union activity. Although union shop clauses still could be negotiated and enforced against existing employees, the employee need only pay dues to abide by that contract clause; no other activity was required. The amendments also allowed state right-to-work laws to outlaw even the union shop requirement.

The union hiring hall is another practice that appears to give equal consideration to union and nonunion personnel. Although a hiring hall operating as a closed shop was technically outlawed by the amendments, a union can still negotiate a contract clause that requires the employer to hire through the union's exclusive referral system. It is then up to the nonunion individual to claim and prove discriminatory referrals. Union security clauses are not the only prohibited behavior violating the individual employee's right to refrain from union activity. The courts consider union intimidation, reprisals, or threats against employees as restraint and coercion. And, as seen in Profile 9-2, even today unions are still trying to overcome some excesses from the past.

Duty of Fair Representation

Under its duty of fair representation, a union must consider all the employees in the bargaining unit when negotiating an agreement and must make an honest effort to serve their interests. This must be a good-faith effort, without hostility or arbitrary

---

PROFILE 9-2

TEAMSTER PRESIDENT HOFFA ANNOUNCES ANTIMOB INITIATIVE

International Brotherhood of Teamsters General President James P. Hoffa announced on July 29, 1999, a new initiative to eradicate corruption and any remaining mafia influences in the Teamsters union. The announcement follows unanimous passage of a resolution endorsing a "Teamsters Anti-Corruption Plan" by the union's General Executive Board (GEB).

"I made the promise that we would take dramatic steps to remove any remaining influence of organized crime from our union, and set new, higher standards for a corruption-free union," Hoffa declared. "I am pleased to announce that the Teamsters General Executive Board unanimously passed a resolution for a comprehensive internal anticorruption plan; a self-policing plan unlike any other union."

Joining Hoffa at a press conference were former federal prosecutor Edwin H. Stier and James M. Kossler, a former FBI official responsible for directing the department's organized crime effort in New York. Stier is a former assistant U.S. attorney and court-appointed Teamster trustee.

"I am convinced that Jim Hoffa and the leaders of this union are committed to running a clean union and are determined to remove any remaining vestiges of organized crime," Stier stated.

Hoffa announced the four-point, anticorruption plan that Stier, joined by Kossler, will assist the general president in implementing. The plan outline is as follows:

- Establish clear, concise, and practical Standards of Conduct;
- Educate officers and members concerning the Standards of Conduct;
- Establish internal procedures to guarantee effective and impartial enforcement of the Standards of Conduct;
- Identify and remove any remaining organized crime influence within the union.

The GEB resolution also declared, "It is time to move toward a process and procedure that will demonstrate that the Union can and will protect itself and its members from corruption and the influence of organized crime and that will lead to an end of outside control of the Union, a goal that is consistent with the fundamental premise of federal law that labor organizations must be maintained as democratic organizations controlled by their members."

SOURCE: Adapted from The International Brotherhood of Teamsters Homepage: www.teamster.org (August 1, 1999).

---

discrimination. But the end result of such negotiations may still unevenly affect one, several, or a class of employees without the union's being considered in breach of its duty, as seen in Case 9-4.

A far more litigious area concerning fair representation is in contract enforcement. Grievance arbitration has become the most common method of enforcing each party's promise to abide by the contract. That promise to arbitrate is enforceable by either the employer or the union. Fitting the individual into that arbitration system involves balancing conflicting interests. The National Labor Relations Act adopted the doctrine of majority rule when it granted a union exclusive representation rights if selected by most unit members. The courts confirmed this doctrine by giving the collective agreement precedence over the individual employment contract. To balance the power of the union, the court recognized the union's duty to represent all its employees.

But there remained a question of whether an individual employee could arbitrate against both or either party. In *Vaca v. Sipes, Hines v. Anchor Motor Co., Inc.,* and *Bowen v. U.S. Postal Service,* the Supreme Court indicated that the individual has no

UNION UNFAIR LABOR PRACTICE

The United Mine Workers of America (UMW) is the exclusive collective bargaining representative for individuals employed in the coal industry throughout the United States and Canada. The union obtained a $1.3 million settlement from the Peabody Holding Company arising from hiring practices at a coal mining facility in Indiana that allegedly were contrary to an agreement between Peabody and the union granting preferential job opportunities to certain active and laid-off miners. The union initially decided to divide the settlement proceeds among the 78 plaintiffs who would have been entitled to employment at the Indiana mine if the agreement had not been breached. But complaints from other plaintiffs, coupled with mass layoffs in the coal industry elsewhere in Indiana, caused the union to reconsider the fairness of that plan. The union then decided to spread the settlement proceeds among the 905 plaintiffs that had employment or recall rights at the Farmersburg facility.

As a result, the original 78 union members who were slated to receive the settlement saw their share decrease from more than $15,000 to about $1,500. Unhappy with the new distribution, 61 of those 78 members (the Plaintiffs) sued the union. The union moved to dismiss the case because the plaintiffs had not appealed the UMW's decision through the union's own grievance procedure.

The lower court granted judgment in favor of the union, finding that the plaintiffs had failed to initiate a proper appeal under the procedures required by the union's constitution and had not demonstrated any basis for their failure to exhaust those procedures. The plaintiffs appealed.

DISCUSSION

The Supreme Court has held that plaintiffs are ordinarily required to exhaust union appeals procedures before bringing suit against their union concerning internal union affairs. The Court recognized, however, that internal procedures may be lengthy and sometimes inadequate to address the employees' grievances and held that, in the context of Labor-Management Relations Act claims against the union, flexibility in imposing the exhaustion requirement is necessary. Balancing the policy of providing a judicial forum to enforce the duty of fair representation against the competing policy of encouraging nonjudicial resolution of labor disputes, the Court held that the courts have discretion to decide whether to require exhaustion of internal union procedures.

The Court identified three factors to guide a court's discretion in deciding whether to excuse exhaustion. First, whether union officials are so hostile to the employee that he could not hope to obtain a fair hearing on his claim; second, whether the internal union appeals procedures would be inadequate either to reactivate the employee's grievance or to award him the full relief he seeks under the Labor-Management Relations Act; and third, whether exhaustion of internal procedures would unreasonably delay the employee's opportunity to obtain a judicial hearing on the merits of his claim. If any of these factors are present, the court may properly excuse the employee's failure to exhaust.

The plaintiffs in this case claim that the first and third factors apply. They argue that it would have been futile to take their case to the union because the union's general counsel stated that the union would

continued

| CASE 9-4 | **UNION UNFAIR LABOR PRACTICE—continued** |

fight the claim "to the end," and the union executives who made the decision to distribute the settlement more broadly were the same people who would hear the plaintiffs' appeal. The plaintiffs conclude that these facts show that the union's decision had become "fixed," rendering any appeal futile.

Plaintiffs next argue that requiring exhaustion would unreasonably delay their opportunity to obtain judicial review of their claim because the international convention to which an adverse decision by a union board must be appealed is required to meet only once every four years.

DECISION

The Court noted that the union's attorney is not a member of any appellate review board within the union. Plaintiffs do not disagree with the district court's observation that she would not be involved in any decision rendered by the board or the international convention. Her statement that the union would fight to the end therefore tells nothing about whether the plaintiffs would receive a fair hearing. Similarly, although one member of the appeal board was involved in the decision to increase the number of recipients of the settlement, there is

no evidence that any other member of the 11-member board was involved in that decision. Plaintiffs complain that the district court failed to take that one member's participation into consideration. But even giving the plaintiffs the benefit of all reasonable inferences, the presence of only one potentially hostile member does not demonstrate hostility so pervasive that the plaintiffs could not hope to receive a fair hearing on their claim.

Furthermore, because the plaintiffs failed to initiate even the first-level appeal with the union—which takes only four months and might have resolved their claim—their delay argument is entirely speculative. To excuse exhaustion on the basis of the possibility that a second-level appeal would be unreasonably lengthy would preempt any opportunity for intra-union resolution at the first level. This is contrary to one of the policies behind the exhaustion requirement—to encourage nonjudicial resolution of labor disputes.

Therefore, the district court was correct in refusing to excuse the failure of the plaintiffs to exhaust their appeal through the union before filing suit on the basis of the union's alleged hostility to the plaintiffs' claims or on the basis of undue delay.

SOURCE: Adapted from *Arnold v. United Mine Workers*, 170 LRRM 2213 (CA 7 2002).

absolute right to have a grievance arbitrated and that the union is liable to the employee only if, in processing and settling that grievance, it violates its fair representation duty.[42]

In contract administration issues, the duty of fair representation is breached when a union's conduct is arbitrary, discriminatory, or in bad faith. A union may not arbitrarily ignore a meritorious grievance or process it in a perfunctory manner. Yet proof of the merit of a grievance is not enough under this test: Arbitrary or bad-faith actions must also be proved.

The subjective nature of the fair representation test has left unions with "Hobson's choice." If a union cannot be reasonably certain that its honest and rational decision not to pursue a grievance to arbitration will withstand a *Vaca* challenge, the arbitration process will be so burdened that its effectiveness and financial viability will be undermined. At the same time, the *Vaca* rule ensures an individual that although there is no absolute right to arbitrate a grievance, the union cannot behave in a capricious fashion.[43]

Due Process

The individual employee has a right to due process of law under a collective bargaining agreement. This process includes a right to *substantive due process,* which is fair treatment by the employer in any action taken against an employee, and a right to *procedural due process*, which comprises a fair hearing on that action.

In general, in substantive due process, the policy or standard invoked must be known by the employee and must be reasonable. In addition, a violation of policies must be proved, and the burden of proof is on the employer. The application of rules and policies must be consistent; certain employees cannot be singled out for discipline. Also, actions must be impersonal and based on fact.

In procedural due process, any contractual procedures for employment actions must be followed. Equally important, the arbitration procedure must be fair. The individual must receive fair representation by the union, a hearing must be held so that the individual can be heard in an unbiased setting, and the employer's reasons for bringing the action must be made known.

Duty to Bargain During the Contract Term

The standards for good-faith collective bargaining contained in the National Labor Relations Act include the duty to bargain during the contract term under certain circumstances. The duty, however, is not absolute. The language of the act provides that a party cannot be required to discuss or agree to terminate or modify the contract during its term. In addition, the contract under which parties operate may limit the duty in the following ways:

1. ***Zipper clause.***   This clause is an abbreviated form of the waiver provision in a collective bargaining agreement, sometimes referred to as a "wrap-up" clause, considered to denote waiver of the right of either party to require the other to bargain on any matter not covered in an agreement during the life of the contract, thus limiting the terms and conditions of employment to those set forth in the contract. A clause of this type would read as follows:[44]

    > This contract is complete in itself and sets forth all the terms and conditions of the agreement between the parties hereto.

2. ***Opener clause.***   This clause allows negotiations to take place during the contract term on certain mandatory items. Most clauses provide for the reopening of negotiations on only one specific issue, whereas the remainder of the contract is closed to discussions. The most common issue specified in reopeners is wages; specific benefits are also common issues.[45]
3. ***Separability clause.***   Most contracts contain a clause that protects the rest of the contract should one section come into conflict with state or federal law. Such a clause usually provides that the offending section becomes null and void or that, as in the following Article XIV from the agreement between duPont Co. and the Neoprene Craftsmen Union, the section must be renegotiated as needed:

    ### Article XIV

    Suspension of Provisions of Agreement
    Section 1. If during the life of this agreement there shall be in existence any applicable rule, regulation or order issued by governmental authority,

which shall be inconsistent with any provision of this agreement, such provision shall be modified to the extent necessary to comply with such law,
rule, regulation, or order.[46]

Union Demand to Negotiate

A question of bargaining during the contract term may arise when the union seeks to
add new items not covered under the contract. This situation highlights the two competing views of collective bargaining. One view is that the collective bargaining agreement does not end the collective bargaining process. It is a continuous process, albeit
with rules as to how the process should proceed. Many people believe that the grievance-arbitration procedures are a part of that process because those decisions shape
the administration of the contract and therefore its terms.

The opposite view is that the collective bargaining process must be completed with
the signing of the contract to give meaning to the contract terms. Because bargaining
should encompass all subjects, the final agreement should settle all subjects either explicitly or implicitly between the parties. Under this view, the grievance-arbitration procedure only interprets the contract and adds nothing to its terms. The NLRB's
attitude to a union demand for bargaining on a new item during a contract term
seems to be that, without a zipper clause, if the item is not contained in the contract
and was not discussed during negotiations, the employer has a duty to bargain on
that item.[47]

Employer's Unilateral Action

Most often the question of the duty to bargain during a contract term arises as a result
of unilateral action by the employer. Depending on the circumstances, such action may
be deemed an unfair labor practice as a breach of that duty to bargain. The questions of
whether a substantive or procedural provision of a contract was violated arise when an
employer takes unilateral action during a contract term and makes a change in some
condition of employment. If the employer's action changes a stated term of the contract, the answer is simple. The employer has committed an unfair labor practice. However, if under a broad management rights clause the employer takes an action that
affects employees in a manner not contemplated by the contract, disagreement as to
breach obviously occurs. As a rule, the NLRB considers charges of unfair labor practice
by a union in this instance a matter for arbitration and, under the *Collyer* decision, will
defer its jurisdiction to the arbitrator.

Even under a management rights clause in which the final decision is the employer's, a contract may contain a requirement that the union must be consulted prior
to any action. An employer who violates this procedural requirement is in breach of the
contract and of his or her duty to bargain during its duration.

Prohibited Economic Activity

The National Labor Relations Act, as amended by Taft-Hartley and Landrum-Griffin,
outlawed four specific economic pressure techniques that unions might try to use during the term of a contract: secondary boycotts, hot cargo agreements, jurisdictional
disputes, and featherbedding.

Secondary Boycotts

Section 8(b)(4) of the National Labor Relations Act prohibits a union from engaging in
or from inducing others to engage in a strike or boycott aimed against the goods or
services of one employer to force the employer to cease doing business with another

employer. This prohibition was a response to the labor movement's use of the **secondary boycott** to affect employer A by exerting economic pressure on those who do business with employer A. Primary economic activity such as a boycott by employees against an employer is not prohibited by this section, nor is a secondary boycott with an objective that is not statutorily forbidden.

The Supreme Court attempted to give guidance on the distinction between a primary and a secondary boycott. A **primary boycott** occurs when persons who normally deal directly with the work involved are encouraged to withhold their services. This type of boycott is not prohibited and includes, for example, appeals to replacement workers or delivery people not to cross a picket line or appeals to employees of subcontractors not to continue work essential to the operation. Even if the picketing takes place at the work site of the secondary employer, it may be protected if the work involved is the object of the dispute.

In 1988, the Supreme Court gave a significant victory to labor unions by ruling that union members may hand out leaflets in a secondary boycott action. The case, *De Bartola Corp. v. Florida Gulf Coast Trades Council,*[48] involved a union's distributing handbills in a shopping mall. The handbills asked customers not to shop at any of the stores in the mall because a construction company hired to build a new mall store was paying substandard wages. The mall was owned by the De Bartola Corporation, which then filed a complaint with the NLRB charging the union with engaging in a secondary boycott against the mall stores. The NLRB and a U.S. circuit court ruled in favor of De Bartola and ordered the union to cease and desist the action. The Supreme Court reversed the decision on the grounds that peaceful handbilling urging a customer boycott was not prohibited by Section 8 of the National Labor Relations Act when unaccompanied by picketing. The key difference between this case and previous cases was the act of handbilling without picketing. The Court declared that picketing was qualitatively different and produced different consequences. Although the Court noted that both picketing and handbilling could have detrimental effects on a neutral third party, prohibiting peaceful and truthful handbilling raised questions of First Amendment rights.[49]

As a result of the Supreme Court ruling, the NLRB overruled a long-standing rule that handbilling dealing with matters unrelated to the labor dispute was an unfair labor practice. In one case, *Delta Airlines, Inc.,* the union and the independent contractor that provided janitorial services to Delta were in a dispute. The union distributed handbills at the airport reporting on Delta's bad safety record.[50] In another case, a union that was protesting a contractor's use of nonunion companies to build housing gave out handbills that pointed out the proximity of the development to an EPA Superfund landfill site.[51] The importance of the board decisions that give unions the ability to affect a labor dispute by marshaling public opinion against their opponent cannot be overstated.[52]

In any event, the secondary employer involved must be neutral for the primary-secondary distinction to be valid. Secondary and primary employers will be considered allied if the secondary employer performs work he or she would not be doing except for the strike or if there is common ownership, control, and integration of operation causing the businesses to be treated as a single enterprise. For example, a union cannot picket a public warehouse that is storing products made by the employer. In the precedent case, *Auburndale Freezer Corporation v. NLRB,* the court overturned an NLRB decision to allow a union to picket a public warehouse. In the case the employer used a public warehouse five miles from its struck plant, and the employer was one of 20 firms storing goods in the warehouse. The court noted that no employees worked at the warehouse and to extend the strike to the warehouse would disrupt other employers not involved in the dispute; therefore the picketing was an unlawful "secondary boycott."[53]

When a union is on strike, it may organize a primary boycott against the employer with whom it is negotiating, such as the one pictured here.

A union may be held liable for any actual damages resulting from an unlawful secondary boycott sustained by the secondary or primary employer.

Shop-ins

A new form of secondary boycotting was demonstrated in 1995 by a union in Massachusetts. The Teamsters union was in a labor dispute with a beer distributor, August A. Busch & Co. of Massachusetts, Inc. The union conducted three **shop-ins** involving three different retail establishments that carried Busch products. The shop-ins involved anywhere from 50 to 125 union members converging on the stores at the same time; buying small items, such as gum or snacks; and paying with large-denomination bills.

The results were crowded parking lots, delays in service, and the loss of regular customers. The union did not engage in any information sharing; that is, it did not leaflet or express an opinion regarding Busch. Nor was it actually picketing. An unfair labor practice charge was made against the union, and the NLRB found this activity to be prohibited as a secondary boycott. Clearly the shop-in was conducted to pressure the retailers to not use Busch products. There was no communication to the public about Busch that would have been protected under the First Amendment.[54]

Hot Cargo Agreement

Hot cargo agreement refers to a negotiated contract provision stating that union members of one employer need not handle nonunion or struck goods of other employers. Court decisions after passage of the Taft-Hartley Amendments basically allowed such agreements, stating that the prohibition against secondary boycotts did not prohibit an employer and union from voluntarily including a hot cargo clause in their agreement, but such a provision was not an absolute defense against an unfair labor practice charge. If inducements of employees prohibited by Section 8(b)(4) of the National Labor Relations Act in the absence of a hot cargo provision occurred, the inducements would still violate the act.

The need to analyze such provisions on a case-by-case basis decreased somewhat after the passage of the Landrum-Griffin Act, which outlawed most hot cargo agreements, except in the garment and construction industries. But there still remain numerous similarly negotiated clauses that may or may not violate the act. A picket line clause protecting employees from discharge for refusing to cross a lawful primary picket line at another employer's premises is not a violation of the hot cargo agreement prohibition. However, a struck-work clause stating that an employer will not do business with a nonunion or struck employer is in violation unless the secondary employer is an ally.

Clauses completely prohibiting an employer from subcontracting are valid. But a clause forbidding subcontracting with nonunion employers may be a violation if it is aimed at a union's difference with another employer and is not designed to protect union standards. A work-preservation clause is lawful if the object of the clause is to protect and preserve work customarily performed by employees in the unit. This is true even if it involves refusing to handle certain cargo as long as it is the cargo that is refused and not the employer making the cargo. The aim of the clause must be to protect the actual employees of the bargaining unit and not union members as a group.

However, NLRB decisions regarding **dual employer** operations must be carefully considered. This "double-breasted" issue arises when a unionized employer establishes a separate, similar company to operate on a nonunion basis. Such employers are often in the construction industry. Because the construction industry was allowed an exception to the act's prohibition against secondary boycotts, the union sought to end dual operations. A contract clause was negotiated that made mere ownership of two ostensibly separate companies sufficient to cover even the nonunion employees of one company under the provisions of the unionized company's contract. The general counsel of the NLRB, however, charged the union with an unfair labor practice for this clause, stating that it violated Section 8(e) of the act and was not covered by the construction industry exception.[55]

Hot Cargo and Sweatshops

The Landrum-Griffin Act clouds union concerns over the operation of foreign sweatshops. The Garment Industry Proviso in Section 8(e) of the National Labor Relations Act allows labor organizations representing the apparel industry to require garment industry employers—known as jobbers—to do business only with union shops. It exempts the garment industry from the provision of the act that makes it an unfair labor practice for labor organizations to force employers to stop handling products of nonunion employers or hot cargo agreements. The garment industry's labor agreement requires jobbers who use contractors to hire union shops. But it also allows those who use nonunion shops or who use low-cost factories outside the United States to pay a "liquidated damage" penalty to the union. Garment unions have collected more than $160 million in liquidated damages since 1970.[56]

Jurisdictional Disputes

Prior to the 1947 Taft-Hartley Amendments, jurisdictional disputes between labor unions competing for the same work assignments caused numerous work stoppages. The amendments and later court decisions made such activities unfair labor practices and gave the NLRB jurisdiction to decide not only the unfair labor practice charge of participating in a jurisdictional dispute but also the underlying question of which union should get the work assignment. Factors the board uses to make its determinations include the skills and work involved; certifications by the board; company and industry practice; agreements between unions and between employers and unions; awards of arbitrators, joint boards, and the AFL-CIO in the same or related cases; the assignment made by the employer; and the efficient operation of the employer's business.[57]

Tips from the Experts

ARBITRATOR

What are the three most common "drafting errors" in collective bargaining contracts that cause problems for an employer or the union?

1. Failure to define a contractual term or phrase. Arbitrators give words their ordinary and usual meaning unless there is an indication that the parties intended a special meaning.

2. Failure to specify the scope of the arbitrator's authority. For example, is the award binding or merely advisory? Does the arbitrator have the usual authority to review the penalty imposed once he or she determines that the grievant did commit the offense with which he or she was charged?

3. Failure to encourage resolution of grievances at the earliest possible step. Such a failure would encourage open and full discovery and exchange of information in the lower grievance steps and could enhance the prospects of settlement or avoid the element of surprise at the arbitration hearing.

Featherbedding

Another prohibited activity is **featherbedding**, which, according to Section 8(b)(6) of the National Labor Relations Act, is "to cause an employer to pay . . . for services not performed or not to be performed."[58] The featherbedding section is rarely used unless a union tries to cause an employer to pay for services neither performed nor intended to be performed. In such cases the NLRB may order the union to reimburse the employer and cease the unlawful activity.[59] The Supreme Court may uphold a negotiated agreement to provide pay for make-work if the work was actually done regardless of its value to the employer.

PUBLIC-SECTOR CONTRACT ENFORCEMENT ISSUES

Reducing the Contract to Writing

For federal government employees, Title VII of the Civil Service Reform Act requires that any agreement must be incorporated into a written document if either party requests it.[60] The subjects covered in a public-sector collective bargaining agreement may differ from those in the private sector. An analysis of the differences can be made using four contract groups: union security and management rights, wage and effort bargaining, job security, and contract administration.

Union security will generally be included in the collective bargaining agreement as an automatic checkoff provision or agency shop. The federal statute mirrors the NLRB in regard to a valid contract as a bar to an election for recognition by a different union. State and local statutes are usually not that comprehensive. The management rights issue is indirectly addressed by detailing procedures to be followed by the employer.[61]

Although often wages and benefits are not subject to negotiation in federal government contracts, such items as merit raise systems and premium pay may be covered. Local government and state contracts may include wage provisions and often include procedures for testing standards of performance.

Job security, seniority, and due process often are covered under merit and civil service systems already in place. If the contract touches on those areas at all, the rights and procedures would be in addition to the civil service system.

In the area of contract administration, federal law requires that a grievance procedure with binding arbitration be part of each contract. Such procedures usually stop at advisory arbitration at the state and local levels.

Contract Enforcement

The Federal Labor Relations Authority (FLRA) performs the same role in federal labor contract enforcement as the private-sector NLRB. If a contract interpretation or violation issue is also an unfair labor practice, the authority has jurisdiction. However, unlike the NLRB, the authority has jurisdiction in all the arbitration awards appealed to it regardless of the issue involved. The authority performs a quasi-judicial role when it determines whether the arbitrator's award is contrary to any law, rule, or regulation or is deficient "on other grounds similar to those applied by federal courts in private-sector labor–management relations."[62]

Duty to Bargain during the Contract Term

In a recent decision, *NFFE Local 1309 v. Department of Interior, et al.*,[63] the Supreme Court ruled that the FLRA had the legal power to determine whether federal agencies and unions must engage in midterm bargaining. The Court noted that the statute that governs federal employment collective bargaining rights was ambiguous or open on the point of midterm bargaining. The Court ruled in reversing a lower court that because the statute did not specifically allow midterm bargaining, it was up to the FLRA to determine whether, when, where, and what sort of midterm bargaining is required. The Court reached its conclusion as supported by the statute's delegation of rule-making, adjudicatory, and policy-making powers to the FLRA and by the similarity of the FLRA's public-sector role and the NLRA's private-sector role.

Duty of Fair Representation

The number of unfair labor practice charges made against unions representing federal employees has risen in recent years. The majority of these charges allege violations of the duty of fair representation.[64] Violations of the duty of fair representation include complaints that the union failed in its duty to represent the employee in a dispute with the employer and that the union somehow discriminated against a nonunion member of the bargaining unit.

Although these issues are similar to a breach of a duty of fair representation in the private sector, there are differences. For example, federal employees often have a right to pursue remedies for job actions in a proceeding before the Merit Systems Protection Board or in litigation. Because of that right, the FLRA does not consider it discriminatory or an unfair labor practice for a union to treat dues-paying union members and nonmembers differently unless the matter in issue falls within the union's exclusive control.[65]

SUMMARY

The parties to the collective bargaining process have a duty to bargain in good faith and, when agreement is reached, to commit that agreement to written form. That written agreement becomes the basis for the labor–management relationship during the contract term.

The contract is enforced at various times and for various purposes by the courts, the NLRB, and the FLRA through arbitration and grievance procedures and through employee job actions.

The NLRB and the FLRA, through their power to prevent unfair labor practices, can interpret, invalidate, and enforce collective bargaining agreements in appropriate cases. The courts also have jurisdiction to enforce the labor agreement as binding on both the employer and the labor organization. As a rule, both the board and the courts defer to a grievance-arbitration process for contract administration whenever possible. The arbitration process allows the parties to resolve their differences during the life of the contract as a continuation of collective bargaining. Resorting to economic activity to enforce contracts cannot always be avoided, and the strike, at least in the private sector, is one aspect of contract enforcement.

Contract administration includes recognition of rights under collective bargaining agreements. Individual workers have the right to refrain from union activity, to be fairly represented by the union, and to receive due process in their dealings with the union and the employer.

The union and the employer operate under a good-faith duty to bargain during the contract term in appropriate circumstances. Neither party has the right to resort to secondary economic activities that violate the collective bargaining agreement or the law.

CASE STUDIES

Case Study 9-1 Contract Interpretation

The collective bargaining agreement contained a provision allowing for double-time pay to be paid as follows: For hours worked on the sixth or seventh consecutive day in a workweek, provided that the employee has worked the full assigned hours in the previous five or six workdays, respectively, in the workweek.

The grievant, a production worker, was 10 minutes late reporting for work on a Thursday morning. He was late because he was a passenger in a car that had a flat tire. As a result of his tardiness, he was only paid time and a half instead of double time for working the following Saturday. The union grieved the issue on the basis that the parties had a different understanding during the negotiating process from the company's current interpretation of the double-time section of the contract. The union stated that at the 14th negotiating session, the company's negotiator had agreed not to count reasonable tardiness against the double-time provision but had refused to change the language used in the contract. The company negotiator, on the other hand, stated that the very purpose of the double-time section was to allow for double-time pay only if there was no absenteeism in the preceding week. The only comment he remembered making regarding "reasonable application" was in response to a maintenance worker on the negotiating committee who thought it was not fair that he worked his regular hours Monday through Friday but would be denied double time on Sunday if he were a few minutes late on Saturday. The company negotiator remembers responding that, in that situation, he would agree to apply a reasonable standard to maintenance workers for Sunday double time following a tardiness on Saturday because the 25 maintenance workers were regularly scheduled for both Saturday and Sunday, whereas the 650 to 675 production workers were rarely, if ever, scheduled to work on Sundays.

The arbitrator was faced with clear contract language but convincing evidence that the parties at the negotiating table had a different understanding of what the contract language meant. The arbitrator had to decide whether the employee should receive double-time pay for the Saturday work or be punished for the Thursday tardiness. The arbitrator could not rely on the "meeting of the minds" concept because obviously the parties disagreed as to what was contained in the collective bargaining agreement. There had been previous grievances on the same issue, but those arbitration awards were inconsistent. Explaining that it is the arbitrator's role to use judgment in a particular grievance not only to reflect what the contract says but also to give effect to the bargain, the arbitrator attempted to discover the purpose for the provision.

The company stated that the double-time provision was added to the contract as a means of combating absenteeism during the week. It was, therefore, both a carrot and a stick provision. The use by the company of the tardiness rule was in and of itself not unreasonable. The question that the arbitrator needed to resolve was whether the grievant in this case would have the incentive to avoid tardiness to get double-time pay under the facts as presented.

SOURCE: Adapted from *Mor Flo Industry, Inc.,* 83 LA 480 (1984).

QUESTIONS

1. As the arbitrator, which fact would you consider most important in deciding this case? Why?
2. Would denying the employee his double-time pay in this instance give "effect" to the bargain of the parties? Explain your answer.
3. If the contract language is clear, why should the arbitrator even hear a case such as this?

Case Study 9-2 Duty to Bargain

The company, prior to 1976, manufactured all its products at a unionized plant in Cleveland. In 1976 it built a nonunion plant in Alabama, originally intending to duplicate the Cleveland operation. Unfavorable economic conditions, however, caused the company to transfer certain operations from Cleveland to Alabama, resulting in the layoff of seven union employees. The union filed unfair labor practice charges that were settled when the company promised not to transfer work from the Cleveland plant without bargaining with the union. The settlement was reached during the same time the company and union were negotiating a new collective bargaining agreement.

During negotiations, the company, despite the previously mentioned settlement, repeatedly submitted to the union a written statement asserting its right to decide what product "is made where by whom" and asked the union to submit any proposal it had to limit the company's right to transfer work. The union made no such proposal. It did, however, submit a severance pay proposal that became part of the contract. That provision provided for severance pay for layoffs as a result of plant closure or operational transfers.

A month after the agreement was signed, and again within a year, the company informed the union of certain operational transfers to the Alabama plant. The actions did not cause layoffs, and the union did not object to either move. However, the next operational move did result in four layoffs, and the union objected and asserted that the company should have bargained before moving. The company disagreed. After 23 more employees were laid off, the union filed unfair labor charges against the company.

The company's position was that the union waived its right to bargain over the work transfers (1) in the language of the collective bargaining agreement, (2) during negotiations of the agreement, and (3) by acquiescing in the previous work transfers.

Language of Agreement

Company Position: The severance pay provision in the contract showed that the union accepted compensation in lieu of bargaining over work relocation. It pointed to the wording of the section. "In the event the company determines to ... transfer ... severance allowances will be payable ..." to show that discretion to relocate was given solely to the company in return for the pay.

Union Position: The severance pay provision was in the supplemental unemployment benefits section, not the management rights section, in which a union waiver would normally be located. In addition, the law required a waiver to be "clear and unmistakable." The company's interpretation of the severance pay section gave too much weight to one word: *determines*. That word was taken out of context as to a clear union waiver of rights.

During Negotiations

Company Position: During negotiations, the company asserted that it had no restraints on its right to relocate work and asked that, if the union wished to restrict the company's right, it should propose constraints. Instead, the union proposed the severance pay provision, definitely a quid pro quo, which constituted a waiver.

Union Position: Because work transfers are a mandatory subject of bargaining, the union did not have to bargain on the subject to avoid waiving it. It was the company's duty to show an unequivocal waiver. In addition, the severance pay proposal during negotiations occurred before the union and the company settled the original unfair labor practice charge in which the company agreed to bargain before relocating work. Obviously the union was still interested in bargaining on the issue and did not waive it by the severance pay proposal.

Failure to Object

Company Position: The union's failure to object to the two initial work transfers constituted a waiver by acquiescence.

Union Position: The union did not object because the first two transfers affected no member of the unit. The union did object when the work relocation resulted in layoffs.

SOURCE: Adapted from *Tocco Division of Park-Ohio Industries, Inc. v. National Labor Relations Board,* 702 F.2d 624 (6th Cir. 1983).

QUESTIONS

1. Did the union waive its right to negotiate transfers? Explain your answer.

2. Do you think the company would have allowed the collective bargaining agreement to remain silent on transfers if it had thought it would have to negotiate each transfer?

3. Should a collective bargaining agreement end the bargaining process, or should the administration of the agreement be part of the process? Explain your answer.

KEY TERMS AND CONCEPTS

- *Boys Market* case
- *Collyer* case
- contract bar
- dual employer
- duty to sign
- *force majeure*
- featherbedding
- hot cargo agreement

- insulated period
- *Lincoln Mills* case
- management rights
- opener clauses
- open period
- primary boycott
- provisional intent test
- reserved rights

- restricted rights
- secondary boycott
- separability clause
- shop-ins
- *Steelworkers Trilogy*
- zipper clause

REVIEW QUESTIONS

1. How can labor negotiators ensure that others will easily understand the agreement reached?
2. What are some common management rights that might be found in labor agreements?
3. Describe the elements of an agreement ensuring that other unions are barred from representing a union's bargaining unit.
4. By what methods can collective bargaining agreements be enforced?
5. Assume that a union wants to end contract negotiations but (1) is concerned that in 18 months the employer may be financially stronger and (2) wants a four-year contract. What should the union do to protect the interests of its members?
6. How did the *Steelworkers Trilogy* help clarify the role of arbitration and court enforcement of contracts?
7. What individual rights do employees have within the collective bargaining process?
8. What kind of economic pressures are illegal?
9. When is distributing handbills that request a boycott considered legal?
10. If a national union seeks to represent members of an independent local union, when can it petition the NLRB?
11. Compare and contrast contract administration in the private and public sectors.

YOU BE THE ARBITRATOR
Reassignment of Job Duties

ARTICLE 5
MANAGEMENT RIGHTS, SECTION A

Unless the Employer agrees otherwise in this collective bargaining agreement, nothing in Chapter 4117 of the Ohio Revised Code impairs the right and responsibility of each public employer to:

1. Determine matters of inherent managerial policy, which include, but are not limited to, areas of discretion or policy such as the functions and programs of the public employer, standards of services, its overall budget, utilization of technology, and organizational structure;

2. Direct, supervise, evaluate, or hire employees;
3. Maintain and improve the efficiency and effectiveness of governmental operations;
4. Determine the overall methods, process, means, or personnel by which governmental operations are to be conducted;
5. Suspend, discipline, demote, or discharge for just cause or lay off, transfer, assign, schedule, promote, or retain employees;
6. Determine the adequacy of the workforce;
7. Determine the overall mission of the employer as a unit of government;
8. Effectively manage the workforce; and
9. Take actions to carry out the mission of the public employer as a governmental unit.

The Employer is not required to bargain on subjects reserved to the management and direction of the governmental unit except as affect wages, hours, terms and conditions of employment, and the continuation, modification, or deletion of an existing provision of a collective bargaining agreement.

ARTICLE II
MISCELLANEOUS, SECTION A

A non–bargaining unit employee shall not do bargaining unit work in order to displace an existing bargaining unit employee.

Facts

The two grievants in this case were employed part time by the Child Support Enforcement Agency (CSEA) and were members of the bargaining unit. Both are attorneys and performed legal services for CSEA, including handling hearings that pertained to establishing paternity and for the collection of child support. The hearings for each grievant would be set for one day a week. Clerical staff would prepare the paperwork, send out notices for the hearings, attend the hearings, and prepare the orders, all under the grievants' supervision. The grievants together worked a total of about 25 hours a week, and both received an annual salary of about $26,000. In addition to the grievants, the CSEA employed one full-time attorney who did the same work as the grievants but was not a member of the bargaining unit. An earlier grievance had resulted in the union accepting that this full-time attorney would not be a part of the bargaining unit but would be doing bargaining unit work. In early 1998, certain state laws were changed that resulted in allowing nonlawyers to conduct the hearings on paternity and child support. As a result of that change, the county undertook an efficiency study of the CSEA, and it was recommended that the number of staff for the CSEA be reduced and it be merged with the Lawrence County Department of Job and Family Services. This reorganization resulted in the grievants being laid off and their hearing duties being assigned to nonlawyers who were in a bargaining unit and their legal duties being assigned to the full-time attorney. The grievants appealed.

Issue

Did management violate the collective bargaining agreement (CBA) when it abolished the grievants' jobs and laid them off and reassigned their job duties to a non–bargaining unit employee?

Position of the Parties

Management argued that it had not assigned bargaining unit work to a non–bargaining unit member to displace the existing bargaining unit employees. As a result of the changes in rules and the reorganization, it could save money and increase efficiency by assigning the work of two part-time attorneys to one full-time attorney. Management noted that much of the nonlegal work of the grievants had gone to members of the bargaining unit. Only the legal work was assigned to a non–bargaining unit employee, and that employee had already been doing that same work with the union's acquiescence. It was also the position of management that it followed state civil service rules in laying off part-time employees before laying off a full-time employee.

The union contended that whether management intended to displace bargaining unit employees or not, its reorganization had done so in violation of the CBA. The union had not objected to the full-time attorney doing what it considered bargaining unit work after the original grievance under the condition that she did not displace any bargaining unit employees. Now that assigning her work meant that the grievants were laid off, they objected. It was clear that the grievants were not laid off for lack of work; individuals in the joint department were still doing the work they had previously done. Under the language of Article II, Section A, reassigning their work outside the bargaining unit was a direct violation of the CBA.

SOURCE: Adapted from *Lawrence County Board of Commissioners v. AFSCME*, 115 LA 789 (2001).

QUESTIONS

1. As arbitrator, what would be your award and opinion in this arbitration?
2. Explain why the relevant provisions of the CBA as applied to the facts of this case dictate the award.

3. What actions might the employer and/or the union have taken to avoid this conflict?

Provisional Intent

PURPOSE:

To become familiar with the concept of provisional intent.

Reducing an agreement to writing, the subject of this chapter, is not an easy task. Although most agreements contain fewer than 100 "short" pages, tens, hundreds, or thousands of people read each article, page, and paragraph in each agreement. Often these many readers are reading from different points of view. Reducing what was intended to be concise, clear language and writing it in a binding contract is not as easy as it may appear. This exercise is designed to help students better understand this aspect of labor relations and collective bargaining and to improve their own writing skills.

TASK:

To best understand the purpose of the exercise, reread the last paragraph of the "Duty" section at the beginning of this chapter. Next the class should be divided into three- or four-member teams. Each team should decide the intent of a new contract clause. The instructor may assign a topic or allow teams to select their own. Once the intent has been decided, each team must reduce it to writing in clear and concise language.

The last step is for teams to exchange written provisions. Now members should play the role of union members or supervisors who must enforce the provision and list any potentially troublesome omissions, vague language, or other enforcement issues. The lists should be returned to their authoring teams for revision. The instructor, in conclusion, will present and discuss the first and second drafts of all provisions to the class.

CHAPTER 10

Grievance and Disciplinary Procedures

Sources of Employee Grievances
Steps in a Grievance Procedure
Functions of Grievance Procedures
Employee Misconduct
Disciplinary Procedures
Grievance Mediation
Public-Sector Grievance Issues

The Hotel Association of New York City reported a 44 percent increase in grievances being filed by the New York Hotel Trades Council in anticipation of contract negotiations to be held in 2006.

Labor News

GRIEVANCES INCREASE 44 PERCENT IN NEW YORK HOTELS

The Hotel Association of New York City negotiates with the New York Hotel Trades Council union that represents thousands of employees at 149 hotels. In September 2005 the Hotel Association reported that the union filed 597 grievances in the previous calendar year—an increase of 44 percent over the total of 416 in 2002. The substantial increase in the number of grievances was largely over increased workloads according to Peter Ward, president of the New York Hotel Trades Council, and foreshadowed the negotiations expected in 2006 as the five-year contract expired. The union president emphasized that the substantial increase in grievances filed during the term of a contract was a strong indication of the area union members would want to focus on in the new contract negotiations. The union strike fund of $13 million was growing rapidly and raised fears of a strike that could cripple the New York tourism industry.

The workload grievances included complaints of unsafe working conditions and employees being required to work through scheduled breaks. The core of the workload issue is the expanded duties including cleaning coffee pots and triple-sheeting mattresses while being required to clean the same number of rooms—14 per day. It is estimated that at $20 per hour, New York's desk clerks and room attendants are among the highest paid in the industry. Ward would like to have more of his approximately 1,000 unemployed union members hired by the hotels. In the previous eight years the union was involved in recovering over $12 million in back pay for members in workload grievance cases.

SOURCE: Adapted from Lisa Fickenscher, "Hotel Union Sets Targets for Contract," *Crain's New York Business* 21, no. 39 (Sept. 26, 2005), pp. 1–3. Used by permission.

In the day-to-day administration of a collective bargaining agreement, the majority of time is spent on grievance handling.[1] The **grievance procedure** is the core of the continuous collective bargaining process. An employer's refusal to process grievances is a violation of the NLRA. The extreme importance of a good grievance procedure has been described as the "lifeblood of a collective bargaining relationship."[2]

Regardless of the completeness and clarity of the labor agreement, disagreements will arise during the life of the contract. Thus, a grievance procedure, a previously agreed-on procedure to resolve such disputes, must be provided in the agreement. The grievance handling process must settle disputes arising during the term of the agreement; if it does not, strikes, lockouts, or other work disruptions may result. One employer, the U.S. Postal Service, has even experienced "grievance gridlock" as described in Profile 10-1.

A **grievance** is often defined as any perceived violation of a contract provision. This definition could be broadened to include any complaint by an employee against an employer and vice versa. One arbitrator provided a classic definition: "If a man thinks he

Postal workers separate millions of pieces of mail each day with letter sort machines. In 2001 the U.S. Postal System had about 210,000 grievances pending, creating a "grievance gridlock" and costing over $200 million per year to resolve.

has a grievance, he has a grievance."[3] However, a more precise definition might include any formal complaint lodged by persons who believe they have been wronged.[4] A grievance is not a *gripe,* which is generally defined as a complaint by an employee concerning an action by management that does not violate the contract, past practice, or law. For example, an employee may only have a gripe if his supervisor speaks to him in a harsh tone, but when the supervisor assigns him work outside his job classification, he may have a grievance.

Fortunately, most collective bargaining agreements contain provisions similar to Figure 10-1 and delineate a grievance procedure that consists of a specified series of four or five procedural steps that aggrieved employees, unions, and management representatives must follow when a complaint arises. Typically, the grievant is provided with a systematic set of appeals through successively higher levels of union and management representatives. The fact that most contracts provide for specific grievance procedures clearly indicates that although both sides try to develop a clear and precise document during the contract negotiation process, some areas will be subject to misunderstanding

PROFILE 10-1

GRIEVANCE GRIDLOCK AT THE U.S. POSTAL SERVICE

In 2001, the U.S. Postal Service had one of its worst financial years—a $2.4 billion loss. The causes for the financial failure included higher fuel costs, revenues that fell short of estimates, and a "grievance gridlock." About 210,000 grievances were pending in 2001. The grievance system that has been negotiated between the National Association of Letter Carriers, the American Postal Workers Union, and the U.S. Postal Service costs more than $200 million per year to operate—about the same amount the Postal Service lost in the fiscal year that ended on September 30, 2000. It requires over 300 outside arbitrators to settle just the grievances that reach the final step in the resolution process, not the hundreds of thousands that are resolved before that step.

Why is the grievance system in a state of gridlock? Some answers provided by those directly involved could be found in many industries—and each side blames the other. Employees say that supervisors are too domineering and that they complain that employees are paid too much and work too little. Supervisors complain that employees file grievances just to annoy them. But Anthony Vegliante, vice president of labor relations for the Postal Service, notes that postal workers, like most public-sector employees, cannot legally strike and do not receive profit sharing or some other private-sector economic perks, and thus they turn to the grievance system to air their complaints. And the significant backlog of cases,

he notes, creates underlying tensions that harm productivity because people feel their issues should be heard in a timely manner.

Sometimes one rule change can cause many grievances. For example, in New York, postal officials at the Morgan Processing and Distribution Center decided that wash-up time could be eliminated, saving 22 to 30 minutes per day. So each time a worker requested a wash-up period and was denied the break, he or she filed a grievance—over 40,000 grievances were filed. An arbitrator ruled that the wash-up time must be restored. But then a second arbitrator reversed the decision and said that wash-up time could be eliminated, saving the Postal Service millions in back pay.

One sad case involved Rick Byrne, a Denver mail handler who was hired under a job program for disabled workers. His supervisor would not let him bring his oxygen tank into the building, forcing Mr. Byrne to walk to his car to use the tank. He filed a grievance, and after three years a federal judge ruled that he had been harassed by six postal supervisors and that the no-oxygen ruling made no sense. The judge noted that the postal service never indicated that Mr. Byrne did not perform his job well. Mr. Byrne was awarded $400,000 but died five months before the final decision was rendered, at age 39, because of a lifelong breathing problem. His mother, Carolyn Byrne, noted that her son "was proud" to work for the Postal Service.

SOURCE: Adapted from Rick Brooks, "Mail Disorder: Blizzard of Grievances Joins a Sack of Woes at U.S. Postal Service," *Wall Street Journal,* June 22, 2001, pp. A1, A4.

during the life of the contract. Indeed, as shown in Case 10-1, the grievance procedure itself is sometimes the subject of a grievance.

The signing of a contract spells out a new relationship between labor and management, and the agreement specifies a new set of rules legally binding labor and management during the life of the contract. The formal grievance process agreed on in the contract provides for the administration of the contract. Although the number and contents of the procedural steps in a formal grievance process vary from contract to contract, most grievance processes involved four or five steps.

A grievance shall consist of a dispute between an employee, the Union, and the Company as to the meaning or application of any provisions of this Agreement.

Step 1. Within five (5) working days after the first occurrence of the situation, condition, or actions of the Company giving rise to the grievance, the employee affected, or a representative of a group of employees affected, shall personally discuss the grievance with the employee's immediate supervisor or the supervisor of the group of employees as the case may be. The employee or representative must clock out (unless it can be discussed on an off-shift hour) and the union steward shall be present. Within twenty-four (24) hours after the grievance is discussed, the supervisor shall give a verbal decision to the aggrieved employee/representative and/or the union steward.

Step 2. In the event that a satisfactory settlement has not been reached at this verbal level, the aggrieved employee, or representative, or the union steward, may within 72 hours present the grievance in writing, and within 72 hours shall receive a written answer from the supervisor.

Step 3. Within five (5) calendar days after the written decision has been given, the Local Union may present the grievance in writing to a representative designated by the Company.

All third step grievances (except discharge grievances which may, if requested by the Union, be discussed at a special meeting to meet deadlines) shall be considered at the next scheduled monthly grievance meeting. Within seven calendar days after the grievance meeting, the Company shall give to the Local Union its written decision. The time limits in this step may be extended by mutual agreement.

The aggrieved employee, or in case of a group grievance, a representative of the aggrieved group, may be present at the meetings at all steps of the grievance procedure if a request to be present is made.

The Union shall certify in writing to the Company, over the signature of the Local Union designated representative, a list of the officers, committee members and stewards who are to be recognized by the Company as the committee for the grievance procedure.

The Grievance Committee shall consist of not less than three (3) union representatives and three (3) representatives of the Company.

In the event the Union is not satisfied with the grievance response, it may pursue arbitration of the grievance through the process outlined in Section X of this Agreement.

FIGURE 10-1   Grievance Procedure

CASE 10-1

WHEN THE UNION FAILED TO FOLLOW THE GRIEVANCE PROCEDURE

The grievance procedure in this case contains four steps with a time period of seven calendar days at each step. For example, step 1 of the grievance procedure states that the union has seven calendar days to present a grievable incident to management. If the grievance is not resolved in step 1, then the union has seven calendar days to prepare a grievance form and move it to step 2 and so on. At step 4, if the grievance is not resolved, the union is required to prepare a written notice of intent to arbitrate and has 14 calendar days to do so. The contract specifies that the notice of

continued

| WHEN THE UNION FAILED TO FOLLOW THE GRIEVANCE PROCEDURE—continued | CASE 10-1 |

intent to arbitrate shall be sent by certified mail with return receipt requested, and the postmark shall govern compliance with the time limit. The union is also required to obtain a listing of possible arbitrators from the Federal Mediation and Conciliation Service (FMCS), meet with the company, and select an arbitrator.

On November 4, 1993, a meeting occurred between the union business agent and the employer's human resources manager (HRM) concerning the discharge of two employees. The meeting was within the seven-day time period required in the contract. During the arbitration hearing, the union business agent testified that on November 9, 1993, he had hand-delivered the "intent to arbitrate" document to the company's HRM. Also, during the arbitration, the HRM testified that he did not remember receiving such a document from the union. On November 15, 1993, the union forwarded a request for an arbitration panel to the FMCS. On December 28, 1993, the union business agent approached the company's HRM with a list of arbitrators. At that time (December 28, 1993), the HRM informed the union for the first time that a grievance had not been properly filed. The union argued that step 1 of the grievance procedure became step 4 because of the nature of the grievance (the

two employees had been discharged) and that an intent to arbitrate had been filed in a timely manner. The parties continued to differ sharply with respect to both whether the grievance was filed and its timeliness.

In November 1994, at an arbitration hearing to resolve this issue, the arbitrator was asked to make a finding as to the timeliness issue. If the grievance was determined to be timely, then the grievance would be heard on its merits. Otherwise, the matter would be dismissed. During the arbitration hearing, the company argued that a written grievance was not filed in a timely manner and that the parties' labor agreement specifically states the following:

> If the grieving party fails to process the grievance in accordance with the requirements of this article, the grievance is waived.

The collective bargaining agreement further states that the "arbitrator may not add to, detract from, or alter in any way, the provisions of the agreement."

DECISION

The arbitrator ruled that the union had failed to follow the requirements of the grievance procedure, and the grievance was denied.

SOURCE: Adapted from *Los Alamos Protection Technology,* 104 LA 23 (1995).

SOURCES OF EMPLOYEE GRIEVANCES

Whatever the subject matter of a particular grievance may be, exactly why the grievance was filed may provide far greater understanding of the union or employee's motives. One or more of the following situations might be a source of employee grievance.

Clarifying Contract Provisions Under Changing Conditions

After contracts are agreed on and signed by both parties, unforeseen circumstances change some operating conditions. Even with the best of intentions, both management and labor may find that they honestly disagree on the contract provision relevant to the new operations. For example, workers at the Diamond Shamrock Corporation normally worked the evening shift from 3:00 to 11:00 PM and received a shift differential under the existing contract. Management changed the hours of the shift to 11:00 AM to 7:00 PM, resulting in a grievance requesting shift differential pay for the four new hours of work overlapping with the old hours for which they received shift differential pay. Management declined, claiming that shift differential was required by contract only when the entire shift was from 3:00 to 7:00 PM. The arbitrator agreed with management that the contract provided shift differential not on a per-hour basis but on a per-shift basis.[5]

Support for Future Negotiations

Unions often encourage their members to file grievances in certain areas to provide a file of supporting evidence during future negotiations. The negotiators may then point to the grievances as evidence of their members' concern over a particular management practice or lack of an employee benefit or service. The union does not intend to prevail in many of these cases but wants to alert management to the issue. Thus, the administration of one contract becomes a basis of negotiation for a future contract.

Rectifying a Contract Violation

Contract negotiators have one primary goal—to sign a contract. Although many contracts are quite lengthy and involved, they cannot cover every possible situation that might arise. For that reason, most contracts specify how each debatable issue should be resolved. Both sides expect that disagreements will occur during the life of the contract, which is why grievance arbitration is included.

One of the most common sources of grievances is the union's honest belief that management has violated a provision of the existing contract. For example, an arbitrator ruled that the contract clause stating that the parties may negotiate necessary schedule changes from the standard workweek did not require the union's consent before changes could be made if negotiations were provided. The union believed that the contract phrase did in fact require management to gain its consent before changes were made.[6]

Show of Power

Sometimes employees and union officials file grievances to demonstrate their authority and influence. Union officials may feel a need to remind employees that they are on their side and work hard to represent their interests. After all, their members elect union leaders, and members expect something in return. Although the union leadership may realize that a particular employee grievance is without substantial merit, they will pursue the issue if it is of great concern to the membership. Individual employees may also, for a variety of reasons, file grievances. Some may simply be letting off steam; others may use the grievance process as a means of settling a score with management. No contract language can eliminate grievances when these kinds of motives are involved. Some management and labor relations personnel claim that such meritless grievances waste time and resources. However, critics should consider that the grievance process is partially designed to provide a safety valve to employees who might otherwise express their normal anxiety and frustration in more harmful ways, such as absenteeism, alcoholism, or even sabotage.

Increased Pay

One of labor's primary motives in bargaining is to provide assurances of pay that might otherwise be at the discretion of management. Labor negotiations have initiated many types of pay incentives and premiums not found in the nonunion sector. Many grievances result from employees' belief that they are entitled to additional pay that management believes is not required.

The union, in one instance, claimed that the contract providing that employees who worked on Sunday would receive double the straight-time hourly rate required double-time pay for all Sunday hours. Management contended that because it had begun opening on Sunday as a regular business day after a state blue law was repealed, the double-time pay was not required because Sunday became a normal workday. The arbitrator agreed with management.[7]

STEPS IN A GRIEVANCE PROCEDURE

Step 1: Employee, Steward, Supervisor

The initial step in a grievance procedure usually instructs the employee to discuss the grievance with the shop steward or go directly to the supervisor. The employee has the legal right to do the latter; the supervisor must resolve the grievance consistent with the contract. The supervisor must also notify the union of the grievance. The shop steward is, however, usually the first person contacted. Therefore, the steward must be experienced in handling grievance matters and be familiar with the terms of the contract and its provisions. The steward must also be able to recognize grievances containing some merit as well as those that are trivial and should be dropped. A steward will encourage and help the employee to pursue a legitimate grievance and in some cases must convince the employee that a grievance contains no merit.

The extent to which grievances are resolved at the lowest possible level is an important indicator of effective grievance handling. One means of attaining resolution at the lowest possible level is the use of feedback from previous grievance cases. The outcome of previous, similar cases provides cues to both parties that tend to focus their discussion and provide a faster resolution of the grievance. In general, the purpose of feedback is not to "set precedent" but to provide both parties with an array of possible likely solutions.[8] In practice, if both sides introduce the results of previous similar grievances at the first level of grievance discussions, a compromise may well be reached more quickly than if they wait until the issue goes to arbitration.

Step 2: Written Grievance

If steward and employee agree that the grievance has some merit and should be pursued, then the grievance is reduced to writing. At this point, the grievance is said to have moved from the informal to the formal stage. The steward and employee complete a grievance form within 48 hours of the occurrence or within the time limit specified in the contract. The process of writing out the complaint forces the grievant to set forth the facts, contract provisions, and contingencies early on in the process.

Most company and union representatives believe it is important to formalize the grievance in written format at this stage.[9] Once the grievance has been reduced to writing, the steward and the employee meet with the supervisor to discuss the grievance in an honest effort to settle the matter quickly. Both sides can assess the strengths and weaknesses of the claim. Most grievances containing little merit will be dropped at this stage.

GRIEVANCE NUMBER _97-003_   DATE FILED _4/23/05_   UNION _Local 1233_

NAME OF GRIEVANT(S) _Davis, Henry_   CLOCK # _0379_

DATE CAUSE OF GRIEVANCE OCCURRED _4/20/05_

CONTRACTUAL PROVISIONS CITED _Articles III, VII, and others_

STATEMENT OF THE GRIEVANCE:

On April 20, Foreman George Moore asked Henry Davis to go temporarily to the Rolling Mill for the rest of the turn. Davis said he preferred not to, and that he was more senior to others who were available. The foreman never ordered Davis to take the temporary assignment. He only requested that Davis do so.

Davis was improperly charged with insubordination and suspended for three days. The foreman did not have just cause for the discipline.

RELIEF SOUGHT:

Reinstatement with full back pay and seniority.

GRIEVANT'S SIGNATURE _____Henry Davis_____ DATE _4/22/05_

STEWARD'S SIGNATURE _____Jim Bob Smith_____ DATE _4/22/05_

<u>STEP 1</u>

DISPOSITION:

Foreman Moore gave Davis clear instructions to report temporarily to the Rolling Mill for the remainder of the shift. Davis refused to do so and was warned that it could result in discipline. When he again refused the foreman's directive, he was disciplined.

The discipline was for just cause. The grievance is rejected.

SIGNATURE OF
EMPLOYER REPRESENTATIVE _____Paul Roberts_____ DATE _4/26/05_
_____Grievance Withdrawn or _____√_____Referred to Step 2

SIGNATURE OF
UNION REPRESENTATIVE _____Jim Bob Smith_____ DATE _4/28/05_

FIGURE 10-2   A Standard Grievance Record Form Step 1

The steward normally investigates the grievance to provide documented facts on the case. The pertinent facts are written on a grievance form such as the one in Figure 10-2. A good rule for remembering the crucial facts in a grievance is the **"5Ws" rule**:

- What happened?
- Where did it happen?
- When did the event take place?
- Why is the complaint a grievance?
- Who was involved? (Witnesses?)

The written grievance is delivered to the supervisor, and a meeting of the three parties is held (the shop steward is occasionally accompanied by a personnel or industrial relations representative). In discussing the grievance, all the parties make an attempt to settle the matter at that point. Research indicates that most grievances are settled in this step of the grievance process. If the grievance cannot be resolved at this stage, the employee may choose to appeal.

Step 3: Shop Steward, Department Head

When the shop steward and supervisor cannot resolve the grievance, then it may be appealed to the next higher level of management and union representative, usually within seven calendar days. At this point, the union representative continues to be the shop steward or business agent. However, the management representative usually represents a higher level and may be a plant superintendent or department head. At this stage, the two sides review the written grievance and try to reach a resolution.

Step 4: Union Grievance Committee, Director of Personnel and Industrial Relations

At this point, a plantwide union grievance committee that may further appeal the answer to step 5, usually within 30 calendar days, reviews the employee's grievance. The plant manager or department head may be assisted by the director of personnel and industrial relations in reviewing the grievance from a management perspective. As with the second step, they review the written grievance and discuss the case with the employee's representatives. The two sides continue to try to resolve the grievance honestly rather than go to the final stage of the process—final and binding arbitration. This final step is more expensive, represents a failure to reach an agreement in the matter, and brings greater tension to the grievance. Both sides realize that they may completely lose the case before an independent arbitrator.

Step 5: Arbitration

Approximately 98 percent of all collective bargaining agreements provide for a binding arbitration as the final step in the handling of grievances.[10] The contract provisions usually include that either management or labor request arbitration as a final step in resolving the grievance. This request must be made within 60 calendar days of the receipt of the answer of step 4. The outside independent arbitrator will study the evidence and listen to the arguments of both sides before rendering a decision. The arbitrator's decision, as agreed on in the collective bargaining contract, is final and binding on both parties and can be appealed to the courts only on the grounds of collusion, if the arbitrator's award exceeded his or her authority, or if the arbitrator's decision was not based on the essence of the labor agreement.[11]

FUNCTIONS OF GRIEVANCE PROCEDURES

Formal grievance procedures have been found to be the most common tool to resolve conflicts arising between labor and management during the life of the agreement. In general, the functions provided by a grievance procedure are as follows.

1. *Conflict management resolution.*   Before grievance procedures and arbitration became popular, employees and unions often used strikes and slowdowns to resolve complaints over the interpretation of labor agreements. Without grievance procedures, questions would probably be resolved by a test of economic strength, harmful both to management and to the union.
2. *Agreement clarification.*   All agreements contain a certain amount of unintentional ambiguity that results in questions requiring contract interpretation. The dynamics of employer–employee relationships cannot be fully anticipated by the

parties at the bargaining table; thus, negotiating language often must be applied to unforeseen situations.

3. *Communication.* Grievance procedures provide a vehicle for individual employees to express their problems and perceptions. They offer employees a formal process to air perceived inequities in the workplace.

4. *Due process.* The most widely heralded function of grievance procedures is that of a third-party intervention. Most grievance procedures provide a fair and

---

CASE 10-2

PERFORMANCE EVALUATION OF A CRANE OPERATOR

The employer operates a metal processing plant that uses cranes of various sizes and capabilities to transport materials. As a result of a bid to fill a vacancy, the grievant, a 20-year employee, was selected to operate a 60-ton crane. After a two-week training program and a 15-year tenure as a crane operator, the grievant was removed from his crane operator position.

During the arbitration hearing, the company argued that the grievant had failed to attain the necessary level of depth perception and motor skills required to perform the duties of a crane operator in a safe and efficient manner. The grievant had received prior warnings that he could be disqualified from his job if his work performance did not improve, and he deliberately failed to take advantage of several training opportunities to improve his performance. Also, at the arbitration hearing, a union employee who had been a crane operator for 20 years testified that two weeks of training was sufficient and that he had trained some 20 to 25 other crane operators. Additional testimony introduced at the arbitration hearing indicated that the grievant had dropped material, hit pilings, and "brushed" employees working on the floor with heavy, dangerous objects. As a result, many of the floor employees refused to work with the grievant.

At the arbitration hearing, the grievant testified that during his first week of training, he was trained by two different crane operators and by two others during the second week of training. The grievant further testified that during the second week of his training, the two training operators refused to ride in the cab with him. The grievant also testified that his supervisor had urged him to "speed up" the operation of the crane to meet production quotas but that he had refused to do so. The grievant testified that he was never told of his unsatisfactory performance and that he was disliked by certain supervisors, several crane operators, and many floor employees. The union argued that the grievant, an African American, had not been properly trained and was disadvantaged by the lack of training in an all-white department.

The parties' labor agreement gives the employer the right to demote and transfer and the right to disqualify. It stipulates, however, that disqualification will not occur in an unreasonably short period of time.

DECISION

The arbitrator ruled that he could find no basis that the grievant's disqualification was based on his race. The arbitrator stated that the overwhelming evidence is that the grievant's disqualification as a crane operator did not violate the parties' labor agreement.

SOURCE: Adapted from *Alloys International,* 94 ARB 449 (1994).

equitable due process containing binding arbitration as a final step. Without this process, management would likely have an upper hand in most grievance situations. However, employee and union strikes would be heightened and economic measures used to balance management's authority.

5. ***Strength enhancement.*** The grievance mechanism helps unions develop employee loyalty and trust. Grievance processing emphasizes union presence and strength during the term of the collective bargaining agreement and reminds employees of the union efforts to protect their interests. The formal grievance also strengthens management and labor's communication skills because first-level stewards and supervisors are almost always involved in the initial step of the grievance procedure. The two sides come to better understand each other's perspectives and develop a closer working relationship.[12]

Case 10-2 describes a grievance regarding a performance evaluation.

EMPLOYEE MISCONDUCT

In labor relations the term "misconduct" applies to a broad spectrum of offenses, ranging from relatively minor ones, such as discourteous behavior, to major ones, including theft and picket line violence. A basic maxim or premise established early in the history of U.S. labor relations is that incidents of **employee misconduct** should be viewed as either (1) *serious offenses,* which under normal circumstances warrant immediate discharge without the necessity of prior warnings or attempts at corrective action, or (2) *minor offenses,* which call for attempts at corrective action and do not call for discharge for the first offense. However, minor offenses can, when repeated despite warnings, lead to discharge.

Employee misconduct cases that are decided by arbitration often are won or lost not because of questions of guilt or innocence but because of (1) management's consistent enforcement of the rules that are involved in the case, (2) management's compliance with the disciplinary procedures in the contract, (3) an employee's work history, and (4) an employee's length of service with the company. According to the Bureau of National Affairs' *Grievance Guide*, 11th ed., 2003, the most common examples of employee misconduct and key factors considered by arbitrators in deciding the cases include the following.[13]

1. ***Damaging company property.*** A person's deliberate and malicious intent is the primary factor in considering the appropriate discipline. The relative value of the damage has relatively little significance. Immediate discharge is usually upheld even in cases of low property value.
2. ***Discourtesy.*** Employees, especially those who serve the public, are expected to be courteous and solicitous toward coworkers and members of the public. Employee discourtesy is generally accepted as just cause for disciplinary action. Customer complaints about rude behavior can be used as sufficient reason for termination.
3. ***Dishonesty.*** Proof "beyond a reasonable doubt" is required to uphold a discharge due to dishonesty. A higher standard of evidence is required because the accused worker has a greater inability to become reemployed (after a discharge due to dishonesty) than for any other cause.
4. ***Dress and grooming.*** Management has the right to set dress and grooming standards for reasons of public image, job safety, and the health of workers, coworkers, and customers. However, workers have the right to unwarranted interference

by management. Thus, dress and grooming standards must be clear and consistently enforced and reasonably related to a "business need," which may include distraction due to revealing attire.

5. ***E-mail and technology issues.*** Employers increasingly use technology to monitor employees' use of e-mail and the Internet in efforts to reduce personal and inappropriate use. Unions have discovered e-mail as a fast and inexpensive means of communicating with members—and workers they are trying to organize. Employers generally should develop and communicate policies that make it clear to all employees that their e-mail communication and Internet use are not private, but instead are property of the employer. In addition policies should clearly state that all computer use is open to employer monitoring. Employees who violate such policies may face discipline, including termination. Arbitrators will expect, however, that employer monitoring of e-mail and Internet use will be consistently applied to all employees and that discipline will be applied to any and all who violate policies.

6. ***Gambling.*** In most organizations gambling, such as sports pools or lunch-hour poker, is ignored. However, employees involved in illegal bookmaking or numbers operations may be discharged, particularly if they have been given prior warning.

7. ***Garnishment.*** Management may discharge employees who violate rules concerning the garnishment of their wages. However, such rules must be based on employer cost, liability, and inconvenience. Less severe penalties may be decided on the basis of the employee's length of service, work record, and efforts to resolve the debt.

8. ***Horseplay.*** Although joking and playing pranks is usually tolerated, acts of horseplay that involve a high risk of serious injury may warrant a serious penalty. Only acts that are premeditated, malicious, and done with evil intent with knowledge of possible injuries or property damage will likely warrant discharge for the first incident (see Case 10-3).

9. ***Off-duty misconduct.*** In general, management may not discipline an employee for off-duty misconduct because employees have a right to privacy in their private lives. However, employees may be discharged or given lesser penalties if their off-duty misconduct either (1) creates publicity that harms the organization's public image, (2) causes the employee to not be able to perform their job, or (3) causes other employees to refuse to work with the employee. Examples of discharges include an employee convicted of manslaughter for fatally beating a 71-year-old woman and an employee who ignored written warnings and continued to park his car on residential streets, invoking the "wrath" of local residents.

10. ***Moonlighting.*** Holding a second job or moonlighting during an employee's off time can be a cause for discharge, particularly if the labor contract includes a relevant provision. Discharge actions are most likely upheld if the case involves (1) an employee's impaired performance, such as absenteeism, tardiness, poor productivity, or inability to work overtime; (2) a conflict of interest due to the second employer being viewed as a competitor; or (3) fraudulently taking a leave of absence to work at another job.

11. ***Sleeping and loafing.*** In general, sleeping on the job warrants discharge, particularly when it causes danger to employees or equipment. However, management in such cases must prove the employee was actually sleeping and not just resting with their eyes closed. In addition, management must strictly and consistently enforce a no-sleeping work rule. Sleeping during lunch breaks or rest periods is generally permissible unless it causes the employee to not return to work on time.

"GOOSEPLAY"

The events in this case occurred in the context of the eighth organizational campaign conducted at the company's Berea, Kentucky, facility. So far as the record shows, no prior unfair labor practices have been committed at this plant.

The company has a pond on its property, and in September there are hundreds of ducks and geese at the pond. A goose wandered into the work area of employee Rowlett, who picked up the goose by its feet and told other employees that it wanted to sign a union card to join the union. Employee Poff wrote "Vote Yes" on a small card, attached it to a string about two feet long, and placed the sign over the goose's head while Rowlett held it. Rowlett then proceeded to drive the goose through the plant on a forklift truck. The record shows that a Canada goose weighs approximately 14 pounds and has a five-foot wingspan.

At the conclusion of the goose escapade, the company sent Rowlett and Poff home early. The company conducted an investigation and collected statements from witnesses. Rowlett and Poff were given the opportunity to explain their conduct, but they declined to participate in the investigation. After considering all the information it compiled, the company discharged Rowlett and Poff. The basic reasons for the discharge decision were that the employees' behavior did not meet adult expectations, posed a safety hazard to them as well as to others, and disrupted production activities of the plant.

The employees sued the company for unfair labor practice in discharging them, claiming that it was because they were union members supporting the organizational campaign.

The administrative law judge (ALJ) appeared to recognize that the National Labor Relations Act did not protect the goose incident because she said that the employees' conduct should have a disciplinary consequence. She concluded, however, that the discipline imposed was unlawfully motivated; that is, she found that antecedent lawful union activity, not the "goose" incident, was the reason for the discharge. As evidence of this, she pointed to antiunion statements in the company's employee handbook and the fact that the only types of dischargeable offenses in the company prior to this had involved dishonesty, attendance problems, and sexual activity on the job.

The company appealed.

DISCUSSION

The National Labor Relations Board (NLRB) found that the record, when fairly considered as a whole, did not contain substantial evidence of antiunion animus. It is true that the company's employee handbook expressed the view that a union "could seriously impair the relationship between the company and the employees and could retard the growth of the company and the progress of the employees." The NLRB has held that statements such as these, although alone not rising to the level of unfair labor practices, may still be used to show animus.

However, the ALJ failed to accord weight to the significant countervailing evidence. No antiunion comments were made to the discharged employees. No unfair labor practices were committed in the previous organizational campaigns conducted at the Berea plant. The same employee handbook that the ALJ relied on as evidence of animus expressly acknowledged the right of the employees to join a union if they wished. In sum, the company's opposition to unionization is not, in the circumstances of this case, sufficient to

continued

"GOOSEPLAY"—continued

warrant the inference that it would unlawfully terminate these employees because of their union support or activities.

The company's officials involved in the investigation and/or decision-making aspects of this incident consistently, albeit in different words, explained their actions as concerns for maintaining safety, production, and discipline in the plant.

Having reviewed the record, the NLRB found no basis for finding that these concerns were not the foundation for the company's decision to suspend and discharge both Poff and Rowlett. Finally, the NLRB rejected the ALJ's finding that these discharges constituted disparate treatment because the only earlier incidents of employee misconduct that resulted in discharge involved dishonesty, attendance problems,

and sexual activity on the job. It is true that the record contains no evidence of previous incidents of "gooseplay" resulting in termination. However, an essential ingredient of a disparate treatment finding is that other employees in similar circumstances were treated more leniently than the alleged discriminatee was treated. The NLRB found no record of a similar incident that the company tolerated. Thus, it concluded that there is no evidence of disparate treatment.

DECISION

The complaint was dismissed because the union failed to establish by a preponderance of the evidence that the company was unlawfully motivated in suspending and discharging Poff and Rowlett.

SOURCE: Adapted for *NACCO Materials Handling Group Inc. v. NLRB,* 170 LRRM 1139 (August 25, 2000).

12. *Violence.* The increased number of workplace violence incidents that have led to the injury or death of coworkers or supervisors has caused employers to take the issue more seriously in recent years. Many employers, therefore, have developed serious or "zero-tolerance" policies covering not only violent acts and fighting, but also threats of violence, bullying, and "uncivil" behavior. Arbitrators have generally held that management has the right to invoke discipline, including termination, in such cases. In cases where the violence was clearly provoked, including fighting, arbitrators have imposed lesser penalties. They also will likely consider other factors, such as the length of service and work record of the employee, whether the act consisted of a single blow or a series of deliberate acts, whether the blow was with a dangerous weapon, the effect of the act on other employees, and the emotional stability of the employee.

Minor Offenses

Incidents of employee misconduct that are generally considered to be minor offenses include loafing during working hours, failure to attend meetings, attending to personal business during working hours, failure to keep a time card, minor insubordination, carelessness, and, perhaps most important, poor work performance. Under most labor agreements the penalty for a minor offense is determined by how often it has occurred. Such a system of **progressive discipline** usually includes several levels of penalties for minor offenses, such as the following:

First offense—oral warning
Second offense—written warning

Third offense—second written warning and suspension without pay

Fourth offense—termination

The objective of a system of progressive levels of penalties is to inform employees of their inappropriate behavior and allow them to correct it without serious consequences. It is assumed that the cause of the problem is lack of awareness or motivation and not ability, and therefore the employee can choose to correct the behavior. Thus, if the behavior is not repeated within a certain period of time, such as six months, the incident(s) usually is removed from the employee's record. However, repeated incidents of even minor offenses can lead to termination because the employee is unwilling or unable to stop their behavior.

Serious Offenses

Contracts often contain provisions that specify that certain actions can lead to immediate discharge for the first offense. Figure 10-3 is an example of such a provision from an agreement between an AFL-CIO carpenters' local union and Anderson Wood Products

FIGURE 10-3 Article XXI Discharge and Discipline

The right of the Company to discharge and discipline employees is recognized, but such action will only be taken for just cause.

Section 1. Commission of the following acts shall constitute just cause for disciplinary action, up to and including discharge:

1. Dishonesty, such as stealing from the Company or other employees, falsification of time records, punching time cards of other employees, or furnishing false information for personnel records.
2. Performing willful destructive acts harmful to persons or property.
3. Interfering with or obstructing production, or attempting to do so.
4. Conviction of a felony or a crime.
5. Gross negligence on Company premises or in line of duty resulting in injury, loss, or damage to persons or property.
6. Insubordination, including refusal or deliberate failure to perform work assignments on instructions given by supervisors.
7. Fighting, horseplay, or any other form of disorderly conduct.
8. Bringing intoxicants onto the Company's premises or consuming intoxicants while on duty, or reporting to work under the influence of intoxicants.
9. Being away from the job or out of work area without the permission of the supervisor.
10. Possessing dangerous weapons on Company property.
11. Excessive unexcused absences and tardiness.
12. Deliberate violations of safety rules or sanitation rules, or repeated refusal or failure to observe such rules.
13. Operating any machine, equipment or vehicle without instruction or permission.
14. Participating in the unnecessary wasting of materials.

Section 2. The list in Sec. 1 of acts which shall constitute just cause for discharge is not exhaustive, and the failure to enumerate any specific act above shall in no way be interpreted to infer that other acts other than enumerated above may not also constitute just cause of discharge.

SOURCE: Agreement Between AFL-CIO Local 2501, Kentucky State District Council of Carpenters and Anderson Wood Products Company, Inc. 1999–2002.

Company, Inc. It lists 14 specific examples that can lead to discharge, but "such action will only be taken for just cause." Section 2 of the agreement also notes that the list of 14 acts is not exhaustive—other acts may also lead to discharge for just cause. The purpose of listing the 14 most common acts is to warn employees about those specific acts and thus, it is hoped, remove any doubt they may have as to the outcome should they commit one of those acts. It is also important to realize that the union has agreed to the acts listed in the contract.

DISCIPLINARY PROCEDURES

A primary objective of a grievance process is to provide employees with a fair review and, if necessary, an appeal of disciplinary actions taken by management. Regardless of size or industry, every company at some time must administer corrective discipline. Certain employees may need such attention only once or twice in their careers and quickly respond to fair procedures; others may never correct their behavior and will exhaust any progressive disciplinary process. However, it is important that other employees believe that the disciplined employee was given a fair chance and equitable punishment. In order to maintain good labor relations, both labor and management should strive for fair and effective disciplinary policies.

Employers need a comprehensive and effective discipline system to maintain control over the workforce. Otherwise, satisfactory employee attendance, conduct, and productivity could not be achieved. A well-structured and uniformly enforced discipline program also may reduce employee discontent, along with any manager's tendency to treat employees in an arbitrary or biased manner. Employees are more satisfied when they know what consequences to expect from rule violations and when they see **disciplinary procedures** consistently administered.[14]

Labor and management officials want to minimize the use of disciplinary actions, but both realize that such actions will be needed in some situations. Therefore, virtually all collective bargaining agreements outline a disciplinary procedure.

Other than the economic benefits of a labor agreement, the disciplinary process may be the most vital aspect of a labor–management relationship. Management views the right and ability to discipline its employees effectively as the heart of maintaining a productive workforce. If one employee can accidentally or willfully violate work rules, the total result could be very costly. For example, if one employee continues to neglect wearing protective goggles because they are uncomfortable or inconvenient, others may follow because they think the rule has been relaxed. The eventual penalty is OSHA citations and fines or possibly an individual's loss of eyesight in an accident because of one minor infraction.

Any degree of discipline—even if it is only an oral warning—is both stressful and embarrassing to the employee because of the economic and psychological penalties of possible layoff or termination. If such discipline was not warranted by the facts of the situation, if the employee was ignorant of any wrongdoing, or if the penalty was unusually harsh, other employees will react very negatively. Protection from biased or thoughtless supervisors in disciplinary matters has been a prime motive behind many union-organizing campaigns.

A variety of disciplinary policies may be provided in the labor contract. The Bureau of National Affairs suggests that these policies should be encouraged and utilized by management and labor officials:[15]

1. ***Explain company rules.*** Orientation courses, employee handbooks, bulletin board notices, and other devices must be used to bring work rules to the attention of employees.
2. ***Get the facts.*** Investigate fairly and objectively by interviewing witnesses to ensure that both sides of a story are presented. Circumstantial evidence, personality factors, and unproven assumptions cannot be easily defended before arbitrators. Determine if substantial evidence is present.
3. ***Give adequate warning.*** Most grievance warning steps are given to the employee in writing; however, all warnings, even oral warnings, should be noted in the employee's personnel record. Copies of warning notices should go to the union.
4. ***Ascertain motive.*** People usually have a reason for what they do. Seldom will employees intentionally and maliciously violate rules. The penalty should be adjusted to the degree the employee's action was intentional.
5. ***Consider the employee's past record.*** Before taking disciplinary action, consider the employee's past record. Take into account both a good work record and seniority, especially in cases of minor offenses. Previous unrelated offenses should not be given heavy consideration.

Minor employee misconduct situations are often subject to an oral warning for a first offense. However, even oral warnings are usually documented in the employee's file and a copy given to the union.

6. *Discipline without discharge.*   Wherever possible, avoid the use of discharge. Only when there is no hope of future improvement or the offense is severe should discharge be used.
7. *Act timely.*   Issue discipline in a timely manner, within a reasonable period after the misconduct.

A critical aspect of the disciplinary procedure is the face-to-face counseling provided by the supervisor. Such encounters can become explosive and often lead to subjective and emotional behavior. Employees may feel that they need a union to provide them protection against what they perceive as unfair supervisory actions. Any corrective supervisory counseling should provide the employee feedback, stating the problem, the preferred action, and future expectations as well as the disciplinary action to be taken.

The Labor-Management Relations Act, in addition to civil and antidiscrimination laws, provides restrictions on employee discipline. The act prohibits disciplinary action against employees for union-related activity. Most related charges of such employer actions arise from union organizing campaigns. The second most common source of unfair discipline charges arises from conflict between the union steward and management. The steward must file the grievances of union members and advocate their point of view. In this situation, the NLRB may view disciplinary actions against the steward as an unfair labor practice. Thus, employers should have a uniformly applied and well-documented disciplinary program they can defend against possible claims of unfair labor practice discrimination.[16]

Grounds for Discharge

Employees may be terminated or discharged for "cause" or "just cause" for specific offenses. Most contracts specify the offenses that are sufficient grounds for immediate discharge, but they also provide for an appeal procedure in that event. The contract may require that the union be notified in advance of a discharge or that a predischarge hearing be held with the employee and union present. The most common grounds for discharge specified in contracts include those listed in Table 10-1. An example of a just-cause grievance is seen in Case 10-4. In cases involving the termination of an employee,

TABLE 10-1   Grounds for Immediate Discharge (expressed as percentage of contracts)

Cause	*Manufacturing*	*Nonmanufacturing*
Violation of leave provision	61	36
Unauthorized strike participation	47	31
Unauthorized absence	62	29
Dishonesty or theft	24	34
Violation of company rules	22	14
Insubordination	18	20
Intoxication	19	33
Incompetence	21	15
Failure to obey safety rules	14	15
Misconduct	20	11
Tardiness	13	5

SOURCE: Reprinted with permission. *Basic Patterns in Union Contracts,* Fourteenth Edition, by The Bureau of National Affairs. Copyright © 1995. The Bureau of National Affairs, Inc., Washington, DC 20037. For BNA Books Publications call toll free 1-800-960-1220 or visit www.bnabooks.com.

JUST CAUSE

The company posted a notice on October 24 scheduling the grievant, along with other employees, to report a half hour early on October 28 to attend a United Way meeting. The half hour would be scheduled overtime and paid as such. The grievant saw the notice, made no attempt to discuss the matter with his supervisor, and failed to report at the time stated in the notice. The grievant reported at his regular work time. The company put a discipline memo in his personnel file for failure to report to work for scheduled overtime. The memo noted that the grievant had not reported to work as scheduled and warned that further disciplinary action would result if he continued to violate the contract. The employee grieved the disciplinary action on the basis that he should not be required to attend a United Way meeting, as he did not agree with the principles espoused by United Way.

It was the company's position that the company was within its rights to require the employee to report a half hour early for work and to attend the United Way meeting on company time. Furthermore, the failure of the employee to report to work on time was in violation of a contract provision. The company adhered to the established principle that the employee should "obey now, grieve later." The company argued that the employee should have attended the meeting and then grieved the factual issue of whether the company had the right to compel attendance at the United Way meeting. It was the union's position that, although the union was supportive of the United Way ac-

tivity and participated with the company in the annual United Way drive, the company did not have the right to compel the attendance of the employee at the meeting.

DECISION

The arbitrator found that the issue in the case was whether the company had the right to compel the grievant's attendance at a United Way meeting. Although it is a well-established rule that the employer has the right to direct the workforce—and this company had the right under its contract with the union to schedule overtime with appropriate notice—the exercise of its management rights must reasonably relate to the operation of the employer's enterprise. It was the arbitrator's belief that the United Way drive was not reasonably related to the company's operation. So, although the company may request attendance by the employees at a meeting and be willing to pay overtime, it did not have the authority to require attendance at the meeting. The arbitrator did not accept the company's position that the grievant should have reported to work and grieved the issue later because that basic premise, "work now, grieve later," is relevant only when it allows the company's operation to continue during a dispute with a grievant. As the United Way meeting was in no way related to the employer's ability to keep his operation going, there was no requirement that the employee delay his disagreement with the requirement.

SOURCE: Adapted from *Green Bay Packing*, 87 LA 1057 (1986).

the union will often insist on taking the case through all the procedural steps to arbitration in an effort to save the employee's job. Management exercises extreme care to exactly follow the steps of the disciplinary process because the decision and process steps are likely to be challenged. Arbitrators generally view a discharge as the "workplace equivalent of capital punishment" and therefore expect both parties to carefully adhere to the letter and spirit of the contract.[17]

Tips from the Experts

ARBITRATOR

What are the three best ways to ensure a fair grievance procedure process if you are the employer or the union?

1. Conduct a full and adequate investigation into the facts and circumstances. The employee should be given an opportunity to explain why he or she should not be disciplined, or the employer should explain why the discipline imposed did not violate the agreement or past practice.

2. Make full disclosures at the earliest possible grievance step. Disclose the issues, the facts, the documents to be presented, and the names of the witnesses and what they will offer as testimony.

3. Do not rely on the other side to make the case for you. Develop a theory of the case, with witnesses and documents ready to support it.

GRIEVANCE MEDIATION

Most collective bargaining agreements include procedures to resolve grievances that arise during the life of the contract, with binding arbitration as the last step. Many, however, also provide for **grievance mediation** as a voluntary last step *before* arbitration. The process provides the opportunity for a neutral, third party, such as a mediator from the FMCS (Federal Mediation & Conciliation Service) to assist the parties in reaching their own settlement of the dispute before it reaches arbitration.

Grievance mediation is a supplement to or a single step in a contractual grievance resolution process but should *not* be viewed as a substitute for the process. The mediator cannot resolve the dispute by making a binding decision but rather works with both parties to achieve a mutually acceptable settlement of the grievance. To request an FMCS mediator, both parties must submit a signed, written request that outlines the issues involved.

Grievance mediation often provides several advantages to the process of resolving disputes: (1) faster resolution of issues compared to arbitration; (2) both parties, grievant and manager, have the opportunity to present their case to a neutral, third party without the possibility of losing as they might in a binding arbitration; (3) even if the process does not lead to a settlement, both parties can better evaluate the strengths and weaknesses of their cases before proceeding to arbitration; and (4) the FMCS provides the service without charge to the parties so that, if a settlement is reached, the costs of arbitration can be avoided. The process utilized by the FMCS in grievance mediation is somewhat different from that of arbitration; thus, the documents prepared and statements made in grievance mediation *cannot* be used during subsequent arbitration proceedings. Both parties must usually agree to the 10 FMCS Guidelines for Grievance Mediation in Figure 10-4.[18]

The process of grievance mediation generally follows one of two formats: (1) the mediator meets with both parties separately and jointly to determine the issues, priorities, and barriers. Then the mediator may present to each side the likely outcome if the grievance progresses to arbitration; or (2) instead of predicting outcomes, the mediator will utilize an interest-based process (similar to interest-based bargaining as discussed in Chapter 5) and seek a settlement agreeable to both parties because their primary priorities are met. For example, a union might trade its demand for back pay (low priority) in exchange for reinstatement (high priority).[19] A 2005 study of 3,387 cases over

1. The grievant is entitled to attend the mediation.
2. Unless the collective bargaining agreement provides for mediation within the grievance procedure, the parties must waive any time limits while the grievance mediation step is being utilized.
3. The grievance mediation process is informal and the rules of evidence do not apply. No record, stenographic or tape recordings, of the meetings will be made.
4. The mediator's noteds are confidential and will be destroyed at the conclusion of the grievance mediation meeting. FMCS is a neutral agency, created to mediate disputes, and maintains a policy of declining to testify for any party, either in court proceedings or before government regulatory authorities.
5. The mediator will use problem-solving skills to assist the parties, including joint and separate caucuses.
6. The mediator has no authority to compel a resolution.
7. If the parties cannot resolve the problem, the mediator may provide the parties in joint or separate session with an oral advisory opinion.
8. If the parties cannot resolve the grievance, they may proceed to arbitration according to the procedures in their collective bargaining agreement.
9. No statement given by either party as part of the grievance mediation process, nor any documents prepared for a mediation session, can be used during arbitration proceedings.
10. The parties must agree to hold FMCS and FMCS mediators harmless for any claim of damage arising from the mediation process.

FIGURE 10-4 Guidelines for Grievance Mediation

SOURCE: *FMCS Grievance Mediation: Problem Solving in the Workplace* (Washington, DC: U.S. Government Printing Office, 2001).

a 24-year period produced significant findings that support the use of grievance mediation in comparison to arbitration:[20]

- *Cost savings.* The average cost of mediation per case was $672 compared to $3,202 per arbitration.
- *Time savings.* The average time required to mediate a case was 43.5 days—compared to 473 days to arbitrate a case.
- *Satisfaction with process.* The participants who were "highly satisfied" with interest-based mediation included: 89 percent management, 68 percent union, and 47 percent grievants.
- *Increased ability to resolve grievances.* Participants (83 percent) indicated they were better able to resolve future grievances because they learned how to communicate better. In addition 65 percent indicated the use of interest-based grievance mediation had led to a better union–management relationship due to a more cooperative atmosphere and the use of mediation techniques.

PUBLIC-SECTOR GRIEVANCE ISSUES

Although differences exist between public- and private-sector labor relations, there are similarities. A major similarity is that the collective bargaining agreements of both sectors are often influenced by the personalities of the negotiators and their abilities to improve their bargaining power relative to the other party.[21] Also, grievances in the two sectors are generally processed in the same manner.

Grievance arbitration in the private sector has proved to be a more effective means of contract enforcement than strikes, in addition to continuing the collective bargaining process through the life of the contract. At the federal, state, and local levels, the grievance arbitration procedure has borrowed heavily from the private sector.[22]

The expense of grievance arbitration is of concern to employers in the public sector just as it is to those in the private sector. A study was done on the attitudes of union stewards toward filing grievances in the public sector to see whether costs could be reduced. It was demonstrated that grievance rates tended to be reduced when management negotiators were perceived as accommodating rather than combative during negotiations. Grievance rates tended to increase or decrease depending on whether union stewards perceived their union members to be combative or cooperative toward their government managers. The study also found that if an informal method of communication existed, fewer grievances were filed. Surprisingly, the clarity of a collective bargaining agreement had little effect on the number of grievances filed. If the relationship between the parties tended to be combative or cooperative, disagreements over contract language followed that same pattern.[23] See Profile 10-2 for some of the approaches being used in the federal government to counter the time and expense of typical grievance arbitration resolution techniques.

In the area of discipline and dismissal, however, public-sector labor law has developed along completely different lines because of the constitutional protection afforded government employees. When government acts at any level to discipline or dismiss an employee, a form of state action has occurred. The power of the state over an individual is curtailed by the Bill of Rights, and if any constitutionally protected right is infringed on by the discipline or dismissal of an employee, that employee has a valid

---

PROFILE 10-2

FLRA COLLABORATION AND ALTERNATIVE DISPUTE RESOLUTION ACTIVITIES

The Federal Labor Relations Authority is actively engaged in the labor–management Collaboration and Alternative Dispute Resolution Program (CADR). CADR is dedicated to reducing the costs of conflict in the federal service. This agencywide program, launched in 1996, provides overall coordination of the use of alternative dispute resolution techniques in every step of labor–management disputes—from investigation and prosecution to the adjudication of cases and resolution of bargaining impasses.

The initiatives include the following:

1. Resolving unfair labor practice and representational disputes by the Office of General Counsel using facilitation, training, and educational services delivered jointly to both management and union representatives on the federal labor relations law, interest-based bargaining, alternative dispute resolution, and relationship building and intervention.

2. Operating an Unfair Labor Practice Trial Settlement Project administered by the Office of Administrative Law Judges, which assigns a judge or a settlement attorney to conduct settlement conference negotiations with the parties before trial. The initial pilot of this project resulted in an 80 percent settlement rate.

3. Resolving impasses in collective bargaining agreement negotiations through the Federal Service Impasses Panel using procedures that include mediation, fact finding, written submissions, and arbitration to move the parties toward voluntarily resolving the impasses short of a written decision and order from the panel.

SOURCE: Adapted from "FLRA News," www.flra.gov (October 15, 1999).

claim against the governmental entity regardless of contractual rights. Examples of constitutionally protected rights include the following:

1. Privilege against self-incrimination
2. Freedom of association
3. Right to participate in partisan politics
4. Freedom of expression

These constitutionally protected rights, as well as specific statutes allowing government employees to appeal to various courts, have assured public employees of multiple forms of relief not available to private-sector employees. Although this protection tends to weaken the grievance-arbitration system, it guarantees the rights of the individual over those of the unions.[24]

SUMMARY

Grievance procedures and the arbitration of disputes provide important tools to collective bargaining. Without such procedures, labor and management, as well as the community, would suffer greatly from economic recriminations, such as strikes and walkouts. Instead, issues such as a supervisor's disciplining an employee, as well as instances of "letting off steam," can be logically decided. Contract provisions that specify how situations involving employee misconduct will be handled are common in contracts. Usually, serious offenses can lead to immediate termination, whereas minor offenses are treated by a progressive discipline policy.

The Supreme Court and the NLRB have given sufficient authority to agreed-on grievance procedures and arbitration as a final step, making the practices commonplace and effective. However, specific steps to be utilized in employee grievances should be detailed in the labor agreement. Grievance mediation reduces the need for arbitration as a final step and should be considered when possible. In addition, in comparison to arbitration, mediation has been found to be less expensive, faster, and produce more satisfactory results.

CASE STUDIES

Case Study 10-1 Insubordination of a Police Officer While in Pursuit of a Stolen Vehicle

The city's police department has a procedure that establishes guidelines for police officers who are in pursuit of the occupants of another vehicle. A section of the pursuit policy states that a shift commander is to be assigned as management supervisor of each pursuit and has the authority to terminate a pursuit when public safety is at risk.

Patrol officers became involved in a pursuit when a man pointed a rifle at his wife, threatened her, discharged the rifle, and then, in a vehicle he had stolen, fled from investigating police officers. Sergeant D, who had been assigned as managing supervisor, monitored the pursuit and finally ordered it terminated. Police Officer A, however, continued to follow the suspect, despite having been told by both Sergeant D and Sergeant C to stop the pursuit. Officer A apprehended the suspect when the suspect's automobile "broke down." The city charged

Officer A with a violation of the pursuit procedure and suspended him for one day without pay.

At an arbitration hearing, Officer A testified that he was concerned that the suspect's automobile would break down and that because the suspect had committed a felony (stealing a vehicle) and was armed, he might engage in a carjacking. Officer A further testified of his oath to protect the public and his belief that the public was in danger from the suspect. Officer A also testified that his emergency lights and siren were not in operation while he followed the suspect, and he never attempted to close the gap on the suspect's automobile; thus, he was not in pursuit.

The city argued that Officer A had failed to obey the orders of two sergeants to terminate a pursuit and should be disciplined for his failure to obey their orders.

SOURCE: Adapted from *City of San Antonio*, 95 ARB 5066 (1995).

QUESTIONS

1. Was Officer A in pursuit of the suspect's vehicle?
2. As an arbitrator, would you uphold or deny the grievance?
3. Would you change the punishment of Officer A from a one-day suspension to that of a written warning?
4. What is the value to the police command in disciplining Officer A?

Case Study 10-2 Grooming Standards at Southwest Airlines

Ramp agents of Southwest Airlines load and unload baggage from aircraft and also collect baggage from customers as they board the aircraft. The union states that Grievant B, a ramp agent with 13 years' experience, is being discriminated against because management at its Love Field Operation in Dallas, Texas, requires him to wear his long hair tucked beneath a cap, but female ramp agents and male maintenance employees are not required to wear caps.

At an arbitration hearing, the company testified that its grooming rules have been enforced on a uniform basis. All male ramp agents have been treated the same, and all female ramp agents have been treated the same. The company argues that discrimination is permissible as long as it is not unlawful and as long as differences in grooming standards that do not unreasonably inhibit work opportunities are permissible under Title VII of the

1964 Civil Rights Act. The company also states that the issue of an alleged discrimination with respect to male maintenance employees is beyond the scope of this grievance because a separate labor agreement exists between maintenance employees and the company.

SOURCE: Adapted from *Southwest Airlines*, 97 ARB 3036 (1996).

QUESTIONS

1. How realistic is the company's argument regarding grooming standards?
2. Can an employer unilaterally impose a grooming rule over the objections of its employees or their bargaining agent?
3. How valid is the company's argument that the labor agreement with maintenance employees is "beyond the scope of this grievance"?

KEY TERMS AND CONCEPTS

- "5 Ws" rule
- disciplinary procedures
- employee misconduct (minor v. serious offenses)
- formal grievance procedures
- grievance
- grievance mediation
- grievance procedure
- progressive discipline

REVIEW QUESTIONS

1. Discuss the relationship that exists between labor and management in the public sector.
2. Explain a typical grievance procedure.
3. Describe how the concepts of authority and influence affect the grievance process.
4. Explain the steps of a grievance. Why do these steps exist?
5. Discuss how disciplinary procedures affect the labor–management relationship.
6. What are advantages and disadvantages of grievance mediation?
7. Why is progressive discipline used in misconduct cases involving minor offenses?
8. What serious misconduct offenses should always result in discharge?

YOU BE THE ARBITRATOR
Employee Writing Threats

SECTION XXIV
COMPANY RULES

Company rules include but are not limited to those listed in APPENDIX "D" of this Agreement. Reasonable changes or additions to these rules may be made from time to time and the Company shall notify the Union of the same prior to the notification to all employees. By the publishing of these rules and notification of changes and additions, it shall be considered that employees will have complete knowledge of the rules. The employees shall abide by the Company's rules and practices; however, the Union may question the reasonableness of any new rule.

APPENDIX D
RULES FOR EMPLOYEE CONDUCT

Rules for acceptable conduct of employees are necessary for the orderly operation of the Courtland Mill and for the benefit and protection of the right, safety, and security of all employees and the Company.

These rules, and others which may be established from time to time, are hereby published to provide and promote understanding of what is considered unacceptable conduct in order to promote a safe, orderly, and efficient operation of the Mill.

Any employee who commits any of the following acts or other acts which are properly and customarily the subject of disciplinary action, may be disciplined, including discharge from employment, either after a warning or immediately without warning, depending on the seriousness, nature, and circumstances of the violation(s). Repeated violations of the same rule, or compounded violations of more than one, shall be cause for accelerated disciplinary action . . .

7. Deliberately damaging, destroying, mutilating, or defacing tools, equipment, or any property of the Company or of another employee . . .

22. Threatening, intimidating, coercing other employees; interfering with the activities of another employee in the performance of his work; or directing abusive, vile or insulting remarks to or about another employee on Company premises at any time.

Supplemental Agreement—Memorandum of Understanding Sub-Foreman Statements (in pertinent part)

A bargaining unit employee set-up to Sub-foreman will continue to have and to accrue all benefits he or she has as a bargaining unit employee during the time he or she is set-up to Sub-foreman.

Facts

The company employed approximately 1,800 production workers represented by three unions. As a result of a change in how its production was done, it announced a downsizing of production workers and some supervisory staff. It accorded the three unions an opportunity to comment on the downsizing plan, which two unions did. One union did not and protested by asking its members not to bid on the sub-foreman jobs as they became available. Employee R, a union member, chose to bid and was given a sub-foreman job. Employee R became the object of union harassment in the form of X-rated graffiti on the bathroom walls. Many of the writings contained threats as well. One bathroom wall had the following: "Watch your back R, you M——F——er. R has an A——whipping coming and soon." The company sent copies of the graffiti and samples of handwritings of a number of workers it suspected to a handwriting expert who determined that the grievant

had written the graffiti. The grievant, a 20-year employee, was notified that he was suspected of writing the threats on the bathroom walls and was suspended. He and his union representative met with management, and after confirming that the handwriting sample the company had provided the expert was the grievant's handwriting, he was told he was terminated. He asked management to reconsider and give him a suspension or a last-chance letter rather than dismiss him. Management declined to do so, stating that his request for leniency was tantamount to an admission of guilt. The grievant denied that he was guilty, but he was dismissed. He filed this grievance. At his hearing, management's handwriting expert testified that the grievant was the writer of the graffiti. But the union's handwriting expert testified that the grievant was not the writer of the graffiti.

Issue

Did the company have just cause to discharge a 20-year employee for writing threats against another employee on bathroom walls?

The Position of the Parties

The company's position was that the grievant was fired for just cause because he violated the company rules regarding threats and destroying company property that were a part of the collective bargaining agreement (CBA). Furthermore, the company's workplace violence policy had a zero-tolerance level. The company had suspected the grievant because he had brought Employee R up on charges with the union for taking the sub-foreman position. After the handwriting expert had identified the grievant as the responsible party and he was told he was fired, his reaction was to ask for a lesser penalty. Only after he was denied a reprieve did he say he was not guilty of the offense. The grievant's actions warranted the ultimate penalty of discharge because the company cannot tolerate the kind of hostile work environment the threats of violence created.

The union's position is that the grievant alone did not create the hostile work environment that existed in the plant. The company had to share responsibility for that because of its downsizing. And, after 20 years of service without incident, the grievant deserved better treatment. First of all, the union's handwriting expert testified that the grievant was not the writer of the graffiti. Second, the grievant had correctly pressed his complaint about Employee R when he brought him up on charges within the union. There was no testimony that the grievant had done anything else that could have been called harassment of Employee R. The union contended that the company had not demonstrated that it had just cause to dismiss the grievant.

SOURCE: Adapted from *Champion International Co. v. Paper, Allied Industrial, Chemical and Energy Workers International Union,* 115 LA 27 (Arb. 2000).

QUESTIONS

1. As arbitrator, what would be your award and opinion in this arbitration?
2. Explain why the relevant provisions of the CBA as applied to the facts of this case dictate the award.
3. What actions might the employer and/or the union have taken to avoid this conflict?

EXERCISE

Source of Grievances

PURPOSE:

To understand the different sources of grievances in the workplace.

TASK:

Divide the class into teams. Each group should survey one of the following types of local businesses to see what types of grievances commonly arise at their workplace. Share the results:

> *Type of business*
> Governmental unit
> Manufacturer
> Retailer
> Professional firm
> Your university

Cause of Grievance	Number of Grievances per Year
Violation of leave provision	
Unauthorized strike participation	
Unauthorized absence	
Dishonesty or theft	
Violation of rules	
Insubordination	
Intoxication	
Failure to obey safety rules	
Tardiness	
Drug or alcohol abuse	
Sexual or racial harassment	
Other	

CHAPTER 11

The Arbitration Process

An arbitrator returned a bus driver to his job after his employer first suspended, then fired him for the same infraction. The arbitrator invoked the principle of "double jeopardy" in ruling that the employer could not punish the employee twice for the same offense.

Labor News

ARBITRATOR CITES "DOUBLE JEOPARDY"

A bus driver departed from his scheduled stop five minutes early and was given a six-day suspension. He accepted the suspension and returned to work afterward. About a week after he returned to his route, he was informed that due to his history of running ahead of schedule and deviating from his route, he was terminated for his record of numerous offenses. The employer's discipline code included specific infractions, including running ahead of schedule, which could result in termination after four offenses in the period of a year. The driver's offense was his fourth within a year.

The union, however, grieved the driver's termination under the principle of "double jeopardy." The union argued that his six-day suspension, which he served, was the disciplinary action decided by management for the last offense, and the termination decision was a second disciplinary action for the same offense, and therefore amounted to "double jeopardy," or two penalties for the same offense.

The arbitrator pointed out that the union did not contest the fact that the driver committed a code violation or that the employer had the right to discipline the driver, and that the disciplinary action chosen could have been termination because it was his fourth offense with a year. However, the union did contest management's decision to impart a second disciplinary action for the same offense. The arbitrator pointed out that the employer knew his record at the time the suspension was imposed and presented no facts to support why a second disciplinary action was justified. The arbitrator noted that the principle of "double jeopardy" is well known in labor and employment relations and is a commonly accepted principle. Thus, the arbitrator applied the principle and concluded that the employer lacked sufficient cause to levy the second penalty of termination.

SOURCE: Adapted from *Transit Authority of River City,* 118 LA 939, (2003); and "Two Penalties for One Offense Prohibited by Double Jeopardy," *2005 Sourcebook on Collective Bargaining* (Washington, DC: The Bureau of National Affairs, 2005), p. 247.

The first mention of labor arbitration in American labor history, according to Professor Edwin Witte, dates to a clause in the constitution of the Journeymen Cabinet-Makers of Philadelphia in 1829.[1] The earliest recorded arbitration hearing occurred in 1865, when ironworkers in Pittsburgh arbitrated their wages.[2] The first known case in which an outside arbitrator was used occurred in 1871 in eastern Ohio. The Committee of the Anthracite Board of Trade (an association of coal operators) and the Committee of Workingmen's Benevolent Association (the coal miners' union) retained the services of Judge William Ewell of Bloomsburg, Pennsylvania, to settle their dispute on "discharging men for their connection with the Workingmen's Benevolent Association." Professor Robban W. Fleming reported that the results were successful in that the parties accepted and implemented Judge Ewell's recommendation. However, in 1874, when the two parties attempted to submit a second dispute to another judge for a decision, one company of the association refused to agree to the process, and a strike developed.[3] Apparently, the other firms in the association were willing to conform to the desires of the dissenting company rather than submit their dispute to an "outside" arbitrator. Professor Jean McKelvey writes that "arbitration" in the period from 1865 to 1931 was a "negotiation" process rather than a third-party decision-making process.[4]

HISTORY AND LEGAL STATE OF ARBITRATION

Four Supreme Court cases (*Lincoln Mills* and the *Steelworkers Trilogy*)[5] have provided the legal foundation for arbitration as it exists today in the United States. The *Lincoln Mills* decision authorized federal courts to fashion a body of law for the enforcement of collective bargaining agreements, and it promoted the view that the agreement to arbitrate is a quid pro quo for an agreement to refrain from striking during the term of a labor contract. This decision was based on the premise that arbitration provided the best route to industrial peace and provided the support necessary for the development of labor arbitration in the United States.

The *Lincoln Mills* concept that the federal courts would mandate the performance of arbitration provisions contained in collective bargaining agreements was given substance in the *Steelworkers Trilogy,* decided by the Supreme Court three years later in 1960. These four cases established the following five principles to govern the arbitration of grievances under collective bargaining:[6]

1. Arbitration is a matter of contract. The parties are not required to arbitrate a dispute that they have not agreed to submit to arbitration. The courts determine whether there is a duty to arbitrate a dispute.
2. In determining whether there is a duty to arbitrate a dispute, the courts should not examine the merits of the underlying grievance, even if it appears to be frivolous.
3. In labor contracts with an arbitration clause, there is a presumption of arbitrability unless there is positive assurance that the arbitration clause is not susceptible to an interpretation that covers the dispute. Doubts should be resolved in favor of coverage.
4. As long as an arbitration award is based on the bargaining agreement, a court should enforce the award without examining its correctness.
5. In interpreting the labor agreement, the arbitrator is not limited to the words of the contract. The arbitrator is empowered to consider factors such as **past practice**, **parol evidence**, and the **common law of the shop**.

Past practice is recognition of the bargaining history of the two parties involved in the dispute. If, for example, the employer allowed employees to use the Friday after Thanksgiving as a "personal day" even though the contract language would indicate otherwise, an arbitrator may rely on past practice to decide in an employee's favor. The *common law of the shop* is recognition of the bargaining history of those in the same industry as opposed to the actual parties in a particular case. Some large manufacturers "schedule" employees' vacations by closing the plant for an established week each year. An arbitrator might uphold a decision by an employer who supplies such a plant to do the same thing, even if the particular labor agreement was unclear on such a right. *Parol evidence* in labor arbitration cases refers to evidence, oral or otherwise, that is not contained within the four edges of the collective bargaining contract. It is usually not admitted for the purpose of varying or contradicting written language recorded in the labor agreement.

Three important issues have evolved from the *Lincoln Mills* and the *Steelworkers Trilogy* cases: the principle of general arbitrability, situations in which the contract has expired or the ownership of the company has changed, and whether the duty to arbitrate survives a change in company ownership:[7]

1. ***General arbitrability.***   The courts have consistently enforced the principle that if the contract provides for the arbitration of grievances, then a grievance is presumed to be arbitrable as long as the agreement does not exclude the topic under consideration.
2. ***Expired contracts or changes in ownership.***   The Supreme Court has ruled that the duty to arbitrate can extend beyond the life of the contract. A postexpiration grievance is arbitrable only when it involves facts and events that occurred before expiration, when the action infringes a right vested under the agreement, or when the normal principles of contract interpretation show that the disputed contractual right survives the remainder of the agreement.
3. ***Successorship.***   The Supreme Court has also ruled that the successor employer is not required to adopt the substantive terms of the predecessor agreement but that the successor inherits the contractual duty to arbitrate as long as there is "substantial continuity" between the old and the new companies.

In summary, the rulings by the Supreme Court on the duty to arbitrate makes it clear that if the parties' labor agreement requires the arbitration of grievances, then it will be difficult to avoid arbitration.

The Supreme Court acknowledged the superiority of arbitration in resolving labor–management disputes under collective bargaining agreements by stating,

> The labor arbitrator performs functions which are not normal to the courts; the considerations which help him fashion judgments may indeed be foreign to the confines of courts. The parties expect that his judgments of a particular grievance will not only reflect what the contract says but, insofar as the collective bargaining agreement permits, such factors as the effect upon productivity of a particular result, its consequence to the morale of the shop, his judgment whether detentions will be heightened or diminished. For the parties' objective in using the arbitration process is primarily to further their common goal of uninterrupted production under the agreement, to make the agreement meet their specialized needs. The ablest judge cannot be expected to bring the same experience and confidence to bear upon the determination of a grievance because he cannot be similarly informed.[8]

The arbitrator's role, however, is not unlimited. Beginning with the *Steelworkers Trilogy,* the Supreme Court limited the arbitrator's role to interpretation and application of the collective bargaining agreement. The Court held that although an arbitrator may look outside the contract for guidance, "he does not sit to dispense his own brand of industrial justice."[9] The courts stressed that arbitrators' decisions, as long as they are based on interpretation of the contract, should be final and binding and not questioned by the courts. For example, in 1986 the Seventh Circuit Court upheld an arbitrator's decision and overturned a district court's reversal of that decision. In this case, an employee of E. I. duPont de Nemours & Company, during a nervous breakdown, attacked fellow employees and damaged company property. The arbitrator had concluded that the incident was a result of a mental breakdown (not drug use as the company contended) and would most likely not recur. The Seventh Circuit Court upheld the arbitrator's decision, which had been vacated by the district court. The court stated, "So long as the arbitrator interpreted the contract in making his award, his award must be affirmed even if he clearly misinterpreted the contract."[10]

Another advantage of arbitration over litigation is the final and binding provision contained in most agreements to arbitrate grievances. This provides a final step for settling labor disputes in comparison with the court process requiring a series of lengthy appeals and many steps before a final decision. In addition, the technical rules of evidence found in the courtroom need not be applied to the proceedings. Arbitration hearings are less formal than litigation, and the advocates need not have legal training.

For most of the 40 plus years since the *Steelworkers Trilogy* cases, judges have refused to review the merits of an arbitration award. Why? Former Michigan Law School Dean Theodore St. Antoine answered that question:

> Put most simply, the arbitrator is the parties' officially designated "reader" of the contract. He (or she) is their joint alter ego for the purpose of striking whatever supplementary bargain is necessary to handle the unanticipated omissions of the initial agreement. Thus, a "misinterpretation" or "gross mistake" by the arbitrator becomes a contradiction in terms. In the absence of fraud or an overreaching of authority on the part of the arbitrator, he is speaking for the parties and his award is their contract.[11]

ARBITRATION OF STATUTORY RIGHTS IN UNION AND NONUNION CASES

The Supreme Court addressed the application of an arbitration clause to the pursuit of an individual's statutory rights even if the individual is covered by an arbitration provision in a collective bargaining agreement in *Alexander v. Gardner-Denver*.[12] In that case the Court ruled that an individual could not be precluded from suing under the civil rights laws just because his claim had gone through arbitration under the collective bargaining agreement. The Court was articulating a public policy exception to labor arbitration provisions.

Title VII Cases

The principle stated by the Court in the *Gardner-Denver* case is clear: Individuals may exercise a legal right based on external law that is independent of their rights under a collective bargaining agreement.[13] An individual who takes a grievance to arbitration that involves an EEO (equal employment opportunity) matter could be entitled to a trial if he or she loses in arbitration.

In 1998, the Supreme Court again took up the issue of whether an employee subject to a collective bargaining agreement with a compulsory arbitration clause is required to take a discrimination dispute to arbitration rather than pursue the claim in federal court. In *Wright v. Universal Maritime Service Corp.*, a longshoreman was refused employment following a settlement of a claim for permanent disability.[14] When he filed suit under the Americans with Disabilities Act, the lower court dismissed the case because the longshoreman failed to pursue his claim under the contract's arbitration procedure. The Supreme Court reversed the lower-court decision on the grounds that the arbitration provision did not contain a "clear and unmistakable" waiver of the employee's right to pursue his antidiscrimination claim in federal court.[15] And at least one federal court has ruled that a waiver of an individual statutory right by a collective bargaining agreement is nonnegotiable, making it an illegal bargaining item.[16]

Although seeming to uphold *Gardner-Denver,* some observers note that the decision follows the reasoning of the Court in *Gilmer v. Interstate/Johnson Lane Corporation*.[17]

In *Gilmer* the Court upheld compulsory arbitration of an age discrimination claim under an employee-signed employment agreement that covered termination for any reason. Although *Gilmer* did not involve an arbitration clause in a collective bargaining agreement, the holding in *Wright* would indicate that if a collective bargaining agreement arbitration provision "clearly and unmistakably" includes antidiscrimination claims, the Supreme Court might require an employee to arbitrate such a claim before resorting to the federal court

The Federal Arbitration Act and Individual Employment Agreements

In the United States, three statutes govern the private-sector arbitration of disputes: The 1947 Labor Management Relations Act (LMRA), which provides for the arbitration of disputes involving collective bargaining agreements as discussed in this chapter; the 1926 Railway Labor Act (RLA), which has jurisdiction over disputes between employees and a carrier in the railroad and airline industries; and the 1925 Federal Arbitration Act (FAA), also called the United States Arbitration Act.[18]

The Federal Arbitration Act[19] governs commercial arbitration situations such as business–business, employer–employee, and buyer–seller. The FAA provides the parties involved with guidelines and enforcement mechanisms for arbitrated disputes. The act enables one party to force the other party to arbitrate a dispute when an agreement to arbitrate exists between the two parties. The U.S. Supreme Court stated that with the 2000 Act Congress "declared a national policy favoring arbitration" over the more expensive, slower court litigation process. The Act also provides that an arbitration award can be confirmed by a court judgment.[20]

The Supreme Court expanded its *Gilmer* decision when it ruled that individual employment agreements that contain arbitration clauses could be enforced under the Federal Arbitration Act (FAA). In *Circuit City Stores Inc. v. Adams,* the employee had signed an employment application with Circuit City that included a provision agreeing to settle any and all "claims, disputes, or controversies arising out of or relating to my . . . employment . . . exclusively by final and binding arbitration.[21] By way of example only, such claims include claims under federal, state, and local statutory or common law, including . . . the Civil Rights Act." Two years later the employee filed an employment discrimination lawsuit against Circuit City, and Circuit City filed suit to require him to submit to final and binding arbitration. The court of appeals ruled that because the FAA excluded coverage of "contracts of employment of seamen, railroad employees, or any other class of workers engaged in foreign or interstate commerce," the clause was not enforceable. The Supreme Court disagreed. It held that the exclusion language of the FAA ought to be narrowly interpreted to apply only to transportation workers. The Court held that

> arbitration agreements can be enforced under the FAA without contravening the policies of congressional enactments giving employees specific protection against discrimination prohibited by federal law; as we noted in *Gilmer,* "[b]y agreeing to arbitrate a statutory claim, a party does not forgo the substantive rights afforded by the statute; it only submits to their resolution in an arbitral, rather than a judicial forum."[22]

As a result of this ruling, it has been estimated that the number of companies with employment arbitration agreements increased from 400 to 700[23] and that as many employees are covered by nonunion arbitration systems as are covered by collective bargaining agreements.[24]

The Supreme Court also upheld a mandatory arbitration provision in a nonemployment case that might have repercussions on employment arbitrations. In *Green Tree Financial Corp.-Alabama v. Randolph*, the plaintiff claimed that because the arbitration clause was silent as to the costs for such arbitration, she was effectively precluded from pursuing her statutory claim under the Truth in Lending Act for fear of incurring excessive costs.[25] The Court ruled that a party seeking to avoid an arbitration agreement must demonstrate the likelihood of incurring prohibitive costs, not just the possibility.

TYPES OF ARBITRATION

Two major types of arbitration exist with respect to labor disputes, interest and rights. **Interest arbitration** occurs over the formation of a collective bargaining agreement or efforts to secure one. **Rights arbitration** involves interpretation of a party's "rights" or the application of a particular provision under existing contract terms. One arbitrator contends that interest arbitration processes are too adversarial and that they are hampered by impediments to settlement.[26] Rights arbitration is found in almost every labor agreement and is used far more today than interest arbitration. Because interest arbitration tends to have a broader scope than rights arbitration, many unresolved issues are present in interest arbitration. Few parties are willing to place such responsibility in the hands of a third-party neutral. Case 11-1 is an example of one dissatisfied participant.

CASE 11-1	ARBITRABILITY IN MAJOR LEAGUE SPORTS

The Major League Baseball Players Association (Association) filed grievances against the Major League Baseball Clubs (Clubs), claiming the Clubs had colluded in the market for free-agent services, in violation of the industry's collective bargaining agreement. A free agent is a player who may contract with any Club rather than one whose right to contract is restricted to a particular Club. The case resulted in a finding of collusion by the Clubs, and damages were awarded in the amount of $280 million. The Association and Clubs entered into a Settlement Agreement (Agreement) regarding the distribution of the fund for claims relating to a particular season or seasons. The Agreement provided that players could seek an arbitrator's review of the distribution plan. The arbitrator would determine "only whether the approved framework and the criteria set forth therein have been properly applied in the proposed Distribution Plan."

Steve Garvey, a retired, highly regarded first baseman, submitted a claim for damages of approximately $3 million, alleging that his contract with the San Diego Padres was not extended because of collusion. The Association rejected Garvey's claim because he presented no evidence that the Padres actually offered to extend his contract. Garvey objected, and an arbitration hearing was held. At the arbitration, he presented a June 1996 letter from the Padres' president that the Padres offered to extend Garvey's contract through the 1989 season but then refused to negotiate with Garvey because of collusion. The arbitrator denied Garvey's claim and in his decision explained that he doubted the credibility of the statements in the letter because, he noted, in the original arbitration the Padres' president had denied collusion and had testified that the Padres simply were not interested in extending Garvey's contract.

continued

ARBITRABILITY IN MAJOR LEAGUE SPORTS—continued

Garvey asked the federal district court to vacate the arbitrator's award, alleging that the arbitrator violated the framework by denying his claim. The district court denied the motion. The Court of Appeals for the Ninth Circuit, however, granted the motion and reversed the arbitrator's decision. The court acknowledged that judicial review of an arbitrator's decision in a labor dispute is extremely limited. But it held that review of the merits of the arbitrator's award was warranted in this case because the arbitrator's refusal to credit the Padres president's letter was "inexplicable" and "border[ed] on the irrational" because a panel of arbitrators in the original proceedings had concluded that the owners' prior testimony was false; that is, the testimony that they did not collude had been rejected by that arbitration. The court found that the record provided "strong support" for the truthfulness of the 1996 letter and directed the lower court to vacate the award. The lower court remanded the case to the arbitration panel for further hearings, and Garvey appealed, arguing that the arbitrator had nothing more to decide since the court of appeals had already found that the 1996 letter was controlling. The court of appeals agreed and directed that the arbitration panel simply enter an award to Garvey in an appropriate amount. Both the Association and the Club appealed the court of appeals' overruling of the arbitrator's award to the Supreme Court, which agreed to hear the case.

DISCUSSION

The Supreme Court noted that Section 301 of the Labor Management Relations Act guided its decision, as the controversy involves rights under an agreement between an employer and a labor organization. Garvey's specific allegation was that the arbitra-tor violated the scheme for resolving players' claims for damages, which was to remedy the Clubs' breach of the collective bargaining agreement. The Court noted that judicial review of a labor-arbitration decision pursuant to such an agreement is very limited. Courts are not authorized to review the arbitrator's decision on the merits even if there are allegations that the decision rests on factual errors or misinterpretation of the parties' agreement. Under the *Steelworkers Trilogy*, it is only when the arbitrator strays from interpretation and application of the agreement that the decision may be held unenforceable by the Court. When an arbitrator resolves disputes regarding the application of a contract and no dishonesty is alleged, the arbitrator's improvident, even silly, fact-finding does not provide a basis for a reviewing court to refuse to enforce the award.

As the Court had previously ruled in *Misco*, even in the very rare instances when an arbitrator's procedural aberrations rise to the level of misconduct, the court must not settle the merits of the case but should simply vacate the award and leave open the possibility of further arbitration proceedings under the terms of the negotiated agreement.

In this case, the court of appeals erred when it overturned the arbitrator's decision because it disagreed with the arbitrator's factual findings with respect to credibility of the 1996 letter. The arbitrator was construing a contract and acting within the scope of his authority and established law precludes a court from resolving the merits of the parties' dispute on the basis of its own factual determinations, no matter how erroneous the arbitrator's decision.

The Supreme Court reversed the court of appeals' decision and sent Garvey back to the arbitrator for further proceedings.

SOURCE: Adapted from *Major League Baseball Players Association v. Steve Garvey*, 532 U.S. 504 (2001).

 American Arbitration Association
Dispute Resolution Services Worldwide

LABOR ARBITRATION RULES
Demand for Arbitration

MEDIATION: Please consult the AAA regarding mediation procedures. If you would like the AAA to contact the other parties and attempt to arrange a mediation, please check this box ☐

Name of Respondent ☐ Employer or ☐ Union	Name of Representative (if known)
Contact Person	Name of Firm (if applicable)
Address:	Representative's Address:

City	State	Zip Code	City	State	Zip Code
Phone No.		Fax No.	Phone No.		Fax No.
Email Address:			Email Address:		

The named claimant, a party to an arbitration agreement dated _____, which provides for arbitration under the Labor Arbitration Rules of the American Arbitration Association, hereby demands arbitration.

Nature of Grievance:

Name of Grievant(s) (if applicable):

Claim or Relief Sought:

REMINDER: You can file your case online by visiting the AAA's website at www.adr.org. Please select "AAA Webfile" from the list of side menu options. You may also wish to visit the "Labor" "Focus Area" for a complete list of our administrative services and procedures, including our Expedited Procedures.

AMOUNT OF FILING FEE ENCLOSED WITH THIS DEMAND (please refer to the rules for the appropriate fee) $

THE FILING PARTY REQUESTS THAT HEARINGS BE HELD AT THE FOLLOWING LOCALE: _____

You are hereby notified that copies of our arbitration agreement and this demand are being filed with the American Arbitration Association office located in _____, with a request that it commence administration of the arbitration. Under the rules, you may file an answering statement within ten days after notice from the AAA.

Signature (may be signed by a representative) Date:	Name of Representative
Name of the Claiming ☐ Union or ☐ Employer	Name of Firm (if applicable)
Address (to be used in connection with this case):	Representative's Address:

City	State	Zip Code	City	State	Zip Code
Phone No.		Fax No.	Phone No.		Fax No.
Email Address:			Email Address:		

To begin proceedings, please send two copies of this Demand and the Arbitration Agreement or relevant contract language, along with the filing fee as provided for in the Rules, to the AAA. Send the original Demand to the Respondent.

AAA Customer Service can be reached at 800-778-7879

FIGURE 11-1   Demand for Arbitration

SOURCE: American Arbitration Association. Used with permission.

Demand for Rights Arbitration

There are no prescribed rules for grievance arbitration as there are in the judicial process. Arbitration procedures should be based on the wishes and the needs of the parties involved to the extent possible within the judgment of the arbitrator. The arbitration process is more private and is therefore unique to the parties, as compared with the public judicial process. Also, the grievance arbitration procedure involves more sophisticated and knowledgeable parties than those in most judicial proceedings, and the arbitrator, in most cases, is more knowledgeable than the judge. Figure 11-1 is a typical example of a demand for a contract interpretation or rights arbitration.

Although many labor disputes are clearly suitable for arbitration, judgment must be exercised in deciding whether to arbitrate a particular dispute. Factors to be considered are the merits of the case, the importance of the issue, the effect of winning or losing the dispute, the possibilities of settlement, and psychological and face-saving aspects. The most popular use of labor arbitration is interpreting applications of the collective bargaining agreements. However, labor arbitration is not always the solution. Management will hesitate to arbitrate issues it considers to be its sole prerogative, such as determining methods of production, operating policies, and finances. Labor likewise considers the settlement of an internal union conflict as a topic in which management should not participate.[27]

SELECTING THE ARBITRATOR

Both labor and management pay the arbitration fees and have a hand in the choice of arbitrator; he or she is not an outside party imposed on them to resolve disputes. The arbitrator's jurisdiction evolves from the contract negotiated by the two parties. Therefore, the arbitrator's performance must generally be satisfactory; the parties can dispense with an incompetent arbitrator. The arbitrator is well aware that he or she provides a service for a fee and is expected to meet certain professional standards. Unlike litigation, both parties have the ability to participate in the selection of the arbitrator. This is recognized as a great advantage over the litigation process, in which the parties have little or no input in the selection of a judge. In fact, both parties can easily access thousands of arbitration awards by arbitrator, by employer, and by union or subject matter. Thus, they know a great deal about possible arbitrator candidates and their thoughts in similar cases.[28]

Because of the very real need to keep both parties satisfied with arbitration decisions, arbitrator decisions and awards are far from uniform on almost any issue.[29] However, no two grievance situations are the same. The arbitrator may be a permanent umpire chosen beforehand by labor and management to decide disputes arising during the life of the collective bargaining agreement. However, most arbitrations take place on an ad hoc basis, with arbitrators selected to hear disputes case by case. Permanent arbitration can help provide a stable union–management relationship. With their knowledge of the specific language of a contract, the personalities involved, and past labor relations, permanent arbitrators can quickly participate, provide immediate assistance, and resolve disputes much faster than the courts in most situations.[30] Collective bargaining agreements with arbitration normally provide for the selection process of arbitrators. If a permanent arbitrator is not designated in the contract, then an impartial agency is often agreed on as a source of arbitrators. The American Arbitration Association and the Federal Mediation and Conciliation Service are the two agencies that are the most frequent sources of arbitrators.

Contract provisions often call for arbitrators (one or a panel) to be selected from the American Arbitration Association.

The American Arbitration Association has developed this process for selecting an arbitrator:

1. On receiving the demand for arbitration or submission agreement, the tribunal administrator (a staff member of the association) acknowledges receipt thereof and sends each party a copy of a specially prepared list of proposed arbitrators. In drawing up this list, the tribunal administrator is guided by the statement of the nature of the dispute. Basic information about each arbitrator is appended to the list.
2. Parties are allowed seven days to study the list, cross off any names objected to, and number the remaining names in the order of preference. If parties want more information about a proposed arbitrator, such information is gladly given on request.
3. Where parties are unable to find a mutual choice on the list, the association will submit additional lists at the request of both parties.
4. If, despite all efforts to arrive at a mutual choice, parties cannot agree on an arbitrator, the association will make an administrative appointment. But in no case will an arbitrator whose name was crossed out by either party be so appointed.[31]

The arbitrator would be required to follow the contract language regardless of any personal opinion as to the reasonableness of the agreement language if the intent of the provision is clear. However, the language is often ambiguous, and the arbitrator must interpret the provision in question.

By interpreting contract language, arbitrators are often sources of future contract language. Collective bargaining agreements can be drafted with general language to be flexible. Sometimes the parties at the bargaining table are purposely vague in some areas to reach agreement in others. At other times, simply because of the size and complexity of an agreement, inconsistent provisions are a source of contention after the contract is signed. Arbitrators therefore are called on to resolve disputes arising from the contract language. In the absence of clear and unambiguous contract language, an arbitrator is guided by basic contract interpretation principles derived from the common law of contracts:

1. Honor the intent of the parties.
2. Interpret the agreement as a whole.
3. Give effect to all terms of the agreement.
4. Give undefined terms reasonable definitions.
5. Avoid absurd results by considering reason and equity.

By following those rules, an arbitrator crafts an "award" that often includes an interpretation of collective bargaining agreement. To some extent, an **arbitrator's award** interpreting contract language becomes part of the contract. A prior arbitration award that contains a well-reasoned opinion and involves the same parties, the same contract, and the same issues is entitled to great weight in subsequent arbitrations. This creates a disincentive for a party dissatisfied with the outcome of arbitration from repeating the same issue before another arbitrator in the hopes of getting a different result.[32]

In addition, in cases where the parties have had the opportunity to negotiate subsequent contracts and to make changes in contract language that has been interpreted in arbitration and fail to do so, the parties may be held to have adopted the award as a part of the contract. Indeed, the binding force of an award may even be strengthened by such renegotiation without change because the opportunity exists in negotiations to alter, amend, or modify any arbitral interpretation that does not reflect the intent of the parties.[33]

For the interpretation of contract language, two role models for arbitrators have been developed. One role model sees the arbitrator as a judge or umpire. Under this model the arbitrator, as a judge, reviews the arguments and proofs presented by the parties and makes a decision according to the rules imposed by the contract.[34] The second role model is much broader. The arbitrator's role is that of a mediator or impartial chairperson and is there primarily to help resolve the dispute rather than to decide which party was right or wrong under the contract. The fact that the future relationship of the two parties would be stronger if they resolved their own disputes is emphasized. The arbitrator issues a binding decision only as a last resort.[35] Today the latter role is more often viewed as proper for a grievance mediator, as discussed in Chapter 10. Arbitrators are more likely to serve as judges.

Arbitration Services

One source of arbitration panels is the Federal Mediation and Conciliation Services' Office of Arbitration Services (OAS). The responsibilities of the OAS include the following:

- Maintaining a roster of arbitrators qualified to hear and decide labor questions in labor–management disputes
- Providing the parties involved in collective bargaining agreements with a list of experienced panels of arbitrators
- Appointing arbitrators following their selection by the involved parties

The OAS maintains a roster of approximately 1,641 private arbitrators. The maintenance of this roster requires establishment of and adherence to high standards of qualification. The OAS boasts of experienced practitioners with backgrounds in

TABLE 11-1   OAS Arbitration Panel Services

Activity	2000	2001	2002	2003	2004	2005
Panel Requests	16,976	16,594	17,282	17,332	16,382	15,370
Panels Issued[a]	19,485	18,275	18,891	19,039	18,033	16,787
Arbitrators Appointed	9,561	8,706	8,335	8,595	7,875	7,592

[a]Frequently, the labor-management parties request more than one panel for arbitration cases, resulting in an increase in the number of panels issued over the number of requests received.

SOURCE: Federal Mediation and Conciliation Service. *Fifty—Eighth Annual Report* (Washington, DC: 2005) p. 9. Available at http://www.fmcs.gov/internet.

collective bargaining and labor–management relations. Panels are selected on the basis of geographical location, professional affiliation, occupation, experience in various industries, and issues or other specified criteria requested by the parties. In 1996, the OAS submitted 30,066 panels to requesting parties in both the private and the public sectors. Table 11-1 shows the number of OAS panel requests from 2000 through 2005.

Qualifications of Arbitrators

Arbitrators are not required to have any specific educational or technical training unless specified in the collective bargaining agreement. But the **qualifications of an arbitrator** are key to a successful system. If rigid qualifications are required, it may become very difficult to find an available arbitrator.

Various characteristics, including experience, education, occupation, and visibility, have been identified as affecting arbitrator selection. Both labor and management prefer arbitrators with specific attributes. Research has shown that age and experience are the most significant demographic factors affecting arbitrator decisions. Surprisingly, though, labor lawyers have not been able to distinguish between the decisions of experienced and inexperienced arbitrators.[36]

In addition to these demographic variables, other variables affecting arbitrator selection include visibility, such as public speaking and professional association membership, and past arbitration decisions. All three appear to determine which arbitrator might be selected for a case. Empirical data indicate that visibility in the community may be the single most important variable.[37] In addition to visibility, a 2000 study of arbitrator behaviors found that arbitrators who use more procedural justice methods (process and procedures used during hearings) are perceived to be more fair (by the participants). In addition, those who use more interactional justice methods (treat the participants with respect, candor, and a lack of prejudice) are more acceptable and likely to be chosen for future cases.[38]

Arbitrators are secured from a wide variety of backgrounds and include attorneys, public officials, judges, and university professors. Elkouri and Elkouri outline some general qualifications of an arbitrator:

1. ***Impartiality.***   Although no one can be absolutely free from bias or prejudice, the arbitrator is expected to divest him- or herself from personal inclinations during an arbitration, even though he or she decides cases according to his or her own judgment. The elements of honesty and impartiality are the most critical qualifications, and the arbitrator must always be able to be up front with both parties. Otherwise, he or she might not be selected again.

2. *Integrity.* Arbitrators are expected to be of the highest integrity. Both parties can review backgrounds and affiliations of prospective arbitrators; personal, financial, or business interests in the affairs of either party are primary considerations. The Code of Ethics for Arbitrators requires the arbitrator to disclose any association or relation that might reasonably bring any doubt to his or her objectivity. Records of past decisions and whether the arbitrator has expressed strong opinions in favor of either labor or management are also reviewed. Arbitrators are expected to exercise fairness and good judgment in issuing awards and not just to please both sides by splitting awards.

3. *Ability and expertise.* A labor–management arbitrator should have a broad background of social and economic experience. Maturity of judgment and a quick, analytical mind are also necessary. The arbitrator is not expected to be a subject-matter specialist; such an expert may be difficult or impossible to find. Both parties may prefer someone with general business or financial expertise, as well as significant arbitration experience.

4. *Legal training.* Labor–management arbitrators often are lawyers. Legal training may help an arbitrator to be objective and to analyze and evaluate facts without personal bias. However, not all lawyers make good arbitrators, nor are all good arbitrators lawyers. The lawyer who is overly concerned with technical rules of evidence may be ineffective.[39] Profile 11-1 describes a labor arbitrator with some unique achievements.

PROFILE 11-1

A. DALE ALLEN, JR., LABOR ARBITRATOR AND PROFESSOR OF LABOR RELATIONS, BAYLOR UNIVERSITY

To my knowledge, I hold the distinction of being the youngest arbitrator to have ever heard a labor arbitration case, and I am among the most published authors of labor arbitration cases in the nation. The manner by which I was selected for my first arbitration cases was most unusual. In 1967, at the age of 31, I was teaching an MBA night class in labor relations at the University of Louisville. Among my students was the vice president of labor relations for a national manufacturing company located in Louisville and the business agent of the large union that represented those employees. Upon completion of the course (and having received good grades), these two men asked me to serve as arbitrator for three of their disputes.

Since that beginning, I have rendered around 1,100 arbitration decisions, of which 350 to 400 have been published in the national arbitration reporting services. In addition, over the years, I have served as permanent arbitrator at various times for about 40 companies and their respective unions. My university education consists of a Doctorate in Labor Relations from the University of Colorado and MBA and BS degrees from Indiana University. Prior to becoming a university professor, I worked in industry for two companies as a line manager and labor relations specialist.

Among my published research are approximately 45 articles that have appeared in the following academic journals: *Employee Relations Law Journal, Labor Law Journal, Labor Studies Journal, Personnel Journal,* and the *Journal of Industrial Engineering,* as well as in numerous management and labor relations proceedings. Despite my heavy involvement in teaching and labor arbitration, I am active in many civic, church, and community projects. I am married and have five children and eight grandchildren at the writing of this profile.

SOURCE: Contributed by A. Dale Allen, Jr.

Tripartite Arbitration Board

The labor agreement may provide for multiple arbitrators. A **tripartite arbitration board** usually has one or more members selected by management, an equal number of members selected by labor, and a neutral member who serves as chairperson. The labor and management members act as partisans or advocates for their respective sides, and in essence, the neutral chairperson becomes a single arbitrator. The panel chair plays a unique role in the arbitration process. It is the chair's duty to keep the other arbitrators informed about all aspects of the case so they can make informed decisions. One panel member may be assigned the duty to outline all issues to be decided and circulate relevant information among the panel members. This outline serves as a "road map" of the issues in dispute.[40]

Tripartite boards sometimes do not reach decisions unanimously. Collective bargaining agreements, therefore, often provide that a majority award of the board is final and binding. Some agreements may even give the neutral member the sole right and responsibility for making the final decision. The advantage of using a tripartite board rather than a single arbitrator is to provide the neutral member with valuable advice and assistance from the partisan members. Each party may be able to give to the neutral arbitrator a more realistic and informed picture of the issues involved than may be given by formal presentation of the issues. The disadvantage of such a board, of course, is the additional time and expense incurred.[41] The following is an example of a panel selection procedure:

ARTICLE 27

Section 2

If the issue cannot be resolved by the Joint Conference Committee, a panel of seven (7) impartial arbitrators will be promptly secured from the Federal Mediation and Conciliation Service. The employer and the union shall each have the right to reject one panel of impartial arbitrators, but they must select an arbitrator from the third panel of arbitrators if they cannot agree to select from the first or second panels. The arbitrator will be selected by each party striking an equal number of arbitrators from the panel. The remaining individual shall be the arbitrator and his decision shall be final and binding on the employer, the union, and the employees. Expenses incurred in any arbitration under the provision of this article will be borne equally by the employer and the union.[42]

DETERMINING ARBITRABILITY

The basic concept of arbitrability suggests that some disputes and conflicts are not subject to arbitration. The power to determine whether arbitration is proper, the breadth of contractual issues, and whether any other issues limit the ability of an arbitrator to resolve a dispute may be called "**arbitrability**."[43] If both parties in a dispute submit the dispute to arbitration, there is no question of arbitrability because a submission by both parties identifies their agreement to go to arbitration. However, if only one party invokes the arbitration clause in a collective bargaining agreement by notice of intent to arbitrate a dispute, the other party may resist the intent to arbitrate on the grounds that the dispute is not arbitrable. Such a challenge to arbitrability is presented either to the arbitrator or to the courts. Although most questions of arbitrability are left in the hands of the arbitrator, they may be taken to the courts. The courts may be involved with arbitrability in one of three ways:

1. The party challenging arbitrability may seek a temporary injunction or stay of arbitration, pending determination of arbitrability.
2. The party demanding arbitration may seek a court order compelling the other party to arbitrate when the applicable law upholds agreements to arbitrate future disputes; the latter party then raises the issue of arbitrability.
3. The issue of arbitrability may be considered when an award is taken to court for review or enforcement unless the parties have clearly vested the arbitrator with exclusive and final right of determining arbitrability or unless the right to challenge arbitrability is held by the court to have been otherwise waived under the circumstances of the case.[44]

The Supreme Court in the ***Warrior & Gulf* case** declared that congressional policy in favor of settlement of disputes through arbitration restricts the judicial process and strictly confines it to questions of whether the reluctant party agreed to arbitrate the grievance in the collective bargaining contract. A labor–management agreement to arbitrate therefore should not be denied unless a court is absolutely positive that the arbitration clause in the collective bargaining contract is not susceptible to interpretation covering the dispute. Any doubt in questions of arbitrability should be resolved in favor of the grievance being arbitrated.[45] Case Study 11-2 at the end of this chapter illustrates a necessary exception to this rule.

In general, the arbitrator may rule on the question of arbitrability. That ruling is not subject to reversal by the courts as long as the arbitrator is applying the contract and acting within the scope of his or her authority. For example, in 2004 the arbitrator in the *Republic Waste Services* case ruled that regardless of the merits of the case, which involved termination of an employee, he did have the authority to arbitrate it. His lack of authority was due to the fact that the prior agreement had expired in January, the employee was fired in April, and the new contract started in July. The new contract did not contain a "retroactivity" clause, and the employer argued the question of arbitrability because the contract was not in effect when the employee was fired, and thus it could not be compelled into arbitration.[46]

HEARING PROCEDURES

The arbitrator fixes the date of the hearing after consulting with both sides and makes the necessary arrangements. The hearing procedure for the arbitration of a grievance normally follows a certain series of steps:

1. An opening statement by the initiating party (except that the company goes first in discharge or discipline cases)
2. An opening statement by the other side
3. The presentation of evidence, witnesses, and arguments by the initiating party
4. A cross-examination by the other side
5. The presentation of evidence, witnesses, and arguments by the defense
6. A cross-examination by the initiating party
7. A summation by the initiating party (optional)
8. A summation by the other side (optional)
9. Filing of briefs (optional)
10. The arbitrator's award[47]

Opening Statement

The opening statement lays the groundwork for the testimony of witnesses and helps the arbitrator understand the relevance of oral and written evidence. The statement should clearly identify the issue, indicate what is to be proved, and specify the relief sought. Sometimes parties will present the opening statement in writing to the arbitrator, with a copy given to the other side. Usually, the opening statement is also made orally so that appropriate points can be highlighted and given emphasis if doing so would be to the advantage of the presenting side.[48]

Rules of Evidence

Strict legal **rules of evidence** are not usually observed unless expressly required by the parties. The arbitrator determines how the hearing is run and how evidence is presented: In arbitration, the parties have submitted the matter to persons whose judgment they trust, and it is for the arbitrators to determine the weight or credibility of evidence presented to them without restrictions as to rules of admissibility that would apply in a court of law.[49]

In general, any pertinent information or testimony is acceptable as evidence if it helps the arbitrator understand and decide the issue. Arbitrators are usually extremely receptive to evidence, giving both parties a free hand in presenting any type they choose to strengthen and clarify their case.[50] The arbitrator decides how much weight to give evidence in making a decision.

Assessing Credibility of Witnesses

Included in the weighing of evidence is the arbitrator's need to assess witness credibility. An arbitrator is both judge and jury in deciding an arbitration. Conducting a fair hearing and at the same time trying to arrive at the truth from the facts presented demands keen analysis. Psychological studies regarding eyewitness testimony offer arbitrators helpful guidelines for such analysis.

An arbitrator must be aware of the following:

1. The most confident witness is not necessarily the most accurate.
2. Demeanor alone cannot reveal that a witness is lying.
3. Biases because of race, sex, or ethnic stereotyping must be eliminated.
4. The occupation or social class of a witness will not guarantee veracity.

In addition, studies indicate the following regarding the ability of a witness to recall information:

1. The more often and the longer an observer sees an event, the more accurate the recall. This factor must be weighed against the possibility that the observer's familiarity with a situation causes him or her to see what he or she expects to see from past experience.
2. Witnesses are not very accurate in estimating the duration of an event or the height, distance, or speed relevant to an event. The more emotionally charged the event, the less accurate the recall.
3. A witness's personal biases may cloud both the memory and the perception of an event.
4. Memory dims as time passes, and "after-acquired" information becomes incorporated into this memory.[51]

Presenting Documents, Photographs, and Videos

Most arbitration cases provide for the presentation of essential documents. Most important, of course, are those sections of the collective bargaining agreement that have some bearing on the grievance. Other documentation would include records of settled grievances, jointly signed memoranda, official minutes of contract negotiation meetings, personnel records, office reports, and organizational information. Documentary evidence is usually presented to the arbitrator, with a copy made available to the other party, but it is also explained orally to emphasize its importance.[52] Photographs and videos can provide excellent evidence as well as written documents. In fact experienced arbitrators encourage the use of visual evidence that can be worth "a thousand words" in understanding a dispute. Visual aids should be carefully identified with date, location, and the identification of key persons involved.[53]

Examination of Witnesses

Each party depends on the direct examination of its own witnesses during an arbitration hearing. The witness is identified and qualified as an authority on the facts to which he or she will testify and is generally permitted to tell his or her story without interruptions and without the extensive use of leading questions as in legal cases. The witness in an arbitration proceeding is rarely cut off, and some arbitrators even ask the witness whether he or she wants to add anything to the testimony as relevant to the case. Arbitrators generally uphold the right of cross-examination of witnesses but not as strongly as courts. The arbitrator also does not usually limit the rights of parties to call witnesses from the other side for cross-examination. However, opinion is split concerning the right of the company to call the grievant as a witness. One side believes that the application of the privilege against self-incrimination should apply in arbitration proceedings, even though there is no applicable constitutional privilege. The opposing view is that the privilege against self-incrimination in the field of criminal law is not present in grievance cases.[54]

Summation

Before the hearing is closed by the arbitrator, both sides are given equal time for closing statements. This is the last chance for each side to convince the arbitrator and to refute all the other side's arguments. Each side can summarize the situation and emphasize relevant facts and issues.[55]

Arbitrator's Award and Opinion

The **award** is the arbitrator's decision in the grievance case. Awards are usually short, are presented in written format, and are signed by the arbitrator. Even if an oral award is rendered, the arbitrator usually produces a written award later. Awards of arbitration boards must be signed by all members if a unanimous decision is required; otherwise, an award must be signed by a majority.

The arbitrator will also often present a written **opinion** stating the reasons for the decision. This opinion is separate from the award and clearly indicates where the opinion ends and the award begins. It is generally felt that a well-reasoned opinion can contribute greatly to the acceptance of the award. The Supreme Court has emphasized the need for arbitrator opinions and encouraged their use. Such opinions should be solidly based on the contract's terms, answer all the questions raised in the arbitration without raising new questions, and address all the arguments raised in the hearing, especially those of the losing party.[56]

CASE PREPARATION

When a grievance has reached the point of arbitration, both parties have probably gone through several steps of discussion in negotiations to resolve the issue. The issues disputed by the parties usually have been fairly well defined by the time the case reaches arbitration. To prepare the case for arbitration, the American Arbitration Association recommends the following steps in hearing preparation:

1. Study the original statement of the grievance and review its history through every step of the grievance machinery.
2. Carefully examine the initiating grievance paper (submission or demand) to help determine the arbitrator's role. It might be found, for instance, that although the original grievance contains many elements, the arbitrator, under the contract, is restricted to resolving only certain aspects.
3. Review the collective bargaining agreement from beginning to end. Often clauses that at first glance seem to be unrelated to the grievance will be found to have some bearing.
4. Assemble all necessary documents and papers at the hearing. When feasible, make postdated copies for the arbitrator and the other party. If some of the documents are in the possession of the other party, ask in advance that they be brought to the arbitration. Under some arbitration laws, the arbitrator has authority to subpoena documents and witnesses if they cannot be made available in any other way.
5. If you think the arbitrator should visit the plant or job site for on-the-spot investigation, make plans in advance. The arbitrator should be accompanied by representatives of both parties.
6. Interview all witnesses. They should certainly understand the whole case and particularly the importance of their own testimony.
7. Make a written summary of each proposed witness's testimony. This summary will be useful as a checklist at the hearing to make sure nothing is overlooked.
8. Study the other side of the case. Be prepared to answer the opposing evidence and arguments.
9. Discuss your outline of the case with others in your organization. Another's viewpoint will often disclose weak spots or previously overlooked details.
10. Read as many articles and published awards as you can on the general subject matter and dispute. Although awards by other arbitrators or other parties have no binding present value, they may help clarify the thinking of parties and arbitrators alike.[57]

Decision Criteria

In surveys conducted by the National Academy of Arbitrators, some interesting facts on how arbitrators decide cases were analyzed. The major criteria used by arbitrators did not change over the 12-year period. The following three factors were used most by arbitrators in both groups:

1. *Labor contract language.* If the labor agreement provides clear and specific directives, obviously this is the first factor used by the arbitrators.
2. *Past practice.* In the absence of clear contract language, arbitrators rely on the parties' past practice to decide.
3. *Fairness.* Arbitrators felt some latitude to decide an issue in a fair and reasonable way regardless of contract language and past practices.

The next five factors were not used by arbitrators in the same order, but they were used often:

1. *Industry practice.*   Even if the parties have no past practice in a particular area, the industry may have some consistent approach to an issue that an arbitrator can use.
2. *Other arbitration awards.*   Precedent does not bind arbitrators but they do often review other arbitrator awards for guidance.
3. *Future labor relations.*   Occasionally an arbitrator decides an issue on what he or she believes will further the labor–management relationship.
4. *State or federal law.*   If relevant, adherence to or violation of state or federal law will determine the outcome of arbitration.
5. *Social mores and customs.*   Seldom is an arbitration award decided on the basis of customs outside the workplace.[58]

As a counterweight to the findings on how arbitrators decide cases, a New York State Bar Association survey of labor and management attorneys found considerable criticism of some arbitrators' styles. Three-fourths of the 345 respondents felt that arbitrators should not consider outside factors in deciding a case. Such factors as the political fallout of a decision, a possible strike, or alleged abuse of power were not appropriate considerations. The respondents also felt that an arbitrator should not help one side even if that side has poor representation at the arbitration hearing.[59] The critical importance of addressing only the precise issue(s) in a dispute cannot be overstated. The arbitrator must avoid *obiter dictum*—remarks irrelevant to the decision—and confine the opinion and award to the case brought to arbitration.[60]

CONTRACTUAL ISSUES

Although both labor and management strive to produce a contract that results in as few disagreements as possible, contractual disputes will arise. Some of these, of course, end up in arbitration after other avenues for resolution have been explored. Historically, certain contractual issues seem to develop an agreed-on solution mechanism that eventually enables both parties to resolve their dispute before arbitration is needed. However, many issues simply cannot be easily resolved with any contractual language and therefore must go to arbitration for final resolution. Table 11-2 lists typical contract issues in arbitration with the Federal Mediation and Conciliation Services' Office of Arbitration Services for the years 2000 through 2005.

Some of the most commonly arbitrated issues are discussed in the following paragraphs.

Just Cause

Most collective bargaining agreements provide that management has the right to discipline or discharge employees for **just cause**. Arbitrator Clarence R. Deitsch noted the importance of just cause provisions in agreements: "Protection from arbitrary and capricious discipline has remained the rock-solid foundation upon which all other negotiated benefits have been based."[61] Thus, he reasoned, bargaining unit members' negotiated wages, benefits, and working conditions are at risk unless the labor contract contains a provision requiring that employees can only lose them for a good, proper or just cause—or simply a good reason. In addition, Deitsch has judged cases in recent years in which employers have pressed for an "end run" around just

TABLE 11-2 Arbitration Issues

	2001	2002	2003	2004	2005
Total Number of Issues	1,902	1,989	2,314	2,581	2,629
General Issues	434	463	506	417	308
Distribution of overtime	34	26	35	41	2
Compulsory overtime	8	12	9	3	2
Other overtime	10	10	12	1	4
Seniority					
Promotion & upgrading	54	52	63	42	26
Layoff bumping & recall	46	48	71	69	57
Transfer	17	21	14	9	0
Other seniority	25	25	35	15	8
Union officers	9	14	13	21	0
Strike & lockout	3	2	1	2	1
Working conditions	35	29	19	20	12
Discrimination	19	24	17	18	18
Management rights	51	63	71	61	72
Scheduling of work	43	67	47	61	62
Work assignments	80	70	99	54	44
Economic Wage Rates & Pay Issues	227	229	233	209	167
Wage issues	29	36	42	95	134
Rate of pay	53	60	60	33	7
Severance pay	6	8	5	1	2
Reporting, call-in & call-back pay	13	7	10	6	0
Holidays & holiday pay	31	26	21	14	8
Vacations & vacation pay	29	39	27	26	0
Incentive rates & standards	13	7	15	9	3
Overtime pay	53	46	53	25	13
Fringe Benefits Issues	69	99	112	104	100
Health & welfare	29	58	61	46	47
Pensions	11	8	11	8	7
Other fringe issues	29	33	40	50	46
Discharge & Disciplinary Issues	849	947	1091	996	937
Technical Issues	81	86	97	69	47
Job posting & bidding	32	38	43	39	43
Job evaluation	18	11	21	14	1
Job classification	31	37	33	16	3
Scope of Agreement	45	65	53	58	50
Subcontracting	29	41	36	44	42
Jurisdictional disputes	8	14	5	7	7
Foreman, supervision, etc.	5	8	9	7	1
Mergers, consolidations, accretion	3	2	3	0	0
Arbitrability of Grievances	109	100	139	96	38
Procedural	76	60	102	62	68
Substantive	14	23	25	18	28
Procedural & substantive	19	17	12	16	10
Not Elsewhere Classified	88	115	83	97	75

SOURCE: Federal Mediation and Conciliation Service, *Fifty-Eighth Annual Report* (Washington DC: 2006) 10–11. Available at http://www.fmcs.gov/internet.

The equal treatment of all employees who may violate a work rule is a critical factor in determining "just cause" for employee discipline. For example, all employees who do not wear required safety goggles on the job should receive the same discipline.

cause clauses by arguing that an employee under a seniority clause should not only lose seniority but employment as well. This most commonly occurs when an employee "walks away" from the job or is absent without notification for three consecutive working days.[62]

Although most labor and management negotiators can agree on the general concept, specifying exactly what constitutes just cause appears impossible. Some contracts will specify the exact grounds that constitute just cause and usually include other less specific provisions that are open to dispute. The inability to specify exactly which employee offenses constitute just cause is a major reason why employee discipline and discharge procedures continue to be one of the most frequently arbitrated contractual issues.[63] The overwhelming majority of discipline cases also involve disagreement over the concept of just cause. Case 11-2 presents an unusual set of circumstances leading to an employee discharge later found to be unjust.

An example of the just cause provisions appears in the 1979 agreement between the National Conference of Brewery and Soft Drink Workers and Teamsters Local No. 745 and the Jos. Schlitz Brewing Company, Longview, Texas:

ARTICLE V

Section 1

The right of the company to discharge, suspend, or otherwise discipline in a fair and impartial manner for just and sufficient cause is hereby acknowledged. Whenever employees are discharged, suspended, or otherwise disciplined, the union and the employees shall promptly be notified in writing of such discharge, suspension, or other disciplinary action and the reason therefore. No discipline, written notice of which has not been given to the union and the employee, nor any discipline which has been given more than twelve months prior

| CASE 11-2 | **JUST CAUSE AT BALL-ICON** |

A 20-year maintenance electrician employed by Ball-Icon Glass Packaging Corporation was discharged after he physically attacked his supervisor, who allegedly had pushed the employee and slapped his face while giving him a new work assignment. Several coworkers prevented the employee from attempting to throw the supervisor over a catwalk railing (the employee and supervisor were on a catwalk approximately 30 feet from floor level).

During arbitration, the supervisor alleged that the electrician previously had threatened to beat him up and also had threatened to kill him. The current plant manager testified that there were morale problems between the supervisor and his employees. The former plant manager testified that the electrician had complained about his supervisor several times and on one occasion had said, "If things don't change, somebody is going to get hurt."

The company contended that the discharge should be upheld because the electrician assaulted his supervisor, who could have been seriously injured or killed. "No employee has the right to physically assault his supervisor with the intent to do serious bodily harm or cause death to him," the company argued.

The union's position was that the electrician was provoked. The supervisor had systematically harassed the electrician over the past four years, the union contended, and the company's inability to control the situation after it was brought to management's attention several times "puts the responsibility squarely on the company's shoulders."

DECISION

Arbitrator Marlin Volz ruled that, although fighting with a supervisor is a serious disciplinary offense, the manner in which the supervisor assigned the work to the electrician had triggered the offense. Arbitrator Volz noted several factors in the employee's favor: an exceptionally good work record for 20 years, no prior disciplinary offenses, three consecutive years of perfect attendance, and no record of difficulties getting along with other supervisors.

Volz ruled that Ball-Icon did not have sufficient just cause to discharge the electrician and restored the electrician to his job with back pay.

SOURCE: Adapted from *Ball-Icon Glass Packaging Corporation,* 98 LA 1 (1992).

to the current act, shall be considered by the company in any subsequent discharge, suspension, or other disciplinary action.

Section 2

If the union is dissatisfied with the discharge, suspension, or other disciplinary action, the questions as to whether the employee was properly discharged, suspended, or otherwise disciplined shall, upon request of the union, be reviewed in accordance with the grievance procedure set forth.

The criteria used by arbitrators for just cause will obviously vary from case to case and from arbitrator to arbitrator. However, the Bureau of National Affairs has provided tests for determining whether a company has just cause for disciplining an employee:

1. *Adequate warning.*   Is the employee given adequate, oral or printed, warning as to the consequences of his conduct? Employees should be warned by the employer as to punishments either in the contract, handbook, or other means in disciplinary cases. Certain conducts such as insubordination, drunkenness, or stealing are considered so serious that the employee is expected to know they will be punishable. Was the rule reasonably related to efficient and safe operation of the organization?
2. *Prior investigation.*   Did management investigate the case before administering the discipline? Thorough investigation should have normally been made before the decision to discipline. When immediate action is required, the employee should be suspended pending investigation with the understanding that he or she will be returned to the job and paid for time lost if found not guilty.
3. *Evidence.*   Did the investigation produce substantial evidence or proof of guilt? It is not required that evidence be conclusive or beyond reasonable doubt, except when the misconduct is of such a criminal nature that it seriously impairs the accused's chances for future employment.
4. *Equal treatment.*   Were all employees judged by the same standards, with rules applied equally? The same penalty, however, may not be always given because it may be a second offense, or other factors may logically suggest a different punishment.
5. *Reasonable penalty.*   Was the penalty reasonably related to the seriousness of the offense and the past record of the employee? The level of the offense should be related to the level of the penalty, and the employee's past record should be taken under consideration.
6. *Rule of reason.*   Is the disciplinary action fairly administered? Even in the absence of specific provisions, a collective bargaining agreement protects employees against unjust discipline. Employees may reasonably challenge any company procedure that threatens to deprive employees of their negotiated rights.
7. *Internal consistency.*   Was management enforcement of the rule or procedure consistent? The company should not selectively enforce codes of conduct against certain employees. Enforcement should be consistent, whether the company disciplines on a case-by-case basis or uses a handbook. An arbitrator will carefully review the past practice of management in similar cases.[64]

The more common remedies used by arbitrators in overturning management actions in discipline and discharge cases often include a "make whole" remedy such as reinstatement with back pay, without back pay, or with partial back pay, with other rights and privileges remaining unimpaired; commuting the discharge to suspension for a specified period of time or further reducing the penalty to only a reprimand or a warning; and reversing management's assessment of suspension because the arbitrator believes the penalty is too severe. Back pay will usually be ordered consistent with the elimination of suspension.[65] Most arbitrators apply accepted common law with contracts not specifying just cause, which usually means that management action is subjected to tests of prior standards and procedural requirements. If the action meets both criteria, it will generally be found to be a valid prerogative of management.[66]

Drug Testing

A current issue regarding disciplining of employees for just cause is the use of **drug testing** as the basis for such discipline. It is certainly an established principle that employees are subject to discipline if they are unable to perform their job while under the influence of alcohol or drugs.[67] Employees will be disciplined because of their impairment under the provisions of the management rights section of an agreement. Proving the fact of drug-related impairment through drug testing provides the just cause test necessary for the employer's action.

In 1986, intolerance of illegal drug use as it related to the workplace entered a new phase. By Executive Order 12564, President Ronald Reagan provided that use of illegal drugs off or on duty makes federal employees unfit for federal employment. The order stated that random drug testing would be initiated in those agencies of the federal government in which the employees' duties involved public safety or law enforcement. Drug testing became a management–union issue separate from the right of the employer to discipline one employee for clearly demonstrated on-the-job impairment.

The Supreme Court upheld the drug-testing programs begun by the Reagan administration. By implication, their decision upholds local and state government programs involving similar personnel.[68] The NLRB has ruled that for the private employer, implementing a drug-testing program for current employees involves a mandatory duty to bargain, at least to impasse. If it is clear that the union has waived that right by contract, the employer may implement a drug-testing program unilaterally. Bargaining is not required, however, prior to implementing a testing program for job applicants.[69] Arbitrators have required employers to meet a higher standard of proof in grievances over discharges for possession and use of drugs because of the stigma attached to an employee so discharged.[70]

Following are issues that are commonly considered by an arbitrator in a drug abuse case.

1. ***Does the drug-testing procedure violate the contract?*** Drug-testing programs instituted unilaterally by employers during the term of a contract have been upheld under the general management rights and health and safety provisions of the contracts. The drug-testing programs, however, must satisfy a just cause test.[71] Sufficient language must be found in the existing contract concerning health and safety, disciplining for drug or alcohol abuse, and management rights to justify the employer's implementing a drug-testing program unilaterally.[72]

2. ***Was the testing of the employee reasonable?*** Random drug screening is generally not allowed for employees not involved in public safety. There must be a reasonable basis for the suspicion or probable cause for the belief that the employee is abusing drugs or alcohol for the employer to require a test.[73]

3. ***Was the test itself fair?*** Management is held to a very high standard to ensure that the test, which might be the basis of discipline, is properly administered. Established procedures regarding "chain of custody" of the specimen, control methods for accuracy, a confirming test, and a certainty on the kinds of drugs being tested are required.[74]

4. ***Was there on-the-job impairment?*** In cases involving discipline as a result of a positive drug test, the union may contend that the tests prove the presence of a drug in the employee's body but not on-the-job use or on-the-job impairment.[75] There is concern that positive drug tests involving illegal drugs might be used to discipline an employee for the illegal activity involved in obtaining and possessing the drug, regardless of the on-the-job effect. Management's position is that an employee who engages in such illegal activity is not a fit employee. To date,

however, arbitrators usually require a nexus between the employee's drug use and the behavior in the workplace before just cause for discipline is found.[76]

5. ***Can an employee be disciplined for refusing to be tested?***   A company can sustain its firing of an employee for failure to take a drug test only if there are reasonable grounds for the belief that the employee had consumed an illegal drug.[77] If there is no probable cause for the test, an employee is within his or her rights to refuse to take the test as a protest against unwarranted invasion of privacy.[78] In addition, just as with other dischargeable offenses, the employee must be warned that failure to submit to a test itself will result in discharge.[79]

Seniority Recognition

The most severe limitation of managerial discretion is the negotiated requirement of **seniority** recognition. It significantly reduces the employer's control over the workforce and the filling of positions. Seniority is commonly understood to mean the length of service with the employer either on a companywide basis or within the particular unit of the organization. People retain their jobs according to their length of service with the employer or within the particular unit and will be promoted to better jobs on the same basis.

The purpose of seniority is to provide maximum security to workers with the longest continuous service.[80] Arbitrators often hear cases involving loss of seniority or management's failure to promote the most senior person. Collective bargaining agreements often provide sections describing the loss of seniority similar to this agreement between General Motors Corporation and the United Auto Workers:

> **SECTION 64**
>
> Seniority shall be broken for the following reasons: (a) if the employee quits, (b) if the employee is discharged, (c) if the employee is absent for three working days without properly notifying the management, unless a satisfactory reason is given, (d) if the employee fails to return to work within three working days after being notified to report for work, and does not give a satisfactory reason, [and] (e) if the employee is laid off for a continuous period equal to the seniority he had acquired at a time of such layoff.[81]

The agreement commonly requires management to prepare seniority lists to be made available to all employees. The seniority list usually contains each employee's name, occupational group, plant seniority date, and new seniority date, if applicable. If the contract does not require the posting of a seniority list, the employer may be held to be under an implied obligation to make proper and reasonable disclosure of seniority. An arbitrator has ruled the following:

> An employee—and the union as his representative—clearly has a right to be informed of a seniority date and length of continuous service credited to him on the company's records. By the same token, since most seniority issues involve a comparison of the relative rights of two or more employees, the employee—and the union as his representative—has a right to know the seniority dates and length of continuous service credited to the other employees in the seniority unit applicable to him at any given time. The only accurate source of such

information is obviously the company. It has the records. It is initiating the various transfers, promotions, demotions, thumps, layoffs, recalls, etc. . . . which are daily causing changes in those records.[82]

Absenteeism

Unexpected employee absences cause major problems for management. Supervisors who receive an employee's call notifying them of his or her absence that day must quickly transfer personnel and possibly call in additional employees. Absenteeism causes several problems:

1. ***Lost productivity.***   Replacement employees usually cannot be as efficient on a job as those who perform it daily. If they are shifted from another area, two or more jobs may be affected by one absence.
2. ***Additional costs.***   Often the use of a replacement employee causes the employer to pay overtime. Thus, even if the absent employee is not paid for hours missed (which is usually not the case), personnel costs increase significantly.
3. ***Benefits.***   Most contracts provide that the absent employee continues to receive almost all benefits. If a replacement employee also receives some additional benefits, the hourly cost can increase significantly.
4. ***Administrative time.***   Several people may be needed to provide replacement help. The immediate supervisor may need not only to contact additional help but also to provide them with more instruction during the day. Personnel department people, department heads, and others may also be required to use part of their day in arranging for replacement help.

Management considers absenteeism a controllable problem and usually seeks to minimize the number of absences through the use of control or disciplinary techniques. Although hesitant to implement new or additional control techniques that may be abused by management, unions recognize the seriousness of the problems caused by unexpected absences and have agreed to a variety of control measures in contracts.

One example of union–management ability to control absenteeism is the case of the H. J. Scheirich Company, a cabinet manufacturer with more than 400 employees. Several years ago, the firm's management concluded that absenteeism was causing major production problems and had inflated labor costs. Together, Scheirich and the union negotiated an innovative "no-fault" absenteeism policy. The new policy centered on the policy statement, "Action may be taken when cumulative time lost from work for any reason substantially reduces the employee's services to the company."[83]

In practice, excessive absenteeism was considered to be about 3 percent above the plant average; however, no exact figure was used. Instead, abuses were examined on a case-by-case basis. In the first six years of the new program, 11 employees were terminated for "unavailability for work." Eight of the 11 grieved their terminations through the union; five went to arbitration. The arbitrators upheld the termination in four of the five cases, and in the fifth case the award was given to the employee only because management failed to notify her with sufficient warnings. In general, the arbitrators issued opinions stating that management has a right to terminate employees for excessive absences even when due to illness or other factors. They found the case-by-case method of comparing the employee's percentage of absenteeism against the company average to be reasonable.[84]

Case 11-3 describes a situation in which an employee was discharged because his absences placed him in the "worst 2 percent" of all employees and the arbitrator decided to reinstate the employee with back pay.

ABSENTEEISM AT WEBER AIRCRAFT

Weber Aircraft's labor agreement contains a no-fault attendance policy that specifies that after 80 hours of absences, an employee is subject to discharge. Vacation time, approved medical leaves, special situation absences, or holidays are not counted against the employee. On February 26, 1992, grievant A received a written notice that his 1990 and 1991 absences placed him "in the worst 2 percent of all employees in the entire plant with respect to attendance and that a failure to maintain an acceptable attendance may result in discharge without any additional warnings." The labor agreement also specifies that an employee is to be notified when 64 of the allowed 80 hours of absences are used.

Beginning in 1990, grievant A experienced heart problems and high blood pressure, which occasioned considerable absence from work during 1990 and 1991 while on approved medical leave. After these absences, grievant A received the February 26, 1992, warning letter. On March 31, 1992, grievant A was granted a medical leave of absence relating to a cyst problem. Grievant A had a cyst removed from his leg and originally believed that this procedure would not result in any loss of work. However, the stitches broke open, and A had to seek and obtain medical leave again. Grievant A's hour bank was not charged for the approved medical leave relating to the cyst problem. Beginning in June 1992, Grievant A experienced considerable discomfort and symptoms (blood in his urine) related to a prostate condition. He continued to work with this discomfort until he left work at approximately 10:30 AM on June 15, 1992, to visit a doctor. A's shift began at 7:00 AM, and he had obtained approval from his supervisor to leave work. His doctor advised him to take off work until June 22, 1992. On the morning of June 16, 1992, A's wife (also a company employee) took a slip signed by A's doctor to the plant nurse, who advised that A should apply for medical leave. The nurse advised A's wife that he probably would not be granted a second medical leave but that the company would charge vacation time for the medical leave and that A would not be charged for an absence. On June 17, 1992, A received a telephone call from his supervisor advising that his medical leave had not been approved, that his allowable absence hours were exhausted, and that he was discharged. The company argued that it could not operate efficiently without the assurance that employees, within reason, will report to work. Numerous arbitral decisions were cited by the company in which an employer has the general right to discharge an employee for chronic excessive absenteeism.

DECISION

Arbitrator Daniel Jennings ruled that the employer was not justified in discharging A because his work record reflected "genuine hard luck and real illnesses" rather than frequently recurring illnesses that would indicate a sickly state that might be permanent. Arbitrator Jennings noted (1) that A's problems (high blood pressure, cyst, and prostate problems) were not permanent and that no evidence was introduced to suggest that the grievant suffered from an illness that would prevent him from returning to work on a regular basis; (2) that although the company had warned A on February 26, 1992, it had failed to discipline him for subsequent illnesses or to warn him that his employment was in jeopardy; in fact, the company had granted a medical leave for the period March 25, 1992, through April 6, 1992; (3) that the company had failed to notify A that he had expended 48 hours of his allowable 80 absence hours; and (4) that the company had failed to honor its agent, the

continued

| CASE 11-3 | ABSENTEEISM AT WEBER AIRCRAFT—continued |

plant nurse, who had given assurances that A's absences since June 15, 1992, would not be counted against him.

The award of arbitrator Jennings was to uphold A's grievance; A was reinstated and received back pay.

SOURCE: Adapted from *Weber Aircraft,* 100 LA 417 (1993).

Incompetence

Arbitrators in general recognize management's right to set reasonable production standards and to enforce such standards through discipline. However, incompetence generally should not be treated the same as a disciplinary problem because proper remedies usually include additional training, transfer, or demotion instead of warnings, suspension, or discharge. In incompetence cases arising over the reasonableness of management's action, arbitrators will consider the adequacy of the employee's training, supervision, and ability to perform the job. The arbitrator must decide whether the contract has been followed. Although both labor and management have the responsibility for producing evidence supporting their case, the burden of proof is usually on management to verify the employee's incompetence.[85]

An arbitrator under the following conditions will not likely uphold the discharge or severe discipline of an employee for incompetence:

1. The charge of incompetence is not properly substantiated thoroughly.
2. The employee is not given adequate warning and opportunity to improve his or her performance.
3. Other employees with equally poor performance records are not treated in the same manner.
4. The employee shows substantial improvement after being warned.
5. The employee was not reassigned to another position where reasonably possible.[86]

Holiday Pay Eligibility

In recent years, most contracts have come to provide for holiday pay eligibility. Certain contract eligibility requirements must be fulfilled to receive pay for the holiday. Since the creation of Monday holidays by the federal government has increased labor's demand for three-day weekends, employers have become even more concerned with attendance problems due to employees' trying to stretch three-day weekends into four days, substantially disrupting production. An example of a common eligibility requirement is provided in the labor agreement between the National Conference of Brewery and Soft Drink Workers and the Schlitz Brewing Company.

ARTICLE XII

Holidays

. . . to be eligible for holiday pay, an employee must work his full shift on the day before the holiday and his full shift on the day after the holiday.

Approved absence on either of these days shall not disqualify the employee for holiday pay. Holiday pay shall be at the straight time rate, excluding shift differentials.[87]

Because paid holidays represent one of the most costly benefits given to the employees, management often will pursue disagreements to arbitration. The most common dispute concerning paid holidays involves the eligibility of employees. Other disputes concern avoidance of holiday stretching, that is, requiring work on the day before or after the holiday. Holiday pay is generally given to workers who fail to meet work requirements through no fault of their own. Also, if a contract provides holiday pay without restriction, laid-off workers continue to be employees of the company and are entitled to the holiday pay. Arbitrators generally agree that the common attendance requirement for employees to work the days before and after the holiday is not limited to the days immediately preceding and following the holiday. For example, a contract stated that holiday pay would be provided if the employee worked the workday previous to and following the holiday. The holiday fell on a Thursday, and the plant was closed for the rest of the week. The employee was denied pay for the holiday because he was absent the following Monday, the next scheduled workday. The arbitration board upheld the company's position that the days preceding and following the holiday do not have to fall on the same workweek.[88]

Management Rights

A common issue in arbitration cases is management rights in the areas not expressly discussed in the contract. Often it is believed that in the absence of restrictive or specific provisions, management retains managerial rights. However, arbitrators do not always take the view that management retains all unstated rights.

The following contract provides a general statement of management rights covering items such as the size of the workforce and operational methods:

ARTICLE V

Management Rights

(a) It is the intent of parties to this agreement that the employee will furnish a full fair day's work for a full fair day's pay. (b) Management shall be the sole determiner of the size and composition of the workforce. Management shall have the prerogative of controlling its operations, inducing new or improved methods or facilities, subject to the limitations set forth in this agreement. (c)Management shall retain all rights and privileges which are not specifically abridged by the terms of this agreement.[89]

Arbitrators usually impose a standard of reasonableness and good faith on managerial actions that adversely affect employees whether or not the contract provides management's discretion in the area. Arbitrators generally agree that the union cannot block technological improvement, even if the workforce is reduced, unless there is a specific contract restriction. Likewise, arbitrators generally give management broad authority in assigning work to employees and in controlling plant operations and procedures unless specifically restricted by the contract.[90]

Tips from the Experts

ARBITRATOR

What are the three most common violations by employers of the "just cause" provision of a collective bargaining agreement?

1. Assuming that the company's rule-making authority abolished the contractual obligation to observe just cause in imposing discipline. It does not necessarily follow that because a unilaterally promulgated rule is reasonable on its face and is uniformly applied that all the just cause requirements have been met and the penalty is automatically justified.

2. Failing to observe an employee's Weingarten rights. Whenever an employee is summoned to an interview with management that he or she reasonably believes is likely to result in discipline, he or she is entitled to union representation if a request is made.

3. Failing to afford the employee procedural due process. This action would include such elements as giving adequate notice of a rule, conducting an adequate and thorough investigation before imposing discipline, and imposing discipline for the purpose of correcting conduct and not punishing.

What are the three most common errors unions make in challenging a "just cause" discharge?

1. Failing to screen the facts and circumstances or to assess properly the company's case. Before deciding to proceed with the grievance, the union needs to be thorough in its investigation and assess the possibility of losing or setting a harmful precedent.

2. Failing to offer successful postdischarge evidence of rehabilitation. In cases involving discharge for drug and alcohol use, a union can demonstrate to the arbitrator the rehabilitation of the employee discharged.

3. Relying on uncorroborated hearsay evidence or bad precedents. A union should carefully screen its evidence for corroboration and its precedents when citing prior arbitration awards to make sure they support the union's position.

The following summarizes points to consider in management rights cases:

1. Management retains all rights not given up in the contract.
2. Management generally is conceded to have the absolute right to make technological improvements, even if some workers are adversely affected, unless contract language restricts management's rights in this area.
3. Similarly, a company normally has the right to eliminate a job for efficiency, if it is not an arbitrary act.
4. Even in the absence of a contract clause forbidding supervisors to do bargaining unit work, arbitrators sometimes have held that they could not do such work if people in the bargaining unit would be adversely affected.[91]

ARBITRATION ISSUES IN THE PUBLIC SECTOR

Interest Arbitration

Legislation that allows public-sector collective bargaining but prohibits strikes often details the procedures available to resolve an impasse. Mediation is provided in almost all states with collective bargaining in the public sector. As with the private sector, the mediator has no independent authority but uses acquired skills to bring the parties back together. It has been suggested that the mediator represent the public's interest at the bargaining table. Such a role does not seem to facilitate resolution of a dispute.

Fact-finding and advisory arbitration can be far more successful in the public sector than the private because of political pressures. Under fact-finding and advisory arbitration, an unbiased third party examines the collective bargaining impasse and issues findings and recommendations. The findings may move the process by simply eliminating the distrust a party feels for the other party's facts or figures. Reasonable recommendations may also pressure a party to accept an offer that otherwise would not have been considered.

Interest arbitration allows a panel to make a *final and binding decision* on a negotiation dispute and has been used in the public sector to resolve impasses. However, the legality of allowing a third party to set the terms of the contract has been questioned in light of the sovereignty doctrine discussed in Chapter 1.[92] The use of a compulsory mechanism such as final and binding interest arbitration seems incompatible with collective bargaining. A fundamental tenet of American industrial relations is that the bargaining outcome be determined by the parties to the greatest extent possible. Interest arbitration violates that tenet by substituting a third party's decision for that of the negotiating parties. Interest arbitration can become a substitute for the arduous demands of bargaining and can discourage the concessions so necessary to negotiations.[93] Furthermore, a third party's decision removes the inherent authority of public officials to determine policies, in this case, concerning public employment issues.

Proponents of interest arbitration, however, believe that the threat of arbitration, like the threat of a strike, provides the necessary incentive to reach a negotiated settlement when the parties understand and appreciate the final offer procedure.[94] The 1984 interest arbitration involving the U.S. Postal Service (USPS) and its two largest unions, the American Postal Workers Union and the National Association of Letter Carriers, was historic. The five-member arbitration panel's award covered more than 500,000 employees, a record number for a single arbitration in the United States. The postal negotiations were the first postal labor talks since the landmark air traffic controllers' (PATCO) strike in 1981. The tone of the talks was set when the USPS Board of Governors proposed a two-tier wage structure with a new scale 33 percent below the current scale. The unions believed the wage concession was unwarranted by the financial condition of USPS. Negotiations quickly went to impasse and led to binding arbitration as provided for in the 1970 Postal Reorganization Act. The central issue was the interpretation of a section of the 1970 act that gives USPS the ability to maintain compensation and benefits "on a standard of comparability" to the private sector. The arbitration award provided for a three-year agreement with 2.7 percent annual increases for incumbent employees. New employees in a two-tier system would start at wage levels below those of current employees.[95]

Rights Arbitration

Rights arbitration in the public sector is treated much like the private sector as shown in Case 11-4. As in Case 11-4, the authority of the arbitrator in rights arbitration is limited by the terms and conditions of the collective bargaining agreement. If a public agency agrees to arbitrate employment decisions using the "just cause" standard, then the arbitrator generally has the authority to reinstate a public employee if that standard is violated. However, courts have overturned an arbitrator's decision to reinstate an employee because the arbitrator felt the discipline was too severe stating, "if an arbitrator finds that one of the enumerated grounds for dismissal has been proved, the arbitrator may not substitute his judgment of what the penalty should be for that of the school district."[96]

<table>
<tr><td>

CASE 11-4

</td><td>

PUBLIC SAFETY AND RANDOM DRUG TESTS

</td></tr>
</table>

Oklahoma City, Oklahoma ("City"), in its collective bargaining agreement ("CBA") with the American Federation of State, County and Municipal Employees ("Union"), required employees with Commercial Driver's Licenses (CDLs) to submit to random drug testing pursuant to Federal Statutes and the U.S. Department of Transportation rules for public employers. Employees who test positive for drugs or alcohol are subject to ". . . suspension, demotion, or termination . . . determined based on the employee's total work record, including but not limited to, any prior drug or alcohol problems." The CBA's Drug Policy also included an Employee Assistance Program to which employees could be required to participate in as a condition of continued employment.

The Grievant had been employed by the City for 19 years and had an excellent work record. As a driver in the Street and Drainage Maintenance Division of the Public Works Department he was required to have a CDL and to submit to random drug tests. In May 2001, he was selected for a random test, for the fourth time in one and a half years, and tested positive for marijuana. Following a predetermination hearing in which the grievant offered no defense to the results of the test, the City discharged the Grievant. The Union appealed the City's action and an arbitration hearing was held.

The City contended that the grievant was required to have a CDL, that the random drug testing policy for CDL drivers was valid, and that the grievant tested positive for marijuana use. The grievant did not challenge the test at the time or avail himself of his right to have the sample tested by a different lab. The City defended its decision to dismiss the grievant as an appropriate act because it cannot tolerate the abuse of controlled substances that represents a threat to public safety and its "accountabil-

ity to its citizens." The City contended that its decision in this case to dismiss the grievant rather than impose a lesser discipline was after due consideration of the grievant's "total work record." The relevant "work record" for the City to consider, according to the testimony of the city officials, was whether the offending employee was or was not required to have a CDL. In other words, nothing in the grievant's 19 years of service was relevant to the City's determination other than the CDL requirement. The City maintained that since 1998 there was a City rule that employees with CDLs who test positive for drug use be dismissed. Therefore, the grievant was not treated differently than other employees. Finally, the City argued that unless the City has violated a specific provision of the CBA or abused its discretion, the Arbitrator should not substitute his decision for the City's as to the proper discipline for a public employee for failing a drug test.

The Union contended that the City's random drug testing procedures were suspect because the grievant was one of 500 employees subject to testing, and yet he was tested four times in one and a half years. More importantly, the drug test did not indicate that the grievant was impaired or under the influence of drugs while at work. The Union further contended that the discharge did not meet the "just cause" test because the City failed to follow progressive discipline and treated the grievant differently from other City employees. The Union presented the Arbitrator with proof that of the forty-eight City employees with CDLs who had tested positively for drugs in the preceding three years, thirteen were demoted to nondriving positions and not discharged. Finally, the Union argued that the City violated the CBA because it did not consider the Grievant's "total work record" of 19 years of exemplary performance, but

continued

PUBLIC SAFETY AND RANDOM DRUG TESTS—continued

only considered the fact that the grievant was required to have a CDL for his position.

The City countered that its decision to demote other employees for the same offense was irrelevant in that some of the demotions were necessary because the procedures followed in those cases were flawed and would not have withstood a challenge by the offending employees. The City noted that even if it had decided that demotion was proper in this case, there was no funded nondriver position available for the grievant.

DECISION

Arbitrator Dr. Daniel F. Jennings declined to take a position on the issues raised by the Union as to the validity of the actual drug test taken by the grievant as there was insufficient evidence presented at the hearing on the test. The Arbitrator did find that there was sufficient evidence to determine that the City *has not always discharged* employees with CDLs who test positive for drugs or alcohol, although there was insufficient evidence to determine whether there was disparate treatment in this case because the circumstances of the other incidents were not presented at the hearing.

The Arbitrator then considered whether the City had "just cause" to impose the severest penalty available to it and addressed the City's contention that the Arbitrator should not substitute his judgment for that of the City in deciding the appropriate punishment. The Arbitrator relied on other arbitration opinions by other arbitrators as justification for overturning the disciplining of an employee. One arbitrator ruled: "Taking the supreme penalty against an employee without due consideration for a long unblemished record goes to the very heart of 'just cause.'" While another held: ". . . most arbitrators exercise the right to change or modify a penalty if it is found to be improper or too severe, . . . This right is deemed to be inherent in the arbitrator's power to discipline and in his authority to finally settle and adjust the dispute before him."

Arbitrator Jennings found that the grievant had an excellent work record for 19 years and the City, in imposing the discipline, should have considered it. Therefore, he held that the City lacked "just cause" to terminate the grievant and ordered that he be reinstated in a nondriving position at the same pay as an Equipment Operator I, even if such a position had to be created for him. He also awarded the grievant back pay, less a two-month suspension, which the Arbitrator deemed the appropriate penalty for the grievant in this case.

SOURCE: *City of Oklahoma City,* 116 LA 1117 (2002).

SUMMARY

The arbitration process has been developed and refined over many years. The selection of an arbitrator or board of arbitrators is generally specified in the labor agreement. The hearing procedure, however, which is not bound by legal precedent, is quite flexible and is subject to the arbitrator's discretion. The courts have generally left the questions of arbitrability and case decisions to arbitrators.

A great variety of important and complex issues end up in arbitration. The issue of just cause for employee discipline or discharge is difficult to define within the contract and in most cases involves emotional situations. Drug testing for substance abuse presents unique problems for an arbitrator to resolve. Seniority and absenteeism are deceptively simple yet important contractual issues. Disagreements over incompetence, holiday pay, and management rights are also common arbitration subjects.

In recent years the number of nonunion employees covered by employment arbitration agreements has rapidly increased until the number may exceed the number of employees who have the right to arbitration under collective bargaining agreements. Thus, the use of arbitration and not litigation to settle employment disputes has become commonplace in the nonunion sector, as it has been in the unionized sector for decades.

CASE STUDIES

Case Study 11-1 Drug and Alcohol Testing

The company is an insulation subcontractor that performs maintenance work for duPont. For several decades, the company had a collective bargaining agreement with a union that included employees who were sent to a duPont plant for maintenance work. The contract in effect between the company and the union had no reference to a drug-testing or substance abuse program. Prior to 1986, the company had never required its employees to submit to drug testing. In 1986, however, the company received a letter from duPont stating that duPont was developing a substance abuse policy and requiring its subcontractors to develop a similar policy to include testing procedures.

The company instituted a drug program similar to duPont's and sent it to the union for its information. The company notified the union that it was willing to meet with it to discuss the plan. At the meeting, the union met not only with its company but also with representatives from duPont concerning the drug program. The written policy stated that "the use, possession of, being under influence of, or the presence in the person's system of prohibitive drugs and unauthorized alcoholic beverages is prohibited on any company work location." Under the policy, all new employees of the company were required to sign consent forms for testing as a condition of employment. The company implemented the drug-testing policy but only as it related to the duPont plant. The union instructed its members to sign the forms consenting to drug testing with the statement that they were signing under duress.

The grievant in this case was referred to the duPont plant by the company for its maintenance work in April 1987. The employee, along with four other fellow employees, submitted to a urine test. The grievant's test was sent to the screening facility, and the initial test resulted in a positive finding of marijuana. The chain of custody for the test was not established, and the level of marijuana found in the test was extremely low. Nonetheless, the grievant was dismissed. The position of the company was that duPont made it mandatory for subcontractors to adopt minimum requirements for drug testing and that such minimum requirements for new employees were not unreasonable. The company further contended that, although it did not agree to negotiate with the union, the company gave the union ample time to study the program's policy.

The union felt that the company's policy was really duPont's policy and was adopted despite the union's disapproval solely because duPont had insisted on it. The union contended that the company made no effort to assure the union that the policy or the enforcement of the policy was reasonable, fair, or accurate. The cutoff level for a positive test result was unreasonable because it did not indicate either on-the-job impairment or consistent use of marijuana. The company did not examine the grievant's prior work record or the fact that there was not prior history or evidence of drug impairment on the job. In fact, the company could not even prove that the specimen tested was the grievant's. The union further contended that even if the results of the test proved that the employee was using marijuana, on the basis of her past work history she should be given an opportunity to correct her conduct and be treated in a fair and consistent way. Discharge was clearly not appropriate.

SOURCE: Adapted from *Young Insulation Group*, 90 LA 341 (1987).

QUESTIONS

1. Did the company have a legitimate business reason for instituting a drug-testing program during the term of a contract?
2. Did the company conduct the drug-testing program properly?
3. As the arbitrator, would you reverse or uphold the dismissal of the grievant? Explain your answer.

Case Study 11-2 Arbitrability

In September 1981, the union grieved the company's announced intention to lay off 79 employees from its Chicago location. The union contended that there was no lack of work at that site and that under the contract the company can lay off from the site only when there is a lack of work. Despite the grievance, the company laid off the employees and transferred approximately 80 employees from other locations to the Chicago location.

The union demanded that the dispute be arbitrated, and the company refused. The company claimed that the "management functions" clause of the contract gives it the prerogative to determine "lack of work" and that as long as it lays off in the order prescribed by the contract, there is nothing to arbitrate. The union contended that certain provisions of the contract modified the "management functions" clause and requested the court to order arbitration.

The lower court found that there were arguable issues to arbitrate and ordered the parties to arbitrate the arbitrability issue; in other words, an arbitrator would decide whether she had jurisdiction under the contract of the issue in dispute.

Before this could happen, the company appealed the lower court's ruling. The company argued that the lower court erred in not simply deciding whether the dispute was subject to arbitration. It contended that under the *Steelworkers Trilogy* cases,

the courts, not the arbitrator, must decide whether the issue is subject to arbitration. The company proposed the following points:

1. Arbitration is a matter of contract, and parties cannot be forced to submit issues to arbitration that they have not agreed to submit.
2. Unless the contract clearly provides otherwise, arbitrability is a judicial determination.
3. In deciding arbitrability, the court is not to decide on the merits of the claim.
4. Where the contract has an arbitration clause, the presumption is for arbitrability.

The lower court pointed out, however, that the exception to the rule is found when deciding the arbitrability of the case would also involve the court in interpreting the substantive provisions of the labor agreement.

The union's position was that the layoffs were subject to arbitration, and they pointed to sections of the labor agreement to prove this. The "management functions" clause, the "adjustment to the working force" clause, and the "arbitration" clause must be read together and interpreted. The court could not decide arbitrability in this case without interpreting these sections and therefore deciding the substantive issue. It is for an arbitrator to decide the substantive issues.

SOURCE: Adapted from *Communication Workers of America v. Western Electric*, 751 F.2d 203 (7th Cir. 1984).

QUESTIONS

1. Should the court decide whether there is an issue to arbitrate, or should an arbitrator? Why?
2. Give the reasons you think arbitration is a superior resolution process to court action in contract disputes.
3. Give the reasons you think a court action is a superior resolution process to arbitration in contract disputes.

KEY TERMS AND CONCEPTS

- absenteeism
- arbitrability
- arbitrator's award
- arbitrator's opinion
- common law of the shop
- drug testing
- holiday pay eligibility
- individual employment agreements
- interest arbitration
- just cause
- *obiter dictum*
- parol evidence
- past practice
- public policy exception
- qualifications of an arbitrator
- rights arbitration
- rules of evidence
- seniority
- tripartite arbitration board
- *Warrior & Gulf* case

REVIEW QUESTIONS

1. Describe how the legal foundation for arbitration as it exists today in the United States was developed.
2. Discuss the five principles that govern the arbitration of grievances under collective bargaining.
3. Explain how the change in ownership of a company affects the duty to arbitrate.
4. What is the process normally utilized in the selection of an arbitrator? How does the selected arbitrator interpret ambiguous contract provisions?
5. How is binding arbitration superior to the courts in settling labor disputes? How does it differ from mediation and conciliation?
6. What information can be presented as evidence during arbitration proceedings? What are the usual hearing procedures?
7. Can a party harm its own case during arbitration proceedings? If it can, explain how.
8. How does an arbitrator determine that a company had just cause for taking a disciplinary action? What remedy might an arbitrator choose if a company did not have just cause?
9. How do labor contracts prevent holiday stretching?
10. Discuss the issues an arbitrator might use in deciding a discharge case involving drug abuse.

YOU BE THE ARBITRATOR
Alleged Theft of Company Property

ARTICLE III
MANAGEMENT RIGHTS

The Company also has the right to establish and require employees to observe company rules and regulations, lay off or relieve employees from duties, to maintain order, and to suspend, demote, discipline, and discharge employees for just cause in line with this Agreement.

Group I. First Violation of These Rules—Discharge

1. Theft or misappropriation of any property or money of employees or the Company.

Facts

The grievant reported to work more than an hour after commencement of his shift. He informed his supervisor that he had stopped by the residence of a friend the night before to watch a basketball game and had overslept, making him late for work. About noon that day, the supervisor was leaving for lunch when he noticed an orange ladder in the back of the grievant's pickup truck that appeared to be a company ladder. He reported this to the human resources manager, and they decided to investigate. They went to the grievant's truck and confirmed that, indeed, it was a company-labeled ladder. They checked with the guard station to determine whether the grievant had obtained a property removal authorization pass granting him permission to take the ladder off company premises. The guards confirmed that the grievant had not presented them with any such pass. The

union vice president was summoned to the scene and was told that they were concerned that the grievant may be planning to steal the ladder. The union vice president suggested that they should wait and see whether the grievant actually left the company's premises with the ladder before reaching any conclusions. The grievant did, in fact, leave with the ladder at approximately 3:30 PM. The grievant does not dispute the fact that he had never obtained a signed authorization pass to remove the ladder from the facility. The grievant returned the ladder to the company facility at 5:40 PM that same day. It was discovered in later discussions that the grievant had originally taken this ladder, without proper written authorization, approximately four months earlier. The grievant indicated that his supervisor had given him verbal permission to take the ladder. His supervisor acknowledged that he did tell the grievant that he could take the ladder, but only if he got an authorization slip. Unconvinced by the grievant's explanations, the company ultimately came to the conclusion that the grievant intended to steal the ladder, and he was terminated. Subsequently, in light of the grievant's 24 years of service with the company, the termination was changed to a six-month suspension without pay. The grievant appealed.

Issue

Did the employer have "just cause" to discipline the grievant for allegedly intending to steal a company ladder?

The Position of the Parties

The company's policy requires employees to obtain a property authorization pass prior to removing any company property from the premises. It is undisputed that the grievant was well aware of this procedure at the time he took the ladder. Indeed, he had utilized this procedure several times in the past. Nevertheless, he did not do so on this occasion, leading the company to believe that he intended to steal the ladder.

The grievant contends that he meant to return the ladder that day but forgot to take it out of his truck before leaving. Later on, he noticed it was still in the back of his truck, so he returned it. The union argued that the employer had no legitimate evidence that the grievant intended to steal the ladder and that the six-month suspension was not warranted and should be overturned. Witnesses testified, with little opposition, that it has been common practice for employees to borrow articles from the company merely by obtaining a supervisor's verbal permission. It has been a "mixed" practice—sometimes a pass is obtained, and sometimes it is not. The supervisor admitted that he had given the grievant verbal authorization to borrow the ladder three or four months earlier. The grievant intended to return the ladder much sooner, but it was stored at his home property. He was prevented from going on that property because of a court order in connection with divorce proceedings. Within days of being released from that court order, the grievant returned the ladder. Surely, if the grievant meant to steal the ladder, he would not be driving in and out of the company's property in front of security guards and the eyes of supervisor with the ladder in plain sight in the back of his pickup truck. If the grievant did not steal the ladder or have that intent, then there exists no just cause for him to be penalized out of nearly $40,000 in back pay. The grievance should be sustained, and the grievant should be made entirely whole.

SOURCE: Adapted from *Rock-Tenn Co.,* 116 LA 1569 (2002).

QUESTIONS

1. As arbitrator, what would be your award and opinion in this arbitration?
2. Explain why the relevant provisions of the collective bargaining agreement as applied to the facts of this case dictate the award.
3. What actions might the employer and/or the union have taken to avoid this conflict?

EXERCISE

Use of the Arbitration Process

PURPOSE:

To enable students to learn how the arbitration process is being utilized in the areas outside of the labor relations field.

TASK:

Using the library, Internet, and other reference sources, identify three fields outside labor relations in which the arbitration process is utilized. Write a two- or three-paragraph summary explanation of each use of the arbitration process. Finally, list the elements of the processes in the fields cited that are similar to the arbitration process discussed in this chapter.

CHAPTER 12

Comparative Global Industrial Relations

Globalization
World Wide Labor Movement
International Labour Organization
Anglophone Countries
European Union Nations
Far East

In 2006 Wal-Mart announced it would not allow it's stores in China to unionize, reversing it's public announcement of 2004. However, the All-China Federation of Trade Unions (ACFTU) with over 130 million members and support of the central government is vigorously trying to organize Wal-Mart as it has other U.S. employers in China. Thus a long, hard struggle between the world's largest union and Wal-Mart may present a historic moment in global industrial relations.

Labor News

WAL-MART WORLDWIDE

In August 2005, Union Network International (UNI), a global coalition of 900 unions in some 140 countries, launched an organizational campaign aimed at the retail giant Wal-Mart. The focus of the unions' efforts is to make Wal-Mart change its posture toward the unionization of its workers. Activities include raising public awareness about Wal-Mart's treatment of its workers, providing information to investors and investment consultants on what the UNI and United Food and Commercial Workers (UFCW) see as violations of workers' rights, and contacts with international authorities and political decision makers around the world to insist that Wal-Mart adhere to all national standards protecting employee rights.

Wal-Mart has a total workforce of 1.5 million people, including over a million employees in the United States. It operates 3,200 U.S. stores and 1,100 outlets in nine other countries. It is a particularly powerful retailer in Canada, UK, and Mexico and also has interests in Germany, Argentina, Brazil, China, Korea, and Puerto Rico and significant interests in Japan. It continues to plan major expansions, both in its home market and internationally. In 2005, it planned to open approximately 230 new Supercenters—on average, a massive 175,000 square feet in size—a hundred of which will be in completely new locations. Internationally, the company expansion includes both new stores (130–140 planned for 2005) and acquisitions. This latter approach, for example, is how it became the second-largest retailer in the United Kingdom.

According to the UFCW, a million workers face a full-scale assault when they clock into work in a Wal-Mart store. Union officials believe that Wal-Mart's employment practices repress workers' wages and health benefits and lower living standards for entire communities. They allege that whenever workers try to organize, the company deploys representatives to implement a systematic campaign of propaganda to deny workers their rights and silence their voices, often through illegal firings. "Wal-Mart fights against increasing the minimum wage, health care reform, job safety measures, and retirement security reform through its lobbying arm, the International Mass Retailers Association," according to a UFCW publication, "Wal-Mart's War on Workers." Because of its size and influence, Wal-Mart would inevitably demand attention from the international trade union movement. However, it is Wal-Mart's way of doing business, and especially its focus on low wages and poor employment conditions, that has gendered most of the UNI's concern. As a report to its membership stated: "[I]t is not a question of how to deal with a single company, bad as that company may be, so much as how to respond to the *Wal-Martization* of the world's economic and business models [that are] becoming a de facto norm which other employers are increasingly obliged to follow."

SOURCE: Adapted from Andrew Bibby, "The Wal-Martization of the World; UNI's Global Response," Report prepared for UNI (March 2005) and "UNI Commerce Global Union, UFCW and Commerce Unions World-Wide Step Up Their Wal-Mart Campaign," UNI, Commerce homepage. http://www.union-network.org

Business conducted on an international scale is commonplace. Its impact on the labor movement, in this country and around the world, is significant. This chapter discusses how the cycle of globalization in the twenty-first century, unlike previous cycles, has resulted in a complex system of worldwide investment, technology, deregulation, and flexible labor markets. These worldwide labor markets have become both competitors with and companions to the U.S. labor movement. A comprehensive review of international labor relations and collective bargaining theories and practices around the world is beyond the scope of this text. However, it is necessary to have a basic understanding of how labor relations developed in representative nations and of the current state of labor relations and collective bargaining around the world. This chapter focuses primarily on industrial relations in Great Britain, Canada, and Australia; on the European Union—Germany and Sweden, France and Italy; and on the Far East nations of Japan, China, and Korea. The International Labour Organization, a common thread for industrial relations in many nations, will also be examined within the context of the worldwide labor movement and globalization.

GLOBALIZATION

Thomas L. Friedman, an award-winning *New York Times* columnist, in his book *The World Is Flat: A Brief History of the Twenty First Century,*[1] argued that the world has gone through three eras of globalization. The first lasted from 1492 until about 1820 and was built around countries colonizing—Spain exploring the New World, Britain colonizing India, the Portuguese, and East Asia. The second great era of globalization, beginning in the early 1800s up to the year 2000, was spearheaded by companies competing internationally for markets and labor. The final era is now, the twenty-first century, in which the world economy is flattening through the activities of individuals and small groups. Mr. Friedman details the ten events he contends launched this current era:

1. *Fall of the Berlin Wall,* which tilted the worldwide balance of power toward democracies and free markets.
2. *Netscape IPO* offering, which sparked massive investment in fiber-optic cables.
3. *Work flow software.* The rise of computer applications that enabled faster, closer coordination among far-flung employees.
4. *Open-sourcing.* Self-organizing communities offering computer operating systems for free.
5. *Outsourcing.* Migrating business functions to Third World economies.
6. *Offshoring.* Moving manufacturing plants to Third World economies.
7. *Supply-chaining.* Creating networks of suppliers, retailers, and customers for increased business efficiency.
8. *Insourcing.* Logistics giants took control of customer supply chains, helping mom-and-pop shops go global.
9. *In-forming.* Internet power searching allowed everyone to use the Internet as a personal supply chain of knowledge.
10. *Wireless.* Wireless technologies pumped up collaboration, making it mobile and personal.[2]

Globalization results in increased competition. U.S. employers, unions, and governments have become increasingly concerned about greater competition from other countries. The production of automobiles, for example, which for nearly a century was concentrated geographically at a national level, is now done at a global level, with cars often being assembled from component parts that are produced by supplier companies in dozens of countries. General Motors has a global presence in more than 200 countries, manufacturing operations in 32 countries, and tens of thousands of supplier companies worldwide, in total employing 317,000 people.[3] The extensive and complex network of suppliers that often exists can lead to situations where a company is no longer able to trace the products it sells, or parts of it, back to its origins.

The internationalization of production directly affects the collective bargaining environment. With companies easily able to operate in the international arena, not only the actual transfer of an enterprise from one country to another adversely affects unionized employees, but the mere threat of doing so can also significantly change power relations at the bargaining table. In addition, workers bargaining at a national level may find that they have inadequate access to information about the international financial position and corporate plans of their employer or that the employer's representative has no real decision-making power. In such circumstances, the real content and meaning of collective bargaining can be seriously reduced. One view is that the effective realization of the right to collective bargaining requires that it too be conducted at the international level.[4] Some unions and multinational corporations are addressing the need for a more global approach to labor relations by entering into international agreements as outlined in Profile 12-1, International Framework Agreements.

PROFILE 12-1

INTERNATIONAL FRAMEWORK AGREEMENTS

What do Volkswagen, DaimlerChrysler, Renault, and BMW, all global automotive industry giants, have in common with IKEA, the Swedish furniture company? These international companies have joined dozens of others in entering into International Framework Agreements as explained in this article from the International Metalworkers' Federation:

International Framework Agreements (IFAs) are negotiated between a transnational company and the trade unions of its workforce at the global level. It is a global instrument with the purpose of ensuring fundamental workers' rights in all the target company's locations. Thus, IFAs are negotiated on a global level but implemented locally. Generally, an IFA recognizes the ILO Core Labour Standards. In addition, the company should also agree to offer decent wages and working conditions as well as to provide a safe and hygienic working environment. Furthermore, there is an agreement that suppliers must be persuaded to comply and, finally, the

IFA includes trade unions in the implementation. Transnational business operations and a global economy raise issues that go beyond the reach of national legislation. Through IFAs, the ILO's Core Labour Standards can be guaranteed in all facilities of a transnational company, which is especially helpful in transitional and developing countries, where legislation is sometimes insufficient, poorly enforced, or antiworker. For transnationals, IFAs can secure good relations with trade unions and contribute to a positive public image. More and more companies increasingly see the need to respond to the growing ethical concerns of consumers and investors. For trade unions, IFAs are a way to promote workers' rights in the global arena. The arrangement guarantees influence and the possibility of a dialogue that is mutually beneficial. Unlike unilateral Codes of Conduct, IFAs emphasize implementation, which paves the way for actual improvements.

SOURCE: International Metalworkers' Federation, *NewsLetter*, January 07, 2003. Available at www.imfmetal.org. Accessed October 1, 2005. Used with permission.

The term **globalization** means many things to many people. For the purposes of this text, it refers not only to the expansion of international trade in goods and services, but also to the degree of interdependence that goes along with the integration of production across national boundaries and the resulting increase in international investment by multinational enterprises.[5] In this section, we will examine the components of globalization that have impacted the employer–employee relationship. These components include foreign investments, multinational enterprises, the import and export of goods and services, deregulation and the technological revolution.

Foreign Direct Investment

International economic interdependence has been driven over the past 30 years by a dramatic growth of **foreign direct investment (FDI)**. FDI is a category of international investment made by a direct investor, a resident entity in one country, in a direct investment enterprise, an enterprise resident in another country, with the objective of establishing a lasting interest. This involves the initial transaction and all subsequent capital transactions between the principles and any affiliated enterprises. Until the 1970s, international economic activity was mostly in the form of *exchange of goods and services* between nation–states where products were made in one country and then transported to another. Since that time, companies have moved production to other countries, resulting in a significant increase in the movement of capital in the global economy. And although worldwide international trade during the 1980s and 1990s grew twice as fast as the Gross Domestic Product (GDP), FDI grew twice as fast as international trade in the 1980s and 1.5 times faster in the 1990s.[6] In other words, FDI is a much more powerful and visible aspect of globalization today than world trade.[7]

Multinational Enterprises

This trend toward foreign direct investment has a concomitant increase in the role multinational enterprises play in the world economy. According to the World Investment Report by UNCTAD (United Nations Conference on Trade and Development), sales by foreign operations of multinationals amounted, in total, to US$18,000 billion in 2002. This was more than twice as high as the value of world exports, which stood at US$8,000 billion. Because an important share of the investment and world trade takes place within multinational enterprises, their operation affects labor relations around the world. A company is not a **multinational enterprise** just because it sells exports overseas; it has to have actually moved part of its operations to another country by investing abroad. Lowering economic barriers between nations opens up enormous new possibilities for multinational companies and the growing number of national businesses connected to them. Parent firms and foreign affiliates of multinational enterprises (MNEs) now account for 25 percent of global output.[8] Although the main impact on employment is on national/local companies that are subcontractors or otherwise linked to MNEs, total direct employment of foreign employees has been increasing. Multinationals lead the way in disseminating new techniques of management and new technologies for production. In many sectors, they are the driving force of a global chain of production, linking companies in one country to consumers in another.

Technology

Today's globalization includes the rapid and massive movement of financial capital. This interdependence and integration is facilitated and accelerated by new technology, particularly information technology (IT). The information technology revolution has not only created a global market for investment finance, but it has also greatly increased the pace and scale of information exchange and dramatically altered production, distribution, and management processes. Just as the industrial revolution challenged the way work was done when machines replaced human physical labor, workplaces are experiencing the impact of intelligent machines that can perform what used to be the uniquely human skill of processing information. For example, by using technology to order, ship, and hold inventory, U.S. wholesalers have boosted output by 20 percent without increasing employment.[9]

The technological revolution in information processing, communications, and transportation made it much easier for companies to

- Create a global production chain and distribution networks
- Integrate subsidiaries
- Build ties with suppliers and customers
- Eliminate the need for proximity as MNEs work from and in any part of the world
- Reduce problems of distance through the use of e-mail, Internet, and videoconferences
- Trade previously untradable services, such as education through *virtual universities*
- Have its employees work at home or in call centers
- Use shorter production runs to create more differentiated and unique products

Financial Markets

The **Bretton Woods exchange rate system** was created after World War II to provide a degree of international exchange rate stability. It resulted in the creation of international financial institutions such as the International Monetary Fund (IMF) and the World Bank. The Bretton Woods exchange rate system collapsed in the 1970s, and flexible exchange rates were introduced.[10] Many national controls on the movement of investment capital were removed, followed by deregulation of the financial sector. The result has been significant movement of capital around the world. Daily financial transactions by thousands of banks and currency traders amount to well over US$1.5 trillion (US$1,500 billion), most of it in the form of speculation.[11] Cross-border lending has exploded, and new financial institutions are developing and restructuring constantly.

National rules have not been replaced by international rules governing these financial markets, as was shown by the economic and financial crisis that began in 1997 in Asia. That crisis stemmed from a combination of inadequate financial sector supervision, poor assessment and management of financial risk, and the borrowing of large amounts of international capital, denominated in foreign currency, which was not backed by real assets. This inflow of foreign capital tended to be used to finance poorer-quality investments.[12]

There is a growing certainty within the international trade union movement that something needs to be done to limit the negative effects of short-term capital investment, such as the layoff of workers. Over the years, the International Federation of Free Trade Unions (ICFTU) has sought to introduce new international regulations of those financial processes to dampen speculation and to reduce the risk of large-scale financial collapse. The ICFTU has suggested reform of the IMF and World Bank, so that their programs promote good governance, respect for human rights and fundamental labor standards, increased employment, poverty reduction, and the provision of public services in key areas.

Deregulation and Liberalization

As a result of global, regional, and bilateral trade and investment negotiations, countries have lowered barriers to trade and investment by liberalizing trade quotas, tariffs, and as discussed earlier, deregulated national capital controls. This deregulation and liberalization trend is worldwide. Major financial institutions, such as the IMF and the World Bank, encourage and facilitate the introduction of free market–based economic policies in their programs. A broadening of the global market saw some developing countries, particularly in Asia, receive a great deal of investment and support for their exports. With the collapse of the Soviet bloc, many Eastern European countries increased their participation in and exposure to the global market as well, with eight former Soviet bloc countries joining the European Union in 2004. The eight countries include the Czech Republic, Estonia, Hungary, Latvia, Lithuania, Poland, Slovakia, and Slovenia.

Developing countries have also moved toward a market economy, many of them under the pressure of structural adjustment programs of the IMF or the World Bank. Economic reforms often involve privatization of large, state-owned enterprises and a reduction of public services. One of the main driving forces responsible for the increase in global trade has been the creation of a framework of intergovernmental trade agreements at global and regional levels, which will be covered later in this chapter.

Trade Unions

All the changes brought about by globalization—the restructuring of production through new technology, the opening of financial and labor markets, deregulation and the liberalization of national laws regarding trade—have allowed organizations to concentrate on their core business and to outsource nonessential functions previously done by in-house workers. Modifications in work organization, spurred by the search for more flexible and responsive work methods, have resulted in more contract and part-time work. These factors are affecting traditional employment relations and the exercise of collective bargaining rights. Flexible work patterns make it more difficult to organize workers; subcontracting arrangements have begun to resemble commercial relationships rather than employer–employee relationships.

Globalization has presented significant challenges to workers and their trade unions.

- Government deregulation has challenged nation-centered systems whose national social and economic policies helped create a degree of social justice and economic equity.
- The international institutions lack a framework in place that can deal effectively with issues of justice and equity.
- Capital is much more mobile than workers, so different forms of business organization and relationships have been created that shift employment and threaten collective bargaining relationships.
- MNEs, which can be rootless, introduce new management methods and sometimes threaten to relocate to countries with lower social or environmental standards and no independent trade unions.
- New forms of work organization have been established such as outsourcing, subcontracting, contract labor, and various other forms of nontraditional employment.
- Competitiveness and flexibility are still the main objectives for most enterprises in the global environment, which put workers into increasingly fierce competition for keeping their jobs; put pressure on social safety nets; and undermine workers' rights.

The international trade union movement is seeking ways to incorporate protections that were achieved in many countries at the national level into the globalization process. The challenge facing trade unions in the era of globalization is to ensure that structural change and adaptation are achieved without compromising the goals of full employment and social justice. Whether at the regional or at the international level, trade unions need to make sure economic integration through human migration, through trade in goods and services, and through movements of capital and integration of financial markets, includes workers' protections.[13]

WORLD WIDE LABOR MOVEMENT

Industrial Revolution

The Industrial Revolution began in England in the early 1800s and developed there and in the United States in similar fashion. In fact, the Industrial Revolution's impact on other nations has certain common features regardless of when the industrialization began, although industrialization was tempered by national experiences and economic influences. The Industrial Revolution, through invention and innovation, substituted machinery for human labor and by using new chemical and metallurgical process harnessed new forms of energy to fuel production. This resulted in the emergence of factories with large concentrations of workers in an interdependent production process that required a hierarchy style of management and a clear division of labor. Later, the emergence of large corporations saw the pooling of capital across borders and the creation of multinational organizations.[14]

The Industrial Revolution caused the widespread movement of people from rural to urban areas, as well as immigration from the Old World to the New World as discussed in Chapter 1. In England and in Europe, employment was characterized as a "status" relationship such as tenant farmers and peasants in feudal relationships with landed gentry or apprentices and indentured servants tied to master craftsmen engaged in cottage industries such as weaving or metallurgy. The migration of labor into urban areas to work in mines, mills, and factories changed the labor market from one of "status" between master and servant to one of "contract" between employer and employee. The need for workers, worker mobility, and the increased proportion of people working for wages caused labor to be seen as a commodity, and its purchase and sale became a cost of doing business.[15]

Democratic Revolution

The political revolutions of the late eighteenth century coincided with the Industrial Revolution. And although England had begun its march toward democracy several centuries earlier by enactment of the *Magna Carta* and by the devolution from monarchy to a representative government, the significant revolutions of this time were in the United States and France. The American colonies threw off the yoke of colonialism, and France sought to rid itself of an oppressive oligarchy of king, nobility, and church. France's revolution had a more dramatic influence in Europe because it shared its feudal tradition with its neighboring nations, and the impact of a new political and social order anchored with the idea of people governing themselves threatened centuries of tradition.

The 'United States' transformation into a democracy was easier because it had no feudal past or rigid patterns of class inequality, with the notable exception of slavery. France's path to democracy, like its neighbors, was one of progress and regression—from the emperor Napoleon's defeat in 1815, a return and demise of the monarchy in 1843, the Paris Commune in 1871 and finally to a limited form of parliamentary democracy in the Third Republic under the Constitution of 1875. The growth of democratic ideas and political liberalization in France as well as Germany, Sweden, Italy, the Austro-Hungarian Empire, and Russia through the nineteenth century, coupled with the development of a middle class through industrialization, led to a demand for *industrial democracy*. Workers, who were questioning the continuation of the "divine right of kings" in the political arena, began to question the autocracy and denial of basic human rights in the mills and factories.[16]

Capitalist Revolution

The third revolution of the late nineteenth century was the rise of capitalism and the spread of the market economy. Adam Smith, in *The Wealth of Nations*[17] published in 1776, the same year as the American Declaration of Independence, challenged the mercantile system of economic monopoly by asserting that a market economy would produce national prosperity. **Mercantilism** is the economic theory that a nation's prosperity depends on the amount of its capital, represented by bullion, and by the volume at which its exports exceed its imports. A mercantile system of economics requires a protectionist role of government in encouraging exports and discouraging imports, generally through the use of tariffs.

According to Smith, however, a nation's prosperity relies on its people as a strategic asset for economic development and a source of prosperity through a more productive use of human capital. Smith believed that a market economy, which is characterized by the principles of free trade, competition, and choice, would spur economic development and reduce poverty. Smith explained that by increasing the division of labor, there would be greater productivity and the development of machinery, as well as the development of new skills and trades among workers. Smith gave the famous example of pins. He asserted that ten workers could produce 48,000 pins per day if each of 18 specialized tasks was assigned to particular workers. Average productivity: 4,800 pins per worker per day. But absent the division of labor, a worker would be lucky to produce even one pin per day.[18] Smith claimed that if given a free hand, an individual would invest a resource, for example, land or labor, to earn the highest possible return on it. Such self-interest, if allowed to flourish, would drive a nation's economy toward prosperity. Smith is credited with creating **capitalism** from his market economy philosophy because capitalism is about allowing self-interest, profit making, and market forces to have free play.

The creation of private property (i.e., private ownership of the means of production and their use for personal profit) was a cornerstone of capitalism and the source of a new labor relationship. Employers paid a group of people—employees—to provide labor in the form of work, and a market for "labor" was created. This **labor market** was the result of the interplay between the employer's demand for labor and the worker's supply of labor. Labor markets could be in geographical areas over which competition for labor took place or within categories of labor such as skilled or unskilled. The **wage relation** was the negotiation, either formal or informal, over what work labor was willing to perform and what the employer was willing to pay for that work. Wages to the employer represented a cost that affected the enterprise's' production cost and profit. Wages to the employees were a source of income and the means for survival. Capitalists wanted to have labor at the lowest possible price, and workers, the suppliers of labor, wanted the highest possible price. This created the basic conflict of interests between capital and labor. However, because without cooperation nothing would be produced and no wages would be earned, capital and labor in a capitalistic economy have an incentive to cooperate.

The need for collective action and the formation of trade unions came about because when the parties are negotiating their wage relation they are "equals," but once the relationship is established, the employer becomes the "boss." The boss has an interest in regulating how the work is performed to make sure it is efficient and effective. And because the effort expended by labor is to a degree discretionary by the employees, the boss will use various methods and practices to elicit the maximum amount of work from labor, such as providing supervision, granting incentives, or imposing penalties. At end of 1800s and in the early 1900s large numbers of unemployed workers in major industrial nations allowed employers to pay little and treat workers poorly. The outgrowth of this mistreatment in the U.K. and Europe, as in the United States, was the rise of collective action, by the creation of trade unions, by the use of worker strikes, and at times, by violence. Capitalism, although the constant economic theory in U.S. labor relations, competed with other economic theories as the industrial revolution spread. Figure 12-1 details such other economic and social theories that influenced the path of other nations' industrial relations.

Growth of Trade Unions

At their conception, trade unions in the United States, United Kingdom, and Europe were seen as having three roles: (1) their market function was to represent and advance the employment interests of its members through collective bargaining as workplace representatives; (2) their class function was to fight battles for the rights and interests of all workers to increase workers' status and power in the economic and political systems; and (3) their social function was to improve the overall quality of life of workers, promoting greater social justice, better schools, and health care. In the United States, unions made the choice to focus on just representation in the workplace, whereas in the U.K. and Europe, they tended to embrace all three to some degree, making the history and direction of the industrial relations in Europe all the more complex.

Most governments have displayed three distinct attitudes in reaction to unionization of workers: suppression, tolerance, and encouragement.[19] Early in the development of their industrial economy, most countries worked to *suppress* unions and the notion of collective bargaining. In Great Britain at the beginning of the industrial revolution, the Combination Acts, passed in 1799 and 1800, made a union of employees illegal as a conspiracy to restrain trade. In France, a 1791 law that forbade employee combinations—ostensibly to prevent any organization from coming between the government and the workers—was actually used to suppress unions. In the late nineteenth and early twentieth centuries, when industrialization reached Germany, Russia, and Japan, these nations passed laws suppressing or banning unions. Some Third World countries just emerging into the industrial world have not directly banned unions but have attempted to suppress collective bargaining. The governments of Ghana, Nigeria, and Singapore, for example, supported unions legislatively but limited their authority.

Great Britain and the United States, however, from as early as the 1830s, began to *tolerate* unions, primarily because unions continued to function despite antiunion attitudes. The ability or desire to keep workers from organizing lost support as these countries experienced economic growth. As representatives of the working masses, unions became powerful political forces that could not be ignored.[20] In addition, both nations had budding middle classes that had embraced progressive moral and political agendas, some from a desire to avoid labor unrest that would threaten their newly found prosperity.

Manchester School	The economic theory that agreed with the noninterference maxim of capitalism, but without an emphasis on human capital.
Capitalism	The economic theory that a nation's prosperity relies on a more productive use of human capital and that by increasing the division of labor there would be greater productivity, the development of new machinery, and of skills and trades among workers. A capitalist or market economy is characterized by the principles of free trade, competition, and choice and noninterference by government.
Mercantilism	The economic theory that a nation's prosperity depends on the amount of its capital, represented by bullion, and by the volume at which its exports exceed its imports. A mercantile system of economics requires a protectionist role of government in encouraging exports and discouraging imports, generally through the use of tariffs.
Neoliberalism	Neoliberalism refers to a political–economic philosophy that deemphasizes or rejects government intervention in the economy, focusing instead on achieving progress and even social justice by encouraging free-market methods and fewer restrictions on business operations and economic development.
Chartism	Chartism was a short-lived political movement in England based on the demand for voting rights and the political representation of the working class in Parliament. It won support from a wide variety of workers and even from lower-middle-class radicals and was regarded a threat to the established order. In 1842 it engineered a General Strike against the proposal of the cotton manufactures to cut wages by 25 percent because of the severe trade depression. The government responded with mass arrests of Chartist leaders, who were put on trial for "levying war against the Queen" and exiled.
Syndicalism	The organizers pre–World War I strikes were inspired by syndicalism, which advocated mass strikes and rapid trade union recruitment as a means to overcome employers' actions.
Fabian Society	The Fabians aimed for democratic socialism. Believing that voters could be persuaded of socialism's justice, they sought to achieve reform by education, stimulating debate through lectures and discussions initiated by democratically accountable and educated professionals. The Fabian Society maintained its independence from the Labour Party, although it helped to create the Labour Representation Committee in 1900. Trade union militancy from 1910–26 and the unemployment climate and depression of the 1930s diminished the attractiveness of Fabian Society, but the seeds for a more political labor movement had been sown.
Progressivism	A broadly based reform movement that reached its height early in the 20th century arose as a response to the vast changes brought by industrialization, the spread of the factory system, and the growth of cities.

FIGURE 12-1 Economic/Social Movements Influencing Global Industrial Relations

Continental Europe, and later Japan among others, continued a policy of union suppression throughout most of the nineteenth century. Feudalism and rigid class distinctions, which had delayed the advent of capitalism, market economies, a large middle class, and democracy, also extended these nations' suppression of working-class political movements and trade unions. Germany enacted an Anti Socialist Law in 1878 that prohibited all political meetings and trade unions associated with socialist groups.[21] These actions caused the workers to become more radical and to move toward socialism and social democracy. The European hierarchy and the smaller European middle class allied against these socialist democrats to preserve the status quo.

Industrial nations fighting World War I, and subsequently World War II, found it necessary to marshal capital and labor for the war effort. Governments found that what "capital" wanted in exchange was money and what labor wanted was collective bargaining. Largely as a result of this need, through law or policy, the United States and Britain mandated collective bargaining, though other countries continued to resist it. As a nation's economy fluctuates, its attitude toward unions and collective bargaining fluctuate. Governments *encourage* collective bargaining when it is perceived as having a positive effect on the economy.[22] But they discourage it when the economy is struggling. This was the case in the interwar period between the World Wars (1919–38), when there was a massive global economic recession. The Great Depression was by far the largest sustained decline in industrial production and productivity in the century and a half for which economic records had been kept. Its impact was felt throughout the entire industrialized world and with their trading partners in less developed nations. Nations' individual responses to trade unions during this period will be discussed later. As for international response to trade unions, the League of Nations attempted to address the need for stability of labor markets by creation of the International Labour Organization.

In 1941, President Franklin D. Roosevelt addressed 250 delegates of the International Labor Organization in the East Room of the White House.

INTERNATIONAL LABOUR ORGANIZATION

The signers of the Treaty of Versailles in 1919, which ended World War I, formed the **International Labour Organization (ILO)** as a parallel organization to the League of Nations. The mission of the League was to keep the peace between nations, and the mission of the ILO was to keep the peace within societies threatened by class divisions within countries. Prior to the war in Europe, the fear that continued worker unrest could lead to increased labor radicalism, support for the Marxist class struggle, and the abolition of capitalism created a Labour Problem that needed to be addressed.[23] A contributing cause for World War I was the imperialistic, territorial, and economic rivalries that had been intensifying from the late nineteenth century, particularly among Germany, France, Great Britain, Russia, and Austria-Hungary. A spirit of nationalism had brought the unification of Germany by "blood and iron"; while France sought to reclaim Alsace and Lorraine, which were lost in the Franco–Prussian War. These issues, imperialist and nationalist, seemed to have been moderated by the advance of industrialization and economic prosperity. Many Europeans counted on the deterrent of war's destructiveness to preserve the peace. But that did not happen.

After the war, these nations hoped to address the humanitarian, political, and economic issues that had been prominent prior to and during the war by the creation of the ILO and by adopting labor standards to improve the conditions of workers.[24] Before the war interrupted it, the *progressive reform movement* hoped to correct the exploitation of workers in industrial nations. Progressivism, a broadly based reform movement that reached its height early in the twentieth century, arose in response to the vast changes brought by industrialization, the spread of the factory system, and the growth of cities. In the United States, men and women of middle-class background, led by women such as Jane Addams in Chicago, social progressives, sought to improve slum life through programs of self-help. The political progressive movement, led in the United States by the Progressive Party, advocated for more government involvement in solving social problems by legislating the end to sweatshops, granting women the vote, and the end of child labor.

The humanitarian goal of the ILO was to end the exploitation of workers in industrialized countries; the political goal was to moderate unrest caused by clashes between workers and the owners; and the economic goal was to establish international standards to improve the workplace so that countries that adopted social reforms would still be competitive.

The creation of the ILO was not without difficulties. Samuel Gompers, president of the American Federation of Labor (AFL), served as chair of the drafting committee charged with formulating the special labor clauses for the Treaty. Consistent with his AFL philosophy, Gompers advocated an international organization that would foster support for the workers' right to organize and collective bargaining as the solution to the Labor Problem, rather than an organization that advocated for political and economic reforms. Many trade unionists and social reformers from Europe believed the ILO had to do more to reform society as well as the workplace if it was to accomplish its purpose of fostering industrial peace. The industrialized countries wanted a set of labor standards that applied to everyone, whereas countries beginning industrialization wanted some leeway to foster their development. There was a question of how colonial territories were going to be affected, and some nations warned that they would not join the ILO unless there was a strong statement condemning racial segregation in participating nations.

A compromise plan proposed by the British gained acceptance.[25] To satisfy the European interests, the ILO was housed in Geneva, Switzerland, and its mission included political lobbying to improve employer–worker relations. All nation–states in the League of Nations were automatic members. The United States never joined the League of Nations, so it was not an initial participant in the ILO.

Nine principles written into the ILO Constitution defined its philosophy:

- Labor should not be treated as a commodity.
- Workers had the right to organize.
- Workers should get a reasonable wage to maintain a reasonable standard of living.
- Work should be limited to an 8-hour day or a 48-hour week.
- One day of rest each week.
- No child labor.
- Equal pay for equal work.
- Equitable treatment of immigrants.
- Enforcement of labor laws.

The ILO was envisioned to be an international "Department of Labor" with a unique **tripartite organizational structure** that brought together representatives of not only the participating governments but also employers and workers as equal parties in its governance. The main work of the ILO was to enact international Conventions and Recommendations regarding labor. *Conventions* would be submitted for ratification to the nation–states and upon ratification would be binding; *Recommendations* were suggested provisions submitted for nation–states to consider. The first annual International Labour Conference took place in Washington and resulted in six International Labour Conventions covering hours of work, unemployment, maternity protection, night work for women, and the minimum age for young workers. Since that time the ILO has issued 185 Conventions and 195 Recommendations.[26]

In 1998, the ILO adopted a *Declaration on Fundamental Principles and Rights at Work* to ensure that social progress goes hand in hand with economic progress and development. The Declaration is a promotional instrument, not a Convention or a Recommendation, but rather a reaffirmation of the central beliefs set out in the organization's Constitution. Excerpts from the Declaration can be found in Figure 12-2.

The Declaration commits member states to respect and promote principles and rights in four categories: freedom of association and the effective recognition of the right to collective bargaining, the elimination of forced or compulsory labor, the abolition of child labor, and the elimination of discrimination in employment. The Declaration and its follow-up provide three ways to help countries, employers, and workers achieve the Declaration's objective. First, there is an Annual Review composed of reports from countries that have not yet ratified one or more of the ILO Conventions that relate to the specific principles and rights stated in the Declaration. This reporting process provides governments with an opportunity to state what measures they have taken toward achieving respect for the Declaration. It also gives organizations of employers and workers a chance to voice their views on progress made and actions taken.

Second, a Global Report each year provides a dynamic global picture of the current situation of the principles and rights expressed in the Declaration. The Global Report is an objective view of the global and regional trends on the issues relevant to the Declaration and serves to highlight those areas that require greater attention. It serves as a basis for determining priorities for technical cooperation. And finally, the ILO offers technical cooperation projects as the third way to give effect to the Declaration. These projects are designed to address identifiable needs in relation to the Declaration

The International Labour Conference,

1. Recalls:
    (a) that in freely joining the ILO, all Members have endorsed the principles and rights set out in its Constitution and in the Declaration of Philadelphia, and have undertaken to work towards attaining the overall objectives of the Organization to the best of their resources and fully in line with their specific circumstances;
    (b) that these principles and rights have been expressed and developed in the form of specific rights and obligations in Conventions recognized as fundamental both inside and outside the Organization.
2. Declares that all Members, even if they have not ratified the Conventions in question, have an obligation arising from the very fact of membership in the Organization, to respect, to promote and to realize, in good faith and in accordance with the Constitution, the principles concerning the fundamental rights, which are the subject of those Conventions, namely:
    (a) freedom of association and the effective recognition of the right to collective bargaining;
    (b) the elimination of all forms of forced or compulsory labour;
    (c) the effective abolition of child labour; and
    (d) the elimination of discrimination in respect of employment and occupation.
3. Recognizes the obligation on the Organization to assist its Members, in response to their established and expressed needs, in order to attain these objectives by making full use of its constitutional, operational and budgetary resources, including by the mobilization of external resources and support, as well as by encouraging other international organizations with which the ILO has established relations, pursuant to article 12 of its Constitution, to support these efforts:
    (a) by offering technical cooperation and advisory services to promote the ratification and implementation of the fundamental Conventions;
    (b) by assisting those Members not yet in a position to ratify some or all of these Conventions in their efforts to respect, to promote and to realize the principles concerning fundamental rights which are the subject of those Conventions; and
    (c) by helping the Members in their efforts to create a climate for economic and social development.
4. Decides that, to give full effect to this Declaration, a promotional Follow-up, which is meaningful and effective, shall be implemented in accordance with the measures specified in the annex hereto, which shall be considered as an integral part of this Declaration.
5. Stresses that labour standards should not be used for protectionist trade purposes, and that nothing in this Declaration and its Follow-up shall be invoked or otherwise used for such purposes; in addition, the comparative advantage of any country should in no way be called into question by this Declaration and its Follow-up.

FIGURE 12-2   ILO Declaration on Fundamental Principles and Rights at Work and its Follow-up

SOURCE: International Labour Organization Web site at www.ilo.org. Used with permission.

and to strengthen local capacities to translate principles into practice. Two of the Global Reports issued since 2000 are of particular significance.

Collective Bargaining

The first Global Report, "Your Voice at Work," issued in 2000,[27] focused on collective bargaining and the standards and principles regarding collective bargaining embodied in the

ILO Convention 87, "Freedom of Association and Protection of the Right to Organize," adopted in 1948, and Convention 98, "Right to Organize and Collective Bargaining," adopted in 1949.

Those Conventions endorsed good-faith collective bargaining as a fundamental right of all workers, private and public, except those in the armed services and the police. Some of the overriding principles can be summarized as follows:

- Collective bargaining should be undertaken by independent workers' organizations not under the control of employers or governments.
- The collective bargaining process should include bargaining over the terms and conditions of employment and the relationship between the parties.
- The agreements reached should be binding on the parties.
- A trade union that represents a majority or high percentage of the workers may enjoy exclusive bargaining rights.
- Conciliation and mediation can be a part of collective bargaining, but compulsory arbitration on the terms and conditions in agreements is contrary to the principle of voluntary collective bargaining.
- Legislation intending to annul, modify, or restrict the agreement of the parties, particularly as it relates to wage agreements, is also contrary to the principle of voluntary collective bargaining.

The Global Report concluded that three interrelated priorities should guide the promotional work by the ILO: (1) ensure that all workers can form and join a trade union of their choice without fear of intimidation or reprisal and that employers are also free to form and join independent associations; (2) encourage an open and constructive attitude by private business and public employers to the chosen representation of workers, including the development of agreed methods of bargaining and complementary forms of cooperation concerning terms and conditions of work; (3) recognition by governments that respect for fundamental principles and rights at work contributes to stable economic, political, and social development in the context of international economic integration, the fostering of democracy, and the fight against poverty.[28]

ANGLOPHONE COUNTRIES

Although the United States, Great Britain, Canada, and Australia have a common heritage, share a language, and legal and political systems, their industrial relations developed in some unique ways. In this section, we will compare their evolution and their status today.

Great Britain

As discussed earlier, the Industrial Revolution began in Great Britain largely because it had the technological means, government encouragement, and a large and varied trade network via its river system. The development of a large inland water-transport network was, perhaps, the most important factor behind the industrial revolution in Great Britain.[29] The first factories appeared in 1740, concentrating on textile production. Such English inventions as the flying shuttle and carding machines and the spinning jenny integrated with a new source of power, the steam engine, resulted in more than 100,000 power looms in Great Britain and Scotland between 1790 and 1830. But the Industrial Revolution had brought with it abuses and hardships on workers. As a medical doctor described such a workplace in the early 1830s:

> The operatives are congregated in rooms and workshops during the twelve hours in the day, in an enervating, heated atmosphere, which is frequently loaded with dust or filaments of cotton . . . They are drudges who watch the movements, and assist the operations of a mighty material force. . . . The preserving labor of the operative must rival the mathematical precision, the incessant motion, the exhaustless power of the machine.[30]

Where previously workers had joined together to form skilled trade unions, the Industrial Revolution spurred widespread unionization of semiskilled and unskilled laborers as a reaction to low wages, long hours, and deplorable conditions. Trade unions developed rapidly, especially in the factory-based textile industry. There were also attempts to form general unions of all workers irrespective of trade as a means for protecting and improving workers' living standards and for changing the political and economic order of society. Figure 12-1 lists a number of movements in Britain's labor history that influenced the path of its trade unionism.

Midcentury, Britain entered into a second phase of industrialization with the construction of a railway network and a growth of the cotton, coal, iron, steel, and engineering industries. Workers in the profitable staple industries were the backbone of the trade union revival that followed the demise of Chartism. These unions were organized nationally and were highly centralized. Negotiation and arbitration gradually came to be accepted practices and were a much more common means of securing improvements in wages and conditions than strike action.

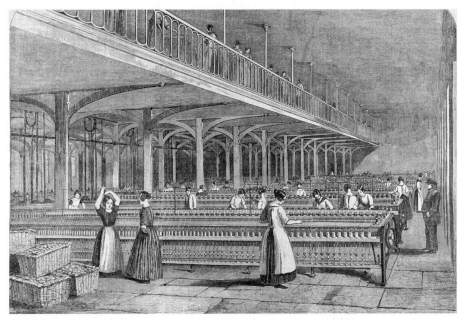

The interior of the doubling-room at Dean Mill, Halliwell, England, in 1851 is an example of some of the innovations in textile production in England at the start of the Industrial Revolution.

In 1868 the **Trades Union Congress** was founded and due to the extension of the right to vote, trade unions began to have success in lobbying for laws protecting workers. The Employers and Workmen Act of 1875 modified the old Master and Servant Law so that employers too could be sued for breach of contract; the 1874 Factory Act set a 10-hour limit on the working day; and the 1871 Trade Union Act recognized unions as legal entities entitled to protection under the law.

Between 1888 and 1918 membership in trade unions grew from 750,000 to six and a half million and unionism within the unskilled, semiskilled, white-collar, and professional workforces spread rapidly. The strength of the movement was seen it its huge May Day 1890 demonstration in favor of the 8-hour day. Employers, threatened by the unions' obvious strength, engineered court decisions outlawing peaceful picketing and enabling employers to sue unions for losses during strikes. Despite these measures, the militancy of unions during the prewar years led to a wave of strikes action, dubbed "'the great unrest'."[31]

Just as Adam Smith's *Wealth of Nations* had articulated the advantages of capitalism brought about by the industrial revolution, two Victorian writers warned of its dangers. Beatrice and Sidney Webb, pioneering social economists and cofounders of the London School of Economic and Political Science, had a profound effect on English social thought and institutions. Their work spread into areas such as historical and social research and educational and political reform. They advocated equal pay for women and universal social insurance and outlined a fledgling welfare state. They led those who believed that the trade unionist movement should include not only their role as the voice of workers with their employers, but also a political voice for all workers in settling national minimum standards of wages.

The First World War accentuated divisions within the labor movement, as labor's rank and file continued to press for economic and political reforms, while labor's leaders aligned more with the government in its war effort. The gulf between the two generated its own structures in the form of the Shop Stewards Movement and Workers' Committees. The role of **shop stewards** of today can trace their origins to this wartime period, during which rank-and-file workers rather than union officials kept effective trade unionism alive in the face of their leaders' preoccupation with the war effort.[32]

The British labor movement in the early 1920s was influenced by the following beliefs: capitalism's decline was inevitable, labor and capital have opposing interests, capitalism should be replaced by socialism, and strikes should be used for both economic and political ends. Great Britain, reacting to what it believed was an untenable position, created the Whitley Committee to study the causes of labor unrest. The committee recommended collective bargaining by independent trade unions and endorsed a system of joint councils to provide for joint consultation by employers and unions.[33]

After WWI the continuing decline of the staple industries and persistent high unemployment culminated in the "'great crash'" or Great Depression at the end of the 1920's. Trade union membership declined from around six and a half million in 1920 to three and a quarter million in 1933. A serious strike wave in 1919 lost 35 million working days. This included strikes by the police and the armed forces. Revolutionary industrial militants and some militant shop stewards were influenced by the theories of Marx and Lenin. When it became clear that British troops were being used with those of other capitalist countries against the revolution in Russia, a powerful solidarity movement emerged in the form of the "'Hands Off Russia'" campaign. This campaign enabled disparate socialist parties to unite as the Communist Party of Great Britain. It was, and for many years remained, small, but it had within its ranks those who had formed the core of the Shop Stewards' Movement during the war.

The first majority Labour government gained prominence as a part of Winston Churchill's coalition government during World War II. In the election of 1945, it gained a majority of the members of Parliament, resulting in a Labour Party Prime Minister and Cabinet. The Labour government inherited the severe economic problems of postwar Europe and responded by passing the following legislation involving labor:

- Nationalized the ailing coal, gas, and electric industries; the iron and steel industry; and the Bank of England, resulting in more than 2 million people becoming public-sector employees.
- Extended social benefits instituting the "cradle-to-grave" welfare system with sick leave and unemployment benefits, workers' compensation, and universal health care.

A fuel shortage and financial crisis in 1947 caused the Labour government to impose a wage freeze and cutbacks in welfare spending. The resulting election put the Tory government in place for the next 13 years.

The trade union movement in the 1950s focused on increasing its memberships, especially among women and young people, and surviving the effects of a sharp recession that caused worker layoffs without notice or pay. These actions were met by union-called strikes, notably against the publicly owned transportation industry, which the government was able to withstand, resulting in a return to work with nothing to show for the strike.

From 1965–1979, the British trade union movement was supported by the creation of a Royal Commission on Trade Unions and Employers Associations (the Donovan Commission), which endorsed collective bargaining rights and Britain's traditional approach to minimal legal regulations of unions and bargaining.[34] This traditional approach, characterized by an absence of statutory regulation, is termed **voluntarism** or a collective laissez-faire system. Under voluntarism a union and an employer or an employers' association can agree to be a party to a collective bargaining agreement, and the contract can extend for as long as the parties agree, although wages are generally negotiated annually. The collective bargaining agreement's terms and conditions cover all the individuals in the bargaining unit, even if they are not in the union. Laissez-faire in British labor relations came to an end with the election of the Conservative government headed by Prime Minister Margaret Thatcher. During Prime Minister Thatcher's term in office, a number of changes occurred in labor–management relations when legislation was passed that:

- Narrowed a union's immunity from labor injunctions
- Outlawed secondary strikes
- Restrained picketing
- Required a secret election of the union membership before calling a strike
- Prohibited a closed shop

With the election of a Labour government in 1997, led by Prime Minister Tony Blair, unions hoped for a change in attitude. But the major aspects of Thatcher's legislation remained in place. Some reforms were instituted, such as the 1999 Employment Relations Act that created a legal mechanism for union recognition to counter some employers' decisions to unilaterally stop bargaining. For the first time these new representation procedures gave statutory support for requiring employers to recognize trade unions that claim at least 40 percent of their eligible workers.

As discussed later in the section on the European Union (EU), Blair's government opted into the EU's protocols on employment standards involving hours of work, parental leave, and the creation of work councils. Most recently, the Employment Act of 2002 was enacted to

- Enhance employees parental leave rights
- Guarantee parental flextime
- Curtail employment appeal rights by requiring the losing party to pay the cost of the appeal
- Establish minimal grievance procedures for collective bargaining agreements to reduce the caseload of employment courts
- Grant fixed-term, or contract, employees protections comparable to regular employees
- Require consultation with employee representatives before layoffs

These legislative enactments have largely supplanted the long-established voluntarism in Britain's labor relation's history.

Canada

Canada in the late 1880s and early 1900s confronted the same labor unrest as the United States and Great Britain due to the deplorable working conditions associated with the early stages of industrialization. The Winnipeg General Strike in 1919 and fears of Bolshevism led to the appointment of Royal Commission on Industrial Relations, which cited as its charge ". . . . the duty of considering and making suggestions for establishing permanent improvement in the relations between employers and employees, whereby, through close contact and joint action, they can improve existing industrial conditions and devise means for their continual review and betterment."[35] The Royal Commission identified unemployment as the most important condition causing industrial unrest; condemned the treatment of labor as a commodity to be bought and sold at a price determined by supply and demand; and endorsed a collective voice for workers, although it had both a majority position, which endorsed independent unions, and a minority position accepting employer-created representation plans.

Up until the Second World War, Canada's economy was still largely rural, centered on resource extraction industries of mining and timber, rather than manufacturing. This inhibited the growth of a large urban-based, wage-earning labor force. And because of Canada's reliance on a few key industries, its economy was more vulnerable to the disruptive effects of strikes and labor conflict. For these reasons, Canada's labor relations developed to discourage the adversarial scheme of trade unionism and collective bargaining and to encourage cooperation and unity of interest between employers and employees to promote efficiency in production and peace in labor relations. This strategy combined British-style voluntarism in union recognition, American-style welfare capitalism, and Australian-style government-mandated mediation and fact-finding.

As the percentage of union membership steadily declined in the United States beginning in the 1940s, the pattern was reversed in Canada, where more collectivist traditions led to more favorable political attitudes toward unions and thus a growth in the union movement. Another contributing factor is Canada's governmental and legal environment. Canada's system of federated government vests most employment matters in the 10 provinces. Its federal authority, except in times of crisis, is limited to about 10 percent of its workers in federal civil service and national industries such as transportation and telecommunications.[36] This fragmented system means that employers and unions have to contend with varying local labor laws. Quebec Province, which still enjoys its French heritage, and Ontario Province have the largest share of Canada's union members.[37]

Canadian law on both the federal and provincial levels mirrors the protections found in the U.S. National Labor Relation Act. Workers have the right to form unions and to elect exclusive bargaining agents, employers must meet with unions for the purpose of collective bargaining, grievance procedures and arbitration are mandated, and strikes during the term of a contract are prohibited. Canadian labor boards have the authority to (1) certify unions without formal elections; (2) make quick, final decisions on unfair labor practice cases; and (3) impose first contracts when employers refuse to bargain with a new union. Canadian labor laws have also provided *public-sector* unions a stronger position by giving them the right to strike (in most instances) and the right to compulsory arbitration.

For many years the Canadian labor movement has been helped by the rise and success of a political party endorsed by organized labor—the Cooperative Commonwealth Federation, renamed the New Democratic Party (DNP) in 1961. So although general public attitudes toward unions have declined similarly in Canada and the United States, Canadian unions were successful in passing favorable labor laws even when the DNP was replaced in the 1980's by more conservative governments. Three provinces of Canada passed labor law reforms that banned the hiring of replacement workers on either a temporary or a permanent basis.[38] The election of an extremely right-wing Conservative Party caused changes in the labor climate against trade unionism.[39] Nevertheless, as late as 1998, a Federal Government Task Force endorsed Canada's collective bargaining system as a

> . . . balance between labour and management; between social and economic values; between the various instruments of labour policy; between rights and responsibilities; between individual and democratic group rights; and between the public interest and free collective bargaining.[40]

Traditionally, the fate of labor relations in Canada followed that of the United States. In fact, in 1966, the percentage of workers in unions in the two countries was almost identical. In recent years, however, that has not been the case. Canadian union density increased and decreased later than the United States or U.K., peaking in mid-1980s and declining less severely, so that by 2000 its density was 30 percent overall and over 80 percent in the public sector, which was higher than in either the United States or U.K. and actually double the United States in overall union density.[41]

Australia

Australia, like Canada, had a long history of British colonial rule and largely reflected British cultural, political, and legal systems. But Australia's industrial relations developed in a unique manner. In opposition to the Anglo-American preference for voluntarism in labor relations, Australia adopted a federal compulsory conciliation and arbitration system in 1904, which gave legal protection to collective bargaining but requires trade union and employer associations to submit disputed contract terms to a state tribunal for conciliation and, if necessary, binding arbitration.[42] This system was in place for most of the twentieth century, but amid the economic difficulties of the 1980s both labor and employers sought to decentralize collective bargaining and adopt enterprise (company or industry specific) bargaining.[43]

After the Federal Coalition Government was elected in 1996, the Coalition government introduced to Parliament its first significant piece of legislation, the **Workplace Relations Act (WRA)**. The key elements of the WRA include

- A streamlined "award" system
- More emphasis on enterprise bargaining

- Curbs on union power
- Restrictions on strikes
- A streamlined unfair-dismissal system, which limits frivolous appeals and compensation claims

Under the WRA, the Australian system of industrial relations is still a centralized model, characterized by industrywide or company **awards** (similar to U.S. collective bargaining agreements), which are negotiated by company, union, and sometimes government officials, and then submitted to the Australian Industrial Relations Commission (AIRC) for ratification or resolution of differences.[44] Such awards establish minimum wages and working conditions for specific categories of workers.[45] Individual companies and their employees or unions may negotiate supplemented "over award" wage benefits based on market conditions. These benefits, when registered with the AIRC, are known as a Certified Agreement if it covers most or all of a company's workforce or Australian Workplace Agreement (AWA) if it covers an individual employee.

The Office of Employment Advocate (OEA) investigates breaches of the WRA's freedom of association provisions and files the AWAs, individual employment agreements. These agreements are subject to far fewer government regulations than are awards and certified or enterprise agreements. An AWA, which is similar to American-style employment contracts, improves on the basic working conditions contained in the award applying to the firm's sector.

The WRA also barred *closed shops,* where an individual has to be a member of a union to be hired, and eliminated preference clauses, which required an employer to give a preference to specified individuals. Under the WRA, unions and workers are prohibited from striking companies engaged in interstate commerce, except when they are negotiating a new enterprise agreement. The strike must also concern a matter specifically related to the negotiations. This is known as "protected action" during a "bargaining period." Industrial disputes are then intended to be settled via conciliation and, if necessary, compulsory arbitration by the AIRC. When unions do strike outside a bargaining period, they can be sued by employers for damages, and union officials and individual strikers can be held personally liable.

Eighty percent of all wage and salary earners are covered by the awards system, with the greatest proportion of employees receiving overaward payments through some form of enterprise agreement. Despite efforts by the federal government to promote the use of AWAs, the vast majority of employers still prefer enterprise agreements or awards.

Although enterprise bargaining is likely to continue to dominate the industrial relations scene for years to come, the ACTU believes that enterprise bargaining has run its course in Australia and has been arguing that workers are unlikely to benefit any further from decentralized bargaining. The union movement sees the future in terms of a return to industrywide bargaining as the only way to provide increased significant new benefits to workers, especially in view of the weakening of the award system.

EUROPEAN UNION NATIONS

The European Union

The **European Union (EU)** is a unique regional body made up of 25 member states that delegate their sovereignty on questions of joint interest to common institutions, which represent the interests of the EU as a whole. However, the EU member states are not one single, new nation. The mission of the EU is to integrate the economies of the member states, to "lay the foundations for an ever closer union," to raise the living standards of its citizens, to remove obstacles to concerted action, and to promote a high level of employment and of social protection. The EU's priority objective has been the political and economic integration of Europe through a gradual elimination of customs barriers and an introduction of common external tariffs. As explained in an EU publication:

> The EU's foundational agreement is a pact between sovereign nations that have resolved to share a common destiny and to pool an increasing share of their sovereignty. It concerns the things that European peoples care most deeply about: peace, security, participatory democracy, justice and solidarity. This pact is being strengthened and confirmed all across Europe: half a billion human beings have chosen to live under the rule of law and in accordance with age-old values that center on humanity and human dignity.[46]

Five EU institutions—the European Parliament, the Council, the Commission, the Court of Justice, and the Court of Auditors—hold responsibility for making and administering EU policy. The EU, headquartered in Brussels, began its cooperative and integrative process in 1951 among Belgium, Germany, France, Italy, Luxembourg, and the Netherlands. Currently it also includes Austria, Denmark, Finland, Greece, Ireland, Portugal, Spain, Sweden, and the United Kingdom. On May 1, 2004, Cyprus, the Czech Republic, Estonia, Hungary, Latvia, Lithuania, Malta, Poland, Slovakia, and Slovenia joined the EU, and the European Council has set 2007 as the date for Bulgaria and Romania to also join. As a politician from one of the new member states put it: "Europe has finally managed to reconcile its history with its geography,"[47] as seen on the map of EU member states in Figure 12-3.

In economic, trade, and monetary terms, the EU has become a major world power. It has considerable influence within international organizations such as the World Trade Organization (WTO), the United Nations (UN), and at world summits on the environment and development. The EU dates its beginning to 1957, when its member states signed the Treaties of Rome, creating the European Atomic Energy Community (EURATOM) and the European Economic Community (EEC), which began removing trade barriers and forming a "common market." In 1967 the institutions of the three European communities were merged. From this point on, there was a single Commission and a single Council of Ministers as well as the European Parliament. Originally, the members of the European Parliament were chosen by the national parliaments but in 1979 the first direct elections were held, allowing the citizens of the member states to vote for the candidate of their choice. Since then, direct elections have been held every five years.

The **Treaty of Maastricht** (1992) created the EU by introducing intergovernmental cooperation to the existing "Community" system and adding new forms of cooperation between the member states, particularly on defense and in the area of justice and home affairs. Economic and political integration within the EU has resulted in member countries developing common policies in a very wide range of fields—agriculture, culture, consumer affairs, the environment, energy, transportation, and trade. The EU negotiates major trade and aid agreements with other countries and is developing a Common Foreign and Security Policy.

It took some time for the member states to remove all the barriers to trade between them and to turn their "common market" into a genuine single market in which goods, services, people, and capital could move around freely. During the 1990s it became

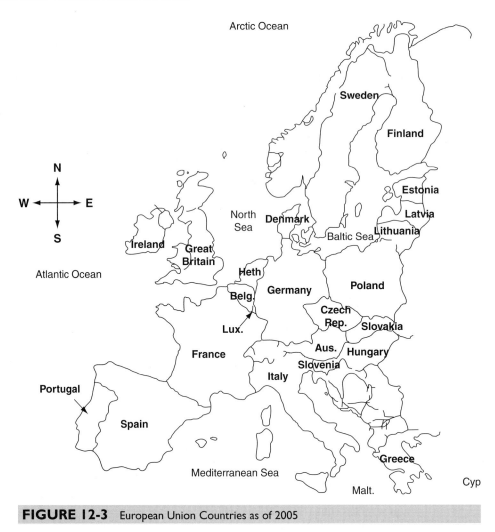

FIGURE 12-3   European Union Countries as of 2005

increasingly easy for people to move around Europe, as passport and customs checks were abolished at most of the EU's internal borders.

The **Single Market** was formally completed at the end of 1992, when the EU decided to adopt economic and monetary union (EMU), through the introduction of a single European currency managed by a European Central Bank. The single currency—the euro—became a reality on 1 January 2002, when euro notes and coins replaced national currencies in 12 of the 15 countries of the European Union (Belgium, Germany, Greece, Spain, France, Ireland, Italy, Luxembourg, the Netherlands, Austria, Portugal, and Finland).

In February 2003, to ensure that the enlarged EU can continue to function efficiently, it established new rules governing the size of the EU institutions and the way they work in the Treaty of Nice. The Treaty will be replaced in 2006 by the new EU Constitution—if all EU countries approve it. The draft Constitution is designed to simplify the Treaties and to make the EU's decision-making system more transparent and clarifies what powers and responsibilities belong to the EU, to its member states, and to regional authorities. It makes it clear that European integration is based on two kinds of legitimacy: the directly expressed will of the people and the legitimacy of the national governments. The nation–state is still the legitimate authority within which European societies operate.

The completion of the Single Market affected the EU's trade policy. The import restrictions that EU countries had been allowed to maintain were steadily abolished, as was the internal distribution of " 'sensitive' " imports such as textiles, steel, cars, and electronic goods. The EU is a single trading bloc, and it is home to nearly half a billion consumers with a relatively high average level of income. As such, it is a very attractive market for exporters in other countries. In terms of trade and investment, the EU is the United States' main partner and the only one with which it enjoys a stable relationship.

The European Commission recognizes three European-wide industrial relations unions as "social partners" in the EU social dialogue: the European Trade Union Confederation (ETUC) for labor and the Union of Industrial and Employers' Confederations of Europe (UNICE) and the European Center of Enterprises with Public Participation and Enterprises of General Economic Interest (CEEP) for employers.[48] ETUC, CEEP, and UNICE are the primary liaison bodies that advise and lobby the European Commission on employment and labor concerns. The Commission is required to consult with its social partners when it wants to submit proposals in a particular social field. ETUC is a European-level labor confederation that represents the national trade union confederations both inside and outside the EU and includes affiliates of the ICFTU and the World Confederation of Labor. Unions within the EU face the challenge of operating at the supranational level, in an effort to influence common EU social and economic policy directly affecting their interests. UNICE consists of 33 principal business federations from 27 European countries, plus 6 federations listed as observers, and CEEP's membership consists of enterprises that are generally state owned but are run on commercial principles.

The **Social Charter** contained in the Maastricht Treaty sets forth an action program to protect workers' rights in employment contracts, collective bargaining, health and safety in the workplace, consultation and participation, parental leave, and social protection. Almost all EU member states elected Social Democratic governments or coalitions in the mid-1990s, which created a political climate conducive to activism in employment and social affairs. Workers' rights, especially during corporate downsizing, became a hot political issue during the 1990s. The EU borrowed from its members' experiences, especially French and German, to guarantee workers and their unions the right to information and consultation before large-scale layoffs could occur and to institutionalize work councils within companies. **Works councils** are permanent elected bodies of workforce representatives, or in some instances joint committees with employers representatives, established on the basis of law or collective bargaining agreements with the overall task of promoting cooperation within the enterprise. Their task is for the benefit of both the employees and the enterprise by maintaining good and stable employment conditions and increasing the welfare and security of employees and their understanding of enterprise operations, finance, and competitiveness. The EU directive on works councils specifies it is to provide employees with rights to information and consultation, and it applies to companies with at least 50 employees or, at the choice of a member state, to companies having at least 20 employees. It directs member states to ensure that the employees' representatives, when carrying out their functions, enjoy adequate protection against dismissal. The information and consultation rights are

- Information on the recent and probable development of the company's activities and economic situation
- Information and consultation on the situation, structure, and probable development of employment within the company and on any anticipatory measures envisaged, in particular, where there is a threat of layoffs

- Information and consultation, with a view to reaching an agreement, on decisions likely to lead to substantial changes in the company or in contractual relations with the company

For a summary of works councils in the EU15 countries see Table 12-1.

Organized labor is well established in the EU throughout its member states,[49] although union membership has dwindled in most EU nations. Changes in the composition of the labor force, including women, temporary and part-time workers, and foreign workers have required trade unions to change from traditional methods of advocacy. At the present time, the overwhelming majority of collective bargaining agreements are still negotiated and signed at the *national level or lower*. However, the increasing integration of the national economies into a European one (including the introduction of the euro) is opening new methods for *transnational labor–management relations.* Steelworkers in Germany and the Netherlands have jointly negotiated a labor contract, and ETUC is developing resources to allow its affiliates and its 11 European industry federations to compare agreements made in other parts of the EU to improve on their negotiations. To date, ETUC, UNICE, and CEEP have signed three European "framework agreements," dealing with parental leave, part-time work, and fixed-term contracts. These agreements are much more general than a normal collective bargaining agreement and only set general frameworks for further negotiations on national levels (see Profile 12-1).

However, member states' retention of sovereignty in broad areas of employment and labor is still a limiting factor in the EU's employment and social agendas. The emphasis of the employment processes is on peer reviews of employment policies and discovering "best practices" (i.e., what has yielded the best results in increasing employment in both the EU and the rest of the world) and disseminating this information to all EU members. And although it is one of the four basic freedoms on which the EU has been built, labor mobility has been underdeveloped. Barriers to labor mobility include linguistic and cultural preferences, the complicated system of social security portability, nonrecognition of diplomas and training and work certificates, and the lack of basic information on work opportunities across borders. With the achievement of the single market and currency, however, the need to be able to redress economic imbalances through movement of labor around the EU has become increasingly clear.

As emphasized throughout this text, the reason the United States adopted the NLRA and established collective bargaining rights was to address the inherent conflict between capital and labor in a peaceful and cooperative manner within a capitalist system. The joint heritage of the United States, Britain, Canada, and Australia resulted in similar understanding of the "labor problem" and similar systems to address that problem. Continental Europe, however, started from a different heritage and, therefore, addressed its labor problem in a different manner. Europe's tradition of severe class differences based on the "divine right of kings," the feudal system, and the union of church and state cause the suppression of worker organizations to be more oppressive than in the Anglo-American countries. That oppression caused a more militant movement that focused not just on industrial equity but also on social equity in a socialist democratic model.

Germany

For Germany the coming of the industrial revolution, democracy, and capitalism was not a gradual transition but was concentrated in the last half of the 1800s. Earlier in that century, the German principalities, ruled by monarchs and supported by a serf system, were

TABLE 12-1	Work Councils in EU 15 Regulations on Employee Information and Consultation
Country	**Definition**
Austria	Elected by the workforce, represents all employees within an enterprise consistently employing five or more workers. Exercises the workplace-level consultation and codetermination rights conferred by law on the workforce as a whole.
Belgium	With the workplace health and safety committee, a works council is the main form of employee participation and representation in an undertaking with 100 or more employees. It is a joint bipartite body composed of representatives elected by workers in the enterprise and representatives appointed by the employer from among managerial staff, who may not outnumber the employees' representatives.
Denmark	Joint body with equal management/workforce representation set up under a cooperation agreement with the purpose of promoting cooperation and employee involvement at individual workplace level. The employee representatives may not be a member of a trade union.
Finland	Works councils are not a part of the national regulation on cooperation within undertakings. The Act on Personnel Representation in the Administration of Undertakings only provides employee representation on the company administrative bodies.
France	Joint body composed of the company's CEO and employee representatives elected by the workforce, of private companies with more than 50 employees. They receive information, respond to formal consultation by the employer, and manage cultural activities for which they have a budget at their disposal.
Germany	Employee representation body that applies to establishments that are organized under private law. The works council has a number of participation rights, consisting of rights to information, consultation, and codetermination.
Greece	Voluntary organs of employee representation and participation in enterprises with at least 50 employees or 20 employees for enterprises that have no trade union. The function of the works councils is participatory and consultative and is aimed at improving working conditions in conjunction with the growth of the company.
Ireland	No statutory work council system.
Italy	Works councils are created by the trade unions, which also define their regulations based on the national sectoral collective agreement. Works councils generally exercise information and consultation rights.
Luxembourg	Employee Committees are made up of employee representatives whose function is to protect employee rights and interest through their right of information and consultation. In addition Joint Works Committees are bodies composed of both employee and employer representatives and exercise codetermination rights over company policy and management decision.
The Netherlands	Body composed of employees within an enterprise that has the task of promoting the interest both of the enterprise and of its workforce. The main rights give to works councils by law are the right of access to information, advisory powers, the right of consent (i.e. the veto right on a number of related matters), and the right to propose initiatives.
Norway	The working environmental committees are compulsory bipartite bodies composed of an equal number of employee and employer representatives. The various duties of these committees include considering questions in areas such as rationalism schemes, work process, and working time arrangements. In addition, work councils are compulsory in companies with more than 100 employees. Employees may also demand the establishment of a work council in companies with fewer than 100 employees.
Spain	The committee is made up of elected worker representatives. It has defined information and consultation rights, but no right to codetermination. Duties include monitoring the implementation of labor laws and related discipline.
Sweden	There is no system of statutory works councils in Sweden, nor are such bodies established on a voluntary basis. Workplace employee participation and representation is based on the role of trade unions and their codetermination rights.
United Kingdom	There is no system of statutory works councils in U.K. Trade unions are the primary vehicle for the consultation of employees. However there is legislation providing for consultation of employees over certain issues. In addition, "joint consultative committees," based on collective agreements or voluntary practice, remain significant.

SOURCE: Mark Carley, Annalisa Baradel, and Christian Welz, *Works Council, Workplace Representation and Participation Structures* (© European Foundation for the Improvement of Living and Working Conditions, 2004): 1–38, 6–8. Used with permission.

challenged by bloody and unsuccessful revolts. The successful uniting of Germany in 1872 did create an elected Parliament, albeit selected by landowners only, and a Chancellor appointed by a hereditary monarch.[50] A severe economic slump in Germany that coincided with its emerging industrialization caused Germany to reject Adam Smith's brand of capitalism and Great Britain's form of democracy for a **state socialism**. This state socialism emphasized the role of government in regulating the market economy rather than the laissez-faire touted by capitalists. In its feudal tradition, Germany's state socialism included a safety net of welfare programs (called *Soczialpoletik*[51]), but such programs failed to suppress the inevitable labor problem that accompanied the abuses of the industrial system. When the working classes began to embrace the socialism of Karl Marx and to form radical anarchist political parties, Germany enacted an Anti Socialist Law that banned all political meetings and trade unions associated with socialist groups.[52] After that the trade unionists adopted the threefold agenda rejected by U.S. unions of representation at the bargaining table, participating within the economic and political systems, and pursuing social justice for all workers.

Nonetheless, just as the United States and U.K. had cooperated with labor when two world wars and a worldwide depression threatened their democracies, German industrialists began to cooperate with trade unions during the First World War, which continued through Germany's defeat and the abdication by the Kaiser. In 1918, trade unions and industrialists signed the Stinnes-Legien Agreement to preserve a representative democracy and a market economy, followed by legislative guarantees for workers rights. But during the Second World War, Adolph Hitler and the Nazi Party abolished labor unions and persecuted its leadership. After WWII, Germany's modern industrial relations system was created.

Briefly, in Germany employees are represented in three ways.

- *Trade unions.* negotiate collective bargaining agreements that are primarily concerned with wages. Collective bargaining takes place on a national or regional basis with a particular industry. These centralized negotiations usually take place annually and result in "pattern" or fairly uniform results.[53] Such collective agreements, however, are only legally binding on the employers who are a part of the association negotiating the agreement and the actual members of the trade union,[54] although employers generally apply the contract to all workers.

- *Work councils.* negotiate working conditions that are location specific and enforce the collective bargaining agreement. Work councils, at the company or enterprise level, participate in the day-to-day operation of the collective bargaining agreement. The members are elected by all employees and represent them in mandated consultations with the particular employer. Employers have to consult with work councils before taking certain employment action such as dismissals, layoffs, or changes in benefits. Work councils can seek wage increases above the collective bargaining agreement entered into on the national level.

- *Codetermination law,* in firms with 2,000 or more employees, requires that the company's supervisory board contain a certain number of employee representatives. **Codetermination** means that unions and employees have a say in company policy, as well as sharing responsibility for the firm.

The German trade unions retained their clout as other unions around the world lost theirs in the 1970s and 1980s. However, in the 1990s, although still one of the world's most powerful union voices, the German trade unions lost political clout and position under the conservative government of former Chancellor Helmut Kohl. Unions were blamed for high labor costs and tighter work rules that caused the country's persistently high unemployment and sluggish growth. German labor unions lost over 3.5 million members from 1991 to 1999, which reduced the percentage of union members in the labor force from 33 to 25 percent in only eight years. This decline in membership was unmatched by any other in German history. Some of the loss was due to the erosion of the system of national contracts negotiated between national unions and national employer associations as more individual employers negotiated directly with individual unions. IBM, for example, dropped out of industry national bargaining in 1991 and negotiated directly with the German union DAG.[55]

The pressure on German trade unions intensified with the fall of the Berlin Wall. Suddenly, an entire country, East Germany, had to be integrated into the economic, political, and social fabric of West Germany. Policy makers underestimated the scope of unemployment, antiquated means of production and infrastructure, and environmental damage in West Germany, as well as the negative impact through the loss of the former Soviet Union's foreign trade system. The East German trade unions, which had been closely aligned with the communist regime, dissolved, and an influx of new members to West German trade unions did not improve working conditions as had been hoped. Globalization and membership in the EU have added more challenges to Germany by the internationalization of employee relations and the creation of European work councils. The range of work councils in the EU can be found in Table 12-1.

Sweden

At the start of the twentieth century, Sweden was still a poor agrarian society with little industry and few unions. The Swedish Trade Union Confederation (LO), formed in 1898, pushed for union rights, which were granted in 1906 after a 1905 strike in the engineering industry. Subsequent strikes through the 1920s kept the unions and employers at odds. However, the relationship changed when the first Social Democrat government was elected in 1932, and with changed government attitudes toward unions came both industrial peace and prosperity. Sweden had enjoyed a reputation for a well-organized and stable unionized workforce that enjoys peaceful and constructive relations with employers.[56] Today 80 to 85 percent of its employees are members of trade unions. The *Saltsjöbaden* agreement between LO and SAF (The Swedish Employers' Confederation) in 1938 laid the foundation for what is usually known as the **Swedish Model**. Under the Swedish Model independent unions and businesses carry out collective bargaining free from government involvement. A high degree of self-regulation, state nonintervention, and the autonomy of the two parties, or "social partners," characterize this model. It is a *single-channel model,* in that the trade unions participate in collective bargaining and in the information, consultation, and codetermination rights granted employees as well.

For 44 years, from 1932 to 1976, the Social Democrats held the political power in Sweden and dominated the policy discussion. Sweden is ruled by a single-chamber Parliament, the Riksdag, with 349 members chosen by proportional representation from 29 constituencies across the country. Sweden is a monarchy in which the head of state, King Carl XVI Gustaf, is the nation's supreme representative but has no political powers.

The Constitution grants citizens a wide range of basic freedoms and rights, including freedom of expression and freedom of association. The *1976 Co-determination Act* regulates the central aspects of collective action and rights—bargaining, information and consultation, codetermination, and the conduct of employers and trade unions. It stipulates that as long as the parties are bound by a collective agreement, industrial action aimed at changing the agreement or its interpretation is prohibited. The Act also provides that when a primary labor action is legal, - sympathy strikes and picketing, or blockades, are permitted as long as they adhere to trade union procedures. The other significant employment law is the *1982 Employment Protection Act* (EPA), which governs the content and termination of employment contracts. The EPA provides that all employers must have just cause for dismissal, must negotiate with a union, and must give notice of layoff.

Collective bargaining agreements often complement statutory regulations and in many cases replace them. Employee representation at the workplace/enterprise level is either through a union club or a union member representative who acts as an ombudsman at each workplace. The union clubs unite to form larger union alliances (*förbund*), which are organized at national level through three main national union organizations: the LO, which represents most of the blue-collar workers; the Swedish Confederation of Professional Employees (TCO) for white-collar workers; and the Swedish Confederation of Professional Associations (SACO). The SAF, which became the Confederation of Swedish Enterprises in 2001, is the dominant employer organization in the private sector. Public-sector employees also have collective bargaining rights.

Following student unrest in1968, there was a call for industrial relations reform to strengthen the voice of the employees and their unions. Laws were passed to increase trade union rights, security of employment, and union representation on company boards. Unions were given the right to bargain not only over wages and conditions of employment, but also on how and what to produce. These changes were strongly opposed by the employers, and the industrial relations climate deteriorated. In 1980 industrial relations were at a low ebb, and by the late 1980s the SAF, which had initiated the establishment of the centralized bargaining structure in the mid 1950s, decided it was time to break away from this system.

The SAF felt there were major disadvantages with centralized bargaining and wanted a system that would permit large wage differences, greater flexibility, and more market influence over wages. The Engineering Employers Confederation (VF) initiated industrywide bargaining in 1983, with the long-term objective of establishing enterprise bargaining, performance-related payment systems, and employee share ownership plans. The trade union movement sought to preserve centralized wage agreements as a framework for local bargaining even though many unions have been unsuccessful in reaching agreements in the 1980s. Performance-related payments systems and employee share ownership systems spread despite union opposition. Since 1984, SAF no longer negotiates the national agreements with LO. Instead, its subdivisions are involved in sector negotiations.

The union movement's ability to withstand the employers' offensive was weakened by internal tensions. Throughout the 1950s and 1960s the LO, which represents the blue-collar workplace, was the dominant union council. Negotiations between the LO and SAF set the standard for the whole labor market. In the 1970s, the white-collar and public-sector unions grew in numbers and challenged LO's position. Nevertheless, unions' ability to recruit members was not weakened. Total union membership has not declined in Sweden.

During the 1990s, partly as a result of EU membership, Sweden has initiated some labor reforms, which are largely aimed at decentralizing and individualizing labor relations with specific regulations and duration limits on fixed-term contracts. Further reforms have been advanced by employers, such as these suggested by Jan-Peter Duker, Deputy Manager of the Confederation of Swedish Enterprise.

1. A legal rule of proportionality (i.e., concerted action, such as a strike) should be in proportion to the effect on the public.
2. A ban of sympathy actions by employees who are not involved in a dispute.

3. Compulsory arbitration to force the social partners to negotiate responsible collective agreements.
4. Give mediators stronger powers to postpone or annul noticed conflict actions.
5. Ban conflicts that are dangerous to society.
6. Ban organizations without collective agreements from starting conflict actions in areas where collective agreements do exist.
7. Prohibit trade union strikes against companies where the union has no member.[57]

Increased decentralization and the increase in individual employment contracts such as fixed-term agreements challenge the continuation of the "Swedish Model" of industrial relations. Traditionally, the terms and conditions of employment have been exclusively regulated by collective bargaining agreements, and individual employment contracts have little or no importance in Swedish labor relations. But the pendulum has begun to swing the other way, and such contracts have begun to replace collective bargaining agreements.[58]

Sweden's membership in the EU may have an impact both on its traditional *neutrality* and on relations with its trade unions. Its Parliament, the Riksdag, approved a bill to transfer decision-making capacities to the EU, and because the key aspect of the new EU is a common security and foreign policy, it is not only the old EC's economic powers that will be decided by EU votes, but also questions of foreign and military engagement. EU membership carries with it a shared obligation to bear the burden of potential military engagements, enforcement of a common sanctions regime, and other policies that are not compatible with neutrality.[59] Sweden's labor unions have also had disagreements with its EU partners concerning the Freedom of Movement policies as detailed in Profile 12-2.

It is interesting to note that when confronted by continuing high levels of inflation and simmering industrial unrest, the Swedish government has suggested the establishment of a national scheme to set wage rates not unlike what has been used in Australia, the Accord on Incomes and Prices. So far, however, the Swedish unions have been cautious about such a development that would represent a move away from their traditional position of keeping at "'arm's length'" from government. However, faced with continued opposition from employers who are unwilling to engage in centralized collective bargaining, the unions may find such an accord a more attractive alternative.[60]

France

Industrial relations in France are characterized by a strong legacy of class conflict, anarcho-syndicalism and communism within the labor movement; employer opposition to power sharing, which caused a slow development of collective bargaining rights; and extensive state involvement through legal regulations. The evolution of French collective bargaining is consistent with its cultural heritage. It has been a grant of power from the State (previously represented by royalty) to the *social partners*—employers (previously represented by the nobility) and employees (previously represented by the feudal system). Industrialization started in the early 1800s, followed by the growth of craft unions and then national federations of labor. After World War I, France enacted favorable collective bargaining legislation that increased union membership. In reaction to the Great Depression, France initiated the Popular Front, which paralleled Franklin Roosevelt's New Deal. After World War II, France emerged as a major economic power with large and technologically equipped companies and an active labor movement.

The French system of employee relations is unique in that it emerged from the anarchists and revolutionary socialists within the labor movement (**anarcho-syndicalism**), which led to a working-class culture distrustful of government and employers and bitter

---

SWEDEN AND THE EU RULES ON FREEDOM OF MOVEMENT

It has become more and more common for foreign companies to bring their own labor to Sweden to do work on a temporary basis. Some of these foreign employers join a Swedish employers' association. In so doing, they accept the valid sectoral collective agreements, including the rules banning lockouts and strikes during the agreement's period of validity. They also have to accept the Swedish pay and conditions laid down in these agreements. In February 2005, LO and the Confederation of Swedish Enterprise started talks over principles and starting points for adding new rules to sectoral collective agreements to address foreign employers coming to Sweden and seeking membership of an employers' association. The two parties wanted to create increased possibilities for free movement on the Swedish labor market, together with equal treatment of Swedish and foreign employees and employers.

In August 2005, the parties agreed to a joint recommendation on the application and adaptation of Swedish national sector collective agreements to foreign employers. With regard to wage levels, it is recommended that if the sectoral social partners fail to reach agreement, the issue will be resolved by LO and the Confederation of Swedish Enterprise.

The need for this agreement was demonstrated in 2004 when the Swedish Building Workers' Union launched a boycott of a Latvian construction company, Laval Un Partneri Ltd, and its daughter company, L&P Baltic. L&P Baltic was then working in Waxholm near Stockholm, with a staff of Latvian workers. This company did not apply for membership in an employers' association affiliated to the Confederation of Swedish Enterprise and was thus covered by Swedish labor laws, which did not protect the company from industrial action by a collective agreement's peace clause. The company refused to pay Swedish wages to the Latvian workers and refused to conclude a Swedish collective agreement wanted by the trade union. The blockade from the Swedish Building Workers Union, joined later by the Swedish Electricians Union, went on for 101 days and was stopped only because the company and its staff left the site and returned to Latvia. The Latvian Company sued the Swedish trade unions before the Swedish Labor Court. L&P Baltic argued that the conflict actions were illegal, as they were contrary to EU law. The trade unions argued, however, that the labor actions are allowed in Swedish law and that labor rules are national and not under EU law.

In April 2005 the Labor Court decided that it was necessary to turn to the European Court of Justice (ECJ) for a preliminary ruling. The issue is whether Swedish trade union blockade actions could be permitted to reach a pay agreement with a Latvian construction company situated in Sweden, working with Latvian employees. The Swedish Labor Court found that the contents of EU law was not clear as to the questions of whether the actions taken toward the Latvian company are in line with the prohibition against the restrictions in the articles of a free movement for services and of a prohibition against all discrimination of nationality in the EU Charter.

SOURCE: Annika Berg, "Social Partners Agree on Treatment of Foreign Employers in Sweden," *European Industrial Relations Observator* (European Foundation for the Improvement of Living and Working Conditions, 2004): (August 22, 2005). Available at http://www.eiro.eurofound.eu.int/structure.html. Accessed October 2005. Printed with permission.

---

that class divisions still existed. Employers have exacerbated the situation by their hold on the reigns of authority as a claim of right unfettered by their need for labor. All French governments of whatever persuasion have advocated for the freedom of social partners to negotiate terms and conditions of employment through collective bargaining, but all have also seriously intervened by passing legislation governing those very terms. Reciprocally, employers' associations and unions exert serious pressure on political parties and the government to obtain through legislation what they cannot get through bargaining.[61]

Collective bargaining legislation names the employers' and employees' bodies that have "representative" status; establishes the terms under which bargaining is valid; specifies what subjects are open to negotiation; and details most bargaining practices, for example, the law places an obligation to negotiate annually on pay and on job classifications every five years. Additionally, the State is directly responsible for a series of decisions regarding the minimum wage, hours of work, employment status, and terms and conditions for layoffs. Frequently, the content of collective agreements is merely a repackaging of the wording of general statutory frameworks.

Negotiations can be carried out at all levels of economic activity, national, sector, or company, as long as recognized bodies take part in them. All employees in a sector or company are covered by an agreement through a State-approved **extension**. Companies that are not even members of the employers' association that entered into the agreement are still covered by a sector-level agreement once the government has extended it. As a general rule, the government always extends sector-level agreements when they comply with statutory criteria and have been signed by recognized bodies. Due to the extension of sector-level agreements by the Ministry of Labour, despite a union membership of less than 10 percent, it is estimated that around 90 percent of private-sector employees in France are covered by sector-level agreements. This system of extension explains the dichotomy for France between **union density**, which is the percentage of workers in the workforce who are union members, and **collective bargaining coverage**, which is the percentage of workers in the workforce who are covered by a collective bargaining agreement (see Table 12-2, Union Density/Collective Bargaining Coverage).

Five union confederations have been recognized as representative bodies to negotiate on behalf of their members and to ensure that labor interests are protected.

CFDT: Confédération française démocratique du travail (French Democratic Confederation of Labor). This trade union confederation is a continuation of the French

TABLE 12-2 Union Density/Collective Bargaining Coverage 2000

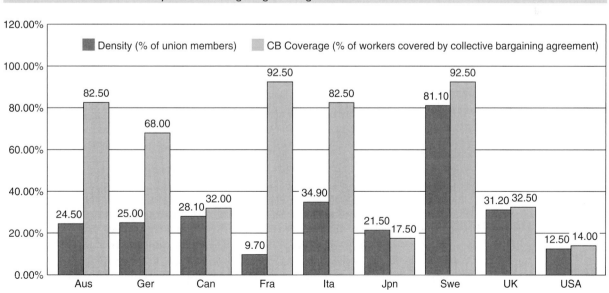

SOURCE OF DATA: *OECD Employment Outlook,* Organization for Economic Co-operation and Development (2004). Available at http://www.oecd.org. Accessed October 2005.

Christian Workers' Confederation, which changed its name in 1964 to mark the wish of the majority of its members to eliminate any religious connotation.

CFTC: Confédération française des travailleurs chrétiens (French Christian Workers' Confederation). Trade union confederation originally formed in 1919, whose name has been preserved by the minority of its members who were opposed to the elimination of the religious connotation and broke away to maintain its traditional image.

CGC-CFE: Confédération générale des cadres-Confédération française de l'encadrement (General Confederation of Professional and Managerial Staff-French Confederation of Professional and Managerial Staff). Trade union confederation that was originally formed in 1946 and is the only one of the five confederations that represents a single occupational category.

CGT: Confédération générale du travail (General Confederation of Labor). Created in two stages, in 1895 and 1906, this is the oldest of the five representative trade union confederations. It still occupies first place among the confederations in terms of the number of votes won in workplace-level elections and, undoubtedly, the number of members.

CGT-FO: Confédération générale du travail-Force ouvrière (General Confederation of Labor-"Force ouvrière"). This trade union confederation (also known simply as FO) was formed in 1947 at the start of the cold war by some CGT's member unions in reaction to CGT's links with the Communist Party. In the spirit of "trade union independence," it rejects all ties with political parties; it focuses only on the promotion of collective bargaining (particularly at multiindustry and industry level). The confederation, whose member unions embrace widely diverse ideological persuasions, claims to be the true heir of a trade unionism whose heritage is free and unfettered collective bargaining.

The low union density in France, 9.7 percent in 2000, may be a result of:

- The change in the French economy caused by a shift from unionized industrial sectors to service sectors
- A growing number of small and medium-sized enterprises (SME)
- High unemployment
- Increase in part-time and temporary workers
- Employers bypassing unions and initiating changes in management styles directly with employees
- Union fragmentation and internal rivalry
- Prohibition of the closed shop
- Union emphasis on "militant" activities as opposed to membership drives
- Extension of union negotiated benefits to nonunion workers
- Lack of financial resources

Employers are represented primarily by *MEDEF* (Mouvement des entreprises de France), which includes 75 percent of all French enterprises. These enterprises are of varying sizes, from different sectors of industry and with diverse ownership structures; however, they share a common interest in modernizing the Labour Code. In March 2004, MEDEF published a report containing 44 proposals on what it views as needed reforms of the Labour Code to make sure " 'the Labour Code no longer constitutes an obstacle to business competitiveness and job creation.' "

The employers' proposals relate to four areas[62]:

Employment contracts	Create a new category of individual employee contracts, "assignment contracts," which would enable employees to be recruited for the duration of a particular project—on an indefinite contract.
	Open up the option of using fixed-term contracts even for jobs linked to the permanent activity of the firm.
	Repeal protections for employees on fixed-term contracts against dismissal on the grounds of physical unfitness for work.
Pay	Annualize the national minimum wage.
	Increases in the minimum wage to be decided on by an independent commission, based on the productivity gains achieved by the least-qualified workers.
Working time	Incorporate only the thresholds set out in the 1993 EU working time Directive, otherwise issues relating to working time—such as when overtime starts, how much of it there should be, and the rate at which it is paid—should be referred to collective bargaining.
Employee representative institutions	Merge current workplace representative structures into a single "social dialogue committee" elected for a four-year term, chaired by the company's chief executive.
	Allow employers to withhold particular information from staff representatives if there is a risk of hampering the operation of the company.
	Reduce the time off for representatives in proportion to the reduction of statutory working time.

Trade unions have unanimously criticized MEDEF's proposals for reform of the Labour Code. One federation calls the document "loudmouth posturing" and sees it as a move by MEDEF to block all genuine discussion with the unions.

None of the topics in the pipeline for bargaining or legislative reform in 2004, however, are more important than addressing the difficult economic situation, pay stagnation, job losses, cuts in civil service employment, layoffs, rises in social security contributions, reductions in medical costs reimbursements, high levels and longer periods of unemployment even for recent graduates, and restrictions in unemployment benefits. All these factors make for a difficult industrial relations environment as evidenced by the reaction to the labor law change in Profile 12-3.

Italy

Modern Italy can be traced to the influence of the French Revolution in 1789, which spurred liberal Italians to push for unification of the various city–states that occupied the Italian peninsula. At the time, Italy consisted of the Kingdoms of Sardinia, the Two Sicilies, the Papal States, Tuscany, and a series of smaller duchies in north-central Italy, all of which had enjoyed self-sufficiency and a strong sense of localism. The Italian unification movement, known as the *Risorgimento,* under the leadership of Camillo Benso, conte di Cavour, and Giuseppe Garibaldi, led Italy to final unification in 1861. Unification combined a group of wealthier northern regions with historical and cultural ties to Austria, Switzerland, and France with a group of southern regions linked to North Africa.

The new nation faced many serious problems. A large debt, few natural resources, and almost no industry or transportation facilities combined with extreme poverty.

YOUTH LABOR LAW IGNITES PROTESTS ACROSS FRANCE

Over a million French teenage workers, union members, and retirees jammed the streets of Paris, France, on March 27, 2006, to protest a new labor law. The protests centered outside the Place de la Bastille, where the historic 1789 French Revolution began over two hundred years before, and followed several weeks of similar protests. The new French labor law that ignited the protests makes it easier for employers to fire young workers. However, some observers, including Serge July, director of the French newspaper *Liberation,* believe the protests are also about the new French "free market system," which is supported by only 36 percent of the French population, compared to 71 percent in the United States and 74 percent in China, according to a poll conducted by the University of Maryland Program on International Policy Attitudes.

The protests coincided with a one-day national strike conducted by French trade unions that closed schools, factories, rail and air traffic, and even the Eiffel Tower. Protests also occurred in other French cities across the country. In Montpellier, a southern French town, protestors took down a statute of former socialist Jean Jaures, claiming it represented their "mourning of the rise of capitalism." Hundreds of protestors were arrested, and in Paris riot police were forced to use water cannons and tear gas to disperse thousands of protestors who began throwing bottles and stones at the police.

French Prime Minister Dominique de Villepin stood firmly behind the new law despite national polls showing his government with only a 20 percent favorable rating. The new law allows employers to fire workers under the age of 26 without reason during the first two years of work. Called "the first contract," the new law is known as CPE in France and is designed to lower national unemployment estimated at 9.6 percent for all workers and 23 percent for workers under age 26. The rationale behind the new law was that employers would be more likely to hire additional workers if they knew they were not required to keep them. The former law made it almost impossible for employers to fire workers unless they committed "grievous mistakes" or the company faced bankruptcy, and even then a worker could go to court where judges usually ruled in favor of the worker.

On April 10, President Jacques Chirac "caved in to" the protesters and canceled the law. The announcement was seen as a major political blow to Villepin, who had hoped to succeed Chirac as president of France.

After over a million French teenage workers, union members, and retirees protested a new labor law in the streets of Paris, President Jacques Chirac cancelled the implementation of the act, which critics say would have made it easier for employers to fire young workers.

SOURCE: Adapted from: Andrew Higgins, "Liberte, Precarite: Labor Law Ignites Anxiety in France," *Wall Street Journal* (March 28, 2006), pp. A1, A8; John Leicester, "Labor Law Protests Widen in France," *Associated Press* (March 29, 2006); and Christine Ollivier, "France Rescinds Labor Law; Protesters Win," *Louisville Courier Journal* (April 11, 2006), p. A4.

Regionalism was still strong, and only a fraction of the citizens had the right to vote. During the 1880s, in Italy as in other European countries, a socialist movement began to develop among workers in the cities. Throughout this period (1870–1915), the nation was governed by a series of coalitions of liberals to the left and right of center who were unable to form a clear-cut majority. Despite the fact that some economic and social progress took place before World War I, Italy during those prewar decades, in an attempt to increase its international influence and prestige, joined in an alliance with Germany and Austria and tried unsuccessfully to conquer Ethiopia and Libya. After the outbreak of World War I in 1914, Italy remained neutral for almost a year, then finally joined the Allies. Aside from a few victories in 1918, Italy suffered serious losses of men, materiel, and morale, and under the treaties that followed the war Italy received only a small part of the territories it had expected. These disappointments produced a powerful wave of nationalist sentiment against the Allies and the Italian government.

Italy was plunged into deep social and political crisis by the war, and the 1919 elections suddenly made the Socialist and the new Popular (Catholic) parties the largest in parliament. In the midst of these unsettled conditions, Benito Mussolini, a former revolutionary socialist, founded a new movement called *Fascism*. Through shrewd political maneuvering and clandestine violence the Fascists gained increasing support resulting in Mussolini becoming a dictator and imposing a totalitarian regime on the country by means of terror and constitutional subversion. In the 1930s, the Italian army invaded and conquered Ethiopia and Albania, sent troops to support Francisco Franco in the Spanish Civil War, established the Rome-Berlin AXIS with Adolph Hitler, and entered World War II on Germany's side. Mussolini's war effort met with setbacks and defeats on all fronts so that when the Allies invaded Sicily, Mussolini was forced to resign. Italy then joined in the war against Germany, and anti-Fascist resistance members fought in the German-occupied north for two years. The Allies pushed the German armies out of Italy with great difficulty, and the war ended for Italy in April 1945.

Between 1945 and 1948, Italians abolished the monarchy in favor of a republic and adopted a new constitution. The Italian nation emerged from the disaster of fascism and war under the leadership of its largest political party, the Christian Democrats. That party stressed industrial growth, agricultural reform, and close cooperation with the United States and the Vatican. With massive U.S. aid, Italy's economy recovered with a rapid industrial expansion and an increase in the standard of living. In the late 1970s and early 1980s Italy, along with other Western nations, experienced chronic inflation and unemployment. Labor unrest, frequent government scandals, and the violence of extremists all contributed to a volatile political situation. In 1981 the Christian Democrats relinquished the premiership first to a Republican and then to a Socialist. The Socialist government was succeeded by two short-lived coalitions and then by a return of Christian Democrats in July 1989. The dominance of the Christian Democratic Party during much of the postwar period lent continuity and comparative stability to Italy's political situation.

However, from 1992 to 1997, Italy faced significant challenges as voters demanded political, economic, and ethical reforms. In 1993 referendums, voters approved substantial changes, including moving from a proportional to a largely majoritarian electoral system. New political forces and new alignments of power emerged in March 1994 national elections, which swept media magnate Silvio Berlusconi and his "Freedom Pole" coalition into office, his first time as prime minister. A series of center-left coalitions dominated Italy's political landscape between 1996 and 2001, when national elections returned Berlusconi to power at the head of the five-party center-right "Freedom House" coalition, comprising the prime minister's own party, *Forza Italia,* the *National Alliance,* the *Northern League,* the *Christian Democratic Center,* and the *United Christian Democrats.* Because of a poor showing in regional elections, he was again forced to resign in April 2005 and form a new government, which was the 60th government since the liberation of Italy.[63]

Industrial relations in Italy are governed by its Constitution, Acts of Parliament, regional laws, customs and practice, and also European Union (EU) measures affecting employment and any adopted Recommendations and Conventions of the International Labour Organization. The Constitution

- Recognizes trade union freedom and collective bargaining (Article 39)
- Recognizes the right to strike (Article 40)
- Recognizes employee participation in enterprises (Article 46)
- Recognizes the right to work (Article 4)
- Charges the republic with a duty to protect labor (Article 35)
- Establishes the right to pay based on quantity and quality of work (Article 36)
- Calls for the registration of trade unions for the purpose of extending the terms of labor agreements to all workers in the industry, union and non-union, known as an *erga omnes* effect.

The Workers' Statute guarantees the freedom of opinion, the right to form and join unions, and the right to carry on union activity at the workplace. It provides trade union representation in firms with more than 15 workers and includes the right to collective bargaining at the company or production facility level, as well as the right to call a strike at company level. Companies may not take actions to suppress union activity. Employers and unions are involved in determining the overall direction of general policy with respect to legislative activity and economic policy and planning.

One can track the historic development of Italian industrial relations through its legislative enactments. Following the adoption of the Italian Constitution in 1944, an effort to exert public control over the labor market resulted in legislation that set minimum standards of employment protection based on a model of open-ended lifelong employment contracts and restrictions on the use of temporary labor and on dismissing employees. These measures were followed by legislation promoting trade unionism with the passage of the Workers' Statute in 1970. At the beginning of the 1980s, to address the serious economic recession, legislation was passed that introduced new working patterns, such as part-time work, work training contracts, and measures governing company restructuring. In the 1990s a new concept of labor law focused on *flexibility*. Acts were passed that aimed not just at safeguarding individual workers in existing jobs, but also at protecting overall employment by supporting the systems of production (i.e., corporate enterprises). These measures included giving greater scope to private collective bargaining, both collective and individual, changing access to employment by expanding the direct hiring of some workers, and abolishing the practice of government monopoly on employment services. Finally, implementation of the EU's employment measures has made the labor market more flexible and modernized the rules governing labor relations.

Reform of Italian labor law to enhance the match between labor demand and supply, relating primarily to job placement services and forms of employment, culminated in June 2003, with the approval of a draft decree enacting a new law on employment and the labor market, the so-called Biagi reform, named after Italian Labor Ministry consultant Marco Biagi, whose assassination in 2002 is linked with the reform law and is discussed in Profile 12-4. The draft decree

- Creates a special register for employment agencies to improve work entry possibilities by the unemployed.

MARCO BIAGI, INTERNATIONAL LABOR MARTYR

In the United States, the violence that accompanied the fledgling labor movement in the nineteenth century produced regrettable but infrequent incidents of deaths among labor leaders. Such incidents, however, are far removed from today's labor movement. But it would seem the same is not true in Italy. On March 19, 2002, terrorists, claiming to be from the "Red Brigades," murdered Marco Biagi, an Italian labor law and industrial relations expert, who was working with the Italian Labor Ministry on labor law reforms. Three years prior to this, terrorists who identified themselves as "Red Brigades" claimed to have murdered Massimo D'Antona, who also advised the government on labor reforms. Biagi was con-

sulting on a proposal to reform the Italian labor market by changing the protections offered laid-off or fired workers under a system that makes a third of Italy's 21 million workers virtually invulnerable to firing. On the day of his death, Biagi had published an article in Italy's leading business newspaper arguing that Italy needed to change its welfare system to catch up with Europe's biggest economies.

The Italian trade unions have always pursued a strategy of protecting employed workers; especially in the first half of the 1970s, when union power was strengthened by economic growth and the mass mobilization of the previous decade, the unions managed to obtain legislation that set restraints on terminations by large firms in the industrial sector. In the 1980s, the use of social shock absorbers (*ammortizzatori sociali*), which cushion the effects of layoffs and restructuring, taxed the wage guarantee fund, introduced in 1945 to be used in situations of temporary crisis, and the extraordinary wage guarantee fund, introduced in 1968, to be used by firms or entire sectors undertaking restructuring as a result of severe structural difficulties. In both cases the benefit paid to workers is 80 percent of the normal wage. This sum is financed by the state and by firms and managed by the National Institute of Social Insurance. The proposal was focusing particular attention on converting these *social shock absorbers* to employment incentives rather than welfare payments, so that those who benefit from the social shock absorbers would have to actively look for a job.

Marco Biagi, 50, was shot dead March 2002 in Bologna, Italy. Biagi worked as advisor for the Italian Labour Ministry on controversial labour reform proposals.

Biagi, a professor of labor law at the University of Modena and a consultant to the EU, was a member of the Italian Socialist Party but had worked with the center-right government of Prime Minister Silvio Berliusconi because he knew that Italy needed to change its labor market. As Biagi biked home from work, he was gunned down by two men on motorcycles outside his home, just steps away from his wife and child and just months after his security escort had been discontinued after threats over his work on a Milan employment pact.[65]

- Places private and public job placement services on an equal footing.
- Extends the right of public and private universities, local authorities, upper secondary schools, employers' associations, trade unions, and certain professional associations to provide job placement services.
- Requires all organizations authorized to offer job placement services to do so free of charge.
- Creates a national continuous labor exchange, an online information system that is freely accessible on the Internet.
- Introduces new types of employment contracts to make the employment relationship more adaptable to the needs of firms and workers, including
  - *Fixed-term or open-ended staff leasing contracts* by which companies may hire temporary workers under a lease with employment agencies.
  - *Permanent staff leasing* for particular kinds of work, such as cleaning, surveillance and security, information technology assistance, and other areas specified by collective bargaining. The staff leasing system, where the company has full managerial authority over the workers, will differ sharply from subcontracting or outsourcing, in which cases it is the subcontractor firm that exercises such authority.
  - *On-call jobs*, where the worker is available to be used by the employer during a preestablished period of time. However, the employer may use the worker for only a limited number of days in this period, depending on production peaks and organizational needs, and must notify the worker that his or her services are needed at least one working day in advance.
- Specifies regulations on job sharing, in which workers may decide—informing the employer on a weekly basis—on substitutions and exchanges and may alter their working hours schedules.
- Encourages the use of part-time work, either "vertical," reducing the number of days worked, or "horizontal," which reduces the hours worked every day, to facilitate the labor-market entry of people who need to juggle family responsibilities, study, or other commitments.
- Forbids open-ended contracts for employer-coordinated freelance work by limiting its use to a project or bringing it under the regulations on subordinate work. This form of employment relationship increased significantly between 1999 and 2003. The most recent estimates on the actual incidence of coordinated freelance work indicate a total of around 500,000 workers. This increase has been matched by a substantial growth, in both quantitative and qualitative terms, of collective bargaining covering such workers, which has led to important agreements being reached not only at the company and territorial level but also at the sectoral and national levels.
- Introduces supplementary work of an occasional nature for no more than 30 days per calendar year using "vouchers" comprising both pay and social security contributions that it issues to the worker.
- Creates joint labor management bodies that may deliver a variety of services to job seekers, to workers concluding work contracts, and to people already employed.

CGIL (Communist and Socialist), one of the three largest trade union organizations, objected to these reforms, maintaining that labor will increasingly become a commodity, so that the work contract will be turned into a form of mere commercial exchange. The other two large union confederations—*CISL* (Christian Democrat) and

UIL (Socialist Republican)—acknowledged that it is necessary to make the labor market more flexible, but maintained that such flexibility should arise from negotiations between the social partners and not from unilateral action by companies.

As a result of the Biagi Law reform measure, collective bargaining negotiations have begun to address and regulate the use of some of these new forms of employment, including an agreement on part-time work negotiated at the local level that provided incentives for companies to increase the number of part-time staff and gave workers time off with pay according to the premium for overtime work established by the sectoral collective agreement, the first national agreement on coordinated freelance contracts in outsourced call centers, and a company-level agreement that established a committee on working hours and an "hours bank" in which workers can accumulate overtime hours.[64]

The involvement of *social partners*—employers and employees—in the design of economic policy, the so-called **concertazione** of the Italian government, has been promoted by the formal adoption of tripartite agreements or *pacts*. Such agreements were signed between labor unions, employers associations, and the government in 1995 to target pension reform; in 1996 to reform the labor market and promote worker education and training; in 1998 to set up a new system of three-way industrial relations, including local authorities; and in 2002, with the goal of reforming the nation's labor market and employment benefits. Employers are represented by three main organizations: Confindustria (industry), Confcommercio (trade), and Confragricultura (agriculture). *Confindustria* represents the interests of small companies at the regional and local level and the private-sector industry at a national level. The three largest trade unions, CGIL, CISL and UIL, although often with competing agendas, are united in a single confederation to work toward common objectives in the interests of all workers. This commitment has been manifested both in requests to the government to introduce—again cooperatively—policies for development and innovation and in the recent creation of a single committee to examine reform of the bargaining structure.

That bargaining structure was established by a tripartite pact as framework for income policy and new rules for the wage bargaining system. The *Protocol on Labour Costs of July 1993* provides for a two-tier wage bargaining system: at the national industry level, collective bargaining agreements are valid for four years on the terms and conditions of employment and for two years for wages and economic benefits and are intended to set minimum wage levels; and at the company or firm level, agreements are valid for four years and may link pay to company profits and increases in productivity.[66] National agreements are binding for all employers in a sector under a principle known as *erga omnes*.[67] In theory, consistent with this two-tiered approach to bargaining, economic decisions at the national level are to be influenced by external measures regarding the competitive position of the affected industry and the rate of inflation. At the company level pay is linked to the performance achieved in relationship to the expectations of the parties.

In the face of continuing difficulties in the Italian economy, Confindustria has proposed new action strategies that require reform of the production system—mainly by means of large investments in research and in the development of infrastructures—and the resumption of meaningful dialogue with the trade unions and the government. Amid the apparent stagnation of Italian industry, these events can be interpreted as signaling a renewed commitment by trade unions and employers' associations to participate with the government in the definition of economic and social policies, which may prove crucial for the Italian economic system to improve its competitiveness.[68]

FAR EAST

Western industrialization took place primarily in a laissez-faire setting, not under direct government direction or patronage. An entrepreneurial middle class moved the industrialization process forward, which in turn created a distinctive and relatively homogeneous working class. This working class was able to organize into trade unions to protect its interests. Western governments did not "create" unions. Western industrial relations systems reached maturity in the twentieth century, long after the commencement of the industrial revolution and at a time when democratic political systems were more or less in place. The industrial relations systems that developed were underpinned by a value system based on democratic principles, a balance between employers and employees, and relatively minimal government intervention. In such an environment collective bargaining and freedom of association were logical developments.

On the other hand, the majority of Asian countries were subject to foreign occupation, so no indigenous entrepreneurial middle class of any significance emerged that could have spearheaded the industrialization process. During the colonial period governments assumed a dominant role, which was maintained by the postindependence governments. Only after the industrialization process had been in operation for some time did an entrepreneurial class emerge to take over some part of the government's role in economic activity. In Japan, China, and Korea, for example, the governments nurtured and assisted in the development of these entrepreneurial classes and provided them with protection from competition until they achieved international competitiveness. The economic development and its imperatives, then, were government and not entrepreneurial driven.

Japan

Contrary to most aspects of Japanese society, the Japanese system of labor relations is not the product of years of tradition. Japan's industrialization began in the 1880s with ownership of a majority of its enterprises concentrated in powerful family groups, which later became the powerful *keiretsu* group of holding companies. Keiretsu is a loose conglomeration of companies organized around a single bank for their mutual benefit. The companies sometimes, but not always, own equity in each other. These families ran their factories in a paternalistic tradition, not unlike U.S. company towns of the same era. Although some trade unions were around prior to World War II, they had very little impact. After WWII during the occupation of Japan by Allied forces, the Japanese labor movement was encouraged, so by 1949, 55.8 percent of the workforce was unionized. In Japan as elsewhere, however, union membership hovered around 30 percent from the 1950s to the 1970s, fell to 20 percent in the early 1980s, and in 2003 unionization rate dropped to 19.6 percent.[69]

The Japanese system of labor relations can be summarized as having three key premises. The first key premise is the concept of lifetime employment. Japan's lifetime employment is not so much a guaranteed benefit as a result of how enterprises are organized. Regular employees enter a firm with the expectation that they will be kept on until they reach the mandatory retirement age of 60. These employees are hired not for specific jobs or occupations but as company employees, knowing that the employer will exhaust all other measures before laying these regular employees off. Japanese firms compete with each other every spring to recruit the best of the new university and high school graduates as regular employees. The desirability of each graduate is normally determined as much by the prestige attached to his/her university or school as by academic record.

The second key premise is the traditional Japanese wage system based on seniority. New employees are given a monthly salary based on the individual's level of educational attainment but not job assignment. This sum automatically rises at least annually in accordance with a published table on the basis of length of service. Japan also has a distinctive bonus system, under which workers are given bonuses twice yearly (June and December). These bonuses are described as a deferred salary payment and constitute a significant portion of the workers' annual income. The amount of the bonus is either negotiated with a union or based on custom and traditionally is not tied to profits.[70]

The third key premise is that although Japanese labor unions are organized into three tiers—enterprise-based unions, industry-level unions, and national federations—over 90 percent are enterprise-based unions. These company unions engage in collective bargaining and consultation with company management. Together, these three management methods, lifetime employment, seniority-based pay, and company unions, served as a mechanism in which both managers and employees could develop their knowledge and ability within the company in the security of the practice of long-term stable employment. The result was that expertise and know-how was accumulated within the organization.

However, there is some evidence to suggest that employment is becoming unstable and that regular employment is giving way to nonregular employees. The U.S. Department of Labor has dubbed the 1990s Japan's "Lost Decade," during which the country's growth in gross domestic product (GDP) averaged less than half the percent average of the preceding decade. Japan has struggled to recover from deflation in the wake of the burst economic "bubble" of the early nineties. In 2001 Japan's unemployment was 5.5 percent, in 2002 it was 5.4 percent, and in 2003, it averaged 5.3 percent, down 0.1 percentage point from the record high set in 2002 and the first improvement in 13 years.[71] The rise in the jobless rate was primarily due to layoffs in manufacturing, construction, and retail.

In the current economic climate, there are few advocates of lifetime employment guarantees, but tradition and inflexible labor laws governing dismissal still cause employers to exercise extreme caution in dismissing workers. In recent years, Japanese companies have shifted toward a wage system that is linked to performance and bonuses to overall corporate profits because Japanese businesses now face increasing global competition and need to motivate their workers.

Japan is increasing the scope of its employment legislation to deal with the new economic and social conditions. A council established by Japan's government called for legal reform in the employment/labor field to encourage labor mobility, industrial structure transformation, and diversified working patterns. Lawmakers in 2003 added an explicit clause that (1) required employers to have just cause when dismissing employees; (2) increased the maximum duration of a fixed-term labor contract from one to three years (five years for workers engaged in highly specialized duties and those aged 60 and above); (3) extended the period from one to three years that a worker may be "dispatched" and the types of job dispatched workers (i.e., temporary workers) can engage in; (4) granted local public bodies the right to provide free job placement services; (5) increased the contribution rate for the unemployment insurance program; (6) lowered the maximum amount of unemployment benefits; (7) enabled a panel of a judge and two labor experts to provide rapid, specific solutions for labor disputes; and (8) extended the retirement age until the age of 65.

The Constitution of Japan provides for freedom of association, the right to organize, and the right to act collectively. The courts have interpreted the right to act collectively as extending to the right to strike. The Trade Union Law protects Japanese workers in exercising autonomous self-organization for the purpose of collective action, defines collective action as the right to engage in union activities and the right to strike, and allows unions and employers to negotiate with each other and to conclude collective bargaining agreements. The Trade Union Law proscribes an employer's refusal to bargain collectively as an unfair labor practice.

The most representative organization of employers is the Japan Federation of Employers Association (Nikkeiren). This association was founded in 1948 to promote harmonious labor management relations and currently has a membership of 47 prefectural employers' associations and 60 industrial organizations. Nikkeiren serves as a liaison with the government and the trade unions, engages in policy study and research, and conducts training programs.

Japanese labor unions basically have a "triplicate structure," enterprise labor unions organized at each business, industrial trade unions organized as loose federations of enterprise union members by industry, and national centers made up of the industry trade unions at the national level, a typical example being the Japanese Trade Union Confederation, *Rengo*.

Collective bargaining is practiced widely in Japan on the terms and conditions of employment. However, issues affecting management and production, such as new plant and equipment and subcontracting, usually are resolved through regular consultations between the unions and management. The Japanese joint consultation system provides a means for continual information sharing and communication. Joint consultation committees are made up of both senior corporate executives and high-level union officials. These committees do not conduct wage negotiations, but it is common for the enterprise to share confidential business and financial information with the union through these committees before wage negotiations. The approach of Japanese employers and unions to a cooperative collective bargaining process through information sharing has resulted in more employment security but more moderate wage increases.[72]

Collective bargaining negotiations normally do not cover wages, which are negotiated separately during the Spring Wage Offensive (**shunto**). The Spring Wage Offensive has occurred annually since 1955. During shunto, enterprise-based unions in each industry conduct negotiations simultaneously with their companies. The objectives of shunto are to provide each individual union with a greater bargaining power and to distribute wage increases proportionally across the industry. Recently, shunto negotiations have shifted away from wages to job security due to the current economic situation.

Rengo, formed in 1989 with the merger of public- and private-sector unions, is the largest national trade union organization in Japan, representing over seven million members, almost two-thirds of Japanese organized labor. In 2000, 11.4 million of an eligible 53.8 million Japanese workers were unionized. The most important role of the national trade unions is their participation in politics. Rengo represents the labor sector on various government advisory bodies and actively takes part in decision-making processes concerning labor policy.

Korea

The Republic of Korea was formally established in 1948 and existed under authoritarian rule for four decades. In 1987, Korea embraced multiparty democratic politics and is now governed by a directly elected president and a unicameral legislature selected by direct voting.[73] In the mid-1960s, Korea's workforce was mobilized to promote export-led development. This strategy brought rapid increases in the gross national product but also left workers with relatively low wages for some of the longest hours in the industrialized world. The government, then as now, played a key role in directing the economy. The government's chosen agency for the country's economic development is in the companies it supports, its *chaebol*. The chaebol are the large, conglomerate family-controlled firms of South Korea characterized by strong ties with government agencies. When the government nationalized the banks of South Korea, it could channel capital to the industries and firms it saw as necessary for achieving national objectives.

Korea's economic structure began to change in the 1990s when export growth slowed considerably and wage hikes priced Korea out of labor-intensive export markets. The Korean economy began to slow down, and by late 1997, the country was fully engulfed by the Asian financial and economic crisis. Since 1997, the government has focused on economic recovery and prevention of another such crisis. The top 30 chaebol contribute about 95 percent of the nation's gross national product, and its top five—Hyundai, Samsung, LG, Daewoo, and Sunkyoung—contribute about 60 percent.[74]

Korea's labor system is a true three-party system, with considerable authority placed in the Ministry of Labor. The Ministry is responsible for formulating labor policy, as well as monitoring compliance with and implementation of the Constitution and the labor law, which govern labor management relations, child labor, forced labor, employment equality, wages and hours of work, and occupational safety and health. The trade union federations and employers' organizations represent their constituents regarding labor matters by giving advice and guidance to the Ministry, as well as actively participating on government *advisory* commissions.

The Korea Employers Federation (KEF), the most representative organization of employers, was founded in 1970 to serves as an umbrella organization representing 13 regional employers' associations and roughly 4,000 enterprises. The KEF advocates its members' interests to the government and the trade unions and participates in national and local bodies concerned with social policy issues; it provides advice to its members with regard to the labor law and industrial relations matters and engages in policy study and research.

Korean trade unions may be organized by company, by occupation, by region, or by industry. Although the majority of unions in Korea are enterprise-based unions, there are 44 industrial federations and 2 national federations: the Federation of Korean Trade Unions (FKTU), which is the largest labor organization in Korea, representing some 950,000 workers in 3,408 unions, and the Korean Confederation of Trade Unions (KCTU), a "dissident" union movement that represents about 600,000 workers in 16 industrial federations. FKTU's objectives include establishing labor rights that are universally recognized and respected, a fairer distribution of resources, and a better quality of life. It provides assistance to member unions in negotiations and also represents its members in consultations with the government and the KEF. The KCTU is committed to employment security, an improvement in working conditions, a living wage, a reduction in working hours, and the elimination of all forms of discrimination. The KCTU also is a proponent of collective action as a means to achieve progress. At the end of 2002, four members of the KCTU trade unionists were being held in prison for instigating violent strikes or illegally disrupting businesses.

The **Korean Tripartite Commission** is a consultative body composed of representatives from government, labor, business, and the public that discusses labor policies and acts as an advisory body to the president of the Republic of Korea. The Tripartite Commission is credited with making recommendations that helped overcome Korea's financial and economic crisis of 1997, promoted laws to guarantee the right of trade unions to undertake political activities, granted teachers the right to organize, and called for the establishment of a 40-hour, 5-day workweek.

Korea has recovered from the Asian economic and financial crisis of 1997 and experienced a 3 percent growth in the wake of the global economic slowdown of 2001 and saw its unemployment rate decreased from 3.7 percent in 2001 to 3 percent in 2002. The country is experiencing a shortage of low-skilled laborers, and as a solution, the government has allowed the entry of migrant workers for three-year terms.

Korea's labor relations are governed by numerous labor laws, including the Constitution of the Republic of Korea and the Trade Union and Labor Relations Adjustment Act (TULRAA), which guarantees freedom of association, the right to bargain collectively, and the right to take collective action. Despite such legal protections, the International Labour Organization's Committee on Freedom of Association has been reviewing an ongoing complaint since 1996 against the government of Korea for the arrest and detention of trade unionists, the government's refusal to register new labor organizations, and the adoption of labor legislation contrary to freedom of association.

Individual and collective labor disputes are adjudicated and mediated or arbitrated by the Labor Relations Commission, a tripartite quasi-judicial government body. The 12 Regional Labor Relations Commissions handle cases concerning labor disputes occurring in their individual regions. The National Commission reviews the decisions made by the regional bodies, mediates labor disputes that fall under the jurisdiction of two or more of the regional commissions, and handles emergency arbitrations.

Workers have the right to form or join trade unions, with the exception of public-sector employees not designated by law. Teachers were legislated the right to organize in 1999 and blue-collar workers in the postal service, railways, telecommunications, and the National Medical Center are allowed to unionize. Other public-sector employees have been able to form workplace councils since 1999. In 2001, Korean trade unions numbered 6,150, with a total membership of 1.57 million, which is 7.3 percent of employed workers.

Only two employees are needed to form a trade union, but the union must register with the proper administrative authorities. In 1997, changes were made to the labor law authorizing the formation of multiple unions at the enterprise level in 2002. However, both trade unions and employers were apprehensive about the repercussions of introducing multiple unions into companies, and therefore, implementation was postponed until 2006 by mutual agreement.

The right to strike is guaranteed by both the Constitution and the Trade Union law, although strikes are prohibited in government agencies, state-owned enterprises, and defense industries. A majority of union members must vote in favor of striking by direct, secret, and unsigned balloting, and the union must report the planned strike in advance.

The Constitution and the TULRAA provide for the right of workers to bargain collectively, which is practiced extensively in Korea. In general, collective bargaining takes place at the enterprise level, but a union may delegate negotiation responsibility to the trade union federation with which it is affiliated. Collective bargaining usually covers wages, hours of work, workers' welfare, and other employment conditions. Negotiations also extend to trade union activities during working hours and issues concerning full-time union officers. Parties must submit the collective agreements to the government authorities, which can determine such a collective agreement unlawful and can order the agreement amended.

The TULRAA protects workers from dismissal for organizing or joining a union, or attempting to do so, and for participating in union activities. A worker may seek relief for any such unfair labor practices by filing a complaint with the LRC or by bringing a civil suit against the employer. Workers more often choose the LRC, as court cases tend to be lengthy and costly. Employers found guilty of unfair labor practices can be required to reinstate workers and provide back pay.

China

For centuries China, the third-largest country in the world occupying one-fifteenth of the world's landmass, stood as a leading civilization, outpacing the rest of the world in the arts and sciences. But in the nineteenth and early twentieth centuries, the country was beset by civil unrest, major famines, military defeats, and foreign occupation. After World War II, the Communists under Mao Zedong established an autocratic socialist system that imposed strict controls over everyday life.

In late 1978 Deng Xiaoping and other leaders began moving the economy from a sluggish, inefficient, centrally planned economy to a more market-oriented system. Although the system still operates within a political framework of strict state control, the economic influence of nonstate organizations and individual citizens has been steadily increasing. China replaced old collectives with a system of household and village responsibility in agriculture, increased the authority of local officials and plant managers in industry, permitted a wide variety of small-scale enterprises in services and light manufacturing, and opened the economy to increased foreign trade and investment. The result has been a quadrupling of GDP since 1978 and an amazing growth in foreign trade (Table 12-3). Measured on a purchasing power parity (PPP) basis, China in 2004 stood as the second-largest economy in the world after the United States.

China has benefited from globalization in the computer Internet industry and has a lead in the absorption of technology and a rising prominence in world trade. China is likely to post a 9.5 percent economic growth for the second half of 2005, slowing to 8.5 to 9.0 percent in the full year of 2006.[75]

The transition toward a market economy has led to changes in the labor relations environment. The starting point of China's industrial relations system was an economy based on the state ownership of the means of production and strict centralized control of wages, prices, and employment. This planned economy was able to reconcile the interests of workers, managers, and the state with an administrative framework guaranteed by the central government. China initially attempted to develop a

TABLE 12-3	Growth of China's Foreign Trade (1995–2004) (Unit USD$ 1 billion)	
Year	*Imports*	*Exports*
1995	148.78	132.08
1996	151.05	138.83
1997	182.79	142.37
1998	183.71	140.24
1999	194.93	165.70
2000	249.20	225.09
2001	266.10	243.55
2002	325.60	295.17
2003	438.37	412.84
2004	593.40	561.40

SOURCE: *China Statistical Yearbook*, China Statistics Press, 1999; General Administration of Customers of the PRC, China's Customs Statistics from Chinability at www.chinability.com.

A Chinese woman sews shirts at the Youngor Group's textile factory in Ningbo, in China's Zhejiang province, June 2005.

"**socialist market economy**" in which state ownership of the means of production would be retained but the control of wages, prices, and employment would be relaxed and a private sector would be allowed to develop.[76] China revised that economic model, much as Korea has done with its chaebol, to strongly favor state-owned enterprises, granting them preferential access to capital, technology, and markets, and, at the same time, to allow foreign investment, resulting in foreign firms claiming much of China's industrial exports.[77] China relaxed its guarantees of employment, wages, and welfare as these **state-owned enterprises** (SOEs) became subject to competitive market pressures, and the central government turned over responsibility for economic management and financial solvency to the SOEs.

This transformation challenged trade unions in China because they had been a part of the socialist system, not as workers' representatives but performing state functions in the workplace. The All-China Federation of Trade Union's constitution had described their role as "transmission belts between the [communist] party and the masses."[78] They focused on the day-to-day shop floor problems to ensure the success of the enterprise, while educating the workers and making sure they were not exploited. With entry into the global economy, jobs and living standards have become subordinate issues to SOEs being competitive. So the growing divergence of interest between employers (the state) and employees has led to increased worker unrest. So in China, as in the countries discussed earlier, the emergence of trade unions as worker representatives, and not the representatives of employers, has been as a result of labor unrest.

Legislatively, China's 1994 Labour Law defines the minimum terms and conditions of labor and replaced guaranteed lifetime employment with labor contracts. The labor contracts could cover wages, working hours, rest and vacations, occupational safety and health, insurance, and welfare. The law was supplemented by regulations from the Ministry of Labour, which stressed that the collective contract should be arrived at by consultation, rather than "bargaining." By the end of 2001, 120 million employees had signed such contracts.[79] The law also created a procedure for dispute resolution in which the union's primary role was to mediate between the employer and employee, not advocate the employee's position. The 1992 Trade Union Law specifies that trade unions may sign collective contracts with managers of enterprises on behalf of the workers, with such contracts being submitted to workers for approval.

Philosophically, China's industrial relations within its socialist market economy have a fundamental difference from industrial relations within capitalist economies. According to the theory of the socialist market economy, state ownership of the enterprise means that the "employers" are really custodians of the interests of the entire society. The trade union, then, is not supposed to represent the employees *against* the employer, but the entire enterprise, just as the employers do. Therefore, collective contracting and resolution of disputes were nonadversarial, resolved on the basis of the common interest of the whole.[80] That philosophy began to change somewhat with the transition to a capitalist market economy, albeit made up primarily of SOEs. These enterprises had to cover their costs and realize a profit to finance future development, which refocused their attention from the collective good to the bottom line. Trade unions found their roles somewhat enhanced as actual representatives of the employees rather than just transition belts between the government and the workers.

But trade unionism in China, as in other "new" economies, suffers from its inability to pressure employers, be they either SOEs or foreign investors, without resorting to conflict tactics that might provoke social unrest and renewed repression, as had been experienced after the Tiananmen Square incident in 1989.

One approach being explored in China is the development of a relatively benign tripartite "collective consultation" between the government, unions, and employers at national, provincial, and municipal levels. The goals of the tripartite consultation are to establish an appropriate legal and regulatory framework for the conduct of industrial relations; to foster collective consultations in all enterprises; to establish a forum for considering the government's social, labor, and welfare policies; and to forestall or resolve labor conflicts that escape the bounds of conflict resolution. The three parties include the All-China Federation of Trade Unions (ACFTU) representing employees, the Ministry of Labor and Social Security (MOLSS) representing the government, and the China Enterprise Confederation (CEC) representing employers. Some observers worry that the goals set for the tripartite consultation cannot be met with the current membership. The MOLSS participation limits the discussion to labor relations and avoids any broader review of government policies and, particularly, its expenditures. The CEC, although originally sponsored by the government, is now a fee organization and is largely dominated by the larger SOEs. Its role has become increasingly limited to a vehicle for employer contacts with the government, rather than an employer representative organization. And ACFTU is a labor organization that is supposed to represent the rights and interests of employees while fulfilling its responsibilities to the government to maintain social stability.[81]

Despite attempts to refocus the role of trade unions within China's economy, the predominant function of trade unions continues to be largely managerial: encouraging workers to increase productivity and enforcing discipline. Its role as protector of employees' interest is largely limited to monitoring managerial practices to ensure compliance with applicable laws, dealing with personal problems, distributing benefits, and arranging celebrations. The trade union's role in arriving at a collective agreement is largely done by a consensus method. The trade union prepares the initial draft of a contract based on the previous contract, which contains general terms and conditions, primarily confined to compliance with existing laws. The draft is shared with members, and then it is discussed with management in a consultation committee. The union defers to management on any contentious issue. The agreed version is referred to the members for endorsement, generally without discussion or debate. Wage negotiation is separate from contract negotiation, and management takes the lead in the process. Wage proposals, generally set by labor market pressures, are submitted to the trade unions whose role is to convey the workers' response to management and to convince the employees of the justice of management's offer.[82]

SUMMARY

Globalization in the twenty-first century has increased competition between nations for investment, technology, and labor. The international trade union movement has been seen as a uniting force, able, perhaps, to institutionalize worker protections within various political and legal systems. In studying labor relations around the world, a comparison can be seen between a number of countries and the United States in the way the labor movement grew from industrialization. Whether the industrial revolution began in the early 1800s, as it did in England, or in Japan a century later, the unskilled workers needed to fuel the industries were vulnerable to being treated as a commodity. So although industrialization brought progress and prosperity, workers found it necessary to band together to make sure they could reap benefits from both.

Great Britain had for years followed a voluntary approach to labor relations, which focused on a union's and an employer's agreement to engage in collective bargaining, rather than legislative fiats. That situation changed somewhat in the 1980s when Prime Minister Margaret Thatcher outlawed secondary strikes, limited picketing and prohibited a closed shop. Australia's industrial relations system uses compulsory conciliation and arbitration to resolve collective bargaining impasses. Prior to the 1980s, most of the time wages and terms of conditions of employment were established across industries once an "award" was arrived at by negotiators or imposed by the arbitrator. Australia modernized its system by streamlining the award system and emphasizing enterprise rather than industry wide bargaining. Canada combined British-style voluntarism in recognition of unions, American-style welfare capitalism in labor benefits laws, and Australian-style government-mandated mediation and fact-finding for its industrial relations.

In Europe, oligarchies and democracies, capitalists and socialists caused the labor movement to embrace a threefold agenda: representing employees and advancing their employment interests through collective action, increasing workers' protections through active engagement in the political process, and improving the lives of workers through the promotion of welfare and education agendas. The EU has become a powerful economic and political entity through its Single Market and Social Charter principles. However, it is still struggling to increase labor mobility despite linguistic and cultural differences, problems with benefit portability, and inconsistent training and education standards.

Japan and Korea had both been subject to foreign occupation so that when the industrial revolution arrived, they had no indigenous entrepreneurial middle class to finance and grow their needed industries. So in those countries powerful families, with the help of the government, became the entrepreneurs and opened and ran the factories with the government's help. The Allied Powers fostered the labor movement in Japan after World War II. In Korea, the labor movement still struggles today against a basically hostile government. China, emerging from its Communist economy, continues to support state-owned enterprises but has opened itself to foreign investment and has become a major contributor to the global economy.

And although it is not a significant player in the history of the labor movement in the United States, the International Labour Organization is a 70-year-old organization dedicated to the key principles of the labor movement: labor is not a commodity, workers have the right to organize into unions, and workers have the right to bargain with their employers about wages and the terms and conditions of their employment. ILO's international standards bring focus and unity to the labor movement around the world, particularly in developing nations.

CASE STUDIES

Case Study 12-1 Insider Trading By Union Official

Mr. Bang is the politically elected general secretary of the Finansforbundet, which is a trade union representing workers employed within the financial sector. Mr. Grøngaard was the employee-elected member of the executive board of the company RealDanmark, a publicly traded company and a major financial institution. Mr. Grøngaard had also been appointed by the union as a member of the corporate liaison committee, established by an agreement between RealDanmark and the union.

Mr. Grøngaard disclosed inside information to Mr. Bang following an extraordinary board meeting of RealDanmark. Mr. Grøngaard disclosed to Mr. Bang the details of a discussion on merger negotiations with Danske Bank, another publicly traded financial institution. Mr. Bang consulted his two deputy general secretaries, Mr. Madsen and Mr. Nielsen, and a colleague in the secretariat of the Union, Mr. Christensen, passing on the same information that he had received from Mr. Grøngaard. Mr. Christensen purchased shares in RealDanmark for approximately EUR 48 000.

Further discussions on merger details were held at a RealDanmark board meeting and at a meeting of the Liaison Committee. Mr. Grøngaard was present at both meetings. He again approached Mr. Bang with a view to helping employees deal with the consequences of the merger. They notably discussed the planned schedule for the merger, as well as the expected increase in the value of RealDanmark's shares of between 60 percent and 70 percent. Mr. Bang passed on information to the head of the secretariat of the Union, Mr. Larsen, and to his colleague, Mr. Christensen, including the planned date of notification of the merger and the anticipated conversion rate. Mr. Christensen purchased additional shares in RealDanmark for approximately EUR 214 000.

When the merger between RealDanmark and Dansk Bank was made public, RealDanmark's stock price increased by 65 percent. Mr. Christensen sold his shares in RealDanmark, making a net gain of around EUR 180 000. He was later sentenced to six-months' imprisonment for insider dealing.

Criminal proceedings were brought against Mr. Bang and Mr. Grøngaard for disclosing privileged information in breach of the Danish Law on Trade in Transferable Securities. Paragraph 36(1) of the Law provides that "... any person in possession of inside information may not disclose such information to any other person unless such disclosure is made in the normal course of the exercise of his employment, profession or duties."

The issue was brought to the attention of the EU Commission because of Mr. Bang and Mr. Grøngaard's contention that their disclosure was protected under the EU's Directive concerning the fundamental rights on the information and consultation of workers. The right of workers to be informed and consulted can conflict with the disclosure requirements imposed by the law on Transferable Securities. The rationale behind the disclosure prohibition is that the more people are entrusted with inside information, the higher the risk is that someone will take advantage of it, thereby affecting the integrity of the market. Any exception to such prohibition risks undermining investors' confidence in the market and should therefore be construed narrowly.

The questions presented to the court as to Mr. Grøngaard were (1) whether an employee-elected board member may seek advice from an expert to perform the specific function of an employee-elected board member; (2) whether the general secretary of a trade union should be regarded as an expert in social and industrial relations; (3) whether he can consult with his appointing authority (i.e., the union) concerning his representation of the workers who might be affected by the planned merger; and (4) whether there is any difference between the role of employee-elected board member and member of the liaison committee as it relates to the disclosure of insider information.

The Danish government acknowledged that an employee-elected board member may consult an expert to exercise his duties toward the company, but insisted that such advice may be sought only if it is being sought in the interests of the company and only if the expert is bound by a duty of confidentiality. All parties thus acknowledge that a member of the board of directors acts within the normal course of his duties when seeking expert advice. However, the Danish government argued that does not amount to authorizing board members to disclose inside information to their advisers. In other words, a board member can disclose inside information within the normal course of his duties only where he seeks advice to perform his duties and limits such disclosure to what is necessary for him to get the relevant expert advice. The Danish government further argued that the general secretary of a trade union cannot be considered an expert in social and industrial relations because in view of his primary mission to protect workers' rights, he cannot be considered unbiased.

As to whether or not all board members had the right to consult their appointing authority, the Danish government contended that it would remain doubtful whether the general secretary of a trade union could be considered the appointing authority of an employee-elected board member, because the latter represents all employees in a company and not only those who are members of the trade union. Finally, the Danish government argued that the roles of board member and liaison member as it relates to disclosure of insider information were the same.

The Union contended that there are interests other than the proper functioning of capital markets, such as the interests of workers, which have to be taken into account. As a result, the interests of workers, and in particular the effects that the transaction may have on their employment situation, will be relevant when assessing whether, in order to perform the specific function of an employee-elected board member, it might be necessary to consult an expert in social and industrial relations. Mr. Grøngaard justified dis-

closing the precise schedule of the planned merger by the need to explain why the Union would have to make resources available to set up a merger task force. He further argued that he had to disclose information on the expected conversion rate to assess whether a competing offer for the company was likely.

The Union further contended that in its interpretation of Danish law, the Danish court will have to take European Community law into account, specifically that the workers' rights to be informed and consulted are protected by Community law. The purpose of that directive, as interpreted by the case law, is "to ensure that the employees of Community-scale undertakings are properly informed and consulted when decisions which affect them are taken in a Member State other than that in which they are employed."

Pointing out that the Danish government attempted to establish a distinction between the advice given by a lawyer and that given by the general secretary of a trade union, the Union argued that to define what may be regarded as an expert consultation would risk unduly restricting the right of a board member, within the performance of his duties, to consult the person he judges the most able. EC law does not in principle appear to debar the general secretary of a trade union from acting as an expert in certain circumstances.

The Union also argued that the liaison committee, which is a specific feature of Danish law, was created by an agreement between RealDanmark and the Union specifically to channel information between a company and a trade union. If the link between the trade union and the liaison committee is sufficiently strong to establish that transmitting information to the liaison committee is equivalent to disclosing it to the trade union, then the disclosure of information by Mr. Grøngaard to Mr. Bang has to be considered lawful.

SOURCE: Adapted from *Anklagemyndigheden v. Grøngaard and Bang,* Case C-384/02, May 25, 2004.

QUESTIONS

1. Do you think Mr. Grøngaard's duty as an employee-elected member of the board of directors should have precluded him from or authorized him to advise the union of the upcoming merger?

2. If Mr. Grøngaard's disclosure to Mr. Bang was protected disclosure because he needed advice

on protecting employees when exercising his vote as a member of the board of directors, is Mr. Bang's disclosure to various union members protected or not protected and why?

3. Is there an inherent conflict for an employee-elected member of a board of directors or a liaison committee member asked to perform his/her representative role without divulging confidential information concerning the enterprises' workers?

KEY TERMS AND CONCEPTS

- anarcho-syndicalism
- awards
- Bretton Woods exchange rate system
- capitalism
- *chaebol*
- codetermination
- collective bargaining coverage
- *concertazione*
- *erga omnes*
- European Union (EU)
- extension
- foreign direct investment (FDI)

- globalization
- International Labour Organization (ILO)
- *keiretsu*
- Korean Tripartite Commission
- labor market
- mercantilism
- multinational enterprise
- shop stewards
- *shunto*
- Single Market
- Social Charter
- socialist market economy

- state-owned enterprise (SOE)
- state socialism
- Swedish Model
- Trades Union Congress
- Treaty of Maastricht
- tripartite organizational structure
- voluntarism
- union density
- wage relation
- Workplace Relations Act (WRA)
- works councils

REVIEW QUESTIONS

1. What are the key components of globalization, and how can they influence collective bargaining?
2. Discuss the challenges globalization presents to trade unions and how trade unions are responding.
3. Why did the industrial revolution, the democratic revolution, and the rise of capitalism result in different labor movements in Anglophone, European, and Far East countries?
4. Using one of the countries described in this chapter, discuss how its government attempted to suppress, then tolerate, and then support unions and why.
5. Why was the International Labour Organization created, and what influenced its structure and its mission?
6. What beliefs of the British labor movement influenced its post–World War I development?
7. Compare and contrast the industrial relations system in the United States, Canada, and Australia.
8. Describe the various ways European work councils are organized and their purpose.
9. Explain the reasons for a dichotomy in European countries between union membership and collective bargaining coverage.
10. Labor union membership dropped in most nations after the 1950s. What were the common reasons in the countries discussed in this chapter, and what were the unique reasons.
11. Why and how is the Japanese tradition of lifetime employment changing?
12. What primary role do trade unions fill in China?

YOU BE THE ARBITRATOR
Minimum Wage

PARAGRAPH I (I)
MINIMUM WAGE

The Law on the Posting of Workers extends certain collective agreements to employers established outside Germany and to their workers posted to Germany. That provision is worded as follows:

The legal rules resulting from a collective agreement governing the construction industry which is declared to be universally applicable ..., which relate to minimum pay, including pay for overtime ... shall also apply ... to an employment relationship linking an employer established outside Germany and his employee working within the territory covered by that collective agreement . . .

[T]he collective agreement on the minimum wage provides that the minimum wage consists of the hourly pay provided for by that agreement and the bonus granted to workers in the construction industry, which together make up the total hourly pay under the agreement. . . . [A]llowances and supplements paid by an employer, with the exception of the general bonus granted to workers in the construction industry, were not to be regarded as constituent elements of the minimum wage. . . . those supplements include in particular allowances in respect of overtime, night and Sunday work or work on public holidays, in addition to bonuses for travel and for heavy work.

Facts

It is an obligation of the member states to the European Union to ensure that employers from other countries that have posted their workers within the member state's borders follow the host country's minimum wage laws. This obligation stems from the promotion of freedom of movement for workers and nondiscrimination against another member state's citizens. The EU Commission investigated a complaint lodged against the Federal Republic of Germany that it was not enforcing the minimum wage law because it was not including in the calculation of the minimum wage all allowances and supplements paid by the employer. By not including those allowances and supplements, the foreign employer was required to pay its workers a higher minimum wage than German employers were required to pay. Specifically, the omitted allowances included: bonuses for a 13th and 14th salary months, holiday pay, contributions to retirement accounts, bonuses for the quality of the work performed, and bonuses for dirty, heavy, or dangerous work.

Issue

Did Germany apply the correct method for comparing the minimum rate of pay due under German law and the amount of pay actually paid by the employer established in another member state to its posted employees?

The Position of the Parties

According to the Commission, employers established in other Member States may be obliged, under the provisions applicable in those States, to provide other elements of pay in addition to the normal hourly pay. For example, an employer in the U.K. may be required to compensate its construction workers posted outside the U.K. for any medical bills they are required to pay because they would not have access to U.K.'s universal health care coverage while outside the U.K. Under the German legislation, such payments cannot be taken into account for the purpose of calculating the minimum wage. The Commission contends that the failure to take into account allowances and supplements results in higher wage costs than those that German employers are required to pay to their employees and that employers established in other Member States are thus prevented from offering their services in Germany. Although the Commission agrees that the Member State to the territory of which a worker is posted is allowed to determine the minimum rate of pay applicable within its borders, a Member State cannot, in comparing that rate and the wages paid by employers established in other Member States, impose its own payment structure on that employer.

According to the German government, it recognizes allowances and supplements paid by an employer that do not alter the relationship between the service provided by the worker and the payment that he receives. By contrast, allowances and supplements that do alter the balance between the services provided by the worker and the consideration that he receives in return cannot, according to the German rules, be recognized as forming part of the minimum wage and cannot be treated as constituent elements of that wage rate. The German government argues that hours worked that involve requirements of a particularly high degree of quality or that involve special constraints or dangers, have a greater economic value than that of normal working hours and that the bonuses relating to such hours must not be taken into account in the calculation of the minimum wage. If those amounts were taken into account for the purposes of that calculation, the worker would be deprived of the economic value corresponding to those hours of work.

SOURCE: Adapted from *Commission of the European Communities v. Federal Republic of Germany,* Case C-341/02, April 14, 2005.

QUESTIONS

1. As arbitrator, what would be your award and opinion in this arbitration?
2. Explain why the relevant provisions of the collective bargaining agreement as applied to the facts of this case dictate the award.
3. What actions might the employer and/or the union have taken to avoid this conflict?

EXERCISE

Attitudes toward Unions

PURPOSE:

To determine whether your attitudes toward unions have changed since originally completing this exercise in Chapter 2.

TASK:

Reconvene the original small groups that completed the survey at the end of Chapter 2. Retake the same survey.

Compare the group's answers before and now. Determine which group has had the most change in attitude and which group the least. Your instructor will ask these two groups to lead a discussion of attitudes toward unions and labor–management relations.

APPENDIX A

Texts of Statutes

National Labor Relations Act

Also cited NLRA or the Act; 29 U.S.C. §§151–169

[Title 29, Chapter 7, Subchapter II, United States Code]

FINDINGS AND POLICIES

Section 1. [§151.] The denial by some employers of the right of employees to organize and the refusal by some employers to accept the procedure of collective bargaining lead to strikes and other forms of industrial strife or unrest, which have the intent or the necessary effect of burdening or obstructing commerce by (a) impairing the efficiency, safety, or operation of the instrumentalities of commerce; (b) occurring in the current of commerce; (c) materially affecting, restraining, or controlling the flow of raw materials or manufactured or processed goods from or into the channels of commerce, or the prices of such materials or goods in commerce; or (d) causing diminution of employment and wages in such volume as substantially to impair or disrupt the market for goods flowing from or into the channels of commerce.

The inequality of bargaining power between employees who do not possess full freedom of association or actual liberty of contract and employers who are organized in the corporate or other forms of ownership association substantially burdens and affects the flow of commerce, and tends to aggravate recurrent business depressions, by depressing wage rates and the purchasing power of wage earners in industry and by preventing the stabilization of competitive wage rates and working conditions within and between industries.

Experience has proved that protection by law of the right of employees to organize and bargain collectively safeguards commerce from injury, impairment, or interruption, and promotes the flow of commerce by removing certain recognized sources of industrial strife and unrest, by encouraging practices fundamental to the friendly adjustment of industrial disputes arising out of differences as to wages, hours, or other working conditions, and by restoring equality of bargaining power between employers and employees.

Experience has further demonstrated that certain practices by some labor organizations, their officers, and members have the intent or the necessary effect of burdening or obstructing commerce by preventing the free flow of goods in such commerce through strikes and other forms of industrial unrest or through concerted activities which impair the interest of the public in the free flow of such commerce. The elimination of such practices is a necessary condition to the assurance of the rights herein guaranteed.

It is declared to be the policy of the United States to eliminate the causes of certain substantial obstructions to the free flow of commerce and to mitigate and eliminate these obstructions when they have occurred by encouraging the practice and procedure of collective bargaining and by protecting the exercise by workers of full freedom of association, self-organization, and designation of representatives of their own choosing, for the purpose of negotiating the terms and conditions of their employment or other mutual aid or protection.

DEFINITIONS

Sec. 2. [§152.] When used in this Act [subchapter]—

(1) The term "person" includes one or more individuals, labor organizations, partnerships, associations, corporations, legal representatives, trustees, trustees in cases under title 11 of the United States Code [under title 11], or receivers.

(2) The term "employer" includes any person acting as an agent of an employer, directly or indirectly, but shall not include the United States or any wholly owned Government corporation, or any Federal Reserve Bank, or any State or political subdivision thereof, or any person subject to the Railway Labor Act [45 U.S.C. §151 et seq.], as amended from time to time, or any labor organization (other than when acting as an employer), or anyone acting in the capacity of officer or agent of such labor organization.

[Pub. L. 93–360, §1(a), July 26, 1974, 88 Stat. 395, deleted the phrase "or any corporation or association operating a hospital, if no part of the net earnings inures to the benefit of any private shareholder or individual" from the definition of "employer."]

(3) The term "employee" shall include any employee, and shall not be limited to the employees of a particular employer, unless the Act [this subchapter] explicitly states otherwise, and shall include any individual whose work has ceased as a consequence of, or in connection with, any current labor dispute or because of any unfair labor practice, and who has not obtained any other regular and substantially equivalent employment, but shall not include any individual employed as an agricultural laborer, or in the domestic service of any family or person at his home, or any individual employed by his parent or spouse, or any individual having the status of an independent contractor, or any individual employed as a supervisor, or any individual employed by an employer subject to the Railway Labor Act [45 U.S.C. §151 et seq.], as amended from time to time, or by any other person who is not an employer as herein defined.

(4) The term "representatives" includes any individual or labor organization.

(5) The term "labor organization" means any organization of any kind, or any agency or employee representation committee or plan, in which employees participate and which exists for the purpose, in whole or in part, of dealing with employers concerning grievances, labor disputes, wages, rates of pay, hours of employment, or conditions of work.

(6) The term "commerce" means trade, traffic, commerce, transportation or communication among the several States, or between the District of Columbia or any Territory of the United States and any State or other Territory, or between any foreign country and any State, Territory, or the District of Columbia, or within the District of Columbia or any Territory, or between points in the same State but through any other State or any Territory or the District of Columbia or any foreign country.

(7) The term "affecting commerce" means in commerce, or burdening or obstructing commerce or the free flow of commerce, or having led or tending to lead to a labor dispute burdening or obstructing commerce or the free flow of commerce.

(8) The term "unfair labor practice" means any unfair labor practice listed in section 8 [section 158 of this title].

(9) The term "labor dispute" includes any controversy concerning term, tenure or conditions of employment, or concerning the association or representation of persons in negotiating, fixing, maintaining, changing, or seeking to arrange terms or conditions of employment, regardless of whether the disputants stand in the proximate relation of employer and employee.

(10) The term "National Labor Relations Board" means the National Labor Relations Board provided for in section 3 of this Act [section 153 of this title].

(11) The term "supervisor" means any individual having authority, in the interest of the employer, to hire, transfer, suspend, lay off, recall, promote, discharge, assign, reward, or discipline other employees, or responsibly to direct them, or to adjust their grievances, or effectively to recommend such action, if in connection with the foregoing the exercise of such authority is not of a merely routine or clerical nature, but requires the use of independent judgment.

(12) The term "professional employee" means—

(a) any employee engaged in work (i) predominantly intellectual and varied in character as opposed to routine mental, manual, mechanical, or physical work; (ii) involving the consistent exercise of discretion and judgment in its performance; (iii) of such a character that the output produced or the result accomplished cannot be standardized in relation to a given period of time; (iv) requiring knowledge of an advanced type in a field of science or learning customarily acquired by a prolonged course of specialized intellectual instruction and study in an institution of higher learning or a hospital, as distinguished from a general academic education or from an apprenticeship or from training in the performance of routine mental, manual, or physical processes; or

(b) any employee, who (i) has completed the courses of specialized intellectual instruction and study described in clause (iv) of paragraph (a), and (ii) is performing related work under the supervision of a professional person to qualify himself to become a professional employee as defined in paragraph (a).

(13) In determining whether any person is acting as an "agent" of another person so as to make such other person responsible for his acts, the question of whether the specific acts performed were actually authorized or subsequently ratified shall not be controlling.

(14) The term "health care institution" shall include any hospital, convalescent hospital, health maintenance organization, health clinic, nursing home, extended care facility, or other institution devoted to the care of sick, infirm, or aged person.

[Pub. L. 93–360, §1(b), July 26, 1974, 88 Stat. 395, added par. (14).]

National Labor Relations Board

Sec. 3. [§153.] (a) [Creation, composition, appointment, and tenure; Chairman; removal of members] The National Labor Relations Board (hereinafter called the "Board") created by this Act [subchapter] prior to its amendment by the Labor Management Relations Act, 1947 [29 U.S.C. §141 et seq.], is continued as an agency of the United States, except that the Board shall consist of five instead of three members, appointed by the President by and with the advice and consent of the Senate. Of the two additional members so provided for, one shall be appointed for a term of five years and the other for a term of two years. Their successors, and the successors of the other members, shall be appointed for terms of five years each, excepting that any individual chosen to fill a vacancy shall be appointed only for the unexpired term of the member whom he shall succeed. The President shall designate one member to serve as Chairman of the Board. Any member of the Board may be removed by the President, upon notice and hearing, for neglect of duty or malfeasance in office, but for no other cause.

(b) [Delegation of powers to members and regional directors; review and stay of actions of regional directors; quorum; seal] The Board is authorized to delegate to any group of three or more members any or all of the powers which it may itself exercise. The Board is also authorized to delegate to its regional directors its powers under section 9 [section 159 of this title] to determine the unit appropriate for the purpose of collective bargaining, to investigate and provide for hearings, and determine whether a question of representation exists, and to direct an election or take a secret ballot under subsection (c) or (e) of section 9 [section 159 of this title] and certify the results thereof, except that upon the filling of a request therefor with the Board by any interested person, the Board may review any action of a regional director delegated to him under this paragraph, but such a review shall not, unless specifically ordered by the Board, operate as a stay of any action taken by the regional director. A vacancy in the Board shall not impair the right of the remaining members to exercise all of the powers of the Board, and three members of the Board shall, at all times, constitute a quorum of the Board, except that two members shall constitute a quorum of any group designated pursuant to the first sentence hereof. The Board shall have an official seal which shall be judicially noticed.

(c) [Annual reports to Congress and the President] The Board shall at the close of each fiscal year make a report in writing to Congress and to the President summarizing significant case activities and operations for that fiscal year.

(d) [General Counsel; appointment and tenure; powers and duties; vacancy] There shall be a General Counsel of the Board who shall be appointed by the President, by and with the advice and consent of the Senate, for a term of four years. The General Counsel of the Board shall exercise general supervision over all attorneys employed by the Board (other than administrative law judges and legal assistants to Board members) and over the officers and employees in the regional offices. He shall have final authority, on behalf of the Board, in respect of the investigation of charges and issuance of complaints under section 10 [section 160 of this title], and in respect of the prosecution of such complaints before the Board, and shall have such other duties as the Board may prescribe or as may be provided by law. In case of vacancy in the office of the General Counsel, the President is authorized to designate the officer or employee who shall act as General Counsel during such vacancy, but no person or persons so designated shall so act (1) for more than forty days when the Congress is in session unless a nomination to fill such vacancy shall have been submitted to the Senate, or (2) after the adjournment sine die of the session of the Senate in which such nomination was submitted.

[The title "administrative law judge" was adopted in 5 U.S.C. §3105.]

Sec. 4. [§154. Eligibility for reappointment; officers and employees; payment of expenses] (a) Each member of the Board and the General Counsel of the Board shall be eligible for reappointment, and shall not engage in any other business, vocation, or employment. The Board shall appoint an executive secretary, and such attorneys, examiners, and regional directors, and such other employees as it may from time to time find necessary for the proper performance of its duties. The Board may not employ any attorneys for the purpose of reviewing transcripts of hearings or preparing drafts of opinions except that any attorney employed for assignment as a legal assistant to any Board member may for such Board member review such transcripts and prepare such drafts. No administrative law judge's report shall be reviewed, either before or after its publication, by any person other than a member of the Board or his legal assistant, and no administrative law judge shall advise or consult with the Board with respect to exceptions taken to his findings, rulings, or recommendations. The Board may establish or utilize such regional, local, or other agencies, and utilize such voluntary and uncompensated services, as may from time to time be needed. Attorneys appointed under this section may, at the direction of the Board, appear for and represent the Board in any case in court. Nothing in this Act [subchapter] shall be construed to authorize the Board to appoint individuals for the purpose of conciliation or mediation, or for economic analysis.

[The title "administrative law judge" was adopted in 5 U.S.C. §3105.]

(b) All of the expenses of the Board, including all necessary traveling and subsistence expenses outside the District of Columbia incurred by the members or employees of the Board under its orders, shall be allowed and paid on the presentation of itemized vouchers therefore approved by the Board or by any individual it designates for that purpose.

Sec. 5. [§155. Principal office, conducting inquiries throughout country; participation in decisions or inquiries conducted by member] The principal office of the Board shall be in the District of Columbia, but it may meet and exercise any or all of its powers at any other place. The Board may, by one or more of its members or by such agents or agencies as it may designate, prosecute any inquiry necessary to its functions in any part of the United States. A member who participates in such an inquiry shall not be disqualified from subsequently participating in a decision of the Board in the same case.

Sec. 6. [§156. Rules and regulations] The Board shall have authority from time to time to make, amend, and rescind, in the manner prescribed by the Administrative Procedure Act [by subchapter II of chapter 5 of title 5], such rules and regulations as may be necessary to carry out the provisions of this Act [subchapter].

Rights of Employees

Sec. 7. [§157.] Employees shall have the right to self-organization, to form, join, or assist labor organizations, to bargain collectively through representatives of their own choosing, and to engage in other concerted activities for the purpose of collective bargaining or other mutual aid or protection, and shall also have the right to refrain from any or all such activities except to the extent that such right may be affected by an agreement requiring membership in a labor organization as a condition of employment as authorized in section 8(a)(3) [section 158(a)(3) of this title].

Unfair Labor Practices

Sec. 8. [§158.] (a) [Unfair labor practices by employer] It shall be an unfair labor practice for an employer—

(1) to interfere with, restrain, or coerce employees in the exercise of the rights guaranteed in section 7 [section 157 of this title];

(2) to dominate or interfere with the formation or administration of any labor organization or contribute financial or other support to it: Provided, That subject to rules and regulations made and published by the Board pursuant to section 6 [section 156 of this title], an employer shall not be prohibited from permitting employees to confer with him during working hours without loss of time or pay;

(3) by discrimination in regard to hire or tenure of employment or any term or condition of employment to encourage or discourage membership in any labor organization: Provided, That nothing in this Act [subchapter], or in any other statute of the

United States, shall preclude an employer from making an agreement with a labor organization (not established, maintained, or assisted by any action defined in section 8(a) of this Act [in this subsection] as an unfair labor practice) to require as a condition of employment membership therein on or after the thirtieth day following the beginning of such employment or the effective date of such agreement, whichever is the later, (i) if such labor organization is the representative of the employees as provided in section 9(a) [section 159(a) of this title], in the appropriate collective-bargaining unit covered by such agreement when made, and (ii) unless following an election held as provided in section 9(e) [section 159(e) of this title] within one year preceding the effective date of such agreement, the Board shall have certified that at least a majority of the employees eligible to vote in such election have voted to rescind the authority of such labor organization to make such an agreement: Provided further, That no employer shall justify any discrimination against an employee for nonmembership in a labor organization (A) if he has reasonable grounds for believing that such membership was not available to the employee on the same terms and conditions generally applicable to other members, or (B) if he has reasonable grounds for believing that membership was denied or terminated for reasons other than the failure of the employee to tender the periodic dues and the initiation fees uniformly required as a condition of acquiring or retaining membership;

(4) to discharge or otherwise discriminate against an employee because he has filed charges or given testimony under this Act [subchapter];

(5) to refuse to bargain collectively with the representatives of his employees, subject to the provisions of section 9(a) [section 159(a) of this title].

(b) [Unfair labor practices by labor organization] It shall be an unfair labor practice for a labor organization or its agents—

(1) to restrain or coerce (A) employees in the exercise of the rights guaranteed in section 7 [section 157 of this title]: Provided, That this paragraph shall not impair the right of a labor organization to prescribe its own rules with respect to the acquisition or retention of membership therein; or (B) an employer in the selection of his representatives for the purposes of collective bargaining or the adjustment of grievances;

(2) to cause or attempt to cause an employer to discriminate against an employee in violation of subsection (a)(3) [of subsection (a)(3) of this section] or to discriminate against an employee with respect to whom membership in such organization has been denied or terminated on some ground other than his failure to tender the periodic dues and the initiation fees uniformly required as a condition of acquiring or retaining membership;

(3) to refuse to bargain collectively with an employer, provided it is the representative of his employees subject to the provisions of section 9(a) [section 159(a) of this title];

(4)(i) to engage in, or to induce or encourage any individual employed by any person engaged in commerce or in an industry affecting commerce to engage in, a strike or a refusal in the course of his employment to use, manufacture, process, transport, or otherwise handle or work on any goods, articles, materials, or commodities or to perform any services; or (ii) to threaten, coerce, or restrain any person engaged in commerce or in an industry affecting commerce, where in either case an object thereof is—

(A) forcing or requiring any employer or self-employed person to join any labor or employer organization or to enter into any agreement which is prohibited by section 8(e) [subsection (e) of this section];

(B) forcing or requiring any person to cease using, selling, handling, transporting, or otherwise dealing in the products of any other producer, processor, or manufacturer, or to cease doing business with any other person, or forcing or requiring any other employer to recognize or bargain with a labor organization as the representative of his employees unless such labor organization has been certified as the representative of such employees under the provisions of section 9 [section 159 of this title]: Provided, That nothing contained in this clause (B) shall be construed to make unlawful, where not otherwise unlawful, any primary strike or primary picketing;

(C) forcing or requiring any employer to recognize or bargain with a particular labor organization as the representative of his employees if another labor organization has been certified as the representative of such employees under the provisions of section 9 [section 159 of this title];

(D) forcing or requiring any employer to assign particular work to employees in a particular labor organization or in a particular trade, craft, or class rather than to employees in another labor organization or in another trade, craft, or class, unless such employer is failing to conform to an order or certification of the Board determining the bargaining representative for employees performing such work:

Provided, That nothing contained in this subsection (b) [this subsection] shall be construed to make unlawful a refusal by any person to enter upon the premises of any employer (other than his own employer), if the employees of such employer are engaged in a strike ratified or approved by a representative of such employees whom such employer is required to recognize under this Act [subchapter]: Provided further, That for the purposes of this paragraph (4) only, nothing contained in such paragraph shall be construed to prohibit publicity, other than picketing, for the purpose of truthfully advising the public, including consumers and members of a labor organization, that a product or products are produced by an employer with whom the labor organization has a primary dispute and are distributed by another employer, as long as such publicity does not have an effect of inducing any individual employed by any person other than the primary employer in the course of his employment to refuse to pick up, deliver, or transport any goods, or not to perform any services, at the establishment of the employer engaged in such distribution;

(5) to require of employees covered by an agreement authorized under subsection (a)(3) [of this section] the payment, as a condition precedent to becoming a member of such organization, of a fee in an amount which the Board finds excessive or discriminatory under all the circumstances. In making such a finding, the Board shall consider, among other relevant factors, the practices and customs of labor organizations in the particular industry, and the wages currently paid to the employees affected;

(6) to cause or attempt to cause an employer to pay or deliver or agree to pay or deliver any money or other thing of value, in the nature of an exaction, for services which are not performed or not to be performed; and

(7) to picket or cause to be picketed, or threaten to picket or cause to be picketed, any employer where an object thereof is forcing or requiring an employer to recognize or bargain with a labor organization as the representative of his employees, or forcing or requiring the employees of an employer to accept or select such labor organization as their collective-bargaining representative, unless such labor organization is currently certified as the representative of such employees:

(A) where the employer has lawfully recognized in accordance with this Act [subchapter] any other labor organization and a question concerning representation may not appropriately be raised under section 9(c) of this Act [section 159(c) of this title],

(B) where within the preceding twelve months a valid election under section 9(c) of this Act [section 159(c) of this title] has been conducted, or

(C) where such picketing has been conducted without a petition under section 9(c) [section 159(c) of this title] being filed within a reasonable period of time not to exceed thirty days from the commencement of such picketing: Provided, That when such a petition has been filed the Board shall forthwith, without regard to the provisions of section 9(c)(1) [section 159(c)(1) of this title] or the absence of a showing of a substantial interest on the part of the labor organization, direct an election in such unit as the Board finds to be appropriate and shall certify the results thereof: Provided further, That nothing in this subparagraph (C) shall be construed to prohibit any picketing or other publicity for the purpose of truthfully advising the public (including consumers) that an employer does not employ members of, or have a contract with, a labor organization, unless an effect of such picketing is to induce any individual employed by any other person in the course of his employment, not to pick up, deliver, or transport any goods or not to perform any services.

Nothing in this paragraph (7) shall be construed to permit any act which would otherwise be an unfair labor practice under this section 8(b) [this subsection].

(c) [Expression of views without threat of reprisal or force or promise of benefit] The expressing of any views, argument, or opinion, or the dissemination thereof, whether in written, printed, graphic, or visual form, shall not constitute or be evidence of an unfair labor practice under any of the provisions of this Act [subchapter], if such expression contains no threat of reprisal or force or promise of benefit.

(d) [Obligation to bargain collectively] For the purposes of this section, to bargain collectively is the performance of the mutual obligation of the employer and the representative of the employees to meet at reasonable times and confer in good faith with respect to wages, hours, and other terms and conditions of employment, or the negotiation of an agreement or any question arising thereunder, and the execution of a written contract incorporating any agreement reached if requested by either party, but such obligation does not compel either party to agree to a proposal or require the making of a concession: Provided, That where there is in effect a collective-bargaining contract covering employees in an industry affecting commerce, the duty to bargain collectively shall also mean that no party to such contract shall terminate or modify such contract, unless the party desiring such termination or modification—

(1) serves a written notice upon the other party to the contract of the proposed termination or modification sixty days prior to the expiration date thereof, or in the event such contract contains no expiration date, sixty days prior to the time it is proposed to make such termination or modification;

(2) offers to meet and confer with the other party for the purpose of negotiating a new contract or a contract containing the proposed modifications;

(3) notifies the Federal Mediation and Conciliation Service within thirty days after such notice of the existence of a dispute, and simultaneously therewith notifies any State or Territorial agency established to mediate and conciliate disputes within the State or Territory where the dispute occurred, provided no agreement has been reached by that time; and

(4) continues in full force and effect, without resorting to strike or lockout, all the terms and conditions of the existing contract for a period of sixty days after such notice is given or until the expiration date of such contract, whichever occurs later.

The duties imposed upon employers, employees, and labor organizations by paragraphs (2), (3), and (4) [paragraphs (2) to (4) of this subsection] shall become inapplicable upon an intervening certification of the Board, under which the labor organization or individual, which is a party to the contract, has been superseded as or ceased to be the representative of the employees subject to the provisions of section 9(a) [section 159(a) of this title], and the duties so imposed shall not be construed as requiring either party to discuss or agree to any modification of the terms and conditions contained in a contract for a fixed period, if such modification is to become effective before such terms and conditions can be reopened under the provisions of the contract. Any employee who engages in a strike within any notice period specified in this subsection, or who engages in any strike within the appropriate period specified in subsection (g) of this section, shall lose his status as an employee of the employer engaged in the particular labor dispute, for the purposes of sections 8, 9, and 10 of this Act [sections 158, 159, and 160 of this title], but such loss of status for such employee shall terminate if and when he is reemployed by such employer. Whenever the collective bargaining involves employees of a health care institution, the provisions of this section 8(d) [this subsection] shall be modified as follows:

(A) The notice of section 8(d)(1) [paragraph (1) of this subsection] shall be ninety days; the notice of section 8(d)(3) [paragraph (3) of this subsection] shall be sixty days; and the contract period of section 8(d)(4) [paragraph (4) of this subsection] shall be ninety days.

(B) Where the bargaining is for an initial agreement following certification or recognition, at least thirty days' notice of the existence of a dispute shall be given by the labor organization to the agencies set forth in section 8(d)(3) [in paragraph (3) of this subsection].

(C) After notice is given to the Federal Mediation and Conciliation Service under either clause (A) or (B) of this sentence, the Service shall promptly communicate with the parties and use its best efforts, by mediation and conciliation, to bring them to agreement. The parties shall participate fully and promptly in such meetings as may be undertaken by the Service for the purpose of aiding in a settlement of the dispute.

[Pub. L. 93–360, July 26, 1974, 88 Stat. 395, amended the last sentence of Sec. 8(d) by striking the words "the sixty-day" and inserting the words "any notice" and by inserting before the words "shall lose" the phrase ", or who engages in any strike within the appropriate period specified in subsection (g) of this section." It also amended the end of paragraph Sec. 8(d) by adding a new sentence "Whenever the collective bargaining . . . aiding in a settlement of the dispute."]

(e) [Enforceability of contract or agreement to boycott any other employer; exception] It shall be an unfair labor practice for any labor organization and any employer to enter into any contract or agreement, expressed or implied, whereby such employer ceases or refrains or agrees to cease or refrain from handling, using, selling, transporting or otherwise dealing in any of the products of any other employer, or cease doing business with any other person, and any contract or agreement entered into heretofore or hereafter containing such an agreement shall be to such extent unenforceable and void: Provided, That nothing in this subsection (e) [this subsection] shall apply to an agreement between a labor organization and an employer in the construction industry relating to the contracting or subcontracting of work to be done at the site of the construction, alteration, painting, or repair of a building, structure, or other work: Provided further, That for the purposes of this subsection (e) and section 8(b)(4)(B) [this subsection and subsection (b)(4)(B) of this section] the terms "any employer," "any person engaged in commerce or an industry affecting commerce," and "any person" when used in relation to the terms "any other producer, processor, or manufacturer," "any other employer," or "any other person" shall not include persons in the relation of a jobber, manufacturer, contractor, or subcontractor working on the goods or premises of the jobber or manufacturer or performing parts of an integrated process of production in the apparel and clothing industry: Provided further, That nothing in this Act [subchapter] shall prohibit the enforcement of any agreement which is within the foregoing exception.

(f) [Agreements covering employees in the building and construction industry] It shall not be an unfair labor practice under subsections (a) and (b) of this section for an employer engaged primarily in the building and construction industry to make an agreement covering employees engaged (or who, upon their employment, will be engaged) in the building and construction industry with a labor organization of which building and construction employees are members (not established, maintained, or assisted by any action defined in section 8(a) of this Act [subsection (a) of this section] as an unfair labor practice) because (1) the majority status of such labor organization has not been established under the provisions of section 9 of this Act [section 159 of this title] prior to the making of such agreement, or (2) such agreement requires as a condition of employment, membership in such labor organization after the seventh day following the beginning of such employment or the effective date of the agreement, whichever is later, or (3) such agreement requires the employer to notify such labor organization of opportunities for employment with such employer, or gives such labor organization an opportunity to refer qualified applicants for such employment, or (4) such agreement specifies minimum training or experience qualifications for employment or provides for priority in opportunities for employment based upon length of service with such employer, in the industry or in the particular geographical area: Provided, That nothing in this subsection shall set aside the final proviso to section 8(a)(3) of this Act [subsection (a)(3) of this section]: Provided further, That any agreement which would be invalid, but for clause (1) of this subsection, shall not be a bar to a petition filed pursuant to section 9(c) or 9(e) [section 159(c) or 159(e) of this title].

(g) [Notification of intention to strike or picket at any health care institution] A labor organization before engaging in any strike, picketing, or other concerted refusal to work at any health care institution shall, not less than ten days prior to such action, notify the institution in writing and the Federal Mediation and Conciliation Service of that intention, except that in the case of bargaining for an initial agreement following certification or recognition of the notice required by this subsection shall not be given until the expiration of the period specified in clause (B) of the last sentence of section 8(d) of this Act [subsection (d) of this section]. The notice shall state the date and time that such action will commence. The notice, once given, may be extended by the written agreement of both parties.

[Pub. L. 93–360, July 26, 1974, 88 Stat. 396, added subsec. (g).]

Representatives and Elections

Sec. 9. [§159.] (a) [Exclusive representatives; employees' adjustment of grievances directly with employer] Representatives designated or selected for the purposes of collective bargaining by the majority of the employees in a unit appropriate for such purposes, shall be the exclusive representatives of all the employees in such unit for the purposes of collective bargaining in respect to rates of pay, wages, hours of employment, or other conditions of employment: Provided, That any individual employee or a group of employees shall have the right at any time to present grievances to their employer and to have such grievances adjusted, without the intervention of the bargaining representative, as long as the adjustment is not inconsistent with the terms of a collective-bargaining contract or agreement then in effect: Provided further, That the bargaining representative has been given opportunity to be present at such adjustment.

(b) [Determination of bargaining unit by Board] The Board shall decide in each case whether, in order to assure to employees the fullest freedom in exercising the rights guaranteed by this Act [subchapter], the unit appropriate for the purposes of collective bargaining shall be the employer unit, craft unit, plant unit, or subdivision thereof: Provided, That the Board shall not (1) decide that any unit is appropriate for such purposes if such unit includes both professional employees and employees who are not professional employees unless a majority of such professional employees vote for inclusion in such unit; or (2) decide that any craft unit is inappropriate for such purposes on the ground that a different unit has been established by a prior Board determination, unless a majority of the employees in the proposed craft unit votes against separate representation or (3) decide that any unit is appropriate for such purposes if it includes, together with other employees, any individual employed as a guard to enforce against employees and other persons rules to protect property of the employer or to protect the safety of persons on the employer's premises; but no labor organization shall be certified as the representative of employees in a bargaining unit of guards if such organization admits to membership, or is affiliated directly or indirectly with an organization which admits to membership, employees other than guards.

(c) [Hearing on questions affecting commerce; rules and regulations] (1) Whenever a petition shall have been filed, in accordance with such regulations as may be prescribed by the Board—

(A) by an employee or group of employees or any individual or labor organization acting in their behalf alleging that a substantial number of employees (i) wish to be represented for collective bargaining and that their employer declines to recognize their representative as the representative defined in section 9(a) [subsection (a) of this section], or (ii) assert that the individual or labor organization, which has been certified or is being currently recognized by their employer as the bargaining representative, is no longer a representative as defined in section 9(a) [subsection (a) of this section]; or

(B) by an employer, alleging that one or more individuals or labor organizations have presented to him a claim to be recognized as the representative defined in section 9(a) [subsection (a) of this section]; the Board shall investigate such petition and if it has reasonable cause to believe that a question of representation affecting commerce exists shall provide for an appropriate hearing upon due notice. Such hearing may be conducted by an officer or employee of the regional office, who shall not make any recommendations with respect thereto. If the Board finds upon the record of such hearing that such a question of representation exists, it shall direct an election by secret ballot and shall certify the results thereof.

(2) In determining whether or not a question of representation affecting commerce exists, the same regulations and rules of decision shall apply irrespective of the identity of the persons filing the petition or the kind of relief sought and in no case shall the Board deny a labor organization a place on the ballot by reason of an order with respect to such labor organization or its predecessor not issued in conformity with section 10(c) [section 160(c) of this title].

(3) No election shall be directed in any bargaining unit or any subdivision within which, in the preceding twelve-month period, a valid election shall have been held. Employees engaged in an economic strike who are not entitled to reinstatement shall be eligible to vote under such regulations as the Board shall find are consistent with the purposes and provisions of this Act [subchapter] in any election conducted within twelve months after the commencement of the strike. In any election where none of the choices on the ballot receives a majority, a run-off shall be conducted, the ballot providing for a selection between the two choices receiving the largest and second largest number of valid votes cast in the election.

(4) Nothing in this section shall be construed to prohibit the waiving of hearings by stipulation for the purpose of a consent election in conformity with regulations and rules of decision of the Board.

(5) In determining whether a unit is appropriate for the purposes specified in subsection (b) [of this section] the extent to which the employees have organized shall not be controlling.

(d) [Petition for enforcement or review; transcript] Whenever an order of the Board made pursuant to section 10(c) [section 160(c) of this title] is based in whole or in part upon facts certified following an investigation pursuant to subsection (c) of this section and there is a petition for the enforcement or review of such order, such certification and the record of such investigation shall be included in the transcript of the entire record required to be filed under section 10(e) or 10(f) [subsection (e) or (f) of section 160 of this title], and thereupon the decree of the court enforcing, modifying, or setting aside in whole or in part the order of the Board shall be made and entered upon the pleadings, testimony, and proceedings set forth in such transcript.

(e) [Secret ballot; limitation of elections] (1) Upon the filing with the Board, by 30 per centum or more of the employees in a bargaining unit covered by an agreement between their employer and labor organization made pursuant to section 8(a)(3) [section 158(a)(3) of this title], of a petition alleging they desire that such authorization be rescinded, the Board shall take a secret ballot of the employees in such unit and certify the results thereof to such labor organization and to the employer.

(2) No election shall be conducted pursuant to this subsection in any bargaining unit or any subdivision within which, in the preceding twelve-month period, a valid election shall have been held.

PREVENTION OF UNFAIR LABOR PRACTICES

Sec. 10. [§160.] (a) [Powers of Board generally] The Board is empowered, as hereinafter provided, to prevent any person from engaging in any unfair labor practice (listed in section 8 [section 158 of this title]) affecting commerce. This power shall not be affected by any other means of adjustment or prevention that has been or may be established by agreement, law, or otherwise: Provided, That the Board is empowered by agreement with any agency of any State or Territory to cede to such agency jurisdiction over any cases in any industry (other than mining, manufacturing, communications, and transportation except where predominately local in character) even though such cases may involve labor disputes affecting commerce, unless the provision of the State or Territorial statute applicable to the determination of such cases by such agency is inconsistent with the corresponding provision of this Act [subchapter] or has received a construction inconsistent therewith.

(b) [Complaint and notice of hearing; six-month limitation; answer; court rules of evidence inapplicable] Whenever it is charged that any person has engaged in or is engaging in any such unfair labor practice, the Board, or any agent or agency designated by the Board for such purposes, shall have power to issue and cause to be served upon such person a complaint stating the charges in that respect, and containing a notice of hearing before the Board or a member thereof, or before a designated agent or agency, at a place therein fixed, not less than five days after the serving of said complaint: Provided, That no complaint shall issue based upon any unfair labor practice occurring more than six months prior to the filing of the charge with the Board and the service of a copy thereof upon the person against whom such charge is made, unless the person aggrieved thereby was prevented from filing such charge by reason of service in the armed forces, in which event the six-month period shall be computed from the day of his discharge. Any such complaint may be amended by the member, agent, or agency conducting the hearing or the Board in its discretion at any time prior to the issuance of an order based thereon. The person so complained of shall have the right to file an answer to the original or amended complaint and to appear in person or otherwise and give testimony at the place and time fixed in the complaint. In the discretion of the member, agent, or agency conducting the hearing or the Board, any other person may be allowed to intervene in the said proceeding and to present testimony. Any such proceeding shall, so far as practicable, be conducted in accordance with the rules of evidence applicable in the district courts of the United States under the rules of civil procedure for the district courts of the United States, adopted by the Supreme Court of the United States pursuant to section 2072 of title 28, United States Code [section 2072 of title 28].

    (c) [Reduction of testimony to writing; findings and orders of Board] The testimony taken by such member, agent, or agency or the Board shall be reduced to writing and filed with the Board. Thereafter, in its discretion, the Board upon notice may take further testimony or hear argument. If upon the preponderance of the testimony taken the Board shall be of the opinion that any person named in the complaint has engaged in or is engaging in any such unfair labor practice, then the Board shall state its findings of fact and shall issue and cause to be served on such person an order requiring such person to cease and desist from such unfair labor practice, and to take such affirmative action including reinstatement of employees with or without back pay, as will effectuate the policies of this Act [subchapter]: Provided, That where an order directs reinstatement of an employee, back pay may be required of the employer or labor organization, as the case may be, responsible for the discrimination suffered by him: And provided further, That in determining whether a complaint shall issue alleging a violation of section 8(a)(1) or section 8(a)(2) [subsection (a)(1) or (a)(2) of section 158 of this title], and in deciding such cases, the same regulations and rules of decision shall apply irrespective of whether or not the labor organization affected is affiliated with a labor organization national or international in scope. Such order may further require such person to make reports from time to time showing the extent to which it has complied with the order. If upon the preponderance of the testimony taken the Board shall not be of the opinion that the person named in the complaint has engaged in or is engaging in any such unfair labor practice, then the Board shall state its findings of fact and shall issue an order dismissing the said complaint. No order of the Board shall require the reinstatement of any individual as an employee who has been suspended or discharged, or the payment to him of any back pay, if such individual was suspended or discharged for cause. In case the evidence is presented before a member of the Board, or before an administrative law judge or judges thereof, such member, or such judge or judges, as the case may be, shall issue and cause to be served on the parties to the proceeding a proposed report, together with a recommended order, which shall be filed with the Board, and if no exceptions are filed within twenty days after service thereof upon such parties, or within such further period as the Board may authorize, such recommended order shall become the order of the Board and become affective as therein prescribed.

    [The title "administrative law judge" was adopted in 5 U.S.C. §3105.]

    (d) [Modification of findings or orders prior to filing record in court] Until the record in a case shall have been filed in a court, as hereinafter provided, the Board may at any time, upon reasonable notice and in such manner as it shall deem proper, modify or set aside, in whole or in part, any finding or order made or issued by it.

    (e) [Petition to court for enforcement of order; proceedings; review of judgment] The Board shall have power to petition any court of appeals of the United States, or if all the courts of appeals to which application may be made are in vacation, any district court of the United States, within any circuit or district, respectively, wherein the unfair labor practice in question occurred or wherein such person resides or transacts business, for the enforcement of such order and for appropriate temporary relief or restraining order, and shall file in the court the record in the proceeding, as provided in section 2112 of title 28, United States Code [section 2112 of title 28]. Upon the filing of such petition, the court shall cause notice thereof to be served upon such person, and thereupon shall have jurisdiction of the proceeding and of the question determined therein, and shall have power to grant such temporary relief or restraining order as it deems just and proper, and to make and enter a decree enforcing, modifying and enforcing as so modified, or setting aside in whole or in part the order of the Board. No objection that has not been urged before the Board, its member, agent, or agency, shall be considered by the court, unless the failure or neglect to urge such objection shall be excused because of extraordinary circumstances. The findings of the Board with respect to questions of fact if supported by substantial evidence on the record considered as a whole shall be conclusive. If either party shall apply to the court for leave to adduce additional evidence and shall show to the satisfaction of the court that such additional evidence is material and that there were reasonable grounds for the failure to adduce such evidence in the hearing before the Board, its member, agent, or agency, the court may order such additional evidence to be taken before the Board, its member, agent, or agency, and to be made a part of the record. The Board may modify its findings as to the facts, or make new findings, by reason of additional evidence so taken and filed, and it shall file such modified or new findings, which findings with respect to question of fact if supported by substantial evidence on the record considered as a whole shall be conclusive, and shall file its recommendations, if any, for the modification or setting aside of its original order. Upon the filing of the record with it the jurisdiction of the court shall be exclusive and its judgment and decree shall be final, except that the same shall be subject to review by the appropriate United States court of appeals if application was made to the district court as hereinabove provided, and by the Supreme Court of the United States upon writ of certiorari or certification as provided in section 1254 of title 28.

   (f) [Review of final order of Board on petition to court] Any person aggrieved by a final order of the Board granting or denying in whole or in part the relief sought may obtain a review of such order in any United States court of appeals in the circuit wherein the unfair labor practice in question was alleged to have been engaged in or wherein such person resides or transacts business, or in the United States Court of Appeals for the District of Columbia, by filing in such court a written petition praying that the order of the Board be modified or set aside. A copy of such petition shall be forthwith transmitted by the clerk of the court to the Board, and thereupon the aggrieved party shall file in the court the record in the proceeding, certified by the Board, as provided in section 2112 of title 28, United States Code [section 2112 of title 28]. Upon the filing of such petition, the court shall proceed in the same manner as in the case of an application by the Board under subsection (e) of this section, and shall have the same jurisdiction to grant to the Board such temporary relief or restraining order as it deems just and proper, and in like manner to make and enter a decree enforcing, modifying and enforcing as so modified, or setting aside in whole or in part the order of the Board; the findings of the Board with respect to questions of fact if supported by substantial evidence on the record considered as a whole shall in like manner be conclusive.

   (g) [Institution of court proceedings as stay of Board's order] The commencement of proceedings under subsection (e) or (f) of this section shall not, unless specifically ordered by the court, operate as a stay of the Board's order.

(h) [Jurisdiction of courts unaffected by limitations prescribed in chapter 6 of this title] When granting appropriate temporary relief or a restraining order, or making and entering a decree enforcing, modifying and enforcing as so modified, or setting aside in whole or in part an order of the Board, as provided in this section, the jurisdiction of courts sitting in equity shall not be limited by sections 101 to 115 of title 29, United States Code [chapter 6 of this title] [known as the "Norris-LaGuardia Act"].

(i) Repealed.

(j) [Injunctions] The Board shall have power, upon issuance of a complaint as provided in subsection (b) [of this section] charging that any person has engaged in or is engaging in an unfair labor practice, to petition any United States district court, within any district wherein the unfair labor practice in question is alleged to have occurred or wherein such person resides or transacts business, for appropriate temporary relief or restraining order. Upon the filing of any such petition the court shall cause notice thereof to be served upon such person, and thereupon shall have jurisdiction to grant to the Board such temporary relief or restraining order as it deems just and proper.

(k) [Hearings on jurisdictional strikes] Whenever it is charged that any person has engaged in an unfair labor practice within the meaning of paragraph (4)(D) of section 8(b) [section 158(b) of this title], the Board is empowered and directed to hear and determine the dispute out of which such unfair labor practice shall have arisen, unless, within ten days after notice that such charge has been filed, the parties to such dispute submit to the Board satisfactory evidence that they have adjusted, or agreed upon methods for the voluntary adjustment of, the dispute. Upon compliance by the parties to the dispute with the decision of the Board or upon such voluntary adjustment of the dispute, such charge shall be dismissed.

(l) [Boycotts and strikes to force recognition of uncertified labor organizations; injunctions; notice; service of process] Whenever it is charged that any person has engaged in an unfair labor practice within the meaning of paragraph (4)(A), (B), or (C) of section 8(b) [section 158(b) of this title], or section 8(e) [section 158(e) of this title] or section 8(b)(7) [section 158(b)(7) of this title], the preliminary investigation of such charge shall be made forthwith and given priority over all other cases except cases of like character in the office where it is filed or to which it is referred. If, after such investigation, the officer or regional attorney to whom the matter may be referred has reasonable cause to believe such charge is true and that a complaint should issue, he shall, on behalf of the Board, petition any United States district court within any district where the unfair labor practice in question has occurred, is alleged to have occurred, or wherein such person resides or transacts business, for appropriate injunctive relief pending the final adjudication of the Board with respect to such matter. Upon the filing of any such petition the district court shall have jurisdiction to grant such injunctive relief or temporary restraining order as it deems just and proper, notwithstanding any other provision of law: Provided further, That no temporary restraining order shall be issued without notice unless a petition alleges that substantial and irreparable injury to the charging party will be unavoidable and such temporary restraining order shall be effective for no longer than five days and will become void at the expiration of such period: Provided further, That such officer or regional attorney shall not apply for any restraining order under section 8(b)(7) [section 158(b)(7) of this title] if a charge against the employer under section 8(a)(2) [section 158(a)(2) of this title] has been filed and after the preliminary investigation, he has reasonable cause to believe that such charge is true and that a complaint should issue. Upon filing of any such petition the courts shall cause notice thereof to be served upon any person involved in the charge and such person, including the charging party, shall be given an opportunity to appear by counsel and present any relevant testimony: Provided further, That for the purposes of this subsection district courts shall be deemed to have jurisdiction of a labor organization (1) in the district in which such organization maintains its principal office, or (2) in any district in which its duly authorized officers or agents are engaged in promoting or protecting the interests of employee members. The service of legal process upon such officer or agent shall constitute service upon the labor organization and make such organization a party to the suit. In situations where such relief is appropriate the procedure specified herein shall apply to charges with respect to section 8(b)(4)(D) [section 158(b)(4)(D) of this title].

(m) [Priority of cases] Whenever it is charged that any person has engaged in an unfair labor practice within the meaning of subsection (a)(3) or (b)(2) of section 8 [section 158 of this title], such charge shall be given priority over all other cases except cases of like character in the office where it is filed or to which it is referred and cases given priority under subsection (1) [of this section].

INVESTIGATORY POWERS

Sec. 11. [§161.] For the purpose of all hearings and investigations, which, in the opinion of the Board, are necessary and proper for the exercise of the powers vested in it by section 9 and section 10 [sections 159 and 160 of this title]—

(1) [Documentary evidence; summoning witnesses and taking testimony] The Board, or its duly authorized agents or agencies, shall at all reasonable times have access to, for the purpose of examination, and the right to copy any evidence of any person being investigated or proceeded against that relates to any matter under investigation or in question. The Board, or any member thereof, shall upon application of any party to such proceedings, forthwith issue to such party subpoenas requiring the attendance and testimony of witnesses or the production of any evidence in such proceeding or investigation requested in such application. Within five days after the service of a subpoena on any person requiring the production of any evidence in his possession or under his control, such person may petition the Board to revoke, and the Board shall revoke, such subpoena if in its opinion the evidence whose production is required does not relate to any matter under investigation, or any matter in question in such proceedings, or if in its opinion such subpoena does not describe with sufficient particularity the evidence whose production is required. Any member of the Board, or any agent or agency designated by the Board for such purposes, may administer oaths and affirmations, examine witnesses, and receive evidence. Such attendance of witnesses and the production of such evidence may be required from any place in the United States or any Territory or possession thereof, at any designated place of hearing.

(2) [Court aid in compelling production of evidence and attendance of witnesses] In case on contumacy or refusal to obey a subpoena issued to any person, any United States district court or the United States courts of any Territory or possession, within the jurisdiction of which the inquiry is carried on or within the jurisdiction of which said person guilty of contumacy or refusal to obey is found or resides or transacts business, upon application by the Board shall have jurisdiction to issue to such person an order requiring such person to appear before the Board, its member, agent, or agency, there to produce evidence if so ordered, or there to give testimony touching the matter under investigation or in question; and any failure to obey such order of the court may be punished by said court as a contempt thereof.

(3) Repealed
[Immunity of witnesses. See 18 U.S.C. §6001 et seq.]

(4) [Process, service, and return; fees of witnesses] Complaints, orders, and other process and papers of the Board, its member, agent, or agency, may be served either personally or by registered or certified mail or by telegraph or by leaving a copy thereof at the principal office or place of business of the person required to be served. The verified return by the individual so serving the same setting forth the manner of such service shall be proof of the same, and the return post office receipt or telegraph receipt therefor when registered or certified and mailed or when telegraphed as aforesaid shall be proof of service of the same. Witnesses summoned before the Board, its member, agent, or agency, shall be paid the same fees and mileage that are paid to witnesses in the courts of the United States, and witnesses whose depositions are taken and the persons taking the same shall severally be entitled to the same fees as are paid for like services in the courts of the United States.

(5) [Process, where served] All process of any court to which application may be made under this Act [subchapter] may be served in the judicial district wherein the defendant or other person required to be served resides or may be found.

(6) [Information and assistance from departments] The several departments and agencies of the Government, when directed by the President, shall furnish the Board, upon its request, all records, papers, and information in their possession relating to any matter before the Board.

Sec. 12. [§162. Offenses and penalties] Any person who shall willfully resist, prevent, impede, or interfere with any member of the Board or any of its agents or agencies in the performance of duties pursuant to this Act [subchapter] shall be punished by a fine of not more than $5,000 or by imprisonment for not more than one year, or both.

LIMITATIONS

Sec. 13. [§163. Right to strike preserved] Nothing in this Act [subchapter], except as specifically provided for herein, shall be construed so as either to interfere with or impede or diminish in any way the right to strike, or to affect the limitations or qualifications on that right.

Sec. 14. [§164. Construction of provisions] (a) [Supervisors as union members] Nothing herein shall prohibit any individual employed as a supervisor from becoming or remaining a member of a labor organization, but no employer subject to this Act [subchapter] shall be compelled to deem individuals defined herein as supervisors as employees for the purpose of any law, either national or local, relating to collective bargaining.

(b) [Agreements requiring union membership in violation of State law] Nothing in this Act [subchapter] shall be construed as authorizing the execution or application of agreements requiring membership in a labor organization as a condition of employment in any State or Territory in which such execution or application is prohibited by State or Territorial law.

(c) [Power of Board to decline jurisdiction of labor disputes; assertion of jurisdiction by State and Territorial courts] (1) The Board, in its discretion, may, by rule of decision or by published rules adopted pursuant to the Administrative Procedure Act [to subchapter II of chapter 5 of title 5], decline to assert jurisdiction over any labor dispute involving any class or category of employers, where, in the opinion of the Board, the effect of such labor dispute on commerce is not sufficiently substantial to warrant the exercise of its jurisdiction: Provided, That the Board shall not decline to assert jurisdiction over any labor dispute over which it would assert jurisdiction under the standards prevailing upon August 1, 1959.

(2) Nothing in this Act [subchapter] shall be deemed to prevent or bar any agency or the courts of any State or Territory (including the Commonwealth of

Puerto Rico, Guam, and the Virgin Islands), from assuming and asserting jurisdiction over labor disputes over which the Board declines, pursuant to paragraph (1) of this subsection, to assert jurisdiction.

Sec. 15. [§165.] Omitted.

[Reference to repealed provisions of bankruptcy statute.]

Sec. 16. [§166. Separability of provisions] If any provision of this Act [subchapter], or the application of such provision to any person or circumstances, shall be held invalid, the remainder of this Act [subchapter], or the application of such provision to persons or circumstances other than those as to which it is held invalid, shall not be affected thereby.

Sec. 17. [§167. Short title] This Act [subchapter] may be cited as the "National Labor Relations Act."

Sec. 18. [§168.] Omitted.

[Reference to former sec. 9(f), (g), and (h).]

INDIVIDUALS WITH RELIGIOUS CONVICTIONS

Sec. 19. [§169.] Any employee who is a member of and adheres to established and traditional tenets or teachings of a bona fide religion, body, or sect which has historically held conscientious objections to joining or financially supporting labor organizations shall not be required to join or financially support any labor organization as a condition of employment; except that such employee may be required in a contract between such employee's employer and a labor organization in lieu of periodic dues and initiation fees, to pay sums equal to such dues and initiation fees to a nonreligious, nonlabor organization charitable fund exempt from taxation under section 501(c)(3) of title 26 of the Internal Revenue Code [section 501(c)(3) of title 26], chosen by such employee from a list of at least three such funds, designated in such contract or if the contract fails to designate such funds, then to any such fund chosen by the employee. If such employee who holds conscientious objections pursuant to this section requests the labor organization to use the grievance-arbitration procedure on the employee's behalf, the labor organization is authorized to charge the employee for the reasonable cost of using such procedure.

[Sec. added, Pub. L. 93–360, July 26, 1974, 88 Stat. 397, and amended, Pub. L. 96–593, Dec. 24, 1980, 94 Stat. 3452.]

Labor-Management Relations Act

Also cited LMRA; 29 U.S.C. §§141–197

[Title 29, Chapter 7, United States Code]

SHORT TITLE AND DECLARATION OF POLICY

Section 1. [§141.] (a) This Act [chapter] may be cited as the "Labor Management Relations Act, 1947." [Also known as the "Taft-Hartley Act."]

(b) Industrial strife which interferes with the normal flow of commerce and with the full production of articles and commodities for commerce, can be avoided or substantially minimized if employers, employees, and labor organizations each recognize under law one another's legitimate rights in their relations with each other, and above all recognize under law that neither party has any right in its relations with any other to engage in acts or practices which jeopardize the public health, safety, or interest.

It is the purpose and policy of this Act [chapter], in order to promote the full flow of commerce, to prescribe the legitimate rights of both employees and employers in their relations affecting commerce, to provide orderly and peaceful procedures for preventing the interference by either with the legitimate rights of the other, to protect the rights of individual employees in their relations with labor organizations whose activities affect commerce, to define and proscribe practices on the part of labor and management which affect commerce and are inimical to the general welfare, and to protect the rights of the public in connection with labor disputes affecting commerce.

TITLE I, Amendments to

National Labor Relations Act

29 U.S.C. §§151–169 (printed above)

TITLE II

[Title 29, Chapter 7, Subchapter III, United States Code]

CONCILIATION OF LABOR DISPUTES IN INDUSTRIES AFFECTING COMMERCE; NATIONAL EMERGENCIES

Sec. 201. [§171. Declaration of purpose and policy] It is the policy of the United States that—

(a) sound and stable industrial peace and the advancement of the general welfare, health, and safety of the Nation and of the best interest of employers and employees can most satisfactorily be secured by the settlement of issues between employers and employees through the processes of conference and collective bargaining between employers and the representatives of their employees;

(b) the settlement of issues between employers and employees through collective bargaining may be advanced by making available full and adequate governmental facilities for conciliation, mediation, and voluntary arbitration to aid and encourage employers and the representatives of their employees to reach and maintain agreements concerning rates of pay, hours, and working conditions, and to make all reasonable efforts to settle their differences by mutual agreement reached through conferences and collective bargaining or by such methods as may be provided for in any applicable agreement for the settlement of disputes; and

(c) certain controversies which arise between parties to collective-bargaining agreements may be avoided or minimized by making available full and adequate governmental facilities for furnishing assistance to employers and the representatives of their employees in formulating for inclusion within such agreements provision for adequate notice of any proposed changes in the terms of such agreements, for the final adjustment of grievances or questions regarding the application or interpretation of such agreements, and other provisions designed to prevent the subsequent arising of such controversies.

Sec. 202. [§172. Federal Mediation and Conciliation Service]

(a) [Creation; appointment of Director] There is created an independent agency to be known as the Federal Mediation and Conciliation Service (herein referred to as the "Service," except that for sixty days after June 23, 1947, such term shall refer to the Conciliation Service of the Department of Labor). The Service shall be under the direction of a Federal Mediation and Conciliation Director (hereinafter referred to as the "Director"), who shall be appointed by the President by and with the advice and consent of the Senate. The Director shall not engage in any other business, vocation, or employment.

(b) [Appointment of officers and employees; expenditures for supplies, facilities, and services] The Director is authorized, subject to the civil service laws, to appoint such clerical and other personnel as may be necessary for the execution of the functions of the Service, and shall fix their compensation in accordance with sections 5101 to 5115 and sections 5331 to 5338 of title 5, United States Code [chapter 51 and subchapter III of chapter 53 of title 5], and may, without regard to the provisions of the civil service laws, appoint such conciliators and mediators as may be necessary to carry out the functions of the Service. The Director is authorized to make such expenditures for supplies, facilities, and services as he deems necessary. Such expenditures shall be allowed and paid upon presentation of itemized vouchers therefor approved by the Director or by any employee designated by him for that purpose.

(c) [Principal and regional offices; delegation of authority by Director; annual report to Congress] The principal office of the Service shall be in the District of Columbia, but the Director may establish regional offices convenient to localities in which labor controversies are likely to arise. The Director may by order, subject to revocation at any time, delegate any authority and discretion conferred upon him by this Act [chapter] to any regional director, or other officer or employee of the Service. The Director may establish suitable procedures for cooperation with State and local mediation agencies. The Director shall make an annual report in writing to Congress at the end of the fiscal year.

(d) [Transfer of all mediation and conciliation services to Service; effective date; pending proceedings unaffected] All mediation and conciliation functions of the Secretary of Labor or the United States Conciliation Service under section 51 [repealed] of title 29, United States Code [this title], and all functions of the United States Conciliation Service under any other law are transferred to the Federal Mediation and Conciliation Service, together with the personnel and records of the United States Conciliation Service. Such transfer shall take effect upon the sixtieth day after June 23, 1947. Such transfer shall not affect any proceedings pending before the United States Conciliation Service or any certification, order, rule, or regulation theretofore made by it or by the Secretary of Labor. The Director and the Service shall not be subject in any way to the jurisdiction or authority of the Secretary of Labor or any official or division of the Department of Labor.

FUNCTIONS OF THE SERVICE

Sec. 203. [§173. Functions of Service] (a) [Settlement of disputes through conciliation and mediation] It shall be the duty of the Service, in order to prevent or minimize interruptions of the free flow of commerce growing out of labor disputes, to assist parties to labor disputes in industries affecting commerce to settle such disputes through conciliation and mediation.

(b) [Intervention on motion of Service or request of parties; avoidance of mediation of minor disputes] The Service may proffer its services in any labor dispute in any industry affecting commerce, either upon its own motion or upon the request of one or more of the parties to the dispute, whenever in its judgment such dispute threatens to cause a substantial interruption of commerce. The Director and the Service are directed to avoid attempting to mediate disputes which would have only a minor effect on interstate commerce if State or other conciliation services are available to the parties. Whenever the Service does proffer its services in any dispute, it shall be the duty of the

Service to promptly put itself in communication with the parties and to use its best efforts, by mediation and conciliation, to bring them to agreement.

(c) [Settlement of disputes by other means upon failure of conciliation] If the Director is not able to bring the parties to agreement by conciliation within a reasonable time, he shall seek to induce the parties voluntarily to seek other means of settling the dispute without resort to strike, lockout, or other coercion, including submission to the employees in the bargaining unit of the employer's last offer of settlement for approval or rejection in a secret ballot. The failure or refusal of either party to agree to any procedure suggested by the Director shall not be deemed a violation of any duty or obligation imposed by this Act [chapter].

(d) [Use of conciliation and mediation services as last resort] Final adjustment by a method agreed upon by the parties is declared to be the desirable method for settlement of grievance disputes arising over the application or interpretation of an existing collective-bargaining agreement. The Service is directed to make its conciliation and mediation services available in the settlement of such grievance disputes only as a last resort and in exceptional cases.

(e) [Encouragement and support of establishment and operation of joint labor management activities conducted by committees] The Service is authorized and directed to encourage and support the establishment and operation of joint labor management activities conducted by plant, area, and industrywide committees designed to improve labor management relationships, job security, and organizational effectiveness, in accordance with the provisions of section 205A [section 175a of this title].

[Pub. L. 95–524, §6(c)(1), Oct. 27, 1978, 92 Stat. 2020, added subsec. (e).]

Sec. 204. [§174. Co-equal obligations of employees, their representatives, and management to minimize labor disputes]

(a) In order to prevent or minimize interruptions of the free flow of commerce growing out of labor disputes, employers and employees and their representatives, in any industry affecting commerce, shall—

(1) exert every reasonable effort to make and maintain agreements concerning rates of pay, hours, and working conditions, including provision for adequate notice of any proposed change in the terms of such agreements;

(2) whenever a dispute arises over the terms or application of a collective-bargaining agreement and a conference is requested by a party or prospective party thereto, arrange promptly for such a conference to be held and endeavor in such conference to settle such dispute expeditiously; and

(3) in case such dispute is not settled by conference, participate fully and promptly in such meetings as may be undertaken by the Service under this Act [chapter] for the purpose of aiding in a settlement of the dispute.

Sec. 205. [§175. National Labor-Management Panel; creation and composition; appointment, tenure, and compensation; duties] (a) There is created a National Labor-Management Panel which shall be composed of twelve members appointed by the President, six of whom shall be selected from among persons outstanding in the field of management and six of whom shall be selected from among persons outstanding in the field of labor. Each member shall hold office for a term of three years, except that any member appointed to fill a vacancy occurring prior to the expiration of the term for which his predecessor was appointed shall be appointed for the remainder of such term, and the terms of office of the members first taking office shall expire, as designated by the President at the time of appointment, four at the end of the first year, four at the end of the second year, and four at the end of the third year after the date of appointment. Members of the panel, when serving on business of the panel, shall be paid compensation at the rate of $25 per day, and shall also be entitled to receive an allowance for actual and necessary travel and subsistence expenses while so serving away from their places of residence.

(b) It shall be the duty of the panel, at the request of the Director, to advise in the avoidance of industrial controversies and the manner in which mediation and voluntary adjustment shall be administered, particularly with reference to controversies affecting the general welfare of the country.

Sec. 205A. [§175a. Assistance to plant, area, and industrywide labor management committees]

(a) [Establishment and operation of plant, area, and industrywide committees] (1) The Service is authorized and directed to provide assistance in the establishment and operation of plant, area, and industrywide labor management committees which—

(A) have been organized jointly by employers and labor organizations representing employees in that plant, area, or industry; and

(B) are established for the purpose of improving labor management relationships, job security, organizational effectiveness, enhancing economic development, or involving workers in decisions affecting their jobs including improving communication with respect to subjects of mutual interest and concern.

(2) The Service is authorized and directed to enter into contracts and to make grants, where necessary or appropriate, to fulfill its responsibilities under this section.

(b) [Restrictions on grants, contracts, or other assistance] (1) No grant may be made, no contract may be entered into, and no other assistance may be provided under the provisions of this section to a plant labor management committee unless the employees in that plant are represented by a labor organization and there is in effect at that plant a collective bargaining agreement.

(2) No grant may be made, no contract may be entered into, and no other assistance may be provided under the provisions of this section to an area or industrywide labor management committee unless its participants include any labor organizations certified or recognized as the representative of the employees of an employer participating in such committee. Nothing in this clause shall prohibit participation in an area or industrywide committee by an employer whose employees are not represented by a labor organization.

(3) No grant may be made under the provisions of this section to any labor management committee which the Service finds to have as one of its purposes the discouragement of the exercise of rights contained in section 7 of the National Labor Relations Act (29 U.S.C. §157) [section 157 of this title], or the interference with collective bargaining in any plant, or industry.

(c) [Establishment of office] The Service shall carry out the provisions of this section through an office established for that purpose.

(d) [Authorization of appropriations] There are authorized to be appropriated to carry out the provisions of this section $10,000,000 for the fiscal year 1979, and such sums as may be necessary thereafter.

[Pub. L. 95–524, §6(c)(2), Oct. 27, 1978, 92 Stat. 2020, added Sec. 205A.]

NATIONAL EMERGENCIES

Sec. 206. [§176. Appointment of board of inquiry by President; report; contents; filing with Service] Whenever in the opinion of the President of the United States, a threatened or actual strike or lockout affecting an entire industry or a substantial part thereof engaged in trade, commerce, transportation, transmission, or communication among the several States or with foreign nations, or engaged in the production of goods for commerce, will, if permitted to occur or to continue, imperil the national health or safety, he may appoint a board of inquiry to inquire into the issues involved in the dispute and to make a written report to him within such time as he shall prescribe. Such report shall include a statement of the facts with respect to the dispute, including each party's statement of its position but shall not contain any recommendations. The President shall file a copy of such report with the Service and shall make its contents available to the public.

Sec. 207. [§177. Board of inquiry] (a) [Composition] A board of inquiry shall be composed of a chairman and such other members as the President shall determine, and shall have power to sit and act in any place within the United States and to conduct such hearings either in public or in private, as it may deem necessary or proper, to ascertain the facts with respect to the causes and circumstances of the dispute.

(b) [Compensation] Members of a board of inquiry shall receive compensation at the rate of $50 for each day actually spent by them in the work of the board, together with necessary travel and subsistence expenses.

(c) [Powers of discovery] For the purpose of any hearing or inquiry conducted by any board appointed under this title, the provisions of sections 49 and 50 of title 15, United States Code [sections 49 and 50 of title 15] (relating to the attendance of witnesses and the production of books, papers, and documents) are made applicable to the powers and duties of such board.

Sec. 208. [§178. Injunctions during national emergency]

(a) [Petition to district court by Attorney General on direction of President] Upon receiving a report from a board of inquiry the President may direct the Attorney General to petition any district court of the United States having jurisdiction of the parties to enjoin such strike or lockout or the continuing thereof, and if the court finds that such threatened or actual strike or lockout—

(i) affects an entire industry or a substantial part thereof engaged in trade, commerce, transportation, transmission, or communication among the several States or with foreign nations, or engaged in the production of goods for commerce; and

(ii) if permitted to occur or to continue, will imperil the national health or safety, it shall have jurisdiction to enjoin any such strike or lockout, or the continuing thereof, and to make such other orders as may be appropriate.

(b) [Inapplicability of chapter 6] In any case, the provisions of sections 101 to 115 of title 29, United States Code [chapter 6 of this title] [known as the "Norris-LaGuardia Act"] shall not be applicable.

(c) [Review of orders] The order or orders of the court shall be subject to review by the appropriate United States court of appeals and by the Supreme Court upon writ of certiorari or certification as provided in section 1254 of title 28, United States Code [section 1254 of title 28].

Sec. 209. [§179. Injunctions during national emergency; adjustment efforts by parties during injunction period]

(a) [Assistance of Service; acceptance of Service's proposed settlement] Whenever a district court has issued an order under section 208 [section 178 of this title] enjoining acts or practices which imperil or threaten to imperil the national health or safety, it shall be the duty of the parties to the labor dispute giving rise to such order to make every effort to adjust and settle their differences, with the assistance of the Service created by this Act [chapter]. Neither party shall be under any duty to accept, in whole or in part, any proposal of settlement made by the Service.

(b) [Reconvening of board of inquiry; report by board; contents; secret ballot of employees by National Labor Relations Board; certification of results to Attorney General] Upon the issuance of such order, the President shall reconvene the board of inquiry which has previously reported with respect to the dispute. At the end of a sixty-day period (unless the dispute has been settled by that time), the board of inquiry shall report to the President the current position of the parties and the efforts which have been made for settlement, and shall include a statement by each party of its position and a statement of the employer's last offer of settlement. The President shall make such report available to the public. The National Labor Relations Board, within the succeeding fifteen days, shall take a secret ballot of the employees of each employer involved in the dispute on the question of whether they wish to accept the final offer of settlement made by their employer as stated by him and shall certify the results thereof to the Attorney General within five days thereafter.

Sec. 210. [§180. Discharge of injunction upon certification of results of election or settlement; report to Congress] Upon the certification of the results of such ballot or upon a settlement being reached, whichever happens sooner, the Attorney General shall move the court to discharge the injunction, which motion shall then be granted and the injunction discharged. When such motion is granted, the President shall submit to the Congress a full and comprehensive report of the proceedings, including the findings of the board of inquiry and the ballot taken by the National Labor Relations Board, together with such recommendations as he may see fit to make for consideration and appropriate action.

COMPILATION OF COLLECTIVE-BARGAINING AGREEMENTS, ETC.

Sec. 211. [§181.] (a) For the guidance and information of interested representatives of employers, employees, and the general public, the Bureau of Labor Statistics of the Department of Labor shall maintain a file of copies of all available collective bargaining agreements and other available agreements and actions thereunder settling or adjusting labor disputes. Such file shall be open to inspection under appropriate conditions prescribed by the Secretary of Labor, except that no specific information submitted in confidence shall be disclosed.

(b) The Bureau of Labor Statistics in the Department of Labor is authorized to furnish upon request of the Service, or employers, employees, or their representatives, all available data and factual information which may aid in the settlement of any labor dispute, except that no specific information submitted in confidence shall be disclosed.

EXEMPTION OF RAILWAY LABOR ACT

Sec. 212. [§182.] The provisions of this title [subchapter] shall not be applicable with respect to any matter which is subject to the provisions of the Railway Labor Act [45 U.S.C. §151 et seq.], as amended from time to time.

CONCILIATION OF LABOR DISPUTES IN THE HEALTH CARE INDUSTRY

Sec. 213. [§183.] (a) [Establishment of Boards of Inquiry; membership] If, in the opinion of the Director of the Federal Mediation and Conciliation Service, a threatened or actual strike or lockout affecting a health care institution will, if permitted to occur or to continue, substantially interrupt the delivery of health care in the locality concerned, the Director may further assist in the resolution of the impasse by establishing within 30 days after the notice to the Federal Mediation and Conciliation Service under clause

(A) of the last sentence of section 8(d) [section 158(d) of this title] (which is required by clause (3) of such section 8(d) [section 158(d) of this title]), or within 10 days after the notice under clause (B), an impartial Board of Inquiry to investigate the issues involved in the dispute and to make a written report thereon to the parties within fifteen (15) days after the establishment of such a Board. The written report shall contain the findings of facts together with the Board's recommendations for settling the dispute, with the objective of achieving a prompt, peaceful, and just settlement of the dispute. Each such Board shall be composed of such number of individuals as the Director may deem desirable. No member appointed under this section shall have any interest or involvement in the health care institutions or the employee organizations involved in the dispute.

(b) [Compensation of members of Boards of Inquiry] (1) Members of any board established under this section who are otherwise employed by the Federal Government shall serve without compensation but shall be reimbursed for travel, subsistence, and other necessary expenses incurred by them in carrying out its duties under this section.

(2) Members of any board established under this section who are not subject to paragraph (1) shall receive compensation at a rate prescribed by the Director but not to exceed the daily rate prescribed for GS-18 of the General Schedule under section 5332 of title 5, United States Code [section 5332 of title 5], including travel for each day they are engaged in the performance of their duties under this section and shall be entitled to reimbursement for travel, subsistence, and other necessary expenses incurred by them in carrying out their duties under this section.

(c) [Maintenance of status quo] After the establishment of a board under subsection (a) of this section and for 15 days after any such board has issued its report, no change in the status quo in effect prior to the expiration of the contract in the case of negotiations for a contract renewal, or in effect prior to the time of the impasse in the case of an initial bargaining negotiation, except by agreement, shall be made by the parties to the controversy.

(d) [Authorization of appropriations] There are authorized to be appropriated such sums as may be necessary to carry out the provisions of this section.

TITLE III

[Title 29, Chapter 7, Subchapter IV, United States Code]

SUITS BY AND AGAINST LABOR ORGANIZATIONS

Sec. 301. [§185.] (a) [Venue, amount, and citizenship] Suits for violation of contracts between an employer and a labor organization representing employees in an industry affecting commerce as defined in this Act [chapter], or between any such labor organization, may be brought in any district court of the United States having jurisdiction of the parties, without respect to the amount in controversy or without regard to the citizenship of the parties.

(b) [Responsibility for acts of agent; entity for purposes of suit; enforcement of money judgments] Any labor organization which represents employees in an industry affecting commerce as defined in this Act [chapter] and any employer whose activities affect commerce as defined in this Act [chapter] shall be bound by the acts of its agents. Any such labor organization may sue or be sued as an entity and in behalf of the employees whom it represents in the courts of the United States. Any money judgment against a labor organization in a district court of the United States shall be enforceable only against the organization as an entity and against its assets, and shall not be enforceable against any individual member or his assets.

(c) [Jurisdiction] For the purposes of actions and proceedings by or against labor organizations in the district courts of the United States, district courts shall be deemed to have jurisdiction of a labor organization (1) in the district in which such organization maintains its principal offices, or (2) in any district in which its duly authorized officers or agents are engaged in representing or acting for employee members.

(d) [Service of process] The service of summons, subpoena, or other legal process of any court of the United States upon an officer or agent of a labor organization, in his capacity as such, shall constitute service upon the labor organization.

(e) [Determination of question of agency] For the purposes of this section, in determining whether any person is acting as an "agent" of another person so as to make such other person responsible for his acts, the question of whether the specific acts performed were actually authorized or subsequently ratified shall not be controlling.

RESTRICTIONS ON PAYMENTS TO EMPLOYEE REPRESENTATIVES

Sec. 302. [§186.] (a) [Payment or lending, etc., of money by employer or agent to employees, representatives, or labor organizations] It shall be unlawful for any employer or association of employers or any person who acts as a labor relations expert, adviser, or consultant to an employer or who acts in the interest of an employer to pay, lend, or deliver, or agree to pay, lend, or deliver, any money or other thing of value—

(1) to any representative of any of his employees who are employed in an industry affecting commerce; or

(2) to any labor organization, or any officer or employee thereof, which represents, seeks to represent, or would admit to membership, any of the employees of such employer who are employed in an industry affecting commerce;

(3) to any employee or group or committee of employees of such employer employed in an industry affecting commerce in excess of their normal compensation for the purpose of causing such employee or group or committee directly or indirectly to influence any other employees in the exercise of the right to organize and bargain collectively through representatives of their own choosing; or

(4) to any officer or employee of a labor organization engaged in an industry affecting commerce with intent to influence him in respect to any of his actions, decisions, or duties as a representative of employees or as such officer or employee of such labor organization.

(b) [Request, demand, etc., for money or other thing of value] (1) It shall be unlawful for any person to request, demand, receive, or accept, or agree to receive or accept, any payment, loan, or delivery of any money or other thing of value prohibited by subsection (a) [of this section].

(2) It shall be unlawful for any labor organization, or for any person acting as an officer, agent, representative, or employee of such labor organization, to demand or accept from the operator of any motor vehicle (as defined in part II of the Interstate Commerce Act [49 U.S.C. §301 et seq.]) employed in the transportation of property in commerce, or the employer of any such operator, any money or other thing of value payable to such organization or to an officer, agent, representative, or employee thereof as a fee or charge for the unloading, or in connection with the unloading, of the cargo of such vehicle: Provided, That nothing in this paragraph shall be construed to

make unlawful any payment by an employer to any of his employees as compensation for their services as employees.

(c) [Exceptions] The provisions of this section shall not be applicable (1) in respect to any money or other thing of value payable by an employer to any of his employees whose established duties include acting openly for such employer in matters of labor relations or personnel administration or to any representative of his employees, or to any officer or employee of a labor organization, who is also an employee or former employee of such employer, as compensation for, or by reason of, his service as an employee of such employer; (2) with respect to the payment or delivery of any money or other thing of value in satisfaction of a judgment of any court or a decision or award of an arbitrator or impartial chairman or in compromise, adjustment, settlement, or release of any claim, complaint, grievance, or dispute in the absence of fraud or duress; (3) with respect to the sale or purchase of an article or commodity at the prevailing market price in the regular course of business; (4) with respect to money deducted from the wages of employees in payment of membership dues in a labor organization: Provided, That the employer has received from each employee, on whose account such deductions are made, a written assignment which shall not be irrevocable for a period of more than one year, or beyond the termination date of the applicable collective agreement, whichever occurs sooner; (5) with respect to money or other thing of value paid to a trust fund established by such representative, for the sole and exclusive benefit of the employees of such employer, and their families, and dependents (or of such employees, families, and dependents jointly with the employees of other employers making similar payments, and their families, and dependents): Provided, That (A) such payments are held in trust for the purpose of paying, either from principal or income or both, for the benefit of employees, their families, and dependents, for medical or hospital care, pensions on retirement or death of employees, compensation for injuries or illness resulting from occupational activity or insurance to provide any of the foregoing, or unemployment benefits or life insurance, disability and sickness insurance, or accident insurance; (B) the detailed basis on which such payments are to be made is specified in a written agreement with the employer, and employees and employers are equally represented in the administration of such fund, together with such neutral persons as the representatives of the employers and the representatives of employees may agree upon and in the event the employer and employee groups deadlock on the administration of such fund and there are no neutral persons empowered to break such deadlock, such agreement provides that the two groups shall agree on an impartial umpire to decide such dispute, or in event of their failure to agree within a reasonable length of time, an impartial umpire to decide such dispute shall, on petition of either group, be appointed by the district court of the United States for the district where the trust fund has its principal office, and shall also contain provisions for an annual audit of the trust fund, a statement of the results of which shall be available for inspection by interested persons at the principal office of the trust fund and at such other places as may be designated in such written agreement; and (C) such payments as are intended to be used for the purpose of providing pensions or annuities for employees are made to a separate trust which provides that the funds held therein cannot be used for any purpose other than paying such pensions or annuities; (6) with respect to money or other thing of value paid by any employer to a trust fund established by such representative for the purpose of pooled vacation, holiday, severance or similar benefits, or defraying costs of apprenticeship or other training programs: Provided, That the requirements of clause (B) of the proviso to clause

(5) of this subsection shall apply to such trust funds; (7) with respect to money or other thing of value paid by any employer to a pooled or individual trust fund established by such representative for the purpose of (A) scholarships for the benefit of employees, their families, and dependents for study at educational institutions, or (B) child care centers for preschool and school age dependents of employees: Provided, That no labor organization or employer shall be required to bargain on the establishment of any such trust fund, and refusal to do so shall not constitute an unfair labor practice: Provided further, That the requirements of clause (B) of the proviso to clause (5) of this subsection shall apply to such trust funds; (8) with respect to money or any other thing of value paid by any employer to a trust fund established by such representative for the purpose of defraying the costs of legal services for employees, their families, and dependents for counsel or plan of their choice: Provided, That the requirements of clause (B) of the proviso to clause (5) of this subsection shall apply to such trust funds: Provided further, That no such legal services shall be furnished: (A) to initiate any proceeding directed (i) against any such employer or its officers or agents except in workman's compensation cases; or (ii) against such labor organization, or its parent or subordinate bodies, or their officers or agents, or (iii) against any other employer or labor organization, or their officers or agents, in any matter arising under the National Labor Relations Act, or this Act [under subchapter II of this chapter or this chapter]; and (B) in any proceeding where a labor organization would be prohibited from defraying the costs of legal services by the provisions of the Labor-Management Reporting and Disclosure Act of 1959 [29 U.S.C. §401 et seq.]; or (9) with respect to money or other things of value paid by an employer to a plant, area, or industrywide labor management committee established for one or more of the purposes set forth in section 5(b) of the Labor Management Cooperation Act of 1978.

[Sec. 302(c)(7) was added by Pub. L. 91–86, Oct. 14, 1969, 83 Stat. 133; Sec. 302(c)(8) by Pub. L. 93–95, Aug. 15, 1973, 87 Stat. 314; and Sec. 302(c)(9) by Pub. L. 95–524, Oct. 27, 1978, 92 Stat. 2021.]

(d) [Penalty for violations] Any person who willfully violates any of the provisions of this section shall, upon conviction thereof, be guilty of a misdemeanor and be subject to a fine of not more than $10,000 or to imprisonment for not more than one year, or both.

(e) [Jurisdiction of courts] The district courts of the United States and the United States courts of the Territories and possessions shall have jurisdiction, for cause shown, and subject to the provisions of rule 65 of the Federal Rules of Civil Procedure [section 381 (repealed) of title 28] (relating to notice to opposite party) to restrain violations of this section, without regard to the provisions of section 17 of title 15 and section 52 of title 29, United States Code [of this title] [known as the "Clayton Act"], and the provisions of sections 101 to 115 of title 29, United States Code [chapter 6 of this title] [known as the "Norris-LaGuardia Act"].

(f) [Effective date of provisions] This section shall not apply to any contract in force on June 23, 1947, until the expiration of such contract, or until July 1, 1948, whichever first occurs.

(g) [Contributions to trust funds] Compliance with the restrictions contained in subsection (c)(5)(B) [of this section] upon contributions to trust funds, otherwise lawful, shall not be applicable to contributions to such trust funds established by collective agreement prior to January 1, 1946, nor shall subsection (c)(5)(A) [of this section] be construed as prohibiting contributions to such trust funds if prior to January 1, 1947, such funds contained provisions for pooled vacation benefits.

BOYCOTTS AND OTHER UNLAWFUL COMBINATIONS

Sec. 303. [§187.] (a) It shall be unlawful, for the purpose of this section only, in an industry or activity affecting commerce, for any labor organization to engage in any activity or conduct defined as an unfair labor practice in section 8(b)(4) of the National Labor Relations Act [section 158(b)(4) of this title].

(b) Whoever shall be injured in his business or property by reason of any violation of subsection (a) [of this section] may sue therefor in any district court of the United States subject to the limitation and provisions of section 301 hereof [section 185 of this title] without respect to the amount in controversy, or in any other court having jurisdiction of the parties, and shall recover the damages by him sustained and the cost of the suit.

RESTRICTION ON POLITICAL CONTRIBUTIONS

Sec. 304. Repealed. [See sec. 316 of the Federal Election Campaign Act of 1972, 2 U.S.C. §441b.]

Sec. 305. [§188.] Strikes by Government employees. Repealed.

[See 5 U.S.C. §7311 and 18 U.S.C. §1918.]

TITLE IV

[Title 29, Chapter 7, Subchapter V, United States Code]

CREATION OF JOINT COMMITTEE TO STUDY AND REPORT ON BASIC PROBLEMS AFFECTING FRIENDLY LABOR RELATIONS AND PRODUCTIVITY

Secs. 401–407. [§§191–197.] Omitted.

TITLE V

[Title 29, Chapter 7, Subchapter I, United States Code]

DEFINITIONS

Sec. 501. [§142.] When used in this Act [chapter]—

(1) The term "industry affecting commerce" means any industry or activity in commerce or in which a labor dispute would burden or obstruct commerce or tend to burden or obstruct commerce or the free flow of commerce.

(2) The term "strike" includes any strike or other concerted stoppage of work by employees (including a stoppage by reason of the expiration of a collective-bargaining agreement) and any concerted slowdown or other concerted interruption of operations by employees.

(3) The terms "commerce," "labor disputes," "employer," "employee," "labor organization," "representative," "person," and "supervisor" shall have the same meaning as when used in the National Labor Relations Act as amended by this Act [in subchapter II of this chapter].

SAVING PROVISION

Sec. 502. [§143.] [Abnormally dangerous conditions] Nothing in this Act [chapter] shall be construed to require an individual employee to render labor or service without his consent, nor shall anything in this Act [chapter] be construed to make the quitting of his labor by an individual employee an illegal act; nor shall any court issue any process to compel the performance by an individual employee of such labor or service, without his consent; nor shall the quitting of labor by an employee or employees in good faith because of abnormally dangerous conditions for work at the place of employment of such employee or employees be deemed a strike under this Act [chapter].

SEPARABILITY

Sec. 503. [§144.] If any provision of this Act [chapter], or the application of such provision to any person or circumstance, shall be held invalid, the remainder of this Act [chapter], or the application of such provision to persons or circumstances other than those as to which it is held invalid, shall not be affected thereby.

Endnotes

CHAPTER 1

1. Foster Rhea Dulles and Melvyn Dubofsky, *Labor in America, A History,* 4th ed. (Arlington Heights, IL: Harlan Davidson, 1984), p. 1.
2. Ibid., pp. 32, 70–73.
3. Robert Asher and Charles Stephens, eds., *Labor Dividend: Race and Ethnicity in United States Labor Struggles 1835–1960* (Albany: State University of New York Press, 1990), pp. 154–58.
4. Maurice F. Neufeld, "The Persistence of Ideas in the American Labor Movement: The Heritage of the 1830s," *Industrial and Labor Relations Review 35,* no. 2 (January 1982), p. 212.
5. John R. Commons, *History of Labor in the United States, Vol. 2* (New York: Macmillan, 1946), pp. 7–8.
6. Joseph G. Rayback, *A History of American Labor* (New York: The Free Press, 1966), pp. 120–22.
7. Dulles and Dubofsky, *Labor in America,* pp. 111–12; Rayback, *A History of American Labor,* 1966, pp. 131–33.
8. Samuel Yellen, *American Labor Struggles* (New York: Harcourt Brace, 1936), pp. 3–38.
9. Joseph Rayback, *A History of American Labor* (New York: Macmillan, 1959), p. 135.
10. Ron Panko, "Underwriting Strike Insurance," *Bests Review 100,* no. 10, pp. 32–33.
11. Yellen, *American Labor Struggles,* pp. 39–71.
12. Richard O. Bayer and Herbert M. Morris, *Labor's Untold Story* (New York: United Electrical Radio and Machine Workers of America, 1955), pp. 98–99, by permission of United Electrical and Radio Machine Workers.
13. Ibid., p. 99; and see Dulles and Dubofsky, *Labor in America,* pp. 116–18.
14. Dulles and Dubofsky, *Labor in America,* p. 135.
15. Sherman Antitrust Act, 15 U.S.C. sec. 1 (1892).
16. Bayer and Morris, *Labor's Untold Story,* p. 131.
17. Ibid., p. 119.
18. J. Robert Constantine, "Eugene V. Debs: An American Paradox," *Monthly Labor Review 114,* no. 8 (August 1991), pp. 30–33.
19. Stuart Bruce Kaufman, "Birth of a Federation: Mr. Gompers Endeavors Not to Build a Bubble," *Monthly Labor Review 104,* no. 11 (November 1981), p. 24.
20. Rayback, *A History of American Labor,* 1966, pp. 194–226.
21. Alice Kessler-Harris, "Trade Unions Mirror Society in Conflict between Collectivism and Individualism," *Monthly Labor Review 110,* no. 8 (August 1989), pp. 34–35.
22. Judith Nielsen, from the papers of Stanley Eston, archived at the University of Idaho.
23. Rayback, *A History of American Labor,* 1966, pp. 238–39, and Gary Chaison, *Unions in America,* (Thousand Oaks, CA: Sage Publications, Inc., 2006) p. 10.
24. Dulles and Dubofsky, *Labor in America,* p. 214.
25. Juliet H. Mofford, "Women in the Workplace: Labor Unions," *Women's History Magazine* (Spring/Summer 1996).
26. Ludlow Massacre (http://222.umwa.org/history/ludlow.shtml). From the United Mine Workers of America, with a link to the Ludlow Monument listing the names of the victims.
27. Rayback, *A History of American Labor,* 1959, pp. 54–57.
28. David P. Twomey, *Labor Law and Legislation* (Cincinnati: South-Western, 1980), pp. 7–8.
29. *Commonwealth v. Hunt,* 45 Mass. (4 Met.) III (1842).
30. Bayer and Morris, *Labor's Untold Story,* p. 131.
31. Erdman Act, 30 Stat. 424 (1898), amended by P.L. 6, 38 Stat. 103 (1913); referenced in 45 U.S.C. sec. 101 (1976).
32. Rayback, *A History of American Labor,* 1966, p. 212.
33. Clayton Act, ch. 323, sec. 1, 6, and 7, 38 Stat. 730 (1914); referenced in 15 U.S.C. sec. 12, 17, and 18 (1982).
34. Theodore Kheel, *Labor Law* (New York: Matthew Bender, 1988), chap. 5, p. 24.
35. *Duplex Printing Press Co. v. Deering,* 254 U.S. 443, 41 S.Ct. 172, 65 L.Ed. 349 (1921), and *Redford Cut Stone Co. v. Journeymen Stone Cutters' Association,* 274 U.S. 37, 47 S.Ct. 522, 71 L.Ed. 916 (1927).
36. Railway Labor Act, 45 U.S.C. sec. 151 (1976).
37. *Texas and New Orleans Railroad Co. v. Brotherhood of Railway & Steamship Clerks,* 281 U.S. 548 (1930).
38. Ibid., 570.
39. David Moberg, "On 75th Anniversary of Railway Labor Act, We Need to Protect Workers' Rights," *The Progressive Media Project* (www.progressive.org), May 15, 2001, and Morgan O. Reynolds and D. Eric Schansberg, "At Age 65, Retire the Railway Labor Act," *Regulation 14,* no. 3 (Summer 1991). (www.cato.org)

40. Davis-Bacon Act, Title 40 U.S.C.A. sec. 276a (1931).

41. Norris–La Guardia Act, 29 U.S.C. sec. 101 (1982).

42. National Industrial Recovery Act, Pub.L. 67, 48 Stat. 195 (1933); referenced in 7 U.S.C. sec. 601 (1982).

43. *Schechter Poultry Corp. v. United States,* 295 U.S. 495, 55 S.Ct. 837, 79 L.Ed. 893 (1937).

44. Patrick Hardin, ed., *The Developing Labor Law,* 3rd ed. (Washington, D.C.: Bureau of National Affairs, 1992), pp. 12–13.

45. Ibid., p. 28.

46. National Labor Relations Act, 29 U.S.C. sec. 151 et seq. (1982).

47. *Associated Press v. National Labor Relations Board,* 301 U.S. 103 (1937), and *National Labor Relations Board v. Jones & Laughlin Steel Corporation,* 301 U.S. 1, 57 S.Ct. 615, 81 L.Ed. 893 (1937).

48. Walsh-Healy Act, Title 29 U.S.C.A. sec. 557, and Title 41 U.S.C.A. secs. 35–45.

49. Fair Labor Standards Act, 29 U.S.C. sec. 201 (1982).

50. War Labor Disputes Act, Pub.L. 89, 57 Stat. 163 (1943).

51. *Thornhill v. Alabama,* 310 U.S. 88 (1940), and *Milk Drivers Local 753 v. Meadowmoore Dairies, Inc.,* 312 U.S. 287 (1941).

52. Small Business Protection Act, H.R. 3448 (August 2, 1996). See also James S. Ray and Barbara Berish Brown, "Federal Leg. Update April–Aug. 1990," *Labor Lawyer 6,* no. 4 (Fall 1990), pp. 1029–30.

53. Fair Labor Standards Act, 29 U.S.C. sec. 206(g) (1996).

54. Darren Bell, "Understanding Recent Changes in the FLSA," *Intercom 52,* no. 4 (April 2005), pp. 25–27.

55. Hardin, *The Developing Labor Law,* p. 35.

56. Labor-Management Reporting and Disclosure (Landrum-Griffin) Act, 29 U.S.C. sec. 401 et seq. (1982).

57. William W. Osborne, Jr. *All You Need to Know About the History of Labor Union Law* (Washington, D.C.: BNA Books, 2003), pp. 56–58.

58. Neil W. Chamberlain, *Sourcebook on Labor* (New York: McGraw-Hill, 1964), pp. 26–29.

59. Labor-Management Reporting and Disclosure (Landrum-Griffin) Act, 29 U.S.C. sec. 401 et seq. (1982).

60. *Transportation Workers Local 525,* 317 N.L.R.B. 62, 149 L.R.R.M. 1222 (1995).

61. *Wirtz v. Hotel, Motel & Club Employees Union, Local 6,* 391 U.S. 492 (1968).

62. "The Labor Movement," *Workforce* 81, no. 1 (Jan. 2002) p. 27.

63. Melaine Payne, "Union Membership Increases in Public Sector," *The Sacramento Be,* (March 11, 2002).

64. P.L. 91–375, 84 Stat. 737, 39 U.S.C. sec. 1209 (1970).

65. Benjamin Aaron et al., *Public-Sector Bargaining* (Washington, D.C.: Bureau of National Affairs, 1979), p. 46.

66. David Lewin and Shirley B. Goldenberg, "Public Sector Unionism in the U.S. and Canada," *Industrial Relations* 19, no. 3 (Fall 1980), pp. 239–56.

67. Jerry Wurf, "Establishing the Legal Right of Public Employees to Bargain," *Monthly Labor Review* 92, no. 7 (July 1969), p. 66.

68. Henry Campbell Black, *Black's Law Dictionary,* 4th ed. (St. Paul, MN: West Publishing, 1968), p. 1568.

69. Robert Wechsler, "The Birth of Modern Public Employees Unions," *New York Labor History Association News Service,* 1995.

70. 5 U.S.C. sec. 7116(a)(1982).

71. 58 Fed. Reg. 52,201 (1993); "Federal Service Labor and Employment Law," *Labor Lawyer* 10, no. 3 (Summer 1994), p. 336.

72. Robert M. Tobias, "The Future of Federal Government Labor Relations and the Mutual Interest of Congress, the Administration and Unions," *Journal of Labor Research* 25, no. 1 (Winter 2004) pp. 19–41.

73. For an overview of state and local legislation, see Aaron et al., *Public-Sector Bargaining,* pp. 191–223, and Nels E. Nelson, "Public Policy and Union Security in the Public Sector," *Journal of Collective Negotiations in the Public Sector* 7, no. 2 (1978), pp. 87–117.

74. *National League of Cities v. Usery,* 426 U.S. 833 (1976).

75. Gregory M. Saltzman, "Bargaining Laws as a Cause and Consequence of the Growth of Teacher Unionism," *Industrial and Labor Relations Review* 38, no.3 (April 1985), pp. 335–51.

CHAPTER 2

1. Robert J. Grossman, "Unions Follow Suit," *HR Magazine 50,* no. 5 (May, 2005), pp. 46–51.

2. Richard Feldman and Michael Betzold, *End of the Line: Autoworkers and the American Dream* (New York: Weidenfeld & Nicolson, 1988), p. 6.

3. "The February Review," *Monthly Labor Review 128,* no. 2 (February 2005), p. 2.

4. Robert J. Flanagan, "Has Management Strangled U.S. Unions?" *Journal of Labor Research 26,* no. 1 (Winter 2005), pp. 33–63.

5. Court Gifford, *Directory of U.S. Labor Organizations, 2001* (Washington, D.C.: Bureau of National Affairs, 2001), p. 1.

6. David Wessel, "Some Workers Gail with New Union Tactics," *Wall Street Journal,* January 3, 2002, p. A1.

7. Lou Dobbs, "Disorganized Labor," *U.S. News & World Report 138,* no. 8, (March 7, 2005), 48.

8. Mark Fitzgerald, "Can't We All Just Get Along?" *Editor & Publisher 136,* no. 27 (July 14, 2003), pp. 10–17.

9. Paul Kennedy, *Preparing for the Twenty-First Century* (New York: Random House, 1993), p. 4.

10. Ralph K. Andrist, ed., *The American Heritage History of the Confident Years* (New York: American Heritage Publishing, 1969), p. 306.

11. Alistair Cooke, *America* (New York: Alfred A. Knopf, 1973), pp. 273–88.

12. Robert B. Reich, *The Work of Nations* (New York: Vintage Books, 1992), p. 35.

13. Foster Rhea Dulles and Melvyn Dubofsky, *Labor in America, A History,* 4th ed. (Arlington Heights, IL: Harlan Davidson, 1984), pp. 343–54.

14. Yang Tianxin, "No More Recession Blues?" *Beijing Review 46,* no. 52 (December 25, 2003) 42.

15. "Fact & Fallacy: Updating the Reasons for Union Decline," *Employment Policy Foundation* (May 1998). Available at http://www.epf.org/pubs/newsletters/1998/ff4-5.asp. Accessed December 2005.

16. Richard W. Judy and Carol D'Amico, *Workforce 2020: Work and Workers in the 21st Century* (Indianapolis, IN: Hudson Institute, 1997), pp. 12–13.

17. See John C. McCarthy, "3.3 Million US Services Jobs to Go Offshore," Forrester Research, TechStrategy™ Research Brief, November 11, 2002; and Paul McDougall, "There's No Stopping the Offshore-Outsourcing Train," *Information Week* (May 24, 2004). Available at www.informationweek.com. Accessed December 2005.

18. Sarah Anderson and John Cavanagh, "Outsourcing: A Policy Agenda," *Policy Brief 9,* no. 2 (April 2004), pp. 1–4. Available at www.fpif.org. Accessed December 2005.

19. Jeff Ball, "UAW's Reception in Alabama Mercedes Plant Is Sour," *Wall Street Journal,* January 31, 2000, p. A15.

20. Yochi J. Dreazen, "Old Labor Tries to Establish Role in New Economy," *Wall Street Journal,* August 15, 2000, pp. B1, B10.

21. Jack Fiorito and William Bass, "The Use of Information Technology by National Unions: An Exploratory Analysis," *Industrial Relations 41,* no. 1 (January 2002) pp. 34–47.

22. David Moberg, "Labor Debates Its Future," *The Nation 280,* no. 10, (March 14, 2005), pp. 11–16.

23. Ed McKenna, "Teamsters Target DHL," *Traffic World* (April 25, 2005), p. 30.

24. Ed Watkins, "Storm Warnings," *Lodging Hospitality 60,* no. 14 (October 2004), p. 4.

25. John E. Lyncheski, "Keeping the Unions at Bay," *Nursing Home Long Term Care Management 51,* no. 5 (May 2002), pp. 44–51.

26. American Federation of Teachers (www.aft.org) October 1, 1999.

27. Robert L. Aronson, "Unionism among Professional Employees in the Private Sector," *Industrial and Labor Relations Review 38,* no. 3 (April 1985), pp. 352–64.

28. John Eckberg, "Union Review Finds Janitors in Poverty," *The Cincinnati Enquirer* (March 9, 2005), D2.

29. Majorie Valbrun, "To Reverse Declines, Unions are Targeting Immigrant Workers," Wall Street Journal, May 27, 1999, p. A1.

30. Mike Bozer, "Union OKs Deal With AK Steel," *The Cincinnati Enquirer* (Sept. 7, 2005), D1.

31. Paul D. Staudohar, "Labor-Management Cooperation at NUMMI," *Labor Law Journal,* January 1991, pp. 57–63; Martha Groves, "Rolling On: GM-Toyota Plant Prospers Amid Auto Industry Slump," *Los Angeles Times,* December 12, 1991, pp. D1–D2.

32. Mike Boyer, "Back from the Nearly Dead," *Cincinnati Enquirer,* June 6, 2000, pp. E1–E2.

33. Lee M. Oyley and Judith S. Ball, "Quality of Work Life: Initiating Success in Labor-Management Organizations," *Personnel Administrator 27,* no. 5 (May 1982), pp. 27–29.

34. Harry C. Katz, Thomas A. Kochan, and Kenneth R. Gobelle, "Industrial Relations Performance and QWL Programs: An Interplant Analysis," *Industrial and Labor Relations Review 37,* no. 1 (October 1983), pp. 3–17.

35. William G. Ouchi, *Theory Z* (Reading, MA: Addison-Wesley, 1981), chap. 11, pp. 1–7.

36. Rosemary Balt, "Who Benefits from Teams? Comparing Workers, Supervisors, and Managers," *Industrial Relations 43,* no. 1 (January 2004), p. 183.

37. Marvin E. Shaw, *Group Dynamics: The Psychology of Small Group Behavior,* 2nd ed. (New York: McGraw-Hill, 1976).

38. S. Dillingham, "Topeka Revisited," *Human Resource Executive 4,* no. 5 (May 1990), pp. 55–58.

39. Jasmine Tata and Sameer Prasad, "Team Self-Management, Organizational Structure, and Judgments of Team Effectiveness," *Journal of Managerial Issues 16,* no. 2 (Summer 2004), pp. 248–65.

40. Ken Murphy, "Venture Teams Help Companies Create New Products," *Personnel Journal 70,* no. 3 (March 1991), pp. 60–67.

41. Sonny S. Ariss, "Employee Involvement as a Prerequisite to Reduce Workers' Compensation Costs: A Case Study," *Review of Business 23,* no. 2 (Spring 2002), pp. 12–16.

42. Richard Wellins and Jill George, "The Key to Self-Directed Teams," *Training and Development Journal 45* (April 1991), pp. 26–29.

43. Frank Shipper and Charles C. Manz, "Employee Self-Management without Formally Designed Teams: An Alternative Road to Empowerment," *Organizational Dynamics 20* (Winter 1992), pp. 48–61.

44. Wellins and George, "The Key to Self-Directed Teams," p. 27.

45. Shipper and Manz, "Employee Self-Management," p. 48.

46. Richard S. Wellins, William C. Byham, and Jeanne M. Wilson, *Empowered Teams* (San Francisco: Jossey-Bass, 1991), pp. 10–13.

47. Joe Ward, "It's a New Day on the Assembly Line," *Courier Journal,* February 7, 1993, p. J4.

48. Steve Jordan, "Union Defies U.P. Quality Concept," *Omaha World Herald,* April 6, 1993, p. M1.

49. The International Brotherhood of Teamsters (www.teamsters.org/98ups/news), August 1, 1999.

50. Harold J. Datz, "Employee Participation Programs and the National Labor Relations Act—A Guide for the Perplexed," presented at the Ninth Annual Labor and Employment Law Institute (1992) at the University of Louisville.

51. *Electromation,* NLRB Case No. 25-CA-19818 (1991).

52. *E. I. duPont de Nemours Company v. Chemical Workers Association, Inc.,* 311 N.L.R.B. 88 (1993), 143 LRRM 1121 (1993) (corrected at 143 LRRM [268]).

53. *General Foods Corp.,* 231 NLRB 1232, 1235 (1977).

54. 334 NLRB No. 92 (2001).

55. Albert Rees, *The Economics of Trade Unions* (Chicago: University of Chicago Press, 1977), p. 30.

56. Jack Fiorito, "Unionism and Altruism," *Labor Studies Journal* (Fall 1992), pp. 19–34.

57. Michael H. LeRoy, "State of the Unions: Assessment by Elite American Labor Leaders," *Journal of Labor Research 13,* no. 4 (Fall 1992), pp. 371–79.

58. Peter A. Bamberger, A. N. Kluger, and Ronena Suchard, "The Antecedents of Union Commitment— A Meta-Analysis," *The Academy of Management Journal 42,* no. 3 (1999), pp. 304–18.

59. Jonathan A. Segal, "Keeping Norma Rae at Bay," *H.R. Magazine* (August 1996), pp. 111–17.

60. *Schultz v. Wheaton Glass Co.,* 421 F. 2d. 259 (3rd Cir. 1970).

61. 29 U.S.C., Sec. 206(d)(1) 1977.

62. Civil Rights Act of 1964, Title VII, 42 U.S.C. sec. 2000e.

63. *Griggs v. Duke Power Co.,* 401 U.S. 424 (1971).

64. Teresa Brady, "The Legal Issues Surrounding Religious Discrimination in the Workplace," *Labor Law Journal 44,* no. 4 (April 1993), pp. 246–51.

65. 42 U.S.C. sec 12112.

66. Paul D. Staudohar, *The Sports Industry and Collective Bargaining* (New York: ICR Press, 1986), pp. 1–7.

67. Ibid.

68. See *Curtis C. Flood v. Bowie K. Kuhn, et al.,* 407 U.S. 258, 32 L.Ed. 2d 728, 92 S.Ct. 2099 (1972).

69. Staudohar, *The Sports Industry,* pp. 20–29.

70. Ronald Blum, "Average Salary for Players in Arbitration Declines," *Associated Press,* (www.sports.com/mlb/news) February 19, 2005.

71. Harris Collingwood, "Did the NFL Owners Gain Yardage?" *BusinessWeek,* February 8, 1993, p. 118.

72. *Brown v. Pro Football,* 152 L.R.R.M. 2513 (1995).

73. *Robertson v. National Basketball Association,* 389 F. Supp. 867 (1975).

74. Staudohar, *The Sports Industry,* pp. 87–118.

75. *Caldwell v. ABA, Inc.,* 66 F.3d 523 (2d Cir. 1995).

76. CBS Sportsline (January 6, 1999).

77. Staudohar, *The Sports Industry,* pp. 119–44.

78. Elizabeth Comte, "Is Hockey the Next Baseball?" *Forbes,* June 7, 1993, p. 44.

79. Stefan Fatsis, "NHL Calls Off Its Entire Season With Labor Face-Off Cold As Ice," *The Wall Street Journal* (February 17, 2005), B2.

80. www.aflcio.org (June 18, 2002).

81. Foster Rhea Dulles and Melvyn Dubofsky, *Labor in America, A History,* 4th ed. (Arlington Heights, IL: Harlan Davidson, 1984), p. 86.

82. Ibid., p. 96.

83. Joseph G. Rayback, *A History of American Labor* (New York: The Free Press, 1966), pp. 122–23; and Norman Hill, "Forging a Partnership between Blacks and Unions," *Monthly Labor Review 100,* no. 8 (August 1987), pp. 38–39.

84. Daniel Guerin, *100 Years of Labor in the USA* (London: Ink Links, 1979), pp. 144–60.

85. Michael Honey, "Fighting on Two Fronts: Black Trade Unionists in Memphis in the Jim Crow Era," *Labor's Heritage 4,* no. 1 (Spring 1992), p. 55.

86. Ibid., p. 59.

87. Michael Flug, "Organized Labor and the Civil Rights Movement of the 1960s: The Case of the Maryland Freedom Union," *Labor History 31,* no. 3 (Summer 1990), pp. 322–46.

88. Hill, "Forging a Partnership," pp. 38–39.

89. Gilfford, *Directory of U.S. Labor Organizations, 2001,* p. 2. See also "Union Members Summary," Bureau of Labor Statistics (www.bls.gov), January 17, 2002.

90. The Coalition of Labor Union Women, *Forging Change for a New Generation of Families, Workers, and Unions* (New York: CLUW, March 1974).

91. Rayback, *A History of American Labor,* pp. 120–22.

92. Philip S. Foner, *Women and the American Labor Movement,* vol. 1 (New York: Free Press, 1979), pp. 290–300.

93. Philip S. Foner, *Women and the American Labor Movement,* vol. 2 (New York: Free Press, 1980), p. 327.

94. Robert Asher and Charles Stephenson, eds., *Labor Divided: Race and Ethnicity in U.S. Labor Struggles 1835–1960* (Albany: State University of New York Press, 1990), pp. 22–23.

95. Timothy Aeppel, "Replacing Picketing Laotians, Company Hires Bosnians; Outbursts of Ethnic Slurs," *Wall Street Journal,* June 12, 2001, pp. B1, B4.

96. Paul Johnston, "Outflanking Power, Reframing Unionism: The Basic Strike of 1999–2001," *Labor Studies Journal 28,* no. 4 (Winter 2004), pp. 1–24.

CHAPTER 3

1. Gerald G. Somers, ed., *Collective Bargaining: Contemporary American Experience* (Madison, WI: Industrial Relations Research Association 1980), pp. 553–56.

2. Scott A. Kruse, "Giveback Bargaining: One Answer to Current Labor Problems?" *Personnel Journal 62,* no. 4 (April 1983), p. 286.

3. "This Is the AFL-CIO," American Federation of Labor and Congress of Industrial Organizations, pamphlet (Washington, DC: AFL-CIO, 1987).

4. U.S. Bureau of Labor Statistics, 1999.

5. U.S. Constitution, art. I sec. 8.

6. 28 U.S.C. sec. 152 (1982).

7. Ludwig Teller, *Labor Disputes and Collective Bargaining,* vol. 2 (New York: Baker, Voorhis & Co., 1940), p. 688.

8. 29 U.S.C. sec. 152 (1) (1982).

9. *Plumbers & Steamfitters Local 298 v. County of Door,* 359 U.S. 354, 79 S.Ct. 844, 3 L.Ed. 2d 872 (1959).

10. *Cincinnati Association for the Blind v. National Labor Relations Board,* 672 F.2d 567 (1982), discussed in *University of Detroit Urban Law Journal 60* (Winter 1983), pp. 324–37.

11. *Brevard Achievement Center, Inc. and Transport Workers Union of America, Local 525,* 342 NLRB No. 101 (2004).

12. Theodore Kheel, *Labor Law* (New York: Matthew Bender, 1988), chap. 8, p. 122.

13. *Asplundh Tree Expert Co. v. NLRB,* 365 F. 3d 168 (3d Cir. 2004).

14. *Res-Care, Inc.,* 280 NLRB 670, 122 LRRM 1265 (1986).

15. *Management Training,* 317 NLRB 190, 149 LRRM 1313 (1995).

16. 341 NLRB No. 138, (2004).

17. U.S. Congress, 39 U.S.C. sec. 1209 (1982).

18. *National Labor Relations Board v. Cabot Carbon Co.,* 360 U.S. 203, 79 S.Ct. 1015, 3 L.Ed. 2d 1175 (1959).

19. *San Diego Building Trades Council v. Garmon,* 359 U.S. 236, 76 S.Ct. 773, 3 L.Ed. 2d 775 (1959); *Amalgamated Association of Street, Electric Railway & Motor Coach Employees v. Lockridge,* 403 U.S. 224, 91 S.Ct. 1909, 29 L.Ed. 2d 473 (1971); *Sears, Roebuck & Co. v. San Diego District Council of Carpenters,* 98 S.Ct. 1745, 56 L.Ed. 2d 209 (1978); and *Tamburelli v. Comm-Tract Corporation,* 67 F.3d 973 (1st Cir. 1995).

20. *Smith v. Evening News Association,* 371 U.S. 195, 51 LRRM 2646 (1962), and Local 174, *Teamsters v. Lucas Flour Co.,* 369 U.S. 95, 49 LRRM 2717 (1962).

21. *Lingle v. Norge Division of Magic Chef, Inc.,* 486 U.S. 399 (1988); Patrick Hardin, ed., *The Developing Labor Law,* 3rd ed. (Washington, DC: Bureau of National Affairs, 1992), pp. 1698–1706; and *Jimeno v. Mobil Oil Corporation,* 66 F.3d 1514 (1995).

22. Jane Byeff Korn, "Collective Rights and Individual Remedies: Rebalancing the Balance after *Lingle v. Norge Division of Magic Chef, Inc.,*" *Hastings Law Journal 1149* (July 1990), pp. 1149–96.

23. *May Department Stores Co. v. National Labor Relations Board,* 326 U.S. 376, 66 S.Ct. 203, 90 L.Ed. 145 (1945).

24. Stephen I. Schlossberg and Judith A. Scott, *Organizing and the Law,* 4th ed. (Washington, DC: Bureau of National Affairs, 1991), pp. 216–17.

25. James L. Perry and Harold L. Angle, "Bargaining Unit Structure and Organizational Outcomes," *Industrial Relations 20,* no. 1 (Winter 1981), pp. 47–59.

26. *Short Stop Inc.,* 192 NLRB 184, 78 LRRM 1087 (1971); *Mock Road Super Duper Inc.,* 156 NLRB 82, 61 LRRM 1173 (1966); *Wil-Kil Pest Control,* 440 F.2d 371 (7th Cir. 1971); and *National Labor Relations Board v. Saint Francis College,* 562 F.2d 246 (3rd Cir. 1977) and *National Labor Relations Board v. Action Automotive,* 469 U.S. 490, 118 LRRM 2577 (1985).

27. *M.B. Sturgis,* 331 NLRB 1298 (2000).

28. Karyn-Siobhan Robinson, "Temp Workers Gain Bargaining Rights," *HR News Online* (Washington, DC: Society for Human Resource Management, September 18, 2000).

29. *H.S. Care LLC, d/b/a Oakwood Care Center and N&W Agency, Inc.,* 343 NLRB No. 76 (2004).

30. Cases cited, in order of listing, are *General Electric,* 107 NLRB 21, 33 LRRM 1058 (1953); *T.C. Wheaton Co.* 14 LRRM 142 (1944); *Safety Cabs, Inc.,* 173 NLRB 4, 69 LRRM 1199 (1968); and *Land Title Guarantee & Trust Co.,* 194 NLRB 29, 78 LRRM 1500 (1971).

31. *Globe Machinery & Stamping Co.,* 3 NLRB 294, 1-A LRRM 1122 (1937), and *Short Stores, Inc.,* 192 NLRB 184, 78 LRRM 1087 (1971).

32. Harold S. Roberts, *Dictionary of Industrial Relations,* 3rd ed. (Washington, DC: Bureau of National Affairs, 1986), p. 243.

33. *Bendix Products Corporation,* 3 NLRB 682 (1937).

34. *National Labor Relations Board v. Delaware-New Jersey, Ferry Co.,* 128 F.2d 130 (3rd Cir. 1941).

35. Schlossberg and Scott, *Organizing and the Law,* p. 219.

36. *Tidewater Oil Co. v. National Labor Relations Board,* 358 F.2d 363 (2d Cir. 1966).

37. Labor-Management Relations Act, sec. 9(b)(1)(2)(3); 29 U.S.C. sec. 159 b (1)(2)(3).

38. *National Labor Relations Board v. Textion, Inc.,* 85 LRRM 2945 (1975), *and Palace Laundry Dry Clean Corp.,* 21 LRRM 1039 (1947).

39. *National Labor Relations Board v. Hendricks City Rural Electric Mem. Corp.,* 108 LRRM 3105 (1981).

40. 444 U.S. 672 (1980); see also Clarence R. Dietsch and David A. Dilts, "NLRB v. Yeshiva University: A Positive Perspective," *Monthly Labor Review 106,* no. 7 (July 1983), pp. 34–37; and Marsha Huie Ashlock, "The Bargaining Status of College and University Professors under the National Labor Relations Laws," *Labor Law Journal 35,* no. 2 (February 1984), pp. 103–11.

41. 64 USLW 4269 (1996), decided April 23, 1996.

42. 64 USLW 4022 (1995), decided November 28, 1995.

43. Hardin, *The Developing Labor Law,* pp. 463–64.

44. 162 NLRB 387, 64 LRRM 1011 (1967); see also *Airco, Inc.,* 273 NLRB 53, 118 LRRM 1053 (1984).

45. Hardin, *The Developing Labor Law,* pp. 464–66.

46. *Stephens Produce,* 515 F.2d 1373, 89 LRRM 2311 (8th Cir. 1975); Hardin, *The Developing Labor Law,* pp. 467–68.

47. *Manor Healthcare Corp.,* 285 NLRB 224 (1987).

48. *Rental Uniform Service,* 330 NLRB 334 (1999).

49. *Trane, an Operating Unit of American Standard Companies,* 339 NLRB No. 106 (2003).

50. *Laboratory Corporation of America,* 342 NLRB No. 140 (2004).

51. *St. Luke's Health System, Inc.,* 340 NLRB No. 139 (2003).

52. Richard R. Carlson, "The Origin and Future of Exclusive Representation in American Labor Law," *Duquesne Law Review 30,* no. 4 (Summer 1992), pp. 779–867.

53. *National Labor Relations Board v. Beck Engraving Co.,* 522 F.2d 475 (3d Cir. 1975).

54. Hardin, *The Developing Labor Law,* pp. 473–89.

55. Joe Ward, "Unions, Nurses Mutually Attracted," *Courier-Journal,* April 16, 1989, pp. E1, E3; Joe Ward, "Hospitals Boost Pay Benefits of Nurses, Other Workers," *Courier-Journal,* April 20, 1989, p. B10; and Associated Press, "Board Issues Final Rules That Unions Say Will Help Hospital Organizing," *Courier Journal,* April 21, 1989, p. F1. See also John Thomas Delaney and Donna Sockell, "Hospital Unit Determination and the Preservation of Employee Free Choice," *Labor Law Journal 39,* no. 5 (May 1988), pp. 259–72; and Cynthia A. Shaw, "Appropriate Bargaining Units in the Health Care Industry," *The Labor Lawyer 5,* no.4 (Fall 1989), pp. 787–823.

56. 111 S.Ct. 1539 (1991).

57. Hardin, *The Developing Labor Law,* pp. 483–85 and 1811–12. See also Stephen A. Mayunk, "The Status of the Employment Relationship: The 1990–91 Supreme Court Term," *The Labor Lawyer 7,* no. 849 (1991), p. 872.

58. *NLRB v. Health Care & Retirement Corporation,* 511 U.S. 571 (1994).

59. *NLRB v. Kentucky River Community Care, Inc.,* 121 S. Ct. 1861 (2001).

60. E. Edward Herman and Alfred Kuhn, Collective Bargaining and Labor Relations (Englewood Cliffs, NJ: Prentice Hall, 1981), p. 101.

61. James E. Martin, "Employee Characteristics and Representation Election Outcomes," *Industrial and Labor Relations Review 38,* no. 3 (April 1985), pp. 365–76.

62. The Associated Press, "Unions Campaigning against Breakup of Los Angeles," *Cincinnati Enquirer,* June 23, 2002, p. A15.

63. James W. Robinson, "Structural Characteristics of the Independent Union in America Revisited," *Labor Law Journal,* September 1992, pp. 567–78.

64. NEA (www.nea.org), October 1, 1999.

65. AFT (www.aflcio.org), October 1, 1999.

66. AFSCME (www.afscme.org), October 3, 1999.

67. Jonathan A. Segal, "Keeping Norma Rae at Bay," *HR Magazine,* August 1996, pp. 111–19.

68. Roberts, *Dictionary of Industrial Relations,* p. 668.

69. Kheel, *Labor Law,* chap. 7A, p. 20.

70. *Trustees of Columbia University,* 2-RC-22355.

71. Ibid. chap. 13, pp. 3–4.

72. *Fessler & Bowman, Inc.,* 341 NLRB No. 122 (2004).

73. *Sunrise Rehabilitation Hospital,* 320 NLRB 28, 151 LRRM 1234 (1996), and *Perdue Farms,* 320 NLRB 64, 151 LRRM 1267 (1996), respectively.

74. *YMCA of San Francisco,* 286 NLRB 98, 126 LRRM 1329 (1987).

75. *Good Shepherd Home,* 321 NLRB 56, 152 LRRM 1137 (1996).

76. *Manhattan Crowne Plaza,* 341 NLRB No. 90 (2004).

77. *Frito Lay, Inc.,* 341 NLRB No. 65 (2004).

78. *Wal-Mart Stores, Inc.,* 339 NLRB No. 153 (2003).

79. *Mailing Service, Inc.,* 293 NLRB 53 (1989).

80. *Midland National Life Ins. Co. v. National Labor Relations Board,* 263 NLRB 24, 110 LRRM 1489 (1982).

81. Herbert G. Heneman, III, and Marcus H. Sandver, "Predicting the Outcome of Union Certification Elections: A Review of the Literature," *Industrial and Labor Relations Review 36,* no. 4 (July 1983), p. 555.

82. Richard N. Block and Myron Roomkin, "Determinants of Voter Participation in Union Certification Elections," *Monthly Labor Review 105,* no. 4 (April 1982), pp. 45–47.

83. Roberts, *Dictionary of Industrial Relations,* p. 101.

84. "University of Baltimore Employees Win Runoff," AFL-CIO (www.aflcio.org), June 17, 2002.

85. Joel Cutcher-Gershenfeld and Patrick McHugh, "Finding That Most New Bargaining Units Achieve Contracts Contradicts Other Reports," *2005 Source Book on Collective Bargaining* (Washington, DC: The Bureau of National Affairs, Inc., 2005), p. 139.

86. Bureau of National Affairs, *Additional Earnings and Union Membership Data (2002).* Unpaged report, 2002.

87. David Wessel, "Some Workers Gain with New Union Tactics," *Wall Street Journal,* January 3, 2002, p. A1.

88. "Serving the Young, Joining AFSCME," AFSCME, (www.afscme.org), June 17, 2002.

89. 227 NLRB 326, 94 LRRM 1135 (1976).

90. "Contract Interpretation, Neutrality Discussed at ABA Meeting," *2005 Source Book on Collective Bargaining* (Washington, DC: The Bureau of National Affairs, 2005), p. 117.

91. Muriel H. Cooper, "Out in the Open: The Richmark Story," *America at Work*, November/December 1996, pp. 10–11.

92. *Dana Corp. & Metaldyne Corp*. 341 NLRB No. 150 (2004).

93. *National Labor Relations Board v. Gissel Packing Co.,* 395 U.S. 575, 71 LRRM 2481 (1969).

94. *Gourmet Foods,* 270 NLRB 578, 116 LRRM 1105 (1984), overruling *United Dairy Farmers* 257 NLRB 772, 107 LRRM 1577 (1981), and *Conair Corp*. 261 NLRB 1189, 110 LRRM 1161 (1982).

95. *Rhode Island State Labor Relations Bd. of City of Woonsocket, 3 Public Employee Bargaining* (CCH) 43,730 (R.I., 1984).

96. Douglas E. Ray, Jennifer Gallagher, and Nancy A. Butler, "Regulating Union Representation Election Campaign Tactics: A Comparative Study of Private and Public Sector Approaches," *Nebraska Law Review 66* (1987), pp. 532–61.

97. *Dana Corp. & Metaldyne Corp*. 341 NLRB No. 150 (2004).

98. James B. Dworkin and Marian Extejt, "Why Do Workers Decertify Their Unions? A Preliminary Investigation," Academy of Management—Proceedings of the 39th Annual Meeting, August 7–11, 1979, p. 244.

99. Clyde J. Scott and Edwin W. Arnold, "Deauthorization and Decertification Elections," *Working USA 7,* no. 3 (Winter 2003–4), pp. 6–20.

100. Ibid.

101. Carlson, "Exclusive Representation in American Labor Law."

102. Shaun G. Clark, "Rethinking the Adversarial Model in Labor Relations: An Argument for Repeal of Section 8(a)(2)," *Yale Law Journal 96* (1987), pp. 2021–50.

103. Bureau of National Affairs, *Grievance Guide,* 11th ed. (Washington, DC: Bureau of National Affairs, 2003), p. 451.

104. Hardin, *The Developing Labor Law,* p. 1496.

105. S. M. Crampton, J. W. Hodge, and J. M. Mishra, "The Use of Dues for Political Activity— Current Status," *Public Personnel Management 31,* no. 1 (Spring 2002), p. 126.

106. *California Saw & Knife Works,* 320 NLRB 11, 151 LRRM 1121 (1995).

107. 373 U.S. 734 (1963).

108. *Collective Bargaining Negotiations and Contracts* (Washington, DC: Bureau of National Affairs, 1981), pp. 87.1, 87.3.

109. *Electrical Workers Local 48,* 342 NLRB No. 10 (2004).

110. *National Labor Relations Board v. Niagara Machine & Tool Works,* 117 LRRM 2689 (2d Cir. 1984), and Local 900, *International Union of Electrical, Radio and Machine Workers v. National Labor Relations Board,* 727 F.2d 1184 (DC Cir. 1984).

111. 108 F.3d 1415 (U.S. 1998); See also The Cornell University Legal Information Institute (supct.law.cornell.edu/supct/html/94.947.25), July 23, 1999.

112. States with right-to-work laws include the following:

Alabama	Nevada
Arizona	North Carolina
Arkansas	North Dakota
Florida	Oklahoma
Georgia	South Carolina
Idaho	South Dakota
Iowa	Tennessee
Kansas	Texas
Louisiana	Utah
Mississippi	Virginia
Nebraska	Wyoming

113. Raymond Hogler, Steven Shulman, and Stephan Weiler, "Right-to-Work Legislation, Social Capital, and Variations in State Union Density," *The Review of Regional Studies, 34,* no. 1 (2004), pp. 95–111.

114. Kheel, *Labor Law,* chap. 42, p. 2; Norman Hill, "The Double-Speak of Right-to-Work," AFL-CIO *American Federationist 87* (October 1980), pp. 13–16.

115. Barry T. Hirsch, "The Determinants of Unionization: An Analysis of Interarea Differences," *Industrial and Labor Relations Review 33,* no. 2 (January 1980), pp. 147–61.

116. Kenneth A. Kovach, "National Right-to-Work Law: An Affirmative Position," *Labor Law Journal* (May 1977), pp. 305–14.

117. Raymond Hogler, Steve Shulman, and Stephan Weiler, "Right-to-Work Laws and Business Environment: An Analysis of State Labor Policy," *Journal of Managerial Issues, 16,* no. 3 (Fall 2004), pp. 289–304.

118. William A. Wines, "An Analysis of the 1986 'Right-to-Work Referendum in Idaho,' " *Labor Law Journal* (September 1988), pp. 622–28.

119. Thomas M. Carroll, "Right to Work Laws Do Matter," *Southern Economic Journal 5,* no. 2 (October 1983), pp. 494–509.

120. Wines, "An Analysis of the 1986 'Right-to-Work Referendum in Idaho,' " pp. 622–28.

121. Emin M. Dinlersoz and Ruben Hernandez-Murilla, "Did 'Right-to-Work' Work for Idaho?" *Review, 84,* no. 3 (May/June 2002), pp. 29–43.

122. Henry S. Farber, "Nonunion Wage Rates and the Threat of Unionization," *Industrial and Labor Relations Review 58,* no. 3 (April 2005), pp. 348–49.

123. Ibid.

124. 323 U.S. 192, 15 LRRM 708 (1944).

125. *Airline Pilots Association v. O'Neill,* 59 USLW 4175, 136 LRRM 2721 (U.S. 1991).

126. 386 U.S. 171, 64 LRRM 2369 (1967).
127. *Marquez v. Screen Actors Guild, Inc., et al.,* 124 F.3d 1034 (U.S. 1998).
128. 112 LRRM 2281 (1983).
129. Rossie D. Alston, Jr., and Glenn M. Taubman, "The Rights and Responsibilities of Employees Confronted with Union Discipline," *Labor Law Journal* (December 1998), pp. 1214–24.

CHAPTER 4
1. 29 U.S.C. sec. 157 (1982).
2. 29 U.S.C. sec. 158(a) (1982).
3. *Cooper Thermometer Co.,* 154 NLRB 502, 59 LRRM 1767 (1965); and *American Freightways Co.,* 124 NLRB 646, 44 LRRM 1202 (1959).
4. *National Labor Relations Board v. Preston Feed Corp.,* 309 F.2d 346 (4th Cir. 1962).
5. *Republic Aviation,* 324 U.S. 793, 16 LRRM 620 (1945).
6. *Lechmere, Inc. v. NLRB,* 112 S.Ct. 841 (1992); see also Roger C. Hartley, "The Supreme Court's 1991–92 Labor & Employment Law Term," *Labor Lawyer 8,* no. 4 (Fall 1992), p. 757.
7. *UFCW Local No. 880 v. NLRB,* 151 LRRM 2289 (1996).
8. 217 F.3d 1306, 2000.
9. "Nonsolicitation Policy is a Non-Starter," *Labor Relations Bulletin,* no. 718 (Jan. 2001), p. 1.
10. 95 F. 3d 457 (6th Cir. 1996).
11. *Malta Co.,* 276 NLRB 171 (1985).
12. *The Cincinnati Enquirer,* 279 NLRB 149 (1986).
13. Christine N. O'Brien, "The Impact of Employer E-Mail Policies on Employee Rights to Engage in Concerted Activities Protected by the National Labor Relations Act," *Dickinson Law Review* (2002), reprinted in *Labor Law Journal 53,* no. 2 (Summer 2002), pp. 69–78.
14. Industrial Workers of the World (www.iww.org), August 2002.
15. Gary Chaison, *Unions in America* (Thousand Oaks, CA: Sage Publications, Inc. 2006), pp. 20–22.
16. *NLRB v. Town & Country Elec., Inc.,* 516 U.S. 85 (1995).
17. "Paid Union Organizers," *Labor Law Reports 107,* no. 468 (August, 1995).
18. John M. Capron, "A Saline Solution to the Salting Problem," *Employee Relations Law Journal 30,* no. 4 (Spring 2005), pp. 12–19.
19. Robert J. Grossman, "Employers Brace for 'Salting' after High Court Ruling," *HR News,* January 1996, pp. 1–5.
20. Capron, "A Saline Solution to the Salting Problem," pp. 12–19.
21. *Fluor Daniel, Inc.* 332 F. 3d 961 (6th Cir. 2003).
22. Christina Binkley, "At Some Casinos, The Worst Enemy Isn't a Card Counter," *Wall Street Journal,* June 7, 1999, pp. A1, A6.
23. Henry S. Farber, "Union Success In Representation Elections: Why Does Unit Size Matter?" *Industrial and Labor Relations Review, 54,* no. 2 (January 2001) pp. 329–348.
24. "Labor Relations and You at the Wal-Mart Distribution Center #6022." Prepared by Orsan Mason, September 1991, United Food and Commercial Workers (www.ufcw.org), August 2002.
25. "Wal-Mart A Manager's Toolbox to Remaining Union Free," United Food and Commercial Workers (www.ufcw.org), August 2002.
26. *Midland National Life Ins. Co. v. National Labor Relations Board,* 263 NLRB 24, 110 LRRM 1489 (1982).
27. *Houston Chronicle Publishing Co.,* 293 NLRB 38 (1989).
28. James P. Swann, Jr., "Misrepresentation in Labor Union Elections," *Personnel Journal 59,* no. 11 (November 1980), pp. 925–26.
29. *U-Haul of Nevada,* 341 NLRB No. 26 (2004).
30. *Crown Bolt, Inc.,* 343 NLRB No. 86 (2004).
31. *National Labor Relations Board v. Gissel Packing Co.,* 395 U.S. 575, 71 LRRM 2481 (1969).
32. Gary L. Tidwell, "The Supervisor's Role in a Union Election," *Personnel Journal 62,* no. 8 (August 1983), pp. 640–45.
33. *Kalin Construction Co.,* 321 NLRB 94 (1996).
34. *Saint Gobain Abrasives, Inc.,* 342 NLRB No. 39 (2004).
35. James H. Hopkins and Robert D. Binderup, "Employee Relations and Union Organizing Campaigns," *Personnel Administrator 25,* no. 3 (March 1980), pp. 57–61.
36. *Automated Products, Inc.,* 242 NLRB 424, 101 LRRM 1208 (1979).
37. Stephen I. Schlossberg and Judith A. Scott, *Organizing and the Law,* 4th ed. (Washington, DC: Bureau of National Affairs, 1991), pp. 316–18.
38. *Struksnes Construction Co.,* 165 NLRB 1062, 1063, 65 LRRM 1385 (1967).
39. 522 U.S. 359 (1998).
40. Peter J. Hurtgen, "Recent Decisions and Current Issues Before the Board," *Labor Law Journal* (June 1998), pp. 1031–36.
41. *MSK Corp.,* 341 NLRB No. 11 (2004).
42. *Rossmore House,* 269 NLRB 1176, 116 LRRM 1025 (1984).
43. Patrick Hardin, ed., *The Developing Labor Law,* 3rd ed. (Washington, DC: Bureau of National Affairs, 1992), pp. 125–26.
44. Schlossberg and Scott, *Organizing and the Law,* p. 301.
45. 107 NLRB 427, 33 LRRM 1151 (1953), and *Rodac Corp.,* 231 NLRB 261, 95 LRRM 1608 (1977).
46. Schlossberg and Scott, *Organizing and the Law,* pp. 298–300.

47. *Federal-Magul Corp., Coldwater Distributors Center Division v. National Labor Relations Board,* 394 F.2d 915 (Mich. Cir. 1968).

48. *RCA del Caribe, Inc.,* 262 NLRB 963, 110 LRRM 1369 (1982), and *Bruckner Nursing Home,* 262 NLRB 955, 110 LRRM 1374 (1982).

49. *Electromation, Inc.,* 309 NLRB 163, 142 LRRM 1001 (December 16, 1992); see also Bennet D. Zurofsky, "Everything Old Is New Again: Company Unions in the Era of Employee Involvement Programs," *Labor Lawyer 8,* no. 2 (Spring 1992), p. 381; and Melvin Hutson, "*Electromation*: Employee Involvement or Employee Domination," *Labor Lawyer 8,* no. 2 (Spring 1992), p. 389.

50. *E. I. duPont de Nemours & Company v. Chemical Workers Association Inc.,* 311 NLRB 88 (1993), 143 LRRM 1121 (1993) (corrected 143 LRRM 1268).

51. Barbara Presley Noble, "A Worker-Involvement Program Violates Labor Law, U.S. Rules" *New York Times,* June 8, 1993, p. A11.

52. 329 NLRB No. 47 (1999).

53. 334 NLRB No. 92 (2001).

54. Lawrence Woods, "Review of NLRB Decisions," delivered at the Thirteenth Annual Meeting of the Carl Warns Labor & Employment Law Institute, Louisville, KY, June 6–7, 1996, p. 10.

55. David Vaughn, "Mixed Motives in Unfair Labor Practices," New York University, 35th Annual National Conference on Labor (New York: Matthew Bender, 1983), pp. 169–94.

56. *Meyers Industries v. Prill,* 268 NLRB 493 (1984), and *Meyers Industries, Inc. II,* 281 NLRB 118 (1986).

57. Hardin, *The Developing Labor Law,* pp. 137–46.

58. Ibid., pp. 148–61.

59. *National Labor Relations Board v. Weingarten, Inc.,* 420 U.S. 251, 88 LRRM 2689 (1975).

60. *Roadway Express, Inc.,* 246 NLRB 1127 (1979); and Neil N. Bernstein, "Weingarten: Time for Reconsideration," *Labor Lawyer 6,* no. 4 (Fall 1990), pp. 1005–27.

61. *New Jersey Bell Telephone Co.,* 308 NLRB 32 (August 18, 1992), and Christopher J. Martin, "Some Reflections on Weingarten and the Free Speech Rights of Union Stewards," *Employee Relations Law Journal 18,* no. 4 (Spring 1993), pp. 647–53.

62. *Barnard College,* 340 NLRB No. 106 (2003).

63. Teamsters (www.org/99resources/), August 1, 1999.

64. *Epilepsy Foundation v. NLRB,* 168 LRRM 2673 (CA DC 2001).

65. *IBM Corp.,* 341 NLRB No. 148 (2004).

66. Hardin, *The Developing Labor Law,* pp. 161–68.

67. *Hussman Corp.,* 109 LA 833 (1998).

68. 473 U.S. 95, 119 LRRM 2928 (1985). For analysis, see Beverly A. Williams, "Pattern Makers' League v. National Labor Relations Board: Individual Autonomy v. Union Solidarity," *Rutgers Law Review 39* (Fall 1986), pp. 197–216.

69. Hardin, *The Developing Labor Law,* pp. 178–84.

70. Schlossberg and Scott, *Organizing and the Law,* pp. 322–24.

71. *United Broadcasting Co.* 248 NLRB 403, 103 LRRM 1421 (1980).

72. "Now That You Have a Union," *HR Briefing* (January 15, 2001), p. 3.

73. 29 U.S.C. sec. 158(a)(5) (1982).

74. *National Labor Relations Board v. Montgomery Ward & Co.,* 133 F.2d 676, 686 (9th Cir. 1943), 12 LRRM 508.

75. Ludwig Teller, *Labor Disputes and Collective Bargaining,* vol. 2 (New York: Baker, Voorhis, 1940), p. 884.

76. 29 U.S.C. sec. 158(d) (1982).

77. *National Labor Relations Board v. General Electric Co.,* 418 F.2d 736, 72 LRRM 2530 (2d Cir. 1969) cert. denied, 397 U.S. 965, 73 LRRM 2600 (1970).

78. *Utility Workers (Ohio Power Co.),* 203 NLRB 230, 83 LRRM 1099 (1973).

79. *U.S. Gypsum Co.,* 200 NLRB 132, 82 LRRM 1064 (1972).

80. Theodore Kheel, *Labor Law* (New York: Matthew Bender, 1988), chap. 16, pp. 26–31.

81. *National Labor Relations Board v. Gellan Iron Works, Inc.,* 377 F.2d 894 (2d Cir. 1967).

82. Hardin, *The Developing Labor Law,* p. 635, n. 317.

83. *Verizon New York, Inc.,* 339 NLRB No. 6 (2003).

84. *National Labor Relations Board v. Katz,* 369 U.S. 736, 82 S.Ct. 1107, 8 L.Ed. 762 (1962).

85. *Saint Gobain Abrasives, Inc.,* 342 NLRB No. 39 (2004).

86. *The Edward S. Quirk Co., Inc. d/b/a Quirk Tire,* 340 NLRB No. 33 (2003).

87. Jeffrey P. Chicoine, "The Business Necessity Defense to Unilateral Changes in Working Conditions under the Duty to Bargain in Good Faith," *Labor Lawyer 8,* no. 2 (Spring 1992), pp. 297–312.

88. *JI Case v. National Labor Relations Board,* 321 U.S. 332, 64 S.Ct. 576, 88 L.Ed. 762 (1944).

89. *National Labor Relations Board v. Truitt Manufacturing Co.,* 351 U.S. 149, 38 LRRM 2024 (1955).

90. Robert E. Block, "The Disclosure of Profits in the Normal Course of Collective Bargaining: All Relevant Information Should Be on the Table," *Labor Lawyer 2,* no. 1 (Winter 1986), pp. 47–74.

91. *Nielsen Lithographing Co.,* 305 NLRB 90, 138 LRRM 1444 (1988), and Reid Canon and Kathryn Ernst Noecker, "The Employer's Duty to Supply Financial Information to the Union: When Has the Employer Asserted an Inability to Pay?" *Labor Lawyer 8,* no. 4 (Fall 1992), p. 815.

92. *Efrain Rivera-Vego, et al. v. Conagra, Inc.,* 70 F.3d 153 (1st Cir. 1995).

93. Donald L. Dotson, "Processing Cases at the NLRB," *Labor Law Journal*, (January 1984), pp. 3–9.

94. Matthew M. Franckiewicz, "How to Win NLRB Cases: Tips from a Former Insider," *Labor Law Journal*, (January 1993), pp. 40–47.

95. William N. Cooke and Frederick H. Gautschi, III, "Political Bias in NLRB Unfair Labor Practice Decisions," *Industrial and Labor Relations Review 35*, no. 4 (July 1982), pp. 539–49; see also Myron Roomkin, "A Quantitative Study of Unfair Labor Practice Cases," *Industrial and Labor Relations Review 34*, no. 2 (January 1981), p. 256.

96. Thomas F. Phalen, Jr., "The Destabilization of Federal Labor Policy under the Reagan Board," *Labor Lawyer 2*, no. 1 (Winter 1986), pp. 1–31.

97. Fred W. Batten, "Recent Decisions of the Reagan Board: A Management Perspective," *Labor Lawyer 2*, no. 1 (Winter 1986), pp. 33–46.

98. Lamont Stallworth, Arup Varma, John T. Delaney, "The NLRB's Unfair Labor Practice Settlement Program," *Dispute Resolution Journal 59, no 4*, (Nov. 2004–Jan. 2005), pp. 22–29.

99. Clifford M. Coen, Sandra J. Hartman, and Dinah M. Payne, "NLRB Wields a Rejuvenated Weapon," *Personnel Journal*, (December 1996), pp. 85–87.

100. Federal Labor Relations Authority (www.flra.gov), October 15, 1999.

101. Joe Swerdzewski, General Counsel, Federal Labor Relations Authority, "Memorandum Regarding Intervention Policy" (www.flra.gov), October 20, 1995.

CHAPTER 5

1. Bureau of National Affairs, *Basic Patterns in Union Contracts*, 14th ed. (Washington, DC: BNA Books, 1995), p. 3.

2. Irving Paster, "Collective Bargaining: Warnings for the Novice Negotiator," *Personnel Journal 60*, no. 3 (March 1981), pp. 203–7.

3. Reed C. Richardson, *Collective Bargaining by Objectives* (Upper Saddle River, NJ: Prentice Hall, 1977), p. 150, and Johanna S. Hunsaker, Philip L. Hunsaker, and Nancy Chase, "Guidelines for Productive Negotiating Relationships," *Personnel Administrator 26* (March 1981), pp. 37–40.

4. 29 U.S.C. sec. 159(a) (1982).

5. *National Labor Relations Board v. Wooster Division of the Borg-Warner Corp.*, 356 U.S. 342, 78 S.Ct. 718, 1 L.Ed. 2d 823 (1958).

6. E. J. Dannin, "Statutory Subjects and the Duty to Bargain," *Labor Law Journal*, January 1988, pp. 442–45.

7. *Allied Chemical & Alkali Workers Local Union No. 1 v. Pittsburgh Plate Glass Company*, 404 U.S. 157 (1971).

8. Mairead E. Connor, "The Dubuque Packing Decision: New Test for Bargaining Over Decision to Relocate,"

Labor Lawyer 8, no. 2 (Spring 1992), pp. 289–95; see also Jay E. Grenig, "The Removal of Work from Bargaining Unit Employees: The Supreme Court, the Board and Arbitrators," *Willamette Law Review 27* (1991), p. 595.

9. Donna Sockell, "The Scope of Mandatory Bargaining: A Critique and a Proposal," *Industrial and Labor Relations Review 40*, no. 1 (October 1986), pp. 19–34.

10. *Fibreboard Paper Products Corp. v. National Labor Relations Board*, 379 U.S. 203 (1964), pp. 210–23, and *First National Maintenance Corp. v. National Labor Relations Board*, 452 U.S. 666 (1981), pp. 677–89. See also *Otis Elevator Company*, 269 NLRB 891 (1984).

11. *W. W. Cross & Co. v. National Labor Relations Board*, 174 F.2d 875 (1st Cir. 1949).

12. Bureau of National Affairs, *Basic Patterns in Union Contracts*, p. 49.

13. Kevin B. Zeese, *Drug Testing Legal Manual* (New York: Clark Boardman Company, 1988), chap. 4, pp. 14–15, and Johnson Bateman Company, 295 NLRB 26 (1989).

14. Bureau of National Affairs, *Basic Patterns in Union Contracts*, p. 4.

15. Roy J. Lewicki and Joseph A. Litterer, *Negotiation* (Homewood, IL: Irwin, 1985), pp. 7–9.

16. Ibid.

17. Patrick J. Cleary, *The Negotiation Handbook* (Armonk, NY: M. E. Sharpe, 2001), pp. 20–21.

18. Theodore W. Kheel, *The Keys to Conflict Resolution* (New York: Four Walls Eight Windows, 1999), pp. 16–17.

19. Frederick Rose, "Longshoremen Are Expected to Reject Contract," *Wall Street Journal*, August 28, 1996, p. A2.

20. Roy J. Lewicki, David M. Saunders, and John W. Minton, *Essentials of Negotiation* (Chicago: Irwin, 1997), pp. 30–36.

21. Ibid.

22. Federal Mediation and Conciliation Service, *Interest-Based Bargaining: A Different Way to Negotiate* (Washington, D.C.: Federal Mediation and Conciliation Service, 1999).

23. Ibid.

24. Mark Estes, "Adversaries Find Common Ground," *Workforce 76*, no. 3 (March 1997), pp. 97–102.

25. Roger Fisher and William Ury, *Getting to Yes* (Boston: Houghton-Mifflin, 1981), p. xii.

26. David A. Bender and William P. Curington, "Interaction Analysis: A Tool for Understanding Negotiations," *Industrial and Labor Relations Review 36*, no. 3 (April 1983), pp. 389–401.

27. Lewicki, Saunders, and Minton, *Essentials of Negotiation*, pp. 55–60.

28. Cleary, *The Negotiation Handbook*, pp. 89–92.

29. Lewicki, Saunders, and Minton, *Essentials of Negotiation*, pp. 55–60.

30. Bruce E. Kaufman, "Bargaining Theory, Inflation, and Cyclical Strike Activity in Manufacturing," *Industrial and Labor Relations Review 34*, no. 3 (April 1981), pp. 333–55, and Bruce E. Kaufman, "Inter-Industry Trends in Strike Activity," *Industrial Relations 22*, no.1 (Winter 1983), pp. 45–57.

31. Michael D. Moberly, "Striking a Happy Medium: The Conversion of Unfair Labor Practice Strikes to Economic Strikes," *Berkeley Journal of Employment & Labor Law 22*, no. 1, (2001), pp. 131–74.

32. Mike Boyer, "Union Thinks Over Smart Talks," *Cincinnati Enquirer,* June 12, 2002, p. D1.

33. Carlos Tejada, "With Jobs and Business at Stake, Labor Talks Are Growing Longer," *The Wall Street Journal* (August 22, 2003), A1.

34. *Noel Corp. v. National Labor Relations Board*, 82 F.3d 1113 (D.C. Cir. 1996).

35. "Breakthrough at Bridgestone," *America at Work*, November/December 1996, p. 5.

36. B. E. Kaufman, J. W. Skeels, M. Paldam, and P. J. Pedersen, "Replies," *Industrial and Labor Relations Review 39*, no. 2 (January 1986), pp. 269–78.

37. Hoyt N. Wheeler, "Comment: Determinants of Strikes," *Industrial and Labor Relations Review 37*, no. 2 (January 1984), pp. 263–69.

38. *Martin J. Mauro, "Strikes as a Result of Imperfect Information," Industrial and Labor Relations Review 35*, no. 4 (July 1982), pp. 522–38.

39. Dennis R. Make, "The Effect of the Cost of Strikes on the Volume of Strike Activity," *Industrial and Labor Relations Review 39*, no. 4 (July 1986), pp. 552–53.

40. Jonathan K. Kramer and Thomas Hyclak, "Why Strikes Occur: Evidence from the Capital Markets," *Industrial Relations 41*, no. 1 (January 2002), pp. 80–93.

41. *North Carolina Fuel Company v. National Labor Relations Board*, 645 F.2d 177 (3d Cir. 1981).

42. Frederick J. Bosch and Paul A. Tufano, "Establishing a Uniform Standard for Striker Misconduct in Arbitration Cases," *Labor Law Journal*, (September 1988), pp. 629–33.

43. 268 NLRB 173, 115 LRRM 1113 (1984).

44. Bosch and Tufano, "Establishing a Uniform Standard," pp. 629–33.

45. John P. Kohl and David B. Stephens, "Labor Relations, Replacement Workers during Strikes: Strategic Options for Managers," *Personnel Journal 65*, no. 4 (April 1986), pp. 93–98.

46. Moberly (2001), p. 138.

47. "Labor Letter," *Wall Street Journal*, June 8, 1993, p. A1.

48. "British Airline Workers Back After Walkout," *The Chicago Tribune* (August 13, 2005), p. 2.

49. Linda Stockman Vines, "High Court Upholds NLRB Strike Replacement Policy," *HR News,* June 1993, p. 10.

50. *NLRB v. Mackay Radio and Telegraph Co.,* 304 U.S. 333 (1938).

51. William T. Krizner, "The Mackay Doctrine," *Labor Law Journal,* June 1998, pp. 997–1007.

52. George S. Roukis and Mamdouhj I. Farid, "An Alternative Approach to the Permanent Striker Replacement Strategy," *Labor Law Journal,* February 1993, pp. 80–91.

53. Paul Johnston, "Outflanking Power, Reframing Unionism: The Basic Strike of 1999–2001," *Labor Studies Journal, 28*, no. 4 (Winter 2004), pp. 1–24.

54. Bureau of National Affairs, *2002 Source Book on Collective Bargaining* (Washington, DC: 2002), p. 34.

55. Robert Manor, "Northwest Says Replacements Ready If Mechanics Walk Out," *The Chicago Tribune* (August 12, 2005), B-1, B-8.

56. Richard L. Lippke, "Government Support of Labor Unions and the Ban on Strike Replacements," *Business and Society Review, 109,* no. 2 (Summer 2004), pp. 127–51.

57. Patrick Hardin, ed., *The Developing Labor Law*, 3rd ed. (Washington, DC: Bureau of National Affairs, 1992), p. 1112.

58. Emily Nelson and J. C. Conklin, "Leary of Strikes, More Workers Stage Sickouts," *Wall Street Journal,* February 12, 1999, pp. B1, B4.

59. Hardin, *The Developing Labor Law*, pp. 1115–20.

60. Goldie Blumenstyk, "Yale University Workers End Strike," *The Chronicle of Higher Education* (October 3, 2003), A27.

61. David S. Bradshaw, "Labor Relations, How to Put Teeth into a Labor Injunction," *Personnel Journal 64*, no. 10 (October 1985), pp. 80–85.

62. Stephanie N. Mehta, "Declining Power of Picket Lines Blunts New York Maintenance Worker's Strike," *Wall Street Journal,* January 17, 1996, p. B1.

63. Joann S. Lublin, "AT&T Walkout Could End by Weekend: Optimism Buoyed by Job-Security Talks," *Wall Street Journal,* August 18, 1983, p. 3.

64. John Breeher and Alexander Still, "Telescabbing: The New Union Buster," *Newsweek 102* (August 29, 1983), pp. 53–54.

65. Peter Perl, "Steel Firms Start Crucial Labor Talks," *Washington Post,* March 9, 1986, p. K1.

66. Rebecca Blumenstein, Nichole Christian, and Oscar Suris, "GM Local Labor Dispute Spins Out of Control," *Wall Street Journal,* March 13, 1996, p. B1.

67. Rick Brooks, "UPS and Teamsters Ready Themselves for Contract Brawl," *Wall Street Journal,* January 28, 2002, p. A2.

68. Mike Boyer, "NuTone Locks Out Union Workers," *The Cincinnati Enquirer* (July 19, 2005), D2.

69. *American Shipbuilders,* 380 U.S. 300, 58 LRRM 2672 (1965).

70. George S. Roukis and Mamdoah Farid, "Balancing Partisan Bargaining Interests Requires More Than Labor Law Reform," *Labor Law Journal,* February 1991, pp. 67–80.

71. *International Paper,* 319 NLRB 150, 151 LRRM 1033 (1995).

72. Bureau of National Affairs, *Basic Patterns in Union Contracts,* pp. 91–93.

73. Ibid, p. 94.

74. Peter Perl, "Steel Firms Start Crucial Labor Talks," *Washington Post,* March 19, 1986, pp. K1, K7.

75. John R. Stepp, Robert P. Baker, and Jerome T. Barrett, "Helping Labor and Management See and Solve Problems," *Monthly Labor Review 105,* no. 9 (September 1982), pp. 15–20.

76. Richard A. Posthuma, James B. Dworkin, and Maris S. Swift, "Arbitrator Acceptability: Does Justice Matter?" *Industrial Relations 39,* no. 2 (April 2000), pp. 94–109.

77. "Labor-Management Tensions High; Need for Mediation Services Strong, FMCS Finds," *2005 Source Book on Collective Bargaining* (Washington, DC: The Bureau of National Affairs, 2005), p. 145.

78. Aaron et al., *Public-Sector Bargaining,* pp. 80–117.

79. *Ellis v. Brotherhood of Railway, Airline and Steamship Clerks,* 446 U.S. 435, 104 S.Ct. 1883, 80 L.Ed. 2d 428 (1984); see also *Abood v. Detroit Board of Education,* 230 N.W.2d 322, 90 LRRM 2152 (1975), and Charles M. Rehmus and Benjamin A. Kerner, "The Agency Shop after ABOOD: No Free Ride, but What's the Fare?" *Industrial and Labor Relations Review 34,* no.1 (October 1980), pp. 90–100.

80. Greg Hundley, "Collective Bargaining Coverage of Union Members and Nonmembers in the Public Sector," *Industrial Relations 32,* no. 1 (Winter 1993), pp. 72–93.

81. Lewin and Goldenberg, "Public Sector Unionism," p. 249.

82. Peter Feuille and John C. Anderson, "Public Sector Bargaining: Policy and Practice," *Industrial Relations 19,* no. 3 (Fall 1980), pp. 309–24.

83. Roger L. Bowlby and William R. Shriver, "The Behavioral Interpretation of Bluffing: A Public Sector Case," *Labor Law Journal 32,* no. 8 (August 1981), pp. 469–73.

84. Eugene H. Becker, "Analysis of Work Stoppages in the Federal Sector, 1962–81," *Monthly Labor Review 105,* no. 8 (August 1982), pp. 49–53.

85. Theodore W. Kheel, "Resolving Deadlocks without Banning Strikes," *Monthly Labor Review 92,* no. 7 (July 1969), p. 62.

86. John M. Capozzola, "Public Employee Strikes: Myths and Realities," *National Civic Review 68,* no. 4 (April 1979), pp. 178–88.

87. Aaron et al., *Public-Sector Bargaining,* p. 151.

88. Bernard F. Ashe, "Current Trends in Public Employment," *Labor Lawyer 2,* no. 2 (Spring 1986), pp. 277–98.

89. Randy Steele, "The Rise of PATCO," *Flying 109* (March 1982), p. 35.

90. Ibid.

91. Herbert R. Northrup, "The Rise and Demise of PATCO," *Industrial and Labor Relations Review 37,* no. 2 (January 1984), pp. 167–84.

92. David Westfall, "Striker Replacements and Employee Freedom of Choice," *Labor Lawyer 7,* no. 1 (Winter 1991), p. 138.

93. Michael Doan, "When Workers Took On Uncle Sam," *U.S. News and World Report,* August 1981, pp. 17–20.

94. Kenneth P. Swan, "Public Bargaining in Canada and the U.S.: A Legal View," *Industrial Relations 19,* no. 3 (Fall 1980), pp. 272–91.

95. Fritz Ihrig, "Labor Contract Negotiations: Behind the Scenes," *Personnel Administrator 31,* no. 4 (April 1986), pp. 55–60.

CHAPTER 6

1. Mitchell Marks and Philip Mirvis, "Wage Guidelines: Impact on Job Attitudes and Behavior," *Industrial Relations 20,* no. 3 (Fall 1981), p. 296.

2. Chris Berger and Donald Schwab, "Pay Incentives and Pay Satisfaction," *Industrial Relations 19,* no. 2 (Spring 1980), p. 206.

3. *UAW-Chrysler Newsgram,* October 1996, pp. 2–3.

4. Michael R. Carrell, "A Longitudinal Field Assessment of Employee Perceptions of Equitable Treatment," *Organizational Behavior and Human Performance 21* (1978), pp. 108–18.

5. Julie Moran Alterio and Jerry Gleeson, "Worker/CEO Pay Gap Widens," *The Cincinnati Enquirer* (December 30, 2002), B6.

6. Scott McCartney, "Livid Over Executive Pay, AMR Unions May Balk at Cuts," *The Wall Street Journal* (April 18, 2002), B1.

7. Bruce E. Kaufman, "Models of Union Wage Determination: What Have We Learned since Dunlap and Ross?" *Industrial Relations 41,* no. 1 (January 2002) pp. 110–58. *UAW-Chrysler Newsgram,* October 1996, pp. 2–3.

8. Lawrence Mishel, "The Structural Determinants of Union Bargaining Power," *Industrial and Labor Relations Review 40,* no. 1 (October 1986), pp. 90–104.

9. Martha Bryson Hodel, "Union Miners Ratify Deal," *Associated Press,* December 23, 2001.

10. Stephen Franklin, "Garbage Strikers Smelling Like Rose," *The Chicago Tribune* (October 12, 2003), 4-1, 4-4.

11. Bureau of National Affairs, *2002 Source Book on Collective Bargaining* (Washington, DC: Bureau of National Affairs, 2002), p. 33.

12. Clare Ansberry, "Union Approves Five-Year Pact With U.S. Steel," *The Wall Street Journal* (May 20, 2003).

13. Lawrence F. Katz and Alan B. Krueger, "The Effect of the Minimum Wage on the Fast Food Industry"; David Card, "Using Regional Variation in Wages to Measure the Effects of the Federal Minimum Wage"; David Card, "Do Minimum Wages Reduce Employment? A Case Study of California 1987–89," *Industrial and Labor Relations Review 46,* no. 1 (October 1992), pp. 6–54.

14. Fair Labor Standards Act, 29 U.S.C. sec. 206(g) (1996).

15. Bureau of National Affairs, *Basic Patterns in Union Contracts* (Washington, DC: BNA Books, 1995), pp. 50–53.

16. Robert A. Zaldivar, "Bills Would End 40-Hour Work Week," Knight-Ridder News Bureau, as reported in *The Herald-Leader,* January 29, 1997, pp. A1, A5.

17. Dan Klepal and Tim Bonfield, "Pact with Nurses Averts a Walkout," *Cincinnati Enquirer,* June 29, 2002, p. B4.

18. "Workers Risk Injury, Illness from Long Hours, Labor Argues," *2005 Source Book on Collective Bargaining* (Washington, D.C.: The Bureau of National Affairs, 2005), p. 121.

19. "DOL Okays Company's Plan to Credit Employees with Advance Overtime Pay," *Payroll Manager's Letter 21,* no. 9 (May 7, 2005), p. 7.

20. "Before You Can Pay for Hours Worked, You Need to Know What Counts as Work Time," *Payroll Manager's Letter 21,* no. 4 (Feb. 21, 2005), p. 3.

21. John C. Richardson, "Prevailing Wage Laws a Boon, Not a Threat," *Los Angeles Times,* March 10, 1991, p. D1.

22. "Davis-Bacon under Attack," *IBEW Journal,* April 2002, pp. 12–13.

23. Charles Hughes, *Making Unions Unnecessary* (New York: Executive Enterprises, 1976), pp. 105–6.

24. Bruce Shearer, "Piece Rates, Fixed Wages and Incentives: Evidence From a Field Experiment," *Review of Economic Studies 71,* (2004), pp. 513–34.

25. Leonard R. Burgess, *Wage and Salary Administration* (Columbus, OH: Merrill, 1984), p. 242.

26. Agreement between UAW and Chrysler Corporation, 1997–1999.

27. Sanford M. Jacoby, "Cost-of-Living Escalators Became Prevalent in the 1950s," *Monthly Labor Review 108,* no. 5 (May 1985), pp. 32–33.

28. Bureau of National Affairs, *2002 Source Book on Collective Bargaining,* p. 37.

29. Louis N. Christofides and Audrey Laporte, "Menu Costs, Nominal Wage Revisions, and Intra-Contract Wage Behavior," *Industrial Relations 41,* no. 2 (April 2002), pp. 287–303.

30. Michael R. Carrell and William A. Hailey, "COLAs: An Analysis of Their Past and Their Relationship with Other Factors," *Labor Law Journal,* October 1989, pp. 658–62.

31. Bureau of National Affairs, *Basic Patterns in Union Contracts,* p. 119.

32. "Pay Day: Typical Ford Worker Gets $1,200 for Profit-Sharing," *Courier-Journal,* March 13, 1986, p. B8, and "Auto Workers Will Feel Pinch of Lower or No Profits," *Bakersfield Californian,* February 20, 1990, p. 87.

33. Douglas Frasier, speech at the University of Louisville, April 22, 1986.

34. Harold S. Roberts, *Dictionary of Industrial Relations,* 3rd ed. (Washington, DC: Bureau of National Affairs, 1986), p. 645.

35. Robert J. Schulhof, "Five Years with a Scanlon Plan," *Personnel Administrator 24* (June 1979), pp. 55–62; see also Shaun G. Clark, "Rethinking the Adversarial Model in Labor Relations: An Argument for Repeal of Section 8(a)(2)," *Yale Law Review 96* (1987), pp. 2021–50.

36. John Savage, "Incentive Programs at Nucor Corporation Boost Productivity," *Personnel Administrator 22* (August 1981), pp. 33–36.

37. "The Revolutionary Wage Deal at G.M.'s Packard Electric," BusinessWeek, August 29, 1983, p. 54.

38. Bureau of National Affairs, *2002 Source Book on Collective Bargaining,* pp. 37–38.

39. The Associated Press, "Workers OK Pact with Unit of Kroger," *Cincinnati Enquirer* (March 8, 2005) p. D2.

40. "The Double Standard That's Setting Worker against Worker," *BusinessWeek,* April 8, 1983, p. 70.

41. Ivan Ross, "Employers Win Big in the Move to Two-Tier Contracts," *Fortune,* April 29, 1985, pp. 82–92; Robert J. Harris Jr., "More Firms Set Two-Tier Pacts with Unions, Hurting Future Hires," *Wall Street Journal,* December 12, 1983, p. A34; Dan Wessel, "Two-Tier Pay Spreads, but the Pioneer Firms Encounter Problems," *Wall Street Journal,* October 14, 1985, p. A1; and Ken Jennings and Earle Trajuham, "The Wages of Two-Tier Pay Plans," *Personnel Journal 67,* no. 3 (March 1988), p. 58.

42. James E. Martin and Melanie M. Peterson, "Two-Tier Wage Structures: Implications for Equity Theory," *Academy of Management Journal 30,* no. 2 (June 1987), pp. 297–315.

43. Thomas D. Heetderks and James E. Martin, "Employee Perceptions of the Effects of a Two-Tier Wage Structure," *Journal of Labor Research 7,* no. 3 (Summer 1991), pp. 279–95.

44. Bureau of National Affairs, *Basic Patterns in Union Contracts,* p. 113.

45. Julia Laulor, "Auto Talks Revive Two-Tier Wage Concept, Concerns," *USA Today,* September 17, 1993, p. 5B.
46. Fay Hansen, "Wages Head South," *Workforce Management 84,* no. 2 (February 2005), pp. 71–72.
47. Bureau of National Affairs, *2005 Source Book on Collective Bargaining,* p. 179.
48. Susan Carey and Scott McCartney, "Airlines Big Profits Raise Unions' Expectations," *Wall Street Journal,* January 10, 1997, p. A2.
49. Reid Carron and Kathlyn Ernst Noecker, "The Employer's Duty to Supply Financial Information to the Union: When Has the Employer Asserted an Inability to Pay?" *Labor Lawyer 8,* no. 4 (Fall 1992), p. 815.
50. David W. Belcher, *Wage and Salary Administration* (Upper Saddle River, NJ: Prentice Hall, 1982), pp. 106–13.
51. Agreement, The Lockheed-Georgia Company and the International Association of Machinists and Aerospace Workers, AFL-CIO, 1968–1971, pp. 86–87.
52. Bureau of National Affairs, *Grievance Guide,* 11th ed. (Washington, DC: BNA Books, 2003), pp. 463–68.
53. Belcher, *Wage and Salary Administration,* pp. 106–13.
54. Ibid., pp. 236–43.
55. Wayne F. Cascio, *Costing Human Resources: The Financial Impact of Behavior in Organizations* (Boston: Kent Publishing, 1982), p. 99.
56. Michael H. Granof, *How to Cost Your Labor Contract* (Washington, DC: Bureau of National Affairs, 1973), pp. 4–5.
57. Ibid., p. 33.
58. Skinner and Herman, "Costing Labor Law Contracts," pp. 500–501.
59. Cascio, *Costing Human Resources,* p. 102.
60. Granof, *How to Cost Your Labor Contract,* p. 34.
61. Frederick L. Sullivan, *How to Calculate the Manufacturer's Costs in Collective Bargaining* (New York: AMACOM, 1980), pp. 23–26.
62. Michael Podgursky, "Unions, Establishment Size and Intra-Industry Threat Effects," *Industrial and Labor Relation Review 39,* no. 2 (January 1986), pp. 277–94.
63. *Auer v. Robbins,* 519 U.S. 452 (1997).
64. *Central State University v. American Association of University Professors,* 160 LRRM 2897 (1999).

CHAPTER 7

1. Olivia S. Mitchell, "Fringe Benefits and the Cost of Changing Jobs," *Industrial and Labor Relations Review 17,* no. 1 (October 1983), pp. 70–78.
2. U.S. Department of Labor, *Employee Benefits Survey* (Washington, DC: U. S. Department of Labor, 1999).
3. The U.S. Bureau of Labor Statistics, *National Compensation Survey* (Washington, DC: 2005) p. 5.
4. Bureau of National Affairs, "Give-Backs Highlight Three Major Bargaining Agreements," *Personnel Administrator 28,* no. 1 (January 1983), pp. 33–35.
5. "Employers Will Seek Concessions in Benefits, May Make Them on Wages, BNA Report Finds," *2005 Source Book on Collective Bargaining* (Washington, DC: The Bureau of National Affairs: 2005), pp. 37–38.
6. Bureau of National Affairs, *Report on Labor Relations in an Economic Recession: Job Losses and Concession Bargaining* (Washington, DC: Bureau of National Affairs, 1982), pp. 56–59.
7. Bureau of National Affairs, *2002 Source Book on Collective Bargaining* (Washington, DC: Bureau of National Affairs, 2002), pp. 71–72.
8. Mark Schuster, "The Impact of Union-Management Cooperation on Productivity and Employment," *Industrial and Labor Relations Review 36,* no. 4 (1983), pp. 415–30.
9. "Negotiated Settlements Called Preferable to Court-Imposed Cuts," *2005 Source Book on Collective Bargaining* (Washington, DC: Bureau of National Affairs: 2005), p. 115.
10. Mark Plovnick and Gary Chaison, "Relationships between Concession Bargaining and Labor-Management Cooperation," *Academy of Management Journal 28,* no. 3 (September 1985), pp. 697–704.
11. Gary N. Chaison and Mark S. Plovnick, "Is There a New Collective Bargaining?" *California Management Review 28,* no. 4 (Summer 1986), pp. 54–61.
12. Joann S. Lublin, "Cost-Cutting Airlines Grapple with Issues of Executive Pay," *Wall Street Journal* (January 29, 2005), B1, 9.
13. Judy L. Ward, "Firms Forcing Employees to Repay Some Costs If They Quit Too Soon," *Wall Street Journal,* July 16, 1985, p. A30.
14. James Pilcher, "Comair's Pilots Vote on Pay Freeze," *Cincinnati Enquirer* (February 20, 2005), A1, 10.
15. "Auto Workers Will Feel Pinch of Lower or No Profits," *Bakersfield Californian,* February 20, 1990, p. B7; Scott A. Kruse, "Giveback Bargaining: One Answer to Current Labor Problems?" *Personnel Journal 62,* no. 4 (April 1983), pp. 286–89; and Douglas Lavin, "Chrysler Aides to Get Bonuses Equal to Salaries," *Wall Street Journal,* February 22, 1994, p. A3.
16. James M. Rosbrow, "Unemployment Insurance System Marks Its 50th Anniversary," *Monthly Labor Review 108,* no. 9 (September 1985), pp. 21–28.
17. Jerry Flint, "The Old Folks," *Forbes 125,* no. 4 (February 18, 1980), pp. 51–56.
18. Dale Detlefs, *1984 Guide to Social Security* (Louisville, KY: Meidinger and Associates, 1984), pp. 6–9.

19. James Pilcher, "Fear Over Pensions: Workers Fret as Systems Bear Strain," *Cincinnati Enquirer* (November 6, 2005), J1, 7.

20. *Inland Steel Co. v. NLRB*, 170 F.2d 247 (CA7 1948).

21. Bureau of National Affairs, *Basic Patterns in Union Contracts*, 14th ed. (Washington, DC: Bureau of National Affairs Books, 1995), p. 27.

22. Bureau of National Affairs, *2002 Source Book on Collective Bargaining*, pp. 51–53, 103.

23. Ellen E. Schultz, "New Pension Plan Attracts Firms Despite Criticism," *Wall Street Journal* (October 5, 2004), D2.

24. Lawrence Meyer, "Many Workers Lose Retirement Benefits Despite Reform Laws," *Washington Post*, September 7, 1982, p. A1.

25. Steven G. Allen and Robert L. Clark, "Unions, Pension Wealth, and Age—Compensation Profits," *Industrial and Labor Relations Review 39*, no. 4 (July 1986), pp. 502–12; see also Steven G. Allen, Robert Clark, and Dan Summer, "Post-Retirement Adjustments of Pension Benefits," *Journal of Human Resources 21*, no. 1 (1986), pp. 118–37.

26. Kenneth H. Anderson, Robert V. Burkhauser, and Jane F. Quinn, "Do Retirement Dreams Come True? The Effect of Unanticipated Events on Retirement Plans," *Industrial and Labor Relations Review 39*, no. 4 (July 1986), pp. 518–26.

27. Vicky Cahan, "Mandatory Retirement Gets Put Out to Pasture," *BusinessWeek*, November 3, 1986, p. 31.

28. Susan Carey, "UAL's Pension Takeover May Prompt a Strike," *Wall Street Journal* (July 1, 2005), B3.

29. Retirement Equity Act of 1984.

30. When Pension Liabilities Dampen Profits," *Business Week*, June 16, 1983, pp. 80–81.

31. Marilyn Schaefer, "Continental Can to Pay $415 Million," *HR Executive 5*, no. 2 (February 1991), p. 10.

32. *Central Laborers' Pension Fund v. Heitz, et al.*, No. 02-891, 541 U.S. ___ (2004).

33. Bureau of National Affairs, *Basic Patterns in Union Contracts*, p. 41.

34. Ibid., p. 44.

35. Quinn Mills, "When Employers Make Concessions," *Harvard Business Review*, May–June 1983, pp. 103–13.

36. Peter Cappelli, "Auto Industry Experiments with the Guaranteed Income Stream," *Monthly Labor Review 107*, no. 7 (July 1984), pp. 37–39.

37. Cristina Pita, "Advance Notice and Severance Pay Provisions in Contracts," *Monthly Labor Review 119*, no. 7 (July 1996), pp. 43–50.

38. Martin Joy Galvin and Michael Robert Lied, "Severance: A Liability in Waiting?" *Personnel Journal 65*, no. 6 (June 1986), pp. 126–31.

39. *UAW v. Roblin Industries*, 114 LRRM 2428 (Mich. Cir. 1984).

40. "ENRON Workers Win Severance Fight," *AFL-CIO* (www.aflcio.org), June 2002.

41. Agreement between Anaconda Aluminum Co. and Aluminum Workers Local No. 130 and the Aluminum Workers International Union, AFL-CIO, 1980–1983, pp. 26–27. Used with permission.

42. The U.S. Bureau of Labor Statistics, *National Compensation Survey* (Washington, DC: 2005), pp. 5–23.

43. Allan P. Blostin, "Is Employer-Sponsored Life Insurance Declining Relative to Other Benefits?" *Monthly Labor Review 104*, no. 7 (September 1981), pp. 31–33.

44. Bureau of National Affairs, *2002 Source Book on Collective Bargaining*, pp. 44–47.

45. Michael R. Carrell, "Employer Provided Health Care—What Are the Alternatives?" *Business Forum 13*, no. 2 (Spring 1988), pp. 4–7.

46. "Health Premiums Rose 9.2% in 2005," *HR Focus*, Vol. 82, Issue 11, (Nov. 2005), pp. 12–21.

47. Bureau of National Affairs, *2002 Source Book on Collective Bargaining*, pp. 43–48.

48. Ellen E. Schultz, "Companies Sue Union Retirees to Cut Promised Health Benefits," *Wall Street Journal* (Nov. 10, 2004), A1, 10.

49. Ibid.

50. William J. Angelo, "Wellness Program Cures Rising Health-Care Costs," *Engineering New-Record 253*, no. 3 (July 19, 2004), p. 13.

51. Jennifer Hutchins, "Labor and Management Build a Prescription for Health," *Workforce 80*, no. 3 (March 2001), pp. 50–52.

52. Richard Feldman and Michael Betzold, End of the Line: Autoworkers and the American Dream (New York: Weidenfeld & Nicolson Publishers, 1988), p. 21.

53. Diane Kirrane, "EAPS: Dawning of a New Age," *HR Magazine 35*, no. 1 (January 1990), pp. 30–34.

54. Ibid.

55. Roger K. Good, "What Bechtel Learned Creating an Employee Assistance Program," *Personnel Journal 63*, no. 9 (September 1984), pp. 80–86.

56. Melissa Praffitt Reese, "Strikes and the Obligation to Continue Group Health Care Coverage under COBRA," *Labor Law Journal 39*, no. 11 (November 1988), pp. 766–70.

57. Bureau of National Affairs, *Grievance Guide*, 11th ed. (Washington, DC: Bureau of National Affairs, 2003), p. 111.

58. The U.S. Bureau of Labor Statistics, *National Compensation Survey*, (Washington, DC: Bureau of Labor Statistics, 2005), pp. 5–23.

59. Ibid., p. 22.

60. Agreement between Anaconda Aluminum Co. and Aluminum Workers Local No. 130 and the Aluminum Workers International Union, AFL-CIO, 1980–1983, pp. 9–11. Used with permission.

61. Granof, *How to Cost Your Labor Contract,* pp. 45–51.
62. Ibid., pp. 50–51.
63. The U.S. Bureau of Labor Statistics, *National Compensation Survey* (Washington, DC: 2005), pp. 5–23.
64. Ibid., p. 22.
65. Ibid.
66. Sandra L. King and Harry B. Williams, "Shift Work Pay Differentials and Practices in Manufacturing," *Monthly Labor Review 198,* no. 12 (December 1985), pp. 26–33.
67. Peter Fritsch, "Bilingual Employees Are Seeking More Pay, and Many Now Get It," *Wall Street Journal,* November 13, 1996, pp. A1, A6.
68. TowersPerrin, Employee Benefits/TowersPerrin Flexible Benefits Research 2005.
69. Michael R. Carrell, Norbert F. Elbert, and Robert Hatfield, *Human Resource Management,* 5th ed. (Upper Saddle River, NJ: Prentice Hall, 1995), pp. 472–75.
70. Carol Ann Diktaban, "Employer Supported Child Care as a Mandatory Subject of Collective Bargaining," *Hofstra Labor Law Journal 8,* no. 2 (1991), p. 385.
71. Richard F. Federico, "Elder Care Benefits Cry Out for Better Communication," *Employee Benefit News 18,* no. 1 (Jan. 2004) pp. 36–41.
72. Bureau of National Affairs, "Growing Demand for Eldercare Programs Ensures Their Survival," *2002 Source Book on Collective Bargaining,* pp. 153–54.
73. Agreement between Ziniz, Inc. and Kentucky State District Council of Carpenters, Millwrights, Conveyors, and Machinery Erectors, 1995–1999, p. 23.
74. Agreement between Ford Motor Company and the UAW, 1996, p. 241.

CHAPTER 8

1. Agreement between Anheuser-Busch, Inc. and the International Brotherhood of Teamsters (1999–2004), (www.teamsters.org), August, 1999.
2. Sumner H. Slichter, *Union Policies and Industrial Management* (Washington, DC: Brooklyn Institute, 1941), pp. 1–5.
3. Agreement between Chrysler Corp. and UAW, 1997–1999.
4. Daniel Cornfield, "Seniority, Human Capital, and Layoffs: A Case Study," *Industrial Relations 21,* no. 3 (Fall 1982), pp. 352–64.
5. William Cooke, "Permanent Layoffs: What's Implicit in the Contract?" *Industrial Relations 20,* no. 2 (Spring 1981), pp. 186–92.
6. Francine Blau and Lawrence Kahn, "Unionism, Seniority, and Turnover," *Industrial Relations 22,* no. 3 (Fall 1983), pp. 362–73.
7. Bureau of National Affairs, *2002 Source Book on Collective Bargaining* (Washington, DC: Bureau of National Affairs, 2002), p. 58.

8. Maryellen Kelley, "Discrimination in Seniority Systems: A Case Study," *Industrial and Labor Relations Review 36,* no. 1 (October 1982), pp. 40–41.
9. Bureau of National Affairs, *Basic Patterns in Union Contracts,* 14th ed. (Washington, DC: BNA Books, 1995), p. 85.
10. Stephen Cabot, *Labor Management Relations Manual,* 1981 Supplement (Boston: Warren, Gorham, Lamont, 1981), chap. 15, p. 1.
11. Agreement between Anaconda Aluminum Co. and Aluminum Workers Trades Council of Columbia Falls, AFL-CIO, 1980, p. 6.
12. Agreement between E. I. duPont Co. and the Affiliated Chemical Workers of Kentucky, 1943.
13. Cabot, *Labor Management Relations Manual,* chap.15, p. 4.
14. Bureau of National Affairs, *Basic Patterns in Union Contracts,* p. 69.
15. "Unqualified Worker Has No Bumping Rights," *Labor Relations Bulletin,* no.746 (May 2003) p. 3.
16. Jonathan Daird Bible, "*U.S. Airways v. Barnett*: Seniority Systems and the ADA," *Labor Law Journal 53,* no. 2 (Summer 2002), pp. 61–68.
17. *Gulton Electro-Voice, Inc.,* 266 NLRB 406, 112 LRRM 1361 (1983).
18. Bureau of National Affairs, *Basic Patterns in Union Contracts,* p. 86.
19. Bureau of National Affairs, Grievance Guide, 11th ed. (Washington, DC: Bureau of National Affairs, 2003), pp. 305–18.
20. Katherine G. Abraham and James L. Medoff, "Length of Service and Promotions in Union and Nonunion Work Groups," *Industrial and Labor Relations Review 38,* no. 3 (April 1985), pp. 408–20; see also D. Quinn Mills, "Seniority versus Ability in Promotion Decisions," *Industrial and Labor Relations Review 38,* no. 3 (April 1985), pp. 421–25.
21. Adapted from Agreement between Anaconda Aluminum Co. and Aluminum Workers Local No. 130 and the Aluminum Workers International Union, AFL-CIO, 1980–1983, pp. 16–17. Used with permission.
22. Bureau of National Affairs, *Grievance Guide,* 11th ed. (2003), p. 231.
23. Ibid.
24. *Bethlehem Steel Co.,* 1924 LA 820 (1955).
25. *Copeo Steel & Engineering Co.,* 12 LA 6 (1979).
26. *Metallab, Inc.,* 65 LA 1191 (1975).
27. Bureau of National Affairs, *Grievance Guide,* 9th ed. (Washington, DC: Bureau of National Affairs, 1995), pp. 207–8.
28. Agreement between Anaconda Aluminum Co. and Aluminum Workers Local No. 130 and the Aluminum Workers International Union, AFL-CIO, 1980–1983, pp. 14–16. Used with permission.

29. *Firefighters Local Union No. 1784 v. Stotts,* 467 U.S. 561 (1984).

30. Valerie Frazel, "Striking a Balance: Temps and Union Workers," *Personnel Journal 75,* no. 1 (January 1996), pp. 103–5.

31. P. L. 100–379, 102 Stat. 895, August 14, 1988.

32. "Reagan Succumbing to Politics, Decides against Vetoing Plant Closings Measure," *Wall Street Journal,* August 3, 1988, p. A3.

33. Wilson McLeod, "Judicial Devitalization of the WARN," *Labor Law Journal 44,* no. 4 (April 1993), pp. 220–29.

34. Bureau of National Affairs, *2002 Source Book on Collective Bargaining,* p. 58.

35. Paul D. Staudohar, "New Plant Closing Laws Aids Workers in Transition," *Personnel Journal 68,* no. 1 (January 1989), pp. 87–90, and comments by Conte Silvio, *Congressional Record,* no. 105, July 13, 1988, p. H5507.

36. Dale Yoden and Paul D. Staudohar, "Management and Public Policy in Plant Closure," *Sloan Management Review 26,* no. 4 (Summer 1985), p. 52.

37. Gillian Flynn, "The Unions' Power to Sue Is Growing," *Personnel Journal* (September 1996), pp.135–41, and *United Food and Commercial Workers Union Local 751 v. Brown Group Inc.,* 116 S.Ct. 1529 (1996).

38. *North Star Steel Co. and Thomas et al. v. USWA,* 115 S.Ct. 1927 (1995).

39. John Zalusky, "Short-Time Compensation: The AFL-CIO Perspective," *Monthly Labor Review 109,* no. 5 (May 1986), pp. 33–34.

40. Frank Elkouri and Edna Asper Elkouri, *How Arbitration Works,* 6th ed. (Washington, DC: Bureau of National Affairs, 2003), pp. 877–79.

41. Bureau of National Affairs, *Grievance Guide,* (2003), pp. 319–25.

42. Adapted with permission from Frank Elkouri and Edna Asper Elkouri, *How Arbitration Works,* 6th ed. (2003), 883–921. Copyright © 2003 by the Bureau of National Affairs, Inc., Washington, DC.

43. Thomas Kennedy, *Labor Arbitration and Industrial Change* (Washington, DC: Bureau of National Affairs, 1963), pp. 1–34.

44. Elkouri and Elkouri, *How Arbitration Works,* 6th ed. (2003) p. 870.

45. Walter Baer, *Winning in Labor Arbitration* (Columbus, OH: Crain, 1982), p. 20.

46. "Union Wins $6 Million Settlement with AT&T," *Louisville Courier-Journal,* January 10, 1987, p. B1.

47. *Fibreboard Paper Products Corp. v. NLRB,* 130 NLRB 1558 (1961).

48. Agreement between UAW and Ford Motor Company, 1996, pp. 236–40.

49. James Pilcher, "Mechanics OK Comair Pact With 2% Raise," *Cincinnati Enquirer* (April 29, 2005), p. 8.

50. Reprinted by permission from Bureau of National Affairs, *Grievance Guide,* 11th ed. (Washington, DC: Bureau of National Affairs, 2003), pp. 409–413. Copyright © 2003 by the Bureau of National Affairs, Inc., Washington, DC.

51. *First National Maintenance Corp.,* 452 U.S. 666 (1981).

52. *Milwaukee Spring Division of Illinois Coil Spring Co.* (I), 718 F.2d 1102 (7th Cir. 1983); (II), 268 NLRB 601 (1984).

53. *Otis Elevator,* 269 NLRB 891, 115 LRRM 1281 (1984).

54. Patrick Hardin, ed., *The Developing Labor Law,* 3rd ed. (Washington, DC: Bureau of National Affairs, 1992), pp. 916–18.

55. *Dubuque Packing Co. v. NLRB,* 303 NLRB 66, 137 LRRM 1185 (1991).

56. Bureau of National Affairs, *Grievance Guide,* (2003) p. 409.

57. *Fall River Dyeing v. National Labor Relations Board,* 107 S. Ct. 2225 (1987).

58. Robert F. Mace, "The Supreme Court's Labor Law Successorship Doctrine after Fall River Dyeing," *Labor Law Journal 39,* no. 2 (February 1988), pp. 102–9.

59. Hardin, *The Developing Labor Law,* pp. 779–80.

60. Steven B. Goldstein, "Protecting Employee Rights in Successorship," *Labor Law Journal 44,* no. 1 (January 1993), pp. 18–29.

61. Celestine J. Richards, "The Efficacy of Successorship Clauses in Collective Bargaining Agreements," *Georgetown Law Journal 79* (1991), p. 1549.

62. *NLRB v. Canteen Company,* 317 NLRB 1052 (1995).

63. *MV Transportation,* 337 NLRB No. 129 (2002).

64. Maria M. Perotin, "Drug Tests for Jobs Waning???????," *Knight Ridder News Service* (May 26, 2003), B5, 8.

65. *Johnson-Bateman Co.,* 295 NLRB 26 (1989).

66. *Minneapolis Star Tribune,* 295 NLRB 63 (1989).

67. David D. Schein, "How to Prepare a Company Policy Abuse Control," *Personnel Journal 65,* no. 7 (July 1986), pp. 30–38.

68. *International Brotherhood of Teamsters No. 878 v. Commercial Warehouse,* 84 F.3d 299 (8th Cir. 1996).

69. *Skinner v. Railway Labor Executives Association,* 109 S. Ct. 1402 (1989).

70. *Pacific Motor Trucking,* 86 LA 497 (1986), and *Amalgamated Transit Union, Local 1433 and Phoenix Transit System,* 87–2 ARB Paragraph 8510 (1987).

71. *Shelby County Health Care Center,* 90 LA 1225 (1988).

72. *Boise Cascade Corp.,* 90 LA 105 (1987).

73. *Warehouse Distribution Centers,* 90 LA 979 (1987).

74. *Gem City Chemicals,* 86 LA 1023 (1986).

75. *Signal Delivery Services, Inc.,* 86 LA 7S (1986).

76. *Consolidated Coal Co.,* 87 LA 111 (1986).

77. Michael H. LeRoy, "The Presence of Drug Testing in the Workplace and Union Member Attitudes," *Labor Studies Journal 16,* no. 4 (Fall 1991), pp. 33–42.

78. Ibid.

79. "Privatization: Pros and Cons," AFSCME (www.afscme.org), October 26, 1999.

80. "Fighting Privatization: Strategies," AFSCME (www.afscme.org), October 26, 1999.

81. "Vouchers and the Accountability Dilemma," American Federation of Teachers (www.aft.org) October 26, 1999, and "Vouchers," National Education Association (www.nea.org), October 26, 1999.

82. Ibid.

83. No. 00-1751, decided June 27, 2002.

84. *National Treasury Employees Union (NTEU) et al. v. Von Raab,* 57 LA 4338 (3-21-89), and *Skinner v. Railway Labor Executive's Association,* 57 LA 4324 (3-21-89).

85. *New York City Transit Authority v. Beazer,* 440 U.S. 568, 99 S.Ct. 1355, 59 L.Ed. 2d 587 (1979).

86. *Consolidated Rail Corporation v. Railway Labor Executives' Association et al.,* 57 LA 4742 (6-20-89).

87. *Dykes v. Southeastern Pennsylvania Transportation Authority,* 68 F.3d 1564 (1995).

88. *Vernonia School District, 47 J v. Acton,* 115 S.Ct. 2386 (1995).

CHAPTER 9

1. *H. J. Heinz Co. v. National Labor Relations Board,* 311 U.S. 514, 51 S.Ct. 320, 85 L.Ed. 309 (1941).

2. 29 U.S.C. sec. 158(b)(1982).

3. David A. Dilts and Clarence Deitsch, *Labor Relations* (New York: Macmillan, 1983), p. 152.

4. Bureau of National Affairs, *Grievance Guide,* 11th ed. (Washington, DC: Bureau of National Affairs, 2003), pp. 443–48.

5. Bureau of National Affairs, *Basic Patterns in Union Contracts,* 14th ed. (Washington, DC: BNA Books, 1995), pp. 1–3.

6. Bureau of National Affairs, *2002 Source Book on Collective Bargaining* (Washington, DC: Bureau of National Affairs, 2002), p. 33.

7. Goldie Blumenstyk, "Yale Workers End Strike," *The Chronicle of Higher Education* (October 3, 2003), p. A27.

8. Marvin Hill, Jr., and Anthony V. Sinicrope, *Management Rights* (Washington, DC: Bureau of National Affairs, 1986), p. 3.

9. Bureau of National Affairs, *Basic Patterns in Union Contracts,* pp. 79–81.

10. Hill and Sinicrope, *Management Rights,* pp. 4–5.

11. Arthur J. Goldberg, "Management's Reserved Rights: A Labor View," Proceedings of the 9th Annual Meeting of the National Arbitration Association, 118 (1956), pp. 120–21.

12. Agreement between the Anaconda Company and United Steel Workers of America, AFL-CIO Local Union No. 4612.

13. Hill and Sinicrope, *Management Rights,* pp. 6–7.

14. Paul Prasow and Edward Peters, *Arbitration and Collective Bargaining: Conflict Resolution in Labor Relations,* 2nd ed. (New York: McGraw-Hill, 1983), pp. 33–34.

15. *Fibreboard Corp.,* 379 U.S. 203 (1964).

16. *First National Maintenance,* 452 U.S. 666 (1981).

17. *Otis Elevator Co.,* 269 NLRB 891, 115 LRRM 1281 (1984).

18. *Dubuque Packing Co.,* 303 NLRB 66 (1991).

19. Mairead E. Connor, "The Dubuque Packing Decision: New Test for Bargaining over Decision to Relocate," *Labor Lawyer 8,* no. 2 (1992), pp. 289–95.

20. Bureau of National Affairs, *Basic Patterns in Union Contracts,* pp. 79–82.

21. Evan Perez, "Delta May Face Costly Rehiring of 1,060 Pilots," *The Wall Street Journal* (April 11, 2004), p. A3.

22. *Auciello Iron Works, Inc. v. National Labor Relations Board,* 517 U.S. 781 (1996).

23. Stephen I. Schlossberg and Judith A. Scott, *Organizing and the Law,* 4th ed. (Washington, DC: BNA Books, 1991), p. 285.

24. Patrick Hardin, ed., *The Developing Labor Law,* 3rd ed. (Washington, DC: Bureau of National Affairs, 1992), pp. 699–701; see also *Bonnell/ Tredegar Industries, Incorporated v. NLRB,* 46 F.3d 339 (4th Cir. 1995), and *NLRB v. Unbelievable, Inc. (dba Frontier Hotel & Casino),* 71 F.3d 1434 (9th Cir. 1995).

25. 29 U.S.C. sec. 158(d) (1982).

26. U.S. Senate, Committee on Labor and Public Welfare, *Committee Report, S. Rep. 105,* 80th Cong., 1st sess., 1947, pp. 16–18.

27. Benjamin Aaron et al., *The Future of Labor Arbitration in America* (New York: American Arbitration Association, 1976), p. 87.

28. *Textile Workers Union v. Lincoln Mills,* 353 U.S. 448, 40 LRRM 2113 (1957).

29. *United Steelworkers v. American Mfg. Co.,* 363 U.S. 564, 46 LRRM 2414 (1960); *United Steelworkers v. Warrior & Gulf Navigation Co.,* 363 U.S. 574, 46 LRRM 2416 (1960); and *United Steelworkers v. Enterprise Wheel & Car Corp.,* 363 U.S. 593, 46 LRRM 2423 (1960).

30. Aaron et al., *Future of Labor Arbitration in America,* p. 56.

31. *Collyer Insulated Wire,* 192 NLRB 837, 77 LRRM 1931 (1971).

32. *Spielberg Manufacturing Company,* 112 NLRB 1080, 36 LRRM 1152 (1955); see also Frank Elkouri and Edna Asper Elkouri, *How Arbitration Works,* 6th ed. (Washington, DC: Bureau of National Affairs, 2003) pp. 534–36.

33. *Paperworkers International v. Misco,* 484 U.S. 29, 108 S.Ct. 364, 98 L.Ed. 2d 286 (1987), and Marlin M. Volz et al., "Labor Arbitration and the Law of Collective

Bargaining Agreements," *Labor Lawyer 5,* no. 3 (Summer 1989), pp. 599–606.

34. Michael H. LeRoy and Peter Feuille, "The Steelworkers Trilogy and Grievance Arbitration Appeals: How the Federal Courts Respond," *Industrial Relations Law Journal 13,* no. 1 (1992), pp. 78–120; see also *American Postal Workers Union, AFL-CIO v. U.S. Postal Service,* 52 F.3d 359 (1995).

35. *Olin Corp.* 268 NLRB 573 (1984), *Combustions Engineering, Inc.,* 272 NLRB 32 (1984), and *Badger Meter, Inc.* 272 NLRB 123 (1984).

36. Benjamin W. Wolkinson, "The Impact of the Collyer Policy of Deferral: An Empirical Study," *Industrial and Labor Relations Review 38,* no. 3 (April 1985), pp. 377–91.

37. *Boys Market, Inc. v. Retail Clerks Union Local 770,* 398 U.S. 235, 90 S.Ct. 1583, 26 L.Ed. 2d 199 (1970).

38. *Sinclair Refining Company v. Atchison,* 370 U.S. 195, 82 S.Ct. 1328, 8 L.Ed. 440 (1962).

39. *Buffalo Forge Company v. United Steelworkers of America,* 428 U.S. 397, 96 S.Ct. 3141, 49 L.Ed. 2d 1022 (1976).

40. *Indianapolis Power and Light Company,* 276 NLRB 211 (1985).

41. *IBEW Local 387 v. NLRB,* No. 85-7129 (9th Cir., May 6, 1986).

42. *Vaca v. Sipes,* 386 U.S. 171, 64 LRRM 2369 (1967); *Hines v. Anchor Motor Co., Inc.,* 424 U.S. 554, 91 LRRM 2481 (1976); and *Bowen v. U.S. Postal Service,* 112 LRRM 2281 (1983).

43. See George W. Bohlander, "Fair Representation: Not Just a Union Problem," *The Personnel Administrator 25,* no. 3 (March 1980), pp. 36–40, 82.

44. Roberts, *Dictionary of Industrial Relations,* 3rd ed. (Washington, DC: Bureau of National Affairs, 1986), p. 285.

45. Bureau of National Affairs, *Basic Patterns in Union Contracts,* pp. 2–3.

46. Agreement between E. I. duPont de Nemours and Company and the Neoprene Craftsmen Union, 1994, p. 28.

47. *Jacobs Manufacturing Company,* 94 NLRB 1214 (1951).

48. *De Bartola Corp. v. Florida Gulf Coast Trades Council,* 56 USLW 4328 (1988).

49. Samuel A. DiLullo, "Secondary Boycotts: Has the Court Gone Too Far or Maybe Not Far Enough?" *Labor Law Journal 40,* no. 6 (June 1989), pp. 376–81.

50. *Delta Airlines, Inc.,* 293 NLRB 67 (1989).

51. *Johnston Development Group v. Local 1578,* 131 LRRM 2417 (N.J. Cir. 1989).

52. Gerard Morales, "Labor Unions' Rights to Handbill Neutral Employers and to Picket on Private Property," *Labor Lawyer 6,* no. 2 (1990), pp. 295–300.

53. Bill Towle, "Strike One, and You're Out," *Warehousing* (May 2002), p. 17.

54. *Pye v. Teamsters Local 122,* 149 LRRM 3089 (1st Cir. 1995).

55. *D'Amico v. Painters District Council 51 (Manganaro Corp. of Md.),* 120 LRRM 3473 (Md. Cir. 1985).

56. Dominic Bencivenga, "1959 Sweatshops Law," *New York Law Journal,* August 13, 1998, pp. 1–4.

57. Hardin, *The Developing Labor Law,* p. 1385.

58. National Labor Relations Act, Section 8(b)(6).

59. Schlossberg and Scott, *Organizing and the Law,* p. 110.

60. 5 U.S.C. sec. 7103(a)(12) (1982).

61. 5 U.S.C. sec. 7106 (1982).

62. 5 U.S.C. sec. 7122 (1982).

63. *National Federation of Federal Employees, Local 1309 v. Department of the Interior et al.,* 526 U.S. 86 (1999).

64. Joe Swerdzewski, General Counsel to FLRA, "Memorandum Re: The Duty of Fair Representation" (www.flra.gov), January 27, 1997.

65. *Fort Bragg Association of Educators, National Education Association,* 28 FLRA NO. 118, 28 FLRA 908 (1987).

CHAPTER 10

1. David Lewin and Richard B. Peterson, "A Model for Measuring Effectiveness of the Grievance Process," *Monthly Labor Review 106,* no. 4 (April 1983), pp. 47–49.

2. Frank Elkouri and Edna Asper Elkouri, *How Arbitration Works,* 6th ed. (Washington, DC: Bureau of National Affairs, 2003), pp. 198–99.

3. *Cudahy Packing Co.,* 7 LA G45, G46 (1947).

4. Elkouri and Elkouri, *How Arbitration Works* (2003) p. 201.

5. *Diamond Shamrock Corp.,* 55 LA 827 (1946).

6. Bureau of National Affairs, *Grievance Guide,* 11th ed. (Washington, DC: Bureau of National Affairs, 2003), p. 494.

7. *Alexander's Personnel Providers, Inc.,* 68 LA 249 (1947).

8. Thomas B. Knight, "Feedback and Grievance Resolution," *Industrial and Labor Relations Review 39,* no. 4 (July 1986), pp. 585–98.

9. Harold Davey, Mario Bognanno, and David Estenson, *Contemporary Collective Bargaining,* 4th ed. (Upper Saddle River, NJ: Prentice Hall, 1982), p. 169.

10. Bureau of National Affairs, *Basic Patterns in Union Contracts,* 14th ed. (Washington, DC: BNA Books, 1995), p. 35.

11. See the *Steelworkers Trilogy* cases: *United Steelworkers of America v. Enterprise Wheel & Car Corp.,* 80 S.Ct. 1358, 34 LA 569 (1960); *United Steelworkers of America v. American Mfg. Co.,* 363 U.S. 566–567

(1960); and *United Steelworkers of America v. Warrior & Gulf Navigation Company,* 363 U.S. 582 (1960).

12. Steven Briggs, "The Grievance Procedure," *Personnel Journal 60,* no. 6 (June 1981), pp. 471–74.

13. Bureau of National Affairs, *Grievance Guide,* (2003), pp. 67–157.

14. Stephen Cabot, *Labor-Management Relations Manual* (Boston: Warren, Gorham, Lamont, 1979), chap. 16, pp. 1–2.

15. Bureau of National Affairs, *Grievance Guide,* (2003) pp. 7–8.

16. Cabot, *Labor-Management Relations Manual,* chap. 16, pp. 3–5.

17. T. L. Stanley, "Running at Peak Performance," *Supervision 66,* no. 3 (March 2005) pp. 10–13.

18. *FMCS Grievance Mediation: Problem Solving in the Workplace* (Washington, DC: U.S. Government Printing Office, 2001).

19. Stephen B. Goldberg, "How Interest-Based, Grievance Mediation Performs Over the Long Term," *Dispute Resolution Journal 59,* no. 4 (Nov. 2004–Jan. 2005), pp. 8–15.

20. Ibid.

21. Richard B. Freeman and Carey Ichniowski, "Introduction: The Public Sector Look of Unionism," in *When Public Sector Workers Unionize,* ed. Richard B. Freeman and Carey Ichniowski (Chicago: University of Chicago Press, 1988), pp. 50–97.

22. Henry Graham and Virginia Wallace, "Trends in Public Sector Arbitration," *Personnel Administrator 27,* no. 4 (April 1982), pp. 73–77.

23. Michael J. Duane, "To Grieve or Not to Grieve: Why Reduce It to Writing?" *Public Personnel Management 20,* no. 1 (Spring 1991), pp. 83–90.

24. David L. Dilts and Clarence K. Deitsch, "Arbitration Lost: The Public Sector Assault on Arbitration," *Labor Law Journal 35,* no. 3 (March 1984), pp. 182–88.

CHAPTER 11

1. Edwin Witte, *Historical Survey of Labor Arbitration* (Ithaca, NY: Cornell University Press, 1952), pp. 29–33.

2. Ibid.

3. Robban W. Fleming, *The Labor Arbitration Process* (Urbana: University of Illinois Press, 1965), pp. 2–8.

4. Jean T. McKelvey, *The Profession of Labor Arbitration: Selected Papers from the First Seven Annual Meetings of the National Academy of Arbitrators* (Washington, D.C.: Bureau of National Affairs, 1957), pp. 42–46.

5. *Textile Workers Union of America v. Lincoln Mills of Alabama,* 353 U.S. 448, 77 S.Ct. 912 (1957); *United Steelworkers of America v. American Mfg. Co.,* 363 U.S. 564, 80 S.Ct. 1343 (1960); *United Steelworkers of America v. Warrior & Gulf Navigation Co.,* 363 U.S. 574, 80 S.Ct. 1347 (1960); and *United Steelworkers of America v. Enterprise Wheel & Car Corp.,* 363 U.S. 593, 80 S.Ct. 1358 (1960).

6. Charles J. Coleman and Theodora T. Haynes, *Labor Arbitration: An Annotated Bibliography* (Ithaca, NY: ILR Press, 1994), pp. 10–22.

7. Arnold M. Zack, *Handbook for Grievance Arbitration: Procedural and Ethical Issues* (New York: Lexington Books, 1992), pp. 76–93.

8. *United Steelworkers of America v. Warrior & Gulf Navigation Co.,* 363 U.S. 574, 80 S.Ct. 1347 (1960).

9. *Steelworkers v. Enterprise Wheel & Car Corp.,* 363 U.S. 593 (1960).

10. *E. I. duPont de Nemours & Co. v. Grasselli Employees Independent Association of East Chicago, Inc.,* No. 85-1577 (7th Cir., May 9, 1986).

11. Theodore St. Antoine, "Judicial Review of Labor Arbitration Awards: A Second Look at *Enterprise Wheel* and Its Progeny," *75 Michigan Law Review 1137,* 1140 (1977).

12. 415 U.S. 36 (1974).

13. *Harrell Alexander, Sr. v. Gardner-Denver Co.,* 415 U.S. 36, 944 S.Ct. 101 (1974), and *W. R. Grace and Co., v. Local Union 759, International Union of the United Rubber Cork, Linoleum and Plastic Workers of America,* 461 U.S. 757, 103, S.Ct. 2177 (1963).

14. *Wright v. Universal Maritime Service Corporation,* 525 U.S. 70 (1998).

15. Ibid.

16. *Airline Pilots v. Northwest Airlines,* 199 F. 3d 477 (D.C. Cir. 1999), reinstated 211 F. 3d 1312 (D.C. Cir. 2000), cert. den. 531 U.S. 1011 (2000).

17. *Gilmer v. Interstate/Johnson Lane Corp.,* 500 U.S. 20 (1991), and George M. Sullivan, "Alexander v. Garner Denver: Staggered but Still Standing," *Labor Law Journal,* March 1999, pp. 43–51.

18. Elkouri and Elkouri, *How Arbitration Works,* 6th ed. (Washington, DC: Bureau of National Affairs, 2003), pp. 49–51.

19. The Federal Arbitration Act, 9 U.S.C. 1-16 (2000), first enacted in 1925.

20. 3 Teresa L. Elliott, "Conflicting Interpretations of the One-Year Requirement On Motions to Confirm Arbitration Awards," *Creighton Law Review 38,* no. 3 (April 2005), pp. 661–89.

21. 532 U.S. 105 (2001).

22. Ibid.

23. Charles Lane, "High Court Backs EEOC Suits in Bias Cases," *Washington Post,* January 16, 2002, p. A1.

24. Ibid.

25. 531 U.S. 79 (2000).

26. Arnold M. Zack, "The Arbitration of Interest Disputes: A Process in Peril," *Arbitration Journal 45* (1985) and 55 (1994).

27. Elkouri and Elkouri, *How Arbitration Works* (2003), pp. 106–7.

28. Theodore W. Kheel, *The Keys to Conflict Resolution* (New York: Four Walls Eight Windows, 1999), pp. 88–89.

29. Elkouri and Elkouri, *How Arbitration Works* (2003), p. 116.

30. Kheel, *The Keys to Conflict Resolution,* p. 90.

31. American Arbitration Association, *Labor Arbitration Procedures and Techniques* (New York: American Arbitration Association, 1978), pp. 12–13.

32. *T.J. Maxx,* 113 LA 533 (1999).

33. *Flathead County Commissioners,* 97 LA 350 (1991).

34. Stephen Cabot, *Labor-Management Relations Manual* (Boston: Warren, Gorham, Lamont, 1979), chap. 18, pp. 4–6.

35. Steven B. Goldberg, "The Mediation of Grievances under a Collective Bargaining Contract: An Alternative to Arbitration," *Northwestern University Law Review 77,* no. 3 (October 1982), pp. 270–73.

36. Nels Nelson and Earl Curry, "Arbitrator Characteristics and Arbitral Decisions," *Industrial Relations 20,* no. 3 (Fall 1981), pp. 312–17.

37. Steven Briggs and John Anderson, "An Empirical Investigation of Arbitrator Acceptability," *Industrial Relations 19,* no. 2 (Spring 1980), pp.163–73.

38. Richard A. Posthuma, James B. Dworkin, and Maris S. Swift, "Arbitrator Acceptability: Does Justice Matter?" *Industrial Relations 39,* no. 2 (April 2000), pp. 313–35.

39. Elkouri and Elkouri, *How Arbitration Works* (2003), pp. 182–88.

40. Judith B. Ittig and Michael J. Baynard, "Thirty Steps to Better Arbitration," *Dispute Resolution Journal 59,* no. 3, (Aug.–Oct. 2004), pp. 41–45.

41. Elkouri and Elkouri, *How Arbitration Works* (2003), pp. 155–158.

42. Agreement between the Mechanical Contractors Association and Plumbers and Gas Fitters Local Union No. 107, 1979–1982, p. 21.

43. Steven C. Bennett, "The Developing American Approach to Arbitrability," *Dispute Resolution Journal 58,* no. 1 (Feb.–Apr 2003) pp. 8–23.

44. Elkouri and Elkouri, *How Arbitration Works* (2003), p. 279.

45. *United Steelworkers of America v. Warrior & Gulf Navigation Co.,* 80 S.Ct. 1347, 1352–1353 (1960).

46. *Republic Waste Services,* 119 LA 1105 (2004).

47. *Labor Arbitration Procedures and Techniques,* pp. 17–20.

48. Ibid.

49. *Instrument Workers v. Minneapolis Honeywell Co.,* 54 LRRM 2660, 2661 (1963).

50. Cabot, *Labor-Management Relations Manual,* chap. 18, p. 6.

51. Margaret A. Lareau and Howard R. Sacks, "Assessing Credibility in Labor Arbitration," *Labor Lawyer 5,* no. 3 (Spring 1989), pp. 151–93.

52. Kheel, *Labor Law,* chap. 24, p. 55.

53. Judith B. Ittig and Michael J. Baynard, "Thirty Steps to Better Arbitration," *Dispute Resolution Journal 59,* no. 3 (Aug.–Oct. 2004), pp. 41–45.

54. Cabot, *Labor-Management Relations Manual,* chap. 18, pp. 7–8.

55. Kheel, *Labor Law,* chap. 24, p. 56.

56. Roger I. Abrams and Dennis R. Nolan, "Arbitral Craftsmanship and Opinion Writing," *Labor Lawyer 5,* no. 2 (Spring 1989), pp. 195–222.

57. Kheel, *Labor Law,* chap. 24, pp. 50–51.

58. Daniel F. Jennings and A. Dale Allen, Jr., "How Arbitrators View the Process of Labor Arbitration: A Longitudinal Analysis," *Labor Studies Journal 18,* no. 1 (Winter 1993), pp. 41–50.

59. Howard Stiefel, "The Labor Arbitration Process: Survey of the New York State Bar Association Labor and Employment Law Section," *Labor Lawyer 8,* no. 4 (Fall 1992), pp. 971–83.

60. Kheel, *The Keys to Conflict Resolution,* pp. 90–91.

61. Clarence R. Deitsch, "Seniority Clauses: An End Run Around Just Cause?" *Dispute Resolution Journal 59,* no. 4 (November 2004–Jan. 2005) pp. 30–34.

62. Ibid.

63. Wallace B. Nelson, "The Role of Common Law in Just Cause Disputes," *Personnel Journal 58,* no. 8 (August 1979), pp. 541–43.

64. Bureau of National Affairs, *Grievance Guide,* 11th ed. (Washington, DC: Bureau of National Affairs, 2003), pp. 3–5.

65. Elkouri and Elkouri, *How Arbitration Works* (2003) p. 1235.

66. Nelson, "The Role of Common Law in Just Cause Disputes," pp. 541–43.

67. Kevin B. Zeese, *Drug Testing Legal Manual* (New York: Clark Boardman Company, 1988), chap. 4, p. 18.

68. *NTEU v. Von Raab,* 649 F.Supp. 380 (ED La 1986), 57 LW 4338 (March 21, 1989).

69. *Johnson Bateman Company,* 295 NLRB 26 (1989).

70. Zeese, *Drug Testing Legal Manual,* chap. 4, pp. 18–19.

71. *N.L.R.B. GC 87-5; Brotherhood of Locomotive Engineers v. Burlington Northern RR. Co.,* 620 F. Supp. 163 (Mont. Cir. 1985).

72. *Maple Meadow Mining,* 90 LA 873 (1988).

73. *Vulcan Materials Co.,* 90 LA 1161 (1988).

74. *Pacific Motor Trucking,* 86 LA 497 (1986), and *Amalgamated Transit Union, Local 1433,* and *Phoenix Transit System,* 87-2 ARB 8510.

75. *Shelby County Health Care Center,* 90 LA 1225 (1988).

76. *Boise Cascade Corp.,* 90 LA 105 (1987); see also Elkouri and Elkouri, eds., *How Arbitration Works,* 4th ed.

1985–1987 Supp. (Washington, DC: Bureau of National Affairs, 1988), p. 131.

77. *Warehouse Distribution Centers,* 90 LA 979 (1987).

78. *Gem City Chemicals,* 86 LA 1023 (1986).

79. *Signal Delivery Service, Inc.,* 86 LA 75 (1986).

80. Nelson, "The Role of Common Law in Just Cause Disputes," p. 551.

81. Agreement, General Motors Corporations and the United Auto Workers, 1970, p. 43.

82. *Bethlehem Steel Co.,* 24 LA 699, 702 (1955).

83. Steve Markham and Dow Scott, "Controlling Absenteeism: Union and Nonunion Differences," *Personnel Administrator 30,* no. 2 (February 1985), pp. 87–102.

84. Ibid.

85. Bureau of National Affairs, *Grievance Guide* (2003) p. 187.

86. Ibid.

87. Agreement, National Conference of Brewery and Soft Drink Workers and Teamsters Local No. 745 and Jos. Schlitz Brewing Co., Longview, Texas, 1979, p. 24.

88. Bureau of National Affairs, *Grievance Guide* (2003), pp. 359–61.

89. Agreement, Mechanical Contractors Association of Kentucky, Inc. and Plumbers and Gas Fitters Local Union No. 107, 1979–1982, p. 6.

90. Bureau of National Affairs, Grievance Guide (2003), p. 389.

91. Ibid., pp. 390–395.

92. Kenneth P. Swan, "Public Bargaining in Canada and the U.S.: A Legal View," *Industrial Relations 19,* no. 3 (Fall 1980), pp. 272–91.

93. David E. Bloom, "Is Arbitration Really Compatible with Bargaining*?" Industrial Relations 20,* no. 3 (Fall 1981), pp. 233–44; see also Patricia Compton-Forbes, "Interest Arbitration Hasn't Worked Well in the Public Sector," *Personnel Administrator 29,* no. 2 (February 1984), pp. 99–104.

94. Angelo S. DeNisi and James B. Dworkin, "Final-Offer Arbitration and the Naive Negotiator," *Industrial and Labor Relations Review 35,* no. 1 (October 1981), pp. 78–87, and John C. Anderson, "The Impact of Arbitration: A Methodological Assessment," *Industrial Relations 20,* no. 2 (Spring 1981), pp. 129–48.

95. J. Joseph Loewenberg, "The 1984 Postal Arbitration: Issues Surrounding the Award," *Monthly Labor Review 109,* no. 6 (June 1986), pp. 31–32.

96. *School Committee of Beverly v. Geller,* 435 Mass. 223 (2001).

CHAPTER 12

1. Thomas L. Friedman, *The World Is Flat, A Brief History of the Twenty First Century* (New York: Farrar, Straus and Giroux, 2005).

2. Ibid., pp. 48–172.

3. General Motors Web site. Available at http://www.gm.com/company. Accessed October 2005.

4. Juhani Lonnroth, "Global Employment Issues in the Year 2000," *Monthly Labor Review 117,* no. 9 (September 1994), pp. 5–15.

5. Helmut Wagner, "Implications of Globalization for Monetary Policy," IMF Working Papers (2001 International Monetary Fund), pp. 1–63. Available at www.imf.org. Accessed October 2005.

6. International Confederation of Free Trade Unions (ICFTU), "A Trade Union Guide to Globalization, Second Edition" (November 2004), pp. 9–18. Available at http://www.icftu.org. Accessed October 2005.

7. Giuseppe Nicoletti, Stephen S. Golub, Dana Hajkova, Daniel Mirza, and Kwang-Yeol Yoo," The Influence of Policies on Trade and Foreign Direct Investment," *OECD Economic Studies No. 36,* (January 2003), pp. 1–77.

8. Stephen J. Kobrin, "Sovereignty@Bay: Globalization, Multinational Enterprise, and the International Political System" in *The Oxford Handbook of International Business,* ed. Alan Rugman and Thomas Brewer (Oxford England: Oxford University Press 2001), pp. 181–205.

9. International Labour Office, *Your Voice at Work* (Geneva, Switzerland: ILO Publications, 2000). Available at http://www.ilo.org/voice@work. Accessed October 2005.

10. Greg Bamber, Russell D. Langsbury, and Nick Wailes, eds., *International and Comparative Employment Relations: Globalisation and the Developed Market Economies* (Thousand Oaks, CA: Sage Publications Inc., 2004), p. 211.

11. *A Trade Union Guide to Globalization,* 2nd ed. (Brussels, Belgium: International Confederation of Free Trade Unions (ICFTU), 2004), pp. 1–172, 13.

12. IMF Staff, "Recovery from the Asian Crisis and the Role of the IMF" (June 2004). Available at http://www.imf.org. Accessed October 2005.

13. Michael Mussa, "Factors Driving Global Economic Integration," Presented in Jackson Hole, Wyoming, symposium sponsored by the Federal Reserve Bank of Kansas City on "Global Opportunities and Challenges," August 25, 2000. Available at www.imf.org. Accessed October 2005.

14. Friedman, *The World Is Flat, A Brief History of the Twenty First Century,* p. 9.

15. Bruce E. Kaufman, *The Global Evolution of Industrial Relations: Events, Ideas and the IIRA* (Geneva: International Labour Office, 2004), p. 16.

16. Ibid. at 20.

17. Adam Smith, *An Inquiry into the Nature and Causes of the Wealth of Nations* (New York: Oxford University Press, 1998).

18. Ibid., pp. 12–13.
19. Roy J. Adams, "Regulating Unions and Collective Bargaining: A Global, Historical Analysis of Determinants and Consequences," *Comparative Labor Law Journal 14,* no. 3 (Spring 1993), pp. 272–300.
20. Ibid.
21. Kaufman, *The Global Evolution of Industrial Relations,* p. 475.
22. Adams, "Regulating Unions and Collective Bargaining," p. 282.
23. Kaufman, *The Global Evolution of Industrial Relations,* at 77.
24. Lee Swepston, "The Future of ILO Standards," *Monthly Labor Review 117,* no. 9 (September 1994), pp. 16–23.
25. Kaufman, *The Global Evolution Of Industrial Relations,* pp. 204–5.
26. Swepston, "The Future of ILO Standards," p. 16.
27. International Labour Office, *Your Voice at Work.*
28. Bernard Gernigon, Alberto Odero, and Horacio Guido, "ILO Principles Concerning Collective Bargaining," *International Labour Review 139,* no. 1 (2000), pp. 33–55.
29. Laurence Waterhouse, "Surveying the British Canal System," *US Hydro* (2001), pp. 1–13. Accessed on September 24, 2005, available at www.thsoa.org/hyo1/5_4.pdf.
30. Kaufman, *The Global Evolution Of Industrial Relations,* p. 25.
31. Ibid., p. 52.
32. Mary Davis, "The Union Makes Us Strong: TUC History Online," *Centre for Trade Union Studies.* Available at London Metropolitan University Web site www.unionhistory.info. Accessed September 2005.
33. Kaufman, *The Global Evolution Of Industrial Relations,* p. 199.
34. Ibid., p. 383.
35. Ibid., p. 278.
36. Ibid., p. 416.
37. *International and Comparative Employment Relations,* pp. 91–115.
38. Joseph B. Rose and Gary N. Chaison, "Canadian Labor Policy as a Model for Legislative Reform in the United States," *Labor Law Journal 46,* no. 5 (May 1995), pp. 259–72.
39. *International and Comparative Employment Relations,* p. 109.
40. Kaufman, *The Global Evolution Of Industrial Relations,* p. 422.
41. Ibid., p. 421.
42. Ibid., p. 290.
43. Joo-Cheong Tham, "The Framework of Australian Labour Law and Recent Trends in 'Deregulation'," Paper Presented at The Japan Institute for Labour Policy and Training (JILPT) Comparative Labor Law Seminar (Tokyo, Japan: 2004), pp. 37–50.
44. Bahman Bahrami, "Australian Labor Relations: The Recent Developments," *Labor Law Journal 47,* no. 5 (May 1996), pp. 327–41.
45. Tham, "The Framework of Australian Labour Law and Recent Trends in 'Deregulation'," at 39.
46. Pascal Fontaine, *Europe in 12 Lessons* (Luxembourg: Office for Official Publications of the European Communities, 2004), pp. 1–68 at 55.
47. Ibid. at 54.
48. "Foreign Labor Trends—European Union," U.S. Department of Labor, Bureau of International Labor Affairs (2003), pp. 1–25. Available at http://www.dol.gov/ILAB/media/reports. Accessed October 2005.
49. Ibid., p. 19.
50. Kaufman, *The Global Evolution Of Industrial Relations,* p. 20.
51. Ibid., p. 474.
52. Ibid., p. at 32.
53. *International and Comparative Employment Relations,* pp. 232–34.
54. Rolf Wank, "The Mechanism for Establishing and Changing Terms and Conditions of Employment," Paper Presented at the Japan Institute for Labour Policy and Training (JILPT) Comparative Labor Law Seminar (Tokyo, Japan: 2004), pp. 59–72, at 65.
55. Cecilie Rohwedder, "Once the Big Muscle of German Industry, Unions See It All Sag," Wall Street Journal, November 29, 1999, pp. A1, A18.
56. Mia Rönnmar, "Mechanisms for Establishing and Changing Terms and Conditions of Employment in Sweden," Paper Presented at the Japan Institute for Labour Policy and Training (JILPT) Comparative Labor Law Seminar (Tokyo, Japan: 2004), pp. 95–107. Available at http://www.jil.go.jp/english. Accessed October 2005. See also Olle Hammarstrom, Tony Huzzard, and Tommy Nilson, "Employment Relations in Sweden," in *International and Comparative Employment Relations,* 4th ed., ed. Greg J. Bamber, Russell D. Lansbury, and Nick Wailes (Thousand Oaks, CA: Sage Publications Inc. 2004), pp. 254–76.
57. Annika Berg, "Employers Call for Changes to Industrial Action Rules," *European Industrial Relations Observatory (EIRO)* Online (May 7, 2005). Available at http://www.eiro.eurofound.eu.int/structure.html. Accessed October 2005.
58. Mia Ronnmar, "Mechanisms for Establishing and Changing Terms and Conditions of Employment in Sweden," p. 104.
59. BHHRG 22 St. Margaret's Road Oxford OX2 6RX UK.
60. Russell Lansbury and Olle Hammarstrom, "Productivity and Industrial Relations: Case Studies in the

Australian and Swedish Automotive Components Industries," July 1991.

61. Christian Dufour, "Questionnaire for EIRO Comparative Study on Changes in the National Collective Bargaining Systems Since 1990—Case of France," *EIROnline,* (May, 2005). Available at http://www.eiro.eurofound.eu.int/2005/03/study/index.html. Accessed October 2005. See also Christian Dufour "Bargaining in France in 2001: The End of an Unusual Era," in *Collective Bargaining in the EU Member-States,* ed. G. Fayertag (Brussels: European Trade Union Institute, 2002); and Christian Dufour, "Mandating: Precursor of a New Practice in Employee Representation or Destructive Force?" in *Lessons Learned from the Reduction of Working Time,* ed. Daugareilh Isabelle and Pierre Iriart, *Maison Des Sciences De l'Homme d'Aquitaine,* pp. 255–65.

62. Maurice Braud "MEDEF Makes Proposals for Modernization of Labour Code," *Institute of Economic and Social Research* (April 7, 2004).

63. *International and Comparative Employment Relations,* pp. 148–53.

64. Diego Coletto and Livio Muratore, "2004 Annual Review for Italy," *EIROnline* (July 2005). Available at http://www.eiro.eurofound.eu.int/about/2005/01/feature/it0501209f.html. Accessed October 2005.

65. David Dukcevich, "Italian Labor Reformer Murdered," *Forbes* (March 20, 2002). Available at www.forbes.com. Accessed September 2005.

66. Michele Tiraboschi and Maurizio Del Conte, "Recent Changes in the Italian Labour Law," Paper presented at the Japan Institute for Labour Policy and Training (JILPT) Comparative Labor Law Seminar (Tokyo, Japan: 2004), pp. 85–93, at 88.

67. *International Reform Monitor, Social Policy, Labour Market Policy and Industrial Relations,* 9th ed. (Gütersloh, Germany: Bertelsmann Stiftung, October 2005). Available at http://en.bertelsmann-stiftung.de/foundation. Accessed October 2005.

68. Diego Coletto, Fondazione Regionale Pietro Seveso, and Livio Muratore, Ires Lombardia, "2004 Annual Review for Italy," *European Industrial Relations Observatory (EIRO).* Available at http://www.eiro.eurofound.eu.int/structure.html. Accessed October 2005.

69. Mitsuru Yamashita "Japanese Labor-Management Relations in an Era of Diversification of Employment Types: Diversifying Workers and the Role of Labor Unions," *Japan Labor Review 2,* no. 1 (Winter 2005), pp. 105–17, 107.

70. "Japan 2002," *Foreign Labor Trends* (U.S. Department of Labor, Bureau of International Labor Affairs: 2002). Available at http://www.dol.gov/ILAB/media/reports. Accessed October 2005.

71. Tetsu Sano, "The Japanese Economy: Current Situation and Outlook for the Future," *Labor Situation in Japan and Analysis 2004/2005* (Tokyo, Japan: The Japan Institute for Labour Policy and Training, 2004), p. 3.

72. Motohiro Morishma, "Information Sharing and Collective Bargaining in Japan: Effects on Wage Negotiations," *Industrial and Labor Relations Review 44,* no. 3 (April 1991), pp. 469–85.

73. "Korea 2003," *Foreign Labor Trends* (U.S. Department of Labor, Bureau of International Labor Affairs: 2003). Available at http://www.dol.gov/ILAB/media/reports. Accessed October 2005.

74. *International and Comparative Employment Relations,* p. 314.

75. "China Economy 'Growing at 9.5%,'" *The China Daily* (November 2, 2005). Available at www.chinadaily.com.cn

76. Simon Clark, "Post Socialist Trade Unions: China and Russia," Industrial *Relations Journal 36,* no. 1 (January 2005), pp. 2–18.

77. George J. Gilboy, "The Myth Behind China's Miracle," *Foreign Affairs 83,* no. 4 (July/August 2004), pp. 33–48.

78. Sarosh Kuruvilla, "Change and Transformation in Asia Industrial Relations," *Industrial Relations 41,* no. 2 (April, 2002), pp. 171–228.

79. Simon Clarke and Chang-Hee Lee, "The Significance of Tripartite Consultation in China," *British Journal of Industrial Relations 42,* no. 2 (2004), pp. 235–54.

80. Clarke "Post Socialist Trade Unions," p. 8.

81. Simon Clarke, Chang-Hee Lee, and Qi Li, "Collective Consultation and Industrial Relations in China," *British Journal of Industrial Relations 42,* 2 (June 2004), pp. 235–54; Clarke and Lee, "The Significance of Tripartite Consultation in China," p. 239.

82. Ibid., p. 239.

Glossary

Ability to pay The financial position of a company and its ability to change its wage rates are general factors involved in negotiations. They are usually a reflection of company profits and will be a basis of a negotiator's wage proposal.

Absenteeism (no-fault) An innovative absenteeism policy, negotiated by management and the union, in which an employer may take action against an employee whose excessive absences from work significantly reduce service to the company.

Absolute rank principle The seniority principle giving employees on merging seniority lists the same ranking that they held on the prior seniority lists, resulting in two employees being ranked first, two employees ranked second, and so on.

Accretion doctrine The practice of allowing the addition of new employees and jobs to existing bargaining units, provided their work satisfies the same criteria of the original unit.

Administrative law judge For the National Labor Relations Board (NLRB), a person who is not a federal judge but rather an employee of the NLRB who conducts hearings under the National Labor Relations Act at which parties present evidence. A ruling of an NLRB administrative law judge can be appealed to the five-member NLRB.

Agency shop A labor contract provision that requires employees to contribute a sum of money equal to union membership dues but does not require the employee to join the union. The employee benefits from collective bargaining by the union and in turn gives financial support to the union for negotiations, contract administration, and other actions.

Albermarle Paper Co. v. Moody The Supreme Court ruling that set standards for back pay awards granted for discrimination, as protected by Title VII of the Civil Rights Act. The Court also ruled that the reliability of employment tests must fall within the EEOC guidelines.

Alcohol testing (See Drug and alcohol testing.)

Alexander v. Gardner-Denver, Co A landmark case in which the Supreme Court ruled that arbitration of a discrimination claim does not bar an employee from filing a Title VII (Civil Rights Act) suit of the same claim. The Court also ruled that great weight would be given to the arbitrator's decision.

Alternative dispute resolution (ADR) Resolving disputes using mediation, interest arbitration, fact-finding, and the like rather than litigation or formal arbitration.

American Federation of Labor (AFL) A federation of unions made up of skilled workers formed in 1886 by Samuel Gompers. The AFL offered trade unions local autonomy because the national union operated as a decentralized organization. Eventually, the AFL merged with the CIO.

American Railway Union (ARU) An industrial union of railway workers founded by Eugene Debs in 1843. It was one of the first unions organized on an industry rather than a craft basis.

Americans with Disabilities Act (ADA) Passed in 1990, this act gave Civil Rights Act protections to people with disabilities and prohibits discrimination in jobs, housing, public buildings and services, and transportation.

Analysis The stage in preparation for collective bargaining negotiations in which the parties gather information and narrow the issues.

Anarcho-syndicalism The anarchists and revolutionary socialists within the labor movement from which the French system of employee relations emerged.

Annual salary A worker's wages based on performing the functions of a job on a yearly basis.

Antiunion animus When an employer's conduct is not motivated, or at least not entirely motivated, by legitimate and substantial business reasons but by a desire to penalize or reward employees for union activity or the lack of it.

Appropriate bargaining unit The number of employees and jobs in an organization determined by the National Labor Relations Board to comprise a bargaining unit for purposes of collective bargaining.

Arbitrability The challenge of whether a disputed issue is subject to arbitration under the terms of the contract.

Arbitration A process in which the parties involved agree to submit an unresolved dispute to a neutral third party, whose decision is final and binding.

Arbitrator's award   The arbitrator's decision in a grievance case, presented in written format and signed by the arbitrator. Examples of awards include back pay and reinstatement of job or benefits.

Arbitrator's opinion   An arbitrator's written statement discussing the reasons for the decision in the case.

Auction bargaining   The willingness to make concessions during negotiations, demonstrated by both parties stating their positions, presenting their proposals, and then trading off the proposals to arrive at agreeable terms.

Authority to negotiate   The duty to bargain in good faith includes sending negotiators to the collective bargaining sessions with sufficient authority to carry on meaningful negotiations.

Awards   In Australia, company or industry awards are negotiated by company, union, and sometimes government officials, to establish minimum wages and working conditions for specific categories of workers and are the approximate functional equivalent of an American collective bargaining agreement.

Back-loaded contracts   A multiyear contract that provides a lower wage adjustment in the first year, with higher wage increases in the later years.

Bargaining items   The issue previously determined to be negotiable in a collective bargaining session. Items are generally either economic or noneconomic in nature.

Bargaining unit   The group of employees determined by the National Labor Relations Board to be an appropriate unit for collective bargaining purposes. After a bargaining unit is identified, the employees of that unit have the right to select their bargaining representative, usually a labor union.

Base compensation   An employee's general rate of pay per unit or hour, disregarding payments for items such as overtime, pension benefits, and bonuses.

Base pay   In the context of a pension plan, usually the average yearly salary for some number of years. The base pay is used to determine an annual pension to be paid to the employee on retirement.

Bilateral bargaining   A typical bargaining situation involving two parties, each with the authority to commit to the negotiated agreement.

Bogey   When union workers informally set a work standard that they will not exceed. Since a "bogey" is usually a level of production that is below normal, or par, the term is similar to a "bogey" on a golf course—not up to par or standard performance.

Borg-Warner doctrine   The 1958 case that outlined three categories of bargaining subjects and the rules governing each. They are (1) mandatory subjects, such as wages and hours; (2) permissive subjects, such as pension benefits of retired employees; and (3) illegal subjects, such as a proposal for a closed shop or discriminatory treatment.

Boulwarism   A collective bargaining approach in which management presents its entire proposal as its final offer, holding nothing back for further negotiations. This approach lacks any "give-and-take" in bargaining.

Boys Market case   A case in which the Supreme Court upheld an injunction against a union that struck an employer despite a no-strike clause in its contract. The Court also ruled that an employer is ordered to arbitrate while seeking a court injunction against a union striking in violation of a no-strike clause.

Bretton Woods exchange rate system   Created after World War II to provide a degree of international exchange rate stability. It resulted in the creation of international financial institutions such as the International Monetary Fund (IMF) and the World Bank.

"Bull pen"   The name given to barracks surrounded by barbed wire where members of the Western Federation of Miners were imprisoned after a strike turned violent with the bombing of a mine in 1899. The term was later used in baseball to refer to the warm-up area for relief pitchers.

Bumping   A procedure commonly used during layoffs, in which employees with greater seniority whose jobs are eliminated displace employees with lesser seniority. Bumping is more often used in companies with plantwide seniority in unskilled jobs.

Business agent   The full-time administrator of a local union paid to handle the negotiation and administration of the union contract as well as the daily operation of the union hiring hall.

Business necessity   A defense to a charge of discrimination when an employer proves that the business would suffer if the complainant were hired or if another person were not hired.

Cafeteria plans   Refers to flexible benefit plans that offer employees a decision on what benefits they want from the employer.

Call-in pay   A supplemental payment given to employees called back to work before they are normally scheduled to return.

Capitalism   The economic theory that a nation's prosperity relies on a more productive use of human capital and that by increasing the division of labor there would be greater productivity, the development of new machinery, and of new skills and trades among workers. A capitalist or market economy is characterized by the principles of free trade, competition, and choice, and noninterference by government.

Card check When a union collects authorization cards from a majority of the unit members and the cards are submitted to a third party to verify the names against payroll.

Certification The determination by the National Labor Relations Board that a union represents the employee's free choice and therefore that the union can become the official bargaining agent for a bargaining unit.

Chaebol Large, conglomerate family-controlled firms of South Korea characterized by strong ties with government agencies.

Charge Under the National Labor Relations Act, an allegation made by an individual, employer, or labor organization of an unfair labor practice.

Cheap riders Employees within a bargaining unit who choose not to join the union which bargains for an agreement but are required to pay a fee to the union to provide their share of the costs associated with negotiations (usually 20 to 85 percent of regular unions' dues).

Checkoff provision A contract provision requiring that the employer deduct union dues directly from union employee paychecks. The collected dues are then deposited in the union treasury.

Civil Rights Act of 1964 A federal law designed to eliminate racial and sexual discrimination. Title VII of the law makes it unlawful for an organization of 15 or more employees to discriminate against an individual because of race, color, religion, sex, or national origin. The act received major amendments in 1972 (Equal Employment Opportunity Act) and 1978 (Pregnancy Discrimination Act).

Civil Service Reform Act of 1978 Signed into law in October 1978, the act was designed to reform the outdated federal civil service structure and was modeled after the National Labor Relations Act. One of the major provisions is a three-member panel, the Federal Labor Relations Authority, whose purpose is to oversee labor-management relations within the federal government, thus acting in a manner similar to that of the National Labor Relations Board in the private sector.

Civil service system A governmental system of employment based on merit. Employee selection is based on examination scores or an assessment of experience and abilities. Promotion, advancement, and discipline are based on job performance.

Clayton Act Passed by Congress in 1914, this law was designed to limit the use of the Sherman Antitrust Act in labor disputes and to limit the court's injunctive powers against labor organizations, stating that labor was not a commodity and union members were not restrained from lawful activities. Strict interpretation by the courts limited the effectiveness of the act.

Closed shop A union security arrangement that requires employers to hire only union members. Closed shops were made illegal under the Taft-Hartley Act.

Coalition of Labor Union Women Founded in 1974, this union was to promote the unionization of women in the workforce.

Codetermination In Germany, in firms with 2,000 or more employees, the company's supervisory board must contain a certain number of employee representatives. Codetermination means that unions and employees have a say in company policy, as well as sharing responsibility for the firm.

Collyer case A 1971 ruling in which the National Labor Relations Board deferred its jurisdiction, ordering the concerned parties to resolve an unfair labor practice dispute through arbitration. The board ruled that cases involving unfair labor practices can be ordered to arbitration if the dispute centers on conditions negotiated in the collective bargaining agreement.

Collective bargaining coverage The percentage of workers covered by a collective bargaining agreement whether or not they are in the union.

Combinations Original organizations of employees who banded together for better wages and working conditions. They were outlawed in most countries as a threat to private property rights of employers and a restraint on trade.

Common law of the shop A recognition of the bargaining history of those in the same industry to determine the respective rights of the parties involved in a labor dispute.

Community-of-interest doctrine Descriptive criteria used by the National Labor Relations Board to evaluate a group of employees and determine whether they constitute an appropriate bargaining unit.

Company unions An employee organization formed by and recognized within a company, initiating reforms such as health benefits and better living conditions. This type of union usually does not meet the requirements of the National Labor Relations Act and thus is not considered a true union.

Complaint Under the National Labor Relations Act, after the regional director investigates a complaint of an unfair labor practice, if merit is found and no settlement is reached, then a complaint is served charging a party with an unfair labor practice. The complaint does not constitute a finding of wrongdoing but rather raises issues to be decided by a judge.

Compressed workweek Any workweek in which the scheduled working days are fewer than the traditional five workdays per week.

Concertazione The involvement of *social partners*—employers and employees—in the design of economic policy with the Italian government, promoted by the formal adoption of tripartite agreements or *pacts*. Such agreements have been signed to target pension reform; to reform the labor market and promote worker education and training; to set up a new system of three-way industrial relations, including local authorities; and reforming the nation's labor market and employment benefits.

Concerted activities Any legitimate action taken by employees to further their common but not individual interests, such as wages, hours, and working conditions.

Concession bargaining Collectively bargained reductions in previously negotiated wages, benefits, or work rules, usually in exchange for management guaranteed employment levels during the term of a contract.

Congress of Industrial Organizations (CIO) A federation of unions made up of industrial workers formed in 1935 by John L. Lewis. The CIO organized unions within industries, such as the auto and steel industries, and included all the workers at a work site rather than restricting membership to one trade. Eventually merged with the AFL.

Consolidated Omnibus Budget Reconciliation Act (CO-BRA) A law passed by Congress in 1986 that provides for the continuation of medical and dental insurance for employees, spouses, and dependents in the event of an employee's death, termination, divorce, or other loss of health care eligibility. Employees may elect to continue health care coverage for up to 18 or 36 months if they pay 100 percent of the cost.

Contract bar The general rule followed by the National Labor Relations Board stating that a current and valid labor contract can prevent another union from petitioning for an election and being certified as the exclusive representative for the term of the existing contract.

Contributory plans A pension plan in which the employer contributes a portion of the funding and the employee contributes the other portion.

Coordinated bargaining The joint bargaining with several unions and/or employers being represented by one negotiating team. The various unions of employers agree to one overall contract.

Cordwainers conspiracy cases A series of court cases that challenged the association of cordwain-ers and their wage agreement, ruling their action to be an illegal conspiracy and a conspiracy to impoverish others. The 1806 Supreme Court ruling that found the mere combination of workers to conspire to raise their wages to be illegal was later overturned.

Corporate campaign A new tactic used by unions to counter company antiunion sentiment in which unions attempt to join corporate boards of directors or contact company bond- and shareholders to put pressure on company management.

Costing wage provisions The methods of determining the financial impact of a contract change such as annual cost, cost per employee per year, percent of payroll, and cents per hour.

Cost-of-living adjustment (COLA) The negotiated compensation increase given an employee based on the percentage by which the cost of living has risen, usually measured by a change in the consumer price index (CPI).

Craft severance The desire of a group of craft employees to break away from an existing union or one that has traditionally represented them.

Craft unions Workers who have been organized in accordance with their craft or skills.

Craft units A bargaining unit composed exclusively of workers with a specific and recognized skill, such as electricians or plumbers.

Current expenditure pension plan A pension plan in which pensions paid to retired employees are funded from a company's current operating income and are treated as a current expense. This type of pension plan cannot guarantee that its current employees will have retirement pensions.

Deauthorization election The bargaining unit members decide if they desire to nullify the union shop provision in their agreement, which must be passed by a majority of the bargaining unit members. Thus if a union loses a deauthorization election (UD), the union still represents the employees in the bargaining unit and the rest of the collective bargaining agreement remains intact, but employees are not required to join the union.

Decertification The process of removing a union as the certified representative of employees within a bargaining unit.

Deferred wage rate increases Wage rate increases that become effective at later dates as specified in the collective bargaining agreement.

Delaying tactics The methods used by either negotiating party to impair the negotiation process, such as the cancellation of meetings, lengthy speeches, or the infrequent scheduling of meetings.

Departmental seniority   A seniority system in which employees accrue seniority according to the time that they work within a specific department, with the seniority credit being valid only in that department.

Departmental units   Similar to a craft unit, a departmental unit is composed of all the members of one department in a larger organization.

Disciplinary procedures   The program of actions that an employer may take, as outlined in a collective bargaining agreement, against an employee who has violated work rules or policies.

Discretionary workweek   A workweek designed to offer employees greater freedom in regulating their lives by allowing them to choose their daily starting and stopping times within certain restrictions.

Distributive bargaining   A type of labor negotiations viewed as a "win-lose" situation. Resources are viewed as fixed and limited, and each side wants to maximize its share.

Doctrine of accretion   As it relates to determining the appropriate bargaining unit, this allows the National Labor Relations Board to add new groups of employees to existing bargaining units if their work satisfies the same criteria without the necessity of an election.

Down-bid   When an employee bids on a job in a lower pay grade or from a specific line classification to a pool classification.

Drug and alcohol testing   The practice of requiring applicants and/or employees to submit to a screening test for chemical substances that can adversely affect their job performance.

Dual-career ladder systems   A dual-pay system within an organization that puts technical, nonmanagerial employees on a separate but comparable pay scale to executive and managerial employees in order to ensure adequate pay increases to keep the technical employees.

Dual employer   A situation involving a unionized employer that establishes a separate, similar operation that is nonunion. Such employers are most often found in the construction industry.

Dual motive discrimination case   A case in which the employer puts forth two explanations for taking an action against an employee—one constitutes a legitimate business reason, and the other is a reason prohibited under the National Labor Relations Act as an unfair labor practice.

Duty of fair representation   The Taft-Hartley requirement that a union must fairly represent all the members of the bargaining unit. This includes the negotiation of the collective bargaining agreement and its enforcement without discrimination or hostility. The requirement includes the pursuit of grievances.

Duty to sign a contract   The obligation of both parties to reduce to writing and sign any agreement reached through the collective bargaining process. Refusal to sign can be declared an unfair labor practice.

Economic strike   An employee strike over the failure to negotiate economic issues such as wages, benefits, or other conditions of employment. During an economic strike, the employer is entitled to replace strikers permanently and need only reinstate those for whom it has vacant positions.

Electromation case   A Supreme Court case in which the Court ruled that the employer-created "work committees" comprised of both employees and managers that met to discuss working conditions were a violation of the National Labor Relations Act.

Employee Assistance Programs (EAPs)   Company-sponsored programs designed to assist employees in resolving personal problems, such as stress, finances, and alcoholism, that may adversely affect job performance and attendance.

Employee Retirement Income Security Act (ERISA)   The first comprehensive reform law, passed by Congress in 1974, to protect employee pensions. Additionally, it places strict regulations on private pension plans and protects the vested rights of employees' beneficiaries. The act also created the Pension Benefit Guarantee Corporation.

Employee stock ownership plan (ESOP)   An employee benefits plan in which the employees are given shares of stock or are allowed to purchase discounted stock. Through this program, the company hopes to develop a pride of ownership among the employees that will result in increased efficiency and production, low turnover, and possibly opposition to outside unionization.

Employer unfair labor practices   Activities by an employer that interfere with an employee's rights as protected by the National Labor Relations Act. Examples include the interference of the formation of a union, discrimination against union member employees, and refusal to bargain with employee representatives.

Equal pay for equal work   The principle that job pay rates should be dependent on relevant factors, such as quantity or quality of work, and independent of irrelevant factors, such as sex or race.

Erga omnes   The literal meaning of the Latin term is "in relation to everyone." It is used to describe collective agreements whose applicability extends to all workers of a certain bargaining unit and that are automatically applicable to all those in the industries covered by it if the trade union has been properly registered.

Escape clause A contract provision that allows either negotiating party to be released from a previously agreed-to provision.

Exclusive bargaining agent/representative (exclusivity rule) Having been certified as the collective bargaining agent for a particular unit, the union has the legal right to bargain for all the employees within the unit, nonunion as well as union.

Executive Order (EO) 10988 The executive order signed by President John F. Kennedy in 1962 allowing federal employees bargaining representation, forms of employee recognition, and the right to collective bargaining.

Exempt Most executive, administrative, professional, and outside sales employees are considered exempt employees and therefore are not subject to the overtime provisions of the Federal Labor Standards Act.

Extension The practice of extending a collective bargaining agreement to all employees in a sector or company through state approval. Companies that are not even members of the employers' association that entered into the agreement are still covered by a sector-level agreement once the government has extended it.

Fact-finding A dispute resolution procedure in which a neutral third party reviews both sides of a dispute and then publicly recommends a reasonable solution.

Falling piece rate A pay system in which an employee is paid more on the basis of how many pieces are produced over an established standard but the rate per piece decreases at predetermined levels.

Family and Medical Leave Act (FMLA) Passed in 1993, it gives employees up to 12 weeks of job-protected, unpaid leave for illness or family emergencies.

Featherbedding A labor practice that unions use to create work for their members, for example, by limiting production, using more workers than a job requires, or paying for work not performed. The practice is prohibited by the Taft-Hartley Act.

Federal Labor Relations Authority (FLRA) The agency created to enforce the labor law giving federal employees the right to collectively bargain.

Federation of unions The uniting of many national unions to increase union power and recognition. The federation serves as a national spokesperson for its members while it itself is not a union. The only existing federation of unions in the United States is the AFL-CIO.

Firefighters v. Stotts The precedent Supreme Court decision that ruled that the affirmative action goals of

a consent decree requiring the hiring of minorities cannot be given greater protection than a seniority system established by a collective bargaining agreement in the event of unanticipated layoffs.

Flexible benefit plans Negotiated in lieu of fixed benefits, employees can choose the benefits that fit their needs among a designated list and within a price established by the contract. Usually includes medical insurance, vacation, pensions, and life insurance.

Flextime An alternative work schedule that allows employees to determine their starting and stopping times each day, provided that they work a set number of hours per day or week and work their scheduled core hours.

Floating holiday A paid holiday that may be used at the employee's discretion or when mutually agreed to by the employee and management.

Follow the Work Principle A seniority principle, used in the merger of two companies, that allows employees to continue previously earned seniority on separate seniority lists when their work with the merged company can be separately identified.

Force majeure Literally means "greater force." This legal concept excuses a party from liability if some unforeseen event beyond the control of that party prevents it from performing its obligations under the contract.

Foreign direct investment (FDI) A category of international investment made by a direct investor, a resident entity in one country, in a direct investment enterprise, an enterprise resident in another country, with the objective of establishing a lasting interest.

Formal grievance The step in a grievance procedure at which the grievance is reduced to writing, usually on a grievance form.

Franks v. Bowman Transportation Co. A 1977 Supreme Court ruling that the normal operation of a seniority system is not an illegal employment practice, as outlined in Title VII, even if it may have some discriminatory results, unless the system was deliberately established for discriminatory purposes.

Free riders Employees within a bargaining unit who choose to not join the union that bargains for an agreement for the unit. While the employees receive all negotiated benefits, they pay no costs associated with the union.

Front-end loading A deferred wage increase in which a larger proportion of the total increase occurs in the first year of a multiyear contract.

Gaman The Japanese tradition of individuals practicing self-denial and perseverance for the greater national cause.

Gissel doctrine The Supreme Court decision that allows the use of authorization cards as a substitute for a certification election when an employer shows unfair labor practices and that the results of an election may be unreliable. The ruling allows an employer both to reject authorization cards as proof of a majority vote and to request a representation election.

Givebacks Collectively bargained reductions in previously negotiated wages, benefits, or work rules, usually in exchange for management-guaranteed employment levels during the term of the contract.

Globalization Refers not only to the expansion of international trade in goods and services, but also to the degree of interdependence that goes along with the integration of production across national boundaries and the resulting increase in international investment by multinational enterprises.

Globe doctrine The policy set by the National Labor Relations Board to help it determine the representation wishes of employees when establishing an appropriate bargaining unit. The board may use the secret ballot election process as a means of giving weight to the desires of a group of employees, such as a smaller craft group within a larger industrial group.

Good-faith bargaining Refers to the reasonable efforts demonstrated by both management and labor during labor negotiations. Generally, it requires both sides to meet, confer, and make written offers. It does not require either side to concede or agree but rather to show reasonable intent to set the terms of employment in a collective bargaining agreement.

Good-faith reasonable doubt A rule by the National Labor Relations Board that provides an employer who entertains a good-faith reasonable doubt that the employees support the incumbent union may request an election, withdraw recognition and refuse to bargain with that union, or conduct an informal poll of employees.

Grievance Any formal complaint filed by an employee or union concerning any aspect of the employment relationship. A grievance is generally a perceived violation of a contract provision.

Grievance categories The types of issues that come up during the grievance process, such as disciplinary actions, seniority, and absenteeism.

Grievance mediation The use of a neutral third party as one step in a grievance procedure to interpret the provisions of a contract in an effort to resolve a dispute and avoid arbitration.

Grievance procedure The step-by-step process, usually outlined in a collective bargaining agreement, available to employees to resolve conflicts arising between labor and management.

Ground rules The general procedures and policies that each party agrees to adhere to during negotiations. These are usually agreed to in writing prior to the negotiations and may include such items as the time, date, and location for the negotiating session.

Guaranteed income stream (GIS) An alternative plan to the traditional supplemental unemployment plans, the GIS plan has three major differences: (1) It furnishes benefits to eligible workers until they retire, (2) worker qualification is based on earnings rather than employment, and (3) benefits are only partially offset by outside earnings.

Hatch Act Passed in 1939, amended in 1993, the Hatch Act limited the political activities of federal employees in order to shield workers from political pressure and ensure that the resources of the federal government were not used to favor a political party.

Haymarket Square Riot A meeting held in Chicago in 1886 to protest the police shooting of striking workers that ended with the bombing of police officers and the subsequent trial and conviction of eight defendants. The Knights of Labor did not participate, but because of their previous violence, they were associated with the riot and began to lose public support.

Health care units Eight basic units identified by the National Labor Relations Board for the health care industry under the 1974 Health Care Amendment to the National Labor Relations Act.

Health maintenance organizations (HMOs) Organizations of physicians and other health care professionals that provide a wide range of health services to employees and their families for a fixed, prepaid fee instead of a fee-for-service basis. HMOs strive to emphasize preventing care, lower total health care cost, and total health care at one location.

Holiday pay Contract provision requiring an employer to pay for time not worked on a holiday.

Homestead Strike An 1892 strike at a steel plant owned by Andrew Carnegie. The plant operator responded with paid police and strikebreakers. The strike ended when martial law was declared and state militia were sent in by the governor.

Hot cargo agreements A negotiated contract provision stating that union members of one employer have the right to refuse to handle nonunion or struck goods of other employers.

Hourly wage A worker's wages based on an established pay rate per hour worked.

Illegal bargaining subjects Items termed illegal and nonnegotiable by the *Borg-Warner* case ruling or the National Labor Relations Board. These items cannot be negotiated even if both parties are in agreement. Examples of illegal subjects are a closed shop, racial separation of employees, or discrimination against nonunion members.

Impasse A stalemate that occurs in negotiations between union and management over the terms and conditions of employment. Impasses are often resolved through mediation or arbitration.

Industrial jurisprudence The system of rules and regulations that labor and management fashion to define their specific rights and obligations in the workplace.

Industrial union A labor union whose membership is composed primarily of semiskilled or unskilled workers, such as automobile workers and steel-workers, who are organized on the basis of the product they produce. Usually all production and maintenance (not management) workers within an organization will belong to the same industrial union.

Insulated period The last 60 days before a collective bargaining agreement is due to expire in which the existing bargaining agent cannot be subject to an employee vote to change bargaining agents.

Interest arbitration A process used to resolve an impasse in negotiations where the parties submit the unresolved items to a neutral third party to render a binding decision.

Intermediate organizational units A level of union organization consisting of regional or district offices that serves to bring the national and local union offices closer together.

International Labour Organization (ILO) Was created as a parallel organization to the League of Nations. The mission of the ILO was to keep the peace within societies threatened by class divisions between capital and labor within countries.

International Workers of the World (IWW) Founded in 1905, this federation hoped to organize all the workers of the world into one union. Its political agenda included the overthrow of capitalism.

Job bidding (up, down, lateral) The process of a company posting notices of new job positions in order to give permanent employees the opportunity to apply. Bids are based on plant seniority and competency and fall into three categories: (1) up-bid, a bid from a lower to a higher pay grade; (2) down-bid, a bid from a higher to a lower pay grade; and (3) lateral bid, a bid from one classification to another classification in the same pay grade.

Job evaluation A systematic method of determining the worth of a job to an organization. This is usually accomplished by analysis of the internal job factors and comparison to the external job market.

Job sharing Generally refers to the division of hours worked in a full-time job into two part-time positions. It often refers to the holding of one full-time position by two employees who are friends or relatives.

Job splitting A method of creating part-time work in which the tasks of a single full-time job are divided into two separate part-time jobs, each having separate duties.

Joint committees Cooperative labor-management committees formed to analyze and solve organizational problems.

Jurisdictional strike A strike called as the result of a dispute between two competing unions over who has the legal authority (jurisdiction) in a specific situation.

Just cause Sufficient or proper reasons for which management has the right to discipline or discharge employees.

Keiretsu In Japan, a loose conglomeration of companies organized around a single bank for their mutual benefit. Keiretsu can trace its beginning to when Japan industrialized in the 1880s and ownership of a majority of its enterprises was concentrated in powerful family groups.

Knights of Labor An organization open to skilled and unskilled laborers, formed in 1869 as the Noble Order of the Knights of Labor (KOL). It sought economic and social reform through political action rather than strikes.

Korean Tripartite Commission A consultative body composed of representatives from government, labor, business, and the public that discusses labor policies and acts as an advisory body to the president of the Republic of Korea.

Labor agreement A phrase referring to a collective bargaining agreement between a union and management.

Labor injunction A court order that prohibits any individual or group from performing any act that violates the rights of other individuals concerned. Until 1932, injunctions were used primarily by employers to end boycotts or strikes.

Labor-Management Reporting and Disclosure Act (Landrum-Griffin Act) Passed in 1959 to help regulate internal union operations, the act amended the Wagner Act and the Taft-Hartley Act and resulted in the limitation of boycotts and picketing, the creation of safeguards for union elections, and the establishment of controls for the handling of union funds.

Labor market Historically, was the result of the interplay between the employer's demand for labor and the worker's supply of labor. Labor markets could be in geographical areas over which competition for labor took place or within categories of labor such as skilled or unskilled.

Labor organization unfair labor practices Any action taken by a union that does not demonstrate the union's desire to negotiate in good faith, such as refusing to sign an agreement previously agreed to by negotiators for the union and management.

Last hired, first fired A seniority-based procedure for determining the order for layoff and recall of employees in the workplace to keep the most experienced employees.

Lateral bid When an employee bids on a job from one classification to another in the same pay grade or from one pool position to another regardless of pay grade.

Layoff recall The order in which employees are recalled to work after being laid off for lack of work.

Length of Service Principle A method used to establish seniority during the merger of two companies in which an employee's length of service is considered regardless of the company for which he or she worked; therefore, the two seniority lists are merged into one with no loss of any previous seniority to any employee.

***Lincoln Mills* case** In a landmark decision, the Supreme Court ordered an employer to arbitrate grievances as provided for in a collective bargaining agreement, stating that an employer's agreement to arbitrate grievance disputes was a trade-off for the union's agreement not to strike.

Local union The union that represents a specific unit or geographic area of unionized workers and is usually affiliated with a national union. One main function of the local union is to negotiate and administer contracts with employers.

Lockout An employer's refusal to allow employees to return to work until an agreement is signed. It is considered the employer's equivalent of an economic strike and is intended to bring pressure on workers to accept management's terms.

Ludlow, Colorado In April 1914 in Ludlow, Colorado, miners on strike were evicted from their company-owned houses. The miners erected a tent colony on public property. The coal operators used the Colorado militia and thugs hired as strikebreakers to attack the camp without warning, killing 20 men, women, and children.

Lump-sum payment A method of providing a general wage increase as a one-time payment rather than adding the increase to the hourly or annual salary of the employee.

Mackay doctrine A court-created rule that construes the National Labor Relations Act as allowing employers to replace striking workers with permanent workers unless it is determined that the strike was an unfair labor strike.

Maintenance of membership A union security provision that requires that those who are union members when a contract is entered into or those who subsequently join the union must remain union members until the contract expires.

Make-whole concept The concept of providing back pay, position, and lost seniority in an attempt to return to the employee those things that he or she may have been deprived of because of discrimination.

Management rights The rights of management to govern the workplace in areas not subject to discussion with the union or to collective bargaining. Included in these rights are production control, price setting, supervision of the workforce, scheduling, and sales.

Mandatory bargaining subjects Those items that must be bargained in good faith, if either party so requests, such as wages, hours, and benefits.

Maryland Freedom Union A union organized by African Americans after the civil rights movement of the 1960s to respond to their union needs.

Master agreement The collective bargaining agreement negotiated between a national union and an industry. The terms and conditions of the contract serve as employment guidelines for the entire industry. Local terms and conditions may be negotiated in addition to the master agreement.

Mediation The introduction of a neutral third party into collective bargaining when the union and management are unable to reach an agreement. While mediators have no decision-making powers, they can make recommendations, suggest new proposals to either or both parties, and actively work to develop compromises.

Mercantilism The economic theory that a nation's prosperity depends on the amount of its capital, represented by bullion, and by the volume at which its exports exceed its imports. A mercantile system of economics requires a protectionist role of government in encouraging exports and discouraging imports, generally through the use of tariffs.

***Misco* case** The Supreme Court case in which it ruled that judicial review of an arbitrator's award under a collective bargaining agreement is limited to a review of fraud or dishonesty and the finding of facts are left to the arbitrator.

Mississippi Freedom Labor Union A union organized by African Americans after the civil rights movement of the 1960s to respond to their members' needs.

Molly Maguires   A group of union organizers who were prosecuted and either executed or imprisoned after an 1875 strike against anthracite mine owners failed.

Monday holiday provision   The provision in a collective bargaining agreement that requires an employee to work the Friday before and the Tuesday after a Monday holiday weekend in order to get paid for the holiday.

Multiemployer units   Collective bargaining conducted between a group of related employers and a single representative union.

Multilateral bargaining   Refers to negotiations in the public sector where the authority to commit to a collective bargaining agreement may be shared by the executive and legislative branches.

Multinational enterprise   An entity that operates in more than one nation for a significant portion of its business, that may exports products, and may have actually moved part of its operations to another country by investing abroad. Also called transnationals.

Multiplant units   Bargaining that occurs between a single employer and a union or unions that represent workers in two or more plants of the employer.

National Colored Labor Union   Organized in 1870, this union was in response to the segregated National Labor Union and the American Federation of Laborers.

National Labor Relations Act (Wagner Act)   Passed in 1935, this act was created to recognize employee rights to organize and bargain collectively through representatives of their own choosing. The act required employers to meet with the certified representatives of a majority of their employees. The act made several unfair labor practices illegal and created the National Labor Relations Board to hold employee elections and to enforce the act.

National Labor Relations Board (NLRB)   An independent agency of the federal government that serves to investigate unfair labor practices, determine appropriate bargaining units, certify unions that legally represent a majority of employees, and administer the provisions of the National Labor Relations Act.

National Labor Union   Founded in 1866, this was the first union to allow skilled and unskilled workers to join in one union. It pursued a political as well as a workplace agenda.

National (or international) union   A union formed by regionally organizing local unions. Its powers, determined by the charter drawn between itself and the local unions it represents, may range from advising the local unions to collective bargaining.

National War Labor Board   An agency formed in 1918 (during World War I) to prevent labor disputes from disrupting the war efforts by providing mediation for labor-management disputes and establishing wage stabilization.

Negotiating with employees   It is a violation of the National Labor Relations Act for an employer to bypass the union by attempting to negotiate directly with employees.

Negotiations   The process by which labor and management meet to determine the provisions of a collective bargaining agreement.

New guaranteed income stream   An innovative provision in the 1982 Ford Motor Company and UAW contract in which laid-off employees with 15 years or more of service were guaranteed 50 percent of their hourly rate of pay until age 62 or retirement.

"No-fault" absenteeism policy   An innovative policy aimed at reducing absenteeism regardless of the cause. Employees are allowed so many absent days in an established period of time, and when those days are exceeded, no matter the reason, the employee is disciplined.

Nonexempt   Employees not considered exempt under the provisions of the Fair Labor Standards Act must be paid time and a half their normal rate of pay when they work over 40 hours per week.

Norris–La Guardia Act   Passed in 1932, this act restricts the federal courts from issuing injunctions in labor disputes except to maintain law and order. The act also made yellow-dog contracts illegal.

Office of Federal Contract Compliance (OFCC)   Created by Executive Order 11246, this office implements equal employment opportunity in the federal procurement process and specifies the regulations applying to all federal organizations, contractors, and subcontractors.

On-call pay   Additional employee compensation given to workers who must remain available to be called in to work if needed.

"One-best-way" theory   A theory of scientific management in which the most efficient way to perform a job is determined by use of a clipboard and a stopwatch.

Open period   The first 30-day period in the last 90 days before the termination of a collective bargaining agreement during which employees can vote to change their bargaining agent.

Open shop   A form of union security in which the workers within a bargaining unit may decide whether to join a union. Those who choose not to join are not required to pay union dues or fees or amounts equal to dues or fees.

Opener clause   A clause in a collective bargaining agreement that allows negotiations to take place during the term of the contract on certain mandatory items, such as wages or insurance coverage.

Organizing drive   A movement initiated by dissatisfied employees or a union organizer to submit a representation petition to the National Labor Relations Board and win a representation election, thus providing union certification and collective bargaining.

Outsourcing   When work that could be performed within a bargaining unit is given by management to outside, nonunion providers. The purpose of such action is to lower costs and/or reduce the number of bargaining unit employees. A similar practice is called privatization in the public sector.

Parol evidence   Evidence that is not contained within the four edges of the collective bargaining agreement and is, therefore, outside the parameters of an arbitration proceeding.

Past practice   A recognition of the bargaining history of the two parties involved in a dispute to determine their respective rights in arbitration.

Pattern bargaining   A collective bargaining practice in which a national union strives to establish equal wages and benefits from several employers in the same industry. The union uses the negotiated contract of one company to serve as a model contract for the entire industry.

Pay equity   A historic union doctrine of "equal pay for equal work" that provides for one standard pay rate for each job and all employees who perform it.

Pay for time not worked   Wages paid to an employee for time away from the job, such as breaks, lunch, vacations, maternity leave, sick leave, jury duty, and personal leave.

Pendleton Act   Also known as the Civil Service Act of 1883, the Pendleton Act created the federal merit system. The act was responsible for (1) the creation of a Civil Service Commission to administer open competitive examinations for selecting federal employees; (2) the right of Congress to regulate the wages, hours, and working conditions of public employees; (3) the merit principle; and (4) the protection of employees from being fired for failure to make campaign contributions and even forbidding some classes of employees from making such contributions.

Permanent striker replacements   Under the National Labor Relations Board, when workers are engaged in an economic strike, management can hire permanent replacements. After the strike, the striking workers cannot claim their jobs back.

Permissive bargaining subjects   Those items not related to wages, benefits, working conditions, or other mandatory subjects that may be negotiated in collective bargaining if both parties agree. However, if one party refuses to negotiate a permissive item, the other party cannot claim bad-faith bargaining or declare an impasse in negotiations over the item.

Personal day   A paid employee holiday (sometimes called a floating holiday) that can usually be selected at the employee's discretion. Personal days often are given in place of sick days, which are more limited in use.

Piece-rate systems   A wage system in which employees receive a standard rate of pay per unit of output. The rate of pay is usually based on the average level of production, with bonus rates given on output units exceeding the average level.

Piecework   Employee wage rate based on the number of units produced.

Pinkerton Agency   A detective agency used by various employers and the government in the late 1800s to infiltrate and spy on unions.

Planning   The stage in the preparation for collective bargaining negotiations when the parties evaluate and set priorities in order to make realistic decisions and to focus on achievable goals.

Plantwide seniority   An employee's length of continuous service with the employer. The employee's accrued seniority in the plant allows for competition for the same position with any other employee within the same unit.

Portability   The right of an employee to transfer tax-free pension benefits from one employer to another.

Posturing   The pattern established during the initial bargaining session in which each negotiating party demonstrates its willingness to negotiate, identifies its basic bargaining positions, and generally sets the tone of the negotiations.

Preemption   A legal theory in which federal law takes precedent over state law if they deal with the same subject and the federal law is determined to be all encompassing.

Premium pay   Wages that exceed the standard or regular pay rate given an employee for work performed under undesirable circumstances, such as overtime hours, weekend work, holiday work, or dangerous and hazardous circumstances.

Pressure bargaining   A negotiating technique in which one side that believes it holds a superior position pressures the other side to accept its position on each issue. As an example, if the union believes the employer cannot withstand even a short strike, it may use its position of strength by threatening to strike over many issues.

Pretext discrimination case   An unfair labor practice charge in which an employer puts forth a legitimate business reason for taking an action but the employee asserts that the true reason is one prohibited under the National Labor Relations Act.

Primary boycott A legally permitted boycott in which persons who normally deal directly with the work involved are encouraged to withhold their services.

Primary strike A strike called by a union for economic reasons to achieve its bargaining objectives.

Principled negotiations A negotiating process developed by the Harvard Negotiations Project in which attention is focused on the merits of the negotiating items rather than on the attitudes of the negotiating parties.

Privatization The practice of governmental entities contracting out public services rather than adding or retaining employees in the public sector.

Probable cause A general term referring to the reasonable possibility that a certain condition exists, such as employer wrongdoing in a discrimination case.

Productivity theory The negotiating position that employees should share in increased profits gained by the greater productivity achieved because of their efforts.

Professional Air Traffic Controllers (PATCO) Strike (1981) The first declared national strike against the federal government resulted not only in the firing of all striking PATCO workers but also in the prohibition of any PATCO striking worker from ever working again as an air traffic controller.

Profit sharing A pay incentive system in which employees receive a share of the employer's profits in addition to their regular wages. A precise formula specifying how profits will be distributed to employees is the heart of a profit-sharing plan.

Prohibited conduct Activities used to interfere with union organizational efforts, such as the threat of loss of benefits, misrepresentation of campaign materials, and interrogation of employees.

Provisional intent test Having knowledgeable but uninvolved parties read the draft of a collective bargaining agreement after the agreement has been reached to test whether the drafting reflects the intent of the parties.

Public policy exceptions Some employee rights under a collective bargaining agreement are also rights enforceable in other forums and may therefore be exempt from the arbitration under such a union agreement.

Public sector union security The ability of a public sector union to grow and to perform its collective bargaining role without interference from management or other unions. Automatic dues deduction is the most commonly allowed public sector union security provision.

Pullman Strike The strike in 1894 by Pullman Car Company employees who were demanding higher wages and lower rents. The strike was honored by other groups of railroad workers who shut down railroads from Illinois to Colorado until the strike was broken by a federal court injunction and the use of federal troops.

Pyramiding of overtime The payment of overtime on overtime that occurs if the same hours of work qualify for both daily and weekly overtime payment. Most contracts prohibit this type of payment.

Qualifications of an arbitrator The attributes or characteristics generally desired in an arbitrator, such as neutrality, honesty, experience, and legal training.

Quality circles (QC) The voluntary meeting of groups of workers with common work interests for the purpose of identification, analysis, and development of solutions to work problems.

Quality of working life (QWL) The process used by the union, the employees, and management to determine how the work environment may be changed to create a better quality of life, with the desired result being increased efficiency and employee job satisfaction.

Railway Strike The railroads' former policies of cutting wages and increasing living costs to their employees resulted in the first general strike in the United States. The bitter and violent strike of 1877 involved railroad workers from Maryland to Missouri who protested 10 percent wage cuts after a 35 percent cut three years earlier.

Ratio-Rank Principle The seniority principle that combines seniority lists according to the ratio established by comparing the total number of employees in the merging groups. If group A has 100 employees and group B has 50 employees, the ratio is two to one. The new seniority list will then give positions 1 and 2 to the highest employees from group A and position 3 to the highest employee from group B.

RC petition The petition filed with the National Labor Relations Board by a group of employees or a union representing employees seeking certification of an appropriate unit for purposes of collective bargaining.

Reasonable accommodation Under the Americans with Disabilities Act (ADA) and the Rehabilitation Act, employers must make changes in the workplace to enable disabled Americans to work. The ADA spells out what accommodation is considered reasonable.

Recall The practice of calling workers back to the job after a company has had to lay off workers as a result of less or no work being available.

Remaining units Employee groups that are separate from the primary production and maintenance units in their job duties, such as professional, technical, guard, and clerical units.

Reporting pay The minimum payment guaranteed for employees who report for work, even if work is not available, provided they have not been given adequate notice not to report to work.

Representation cases Cases in which the National Labor Relations Board determines the appropriate unit of employees for purposes of collective bargaining.

Republic Aviation **case** A 1945 court case in which the Supreme Court upheld an employee's legal right to seek union support during personal time. The Court ruled that union solicitation by employees outside their work time, even on company property, was legal.

Reserve clause A practice in professional sports whereby only one team is given the right (by the league) to negotiate a contract with a player. Thus, the player is not free to negotiate a better contract with another team.

Reserved rights The theory generally contending that all rights not specified in an agreement or shared with a union remain the unwritten or implied rights of management.

Residual units Employees who do not fit into the major job units except by their common working situations, such as janitors and salespeople, may be grouped together to form a unit. Employees left unrepresented after the bulk of the employees are organized may be entitled to separate representation by a residual unit.

Restricted rights The union's use of contract clauses to impose specific restrictions on management's decision-making rights, such as plant relocation or subcontracting.

Rights arbitration The submission to arbitration for the interpretation or application of current contract terms. In grievance cases, the arbitration involves the rights of the parties involved under the terms of the contract.

Right to strike For employees in the private sector, the right to strike is guaranteed by the National Labor Relations Act, but public employees are generally prohibited from striking, making the right to strike a major issue for public sector unions.

Right-to-work laws The laws permitting states to prohibit agreements requiring membership in a labor organization as a condition of employment.

Rising piece rate A pay system in which an employee is paid on the basis of units produced but the rate per unit increases when the employee goes over the standard level.

Robotics The operation of programmable robots (computer-controlled machines) to perform routine operations such as assembly, painting, welding, and inventory.

Rolling strike A strike technique used by unions that moves a strike against an employer from location to location so that hiring replacement workers becomes more difficult.

Roll-up The direct increase in the cost of benefits that results from a negotiated increase in wage rates, such as social security, overtime pay, and pensions.

Rules of evidence An arbitrator's determination of how a hearing will be conducted, how evidence will be presented, and how much weight or credibility will be given to the evidence presented.

Runoff election The successive election held when a representation election involving three or more choices results in no one choice receiving the majority vote. The choices receiving the most votes are again voted on until one receives the majority of the votes cast.

Salting Members are encouraged by their union to seek employment at a nonunion company. Once hired, they promote unionization. The union may supplement their regular pay with a supplement to provide equity with a "union" wage.

Saturn agreement The agreement between the UAW and the General Motors Corporation that included several innovative joint labor-management practices and was arrived at before the new Saturn plant in Tennessee began production.

Scabs A derogatory term to describe workers who cross a union picket line to perform the jobs of striking workers.

Scanlon plans A group incentive plan designed by Joseph Scanlon in which greater production is achieved through increased efficiency with the accrued savings being distributed among the workers and the employer.

Scope clause A provision in a collective bargaining agreement that prohibits the company from outsourcing bargaining unit work while any member of the union is in a layoff status.

Secondary boycotts Union pressure exerted on a neutral party indirectly related to the primary employer. The neutral party then exerts pressure against the primary employer.

Section 10(j) The section of the National Labor Relations Act that allows the board to seek a federal court injunction in situations in which the action of a union or the employer might cause substantial harm to the other side.

Selective strike A strategy used by a union to have a strike at one location that supplies many other locations, resulting in an industrywide shutdown.

Self-managed employee teams A small group of employees given responsibility for an entire segment of a work process.

Seniority The length of service an individual employee has with an employer or unit.

Seniority list A company list used to identify employees in a bargaining unit according to their length of continuous employment.

Separability clause A contract clause stating that any portion of a contract declared invalid by state or federal law shall be declared null and void while still holding the remainder of the contract valid.

Severance pay A lump-sum or a dispersal of payments given to employees who are permanently separated from the company through no fault of their own.

Sexual harassment Unwelcome sexual advances, requests for sexual favors, and other verbal or physical conduct having the purpose or effect of unreasonably interfering with an individual's work performance or creating an intimidating, hostile, or offensive working environment.

Shared work The reduction by management of employee work time and, consequently wages, in an effort to reduce personnel costs without reducing personnel.

Shift differential Additional hourly rates of pay provided to employees who work the least desirable hours.

Shop-in Slang term referring to a union method of conducting a secondary boycott. Several union members converge on retail establishments, that sell a boycotted product and cause disruptions in service by overcrowding the stores and parking lots and thus a loss of regular customers. The result desired by the union is to pressure the retailers into not stocking the boycotted product.

Shop stewards A term that can trace its origin to the First World War, when divisions between labor's rank and file, who pressed for economic and political reforms, and labor's leaders, who were more aligned with the government in its war effort, caused the formation of the Shop Stewards Movement and Workers' Committees.

Showing of interest The demonstration of employee support, usually in the form of petitions or authorization cards, that a union is required to compile before a representation election can be considered.

Shunto The Spring Wage Offensive in Japan, at which wages are negotiated separate from other collective bargaining. During *shunto*, enterprise-based unions in each industry conduct negotiations simultaneously with their companies. The objectives of *shunto* are to provide each individual union with a greater bargaining power and to distribute wage increases proportionally across the industry.

Sick leave Time off allowed an employee because of illness or injury, with the provision of continued employment when the employee is able to report back to work.

Sick-out An illegal, partial strike in which employees call in sick to protest a working condition.

Single Market Created by the European Union when it adopted economic and monetary union through the introduction of a single European currency managed by a European Central Bank.

Social Charter Contained in the Maastricht Treaty, it sets forth an action program for the European Union to protect workers' rights in employment contracts, collective bargaining, health and safety in the workplace, consultation and participation, parental leave, and social protection.

Socialist market economy An economic theory in China in which state ownership of the means of production was retained by the government but the control of wages, prices, and employment was to be relaxed to allow a private sector to develop.

Social Security The U.S. government–created pension plan to provide supplemental income to retired workers. The system is financed through an extra tax placed on both the employer and the employee.

Sovereignty doctrine The unrestricted and paramount power of the people to govern. In the public sector, this is presented as a basic reason for not allowing employees to have collective bargaining rights or the right to strike their public employers.

Spillover The duplication of wage and benefit increases for nonunion and management personnel that an employer provides as a result of negotiated union increases.

Spoils system In the early 1800s, this patronage system for the federal government meant that workers were hired on the basis of who they supported in elections and employees were expected to support political candidates or lose their job.

Staggered start An example of the discretionary workweek system in which the employee chooses one of several alternative starting times and works an eight-hour day.

Standard hour plan A pay plan based on paying an employee on the basis of a "standard time" to complete a particular job.

Standard rate The flat or hourly rate of pay established for each job classification or occupation within a plant or industry, effective for the duration of the collective bargaining agreement.

State-owned enterprises (SOEs) Chinese businesses granted preferential access to capital, technology, and markets. China relaxed its guarantees of employment, wages, and welfare as these state-owned enterprises (SOEs) became subject to competitive market pressures, and the central government turned over responsibility for economic management and financial solvency to them.

State-socialism In Germany, an economic system that emphasized the role of government in regulating the market economy rather than the laissez-faire touted by capitalists.

Steelworkers Trilogy **cases** Three 1960 Supreme Court rulings that upheld the grievance arbitration process and limited judicial intervention.

Steps of a grievance procedure The detailed procedure an employee must follow when filing a grievance. The grievance must be (1) discussed with the supervisor, (2) put in writing, (3) taken to the union-management level, (4) reviewed by a plantwide grievance committee, and (5) taken to arbitration.

Steward An on-the-job union representative who carries out the responsibilities of the union in the plant at the departmental level.

Stipulated units A bargaining unit agreed to by an employer and a union that cannot be altered by the National Labor Relations Board.

Subcontracting The arrangement by a company to have another firm make goods or perform work that could be accomplished by the company's own employees, usually because the work can be done more efficiently or for less cost.

Substantially equal The conclusion that two jobs, although not identical, may be considered generally equal and thus require equal pay. Evaluations of effort, skills, working conditions, and responsibility are necessary to compare the jobs.

Successorship The status of the collective bargaining relationship between an employer and the union when a change in the ownership of the organization or a change in a union occurs.

Sunshine laws Statutes requiring that public sector collective bargaining sessions be open to the public.

Superseniority The special seniority rights granted to union officers and committee personnel that override ordinary seniority during layoffs and recall situations in order to maintain active union representation within the company.

Surface bargaining The act by either negotiating party of simply going through the motions without any real intention of arriving at an agreement.

Surviving Group Principle A principle used for the determination of seniority in merging companies in which seniority lists are merged by adding the names of the acquired company employees to the bottom of the list of names of employees of the acquiring company.

Swedish Model In Sweden independent unions and businesses carry out collective bargaining free from government involvement. A high degree of self-regulation, state nonintervention and the autonomy of the two parties, or "social partners," characterize this model. It is a *single-channel model,* in that the trade unions participate in collective bargaining and in the information, consultation and codetermination rights granted employees as well.

Taft-Hartley Amendments Also known as the Labor Management Relations Act of 1947, it generally was created to counterbalance the provisions of the National Labor Relations Act of 1935. The law declared closed shops and automatic checkoffs illegal, cited unfair labor union practices, and protected the rights of employees who chose not to unionize. The law also created the Federal Mediation and Conciliation Service, restricted secondary boycotts and strikes, and gave states the right to outlaw union shops.

Teamwork for Employees and Managers Act (TEAM) A law passed by Congress in 1996 but vetoed by President Clinton that would have allowed employers to establish employee-management teams that otherwise violate the National Labor Relations Act.

Technological change and retraining A company's need to increase productivity through the use of new machinery and equipment often results in employee reduction or termination. Many companies have developed employee assistance programs that provide testing, vocational training, and job placement assistance in a conscientious effort to help employees affected by technological change reenter the labor market.

Telecommuting Work scheduling that allows employees to do some or all of their work at home, usually involving the use of computers.

Telescabbing The use of modern technology, such as automated equipment, as a substitute for labor during a strike instead of hiring scab labor. The term was first applied to the 1983 AT&T strike when management relied on automated equipment to process 97 percent of all telephone calls.

Termination at will The termination or discharge of an employee by an employer for any reason or no reason.

Terms of employment Those items generally negotiated between union and management, including wages, benefits, work rules, job classifications, work practices, seniority, promotions, and management and union rights.

Title VII of the Civil Rights Act A section of the Civil Rights Act of 1964 that prohibits an employer from discriminating against an individual because of the individual's race, color, sex, religion, or nationality and that delegates authority to the Equal Employment Opportunity Commission to investigate an employee's complaints and act as his or her attorney.

Totality-of-conduct doctrine A test or review of the total bargaining process used to determine whether a negotiating party has acted in good faith as opposed to isolated acts that may have occurred during negotiations. Generally requires some "give-and-take" by a negotiating party to warrant good faith.

Trade unionists Like-skilled workers, such as printers, shoemakers, tailors, and bakers, who organized the earliest unions in the United States.

Trades Union Congress Founded in Great Britain and due to the extension of the right to vote, trade unions began to have success in lobbying for laws protecting workers.

Transnational A corporation that operates in more than one nation for a significant portion of its business. Also called multinationals.

Treaty of Maastricht (1992) Created the European Union by introducing intergovernmental cooperation to the existing "Community" system and adding new forms of cooperation between the member states, particularly on defense and in the area of justice and home affairs.

Tripartite arbitration board An arbitration board composed of one or more members representing management, an equal number representing labor, and a neutral member who serves as chairperson.

Tripartite organizational structure of ILO. The ILO brought together representatives of not only the participating governments but also employers and workers as equal parties in its governance.

24-hour rule This rule by the National Labor Relations Board prohibits employers and unions from making organizational campaign speeches on company time to assemblies of employees within 24 hours of a scheduled election.

Two-tier wage systems A wage system that pays newly hired workers less than current employees performing the same or similar jobs.

Undue hardship Under the Americans with Disabilities Act, an employer can refuse to accommodate a disabled person if it will be too expensive or will change the operation significantly.

Unemployment insurance Established under the Social Security Act of 1935 and funded through payroll taxes paid by employers, the program is designed to provide compensation, after a brief waiting period, to those employees who have been laid off from employment. Recipients are expected to seek employment actively.

Unfair labor practice strike A strike called over an employer's action determined by law to be an unfair labor practice, such as employee discrimination because of union activity.

Unilaterally changing conditions Any method an employer may use during contract negotiations, such as changing wages or hours of employment, in an effort to bypass the union and deal directly with the employees.

Union density rate The percentage of workers belonging to unions within a defined population.

Union hiring hall A local union office that coordinates workers seeking employment with available jobs. Since closed shops are illegal under the Taft-Hartley Act, hiring halls today must serve both union and nonunion members.

Union organizer A full-time, salaried staff member of a union who generally represents a national union and organizes workplaces to increase union membership.

Union security The provisions of collective bargaining agreements that directly protect and benefit the union, such as dues checkoff and union shops.

Union shop A union security provision that all new employees must join the union and pay dues within a specified time.

United Farm Workers A union formed by Cesar Chavez with the merger in 1962 of the National Farm Workers Association and the Agricultural Workers Organizing Committee, to gain collective bargaining rights for agricultural workers even though they were excluded from coverage by the NLRA.

Up-bid When an employee bids on a job in a higher pay grade or from a pool classification to a specific line classification.

Value-added concept The theory that wages should equal the contribution of labor to the final product.

Variable hours A method of employment in which the employee contracts to work for a specified time each day, week, and so on, with the option of varying the schedule daily if both parties agree.

Vested rights The time required for employees to accrue an irrevocable right to pension contributions made by their employer.

Voluntarism   A collective laissez-faire system is when a union and an employer or an employers' association can agree to be a party to a collective bargaining agreement and the contract can extend for as long as the parties agree, although wages are generally negotiated annually. The collective bargaining agreement's terms and conditions cover all of the individuals in the bargaining unit even if they are not in the union.

Voluntary recognition   In rare occasions an employer recognizes a union as the bargaining agent of the employees without requiring a union vote.

Wage employment guarantees   A contract negotiation assuring employees a minimum amount of work or compensation during a specified amount of time.

Wage relation   The negotiation, either formal or informal, over what work labor was willing to perform and what the employer was willing to pay for that work. The wage to the employer was a cost that affected the enterprises' production cost and profit. The wage to the employee was a source of income and the means for survival.

Wage reopener   A collective bargaining provision, effective for the term of the contract, that allows contract talks to be reopened only for the renegotiation of wage rates.

Wage survey   The collection and appraisal of data from various sources used to determine the average salary for specified positions in the job market.

Weingarten rule   Under this case decision, a union employee may request the presence of a union official during questioning by management in a disciplinary situation.

Wellness program   Any of a variety of company-sponsored programs designed to enhance the employee's well-being, such as stress management, cancer detection, exercise programs, and complete physical fitness centers.

Wildcat strike   Any work stoppage not authorized by the union.

Wobblies   Nickname for members of the Industrial Workers of the World (IWW) organization.

Women's National Trade Union League   The original name of the National Woman's Trade Union League, this union was begun between 1903 and World War I by middle-class reformers and working-class women to support unionization of women workers.

Work councils   Within the European Union member states, work councils are permanent elected bodies of workforce representatives, or in some instances joint committees with employers' representatives, established on the basis of law or collective bargaining agreements with the overall task of promoting cooperation within the enterprise.

Work sharing   A method of reducing the number of employees to be laid off by asking all employees to work fewer hours.

Workers Adjustment and Retraining Notification Act (WARN)   Commonly known as the Plant Closing Act, WARN became effective in 1989 and generally requires employers to provide 60 days' advance written notice to employees and communities of either a plant closing or mass layoffs.

Workers' compensation   A program designed to provide employees with assured payment for medical expenses or lost income due to injury on the job.

Workplace Relations Act (WRA)   Australian labor law reform that includes streamlined "award" system; emphasis on enterprise bargaining; curbs on union power; restrictions on strikes; and a streamlined unfair-dismissal system, which limits frivolous appeals and compensation claims.

Zipper clause   A provision of a collective bargaining agreement that restricts either party from requiring the other party to bargain on any issue that was not previously negotiated in the agreement for the term of the contract.

Photo Credits

Index

HR Related Web Sites

FEDERAL GOVERNMENT

U.S. Department of Labor
www.dol.gov
Family and Medical Leave Act
www.dol.gov/compliance/laws/comp-fmla.htm
Bureau of Labor Statistics
www.bls.gov
U.S. Census Bureau
www.census.gov/
U.S. Government
www.firstgov.gov
OSHA
www.osha.gov
Federal Statistics (non DOL)
www.fedstats.gov
Employment Laws (DOL)
www.dol.gov/elaws
National Labor Relations Board
www.nlrb.gov
EEOC
www.eeoc.gov
Federal Mediation and Conciliation Services
www.fmcs.gov
U.S. Department of Justice
www.usdoj.gov
Federal Sector Labor Relations and H.R.
www.members.aol.com/cfr5
U.S. Employment and Training Administration
www.doleta.gov
Veterans Employment and Training Service
www.dol.gov/vets

PROFESSIONAL ORGANIZATIONS AND ASSOCIATIONS

Society for H.R. Management
www.shrm.org
American Society for Training and Development
www.astd.org
American Compensation Association
www.worldatwork.org
Employee Benefit Research Institute
www.ebri.org
International Personnel Management
www.ipma-hr.org/
Training Forum
www.trainingforum.com
College and University Professional Association for Human Resources
www.cupa.org

American Arbitration Association
www.adr.org
Equal Employment Advisory Council
www.eeac.org
National Business and Disability Council
www.business-disability.com
AFL-CIO
www.aflcio.org
Institute of Management and Administration
www.ioma.com
Families and Work Institute
www.familiesandwork.org
American Management Association International
www.amanet.org
International HR Information Management Association
www.ihrim.org
International Foundation of Employee Benefit Plans
www.ifebp.org
World Federation of Personnel Management Associations
www.wfpma.com

HR PUBLICATIONS

HR Magazine
www.shrm.org/hrmagazine
Workforce Management
www.workforceonline.com
Human Resource Issues
www.hrpapers.com
HR Live
www.hrlive.com
HR/PC (from HR world)
www.hrworld.com
MCB UP Limited
www.managementfirst.com
Up-To-Date Library
www.utdlibrary.com
Benefits and Compensations Solutions
www.bcsolutionsmag.com
Employment Law Central
www.employmentlawcentral.com
Human Resource Executive Magazine
www.workindex.com

PRIVATE RESEARCH AND CONSULTING COMPANIES

Bureau of National Affairs
www.bna.com

Commerce Clearing House
www.cch.com
Mercer Human Resources Consulting
www.mercerhr.com
Clayton Wallis Company
www.claytonwallis.com
Ernst and Young
www.ey.com
Towers Perrin
www.towers.com
ERI Economic Research Institute
www.erieri.com
PeopleSoft
www.peoplesoft.com
Best Practices, LLC
www.best-in-class.com
Families and Work Institute
www.familiesandwork.org

NEGOTIATION SOURCES

Negotiation Resources
www.negotiationresources.com
Arrow Plan
www.arrowplan.com
International Negotiation & Consultancy
www.international-negotiation.com
Center for Negotiation Analysis
www.negotiations.org
Win Squared Negotiation Software
www.winxwin.com
The Negotiation Institute
www.negotiation.com
The Consortium of Negotiation and Conflict Resolution
www.law.gsu.edu/CNCR
Alternative Dispute Resolution Sources: Global Arbitration and Mediation Association
www.gama.com
ADR Resources, INC.
www.adrr.com
Mediate.Com
www.mediate.com
Alternative Dispute Resolution Locator
www.adr.martindale.com
National Arbitration Forum
www.arb-forum.com
Hieros Gamos'
www.hg.org/adr.html
American Bar Association
www.abanet.org/dispute
Institute for the Study of ADR
www.ilr.cornell.edu/icr